D0085164

Encyclopedia of African History

BOARD OF ADVISORS

ENCYCLOPEDIA OF AFRICAN HISTORY

VOLUME 2
H–O

Kevin Shillington, Editor

Fitzroy Dearborn
An Imprint of the Taylor & Francis Group
New York • London

Published in 2005 by
Fitzroy Dearborn
Taylor & Francis Group
270 Madison Avenue
New York, NY 10016

Printed in the United States of America on acid-free paper.

10 9 8 7 6 5 4 3 2

Library of Congress Cataloging-in-Publication Data
Encyclopedia of African history / Kevin Shillington, editor.
p. cm.
Includes bibliographical references and index.
ISBN 1-57958-245-1 (alk. paper)
1. Africa—History—Encyclopedias. I. Shillington, Kevin.

DT20.E53 2004
960'.03—dc22 2004016779

Contents

List of Entries A–Z

(with chronological sublistings within nation/group categories)

VOLUME 1

D

E

F

G

VOLUME 2

L

M

VOLUME 3

P

Q

R

S

U

V

W

Y

Z

Hadya: ***See*** **Ethiopia: Muslim States, Awash Valley: Shoa, Ifat, Fatagar, Hadya, Dawaro, Adal, Ninth to Sixteenth Centuries.**

Hafsids: ***See*** **Maghrib: Marinids, Ziyanids, and Hafsids, 1235–1359.**

Haile Selassie I (1892–1975)

Emperor of Ethiopia

Ethiopian monarch from 1930 to 1974, Emperor Haile Selassie, the 225th ruler of his country, was the son of *Ras* (Prince) Makonnen, the cousin of Emperor Menelik II. He was a direct descendant of King Solomon and the Queen of Sheba, hence his epithet, "Conquering Lion of Judah." Originally named Ras Tafari Makonnen, he bore that name until 1930, when the empress died and the thirty-eight-year-old prince was crowned *Negusa Negast* (King of Kings), Emperor of Ethiopia and the Elect of God with the title of Haile Selassie I, meaning "Might of the Trinity."

Before he became regent in 1916, Ras Tafari was an educated and experienced administrator. His early education was provided by private lessons at the royal court and under French Jesuit missionaries, followed by formal schooling at Menelik School in Addis Ababa. The Emperor Menelik II recognized his intelligence and appointed him governor of Gara Muleta province in 1906 at age thirteen. At fourteen he became governor of Selalie, at sixteen governor of Sidamo, and governor of Harar in 1910. As governor of Sidamo and Harar in particular, which were then Ethiopia's richest provinces, Ras Tafari tried to introduce a program of cautious modernization, economic development and social transformation without damage to the sovereignty, culture, and tradition of his country. His ideas were challenged by the powerful conservative forces of oligarchy; yet despite stiff opposition, he did much to reduce feudal influence.

In 1923 Ras Tafari engineered the admission of Ethiopia into the League of Nations (and later, to its successor, the United Nations). In 1924 he outlawed domestic slavery and slave trading in Ethiopia and attempted to expose his country to modern economic forces by granting concessions and monopolies to various nationalities. In that year, he visited several European countries to secure foreign investments and financial assistance for his developmental plans in Ethiopia, as well as better terms for his country's export and import through Djibouti. He promoted education by encouraging promising young Ethiopians to study abroad. He allowed French, Swiss, German, Belgian, and American teachers and doctors to open schools and hospitals in Ethiopia. In 1928 Ras Tafari signed a twenty-year treaty of friendship and arbitration with Italy. The convention provided for economic cooperation with regard to import and export through the Italian port of Aseb, as well as road construction linking Aseb with Dassieh in the northeast of Ethiopia to be jointly owned by Italy and Ethiopia. Following the death of Empress Zewditu in 1930, Ras Tafari took over full power as head of state in Ethiopia.

As emperor, Haile Selassie embarked on further modernization schemes. Within a year of his ascension, he introduced a modern constitution, appointed ministers, and created a parliament of two deliberative chambers. Though the parliament had only advisory functions, it served as a forum for criticizing his regime.

Emperor Haile Selassie's remarkable success at introducing socioeconomic reforms and establishing a universally respected independence and equality with other nations frustrated Italy's imperial ambitions. By

October 18, 1935: Emperor Haile Selassie I in the field with his troops in the war against the Italian invasion. © SVT Bild/Das Fotoarchiv.

the early 1930s, Italy under Benito Mussolini had sought to conquer Ethiopia, to make up for an earlier defeat at the Battle of Adowa in 1896 and to establish a North African empire. In 1934 Italian forces were repulsed at the border wells at Walwal in Ogaden Province of Ethiopia. Mussolini used this incident as a pretext for war, portraying Ethiopia as the aggressor. Haile Selassie's trust in collective security, under the aegis of the League of Nations, was betrayed on October 3, 1935, when Italy, in violation of international law, attacked Ethiopia. Italy was victorious against the ill-prepared and virtually helpless Ethiopians and on May 2, 1936, Haile Selassie left Addis Ababa for exile in Jerusalem, and then London. He remained abroad until 1940, when Italy joined the Axis side in World War II and Ethiopia's government in exile joined with the Allied forces. With the support of the Allies, the Italians were driven out of Ethiopia and on May 5, 1941, the emperor returned to Addis Ababa in triumph.

On his return, Haile Selassie immediately established a bilateral relationship with the United States, from whom he secured military and technical assistance with which he strengthened Ethiopia's independence. By 1945 he had firmly established the supremacy of the central government, and in the 1950s established the federation of Eritrea. Ethiopian's constitution was revised in 1955 to provide for the direct election of the Assembly of Deputies by the people; in 1957 the first general elections took place. He introduced a program for the extension of education to university level, improvement of transport and communication, massive industrialization, and the development of more opportunities for employment.

Meanwhile, after the end of World War II in 1945, Ethiopia under Haile Selassie had become an active participant in international affairs. The country became a staunch supporter of the United Nations, and Ethiopian troops formed part of the United Nations contingent in Korea in 1950 while a similar contribution was later made to the Congo. When the United Nations economic commission for Africa was established in 1958, Addis Ababa became its permanent headquarters. From the early 1960s, Africa became the focal point of Haile Selassie's foreign policy. He played a leading role in the movement for African unity by convening the first conference of African heads of state at Addis Ababa in 1963, at which the Orgnization of African Unity (OAU) was formed. Similarly, he visited many African capitals, participating in successful mediation of interstate disputes such as the Algerian-Morocco border war of 1963.

As the years went by, there was serious domestic political opposition, sometimes violent, to the authority of the aging emperor. Economic development in Ethiopia slowed due to a lack of capital, technical know-how, and adequate personnel. Haile Selassie's approach to educational, political, and economic reforms was deemed slow and overly cautious by the country's young intelligentsia. The hostility generated by the growing impatience culminated in an attempted coup, which his loyal troops successfully crushed. Following incessant inflation, coupled with serious drought and famine in the 1970s which claimed several thousands of lives, students, workers, and segments of the army became increasingly restless. From January 1974, there were violent demonstrations. Thereafter, army officers under the chairmanship of Major Mengistu Maile Mariam gradually took over, and on September 12, 1974, they deposed the emperor. Haile Selassie died in Addis Ababa while under house arrest on August 27, 1975.

S. Ademola Ajayi

See also: **Ethiopia.**

Biography

Haile Selassie I was born in 1892. Appointed governor of Gara Muleta province in 1906. Became governor of Selalie in 1907, governor of Sidamo in 1909, and governor of Harar in 1910. Regent and heir apparent to the throne from 1916 to 1930. Following the death of Empress Zewditu in 1930, he was named Emperor of Ethiopia.

Left for exile in Jerusalem and then London on May 2, 1936, following Italy's invasion of Ethiopia. He returned on May 5, 1941, after joining the Allied forces and forcing Italy out of Ethiopia. Deposed by army officers led by Major Mengistu Maile Mariam on September 12, 1974. Died in Addis Ababa while under house arrest on August 27, 1975.

Further Reading

Greenfield, R. *Ethiopia: A New Political History*. Pall Mall, 1965.

Lockot, H. W. *The Mission: The Life, Reign, and Character of Haile Selassie I*. New York, 1989.

Marcus, H. G. *Haile Selassie I: The Formative Years, 1892–1936*. Berkeley, Calif. 1987.

Mosley, L. *Haile Selassie: The Conquering Lion*. Weidenfeld and Nicolson, 1964.

Pankhurst, R. *Journeys in Ethiopia*. Oxford: Oxford University Press, 1960.

Sandford, C. *The Lion of Judah Hath Prevailed*. Dent, 1955.

Hailey: An African Survey

It is impossible to study the colonial question without becoming aware of the immense influence exerted by Lord Hailey. Undoubtedly, Lord Hailey was one of the most important personalities connected with British imperialism and colonialism in Africa in the twentieth century. He was a typical colonial bureaucrat who had served the crown as governor of the Punjab and the United Provinces in India. During the 1930s, Hailey launched a massive research study on Africa and its problems in relation to colonialism. The outcome of this study was the publication of *An African Survey,* a major treatise on British colonial rule in Africa, in 1938, which made him a noteworthy historical personality in the era of colonialism in Africa.

Hailey's *An African Survey* refers, essentially, to the body of reports that Hailey compiled on colonialism in Africa, in which emphasis was placed on the need for political change, economic reforms and development, and above all, a review of the "indirect rule" system, which was the prevailing system of local administration in British Africa colonies. To appreciate the importance of Lord Hailey's *An African Survey*, it is important to note that scholars of British imperial disengagement from the African colonies have tended to categorize it as part of the evidence of independent metropolitan initiatives on the need for colonial reforms in the immediate prewar years (late 1930s). In this regard, *An African Survey* is often seen as belonging to the category of intellectual and liberal tradition calling for a review of the system of managing African colonies during the interwar and World War II years. Others in the category of Hailey's *An African Survey* included the desultory minutes and opinions expressed by colonial office staff responsible for overseeing the African colonies, such as O. G. R. Williams, Andrew Benjamin Cohen, and Sir Charles Jeffries, among others.

Yet the strength of *An African Survey,* as far as the history of European colonialism in Africa is concerned, lies in its status as a singular, sustained effort by a respected British technocrat to itemize, and then bring into sharp focus, the major projects that he believed the colonial administration should undertake in the aftermath of the then-looming war. Not surprisingly, Lord Hailey's *An African Survey* has been categorized by many scholars of this period of British policy in Africa in the same class as the *Report of a Commission of Inquiry* (headed by Lord Moyne), published in 1938, on the labor problems in the West Indies. Together with the Moynes Commission Report, Hailey's survey provided one of the earliest indictments of the colonial system, pointing out many of its inadequacies. In the aftermath of the publication of *An African Survey*, Lord Hailey continued to publicize his interest in colonial affairs, especially the need to reassess the strategy of managing British African colonies and bringing some modicums of reforms to these areas.

A particularly significant aspect of *An African Survey* was the meticulously thought out conclusions offered by the author, which suggested a great intellectual engagement with the pressing issues at hand. Hailey traveled extensively across Africa and served on the League of Nations Permanent Mandates Commission, which, in the interwar years, managed some of the dependent territories in Africa, and elsewhere. The importance of Lord Hailey's *An African Survey,* therefore, lies in the fact that it was a major synthesis of a kaleidoscope of information on the resources and opportunities, as well as the socioeconomic problems, of emergent Africa in the first decades of the twentieth century. Clearly, *An African Survey* devoted considerable attention to British administration of its colonies, yet it said much for the way and manner in which other European colonial powers managed their colonies in Africa. Since the end of World War II, Hailey's *An African Survey* has remained a major reference material for scholars interested in the general history and fortune (or misfortune?) of colonialism, especially in British African colonies in a postwar world.

KUNLE LAWAL

Further Reading

Easton, S. C. *The Twilight of European Colonialism*. New York, 1960.

Hailey. *An African Survey*. London, 1938.

———. *The Position of Colonies in a British Commonwealth Nation (The Romanes Lectures)*. London, 1941.

Hancock, W. K. *Survey of British Commonwealth Affairs (1937–42)*. London, 1942.

Kunle, L. *Britain and the Politics of Transfer of Power in Nigeria: 1945–60*. 1999.

Lee, J. M. *Colonial Development and Good Government: A Study of the Ideas Expressed by the British Official Classes in Planning Decolonization 1939–1964*. London, 1967.

Louis, W. R. *Imperialism at Bay: The United States and the Decolonization of the British Empire*. New York, 1978.

al-Hajj Umar. *See* Tukolor Empire of al-Hajj Umar.

See Tukolor Empire of al-Hajj Umar.

Hamdallahi Caliphate, 1818–1862

The jihad that created this caliphate occurred in Macina, in the fertile region of the Niger River bend, in the early nineteenth century. Macina was then controlled by Fulani overlords, vassals of the Bambara of Segu. The government was animist in practice, although the ruling king (*ardo*) of Macina was a Muslim. At all levels of society, Islam was amalgamated with traditional African beliefs. Reformers preached a jihad that would restore genuine Islam. They also promised to put an end to the oppressive rule of Segu, liberate slaves if they converted, free pastoralist Fulani from the cattle tax and merchants from market taxes, which, they pointed out, were illegal under Qur'anic law. They attracted a large following. Encouraged by the success of earlier Islamic jihads in the Western Sudan, several Macina marabouts vied for leadership. It was Ahmadu Lobbo who succeeded in overturning the ruling Fulani dynasty and transforming Macina into a powerful Muslim state.

Ahmadu was born in 1775. He spent his youth tending cattle and studying Islamic law. He drew inspiration from another follower of the Qadiriyya brotherhood, Uthman dan Fodio, creator of the neighboring Sokoto caliphate, but maintained his independence from him. Between 1810 and 1815, with ardent support from Fulani pastoralists, Ahmadu won a long war against Segu. The jihadists then captured Djenné (1818). Next, the Fulani Sangare clan revolted against the *ardo* and invited Ahmadu to rule. Other Fulani chiefs quickly declared loyalty. Ahmadu, realizing that they were motivated by self-interest rather than religious conversion, overthrew them one by one. In 1823 he defeated the Fulani of Fittuga (1823) who wanted to launch their own jihad. In 1826–27 he conquered Timbuktu and established a Fulani garrison in the city. Thus, the power of the Macina caliphate extended from Djenné to Timbuktu.

Ahmadu's caliphate was remarkably well organized. The shari'a (Islamic law) was applied to all aspects of life. Ahmadu formed a governing council of forty scholars with executive, legislative, and judicial powers. Important issues were taken up by this council. Since convening a body of this size was cumbersome, he selected two especially outstanding scholars to consider state business prior to submitting it to the council. He furthermore appointed administrators, selected for their high moral standards, to keep a watch on public servants. Courts banned many non-Islamic practices. Punishments were severe. Conversion and education were emphasized. State-sponsored schools were founded throughout the caliphate. Yet, under this autocratic regime, the needs and rights of individuals and groups within the caliphates were protected.

While mainly concerned with the regulation of cities, Ahmadu also provided for his own pastoral Fulani, who had formed the bulk of the fighting forces during the jihad, and arranged to give them military protection during their annual migration with their herds. He also encouraged them to settle. Slaves who had participated in the jihad were freed; those who did not remained slaves, while more slaves were captured in raids across frontiers and in suppressing rebellions. They were made to cultivate fields for the state, enabling Macina to produce large quantities of grains and vegetables and guarantee a sufficient food supply. Ahmadu founded his own capital, which he called Hamdallahi ("Praise God"). Its mosque was unadorned. An area near the council's meeting hall was reserved to lodge those without means of support. Standards of hygiene were high. Clerics concerned not only with crimes but also with private morality were in charge of policing the city.

Through a combination of diplomacy and force, Ahmadu was able to preserve the frontiers of the caliphate from external aggression. He also succeeded in maintaining peace internally, though the austerity of the rules he imposed brought him into conflict with Djenné and Timbuktu. Here merchants incurred financial losses because Ahmadu's stand against luxury and practices forbidden by Islam, such as the use of alcohol or dancing, strictly enforced by the Censor of Public Morals, made the city less attractive to visitors, and because the wars between Macina and Segu cut them off from gold supplies.

Djenné lost much of its importance when Ahmadu built his own new capital nearby. Timbuktu, on the other hand, persisted in fighting for a measure of self-determination. The Kunta inhabitants, who had produced many great religious leaders themselves, considered Ahmadu an upstart, and led a number of uprisings against him. In the 1840s the governing council of Hamdallahi starved Timbuktu into submission.

Ahmadu died in 1844, and was succeeded by his son Ahmadu II (1844–52), and then his grandson, Ahmadu III (1852–62). Ahmadu II was less skillful than his father had been, and problems soon surfaced. Timbuktu rebelled and succeeded in gaining control of its internal affairs. Ahmadu III deepened the crisis by replacing old respected religious leaders with younger, more liberal men. The caliphate was permeated with intrigues when al-Hajj Umar, leader of the Tukulor jihad, attacked.

Umar, stopped by the French in his northward empire-building drive, had turned east against the kingdom of Segu. So far Umar's victories had been against animists, but his attack on Segu created a confrontation with Macina, a major Muslim power. He had hoped that Macina would align itself with him against Segu, but Ahmadu III refused, arguing that the Segu kingdom lay within Macina's sphere of influence, and that the responsibility for converting it was Macina's alone. Besides this political dispute, there was also a doctrinal disagreement. Umar, representing the Tijaniyya brotherhood, argued that Macina's scholarly Qadiriyyi elitism did not spread Islam efficiently. Umar's invasion of Segu provoked a violent reaction from the Macina Fulani, who joined forces with the Bambara and Kunta Berbers against him. In 1861 Umar defeated Segu and in the following year marched against Macina. He won, destroyed Hamdallahi, took Timbuktu, and put an end to the Hamdallahi caliphate.

NATALIE SANDOMIRSKY

See also: **Mali (Republic of): Economy and Society, Nineteenth Century.**

Further Reading

Ajayi, J. F. A., and M. Crowder, eds. *History of West Africa. Vol. 2.* Burnt Mills, Essex: Longman, 1987.

Bâ, A. H. *L'Empire peul du Macina: (1818–1853).* Paris: Les Nouvelles Editions Africaines, 1975.

Coulon, C. *Les musulmans et le pouvoir en Afrique noire: religion et contre-culture* [Muslims and Power in Black Africa: Religion and Counter-culture]. Paris: Editions Karthala, 1983.

Djata, A. *The Bamana Empire by the Niger, Kingdom, Jihad and Colonization 1712–1929.* Princeton: Markus Wiener, 1997.

Martin, B. G. *Muslim Brotherhoods in Nineteenth-Century Africa.* Cambridge: Cambridge University Press, 1976.

Monteil, V. *L'Islam noir* [Black Islam]. Paris: Le Seuil, 1964.

Sanankoua, B. *Un empire peul au XIXe siècle* [A Peul Empire in the 19th Century]. Paris: Editions Khartala-ACCT, 1990.

Harare

Harare (formerly Salisbury) is the largest urban center in, and capital city of, Zimbabwe. It is the seat of government and the administrative center for three Mashonaland provinces. It is a focal point of rail, road, and air transport, and has an international airport.

White settlers occupied Harare in September 1890 and named the settlement Fort Salisbury, after Robert Gascoyne-Cecil, then prime minister of Great Britain. In occupying this site, the settlers displaced Chief Gutsa, a Shona leader. The area for settlement was chosen because of the Mukuvisi River's adequate supply of water, reliable rainfall, a considerable expanse of fertile land for cropping, grazing, and hunting, an easily defensible site because of the surrounding hills, and significant supplies of traditional building materials.

The original town center was around the Kopje area, but this formally moved to the Causeway area in 1910. The first buildings were of a pole and dagga nature. Salisbury got its first newspaper on June 27, 1891, and first magistrate Major Patrick Forbes arrived in the same year. Also, 1891 saw the settlement's first formal town plan and the establishment of a "location" for Africans, about a kilometer south of the Kopje at the site of the present-day residential area of Mbare (called Harari at that time).

Municipal administration came in the form of the Salisbury Sanitary Board, which was established in 1892 with a mandate to provide water and dispose of sewage. It was also to maintain and regulate streets and traffic, deal with obstructions, noises, filth, pollution of water, and fires. In 1897, when Salisbury's white population was well over 1,000, the Sanitary Board gave way to the Municipality of Salisbury. The latter formally established Harari African township, away from the city center because Africans were considered "bad neighbors" for whites.

Although the telegraph line from South Africa had reached Salisbury in February 1892, it was not until August 1897 that the town, now with its first mayor, had its first telephone put into operation. In the same vein, it was only on May 1, 1899, that the railway line from Beira reached Salisbury, well after Bulaweyo had received the line. In fact, by the end of 1899, Salisbury, with its population of 1,600 whites, was still essentially a village. Although it was the capital of Southern Rhodesia, it lacked basic amenities, such as electricity, which Bulaweyo already had. In 1902 Salisbury was linked by rail with Bulaweyo. In 1913 and 1914, it witnessed the opening of the Cleveland Dam and the attendant provision of diesel-generated electricity for improved water and electrical supplies.

In 1935 Salisbury was elevated to city status. This occurred in the wake of the passage of the 1930 Land Apportionment Act, which prohibited blacks from acquiring land outside the "reserves." The act contained a provision that set aside land for African townships, which were to be run by advisory boards with consultative, not decision-making, powers.

The city expanded considerably after World War II due to two primary factors. First, the successful development of the manufacturing sector brought with it a significant amount of financial investment. Second, Salisbury became the capital of the Federation of Rhodesia and Nyasaland. This led to a marked increase in development in the Salisbury city center. Since they were providing essential labor services for the colonial administration, Africans were provided with housing in areas like Highfield in 1935, Mabvuku in1952, and Mufakose in 1959. These residential areas were conveniently situated close to industrial areas to ease labor provision. However, the breakup of the federation in 1963 and the subsequent Unilateral Declaration of Independence (UDI) in 1965 brought about a recession and the flight of capital, negatively impacting Salisbury's development. UDI attracted sanctions from the international community, further slowing the city's development. The intensification of the struggle for independence did not make matters any better for Salisbury. The city's situation was worsened by an influx of people from the war-torn rural areas, straining Salisbury's ability to provide basic services.

Since the 1969 Land Tenure Act had sanctioned the "right" of housing for Africans in "white" areas like Salisbury, provision of housing for the growing black population in the 1970s was augmented by the creation of more residential areas like Glen Norah and Glen View. Toward the end of the 1970s, some Africans started moving into "white" suburbs, as some of the houses had been vacated by whites fleeing the war.

From 1980 the independent Zimbabwean government set out to redress the imbalances including those involving the city of Salisbury. In the health sector, the former African residential areas, now high density residential areas, were provided with more clinics, at least one per area. In keeping with the postcolonial government's policy of education for all, Harare City Council built primary and secondary schools. It undertook more or less equitable waste collection and disposal in the city. More residential areas were established, including eWarren Park, Kuwadzana, Hatcliffe, Budiriro, and Sunningdale, in the 1980s. The water supply situation was stable, with Lake Chivero, the Manyame River, and Cleveland and Seke dams providing adequate water, except in the drought years of 1983–84 and 1991–92. The city faces the increasing problem of "squatters" and "street kids." Public transport remains inadequate, but more worrying is the widening gap between the rich and the poor. Race, however, is no longer as divisive an issue as it was in the period up to 1980.

GOVERNMENT CHRISTOPHER PHIRI

See also: **Zimbabwe.**

Further Reading

Drakakis-Smith, D., ed. *Urbanisation in the Developing World.* London: Croom Helm, 1986.

Encyclopedia Zimbabwe. Harare: Quest Publishing, 1987.

Kay, G., and M. A. H. Smout, eds. *Salisbury: A Geographical Survey of the Capital of Rhodesia.* London: Hodder and Stoughton, 1977.

Kileff, C., and W. D. Pendleton, eds. *Urban Man in Southern Africa.* Gwelo: Mambo Press, 1975.

Potter, R. B., and A. T. Salau, eds. *Cities and Development in the Third World.* London: Mansell, 1990.

Rakodi, C. *Harare: Inheriting a Settler-Colonial City: Change or Continuity*? Chichester, Sussex: Wiley, 1995.

Simon, D. *Cities, Capital and Development: African Cities in the World Economy.* London: Belhaven, 1992.

Stren, R. E., and R. R. White. *African Cities in Crisis: Managing Rapid Urban Growth.* Boulder, Colo.: Westview Press, 1989.

Tanser, G. H. *A Scantling of Time: The Story of Salisbury—Rhodesia: 1890 to 1900.* Salisbury: Stuart Manning, 1965.

Zinyama, L., et al., eds. *Harare: The Growth and Problems of the City.* Harare: University of Zimbabwe Publications, 1993.

Harris, William Wade (*c.*1865–1929)
Religious Leader

William Wade Harris was a prominent religious leader in twentieth-century West Africa. His formal entry into the Episcopal Church opened up opportunities for Harris. Less than a year after his confirmation, he became a part-time unpaid teacher's aide at the boarding school operated by the Episcopal Church at Half Graway. A few years afterward he became a salaried employee of the church, as assistant teacher at the school and catechist at the mission. In 1907 he was appointed head of the school, a position he continued to hold long after he became the interpreter for the Liberian government for the Graway area the following year. Seemingly emboldened by his improved social and economic status, Harris became involved in political affairs. Some traditional authorities asked him to intervene with the government on their behalf. At other times, he interceded with national and local leaders on his own volition. He became sufficiently politically prominent to gain audiences with Liberian President Arthur Barclay and other high officials. Before long however, his activities got him into difficulty with the president, who had Harris arrested in 1909 during a roundup of alleged plotters against the state. He spent more than three years in prison following his conviction.

Harris underwent a religious transformation while he was incarcerated. According to him, an angel, who anointed him "the last prophet" and instructed him to prepare the world for the imminent coming of Jesus Christ, visited him. On his release from prison, the prophet set out on his "duty" as commissioned by the angel. Between 1912 and 1920 he walked across much of the coastal regions of Liberia, the Côte d'Ivoire, and the then British Gold Coast preaching to those who would listen. His message was simple: followers of traditional religions should abandon their fetishes and take up the true religion, the message of Christ. He baptized those who accepted his message. For himself, he requested only food and shelter. He converted an estimated 200,000 West African practitioners of indigenous religions. A separate campaign in Sierra Leone in 1916–17 and continuous work in Liberia between 1920 and 1922 swelled the number of his converts by tens of thousands. He also spawned a number of apostles who took his message deep into the interior of the Côte d'Ivoire and won thousands of converts.

The volume of his conversions was truly remarkable, especially in the Côte d'Ivoire, the site of more than half of the conversions. Harris was in the Côte d'Ivoire from September 1913 to January 1914 and again from August 1914 to January 1915. On the intervention of the Society of African Missions (SAM), French authorities arrested him for preaching without a license and ordered his expulsion. However, upon discovering that he had been successful in getting indigenes to abandon traditional religions, stop drinking alcohol, and work their fields or seek paid employment, the lieutenant governor ordered his release. With its base of returning Africans, Liberia had started with a Christian base that was expanded upon by American missionaries. The Gold Coast also had a strong Christian presence, the results of the work of Anglican and Methodist missionaries. In contrast, the Christian community in the Côte d'Ivoire was meager even after two decades of continuous effort by the SAM, a French Roman Catholic order. The first Protestant missionary, Rev. H. G. Martin of the Wesleyan Methodist Society, arrived in the Côte d'Ivoire shortly before the outward voyage of Harris.

Harris had not intended to create a new denomination. At home in Liberia, he expected his converts to join the existing Christian community. Markedly, he did not direct them to do so. Guided by his intention to return to his family in Liberia, he directed the followers in the Côte d'Ivoire "to go to the Christian Church." Roman Catholic missionaries and some converts interpreted "Christian Church" to mean Catholic, while Wesleyan missionaries and some of the Harris converts decided that it meant the Wesleyan Methodist Church. Thus some of the converts flocked to the Catholic Church while others turned to the Wesleyan Church. However, after clerics and missionaries of the two denominations insisted that the converts had to be instructed properly in the tenets of their respected religion and to be baptized before they could be accepted fully into the faith, the vast majority of the converts banded together and created the Harriste Church. Many had associated baptism with a rite of passage, and as with other such rites with which they were more familiar, a person could experience it only once. In Liberia, the prophet's continued evangelization kept his followers under his direction. Eventually, that community also evolved into the Harrisite Church. It views itself as the true Christian Church and continues to exist as a vibrant sizeable denomination in both countries.

ASHTON WESLEY WELCH

See also: **Côte d'Ivoire; Liberia; Religion, Colonial Africa: Independent, Millenarian/Syncretic Churches; Religion, Colonial Africa: Prophetic Movements.**

Biography

Born to Grebo parents in Liberia. In his early teens, moved from his parents' home in Glogbale to live with the Reverend Jesse Lowrie in the nearby town of Sinoe. Tutored in Grebo and English and baptized. Returned home as an adolescent but soon left again to become a crew boy working on ships along the West African coast. Attended Anglican services during stopovers in Lagos. Married Rose Badock Farr in 1884. Confirmed in the Protestant Episcopal Church. Died 1929.

Further Reading

Haliburton, G. M. *The Prophet Harris.* London: Longman, 1971.
Hayford, J. C. *William Waddy Harris the West African Reformer: The Man and His Message.* London: Phillips, 1915.
Platt, W. J. *An African Prophet: The Côte d'Ivoire Movement and What Came of It.* London. S. C. M. Press, 1934.
Walker, F. D. *The Story of the Côte d'Ivoire.* London: The Cargate Press, 1926.

Hassan, Abdile: *See* Somalia: Hassan, Muhammad Abdile and Resistance to Colonial Conquest.

Hausa Polities: Origins, Rise

The Hausa states were found between the Niger River and Lake Chad, between the kingdom of Bornu and Mali. Immigration and conquest mark Hausa history. The Hausa people themselves are a conglomerate of a number of different people who have been incorporated into the "original" stock through conquest or merger. A common language, Hausa, and a common religion, Islam, tend to blend the people into a more homogeneous group. Hausa tradition states that there are seven "true" Hausa states, the "Hausa bakwai," and seven derived or illegitimate states, the "Hausa banza." Tradition further states that all Hausa people derived from the Hausa bakwai, the "true" seven states. Daura, founded by Daura, a woman, is the senior city among the Hausa states. The Hausa origin myth recognizes this seniority by noting that the culture hero Bayajidda, the son of the king of Baghdad, arrived in Daura after visiting Bornu. A snake had made its dwelling place in the town well, making it difficult for people to drink from it. Bayajidda managed to kill the snake, and he took the queen in marriage as his reward. Their marriage produced a son, Bawo. In turn, Bawo fathered six sons of his own. These sons founded the six true Hausa states: Daura, Katsina, Zazzau (Zaria), Gobir, Kano, and Rano. Bayajidda had another son, a child with his first wife, Magira, a Kanuri. That son founded Biram, the seventh state of the Hausa bakwai.

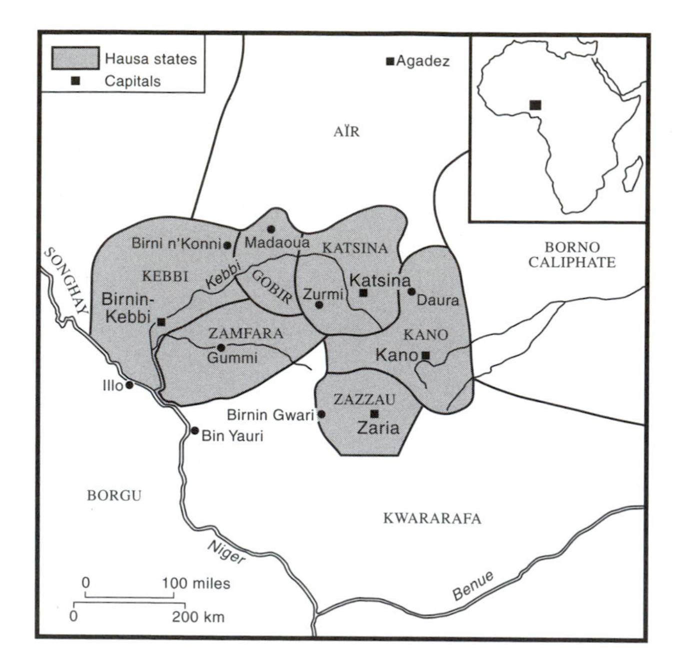

Hausa states, thirteenth–eighteenth centuries.

History does not yet yield an exact date for the migration and merger of peoples that led to the development of the Hausa people. What is known is that the seven kingdoms resulted from a mixture of newly arrived foreigners and local people because of urbanization in northern Nigeria. Capital cities became centers of power and rule. These new cities were walled and fortified and marked the rise of kingship in the region. Over time, these kings controlled trade in the region along the Niger River in what became northern Nigeria. The Habe rulers turned to Islam to aid their government organization. However, until the Fulani jihad of the nineteenth century, the Habe continued to worship their traditional gods. The Habe reign lasted until 1804 when the Fulani conquered the area.

The Hausa states specialized in various crafts and trade goods. Kano, for example, was known for its dyed cotton fabrics and so-called Moroccan leather, while Zaria specialized in slave trading. Slaves, who were generally captured warriors, built the walled towns, which enabled the Hausa to resist their various enemies and protect their control of much of the trans-Saharan trade. Katsina and Kano became centers of caravan routes. Hausa traders established *sabon gari* (strangers' quarters) all over Nigeria. These *sabon gari* helped the Hausa to set up efficient trade networks, securing access to markets in other parts of West Africa.

The Hausa organized areas surrounding their walled capitals into residential clusters of wards or hamlets. Each of these political and residential units had a head. In turn, the wards were part of a village which itself was under the control of a village head. Villages were organized and controlled under the leadership of a titled official who held the land under the Emir or chief. The official lived in the capital where he could serve the Emir and be under his control. Fiefs were attached to particular tribes and were granted by the emir, or head of the state. The fief holder chose officials to administer the lands under his care. These officials were responsible to him. The village chief was the most important local administrator. His responsibilities included collection of taxes, recruiting men for military service, organizing road labor, and settling minor disputes.

Hausa trading centers became the center of a new urban Muslim Hausa culture, succeeding pre-Hausa states, and the Mbau kingdoms that formed part of a series of shrines, which featured fairs at which disputes were mediated. These early kingdoms seem to have been formed around 1500, around the time the Habe rulers converted to Islam. Islam certainly enabled the Hausa to oversee the flowering of a powerful culture whose height was about the middle of the seventeenth century. Kano and Katsina became centers of Islamic scholarship and trade, profiting from the rivalry between Morocco and the Ottoman Empire. From the mid-seventeenth century on, the Hausa states were engaged in a series of military conflicts, ending with the victory of the Fulani in the nineteenth-century jihad.

FRANK A. SALAMONE

Further Reading

Adamu, M. *The Hausa Factor in West Africa.* London: Oxford University Press, 1978.

Paden, J. *Religion and Political Culture in Kano.* Berkeley: University of California Press, 1974.

Pellow, D. "Hausa." In *Africa and the Middle East*, edited by John Middlton and Amal Rassam. Boston: G. K. Hall, 1995.

Hausa Polities: Urbanism, Industry, and Commerce

There are several myths and theories relating the origin of the Hausa people. According to one, the founder of the Hausa came from Iraq; this myth highlights the source of Islam, across the Sahara. Other theories maintain that the Hausa moved to their land following the desertification of the Sahel regions. One more theory argues that the Hausas originated from the Lake Chad region and subsequently spread westwards. Hausaland eventually developed into an area marked by highly urbanized city-states. The *hausa bakwai*, or original Hausa cities, include Biram, Daura, Gobir, Kano, Katsina, Rano, and Zazzau. The later settlements include Jukun, Gwari, Kebbi, Yoruba, Nupe, Yoruba, Yawuri, and Zamfara.

The earliest immigrants to Hausaland arrived from the Sahel regions. They inhabited the Fulbe settlements in Hausaland from the fifteenth century. Tuareg followed in the footsteps of the Fulbe. People form Bornu and Songhay also settled in small communities. Arab traders, settling primarily in cities, were another group.

Families (*gidaje*), under chiefs (*maigari*), formed small rural communities (*kauyuka*). These constituted the villages, which were permanent settlements, headed by the *sarkin gari* or village chiefs. The *birane* or district capital was in most cases a walled city of a considerable size that functioned as the seat of political power and the center of commercial activities. These centers were generally understood to include regions of authority, usually called *kasas.* At the head of the *kasa* was the ruler or *sarki* who, in theory, had absolute power, and was considered as sacred in the early period. This was not necessarily a hereditary position, as a council of the nine, or the *Tara,* most often elected someone to the post. In Kebbi, soldiers rose to this position, while in other places it was generally filled by a member of the local aristocracy. The *sarki*'s authority was exercised through a body of officials, comprised of family members and town officials. Guilds, immigrants, and Islamic scholars had their own representatives and exercised some forms of authority and influence over the *sarki*'s decisions that related directly to them.

Present-day Hausaland includes vast resources of iron ore and stretches over a region characterized by fertile and rich soil. While the former factor encouraged the development of refined iron-working, leading to the production of excellent weapons, tools, and utensils, the latter fact enabled a rich agricultural program. The produced goods included crops like millet, sorghum, rice, maize, peanuts, cotton, and indigo.

By far the largest component of Hausa society was the free peasants, living in the *kauyuka*, centered in the villages or the *garuruwa*, which were scattered around the *birane*. They were the primary agriculturists and formed the largest body of taxpayers, contributing the *kudin kasa*, or land tax. As in the economic and social structure of the society, the family came to represent the unit of taxation too.

Although some ethnic groups were enslaved, usually as a result of wars on the frontiers, slavery was not widespread, although palace slaves were found in major cities. The first slave settlements seem to have originated from Fulbe herders who bought or captured slaves and formed agricultural estates driven by slave labor, possibly as early as the eighteenth century. Based on the available evidence, it is currently assumed that Hausaland never became a slave-exporting region, with the exception of Kawar and Zawila, which participated in the slave trade probably in the fourteenth, fifteenth, and sixteenth centuries.

Craftsmen were usually centered in either the *garuruwa* or the *birane*. By the sixteenth century, highly specialized groups of artisans were formed who eventually came to be represented by guilds in local political affairs. Makers of leatherwork, saddles, sandals, and jewelry were all represented.

The Hausa traders (*bahaushe*) and trading networks penetrated the Western Sudan, distributing domestic products like textiles, fabrics, hides, and salt, as well as handcrafts and slaves. They imported European goods, and the natural stimulant of kola nuts. The regional trade, represented to a great extent by the *bahaushe*, used caravans and relied on a regular network of markets. Their role in urban development was key, as they came to form in many places the prosperous and established middle class.

The upper echelons of society included the nobility, the city governments, and the representatives of integrated ethnicities like the Fulbe. These, however, never formed a universal class of rulers and authority was maintained through various bodies of institutions. Taxation was levied on all elements of the society, including the free peasants and the herdsmen paying to the nobility, while the craftsmen and traders paid direct and indirect taxes (custom duties or the *kudin hito*) to cities. Most high-ranking officials, governors, and dignitaries regularly received gifts from all elements of the local society. The turbulent inter-city rivalries brought about frequent raiding and pillaging of the neighboring *kasa*. The captured slaves, horses, and cattle were incorporated into local economies, although, as has been noted, the sale of slaves was rare.

By the early nineteenth century, even the economically strong states of Kano and Katsina had grown politically weak. They were integrated into the largest state in the modern Western Sudan, the Sokoto Caliphate, which was the result of the Fulbe jihad.

LÁSZLÓ MÁTHÉ-SHIRES

See also: **Rumfa, Muhammad.**

Further Reading

Adamu, M. *The Hausa Factor in West African History.* Zaria, Nigeria: Ahmadu Bello University, 1978.

Hill, P. *Rural Hausa: A Village and a Setting.* Cambridge: Cambridge University Press, 1972.

Lovejoy, P. E. *Caravans of Kola: The Hausa Kola Trade, 1700–1900.* Zaria, Nigeria: Ahmado Bello Univeristy, 1980.

———. *Transformations in Slavery: A History of Slavery in Africa.* Cambridge: Cambridge University Press, 1997.

Oshomha, I. *The Hausa and Fulani of Northern Nigeria.* Ibadan: New-Era, 1990.

Hausa Polities: Warfare, Nineteenth Century

The Hausa had ruled much of what became Northern Nigeria since before the thirteenth century. In the

1790s, however, a Fulani Muslim teacher, Usman dan Fodio (1751–1817), disputed with the rulers of the northern city of Gobir. The dispute concerned their practice of Islam. dan Fodio argued that the rulers, following common Hausa practice, had mixed "pagan" practices with Islamic ones and did not adhere closely enough to Islam.

dan Fodio was the leading Fulani Muslim leader in Gobir, the northern most Hausa state and the most militant of the states. The political situation at the time was quite sensitive. The Taureg's had become a dominant military force in the region, and the Gobir rulers had turned south to spread their power, spreading into Zamfara and Kebbi.

The dissolution of the Songhai Empire left a power vacuum, and the Fulani pastoralists rushed into the area. The Muslim Hausa rulers of Gobir hired dan Fodio as a court cleric. However, he used that position to gain control over a Muslim community he developed away from Gobir. He enforced the strict principles of the Qadiriyah on his followers. Gobir's kings realized that dan Fodio's community threatened their power. They tried to control the group but dan Fodio declared himself an independent Muslim ruler (*amir al-mu'minin*) or, in Hausa, *sarkin musulmi*.

dan Fodio gathered a large following of Fulani pastoralists, who had their own feud with Gobir's rulers concerning the cattle tax (*jangali*). A number of Hausa commoners (*talakawa*) also participated in the holy war or jihad. The jihad moved relentlessly through all of the Hausa states and captured the walled cities (*birni*) of the Hausa, sweeping south into the Nupe and Yoruba areas.

In 1804, then, the Fulani launched their jihad against the Hausa people of Gobir, Zamfara, Kebbi, and Yauri. By 1808 the Fulani had defeated the Hausa peoples of Gobir. The Fulani leader Shehu (Sheik) Usman dan Fodio divided his conquest into two areas. He knew that he was more a scholar than a political leader. Therefore, he turned over the day-to-day control of the eastern part of the empire to his son Muhammad Bello. Bello ruled from Sokoto while dan Fodio's brother Abdullahi was given the western area. Abdullahi settled in Gwandu.

In 1809, then, dan Fodio made his son, Muhammad Bello, emir of Sokoto and overlord of the eastern emirates. When his father died in 1817, Bello became leader of the faithful (*sarkin musulmi*) and first sultan of Sokoto. This control made him both the spiritual and political leader of the Fulani Empire, and the empire reached its highest political and spiritual point under his direction.

The Hausa, or Habe, made numerous attempts to overthrow the Fulani usurpers. Muhammad (1817–37), however, was able to turn the Hausa attempts back and rally the Sokoto Empire behind him. For example, the southern area of the empire in Yauri was the scene of a number of revolts. Nevertheless, Bello managed to quell them with his uncle's help from Gwandu. In 1853 Sokoto further consolidated its power by joining the British in a trade treaty, one the Fulani strengthened in 1885. Although Bello and his successors opposed British domination, the British defeated the Fulani in 1903.

FRANK A. SALAMONE

See also: **'Uthman dan Fodio.**

Further Reading

Hogben, S. J., and A. H. M. Kirk-Greene. *The Emirates of Northern Nigeria.* London: Oxford University Press, 1966.
Last, M. *The Sokoto Caliphate.* London: Longmans, 1967.
Smith, M. G. *Government in Zazzau.* London: Oxford University Press, 1980.
———. "The Hausa of Northern Nigeria." In *Peoples of Africa*, edited by James L. Gibbs, Jr. New York: Holt, Rinehart, and Winston.

Hay, Edward, and John Drummond: *See* Morocco: Hay, Edward and John Drummond, British Diplomatic Protection, 1829–1903.

Health: Medicine and Disease: Colonial

Disease and medicine played an important role in the process of European colonization of Africa in the nineteenth and twentieth centuries. Until the mid-nineteenth century, when the activities of the European merchants were limited to the coastal regions, the image of Africa that emerged from European travelers' accounts was that of the "white man's grave" because of the high rates of mortality and morbidity from infectious and parasitic diseases, including yellow fever, malaria, typhoid, typhus, and cholera. The main underlying assumption was that the Africans were believed to have inherited or naturally acquired immunity against several diseases because, although they too died from these diseases, they often exhibited mild to moderate symptoms.

The development, after 1871, of the exploration movement by various European geographical societies using faster ships increased the incidence and prevalence of infectious and parasitic diseases. The 1878 yellow fever pandemic, which struck most Atlantic societies ranging from West Africa to Brazil and New Orleans, shut down the French administration in Saint-Louis during the summer months and early fall. Subsequent malaria, yellow fever, and cholera epidemics slowed down European commercial activities along the coast and the exploration of the interior of Africa.

Colonial wars during the "scramble for Africa," through the movement of troops and refugee populations, spread viruses, parasites, and bacteria from contact with previously isolated or unexposed people.

Colonial medicine was linked to the colonial state itself and early on focused on preserving the health of the European troops and civilians and the natives who were in contact with them in various capacities (interpreters and other employees, prostitutes, and prisoners) in urban centers, mining compounds, plantations, and missions. But doctors did not have a clear understanding of the etiology and epidemiology of many diseases and, until the mid-nineteenth century, remedies and cures were mainly based on either misinformation or incorrect assumptions. No surgery could be safely performed before the invention of antiseptics (1864). The modus operandi of the major scourges was not known until 1880 for typhoid fever, 1881 and 1901 for yellow fever (vector and virus), 1882 for tuberculosis, 1883 for cholera, 1892 for malaria, and 1894 and 1898 for plague (organism and vector). Only vaccination against smallpox, despite technical problems of transportation and preservation and popular opposition, had some success. Quinine prophylaxis became more effective only with the implementation of vector control measures in the 1890s.

In the absence of effective cures for these diseases, health officials adopted an environmental approach to disease causation and explained the causes of most diseases in terms of contagion and miasmas generated by decaying matter in the tropical environment because tropical Africa was perceived as disease-stricken. Doctors also attributed high mortality to the living and working conditions of the African poor, including overcrowding, unhealthy living conditions, "offensive trades" (slaughtering, tanning, dyeing), inadequate waste disposal, and cemeteries. These miasmatic theories led to strategies of avoidance and segregation (evasive measures, temporary camps in more salubrious locations) as protective measures against disease threats. Military garrison and prisons became the primary sites of medical observation and experimentation. Thus, at the time of growth of the sanitary movement in Europe, colonial officials defined health problems as engineering problems that called for engineering solutions.

Despite its early weaknesses, colonial medicine struggled to establish itself as the official or legal medicine among the Africans who continued to rely on their own theories and perceptions of health and disease. Doctors, missionaries, and administrators waged a propaganda war against indigenous healers, diviners, and other rainmakers, perceived as the main obstacle to the progress of Western medicine, and they eventually drove healers underground.

The bacteriological revolution or the germ theory of the 1880s–1890s provided doctors with a more scientific approach to public health and with the means of social control through the control of crucial techniques (drugs, spectacular surgical interventions), access to "taboo" areas, and participation of physicians in the decision-making process involving the administration of the colonial society. Colonial officials used medicine as a key tool in their "civilizing mission." Missionaries, who saw disease as a tangible manifestation of the evil, approached cure as just the first step in the long process of conversion. The germ theory also inspired policies of separation between white residential areas and "native" quarters in colonial cities.

The expansion of the colonial state in late nineteenth and early twentieth centuries also contributed to the spread of disease, mortality, and morbidity. In Belgian Congo and French Equatorial Africa, for example, the forced collection of rubber and ivory in remote rain forest exposed people to new strains of infectious agents. Sleeping sickness spread along the major waterways and took epidemic proportions. The forced peasant cultivation of commercial crops at the expense of subsistence agriculture led to malnutrition, which compromised people's immune systems and made them vulnerable to diseases. In Southern Africa overcrowding, low wages, poor diets, and unsanitary conditions resulted in the spread of tuberculosis among labor migrants, who brought the disease to rural areas. Nowhere were social tensions and resentments greater than in the colonial cities, whose growth resulted in serious health problems of sewerage, breeding places for mosquitoes, and garbage collection. However, improvements in sanitation, working and living conditions, and nutrition led to the reduction of mortality and morbidity.

World War I disrupted the existing disease control programs. War effort, including labor conscription, the collection of forest products for export, and forced cultivation of cotton and rice, affected the health of millions of Africans and reduced their resistance to malaria, influenza, typhoid fever, and plague, which killed millions of people. Although during the interwar period better public health measures and the development of medical services reduced the incidence of disease and mortality, World War II saw the deterioration of public health conditions.

In the 1940s and 1950s medical advances, especially the widespread use of sulpha drugs and antibiotics, and the research undertaken in the discipline of "tropical medicine" helped reduce the incidence of infectious and parasitic diseases and improve living conditions among the urban residents and an increasing number of rural Africans.

KALALA J. NGALAMULUME

Further Reading

Arnold, D., ed. *Imperial Medicine and Indigenous Societies.* New York: Manchester University Press, 1988.

Curtin, P. D. *Disease and Empire: The Health of European Troops in the Conquest of Africa.* New York: Cambridge University Press, 1998.

Feierman, S., and J. M. Janzen, eds. *The Social Basis of Health and Healing in Africa.* Berkeley: University of California Press, 1992.

Gallagher, N. E. *Egypt's Other Wars: Epidemics and the Politics of Public Health.* New York: Syracuse University Press, 1990.

Lyons, M. *The Colonial Disease: A Social History of Sleeping Sickness in Northern Zaire, 1900–1940.* New York: Cambridge University Press, 1992.

Packard, R. M. *White Plague, Black Labor: Tuberculosis and the Political Economy of Health and Disease in South Africa.* Berkeley: University of California Press, 1989.

Health: Medicine and Disease: Postcolonial

In nearly every statistic, Africans, especially in the sub-Saharan regions, fare worse than any other peoples in rates of mortality, life expectancy, access to clean water and health care. Africa is not a naturally diseased continent, but it is a continent with a great deal of poverty, and Africans' poor health has primarily been a result of poverty. People's health status, the diseases to which they are subjected, and the medical systems upon which they can rely are greatly dependent on their economic status. Africans have suffered and continue to suffer and die from diseases and illnesses which in other places would be preventable and treatable. Infectious and parasitic diseases account for the majority of illness and mortality, and consequently adults in Africa are more likely to die from malaria or tuberculosis while adults in industrialized countries die more often from cancer and heart disease. As a result of economic difficulties African governments in the late 1990s were spending less than ten dollars U.S. per person annually on health.

Nurses in the missionary hospital of Kikoko, Kenya, 1999 © Andrea Kuenzig/Das Fotoarchiv.

Even small amounts of money properly directed can have a significant impact on public health. Unfortunately, the public health and medical systems in most of Africa in the immediate postcolonial period were continuations of the colonial systems and were exactly opposite of what was most needed. Rather than focus on public health, disease prevention, and primary care for all citizens, health policies privileged clinics and hospitals whose purpose was curative medicine. Some countries have continued this focus: as of the late 1990s Liberia, Malawi, Sierra Leone, Tanzania, and Togo all spent over 80 per cent of their national health budgets on hospitals (Turshen, 1999, p.15).

Under the leadership of the World Health Organization, African countries dedicated themselves to a program of Primary Health Care (PHC) with an optimistic goal of Health for All by 2000. The key concept of the PHC initiative has been to move away from hospital-based medicine and toward rural clinics and effective public health measures. Health policy planners in the 1990s, recognizing the influence of indigenous practitioners, tried to incorporate traditional healers, herbalists, and traditional birth attendants into health care efforts and public health campaigns. As a result of policy changes and the impact of antibiotics and immunizations, between 1960 and 1990 the infant mortality rate in Sub-Saharan Africa fell by 37 per cent while the life expectancy increased by twelve years to fifty-two.

African governments and international agencies have recognized the importance of a population's health for the overall development of African countries, but the multiplicity of projects and programs has left a mixed record. While the World Bank and International Monetary Fund in the 1980s were proclaiming themselves dedicated to health for development, they were also insisting that as a component of structural adjustment programs some African countries limit medical care. Large development projects like dams, while intended to be development motors, have often had the unintended consequences of aiding the spread of water-related diseases such as schistosomiasis and malaria.

Projects that focus on individual diseases, such as HIV/AIDS and other sexually transmitted infections, tuberculosis, and smallpox, often come at the detriment of attention to overall health problems, but they have had quite positive effects. International efforts resulted in the eradication of smallpox by 1980, and impressive gains toward the eradication of polio and dracunculiasis/Guinea worm are being made. In the meantime research continues on the development of vaccines to combat malaria and HIV/AIDS. The problem of HIV/AIDS requires special mention, as the preeminent health and development problem facing the continent. By 2002 infection rates in Southern Africa

Ogunlola, a well-known Benin natural healer, and his helpers mixing a lotion; the fat used is shea butter (from the shea nut). He mixes three plants into the fat—his own recipe for curing a variety of skin diseases. Porto Novo, Benin, 2000. © Henning Christoph/Das Fotoarchiv.

in particular had reached astronomical levels, including 20 per cent of adults in South Africa, and over 30 per cent of adults in Botswana, Swaziland, Zimbabwe, and Lesotho. The response to HIV/AIDS by African countries has been mixed, with some leaders like Presidents Moi and Mbeki being slow to deal with the problem. In contrast, Yoweri Museveni of Uganda dedicated his government from the late 1980s to broad public information and prevention efforts that led to a decrease in infection rates, the only country in Africa to show this kind of success. Organizations like UNAIDS, and the Global Fund to Fight AIDS, Tuberculosis, and Malaria, have assisted African health professionals with prevention campaigns, but the cost of drugs for HIV/AIDS limits treatment options.

There are some notable regional differences in health status across the continent. Health conditions for people in North Africa are the best on the continent, excepting the effects of the Algerian violence in the 1990s and the continuing problem of schistosomiasis in Egypt that has been exacerbated by the Aswan High Dam. Across sub-Saharan Africa people in East Africa have enjoyed lower adult mortality and higher life expectancy at age fifteen than people in West or Central Africa. Southern Africans also have lower life expectancies than East Africans, due in large part to the influence of South Africa. South Africa is only just beginning to overcome the legacy of apartheid on health for the majority of its citizens, and the majority of the African population continues to suffer the worst health, with poor housing, unsafe working conditions, and fewer resources for medical care. In addition, countries surrounding South Africa have higher rates of adult male mortality due to illnesses, especially tuberculosis, contracted by migrant laborers who work in South Africa and then return home infected.

In spite of some positive trends on the continent many troubles remain. The biggest difficulties are in areas where armed conflicts continue: the Lakes region of Central Africa and the neighboring Democratic Republic of Congo; Liberia and Sierra Leone; and Sudan. The unrest in these regions is destroying people's ability to farm and has a detrimental impact on their livelihood and health. Hunger and even starvation often result. Troops and refugees moving across wide areas spread disease with them and cause further disruption. Refugee camps are breeding grounds for cholera and other intestinal diseases, while the weakened state of the refugees leaves them vulnerable to common infections. Africans also have some of the same health problems as the rest of the world, including with alcohol, recreational drugs, and tobacco, and the highest rate of mortality from motor vehicle accidents in the world.

Even in relatively stable countries there exist segments of the population whose health suffers and who have less access than others to health care. In most countries the rural populations are at a distinct disadvantage in public health and health care programs. Urban areas are more likely to have sanitation systems and safe water, although these became strained by the large urban growth of the 1980s. Larger cities have also boasted the most extensive health care facilities. Many politicians used government resources, including health care, to reward urban voters, robbing people in the rural areas of their share of medicine and health care.

Women and children have been and continue to be the most vulnerable to illness, and yet the least likely to receive the health care they need. Since women are more likely than men to be mired in poverty they are more susceptible to nearly all health problems and are less able to pay for medical care. Many women are left in the relatively unhealthy rural areas without support while men head to the cities to find work. Women are also hit harder by food shortages and famines, and illness among any in a community increases the burden on women because they are the primary caregivers for sick family and neighbors. Maternal mortality, including deaths from unsafe abortions, is higher in Africa than anywhere. In sub-Saharan Africa "a woman has a 1 in 21 chance of dying of pregnancy-related causes during her reproductive life, compared with 1 in 54 in Asia and 1 in 2,089 in Europe" (Graham, p.106). Recent studies have begun to point attention to domestic violence, rape, and female circumcision/genital mutilation as health issues affecting women across Africa.

African children still suffer from the highest under age five mortality in the world. While diseases like diarrhea, measles, HIV/AIDS, and malaria continue to take their toll, it is recognized that a major underlying cause of high child mortality is overall malnutrition. Researchers are also coming to recognize that special problems exist in deficiencies of protein, iron, vitamin A, and iodine. One response to infant malnutrition has been to promote breastfeeding of children for at least the first six months of life. Breastfeeding has many benefits, helping to protect infants from disease, and as a healthy and safe alternative to expensive, incorrectly prepared commercial infant formulas. One problem with breastfeeding in the last decade has been the recognition of HIV transmission via breast milk. However, given the benefits of breastfeeding, mothers in regions with very high HIV infection rates are urged to continue breastfeeding even with the possible transmission of HIV to the child. Better than any other example, this demonstrates the difficult decisions Africans make daily in their struggle for healthy lives.

MICHAEL W. TUCK

Further Reading

Dugbatey, K. "National Health Policies: Sub-Saharan African Case Studies (1980–1990)." *Social Science and Medicine.* 49 (1999): 223–239.

Falola, T., and D. Ityavyar, eds. *The Political Economy of Health in Africa.* Athens, Ohio: Ohio University Press, 1992.

Garrett, L. *The Coming Plague: Newly Emerging Diseases in a World Out of Balance.* New York: Farrar, Straus and Giroux, 1994.

———. *Betrayal of Trust: The Collapse of Global Public Health.* New York: Hyperion, 2000.

Turshen, M. "African Women and Health Issues." In *African Women South of the Sahara.* 2nd ed. Edited by M.J. Hay and S. Stichter. Harlow, England: Longman, and New York: John Wiley and Sons, 1995.

———. *Privatizing Health Services in Africa.* New Brunswick, N. J., and London: Rutgers University Press, 1999.

Watts, S. "Perceptions and Priorities in Disease Eradication: Dracunculiasis Eradication in Africa." *Social Science and Medicine*, 46, no. 7 (1998): 799–810.

Herding, Farming, Origins of: Sahara and Nile Valley

Africa developed original forms of neolithization, rather than mere diffusion of models from the Middle East. Cattle were locally domesticated, and at least as early as in the Levant, from the aurochs, which were living throughout the whole northern Africa since the beginning of the Quaternary (the current geological period of the last 2 million years). For ovicaprids the issue is less sure, however, imports from the Middle East seem very unlikely. Moreover, the early type of the Saharan sheep is an archaic one, and linguists point out that some very old roots for naming ovicaprids can be found in (reconstructed) African languages from the Afro-Asiatic and Nilo-Saharan blocks. Pastoral nomadism in order to exploit the steppe seems to be a local invention of the Saharan people. As for cultivated plants, the southern Sahara and the Sahel adopted particular African species (millet, sorghum, yam, African rice). Even ceramic was invented in Africa around 8500BCE,[1] approximately 1500 years before it was adopted in the Middle East.

Nile Valley: Egypt and Nubia

Early evidence is lacking for Lower Egypt, where the living sites have been overlaid by recent alluvial deposits. But in Upper Egypt and in Egyptian or Sudanese Nubia, many sites dating from the very end of the Palaeolithic toward 15,000 to 10,000BCE can be found. Their flints are of microlithic type (a type called "epipalaeolithic" or "Late Stone Age") and diverse. Some social features already point to the neolithic way of life. This is called the "Nilotic Adjustment," a broad-spectrum economy notably characterized by semi-sedentism. The sites were specialized—some in collective hunting of the hartebeest or the aurochs, others in bird-hunting, fishing, or in intensive gathering of wild cereals—and people seasonally returned to the same place for the same activity. The notion of "territory" was emerging. The territory now allowed the local accumulation of capital, either material, technical, linguistic, or spiritual, which constituted the identity of an ethnic group spatially confined. It seasonally exploited, with its own culture, the diverse resources of a unique biotope, but with exclusive rights in it. As a consequence, a new social phenomenon developed: war, in the modern meaning, between important groups able to conquer or defend the more advantageous biotopes.

After 10,000BCE, a dark age of several millenia occurred. During the "Great Wet Phase" of the early Holocene (or, the last 10,000 years) the Nile flooded, the alluvial flat was under water, and the sites of the "Nilotic Adjustment" were often swept away. But around 6,000BCE, sedentary groups appear again, population densities are obviously increasing, the first ceramic sherds are visible in the assemblages, and toward 5,000 to 4,000BCE real villages suddenly come to light, fully neolithicized, totally sendentary, and with cemeteries. The villagers raised various domestic animals, such as cattle, sheep, goats, donkeys, and pigs. On the sites of Lower Egypt, wheat, barley, and flax were commonly cultivated, as illustrated by the presence of charred grains, store pits, sickles, and threshing tools. Near 3,800BCE the urban phase (the "Amratian" phase) began, with the foundation of Hierakonpolis in Upper Egypt. This initiates the predynastic period, which will end around 3,000BCE, with the advent of the first pharaohs.

Sudan

As the Great Wet Phase came to an end, the whole southern Sudan was interspersed with lakes and permanent rivers, as were also the whole southern Sahara and the Sahel. Sites were numerous, and the inhabitants were already sedentary or quasi sedentary with a frequent return on the same place. Fishers, mollusk, and land turtle gatherers, and hippopotamus hunters were living there. The archaeological remains include harpoons and fishhooks, as well as pottery from 6,000BCE onward. The latter is usually linked with gathering of wild cereals. However, neither trace of domestic animals nor cultivated cereals has yet been found. These sites have been given the collective name of Aqualithic. According to some linguists, the Aqualithic could have been the origin of the linguistic block of the Nilo-Saharans.

In the upper layers of these Sudanese sites, around 5,000 to 4,500BCE, the first domesticated animals appear. This is the period known as the Shaheinab Neolithic.

Sahara

In the Sahara, the long climatic episode of the Postaterian Hyperarid Phase came to an end around 12,000BCE. At that point, animals repopulated the desert, and toward the beginning of the Holocene, approximately 9,000BCE, humans returned as well. This is the starting point of the Great Wet phase. Until its end, around 6,000BCE, water sources were numerous, and much of the Sahara became a steppe that could be easily traveled in all directions. Traces of hearths or small campsites are found, even in the large plains. However, the living sites are more numerous in the massifs, which received more rain. Hunting was becoming very specialized, often focused upon a single species: mainly the Barbary sheep (*Ammotragus lervia*) or the hartebeest. The collection of wild cereals was increasing, attested to by the abundance of heavy or small grinding stones and pestles. Sedentism was becoming the rule, as in the villages excavated at Amekni (Ahaggar), Ti-n-Torha (Acacus), and Nabta Playa (Egyptian Western Desert), with sometimes constructions in durable materials. Pottery appeared here very early: as soon as 8,500BCE at El Adam (Egyptian Western Desert), and Tagalagal (Air), and around 8,000BCE at Amekni, Ti-n-Torha, and Wadi Akhdar (Gilf Kebir, Egypt).[2]

These early sites, characterized by the presence of pottery but a lack of domestic animals, are grouped by Francophone researchers into a unit named "Saharo-Sudanese Neolithic," which includes the many sites of the Aqualithic in the southern Sahara. Both terms are the names, not of a discrete ethnic group, but of a somewhat artificial set of sites that have some neolithic features in common, notably a frequent pottery with decorations impressed before firing.

After the Great Wet phase, a short arid period occurred, followed by the Neolithic Wet phase (*c*.5,000–3,000BCE). Many sites from the Atlantic up to the eastern Sahara bones of cattle and ovicaprids, both surely domestic, have been found. This period also marks the arrival of rock art throughout the Sahara. Contrary to previously held views, which claimed that the beginnings of the Saharan rock art would go back to preneolithic or even palaeolithic times, the earliest schools date only from the Neolithic Wet phase.

Between approximately 3,000 and 1,500BCE, a severe arid episode occurred: the Postneolithic Arid phase. It put an end to the Saharan pastoral societies. A short wet period around 1,000BCE allowed some Berber groups to reoccupy the massifs. Afterward, aridity steadily increased, and the actual desert became established. During the first millennium BCE, a prestigious domestic animal, the horse, was introduced from an unspecified Mediterranean region, but only for a few centuries. The horse was used for pulling chariots, mainly for racing. More significant was the introduction of the camel, shortly before the beginning of the Common Era. This animal brought a radical transformation in the relations between populations, whether through peaceful exchanges or war.

In terms of cultivated plants, only the palm tree was exploited at an early stage, as illustrated in rock art dating to the Neolithic Wet phase. Even in the oases, the earliest traces of cultivated cereals only go back to dates approaching the first millennium BCE, and evidence is scanty. It seems likely that wheat and barley were cultivated in the Wadi el-Agial (Fezzan), as was millet at Tichitt (Mauritania), and sorghum, millet, and African rice at some sites in the Sahel.

ALFRED MUZZOLINI

Notes

1. All 14C dates in this entry are "calibrated" (i.e., translated into usual calendar years).
2. For French-speaking researchers the criterion of the Neolithic is pottery, for English-speaking researchers it is food-production, i.e., domestic animals or cultivated plants. The two criteria do not necessarily coincide.

See also: **Egypt, Ancient: Agriculture; Egypt, Ancient: Predynastic Egypt and Nubia: Historical Outline; Hunting, Foraging; Iron Age (Early): and Development of Farming in Eastern Africa; Iron Age (Early): Farming, Equatorial Africa; Iron Age (Early): Herding, Farming, Southern Africa.**

Further Reading

Aurenche, O., and J. Cauvin, eds. *Neolithisations*. Archaeological Series, no. 5: Oxford, BAR International Series 516: 1989.

Connor, D. R., and A. E. Marks. "The Terminal Pleistocene on the Nile: The Final Nilotic Adjustment." In *The End of the Palaeolithic in the Old World*, edited by L. G. Strauss. Oxford: BAR International Series 284, 1986.

Gautier, A. "Prehistoric Men and Cattle in North Africa: A Dearth of Data and a Surfeit of Models." In *Prehistory of Arid North Africa*, edited by A. E. Close. Dallas: Southern Methodist University, 1987.

Muzzolini, A. "The Sheep in Saharan Rock Art." *Rock Art Research* 7, no. 2 (1990): 93–109.

Shaw, T., P. Sinclair, B. Andah, and A. Okpoko, eds. *The Archaeology of Africa: Food, Metals, and Towns*. London: Routledge, 1993.

Sutton. J. E. G. "The African Aqualithic." *Antiquity*. 51 (1977): 25–34.

Wendorf, F., R. Schild, and A. E. Close. *Cattle-keepers of the Eastern Sahara: The Neolithic of Bir Kiseiba*. Dallas: Southern Methodist University, 1984.

Herero: *See* Namibia (Southwest Africa): Nama and Herero Risings.

Hieroglyphics: *See* Egypt, Ancient: Hieroglyphics and Origins of Alphabet.

Historiography of Africa

Historiography, in the strict sense, is concerned not with what happened in the past, but with what people believed happened in the past, and most especially, what historians have written about the past. The historical study of Africa has witnessed several phases, notably precolonial, colonial, postcolonial, Marxist, and postmodernist historiographies. These divisions are neither exhaustive nor mutually exclusive.

Precolonial Historiographies

The study of African history dates back to the beginning of history writing itself. Herodotus (484–*c*.424 BCE) visited Egypt and wrote about Egyptian civilization in his seminal work, *The Histories* (*c*.455 BCE). Similar references to Egypt, Ethiopia, and the Maghreb occurred in the works of other classical writers such as Pliny, Strabo, and Ptolemy. These writings, however, had their limitations. They were eclectic and perfunctory, byproducts of occasional journeys, military incursions, and maritime voyages. Besides, the authenticity of their sources and conclusions remain doubtful and questionable. The most valuable of these early accounts was *The Periplus of the Erythraean Sea* (The Voyage of the Indian Ocean), written by an Alexandrian Greek around the year 100. It provided the most comprehensive and illuminating report on the east African coastal trading cities of Azania before the Islamic era.

The advent of Islam brought literacy to many parts of Africa. Notable Islamic scholars like al-Masudi (950), al-Idrisi (1154), and Leo Africanus (1494–1552) all left accounts about African societies that they visited or heard about. Our knowledge of Sudanese empires would be much less comprehensive, but for the works of scholars like al-Bakri (1029–1094) on Ghana, ibn Battuta on Mali, and ibn Fartuwa on Borno, to mention just a few. Added to these are works in African languages, such as Akan, Fulfulde, Yoruba, Hausa, and Swahili, written in the Arabic script.

Alhough the Arabic writers were generally better informed than their classical forbears, their writings had major limitations. They depended mainly on current data and were thus more valuable on contemporary events than past ones, on which they carried out no systematic investigation. Since they obtained much of their information by chance or through hearsay, their accounts were haphazard, presenting a static picture of society, with no attempt made to analyze change over time. Furthermore, since they left no references, it is impossible to check the authenticity of their sources and thus the plausibility of their accounts.

The singular exception was ibn Khaldun of Tunis (1332–1406), who proposed a cyclical concept of history and developed a theory of historical criticism and comparison that was superior to any of his time, thus ranking him among the leading historiographers of all time.

From the fifteenth century, European explorers, traders, sailors, missionaries, and other travelers provide the first dated evidence. Most of these accounts were firsthand observations; a few, like those of Dapper on Dahomey, were compiled from the observations of others. In places like Ethiopia, where an indigenous literacy tradition had flourished for close to two millennia, European missionaries simply plugged themselves into the preexisting traditions of historiography in the indigenous Ge'ez and Amharic languages. In 1681 Job Ludolf, a leading European Orientalist published his full-scale history, *Historia Aethiopia* (History of Ethiopia), at Frankfurt, Germany, the same year that Oliveira de Cadornega produced his *History of the Angola Wars*. While most of these works focused largely on contemporary situations, they contain a great deal of history. By the beginning of the eighteenth century, enough information existed on African history in the records and libraries of Europe for works such as *Universal History*, published in England in the mid-eighteenth century, to give Africa its fair share of space in world history.

The publications of these works occurred at a time when a major shift was taking place in the attitude of

Europeans toward non-European peoples. Centuries of social and economic progress led to a European conception of history in which Europe was the only region of the world that mattered. The most quoted representative of this view was Friedrich Hegel (1770–1831). Writing in his influential book, *Philosophy of History*, he stated categorically that Africa "is not a historical continent," because "it shows neither change nor development," and that its inhabitants were "capable of neither development nor education. As we see them today, so they have always been."

In nineteenth-century Europe, under the influence of the German historian Leopold von Ranke (1795–1886), history ceased to be merely a branch of literature to become a science based on the rigorous analysis of written sources. For Europe, with a plethora of written sources, this was not an issue. However, for much of Africa, where written sources were either entirely lacking or, where they existed, very weak, the possibility of history was thus foreclosed. It is not surprising then that when Professor A. P. Newton was invited in 1923 to give a lecture by the Royal African Society of London, on "Africa and Historical Research," he had no hesitation in promptly informing his august audience that Africa, had "no history before the coming of the Europeans," because, "history only began when men take to writing." Whatever past Africans might have had, before the arrival of white men on their shore, he continued, can only be gleaned "from the evidence of material remains and of language and primitive custom," and such fancies are outside the concerns of historians. Denied recognition and validity in the exclusive club of historians, the study of the African past was thus relegated to archaeologists, anthropologists, linguists, and others. While these disciplines would significantly contribute to the understanding of the African past, they had their limitations. With regard to archaeology, Africa, especially beyond the Nile River valley civilizations, was not an attractive field for archaeological research. This was due to the fact that archaeology as practiced in Europe at this time focused on discovering more about literate societies such as Greece, Troy, and Egypt, which were already well known from abundant written sources. Such societies were not known to be many in Africa. When eventually the archaeologists, such as Louis Leakey and Raymond Dart, became actively involved with Africa, they were preoccupied with finding the origin of man, discovering the missing link in the chain of human evolution. Their concern was more geological than historical. The past that interested them was so distant in time, sometimes dating to two or three million years ago, as to be almost entirely irrelevant to the history and cultures of the peoples and societies of today. Similarly, the existence of a wide variety of groups, cultures, and languages on the continent made Africa a major attraction to anthropologists and several of them soon became actively engaged there. Nevertheless, most of these works suffer major limitations as means for the understanding of the African past. In the first place, anthropologists' main concern was with the timeless ethnographic present. Their representation of the past was often narrow and perfunctory, meant to provide mere background information for the present day societies being studied. More damaging to scholarship was that their writings were often highly speculative and hypothetical, more a reflection of the prevailing prejudices of the European society of their time, than an accurate interpretation of the data. They propounded theories of civilizations and of the direct correlation between race, language, and culture that could not be supported by the available evidence.

The most pernicious of these was the Hamitic hypothesis, which has been soundly refuted. Simply put and as stated by its leading proponent, C. S. Seligman, it espoused the superiority of light-skinned peoples over dark-skinned ones. It argued that "the civilizations of Africa are the civilizations of the Hamites," meaning that all the major advances and innovations in Africa, such as in the areas of iron working, kingship, pastoralism, and architectural forms, were the works of the "better armed as well as quicker witted" conquering Hamites vis a vis the dark and thus (in their view) inferior "agricultural Negroes," who had invented little but were always being impacted upon by their light-skinned and thus superior pastoralist-invaders and rulers. The anthropologists' ethnocentrism, their concern with exotic societies, usually presented as static and unchanging, their readiness to always seek for external explanations and their contempt for oral traditions combined to weaken the usefulness of their work in the attempt to understand the past of Africa. In the same vein, the linguists, who pioneered the study of African languages, were also infected with the same virus that plagued the works of the anthropologists. Unable to transcend the racial and cultural prejudices of their time, they bequeathed to posterity conflicting classifications of African languages that were as eccentric as they were pernicious. These, then, were the scholars and the presuppositions that dominated European-colonial historiography.

Indigenous Historiography and the Era of Decolonization

Partly in response to this attempt to remove Africans from history and partly as expressions of local initiatives and identities, a tradition of indigenous written historiography developed in many parts of Africa. The most famous of these new works was Samuel Johnson's

History of the Yorubas (1897). The measure of Johnson's influence can be seen even today; it is still virtually impossible to carry out any major study of Yoruba history before the colonial period without due reference to his work. Another was Carl Christian Reindorf's *A History of the Gold Coast and Asante*, published in 1895. In Buganda, Appollo Kagwa produced *The Kings of Buganda* in 1901.

These works had many things in common. Their authors were either ministers of the new religion of Christianity or had been much influenced by it. Moralistic in tone and political in orientation, these works were written for a narrow literate elite. Nevertheless, by focusing on individual communities and groups, emphasizing cultural glories and personal initiatives, they reaffirmed the authenticity of oral sources and rejected the colonial monolithic vision of African history.

The triumph of nationalism following the end of World War II added new impetus to this attempt to affirm the authenticity of African history. In England, the School of Oriental and African Studies (SOAS) was established at the University of London in 1948 to meet the growing demand for teaching and research on African history. That same year, Roland Oliver was appointed by SOAS to its first lectureship in African history. Working with Joseph Fage, who joined him at SOAS in 1959, and with the aid of a grant from the Rockfeller Foundation, Oliver started the *Journal African History* (*JAH*) in 1960, the same year the *Cahiers d'etudes Africaines* began its long history as the premier Francophone scholarly journal on Africa. The *JAH* became immediately the combined manifesto and charter for the field. In 1965 Oliver and Fage started editing the eight-volume *Cambridge History of Africa* (1975–1986). By dedicating much of the first volume to the prehistory of the Lower Nile, they ensured that the civilization of ancient Egypt would be seen for the first time in its African context. At about the same time (1963), UNESCO accepted the recommendations of the International Congress of Africanists (1962) and of the OAU (1963) to undertake the writing of a multivolume *General History of Africa*, which would be written from an African-centered perspective and would focus on African peoples rather than Europeans activities in Africa.

From England the study of African history spread rapidly to Europe and the United States. In France the growing interest in African study led to the establishment of the *Institute Francais d'Afrique Noire* in Dakar in 1938. Beginning from 1958 with a series of publications, Jean Suret-Canale, the Marxist geographer, would do in France what Basil Davidson was doing in England: establishing and popularizing the idea of the possibility and validity of the African past. In the United States, the anthropologist Mervin Herskovits, based at Northwestern University in Chicago, Illinois, espoused the study of the African culture. Other scholars, European immigrants, or Americans converted from other specialties, would soon distinguish themselves as pioneers, such as Jan Vansina on oral tradition and Philip Curtin on the slave trade.

Variants in Regional Historiographies: North and Southern Africa

Prior to the nineteenth century, historical writing in North Africa centered on the chronicle of local events, dynasties, and geneologies as well as on hagiographies of rulers and saints. The most valuable exception to this provincial outlook was Ibn khaldun.

By 1800, after centuries of European pressures, a widening of historical imagination began to occur. The onset of French imperialism, which began in Algeria in 1830, Tunisia in 1881, and Morocco in 1912, would inaugurate a new era of Maghrebian historiography, conceived to legitimize French conquest, which was presented as liberation from Turkish oppression and as the triumph of Christian civilization over barbarism. Through the journal, *Revue Africaine*, published at the University of Algiers from 1856 onward, the precolonial history of the Maghreb was presented as one characterized by political regression, economic backwardness, and destructive warfare in contrast to the progressive era of state building and law and order inaugurated by French colonization. In his eight-volume *Histoire ancienne de l'Afrique du Nord* (Early History of North Africa) published in Paris from 1913 and 1928, Stephane Gsell, pioneered the study of ancient history in which French colonialism was presented as the successor to Rome. Maghrebian history was presented as a mortal struggle between the *bled el-makhzen* (the territory of the state) and the *bled es-siba* (the territory of dissidence). The Arabs, Greeks, and Romans represented the former and the Berbers the later; now the French represented the former and the Maghrebian resisters the later. Most European writers glorified the civilization of ancient Egypt but denigrated the Maghreb, which a French writer described in 1958, as "one of those rare Mediterranean countries which made no original contribution to civilization" (J. Despois, *L'Afrique du Nord*, 1958). The only discordant note in this seemingly monolithic colonial disourse was Charles-Andre Julien's *Histoire de l'Afrique du Nord* (1931), but its critical and liberalist perspective ensured its unpopularity during this period.

During the era of decolonization (1956–1970), Maghrebian historians, inspired by the successes of the nationalists, rejected several of the premises of French colonial historiography, casting doubts on its sources, questioning its explanations for economic and political decline, and challenging its understanding of pastoral and Islamic societies. They criticized the *bled al-makhzen/bled es-siba* dichotomy and, like their peers to the south, argued for a new approach focused on "modes of production" in an essentially feudal society.

A multidisciplinary area-study approach that drew inspirations from modernization theories became dominant. The post-1970 period was one of disillusionment, a consequence of the pathetic failure of the nationalist and socialist governments all over the region. Analysis of issues shifted emphasizing the "relations of exploitation" and "underdevelopment" paradigms. As in other parts of Africa, the pervasiveness of dependency, and the persistence of traditional structure and values, led to the decline of the modernization paradigm and of the area-study approach. New questions were asked and grappled with the meaning of the Maghreb (occident, west): who should write its history, and on whose terms and for what purpose? How should the history of North Africa be articulated in relation to the Arab, European, and African worlds? As the issue of identity and religion came to the fore, with militant Islam triumphing in Iran and warring in Algeria, the end result was that North African intellectuals became ever more integrated into the "Arab" and "Islamic" world and more distanced from "Africa." In the last three decades of the twentieth century, North African historiography grew and expanded with hardly any cognizance of relations to other African peoples, and with practically no reference to the massive continental scholarship to the south.

In Southern Africa, the pioneers of colonial historiography were Alexander Wilmot, John Chase, George Theal, and Harry Johnston. Their writings were pro-empire and pro-British settlers. Afrikaners were presented as obscurantist oppressors of the indigenous peoples. This orthodoxy was soon challenged by a series of publications by Afrikaners documenting British injustices and the accumulative grievances of the Boers. Most notable of these were S. J. du Toit, *The History of Our Land in the Language of Our People*, published in Afrikaans in 1877 and the scathing criticism of British policies to the Afrikaners by J. C. Smuts, *A Century of Wrong*, published at the end of the Anglo-Boer war (1899–1900).

In the succeeding decades, more historical works would appear. The main features of these histories are clear. Almost without exception, they all focus on the South African white settlers, their conquests, and industrialization. The African majority was regarded as non-population, a part of the landscape to be occupied, used, dispossessed, and discarded. Its history was either completely ignored or, as in C. F. J. Muller's *500 Years: A History of South Africa* (1969), relegated to a 20-page appendix in a 467-page book.

In the rare cases where African societies received attention, their history was distorted. Their ways of life were presented as monolithic, static, and unchanging. Overworked clichés such as listless, impudent, fractious, thieving, savage, harmless, docile, and others were applied to describe black Africans. The oppressive, dehumanizing, and racist nature of white rule was often ignored, while its debt to the indigenous population, most especially the Khoisans, was rarely acknowledged. The publication of the two-volume *The Oxford History of South Africa* (1969, 1971), edited by Leonard Thompson and Monica Wilson, signaled, especially among historians resident outside apartheid South Africa, a new departure in the representation of the south African past.

Postcolonial Africanist Historiography

Upon independence, one of the immediate challenges facing the new African elite was to achieve in the historical field what they had achieved in the political one: restore Africa to history and history to Africans. Achieving this required, and still requires, reasserting once and for all the authenticity of nonwritten sources, establishing the historicity of African societies before the coming of the Europeans, and seizing the initiatives in the rewriting and teaching of African history from an African perspective.

Within Africa, the new radical approach was pioneered by a crew of newly trained young historians working mostly in the recently established University Colleges on the continent. They produced a stream of historical works during the 1960s and 1970s that remarkably demonstrated that Africans were not a "people without history." By amassing (and utilizing) a wealth of data on ancient civilizations and powerful kingdoms in Africa, they showed that African societies like other societies had well-developed historical consciousness that were conceptualized, preserved, and transmitted through oral traditions, as well as, in some cases, through hieroglyphics or Arabic writings. The most influential of these schools of history was the Ibadan History Series, published under the leadership of Kenneth Dike and Jacob Ade Ajayi. Similarly, the Legon History Series, based at the University of Ghana, published a number of pioneering works on the history of the Akan-speaking peoples and their neighbors. In East Africa, Terence Ranger and a coterie of scholars such as Alan Ogot, Arnold Temu, Isara Kimambo, and others made significant progress in the study of precolonial history. The works of these scholars were ably complemented by those of others based outside of Africa, such as Basil Davidson, John Hunwick, Ivor Wilks, Catherine Coquery-Vidrovitch, Shula Marks, and Robin Law. With regard to prehistory, a chain of archaeological discoveries by and writings of Leakey, Desmond Clark, Peter Shinnie, and others have significantly improved our understanding of early man, while pushing further back the antiquity of the African past.

In addition to turning colonial history on its head, these scholars also made significant impact in the area of methodology. By combining the techniques of the anthropologist, the historical linguist, the oral historian, the archaeologist, the paleontologist, the plant geneticist, the art historian, and others, they demonstrated the complexity and multidimensional nature of the African past, while setting a new charter and providing a new guideline for the recovery and reconstruction of the history of nonliterate societies everywhere. The groundbreaking work, *Oral Tradition* (1961), by Vansina, the result of his fieldwork among the Kuba of equatorial Africa, became a classic, the standard work in the field, widely used and cited by scholars working in and on many societies all over the world. Despite the vigorous assault mounted by the structuralists, inspired by the writings of Claude Levi-Strauss and Luc de Heusch in France, on the validity of oral traditions as sources, they were continually relied upon in the reconstruction of the African past. For the African of the newly independent nations, the affirmation that African peoples and societies were just like those of Europeans, in the sense that they created states, empires, and kingdoms, built civilizations, invented writings, practiced democracy and commerce, had religion and art, filled him with confidence for the present and hope for the future.

Nevertheless, while it is important to underscore the achievements of these pioneer Africanists, their contribution must not be overemphasized. As an ideological response to western historiography, the new Africanist history succeeded in destroying the picture of tribal stagnation and lack of initiatives in Africa, but beyond this it did not go far enough. Its definition of what constitutes history was still defined in Western terms. It proved that Africa had a history and deserved the respect of others because it did what Europeans did and had what Europeans had. This approach led to the privileging of large-scale societies and the denigration of small-scale ones. The former were considered more advanced along the stages and path of human progress, while the later variously described as stateless or acephalous and presented as "anachronisms" and "survivals," considered to be at the lowest level of social evolution. Thus, we now know more about rulers rather than the subjects, about cities rather than the country. Moreover, a perusal of the published titles showed that in the early years, the major attraction was interactions with Europeans and on the post-1800 period, on which a plethora of missionary and colonial archival written sources exist. In spite of Vansina, only a few scholars like Ogot in East Africa or Ebere Alagoa in West Africa focused on topics requiring exclusive use of oral traditions.

The nationalistic need to promote patriotism, national unity, and nation building in the newly independent states, led to a focus on unity rather than discord in the selection and analysis of data. In their sustained search for a useable past, the nationalist historians moved roughshod over the terrain of evidence, extrapolating firm evolutionary trends, ignoring awkward facts, or dismissing them as extraneous and anomalous. The problem was not one of deliberate distortion. It was, rather, a problem of conscious selection determined by value-laden criteria of what history should be taught to meet the needs of the new nations and which history should rather be forgotten. In this brave new world, badly in need of models, archetypes, and heroes, everything hinged on interpretation. The rebels of the colonial era became protonationalists, those who fought European conquests like Jaja of Opobo, Urabi Pasha of Egypt, and Samori Toure of the Madinka became the first nationalists; slavery became a "form of social oppression"; slave raids and conquests became state formation efforts; and authoritarianism became a strategy of nation building. In the attempt to emphasize Africa, the new history dismissed European colonialism as a mere episode in the long stretch of African history, a view that failed to underscore how consequential and far-reaching has been the transformation occasioned by this "brief" encounter with the West. Similarly, in spite of pretensions to the contrary, this was still history from above, focused largely on the male and ruling political elites, with little acknowledgement of the role of women and the importance of gender and class. By concentrating on narrow political themes, the new history ignored social and economic forces.

Era of Disillusionment and the Onset of Marxist Historiography

The sociopolitical crises of the 1960s also created a major crisis in Africanist historiography. The failure of the new African political elites to deliver on the promises of independence, the rampart corruption, the gross economic mismanagement, the political instability, the social malaise, as well as the resilience and pervasiveness of the force of neocolonialism, resulted in a profound sense of disillusionment that had major reverberations in the perception of the African past. The idea of progress in history began to give way to a feeling of nihilism; the optimism offered in the works of scholars like Omer-Cooper and Ajayi began to turn to pessimism; and where there had been consensus, discord and confusion began to reign. In a queer paradox, the term "Africanist" became a term of opprobrium. In place of the celebration of the African achievement, came stinging indictment of the new ruling elite and their neocolonialist collaborators. The experiments with European economic and political models had not worked; Europe could no longer serve as the epitome of historical progress and self-definition. The golden age of Africanist historiography had come home to roost.

With the preoccupation with the dual problem of continuing poverty and dependency, a new historiography inspired by the ideology of development came to the fore. The most powerful statement of the new Marxist school was issued with the publication of Walter Rodney's *How Europe Underdeveloped Africa* in 1972. Rodney's thesis was as radical as it was far-reaching. In the preface to the book, Rodney stated, unequivocally that "African development is possible only on the basis of a radical break with the international capitalist system, which has been the principal agency of underdevelopment of Africa over the last five centuries." The new theory of the development of underdevelopment insisted that the West had gained an undue advantage through its domination (by means of the slave trade and colonialism) by which it had crippled and continued (through neocolonialism) to compromise Africa's ability to progress. Confronted with the problem of defining what constitute "class," Coquery-Vidrovitch suggested that since classes were unknown in precolonial Africa, the terms "mode of production" and "relations of exploitations" should be applied to the African experience, even though the specific features and varieties of these expressions remained in dispute. This new school focused on colonial rather than precolonial history, except as a background to understanding the present. It is also reductionist in two ways. First, while it illuminates widespread patterns, it obscured specific and concrete historical situations and failed to account for the wide range of varieties in African social and economic formations. Second, its sweeping generalization led it to ignore or even deny the relevance of African cultural makeup in the formation of their class and historical consciousness. These weaknesses would, among other factors, draw African scholars to the works of Antonio Gramsci, in whose recognition of the centrality of the manipulation of cultural norms in the maintenance of power hegemony and relations of oppression, they found more plausible.

Nevertheless, with its much greater elucidatory models and its materialist insights, the success of the Marxist approach to the study of the African past can be seen first in provoking a more critical and more holistic approach to the study of colonialism and African relations with the West, and second in the broadening of the field of historical production to areas that were shortchanged by the nationalist-liberalist approach. The works of Claude Meillassoux on *Maidens, Meal, and Money* (1981), Lucette Valensi's innovative *Tunisian Peasants in the Eighteenth and Nineteenth Century* (1985), Judith Tucker's trailblazing *Women in Nineteenth Century Egypt* (1985), Charles van Onselen on sharecropping in apartheid South Africa (*The Seed is Mine*, 1996), Steven Feierman on peasant intellectuals, John Iliffe's *The African Poor: A History* (1987), Isichei's groundbreaking survey, *A History of African Societies to 1870* (Cambridge, 1997), as well as the price-winning Heinemann Social History of Africa series, edited by Allen Isaacman and Jean Hay, continue to attest to the resilience of this new and vigorous attempt to write history from below.

The eclipse of a Marxist-inspired view of history did not mean an end to the crisis in Africanist historiography. The discovery by the embattled historical materialists during the late 1980s of Michael Foucault, with his insistence on the centrality of ideology in the imposition and maintenance of hegemony, once again jolted the field and challenged the attempt to dismiss Marxist interpretation as a mere "superstructure" or "false consciousness." The result was a series of introspective essays by leading historians on the continuing crisis in the field. Most notable among these essays, some of which began to appear in the *African Studies Review* from 1981, were written by Fredrick Cooper on the economy, John Lonsdale on social processes, Bill Freund on labor (1984), Sara Berry on agriculture (1984), Ranger on religion (1985), Joseph Miller (1980) and Bogumi Jewsiewicki (1989) on historiography, and Isaacman on rural protests (1990). Similarly, Abdallah Laroui's *The Crisis of the Arab Intellectual: Traditionalism or Historicism?* (1976) underscored the continuing soul-searching and crises of identity among North African scholars, many of whom began to advocate a more rigorous exploration of "Maghrebian Islam" as an antidote to the continuing realities of neocolonialism and dependency.

Postmodernist Historiography

The widespread mood of introspection, combined with the resurgence of ideological underpinnings of historiography and power relations, led to the emergence of a new approach, "deconstruction" or "postmodernism." In its basic form, the new theory states that the past or consciousness of it does not exist by itself, except as an ideological product of the present, whose power relations and realities it reflects. And even if the past exists, it is directly unknowable, since only traces of it are accessible to readers for their interpretation, "invention," or "deconstruction," a process that can never be truly objective, since it is constrained by the individual's necessarily subjective experience and perceptions. In such a situation, the line separating fact from fiction is very thin and the search for consensus is both hypocritical and dangerous, an attempt to create a false hegemony in the subjective and conflicting myriads of views constituting the archaeology of knowledge. The application of these ideas to oral traditions led to their dismissal by anthropologists as nothing more than subjective expressions of contemporary realities. As this debate intensified, and as notable scholars of African history like David Cohen and Ranger began to subscribe to the postmodernist thesis, others like Joseph Miller suggested that oral traditions be viewed as valuable expressions of African mentalities, rather than as objective mirrors of a collective, historical past.

Following in the wake of the anthropologists and the literary critics were the philologists and the philosophers. The most notable of these was Valentine Mudimbe, a Zairian, driven into exile in the United States by the terror campaigns of Mobutu Sese Seko in 1981. In a series of essays, of which the most influential was *The Invention of Africa: Gnosis, Philosophy, and the Order of Knowledge* (1988), he argued that the ideas and interpretations of African scholars were the product of Western academic discourse, whose notion of what constitute scientific knowledge lacked any universally acceptable validity and should be rejected. It is yet to be seen how significantly the postmodernist view will affect the research and writing of African history; nothing so far has come to indicate that its impact will be as threatening as the materialist approach, whose ferocity it has somehow muted.

Afrocentricity

In the meantime, in the United States, following closely in the literary and ideological traditions of *négritude*, espoused by Aime Ceasaire and Leopold Senghor, and of Pan-Africanism, espoused by Marcus Garvey and William E. B. Du Bois, African Americans from the 1960s onward began to associate themselves more closely with Africa. This growing interest led to the formulation of a new theoretical approach to the study of Africa, Afrocentrism, or Afrocentricism. The new approach was conceived as a radical critique of the dominant Eurocentric epistemology, with its tendentious claim to universality and its representation of the African experience as by-product of European experience, and as tangential to the historical process. Afrocentrism insists that for a form of historical discourse to have meaning and relevance to Africa, it must assault Eurocentric intellectual hegemony and discard its modes of explanation, and become Africa-centered, meaning it must make African ideas, interests, and presuppositions the core of its analysis. Furthermore, especially as enunciated by its leading exponent, Molefi Kete Asante, the new approach must have as its intellectual foundation and source of inspiration the civilization of ancient Egypt, in the same way as Greece and Rome serve as the basis of European scholarship.

The cultural and intellectual appropriation of ancient Egypt did not begin with the Afrocentrists. Cheikh Anta Diop, the Senegalese historian and Egyptologist, was the first to set out, in a series of works, the most notable of which was *The African Origin of Civilization: Myth or Reality* (1974), to prove that the "ancient Egyptians were Negroes," and that "ancient Egypt was a Negro civilization." More recently, the Afrocentric claim was strengthened by the publication of Martin Bernal's *Black Athena: The Afroasiatic Roots of Classical Civilization: The Fabrication of Ancient Greece, 1785–1985* (1987). Bernal argued that Eurocentric scholars have over the years deliberately refused to acknowledge that ancient Greece derived a lot of inspiration from ancient Egypt. Consequently, he agreed with Diop that since Europe owes its civilization to Africa, the black world should reject its current representation "as an insolvent debtor" to the West and should see itself as "the very initiator of western civilization."

The postulations of these ideas have generated heated controversies among scholars. Few will argue with the need for African studies to be African-centered, but many have warned against replacing a discredited theory of white supremacy with an equally disreputable black supremacy discourse. The growing popularity of the Afrocentric tenets among African Americans is largely a function of the continuing relevance and salience of race in Africa's struggle for respect, equality, and empowerment in the Americas, nearly a century and a half after the formal abolition of slavery. On the other hand, the perfunctory interest shown by most African scholars in the debate is indicative of the limited relevance of race to their current preoccupation with other more pertinent sociopolitical challenges on the continent. There is also the fear that privileging ancient Egypt as the reference point for validating African culture will be to subscribe to a Eurocentric definition of what constitute civilization, and its assumption that ancient Egyptian civilization was superior to that of black Africa.

Conclusions: "What History for Which Africa?"

The combination of all these challenges has strengthened the development of African historiography. Old themes are being reinterpreted, while new and neglected issues are receiving attention. There is a new emphasis on the study of biographies, an approach to the study of the past that was part of the casualties of the assault on the nationalist historiographical focus on "great men." The study of women, their role in industrialization and the anti-apartheid struggle in South Africa, the intersection of gender and Islam in western and northern Africa, the impact of structural adjustment programs on women, and the need for a fully gendered history of men has received attention. The study of peasants as farmers and as intellectuals, of historical demography, of liquor and leisure, of the history of health and diseases as well as of climate and ecology show how far scholars have gone to push the boundaries of African historical universe.

In South Africa, the end of apartheid and the onset of majority rule in the mid-1990s, led the Afrikaners to begin to repudiate their own history, while the debates continue as to how the past of this troubled region of Africa should be written as it strives to heal its wounds and reconcile its peoples. The collapse of communism in Eastern Europe and of the Soviet Union as well as the failure of socialist experiments in Africa started to elicit revisionist responses from neo-Marxist historians of Africa. The resurgence of ethnosectarian crises and violence in multiethnic nations like Rwanda, Algeria, and Nigeria and in monoethnic countries like Somalia has led to the questioning of earlier assumptions about "tribalism" and has resuscitated ethnicity as a major specialty in African study.

More pertinent to the future of the profession is the fact that the gnawing economic and political problems facing most African countries today have led to the migration of many talented scholars from Africa to the United States, in search not so much of "greener pastures" but of security and freedom. With Europe increasingly turning its back on African studies, scholars in North America are now taking the lead in determining the agenda and future directions of African historiography. The emergence of many robust subfields and specialties, and the seemingly bewildering fragmentations, especially from the 1980s onward, should be seen as a sign of growing strength, though this should not be allowed to degenerate into abstruse specializations, resulting in tunnel vision and arcane isolation. The greatest danger, at least before a turn around is witnessed in the fate of the African continent, will be for scholars of African history, now mostly based in Western institutions, to continue to write "esoteric" or "academic" history, meant principally to be read by their peers in the West, a history oblivious to the needs and realities of Africa and totally inaccessible and thus irrelevant to the Africans themselves. Today the study of the African past may appear to be in a state of flux, but this should not necessarily be seen as a sign of crisis or as an untoward development. After decades of progress, occasional pause for critical questioning and soul-searching to assess progress and chart a new course in response to our understanding of the past, the challenges of the present and our hope for the future—is a welcome and necessary development.

FUNSO AFOLAYAN

Further Reading

Asante, M. K. *The Afrocentric Idea.* Philadelphia: Temple University Press, 1997.

Bernal, M. *Black Athena: The Afroasiatic Roots of Classical Civilization: The Fabrication of Ancient Greece, 1785–1985.* New Brunswick: Rutgers University Press, 1987.

Davidson, B. *The Search for Africa: History, Culture, Politics.* New York: Times Books, 1994.

Diop, C. A. *The African Origin of Civilization: Myth and Reality.* New York: Lawrence Hill, 1974.

Falola, T., ed. *African Historiography: Essays in Honour of J. F. Ade Ajayi.* London: Longman, 1993.

Howe, S. *Afrocentrism: Mythical Pastsa and Imagined Homes.* London and New York: Verso, 1998.

Isichei, E. *A History of African Societies to 1870.* Cambridge: Cambridge University Press, 1997.

Jewsiewicki, B., and D. Newbury, eds. *African Historiographies: What History for Which Africa?* Beverly Hills, Calif.: Sage Publications, 1986.

Mudimbe, V. I. *The Invention of Africa: Gnosis, Philosophy, and the Order of Knowledge.* Bloomington: Indiana University Press, and London: James Currey, 1988.

Neale, C. *Writing "Independent" History: African Historiography, 1960–1980.* Westport, Conn.: Greenwood Press, 1985.

Newton, A. P. "Africa and Historical Research." *Journal of African Society.* 22 (1922–1923): 267.

Nuttall, S., and C. Coetzee, eds. *Negotiating the Past: The Making of Memory in South Africa.* Cape Town: Oxford University Press, 1998.

Oliver, R. *In the Realms of Gold: Pioneering in African History.* Madison: The University of Wisconsin Press, 1997.

Ranger, T., ed. *Emerging Themes of African History.* Nairobi: East African Publishing House, 1968.

Vansina, J. *Living with Africa.* Madison: The University of Wisconsin Press, 1994.

Historiography of Western Africa, 1790s–1860s

The foundation of European historiography of Western Africa was laid in the sixteenth century by Leo Africanus and Luis del Mármol Carvajal. According to them, the inhabitants of Sudanic West Africa had been uncivilized until they were subjugated by "King Joseph" of Morocco, reflecting the historical Almoravid ruler Yūsuf bin Tāshfīn (d. 1106). Subsequently the "Land of the Blacks" was divided up among five "Libyan" tribes, referring to Berbers, nomads of the Sahara, who converted the Africans to Islam and taught them various useful skills, including agriculture and commerce. The Libyan tribes ruled until they were driven to the desert by Sunni Ali (*c.*1464–92), who established the Songhay Empire in the Niger bend area. He was succeeded by his general

Abuacre Izchia (Askia Muhammad Ture, 1493–1528), who reigned the powerful and prosperous "Empire of Timbuktu." This interpretation of West African history before the Portuguese discoveries was repeated in all European works describing Africa.

Interest in West African history started increasing in Europe toward the end of the eighteenth century. There were two reasons for this. One was the more widespread interest in African geography and nature; the interior of the continent was still an unknown territory. This interest culminated in 1788 in the founding of the African Association, which equipped many explorers to unveil the secrets of West Africa, the greatest of which were considered to be the course of the Niger and the mysterious Timbuktu. Although most of the explorers proved to be unsuccessful, the reports sent by Simon Lucas, Daniel Houghton, Mungo Park, and Frederick Horneman contained significant new information.

Another reason for increased interest in Africa was the contemporary development of Oriental studies in Europe. The earliest example of medieval Arabic sources for African geography to become available in Europe was the "Book of Roger," written in 1154 in Sicily by al-Idrīsī. Its abridged Arabic version was printed in 1592 in Rome; a Latin translation of the same text appeared in 1619 in Paris. al-Idrīsī described the conditions of Sudanic Africa as they were in his time. European readers, however, were incapable of combining his information with the existing picture of West African geography, as they had no clear ideas on the exact locations of the towns and kingdoms al-Idrīsī described (such as Ghana, Takrur, Wangara, and Awdaghust), which were not mentioned by Africanus and Mármol. Other medieval Arabic sources for African geography, which were available to eighteenth-century European scholars, were extracts from the works of Abū 'l-Fidā', Ibn al-Wardī, al-Mas'ūdi, al-Bakuwī, and al-Maqrīzī. A critical study of al-Idrīsī's description of Africa was published in 1791 by Johannes Melchior Hartmann.

The first European writer who tried to reconstruct the history of Sudanic West Africa with the help of Arabic material was Francis Moore, who spent five years on the Gambia. Moore's journal, *Travels into the Inland Parts of Africa*, appeared in 1738. Moore believed that the kingdom of Ghana, described by al-Idrīsī as the paramount kingdom in the "Land of the Blacks," was the same as the kingdom of Yany on the upper Gambia River. This identification was based on the phonetic resemblance between the two names, Ghana and Yany. Otherwise Moore repeated the story of King Joseph and the five Libyan tribes, which he took as historical fact.

The "Question of Ghana"—that is, its location and existence—reentered public debate some fifty years later. In 1790, James Rennell (1742–1830) completed a short essay, *Construction of the Map of Africa*, in which he attempted to summarize the existing knowledge on the interior geography of West Africa. Rennell followed the seventeenth-century cartographic tradition of placing the Ghana of al-Idrīsī to the east of Timbuktu, where it was identified, on the ground of phonetic resemblance, as the kingdom of Cano described by Africanus and Mármol. (European geographers were still unaware of the existence of the real Kano in Hausaland; the location of Cano was based on Leo's description of the fifteen kingdoms that he placed along the imaginary West African branch of the Nile.) Rennell returned to the subject eight years later in his more detailed paper, *Geographical Illustrations of Mr. Park's Journey*, in which he elaborated his hypothesis about the location of Ghana. He believed that the Ghana of al-Idrīsī was the mighty Ogané, whose domination was recognized (according to the sixteenth-century Portuguese author João de Barros) by the king of Benin near the Atlantic coast. Thereafter, Ghana had declined and eventually became a province of the kingdom of Katsina. The paramount state of the West African interior was the kingdom of Timbuktu; this was confirmed by Mungo Park who had reported that its ruler possessed "immense riches." Of ancient Mali, Rennell wrote hardly anything. This is understandable, for the available Arabic sources did not mention Mali at all, and the descriptions of Melli by Africanus and Mármol suggested that it was a kingdom of minor importance. According to Rennell, Melli was to the east of Timbuktu.

The key that makes medieval Arabic sources for the history of Sudanic West Africa understandable is the *Book of the Routes and Realms*, written in about 1068 in Islamic Spain by al-Bakrī. The importance of this book is that al-Bakrī is the only Arabic author who described ancient Ghana and its location in details. A copy of his book was acquired in Tripoli by the Swedish consul Jacob Gråberg af Hemsö. A brief French translation of al-Bakrī's description of Ghana appeared in 1825. It was followed in 1831 by a much longer French translation based on a manuscript copy preserved in the Bibliothèque Nationale, covering the entire Sudanic Africa and the Maghrib. An Arabic edition was published in 1857. A new French translation appeared in 1858–1859, which finally made al-Bakrī a popular source among European historians of Western Africa.

The first scholar to use the work of al-Bakrī was Friedrich Stüwe, whose study on the long distance trade of the Arabs during the 'Abbasid period was published in Germany in 1836. The emphasis in Stüwe's study is on Arab commercial enterprise in Eastern Europe and Asia, but it also deals with the development of trans-Saharan trade. Stüwe was, however, incapable of finding the correct parallels between current geographical knowledge of the West African interior—which had increased considerably on account of the journeys of exploration by René Caillié, Dixon Denham, Hugh Clapperton, and the brothers Laing—and the information provided by the medieval Arabic authors. The greatest weakness in Stüwe's study (and certainly the reason why it was so rapidly forgotten) was that he stuck to the old hypothesis of Ghana being identified as the city of Kano in Hausaland. Stüwe combined the few dates he could glean from the works of al-Bakrī and al-Idrīsī with the interpretation of West African history by Leo Africanus. He correctly noticed that Ghana had been the paramount kingdom, but it had declined during the Libyan domination. The most original part in Stüwe's book was his hypothesis that Islam had spread in Sub-Saharan Africa peacefully through the trans-Saharan commercial contacts. This hypothesis was contrary to the tradition that it was the Libyan conquerors that introduced Islam and the basic elements of civilization to the blacks. Of ancient Mali, Stüwe said nothing (nor could he, as he had no relevant sources available to him).

The honor of establishing the modern historiography of West Africa belongs to William Desborough Cooley (1795–1883) whose *Negroland of the Arabs* appeared in 1841. It is difficult to say how Cooley had became interested in this subject, even though he had already distinguished himself by producing several publications on the geography of Eastern Africa. We may assume that Cooley was influenced by his friend Pascal de Gayangos, a Spanish Orientalist, who owned a large collection of Arabic geographical manuscripts. Another reason might have been that the recent European voyages to Timbuktu, Bornu, and Hausaland, together with the appearance of the works of al-Bakrī and Ibn Baţţūţa (an abridged Latin translation in 1818; an abridged English translation in 1829), had made speculation on the early history of West Africa fashionable. It is noteworthy that the three pioneering works, written by Stüwe (1836), Cooley (1841), and Wappäus (1842), were published almost simultaneously.

Cooley's aim was to establish the historical geography of Sudanic Africa on a solid basis by carefully examining all the available Arabic material and by comparing it to the existing European knowledge of the area. Cooley abandoned all the previous hypotheses concerning the locations of Ghana and Mali; that is, he gave up Leo Africanus who had dominated European geography of Sudanic Africa for three centuries. The real novelty was Cooley's method, which he referred to as the "principle of rectification of sources." In practice this meant that the interpreter of sources had to understand not only the language of the original text (not to mention the other languages through which the information had been transferred) but also the theoretical and other preconceptions of the original author: today, this would be called contextual consideration.

Following his method, Cooley preferred to rely upon Arabic manuscripts rather than their often inaccurate and abridged translations. This was possible with the help of his learned friend Gayangos. The basis of Cooley's sources was the works of the three Arabic authors: al-Bakrī, Ibn Baţţūţa, and Ibn Khaldūn. The importance of al-Bakrī is noted above; the importance of Ibn-Baţţūţa is the fact that he provides us with an eyewitness account of Mali in the 1350s, whereas Ibn Khaldūn provides us with a chronology of Malian rulers from the mid-thirteenth century to the year 1396.

Cooley managed to make order out of the early history of Sudanic West Africa and this is what makes his work valuable. His work provided what was then the only reasonably reliable account of the West African empires and his readers had a good cause to doubt that African society was a changeless barbarism. Although Cooley's conclusions on the locations of the Sudanese kingdoms and cities were later proved to be false (he placed Ghana to the west of Lake Faguibine, Takrur close to Jenne, and Awdaghust in the oasis of Mabrouk), his chronology for the history of ancient Ghana and Mali is still accepted with minor corrections. Cooley also established several important hypotheses, such as the three conquests of Ghana by the Almoravids (1076), the Susu (1203), and Mali (1240). The fact that some of these hypotheses are erroneous is not Cooley's fault: in relation to the available sources his reasoning is sound. We can only blame the succeeding generations of historians of Western Africa who did not bother to evaluate the reliability of Cooley's hypotheses, despite possessing much a broader body of evidence.

In 1842 the German geographer Johann Eduard Wappäus (1812–79) published his study, which bore a title almost identical to that of Cooley's, *Untersuchungen über die Negerländer der Araber*, although the latter part of this book examines the Italian, Spanish, and Portuguese overseas trade in the late Middle Ages and the subsequent Portuguese discoveries. Wappäus was aware of Cooley's *Negroland*, for he refers to it in his preface. Nevertheless, he had apparently received Cooley's book too late to be able to discuss its contents properly in his own study. On the other hand, Wappäus praised Stüwe's *Handelszüge* for being the first serious study in this field, even if he considered it gravely mistaken in many details. In reality, Cooley's *Negroland* made Wappäus's work outdated even before its publication.

The Arabic sources used by Wappäus were almost the same as those familiar to Cooley, although he relied upon printed translations only. Wappäus considered al-Bakrī to be the most important source for Ghana, which (according to Wappäus) was the existing city of Jenne in the middle Niger valley. Sufficient proof for this identification was the congruence between al-Idrīsī's information about the riverine location of Ghana and René Caillié's recent description of Jenne. Regarding the early history of West Africa, Wappäus said surprisingly little. There is no clear chronology in his work, nor could there be, since he did not know Ibn Khaldūn's universal history, *Kitāb al-'Ibar* (Arabic and French editions were published in 1847–1851 and 1852–1856, respectively).

Another early German interpretation of early West African history was written by Friedrich Kunstmann, whose lectures on the subject at the Royal Bavarian Academy of Sciences were published in 1853 with the title *Afrika vor den Entdeckungen der Portugiesen*. There is nothing that suggests that Kunstmann knew Cooley's *Negroland*, although he cited Wappäus and hence he must have seen the latter's reference to Cooley in the preface. Likewise, *Negroland* was unfamiliar to the American Revered J. Leighton Wilson, who claimed in his *Western Africa: Its History, Condition and Prospects* (1856) that black Africans were quite unable to establish any large political organizations, with the exception of Ashanti and Dahomey.

Cooley's ideas were developed further and popularized by the German explorer Heinrich Barth (1821–1865) who traveled in Bornu and Hausaland in 1849–1855 and spent nearly a year in Timbuktu. Barth's journal, *Travels and Discoveries in North and Central Africa*, was no bestseller, but the few European scholars interested in African geography and history recognized its value. Barth's information about West African history is both in the main text and the numerous appendices, which are attached to each of five volumes of his journal. The most important is the "Chronological Table of the History of Songhay and the Neighboring Kingdoms" in volume four. This lengthy table follows the history of Western and Central Sudan from 300 to 1855 without any major interruptions. Most of Barth's information about Ghana and Mali is taken directly from Cooley, but Barth was able to supplement the latter's chronology with his own speculations about the origins of Ghana and with a few details on the decline of Mali in the fifteenth century. Barth's greatest achievement, however, was that he uncovered the history of the two other great Sudanese empires that had been flourishing in the sixteenth century: Songhay and Bornu. This was possible because Barth had managed to obtain some copies of the hitherto unknown Arabic chronicles written by local Muslim scholars. The most important of these chronicles were a list of the kings of Bornu and the *Ta'rīkh al-Sūdān*, written in about 1652/55 in Timbuktu by 'Abd al-Rahmān al-Sa'di, which describes the history of Songhay Empire under the Askia-dynasty. German translations of these two sources appeared in 1852 and 1855, respectively.

If Barth's journey to the African interior completed the ancient European exploration into Timbuktu and Niger, his chronological table did the same for the historiography of the ancient Sudanese empires. Nineteenth-century Africanists were content with his conclusions for the next five decades. It was impossible to add anything new to Barth's table of early West African history by using the existing Arabic and European material. It also appears that speculation about the history of Sudanese empires became a less popular and intriguing topic after the emphasis in European exploration of Africa shifted from the Niger to the Nile. Only the discovery of local West African oral historical traditions and the beginning of the first archaeological excavations in the western Sahel at the turn of this century brought about significant changes in historiography.

PEKKA MASONEN

Further Reading

Barth, H. "A General Historical Description of the State of Human Society in Northern Central Africa." *Journal of the Royal Geographical Society.* 30 (1860): 112–128.

———. *Travels and Discoveries in North and Central Africa Being a Journal of an Expedition Undertaken under the Auspices of H. B. M's Government in the Years 1849–1855.* London: Frank Cass, Centenary Editions, 1965.

Cooley, W. D. *The Negroland of the Arabs Examined and Explained; or An Inquiry into the Early History and Geography of Central Africa.* London, 1841; 2nd ed. with a bibliographical introduction by John Ralph Willis, London: Frank Cass, 1966.

Masonen, P. *The Negroland Revisited: Discovery and Invention of the Sudanese Middle Ages.* Helsinki: Finnish Academy of Science and Letters, 2000.

Moore, F. *Travels into the Inland Parts of Africa.* London, 1738.

Rennell, J. "Construction of the Map of Africa" and "Geographical Illustrations of Mr. Park's Journey." *Proceedings of the Association for Promoting the Discovery of the Interior Parts of Africa.* Vol. 1. London, 1810; facsimile reprint with an introduction by Robin Hallett, London, 1967.

History, African: Sources of

Four periods emerge in considering the periodization of written sources of African history. The first is from about 1580BCE, the beginnings of historical records in ancient Egypt, to the seventh century of the common era, that is the pre-Islam antiquity. The second is the period dominated by Arabic documents from the seventh to the fifteenth centuries. Third, the period from the late fifteenth to the eighteenth centuries saw the predominance of European works on Africa. Finally, in addition to Arabic and European works, in the nineteenth and twentieth centuries, Africans in most parts of the continent increasingly kept their own records in Arabic and European languages, and even in their vernaculars using Arabic script for example Kiswahili, Hausa, Fulfulde, and so on, and later the European script.

These written sources of African history were produced in many different languages of their authors. The historian of Africa may, therefore, require linguistic versatility in order to succeed in a research because of the diversity of the languages of the sources. But to the rescue of such researchers, translations, for instance, of important Arabic, or Greek sources into English or French, as well as French into English and vice versa, are continually being published. A few examples of such translations will suffice here: (1) Muhammad ibn 'Abdullah ibn Battuta, *Travels in Asia and Africa 1325–1354*, edited by H. A. R. Gibb (1929), Arabic text and French translation by C. Defremery, and B. R. Sanguinetti, *Voyages d'ibn Battuta* (Paris, 1922), volumes 1–4, reprinted with preface and notes by Vincent Monteil, (Paris, 1969); (2) Abd al-rahmam ibn Khaldum, *Kitab ta'rikh al-duwal al-Islamiyya bi l-Maghrib min Kitab al-'ibar*, translated by M. G. de Slane as *Histoire des Berberes et des dynasties musulmanes de l'Afrique du Nord* (Paris, 1925–1956), volumes 1–4.

Pre-Islamic Antiquity (c.1580BCE–Seventh Century)

In Egypt, the cradle of civilization in Africa, written sources are found in the form of hieratic papyri and ostraco for the pre-Islamic antiquity. They include archival materials dealing with the official and private life of Egyptians and even stories and novels during the New Kingdom (*c*.1580 to 1090BCE). The British Museum has some extensive collections of these documents some of which have been published as *Select Papyri in the Hieratic Character from the Collections of the British Museum* (London, 1860). This papyri tradition continued up to the end of the Pharaonic period (332BCE) and even beyond only in Egypt.

External narrative sources shed some light on events in Egypt and the Nile from the seventh century BCE. The authors were historians, travelers, and geographers. The sources include some Greek and Latin works of Aristodemus, Herodotus, Polybius, and Strabo. The *Natural History* by Pliny the Elder gives information about Ethiopian trade, trade routes, and other aspects of the Ethiopian world. These narrative sources should be used with caution as some of the foreign authors did not write as eyewitnesses, nor crosscheck their data.

More accurate information about Egypt, Ethiopia, and the Horn of Africa, and even the east coast appeared in the years after the advent of Christianity. The most outstanding include: Ptolemy's *Geography* (*c*.140) edited by Y. Kamal as *Monumenta cartographica Africae et Aegypti* (16 volumes, Cairo/Leyden, 1926–1951); *The Periplus of the Erythraean Sea* (*c*.230), edited by F. Muller as *Geographi Graeci Minores* (Paris, 1853), and *Topographica Christiana* (*c*.535) by Cosmas Indicopleustes who traveled as far as Ethiopia and Socotra Island. His work appears in Migne's *Patrologia Graeca* (vol. 38), which should be consulted along with the same editor's *Patrologia Latina* (H. Djait, 1981).

Unlike Egypt, ancient Maghrib produced no autochthonous writers before the romanization of the area. The result is that for the history of the Maghrib before the Roman period, scholars depend on archaeology, epigraphy, and some references in Herodotus, and other Greek writers. The conflict between Carthage and Rome, the Punic wars, attracted non-African historians and geographers who wrote about the Maghrib in Greek and Latin. Many of such works by Greek and Latin authors are useful sources for Maghribi history of the period extending from 200BCE to 100CE. Among them, Polybius is acclaimed the chief source because of the quality of information and details in the *Pragmateia*. Others include Strabo, Sallust, Caesar (*Bellum Civile* and *Bellum Africum*), and Ptolemy's *Geography*. As North Africa became romanized, African-Roman writers sprang up. Among them were Tertulian, Cyprain, and Augustine. Although they produced Christian works that were colored by religion, and should be approached with caution, they are important sources for their respective times.

The western Africa south of Maghrib, that is, the Sahara and West African area, was not actually covered in the writings of the ancient Carthaginians, Greeks, and Romans. Even the authenticity of the Carthaginian document, *Periplus of Hanno*, is in doubt and serious debate among scholars; some see it as "entirely spurious" and with jumbled borrowings from earlier writers, and others as "enigmatic." The information about the area in the written sources probably refers to the southern extremity of Morocco and it is peripheral in the documents. Herodotus has some references to their silent trade in gold with Carthaginians. Polybius made more accurate reference to the area as interpolated in Elder Pliny's *Natural History*; while the Alexandrian geographer, Ptolemy, in his *Geography* gave a revised resume of his predecessors' information and provided antiquity with more reliable data on names of peoples and places in the western coast of the Sahara, Fezzan, and Lybian desert.

Written Sources from the Seventh Century Onward: External Narrative Sources in Arabic

During the period between the ninth and the fifteenth centuries, external sources of African history were predominantly written in Arabic, making those centuries to be sometimes referred to as "the era of Arabic sources." Although the Arabic materials were in decline from the sixteenth century, yet they continued to be the main source for the history of Muslim areas of Africa such as North Africa until the colonial era. They were, however, supplemented by Spanish, Portuguese, and Ottoman Turkish sources.

No Arabic chronicles appeared before the ninth century when the great histories *(ta'rikhs)* of the Islamic world made their debut. These were focused on the East as center of the Islamic world. Egypt, the Maghrib and the Sudan received peripheral coverage in the great *tarikhs* with the exception of the *Ta'rikh* of Khalifa b.Khayyat (d.*c*.862CE). Khalifa provides very important information on the conquest of the Maghrib. H. Djait's critically annotated inventory (1981) of these Arabic sources has shown that the history of Egypt and the Maghrib are well covered in the Arabic works of the tenth through fourteenth centuries.

The historian of black Africa would depend more on geographical and travel works than on the chronicles of Arabic writers for valuable information especially for areas which had come under Islamic influence. The most important geographers in the period from the ninth to the eleventh centuries were al-Ya'qubi (d.897), Mas'udi, ibn Hawqal, and al-Bakrih (1040–94). Yaqubi traveled widely in the Islamic world, especially Egypt and the Maghrib, and in his *Tarikh* and the *Kitab al-buldan*, a geographical compendium, he provides a great deal of information about Egypt, the Maghrib, and the black world: Ethiopia, the Sudan, Nubia, the Beja, and Zandj. Mas'udi's *Fields of Gold* provides information on Zandj and the east coast of Africa. Ibn Hawqal, who visited Nubia and possibly the western Sudan, provides useful information in his *Kitab surat al-ard*, especially about the trans-Saharan trade.

Three of the Arab geographers of the eleventh to the fourteenth centuries, al-Bakri, al-'Umari (d.1336), and Ibn Battuta (1304–1368/9) distinguished themselves by the high quality of their information. Al-Bakri lived in Cordova and produced his *Masalik wa'l-Mamalik*, which Arabists and Africanists hail as providing materials for detailed study of the political, economic, and religious aspects of the Sudan and its relation with the Maghrib. Likewise, Djait has described al-'Umari's *Masalik al-Absar* as "the major work" for Islamized black Africa, the "main source for the study of the Mali kingdom" and "the richest Arabic account" of fourteenth-century Ethiopia and its Muslim states. Similarly, the work of the Moroccan Ibn Battuta is hailed as the most valuable source for the history of the Maghrib and the Sudan. His *Voyages d'ibn Battuta*, already mentioned above, represents a firsthand account of a direct observer during his travels in China, Ceylon, the East African coast as far as Kilwa in 1329, and from the capital of old Mali kingdom back to North Africa via Timbuctu, Gao, and the central Sahara.

In the period from the sixteenth century onward, Arabic chronicles, annals, and geographical and travelers' reports continued to be produced, but at a very reduced level both in quantity and quality. Egypt, for instance, produced only two great historians between the sixteenth and the early nineteenth centuries: Ibn Iyas (d.1524) brought the history of Egypt from under the Mamluks to the beginning of Ottoman control, while al-Jabarti (d.1822) covered the twilight of Ottoman control of Egypt, the French conquest and occupation under Napoleon (1798–1801), and the rise of Muhammad Ali. European travelers' accounts also become important and abundant during this period. The most important is *Description de l'Egypte* (24 vols., Paris, 1821–24), compiled by the scientific staff of the French invaders. These volumes have been acclaimed as "an inexhaustible source for every kind of information on Egypt," (I. Hrbek, 1981) and that in spite of the anti-Islamic bias, the European accounts of travels in Muslim Maghrib and Egypt provide many interesting insights and observations not to be found in the indigenous works.

It was only in Morocco that the decline of Arabic narrative sources did not take place from the sixteenth century to the present. Detailed histories of the Moroccan dynasties continued to be chronicled up to the present. Hrbek (1981) has produced a list of many distinguished historians of Morocco, placing al-Zayyani (d.1833) as the greatest since the Middle Ages, and al-Nasiri al-Slawi (d.1897), who wrote a general history of Morocco, as having used both traditional and modern methods as well as archival sources. Al-Nasiri al-Slawi's geographical work also provides valuable information for social and economic history.

Genealogies of various Arab groups in the eastern Sudan, in addition to the biographical dictionary of Sudanese scholars, the *Tabaqat* by Wad Dayfallah, form the main source of the history of eastern Sudan. The *Funj Chronicle* is a publication of oral tradition in the early nineteenth century, the beginning of local historiography in eastern Sudan. Among the useful travelers' accounts are narratives of al-Tunisi (1803). In his *Voyage au Ouaday*, al-Tunisi narrated his visit to Wadai and also reported on the Darfur. He wrote in Arabic translated into French by Dr. Perron (Paris, 1851). European travelers of the eighteenth century with useful narratives about the eastern Sudan include James Bruce (1773) and W. J. Browne (1792/8). Many more travelers followed in the Sudan in the early nineteenth century in search of the Nile and left narratives, some of which are the earliest written sources about the upper reaches of the Nile.

External Narratives in European Languages

Some European nations maintained ascendancy at various periods in the African enterprise and during such periods, nationals of the predominant European nation produced most of the narratives. The Portuguese who pioneered the European enterprise in Africa wrote most of the narratives in the sixteenth century. Those narratives, maps, sea route surveys, and other navigational aids were produced to assist their nationals to know the African situation and thus participate more actively to maintain Portuguese monopoly in the African business. This explains why Portugal imposed strict censorship on any Portuguese work that could help its trade rivals. This censorship, according to F. Wolfson (1958), accounts for the scantiness of Portuguese narratives that survived. The competition of other nations to participate in the African enterprise also led to translations of early narratives into the languages of other Europeans. For instance, Olfert Dapper, a Dutch medical doctor and historian published his narrative in Dutch language in Amsterdam, 1668, and in 1670 J. Ogilby published the English translation *Africa* in London, while the French translation, *Description de l'Afrique* was published in Amsterdam in 1686. The seventeenth-century authors of the European narratives on Africa were predominantly Dutch, French, and British; the eighteenth-century, British and French; and the nineteenth century, mainly British, German, and French. Other nations of Europe participated in producing the narratives to some minor extent.

The most relevant of the authors and their works can be gleaned from various historical anthologies now available: Thomas Hodgkin, *Nigerian Perspectives: An Historical Anthology* (London, 1975); Freda Wolfson, *Pageant of Ghana* (London, 1958); G. S. P. Freeman-Grenville, *The East African Coast: Select Documents from the First to the Earlier Nineteenth Century* (Oxford, 1962). Even collections of some of these early narratives are also available, for example, A. and I. Churchill, *Collection of Voyages and Travels* (3rd ed., 1744–46, and the ones by Hakhuyt Society, London. While the collections ease the researcher's problem of location and accessibility of the materials, the translations solve his language problems by providing the materials in more popular languages.

The British contribution is very impressive in the nineteenth century with the *Narratives* and *Journals* of the various expeditions into the interior of Africa undertaken by Mungo Park (1805), Dixon Denham and Hugh Clapperton, Richard and John Lander, Macgregor Laird and Oldfield, William Baikie, Henrich Barth, Allen and Thompson, David Livingstone, H. M. Stanley, John Speke, Mary Kingsley, and other minor ones.

Like the Arabic narratives, these European ones provide some absolute chronology and thus solve one serious problem of African history. Moreover, one main aim of most European travelers, explorers, traders, missionaries, and officials was often the promotion of trade. Thus the narratives are reliable as sources for economic history in dealing with such issues as available trade goods, routes, and markets, sources of supply, variation in price levels, and types of currency, African consumption habits, control of trade, production techniques, and so on. It is reasonable to conclude that the reconstruction of the history of some parts of Sub-Saharan Africa would have been nearly impossible without the European narrative sources. Their weaknesses are normal problems that historians know how to resolve. The Christian missionaries made so many contributions through their narratives that they require further mention here.

During the period from the fifteenth century onward, especially from the nineteenth century, Christian missionaries participated in the African enterprise to convert Africans to Christianity. But in many cases, they were ill-equipped to understand and report meaningfully on African religion and systems of government. Some rather concerned themselves with exposing what they regarded as "errors" and "barbarisms" of African religion, and as "marvels" and "crudities" of African culture. Apart from such negative problems of the earliest periods, the Christian missionaries provide positive sources of African history. From the nineteenth century in particular, those of them who had stayed long enough and learnt the local languages, or understood the African society, contribute data for social history of some African communities as well as for the study of African languages, some of which the missionaries helped to reduce into writing for the first time. For example, Archdeacon T. Dennis of the Church Missionary Society (CMS) in Southern Nigeria translated the Christian Bible into Igbo language, while H. Goldie's Efik-English dictionary is still a standard work today also in southern Nigeria.

Internal Narrative Sources

Africans have been producing narrative materials from the beginning of Egyptian historical writing in the form of hieratic papyri, ostracon, and demotic. Later on romanized Africans such as Tertullian, Cyprain, and Augustine (*d.*430) also produced in Latin written works on the Roman Church with some sidelights on North African problems. From the ninth century, Arabized Africans in Egypt and the Maghrib including Ibn Battuta, Ibn Khaldun, and others wrote their narratives in Arabic.

But Sub-Saharan Africans did not produce written histories until the sixteenth century. From then onward, the writing of history in the form of Arabic chronicles, biographies, and the sort began in earnest in the Sudan and the East African coast, that is, in parts of Africa that had been under prolonged influence of Islam. Later they also produced similar works in African languages, such as Hausa, Fulfulde, Kanuri, Swahili, and so forth, using Arabic script. Two centuries later, precisely from the late eighteenth century, Africans from the non-Islamized areas also started writing their own histories in European languages, and later finally in their own languages using the European script, a result of the educational efforts of Christian missionaries. A survey of these works written in Arabic and European languages shall deal with what materials they produced and of what relevance as sources of African history. Already fuller inventory of such written sources is available (Hrbek, 1981).

The autochthonous African writers provide the black African views. Such works came from the scholars from the Jenne and Timbuktu seats of Islamic learning from the sixteenth century. The first notable one was *Ta'rikh al-Fattash*. It was the work of three generations of Ka'ti family of Jenne that was started by Mahmud Ka'ti about 1519 and subsequently enlarged and edited by one of his grandsons. It provides a compendious history of the Songhay empire of Gao down to the Moroccan conquest in 1591, plus other events of earlier periods recorded from oral traditions. A more comprehensive history of the same empire, *Ta'rikh al-Sudan*, by the Timbuktu historian, al-Sa'di appeared later, covers the same period, and carries the narrative down to 1655. There is also the biographical dictionary of the learned men of the western Sudan compiled by the Timbuktu scholar, Ahmad Baba (*d.*1627) and published in Fez (1899), and Cairo (1912).

In Central Sudan, Ahmad Ibn Fartuwa provides useful works on the campaigns of Mai Idris Aloma of Borno including the expedition against the Bulala about 1575, translated and edited by H. R. Palmer, *Sudanese Memoirs* (3 vols., Lagos, 1928). Another of Ibn Fartuwa's works was also translated and edited by H. R. Palmer as *History of the First Twelve Years of the Reign of Mai Idris Aloma* (1926).

The tradition of chronicle writing did spread from Timbuktu and Jenne toward the south and west. In those areas local chronicles, clan genealogies, king lists, biographies, and religious books by Muslim scholars started to emerge from mid-eighteenth century. They were written in Arabic or in local languages. *Kitab al-Ghunja*, the chronicle of Gonja kingdom in northern Gold Coast (now Ghana), is an outstanding example of the spread of the tradition to the south. And in Futa Toro and Futa Jalon such works have been collected by Gilbert Vieillard and kept in the IFAN library in Dakar (Hrbek 1981).

The nineteenth century saw a resurgence of literature in central and western Sudan in Arabic and the local languages such as Hausa, Fulfulde, Kanuri, Mandara, and so on, written in Arabic script. For example, the social and intellectual life in the Hausa states in the eighteenth and nineteenth centuries can be reconstructed from the numerous works of the leaders of the Fulani jihad in northern Nigeria. Some chronicles and king-lists of Hausa cities and Borno compiled in the later nineteenth century from earlier documents and oral tradition provide information for the history of those areas. The *Kano Chronicle* is a valuable source for Kano and the neighboring states.

Similarly, the East African coast shared the same tradition of chronicle writing in Arabic language or Swahili written in Arabic script. Of importance as sources of history are the chronicles of individual coastal towns such as the *Chronicle of Pate* and the earliest known *Kitab al-Sulwa fi akhbar Kulwa* ("The Book of Consolidation of the History of Kilwa" or simply, *Chronicle of Kilwa)*. The author stated that he was commissioned by the sultan of Kilwa to write the history of Kilwa. It may have been written in 1520 or 1530 and a summary of the work in Portuguese language was printed in 1552.

The ability to read and write in European languages developed first among Africans in diaspora and those exposed to the liberal education policies of Christian missionaries especially in western African coastal communities, and in southern Africa. By 1750s some Fante had received Christian education, and even became missionaries themselves. Such men as Jacobus Capitein and Philip Quaque (1741–1816) published English narratives of little historical significance. It was the African liberated exslaves from Freetown, Liberia, and Europe that blazed the trail in producing narratives of historical importance in European languages, for instance, Ottobah Cugoano's *Thoughts and Sentiments on the Evil and Wicked Traffic of the Slavery and Commerce of the Human Species* (1787), Olaudah Equiano's *The Interesting Narrative of the Life of Olaudah Equiano or Gustavus Vasa, the African* (1789), to mention only a few. They wrote mainly for a European audience against the slave trade and on the conditions of Africans in Africa and in Europe and to justify African culture.

Of equally high value as sources of African history are the nineteenth-century narratives of black Africans in European languages: those of African-Americans; a Liberian, Benjamin Anderson; Samuel Crowther's description of his journeys up the River Niger as part of Niger expedition of 1854 and 1857; and African leaders Edward W. Blyden and James Africanus Horton in their explanation and justification of African culture as well as their proposals for the political development of West Africa.

Thus from the late nineteenth century other indigenous black African writers followed in the production of histories of their own countries. The first historian of the Gold Coast (now Ghana) a Ga missionary, Rev. Carl Christian Reindorf, compiled the history of his country in 1895 mainly from traditional sources. His *History of the Gold Coast and Ashanti* (1895) is invaluable for information on the early history of the people of Gold Coast and Ashanti including the reconstruction of the Ashanti defeat at Dodowa in 1826. About the same time Rev. Samuel Johnson (1846–1901), who migrated from Sierra Leone to Lagos, later Ibadan, and finally as a CMS pastor in Oyo, completed *The History of the Yorubas* in 1897, but it was not published in Lagos until 1921. This work was based mainly on Oyo traditions only in its earlier sections as the author was an eyewitness of the events of the later nineteenth century. It has since been the main source for early Yoruba history. These works started the "chain of African historians, at first amateurs (in majority missionaries), later professionals" (Hrbek, 1981).

In South Africa indigenous written sources of African opinion against white racial domination also emerged in the nineteenth century. Apart from written petitions and complaints of Africans against their plights now preserved in South African archives and in London, vernacular newspapers also emerged in the nineteenth century: the weekly *Isidigimi* was published between 1870 and 1880 critical of European policies and their negative impact on Africans. John T. Jabavu's vernacular newspaper *Imvo Zabantsundu* (The Voice of Black People) since 1884 discussed African plight under white domination. Jabavu (d.1921) also published *The Black Problem* (1920), like that of the self-educated African journalist, S. T. Plaatje, author of *Native Life in South African before and since the European War and Boer Rebellion* (1916). These African voices in South Africa continued to be heard in increasing volume and Christian missionary activities and records were also in support of African rights. From the early twentieth century precisely in January 1912, the South African Native Congress (later African National Congress, ANC) was formed by the indigenous elite with more organized protest against the settler dominance.

Archival Sources

Archival sources of African history appeared first in ancient Egypt. The *Select Papyri in Hieratic . . .*, already mentioned, includes some civil service and legal reports, accountancy records, private letters, and the like, covering the period from 1580BCE to the end of the Pharaonic Egypt 323BCE and even beyond. During the Christian era, the Greek and Coptic papyri appeared, and the Arabic papyri from the Muslim era. From the twelfth century CE, Egyptian archival sources became more plentiful especially under the Mamluks. But they still took the second place after narrative sources for historical reconstruction as they remained scattered and insufficient for creating a coherent picture of the past. Some of the European treaties, contracts, and letters, preserved in government and private archives in Venice, Genoa, Pisa, and Barcelona, which deal mainly in European business relations with Egypt and the Maghrib, have been published and studied: *L. Mas-Latrie, Traites de paix et de commerce et documents divers concernant des relations des chretiens avec les arabes d'Afrique șeptentrionale au moyenage* (Supplement, 1872, 1866, 1872).

The Maghrib produced its own archival materials from the Almoravid era. New light has been thrown on the institutions and ideology of the Almoravid and Almohad empire movements by some of their official records published and edited by H. Mu'nis and A. M. Makki as *Lettres officielles almoravides*; and al-Baydaq's *Documents inedits d'histoire almohade* (translated and edited by E. Levi-Provencal, 1928). North Africa continued to produce more archival records in Arabic and Turkish in the sixteenth to the eighteenth century, now preserved in Cairo, Tunisian, and Algerian archives. Some have been translated and published: R. le Tourneau, "Les archives musulmanes en Afrique du Nord" in *Achivum*, volume 4 (1954). The administrative and judicial documents of independent Morocco have been preserved in Moroccan archives while other related materials in some European archives have been collected and published: by Henri Castries, *Les Sources inedits de l'histoire du Maroc* (24 vols., 1905–1951).

From the nineteenth century onward archival sources became as abundant for North Africa as in European countries. They now occupy the first place as the primary and more objective sources for historical reconstruction, pushing the narrative sources to the second position. Thus archival sources in Arabic and also European languages for North African history defy enumeration.

For black Africa only a few isolated correspondences of the pre-nineteenth-century period in Arabic are now known: the 1578 dispatch from the Ottoman sultan to Mai Idris Aloma of Borno preserved in the Turkish archives; and the ones from the sultan of Morocco to Askiya of Songhai and to the Kanta of Kebbi. There was also the letter from Borno to Egypt dated 1391.

In the nineteenth century there was an explosion in diplomatic and administrative activities in the Sokoto caliphate between the caliph and the various emirs and in the Borno Empire. Archival materials in Arabic from Muslim leaders in the Sudan such as al-Hajj Umar, Samori Touré, Rabih, among others, are to be found in the archives of West African countries. Despatches were also exchanged between the various empires, for instance between Sheikh al-Kanemi of Borno and Muhammad Bello of Sokoto on the justification for the Fulani jihad against Borno, a fellow Muslim empire.

Archival materials in European languages have been accumulating since the sixteenth century. They are now too numerous for an inventory. And they are scattered all over the world in archives, libraries, and private collections to which access in extremely difficult in terms of time and resources. To make the existence of these archival sources known to researchers in African history, the International Council of Archives is preparing a series of guides to source materials in public and private repositories as well as in libraries and museums. It is planned that the series in twelve volumes will cover archival records in Africa South of the Sahara, western Europe and the United States of America. This project for the *Guide to the Sources of the History of Africa* will certainly expose more valuable sources to researchers. Other categories of catalogs and lists of archival sources have been provided to ease the work of the researcher and also enrich African history: missionary documents from the Portuguese and some other archives collected by A. D. Brasio, *Monumenta missionaria africana* (9 vols., Lisbon, 1953); G. E. Metcalfe, *Great Britain and Ghana Documents of Ghana History, 1807–1957* (1964). The need for more catalogs and inventories is still being felt.

It should also be noted that every independent African state has now established government archives in which materials left by former colonial governments are preserved. Since some records may be missing in such archives in Africa, researchers should use them in combination with the archives in the metropolis in Europe in order to get a fuller picture of the events. The national archives in Africa should also publish lists of the holdings of their repositories, catalogs of major subject matters and other search aids. They could also arrange international cooperation with archives of related countries in the line being taken by the Portuguese and Zimbabwean archives to publish the original and English translation of all Portuguese documents concerning South-East Africa. African history would benefit from such combined effort between, for instance, Nigerian and Portuguese archives; or the Cameroonian and German archives could collect and publish all German documents concerning the Cameroons in original form with French and English translations as Cameroon is a bilingual state. South Africa is in a unique historiographical case.

Similar combined efforts between South African and Dutch archives will be fruitful for producing a true history of Africans in South Africa. Some official documents of the Dutch colonial period are now kept in archives in South Africa, in London, and The Hague, though some are still not accessible. Extracts of journals and other documents have also been edited and published by D. Moodie as *The Record: or A Series of Official Papers Relative to the Conditions and Treatment of the Native Tribes of South Africa* (1960). Also useful are the records published by G. M. Theal as the *Basutoland Records*, 3 volumes (1883), *Records of the Cape Colony*, 36 volumes (1897–1905), and *Records of South-Eastern Africa*, 9 volumes (1898–1903).

Pictorial and Film Evidence

Pictorial and film sources of history can be categorized as written sources. Nonliterate societies cannot produce them, though some external narrative sources from the sixteenth century such as William Bosman's *A New and Accurate Description of the Coast of Guinea* (1705) provides some maps and drawings. The main pictorial and film sources are for the contemporary period, when Africans have acquired the capability to produce and use them as source for research into and teaching of African history. Such sources include all types of photographs, the photostat, microfilm, the moving pictures, old maps, sketches, and drawings.

The illustrative old maps, pictures, sketches, and drawings are also published in some old narratives of early travelers, explorers, geographers, historians, and missionaries like the ones in William Bosman's *Description . . .*, or A. and I. Churchill's *Collection of Voyages and Travels* (1744). These provide their own factual data about the architecture, market scenes, dressing styles, means of transport, settlement patterns, and so on, of those centuries for social history.

Films, like pictures, depict the reality of anything: situations, activities, and the portrait of individuals. Films are useful visual aids in teaching history using projectors and the screen before the class. The profiles of important late political figures, such as, Nnamdi Azikiwe, Obafemi Awolowo, Ahmadu Bello, Leopold Seda Senghor, Kwame Nkrumah, Julius Nyerere, and the like, will benefit much from the use of films in teaching them. The various kinds include newsreel, documentary, and feature films.

The quality of the pictorial and film evidence, however, is the problem. They are usually produced by journalists, businessmen, cameramen, editors, and other technologists, who may at best produce only pop history films. Though that quality is still history all the same, academic historians should as much as possible be involved in the making of history films and historical programs on radio and television to improve the quality. An advisory committee of experts for history and programs will certainly help to improve the situation.The premier and conventional source for writing history remains the contemporary written sources both narrative and archival types. But in Africa, as already stated, there was a dearth of such sources. For the Sudan and the coastal parts of Africa no written documents for history writing were available until from the Portuguese period, and for most parts of the hinterland areas until the colonial period. Moreover, those available written sources were produced by non-Africans. Most of the authors were not familiar with Africa and the Africans, nor did they write without bias and superiority complex against Africans. There is, therefore, the necessity to seek for historical information about especially precolonial period of African history from other sources: oral, archaeological, artifacts, as well as from other disciplines like linguistics, anthropology, geography, and literature.

Oral Sources

An oral source of history can be defined as evidence transmitted through the word of mouth whether it has already been committed to writing, or even published. The two most important types of oral sources are oral tradition and oral history. Oral history is one of the sources for the study of contemporary history. The evidence is collected through interviews in which informants speak of their own experience about the recent past whether as participant, eyewitness, or not. For example, the study of recent topics such as economic or political development, or military intervention in politics in any country, must derive very valuable evidence through oral historical research by means of interviews of participants and activists in the events. Such participants give more useful information, comments, and elucidations in oral interviews than a researcher would be able to glean from their private published diaries, memoirs, and other papers, which persons publicize after they may have rationalized their roles in those events.

Oral traditions, on the other hand, could be defined as the form in which man relates by word of mouth the past of his people, the rulers, and the ancestors, as far back in time as possible, or simply, a testimony about the past transmitted orally from one generation to another. Oral traditions are of two main types: the factual or historical traditions, and the literary and philosophical types. The historical traditions deal mainly with origins, migrations, settlement, the establishment of dynasties, chronicles of each reign, genealogies, praise names, and so forth, of each king or great chief, and certain laws and customs. They deal with remote and recent past but are more reliable when they give account of events of last few centuries. The factual traditions are very useful as sources of African history after they have, like the written sources, undergone the historian's usual critical examination.

The literary and philosophical traditions may include proverbs and sayings, songs and lyrics of various are-grades, guilds, or those of religious organizations such as the sacred verses of the gods, divination poems, funeral dirges, liturgies and sacred hymns. They are useful for, among other things, the religious history, the worldview and culture of the people. Myths and legends have both factual and literary aspects but are less reliable as sources of history.

Some major traditions in the Nigerian region include the Oduduwa tradition of Yoruba origin, the Bayajidda of the origin of Hausa states, the Eri tradition of Igbo origin, the Tsoede among the Nupe, and the Ogiso and Oranmiyan among the Bini. These are mainly in the area of myths and legends, and many of them have variants in the question of details. The most outstanding of these traditions in Sub-Saharan Africa, however, is the "traditions of Sundiata of Mali," collected and published by Djibril T. Niane in *Presence Africaine*, translated by G. D. Pickett and published by D. T. Niane as *Sundiata: An Epic of Old Mali* (London, 1965).

The use of oral sources has a long history. Oral evidence was used as a valid source of history even among ancient European writers. Latin and Greek historians, such as Homer in the *Iliad*; Herodotus, the "father of history"; and Thucydides (*c*.455–*c*.400BCE), made extensive use of oral sources in their works. Similarly, medieval western European historians, like their Islamic counterparts, also relied on both written and oral sources. By the seventeenth and eighteenth centuries, however, the use of oral sources was no longer in vogue among European historians. Compilers rather collected and published edited texts of charters, treaties, and so on, especially in England, France, and Italy.

The use of oral sources, however, continued among the oral societies. Oral tradition was the mode in which preliterate Africans recorded their past. It was the only important source of history for them. Those of them who learned to write in the European languages continued to base their works of history on oral sources; for example, Carl Christian Reindorf in Ghana, Apollo Kagwa in Uganda, Samuel Johnson in Nigeria, and others. In the 1950s and 1960s trained Africanist historians joined them in the use of oral sources. Even European colonial officials appreciated the place of oral traditions during their prolonged contact with oral societies of Africa. They subsequently joined in producing works they regarded as history sourced mainly from oral evidence they collected during colonial service.

With the publication of Jan Vansina's *Oral Tradition: A Study in Historical Methodology* (1965), the case for oral evidence as a valid historical source became further strengthened. Since then more scholarly works on how to further refine the technique for dealing with oral sources of history have continued to be published: for instance, the works of Jan Vansina, Yves Person, P. D. Curtin, D. Henige, D. F. McCall, E. J. Aloagoa, and others in that regard.

Some of the scholars have shown that oral traditions are very important and "essential source" of African history. They are in general agreement that the traditions require cautious and careful scrutiny, for they have structural problems and limitations that make them fundamentally subjective. Hence the use of oral traditions as valid historical source has many detractors. To save the situation the exponents insist that oral traditions should be analyzed with the general rules of textual criticism, both external and internal, as in the case of written documents, and even more. It remains, therefore, to survey briefly some of these problems and limitations of oral traditions: chronology, collection and evaluation, as well as preservation and publication.

Chronology The greatest problem of oral traditions is its lack of absolute chronology. This is one of the major reasons for the unjust scorn in which detractors hold oral traditions as valid source of history. For history deals with every issue or change in time perspective and without that time dimension history will look like sociology. But oral traditions have only relative chronology, distinguishing events in terms of reigns of kings, great chiefs, or queen-mothers; genealogies, and generations of age-grade; or occasionally notable natural disasters such as epidemic (the Spanish influenza of 1918), or periodic natural phenomena such as eclipse of the sun, or volcanic eruptions. Where these events are recorded in other sources especially written with specific dates, such relative chronology of oral tradition becomes absolute chronology. However, this is unusual since the sponsors of oral traditions are oral societies, unless the exact dates were written down by literate visitors of the community.

Historians have, however, endeavored to work out a system of absolute dating for oral traditions. The most popular method has been "to work out a mean length of reign from the dated portion of a king-list" (E. J. Alagoa, 1972), or length of a generation, and then apply the average to the rest of the king-list by projecting the average length of reign backward in time to determine the possible date of each reign, at least approximately. Alagoa used average reign-length of 13.6 years for the Ijo kings, a close figure to the mean reign of 13 years obtained for 71 African dynasties. He still warned that the result is estimated absolute dating. The social, political, and cultural factors affecting the length of reigns such as succession and interregnum problems, distortions of the lists, and such other limitations of oral transmission, may have made the list fundamentally unreliable, since these factors may not have been constant over the years. Hence it has been suggested that such calculated dates should be indicated with a siglum showing a wide span, thus around 1650CE and not just 1650 (J. Vansina, 1981).

It must, however, be stated that the relative chronology was usable and satisfactory to oral societies as it provided a sequence of events for each kingdom but not useful in recording the relationship between such events and ones in the traditions of other kingdoms, or with ones in the written sources. Historians are still actively involved in the efforts to rescue their oral tradition from its lack of absolute chronology since history is not possible without time dimension.

Preservation and Publication The preservation of oral traditions is in fact more important than their publication. Every oral tradition collected should be processed, indexed, and preserved in the documentation centers, libraries, or archives in their countries of origin. Traditions recorded on tapes should also be indexed, transcribed, and preserved. Publication should be for the interest of the international world of scholars and other users. What should be published are not the enormous volumes of the traditions collected but detailed catalogs and lists of the holdings of the preservation centers. The catalogs and lists may include the index numbers, topics, informants' names, and other particulars, as well as brief abstracts of the oral traditions, and any other notes to enable scholars to evaluate the traditions and as guides to the locations of the preservation centers.

Auxiliary and Related Disciplines

History has auxiliary relationship with a number of independent disciplines, which, in one way or the other, contribute information and techniques for the historian's reconstruction of the past. The African past, which lacks most of the conventional sources of history, relies on those other disciples for evidence especially about the pre- and protohistoric eras. The related and supportive disciplines to history include archaeology, linguistics, anthropology, geography, political science, economics, psychology, and even literature, that is, the social sciences.

These disciplines are not sources of African history per se. Rather, depending on the theme of the research, the historian borrows relevant information from the discoveries, inferences, and conclusions of experts in the related disciplines for solving historical problems.

For instance, the inferences and conclusions that the archaeologists arrive at from the study of excavated materials, archaeological surveys, and so forth, make useful evidence for the historian researching into the same, or a related community. Historians also adopt some appropriate tools or methods of some of the related disciplines in historical analysis.

The economic historian, for instance, needs some knowledge of certain economic tools, such as principles and theory of economics, for clear and intelligible conclusions about human social and economic affairs in the past. The traditional historian borrows, for instance, the "location theory" of economics for analyzing the consequences in profitability of, say, the brewery industries established in two different towns, one rural, and the other urban locations. With its locational advantage of larger home market, the urban industry survived better. Some knowledge of the principles of political science enables the historian to explain group relations in modern institutions of civil government. The knowledge of, for example, group behavior in psychology helps the historian to understand and analyze historical issues such as revolutions, character of labor union leaders, and so on.

Borrowing from the social sciences and others by the historian is clearly demonstrated by Thomas C. Cochran who is said to have consulted economists, sociologists, political scientists, and psychologists for his study, *Railroad Leaders, 1845–1890: The Business Mind in Action* (1953). The historian should have broad knowledge and interests, but if he has to be an expert in all the auxiliary disciplines necessary for his research, his work will be delayed beyond measure, and little time would be left for his main work of studying and writing history. Hence he borrows from other experts but also acquires enough rudimentary knowledge of the auxiliary disciplines in order to understand their conclusions and to borrow intelligently from them.

Archaeology The most intimately related discipline to history is archaeology. It has already served the interests of history especially about ancient Rome, Greece, the Orient, and in recent times Africa, more than any of the other auxiliary disciplines. Archaeology is the method or science of studying through excavation and examining and describing the material remains of man in the past, and thereby making relevant inferences about his social, economic, and technological achievements. Apart from the contemporary period and the recent past, archaeology covers the whole of human past beginning from the early man.

Excavation is the most essential task of the archaeologist. It is the skilled digging up of material remains of earlier man from the soil where years have buried them. These materials are the artifacts—the remains of man himself and of everything man had produced and used usually in a vanished culture or civilization. The artifacts include his physical remains such as his skeleton, teeth, and hairs; his tools, weapons, pots and remains of his habitation, houses or huts, and other structures; as well as his objects of art and religious rituals, and so forth. When the archaeologist has carefully unearthed the artifacts, he classifies their types, the frequencies, distribution, and sequence. He studies the artifacts and produces his archaeological or excavation report.

Artifacts are probably the most important source of human history especially for the millennia between the origin of man and the invention of writing and record keeping, about 6,000 years ago. The use of artifacts has enabled archaeologists to acknowledge that Africa was probably the cradle of mankind. Only the artifacts are available as sources of history for that very long period of human existence, since oral traditions do not go far back to more than four or five hundred years even where their preservation and transmission methods are exceptionally good. The writing of history, sourced only from artifacts is, therefore, the task of archaeologists who are very familiar with, and facilitators of artifacts.

Even for African history during the later period after the invention of writing and record keeping, artifacts are still very relevant. Where other sources of history such as written records and oral traditions are available, artifacts still help in filling the gaps in the evidence, and to supplement, corroborate, or authenticate the data from those other sources and vice versa, or to revise existing conclusions for a fuller picture of the human past to emerge.

A glaring instance of revision of conclusions through the result of excavations is the controversy over the origin of the stone buildings of Great Zimbabwe. Europeans had assigned the construction to exotic, non-African, forgotten "whites" probably Phoenicians and some others. Excavations in the 1900s and another in the 1920s by professional archaeologists revealed that the site was the headquarters of an indigenous African state. But the controversy and speculations based on the now discredited "Hamitic hypothesis" raged on, until the recent excavations of Roger Summers and Kenneth Robinson plus "carbon dating have fully confirmed . . . that these stone buildings were the work of Iron Age Africans," (R. Gray 1970). That was a case of the science of archaeology using artifacts to restore African initiative. The excavations at the ancient Ghana site of Koumbi Saleh (Mauritania) and at Lake Kisale (Katanga/Shaba, Zaire/Democratic Republic of Congo) have corroborated and validated the oral sources that located them (J. Vansina, 1981).

Thus artifacts enable historians to get a fuller picture of the human past, especially in Sub-Saharan Africa where artifacts remained almost the sole source of history until the European written sources appeared from the sixteenth century, though areas that came under Muslim influence (the Sudan and east coast of Africa) experienced written sources much earlier. In the case of Egypt, the dry climate favors the survival of even perishable objects of wood, bone, and the like, made by the early man, as well as the almost indestructible artifacts made of stone and pottery. Consequently, early Egyptian written records of hieratic papyri and ostraco also survived. And with detailed information from these written sources and the artifacts, Egyptologists have reconstructed the history of ancient Egypt. The east coast of Africa, like the Sudan, has external written sources from the first millennium CE and some later Swahili documents written in Arabic script. Neville Chittick (1968) has used information from these written sources including the eyewitness accounts of early Portuguese visitors supplemented with artifacts excavated from some coastal trading towns to reconstruct a history of "The Coast Before the Arrival of the Portuguese."

In most parts of Sub-Saharan Africa, however, archaeological investigations are yet to accumulate enough data for meaningful reconstruction of the past, be it prehistory or protohistory of the various regions. Hence Thurstan Shaw (1971) has assessed his pioneer study of "The prehistory of West Africa" as an "outline summary of the rather disjointed information" about the subject matter, because of the dearth of archaeological data. He suggests further archaeological research and accumulation of data as the only way out.

Archaeology brings with it its own set of difficulties. For instance, the location of archaeological sites often depends very much on chance and this helps to slow down the progress of the research. Archaeology in itself is an expensive discipline because of the amount of money and time required for the team to excavate a known site and to fully study and report on it. There are also a few archaeologists in Africa outside Egypt and North Africa. The number, however, is increasing as fully trained ones are being attached to the universities, research institutes, and antiquities commissions in various African countries. But some are not committed, while some governments, foundations, and even philanthropists are yet to realize the importance of archaeological research for history, and so encourage its execution with handsome grants.

The use of artifacts has also given rise to other subsidiary sources of African history: numismatics, epigraphy, and chronological systems. Numismatics is the study of coins and coinage, as well as their description and classification according to countries of origin and periods. The legends on coins often afford useful historical data especially on chronology of reigns, dynasties, or significant events, as well as indicating the directions of trade links. Although numismatic data do not supply details, they have afforded insights into the history of Greece and Rome, for example, and their empires as far afield as the Greek kingdoms set up in northwestern India by Alexander the Great. (Garraghan, 1946) However, they are not an important source for Sub-Saharan Africa, with the possible exception of the East African coast, where even coin-hoards have been found, and Gao in Sudan, and probably along the fringes of Muslim influence.

Epigraphy or science of inscriptions made on stone, or statue, and so forth, is another aspect of archaeology. It studies inscriptions on artifacts and their physical characteristics and makes collections of their text according to language, country, and period. It is important for the ancient history of literate societies such as the Orient, Greece, or Rome, and to a little extent, in Egypt, Maghrib, and Axum. G. W. B. Huntingford has even used the inscriptions of Ezana, king of Axum, who was converted to Christianity in the fourth century CE to reconstruct part of the history of the kingdom of Axum and Ethiopia. (R. Oliver, 1971). Like numismatics, it is not important as a source of the history of black Africa. However, epigraphical sources could be obtained in the Sudan as a *tarikh* is reported to have been found in the walls of Koumbi Saleh (D. McCall, 1964).

Archaeological systems of chronology constitute a very important source of African history. Both archaeology and history all over the world experience great difficulties in knowing exactly when different events took place in the past. Archaeology has devised stratigraphy that yields relative chronology: items deeper in the earth stratum are older than those above them in the same soil. Some idea of the date could also be worked out through dendrochronology: the counting of tree rings; and from objects imported to Africa and found in excavations such as clay pipes for tobacco smoking, glass beads, or Chinese porcelain.

The best-known method devised by archaeology and its subsidiaries, however, is the radiocarbon fourteen (C14) dating. If bone, wood, charcoal, or shell from an excavation is dated by this method, and 1,400 ± 120 years before the present is obtained, the two possible chances are that the actual time lies between 1,520 and 1,280 years ago. This is the archaeological discovery of absolute dating; though far from being exact, historians adopt it. Archaeologists have a new method for dating pottery shards: the thermoluminescent dating. This system also depends on physics and is very promising as it uses one of the commonest artifacts: pottery (T. Shaw 1970).

Linguistics In their degree of support to history, linguistics is next to archaeology. Linguistics is the scientific study of the development of languages including such items as their rate and pattern of change and divergence in time and space, their borrowing and diffusion patterns, their relationships and classification, and so forth. Linguistics contributes valuable data to the historian who is researching on the prehistoric era. According to P. Diagne (1981), it "supplies history with at least two kinds of data; first, linguistic information properly speaking; and secondly, evidence which might be termed supra-linguistic."

Similarly, in his "Linguistics as an Instrument of Prehistory" Morris Swadesh (1959) explains some ways linguistics can contribute to prehistory: it establishes common origin and subsequent divergence of languages, inferring that originally united peoples later separated some thousands of years ago; it also suggests prehistoric culture contacts, physical environments, and contents of such pristine cultures through conclusions and deductions from diffused features and reconstructed old vocabularies especially culture words (such as horses, or iron, or chief, or chicken, etc.) among languages.

These possibilities of linguistics raise the hope that it is a very essential source of African prehistory, and that in collaboration with archaeology and oral tradition, it would help solve the problem of scarcity of evidence for the prehistory of Africa. But the full realization of this hope is being hampered by the present problems of linguistics in Africa. For instance, only a few language experts are interested in the enormous fields of research in African languages. There are also the good deal of controversies, arguments, reservations, and even outright rejection of reconstructions, deductions, and other results of research in African languages, especially on the issue of African linguistic classification among linguists themselves. These hinder some historians from the use of such data. Moreover, the results of research could be ideologically distorted and thus falsified. The Hamitic hypothesis is a case in point, whereby some European scholars seek to explain interesting achievements and cultural features in black Africa in terms of external influence. For instance, C. G. Seligman, C. Meinhof, and others present Bantu as a mixed language "descended of a Hamitic father and a Negro mother" (Diagne, 1981).

In the light of these problems, historians make use of linguistic data with caution and careful consideration. They often make allowance for the provisional nature of the evidence, and the possibility of revising the conclusions, when, and if, a consensus is reached among linguistics on a particular issue, or further research provides a more solid evidence. Take for example the issue of Bantu "homeland" and expansion. In reconstructing this prehistory of the Bantu-speaking people of Central and Southern Africa, Roland Oliver (1966) has used mainly the research reports of linguistic authorities (Joseph Greenberg 1955, and Malcolm Guthrie 1962) together with some cultural and additional evidence, while archaeology also provides the chronology. He recognized the possibility of revision when he states that he had relied on "evidence available in 1966." Similarly while using linguistic evidence to reconstruct the migrations and early inhabitants of the "Windward Coast" that covers the coasts of the states of Guinea, Sierra Leone, and Liberia, Christopher Fyfe (1965) also calls attention to the "argument among them" (linguists) over language grouping in the area.

Thus by combining evidence from linguistics, archaeology, oral tradition, and anthropology our knowledge of the preliterate period of African history is being expanded, especially where the linguistic evidence is not contentious. I. A. Akinjogbin (1971) for instance, has on the strength of solid evidence from linguistics, religion, social, and economic organization firmly declared that the Aja and the Yoruba form "one distinct cultural area."

Anthropology Apart from anthropology and perhaps geography, other social sciences offer peripheral support as sources of African history. Anthropology is the scientific study of man especially his racial and tribal development, customs, manners, arts, religious beliefs, and other cultural traits. Like ethnologists, early anthropologists originally presumed, on the basis of their ethnocentric considerations, that Europeans pioneered civilization, and therefore, are in the van of human progress while the "primitive natives" of Oceanian, Amazonia, and Africa bring up the rear. Anthropology thus became a tool for European colonizers to study their colonial victims and achieve greater understanding and control. As colonialism transformed the "primitive natives" into producers for the world markets, anthropologists began investigating the original structures in African societies without preconceived ideas such as the Hamitic hypothesis. Joseph Ki-Zerbo's (1981) warning that "if it is to be useful to history, anthropology must avoid theoretical reconstructions in which ideology outweighs concrete facts" is timely enough for the historian to use anthropological information with caution.

Anthropology is a source of African history. Historians borrow from the reports of the field investigations and the synthesis of anthropologists on particular African societies. Such borrowings help historians in fuller understanding and analysis of social and political relationships, events, and the cultural traits of the people under study especially for the preliterate era and the early period when written documents are available. In researching into the history of an African people, for instance, one should wish to study, first, the general works in anthropology and even ethnography of Africa such as E. E. Evans-Pritchard and M. Fortes (eds.), *African Political Systems* (1940); A. U. Richards (ed.), *East African Chiefs* (1960), and so forth; and second, any monographs on the particular area of study, for example, the Bantu: J. F. M. Middleton, *The Kikuyu and Kamba of Kenya* (1953); R. P. P. Tempels, *Bantu Philosophy* (translation by Colin King, 1959); J. H. M. Beattie, *Bunyoro, an African Kingdom* (1960), and so on; or the Asante: R. S. Rattray, *Ashanti* (1923); *Religion and Art in Ashanti* (1927); A. W. Cardinall, *In Ashanti and Beyond* (1927); K. A. Busia, *Position of the Chief in the Modern Political System of Ashanti* (1951).

It is with the knowledge acquired from the study of such appropriate anthropological sources that the historian will be in a position to proceed in the research: first, to understand and adequately write about the early political or economic structures of the people under study as may be required in the research report; and second, to appreciate how some modern institutions of government such as the chieftainship may have actually functioned in the past, and be able to explain their transformations, for example, in terms of the arrival of immigrant rulers, evolution from within the system, or the impact of colonialism. Proper understanding of the dynamics of political, economic, and kinship organizations will equip the historian with more evidence to understand and perhaps discredit the Hamitic hypothesis on state formation in West Africa (R. Horton, 1970) or any other ideological distortions.

The library study of the anthropological materials should be enough for the historian to pick up the required background knowledge of the people being studied. For the historian cannot afford the time to undertake the anthropological fieldwork by himself as it takes too much time; since the task requires the student to live among the people being studied for two or more years, celebrating with them as a member of the society and collecting details for the monograph. Moreover, the monographs on many parts of Africa are not in short supply as many were produced by colonial government anthropologists, ethnographers, and other scholars.

Geography The main branches of geography contribute data in some degree to the historical study of the development of man. The physical geography, which deals mainly with topography, climate, and potential wealth in soil, minerals, flora, and fauna, makes the maximum contribution to history, followed by human geography with minimal contribution from the other branches. However, all the branches of geography contribute their illustrative devices (maps, diagrams, and tables), which the historian borrows to make history more real and understandable. The maps, for instance, set the historical events in their real context on the ground, and thus aid the student to report the historical findings with precision. Hence, most national and regional works in history begin with an introductory chapter on the "land and people" with maps and relevant illustrations.

The elements of physical geography provide data for the understanding of the influence of geography on man and his social evolution, for example, grassland and woodland vegetations encourage more population increase and human mobility than the humid forests; the desiccation of the Sahara from about 3000BCE may have caused the flight of the Saharan peoples into Egypt and southward into the more humid forest regions; the desiccation eventually left the great sandy barrier between North Africa and Sub-Saharan Africa, making black Africa to miss out in the diffusion of the fertilizing innovations of copper and bronze metallurgy and the wheel, which reached Britain by the first half of the second millennium BCE. (T. Shaw, 1971). The open woodlands south of the Congo forests into which the Bantu migrated and settled is believed to have favored the increase of their population which in turn may have encouraged their further migration into the rest of southern Africa.

Nevertheless, other contributory factors apart from the geographical influences must be taken into due consideration. Whatever favorable geographical conditions do exist for expansion, or growth, or the like, or may have induced migration, the actual movement or actions that favored growth arose also from the free will decision of the population, who, for example, built the irrigation channels in Egypt, or took the decision and undertook the movement to new sites.

Literary Sources Among the literary sources of history are novels, plays, and poems that introduce historical facts and persons often with fictitious names. The aim of the literary authors is primarily to stimulate emotional enjoyment, aesthetic pleasure, and entertainment. To achieve such aims, the dictum "facts are sacred" no longer applies, rather exaggerations of events and characters, fictitious details, and the like, to stimulate the sensibilities of readers or the audience are employed. As such, these literary types, like such other discourses as funeral orations, eulogies, and public declarations of diplomats, are not strictly sources of factual data for the historian. One should not trust or take the words of a novelist, poet, or playwright about an event unless such event is confirmed by sources of factual data.

The historian should, however, study many such historical novels, poems, and plays (if any is available) on the subject and period of his research. From such wide reading one would derive not the factual data for his research report, but the general insight, picture, and balanced estimate of the period about which the works were written. Such insight could even suggest to the historian more themes and issues to be investigated from the sources of factual data like government records, commercial company papers, and so forth. The historian could, however, use any vivid example from novels, poems, and plays to illustrate and support the factual data.

A few examples will suffice here. A historian researching into the life of Africans under the policy of racial discrimination in South Africa will have many literary sources to study for the general picture of color bar in the country. Peter Abrahams' pioneer novel, *Mine Boy* (published by Faber and Faber in London, 1946, and first published in the African Writers Series in 1963), was one of the first books to depict the miserable lives of blacks in the racially segregated, white-dominated country. *Tell Freedom*, his autobiography about his childhood and youth in the slums of Johannesburg (published by Faber and Faber, 1954) also depicts the wretched lives of blacks in South Africa even more boldly. These and other novels, poems, and plays will provide the researcher with the general picture. For the factual data for the research, he turns mainly to the archival sources, and the external and internal narrative sources on South Africa already mentioned above.

Again the main themes of most novels, poetry, and plays published in the African Writers Series are European colonial encounters with Africans and their impact on African societies. Most poets, novelists, and playwrights in that series create in bold relief the picture of the devastation of African institutions and traditional societies in the colonial encounter in which life is falling apart. But historians from the sources of factual data are enabled to emphasize continuity and change, or even continuity of African institutions under colonialism. However, some works in the series written as biography or autobiography such as Elechi Amadi's *Sunset in Biafra, A Civil War Diary* (1973) should be treated as a source of factual data, not for mere entertainment; however, data from such sources should be subjected to proper criticism before use.

Conclusion

There are certain problems that still impede research and publication in African history. Research is seriously hindered by some difficulties in getting reliable sources of information. Some of the sources discussed in this essay are not readily available for scholars to consult nor are they all easily accessible. In addition, the problems of language of the narrative as well as archival sources, which are scattered throughout many European cities, have been mentioned. Some solutions have already been suggested such as translations from the obscure or dead ancient languages to modern international languages and the retrieval of publications, microfilm, and electronic to African states. Even most of the auxiliary sciences such as archaeology, linguistics, and the like, which provide their results of research as the historians' data, are yet to accumulate enough data on various parts of Africa for solid historical conclusions to be based on them.

The result of the problems of sources is that certain periods and regions in African history are unpopular among research scholars. For example, while the history of Africa since the colonial era is popular to all including young researchers even for doctoral studies, the history of Africans before that period is unattractive to research scholars. Sometimes the earlier periods from the period of emergence of European narratives on Africa from the sixteenth century are only cursorily treated as introductory in the colonial studies.

The publishing policy of selective acceptance of jobs for publication is the most serious impediment to publication of monographs in African history. Most publishers are ready to publish textbooks, examination notes and aids, and the like whose markets are fully assured, while they reject serious historical monographs whose market, they argue, is usually restricted. The only possible exceptions to this policy are university presses. Some publishers even frown at the detailed documentation that historians stick to in historical works. But history does not worship documents as such. It only insists on full documentation because it deals with human reality in the past. This makes it mandatory that the sources of information on which historical statements are based should be fully stated to facilitate verification.

The most serious modern problem impeding research and publication in history is underfunding. This is a result of the short-sightedness of the educational policies of mainly some third world countries in Africa that look down on history and other humanities while promoting almost only science-and-technology-based disciplines. Proper funding of research and publication in African history by governments and philanthropic individuals and organizations will go a long way in removing most of the hindrances. It will enable more sources to be collected in Africa, thus making them available in better-equipped libraries of the universities and research institutes and the state archives; adequate research grants would be available, and university presses would be able to publish research reports. Thus, more research scholars would be attracted to participate in the field of African history.

JOSEPH B. C. ANYAKE

See also: **Crowther, Reverend Samuel Ajayi and the Niger Mission; Equiano, Olaudah; Ibn Battuta, Mali Empire and; Ibn Khaldun: Civilization of the Maghrib; Livingstone, David; Portugal: Exploration and Trade in the Fifteenth Century; Religion, Colonial Africa: Missionaries; Yusuf ibn Tashfin: 1070–1147. Almoravid Empire: Maghrib:**

Further Reading

Afigbo, A. E. *K.O. Dike and African Historical Renascence*. Owerri: Rada Publishing Company, 1986.

Alagoa, E. J. *A History of the Niger Delta: An Historical Interpretation of Ijo Oral Tradition*. Ibadan: Ibadan University Press, 1972.

Biobaku, S. O. (ed.). *Sources of Yoruba History*. Oxford: Oxford University Press, 1973.

Chittick, N. "The Coast Before the Arrival of the Portuguese" in *Zamani: A Survey of East African History*, edited by B. A. Ogot and I. A. Kieran. New York: Humanities Press Inc. and London: Longman, 1968; revised edition, Nairobi: East African Publishing House, 1974.

Curtin, P. D. "Field Techniques for Collecting and Processing Oral Data." *Journal of African History*, 9/3 (1968): 367–385.

Dalby, D. (ed.). *Language and History in Africa*. London: Frank Cass, 1970.

Diagne, P. "History and Linguistics" in *UNESCO General History of Africa*, Vol. 1: *Methodology and African Prehistory*, edited by J. Ki-Zerbo. Paris: UNESCO, 1981.

Dike, K. O. and J. F. Ade Ajayi. "African Historiography" in *International Encyclopaedia of the Social Sciences*, Vol. 6, New York: Macmillan and Free Press, 1968.

Fage, J. D. (ed.). *Africa Discovers Her Past*. London, Ibadan and Nairobi: Oxford University Press, 1970.

Garraghan, G. T. *A Guide to Historical Method*, edited by J. Delanglez. New York: Fordham University Press, 1946.

Gray, R. "Historians and Central Africa" in *Africa Discovers Her Past*, edited by J. D. Fage. London: Oxford University Press, 1970.

Greenberg, J. H. *Studies in African Linguistic Classification*. New Haven: Compass Publishing Company, 1955.

_______. "Linguistic Evidence for the Influence of the Kanuri on the Hausa." *Journal of African History*, 1/2 (1960): 205–212.

Guthrie, M. "Some Developments in the Prehistory of the Bantu Languages." *Journal of African History*, 3/2 (1962): 273–282.

Henige, D. P. *The Chronology of Oral Tradition: Quest for a Chimera*. Oxford: Clarendon Press, 1974.

Hunwick, J. "Arabic Sources for African History" in *Africa Discovers Her Past*, edited by J. D. Fage. London: Oxford University Press, 1970.

Ki-Zerbo, J. (ed.). *UNESCO General History of Africa*, Vol. 1: *Methodology and African Prehistory*. Paris: UNESCO, 1981.

Lawrence, A. W. "Some Source Books for West African History. *Journal of African History*, 2/2 (1961): 227–234.

Marwick, A. *The Nature of History*. London: Macmillan, 2nd Edition, 1981.

McCall, D. F. *Africa in Time-Perspective: A Discussion of Historical Reconstruction from Unwritten Sources*. Boston (USA): Boston University Press, Legon: Ghana University Press, 1964, New York: Oxford University Press, 1969.

Oliver, R. "The Problem of the Bantu Expansion." *Journal of African History*. 7/3 (1966): 361–376.

Person, Y. "Tradition Oral et Chronologie," *Cahiers d'etudes Africaines*, 7/2 (1962): 462–476, translated by S. Sherwin, "Chronology of Oral Tradition" in *Perspectives on the African Past*, edited by M. A. Klein and G. W. Johnson. Canada and Boston: Little, Brown and Company, 1972.

Shaw, T. "Archaeology and the Dating of African History" in *Africa Discovers Her Past*, edited by J. D. Fage, London, Ibadan and Nairobi: Oxford University Press, 1970.

_______. "The Prehistory of West Africa" in *History of West Africa*, Vol. 1, edited by J. F. Ade Ajayi and M. Crowder. London: Longman Group, 1971.

Vansina, J. *Oral Tradition: A Study in Historical Methodology*, translated by H. M. Wright, Chicago.

_______. "Oral Tradition and Its Methodology" in *UNESCO General History of Africa*, Vol. 1: *Methodology and African Prehistory*, edited by J. Ki-Zerbo. Paris: UNESCO, 1981.

Hominids: *See* Humankind: Hominids, Early, Origins of.

Horton, James Africanus Beale (1835–1883)

Sierra Leonean Scientist and Patriot

Medical doctor and researcher, army officer, administrator, geologist, mining entrepreneur, banker, and political scientist, Horton grew up in a society in which skin color was no barrier to advancement. Senior official posts, including that of governor, were held at this period by men of African descent. In London, the War Office, alarmed by the high mortality rate among army medical officers in West Africa, decided to recruit Africans. Horton was chosen with two others (one died in England) to study medicine at King's College, London. From there he went on to Edinburgh University where in 1859 he graduated with a doctorate. He at once published his doctoral thesis, *The Medical Topography of the West Coast of Africa*, adding on the title page the name "Africanus" (Beale, his former headmaster's name, he had already adopted), to identify himself as an African.

Horton and his fellow student William Davies were then given commissions in the army. He was posted to the Gold Coast (Ghana) where he spent most of his army career. In the early years he was ill treated by his fellow officers, who resented his presence and persuaded the War Office not to appoint any more African medical officers. But it could not be denied that he carried out his military duties efficiently, including service in the Anglo-Asante wars of 1863–64 and 1873–74. He also acted regularly as an administrative officer in the districts where he was stationed. Wherever he went he conducted medical, botanical, and geological research.

During this time, the British government was considering a political reorganization of the West African colonies, and possibly a withdrawal from them. Horton began formulating his political ideas in a brief pamphlet published in 1865. In 1866 he went on leave to England, and there published three books; two were medical: *Physical and Medical Climate and Meteorology of the West Coast of Africa* (1867) and *Guinea Worm, or Dracunculus* (1868). The third was his best-known work, *West African Countries and Peoples* (1867). He subtitled it *A Vindication of the African Race* and began by contesting the theories of white racial supremacy that were then becoming prevalent. These he refuted empirically and showed to be groundless. There next followed a blueprint for the political reorganization of West Africa. He envisioned its peoples developing as self-governing nations and outlined appropriate constitutions for each, based on his own estimates of their political and economic potential. They included those under not only British rule but the Yoruba country, already under Christian missionary influence, and even his own ancestral Igbo country, still virtually unknown to Europeans. They would at first be under British protection but ultimately form a united West Africa, with its own government and legislature, a proposal for which he has been hailed as a pioneer of Pan-Africanism. For his plans to succeed, the rich, neglected, economic resources of West Africa would have to be developed, and the proceeds spent on sanitary and health measures as well as providing universal education.

On return, he was able to make a start toward putting his plans into practice. The Fante peoples were becoming dissatisfied with the British authorities, and in 1868 the leading chiefs and businessmen formed a "Fanti Confederation" to protect their interests. Horton saw in their initiative the nucleus of his self-governing West Africa and sent the Colonial Office a series of letters, published as *Letters on the Political Condition of the Gold Coast* (1870), urging that the confederation be officially recognized and drafting for it a constitution, which was adopted in modified form. However, the British authorities refused to recognize the confederation, and its members fell to quarreling; within a couple of years it had dissolved.

Horton gave up political writing. In 1874 he published a comprehensive medical reference work, *The Diseases of Tropical Climates and their Treatment*, with a revised edition appearing in 1879. His activities had now become increasingly entrepreneurial. Using his knowledge of geology, he located potential goldfields, obtained mining concessions from chiefs, surveyed a potential railway line to link them and, with an associate in London, floated companies to exploit them. In 1880 he retired with the rank of lieutenant colonel and returned to Freetown, where he had bought a large mansion, to devote himself to his business interests. He also opened a bank. His years of service had been regularly punctuated with illness. His health worsened, and on October 15, 1883, he died of the infectious disease erysipelas.

Horton married twice: in 1862 to Fannie Pratt, daughter of a wealthy recaptive, who died in 1865, and again in 1875 to Selina Elliott, a member of one of the old Freetown settler families. He left an elaborate will, endowing with his substantial fortune an institution to provide scientific and technological education in Freetown. But for the next thirty years his relatives contested it, the value of his mining investments collapsed, and his institution was never founded. Meanwhile his dreams of West African self-government were swept away by the racially stratified colonial rule of the early twentieth century. Only in the era of decolonization was his work again recognized. His emphasis on the need for governments to invest in economic development, public health, and education, and his pioneer Pan-Africanism fitted the policies and aspirations of the new African states; he was recognized belatedly for his achievements and vision.

CHRISTOPHER FYFE

See also: **Du Bois, W. E. B., and Pan-Africanism; Organization of African Unity (OAU) and Pan-Africanism.**

Biography

James Africanus Beale Horton was born on June 1, 1835, in Sierra Leone, at Gloucester village, in the mountains above Freetown. His parents, James and Nancy Horton, were Igbo recaptives, among the thousands captured by the British navy from slave ships in transit across the Atlantic and liberated in Sierra Leone. His father was a carpenter who, like most recaptives, took a European name and became a Christian. He attended the village school and in 1847 was given a scholarship to the Church Missionary Society Grammar School in Freetown. In 1853 he left for Fourah Bay Institution (later College) to study for the Anglican ministry. He published several books and is generally considered a pioneer of Pan-Africanist thought. He died of the infectious disease erysipelas on October 15, 1883.

Further Reading

Fyfe, C. *Africanus Horton: West African Scientist and Patriot.* New York: Oxford University Press, 1972.
———. "Africanus Horton as a Constitution-Maker." *The Journal of Commonwealth and Comparative Politics.* 26, no. 2 (1988): 173–184.
———. *A History of Sierra Leone.* London: Oxford University Press, 1962.
Geiss, I. *The Pan-African Movement.* London: Methuen, 1974.
Horton, A. B. *Letters on the Political Condition of the Gold Coast.* London: Frank Cass, 1970.
———. *West African Countries and Peoples.* Edinburgh: Edinburgh University Press, 1969.
Nicol, D. *Africanus Horton: The Dawn of Natzonalism in Modern Africa.* London: Longman, 1969.

Houphouët-Boigny, Félix (1905–1993)
President and Politician

Felix Houphouët-Boigny was the dominant political figure in Côte d'Ivoire and West Africa until his death in November 1993. Born into a chiefly Baoulé family in Yamoussoukro on October 18, 1905, Houphouët-Boigny followed the typical path of someone from a prominent African tribe in the French colonial system. Unlike the vast majority of his countrymen, he received a primary and secondary education. Between 1925 and 1940, he traveled throughout Côte d'Ivoire as a practitioner of pharmacy medicine.

In 1940 he became a district officer in the colonial administration. He was also a planter of cocoa and coffee. In fact, by the 1930s, he was one of the country's largest cocoa producers. He rose to political prominence with the creation of the *Syndicat Agricole Africain* (SAA)—the country's first African led rural union. Elected as Côte d'Ivoire's deputy to the French Constituent Assembly in 1945, he was instrumental in getting the French parliament to abolish a forced labor law that was hated widely by Africans, especially farmers who were deprived of needed labor because of the law. With this success, he, along with other prominent members of SAA, launched the country's first independent political party, the *Parti Démocratique de la Côte d'Ivoire* (PDCI), which became part of a larger federation of parties in French-speaking West Africa, *Rassemblement Démocratique Africain.*

While the PDCI-RDA was initially positioned on the left with the support of the French Communist Party, Houphouët-Boigny broke with the Communists in 1950 and became one of France's staunchest supporters in West Africa. He served first as a minister attached to the French prime minister's office between 1956 and 1957 and then minister of health in 1957 to 1958. From 1958 to 1959, he was minister of state in three successive French cabinets, those of Pflimlim, De Gaulle, and Debré. Even after Côte d'Ivoire gained independence in 1960, Houphouët-Boigny maintained extremely close ties with the country's former colonial power.

The constitution that was adopted in 1960 gave the president preeminence over the legislature and judiciary. The president is elected for five years by direct universal suffrage and able to renew his mandate an unlimited number of times. Felix Houphouët-Boigny was elected president. In subsequent elections, he was reelected with more than 90 per cent of the popular vote. Along with the presidency, he headed the ministries for foreign affairs (1961), the interior, education, agriculture (1963), and defense (1963–74).

Houphouët-Boigny's main objective was to keep full control over the political dynamics in the country. He was able to do this by utilizing the broad powers provided to him by the constitution and one-party rule to push through legislation without any significant opposition. Thus, there was no real separation of powers between the various branches of government. Power and decision making was in the hands of the president and the ministers that he personally selected. He used his broad powers to satisfy the political elite with patronage positions in the bureaucracy and party. He diffused potential ethnic tension by maintaining a rough balance among the country's major ethnic groups in his appointments to the cabinet, and when necessary, he jailed or exiled opponents.

Probably more than any other postcolonial African leader, Houphouët-Boigny continued to seek legitimacy of his personalization of power from the public. Unlike Sekou Touré in Guinea and Kwame Nkrumah in Ghana who explicitly developed their own ideological systems as a guide for their countrymen and other Africans in a broader Pan-African context, Houphouët-Boigny never explicitly set out to directly expose his thoughts. For example, he never advocated a form of "Houphouëtism" in the way that Touré and Nkrumah did. He refused to have his thoughts published and disseminated to the masses and publicly disavowed any official cult of personality.

Despite these apparent limitations on fostering a cult of personality, Houphouët-Boigny cultivated a highly personalized image of himself as the father of the Ivorian nation. He reinforced the country's close identification with him by the holding of periodic national dialogues. These were occasions for the president to invite the nation's major socioprofessional groups together to listen to their complaints about the government, social issues, and economic concerns. More specifically, as Michael A. Cohen in *Urban Policy and Political Conflict in Africa* noted, they permitted the president "to emphasize the difference between himself and members of his government." This strategy worked as the following comment indicates: "The ministers don't mean anything. It is the President who acts."

The same thing was true for the country's only political party. Until the reintroduction of multiparty competition in 1990, the PDCI served as the political guardian for the Houphouët-Boigny regime. No other parties were permitted and the country's major socio-professional associations were obligated to associate themselves with the party. The party quickly lost its function as a mass mobilization machine. Rarely did it mobilize Ivorians for ideological purposes; its primary task was to ensure that opposition forces did not take root in Ivorian society.

After decades of spectacular economic growth under his leadership, the economy declined in the 1980s. As the economic crisis deepened, the International Monetary Fund, the World Bank, and popular forces demanded economic and political reforms. Reluctantly, President Houphouët-Boigny introduced a number of changes in the early 1990s. First, as mentioned above, new electoral rules opened the system to multiparty politics. Second, the government attempted to decentralize decision making by creating municipal governments. Before 1980, there were only two municipalities, Abidjan and Bouaké. Afterward there were over 100 municipal governments. Third, in 1990, President Houphouët-Boigny appointed a prime minister to manage the day-to-day affairs of the country. And finally, he revised the constitution and designated the speaker of the assembly as his successor.

In search of immortality, Houphouët-Boigny built the world's largest basilica in his birthplace, Yamoussoukro, which had become the nation's capital in 1983. On the stained glass in the basilica, one can see Felix Houphouët-Boigny, a fervent Catholic, ascending to heaven.

DWAYNE WOODS

See also: **Côte d'Ivoire.**

Biography

Born into a chiefly Baoulé family in Yamoussoukro on October 18, 1905. Studied pharmacy at the elite William Ponty School in Dakar, Senegal. In 1940 he became a district officer in the colonial administration. Elected as Côte d'Ivoire's deputy to the French Constituent Assembly in 1945. As a minister attached to the French prime minister's office between 1956 and 1957, as minister of health from 1957 to 1958, and as minister of state in three successive French cabinets. Elected president in 1960. Also headed the ministries for foreign affairs (1961), the interior, education, and agriculture (1963), and defense (1963–1974). Died 1993.

Further Reading

Toungara, J. M. "The Apotheosis of Côte d'Ivoire's Nana Houphouët-Boigny." *The Journal of Modern African Studies.* 28, no. 1 (1990).

Woods, D. "Ethno-Regional Demands, Symbolic and Redistributive Politics: Sugar Complexes in the North of the Côte d'Ivoire." *Journal of Ethnic and Racial Studies.* 12 (1990): 470–88.

_______. "The Politicization of Teachers' Associations in the Côte d'Ivoire." *African Studies Review.* 39 (1996): 113–29.

Zolberg, A. *One-Party Government in the Côte d'Ivoire.* Princeton, N.J.: Princeton University Press, 1964.

Human Rights: Postcolonial Africa

Human rights concepts are notoriously subjective, and their interpretation is at the core of recent controversies in Africa. Despite lapses, in general Western governments are usually judged by Western observers to have better human rights observance records than virtually all African states. Why should this be the case? Many African governments would, in fact, deny that this is the case and, when charged with a poor human rights regime, might argue that their society's conception of rights is different from, rather than inferior to, that of the West. Consequently they would contend that, where human rights are concerned it is difficult, if not impossible, to compare like with like. In addition, some African governments have sought to defend what many (not only Western) observers have judged to be arbitrary or harsh treatment of individuals by arguing that such actions are occasionally justified in the name of the collective (or national) good.

Because of their nature, human rights have long since ceased to be the exclusive preserve of individual governments. Over time, human rights concerns have become of universal significance. Since the end of World War II, the United Nations (UN) has sought to promote human rights observance with the aim that regional institutions are needed to oversee improvements in human rights regimes in individual countries. The Organization of African Unity adopted the African Charter of Human and People's Rights (ACHPR) in 1981, with a commission based in Banjul, Gambia, established to promote improved human rights in the continent. However, while citizens in some African countries, including Ghana, Nigeria, and Cameroon, have sought to establish national organizations to seek compliance with the ACHPR, its provisions have remained substantially unenforced for two decades in many continental countries.

Despite slow progress, the existence of the ACHPR highlights the desirability of a better human rights regime in Africa. It also suggests signs of a gradual shift from the principle that state sovereignty must be safeguarded, irrespective of its consequences for individuals, groups, and organizations, toward a presumption that citizen preferences must be taken into account. A continental search for enhanced respect for the autonomy of the subject, as well as for a more extensive range of human rights, is helping create a new set of ordering principles in political affairs in Africa. It is hoped that this development will, in time, delimit and curtail the principle of state sovereignty itself when the latter is used to abuse human rights.

It is often argued that the end of the Cold War in 1989 ushered in conditions favorable to a new respect for universally recognized human rights, and the emphasis on such rights in the new world order rhetoric of the early 1990s reinforced this impression. Moreover, since the superpowers had, for Cold War reasons, been supporters of African regimes that had notoriously violated their own citizens' rights, for example, the governments of Congo (Kinshasa) and Ethiopia, then the removal of this structural condition appeared favorable to a general improvement in human rights for Africans. In addition, determination on the part of the international community to implement war-crime tribunals, for example following the conflicts in Rwanda and Burundi, was symptomatic of the rediscovered universalism that had first been encouraged in the aftermath of World War II. Further evidence of a move in this direction was the greater emphasis on human rights issues in North-South relations. Not only was liberal democracy triumphant in the Cold War competition, but the West became increasingly assertive in demanding change in political behavior in Africa and elsewhere in the South. Political conditionality—the imposition of political tests of multiparty democracy and human rights performance—emerged as a major element in Western thinking. International Monetary Fund, World Bank, and the European Union aid policies were contingent upon African governments' having a certain concern for political and human rights norms. These developments augmented the development of international law that, over time, has placed African individuals, governments, and nongovernmental organizations under new systems of legal regulation.

Another important issue in relation to human rights in Africa is the relative position of individual and collective conceptions of human rights. Individualistic conceptions of human rights have long been dominant in the West, while collective interpretations have long been to the fore in most African countries. However, it must not be overlooked that there are many numerous cultures, traditions and religions in Africa making it impossible to talk meaningfully about a unitary "African" culture. However, despite this diversity, Africans, it is sometimes claimed, have traditionally been more prepared to accept authoritarian governments and are less concerned with political and civil freedoms than people elsewhere. "African" notions in this regard are said to be primarily characterized by societal concern with collective rather than individual rights. The result is said to be that individualistic conceptions of human rights in Africa are products of Western history and derive in part from experiences of European colonial rule. To a large degree, individualistic values are said not to have been widely respected by Africa's precolonial societies but rather introduced into the region following the instigation of colonial rule in the late nineteenth and early twentieth centuries. At the same time, however, Africans are thought not to be traditionally more tolerant of arbitrary power. Events since the early 1990s, when many African countries adopted multiparty political systems, served to cast serious doubts not only on the assumption that Africans are more tolerant of authoritarian government than people elsewhere but also that African conceptions of human rights are not concerned with individual rights. In general, the poor performances of authoritarian African governments in relation to both human development and democracy are believed to have been instrumental in stimulating challenges to nondemocratic rule and to demands for more and better human rights.

The social importance of Islam cannot be denied in North Africa. Islam is rooted in the emphatic importance of collective over individual rights; in other words, there is a high regard for social solidarity within North African Muslim countries. The Muslim community (the *umma*) is a compact wall whose bricks support each other. While the role of the individual is not merely to act so as to ensure the community's preservation, it is also to recognize that it is the community that provides for the integration of human personality realized through self-abnegation and action for the good of the collectivity. As far as girls and women are concerned, if they do not wish to court social opprobrium they must act within norms of behavior sanctioned by Muslim conventions.

In Islam, the language of collective duty seems more natural than that of individual rights. Because of the primary importance attached to obedience to God, in Islam rights are seen as secondary to duties. Rules of conduct were laid down by God fourteen centuries ago through his mouthpiece, the Prophet Muhammad. Since then, Muslims have sought to serve God by thorough obedience to divine rules. The consequence is that if rights are thought of as "freedoms," then in Islam, true freedom consists in surrendering to the divine will rather than in some artificial separation from the community of God. Human rights remain subordinate to and determined by duties.

Governments of North African Muslim countries typically claim divine sanction for their existence and for what they do; that is, their rule is God's will and their policies are, implicitly, sanctioned by God. This is, of course, a potential justification for harsh or arbitrary rule, which has been used to justify denials of democracy, freedom of speech, and harsh treatment of women. There is, however, an emergent trend among some educated Muslims and revisionist *ulama* (theological teachers) questioning the poor position of women and of non-Muslim minorities in some North African Muslim countries, such as Egypt. These are social areas, it is claimed, that have seemed for a long time to be outside the Islamic critical gaze. The Islamic revisionists believe that many Muslims confuse some inherited traditional cultural values with Islamic values.

Despite Western concern with human rights abuses in North Africa—with the position of females and minorities especially criticized—there are several reasons why it is unlikely that individual rights will soon take precedence over collective rights in North African Muslim countries. First, their societies are mostly conservative. Second, incumbent political elites do their best to ensure the continuity of the status quo. Since independence, political elites in North Africa, often in alliance with the military, have striven to modernize their political systems, while retaining a tight grip on power. The avowed aim in, for example, Tunisia and Egypt, has been to build nation states along Western lines. As a result, the status of Islam was at least temporarily downplayed and religious professionals were either incorporated into the state elite or, if not, their power was neutralized. The result was a modernist superstructure balanced uncomfortably upon a substructure deeply rooted in traditional beliefs, with Islam the cement holding the social system together. Elsewhere, in the region's more socially and religiously traditional countries, such as Morocco, governments have sought to deepen their Islamic credentials and to limit the spread of Western ideas.

The core dynamic relating to human rights in both Muslim North Africa and elsewhere in the continent lies not in differing cultural approaches but in the processes of social change and economic development, which create new political realities and tensions. The most important tension seems to be not between Western and Islamic or African values but between modernization and tradition. There is some (limited) evidence that, in Africa, demands for political reform and economic growth have helped create added space for groups and political movements to seek a new human rights culture. However, the important dynamic is not necessarily between Western and African or Islamic values. Most regional governments view opposition groups with suspicion and, even under their own laws, regional regimes are prone to commit human rights violations.

JEFF HAYNES

Further Reading

Black, D. "The Long and Winding Road: International Norms and Domestic Political Change in South Africa." In *The Power of Human Rights: International Norms and Domestic Change*, edited by T. Risse, S. C. Ropp, and K. Sikkink. Cambridge: Cambridge University Press, 1999.

Haynes, J. "Human Rights and Democracy: The Record of the Rawlings Regime in Ghana." *African Affairs*. 90, no. 3 (1991): 407–425.

Jackson, R. *Quasi-states Sovereignty, International Relations and the Third World*. Cambridge: Cambridge University Press, 1990.

Risse, T., and S. C. Ropp. "Conclusions." In *The Power of Human Rights: International Norms and Domestic Change*, edited by T. Risse, S. C. Ropp, and K. Sikkink. Cambridge: Cambridge University Press, 1999.

________. "The Power of Norms Versus the Norms of Power: Transnational Civil Society and Human Rights" In *The Third Force: The Rise of Transnational Civil Society*, edited by A. Florini. Tokyo and Washington, D.C.: Japan Center for International Exchange/Carnegie Endowment for International Peace, 2000.

Humankind: Hominids, Early, Origins of

The first hominid fossil was found in Asia (*Homo erectus*, from Java, 1891; China, 1929), but Raymond Dart's 1924 description of the first specimen of *Australopithecus* (*A. africanus*) moved human origins to Africa. The Leakeys' 1959 find at Olduvai Gorge, "Zinjanthropus" ("East African man"), was a nonancestral robust australopithecine (now "paranthropine" *Paranthropus boisei*). But two years later the site produced the earliest protohuman: *H. habilis*, dated to 1.8 million years ago (hereafter *mya*) and believed, from hand bones evidencing a precision grip, to be the first tool maker, though not found in association with tools. Soon after *H. erectus/ergaster* (1.4 *mya*) was discovered. Among other finds between Eritrea and Gauteng *about* 4 > 1.5 *mya*, most important was "Lucy" (*A. afarensis* 3,2 *myo* from Hadar, Ethiopia), not fully bipedal and with apelike skull but accepted as a distant Homo relative.

Before the 1990s, eight African hominid species before *H. erectus* were known from the period 5 > 1 *mya*; thirteen are now described. Finds from beyond the eastern Rift (from Chad, 1995, a new australopithecine *A. bahrelghazali*) seem unlikely to invalidate the "East Side Story" of origins: the oldest fossils still come from East and southern Africa during periods of climate change within the past six million years.

"Find of the century" was 1992–1993's earliest part: bipedal hominid *A. ramidus* from 4.4 *mya*, producing a new genus, *Ardipithecus* ("earth ape"), possibly an early offshoot of the human lineage lacking any known descendants. (2001: fragments dated 5.2 > 5.8 *mya* have suggested a subspecies, *A. ramidus kadabba*, very close to the human-chimpanzee divergence dated

5.5 > 6.5 *mya* by molecular studies.) The early 1990s' find at Kanapoi dated 4.2 > 3.9 *mya* was named *Australopithecus anamensis* ("Lake [L.Turkana] australopith"), primitive enough to be distinct from *A. afarensis*, and too close in time to *A. ramidus* to be its descendant.

Kenyanthropus platyops ("flat-faced Kenya man," found 1995) introduces more complexity to the origins puzzle: at 3.5 > 3.2 *mya* it is contemporary with *A. afarensis* but flatter—faced with smaller teeth, indicating a different adaptation (possibly a sister species to *A. ramidus*). It shares no key features with the earlier *A. anamensis* but strongly resembles a primitive Homo, *H. rudolfensis* (2.5 *mya*), to which it may therefore be ancestral if it is not an entire new genus as proposed—*Kenyanthropus*—which would bifurcate the human lineage.

The most recent find is the "'Millennium Ancestor'" (announced in 2000), *Orrorin* ("original man") *tugenensis*, at six million years ago, from when molecular clocks show apes and hominids diverging. One and a half million years older than *A. ramidus*, its partial bipedalism and modern teeth make it a possible "earliest hominid," though it could be ancestral to humans, to chimps, to a common ancestor of both, or just an extinct side branch.

"Find of the millennium," announced in 2000, was the near-complete Sterkfontein australopithecine skeleton named "'Little Foot." At 3.3 *mya*, it is pene contemporary with Lucy, though its longer arms, short legs, and divergent big toe suggest it was possibly a more arboreal sister species to a more terrestrial *A. afarensis*. Still debated is whether early Homo is descended from *A. afarensis, A. africanus*, both, or neither. *A. africanus* has a larger brain and more human teeth and face, meaning Lucy may be ancestral to the robust hominids. *A. garhi* ("surprise pith") from Bouri, Afar (1997), is a "scaled—up *afarensis*" except for brain size; at 2.5 *mya* it is on the Homo threshold, thus possibly the link between the graciles and Homo, but its morphological mix (long forearms, big molars) suggests another possible ancestor of the paranthropines (see below).

These multiple discoveries have created confusion, replacing the hierarchical ladder model created by the Lucy discovery with a "tangled bush" image denoting several evolutionary experiments underway. It is probable that not all of the known australopithecines are our ancestors, and at least possible that none is.

The mid-Pliocene cooling/drying turnover pulse of 3 > 2.4 *mya* opened extensive new savannas, and the woodland-adapted "gracile" human ancestor becomes an opportunistic omnivore, leading to increased stature and larger brain size than the contemporary big-toothed, massive-jawed "robust" genus (now "paranthropines" [near-men], *Paranthropus aethiopicus, P. robustus, P. boisei*). These largely vegetarian but non-massive woodland browsers, with dish-shaped faces and skull crests, diverge from the graciles *c*.2.7 *mya*. Possibly also toolusers, they were long coeval but a "deadend" side branch, extinct by 1.1 *mya*.

No clear dividing lines show between some of the later gracile australopithecines and early Homo (now called "habilines" following the definition of humanity by tool making). But the habiline stock has been controversial; *H. habilis* is a very complicated "mixed bag," widely variable in brain and body size; few agree on what traits define it. Some are unsure whether it belongs in the genus Homo or Australopithecus; others believe all habiline specimens should be assigned to either australopithecine or *H. erectus*, or subdivided into large and small taxa: the eponymous small *H. habilis* (brain 500–650 cm^2), the large called *H. rudolfensis* (brain 600–800 cm^2) represented by the 1972 find "1470" at Koobi Fora (L. Rudolf), 1.9 *mya*. The subsequent find of *H. rudolfensis* in Malawi (Uraha, early 1990s) makes this species the oldest habiline yet (2.4 > 2.1 *mya*), and the best candidate for the oldest stone tools, apart from hominids that may be associated with artifacts found in the Gona sediments (Omo, Ethiopia, 1997) dated 2.6 > 2.5 *mya*. (Before this, the Leakeys' Olduvai finds, 1.8 million years old and designated Olduwan, were among the oldest tools known.) Though so far only cranial remains are known, *H. rudolfensis* may be a "missing link"—first member of the genus Homo on a path to modern humans—or, a more Homo-like australopithecine with no direct bearing on the evolution of *H. sapiens*. The Uraha find may also help resolve questions about East-South hominid links, Malawi being the one region to provide a link between the Plio-Pleistocene faunas of East and South Africa.

The initial stage of *Homo* emergence may therefore have seen a number of short-lived experiments producing several contemporaneous habiline forms and two or more successive species ancestral to early and later *H. erectus*, with only one later becoming human. But recent postcranial finds of *H. habilis* show a body too primitive (apelike long arms, short legs) for an *erectus* ancestor.

Key anatomic changes leading to moderns were cranium enlargement, lightly built face, changes to hands and teeth, and reduced sexual dimorphism. These occur in the stressful Plio-Pleistocene transition 2 > 1.5 *mya*, when *H. ergaster* (an early form of *H. erectus* geographically confined to Africa) emerges about 1.9 *mya*, with a modern skeletal anatomy very different from habilines but a smaller average brain size than *H. erectus* and more flaring brow ridges. He is nevertheless considered by some to be directly ancestral to *H. sapiens*, with *H. erectus* a dead end. The most complete early Homo skeleton yet discovered, the 1984 "Nariokotome boy" from West Turkana, 1.6 *mya*, is probably *H. ergaster*. As an open savanna adaptation, the species is built for covering great distances: long torso and limbs and narrow hips for a striding gait facilitate his dispersal from East Africa's mountain valley systems from about 2 *mya*, then radiation into Eurasia 1.8 > 1.5 *mya*.

Within Africa, no clear dividing lines show between *H. ergaster* and archaic *Homo sapiens* such as *H. heidelbergensis*, who is thought to have left Africa around 800 *mya*. A cranium find from Eritrea about 1 *myo* is a mix of *erectus* and *sapiens* characters. Though Acheulean tools are found everywhere, the African fossil record from 1.5 *mya* > 500 *mya* is largely empty (the so-called million year gap) with a dearth of archaic *sapiens* specimens. All the finds—from Kabwe, Ndutu, Bodo, Ngaloba, Omo 2, Eliye Springs, Saldanha, Florisbad, and Jebel Irhoud—have modern characteristics (larger, more rounded crania, higher foreheads, smaller brow ridges), but these are highly variable until 200 *tya* (thousands of years ago). Nor do grades show between archaic and modern *sapiens*: several "late archaics" flourished 150 > 100 *tya*, after which anatomical moderns are everywhere.

The "genetic African" Eve hypothesis (all moderns descended from a single woman *c.*200 *tya*) was shown to be statistically flawed in 1992, but the "Out of Africa" explanation of modern origins, though challenged by the "multiregional model" (moderns arose gradually in many global regions), is still supported by the fossil record, and by current genetic studies showing Africans have greater diversity than any other continental population—meaning modern man has lived in Africa longest, arising 200 > 100 *tya*.

New dating techniques show gracilization and brain size increase in extreme southern Ethiopia (the Omo skull, 100 *tya*) and the eastern Cape coast fossils from Klasies River mouth 120 > 100 *tya*, which are supported by finds of early moderns at the Equus and Border Caves (the latter with first evidence of symbolism—grave ochre and ornament—at 100 > 80 *tya*). Faunal material from the Klasies, Die Kelders, and Blombos caves and from Hoedjiespunt supplies evidence of a shore-based diet in the Late Pleistocene.

Anatomically modern humans were evolving in coastal southern Africa and the Rift Valley when Eurasia was inhabited by archaic hominids (including Neanderthals). Africa is therefore cradle of not only the first hominids and first Homo but also the first true humans.

There is little consensus presently on human origins, other than that four hominid genera existed (*Ardipithecus, Australopithecus, Paranthropus,* and *Homo*, the new *Kenyanthropus* making five), and that considerable species diversity may mean that many evolutionary experiments occurred in the last 5 *my*, with parallel evolution bringing diverse lineages to different stages at different times.

For skeptics, reconstructions of ancestor-descendant relationships are implausible because each new fossil presents a mosaic of features, meaning that such relationships are perhaps unlikely ever to be determined. For now at least, naming ancestors is therefore to be avoided, and instead a simple division maintained between hominids of archaic aspect (*Orrorin*, *Ardipithecus*, *Australopithecus* including *Paranthropus* and *Kenyanthropus*) and those of modern aspect (the *Homo* spectrum, including archaics).

ROBERT PAPINI

See also: **Olduwan and Acheulian: Early Stone Age.**

Further Reading

Aitken, M. J., C. B. Stringer, and P. A. Mellars, eds. *The Origins of Modern Humans and the Impact of Chronometric Dating*. Princeton, N.J.: Princeton University Press, 1993.

Berger, L., with B. Hilton-Barber. *In the Footsteps of Eve: The Mystery of Human Origins*. Washington, D.C.: National Geographic Adventure Press, 2000.

Brauer, C. "Africa's place in the evolution of Homo sapiens." In *Continuity or Replacement? Controversies in Homo sapiens Evolution*, edited by C. Brauer and F. H. Smith. Rotterdam: Balkema, 1992.

Caird, R. *Ape Man—The Story of Human Evolution*. London: Boxtree Publishing, 1994.

Deacon, H. J., and J. Deacon. *Human Beginnings in South Africa: Uncovering the Secrets of the Stone Age*. Cape Town: David Philip, 1999.

Johanson, D. C., and B. Edgar. *From Lucy to Language*. New York: Nevraumont, 1996.

Jones, S., R. Martin, and D. Pilbeam. *The Cambridge Encyclopaedia of Human Evolution*. Cambridge University Press, 1992.

Leakey, R., and R. Lewin. *Origins Reconsidered: In Search of What Makes Us Human*. London: Little Brown, 1992.

Rasmussen, D. Tab, ed. *Origin and Evolution of Humans and Humanness*. Boston: Jones and Bartlett, 1993.

Stringer, C., and R. McKie. *African Exodus: The Origins of Modern Humanity*. London: Jonathan Cape, 1996.

Tattersall, I. *The Fossil Trail*. Oxford: Oxford University Press, 1995.

Walker, A., and P. Shipman. *The Wisdom of Bones: In Search of Human Origins*. London: Weidenfeld and Nicholson, 1996.

Hundred Years' War, 1779–1878

The frontier between the Cape Colony and Xhosa chiefdoms was the first arena in which white colonists partially dispossessed Bantu-speaking Africans. The relations involved are conventionally described as the Hundred Years' War, but they were far more complex than merely a series of armed conflicts between colonists on the one side and Africans on the other. Throughout the extended periods of peace on the frontier, there were mundane exchanges of commodities, labor and even political allegiance between those of different "ethnicity," and even during the episodes of warfare, alliances were forged between groups of colonists and Xhosa as well as Khoi. It was only as colonial imperatives shifted toward agrarian capitalist expansion in the mid-nineteenth century that the balance of power swung against the Xhosa's continued autonomy.

Dutch-speaking colonists occupied the Zuurveld, between the Bushmans and Fish Rivers, from the 1770s. During the first two frontier wars (1779–81 and 1793), these sparsely settled farmers acted in a loose alliance with the Xhosa chief Ndlambe, who was seeking to establish his authority over the Zuurveld chiefs. In 1795, however, Ndlambe's nephew Ngqika rebelled in order to claim authority in his own right. Ndlambe was able to escape Ngqika's control only by moving west of the Fish River himself. As the Zuurveld filled up with increasing numbers of both colonists and Xhosa, differences between colonial and Xhosa modes of authority, for the first time, became critical.

In 1778 the Dutch authorities had attempted to negotiate a discrete border between colonial and Xhosa territory. Through a treaty reached with the Gwali chiefs, they settled on a line partially following the Fish River. Despite the fact that other Xhosa chiefdoms did not consider themselves subject to this treaty, both Dutch and later British colonial governments thereafter assumed that they were entitled to exclusive control of the Zuurveld. The mercantilist Dutch showed little enthusiasm for exercising such control, but after 1795 British authorities adopted a more forceful approach. The "Third Frontier War" (1799) was the result of a British governor deciding to convert a theoretical claim to the Zuurveld into an exclusive occupation. British action was directed particularly against the Gqunukhwebe chiefs, but facing a simultaneous uprising of Khoi servants, the governor was forced to concede the Xhosa's continued presence.

With a struggle being waged between Ndlambe and Ngqika, and between Ndlambe and the other Zuurveld chiefs, it proved impossible for either Xhosa or colonial authorities to prevent an escalation in mutual cattle raiding. Frustrated in their attempts to administer a zone of political instability and conflict, British officials represented the Xhosa as being imbued with a "thirst for plunder and other savage passions." Arising from this construction was the more fervent desire to separate colonial and Xhosa territory. In 1809 small chiefdoms along with individual Xhosa farm workers, were expelled to the east of the Sundays River, but it was in 1812 that the "Fourth Frontier War" was launched by British, colonial, and Khoi troops. Those Xhosa chiefdoms long established in the Zuurveld, together with the Ndlambe, were forced across the Fish River. The expulsion threw the Ndlambe on top of the rival Ngqika in congested lands just across the frontier. Far from desisting, members of both chiefdoms now intensified their raids against the colony.

Faced with the prospect of "endless expense without compensatory returns," Governor Somerset attempted to cultivate Ngqika as a colonial ally. At the same time he pressured Ngqika into vacating further land between the Fish and Keiskamma Rivers. This "neutral territory" was to be maintained purely as a buffer for the colony. But it soon became known as the "ceded territory" and colonists were permitted to move into it. Certain Xhosa chiefdoms were also "tolerated" within it on the condition of their "good behavior." In order to retain Ngqika as a colonial client, the British authorities went to war again in 1818–1819 (the "Fifth Frontier War"), when Ndlambe defeated Ngqika's forces. A British commando came to Ngqika's aid, and Ndlambe's soldiers, spurred on by the war doctor Nxele, almost overran the British garrison at Graham's Town. Only the arrival of Khoi troops saved the defenders and allowed colonial forces to effect Ndlambe's surrender.

Between 1809 and 1820, Xhosa grievances against the British colony had steadily mounted. A balanced, if sometimes violent, interaction between isolated colonists and Xhosa chiefdoms had been possible in the late eighteenth century, but British officials' attempts to instill "order" had brought cumulative land loss, frequent humiliation, and greater competition for scarce resources to a number of Xhosa chiefdoms. The establishment of 4,000 British settlers in 1820 was to precipitate a further shift in the overall balance of power. The "1820 settlers" had taken passages to the Cape in order to improve their material situation, not knowing that the colonial authorities required them as a defense against Xhosa "intrusion." By the 1830s they were broadly united around a program of colonial expansion. Alienated by Xhosa raids, and enthused by the profits to be made from wool production, many settlers envisaged the Xhosa's territory becoming sheep farms. Settler spokesmen directed propaganda against the "irreclaimable" Xhosa in the press and criticized the "futile" efforts of missionaries to civilize them, while local officials occasionally expelled Xhosa chiefdoms from the "ceded territory" on the pretext of continuing raids.

Ngqika's son, Maqoma, was especially enraged by arbitrary acts of expulsion and re-admittance. In 1829 his followers were decisively expelled from the Kat River area and a humanitarian "experiment" was carried out on their land. Khoi and "Bastaards" were assigned cultivable plots with the aim of generating a loyal and productive peasantry—which would also act as a buffer against Xhosa raids. "Hostile" frontier chiefdoms were provoked yet more by colonial commandos which were allowed to "reclaim" cattle reported stolen from the colony by raiding the first kraal to which the tracks were traced. In 1834 it was Maqoma, in alliance with other chiefs, who launched the "Sixth Frontier War" or "War of Hintsa." (Hintsa was a Gcaleka paramount who was first taken captive after entering the British camp to negotiate, and then killed and mutilated by colonial troops.) For Maqoma the war was an attempt to reclaim lost land and reassert Xhosa independence. However, not all the frontier chiefs were behind him. The Gqunukhwebe now assisted the British forces, while Khoi troops, especially those recruited from the Kat River settlement, did most of the colony's fighting. In 1835 British forces also persuaded thousands of "Mfecane" refugees, who had accepted clientship under the Gcaleka Xhosa, to turn against their patrons. Together with Xhosa who chose to desert their chiefs, these new allies became known as the Mfengu. Some were favored with land grants within and just beyond the colony and others encouraged to take employment with colonists.

During the 1834–1835 war, spurred on by settlers, Governor D'Urban declared the annexation of Xhosa territory up to the Kei River. However, the military proved unable to effect the expulsion of the "hostile" Xhosa from within the new territory, and in 1836 a humanitarian and economically minded Colonial Office instructed that the Xhosa chiefs' autonomy be restored. Nevertheless, British settlers continued to agitate for colonial expansion. Attempts by the Colonial Office to pursue a policy based on treaties with the chiefs were undermined by exaggerated settler complaints of Xhosa raids and, when a minor incident involving the "rescue" of a Xhosa prisoner took place in 1846, the next assault on Xhosa independence was launched.

During the "Seventh Frontier War," or "War of the Axe" (1846–1847), Xhosa territory up to the Kei was annexed once more and named British Kaffraria. The Cape government was determined to extend its military power over the Xhosa while allocating much of their land to settler capitalists. Converted to a free trade economic policy and disillusioned with humanitarian policies, the Colonial Office now proved willing to endorse the scheme. By 1850 settler pressure on the land and labor of both the Kat River Khoi and Xhosa chiefdoms were sufficient to create the conditions once more for mass "rebellion." Between 1850 and 1852, Xhosa from British Kaffraria united with Khoi from the Kat River Settlement in a final effort to resist subordination within a settler-dominated, capitalist system (the "Eighth Frontier War," or "War of Mlanjeni," a Xhosa war doctor). After the "rebels'" defeat, British military control was tightened and settler land grabbing further encouraged within British Kaffraria. When, from 1856 to 1858, the cattle-killing movement spread through the Xhosa's remaining "locations," Governor Grey was able to use the ensuing famine and the dramatic decline in British Kaffraria's Xhosa population in order to increase dependency on colonial wages and consolidate settler landholding.

Although the Rharhabe Xhosa were effectively colonized in the wake of the cattle-killing, the conquest of the Gcaleka to the east of the Kei River was delayed, taking place only in the context of South Africa's mineral revolution. In 1877 British authorities intervened in a struggle between Gcaleka and some of the colony's Mfengu clients, precipitating the "Ninth Frontier War." Despite an uprising in British Kaffraria in support of the Gcaleka, the colonial state was now able to bring the entire Xhosa people within the imperial framework on which South Africa's industrialization would be based.

ALAN LESTER

See also: **Boer Expansion: Interior of South Africa; Cape Colony: British Occupation, 1806–1872; Nonqawuse and the Great Xhosa Cattle-Killing, 1857.**

Further Reading

Crais, C. *White Supremacy and Black Resistance in Pre-Industrial South Africa: The Making of the Colonial Order in the Eastern Cape, 1770–1865.* Cambridge: Cambridge University Press, 1992.

Galbraith, J. S. *Reluctant Empire: British Policy on the South African Frontier, 1834–1854.* Berkeley: University of California Press, 1963.

Keegan, T. *Colonial South Africa and the Origins of the Racial Order.* London: Leicester University Press, 1996.

Le Cordeur, B. *Eastern Cape Separatism, 1820–54.* Cape Town: Oxford University Press, 1981.

Legassick, M. "The State, Racism and the Rise of Capitalism in the Nineteenth Century Cape Colony." *South African Historical Journal.* 28 (1993): 329–368.

Lester, A. "Reformulating Identities: British Settlers in Early Nineteenth-Century South Africa." *Transactions of the Institute of British Geographers.* 23, no. 4 (1998): 515–531.

Maclennan, B. *A Proper Degree of Terror: John Graham and the Cape's Eastern Frontier.* Johannesburg: Ravan Press, 1986.

Macmillan, W. M. *Bantu, Boer and Briton: The Making of the South African Native Problem.* Oxford: Clarendon Press, 1963.

Mostert, N. *Frontiers: The Epic of South Africa's Creation and the Tragedy of the Xhosa People.* London: Jonathan Cape, 1992.

Newton-King, S. "The Enemy Within." In *Breaking the Chains: Slavery and its Legacy in the Nineteenth-Century Cape Colony,* edited by Nigel Worden and Clifton Crais. Johannesburg: Witwatersrand University Press, 1994.

Peires, J. *The House of Phalo: A History of the Xhosa People in the Days of Their Independence.* Berkeley, Los Angeles, and London: University of California Press, 1981.

———. *The Dead Will Arise: Nongqawuse and the Great Xhosa Cattle-Killing Movement of 1856–7.* Johannesburg: Ravan Press; Bloomington and Indianapolis: Indiana University Press; and London: James Currey, 1989.

Stapleton, T. *Maqoma: Xhosa Resistance to Colonial Advance.* Johannesburg: Jonathan Ball, 1994.

Hunting, Colonial Era

Hunting served as a fundamental component of European colonialism in Africa. During the early colonial reconnaissance of the nineteenth century, hunting was a basic necessity for explorers, missionaries, and settlers trying to survive in an unfamiliar and challenging environment. As Europeans began to establish themselves and push more deeply into the interior during the mid-nineteenth century, a group of rugged professional hunters emerged, taking prominent positions in local trading networks and entangling themselves in local politics. In Ndebele-land in Central Africa, for example, white hunters first appeared during the 1850s and began to arrive in large numbers by the 1870s. The Ndebele kings solicited the hunters for diplomatic favors, firearms, and ammunition, in return for granting them access to the area's rich game. The white hunters wasted no time in decimating elephant populations, to such an extent that hunters were forced within twenty years to shift from their preferred method of hunting on horseback, to tracking the few remaining elephants on foot through the dense brush to which they had retreated. Frederick Selous, perhaps the most famous white hunter of them all, made his first fortune in Ndebele-land. Selous became the real-life model for Rider Haggard's literary hero Allan Quartermain, anticipating by a few decades the peak of British cultural fascination with the heroic image of the white hunter.

During the consolidation of European rule in the late nineteenth and early twentieth centuries, hunting continued to serve practical purposes. Colonial troops sent to "pacify" African resistance were regularly provisioned with whatever wildlife they could shoot. Individual colonial pioneers, such as Frederick Lugard and Frederick Jackson in East Africa, used profits from their impressive hunting ventures to finance the extension of British colonial influence into the interior. When the railways of East, Central, and Southern Africa were being built, colonial engineers wrote into their financing calculations the practice of shooting game to feed their laborers. Once the railways were completed, tourists then used the trains as mobile hunting platforms, gunning down animals as they rolled by. At the same time, Africans were now beginning to acquire guns for themselves, and found themselves in economic circumstances which often necessitated hunting for food. During the 1890s wildlife became noticeably scarce, and by the turn of the century the devastating impact of hunting was so obvious to anyone who cared to look, that colonial administrators began to take seriously the idea of establishing game reserves.

The cultural mythos surrounding "the hunt" evolved simultaneously with the consolidation of the colonies. As the wars of "pacification" settled into the routine of administration in the early twentieth century, a new cultural phenomenon emerged, that of the recreational hunting safari. The hunting safari became a status symbol for upper-class men who could afford to hunt at their leisure, a lifestyle glamorized by countless juvenile adventure stories, as well as popular novels such as Isak Dinesen's *Out of Africa* (1937) and Ernest Hemingway's *The Green Hills of Africa* (1936). This "Golden Age" of hunting between world wars drew prominent men from around the world to enjoy their own safaris, and merely compounded the devastating effects of earlier colonial hunters on Africa's wildlife. Perhaps the most celebrated safari was that of Theodore Roosevelt through East Africa in 1909, guided by Frederick Selous. In the course of this single journey, Roosevelt's entourage killed more than ten thousand animals for shipment home to the Smithsonian.

This new kind of hunting sportsman was no less involved with colonial domination than the earlier imperialist who hunted out of necessity, an unfortunate connection that would deeply affect the rise of the conservation movement in Africa. White hunters such as Roosevelt and Selous were portrayed as free individualists, adventurous and masculine, the very embodiment of European triumph over the "Dark Continent" and its peoples. Since the early days of British imperialism in India, hunting in the colonies had been explicitly linked to military training, and young boys were taught to see themselves growing into heroic soldiers for the empire. Lord Baden-Powell, the founder of the Boy Scouts, touted the virtues of the hunt in South Africa as preparation for combat against Africans. In some ways, whites held hunted game animals killed through ritualized sport in higher esteem than African casualties of colonialism, killed in response to their anticolonial resistance. The establishment of game reserves in colonial Africa during the early twentieth century was closely linked to the desire that these wildlife sanctuaries would also provide whites with sanctuary from the harsh political realities of colonialism in Africa.

Thus, the wildlife conservation movement that grew during the early the twentieth century maintained, on the one hand, a professed concern for "natural" environments, and on the other, a deep-seated refusal to acknowledge African rights or involvement in their own lands. Colonial conservationists began to bolster their attitudes with pseudoscientific arguments, and many hunters made a great show of pretending to be naturalists on their safaris, dutifully collecting and classifying the various species they shot. But despite this intellectual posturing, the primary goal of early conservationists was clearly to protect and restrict the practice of hunting as the domain of white sportsmen. The separation of Africans from hunting was supported by colonial law, which criminalized African hunters as poachers, even when hunting seemed to be a necessary measure. When cyclical droughts struck African communities, Africans often were not allowed to hunt for food as they had during times of famine before colonial rule, sometimes producing tragic results. The conservation movement in Africa would not fully outgrow its colonialist background until the late twentieth century, and even today, many of the attitudes that shaped colonial conservationism still inform policy decisions on environmental issues.

CHRISTIAN JENNINGS

Further Reading

Adams, J. S., and T. O. McShane. *The Myth of Wild Africa: Conservation Without Illusion.* Berkeley: University of California Press, 1992.

Mackenzie, J. M. "Chivalry, Social Darwinism and Ritualised Killing: The Hunting Ethos in Central Africa up to 1914." In *Conservation. in Africa: People Policies, and Practice,* edited by D. Anderson and R. Grove. Cambridge University Press, 1987.

Hunting, Foraging

The hunting-foraging model is the earliest form of human food production. Until about twelve thousand years ago, with the possibility of cultivation, it was the only means of survival and therefore deserves unique recognition as mankind's earliest adaptation to the world in which we live. The ability to hunt-forage meant survival for humans from their very conception, and it is, therefore, not only the first but also the most important adaptation of all. Hunting-foraging has over time existed in all possible environments and not just in areas of geographical necessity, as has been frequently argued. The presence of such a lifestyle in deserts and mountainous regions, for example, used to be taken as evidence that early man was simply not sufficiently advanced to live otherwise. However, we now know of many instances of its wide usage in areas where agriculture was also present, the concurrent presence of pastoralists and agriculturalists in East Africa being a good example.

In Africa today there are estimated to be half a million people who are, or consider themselves to have been recently, hunters or foragers. Of these there are no more than about 30,000 who actually live primarily by these means. These groups have always had some contact with settled peoples. The dwindling numbers are more often due to the loss of traditional hunting grounds, through the spread of agricultural, and should not be taken as a sign of any inherent or fundamental flaw in the means of production itself. That said, it is equally true that the world's population today is too large for hunting-foraging to be globally viable. That possibility probably disappeared perhaps as long as 10,000 years ago, the result of three interrelated factors: the rise of cultivation, the growth of cities, and significant rises in population, made possible as a result of the first two factors.

The future survival of those groups who continue to pursue this mode of living is, for largely the same reasons as above, not entirely up to them but will rather depend on how they are perceived and treated by their respective neighbors and national governments. Positive images are often patronizing, with hunter-foragers being seen as "purer" due to their lack of material possessions or their perceived closeness to nature. They are also often characterized as harmless, peaceful, innocent "savages." The negative images can be surprisingly close to the supposed positive ones, where simplicity and closeness to nature are substituted for primitiveness, ignorance of the modern world, and backwardness.

The fact that hunter-foragers have traditionally lived outside of any central authority leads to their being viewed with a great deal of suspicion, as being diametrically opposed to systems of bureaucracy. If they cannot be found, they are hard to count, and hard in consequence to tax or conscript should the need arise. They tend to fall through (or ignore) the net of any government policies or plans, whether agricultural, educational, or developmental. The suspicion that exists between settled and wandering peoples is mutual however, and based on a long history of conflict that appears to stretch back as far as their first encounters.

The attitude of some national governments to their nonsettled citizens has been criticized by the wider world, largely through the successful efforts of pressure groups to raise awareness of the plight of these peoples. It is as yet unclear whether these unprecedented levels of interest will lead to any long-term benefits in the preservation of these ways of life. One positive result has been to highlight the fact that the hunter-forager mode of living is not necessarily entirely negative and indeed may actually be able to be of benefit to a country, most notably in the area of working otherwise marginal land.

The flexibility and diversity of hunter-forgers are two elements that have ensured their survival into modern times, in addition to proving to be one of their weaknesses. They enjoy the advantage over sedentary peoples of being able to move quickly if they come under threat, due to invasion or crop failure, for example. This freedom and lack of centralized control also means that concerted efforts on the part of an organized opposition should, in time, be able to defeat the more loosely affiliated and less militarily organized force.

The greatest threat to the continuing viability of hunter-foragers, and an area of perpetual conflict between settled and nonsettled peoples, is the question of land rights. The acuteness of this issue grows annually as population increases place greater demands on available arable land. The problem revolves around legal ownership of land as applied across African today—legal systems adapted from non-African backgrounds. A significant number of African cultures traditionally held land as a common resource, rather than as something subject to private ownership. To European colonists this rather suggested that the land was not owned and, therefore, they were entitled to claim it for themselves. Independent governments across African have adopted this model, which means that hunter-foragers do not own any land, regardless of long term, seasonal usage or occupancy. Land instead is seen as belonging to the country, over which the government has full control to do with as it sees fit.

The strongly felt distrust that exists between settled peoples and hunter-foragers, who are largely seen as unnecessary in a modern setting, or an embarrassing remnant of some primitive past, leaves the future existence of the relatively small number of these nonsettled people in a great deal of doubt. The modern world, with its view of land ownership, national borders, and pressures resulting from population increases, does not sit well with the needs of hunter-forager populations. The best chance for their future survival would seem to be decisions made at a national, country-by-country level, that accord them a legal status they have never before possessed.

EAMONN GEARON

Further Reading

Barfield, T. J. *The Nomadic Alternative.* New Jersey: Prentice Hall, 1993.

Bettinger, R. L. *Hunter–Gatherers: Archaeological and Evolutionary Theory.* New York: Plenum Press, 1991.

Ehret, C. *The Civilizations of Africa: A History to 1800.* Charlottesville: University Press of Virginia, 2002.

Salzman, C., and J. G. Galaty, eds. *Nomads in a Changing World.* Naples: Istituto Univeritario Orientale, 1990.

Stewart, H., A. Barnard, and K. Omura, eds. *Self- and Other-Images of Hunter-Gatherers.* Osaka: National Museum of Ethnology, 2002.

I

Ibadan

The capital of Oyo State in Nigeria, Ibadan is situated in the southwestern part of the country. It is the chief urban center of the Yoruba people (one of the three principal ethnic groups in Nigeria), and the largest indigenous city in West Africa.

Ibadan is an ancient city in the history of the Yoruba, and its rise to prominence has been gradual. The town was initially a small settlement into which people from the Yoruba subgroups of Ijebu, Ife, Oyo, Egba, and Ijesha settled in the nineteenth century, to form the nucleus of the modern city. Several factors contributed to its rise to prominence, the most salient of which was the collapse of the Old Oyo Empire, the most powerful Yoruba state. This was followed by a fratricidal warfare that engulfed all of Yorubaland. With its military might, Ibadan rose to fill the power vacuum created by Oyo's collapse. It checked the southward advance of the Muslim Fulani jihadist forces from Sokoto, which had penetrated Yorubaland through Ilorin, a northern Yoruba town, at the celebrated Battle of Osogbo in 1840. Similarly, in 1862 Ibadan successfully crushed Ijaye, its archrival, in the struggle for supremacy. By 1877, however, revolts by eastern Yoruba groups against Ibadan's tyranny and oppression precipitated an anti-Ibadan coalition in a confederacy called Ekitiparapo, culminating in the Kiriji War. It took the intervention of the British in 1886 to restore peace. In 1893 the British imposed a treaty that formally absorbed Ibadan, like other Yoruba states, into the British colonial system.

In spite of hindrances to Fulani expansion into Yorubaland that followed the nineteenth-century Sokoto jihad, Islam wielded (and still wields) a considerable influence in Ibadan. Christianity also became a remarkable force of change in the town from the second half of the nineteenth century.

Since the original population of Ibadan was drawn from several parts of Yorubaland, especially from the late 1820s, the town evolved an open social and political system in which title and rank depended largely on a man's strength and talent, rather than on heredity. This system, which attracted many people with administrative and military skills, has to a large extent continued to this day in the appointments and promotion of candidates within the political sphere.

Ibadan has undergone a consistent process of urbanization over the course of the last 150 years. The establishment of British rule in the 1890s, after which the city was made a seat of government in the new colonial dispensation, gave it a cosmopolitan outlook that aided its sociopolitical and economic development. After World War II, Ibadan began to witness tremendous growth, which created massive socioeconomic problems in the areas of housing, transportation, and employment.

Throughout the nineteenth century and the first half of the twentieth century, agriculture was the mainstay of the economy. However, Ibadan's location near the boundary between the tropical rain forest and the savannah made the town an ideal center for trade and commerce, with several large markets coming into existence. The city's commercial development gathered momentum with the construction of railway lines from Lagos, reaching Ibadan in 1901, and extending to Kano, in northern Nigeria, in 1912. The increasingly cosmopolitan nature of Ibadan has, over the years, necessitated the establishment of a number of businesses and banks, handcrafts, manufacturing, and service industries.

The University of Ibadan, established in 1948, was the first university in Nigeria, and still retains its stature as one of Africa's foremost centers of academic excellence. There are a number of specialized institutions, such as the National Institute for Horticultural Research and Training, the Cooperative College, Cocoa Research Institute of Nigeria, the Nigerian

Cereal Research Institute, the Nigerian Institute of Social and Economic Research (NISER), and the International Institute of Tropical Agriculture (IITA) in Ibadan. There is also a branch of the National Archives located within the premises of the university.

Since Nigeria's independence in 1960, Ibadan has retained its political position as the headquarters, first of the western region, then the Western State, and currently Oyo State. As the seat of government, it houses administrative as well as federal ministries, parastatals, and agencies such as army, police, fire services, and the central bank. Ibadan, which initially had a central city council, is now divided into five local administrative units: North, Northeast, Northwest, Southeast, and Southwest.

S. Ademola Ajayi

See also: **Education, Higher, in Postcolonial Africa; Nigeria.**

Further Reading

Ajayi, J. F. Ade., and R. S. Smith. *Yoruba Warfare in the Nineteenth Century*. 2nd ed. Cambridge, 1971.

Awe, B. "*The Rise of Ibadan to Power in Yorubaland*." D. Phil. thesis, Oxford University, 1964.

Falola, T. *The Political Economy of a Pre-Colonial African State: Ibadan, 1833–1900*. Ile Ife, Nigeria, 1984.

Filani, M. O., F. O. Akintola, and C. O. Ikporukpo, eds. *Ibadan Region*. Ibadan: Rex Charlex Publications, 1994.

Johonson, S. *History of the Yorubas*. Lagos: C. S. S. 1976.

Ladigbolu, A. G. A. *Olubadan of Ibadanland*. Lagos: Lichfield, 1999.

Lloyd, P. C., A. L. Mabogunje, and B. Awe, eds. *The City of Ibadan*. Cambridge, 1968.

Morgan, K. *Akinyele's Outline History of Ibadan*. Parts 1, 2, and 3. Ibadan: Caxton Press, n.d.

Ibn Battuta, Mali Empire and

By 1324 Mali had acquired a reputation as a fabulously wealthy empire, ruled by a generous and pious sultan, Mansa Musa, who, ruling some one hundred years after Sundiata, followed the great leader's example. He extended the borders of his empire in all directions, incorporating the trading cities of Gao and Timbuktu into the empire, extending his control over the salt-rich lands of the Taghaza region to the north, expanding eastward to the borders of the Hausa lands and westward into the lands of the Fulani and the Tukulor.

In addition to military conquest, Mansa Musa sent diplomatic agents to lands further away, such as Morocco and Egypt. He also strove to secure Mali's place in the world of Islamic learning by importing scholars from Egypt and establishing them in major cities and towns in Mali and by building numerous mosques in the empire. But it was perhaps Mansa Musa's conduct in Cairo, on his way to perform the *hajj* (pilgrimage) in Mecca during the summer of 1324, that made him and his empire famous. Arriving in Egypt with an entourage that numbered in the thousands and included wives, slaves, soldiers, court officials, and one hundred camels bearing loads of gold to cover expenses, the sultan of Mali spent so lavishly that he singlehandedly caused the price of gold in Cairo to fall significantly; tradition has it that it was depressed for years afterward.

In 1325 another traveler set out for Mecca with the same objective; this man was Abu 'Abdallah Ibn Battuta (1304–*c*.1369), a Moroccan scholar who became one of the most noted travelers of the fourteenth century. His trip to Mecca began a long series of voyages for Ibn Battuta, who faithfully recorded his observations on the governments, peoples, and lands he visited, making his writings immensely valuable to historians, and in some instances, the only available documentation of certain periods in certain countries. Ibn Battuta seemed to travel for the sheer pleasure of it; his studies under respected scholars and Sufi saints in the Middle East and his judicial training not only made him an attractive and interesting visitor to the courts and palaces he visited but also qualified him for certain governmental posts throughout the Islamic world. After traveling to Mecca, by way of North Africa, Egypt, Palestine, and Syria, the young scholar journeyed to Iraq, Persia, East Africa, Oman, the Persian Gulf, through central Arabia, to Delhi, Asia Minor, west Central Asia, China, Ceylon, the Maldives, Burma, Sumatra, and Granada. Not until 1353 did he make his final voyage, this time by camel caravan across the Sahara desert to the empire of Mali.

It is unclear why Ibn Battuta decided to journey to Mali. Some scholars argue that Ibn Battuta undertook the trip at the behest of the Marinid sultan Abu 'Inan; others suggest he may have been seeking an appointment and the favor of yet another Muslim ruler, as he had done so many times in his travels; still others believe Ibn Battuta wished to see the Muslim lands of West Africa simply because they were an important part of the Islamic world that he had not yet visited.

Ibn Battuta's initial impressions of Mali were not positive. Arriving in the northern-most town of Walata, he was offended by the behavior of the local governor, who spoke to him through an intermediary, rather than addressing him directly. He was also taken aback at what he perceived as the scantiness of the welcoming meal, a bowl of millet with yogurt and honey, remarking that after this meal "I knew for certain no good was to be expected from them and I wished to depart." Ibn Battuta did not depart, however, but stayed on in Mali for almost a year. He continued to be, at times, shocked, dismayed, and disappointed in the customs of the people of Mali, particularly with respect to gender relations. The traveler was appalled to find his judicial colleagues in Mali freely speaking with and inviting to their homes women who were not relatives, and even more so by seeing their wives conversing with strange men.

The Moroccan jurist was also critical of the continued adherence to Malinke traditional practices, such as the humility with which the subjects treat the ruler, dressing in rags before appearing at the palace, hitting the ground with their elbows, and throwing dust on themselves; the strange feathered costumes of the poets; the custom of slave women, female servants, and occasionally even the daughters of the sultan appearing in public naked; and the consumption of the meat of animals considered unclean (such as dogs) and the meat of animals not ritually slaughtered. He was also disgruntled by the sultan's failure to offer him what he considered proper hospitality to a man of his stature. He dismissed the sultan's original hospitality present ("three circular pieces of bread, a piece of beef fried in gharti, and a calabash of sour milk") with laughter and deprecating comments at "their weakness of mind and their magnifying of the insignificant." When several months elapsed without the sultan offering the traveler any further recognition, Ibn Battuta chastised the sultan, saying that his image among other Muslim rulers would not be good when it was known how he treated foreign guests. At this, the sultan presented his guest with a house and an allowance. However, this was not enough to prevent Ibn Battuta from labeling Mansa Sulayman "a miserly king."

Ibn Battuta's observations on the country were not wholly negative however; on the contrary, he praised the order and safety of the country under Mansa Sulayman. He also praised the sultan as a just and fair ruler, noting that "their sultan does not forgive anyone in any matter to do with injustice," and saying that when a foreigner dies in Mali, the sultan does not appropriate the foreigner's property, but rather guards it until a "rightful claimant" arrives. He also remarked on the elegance and attractiveness of the palaces and mosques of the capital city (whose exact location is not known). He was also favorably impressed by the piety of the sultan and of the people, the wearing of clean white clothes for Friday prayers, and the attention paid to memorizing the Quran. After leaving the capital city, Ibn Battuta had more positive experiences. He lavishly praised the good character and generosity of the local rulers he encountered and was very pleased with the abundance of food and the fertility of Gao.

Ibn Battuta began his return trip after staying in Gao for about a month; he arrived in Fez in early 1354. After reporting on his journey to the sultan, the sultan commanded that he remain in Fez and record his travels and experiences. With the help of his secretary, Ibn Juzayy, the report was prepared in the space of about two years and given the title "A Gift to the Observers Concerning the Curiosities of the Cities and the Marvels Encounters in Travels." Little is known about the traveler's life after this work was completed. He appears to have been appointed as a judge (*qadi*) in some provincial town, where he lived out his life in relative obscurity until his death in 1368 or 1369. Ironically, his chronicles, so valued by the modern historian, received little attention until some five hundred years after his death.

Mansa Sulayman, the ruler of Mali during Ibn Battuta's journey there, succeeded his brother Mansa Musa as ruler when the latter died around 1341. Mansa Sulayman presided over the empire's twilight years. Like his brother, Mansa Sulayman was known for his piety and religious leadership and under his effective leadership, Mali's trans-Saharan trade continued to flourish. However, after Mansa Suleyman's reign ended, the empire began a slow decline. By 1400 various parts of the empire began rebelling against central control (such as Gao), others became targets of invasion (such as Walata and Timbuktu, taken by the Tuareg). By the mid-sixteenth century, Mali was no longer an important political, economic, or cultural center in West Africa.

AMY J. JOHNSON

See also: **Mali Empire; Mansa Musa, Mali Empire and.**

Further Reading

Abercrombies, T. J., and J. L. Stanfield. "Ibn Battuta." *National Geographic*. 180, no. 6 (December 1991): 2–50.

Dunn, R. E. *The Adventures of Ibn Battuta: A Muslim Traveler of the 14th Century*. Berkeley: University of California Press, 1989.

Hamdun, S., and N. King. *Ibn Battuta in Black Africa*. Princeton: Markus Wiener Publishers, 1994.

Ibn Batuta. *Travels in Asia and Africa, 1325–1354*. Translated by H. A. R. Gibb. London: Routledge, 1939.

Levtzion, N. *Ancient Ghana and Mali*. New York: Africana Publishing, 1980.

Levtzion, N., and J. F. P. Hopkins, trans. and eds. *Corpus of Early Arabic Sources for West African History*. New York and Cambridge: Cambridge University Press, 1981.

Niane, D. T. *Sundiata: An Epic of Old Mali*. G. D. Pickett, trans. London: Longman, 1970.

Ibn Khaldun: Civilization of the Maghrib

One of the outstanding figures of medieval Muslim culture, 'Abd al-Rahman Ibn Muhammad Ibn Khaldun was an incisive witness to the political fragmentation and warfare that followed the late-thirteenth-century collapse of the Almohad Empire in North Africa. Born in Hafsid, Tunis, in 1332 to an Arab family with roots in al-Andalus, his career as a scholar, teacher, and judge was spent in the service of various regional princes.

His youth coincided with the domination of Tunis by the Marinids, a Zanata Berber dynasty based in what is currently Morocco, who sought to recreate the vanished glory of the Almohads. Taking advantage of opportunities provided by the conquest, Ibn Khaldun left the troubled environment of Tunis for Fez, the Marinid capital, where he eventually entered into the service of the Marinid ruler, Abu Inan. Soon after his arrival, however, Ibn Khaldun was implicated in a conspiracy to aid the exiled Hafsid *amir* of Bijiya regain his throne and as a consequence was imprisoned for two years (1357–1358). Following his release, he spent two decades serving courts at Granada, Bijaya, and Tunis, and in each case involved himself in dynastic intrigues.

Weary of the turmoil of Maghribi politics, and eager to distance himself from his enemies, he made his way to Mamluk Cairo in 1382, where his scholarly reputation gained him postings as head of the Sufi *khanqah* (convent) of Baybars and chief *qadi* (judge) of Egypt's Maliki legal school. Although Ibn Khaldun remained in Egypt until his death in 1406, he relinquished neither his Maghribi identity nor his fundamental concern with the trajectory of North African politics and society.

In 1375, while still in the Maghrib, Ibn Khaldun temporarily withdrew from public life and settled among the Awlad Arif at the castle of Ibn Salama, in what is now the Oran province of Algeria. There he composed the first draft of his justly famous *Kitab al-Ibar* (Book of Exemplaries), which analyzed and documented the history of the Islamic world up to his own time, especially the history of the medieval Maghrib. The work is notable for its Introduction (*al-Muqaddima*), which claims to put forward principles capable of elucidating the nature of the dynastic state, the prime object of its author's investigations. Following the political wisdom common to his age, Ibn Khaldun begins the *Muqaddima* by explaining how human beings must form communities and appoint chieftaincies in order to survive and prosper. He distinguishes between two types of social organization: primitive, which is the state organized according to modes of natural livelihood, such as agriculture and animal husbandry, and civilized, which is the state based upon characteristic forms of urban life. According to Ibn Khaldun, civilized society has its origin in its primitive counterpart: out of teleological necessity, primitive society is bound to develop into more complex forms of social organization. He explains the transition from primitive to civilized society as a function of *'asabiyya*, identified with tribal consanguinity, and often translated as "group solidarity." The primitive community which demonstrates the greatest *'asabiyya* will, in accordance with man's aggressive instincts, overcome other communities in a snowballing effect that terminates when its dominion finally comes to encompass a region characterized by civilized urban life. The process is strengthened if a powerful religious message is grafted onto the *'asabiyya* of the expanding tribal core. This is what allowed, for instance, the Arab armies under the caliph Umar to defeat the superior forces of Byzantium at the Yarmuk. The ventures of the North African Almoravids and Almohads were each similarly propelled by a combination of *'asabiyya* and religious zeal.

However, according to Ibn Khaldun, the attainment of civilized life also leads to its decline, in that luxuries and riches, once irresistible attractions for the primitive community, now work to weaken its *'asabiyya*. The process of decline begins when an element within the dominant group detaches itself from the grand *'asabiyya* and establishes a centralized administrative bureaucracy protected by a cadre of slave soldiers recruited from the outside. Decline continues as the courage and moral rectitude of the original tribal grouping is progressively eroded by the temptations of the city, and by the emergence of new distinctions of wealth and status. In consequence, the civilized state becomes prey for the next fresh group of tribesmen, with origins in the countryside, who possess *'asabiyya* in its uncorrupted form.

The cyclical theory of history put forward in the *Muqaddima* was closely linked to the fourteenth century political fragmentation of the Maghrib, of which Ibn Khaldun had firsthand knowledge. According to Ibn Khaldun, dynasties have life spans of no more than three generations, or 120 years. The Maghribi dynasties with which he had been associated must have appeared to him to be approaching the final decadent stages of their existence.

Ibn Khaldun's appreciation of a nonreligious impulse (i.e., *'asabiyya*) as the motive force of history and politics was unique in the medieval Islamic world. Ibn Khaldun was aware of having created a new science and prides himself as the first to have treated culture (*'umran*) as a subject of inquiry. The Muqaddima's sociological focus prompted some scholars in the contemporary period to regard Ibn Khaldun as having anticipated modern ideas regarding state formation. Studies, however, have shown how Ibn Khaldun's study was based firmly upon the intellectual resources of his own culture, including political wisdom literature, the positive sciences of religion, and the deductive logic of peripatetic philosophy. He is, therefore, no founder of the social sciences, but rather a medieval man who combined aspects of his intellectual milieu in a way unique to his times.

JOHN CALVERT

Biography

Ibn Khaldun was born in Hafsid, Tunis, in 1332. He moved to Fez and was employed by the Marinid ruler,

Abu Inan. He was implicated in a plot to overthrow Inan and reinstate the exiled Hafsid *amir* of Bijiya and was thus imprisoned from 1357 to 1358. For the next twenty years, he served in the courts at Granada, Bijaya, and Tunis. In 1375 he settled among the Awlad Arif at the castle of Ibn Salama and wrote the first draft of *Kitab al-Ibar* (Book of Exemplaries). In 1382 he moved to Mamluk Cairo, where he was named head of the Sufi *khanqah* (convent) of Baybars and chief *qadi* (judge) of Egypt's Maliki legal school. Ibn Khaldun died in Egypt in 1406.

Further Reading

Al-Azmeh, A. *Ibn Khaldun: An Essay in Reinterpretation*. London: Frank Cass and Co., 1982.

Brunschivg, R. "Ibn Khaldun." *The Encyclopaedia of Islam*. 1981.

Fischel, W. *Ibn Khaldun in Egypt: His Public Functions and His Historical Research*. Berkeley: University of California Press, 1967.

Khaldun, I. 'Abd al-Rahman Ibn Muhammad. *The Muqaddimah: An Introduction to History*. 3 vols. Princeton: The University of Princeton Press, 1967.

Mahdi, M. *Ibn Khaldun's Philosophy of History: A Study in the Philosophic Foundations of the Science of Culture*. Chicago: University of Chicago Press, 1957.

Ibn Khaldun: History of the Berbers

Ibn Khaldun (1332–1405), a noteworthy figure in the history of Islamic thought, was the only medieval Muslim historian to have encompassed within a single sweep the history of the Berber peoples of North Africa. His narrative of Berber history is contained in his *Kitab al-Ibar* (Book of Exemplaries), a dissertation on the history of the world, written in the late fourteenth century, is notable for the theoretical discussion contained in its introduction (*al-Muqaddima*). The narrative portion of the work, which includes along with the Berber materials a discussion of Arab history, aroused less interest among European Orientalists than did the *Muqaddima*. It did, however, find an early translator in the Baron de Slane, who from 1852 to 1856 published extracts under the title *Historie des Berberes et des dynasties musulmanes de l'Afrique septenrionale* (History of the Berbers and the Muslim Dignitaries of North Africa). For many decades de Slane's translation remained the principle source in Europe for the history of the medieval Maghrib.

Ibn Khaldun was born in Tunis in 1332 into an old Arab family, which, prior to arriving in the Maghrib in the thirteenth century, had lived for many generations in al-Andalus. He spent his career as a scholar and served several North African princes before finally migrating to Egypt, where he died in 1406. Between 1375 and 1379 he abandoned his royal connections and lived in relative solitude at the castle of Ibn Salama, in what is now western Algeria, where he composed the first draft of *Kitab al-Ibar*. His main purpose in composing the work was to record the histories of those peoples of the earth, especially in the Islamic world, who had attained state power, which for him was the prime criterion for historical significance. In the *Muqaddima*, Ibn Khaldun treated this subject discursively by analyzing the social and economic forces underlying the development of the state. In the narrative portions of the work he did so by tracing the fortunes of the various Muslim dynasties that, up to his own time, had dominated the Maghrib's political landscape. While Ibn Khaldun may, in part, have written his Berber history in order to flatter the Berber princes whom he served, his chief encouragement in doing so came from the Berber peoples' attested ability to unite and to prosper politically. As Ibn Khaldun says in *Kitab al-Ibar*, the Berbers "belong to a powerful, formidable, and numerous people; a true people like so many others the world has seen—like the Arabs, the Persians, the Greeks and the Romans."

In *Kitab al-Ibar*, Ibn Khaldun followed the established Muslim practice of tracing the genealogies of the world's peoples to the progeny of Noah. He relates to his readers the claim that the Berbers are the descendants of Ham and, more recently in history, of the Canaanites, who were said to have migrated to North Africa in antiquity. He goes on to relate how these transplanted Canaanites subsequently divided into two, mutually antagonistic, tribal moieties, the Butr and the Baranis, each of which is said to have spawned the Berber tribal groupings known to history. Although Ibn Khaldun was as aware as any modern day anthropologist that the contents of genealogical schemes were notoriously unreliable, he also understood the function of genealogy in providing social collectivities, such as the Berbers, with a sense of their integrity and historical continuity.

Of those Berber peoples purportedly descended from the Baranis, Ibn Khaldun devotes considerable attention to the Sanhaja, among whom he distinguishes four major divisions, or "classes," each of which represents a chronological moment in the history of the grouping. The first of these is represented by the Zirid dynasty, which, in the eleventh century, ruled what is currently Tunisia in the name of the Fatimid caliph. The second class is that of the Almoravids, who carved out a religiously inspired empire encompassing the western Sahara, the extreme Maghrib and al-Andalus in the late eleventh and early twelfth centuries. The Almoravids are followed by the Almohads, who supplanted the Amoravids and extended their rule to encompass Tunisia. The fourth and final class comprises the Hafisds of Tunis, under whose dominion Ibn

Khaldun was born. Juxtaposed to the Sanhaja is the other major Berber tribal grouping, the Zanata, the first class of which includes the tenth century movement of Abu Yazid, followed by a second represented by the Abd al-Wadids of Tlemcen, and a third consisting of the Merinids of Fez, in Morocco. The Abd al-Wadids and Merinids, Ibn Khaldun tells his readers, each emerged in the wake of the Almohad decline.

On the authority of the medieval Arab historians Ibn Muyassar and Ibn al-Athir, Ibn Khaldun relates at the beginning of Book IV of *Kitab al-Ibar* the story of how the eastern Maghrib had been invaded by Arab nomadic tribes, the Banu Hilal and Banu Sulyam, in the mid-eleventh century. The nomads, he goes on to explain, were sent in 1051 by the Fatimid caliph in Cairo, in order to punish his rebellious Zirid vassal, al-Mu'izz Ibn Badis. According to Ibn Khaldun, the Arab nomads swarmed over the eastern Maghrib like locusts, and destroyed a region once renowned for its agricultural and urban prosperity. Some modern historians have attributed to the Banu Hilal and Banu Sulaym an important role in the arabization of the Maghrib. Recently, however, critical scrutiny of *Kitab al-Ibar* and other Arabic sources has determined that the processes of arabization and decline in the eastern Maghrib were consequences of general pattern of political decentralization and Arab infiltration, which the Arab nomads accelerated but did not initiate.

John Calvert

See also: **Maghrib.**

Further Reading

Al-Azmeh, A. *Ibn Khaldun: An Essay in Reinterpretation.* London: Frank Cass and Co., 1982.

Brett, M. "Ibn Khaldun and the Arabization of North Africa." *The Maghreb Review.* 4, no. 1 (January–February 1979: 8–16.

Brett, M., and E. Fentress. *The Berbers.* Oxford and Cambridge, Mass.: Blackwell, 1996.

Khaldun, I. 'Abd al-Rahman Ibn Muhammad. *Histoire des Berberes et des dynasties musulmanes de l'Afrique septrionale* [History of the Berbers and the Muslim Dynasties of North Africa]. W. de Slane., trans. 3 vols. Paris: Librairie orientaliste Paul Geuthner, 1925.

Lacoste, Y., trans. *Ibn Khaldun: The Birth of History and the Past of the Third World.* London: Verso, 1984.

Ibn Tumart, Almohad Community and

Our knowledge of the early life of Ibn Tumart, religious reformer and founder of the Almohad movement, is patchy. He is thought to have been born in or around 1075, in a remote village of the Anti-Atlas whose dwellers belonged to the Hargha tribe, one of the branches of the Masmuda confederation. References to his activity prior to his journey to the East in search of enlightenment seem to be legendary fabrications spread by his acolytes to enhance his reputation. Not even the accounts relating to his studies in the East during his pilgrimage to Mecca are entirely reliable. He is said to have studied with a number of leading scholars both in Baghdad and Damascus. Claims that he encountered Al-Ghazali, whose teachings later exerted enormous influence on his doctrines, are, however, spurious. Ironically, it was by following one of Al-Ghazali's most famous teachings, regarding the need to fight against immoral behaviors (*taghyir al-munkar*), that Ibn Tumart achieved widespread recognition. His activity as a moral censor began as soon as he decided to return to the Maghrib. After receiving a rather lukewarm response in towns like Bougie (where he was joined by 'Abd al-Mu'min, first Almohad caliph), Fez, and Meknes, he ended up in Marrakesh. His public sermons in the Almoravid capital, full of admonitions and rebukes to the moral laxity prevalent at the time, soon provoked animosity among the judicial hierarchy. Fearing reprisals, Ibn Tumart and his followers fled Marrakesh and settled in the village of Tinmal, in the High Atlas, in approximately 1125. The embryonic religious community later known as the Almohads was thus formed.

Ibn Tumart's doctrine is both eclectic and sophisticated, in contrast to the ideological simplicity often attributed to the Almoravids. It incorporates elements of some of the intellectual trends then dominant in the Muslim East. Its main tenet is the reaffirmation of the oneness of God (*tawhid*), a feature so central to Ibn Tumart's thought that it was ultimately used as a designation for the religious movement it spawned: the "Unitarians" or Almohads (*muwahhidun*). This insistence on the oneness of God was probably a response to the literal interpretation of the Quran advocated by the Almoravids and, according to Ibn Tumart, its most damaging corollary, anthropomorphism. In this regard, he adopted the Mu'tazilites' position and favored an allegorical exegesis of the sacred text. He advocated a return to the traditional sources of Islam, Quran and *hadith*, in an attempt to end the restrictive legalism of the Maliki school of jurisprudence. He condemned the excessive reliance on legal manuals (*furu'*) and adopted Zahiri views in legal issues, supporting both the use of traditional sources and, when necessary and always with extreme caution, judicial consensus (*ijma'*) and reasoning by analogy. In sum, Ibn Tumart's ideology evinces the strong influence of the theological doctrines of Al-A'shari (d.935) with which he became acquainted during his stay in the East.

Ibn Tumart strove for religious legitimacy, and Almohad propaganda reflects his continuous efforts to resort to popular imagery to convey his message. He took advantage of the millenarian expectations latent among the peoples of southern Morocco and claimed to be the Mahdi, or "awaited one," a figure of redemption thought to emerge in times of moral decadence in order to restore justice and punish idolaters. The fact that he referred to the ruling Almoravids as polytheists (*mushrikun*) was not, therefore, fortuitous. He cultivated an image of himself that often resembled an exact replica of the Prophet Muhammad. He made up a family genealogy that linked him directly to Muhammad (a somewhat far-fetched idea, as both his name and mother tongue clearly showed his Berber origins), and he retreated to a cave during times of tribulation and referred to his followers as "companions" (*ansar*), in imitation of Muhammad. He also claimed to possess infallibility (*'isma*) and to be immune from error.

In spite of its complexity, the Almohad program of moral reform gained numerous followers among the Masmuda of the High Atlas. Its universalist scope remained purely nominal and the movement was always ethnically based. The transformation from a group of religious dissidents to political adversaries was rapid. From his hideout in Tinmal, Ibn Tumart devoted his energies to providing his movement with a solid organization and military capability. Its structure was hierarchical, based on categories of command of descending order: the privy council (*jama'a*) that included the first "converts," like 'Abd al-Mu'min; an advisory assembly (*ahl al-khamsin*) comprising the leaders of the main tribes; the so-called *talaba*, a group of propagandists also in charge of instruction and military training and the "rest of the community" (*kaffa*), organized in groups of ten to increase their cohesion and efficiency in the relentless skirmishes launched against the Almoravids.

The Almohads' military strategy was aimed at occupying the capital, Marrakesh, as quickly as possible. Its proximity to the Atlas Mountains, from where they raided the plains, gave them an advantage. After several clashes, Aghmat was taken in 1130, leaving Marrakesh dangerously exposed. The first expedition against the capital ended in defeat. Ibn Tumart died in August of the same year, but his death was kept secret in order not to demoralize the Almohad army. After three years, the stratagem was no longer viable, and 'Abd al-Mu'min secured the support of the main Almohad grandees and was recognized as Ibn Tumart's successor, adopting the title of caliph.

FRANCISCO RODRIGUEZ-MANAS

See also: **'Abd al-Mu'min: Almohad Empire, 1140–1269; Maghrib.**

Further Reading

Bourouiba, R. *Ibn Tumart*. Algiers, 1982.
Goldziher, I. "Mohammed ibn Toumert et la theologie de l'Islam dans le nord de l'Afrique au XIe siecle." In *Le Livre de Mohammed Ibn Toumert, by R. Luciani*. Algiers, 1903.
Tourneau, R. Le. *The Almohad Movement in North Africa in the Twelfth and Thirteenth Centuries*. Princeton, 1961.
Urvoy, D. "La pensee d'Ibn Tumart." *Bulletin d'Etudes Orientales*. 27 (1974): 19–44.

Identity, Political

The colonization of Africa by the major European powers in the late nineteenth century was caused by many factors, political, economic, and nationalistic. Colonial hegemony brought on by colonization was partly constructed on the idea of race difference, the assumption was that blacks were inferior and needed new tools and ideas to uplift themselves. The advent of anthropology helped to provide many middle- and upper-class Victorians with scientific justification for believing that they had a divine duty to "civilize" Africans. The idea of race was made respectable by reports of missionaries and gentlemen explorers and travelers of the nineteenth century.

Once colonial rule was established, class and race became inseparable.

Race constituted a group identity that had certain predetermined advantages. Nowhere was this more manifested than in the settler colonies of South Africa, Algeria, Kenya, and Zimbabwe. Wages, residential locations, as well as access to education and health care facilities were determined by one's race. While the foundation for a segregated South African society was laid in the decades before and immediately after the dawn of the twentieth century, it was the victory of the Nationalist Party in the 1948 election that led to the adoption of apartheid, that is, racial segregation, as the official government policy. As a result, the South African apartheid regime classified all the people in South Africa into the following "racial" categories: Caucasians, Asians, Colored, and Black. Each race had its own place in the society. The significant point to note here is the way the apartheid regime defined and constructed the idea of race for the purpose of control of the majority by the minority. Furthermore, it is also instructive that the regime created a distinctively capitalist nation whose economy was based officially on racial oppression and exploitation.

In Algeria the victorious French armies imposed French civic codes on the Muslim society. In British colonial Kenya, the Devonshire Declaration of 1923 upheld the view that Kenya was primarily an African country, but the British had the authority to hold and govern the country in trust for the Africans. This view was the cornerstone of the principle of the British trusteeship mandate by which it justified its governance of the country until Africans would be "guided" to independence.

In all these cases Africans were dispossessed and considered in the new milieu to be inferior to the Europeans. Colonialism was a system that buttressed race thereby exerting pressure on all Europeans in the colonies to maintain a pretense of race preeminence and class snobbery so as not lose face in front of the Africans.

Besides race, ethnicity was another critical group identity in the colonial plan and scheme of governance. Ethnicity represents a sense of collective identity that rests on claims of common descent, shared attributes such as language and cultural traditions, as well as territoriality and political organization. In the context of most African societies ethnicity was not unchanging identity. Before the onset of colonialism, ethnic groups in Africa were involved in fruitful mingling and migration. In the process ethnic identity went through constant redefinition as some communities split and were either absorbed by the dominant groups or simply moved away into new terrain to assume new identity. What is important in the history of evolution and development of most ethnic groups in Africa is not how they are, but how they came to be. Most communities operated on the notion that their continuity and long-term survival depended less on its purity or single origin than on its ability to accommodate and assimilate diverse elements. Ethnicity, then, may represent one of the most accessible and easiest levels of discourse on the complex issue of identity, in both colonial and postcolonial Africa, but it is not the most accurate, nor is it explanatory.

With the onset of colonialism and institutionalization of the colonial state, African societies were forced to exist within defined boundaries and borders of the artificial construct of nation-state. The construction of the borders of the African colonial state was so arbitrary that some communities, clans, and even lineages were torn apart and placed under different nation-states. In the same vein, many and varied societies, with little in common, were lumped together, given new names, and depicted as ethnic groups. Ethnicity in the colonial system became relational markers of differences between groups. It served the colonial state as its premier instrument of divide and rule. Ethnicity was used to emphasize differences in culture, economy, and politics among the various communities. Terms that were hitherto merely expressive of ethnic identity became transformed into stereotypical prisms of ethnic differences. Indeed, the colonial state nurtured and promoted ethnic schism by privileging myths in which some communities were adulated as superior and enlightened, while others were dismissed as indolent and inferior. This sowed the seeds of rivalry, hatred, and destruction that flowered in the postcolonial period. In essence, the colonial state nurtured ethnic and racial parochialism for the purpose of maintaining order by emphasizing difference. Individual identities were sacrificed at the altar of group identities, race, and ethnicity.

African elites have confronted the variables of race and ethnicity in many different ways, both in the colonial and postcolonial period. While colonial powers promoted Western education and developed health care facilities, these developments occurred against the backdrop of African political marginalization and cultural disinheritance. Some of the Africans who had acquired Western education attacked racist ideas and presented significant historical evidence on the consequences of African civilization and contributions to human progress. In the French colonies, this critique of colonialism and race coalesced into the Negritude movement. The movement spearheaded by Leopold Senghor of Senegal emphasized pride in African culture but not the dismantling of the colonial system.

However, in some cases, particularly after World War II, the critique of preferential treatment based on race led to the formation of nationalist movements, which challenged and sought to change the status quo. The African elite found out that the colonial pecking order prevented them from assuming certain positions in the colonial public service, denied them access to state resources, and confined them to eternal subjugation. Since racism endowed the settler with class-race cohesion, the African elite mobilized the masses in their determination to dismantle colonialism. In essence, African elite viewed colonial oppression and exploitation as situations reinforced by race difference. Africans were united by their common desire to attain independence. In the course of struggle for independence, ethnicity was temporarily suppressed, and they rose above ethnic parochialism in the determination to present a united and formidable front against the colonial state. The attainment of independence and dismantling of colonial rule signaled the end of race as a dominant factor in the domestic politics of postcolonial African countries. The paradox, though, is that no sooner had the independence been won than ethnicity resurfaced as a destructive force in African politics. The end of colonial rule unleashed forces of cultural, ethnic, economic, and national intolerance with untold suffering to the citizenry. The critical issue in post-colonial Africa has been the persistence of ethnicity as a portent force in national politics.

African elites inherited the colonial state structures intact. The institutions of governance had been anything but democratic. Furthermore, few political parties were developed on the basis of interests that transcended ethnic interests. The African elite and leadership focused more on using the inherited state apparatus and structures to accumulate wealth and reward their cronies and less on democratizing the political institutions for better governance. As a result, the African elite perpetuated the colonial state's authoritarianism as well as agenda of divide and rule by using ethnicity to rally members of their ethnic groups in support of self-centered narrow political and economic interests. Thus ethnicity in the postcolonial period has been used within the wider political field as an instrument in the exercise of power and accumulation of wealth as well as a mechanism for rallying members of an ethnic group to support their elite in their struggles on the national stage.

In the wake of weak economies and fragile institutions, the competition for access to state resources has intensified ethnic tensions leading to military coups, political instability, and incessant civil wars. Ethnicity has become the crushing burden that most postcolonial African states have to contend with. This is not to imply that ethnic conflicts were nonexistent in Africa before European colonization. Nothing could be further from the truth. The contention is that the intensity of ethnic conflicts that have characterized most African countries in the postcolonial period have been destructive and severe in the extreme. Also, the unbridled competition for access to state resources within the boundaries of the nation-state is a unique phenomenon that can be partly attributed to colonialism since the boundaries of the nation-state are fixed. Power struggle and competition for resources usually takes place within the defined boundaries of the nation-state. When rivalry gets out of control the stability of the state is compromised. And in cases where members of an ethnic group were split and live in two or three adjacent nation-states the turmoil spills over to those countries as well. Furthermore, when the state collapses or its institutions are mobilized by the elite and directed against members of a rival group, the consequence is usually catastrophic in terms of human lives lost and the number of people who are displaced from their homes. Indeed, Africa has the largest number of refugees. The situation in the Great Lakes region of Africa best exemplifies the intricacies of the legacy of colonialism, ethnicity, power struggle, and competition for resources and international economic interests in postcolonial Africa.

GEORGE ODUOR NDEGE

See also: **Martial Races.**

Further Reading

Boahen, A. A. *African Perspectives on Colonialism*. Baltimore: Johns Hopkins University Press, 1987.

Chretien, J. P. *The Great Lakes of Africa: Two Thousand Years of History*. New York: Zone, 2003.

Clapham, C. *Africa and the International System: The Politics of State Survival*. Cambridge: Cambridge University Press, 1996.

Davidson, B. *The Black Man's Burden: Africa and Curse of the Nation State*. New York: Random House, 1992.

Magubane, B. M. *The Making of a Racist State: British Imperialism and the Union of South Africa, 1875–1910*. Trenton, N.J.: Africa World Press, 1996.

Mamdani, M. *When Victims Became Killers: Colonialism, Nativism, and Genocide in Rwanda*. Princeton, N.J.: Princeton University Press, 2002.

Ottaway, M. *Africa's New Leaders: Democracy or State Reconstruction*. Washington D.C.: Carnegie Endowment for International Peace, 1999.

Wilmsen, E., and P. McAllister. *The Politics of Difference: Ethnic Premises of a World Power*. Chicago: University of Chicago Press, 1996.

Ifat: *See* Ethiopia: Muslim States, Awash Valley: Shoa, Ifat, Fatagar, Hadya, Dawaro, Adal, Ninth to Sixteenth Centuries.

Ife, Oyo, Yoruba, Ancient: Kingship and Art

Yorubaland is made up of a collection of people who are bound together by a common cultural heritage and language (there are dialectal variations from one group to another). They include the Ife, Oyo, Ijebu, Remo, Awori, Egba, Ijesa, Ekiti, Ilaje, and Ondo. The Yoruba have their original homeland in western Nigeria. These Yoruba-speaking people appear to have adapted to a sedentary lifestyle quite early in Sub-Saharan Africa when compared to many other parts of the continent.

From about the tenth or eleventh century, the Yoruba seem to have evolved a political system that became sophisticated over time and bore similar peculiarities across the area of western Nigeria. The similarity of the political system has generally been attributed to the fact that nearly all the states and kingdoms developed by the Yoruba people claim common ancestry and descent from Ile-Ife (Ife for short).

To the Yoruba, the origin of the world is Ile-Ife, from which all the people of the world dispersed. Ife in ancient and contemporary Yoruba societies is unique because it is believed that a successful linkage of ancestry to Ife automatically confers legitimacy on any Yoruba traditional ruler. Ife is held to be the cradle of Yoruba civilization. It played a key role in the evolution and development of political centralization, with its auxiliaries, which included many sociopolitical and economic chieftaincies. The concept and principle of political centralization seem to have evolved quite early in Ife and diffused to other parts of Yorubaland subsequently. Essentially, the great strides in the area of centralized government have been attributed to a great historical personality, Oduduwa, who in contemporary times is referred to as the purveyor of Yoruba civilization.

To Ife, therefore, is granted the acknowledgement of the beginning of kingship and the institution of monarchy as it is found today in different parts of Yorubaland. Yet scholars are agreed that if the real growth of monarchy, with its additive of checks to prevent absolutism, were to be located, the search must focus on a later kingdom, founded by a group that migrated from Ife and established to the far northwest of the cradle, and which is generally agreed to be its successor. This was the kingdom of Oyo, which seemed to have reached a peak of political centralization in the twelfth or thirteenth century.

Although an offshoot of Ife, Oyo's importance lies in its original development of the principle of checks and balances as a key component of any political structure. While the central political authority of the Oyo kingdom resided with the *alaafin*, his exercise of his theoretically absolute powers was moderated by the institution of the *oyomesi*. The *oyomesi* was the cabinet, which also doubled as the legislature, and could challenge an *alaafin*'s decree. The *oyomesi*, a seven- or eight-member political oligarchy with a *bashorun* as its head could (and actually did on a number of occasions) even force an *alaafin* into exile or advise him to commit suicide.

The powers of the *oyomesi* could be moderated by the military, which was headed by the kingdom's military leader, the *are-ona-kakanfo*, who could lead his troops to challenge any undue affront or disobedience to the person and office of the *alaafin*. There is evidence that such moderating influence was exercised during the Oyo kingdom.

Similarly, the Oyo kingdom developed the institution of *ogboni*, a quasijudicial body of elites who reserved the power to pronounce judgment on individuals convicted of crimes. In a way, therefore, Oyo evolved as a society with many of the paraphernalia of modern political administration, with emphasis placed upon the separation of powers. These ideas were soon transferred to many settlements that were founded by former members of the Oyo community, or conquered by Oyo's forces. Oyo collapsed when the value placed upon separation of powers eroded, as powerful individuals began to exercise overbearing influence on the system that had sustained the kingdom over the centuries.

It is important to note that at Ife, Oyo, and throughout Yorubaland, the evolution of a political civilization also brought considerable socioeconomic and cultural growth. An important dimension of this was the development of art and artistic traditions. Yorubaland remains a rich zone of African arts of considerable antiquity; these are enormous in quantity and vary in forms and materials.

Different parts of Yorubaland have yielded considerable archaeological materials that testify to the great antiquity of Yoruba arts. Ife and Oyo, especially, have rendered considerable evidence of a glorious artistic past. In Ife, for instance, there developed an art industry that specialized in the use of clay or bronze to produce figurines. Ife artists developed an early expertise in bronze and terracotta works, as well as in wood and stone carvings and glass beadwork. The Yoruba are probably the most prolific wood carvers in West Africa, and this has contributed to the greatness of Ife art. Many wood artifacts unearthed at Ife, which are associated with religious worship, seem to constitute the bulk of precolonial traditional Yoruba wood works.

Stone carving discovered at Ife indicate, also, that they served similar historical and religious purposes as the bronze and terra cotta works earlier mentioned. Stone works certainly predated metal works in Ife. Stone carvings discovered have revealed that Ife experts carved human, fish, animal, reptile, and bird figures. Glass beads excavated at Ife were a translucent bluish-green color, quite distinct from the coral beads which are of more recent and contemporary development.

The great arts of Ife have been examined not only in relation to later Yoruba sculptures but also to other sculptural traditions of West Africa, particularly seemingly older ones from areas such as the Nok area to the north of Ife (Central Nigeria). In fact, the antiquity of Ife art has been brought to world attention since the 1910 excavation by the German ethnographer, Leo Frobenius, which contributed immensely to the global knowledge of Ife art and the fame of the Yoruba race.

Similarly, Oyo developed similar arts and improved upon the traditions seemingly inherited from Ife, although there is also evidence of a contemporaneous development with Ife art. Yet, apart from stone and metal working, which have been generally acknowledged as the legacy of the Yoruba, the Oyo also developed a respected expertise in calabash carving, which still exists today.

KUNLE LAWAL

Further Reading

Adediran, B. *Yorubaland up to the Emergence of the States in Culture and Society in Yorubaland.* D. Ogunremi and B. Adediran, eds. Ibadan: Rex Charles, 1998.

Adepegba, C. O. *Yoruba Art and Art History in Culture and Society in Yorubaland.* D. Ogunremi and B. Adediran, eds. Ibadan: Rex Charles, 1998.

Akinjogbin, I. A., ed. *The Cradle of a Race: Ife from the Beginning to 1980.* Lagos: Sunray, 1992.

Olapade, O. *Ife Classical Art in the Cradle of a Race: Ife From the Beginning to 1980.* I. A. Akinjogbin, ed. Lagos: Sunray, 1992.

Ifriqiya: *See* **Aghlabid Amirate of Ifriqiya.**

Igala: *See* **Igbo and Igala.**

Igbo and Igala

The Igbo are the third largest ethnic group in Nigeria and share borders with the Igala, Idoma, Ogoja, Edo, Efik, Ibibio, and the Ijo of the Niger Delta. The origins of the Igbo are shrouded in myths and legends, but oral traditions and archaeological evidence suggest that they have lived in their present abode for several millennia.

Their social and political organization was not uniform; there were variations from one location to another. Many communities were segmented, while others were centralized. Igbo communities west of the Niger were generally chiefdoms with titles and chieftaincy paraphernalia. East of the Niger, towns such as Onitsha, Oguta, Arochukwu, and Nri had monarchical institutions, with an *eze* (king), as the overall head of the particular community. A large part of Igboland had title associations. Men and, in some cases, women were either conferred with titles or they bought them from existing title members. Initiation into these associations conferred on members some privileges and obligations in society. People from Nri town were involved in the conferment of titles and cleansing of villages when abominations were committed and epidemics afflicted the communities. Age-grade organizations and the deities acted as centralizing agencies in Igbo communities.

The Igbo displayed dynamism in their technology and their quest to improve their situation and environment. They learned ironworking, which helped them overcome the difficulties of the forest environment. They engaged in other crafts and industries as well. The smiths, carvers, weavers, and potters produced farming, hunting, and fighting implements, household items, and utensils. Weaving and pottery were usually undertaken by women. The mainstay of the Igbo economy, however, was agriculture, as attested to by Olaudah Equiano, the Igbo ex-slave, and other observers in the eighteenth century. Land was held in sacred trust by the elders and heads of the families on behalf of their people.

The people also engaged in local and regional trade. Markets were held during the cycle of a four-day week (the days being designated as *orie*, *afor*, *nkwo*, and *eke*). There was a temporal and spatial organization of markets in Igbo communities to reduce the incidence of clashes and the cost of both collection and distribution of goods. An Igbo group that took full advantage of the trading activities were the Arochukwu people. They charted trade routes throughout the length and breadth of what later became southeastern Nigeria and established many settlements and colonies. In order to have a free flow of trade, they entered into covenants (*igbandu*) with the leaders of the communities they passed through or settled in. Their famous oracle, *Ibiniukpabi*, also provided them with additional safe conduct.

One of the principal neighbors of the Igbo were, and still are, the Igala. Their geographical position brought them into contact with the Igbo, Yoruba, Edo, and the Jukun, among others. Idah, the capital, is situated on the Niger. The Igala evolved a centralized political organization at the head of which was the king (*ata*). There are divergent views on the origin of the Igala monarchy, deriving it variously from Jukun, Yorubaland, and Benin. The king ruled with a number of officials and exercised control over appointments to the headships of the provincial royal subclans, but his own office was subject to the control of the "king-makers" (*igala mela*) who controlled the election of a new king and saw to the smooth transfer of power in rotation among the ruling houses. He was attended by non-hereditary officials (*edibo* and *amonoji*).

The *ata* was not only a ruler; he was the embodiment and earthly representative of the ancestors. He played the role of intermediary between the living and the dead through daily prayers, offerings, and sacrifices. Contrary to the picture painted by some European visitors in the nineteenth century, the *ata* was not an autocrat. The checks and balances of Igala's political setting militated against despotism. In fact, an *ata* was assassinated in the first half of the nineteenth century for showing signs of autocracy.

The strategic location of Igalaland in the forest-savannah interface meant that both forest and savannah crops could and did flourish in the area. Their traditional economy was based on farming, although they also engaged in hunting, fishing, and canoe building. In spite of the riverine network, the bulk of the people lived inland away from the Niger whose control was vested in the heads of three leading riverine clans. These heads acted as the *ata*'s chief lieutenants on the Niger, maintaining peace, providing canoes for the *ata*'s service and acting as intermediaries between the king and the alien groups that used the Niger. Indeed, the Niger was, for centuries, a major channel of communication between the Igbo and the Igala. Up till the mid-nineteenth century, Igala appears to have controlled the Lower Niger up to the Onitsha/Asaba sandbank, while the west Niger Igbo kingdom of Aboh controlled the region to the apex of the Niger Delta.

Contact between the Igbo and the Igala appears to originate in antiquity. As neighboring communities, there are traditions of wars and skirmishes as well as of trade and other peaceful links. Igala sources speak of the conquest of some northern and riverine Igbo towns by a legendary war leader and giant, Ogboni Onojo. There are earthworks and moats (*okpe Igala*) on the Nsukka escarpment reputed to have been constructed as a defense against Igala raids. On the other hand, the peaceful Igbo-Igala contacts are mirrored in the traditions of Onitsha people; their folklore claims that Igala fishermen ferried the first Onitsha immigrants from the west of the Niger to the east bank, where the people now settle. There are also claims that some Igbo communities were founded by scions of the Ata or Igala fishermen. Nri oral tradition asserts that it was a Nri or Umueri prince that founded the Igala kingdom. The Achadu, the head of the kingmakers, is said to have been an Igbo hunter who rescued the Igala people from the menace of a dangerous snake. In order to reward this gallant Igbo hunter, he was made the consort of the predynastic female *ata*, Ebelejonu, and the head of the kingmakers. These Igbo and Igala traditions underscore centuries of social, political, economic, and cultural ties between the Igala and the Igbo border towns as well as those on the Niger.

The long interaction between the Igbo and the Igala is manifested today in the vocabulary, masquerades, and facial marks prominent among Nsukka (Igbo) people.

J. Okoro Ijoma

See also: **Equiano, Olaudah; Niger Delta and its Hinterland.**

Further Reading

Afigbo, A. E., ed. *Groundwork of Igbo History*. Lagos: Vista Books, 1992.
Andah, B. W., and A. I. Okpoko, ed. *Some Nigerian Peoples*.
Boston, J. S. "Notes on Contact Between the Igala and the Ibo." *Journal of the Historical Society of Nigeria*. 2 no. 1 (1960).
———. *The Igala Kingdom*. Ibadan: Oxford University Press, 1968.
Edwards, P., ed. *Equiano's Travels*. London, 1967.
Ikime, O., ed. *Groundwork of Nigerian History*. Ibadan, 1980.
Isichei, E. *A History of the Igbo People*. London, 1976.
Shelton, A. J. *The Igbo-Igala Borderland*. New York: State University Press, 1971.

Igboland, Nineteenth Century

The Igbo of southeastern Nigeria were a culturally heterogeneous group. Igboland was not a centralized state but consisted of a very large number of independent and relatively small polities, united by the Igbo language, customs, and life style, and by a network of trade routes and markets that had developed centuries before.

Nineteenth-century Igboland was shaped by the decline in the Atlantic slave trade; trade in palm produce; European penetration and the activities of the trading firms, missionaries, and colonizers; and wars and subjugation of the people. During this time, trade in slaves overshadowed every aspect of Igbo life. The means of capturing slaves or enslavement generated fundamental insecurity, increasing militarization of life and continuous war in the region. The increasing European activities also generated tension and open conflicts. Most important Igbo wars were fought in the nineteenth century partly because of the above factors and partly due to the increasing use of firearms. As the century progressed, and population pressures increased, wars over boundaries became more frequent.

Abo and Osomari were the leading slave raiders on the Lower Niger in the nineteenth century when the Niger route saw the transportation of an increasing number of slaves, the victims of the Islamic jihad from the north. Abo evolved a canoe-house system that was similar to that of the city-states of the Delta. The king of the town and his leading chiefs recruited slaves to man the canoe-houses equiped with firearms. In 1831 the Lander brothers captured at Asaba were sent to the Abo king, Obi Ossai, who released them after a ransom was paid. Other famous slave dealers were the Aro, Nike, Bende, and Uzoakoli who got most of their supplies from communities that engaged in wars and kidnapping.

The mid-nineteenth century saw the beginning of European penetration of the hinterland. Igboland witnessed extensive European activities, which were resisted by most Igbo states. This resulted in hostility, which escalated into open conflicts and wars following the granting of a royal charter in 1886 to the National African Company (subsequently, Royal Niger Company, or RNC). The royal charter gave the company right to administer the Niger from Abo northward to Nupe until 1900, when the charter was revoked and the British Protectorates of Northern and Southern Nigeria were established. Between 1892 and 1899, the RNC with its constabulary forces embarked on many punitive expeditions against the Igbo. From the 1890s, the Aro defiantly fought back British efforts to penetrate into the hinterland and resorted to anti-British intrigues with other local communities such as the Ikwo, Izzi, and Ezza, and against local groups friendly to the British. In 1898 the Ekumeku mounted ruthless reprisals against the European and their local agents in the western Igboland.

While the external slave trade declined, export of palm produce witnessed a vast increase. Export of slaves ceased at most Delta ports in the 1830s, but the last slave ship left Brass in 1854. The growth of the palm oil trade existed simultaneously with internal slave trade. The internal slave trade continued among Igbo groups, who were geographically disadvantaged with regard to the new trade in palm produce. The continued trade in slaves, as well as the decline in external trade, had implications for the Igbo and their society. One was an increased number of slaves to be absorbed internally. Slaves became cheaper. There was a tremendous influx of Igbo slaves into the Delta resulting in increased number of the Igbo in places like Bonny, Calabar, and Brass. The Delta became increasingly Igbo in terms of population and language. There was also an increased incidence of human sacrifices due to this loss of the external outlets for slaves. These dehumanizing treatments meted to slaves resulted in series of slave revolts in Igboland. For instance, in the mid-nineteeth century, a large number of slaves left the town of Abara-Uno and settled at Abara-Ugada, an independent settlement. Osomari and Abo also witnessed a series of slave migrations during this period.

Palm oil and kernel production was labor-intensive and was performed mostly by women and children. From the 1830s and throughout the colonial period, Igboland's major export became palm produce (initially, palm oil, and later, palm kernel) needed by the industries in Europe. Igboland became an economic satellite of the European industrial economy, a dependent monoculture. In the 1870s the demand for palm oil declined and palm kernels were processed, used first for soap, later for magarine and residue for cattle feeds by Europe's growing industries. Igboland also provided a market for European industrial products.

To meet the labor demand, the incidence of slavery and polygyny increased in Igboland. Palm produce, a bulky commodity could only be transported by canoe in nineteenth-century Igboland. Thus, its trade was confined to areas with navigable waters and links with the Delta. Trading factories were opened up along the Niger in Abo in 1843, Onitsha in 1857, Asaba in 1863, Osomari in 1877, and Oguta, Atani, and Aguleri in 1884. Oguta Lake was discovered by the RNC in 1885, and it served as an inland port and a base for palm produce from the interior. Oguta was linked to both the Niger and the Delta by navigable waterways. Ohambele, Azumini, Akwete, and Owerrinta developed to become major palm produce markets as a result of the Imo River, which linked them to the Delta. Individual producers carried their palm oil in calabashes to these collecting centers where they were sold.

Following a fall in oil prices and foreign firms' attempts to retain their profit margins by cutting prices, a chronic conflict of interest ensued between the firms and the Igbo producers, who resorted to collective action of trade stoppages. The firms responded through collective action of forming amalgamations in the name of the Royal Niger Company. With full monopoly and authority to administer Igboland, the RNC became more ruthless and formed the worst government in the history of the Igbo (1886–99). Its attempt to establish botanical gardens to increase the range of products for export failed. Thus, the 1870s witnessed sporadic outbreaks of violence, deep-seated and endemic hostility, and even wars between the trading firms and the local people. Trading factories at Abo, Oko, Alenso, and Osomari were attacked by the local people. These states were silenced by the British naval force, including Abo, which was bombarded twice in 1862 and 1893, Onitsha in 1879, Atani in 1880, and Aguleri in 1892.

Other economic activities of the Igbo included smithing, salt manufacture, pottery, cloth weaving, carving, mat making, basket weaving, soap-making, and food processing. Most of these crafts and industries were governed by guilds, which exercised control over methods and standards of production and prices and entry into the industry. Iron technology, an important industry, was associated with the Awka, Udi, Nkwerre, Abiriba, Afikpo, and Nsukka. Smiths produced a wide range of agricultural tools, war implements, household utensils, tools and monetary objects, as well as objects used for rituals and ceremonies. Notable cloth-weaving areas were Nsukka, Abakaliki, Akwete, and the Aniocha and Oshimili areas in western Igboland. Apart from Abakaliki, where men wove, weaving in other areas was done by women.

Salt production was associated with women in Igboland and was limited to the Okposi, Uburu, and Abakaliki areas. Salt served as food, medicine, and currency. The industry was adversely affected by an influx of imported salt into Igbo markets.

Carving was a very lucrative occupation among the Northern Igbo of Umudioka near Awka. Carving products included stools, doors, panels, wooden utensils, and other domestic property, as well as products used for ritual purposes and as insignia. Leather and ivory works were important in Abakaliki, Nsukka, and Anambra areas.

Pottery was another local industry associated with women. The Inyi, Nsukka, Ishiagu, Unwana, Isuochi, Okigwe, Udi, and Umuahia achieved regional recognition as pottery specialists. The sizes, designs, and shapes of the earthen wares depended on the purposes for which they were intended. These included household utensils, musical instruments, and ritual objects. This industry suffered as a result of the importation of more durable European enamel substitutes.

From the mid-1880s, the process of colonial conquest began in Igboland. No Nigerian people resisted colonialism more tenaciously than the Igbo. The conquest of Igboland took over twenty years of constant military action. In 1891 the Oil Rivers (later, renamed in 1893 the Niger Coast) Protectorate was established. In 1896 the officials of this government began the penetration of southern Igboland, which the Igbo resisted. The Igbo fought with capguns, dane guns, matchetes, and occasionally rifles, suffering from a chronic shortage of ammunition, and a British unlimited supply of sophisticated weaponry. Igboland lost its sovereignty to the British colonizers in 1918, when the last Igbo group were subjugated.

Igboland witnessed a decline in the influence of its oracles—Ibiniukpabi, Agbala, Igwekala, and Kamalu—which was attributed to the activities of the Christian missionaries.

The Christianization of Igboland began in 1841 with the work of Simon Jonas, a Sierra Leonian of Igbo parentage, at Abo. The first Christian mission in Igboland was established at Onitsha in 1857 by the Church Missionary Society (CMS), under the leadership of Rev. John C. Taylor. In 1885 the Roman Catholic Mission followed. The Presbyterians built their first station in 1888 at Unwana. This period also saw the emergence of Igbo missionaries who helped in spreading Christianity throughout Igboland. Schools were established. The CMS was the first body to provide any form of postprimary education in Igboland. In 1895 it established the Onitsha Girls School. In the late nineteenth century, it opened a training school for catechism at Lokoja, which was later moved to Asaba, then to Iyienu and finally to Awka in 1904.

GLORIA IFEOMA CHUKU

See also: **Nigeria: Colonial Period: Christianity and Islam; Royal Niger Company, 1886–1898; Yoruba States: Trade and Conflict, Nineteenth Century.**

Further Reading

Afigbo, A. E. *Ropes of Sand: Studies in Igbo History and Culture*. New York and Toronto: Oxford University Press, 1981.

Afigbo, A. E., ed. *Groundork of Igbo History*. Lagos: Vista Books, 1991.

Basden, G. T. *Among the Ibos of Nigeria*. Ibadan: University Publishing, 1982.

Isichei, E. *The Ibo People and the Europeans: The Genesis of a Relationship to 1906*. London: Faber and Faber, 1973.

———. *A History of the Igbo People*. London: Macmillan, 1976.

Uchendu, V. C. *The Igbo of South Eastern Nigeria*. London and New York: Holt, Rinehart and Winston, 1965.

Igbo-Ukwu

Situated about twenty-five miles southeast of Onitsha in eastern Nigeria, Igbo-Ukwu was an accidental discovery. In 1938 a man digging a cistern struck a hard object, which turned out to be a highly decorated bronze bowl. Further digging revealed many more bronze materials that eventually came to the notice of the colonial district officer and Professor Thurstan Shaw, a Cambridge archaeologist.

In December 1959 and February 1960, Shaw carried out excavations on two sites. In April 1964, Shaw investigated a third site. These sites were located on farmland owned by farmers with the surnames Isaiah, Richard, and Jonah; thus the sites were code-named Igbo-Isaiah, Igbo-Richard, and Igbo-Jonah respectively.

Igbo-Isaiah yielded a bronze roped pot, a tusk holder, a pile of iron knives, a copper spiral snake ornament, some globular pots, bronze bowls, an ornate pedestal pot, and thousands of beads of different types. This site also yielded a bronze bell, an elephant head pendant, some copper chains, and many other small bronze objects. It was the cultural richness of this site and the ornamental nature of the finds that made Shaw refer to it as a storehouse of regalia.

A few meters west of the first site was Igbo-Richard. The discovery of a human skull and limb bones made it clear that his site was a burial chamber. At the top of this chamber was a shrine identified by shaped piles of pots and broken pottery shards. Prominent among the artifacts found in the burial chamber were a decorated copper plate, a crown, three elephant tusks, decorated copper roundels, a copper fan holder and a bronze horseman hilt. About 100,000 beads were recovered from the chamber. The contents of the burial chamber suggested that the individual buried there had been a rich and prominent member of a society.

Igbo-Jonah was adjacent to Igbo-Isaiah, on its eastern side. This site yielded a copper chain with about one hundred links, two iron blades, two cylindrical bronze staff ornaments, fifteen bronze wristlets, and a small bronze bell. Found intact in this site was a giant globular pot with five strap-like handles decorated with projecting bases, concentric grooves, and decorated with snakes and tortoise.

The Igbo-Ukwu site has been dated to approximately the ninth century, although this date is by no means certain, and remains contested and controversial. As the ancestors of the present-day Igbo, the people of Igbo-Ukwu are currently considered the earliest smiths of copper and its alloys in West Africa. The art of metalworking is still widespread among the Igbo and Igboland.

An examination of Igbo-Ukwu, and a general ethnoarchaeological study of the area, suggest that the culture of the ancient predecessors of the Igbo was associated with the traditional chieftaincy institution, the *Eze Nri*. This figure was the priest-king of one of the clans, the Umuer. The find therefore signifies a concentration of wealth, a specialized metalworking industry, skilled metalworking specialists, and extensive trade. The Igbo-Ukwu discovery stands as a good example of indigenous processes of trade expansion, social stratification, and urbanism in Igboland in the ninth, tenth, and eleventh centuries.

BENEDICTA N. MANGUT

Further Reading

Andah, B. W., and A. I. Okpoko, eds. *Foundations of Civilization in Tropical Africa*. Ibadan: 1987.
Anozic, F. N. *Archaeology of Igbo Land*. Nimo, Nigeria: Esele Institute, 1985.
Shaw, T. *Igbo-Ukwu: An Account of Archaeological Discoveries in Eastern Nigeria*. 2 vols. London, 1977.
———. *Unearthing Igbo-Ukwu, Archaeologing Discoveries in Eastern Nigeria.* Oxford University Press: Ibadan, 1977.

Ikhshidids: *See* Egypt: Tulunids and Ikhshidids, 850–969.

Ila: *See* Tonga, Ila, and Cattle.

Ile de France: *See* Bourbon, Ile de France, Seychelles: Eighteenth Century.

Imbangala: *See* Angola: Ambaquista, Imbangala, and Long-Distance Trade.

IMF: *See* World Bank, International Monetary Fund, and Structural Adjustment.

Imperialism: *See* Europe: Industrialization and Imperialism.

Indentured Labor: *See* Mauritius: Indentured Labor and Society, 1835–1935.

Independent Churches: *See* Angola: New Colonial Period: Christianity, Missionaries, Independent Churches.

Indian Question: *See* South Africa: Gandhi, Indian Question.

Indigenous Religion: *See* Religion, Colonial Africa: Indigenous Religion.

Indirect Rule: *See* Ghana; (Republic of) (Gold Coast): Colonial Period: Administration; Nigeria: Lugard, Administration, and "Indirect Rule."

Industrialization and Development

In the year 2000 Africa remained the least developed region of the world, following forty years of varying development policies that broadly commenced with the beginning of the independence era in 1960. At that time, newly independent African states faced three options: expanding and increasing the range of their primary agricultural and mineral exports, focusing on industrialization to create the means for sustained growth, and promoting tourism. Unfortunately, most of the approaches adopted, with every kind of advice from aid donors and international bodies such as the World Bank, hindered rather than promoted industrialization.

Much effort was initially put into maximizing the export of raw materials in order to earn the means with which to industrialize. Agreements with the former metropolitan powers and other pressures from advanced economies tied the newly independent countries to the industrial world as suppliers of raw materials, with the result that little industrial or other development took place.

The next strategy attempted was import substitution, with emphasis placed upon the creation of industries to produce basic manufactures required for development. One aspect of this policy, which proved costly and counterproductive, was to establish plants for the assembly of imported knocked-down kits, for example, for vehicles. Peugot did this in Nigeria. In fact, these assembly plants did not provide the expected employment, nor did they contribute much to African industrialization by providing real skills. If anything, such substitution policies impeded development, while the end products were often more expensive than direct imports would have been since they ignored the laws of economy of scale.

However, there were exceptions. South Africa and Egypt had reasonably developed infrastructures and a range of relatively sophisticated industries, while the oil-producing states of Algeria, Libya, Gabon, and Nigeria were in the best position to create new industries as a spin-off from the petroleum sector. Some processing of raw materials, usually agricultural, took place in countries like Kenya, Malawi, or Côte d'Ivoire—although fruit canning, for example, hardly represented an industrial leap forward.

The failure to achieve industrial breakthroughs during the 1960s—a decade of reasonable growth for Africa, when it might have been expected that surplus labor would be removed from the agricultural sector and attracted into industry—meant that the 1970s and 1980s witnessed something of a reverse shift back to agriculture. Ironically, sanctions against Zimbabwe, or Rhodesia, following its Unilateral Declaration of Independence (UDI) in 1965, led the illegal government to embark upon a policy of forced industrial self-sufficiency wherever this was possible, although this was usually only achieved at high costs.

Throughout these years, the failure to attract major investments was compensated for, in part, by inflows of aid from both bilateral donors and multilateral organizations such as the World Bank. On balance, however, the negative effects of this aid have far outweighed its positive contributions. Aid inflows have been more than matched by outflows of resources in the form of repayments, debt servicing, and repatriation of profits by multinational corporations. International aid debts have imposed intolerable burdens upon some of the world's poorest countries. And perhaps worst of all, African countries, or at least their governments, have become dependent upon aid, and turning to the international community to solve problems has taken the place of making hard and unpopular decisions.

The general pattern of industrialization in Africa has followed the same lines throughout most of the continent: the development of the mining industries, which, in most cases, had been created by the colonial powers, the establishment of oil-related industries to service the petroleum sector, an emphasis upon the production and export of agricultural and mineral raw materials, and, where conditions made it attractive, the development of tourism.

The yardstick for measuring industrial output is manufacturing value added (MVA) and by world standards, Africa's MVA is minuscule. In 1996 South Africa had an MVA equivalent to $25 billion, which was $10 billion higher than any other African country. Egypt came next with an MVA equivalent of $15 billion, with Morocco in third place at $5.5 billion. These three were followed by four Arab African states (Algeria, Libya, Tunisia, and Sudan) with MVA equivalents to $3 billion each. They were followed by Cameroon and Côte d'Ivoire with MVA equivalents of $2 billion each, and in tenth place came Zimbabwe, with an MVA of $1.5 billion. During the 1990s a few other African countries had a high rate of industrial growth (13% in Uganda, for example) but they were beginning from very small bases. In 1997 Africa as a whole accounted for less than 1 per cent of world MVA, as opposed to Latin America at 5 per cent, Asia (excluding China) at 8 per cent, North America at 27 per cent, and Western Europe at 31 per cent. In 1997, apart from South Africa, the rest of Africa's MVA came to $54 billion.

Only South Africa and, to a lesser extent, Egypt stand out from this dismal performance. Industrial development in South Africa took off in the post-1945 period, although later it slowed as a consequence of the country's apartheid policies. The end of apartheid and the decision of the African National Congress to embrace an open market approach to industrialization opened up the prospects of much more rapid development. South Africa, in any case, had the advantage of the most advanced infrastructure on the continent. Egypt, too, possesses a reasonable industrial and commercial infrastructure but both countries have a long way to go if they are to compete effectively outside the continent with their industrial products.

In 1999, in response to this lack of industrial development, a UNIDO sponsored conference backed by the African Development Bank (ADB), the Organization of African Unity (OAU), and the United Nations Economic Commission for Africa (ECA) was held at Dakar in Senegal. This was the Conference for Industrial Partnerships and Investment in Africa (CIPIA); it pinpointed the crucial need that was to attract external investment for the continent's industrialization. UNIDO, meanwhile, had been involved in creating integrated industrial development programs for African countries and at the end of the century was involved in doing so in Algeria, Burkina Faso, Guinea, Kenya, Rwanda, Sudan, Tanzania, and Uganda.

The failure of Africa to industrialize is reflected in the statistics of the 1990s: thirty countries containing half the continent's population had per capita incomes of less than $350, while only seven countries containing 10 per cent of the population had per capita incomes above $1,000.

As globalization accelerates, African countries face ever more daunting economic challenges; if they are to succeed they need to achieve sustainable industrialization. At the beginning of the twenty-first century, few countries had even begun to industrialize on anything like the scale that would make them competitive with the rest of the world.

Guy Arnold

See also: **African Development Bank; Mining; Multinationals and the State; Oil; Organization of African Unity (OAU) and Pan-Africanism; Tourism.**

Further Reading

Akinrade, O., and J. K. Barling. *Economic Development in Africa*. London: Pinter Publishers, 1987.

Arnold, G. *Aid in Africa*. London: Kogan Page, 1979.

Bauer, P. T. *Dissent on Development*. London: Weidenfeld and Nicolson, 1971.

Cheru, F. *The Silent Revolution in Africa: Debt, Development and Democracy*. London: Zed Books, 1989.

Dinham, B., and C. Hines. *Agribusiness in Africa*. London: Earth Resources Research, 1983.

Dumont, R. *False Start in Africa*. London: Andre Deutsch, 1966.
Husain, I. *Trade, Aid, and Investment in Sub-Saharan Africa* (Policy research working paper 1214). Washington, D.C.: Africa Regional Office, World Bank, 1993.
Marsden, K. *African Entrepreneurs: Pioneers of Development* (IFC discussion paper no. 9). Washington, D.C.: World Bank, 1990.
UNIDO. *Official Development Assistance to Manufacturing in Sub-Saharan Africa*. Prepared by the Regional and Country Studies Branch, UNIDO.IS.647, 1986.
World Bank. *Financing Adjustment with Growth in Sub-Saharan Africa 1986–1990*. Washington, D.C.: World Bank, 1986.

Industry: *See* Colonial Imports versus Indigenous Crafts.

Ingombe Ilede

Ingombe Ilede is an Iron Age prehistoric site on the highest point of a ridge of the same name, on the left bank of the Lusitu River, a tributary of the Zambezi River in southern Zambia. In the local Tonga language the name means "the place where the cow sleeps or lies down." The ridge itself is named after a fallen baobab tree in the immediate vicinity of the site, which resembled a cow lying down. The site was discovered while digging foundations for a water tank in 1960. It was then excavated by J. H. Chaplin, of the National Monument Commission, that same year. Then in 1961 and 1962 Brian Fagan of the Livingstone Museum carried out further excavations at the site. Altogether over forty-nine burials of adults, infants, and adolescents were discovered during these excavations. The burials were associated with several grave goods ranging from gold beads, glass beads, copper bangles, cotton cloth, copper crosses, iron gongs, hammerheads, tongs, hoes, razors, spokes, and bangles. Several pottery shards from 1,447 vessels were also excavated from the site. Several other items like animal bones, carbonized seeds of sorghum, grind stones and rubbers, fish bones, and shells were also excavated.

The site was first settled between the late seventh and the late tenth centuries, then abandoned and resettled in the early fifteenth century. Most of the graves and their goods date to the fifteenth century.

The earlier occupation of Ingombe Ilede was carried out by mixed agriculturalists with characteristic pottery styles, appearing for the first time in the area. The pottery of this period has two dominant vessel types: a recurved, straight-to-inward-sloping vessel with a band of oblique stamping on the upper neck, a space, and then stamped triangles or hatching on the upper shoulder, or with single and multiple stamped bands on the neck with or without stamped triangles; and a hemispherical vessel with a stamped band below the rim. This pottery type occurs at several other contemporary sites in southern Zambia such as Sebanzi and Kangila in the Kafue River valley, and Ndonde, Isamu Pati, Kalundu mound, and Matobo on the Tonga plateau to the south. The pottery at these sites could be forerunners to that dating from the fifteenth-century site at Ingombe Ilede. Ancestral pottery of this assemblage was discovered at Naviundu near Lubumbashi in the Democratic Republic of Congo dated to the fifth century, perhaps evidence of the origin of this assemblage in Zambia. During this early period, the communities responsible for these ceramics seem to have been decentralized, and possessing goats but not cattle—a typical feature of economies in the forest areas of the Congo at that time.

The fifteenth century occupation of Ingombe Bede was marked by several practices: agriculture, livestock-breeding (both goats and now cattle), hunting, fishing, food-gathering, and extensive trading. An exceptional array of iron tools and implements were found at the sites, some ceremonial in nature and some basically utilitarian. Evidence of trade at the site includes copper cruciform ingots, bars, and wire forms, gold beads and bracelets, glass beads, and amulet-holders, lead, cloth, and ivory. Characteristic pottery vessel forms of the period were flattened sphere-shaped, shallow vessels with filled comb-stamped triangles mostly pendant, straight-necked vessel forms with filled comb-stamped triangles in the necks, necked vessels with everted rims with filled comb-stamped triangles or comb-stamped chevron lines on the necks, straight-sided beaker vessels with zig-zag or chevron comb-stamped bands below the rim. There were also vessels with filled comb-stamped single or multiple triangles just below the rims, and hemispherical shallow vessels with bands of filled comb-stamped triangles or diagonal forms. Pottery of this type forms an important component of the ceramics of early Tonga (sixteenth through eighteenth centuries) communities in a wide area along the Kaftie River valley and on the plateau to the south. Its decorative motifs continue to appear present-day Tonga ceramics. Its origins, however, seem to be firmly placed among the earlier assemblages in the area, such as Gundu and Fibobe.

It is this fifteenth-century settlement of the site, associated with extensive trading and symbolic items, that has made it significant in the later Iron Age prehistory of Zambia. Skeletons buried with gold ornaments, copper crosses, iron gongs, and metal working tools such as anvils and hammers are widely recognized as symbols of leadership among western Bantu peoples. Most burials, however, did not depict such grave goods, a symbol of commonality. The site therefore portrays a stratified society, with members of a wealthy elite buried among members of the lower classes, a new development at that time among Later Iron Age people in Zambia.

No other site in Zambia depicts evidence of gold ornaments at that time as does fifteenth-century Ingombe Ilede, perhaps an indication of wealth acquired through trade with communities in Zimbabwe, south of the Zambezi where gold mining was common. Copper crosses of the type found at site bear close resemblance to those at Kipushi site in the Copperbelt area of Zambia. There, the growth of copper mining and trading appeared earlier, concurrent with the local rise of centralized states in that area. The presence of copper crosses at Ingombe Ilede is perhaps an indication of the spread of a centralized state concept to the Zambezi area. The rise of Ingombe Ilede seems also to coincide with the demise of Great Zimbabwe, a major trading focus south of the Zambezi, an indication that the focus of trade was now the Zambezi valley. The Zambezi became a commercial channel to the east coast, as suggested by the presence of Indian glass beads at the site.

Its geographic position, in a valley rich in animal life and ivory (from elephants), and its close proximity to mines producing copper in the north and gold in the south, with rich local salt deposits, made Ingombe Ilede an unrivaled trading post of the fifteenth century. Portuguese documents of the sixteenth century identified the Ingombe Ilede group as Mbara, who according to oral traditions were either of Tonga or Soli origin, who are matrilineal western Bantu. In subsequent centuries slavery and the ivory trade became more prominent than gold and copper in the valley, but Ingombe Ilede was no longer the focal point of trade. Today the area continues to be settled by matrilineal Gwembe valley Tonga peoples, with loosely centralized kingship systems, who tend cattle and goats and grow subsistence crops (maize) and commercial crops (cotton). Most of them were translocated from the valley upon its flooding by Kariba Dam water in the late 1950s.

NICHOLAS KATANEKWA

See also: **Sena, Tete, Portuguese, and Prazos.**

Further Reading

Derricourt, R. *Man on the Kafue*. London: Ethnographica, 1980.

Fagan, B., D. Phillipson, and G. Daniels, eds. *Iron Age Cultures in Zambia*. Vol 2, of *Dambwa Ingombe Ilede and the Tonga*. London: Chatto and Windus, 1969.

Huffiman, T. *Iron Age Migrations*. Johannesburg: Witwaterrand University Press, 1989.

Phillipson, D. "Iron Age History and Archaeology in Zambia." *Journal of African History*. 15 (1974): 1–25.

———. *The Prehistory of Eastern Zambia*. Nairobi: British Institute in Eastern Africa, 1976.

Iqta' System: *See* Egypt: Mamluk Dynasty (1250–1517): Army and Iqta' System.

Iron Age and Neolithic: West Africa

In much of Sub-Saharan Africa, most notably the Bantu-speaking regions, the beginning of ironworking appears to have been associated with a pronounced cultural discontinuity. This was not the case in West Africa—a generalization that remains true whether ironworking is seen as a local development or one stimulated by external contacts.

In West Africa there appear to have been two successive and distinct economic transitions. The first of these saw the widespread adoption of cultivation and, particularly in more northerly areas, herding. Herding and cereal cultivation were both probably established in what is now the southern Sahara before they were adopted in West Africa proper. Desiccation of the Sahara between the fourth and second millennia BCE may well have contributed to these developments. In the West African forest, however, especially in what now comprises eastern Nigeria and Cameroon, the propagation of yams is now of great economic importance; the date of origin of this practice is not yet known and there is no reason to assume that it was necessarily subsequent to the inception of cereal cultivation in more northerly latitudes. The archaeological evidence indicates that there may have been some movement of people into West Africa from the north around the second millennium BCE, but that otherwise there was much continuity of population from hunter-gatherer stages of the "Late Stone Age."

The same appears largely true of subsequent periods. Despite the fact that well-developed ironworking seems to have appeared in several areas at more-or-less the same time (although variation in the radiocarbon calibration curve at this crucial period renders precision unattainable), it was many centuries before it was adopted throughout West Africa. Little significant change in population seems to have accompanied this process.

Discussion of these phases of West African prehistory is hindered by use of confusing terminology. The conventional terms "Late Stone Age" and "Iron Age" carry the implication that they refer to finite periods of time. The concepts of gradual transition, of overlap, and of disparity between neighboring regions or populations are incompatible with the logical use of these terms. Occasional use of the term "Neolithic" to denote those parts of the "Late Stone Age" where there is evidence for cultivation and/or herding and/or pottery and/or ground-stone artifacts has added to the confusion. Recognition of the essential continuity at this time in West Africa has led some writers to refer to a "Stone to Metal Age"; this has not been widely adopted and has proved of very limited benefit. It seems best to avoid the use of such general terms altogether (e.g., Phillipson 1993).

Remarkably little concerted archaeological research has yet been undertaken in West Africa to investigate this general period. Most investigations have been on a small scale, focusing on individual occupations. The reconstruction of comprehensive regional sequences is correspondingly difficult. The best sequences so far available are those from the plains of northeastern-most Nigeria bordering on Lake Chad, and in northwestern Cameroon.

In the alluvial plains of northeastern Nigeria settlements comprising wooden-walled buildings with clay floors were present from at least the second millennium BCE. The inhabitants herded cattle and goats, being engaged also in fishing and hunting. In the local absence of stone, many tools were made of bone. It is not until early in the first millennium CE that there is clear evidence for the working of iron, despite the much earlier attestation of this practice in other parts of Nigeria. By this time, if not before, sorghum was cultivated on the Lake Chad plains. Throughout this long sequence, the locally produced pottery showed steady stylistic development, with no discontinuities such as might suggest breaks in the sequence.

The Cameroon sequence is longer but less complete. At the Shum Laka rockshelter near Bamenda, chipped-stone hoelike implements (perhaps used for forest clearance) and stamp-decorated pottery were in use as long ago as 5,000 BCE. Somewhat more informative are village sites located in a former forest clearing at Obobogo near Yaounde. By at least the first millennium BCE flat-based pottery and ground-stone axe or hoes were in use alongside flaked stone artifacts. Nuts of oil palm and canarium were preserved, and iron probably came into use around the fourth century BCE. Once again, there is evidence for strong local continuity through the time that these cultural innovations took place.

It is also pertinent to consider evidence for continuity from the earliest West African metal-working societies into more recent times. The so-called Nok Culture provides a convenient starting point. Its sites are concentrated on the Jos Plateau to the north of the Benue-Niger confluence. There is evidence for the working of iron from about the mid-first millennium BCE, as at the Taruga settlement, but most discoveries have been made without archaeological context during tin-mining operations. Highly distinctive terracotta figures, mostly anthropomorphic, have been discovered and dated between the mid-first millennium BCE and the mid-first millennium CE. The style of these figures appears ancestral to the later terracottas and cast bronzes of Ife, to which the later castings of Benin probably owe their inspiration. The elaborate Benin heads of the early nineteenth century depict associated items including ground-stone axe or hoes that were preserved as magical when discovered in the earth in several regions of West Africa. Here, and in the continued use of wooden digging sticks at the New Yam Festival, is further evidence for cultural continuity in West Africa from before the use of metal into recent times.

David W. Phillipson

See also: **Urbanization and Site Hierarchy: West Africa: Savannah and Sahel.**

Further Reading

Connah, G. *Three Thousand Years in Africa*. Cambridge 1981.
Jemkur, J. F. *Aspects of the Nok Culture*. Zaria 1992.
Lavachery, P. "Shum Laka Rockshelter Late Holocene Deposits: From Stone to Metal in Northwestern Cameroon." In *Aspects of African Archaeology*, edited by G. Pwiti and R. Soper. Harare.
McIntosh, S. K., and R. J. "From Stone to Metal: New Perspectives on the Later Prehistory of West Africa." *Journal of World Prehistory.* 2 (1988): 89–133.
Phillipson, D. W. *African Archaeology*. 2nd ed. Cambridge 1993.

Iron Age (Early) and Development of Farming in Eastern Africa

In Eastern Africa, the Early Iron Age (EIA) is generally associated with the first appearance of settled, iron-using agricultural communities. Historical linguists believe these communities were also the first speakers of proto-Eastern Bantu (also referred to as "Mashariki") to have occupied the region, having spread, originally, from a proto-Bantu "homeland" in northern Cameroon or southern Nigeria. The date of inception of the EIA varies across Eastern Africa, with the earliest sites being situated in the interlacustrine zone. Archaeologists have sought to classify the various EIA communities principally in terms of formal and stylistic variations in the different types of pottery found across the region. Since at least some of the chronologically later types are found further south and/or east of the earliest dated EIA ceramics, this has tended to reinforce a view that the expansion of early farming communities across the region was, principally, as a consequence of population growth and subsequent settlement migration and that, in turn, this provided the primary mechanism by which Eastern Bantu languages were introduced into southern and east-central Africa.

Depending on the locality, most of the region stretching from eastern Zambia to the East African coast had been settled, at least in part, by early farming populations by the year 500, and in some cases several centuries earlier. In certain areas, most notably along the eastern Rift, the establishment of Bantu-speaking, agricultural populations was never fully realized, and the economic exploitation of these zones remained very much in the hands of the stock-keeping and hunter-gathering populations that were already well established prior to the appearance of farming. It is conventional to think of the pastoral groups as being derived, essentially, from the various stock-keeping speakers of proto-Cushitic languages who entered the northern end of the eastern Rift at sometime between 3,000 and 2,000BCE, and the hunter-gatherer populations as descendants of different Later Stone Age, proto-Khoisan populations. However, most scholars recognize that this is a gross over-simplification of what must have been a much more fluid pattern of population distribution. Thus, for instance, the influence of Central Sudanic and Eastern Sahelian speakers on the EIA Mashariki populations during the last millennium BCE is clearly attested by the presence of a wide range of Sudanic and Sahelian loanwords in Eastern Bantu languages for livestock, items of material culture, cereals, and various economic practices. Equally, exchange and interaction between the so-called EIA, LSA, and Pastoral Neolithic (PN) communities during the last few centuries BCE and the first half of the first millennium, can be demonstrated archaeologically at a number of sites. However, although such data call into question the value of earlier attempts at simple, one-to-one correlation between the presumed language affiliations and subsistence strategies of different groups, the Bantu migrationist paradigm still dominates many archaeological and historical interpretations of the emergence of farming communities.

From an archaeological perspective, the earliest dated sites associated with the adoption of iron metallurgy and crop cultivation are those on which Urewe ware, previously known as "dimple-based" pottery, occurs. The term is derived from the type site of Urewe, situated in Siaya District close to the Yala River in western Kenya, where examples of this type of EIA pottery were discovered by Archdeacon W. E. Owen (and his seminary students) in the early part of the twentieth century, and later described and classified by Mary Leakey. Additional reconnaissance in the vicinity led to the discovery and partial investigation of several other sites with similar ceramics, including Yala Alego, Ulore, Mbaga, and Seludhi. Subsequent research throughout the region has demonstrated that Urewe ware had a fairly wide distribution across much of Rwanda, Burundi, and neighboring parts of southwestern Uganda and northwestern Tanzania.

Based on present evidence, the earliest sites all lie to the west of Victoria Nyanza and are especially concentrated around Buhaya in Tanzania and the Kivu-Rusizi River region in Rwanda-Burundi. Radiocarbon dates from a number of sites in these areas suggest an initial appearance between the eighth and sixth centuries BCE. The earliest Urewe sites on the eastern side of Victoria Nyanza, on the other hand, all appear to be younger by a factor of 700 to 1,000 years. Recent systematic surveys have also shown some areas to be devoid of Urewe sites, such as Mawogola, southern Uganda and Karagwe in northern Tanzania, despite their proximity to areas with a high density of Urewe sites. It is also evident from recent surveys that Urewe sites show a preference for particular topographic settings and habitats, notably the better watered areas such as riverine or lacustrine environments and along the intersection between submontane forest and woody savanna. Moreover, with their demands for fields and fuel, EIA populations ultimately altered the distribution of forests, and may well have induced a number of other environmental changes, at least in some areas such as Buhaya where this activity appears to have been particularly intense.

It is generally assumed that EIA populations were mixed farmers, who placed more emphasis on farming than on herding. Due to the acidic nature of the soils on which many Urewe ware sites are found, faunal remains survive only rarely. An important exception is the Gogo Falls site in South Nyanza, where Urewe ware pottery possibly associated with cattle bones, were recovered from a horizon above an earlier PN, Elementeitan midden. Urewe ware sites are also closely associated with the first appearance of iron-working in the Great Lakes region, and considerable research efforts have been directed at elucidating the origins and nature of this technology. Of these, the most wide-ranging studies have been conducted by Schmidt and colleagues in Buhaya, the eastern part of the Kagera region of northwestern Tanzania. In particular, the accumulated archaeological evidence from the many smelting furnaces excavated at sites such as KM2 and KM3, near Kemondo Bay, in conjunction with the results of experimental and ethnographic studies, indicate that EIA smelters had a sophisticated knowledge of the physical and chemical processes involved, and by the first millennium were capable of generating furnace temperatures sufficiently high enough to produce carbon steel.

As indicated above, typological links have drawn between Urewe ware and other Iron Age ceramics across eastern and south-central Africa. Multidimensional analyses of these assemblages suggest that two broad facies can be identified. Following the most recent studies by Huffman, these are referred to as the

Nkope (formerly Highland) and Kwale (formerly Lowland) Branches of the Urewe Tradition (formerly Eastern Stream). Kwale ware is named after the type site in the Shimba Hills southwest of Mombasa located by Robert Soper in the 1960s and dated to the third century. Other, broadly contemporary sites with Kwale-type pottery have been found in similar areas of good grazing and permanent surface waters in the hills immediately inland from the Kenya-Tanzania coast, and in the Usambara-Pare corridor.

Recent surveys further south along sections of the Tanzanian coast indicate that early farming communities had also settled the central coastal hinterland, as at the site of Limbo, and the lower stretches of the well-watered valleys of the Ruvuma, Wami, and Rufiji by the second or third century, and possibly even earlier. In general terms, pottery from these sites share affinities with Kwale ware proper, although as more sites have been investigated it has become clear that there were probably several local spatial and temporal variants. Around the sixth century, a new pottery style emerged in this area, and elsewhere along the East African littoral as far north as southern Somalia and on the offshore islands of the Zanzibar archipelago. Known by a variety of terms, of which Tana Tradition (TT) and Triangular Incised Ware (TIW) are the most current, this pottery type has been found in the basal levels at a number of the early trading settlements, including Shanga in the north and Kilwa in the south, that began to emerge along the East African coast from the eight or ninth century. Partly because of this, some scholars have begun to equate the appearance of TT-TIW pottery with the emergence of a distinctive Swahili identity. This hypothesis is complicated, however, by the fact that TT-TIW pottery has also been found in the lower levels of some of the *kayas* (sacred, forest-protected homesteads) occupied by Mijikenda communities who have different histories and linguistic origins from the Swahili.

Inland of the main distribution of Kwale wares, much less research has been conducted on the spread of early farming communities. The main pottery variant in west-central Tanzania, known as Lelesu ware, although broadly contemporary with the main Kwale variant, is generally regarded as part of the Nkope Branch. Further south, around Kalambo Falls in northern Zambia, several sites with deep pits containing settlement and ironworking debris indicative of an early farming presence by the early fourth century, have been excavated. Nkope wares, some of which share certain similarities with the early coastal ceramic traditions, are also present on various sites in Malawi by the third century. As with the evidence from northern Zambia, while these early dates are suggestive of a fairly rapid southerly spread of pioneer farming, renewed fieldwork in these areas could help to resolve a wide range of issues concerning the cultural origins of these communities.

PAUL LANE

Further Reading

Chami, F. A. "A Review of Swahili Archaeology." *African Archaeological Review*. 15, no. 3 (1998): 199–218.

Ehret, C. *An African Classical Age: Eastern and Southern Africa in World History, 1000 B.C. to A.D. 400*. Oxford: James Currey, 1998.

Phillipson, D. W. *The Later Prehistory of Eastern and Southern Africa*. London: Heinemann, 1977.

Schmidt, P. R. "Archaeological Views on a History of Landscape Change in East Africa." *Journal of African History*. 38 (1997): 393–421.

Sutton, J. E. G., ed. *The Growth of Farming Communities in Africa from the Equator Southwards*. Nairobi: British Institute in Eastern Africa, 1995.

Iron Age (Early): Farming, Equatorial Africa

The equatorial region of Africa remains one of the least known in archaeological and historical terms. This area of dense forest threaded through with great river systems has presented a physical, political, and conceptual barrier to scholars for many years.

The majority of current knowledge of the Iron Age of the equatorial region was the result of a groundbreaking field project, the River Reconnaissance Project (RRP), initiated and led by M. Eggert. Between 1977 and 1987, when the deteriorating political and economic situation caused this project to be abandoned, small teams explored various river systems within the inner Zaire basin, examining river banks and the forest fringe for archaeological evidence. They successfully recorded the first systematic body of archaeological data from the equatorial region, analysis of which enabled Wotzka to compile the first ceramic sequences. In justification for the potential bias introduced into this survey by the restriction to rivers and their immediate hinterland, Eggert (1992, 1993) has convincingly argued that these waterways have always presented a natural network of communication routes and that today they constitute a major element of the traffic network. He has suggested that the first settlers took advantage of this ready-made system to penetrate deep into the rainforest region, only then additionally exploiting the hinterland.

The antiquity of human activity in the forests has always been a subject of debate, and it had been claimed that farming populations only settled this area in the last millennium. Much of this argument has revolved around the issue of foraging, or hunting and gathering, in the tropical forest environment. It has been argued that the tropical environment cannot support a purely hunting and gathering lifestyle, and that some form of relationship with an agricultural community is essential for survival. This claim remains disputed. The ceramic typology compiled by Wotzka and associated radiocarbon dates have, however, pushed back this occupation of the region by pottery producing and thus, by inference, potentially farming groups to the last half of the first millennium.

Although there are instances of foraging groups using ceramics in some parts of Africa, it is generally assumed that the production and use of ceramics of the quality and on the scale revealed by the RRP is characteristic of a food-producing society. However there is, as yet, very little actual evidence of the food plants or subsistence methods employed by these early Iron Age communities. It is particularly difficult to identify past food crops in the equatorial environment. The warm, wet conditions that ensure rapid decay of organic matter, and the reliance upon tubers and plantains—crops which have, until recently, been largely archaeological unidentifiable—have resulted in a lack of evidence. Recent developments in the study of phytoliths, minute particles of silica derived from plant cells, are seen as possessing great potential for future research. Phytoliths are characteristic of different species and survive after the plant has decayed. In Cameroon very early evidence for the use of Musaceae has been identified by these methods and has added to the expectation that early food crops could also be identified in the equatorial forests.

The antiquity of the production of plantains or bananas in Africa has been a controversial issue because of the lack of archaeological data. The edible banana, a plant that originated in Asia (wild inedible bananas are found in Africa), is thought to have rapidly become the staple food crop in the equatorial forest some 1,500 to 2,000 years ago, its far greater suitability to the tropical forest environment than either root or cereal crops allowing the first settlement of the forest zone in any great numbers. However, this argument has been based upon the study of cultural lexicons (the names given to different bananas in different languages) and of the various types and distributions of cultivars; it has not derived from archaeological evidence. The early radiocarbon dates obtained in Cameroon suggest that the banana may have been a food crop grown by the first Iron Age rainforest settlers.

The yam is today a dietary staple in many equatorial communities, although it too is not a true native of the tropical forests. Wild yams originated in the savanna yet may already have been grown, together with the banana, by these earliest equatorial farmers. Again, it is hoped that the study of phytoliths will provide archaeological evidence for such a practice.

Eggert (1996) reports that excavations conducted by the RRP found associations between early ceramics and the oil palm (*Elaeis guineensis*) and the fruits of a wild tree, *Canarium schweinfurthii*, associations that have been recorded in other parts of central Africa. He stresses that, while it cannot be assumed that the oil palm represents a farming complex, it must nevertheless be seen as an important food crop, and may have been the main source of dietary fat.

The RRP was also successful in identifying evidence for early ironworking in the equatorial forest. At the site Munda, which lay on the Likwala-aux-Herbes River, a bowl-like, slag-containing feature was partly excavated and was interpreted as a bloomery furnace. Partially lined with clay, it had been subjected to intense burning and contained elements of the earliest pottery identified by Wotzka of a Northeast tradition (which he named the Pikunda-Munda horizon). It was also superimposed upon a shaft containing the same pottery. Four radiocarbon dates obtained from the excavation dated the features to the end of the last millennium BCE and the beginning of the first millennium CE (106BCE to 420CE). This would suggest that the earliest Iron Age settlers of the equatorial forests, in addition to producing a variety of good quality pottery and beginning to cultivate a variety of food crops, were also working and using iron.

RACHEL MACLEAN

Further Reading

De Langhe, E., R. Swennen, and D. Vuylsteke. "Plantain in the Early Bantu World." *Azania.* 29–30 (1996): 147–160.

Eggert, M. K. H. "The Central African Rain Forest: Historical Speculation and Archaeological Facts." *World Archaeology.* 24, no. 1 (1992): 1–24.

———. "Central Africa and the Archaeology of the Equatorial Rain Forest: Reflection on Some Major Topics." In *The Archaeology of Africa*, edited by T. Shaw, P. Sinclair, B. Andah, and A. Okpoko. London: Routledge, and New York: Routledge, 1993.

———. "Pots, Farming, and Analogy: Early Ceramics in the Equatorial Rainforest." *Azania.* 29–30 (1996): 332–338.

Rossel, G. "*Musa* and *Ensete* in Africa: Taxonomy, Nomenclature and Uses." *Azania.* 29–30 (1996): 130–146.

Iron Age (Early): Herding, Farming, Southern Africa

Based on present evidence, it seems likely that the initial introduction of animal husbandry and seed plant cultivation into Southern Africa took place on its northern margins, in the drainage zones of the Okavango and Zambezi Rivers, while portions of coastal Moçambique received food crops from Asian sources. Proximity of the inland zones to earlier experience of these economies in Central Africa was no doubt crucial, as was that of the coastal sites to seafaring trade. Prior developments in the entire region had prepared its inhabitants for domesticated economies. About 15,000 years ago, Late Stone Age peoples had developed hunting-fishing-gathering economies adapted to the highly diverse local ecologies of the subcontinent. These peoples are thought to have been the ancestors of proto-Khoisan speakers, whose descendents speak the extant Khoisan languages.

About 2,000 years ago, cattle and sheep were introduced from the north and incorporated into these local foraging economies. A distinctive pottery called Bambata—thin and decorated with a comblike tool, and also found to the north—accompanied this introduction of livestock. The economy that emerged is best thought of as pastro-foraging, with wild foods continuing to be as important as before. Sites with these characteristics are thinly spread across the northern parts of Botswana, Namibia, and Zimbabwe. These sites begin to fill the geographical vacuum that has existed between Central Africa and the Cape coast where domestic animals dating before the year 500 have previously been known to be present at Die Kelders, Nelson's Bay, and Byneskranskop. We can be confident that people who spoke a Khoe variant of proto-Khoisan played an important role in this transfer because the cattle pastoral vocabulary of most southern African herders—including most southeast Bantu-speakers—is derived through a Khoisan intermediary. In addition, terms for cattle have undergone a regular sound shift from proto-Khoisan in Khoe languages, indicating that they have not been re-borrowed in recent times.

We do not know if the appearance of Bantu-speaking peoples coincided with this first introduction of cattle and pottery. But it is clear that such peoples were moving down from central Africa shortly thereafter. A large number of sites were established by these people during the seventh to the eleventh centuries in the Limpopo and Zambezi valleys, and on the eastern hardveld of Botswana. They brought horticulture (sorghum, millet, cowpeas, and perhaps melons) as well as iron and copper metallurgy with them. They also introduced goats into the region, and probably different varieties of cattle; both hump-backed (*Bos indicus*) and flat-backed (*Bos taurus*) varieties appear in early archaeological sites while long- and short-horned taurines are reported in early European records. Humped cattle originated in India and are known to have been introduced into East Africa before the common era began; their presence in southern Africa (along with that of chickens, southeast Asian in origin) reinforces other evidence (the presence of coconuts and bananas, also Southeast Asian, somewhat earlier in East Africa) suggesting that domesticated animals and plants were brought into the region through complex social and economic networks rather than by migrations of detached peoples. Cattle, sheep, and goats remains at some of the larger sites make up 80 per cent of the faunal assemblage, the remaining 20 per cent being of hunted wild animals. At large sites in the interior, dung vitrified by burning, as much as 150 centimeters deep, marks the presence of kraals, evidence that sizable herds were kept.

Houses of the kind still commonly made in the region of a cowdung-clay plaster applied to wattle frames are preserved at some places. Iron and copper tools and ornaments are abundant, most if not all of which were manufactured locally. Finally, glass beads along with cowrie and conus shells are found at the largest sites; before 1000 the greatest number are found in Botswana. This is certain evidence that before that date agro-pastoral peoples in the interior participated in exchange networks that reached the east coast of the continent.

In Botswana, where the majority of pertinent data have been recovered, a tripartite hierarchy of settlements may be discerned in terms of site size, location, length of occupation, proportion of exotic trade items, and relative numbers of domestic stock; social stratification of the inhabitants seems to be clearly indicated. Toutswemogala and Bosutswe, the largest of these sites were situated on hilltops, were occupied (perhaps with interruptions) for over 500 years, and contain very large kraal deposits as well as many trade items. Second level sites, such as Taukome and Thatswane, are also on hilltops but have much smaller kraals and appear to have been occupied for only 200 to 300 years. At the tertiary sites, all on the plains surface, kraals are very small or absent, stone artifacts typical of the Late Stone Age are numerous, and hunted animal remains usually approach in number those of domesticates. This is in contrast to the larger sites where stone artifacts are virtually nonexistent and hunted animals comparatively few; foraging appears to have been more important at these smaller settlements compared with larger centers. A fourth, solely foraging, level probably exists, but its remains will be very difficult to find.

A further indication of social stratification is provided by analysis of the age at slaughter of cattle at these sites. At Bosutswe, as also at the later, much larger chiefdoms established at K2 and Mapungubwe in the Limpopo valley, prime young-to-middle-adult animals were killed in far higher proportion than were juvenile and aged animals. These animals are most desirable as food, but they are also the reproducing cohorts of a herd. In contrast, juveniles (probably yearling bull culls and runts) and old, postreproductive animals were most often slaughtered at Taukome; this is the slaughter strategy practiced in rural Botswana today by subsistence farmers who emphasize herd size maintenance at the expense of meat production. It appears that, at this early date, members of an elite social stratum were already able to extract prime food resources—along with a surplus product distilled in value as exotic trade goods—for their own use from subordinate classes. Many, if not most, of the prime animals slaughtered at Toutswe and Bosutswe must have been obtained from lower ranked locations, for a sustained off-take of breeding stock would lead quickly to reduction of a resident herd to unsustainable numbers. It may be appropriate to think of tertiary site herders as cattle managers for centralized elites rather than cattle owners in their own right.

The process of social differentiation may be traced in languages as well as materials. Kizulu, Isixhosa, and Sindebele (and Sesotho to a lesser extent), while Bantu in structure and basic lexicon, incorporate many click consonants and a large vocabulary from Khoisan sources. However, the fact that Bantu languages, though radically altered, continued to be spoken while Khoisan languages declined (sometimes losing their clicks) and Bantu social forms became the norm for all suggests that Bantu-speakers, though increasingly absorbing Khoisan persons and cultural elements into their social units, were politically hegemonic in the eastern region.

The history of pastoralism in the western half of the region has a similar chronology although it differs in a number of significant social and economic details. Bantu peoples arrived at roughly the same time, bringing essentially the same economic suite; they too encountered Khoisan pastro-foragers. Again subsequent processes are visible in linguistic as well as material form: the Bantu language, Shiyei, incorporates a large click inventory of Khoisan origin and, therefore, the Wayei people of the Okavango Delta must have a long history of intimate association with Khoisan peoples. But here similarities give way to differences, the most salient being that until recently Khoisan social forms were predominant in much of this area from the Kunene-Okavango to the Cape. This is strong evidence that, in contrast to the east, during the early centuries of association ideological values and political power were the prerogatives of Khoisan peoples and Bantu were drawn into their social networks through marriage and other kinds of alliances rather than the reverse.

Divuyu, the name given to an agro-pastoral occupation of the Tsodilo Hills during the seventh and eighth centuries, is a fully developed Early Iron Age site rich in ceramics as well as iron and copper tools and ornaments. Sheep and goats were mainstays of the economy, but cattle appear to have been rare and to have been kept elsewhere and possibly were obtained from Khoisan. Divuyu ceramics have design affinities to sites roughly contemporary with it in central Angola. They also appear to be related in design to the site of Madingo-Cayes north of the Congo. Two marine shells of Atlantic Coast origin and two iron pendants were found at Divuyu; the pendants are virtually identical to specimens of the same age found in Shaba Province, Zaire. These items indicate that exchange systems with the coastal and interior areas from which they had recently moved were maintained by Divuyu peoples. Thus, during the middle of the first millennium, this northern margin of the Kalahari was already actively part of a wider sphere of production and exchange extending throughout a large portion of the Angolan and Kongo river systems. Fish bones and river mussel shells found at Divuyu are further evidence for such exchange. Relatively small communities of Bantu- and Khoisan-speakers appear to have intermingled throughout this entire region on relatively equal terms. Economic and linguistic—and therefore, social—transfers appear to have flown freely among these communities with the result that pastoral economies became well established in the Kalahari.

Nqoma, also in the Tsodilo Hills, the main components of which are dated to the ninth to eleventh centuries CE, followed Divuyu. Cattle, some of which were of a hump-backed variety, were paramount in the economy, but sheep and goats were also common. Sorghum, millet, and possibly melons were grown, but wild nuts and berries, along with wild faunal remains, indicate that foraging continued to be important. Dung-clay houses were constructed and an elaborate variety of ivory, iron, and copper ornaments, along with iron tools were made on the site. Nqoma people would also have controlled the specularite mines found in the Hills. Glass beads and marine cowrie and conus shells provide firm evidence that Nqoma was an important local center in intercontinental trade networks that extended from the Indian Ocean coast. Fresh water mussels and fish continue to have been imported from Okavango communities.

Another site, Matlapaneng, northeast of Maun on the eastern side of the Okavango Delta, is contemporary with Nqoma. Cattle, sheep, and goats were kept here and sorghum, millet, and cowpeas were grown. Matlapaneng had all the material characteristics of Nqoma, but there are two quite significant differences between them. Matlapaneng is not nearly so rich in metal ornaments or East Coast trade goods; in this respect, it resembles the secondary sites of the eastern hardveld, such as Taukome, rather than Nqoma. In addition, Matlapaneng ceramics are largely allied with those of the hierarchical east, and this must mean that their social, economic, and political ties were in that direction rather than northward as those of the Tsodilo sites had been until this time. It appears that the dominant centers of the hardveld, Toutswe and Bosutswe, were extending their economic interests into the western sandveld at this time; indeed, some Nqoma ceramic motifs display eastern influence, evidence that these interests were penetrating deeply into the west. It would seem that this was the beginning of hegemonic domination from the east that was consolidated by about 1000.

A series of smaller sites is assignable to the general time span of the eighth through eleventh centuries. At CaeCae, ceramics, iron, and cattle are contemporary with Nqoma and Matlapaneng. At the nearby sites, Qubi, Magopa, and Qangwa similar ceramics as well as iron occur in small quantities. All of these shards appear to have come from small bowls or dishes. Just across the border in the NyaeNyae area of Namibia, similar ceramics may be related. In the Delta area, small undated components containing ceramics similar to those of Matlapaneng are present at Lotshitshi and near Tsau.

A hierarchical site structure may be discerned in the foregoing description, a structure that is not unlike that described for the eastern hardveld during these same centuries, but one that is not so elaborate. Nqoma appears to be at the apex of this western settlement hierarchy and seems to have been occupied (perhaps intermittently) for about three hundred years. Nqoma yielded a predominately pastoral fauna with an even higher proportion of cattle to sheep and goats than found at the larger centers in the east; it contained moderate numbers of exotic trade items. In addition, Nqoma has the richest (both in quantity and variety) and most elaborate metal ornament inventory presently known for any site of its time in the entire southern African region.

At CaeCae, on the other hand, although occupation debris is found throughout an area of more than a square kilometer, settlement seems to have occurred in small clusters similar to present-day homesteads in the area, which also are spread over more than a square kilometer. There is no way to determine how many of these clusters may have been occupied simultaneously, but it is unlikely that aggregate occupation area at any given time would have exceeded 2,000 square meters. The other sandveld locations, though known only by isolated, small test excavations, appear to be similar in most respects. Contemporary levels at Lotshitshi are also in this range. As already noted, ceramics and metal occur in very small numbers in these sites, cattle are known from CaeCae, Lotshitshi, and Toteng, but exotic trade items are absent from all current inventories.

It appears that an elite was established at Nqoma that was able to exercise sufficient hegemony over the inhabitants of secondary settlements to appropriate to itself the overwhelming preponderance of imported goods (glass beads and marine shells) that entered the western sandveld as well as the bulk of locally manufactured surplus product (metal and ivory ornaments) that was not exported. Some local products must have been exported, for we may assume that imports were desired, thus were expensive and had to be obtained for value; otherwise, they would be more widely distributed among many sites. It seems likely that Nqoma elites were also able to extract the required exchange value from their subordinates, probably from as far afield as CaeCae, Qubi, and the other sandveld communities, to judge from the presence of contemporary ceramics at these sandveld places.

Thus, in the earliest well documented period (600–1000) of agro-pastoral penetration into the Kalahari, a regional differentiation of settlement organization and an associated difference in social formations can already be discerned in the archaeological record. In the east there was clearly an appropriation of indigenous Khoisan forager, and possibly pastro-forager, systems by Bantu-speaking peoples who colonized the area in numbers and quickly established a hierarchy of settlements around their central towns. The smaller, tertiary, sites in this organization accurately reflect in their size and content the domains of pastro-foragers whose position in the imposed social hierarchy into which they were incorporated was economically subordinate to that of pastoral elites. It appears that by the end of the first millennium CE eastern Kalahari communities were differentiated socially and economically in a manner similar to that of historically known and contemporary social formations found in that same region. This picture conforms to what is known for the rest of the eastern half of southern Africa.

In the western half of the subcontinent, full agropastoralist economies with iron working and transcontinental exchange networks were introduced at the same time as in the east. Bantu-speaking peoples were surely involved in the process in the northern peripheral zones where transmission must have taken place, and there is some historical evidence to suggest that they penetrated much farther south. But Bantu hegemony as it now exists was not reestablished in the western Kalahari until mid-nineteenth century, and at first only to a limited extent. It appears, rather, that early agropastoral economies were transferred among indigenous pastro-foragers, who could only have been Khoisan speakers, and entering Bantu-speaking herding and horticultural ironworkers. Mechanisms for these transferals are not yet entirely clear but probably followed long established lines of interaction and then became internally differentiated according to local conditions. Forager and herder polities were less hegemonically structured in this area than in the east, as they are known not to have been in historic time until disrupted in the nineteenth century, first by Tswana state expansion and then by European capitalism.

As trade with the Indian Ocean grew in scale, however, and gold became a major export from the interior while fine India cloth was imported to places like Ingombe Ilede on the Zambezi River (and possibly Toutswe, where clay figurines of women appear to be wearing wrapped loin cloths of woven material rather than hanging skins), the nearer peoples on the eastern highlands of present day Zimbabwe reorganized trading networks to their own benefit. The routes to the ocean from the west were truncated beginning in the eleventh century by Mapungubwe followed by the developing Great Zimbabwe and Khami states, which established major outposts in the eastern hardveld of Botswana. From then on, the western half of the subcontinent was reduced to the status of producer rather than receiver in the Indian Ocean trade, a status from which it emerged, and then only briefly and partially, with the establishment of Portuguese trade on the Atlantic coast.

EDWIN N. WILMSEN

Further Reading

Denbow, J. "Congo to Kalahari: Data and Hypotheses about the Political Economy of the Western Stream of the Early Iron Age." *African Archaeological Review.* 8 (1990): 139–176.

Ehret, C. "The First Spread of Food Production to Southern Africa." In *The Archaeological and Linguistic Reconstruction of African History*, edited by C. Ehret and M. Posnansky. Berkeley: University of California Press, 1982.

Hall, M. *Farmers, Kings, and Traders: The People of Southern Africa, 200–1860.* Chicago: University of Chicago Press, 1987.

Huffman, T. *Iron Age Migrations.* Johannesburg: Witwatersrand University Press, 1989.

Lane, P., A. Reid, and A. Segobye. *Ditswammung: The Archaeology of Botswana.* Gaborone: Pula Press and the Botswana Society, 1998.

Morris, A. *The Skeletons of Conquest: A Study of Protohistoric Burials from the Lower Orange River Valley, South Africa.* Johannesburg: Witwatersrand University Press, 1992.

Plug, I. "Seven Centuries of Iron Age Traditions at Bosutswe, Botswana: A Faunal Perspective." *South African Journal of Science.* 92 (1996): 91–97.

Sealy, J., and R. Yates. "The Chronology of the Introduction of Pastoralism to the Cape, South Africa." *Antiquity.* 68 (1994): 58–67.

Thomas, D., and P. Shaw. *The Kalahari Environment.* Cambridge: Cambridge University Press, 1991.

Wilmsen, E. *Land Filled with Flies: A Political Economy of the Kalahari.* Chicago: University of Chicago Press, 1989.

———. ed. *The Kalahari Ethnographies (1896–1898) of Siegfried Passarge.* Köln: Rüdiger Köppe, 1997.

Iron Age (Later): Central Africa

Outside of the Upemba Depression, little is known of central Africa during the Late Stone Age. The following is more reflective of the scattered and disparate nature of archeological research, than any coherent image of Late Stone Age societies in central Africa.

Southwest Africa

This area principally covers two present-day nations, the Democratic Republic of Congo and Angola; the Republic of the Congo (Brazzaville) is also slightly covered by this region.

In the Democratic Republic of Congo, a series of pottery traditions associated with the Late Iron Age are found in Lower Congo and in Kinshasa. These are represented by the objects classified under the name Group II, found in, among other places, Dimba cave and the Kovo cemetery, as well as at Kingabwa (in Kinshasa).

Dated from the eighteenth century, Group II pottery includes both tall and squat vessels. The clay is generally thin-walled, light-colored, and rings clearly when tapped. The decoration is embossed, with triangular or lozenge shapes. At Dimba, the pottery is accompanied by metal goods. At Kingabwa, in addition to objects displaying Group II stylistic characteristics, a whitish ceramic is found, notable for the richness of its decoration. The ceramic has also been found at Mafamba in the Republic of the Congo, at Bandundu, in the vicinity of the Kwango River, and near Lake Maï-Ndombe (all in the Democratic Republic of Congo).

The geographical location of the ceramic and the Group II pottery indicates that the Kinshasa area on Malebo Pool served as the crossroads of interregional trade for Mafamba in the Republic of Congo, as well as for various locations in the Democratic Republic of Congo.

In Angola the site of Mpangala I at Mbanza Soyo, near the mouth of the Congo River, has yielded pottery shards associated with the bones of wild game and seashells. Unfortunately, there is no firm dating available for these artifacts. At Kamabanga to the south of Luanda, a pottery with fine decorations has been exhumed: the animal bones and remains associated with it include zebra, buffalo, warthog, clams (*Anadera senilis*), fish, and domestic cattle. Kamabanga dates from the period when the Early Stone Age gave way to the Late. To the south of Luanda, the deposits grouped under the name Captiously II have yielded a thick bed of shells surrounding a pot filled with honey, the site dating from the eighteenth century. To the east of Luanda, the station of Cabbies has provided abundant pottery representing a mixture of elements from two phases of the Iron Age.

Northwest

In addition to the whitish ceramic already mentioned, other traces of the Late Iron Age have been found throughout the Democratic Republic of Congo: on the plateaus (notably the Mbé Plateau), in the zone of high hills (the site at Masamasa), in the forest at Chailu and in the Niari valley (Ntadi Yomba shelter), and in the

Copperbelt. Archeological remains consist essentially of smelting debris (iron and copper) plus terra cotta (vases, pipes, etc.), low smelting furnaces, broken tuyeres from the bellows, and glass beads. Available dates range from the ninth to the nineteenth century: the oldest from the plateaus, the most recent from the high hills.

In Gabon iron ore was smelted in the Léconoie area in the Upper Ogooné during the tenth and eleventh centuries.

Several Late Iron Age sites exist in Cameroon, particularly Fundong in the Grassfields and Mbongué, the latter yielding ceramics and palm nuts. Fundong's remains are generally smelting debris.

Southeast

This district coincides with the southern part of Katanga. Leaving aside the Upemba Depression, evidence of the occupation of these lands during the Late Iron Age has come from the Kafubu River, from Kipushi (on the Zambian side of the watershed and the modern border), from the Kamoa stream, and from the Lubumbashi area along the Lubumbashi, Lwano, Naviundu, Kilobelobe, Luowoshi, and Karavia streams. The as-yet undated ceramic from around Lubumbashi differs little from that of Kipushi on the frontier of the Democratic Republic of Congo and Zambia, dated between the ninth and thirteenth centuries. This consists generally of shards decorated by impression with a comb, string, or metal bracelets. The Lubumbashi sites, like Kipushi, also share other traits, such as the fabrication of small crosses in molds and the presence of iron and copper slag. In Lubumbashi, furnaces and tuyeres have been found for copper and iron smelting and making bracelets. At the Kafubu, the ceramics are associated with *dagga* (worked clay), attesting to the construction of dwellings. The findings along the Kafubu, at Kipushi and around Lubumbashi belong to the complex called either "Copperbelt" or "Chondwe."

The inhabitants of the site along the Kamoa smelted both copper and iron in the sixteenth century. Copper was used for small crosses and beads, iron for tools such as knives. The Kamoa crosses resemble those found at the Upemba Depression in their miniature size and their form (in an irregular H). Ceramics have been found, but their fragmentary condition makes them difficult to correlate with any defined tradition. Lastly, the presence of upper and lower grindstones alongside the pottery and metal objects suggests that the inhabitants practiced agriculture.

East (Kivu, Burundi, Rwanda)

Mikweti, in the Kivu area of the Democratic Republic of Congo, is presently the only site in the eastern region belonging to the Late Iron Age. A problem remains, nonetheless. By the carbon date of 1870–80, the Mikweti deposits belong to the Late Iron Age, but by its pottery it is tied to the Early Iron Age. It evokes, for example, the basal cavity of Urewe ware and is characteristic of the Early Iron Age in the interlacustrine region.

Burundi, and especially Rwanda, are rich in recent Iron Age sites, including in Rwanda the caves of Cynkomane and Akameru, the sites of Masanganio, Murunda, Mucucu II, Nyirarubona, Bugarama and Kandolo, and in Burundi that of Miramba II. In both countries, the pottery is characterized by rouletted pattern and smelting with the use of low furnaces.

Remains collected at Cynkomane and Akameru include wild game as well as domestic livestock. The first category includes rodents, elephant, sitatunga, and duiker. Domestic livestock included chicken, cow, sheep, and goat with a majority of bovine stock; among the smaller livestock, sheep predominate over goats.

Whether or not agriculture was practiced in the region has not yet been determined in a conclusive way. However, since there are indications of agro-pastoral activity during the Early Iron Age, one can suppose that both continued in the Late Iron Age, with agriculture based on eleusine and sorghum. The consumption of cereal grains was likely to have been accompanied by use of inorganic salt, such as was the case in the Early Iron Age.

Conclusion

Data from the Late Iron Age in Central Africa is unequal and fragmentary; there are still far too many gaps in the knowledge, and uncertainty. Nonetheless, it is generally accepted that by this period, human populations made pottery, produced charcoal, smelted iron and copper, built housing in thatch, hunted, farmed, raised livestock, and fished. Moreover, these groups carried out long-distance trade. Despite worldviews including much that could be called superstitious and non-objective, the evidence implies a minimum of socio-economic organization auguring well for the emergence of large states in the region, such as the Kongo and Teke kingdoms.

MUYA BUTANKO

Further Reading

Lanfranchi, R., and B. Clist, eds. *Aux Origines de l'Afrique Centrale*. Paris: Centres Culturels Français d'Afrique Centrale et Centre International des Civilisations Bantu, 1991.

Noten, F. van, ed. *The Archaeology of Central Africa*. Graz: Akademische Drück-und-Verlagsanstalt, 1982.

———. ed. *Histoire archéologique du Rwanda*. Coll. Annales: Sciences Humaines 112. Tervuren: Musée Royal de l'Afrique Centrale, 1983.

Iron Age (Later): Central Africa: Luangwa Tradition

"Luangwa" is the designation given to a pottery tradition practiced by diverse ethnic communities in Zambia. Among these are the Ambo, Cewa, and Nsenga in eastern Zambia, the Lala in central Zambia, the northern Lunda, Ushi, Chishinga, Bwile, Shila, Mukulu, and Ngumbo along the Luapula River valley, the Bisa and Bemba in northern Zambia, the Lenje and Soli in central Zambia, Tonga and Ila of southern Zambia, the western Lunda and Kaonde of northwest Zambia, and the Lamba and Lima of Copper Belt Zambia.

Geographically, the Luangwa tradition spans the entirety of Zambia, from the borders with Angola in the northwest, the Democratic Republic of the Congo in the north and Tanzania in the northeast, into Malawi in the east, and Mozambique and Zimbabwe in the south. The name "Luangwa" is derived from the Luangwa River, which was central to the distribution of this pottery tradition. The above-mentioned ethnic groups (excluding the Cewa) with which the tradition is associated are all matrilineal communities who originated in the region of the Democratic Republic of Congo at varying periods in the past. In these communities, pottery is invariably made by women.

The distinguishing characteristic of this pottery is its almost total dependency on comb-stamped decorative motifs and combinations applied above the necks and on shoulders of necked pots and near the rims of shallow bowls, globular pots, beakers with straight sides, and gourd-shaped vessels. The most common decorative motif consists of horizontal bands of diagonal comb-stamping, commonly made with light incisions. Single or interlocking triangles of diagonal comb-stamping in parallel rows, a single row, a vertical zigzag pattern, pendant triangles or intertwined triangles and panels are also very common, especially in central and southern Zambia. In northern Zambia diagonal or crossed incisions and false relief chevrons also occur as regional variations. In the south, incised chevrons are also present.

According to the available archaeological dating, ancestral pottery of this tradition makes its first appearance in southwest Zambia in the mid-sixth century, in northwest Zambia from the twelfth century; in southern and central Zambia from the eighth century, in eastern Zambia from the eleventh century, and in most of northern Zambia from the seventeenth century. Archaeological sites associated with the Luangwa tradition in Zambia are: Nakapapula (eleventh century), Fibobe (ninth/tenth centuries), and Twickenham (seventh to ninth centuries), all in Central Zambia, Ingombe Ilede (fifteenth century) and Gundu (eighth to eleventh centuries) in southern Zambia, Namakala (sixth century) in southwest Zambia, Kumusongolwa hill (twelfth century) in northwest Zambia, and Chondwe (twelfth century) in the Copper Belt.

In its earliest incarnations in Zambia, the tradition existed side by side with other pottery traditions practiced by cattle-keeping, patrilineal, Bantu communities. Its practitioners gradually, however, assimilated into these communities, as evidenced by some decorative motifs derived from the Bantu works, discovered in more recent Luangwa tradition pottery.

The Luangwa tradition manifests a strong continuity of style throughout most of the area in which is was produced. It also portrays regional variations as noted above, which are due to various factors such as its age and specific location. In the north, where it first appeared in the seventeenth century, it shows great uniformity, although because it assimilated other pottery traditions in the area, it displays incorporated elements from those traditions. In the south, parts of central, Copper Belt, and eastern Zambia, where it has an especially long presence, it has evolved some exclusive features and also incorporated aspects from other traditions in those areas.

When the Luangwa tradition originated, its practitioners were mixed agriculturalists who herded and maintained goats and sheep. Gradually, they incorporated cattle as they acquired the holdings of neighboring peoples. This occurred especially in south, central, and eastern Zambia. In the north, where the tradition's practitioners arrived more recently, they owned very few cattle but large numbers of goats. The northern peoples composed highly centralized societies with strong kingship systems, unlike in the south, where the tradition's adherents retained their original decentralized system, with its weak kingship system. In the east and parts of central Zambia, kingship systems were gradually introduced by Luangwa practitioners who were new arrivals to earlier, decentralized communities. Today these areas also have strong, highly centralized systems. In the northwest, the Luangwa tradition communities either evolved or arrived with centralized kingship systems which persist to date.

NICHOLAS KATANEKWA

Further Reading

Derricourt, R. *Man on the Kafue*. London: Ethnographica, 1980.
Fagan, B., D. Phillipson, and G. I. Daniels, eds. *Iron Age Cultures in Zambia*. Vol. 2, *Dambwa, Ingobe Ilede and the Tonga*. London: Chatto and Windus, 1969.
Huffinan, T. *Iron Age Migrations*. Johannesburg: Witwatersrand University Press, 1989.

Phillipson, D. "Iron Age History and Archaeology in Zambian." *Journal of African History XW* (1974): 1–25.
———. *The Prehistory of Eastern Zambia*. Nairobi: British Institute in Eastern Africa, 1976.

Iron Age (Later): Central Africa: Peoples, Forest

The equatorial forest was long outside the research interests of archaeologists. In part this was due to conceptions about the peopling of the forest and savanna south of the Equator, centered on the notion that pygmies and bushmen were the first and only inhabitants before the Bantu migrations. The lack of interest was also due in part to the fact that the forest was considered unlikely to yield adequate returns from research. Archaeological research carried out since 1970 in the Democratic Republic of Congo, Central African Republic, Gabon, and Cameroon put an end to this neglect.

Democratic Republic of Congo

Ashes and pottery have been found in Matupi Cave in the Ituri, with polished stones, iron slag, tuyeres from furnaces, and unusual pottery near the Buru Stream in the Uele. While the Matupi ceramics are not yet studied thoroughly, they are dated to the thirteenth century; the Buru site is dated to the seventeenth century. Elsewhere in Ituri, the Malembi, Nduye, and Epulu sites indicate that pottery, stone tools, and iron coexisted for a time, then only the pottery and iron technologies continued on to the present day. The pottery labeled as Mukubasi has not yet received absolute dating or been published. Clay was also used to make beads; iron was used, among other things, to produce knives and needles. The consumption of *Elaeis* (oil palm), *Canarium*, and mollusks is attested throughout the Ituri, but clear proof of agriculture is lacking. The burial of the dead with grave goods has been demonstrated.

In the western part of the forest, the most recent phase of the Iron Age began with the pottery tradition known as Bondogoid, that is, the "Bondongo group." This is characterized by pots with a pronounced shoulder, dating from 1000 to 1400. Form and decoration grew more and more simplified through the Bokone phase (around 1600), with the tendency continuing on to the present style. Bondongo potters exported their goods to the Malebo Pool (modern Kinshasa). Their diet included plantains, yams, *Elaeis*, and *Canarium*, although it is not known which were gathered in the wild and which were cultivated.

Central African Republic, Gabon, and Cameroon

One single decorative technique unites the three modern countries. The Late Iron Age has been identified at Tazunu Butume in the Bouar Region and in Ouhan Taburo. The pottery of Tazunu consists of shards decorated with a wooden roulette and is accompanied by metal knives and bracelets, iron slag, and tuyeres. The population that produced it fished, hunted palm rats, porcupines, antelope, and birds, gathered land snails, and farmed sorghum and yams. The sites from the Ouhan have yielded a pottery called Nana Modé, composed of cooking pots and storage jars with convex bases and decorated with a wooden roulette. One of the sites contains, in addition to the shards, a skeleton in bent position and two iron objects. The population group to which the skeleton belonged is unknown.

The Lopé Game Reserve in Gabon has yielded a pottery from the eleventh century composed of pots and bottles, of fairly fine lines and decorated with a basketry roulette. The base is convex, the neck angular. Iron ore was smelted at Léconi on the upper Ogooué in the tenth and eleventh centuries. Finally, the Angondjé and Group IV industries belong to the most recent period. Group IV is composed of crude pottery, without decoration, and with a beveled rim. The Angondjé industry includes tuyeres, cylindrical terra cotta beads, as well as recipients with a small flat lip; the decoration is impressed with a comb or incised with a stick; the bases are flat or convex. Angonjé ware has been dated from 1000 to 1500, and Group IV from 1500 to 1900. The pottery from the second phase of the Iron Age at Shum Laka in Cameroun is from the eighteenth century; containers are decorated with a roulette of braided or, rarely, twisted fiber.

Negroids, Pygmoids, and the Late Iron Age in the Rain Forest

The forested portions of Central Africa are inhabited today by pygmoids and negroids. No human remains of any age have yet been recovered in the equatorial forest. On the other hand, archaeological work has greatly increased the volume of artifacts and structures, some of which argue for the occupation of the forest since the Late Stone Age not only by pygmoids but also by other groups, including negroids, particularly since it is well established that humans have occupied the northern fringes of the forest for a very long time. Moreover, the presence of negroid groups east of the Democratic Republic of Congo and in East Africa, Zambia, and Malawi dates from the Late Stone Age, thus long before the period of Bantu expansion.

Human skeletons found in the forest and associated with Late Stone Age artifacts are rare and not yet attached to any known human groups. Nothing can thus be proved about which group among the pygmoids and negroids was responsible for the last phase of the Iron Age in the forest. However, pygmoids are often neither potters, smiths, nor farmers; negroid populations, on the other hand, generally know all three technologies, thus encouraging an attribution of the Late Iron Age to the negroids (taller black farmers) rather than to the pygmoids (hunter-gatherers). These negroids were probably Bantu-speakers.

The African forest is now beginning to speak about its human occupation through archeology. Nonetheless, if several answers have been, there still remain many more questions. This is especially true for the Late Iron Age, a crucial period if we wish to better understand both early and contemporary African societies.

MUYA BUTANKO

Further Reading

Eggert, M. K. H. "Equatorial African Iron Age. In *Encyclopedia of Precolonial Africa: Archeology, History, Languages and Environments*, edited by J. O. Vogel. Walnut Creek: Altamira Press, 1997.

Kanimba, M. *Aspects écologiques et économiques des migrations des populations de langues bantu*. Frankfurt-am-Main: Peter Lang, 1986.

Iron Age (Later): Central Africa: Upemba Basin

Also known as the Upper Lualaba Valley, the Upemba Basin in Katanga has known three cultural traditions during the Late Iron Age: classic Kisalian, Katotian, and Kabambian. These three traditions have been identified on the basis of six abandoned cemeteries.

Classic Kisalian

This culture probably began around the eleventh century. Grave goods include fine and diversified ceramics, personal adornment items in limestone, ivory, and mollusk shell; glass beads, and cowries. They also include tools, arms, and decorative objects in iron and copper, such as lance points, fishhooks, harpoons, knives, necklaces, and bracelets.

The metal and ivory objects as well as the pottery reflect the great technical mastery and skill of Kisalian artisans. For example, they drew, twisted, and braided iron and copper wire; such mastery implies the existence of a social and political organization promoting the development of specialists. Funeral ritual connotes the existence of a certain social stratification and of human sacrifice. The cowries are evidence of trade with the Indian Ocean; the copper goods show exchange with the copperbelt of southern Katanga.

The population along the river was very dense. Nonetheless, this demographic achievement was limited by a high level of infant mortality. The growth of the population would have been primarily due to the availability of protein from fishing in addition to the usual resources from agriculture, herding goats and chickens, and hunting (primarily antelope and hippopotamus).

The Katotian

While the classic Kisalian flourished on the north side of the basin, the Katotian developed on the southern side from the twelfth century. The Katotian culture distinguished itself with group burials containing as many as seven bodies per tomb. Grave goods are made up of iron weapons and tools (points, fishhooks, hoes, fancy axes, anvils, bells), as well as ornaments in iron or copper, jewelry in ivory, achatina shells, or iridina mother-of-pearl. The grave pottery is remarkable for the vertical neck of the containers.

The anvils, bells, and decorated axes are among the indicators of hierarchical ranks in Katotian society. The seashells witness trade with the Indian Ocean coast. The inhabitants of Katoto were also in contact with the Kisalian culture, for Kisalian ceramic is found in Katotian tombs and vice versa. Moreover, Katota had trade links with the Atlantic Ocean for *conus* shell.

The food supply was derived from hunting, fishing, and agriculture.

Kabambian

Classic Kisalian culture prospered until the period of the thirteenth or fourteenth century, when it was replaced by the Kabambian.

Kabambian funerary goods include copper and iron objects: crosses, pins, fishhooks, knives, awls, bracelets, lance and arrow heads, and bells. In addition, glass beads are found as well as ornaments in ivory and stone (malachite, granite, etc.); cowries, other marine shells, and ceramics are well represented. Kabambian ceramics are characterized by their red slip on the interior surface of the upper part of the pottery. The clay and the finish are similar to classic Kisalian, but the walls of the pottery object are thinner.

The Kabambian population maintained a similar density to that of the classic Kisalian period. On the other hand, metal objects became less numerous. With the exception of one bell with clapper, no symbol of political power has been excavated from the Kabambian culture. Interregional trade increased through the period, and the commercial expansion translated in the decreased size of copper crosses, a decrease that corresponded to the standardization of the cross as a currency. However, crosses were not the only currency, for the copper pins and cowries must also have known the same use. The Kabambians traded with the southern Katanga copperbelt to obtain copper objects as well as with the Indian Ocean for their cowries and glass beads.

The Kabambian culture developed into a vast political-economic formation known to European ethnographers during the last part of the seventeenth or the early eighteenth century as the Luba state system.

The Upemba Basin has known three cultural traditions during the New Iron Age. The study of the grave goods associated with these traditions has permitted sketching the general lines of sociopolitical organization, economic systems, and conceptual worlds. This makes the Upemba Basin one of the best known regions of Central Africa at the dawn of large African political constellations: namely, states, empires, and political models.

MUYA BUTANKO

See also: **Luba.**

Further Reading

Nenquin, J. "Excavations at Sanga, 1957: The Protohistoric Necropolis." *Annales du Musée Royal de l'Afrique Centrale.* 45 Tervuren: Sciences Humaines, 1963.

Reefe, T. Q. "A History of the Luba Empire to c.1885." Ph.D. thesis, University of California, Berkeley, 1975 (published by University Microfilms, 1976).

Iron Age (Later): East Africa: Cattle, Wealth, Power

In many parts of the East African interior today, and particularly in the area that lies between the Great Lakes, cattle carry a disproportionately high value and have become inherently linked to social prestige and political power. In certain areas cattle ownership has been restricted to elite ruling classes. This is not a new development. In the mid-nineteenth century, the first Arab and European traders to travel into the interior recorded the existence of complex kingdoms and states in the Great Lakes region and, in the Rift valley and highlands, successful specialist pastoral groups, in all of which cattle played a pivotal role. Moreover, the many breeds of cattle found throughout the region today, and the more spectacular examples like the magnificently horned Ankole cow, speak of many generations of selective breeding.

There is archaeological evidence for the presence of domestic cattle in East Africa from a very early date (at least the third millennium BCE). It is agreed that the many breeds of cattle found today originate from the introduction of unhumped cattle (*Bos taurus*, originally from Eurasia) and humped cattle (*Bos indicus*, originally from Asia) into the region, but it is also thought that the "Sanga" breed (sometimes called *Bos africanus*), a large, long-horned breed of which the Ankole cow is one example, is of very ancient African origin.

Cattle were exploited in the region long before the first appearance of the settled, food-producing communities in the Great Lakes region that are seen as marking the start of the Early Iron Age in the first millennium BCE. It is not yet apparent whether these first food producers were also cattle keepers (there is very little faunal evidence from this early period) but the increasingly important role played by cattle becomes evident in the Later Iron Age. An important factor throughout this period has been the numerous challenges and opportunities that the adoption of cattle has presented to East African communities. Throughout the region, large areas of ranker grasses and bush are home to the tsetse fly (*Glossina* spp.) and the brown ear tick (*Rhipicephalus appendiculatus*), carriers of trypanosomiasis (sleeping sickness) and theileriosis. Some degree of environmental management could control these threats, but their presence did determine the areas in which cattle keeping could flourish. Predators, such as hyenas and the large cats, demanded constant vigilance and protective measures. Successful cattle rearing, however, enabled new economic and social developments, leading eventually to economic and political centralization and the creation of a social elite.

The only comprehensive archaeological study of the role of cattle in the Iron Age, and the earliest evidence for the intensive exploitation of cattle, comes from Reid's work at the site of Ntusi in western Uganda (1990, 1996). He analyzed a considerable faunal assemblage from this site, dating from the eleventh century to the fifteenth century, and was able to identify herd-management strategies that involved large quantities of immature animals. At its height in the fourteenth century, Ntusi had grown to cover an area of approximately 100 hectares (247 acres), and clearly dominated its hinterland. Excavations at the site recovered glass beads and cowry shells, objects that had traveled along complex trade routes from the distant East African coast and clearly indicate the economic importance of the site. Survey of the grasslands around Ntusi revealed a number of much smaller sites that Reid identified, following excavation, as single livestock enclosures. Faunal evidence at these sites showed the culling of animals at a younger age than at Ntusi. Reid has concluded that the control of cattle was central to the Ntusi economy, with more mature animals being removed from the small outlying settlements and taken to the dominant site at Ntusi. Cattle were clearly linked, at this early date, with both economic and political power, but there is not yet any evidence for the restriction of cattle to elite social groups suggesting this was a later development.

The evolving role of cattle in the East African Iron Age has also been explored by Schoenbrun (1998), who has supplemented his own exhaustive study of historical and comparative linguistics with evidence from environmental studies, ethnography and archaeology to create a dynamic picture of past power relationships. He has associated the gradual development of cattle mastery, evidenced by the emergence of cattle color and horn shape terminologies, with the emergence, first of technical expertise and new social relationships, and later of social, economic and political inequality, conclusions which concur with the archaeological picture suggested by Reid.

Several large earthwork sites dating from the Iron Age are found in modern Uganda, and their large size is seen as suggesting some degree of centralized political and social control. Radiocarbon dates have only been obtained for two of these sites, Bigo and Munsa: fifteenth to the nineteenth and fourteenth to the fifteenth centuries, respectively. Bigo, the largest site, consists of some 10 kilometers (6 miles) of ditches, with depths of up to 4 meters (13 feet), and encloses approximately 300 hectares (741 acres). While these earthworks appear to have been built as barriers and enclosures, many of them are not defensive as the interior is often lower than ground outside the ditches and Reid has suggested that they may have functioned as enclosed pasturage. This idea is also echoed in the oral traditions attached to Bigo, which claim that Mugenyi, one of the legendary Cwezi, kept his cattle here.

In the western highlands evidence for the presence of past cattle keepers can be seen scattered across the landscape in the form of groups of small, saucer-shaped depressions, approximately 10 meters (33 feet) in width. These groups may contain anything from 5 to 50 hollows. These depressions have been interpreted as the remains of former cattle pens, or stockades, and their use has been tentatively dated to the twelfth to the eighteenth centuries. In the eighteenth century, an increase in aggression and a new exploitation of iron weaponry has been linked with the rise of the Maasai, a successful confederation of pastoralist groups which occupies the area today.

RACHEL MACLEAN

See also: **Great Lakes Region.**

Further Reading

Clutton-Brock, J. "The Spread of Domestic Animals in Africa." In *The Archaeology of Africa*, edited by T. Shaw, P. Sinclair, B. Andah, and A. Okpoko. London: Routledge, and New York: Routledge, 1993.

Reid, A. "Ntusi and its Hinterland: Further Investigations of the Later Iron Age and Pastoral Ecology in Southern Uganda." *Nyame Akuma*. 33 (1990): 26–28.

———."Ntusi and the Development of Social Complexity in Southern Uganda." In *Aspects of African Archaeology*, edited by G. Pwiti and R. Soper. Harare: University of Zimbabwe Publications, 1996.

Schoenbrun, D. L. *A Green Place, A Good Place*. Oxford: James Currey Publishers, and Portsmouth, N.H.: Heinemann, 1998.

Sutton, J. *A Thousand Years in East Africa*. Nairobi: British Institute in Eastern Africa, 1990.

Iron Age (Later): East Africa: Labor, Gender, Production

The present lack of historical and archaeological evidence from the East African interior makes it particularly difficult to examine the very many relationships between labor, gender, and production which must have existed in the Iron Age. The first written accounts of this region date from the mid-nineteenth century, when Arab and European traders first penetrated the East African interior. These relatively modern records are supplemented by a rich body of oral history and traditions, the antiquity and meaning of which are the subject of continuing debate. Studies, such as Peter Schmidt's (1997) of the Haya in northwestern Tanzania, have employed a multidisciplinary approach to the oral records, examining them in association with archaeological and ethnographic data and have suggested that some of these traditions may indeed be of great antiquity and may help to explain aspects of the region's past.

The archaeological record of the East African interior is also patchy and, perhaps because of colonial concerns, much earlier work was concerned largely with prehistory and the very distant past. Increasingly, however, archaeologists are examining Iron Age material and attempting to examine issues of labor and production, of which gender must be seen as an integral element.

Rachel MacLean (1998) has suggested that the division of activities between different sections of the Early Iron Age (EIA) community may enable us to see the presence of these groups in antiquity. In the area to the west of Lake Victoria the archaeological record, supplemented by palaeoecological data, gives direct or indirect evidence for the appearance of five new activities in the EIA communities that settled the area: the production of ceramics and the working of iron, and land clearance, agricultural production, and pot cooking (cooking in a ceramic vessel). Today these activities are not undertaken indiscriminately by all members of the community, and in most cases there is a restriction to a particular gender. Although it is simplistic to project modern patterns of labor division back into the past, it is almost certain that labour division did occur. MacLean argued that iron production and pot cooking were, in this context, inherently gendered activities, being considered male and female aspects of interlinked pyrotechnologies. In addition she suggested that land clearance, which in this area is today a male activity establishing a male interest in future food production, and agricultural production, today a female activity establishing control of the food supply, may have been so in the EIA. Schoenbrun (1998) has also made similar suggestions following his analysis of comparative and historical linguistics in the region.

Such approaches to past labor and gender relations have been criticized, but they do at least begin to see the Iron Age community as a multifaceted one in which different identities, and ultimately differential access to economic, political, and social power, were functioning. Schoenbrun's work, which draws upon environmental studies, ethnography, and archaeology to supplement his linguistic arguments, has also begun to suggest a dynamic picture of past power relationships in which the control and restriction of different resources and activities resulted in the complex relationships that exist today.

From the end of the first millennium, there is archaeological evidence for increasing economic specialization. At Kibiro, on the eastern shore of Lake Albert, Graham Connah (1996) has uncovered evidence for salt production from the twelfth or thirteenth century until the present day. Today salt production is a female activity, the areas in which the salt-rich mud is extracted and processed are known as the women's "salt gardens." Men engage in fishing and other specialized, gender specific tasks. Again, it would be naive to suggest a simple continuity of labor division, but it is interesting to note current practice and to speculate that labor division along gender lines was a valuable economic strategy throughout the Iron Age.

There is also evidence from across the region for the presence of pastoralist groups. At Ntusi, a site dating from the eleventh to the fifteenth century located in the western grasslands of Uganda, Andrew Reid (1990) has suggested that the control of cattle was central to the economy. Ntusi itself grew to some 100 hectares (247 acres) at its height in the fourteenth century and appeared to be obtaining large numbers of relatively mature cattle from the many small sites that lay scattered throughout its hinterland. Although cattle clearly played a dominant role in the economy, evidence for agricultural production was also common at these sites (crops included sorghum and finger millet), ceramic production and use was occurring, as was iron production. There is also some evidence for the manufacture of ivory beads. Increasing economic specialization would suggest that some forms of activity specialization were also developing, ultimately resulting in the social and economic inequalities evident in the later kingdoms.

Schmidt's (1997) study of recent Haya ironworking methods, the symbolism surrounding the technological process, and the role of iron, ironworkers, and ironworking in recent Haya society presented a detailed picture of a technology viewed as explicitly gendered; the smelter being male and the furnace female. He was able to interpret the symbolic landscape of the Kyamutwara capital of Rugamora Mahe (dated by radiocarbon to the seventeenth century) using the insights gained from his ethnographic work, and to identify, through excavation, ironworking features dating from the third century BCE indicated by these traditions. Kyamutwara was located in northwestern Tanzania, on the western shore of Lake Victoria. This work suggests that iron production may have been similarly gendered, certainly in the Later Iron Age kingdom of Kyamutwara, and possibly also in the EIA. Schmidt argues that control over iron production and the symbolism associated with iron production enabled new dynasties to gain both economic power and political legitimacy in Kyamutwara.

RACHEL MACLEAN

Further Reading

Connah, G. *Kibiro*. London: British Institute in Eastern Africa, 1996.

MacLean, R. "Gendered Technologies and Gendered Activities in the Interlacustrine Early Iron Age." In *Gender in African Prehistory*, edited by S. Kent. Walnut Creek: AltaMira Press, 1998.

Reid, A. "Ntusi and its Hinterland: Further Investigations of the Later Iron Age and Pastoral Ecology in Southern Uganda." *Nyame Akuma*. 33 (1990): 26–28.

Reid, A., and R. MacLean. "Symbolism and the Social Contexts of Iron Production in Karagwe." *World Archaeology*. 27, no. 1 (1995): 144–161.

Schmidt, P. R. *Iron Technology in East Africa*. Oxford: James Currey Publishers, and Bloomington: Indiana University Press, 1997.

Schoenbrun, D. L. *A Green Place, A Good Place*. Oxford: James Currey Publishers, and Portsmouth, N.H.: Heinemann, 1998.

Sutton, J. *A Thousand Years in East Africa*. Nairobi: British Institute in Eastern Africa, 1990.

Iron Age (Later): East Africa: Societies, Evolution of

The communities that were living in the East African interior at the beginning of the first millennium appear to be a mix of foragers, or hunter-gatherer-fishers, simple farming communities, and nomadic pastoralists. The archaeological record of the East African interior indicates that a major cultural and economic change occurred across the region toward the end of the first millennium and the beginning of the second millennium—a change that marks the division between the periods archaeologists have labeled the Early Iron Age and the Late Iron Age (EIA and LIA). The most archaeologically ubiquitous marker of this change is a widespread change in pottery styles. In the Great Lakes region this was marked by the new use of roulettes to decorate pottery. Roulettes are made either of carved wood, or twisted or knotted plant fiber, and are rolled across the surface of a wet pot to create an impressed, continuous design. There are, however, other new developments, including the construction of large earthworks in what is now Uganda, monuments that suggest the evolution of more complex societies. When Arab and European traders were finally to travel into the interior of East Africa in the mid-nineteenth century they recorded a number of complex states or kingdoms lying in the Great Lakes region, sophisticated political entities that they had to recognize as truly indigenous African developments. The evolution of these entities from their simple Early Iron Age beginnings continues to be a little known subject.

It has been argued by Peter Schmidt (1997) that the roots of these complex societies lie in the early iron-producing communities that lived and worked on the northwestern shores of Lake Victoria, in Buhaya. The size of these communities and the complexity and scale of their iron industry has been disputed, but it is plausible that the control of important resources such as iron may have enabled the development of economic and political inequality from which the Later Iron Age kingdoms developed. The kingdoms encountered by the first traders were, in many cases, exercising control over iron production, and in some, such as Karagwe (which lies to the west of Buhaya), and in Rwanda, the working of iron was intimately and symbolically linked to royal power.

The control of cattle, and the symbolic value placed upon them, was also common to many of these nineteenth-century societies; indeed, in Karagwe the royal insignia included several iron cows representing the association of both these resources with political control. Andrew Reid and John Sutton's excavations at the site of Ntusi, in southern Uganda, indicated that from its beginnings in the eleventh century the production of cattle was central to its economy. At its height, in the foureenth century, Ntusi covered an area of approximately 100 hectares (247 acres) and clearly dominated its hinterland, yet Reid argues that the control of cattle by a small elite had not yet emerged at Ntusi, which therefore had not reached the socio-political complexity of the later kingdoms.

The large earthwork sites—the most notable of which is Bigo with some ten kilometers (6 miles) of ditches, up to four meters (13 feet) in depth—attracted the attention of the first archaeologists to work in the region. These earthworks appeared to have little association with the later kingdoms but were associated, or were associated by archaeologists, with oral traditions of the Cwezi, a mysterious group of royal heroes and godlike characters who ruled the region in antiquity. The Cwezi remain controversial figures, hovering between myth and distant historical reality, but their influence on archaeology has been actual. The early excavations in Uganda, and particularly the excavation of Bigo by both Shinnie and Posnansky, were attempts to verify the truth of the Cwezi traditions and the function of these earthworks remains poorly understood. The ditches are not defensive, little cultural material has been recovered from large areas of the sites, and only Bigo and Munsa have produced radiocarbon dates (fifteenth to nineteenth centuries and fourteenth to fifteenth centuries, respectively). Reid has suggested that they may have been used for either agriculture or pasturage.

The control of a third resource, salt, is also known, both historically and archaeologically. At the site of Kibiro, on the eastern shore of Lake Albert, Connah has uncovered evidence for occupation and salt production beginning in the twelfth or thirteenth century and continuing to the present day. The recovery of glass beads and cowry shells, imported luxury goods, suggests the economic importance attained by Kibiro during the Iron Age. At some unknown date Kibiro became incorporated into the Bunyoro state and played such an important economic role in the region that the British launched several punitive expeditions to destroy it at the end of the nineteenth century.

Survey work by Peter Robertshaw (1994) in western Uganda has also indicated a period of social and economic change. He has identified the appearance of settlements from at least the twelfth century in areas previously unoccupied by iron-using communities, indicating a shift from the wetter, more fertile margins of Lake Victoria where the EIA settlements were clustered. He has also found some evidence for the appearance of larger sites, site hierarchies, and defensive locations by the fourteenth century, all factors that would indicate increasing social tension.

Reid has argued that the archaeological evidence shows a period of increasing regional diversification and economic specialization, economic changes that would have required or initiated the creation of new forms of physical storage, social support, and extensive trade networks. In turn these social changes would have been fundamentally linked to the political changes that resulted in the development of the politically complex, economically specialized kingdoms recorded in the nineteenth century. These archaeological arguments are paralleled by the linguistic arguments of David Schoenbrun (1998), who has suggested the evolution of increasingly complex forms of power in the region from the eighth century onward. The possible social changes first evidenced by a widespread change in pottery decoration finally culminated in the development of a mosaic of inter-related and incontrovertibly East African states.

RACHEL MACLEAN

Further Reading

Connah, G. *Kibiro*. London: British Institute in Eastern Africa, 1996.

Reid, A. "Ntusi and the Development of Social Complexity in Southern Uganda." In *Aspects of African Archaeology*, edited by G. Pwiti and R. Soper. Harare: University of Zimbabwe Publications, 1996.

Robertshaw, P. "Archaeological Survey, Ceramic Analysis and State Formation in Western Uganda." *African Archaeological Review.* 12 (1994): 105–131.

Schmidt, P. R. *Iron Technology in East Africa*. Oxford: James Currey Publishers, and Bloomington: Indiana University Press, 1997.

Schoenbrun, D. L. *A Green Place, A Good Place*. Oxford: James Currey Publishers, and Portsmouth, N.H.: Heinemann, 1998.

Sutton, J. *A Thousand Years in East Africa*. Nairobi: British Institute in Eastern Africa, 1990.

Iron Age (Later): East Africa: Salt

One consequence of the adoption of agriculture in Africa, as elsewhere, was an increased demand for salt as a dietary supplement. A variety of different sources came to be exploited. The purest of these, natural rock salt, has a fairly limited distribution in Africa, being found only at a few places in the Sahara. Other sources include sea salt; naturally occurring salt crusts produced by solar evaporation; brine springs; salt impregnated soil; termite runs; and various salt-bearing plants. With the exception of natural salt crusts, some form of processing is necessary before the salt can be utilized. Typically, this involves either the straining of brine or other salt-rich solutions, or their evaporation by boiling or exposure to solar energy.

The practice of extracting salt from plants may have been quite widespread among early African agriculturists, and was possibly one of the commonest methods used. The technique is well documented ethnographically for Malawi, where a wide range of reeds, sedges, swamp grasses, and other waterside plants were used, as well as some dry-land trees and shrubs. The technique here, as elsewhere on the continent, entailed the production of a salt-rich ash by burning appropriate plant material. Water was then strained through this and the resultant brine boiled until the water had evaporated. Perforated ceramic vessels, various kinds of baskets, and woven mats were employed as strainers.

A somewhat similar technology was used to process salt-rich earth, such as that found around the margins of salt pans and hot springs. Salty earth was first collected and placed in perforated pots or gourds with water, which filtered through to a vessel placed underneath. The filtrate could then be used either directly for cooking, or evaporated over a hearth, with more and more brine being added to the boiling pot until the vessel was completely filled with salt. Since the pots had to be broken to extract the salt, the resultant mounds of shards of salt-boiling vessels (*briquetage*) can make this type of extraction sites highly visible in the archaeological record. Around the Ivuna salt pans, near Lake Rukwa in southern Tanzania, for example, up to seven meters (21 feet) of deposits containing a mass of pottery, food bones, the remains of house floors and other debris, as well as several burials have survived. Dating to between the thirteenth to fifteenth centuries, the extent of these deposits suggest salt extraction was being undertaken here on quite an intensive scale, most probably for long-distance exchange, although only a handful of imported glass beads were recovered from the excavations.

Examples of perforated pots that could have been used in the domestic production of salt have also been found on various archaeological sites in the region. One of the earliest examples comes from the fifth-century site of Kapwirimbe in Zambia; others are known from the eighth-century site of Dakawa in east-central Tanzania, and from various sites around Lake Malawi, including the eighth–eleventh century sites at Namaso Bay, the mid-eighteenth-century site at Nfera Lagoon, and the Later Iron Age site of Kyungu at the northern end of the lake. Typological similarities between the pottery from this latter site and that recovered from Ivuna, suggest cultural links between the two areas, although Kyungu was occupied significantly later than Ivuna.

Salt extraction was also undertaken on an even larger scale at a number of locations in eastern Africa. In western Uganda, the salt works at Katwe, near Lake Edward, and Kibiro on Lake Albert were especially important during the nineteenth century when they fell within the boundaries of, respectively, the Toro and Bunyoro kingdoms. In both cases, the trade in salt made important contributions to the economy of the state, and the maintenance of centralized authority. Of the two, Kibiro was probably the more significant; the long-distance trade in salt from here may have been instrumental in the massive expansion of the Bunyoro state during the seventeenth century. Even so, although Kibiro was under Bunyoro authority and its inhabitants liable to pay tribute to their king, the local population was able to retain control over the resource. Most of the actual production was left to women, and probably organized on a household or kin-group basis. Each woman was allocated her own space, and once ready the salt was made up into small loads to be carried to local markets.

At Katwe, salt was extracted by trapping brine from hot springs in specially constructed clay-line hollows and evaporating the water. In the 1920s, salt was still being taken overland by porters to Ankole and Toro on a regular basis. At Kibiro, up to three meters (10 feet) of deposits associated with salt working spanning the last 700 to 800 years have survived. Extraction, as at Ivuna, involved filtering deposits of saline earth, but with an additional, and unusual, feature: the re-use of the saline earth. This involved spreading the earth from each filtration over "salt-gardens." After a number of days, the earth would absorb salty moisture from the underlying salt-rich deposits and was thus readied for repeated use. It is conceivable that it was the development of this technique that made the industry sustainable for so long.

Another important salt-trading center during the nineteenth century was Uvinza, in western Tanzania. By the end of the century production was on a massive scale, with different sections of the labor force being engaged in carrying and boiling the brine; making pots; cutting and fetching firewood; and packing salt. In 1898 German records suggest that annual output had reached 350,000 kilograms (345 tons) and that up to twenty thousand individuals were engaged in the industry. Much of this workforce was made up of seasonal itinerants, who traveled from as far afield as Burundi. Salt was exchanged locally for food and fuel, but the main stimulus for the growth of the industry from at least 1850 onward was the expansion of the long-distance caravan trade between the coast and the interior. Once obtained, the traders would exchange the salt for food as well as cloth, ivory, iron hoes, and other commodities along the caravan routes. The three Vinza chiefs who controlled the springs also profited from this trade by levying a tax amounting to one-tenth of the annual output and charging road tolls and ferry charges.

Excavations at several of the brine springs at Uvinza have uncovered a number of clay-lined, U-shaped pits used to trap the brine. Many of these also contained hearth stones and the remains of broken salt-boiling pots, and virtually all of them can be dated to the nineteenth century. However, traces of earlier Iron Age ceramics, some dating to as early as the fifth century, were also recovered from lower horizons. It is likely that these remains were also associated with earlier salt processing activities and its subsequent exchange, although details of the techniques used during these phases have yet to be determined.

PAUL LANE

See also: **Sahara: Salt: Production, Trade.**

Further Reading

Connah, G. *Kibiro: The Salt of Bunyoro, Past and Present.* London: British Institute in Eastern Africa.

Davison, S. "Saltmaking in Early Malawi." *Azania.* 28 (1993): 7–46.

Fagan, B. M., and Yellen, J. E. "Ivuna: Ancient Salt-working in Southern Tanzania." *Azania.* 3 (1968): 1–43.

Sutton, J. E. G., and A. D. Roberts. "Uvinza and its Salt Industry." *Azania.* 3 (1968): 45–86.

Iron Age (Later): East Africa: Trade

In Eastern Africa, archaeological evidence indicates that long-distance exchange networks existed well before the establishment of settled farming some 2,000 to 2,500 years ago. Thus for example, many Late Stone Age and Pastoral Neolithic sites located to the west and east of the Rift Valley contain stone tools made from obsidian that originated from sources up to 150 kilometers (95 miles) away, around Lake Naivasha. With the emergence of farming, the level of trade seems to have intensified, and by the mid-first millennium, at least three distinct exchange arenas were in operation. These were the maritime trade along the East African littoral and with other lands bordering the Indian Ocean; various east-west trading links between these coastal communities and those occupying parts of the interior; and, the north-south trade between different groups in the interior. Each sphere had different origins and, at least initially, was concerned with the circulation of different products. Ultimately, however, all three were linked to each other, and, through other external ties, to the economies of the Middle East, Asia, and Europe.

In the early centuries of its development, trade between the coast and the interior probably took the form of a series of loosely organized networks along the main river valleys and other suitable routes. Movement of people was probably over relatively short distances to barter for goods from neighboring communities. The goods themselves could easily have passed from one market to another, thereby moving steadily further away from their point of production. This type of "down-the-line" exchange probably accounts for the finds of limited numbers of exotic items, such as cowrie shells and trade wind beads, on Iron Age and earlier sites in the interior. In exchange, ivory, rhinoceros horn, leopard and other skins, and perhaps iron were among the main items being sent to the coast, and, with the exception of iron (which would have been used locally) then on to markets in Persia, India, China, and Europe. Slaves were another important export at various times. It is estimated, for example, that between the seventh and ninth centuries some fifteen thousand were shipped to southern Iraq to assist with the drainage of the Shatt al-Arab marshes; a proportion of these would have come from the interior.

It is likely this early trade also incorporated different "spheres of exchange," such that subsistence goods, especially foodstuffs, but also items like pottery and perhaps salt and iron, while being exchangeable for one another could not be exchanged for scarcer or more prestigious items. In the interior, the latter would have included items only available from the coast, but also finer pieces of metalwork made from copper, iron, and gold. The display and/or consumption of such items probably played a prominent role in signaling elite status and more generally as symbols of power. However, whereas access to these long-distance trade routes was an integral component of the rise to prominence of centers such as Sanga, Ingombe Ilede, and Great Zimbabwe in southern and central Africa, it seems to have been of less of a contributory factor in the interlacustrine zone, even though examples of coastal imports have been from sites, such as Ntusi and Munsa, in this area. Instead, intensification of grain and cattle production, and economic diversification in other areas—such as salt production on Lake Albert at Kibiro, and ironworking further to the south—and control of the local trade in these products seem to have been more important.

From around the fifteenth century onward, however, various communities in the interior began to take a more prominent role in the organization and control of long-distance trade with the coast. In the immediate coastal hinterland, the Mijikenda and subsequently the Akamba and Zigua were among the most important traders; whereas in the south it was the Yao and Makua, and in the central and northern parts of the region the Nyamwezi, Banyoro, and Baganda achieved greatest dominance. A major focus of this later trade was the supply of ivory and slaves to Swahili and Arab traders on the coast. Elephant hunting parties became a common feature across the region, and members of these different communities began to venture well beyond the territorial boundaries of their own societies. Yao trading parties, for example, went as far as Central Africa in search of ivory and slaves, while Akamba expeditions traveled from their homeland in what is now southern Kenya to the areas around Kilimanjaro and the Usambara-Pare Mountains and also northwest as far as Mount Kenya and the Laikipia Plateau.

As the volume of trade increased, it became more market oriented in nature with greater emphasis being placed on the realization of profit, rather than the use of exchange as a means to establish and reinforce social relationships. Furthermore, whereas most trade in the earlier centuries had been essentially between individuals or communities seeking to satisfy local needs created by the uneven distribution of natural resources, trading expeditions became steadily more organized and subject to control by local chiefs, many of whom rose to even greater prominence during the height of the nineteenth-century caravan trade.

PAUL LANE

See also: **Neolithic, Pastoral: Eastern Africa.**

Further Reading

Alpers, E. A. *Ivory & Slaves in East Central Africa.* London: Heinemann, 1975.

Gray, R., and D. Birmingham, eds. *Pre-Colonial African Trade.* London: Oxford University Press, 1970.

Muturo, H. W. "Precolonial Trading Systems of the East African Interior." In *Transformations in Africa*, edited by G. Connah. Leicester: Leicester University Press, 1998.

Sutton, J. E. G. "The Antecedents of the Interlacustrine Kingdoms." *Journal of African History.* 34, no. 1 (1993): 33–64.

Iron Age (Later): Southern Africa: Characteristics and Origins, South of Zambezi

The Iron Age prehistory of southern Africa has traditionally been divided into two periods, the Early Iron Age and the Later Iron Age. Chronologically, the division was put at the year 1000. Culturally, it was based on a number of changes observable in the archaeological record, including economic, social, and political organization. Because of this, the two periods were seen as bracketing separate cultural phenomenon and interpreted as reflecting new population movements into southern Africa from the north. In fact no new population movements into the region took place. The cultural changes that took place around the turn of the millennium and the origins of the Later Iron Age in southern Africa are seen mainly as a result of local developments, although scholars offer different explanations.

Using ceramic typology, archaeologists have recognized the earliest Later Iron Age communities as represented by the Leopard's Kopje Tradition, which divides into two main phases, Phase A and Phase B, as well as a north and south geographical division. Phase A is best known from the site of K2 just south of the Limpopo River. In the north it is best known from the sites of Leopard's Kopje and Mambo in the Matebeleland region of southwestern Zimbabwe. Phase A is dated around the tenth or eleventh century.

The north-south geographical division of Leopard's Kopje continues into Phase B, with Woolandale in the north and Mapungubwe in the south. This phase is broadly dated to the twelfth or thirteenth century. In northeastern Botswana, the Leopard's Kopje Tradition has been identified at such sites as Mmamagwe and Bobonong. Further to the north in Zimbabwe are several other Later Iron Age cultural units such as Gumanye in south-central Zimbabwe, Harare in central Zimbabwe, and Musengezi in the north. Their relationship to the Leopard's Kopje Culture is unclear.

There are two main views that dominate the explanation for the appearance of these cultural entities during the early part of the second millennium. One view sees the Leopard's Kopje culture as originating from the Early Iron Age cultures around the Lydenburg area in the southeast in South Africa, which then spread out into the different parts of the region. It has been argued that this was the result of the build up of cattle and human populations that then forced people to expand northwards. This was termed the Kutama Tradition after the Shona word "*kutama*," meaning migration. This movement saw the establishment of ancestral Shona speakers in the Shashi-Limpopo area and parts of Zimbabwe. However, there are no clear antecedents of the Leopard's Kopje Tradition in the presumed area of origin, and the evidence for climatic changes leading to cattle and human population buildups remains inconclusive.

Alternative explanations emphasize internal change among the local Early Iron Age communities. Some scholars see the transformations as the result of changes in social organization from matrilineal to patrilineal society. This should explain for example the change in the ceramics from the more complex styles of the Early Iron Age to the simpler ones of the Later Iron Age in the region. Early Iron Age ceramics are of better quality and more elaborately decorated because, it is argued, they were made by male specialist potters for wider distribution. On the other hand, Later Iron Age ceramics were made by women for local household use, hence their diversity and simplicity. The sociocultural transformations that characterize Later Iron Age societies discussed below are thus interpreted as a reflection of this major change in the social systems. It has been observed that the explanation that argues for population movements is inconsistent with the archaeological evidence such as that from the site of K2. Here, the evidence suggests that the features characterizing Leopard's Kopje originated from the local Early Iron Age Zhizo culture, with no intrusive elements from the south.

More recently, the change from the Early Iron Age to the Later Iron Age has been viewed in terms of change in ideology amongst the local early farming communities. This ideological change is argued to have been occasioned by new economic conditions rather than by population movements. The archaeological record indicates that the early farming communities possessed an ideology of equality. This is partly evident from the spatial organization within and between sites. The ideology is evident for a greater part of the first millennium. However, as cattle herds increased and as long as distance trade developed towards the end of this millennium, this ideology changed to one that allowed or encouraged inequality, resulting in economic and social differentiation in society.

Although some archaeologists have recently argued that Early Iron Age societies at such sites as Broederstroom in South Africa show indications of social complexity, the evidence for this is rather limited. Most archaeologists believe that they were small-scale egalitarian village communities. The Later Iron Age is characterized by greater material diversity and increasing cultural complexity that saw the growth of stratified societies either at the chiefdom or state level of organization in the region. Some of the changes that signaled the development of this period include a shift in settlement location from low-lying river or stream or valley locations to hilltops. The construction of stone walls on hilltops is another important change in spatial behavior. While some of the stone walls were functional, many, especially the later ones such as at Great Zimbabwe, are generally agreed to have been symbols of the power and prestige of the ruling classes.

One of the most important developments in the Later Iron Age was economic growth. Although changes are traceable back to the terminal stages of the Early Iron Age, two notable economic transformations are noted during the early part of the second millennium. First, there is considerable increase in cattle herds and their growing importance in social and ideological terms. Sites such as K2, Toutswemogala in northeastern Botswana, and later, Great Zimbabwe, have yielded vast quantities of cattle bone compared to any other domestic animals. In this regard, it would appear that cattle acted as important avenues to social and political power. Their importance in marriage transactions among contemporary southern Bantu people probably dates back to this period. As a source of social and political power, their possession no doubt saw the entrenchment of sociopolitical stratification in different parts of the region. Another important economic development was the increase in the volume of external trade. Several sites have yielded large quantities of exotic trade goods such glass beads in a variety of types and colors as well as ceramics. These were traded via the Indian Ocean coast and have been sourced from as far away as Persia and India. Possession of rare goods from distant sources also contributed significantly to the growth of social stratification and the rise of complex social formations in the region. Indeed, for some archaeologists, the introduction of external trade was the single most important factor in the growth of complexity in the region. Others however prefer to examine this process in much broader terms involving other factors.

However the process is explained, what is notable is that the Later Iron Age communities were characterized by the development of stratified societies. Initially, these were in the form of large chiefdoms such as Toutswe in Botswana, and what appear to have been several small chiefdoms associated with the Musengezi Tradition in the northern part of Zimbabwe.

With time, we see the development of a succession of state systems in the form of the Mapungubwe State with its capital at the site of Mapungubwe. This was succeeded by the Zimbabwe State with its center at Great Zimbabwe. Zimbabwe was in turn succeeded by the Torwa State based at the site of Khami in southwestern Zimbabwe and the Mutapa State in northern Zimbabwe. These complex systems are all characterized by a similar ceramic style that emphasized graphite burnishing and the construction of capitals of elaborate dry stone buildings in a variety of styles. The capitals share a similar spatial arrangement called the Zimbabwe culture pattern. In part, this spatial organization divides into binary opposites such as high-low and inside-outside as symbolic representations of status. It is also argued that the systems shared a similar ideology based on the manipulation of symbols of gender and power linked to the world of the ancestors.

GILBERT PWITI

See also: **Iron Age (Early): Herding, Farming, Southern Africa.**

Further Reading

Denbow, J. "A New Look at the Later Prehistory of the Kalahari." *Journal of African History.* 27 (1986): 3–28.

Garlake, P. S. *Prehistory and Ideology in Zimbabwe. In Past and Present in Zimbabwe*, edited by J. D. Peel and T. O. Ranger. Manchester: Manchester University Press, 1982.

Hall, M. *The Changing Past: Farmers, Kings, and Traders in Southern Africa 200–1860.* Cape Town: David Philip, 1987.

Huffman, T. N. "Ceramics, Settlement, and Late Iron Age Migrations." *African Archaeological Review.* 7 (1989): 155–182.

———. *Snakes and Crocodiles: Power and Symbolism in the Zimbabwe Culture.* Johannesburg: Witwatersrand University Press, 1997.

Maggs, T. O. C. "The Iron Age South of the Zambezi." In *Southern African Prehistory and Palaeoenvironments*, edited by R. Klein. Rotterdam: A. A. Balkema, 1984.

Phillipson, D. W. *The Later Prehistory of Eastern and Southern Africa.* London: Heinemann, 1977.

Pwiti, G. *Continuity and Change: An Archaeological Study of Early Farming Communities in Northern Zimbabwe.* Uppsala: Department of Archaeology, 1996.

———. "Peasants, Chiefs, and Kings: A Model of the Development of Complexity in Northern Zimbabwe." *Zambezia.* 27 (1996): 31–52.

Whitelaw, G. J., "Southern African Iron Age." In *The Encyclopedia of Precolonial Africa*, edited by J. Vogel. Altimira Press, 1997.

Iron Age (Later): Southern Africa: Toutswemogala, Cattle, and Political Power

One of the most complex states in Later Iron Age southern Africa arose in the region today covered by modern Botswana, starting in approximately 900.

The state is a political form more stable than that of the chiefdom. It is normally characterized by a new political and economic order, in which one group is able to hold power over the entire society for several generations, avoiding the tendency to fission common in chiefdoms. States maintain power through the idea of symbolic consensus created through a common ideology and the successful resolution of conflict through force if necessary. The transition from a society organized around chiefdoms to one that can be characterized as a state was probably achieved through the accrual of wealth in cattle, which gave rise to a more differentiated and complex set of social relations.

This occurred in a few cases in southern Africa towards the end of the first millennium. One of the first states in this tradition is often referred to through its association with its principal site, Toutswemogala. Its society is sometimes referred to as the Zhizo tradition.

Until about the middle of the first millennium, Botswana was not extensively populated by farmers. Although Botswana is currently beset by severe environmental degradation, mostly as a result of overgrazing, about 1,100 years ago the climate in the east was marked by more rainfall and was consequently more capable of supporting livestock. Around the year 700, pastoralists began to move into the area in greater numbers, taking advantage of the ability of local pasturage to support larger cattle herds. Here they came into contact with the Khoisan people already resident in the area, some of whom were themselves cattle keepers. By 900 a stratified and hierarchical society was emerging on the fringes of the Kalahari Desert, linked regionally to other emergent states like that at Mapungubwe.

Toutswemogala society was organized into settlements of different sizes. The evidence for this comes from aerial photographs that show changes in vegetation and ancient accumulations of dung. As a result of this, archaeologists have been able to plot the existence of three different kinds of settlement. The smallest range is between 100 and 5,000 square meters in size. These sites have small kraals (cattle pens), or no kraals at all. They contain Later Stone Age artifacts, and the remains of wild animals, likely hunted as food supplements. These sites appear not to have been reused and were probably abandoned after one generation.

Other sites, like those at Taukome and Thatsane, range in size up to 10,000 square meters. They contain kraals, and show evidence of having been occupied for between 200 and 300 years. It is thought that these sites supplied cattle to the larger central site at Toutswemogala, which is calculated to have been 100,000 square meters in extent. Toutswemogala was occupied for approximately 500 years until the fourteenth century. The site was home to a very large kraal.

Excavated artifacts and material include shells from the Indian Ocean and glass beads made in Arabia. These are evidence for Toutswemogala's links with greater southern African society. All the sites contain pottery similar in style to that found in Zimbabwe and Northern Province, South Africa, for the period between 680 and 1300, indicating cultural affinities between the groups resident in this area, as well as contact with the Mapungubwe state.

The bones of mature cattle of reproductive age have also been found in the deposits at Toutswemogala. These provide one source of evidence about the importance of the site. These bones would indicate that Toutswemogala was an important and rich state because its rulers could afford to kill their most valuable cattle. This would only be possible if mature cattle of reproductive age were a resource in great abundance.

The power of Toutswemogala developed firstly out of the accumulation of wealth in cattle. The ability to control the breeding and distribution of cattle gave the elite of the emergent state access to stores of wealth. These stores of wealth could be used to barter for more wealth or to secure the allegiance of outer lying groups. Few trade goods and no gold have been found in the deposits at Toutswemogala, indicating that these goods did not play a role in the accumulation of wealth, unlike the case at Mapungubwe. Being further away from contact with the east coast than the Mapungubwe state, Toutswemogala did not gain its wealth from trade.

The focus on cattle in Botswanan society at this point, together with the evidence of hierarchical settlement patterns, points to a social system with features of the Central Cattle Pattern. Cattle would have held both symbolic and literal wealth, and society would have been organized around a structure of oppositions which gained their meaning from references associated with cattle. The meaning of cattle was carried over into the successor societies to Toutswemogala. The power of the state diminished during the thirteenth century, probably as a result of overgrazing and drought and the state went into a decline.

NATASHA ERLANK

Further Reading

Denbow, J. "Cows and Kings: A Spatial and Economic Analysis of a Hierarchical Early Iron Age Settlement System in Eastern Botswana." In *Frontiers: Southern African Archaeology Today*, edited by M. Hall, G. Avery, M. Avery, M. L. Wilson, and A. Humphreys. Oxford: British Archaeological Reports, 1984.

Hall, M. *The Changing Past: Farmers, Kings, and Traders in Southern Africa 200–1860*. London: James Currey, 1987.

Iliffe, J. *Africans: The History of a Continent*. Cambridge, Cambridge University Press, 1995.

Shillington, K. *The Colonisation of the Southern Tswana 1870–1900*. Johannesburg: Ravan, 1985.

Wilmsen, E., and J. Denbow. "Paradigmatic History of San-speaking Peoples and Current Attempts at Revision." *Current Anthropology*. 31, no. 5 (1990): 489–524.

Iron Age (Later): Southern Africa: Leopard's Kopje, Bambandyanalo, and Mapungubwe

By the ninth century, Arab traders from Yemen and the Persian Gulf, as well as local Swahili coastal traders, had extended their trade networks down the east coast of Africa, as far as Chibuene on the Mozambican coast. Their presence was to have a significant impact on developments in the interior of southern Africa, prompting the growth of the first complex state in the region, a precursor to Great Zimbabwe. The most important site linked to this state has been found at Mapungubwe, on the south side of the Limpopo River (the South Africa/Zimbabwe/Botswana border) in the Limpopo River valley. However, there are a number of sites linked to this state, and their evolution reflects the growing importance of trade with the east coast.

The Limpopo valley region was inhabited from the second century, probably by ancestors of modern Shona-speakers. However, it was not settled extensively by Iron Age farmers until the eighth century, when climate changes made more extensive farming possible. When larger settlements were formed they were characteristic of the Central Cattle Pattern, with stone huts and kraals (cattle pens). One of the earliest sites excavated for this period is Schroda, close to Mapungubwe and dated to the ninth century. Archaeological deposits at Schroda contain imported glass beads and ivory, import and export goods that point to the development of a trade with the east coast, if only indirectly.

From the tenth century, sites in the region became more complex, showing evidence of larger cattle herds and a new pottery style. This is evident at Leopard's Kopje (dated to 980), near modern Bulawayo. The site's name is often used to refer to a Later Iron Age phase covering the period between 1000 and 1300, which includes the period when the Mapungubwe state was in its ascendancy. These shifts are taken to indicate the beginnings of more complex social structure in the area, prompted by a developing trade in gold.

Gold was present in alluvial and surface deposits on the Zimbabwean plateau. However, the local people disregarded it, until Arab traders on the East African coast expressed an interest in it, and the demand for gold became apparent. The start of this trade can be dated accurately, because it was reported by the Arabian chronicler, Al-Masudi, in 916.

By the end of the tenth century, people of the Leopard's Kopje tradition had settled at Bambandyanalo (known in some of the literature as K2) at the base of Mapungubwe hill. The large amount of cattle bones found confirms the importance of cattle to this society. The presence of imported glass beads indicates a flourishing trade with the coast. The beads are found throughout the deposits for Bambandyanalo and Mapungubwe, attesting to the importance of trade until Mapungubwe's decline. At Bambandyanalo there is also evidence of specialized craft working, resulting in ivory bracelets and spindle whorls.

By 1075 a small part of the settlement had relocated to the top of Mapungubwe hill. It is thought that the Mapungubwe rulers and religious elite occupied the hill as a direct result of growing hierarchical distinctions in Mapungubwe society, the literal placement of different classes at the top or bottom of the hill reflecting symbolic status. Thereafter, livestock and the majority of people lived at the bottom of the hill. Remains from the top of the hill include richly endowed burials and evidence of successive phases of building that incorporated more elaborate stone walling than at Bambandyanalo. (Mapungubwe's famous gold rhinoceros was found here.)

Some of the information about Mapungubwe is gathered from the skeletons (over 100) buried in the complex. These skeletons comprise the largest collection of Iron Age human remains found to date in southern Africa. Most were buried in flexed positions, together with material goods such as beads, bangles, and pottery shards.

Mapungubwe has been identified as the center of a state that emerged on the southern bank of the Limpopo at the end of the tenth century, and which extended its rule over the Zimbabwean plateau and into modern Botswana. Smaller settlements, with layouts similar to Mapungubwe, are to be found around the bases and summits of hills of the surrounding region. This pattern of a hierarchy of settlements, modeled on the main settlement, is similar to that of Toutswemogala.

Shifts in the nature of power relations at Mapungubwe have been linked to control over external trade. The precondition for the emergence of the state would have been control of internal resources, such as cattle. Thereafter, those groups who controlled the production and distribution of trade items like gold and ivory would have been able to accumulate the resources necessary to assert power over others. This would have encouraged the emergence of a more hierarchical social system. Social stratification is necessary for the emergence of states, which are more permanent social arrangements than chiefdoms. States also rely on additional means as sources of authority. The continual rendering of tribute, necessary for the reproduction of the state, was achieved through social contract. This was achieved through the creation of a symbolic order binding the state together. This, in turn, called into existence the need for a religious elite. Analyses of the use of space at Mapungubwe indicate that its leaders combined secular leadership with sacred power. States of this kind are also characterized by a social division of labor, which was present at Mapungubwe through the evidence of specialized craft working.

By the thirteenth century, the Mapungubwe state was in decline, probably as a result of its loss of control of the gold trade. Arab traders were locating themselves further north along the east coast and trading directly with a newly emergent state on the Zimbabwean plateau. This state became known as Great Zimbabwe.

NATASHA ERLANK

See also: **Great Zimbabwe: Origins and Rise.**

Further Reading

Hall, M. *The Changing Past: Farmers, Kings, and Traders in Southern Africa 200–1860*. London: James Currey, 1987.

Huffman, T. *Snakes and Crocodiles: Power and Symbolism in Ancient Zimbabwe*. Johannesburg: Witwatersrand University Press, 1996.

Iliffe, J. *Africans: The History of a Continent*. Cambridge, Cambridge University Press, 1995.

Maggs, T., and G. Whitelaw. "A Review of Recent Archaeological Research on Food-Producing Communities in Southern Africa." *Journal of African History*. 32 (1991): 3–24.

Maylam, P. *A History of the African People of South Africa: From the Early Iron Age to the 1970s*. London and Johannesburg: Croom Helm and David Philip, 1986.

Sinclair, P., and I. Pikirayi, G. Pwiti, and R. Soper. "Urban Trajectories on the Zimbabwean Plateau." In *The Archaeology of Africa: Food, Metals and Towns*, edited by T. Shaw, P. Sinclair, B. Andah, and A. Okpoko. London: Routledge, 1993.

Iron Age (Later): Southern Africa: Highveld, Emergence of States on

Toward the end of the first millennium, a number of major shifts occurred in southern African history, signified in the archaeological record by a break in ceramic traditions, different settlement patterns, more settled dwellings, more extensive cattle-keeping, and the initial development of more complex social formations. This forms the start of the period known as the Later Iron Age. Previous to this date, the highveld (which covers central South Africa) had seen little concerted occupation by the Early Iron Age mixed farmers, because the highveld soil was not suited to Early Iron Age farming techniques. The northern highveld was the first part of this region to be occupied, during the eleventh century. The occupation of the southern highveld occurred from approximately 1400 onward.

The move to the highveld occurred as a result of an increased dependence on cattle-keeping. This shift is visible in the remains of fossilized dung and the presence of cattle pens (kraals) that are prominently positioned in the settlements built by the new inhabitants of the highveld. The absence of trees on the highveld meant that its inhabitants had to build in stone. As a result, the area is characterized by different types of stone remains, the presence of which has made it significantly easier to reconstruct the history of these areas because of the durability of the ruins (coastal dwellers built dung and straw huts).

Highveld settlements consist of huts and kraals built out of stone, some linked together by dry-stone walling. The settlements exist in both relatively simple and complex forms (referred to as Type N and Type V): a few huts and one central pen, or several huts linked together by intricate walling. The kraals are always in the middle of these settlements. Their central position points to the importance of cattle-keeping in these societies.

This importance is echoed in the modern ethnographic record. The study of modern cattle-keeping societies and the arrangement of their homesteads has allowed anthropologists to show symbolic links between settlement patterns and social arrangements. The front of a settlement was for public, secular, and dangerous activity, the back for private, religious, and safe activity. Women's huts were on the left-hand side and men's on the right-hand side. The position of huts also reflected the status of its occupants. The use of space reflected a particular worldview. This is sometimes called the Central (or Bantu) Cattle Pattern. Some archaeologists have suggested that the presence of archaeological ruins showing this pattern is evidence for similar social relations in Later Iron Age societies, including those at Mapungubwe and Great Zimbabwe.

Remains of large, densely populated settlements dominate the west Highveld, while smaller settlements are more characteristic of the east. Smaller Type N remains have been linked to societies who were resident in the Highveld from the fourteenth century onward. Type V settlements dominate the period from the sixteenth to the nineteenth century. Highveld farmers subsisted on agriculture, herding, and hunting. They used items made from iron, copper, pottery, and ostrich egg shell. The absence of evidence for iron smelting at such sites points to trade in iron from places on the edge of the Highveld in Mpumalanga province, South Africa. It is likely that iron was exchanged for cattle. Copper was re-smelted locally.

Highveld societies were hierarchically organized and ruled by chiefs. A chief would command the allegiance of the senior homestead heads in his region, cementing their support through the distribution of cattle and the provision of access to land. Homestead heads, in turn, commanded the labor and resources of their homesteads. Homesteads were often polygynous. Alliances between homesteads were cemented through marriage and bridewealth exchanges (*bohali*), where a young man acquired a wife through the payment of cattle made on his behalf by his father or senior male relatives. These societies were patriarchal, although unlike among the more southerly herding societies in southern Africa, women could become chiefs. This social pattern appears to have been present to some degree since the fourteenth century, if the record of settlement patterns is reliable. Its longevity is attested to by similarities in the layout of homesteads dated to this period and to the nineteenth century.

These settlements can be linked to the ancestors of the Sotho-Tswana people, a term developed to encompass a range of diverse peoples. Sotho-speakers consist of the Northern (Pedi) and Southern Sotho (Basotho), while the Tswana are today found in Botswana and North-West Province, South Africa. The history of some of these communities can be traced in the oral traditions of contemporary Sotho communities. From the nineteenth century, these records are supplemented by the recorded evidence of missionaries and other Europeans in the interior.

The major Tswana chiefdoms had emerged by 1600, including the Hurutshe and Kwena. A process of fragmentation led to the development of a number of smaller polities, which had amalgamated into larger units like the Rolong and the Thlaping by the eighteenth century. In 1806 the Thlaping capital was estimated to contain 10,000 to 15,000 people and, according to the English traveler John Barrow, it was as large as contemporary Cape Town. Furthermore, it had "a well-developed administrative order, and a strong 'king' who owned large herds and regulated trade, supervised rainmaking and other rites, controlled the allocation of land and public meetings, and derived considerable wealth from tributary labor and the spoils of the hunt" (Comaroff and Comaroff 1991, p.27). The size of these towns is confirmed in the archaeological evidence, where they are referred to as Type V settlements.

Denser settlement in the west can be explained by the more arid conditions of the region. These chiefdoms were bigger than any other contemporary ones in southern Africa. The emergence of large Tswana chiefdoms by the late eighteenth century is given as evidence for the development of states on the southern Highveld. A state was a more complex form of political organization than the chiefdom, more stable, and long lived. Tswana chiefdoms consisted of a hierarchy of social forms, beginning with the homestead. A number of homesteads formed a family unit. A number of family groups made up a ward, which was governed by a hereditary headman. These headmen had considerable authority but ultimately deferred to the chief. The need to exploit environmental resources efficiently is provided as the reason for this concentration of authority in the person of the chief. However, state formation did not proceed beyond this level.

NATASHA ERLANK

Further Reading

Comaroff, Jean and John. *Of Revelation and Revolution: Christianity, Colonialism, and Consciousness in South Africa*. Vol. 1. Chicago, Chicago University Press, 1991.

Hall, M. *The Changing Past: Farmers, Kings and Traders in Southern Africa 200–1860*. London: James Currey, 1987.

Lye, W., and C. Murray. *Transformations on the Highveld: The Tswana and the Southern Sotho*. Cape Town and London: David Philip, 1980.

Maylam, P. *A History of the African People of South Africa: From the Early Iron Age to the 1970s*. London and Johannesburg: Croom Helm and David Philip, 1986.

Shillington, K. *The Colonisation of the Southern Tswana 1870–1900*. Johannesburg: Ravan, 1985.

Iron Age (Later): Southern Africa: Southeastern Lowveld, Emergence of States on

In the late eighteenth and early nineteenth centuries, African societies in the region between the Drakensberg and the Indian Ocean went through a series of wide-ranging and sometimes violent political and social transformations. In certain parts of the region, the ruling groups of particular chiefdoms were able to bring neighboring chiefdoms under their domination on a wider scale than seems to have been the case beforehand. Inside these expanding polities, rulers worked to establish a greater degree of authority over their adherents. As late as the mid-eighteenth century, there had been several hundred independent chiefdoms in the region, most of them not more than a few hundred square kilometers in extent and with populations of not more than a few thousand. The powers that chiefs were able to exercise over their followers were relatively limited. By the 1820s the region was dominated by a handful of much larger emerging states, some of which covered several thousand square kilometers and numbered scores of thousands of inhabitants. The kings ruled with a strong and sometimes despotic hand.

It was not until the late nineteenth and early twentieth centuries that colonial historians, both white and black, began trying to put together coherent accounts of these changes. As sources, they used mainly scraps of African oral histories recorded by European traders, travelers, officials, and missionaries. For several decades their explanations of events placed strong emphasis to the doings of "great men," particularly the Zulu king Shaka, whose supposedly widespread conquests in the 1810s and 1820s were seen as the prime source of a chain reaction of population movements and political violence that had led to the consolidation of numbers of large kingdoms over much of southeastern Africa. From the 1940s a new generation of academic writers began to explore the possible effects of more "structural" factors, such as human population growth, the expansion of external trade, climatic and environmental change, and the introduction of a new crop in the form of maize. The paucity of evidence kept their hypotheses very much at the level of speculation.

In the 1960s and 1970s historians of the region began to make more systematic use of two major sources of evidence. One consisted of Portuguese documentary records housed in archives and libraries in Lourenço Marques (now Maputo) and Lisbon. The other was the rich collection of African oral histories that had been made early in the century by Natal colonial official James Stuart and which had been available to the public in a Durban library since the late 1940s. At the same time, historians inside and outside southern Africa began to subject to more critical scrutiny many of the assumptions about the history of African societies that had been entrenched in the literature since colonial times.

Since the last decades of the twentieth century, a number of historians have edged toward accepting the expansion of international trade through Delagoa Bay as the most likely prime cause of the emergence of African states east of the Drakensberg. The evidence is clear that from the 1760s onward, European and Indian merchants were buying increasing quantities of ivory from chiefdoms at the bay in exchange for cloth, beads, and brass. By the 1790s American whalers were docking at the bay in increasing numbers and, it seems, trading for cattle as provisions. Foreign goods had been circulated in the region by Portuguese traders since the mid-sixteenth century but never in the quantities that now became available. Historians who favor the "trade hypothesis" argue that increasing competition for these highly prized commodities between and within chiefdoms at Delagoa Bay and in its hinterland was a prime cause in stimulating both the territorial expansion and the political centralization which were taking place at this time.

The available evidence indicates that among the first chiefdoms to begin expanding its power was that of the Maroteng, who lived three hundred kilometers to the northwest of Delagoa Bay. The polity, which they eventually dominated, became known as the Pedi kingdom. At much the same time a cluster of rival statelets emerged around Delagoa Bay itself. The largest of these seems to have been the Mabhudu or Maputo kingdom to the south of the bay. Further south still, in the northern parts of what is now the KwaZulu-Natal province of South Africa, the Nxumalo and the Nyambose were consolidating their hold on what became the Ndwandwe and Mthethwa kingdoms respectively. In the vicinity of all these budding states, there emerged numbers of smaller and more loosely organized amalgamations of chiefdoms, often formed in defensive reactions against the expansion of their more powerful neighbors. Among them were the polities dominated by the Dlamini in what is now southern Swaziland, the Hlubi in northwestern KwaZulu-Natal, and the Qwabe on the coast north of the Thukela River in central KwaZulu-Natal.

Rivalries between developing states seem to have been most pronounced in the region to the south of Delagoa Bay. By the 1810s a confrontation was building up between the Ndwandwe under Zwide kaLanga and the Mthethwa under Dingiswayo kaJobe. Both chiefs were actively expanding the territories under their authority, partly, it seems, to acquire areas of good agricultural and grazing land, and partly to extend their control over trade routes to Delagoa Bay, where the Portuguese had recently established a small garrison. Portuguese interventions in the politics of neighboring chiefdoms, aimed largely at controlling the trade in ivory and at trying to expand a trade in slaves, may also have affected relations between the Ndwandwe and the Mthethwa. In the late 1810s the rivalry between them broke out into warfare. The upshot was that the Mthethwa were defeated, Dingiswayo was killed, and his kingdom rapidly broke up.

The disintegration of the Mthethwa polity opened the way for the emergence of a new local power in its place. This was the Zulu chiefdom, previously a minor polity whose ruler, Shaka kaSenzangakhona, had been subordinate to Dingiswayo. Through a combination of diplomacy and force, Shaka was able to establish himself as the leader of a defensive alliance of smaller chiefdoms against the Ndwandwe. His subsequent success in warding off several Ndwandwe attacks may have been a factor in triggering the breakup of the Ndwandwe kingdom, which for some time seems to have been experiencing increasing internal political tensions. The main Ndwandwe house under Zwide moved off northward into southern Swaziland and subsequently further northwest into what is now the Mpumalanga province of South Africa, where it began to reconsolidate its power. Other sections that hived off to the northwest and northeast formed the nuclei of what subsequently became the Ndebele, Gaza, Ngoni, and Jele kingdoms.

These events left the way open for Shaka to extend his authority northwards into Zwide's former territories. By the early 1820s the emerging Zulu kingdom dominated most of what is now KwaZulu-Natal, though, contrary to the common stereotype, Shaka's power rested on shaky political foundations throughout his reign.

JOHN WRIGHT

See also: **Mfecane.**

Further Reading

Bonner, P. *Kings, Commoners and Concessionaires: The Evolution and Dissolution of the Nineteenth-Century Swazi State*. Cambridge: Cambridge University Press, 1983.

Delius, P. *The Land Belongs to Us: The Pedi Polity, the Boers and the British in the Nineteenth-Century Transvaal*. Johannesburg: Ravan Press, 1983.

Guy, J. "Ecological Factors in the Rise of Shaka and the Zulu Kingdom." In *Economy and Society in Pre-Industrial South Africa*, edited by S. Marks and A. Atmore. London: Longman, 1980.

Smith, A. "The Trade of Delagoa Bay as a Factor in Nguni Politics 1750–1835." In *African Societies in Southern Africa*, edited by L. Thompson. London: Heinemann, 1969.

Wright, J., and C. Hamilton. "Traditions and Transformations: The Phongolo-Mzimkhulu Region in the Late Eighteenth and Early Nineteenth Centuries." In *Natal and Zululand from Earliest Times to 1910: A New History*, edited by A. Duminy and B. Guest. Pietermaritzburg: University of Natal Press and Shuter and Shooter, 1989.

Webb, C. de B., and J. B. Wright, eds. *The James Stuart Archive of Recorded Oral Evidence Relating to the History of the Zulu and Neighbouring Peoples*. 4 vols. Pietermaritzburg: University of Natal Press, 1976.

Iron Age (Later): Southern Africa: Ethnicity, Language, Identity

Southern African societies can be distinguished on the basis of a range of characteristics, including language, ethnicity, political affiliation, and cultural identity, some of which still have currency. These group identities do not always overlap and all these identities have a discernable history. Many of these identities emerged in the Later Iron Age (*c*.1000–1800). None of these identities has remained unchanged since this period, while some forms of political identification no longer exist.

All Africans languages in southern Africa fall into two groups. The Sarwa (Bushman) of Botswana speak a language that, together with historically recorded Khoekhoen dialects, formed one group. The other group consists of Bantu-speakers, whose languages have their origin in the Niger-Congo region of Africa many thousands of years ago. Today this family consists of about three hundred languages, spoken by roughly 200 million people. Speakers of these languages reached Africa's southernmost tip approximately two thousand years ago.

In southern Africa, most Bantu-speakers are members of one of two language groups: Sotho and Nguni. Among the former are speakers of South Sotho, currently spoken in South Africa and Lesotho; Tswana, currently spoken in South Africa and Botswana; and North Sotho, or Pedi, which is spoken in South Africa. Nguni languages include Xhosa, Zulu, Swati, and Ndebele, spoken in South Africa, Swaziland, and Mozambique. Contemporary speakers can trace their ancestry to a number of chiefdoms whose residence in particular regions dates back to the Later Iron Age. During that era, several different chiefdoms spoke the same language; language units generally extended beyond social and political boundaries.

Chiefdoms were the most common form of political organization and one of the most easily distinguished social units, in southern Africa. Their presence is attested to by oral history, European travel narratives, and archaeological evidence. A chiefdom is generally defined as a group of people who comprise an independent polity, having a distinct territorial base, principles of hierarchical arrangement based on lineage (often male-descent based), and reliant on subsistence agriculture together with some craft specialization. There is often ambiguity and little consensus about what this term means. Some anthropologists see chiefdoms as "segmentary societies," referring to political integration derived from relations between descent groups whose status with respect to each other is defined precisely and hierarchically. Other anthropologists stress the limited authority of kin groups, pointing to the fact that the chiefdom refers to a group constituted by political ties, where the chief exercises authority over all who live within his territory. Membership of a chiefdom may have been linked by ancestry, but it only had meaning when it acted as a political unit.

It is possible to trace the history of southern African chiefdoms back to the middle of the last millennium. Contemporary Xhosa-speakers are the descendents of a number of powerful chiefdoms that occupied the southernmost part of southern Africa as independent units until European conquest in the nineteenth century. These chiefdoms, the Rharhabe and the Gcaleka for instance, trace their ancestry back to the rule of Chief Tshawe in the sixteenth century. Tswana-speaking chiefdoms were descended from political units based on descent, whose history can be traced back to the fourteenth century. All Tswana ruling families can be linked to three founding ancestors from this period. Out of one of these emerged the Kwena chiefdom, one of the most powerful during the seventeenth and eighteenth centuries. During the eighteenth century, the Ngwaketse and the Ngwato chiefdoms, beginning processes of consolidation common to most Tswana chiefdoms, broke away from the Kwena. Today, no traditional chiefdoms survive as independent political entities.

In some historical writing, the concept of a chiefdom is often collapsed into the notion of a tribe. During the colonial era government officials, missionaries, and anthropologists divided African people into conveniently sized groups to facilitate the process of study and rule. The boundaries of these groups were defined according to a common culture, language, and territory. The result was the "invention" of tribes—units that would not have recognized themselves as cohesive entities before this process of description occurred. Colonial powers considered tribes to be a primitive form of political organization and to be culturally and racially inferior to Europeans. Subsequently, the concept of a tribe formed one of the cornerstones of apartheid policy in South Africa. Government ethnographers drew up lists of the different tribes living in South Africa, ascribed to them particular characteristics, and used these to justify separate development. The term has now fallen into disuse because of its association with a retrogressive artificiality.

Ethnicity or ethnic self-identity is also a means for distinguishing groups. Ethnic affiliations go beyond the political to refer to a shared cultural identity. Characteristics of ethnic groups include cultural affinity (language, values, rituals, traditions), the idea of a common historical origin, and the idea that these features distinguish the group from other ethnic groups.

In contemporary use, ethnicity also includes some notion of hierarchy. This notion of hierarchy means that ethnicity provides the conceptual basis for groups to assert asymmetric relations against others. The focus on common historical origins often leads to political mobilization of a conservative type. The Inkatha Freedom Party (the Zulu nationalist party in South Africa) stresses political mobilization at the expense of other groups on the basis of a common cultural identity. This identity draws on the symbol of the Zulu warrior, supposedly triumphant during the nineteenth century, in order to appeal to its male members and to craft Zulu unity.

It is possible, to some extent, to trace ethnicities into the past. Groups used culture, language, and history to distinguish themselves from one another, as is evident from the nineteenth century. However, the reconstruction of the content of particular ethnicities is difficult to detect further back into the past. Archaeologists have made some progress in this respect, as is the case with the detection of social relations characteristic of the Central Cattle Pattern as far back as the first millennium. It is also difficult to determine the value of an ethnic identity to, for instance, seventeenth century Tswana chiefdoms.

Ethnicity, therefore, is perhaps a problematic concept to use when attempting to define Iron Age group identities. Definition on the basis of shared cultural characteristics may be easier. Culture, however, is also problematic given the tendency of archaeologists to talk about the existence of distinct cultural entities in the past, on the basis of the distribution of ceramics of a similar type. The past, then, becomes populated by cultures, rather than people.

NATASHA ERLANK

Further Reading

Comaroff, J. "Of Totemism and Ethnicity: Consciousness, Practice, and the Signs of Inequality." In *Perspectives on Africa: A Reader in Culture, History and Representation*, edited by R. Grinaker and C. Steiner. Oxford: Blackwell, 1997.
Grinaker, R. R., and C. B. Steiner. "Introduction: Africa in Perspective." In *Perspectives on Africa: A Reader in Culture, History and Representation*, edited by R. Grinaker and C. Steiner, Oxford: Blackwell, 1997.
Lye, W., and C. Murray. *Transformations on the Highveld: The Tswana and the Southern Sotho*. Cape Town and London: David Philip, 1980.
Maylam, P. *A History of the African People of South Africa: From the Early Iron Age to the 1970s*. London and Johannesburg: Croom Helm and David Philip, 1986.
Vail, L. "Ethnicity in Southern African History." In *Perspectives on Africa: A Reader in Culture, History and Representation*, edited by R. Grinaker and C. Steiner. Oxford: Blackwell, 1997.

Iron Age (Later): Southern Africa: Peoples

Before the arrival of the Dutch in 1652, southern Africa remained the home of diverse and numerous indigenous groups who were hunters and wanderers. The mid-seventeenth century to the close of the eighteenth century, however, witnessed the growth not only of a settlement of Europeans of various nationalities but of a totally new and unique society of different races, colors, and cultural attainments, fashioned by conflicts of racial heredity and the apposition of unequal social groups.

The Indigenous Peoples

The first known inhabitants of southern Africa up to the Iron Age era were the Bushmen (or San) and Hottentots (or Khoikhoi), both of who lived by hunting or fishing and gathering of wild foods. They are collectively called the "Khoisan" peoples—a term used by linguists to classify their languages of Khoi and San. The other indigenous groups are the larger Bantu group of peoples.

The Bushmen The Bushmen or San were to be found in the area of the Kalahari Desert of present-day Namibia, and in the interior of the Orange Free State and the Cape Province. Pockets of them were located in Angola. It is widely believed that the Bushmen had lived in southern Africa for at least a thousand years before the arrival of the Dutch. The origin of the Bushmen is not specifically known. However, available evidence indicate that their original homes were to be found somewhere in East and Central Africa, and that probably because of local pressure with the powerful tribes in the area, they were forced to migrate further south. It was in the region of southern Africa that they finally settled. The Bushmen were probably not the first group of people to have lived in southern Africa.

Be that as it may, the way of life of the Bushmen was very rudimentary and in many respects similar to that of the early man of the Late Stone Age. The Bushmen were basically nomadic hunters and gatherers of food and their social organization was suited to that life. Their itinerant way of life in a semidesert country did not make it easy to provide food for a large number of people in a small area; hence they lived in small groups known as hunting bands that were constantly on the move after herds of wild life. Each unit or band shared a common life and had a definite area within which its members moved. They jealously guarded such area, and had little or no contact with others. At a particular point during the Iron Age, the Bushmen had a considerable part of the southern Africa region as their hunting grounds. This is established from the fact that their skulls, stone implements, and rock paintings are found in most parts of southern Africa, and as far north as Uganda.

The Bushmen had high regard for their way of life and culture and resisted changes even for material rewards. Apart from ornamental materials such as beads and hunting instruments, they kept no private properties.

The Bushmen clothes were animal skins. They had no permanent houses but slept in temporary shelters in branches of trees and caves which they usually decorated with beautiful pictures of hunting scenes and animals. Marriage among the Bushmen was essentially endogamous.

The political life of the Bushmen was equally rudimentary. With no clearly defined clans but only hunting parties, they had no particular chief or other formal system of government but older men took whatever decisions were necessary after due consultation with one another.

It is instructive to note that in spite of their primitive nature, the Bushmen were known to exhibit remarkable artistic talent and abilities. They were noted to be very skilled in rock engravings and paintings. They chose as their subjects hunting and battle scenes, domestic life, cattle raids, and scenes from their mythology.

The Hottentots The Hottentots, also known as the Khoikhoi, belong to the same family of Khoisan people of southern Africa. They probably came from the region of the Great Lakes in Central Africa. Like the Bushmen, the Hottentots worshipped the moon and personified natural forces, particularly those connected with water and rain. Similarly, they practiced no agriculture while enriching their diet by hunting and gathering. Besides, each Hottentot group laid claim to a particular area of land as its tribal territory.

Despite these similar features, there are considerable differences between the cultures of the two Khoisan peoples. The Hottentots were pastoralists who kept cattle and sheep, and these in fact mirrored the prosperity of their owners. There are indications also that those of them living along the coast and river basins engaged in fishing. Their standard of living was evidently higher than that of the nomadic Bushmen particularly with the relative availability of food supplies and the much treasured sheep and cattle. Besides, while the Bushmen still made use of stone implements, the Hottentots knew how to smelt iron and copper. This variety of economic activities ensured that the Hottentots were organised in bigger political units than the Bushmen. Their political organization was more advanced, the basic political unit being the tribe. The tribe consisted of a number of related clans with the chief of the central or senior clan as the overall tribal chief.

Their dwellings were simple and not of a permanent nature, though more permanent than those of the Bushmen. Houses were built of materials that could easily be transported during the frequent movement from place to place in search for pasture.

Although the Hottentots had a definite sense of territorialism, the necessity to move along in search of water, better pastures, and better homes was a great limitation on tribal cohesion and unity. Internal conflict over grazing land, more often than not, led to political fragmentation.

It is worth noting that while the Hottentots and Bushmen were neighbors, the relations between the two peoples were often hostile. The Bushmen extremely resented the intrusion of the Hottentots on areas they regarded as their own. They resisted this by killing the Hottentots' animals or kidnapping them. In retaliation of such brutality of the Bushmen, the Hottentots too made attempts to wipe out the Bushmen.

The Bantu By about 1600 both the Bushmen and Hottentots had been submerged in most parts of southern Africa by a third and much more numerous group, known as the Bantu. Bantu is a general name given to a vast group of peoples who speak several hundreds of different but related languages. Among them are the Zulu, Xhosa, Swazi, Twana, Venda, Ndebele, and Nguni. Others include the Sotho, Herero, Ambo, Thonga, Shona, Rozwi, Kalanga, Ndwandwe, Ngwane, Qwabe, and Mthethwa.

The Bantu-speaking peoples who could be broadly divided into two groups—namely, southern and central Bantu—had been settling in the region south of the Limpopo from about the fifth century, spreading out gradually over the years to occupy most parts of Southern Africa. Their movement and spread into southern Africa was part of the wider expansion of Iron Age culture. The Bantu intermarried with other peoples, established a basic pattern of settlement, and developed a wide variety of cultures and political systems. Most of the later Iron Age communities appear to have shared a common culture, with very little or no variation.

The southern Bantu depended heavily on agriculture as their principal means of livelihood. They accumulated cattle as a major expression of wealth and power in their societies. The material standard of living of the Bantu-speaking peoples was generally simple. Usually, the family possessed a few simple tools, some mats, cooking pots, and clothes made of animal skins. Their construction of building and shelter was equally simple. Among the cattle-keeping tribes, the cattle enclosure was the center of every settlement and grain was carefully stored to last until the next harvest.

Despite their simple material standard of living, the social organization of the Bantu was rather complex. They had a strong belief in law and a respect for traditional ways, with complicated rules that governed the conduct or behavior of individuals. They held the belief that the spirits of their ancestors took a close interest in, and exerted a considerable influence on their daily life. Consequently, the spirits of the ancestors were constantly venerated before important decisions were taken.

The Bantu lived in larger groups than the Bushmen and Hottentots and their tribes contained several thousand members. This was due partly to the fact that they were predominantly farmers and cattle rearers who needed a more settled life. However, they too sometimes shifted their homes to find new land and grazing ground. At any rate, the governmental apparatus of the Bantu differed slightly one from the other. The southern Bantu operated tribal system of government. At the head of each tribe was a hereditary chief, *nkosi*, who was the supreme head of the community. The *nkosi* came from the central clan and had the last word in all political matters. He was the final judge in all legal disputes. He was the link between the community and its ancestors and took the lead in all important ceremonies. The *nkosi* was assisted by officials called *indunas*, among whom there was a senior *induna* who performed many functions including deputizing for the *nkosi* with full powers, when the *nkosi* was unavailable.

The Arrival of European Immigrants

The first contact of Europeans with southern Africa could be dated back to the late fifteenth century, when Portuguese sailors and adventurers visited the coastal areas of the region. Such early contacts were, however, merely exploratory. From the mid-seventeenth century onward, large areas of Southern Africa began to experience invasion and conquest by groups of Europeans. European interest in this area was encouraged by the Dutch East India Company, which arrived at a settlement at Table Bay, on the site of the present-day Cape Town, in 1652. The initial desire of the company was to utilize the Cape as a cheap and efficient means through which it intended to support its needed base to control entry to the Indian Ocean as well as to supply its ships sailing to and from the East Indies. When the Dutch East India Company at last took action to establish a permanent post at the Cape, a new element was added to the pattern of southern African peoples. It was soon decided that farmers growing crops for their own profit would perform the task more efficiently than company servants working for salaries. Consequently, a small number of the company's men were released from their service agreements and given land on which to set up as free burghers growing crops on their own account for sale to the company. The nucleus of the future white population in southern Africa in general, and South Africa in particular, had thus been created.

The territorial expansion of white settlement in southern Africa took place at the expense of the indigenous people. With the increase in white population, more immigrants sought their means of livelihood in agriculture, leading to more rapid expansion of the settler enclave. The indigenous southern African peoples continually resisted the white advance. Inevitably, conflicts erupted. Such conflicts and clashes characterized the history of southern Africa up to the close of the eighteenth century, and beyond.

S. Ademola Ajayi

Further Reading

Marks, S., and A. Atmore, eds. *Economy and Society in Pre-Industrial South Africa*. 6. Harlow, Essex: Longman, 1980.

Parsons, N. *A New History of Southern Africa*. London: Macmillan, 1993.

Uzoigwe, G. N. *A Short History of South Africa*. Owerri, Nigeria: Esther Thompson, 1988.

Iron Age, Origins: *See* Metalworking: Origins of Ironworking.

Irrigation: *See* Sudan: Cotton, Irrigation, and Oil, 1970s.

Islam in Eastern Africa

Archaeological and documentary evidence suggests that the first appearance of Islam in sub-Saharan Africa occurred on the East African coast. Mosques dating to the eighth century have been discovered at Shanga, in the Lamu Archipelago, and at Mtambwe Mkuu on Pemba Island. The latter site probably corresponds to the Muslim settlement of Qanbalu, frequently mentioned in Arabic sources dating from the eighth to the tenth centuries. Historians and archaeologists have found coins from the coast issued in the names of Muslim rulers, as well Islamic burials in several locations, which further indicate that the origins of Islam in East Africa date from the late first millennium.

It was not until after the eleventh century, however, that Islam began winning significant numbers of converts among coastal East Africans. Mark Horton found evidence that, despite an early appearance at Shanga in the Lamu Archipelago, it was not until the eleventh century that Muslims became a majority there. The same appears to have held true for a handful of other northern and central coastal sites. Conversion progressed very unevenly along the coast, making its greatest gains at the major commercial centers like Shanga, Manda, Mombasa, Pemba, Zanzibar, and Kilwa. An Islamic presence developed much more slowly in the dozens of less dynamic urban and rural Swahili towns and villages that appeared between 1000 and 1500. Islam made no significant or permanent advances among inland East Africans until the nineteenth century.

Like elsewhere on the continent, "conversion" to Islam in East Africa until the late nineteenth century carried a number of meanings. While there were those who resisted Islamization and the power of Muslim rulers outright, and those who eventually converted to the full written tradition, most Muslims combined imported Islamic with local African beliefs and practices. For example, conversion did not rule out continued veneration of the spirits of the hearth, home, and clan. Available evidence suggests that, while coastal Muslims won converts among their trading partners inland from Sofala, once regular trade was discontinued after the sixteenth century, converts reverted to local beliefs. Ibn Battuta reported hostilities between the sultans of Kilwa and their non-Muslim neighbors, and later Portuguese accounts bore witness to similar confrontations.

Even in the major coastal centers, scholarship appears to have remained at a generally low level until the nineteenth century. Although commercial contacts with the Red Sea religious centers were frequent, pilgrimage was not widely undertaken; hence, books remained rare (and in Arabic only) and few were trained in the advanced sciences. There is no evidence that the Sufi brotherhoods played a significant role in East Africa before the late sixteenth century.

Despite official Portuguese persecution, between 1500 and 1800 Islam continued to win converts and experience intellectual growth in East Africa. As in its previous phase, commercial contacts provided the key stimulus. Present evidence suggests that the Inquisition was somewhat active in East Africa during the seventeenth century. However, as in the case of trade, local Muslims found ways of circumventing Portuguese interference. Channels of trade and communication through Mogadishu with the Hijaz and Hadhramawt were maintained. The sixteenth and seventeenth centuries saw Arab sharifs and scholars settling in the region of Pate and Lamu. Subsequent remigrations of these Hadhramawt scholarly clans southwards brought new standards of literacy and learning along the coast as far as the Comoro Islands and Madagascar.

The seeds for greater and more widespread attention to the universal written law (Shari'a) were sown with the rise, in both numbers and influence, of Umani Arabs, who immigrated in the eighteenth and nineteenth centuries. Helping to cement this change were renewed Hadhramawt immigration, assertions of Busaidi control, and later British colonial policies. As long as Umanis remained Ibadis, they remained aloof from local practices. Inevitably for most, conversion to Shafi'ism came and with it, attention to the stricter standards of religious observance that were common among the Arab social elite. Sultan Barghash's (1870–1888) creation of a system of official *qadis* (judges) to enforce the Shari'a was a further, decisive development. In the 1890s British administrators imposed the policy of "indirect rule," endowing Islam with the undeclared, augmented status of an official religion enforceable by "native administrators" and judges. Simultaneously, however, throughout East Africa the colonial administrations gradually decreased Muslim officials' salaries and curbed their powers of sanction.

The years of the Zanzibar sultanate and colonial rule were also the era of the first significant spread of Islam inland. Again, this development occurred in the wake of trade that was a part of the wider development of the region in the nineteenth century. In the last 150 years, Islam moved out from the coastal urban centers and won converts among inland rural Africans. This seems to have been true especially in Tanganyika and eastern Uganda. Prior to this, sufi brotherhoods (*tariqas*) like the Qadiriyya and the Shadhiliyya had succeeded in winning many converts among the urban lower classes on the coast. This phenomenon repeated itself during the years of colonial administration, where *tariqa* shaykhs, representing their religious orders, turned up in increasing numbers at key villages along the main travel lanes. There, they converted large numbers to their religion and the particular sodalities they represented. In Mombasa, where the Mazrui virtually monopolized qadiships and resisted rival shaykhs, the *tariqas* were not successful in their conversion attempts. Islam, therefore, was far less successful in penetrating the Kenyan interior than the interiors of Tanganyika, Mozambique, Malawi, Zambia, and the Congo. In Uganda, Islamization largely (though not exclusively) remained restricted among the Buganda elites.

In the late twentieth century, there was a slowing of Islam's advance in East Africa. Intense rivalries with Christian and traditionalist religious communities contributed to this. More relevant has been the slow response of Muslims in the past to changing conditions and opportunities, especially in education. Further difficulties have arisen from the undefined place of religious communities in modern, secular nations.

RANDALL L. POUWELS

See also: **Law, Islamic: Postcolonial Africa; Religion, History of; Religion, Colonial Africa: Islamic Orders and Movements; Religion, Postcolonial Africa: Islam.**

Further Reading

Freeman-Grenville, G. S. P. *The East African Coast: Select Documents*. Oxford: Clarendon, 1962.

Horton, M. "Early Muslim Trading Settlements on the East African Coast: New Evidence from Shanga." *Antiquaries Journal*. 68 (1986): 290–323.

Levtzion, N., and R. L. Pouwels. *The History of Islam in Africa*. Athens, Ohio: Ohio University Press, forthcoming.

Martin, B. "Arab Migrations to East Africa in Medieval Times." *International Journal of African Historical Studies*. 5 (1974): 367–390.

Randall L. P. *Horn and Crescent: Cultural Change and Traditional Islam on the East African Coast, 800–1900*. Cambridge: C. U. P., 1987.

Ivory Coast: *See* Côte d'Ivoire; Houphouët-Boigny, Félix.

J

Jabavu, John Tengo (1859–1921)

South African Newspaper Editor and Politician

John Tengo Jabavu was born in 1859 near the Methodist mission school of Healdtown in the eastern districts of the Cape Colony. Both his parents were Mfengu (or Fingo), which was a Xhosa-speaking group that had been closely associated with European colonial officials and missionaries since the Cape-Xhosa War of 1835 when some of them allegedly took an oath to "become Christians, educate their children, and be loyal to the government."

Typical of the industrious reputation that the Mfengu had acquired in the eyes of colonial society, Jabavu's father alternated between working as a mason and on road construction while his mother was a laundress and a seller of maize meal. When Jabavu turned ten, he began herding his family's cattle but shortly thereafter began attending school at Healdtown. In 1875 he obtained a government certificate of competency from nearby Lovedale, a missionary high school and teacher training college. At the age of seventeen he became a teacher and Wesleyan Methodist lay preacher in the colonial town of Somerset East. It was also here that Jabavu's interest in journalism was sparked when he worked in the printing shop of a local newspaper and began sending letters to the editor of the "Cape Argus," a major Cape Town newspaper, some of which were published under a *nom de plume*. In 1881 Dr. James Stewart, head of Lovedale, offered Jabavu the editorship of *Isigidimi samaXhosa* (The Xhosa Messenger), which was an official missionary publication aimed at the emerging community of African Christians. While working in this position, Jabavu continued his own studies and taught classes in Xhosa and Latin, and in 1883 he became only the second black South African to matriculate.

Jabavu fell out with Stewart when the former began publishing articles in *Isigidimi,* which were critical of some white politicians who had been elected by African voters (the Cape had a qualified nonracial franchise up to 1936) but did nothing to advance their interests. In 1884 he worked as a canvasser among the Xhosa people for James Rose Innes who was elected to the Cape parliament. Later in the same year, Jabavu obtained financial sponsorship from Richard Rose Innes, a King William's Town lawyer and brother of James Rose Innes, and some white merchants from the same town. As editor of *Imvo Zabantsundu* (Views of the Bantu People), Jabavu published the first independent newspaper aimed primarily at an African audience. With articles in both Xhosa and English, Jabavu's paper supported white English-speaking "liberal" politicians such as Rose Innes, whom he considered "friends of the natives." He tended to oppose the Afrikaner Bond, which was supporting proposed laws that would make it more difficult for Africans to vote.

Jabavu was also involved in the formation of early African political organizations in the eastern Cape. He was vice president of the Native Education Association (NEA), which was formed in 1880. Although originally a teachers' organization, Jabavu transformed the NEA into a political group that registered African voters, protested pass laws, and insisted that African jurors be allowed to sit in court cases involving Africans. However, by 1887 the NEA had returned to its role as a teacher organization because of a lack of success with political aims and division within its ranks. Responding to the 1887 Voter Registration Act, which eliminated 20,000 potential African voters, Jabavu became head of the executive of the first regional African political organization, Imbumba Eliliso Lomzi Yabantsundu (Union of Native Vigilance Associations). This would be a coordinating agency for the various local "iliso lomzi" (literally, "eyes of the house," or vigilance associations). In practice, the 1887 Imbumba did not meet again until 1898, and

Jabavu's local vigilance association in King William's Town became a de facto executive of the other associations throughout the Ciskei region. In 1892 Jabavu declined to protest the Franchise and Ballot Act, which further raised the qualifications of the franchise to the detriment of Africans, because some of his white "liberal" allies such as James Rose Innes were members of Cecil Rhodes's coalition government, which had passed it. Disillusioned with Jabavu's leadership, other members of the emerging African elite of the eastern Cape such as Walter Rubusana, a Congregationalist minister, formed the South African Native Congress (SANC) in 1891. Jabavu refused to attend the inaugural meeting, believing that the members of this new organization were too inexperienced to be effective in Cape politics.

In the Cape election campaign of 1898, Cecil Rhodes, leader of the Progressive Party, was determined to regain the premiership, which he had lost because of the unsuccessful Jameson Raid. After failing to gain Jabavu's support, Rhodes sponsored the creation of another Xhosa language newspaper called *Izwi Labantu* (Voice of the People), which was based in East London and operated by SANC members such as A. K. Soga and Walter Rubusana. At this time Jabavu changed his usual political stance and began favoring the Afrikaner Bond because its leader, J. H. Hofmeyer, had hinted that the party might change its opinion on "native policy." While the Bond won the election, Jabavu's support for them alienated him from many Xhosa people.

From August 1901 to October 1902, *Imvo* was closed by the government because Jabavu had published pacifist articles in response to the Anglo-Boer War.

Recovering some of his lost popularity, Jabavu became part of the 1909 delegation—which also included his old rival Rubusana—that went to London to protest the clauses of the proposed Union of South Africa that excluded blacks from the national parliament and failed to safeguard the Cape's nonracial franchise. However, the officials of the British government refused officially to meet the delegation.

When the South African Native National Congress (SANNC) was formed in 1912 (renamed the African National Congress in 1923), Jabavu refused to join because of the presence of many of his SANC rivals in its ranks. Instead, Jabavu formed his own South African Races Congress that was made up primarily of Mfengu from the eastern Cape and was not successful.

Perhaps Jabavu's greatest political mistake was his support for the Natives Land Act of 1913, which prevented Africans from acquiring land outside a system of designated reserves. He probably did this because the bill had been introduced by J. W. Sauer who had been a supporter of the Cape liberal tradition and African voting rights. Sol Plaatje, a Tswana newspaper editor and member of the SANNC, attacked Jabavu for dishonestly inventing support for the Land Act in order to please his masters in the ruling South African party.

In 1910 Jabavu had criticized Walter Rubusana's candidacy in the Cape elections, as he thought it would drive whites to further curtail African political participation. Rubusana won the Thembuland constituency and became the first African to sit in the Cape parliament. However, when Rubusana was up for reelection in 1914, Jabavu ran against him, thereby splitting the African vote and allowing a European, A. B. Payn, to win. Jabavu was now discredited, and his political career came to an end.

Jabavu was also active in establishing a university for Africans. Although Rubusana was the first to form a group with this aim, the Queen Victoria Memorial Fund, he and his supporters were considered too radical by the white establishment. Therefore, when Jabavu and other moderates became involved in the Inter-state Native College Scheme, they received support from white missionaries and the government. This led to the founding of the South African Native College (later the University of Fort Hare) in 1916 near the Lovedale institution. That same year D. D. T. Jabavu, J. T. Jabavu's son and only the second black South African to obtain a university degree, became the first lecturer at what some people called "the College of Jabavu."

TIMOTHY J. STAPLETON

See also: **Dube, John, Langalibalele; Plaatje, Sol T.; South Africa: Peace, Reconstruction, Union: 1902–1910.**

Biography

Born in South Africa's eastern Cape region in 1859. Earned a teaching certificate from Lovedale mission in 1875. After working as a teacher, he became editor of the Lovedale based newspaper *Isigidimi samaXhosa*. In 1883 he became the second black South African to matriculate. In 1884 he became editor of the first independent African language newspaper in South Africa, *Imvo Zabantsundu*, with financial support from white liberal Cape politicians. He was instrumental in forming some of the first African political organizations in the Cape such as the Native Educational Association in 1880 and the *Imbumba Eliliso Lomzi Yabansundu* in 1887. Through his newspaper and involvement in political organizations, he opposed many laws that attempted to make it more difficult for Africans to qualify for the Cape's nonracial franchise. In 1909 he was part of a delegation that went to London to protest the proposed Union of South Africa as it did not safeguard that same franchise. In 1912 he refused to join the new South African Native National Congress (later renamed the African National Congress) because many of his rivals were in it. Perhaps his greatest mistake was supporting the notorious Natives Land Act of 1913. In 1914 he ran for election to the Cape legislature in the Thembuland constituency but lost because the African vote was split between himself and Walter Rubusana. He was also instrumental in the opening of the South African Native College (later the University of Fort Hare) in 1916. He died in 1921.

Further Reading

Higgs, C. *The Ghost of Equality: The Public Lives of D. D. T. Jabavu of South Africa, 1885–1959.* Cape Town: David Phillip, 1997.

Jabavu, D. D. T. *The Life of John Tengo Jabavu, Editor of Imvo Zabantsundu, 1884–1921.* Lovedale, South Africa: Lovedale Press, 1922.

Ngcongco, L. D. "Imvo Zabantsundu and Cape 'Native' Policy, 1884–1902." Master's thesis, University of South Africa, 1974.

———. "Jabavu and the Anglo-Boer War." *Kleo Bulletin.* 2 (October 1976): 6–18.

———. "John Tengo Jabavu, 1859–1921." In *Black Leaders in Southern African History*, edited C. Saunders. London: Heinemann Educational Books, 1979.

Odendaal, A. *Vukani Bantu: The Beginnings of Black Protest Politics in South Africa to 1912.* Cape Town: David Phillip, 1984.

Switzer, L. *Power and Resistance in an African Society: The Ciskei Xhosa and the Making of South Africa.* Madison: University of Wisconsin Press, 1993.

Jaga: *See* Kongo Kingdom: Jaga Invasion to 1665.

Jameson Raid, Origins of South African War: 1895–1899

The nineteenth-century struggle for supremacy in South Africa between British imperialists and Boer republicans culminated on October 11, 1899, with the outbreak of the South African War (Second Anglo-Boer War). British suzerainty over the landlocked, impoverished Boer republic of the Transvaal had seemed reasonably in hand until September 1886, when the world's richest gold deposits were discovered there. Suddenly the agrarian republicans, who had only a generation before migrated into the African interior to escape British rule and culture, gained international economic and political power at British expense.

Cape Premier Cecil Rhodes quickly responded by using railways as tools of imperialism. His agents attempted to purchase the Delagoa Bay railway concession from the Portuguese, whose short section the Transvaal's projected eastern line needed to connect at the frontier to reach the British-free port of Loreno Marques. He promoted the construction of a northwestern line that threatened to leave the Transvaal out of much northern traffic. When in 1891 the Transvaal became virtually bankrupt, Rhodes offered to help President Paul Kruger. In return for a two-year railway monopoly on traffic to the gold fields, the Cape loaned the Transvaal funds to construct its southern line from the Vaal River to Johannesburg, which opened in September 1892 and connected the gold fields to Cape ports via the Orange Free State. The Sivewright Agreement gave mine owners access to heavy mining equipment, restored investor confidence, and enabled the Transvaal to float the Rothschild loan to complete Pretoria's eastern line. Its opening in January 1895 and the Transvaal's success at aggrandizing colonial animosity between the Cape and Natal, of which the latter was constructing the rival Durban-Johannesburg line, were major victories for railway republicans.

As the Sivewright Agreement drew to an end in late 1894, the Cape began a railway and customs rate war. The Transvaal retaliated by raising railway rates on its 51-mile section of the Cape ports-Johannesburg line. The Cape circumvented this increase by offloading some goods onto ox wagons at the Transvaal's Vaal River border. These goods were then transported across the drifts (shallows) and delivered directly to Johannesburg merchants without traversing a single mile of the Transvaal's southern line. Kruger was furious.

When Kruger closed the drifts to ox wagons carrying overseas goods on October 1, 1895, the Cape protested that Kruger had violated British suzerainty. As the Drifts Crisis deepened, Rhodes secretly adapted the Loch Plan, which High Commissioner Sir Henry Brougham Loch had conceived in mid-1893. Loch had envisioned direct imperial intervention, sparked by civil unrest in Johannesburg, to force the Transvaal into a union of South Africa under the British flag. During 1895 Rhodes and his agents conspired with and armed supporters in Johannesburg to help him overthrow the Boer government. On October 18, just two days after a private British ultimatum demanded that Kruger open the drifts, Rhodes's Chartered Company acquired a six-mile wide strip of land in Bechuanaland Protectorate along the Transvaal's western frontier. Pitsani, an isolated settlement in the strip proximate to Johannesburg, was selected as a base camp at the height of the Drifts Crisis by the administrator of Rhodesia and trusted friend of Rhodes, Dr. Leander Starr Jameson, should force be necessary to carry out the ultimatum. Unfortunately for Rhodes, Kruger reopened the drifts and ended the crisis.

The Cape remained threatened with bankruptcy. As long as Kruger controlled the golden hub of Johannesburg, he could play the Cape off against Natal and both off against his eastern, British-free line. Thus, an important economic and political cause of the South African War can be found in the opposing policies of railway imperialists and railway republicans, exacerbated and left unresolved by the Drifts Crisis.

On December 29, 1895, just seven weeks after the Drifts Crisis, Jameson invaded the Transvaal from Pitsani. A smaller force forayed from Mafeking, some 30 miles south in British Bechuanaland, and joined Jameson at Malmani. Together about 500 men from Chartered Company police rode toward Johannesburg.

By December 30, the Boers knew Jameson had invaded. Jameson's allies in Johannesburg refused to help. Scouts betrayed him. Imperial authorities in London and South Africa ordered him to retire. He refused.

On New Year's Day the Boers ambushed Jameson's raiders in a valley three miles from Krugersdorp. Encircled, Jameson surrendered at Doornkop, about twenty miles west of Johannesburg. His forces had suffered 17 killed and 55 wounded; the Boers lost one dead. The Boers also recovered Jameson's correspondence and code books that revealed both the depth and the supporters of the conspiracy. After three weeks in Pretoria's jail and after Rhodes had paid a handsome ransom, Kruger turned Jameson over to British authorities. Tried, convicted, and sentenced to 15 months in prison, the doctor was released early due to ill health. He survived Rhodes and became a Cape premier.

The Drifts Crisis and the Jameson Raid poisoned imperial-republican relations in South Africa, diminished Boer opposition to Kruger, and estranged the Cape's railway ally, the Orange Free State, which purchased its section of the Cape's trunk line to Johannesburg and signed a military treaty with the Transvaal. Distrust, jingoism, and inflexibility combined to ignite war on October 11, 1899, publicly over Uitlander (immigrant) political rights in the Transvaal. When the Treaty of Vereeniging was signed on May 31, 1902, England had spent about £230 million pounds. Of the approximately 450,000 imperial and colonial soldiers who served in the war, over 22,000 lay dead. At least 7,000 Boer soldiers were killed out of the 87,000 who fought. An estimated 28,000 of 136,000 Boer men, women, and children met their deaths in 50 British concentration camps; 22,000 were children under 16 years of age. Approximately 15,000 Africans died assisting both sides.

The historiography of the causes of the raid and war is rich and unsettled. Grand theories and case studies have focused on economic, political, diplomatic, strategic, and cultural causes, as well as the motivations of individual actors. Joseph Schumpeter (1951) suggested that the atavistic (feudal) nature of British culture and society was responsible. Ronald Robinson and John Gallagher (1961) argued that only by balancing policies, events, and actors at the metropole (London) with those on the periphery (southern Africa and elsewhere) could primary causes be identified.

Capitalism and gold have been examined from a number of perspectives. In 1900 John Hobson argued that the conflict was a capitalist war fought to protect British investors and South African millionaires. More recently, Shula Marks and Stanley Trapido (1992) have argued from the perspective of political economy that access to Transvaal gold, so crucial to the health of the international economy, was critical as well to London's position as the world's financial capital. Jean Jacques Van-Helten (1982) has investigated the impact of the gold policies of the Bank of England on the outbreak of the war.

In contrast to economic arguments, in 1900 Leo Amery believed that the war was caused by political differences between governments. Andrew Porter (1980, 1990) has found the causes of the war in the politics of the metropole and the consequences of those policies on South Africa. Iain Smith (1990) has argued similarly, stressing the maintenance of British supremacy in South Africa and the security of the sea route to India.

Mordechai Tamarkin (1997) has pointed to Alfred Milner, the inflexible high commissioner of South Africa, while Ethel Drus (1953) has criticized Joseph Chamberlain, the secretary of state for the colonies in the Salisbury cabinet, for collaborating with Rhodes during the Drifts Crisis and in the preparations for the raid fiasco; both officials, these historians have maintained, bear heavy responsibilities for the war, whether due to political or economic motivations. Boer historiography, exemplified by J. H. Breytenbach (1969–77), has usually seen the war as a conflict between an aggressive, capitalist, imperial power seeking to wrest the independence of a virtuous, agrarian republic for its own material ends.

The war continues to intrigue scholars. Ian Phimister (1993) has suggested that future work concentrate on regional issues in southern Africa, the nature of Kruger's government and economic policies, and the character of British paramountcy. On the centennial of the South African War, consensus among historians remains elusive.

KENNETH WILBURN

See also: **Johannesburg; Kruger, Paul; Rhodes, Cecil J.; Rhodes, Jameson, and Seizure of Rhodesia; South Africa: Gold on the Witwatersrand, 1886–1899; Zimbabwe: Incursions from the South, Ngoni and Ndebele.**

Further Reading

Breytenbach, J. H. *Die Gieskiendenis van die Tweede Vryheidsoorlog in Suid-Afrika.* 5 vols. Pretoria: Die Staatsdrukker, 1969–1977.

Drus, E. "The Question of Imperial Complicity in the Jameson Raid." *English Historical Review.* 58, no. 269 (October 1953): 582–587.

Marks, S., and S. Trapido. "Lord Milner and the South African State Reconsidered." In *Imperialism, the State and the Third World*, edited by M. Twaddle. London and New York: British Academic Press, 1992, 80–94.

Phimister, I. "Unscrambling the Scramble for Southern Africa: The Jameson Raid and the South African War Revisited." *South African Historical Journal.* 28 (1993): 203–220.

Porter, A. *The Origins of the South African War: Joseph Chamberlain and the Diplomacy of Imperialism, 1895–99.* Manchester: Manchester University Press, 1980.

———. "The South African War (1899–1902): Context and Motive Reconsidered." *Journal of African History.* 31, no. 1 (1990): 43–57.

Robinson, R., and J. Gallagher with A. Denny. *Africa and the Victorians: The Official Mind of Imperialism.* London: MacMillan, 1961.

Schumpeter, J. A. *Imperialism.* Oxford: Blackwells, 1951.

Smith, I. "The Origins of the South African War (1899–1902): A Reappraisal." *South African Historical Journal.* 22 (1990): 24–60.

Tamarkin, M. "Milner, the Cape Afrikaners, and the Outbreak of the South African War: From a Point of Return to a Dead End." *The Journal of Imperial and Commonwealth History* 25, no. 3 (September 1997): 392–414.

Van-Helton, J. J. "Empire and High Finance: South Africa and the International Gold Standard, 1890–1914." *Journal of African History.* 23 (1982): 529–546.

Wilburn, K. "Engines of Empire and Independence: Railways in South Africa, 1863–1916." In *Railway Imperialism*, edited by C. B. Davis and K. E. Wilburn. New York: Greenwood Press, 1991.

———. "The Drifts Crisis and the Jameson Raid: A Centennial Review." *The Journal of Imperial and Commonwealth History.* 25, no. 2 (May 1997): 219–239.

Johannes IV: *See* Ethiopia: Johannes IV, Era of.

Johannesburg

The spectacular growth of Johannesburg, from a tented village of a few thousand prospectors to the second or third largest metropolitan region in Africa (after Cairo, and possibly Lagos), took little more than a century and was triggered by the discovery of gold in early 1886 at Langlaagte farm, on the bleak Witwatersrand ridge in the southern Transvaal. The town was proclaimed in September 1886 and within six months three main streets had been laid out. By early 1888 the population was around 6,000, and with a massive influx of black and white labor to work in the rapidly expanding mining industry, as well as associated services and manufacturing, the population grew to about 100,000 by 1896 and reached 237,000 by 1911, when the city was the largest in Sub-Saharan Africa.

Defining Johannesburg's boundaries has always presented problems. A fairly continuous ribbon of settlement developed for 65 kilometers along the line of the Witwatersrand (or Rand) gold reefs, from Krugersdorp in the west to Springs in the east; and at the center of this belt, the city itself was increasingly fringed by black African townships like Alexandra and Soweto during the twentieth-century peak of apartheid. The latter were excluded from earlier census counts, but the postapartheid constitution of 1994 extended municipal boundaries and by 1997–99 estimates of greater Johannesburg's population ranged from four to six million.

With the Rand's share of world gold output rising from 7 to 40 per cent between 1890 and 1913, long lines of mine dumps and headgears dominated an increasingly diverse but sharply segmented city. At this time, half Johannesburg's inhabitants were migrant black laborers, crowded into unsanitary compounds on the mines, while a highly disparate white community was dominated by *uitlanders*— mostly Europeans and Americans—who uneasily shared the city with landless Boers, often drawn there as transport drivers, and numerous Asians. Even among whites, sharply demarcated suburbs developed: the elite escaped into the leafy northern ridges of Parktown, the lower middle and working classes into areas like Braamfontein and Jeppestown, while poor whites lived in developments nearer the mines like Burgersdorp and Vrededorp.

Johannesburg's character before the 1920s was in many respects typical of mining boom-towns around the world: a heavy preponderance of males, flourishing saloons (licensed establishments on the Rand growing from 147 in 1888 to 552 in 1892) and brothels, as well as an infamously high cost of living, although railway links to the distant coastline, opened 1892–1895, helped reduce transport rates. The local economy also experienced frequent fluctuations, especially during the South African War, when gold production virtually ceased and an *uitlander* exodus left only about 40,000 in the city between October 1899 and June 1900. The economy was also shaken during the Rand Revolt of 1922, when racially motivated labor disputes left over 200 dead.

The seeds of longer-term tensions were sown with a progressive tightening of racial segregation, particularly from the 1920s onward. Major outbreaks of bubonic plague in 1905 and influenza in 1919 provided excuses to burn down black slum housing within Johannesburg and forcibly relocate their residents to fringe townships, the first such large-scale development being Alexandra, established outside the northeastern city limits in 1905. Successive legislation reinforced this process, especially the 1923 Urban Areas Act, which prohibited black Africans from buying land, and the 1950 Group Areas Act, which designated single ethnic groups for specific suburbs. Before the 1923 act, blacks were able to buy land and build houses in a number of Johannesburg suburbs: by the 1940s and early 1950s the only such area to have retained a large black African community was Sophiatown. This was a highly overcrowded, unsanitary township with an estimated population of 24,000 in 1934, when up to 40 inhabitants typically shared one or two toilets and a single water tap. Unsurprisingly, such conditions in this and other black communities in Johannesburg were reflected in an enormous racially determined health gap: in 1939–1944, for example, white infant mortality rates in the city were 52 per 1,000 while black rates were 580 per 1,000, the differential actually having widened since the early 1920s.

Government policies aimed at relocating black Johannesburg residents intensified after the 1923 act, and in 1932 a new township was established at Orlando, the first stage in the mushroom development of Soweto (southwestern townships). Between 1955 and 1963, Sophiatown was demolished, and its residents were forcibly relocated to the new township of Meadowlands, in Soweto; the official rationale highlighted rising crime and unrest within the old black suburb. By 1955 the official population estimate for Orlando and four adjacent townships was 200,000, but with a continuing influx of migrants from both within and outside South Africa, by the 1970s and 1980s unofficial estimates put Soweto's population at a million or more. Under the strict regime of apartheid, at least a quarter of a million Sowetans daily commuted by overcrowded trains and buses into the adjacent city, which relied on their labor but denied them residence. Tensions within the townships frequently escalated into widespread violence, especially during the Soweto student protests of 1976, when a state of emergency was declared, and in the ANC-Inkatha conflicts preceding the first free South African elections in April 1994.

Postapartheid Johannesburg remains a city of intense contrasts: between the ostentatious affluence of shopping mall crowds in chic northern suburbs like Sandton, and the abject poverty of recent migrants inhabiting the most squalid sections of Soweto. The city and its hinterland have diversified widely into manufacturing and services since the 1930s, but general economic problems have been exacerbated by recession in the still-important gold industry. Unemployment and crime are endemic, especially in such deprived neighborhoods as Eldorado Park, where gangs like the *Majimbos* dominate the streets, and black infant mortality rates remain considerably above the national average. The ubiquitous middle-class obsession with violent crime and the increasing squalor of the city center, especially the central business district, has prompted a mass exodus of businesses and affluent residents into distant suburbs, most notably Sandton, where villas sit behind reassuring security-patrolled fences. Racial distinctions may no longer be enforced by statute and there are numerous mixed suburbs, such as Hillbrow, but widespread segregation persists, largely deriving from inherited employment differentials. The present century presents great challenges for a city that some estimates suggest is now one of the fastest-growing in the world, with a seemingly unstoppable influx of migrants from Mozambique and other parts of southern Africa, crowding into ever-expanding fringe shanty settlements. Nevertheless, Johannesburg remains a vibrant cultural focus for the new South Africa, a tradition inherited from communities like Sophiatown, and this allows a degree of optimism for the city's future.

CHRISTOPHER SCHMITZ

See also: **South Africa.**

Further Reading

Bozzoli, B., ed. *Labour, Townships, and Protest: Studies in the Social History of the Witwatersrand.* Johannesburg: Ravan Press, 1979.

———. *Town and Countryside in the Transvaal.* Johannesburg: Ravan Press, 1983.

Cammack, D. *The Rand at War 1899–1902: The Witwatersrand and the Anglo-Boer War.* London: James Currey, 1990.

Hellmann, E. *Soweto: Johannesburg's African City. Johannesburg*: Institute of Race Relations, 1971.

Kallaway, P., and P. Pearson, eds. *Johannesburg: Images and Continuities: A History of Working Class Life Through Pictures, 1885–1935*, Johannesburg: Ravan Press, 1986.

Ricci, D., ed. *Reef of Time: Johannesburg in Writing.* Craighall: A. D. Donker, 1986.

Themba, C. *The Will to Die.* London: Heinemann, 1972.

Van Onselen, C. *Studies in the Social and Economic History of the Witwatersrand, 1886–1914.* 2 vols. Harlow: Longman, 1982.

Venter, P. C. *Soweto: Shadow City.* Johannesburg: Perskor, 1977.

Johnston, Harry H. (1858–1927)

British Explorer, Artist, Naturalist, Linguist, and Colonial Administrator

Harry H. Johnston was perhaps the leading Africanist of his generation. His travels took him to every region of the continent and enabled him, better than any of his contemporaries, to see Africa whole. Son of a London company secretary, his education was directed to developing his obvious talents in painting, natural history, and modern languages. In 1879–1880 he spent eight months in Tunis painting and studying Arabic, but also observing French preparations to take over the country as a protectorate. In 1882–1883 he accompanied a geographical and sporting expedition to southern Angola and afterward made his own way northward to the Congo estuary, where H. M. Stanley was preparing the ground for King Leopold's future colony by building a railway round the river's cataracts so as to open up the 4,000 miles of navigable waterways that lay beyond. It was a highly secret operation, but Stanley enabled him to visit the stations being built on the upper river and to return home with the materials for an attractively written and illustrated travel book, which would establish him as an African explorer.

Soon Johnston was off again, this time to East Africa, where the Royal Society had invited him to investigate the flora and fauna of Kilimanjaro. With the help of 120 Swahili porters, he set up a collecting base in the foothills of the mountain near Moshi, where plants, insects, stuffed birds, and animal skins were identified and specimens sent home to Kew and the British Museum. He was already deeply involved in the recording and comparison of Bantu languages, which was to dominate the rest of his intellectual life. But his concern for the political future of Africa had also deepened to the point that he sent to the Foreign Office a madcap proposal for the establishment of a self-supporting colony of British farmers on the uninhabited upper slopes of the mountain, which would quickly mature into an "East African Ceylon." Incredibly, but for the diplomatic pandemonium caused by the German annexations of 1883–1884, his scheme was approved by the Colonial Committee of the Cabinet and scotched only by the personal intervention of the prime minister, William E. Gladstone.

Nevertheless, "Kilimanjaro Johnston" was soon rewarded with a vice consulship in the recently declared Oil Rivers Protectorate in eastern Nigeria, which was combined with the representation of British interests in the adjoining German protectorate of Cameroon. From a base on the offshore island of Mondole, he made frequent visits to the Cross River, studying the northwestern Bantu languages and their relationship to the adjacent languages of eastern West Africa and preparing grandiose proposals for the projection inland of the colonial enclaves thus far created around the coasts of Africa. His views somehow reached the eyes of the new British prime minister and foreign secretary, Lord Salisbury, who, on his return to England in 1888–1889, used him as a confidential adviser in his reshaping of British aims in the partition of the African interior, which were to be implemented in the crucial agreements with Germany, France, and Portugal of 1890–1891. Johnston returned to Africa in 1889–1990, ostensibly as consul in Mozambique but in reality to obtain the treaties with African rulers that would enable Salisbury to claim as British the territory which would later become Nyasaland (Malawi) and Northern Rhodesia (Zambia).

Between 1891 and 1896 Johnston presided as commissioner over the beginnings of colonial administration in what was at first known as British Central Africa. His initial funding was provided by Cecil Rhodes, in the expectation that most of the region would soon be transferred to his newly Chartered British South Africa Company. It enabled Johnston to employ just ten European officials, seventy Punjabi soldiers, and eighty-five Zanzibari mercenaries, and to occupy effectively a few hundred square miles at the center of his vast domain. Such were the realities of early colonial government, which left him plenty of time to pursue his scientific and linguistic interests, and to produce an encyclopedic account of Britain's latest acquisition. Only in 1894 was Nyasaland separated from Northern Rhodesia, and only then did he gain an imperial grant-in-aid sufficient to enable him to occupy Nyasaland as a protectorate. His proconsulship ended tragically in 1896 with a third attack of the dreaded blackwater fever, which should have precluded his further residence in the tropics.

In 1898–1899 Johnston served in the undemanding post of consul general in Tunis, which gave him the opportunity to complete much scholarly work, including a *History of the Colonization of Africa by Alien Races*, which remained without a rival until the 1950s. In 1899 came the tempting offer to go for two years as special commissioner to Uganda, to establish civilian administration after seven years of disastrous and very expensive military rule. He succeeded by concluding a formal alliance with the ruling chiefs of Buganda, which turned them into the privileged allies of the British, thereby enabling him to halve the military expenditure incurred by his predecessors, before two more attacks of blackwater fever drove him permanently from the African scene.

There followed 27 years of retirement, devoted first and foremost to the *Comparative Study of the Bantu and Semi-Bantu Languages*, completed in 1922, which set out the equivalents of some 250 words in 300 languages, for many of which he had himself collected the primary data. Although now outdated, its classificatory analysis and historical interpretation of the evidence were remarkable. He understood the relationship between Bantu and the languages now called Niger-Congo that are spread across southern West Africa. He understood that the oldest of the Bantu languages were those spoken in the northwestern corner of the present Bantu sphere. And he saw that the eastern Bantu languages descended from ancestors that had crossed the continent to the north of the equatorial forest. It is remarkable that, although starting as a social Darwinist, his political outlook moved faster than that of most of his contemporaries. In *The Negro in the New World*, which followed a journey to the United States and the Caribbean in 1908–1909, he stressed the importance of treating individuals as equals, regardless of race.

ROLAND OLIVER

See also: **Rhodes, Cecil J.; Stanley, Leopold II, Scramble.**

Further Reading

Johnston, H. H. *The Kilimanjaro Expedition*. London: Kegan Paul, 1886.
———. *British Central* Africa. London: Methuen, 1903.
———. *The Colonization of Africa by Alien Races*. 2nd ed. Cambridge: Cambridge University Press, 1913.
———. *Comparative Study of the Bantu and Semi-Bantu Languages*. 2 vols. Oxford: Oxford University Press, 1919–1922.
———. *The Story of My Life*. London: Chatto and Windus, 1923.
Oliver, R. *Sir Harry Johnston & the Scramble for Africa*. London: Chatto and Windus, 1957.

Jolof Empire: *See* Wolof and Jolof Empire.

Jonathan, Chief Joseph Leabua (1914–1987)
Prime Minister of Lesotho

With no prospects for further education, the future Chief Leabua joined hundreds of thousands of other Basotho young men and left to go and work in a South African gold mine. He remained there until 1937. He first held public office in 1937, when Chief Mathealira appointed him to an administrative post in the Tsikoane ward. Over time he performed more significant functions in the ward and ended up as a member of a panel that presided over customary court cases. Experience and knowledge gained in this role soon earned him a position as an assessor to the roving Judicial Commissioner in 1951. In 1956 Leabua was appointed to two significant political roles. He became a member of the Basutoland National Council (BNC), a body set up in 1903 and dominated by the chiefs, their nominees, and appointees of colonial authorities. He was also appointed to a panel of advisers to Chieftainess 'Mantsebo Seeiso, who ruled Lesotho between 1940 and 1960 as regent for Prince Bereng Seeiso (later King Moshoeshoe II). It was during this time that he left the Protestant Lesotho Evangelical Church to join the Roman Catholic Church.

Besides being a member of a 1957 deputation sent by the BNC to England to protest against the Colonial Office's appointment of South African-born A. G. Chaplin as a resident commissioner in Lesotho, Leabua joined a number of missions that went to England in connection with Lesotho's move to independence. In 1958 he was a member of another delegation that the BNC sent to England to present the Report of the Constitutional Reform Committee (to which he had been nominated in 1956).

In 1959, on the advice of Patrick Duncan, Chief Leabua formed a political party with a view to contest the 1960 District Council and the 1965 parliamentary elections on a more conservative, religious, anticommunist, and prochieftainship ticket, to counter the radical and antichieftainship Basutoland Congress Party (BCP, formed in 1952). At that time, the Roman Catholic Church was assisting in the formation of a political party (the Christian Democratic Party) with a similar program to that of Leabua. The church agreed to abandon her plan, and gave her support to Leabua. His Basutoland National Party (BNP) was launched on April 4, 1959, in Maseru.

In the 1960 District Council elections where he competed against the much more established BCP, Leabua and his young party won 22 of the 162 district councils, although this translated into only 1 out of 40 seats in the Legislative Council. In the 1965 elections, his party won 31 of the 60 seats. This advancement was ascribed to Leabua's tireless campaigning, church assistance, aid from the South African government, and Mokhehle's complacency (due to the BCP's resounding victory in the 1960 elections). However, Leabua himself failed to win his constituency and when Parliament met it was his deputy, Chief Sekhonyana 'Maseribane, who was elected the first prime minister of Lesotho. The party made arrangements for John Mothepu, a BNP member of Parliament from the safe constituency of Mpharane, to resign his parliamentary seat so that a by-election could be held in the constituency, which Leabua easily won in July 1965. He then took over the premiership from Chief 'Maseribane.

Chief Leabua remained in power for 21 years. He developed into a shrewd politician. In the 1970 elections, Mokhehle and his BCP were victorious, but Leabua refused to hand over power, declared a state of emergency, and suspended the constitution. He sent Mokhehle to prison and later tricked him into signing a document by which Mokhehle accepted that the 1970 elections had not been free, that they should be annulled and new elections should be held. The king refused to cooperate with Leabua's government; the chief reacted by exiling him. Mokhehle was forced to flee Lesotho in 1974.

Chief Leabua tried to appease the international community, which was threatening to withdraw aid, by establishing an Interim Parliament in 1973, and setting up a government of national unity and reconciliation in 1975. But these concessions fell far short of the demands of the opposition and the international community. In the mid-1970s the chief took advantage of Cold War politics and, while maintaining and intensifying repression in the country, adopted a progressive foreign policy. Elements of this policy included a vociferous anti-apartheid stance and the acceptance of refugees fleeing South Africa. By the late 1970s the military wing of the BCP, the Lesotho Liberation Army (LLA) was engaged in attempts to unseat Chief Leabua. These attacks began at the same time that the chief's government became a target of South Africa's destabilization policy because of its foreign policy, primarily by military incursions into Lesotho. Soon a faction of Mokhehle's LLA was working with the South Africa security establishment against Lesotho. Leabua established diplomatic relations with the People's Republic of Korea, the People's Republic of China, Cuba, the USSR, and other East European countries.

These initiatives bore a bounty of political fruits. The opposition was split over some members joining Leabua's interim parliament and accepting his offer of cabinet posts. Mokhehle became discredited as an apartheid collaborator. The chief's government received various forms of aid from socialist countries as well as from Western governments eager to keep Lesotho free of Communist influence. The UN and nations opposed to apartheid dispensed aid freely, and Leabua and his regime gained some legitimacy and acceptability locally and internationally.

One of the most important causes of Chief Leabua's downfall in 1986 was the development of a personality cult around him. Individuals controlling the party's Youth League turned it into a vigilante group that determined civil service appointments, promotions, and dismissals, took over some of the functions of the army and the police, and unleashed a reign of terror in public institutions and civil society. All this was done to achieve absolute acquiescence and loyalty to the chief throughout the country. However, the activities of the Youth League alienated the more moderate elements within both the army and the chief's cabinet. It is individuals from this group who engineered the chief's downfall, with the help of South Africa, in January 1986. Chief Leabua died in Pretoria the following year of cancer.

MOTLATSI THABANE

See also: **Lesotho; Mokhehle, Ntsu.**

Biography

Born in 1914, Leabua was the fourth of Chief Jonathan Molapo's seven children with one of his junior wives, 'Makatiso. His grandfather, Chief Molapo, was the second son of Moshoeshoe I and his first wife, 'Mamohato. He completed his primary education at a Protestant Paris Evangelical Missionary primary school, Maoana Masooana, in 1933. He married a distant cousin, Paleo Molapo and the couple had seven children. Leabua launched the Basutoland National Party (BNP) on April 4, 1959. Leabua himself failed to win his constituency and when Parliament met it was his deputy, Chief Sekhonyana 'Maseribane, who was elected the first prime minister of Lesotho. The party made arrangements for John Mothepu, a BNP Member of Parliament from the safe constituency of Mpharane, to resign his parliamentary seat so that a by-election could be held in the constituency, which Leabua easily won in July 1965. He then took over the premiership from Chief 'Maseribane. Leabua remained in power for 21 years. The more moderate elements within both the army and the chief's cabinet engineered Leabua's downfall, with the help of South Africa, in January 1986. He died in Pretoria in 1987 of cancer.

Further Reading

Khaketla, B. M. *Lesotho 1970: An African Coup Under the Microscope.* Berkeley: University of California Press, 1972.

Leeman, *Lesotho and the Struggle for Azania.* 3 vols. University of Azania, 1985.

Macartney, W. J. A. "The Lesotho General Election of 1970." *Government and Opposition.* 4 (1973): 473–94.

Sixishe, T. D. *"But Give Him an Army Too": Leabua Jonathan, a Biography.* Maseru, 1984.

Weisfelder, R. F. "The Basotho Monarchy: A Spent Force or a Dynamic Political Factor." *Papers in International Studies.* Athens, Ohio: Ohio University, 1972.

Journalism, African: Colonial Era

Newspapers, having become a feature of life in Europe in the eighteenth century, were started in colonies of settlement in Africa in the following century, beginning with South Africa. White settlers later established their newspapers in newly occupied parts of Africa in the late nineteenth and twentieth centuries, in Southern Rhodesia and Kenya, for example. At the same time, Africans began publishing newspapers in the nineteenth century in those West African areas where colonial rule or European influence, missionary teaching, and Western education spread at an early stage: the Gold Coast (Ghana), Lagos (later part of Nigeria), and especially Sierra Leone under British rule, and Senegal (i.e., the coastal "Four Communes" of Senegal) under French rule.

The first newspaper in Sierra Leone, apart from the government *Gazette,* was the *Sierra Leone Watchman* (1841–1851). Others followed, and in 1884 the most famous newspaper, the *Sierra Leone Weekly News*, was founded by the famous educationist and writer Edward Wilmot Blyden and the Rev. Claudius May; May's brother Cornelius was the first editor. The *Weekly News*, celebrated all over West Africa, continued publication until 1951.

In Gold Coast, the pioneer newspaper was the *Accra Herald*, founded in 1857 by Charles Bannermann and renamed in 1859 the *West African Herald*. James Hutton Brew founded the *Gold Coast Times* (1874–1885) and then the *Western Echo* (1885–1887). Such short lives for newspapers were quite common.

The founders and editors of these early West African newspapers were men of the educated elite: teachers, clergymen, merchants, lawyers, doctors, and others. They operated all along the West Coast and had roots and links in all the British territories and independent Liberia, which also had its early African-owned newspapers. The newspapers expressed the general outlook of the Sierra Leone Creoles and others of the elite: generally loyal to Britain, indeed often favorable to further British expansion but still critical of the British, who generally disliked their attitude, which became more critical after the great expansion of colonial rule in the "Scramble for Africa."

There was commonly a close link between journalism and politics, as when the nationalist leader J. B. Danquah published the *West African Times*, renamed the *Times of West Africa*, in 1931–1934, as a daily—something rare in the first decades of the African press, although the *Gold Coast Spectator* had preceded it as a daily in 1927. Most editors and journalists were still amateurs then, but they often produced newspapers of high standard. There were some experienced journalists, such as R. B. Wuta-Ofei, for long editor of the *Spectator*. A new and daring approach was brought in when the U.S.-trained Nigerian Nnamdi Azikiwe (1904–96) edited the daily *African Morning Post* in 1935–1936, and ran into trouble with the usually tolerant British authorities.

In Nigeria the African-owned press, centered in Lagos at first, developed as in other parts of West Africa; 51 newspapers appeared between 1880 and 1937, including 11 dailies. For much of that period the *Lagos Weekly Record* was a leading newspaper; others included the *Lagos Standard*, the *Nigerian Times*, and the *Nigerian Pioneer*. The regular political links were illustrated by the *Lagos Daily News,* which supported the Nigerian National Democratic Party in the 1920s. European businessmen, hardly involved in the press in West Africa until then, started the *Daily Times* in 1926 to compete with the *Lagos Daily News*. It was made an independent paper, and more like a typical modern newspaper, by its first editor, Ernest Ikoli (1893–1960), whose *African Messenger* had been taken over by the new newspaper; he later (1938–1944) edited the *Daily Service*, organ of the nationalist the Nigerian Youth Movement, with S. L. Akintola who became a major political leader in later years. But the leading journalist-politician was Azikiwe who, after his editorship in Accra, founded a group of newspapers based on the daily *West African Pilot* in Nigeria in 1937. These hard-hitting nationalist organs backed him in his campaign against British rule as leader of the National Council of Nigeria and the Cameroons (NCNC) from 1944.

Azikiwe spread newspaper publishing to other parts of Nigeria, where, independently, a pioneering Hausa-language newspaper, *Gaskiya ta fi Kwabo* (Truth Is Worth More Than a Penny), was founded in the north in 1939. In the era of mass politics developing in Nigeria and elsewhere from the 1940s, the press played a major role. It underwent expansion and modernization, with some involvement of European capital. Britain's *Daily Mirror* group, the International Publishing Corporation (IPC), bought the *Daily Times* in 1947. It was developed rapidly and vigorously, with sister publications added, under the dynamic direction of Alhaji Babatunde Jose, the most prominent of many journalists who emerged in Nigeria; eventually the *Daily Times* sold 200,000 and *Sunday Times* 350,000 at their peak. Professional journalists were now common, in contrast to the earlier period. Many also worked in radio, also rapidly developed in Africa from the 1940s.

The IPC developed the *Daily Graphic* in the Gold Coast from 1950 on Western tabloid lines, with great success, to make it the leading daily when the country became independent in 1957. Kwame Nkrumah and his Convention People's Party (CPP) published from 1948 their own daily, the *Evening News*, to rival the *Graphic* and the *Ashanti Pioneer*, which was against the CPP. Many older newspapers ceased publication in those years in Ghana and Sierra Leone. In the latter country the *Daily Mail* was founded in 1933 as successor to *The Colony and Provincial Reporter* (1912), renamed *The Colonial and Provincial Reporter*, and in 1920 *The African Mail and Trade Gazette*. Taken over by the IPC in 1952, the *Daily Mail* was developed into the country's only significant daily newspaper.

In eastern and southern Africa there was no parallel to the early West African development of African-run newspapers, with the significant exception of South Africa, where there were several such newspapers in the nineteeth century. There, too, the role of Christian missions in starting various publications, not always narrowly religious in outlook, was important. But in the twentieth century, the press in South Africa, the Rhodesias, Nyasaland, and East Africa was very largely in white hands.

The *East African Standard*, the settler newspaper of Kenya, was originally founded by an Asian, J. M. Jeevanjee, as the *African Standard* in Mombasa in 1902. It was renamed and moved to Nairobi, and became a daily, under two English owners in 1910. It launched the *Tanganyika Standard* in 1930. This was the only significant newspaper in Tanganyika until independence. In Kenya, however, there were well before then some Asian-owned publications: the *Kenya Daily Mail* of Mombasa, the *National Guardian* of Nairobi, and the *Daily Chronicle* of Nairobi. And there were some early African publications in the era of the nationalist upsurge, such as the *Coast African Express*, the *Nyanza Times*, and the leading Kikuyu paper around Nairobi, the weekly *Mumenyereri.* A liberal European, Charles Hayes, founded *Taifa Kenya*, which was taken over, not long before independence, by the Aga Khan and replaced by *Taifa Leo* in Swahili, while the new owners then launched, in 1960, the famous *Daily Nation* and *Sunday Nation*.

Uganda in the colonial era had the *Uganda Argus*, part of the Standard group, but also some African newspapers, missionary education having spread early in that country. *Ebifa mu Uganda* was founded in 1907, *Gambuze* and *Dobozi Iya Buganda* in the 1930s. The first significant African newspaper, however, was *Uganda Eyogera*, founded in 1953; it was the voice of a nationalist party, the Uganda National Congress.

In Nyasaland (now Malawi) there was effectively one newspaper in the colonial period, founded as the *Central African Planter* in 1895, renamed the *Central Africa Times* soon after 1900, and then given its best-known name of the *Nyasaland Times*. In Northern Rhodesia (Zambia) the settler newspaper *Livingstone Mail* was founded in 1906, and in the 1940s the young Roy Welensky (later prime minister of the Federation of Rhodesia and Nyasaland) started the twice-weekly *Northern News* at Ndola, as his mouthpiece; it was taken over by the Johannesburg-based Argus empire in 1951 and turned into a daily in 1953. Alexander Scott founded the weekly *Central African Post* at Lusaka in 1948, and the short-lived *African Times*, in 1958; then he joined with David Astor to start the weekly *African Mail*, edited first by the late Richard Hall (one of many journalists from Europe who helped to build up African newspapers), and independent of both the settlers and the African nationalists.

Southern Rhodesia (now Zimbabwe) had two pre-eminent settler newspapers for decades: the *Rhodesia Herald*, founded in 1892 by the Argus Company, and the *Bulawayo Chronicle* launched by the same South African company in 1894. They had their companion Sunday papers and the Argus group also published the *Umtali Post*. Among other newspapers the Salisbury *Daily News* was taken over by the Thomson newspaper empire in 1962 and sought to cater for Africans, supporting legitimate African aims. It was banned in August 1964 and its African editor, Willie Musarurwa, was imprisoned without charge for 11 years. This was one episode in the long struggle of the press against the settler regime that unilaterally declared independence from 1965 to 1980. The Catholic-owned Mambo Press, publishing in the 1960s the monthly *Moto*, which was popular with Africans, also fought a long battle against the Smith regime.

In French Africa, censorship was more strict than in most British colonies, and early development of the press was largely confined to Senegal. Several newspapers were founded in the 1880s and 1890s, but of them only *L'Afrique Occidentale*, founded by the Creole Louis Huchard in 1896 and the first modern Senegalese newspaper, had more than a short life. Later newspapers were started both by European entrepreneurs and by local politicians. Jean Daramy, a globe-trotting adventurer, briefly made *Le Petit Sénégalais* a major scandal sheet in 1912; dismissed from there, he stayed in Senegal with the new name of D'Oxoby and founded in 1913 *La Démocratie du Senegal*, one of the first independent, satirical newspapers in French Africa.

A Frenchman, Charles de Breteuil, founded *Paris-Dakar* in 1933, initially as a weekly; it became a daily two years later and was subsequently renamed *Dakar-Matin*. De Breteuil founded a French-African newspaper empire later run by his son Michel. It included *France-Afrique* founded in 1938 in Côte d'Ivoire, later renamed *Abidjan-Matin* in 1954; this was one of the first newspapers founded in French West Africa outside Senegal and Dahomey (today the Republic of Benin), where, exceptionally, African-owned newspapers flourished in the 1920s. Later, after World War II, de Breteuil founded *La Presse du Cameroun*, taking over a European newspaper, *L'Eveil du Cameroun*, almost the only newspaper that country had had. In some French-speaking African countries, mission-founded newspapers played a major role, especially *La Semaine* in Congo-Brazzaville and, notably, *L'Afrique Nouvelle*, founded by the White Fathers, a Roman Catholic religious order, in 1947 and for decades a leading independent journal based in Senegal.

In Portuguese Africa the press was under strict control under the fascist dictatorship (1926–1974), but it did retain some degree of independence. Toward the end of Portuguese rule Angola had an evening paper, the *Diario de Luanda,* and a morning paper, *A Provincia de Angola*, founded in 1923. In Mozambique *Noticias* was founded in 1926; it was virtually an official government newspaper. Mozambique also had the *Lourenço Marques Guardian*, founded by the local British community in 1905; it was bought by the Catholic archbishop of Lourenço Marques in 1956 and renamed the *Diario*. Church influence, important in the development of the press in much of Africa, was particularly important in Mozambique; the Catholic bishop of Beira, more sympathetic to the Africans than the archbishop, provided assistance for the weekly *A Voz Africana* founded in 1932, with an African editor, and also founded the relatively liberal *Diario de Moçambique* in 1950. But censorship after 1933 largely emasculated the weekly *O Brado Africano*, a weekly founded by the Associação Africana (an organization for people of mixed race). *Voz Africana* was bought out in the late 1960s by the financial interests behind the right-wing European *Noticias de Beira*. Two relatively liberal newspapers, *Tribuna* and *A Voz de Moçambique*, were tolerated for a time in the 1960s.

The Portuguese territories were unusual in that press freedom was very limited or nonexistent in the last decades of colonialism. The rest of colonial Africa saw a large degree of press freedom, which imparted training and journalistic experience to African journalists. After the end of the colonial era, African journalists and newspapers in most countries faced independent governments that quickly sought to control and restrict the press.

JONATHAN DERRICK

See also: **Colonialism: Impact on African Societies; Media as Propaganda; Press.**

Further Reading

Ainslie, R. *The Press in Africa.* Gollancz, 1966.
Azikiwe, N. *My Odyssey.* London: Hurst, 1970.
Barton, F. *The Press of Africa: Persecution and Perseverance.* Macmillan, 1979.
Cole, B. *Mass Media, Freedom, and Democracy in Sierra Leone.* Freetown: Premier Publishing House, 1995.
Fyfe, C. *A History of Sierra Leone.* London: Oxford University Press, 1966.
Jones-Quartey, K. A. B. *History, Politics, and Early Press in Ghana.* Legon: University of Ghana, 1975.
King, C. *Strictly Personal.* Weidenfeld and Nicolson, 1969.
Omu, F. *Press and Politics in Nigeria, 1880–1937.* Longman, 1978.

Jugnauth: *See* Mauritius: 1982 to the Present.

Juhayna: *See* Nubia: Banu Kanz, Juhayna, and the Arabization of the Nilotic Sudan.

Jukun: *See* Benue Valley Peoples: Jukun and Kwarafa.

Juula/Dyula

"Juula" (or "Dyula"), a Mande (Mandingo) word meaning simply "merchant," is used to refer to the trading caste that spread throughout the former area of Mande culture and influence, from the Atlantic coast of Senegambia to the Niger, and from the southern edge of the Sahara to the fringes of the forests further south. These Mande merchants made their appearance under the empire of Mali and, as specialists in trade, built up a mercantile economy in parallel with the construction of that empire and its successors.

Even earlier, merchants in the empire of Ghana, who were known as "Wangara" among the Sarakolle and the Soninke, had kept up the links between the trading cities of the Sahel and the savanna and forest regions to the south. The Mande first embarked upon trade in the shadow of the Sarakolle and then, when hegemony over the region passed to them following the foundation of the Malian empire, the Juula took up the baton from the Wangara. The Wangara did not disappear, however; together with the Juula, they maintained a presence in all the cities of the Malian empire.

The Juula then spread out toward the West, where they introduced Islam into the city of Kano, in the land of the Hausa, as well as toward the forests of the south, where they went in search of cola nuts, which they obtained in exchange for millet and salt. The Juula organization was based on a vast commercial web spun across the savanna and the Sahel and then extended into the forest, as the Juula deployed their skills in buying and selling in order to regulate prices. There were fully fledged Juula trading companies built around family structures: the members of a given family, dispersed from the savanna to the forest, saw to the circulation of merchandise and information, placed orders, and controlled the mechanisms of supply and demand. The Juula were converted to Islam at an early stage, through contact with the Soninke and with Arab and Berber merchants, and they became active in diffusing the religion across the savanna. As the form of Islam that they tended to practice was relatively tolerant, and capable of accommodating traditional cults, they often served as priests, soothsayers, and counsellors at the courts of animist rulers.

In addition, the Juula spearheaded the penetration by the Mande of the forested areas in the south by taking their caravans of donkeys there and collecting the cola nuts that were much sought after throughout the savanna and the Sahel. As Moslems, the Juula were able to link up with the trans-Saharan trade conducted by the Arabs and the Berbers, whom they met in such cities of the Sahel as Djenn, Timbuktu, Takrour, and Walata. They sold slaves, gold, millet, and other commodities to the Arabs, in exchange for fabrics, incense, weapons, and books. They controlled the savannah as far as the lands of the Hausa, where their merchandise was passed on to Hausa merchants who were as expert in the trade as the Mande themselves.

Many of the staging posts that the Juula established en route to the cola-producing areas developed into market villages, or even cities, such as Kong in what is now northern Côte d'Ivoire. Kong traced its origins back to the fourteenth century and the Malian empire, under which it was established by a number of merchants from Djenn. Although it began as just another stopover for the Juulas' donkey caravans heading toward the lands of the cola nut, it rapidly became a commercial center, far removed from the heartlands of the Mande people, handling large-scale trade between the dry savanna and the humid savanna. It was a center as much for religion as for commerce and was home to a large number of Moslem scholars pursuing Quranic studies, with palaces and mosques built in the traditional Sudanese style. However, it faced competition from Bobo Julasso, in what is now Burkina Faso, another city founded by Juula from Kong itself within the same geographical area. As was the custom among the Juula, one of a set of brothers established himself at this intersection of trading routes, a location well-suited to the founding of a market. Thus, Bobo Julasso too began as a staging post and gradually grew as more and more merchants set up business there.

The city of Kong enjoyed its golden age from the turn of the eighteenth and nineteenth centuries onward. At its peak, in the early nineteenth century, it was the meeting place for Juula from Djenn, on the Middle Niger, and from Kankan (now in Guinea), on the Upper Niger, a city that had been founded by Juula from Diafunu and that controlled the savanna as well as the sources of the Niger as far as the mountains of the Guinea range, which borders on the forests of what is now Côte d'Ivoire. Both groups went to Kong to exchange rock salt, millet, and cotton fabrics from the savanna for gold, slaves, and cola nuts. The Juula of Kong also maintained links with the European trading posts set up on the Atlantic coast, around the Gulf of Guinea, from which they could easily obtain highly prized European goods, notably rifles, gunpowder, and textiles. The acquisition of rifles allowed the city to create its own militia in order to protect the caravans passing along the established routes through the territories of the various minor rulers. However, Kong was badly affected by the slave trade, since the hunt for slaves gradually led to the depopulation of the open country of the savanna. At the end of the nineteenth century, on the eve of the colonial conquest, Kong was still a beautiful city of fifteen thousand people, but now that there is no trade in its hinterland it is practically in ruins.

The Mande conquerors of the nineteenth century frequently made use of the routes established by the Juula. Indeed, it was his exploitation of their commercial network that allowed Samori Touré (1830–1900) to rise to a dominant position in the regions of the Upper Niger. He himself was a member of a Juula family from Sanankoro in Guinea and had started his adult life as a Juula pedlar, traveling from village to village with his merchandise on his head. Through a series of unforeseen events, this merchant became first a warrior, then the head of a warrior band, and went on to use the merchant network to extend his rule, not only over the Upper Niger region of Guinea, but over the whole of the savanna. Having created an empire, he adopted the religious title of "Almamy" and recreated the Malian realm. The Juula had never enjoyed as much prosperity as they did under the Almamy, for he was one of their own, and took care to protect their routes, thus promoting the free circulation of people and goods. He put up the strongest resistance to the colonial penetration of West Africa, fighting both the French and the British for 17 years up to his final defeat in 1898.

The Juula had long been accustomed to surrounding their cities with fortifications and taking up arms when it seemed necessary in order to defend themselves and maintain the flow of caravans. As a result, they became closely associated with the warrior class. At the same time, given the Mande tradition of combining trade and warfare with farming, they were not averse to taking up the hoe and working the ground whenever the rains came.

The infiltration of the Juula into the forests of modern Guinea and Côte d'Ivoire proceeded slowly and, more often than not, peacefully. They established numerous markets and caravansarais that ended up as permanent settlements and thus created new population centers. Their descendants are among the inhabitants of part of the northern savanna in Côte d'Ivoire; and, while they are Mande, and not a separate ethnic group, they are known to their neighbors as Juula even today.

Djibril Tamsir Niane

See also: **Mali Empire; Religion: Islam, Growth of: Western Africa.**

Further Reading

Delafosse, M. *Le Haut Sénégal-Niger.* 3 vols. Paris: Maison Neuve, 1972.

Devisse, J. *Routes de commerce et échanges en Afrique occidentale en relation avec la Méditerranée* [Commerce and Trade Routes in Western African in Relation with the Mediterranean]. Paris: Revue Historique, 1972.

Mauny, R. *Tableau géographique de l'ouest africain au moyen Age* [Geographical Picture of West Africa in the Middle Ages].

Person, Y. *Une Révolution Dyula.* Samori. Mémoire 80. Dakar: IFAN, 1968.

Kaarta: *See* Massassi and the Kaarta State.

Kabarega and Bunyoro

Nineteenth-century Europeans depicted Kabarega (1869–1899; d.1923) as an oppressive ruler, a brutal savage, and a proponent of the slave trade. However, his reputation was rehabilitated by Nyoro historians during the colonial period who saw his reign as Bunyoro's last moment of glory. After independence, Ugandan politicians and academics depicted Kabarega as a great protonationalist leader whose revolutionary reforms had transformed his kingdom. Bunyoro today sees Kabarega as one of its greatest kings, a modernizer who united and expanded the kingdom, although his reign is also remembered as a time of violence and exploitation.

Kabarega ascended to the throne in 1870, while still a young man. He was his father Kamurasi's chosen heir and was popular among the military and peasantry, but his elder brother, Kabigumire, was supported by most of the elite. A bloody succession war was prolonged by the intervention of neighboring kingdoms and Sudanese slavers. The rest of Kabarega's reign was dominated by the struggle to limit the power of Bunyoro's great families and to preserve his kingdom's independence.

Kabarega's internal reforms were concerned with the centralization of power and the extension of the political structures of the core of the kingdom to the semi-autonomous periphery. A series of foreign campaigns were embarked upon to heighten the prestige and the coercive power of the state, to bring in booty to reward followers, and to provide new tax resources and offices to be redistributed. Royal absolutism increased as competition for royal favor became institutionalized, and centers of opposition were removed, primarily through the execution or destitution of most hereditary chiefs. Delegated authority was given precedence over inherited status, as commoner chiefs were entrusted with disciplining the destructive ambitions of royal kin.

What was most striking about Kabarega's reign was the violent transformation of administrative personnel. Aristocratic pastoralists and princes who were only distantly related to the current ruler viewed themselves as feudal lords and increasingly challenged royal authority. Kabarega's new men displaced these provincial lords, drawing on both traditional and modern sources of authority. One military chief's elevation derived from his reputation as a famous medium as well as his success as a general. Kabarega, moreover, replaced many holders of hereditary chiefships with closely related kinsmen or members of his mother's pastoralist clan. Nonetheless, Kabarega's most powerful chiefs were commoners who had displayed unusual ability in war and trade.

Kabarega made innovations in the structure as well as the personnel of the state. *Barusura* regiments were garrisoned in the various districts to counter any tendency toward fission while the development of the new office of prime minister was an indication of growing centralization of power. Kabarega's creation of the *Barusura* underlay the revival of Bunyoro's power. The *Barusura* should be viewed as a response to unprecedented threats to the Kinyoro state, from Europeans and traders as well as Buganda's growing aggression. Elsewhere in East Africa, nineteenth-century leaders relied increasingly on the use of force to maintain themselves in power, in the face of expanding trade, new epidemics, and the appearance of firearms. In few cases were the destruction of internal dissension and the expansion of territory so successful as in Bunyoro. Within Bunyoro, the *Barusura* enabled the royal government to achieve closer control over the population. The new warbands overawed powerful chiefs, and *Barusura* leaders were given chiefships over areas with a history of rebelliousness. *Barusura* were used to punish criminals and to discipline rebellious peoples, but their reputation for lawlessness, brutality, and plundering made them universally feared.

Bunyoro built on existing regional trading links to maximize profit from the expanding coastal trade. Kabarega passed on imported copper, brass, and beads to the Langi, as well as traditional iron products, in exchange for ivory. Ivory was also brought in from Alur, Bulega, and Acoli, the latter area receiving guns in exchange. Bunyoro's access to immense resources of ivory became its strongest advantage over Buganda, whose supplies were fast declining. Kabarega wanted guns above all from long-distance traders. A musket worth one dollar in Zanzibar was exchanged in Bunyoro for ivory worth fifty pounds. Nonetheless, the same firearm could be sold on north of Bunyoro for much more. Firearms enriched Bunyoro, greatly increased its military power, and served to cement political alliances.

Bunyoro's wealth, unity, and military strength enabled her to overcome the unprecedented challenges that faced Kabarega when he came to power. Sudanese slave traders fostered local conflicts for material gain and sought to make Kabarega militarily dependent on their mercenaries. The Egyptian empire attempted to annex Bunyoro and replace Kabarega with one of his rebellious cousins, while immense Ganda armies began attacking Kabarega's capital instead of merely raiding Bunyoro's borderlands. While Kabarega's stubborn resistance and diplomatic skills contributed to the downfall of the slavers and the Egyptian Empire, his greatest military achievement was in bringing about some kind of parity with Buganda. For generations the Baganda had been free to raid almost at will across Bunyoro's borders.

Kabarega's military reforms brought Bunyoro victory in the Battle of Rwengabi in 1886, which transformed the balance of power in the interlacustrine region. By 1888 the Egyptian Empire had collapsed, all internal rebels had been defeated, and Buganda's armies had turned in on themselves. Nyoro armies had conquered thousands of square miles of territory and captured numerous livestock and slaves. Kabarega's very success, however, led to catastrophe.

In 1893 British forces invaded Bunyoro in order to secure the Nile. No serious attempt at negotiation was attempted because Kabarega was perceived as an uncompromising opponent of European intervention in the region. Kabarega's military skills meant that conquest in Bunyoro would be more destructive than anywhere else in East Africa. It took six years of sustained fighting before Kabarega was finally captured. Nyoro armies became proficient at guerilla warfare, constructed stockades and trenches, and allied with the king of Buganda and mutinying imperial forces. Imperial forces in Bunyoro were larger than those employed anywhere else in the conquest of East Africa while nowhere else were scorched earth policies followed for so long. Defeat only came when the kingdom was utterly devastated and almost entirely depopulated. Kabarega was exiled to the Seychelles and one of his sons put on the throne. He was allowed to return to Uganda in 1923 but died before reaching his kingdom.

SHANE DOYLE

See also: **Uganda: Colonization, Resistance, Uganda Agreement, 1890–1900.**

Further Reading

Baker, S. *The Albert N'yanza: Great Basin of the Nile and Explorations of the Nile Sources.* 2 vols. London: Macmillan, 1867.

Beattie, J. *The Nyoro State.* Oxford: Oxford University Press, 1971.

Casati, G. *Ten Years in Equatoria and the Return with Emin Pasha.* London: Warne and Co., 1891.

Colvile, H. *The Land of the Nile Springs: Being an Account of How We Fought Kabarega.* London: Edward Arnold, 1895.

Dunbar, A. R. *A History of Bunyoro-Kitara.* Nairobi: Oxford University Press, 1965.

Fisher, R. *Twilight Tales of the Black Baganda.* London: Marshall Brothers, 1911.

Gray, J., ed., "The Diaries of Emin Pasha—Extracts II." *Uganda Journal.* 25, no. 2 (September 1961): 149–170.

———. The Diaries of Emin Pasha—Extracts VII." *Uganda Journal.* 28, no. 1 (March 1964): 75–97.

Low, D. A. "Warbands and Ground-level Imperialism in Uganda, 1870–1900." *Historical Studies.* 16 (1975): 584–597.

Nyakatura, J. *Anatomy of an African Kingdom: A History of Bunyoro-Kitara*, edited by G. N. Uzoigwe. New York: NOK, 1973.

———. *The Customs of the Banyoro.* Nairobi: East Africa Literature Bureau, 1970.

Perham, M., and M. Bull, eds. *The Diaries of Lord Lugard.* 4 vols. London: Faber and Faber, 1959.

Schweinfurth, G., et al., eds. *Emin Pasha in Central Africa: Being a Collection of his Letters and Journals.* London: George Philip and Sons, 1888.

Steinhart, E. *Conflict and Collaboration: The Kingdoms of Western Uganda 1890–1907.* Princeton: Princeton University Press, 1977.

Ternan, T. *Some Experiences of an Old Bromsgrovian: Soldiering in Afghanistan, Egypt and Uganda.* Birmingham: Cornish Brothers, 1930.

Thruston, A. B. *African Incidents.* London: John Murray, 1900.

Uzoigwe, G. N. "Kabarega and the Making of a New Kitara." *Tarikh.* 3, no. 2 (1970): 5–21.

Kagwa, Apolo Kafibala Gulemye (*c.*1865–1927)

Chief Minister of Buganda, 1889–1926

Kagwa was born about 1865 at Kasozi in Busiro county. His father was the son of an important chief, but held no significant office himself. Nevertheless, he was able to place the child Kagwa with an influential relative, who recommended the boy to the keeper of Kabaka Mutesa's mosque, which was inside the royal compound. There Kagwa served as a water bearer, learning the ways of the palace. In 1884 Kagwa managed to secure a transfer to the royal storehouse, where he had a number of friends studying Christianity and Christian texts with the Church Missionary Society (CMS) missionary Alexander Mackay. Kagwa was attracted to the mission by the offer of free food, and soon began to learn to read there. At the palace Kagwa was given responsibility for carrying medicine to the ailing Kabaka (king). When the *kabaka* died in October 1884, he was succeeded by Kabaka Mwanga, a young man who favored the youths of his generation.

Kagwa, soon baptized as Apolo, was tall and heavily built; he became popular as a champion wrestler, a sport much admired in Buganda. In the 1886 persecution of Christian converts, Apolo escaped execution but was struck with a spear by the angry Kabaka Mwanga. Perhaps his athletic fame saved his life; at any rate a year later Mwanga promoted Kagwa to be in charge of the royal storehouse. Thus Kagwa came to command a sizeable group of young Christian converts who had access to firearms. When civil war broke out in 1888, Kagwa became second in command of the Christian army fighting the Muslims for control of Buganda after Kabaka Mwanga had been deposed.

The war sealed Kagwa's military reputation. He became known for his fearless assaults on the enemy in an era when inaccurate muzzle loaders meant most engagements were fought at very close quarters. In one battle, Kagwa was wounded in the shoulder and almost died, but he recovered to fight again. A song was composed that praised Kagwa's courage but pointed out he was prone to rush headlong into ambush. On the death of the respected Christian commander, a Roman Catholic, Kagwa assumed leadership, but he lacked the tact of his predecessor. Christian victory in 1889 brought Kagwa the position of chief minister of Buganda; he was now more powerful than any previous holder of that office because the restored Kabaka Mwanga was a mere figurehead. Though a battle hardened leader, Apolo Kagwa was only twenty-four years old.

The "Scramble for Africa" reached Buganda in the form of rival imperialist expeditions. Carl Peters promoted German aspirations while Fredrick Jackson, and later Captain Lugard, represented British interests. Kagwa and the Protestants, advised by the CMS missionaries, favored the British, while Catholic converts and Kabaka Mwanga sought any alternative. Kagwa announced that if the British were rejected the entire body of Protestant converts would depart the country. Ultimately the Battle of Mengo in January 1892 decided Buganda's fate in favor of British overrule, with a dominant position enjoyed henceforth by Protestant Ganda allies under Kagwa. The rebellion of Kabaka Mwanga in 1897 tested that alliance but Kagwa and the Protestants, along with many Roman Catholics, were prepared to defend the new order on the battlefield. A grateful British government awarded Kagwa a knighthood in 1903.

Meanwhile, Kagwa was enthusiastically "modernizing." He built a two-story house (which was burnt by arsonists) and then another, stronger building called Basima House (meaning "they are pleased"). Many of his countrymen were not pleased with the power that Kagwa had acquired through his British alliance. They particularly resented Kagwa's overbearing role as chief regent ruling in the name of the child Kabaka Daudi Chwa, who was only four years old in 1900. They noted that after negotiations of that year resulted in the Uganda Agreement with the British, Kagwa and his friends emerged with vast holdings of private land. A new song called *buto dene* ("big belly") was anonymously composed. It proclaimed: "The man with the big belly has gone to Entebbe (British headquarters) to sell his children." An attempt was made to revoke Kagwa's clan membership by claiming that he was not a true Ganda citizen but had been captured as a child slave on a raid in neighboring Busoga. Kagwa fought back, marshalling his allies, and attacking his accusers mercilessly.

Despite his considerable unpopularity, Kagwa energetically promoted school construction, awarded prizes to top students, and hired those skilled in English to serve as translators for, and spy on, British colonial officers. Kagwa's trip to Great Britain for the coronation of Edward VII in 1902 brought him prestige and a small but efficient printing press. He churned out in rapid succession his five books in the Luganda language on Ganda history *(Basekabaka be Buganda),* customs *(Empisa za Baganda),* clans *(Ebika bya Buganda),* his own grasshopper clan *(Ekika kye Nsenene),* and folklore *(Engero za Baganda).* Several of these appeared in multiple editions and reprints and are still in demand today. His promotion of Buganda's oral-historical heritage was a sign that he wanted to preserve national identity while engaged in Westernization.

When the young Kabaka Daudi Chwa reached adulthood in 1914, many thought Kagwa would step down, but they were wrong. He was too entrenched and the kabaka, who also had progressive plans for his country, remained on the sidelines. Kagwa survived attacks by both traditionalists who objected to the loss of clan burial sites on privately owned estates, and a young generation of school leavers who could speak to the colonial officials in their own language. It was those British officials, augmented by an influx of World War I officers, who began in the 1920s to press for Kagwa's retirement. Their watchword was "efficiency" and their test was financial accounting, which no chief of Kagwa's generation could hope to pass. In vain Kagwa pointed out his decades of support for the British Empire, including mobilizing Buganda wholeheartedly for the war effort in 1914–1918. In 1926 at the age of sixty-one, Sir Apolo was forced to resign on "medical" grounds; depressed and feeling betrayed, he died within a year.

Although a collaborator with colonial rule, Apolo Kagwa was a Ganda patriot determined to see his country (as well as himself) benefit from the opportunities made available by an alliance with the British. That alliance doubled Buganda's territory at the expense of neighboring rival Bunyoro.

Sharp bargaining in the 1900 agreement also ensured all the arable land went to Ganda owners while the British were left with swampland and bush. The primary goal was to preserve Buganda's identity and autonomy, which was achieved but with serious implications for the future unification of Uganda.

JOHN ROWE

See also: **Uganda: Colonization, Resistance, Uganda Agreement, 1890–1900.**

Biography

Born about 1865 at Kasozi in Busiro county. Baptized Apolo. Placed in charge of the royal storehouse in 1887. Named second in command of the Christian army when civil war broke out in 1888. Appointed Chief minister of Buganda in 1889. Knighted by the British in 1903. Attended the coronation of Edward VII in Britain in 1902. Awarded a small printing press, on which he published his five books in rapid succession. Forced to resign on "medical" grounds in 1926. Died in 1927.

Further Reading

Hansen, H. B. *Mission, Church, and State in a Colonial Setting: Uganda 1890–1925*. New York: St. Martin's Press, 1984.

Kiwanuka, M. S. M. "Sir Apolo Kagwa and the Precolonial History of Buganda." *Uganda Journal*. 30, no. 2 (1966): 137–152.

Low, D. A., and R. Cranford Pratt. *Buganda and British Overrule: Two Studies*. London: Oxford University Press, 1960.

———. *The Mind of Buganda: Documents of the Modern History of an African Kingdom*. London: Heinemann, 1971.

Rowe, J. A. "The Baganda Revolutionaries." *Tarlkh*. 3, no. 2 (1970): 34–46.

Twaddle, M. *Kakungulu and the Creation of Uganda*. Athens: Ohio University Press, 1993.

Kakungulu and the Creation of Uganda

Kakungulu (1868–1928) was born in Koki, a small state that had just broken away from the kingdom of Bunyoro. In 1884 Kakungulu went to Buganda to take up service at the court of Mutesa I. This was a crucial period in the history of Buganda, as the European partition of Africa was gaining momentum. By 1890, when the Anglo-German Agreement placing Buganda in the British sphere of influence was signed, Kakungulu had become one of the most important generals of Buganda. His failure to establish a power base in Buganda, coupled with his military prowess and great ambition, made him a potentially useful tool for the new colonial administration in pacifying the protectorate.

The officials of the British East African Company, then in charge of Buganda, were faced with a number of problems. Buganda was polarized into Protestant, Catholic, and Muslim factions. The Muslims, who had been pushed out of Buganda in 1888, were in Bunyoro and threatening Buganda. In 1893 the Muslims again rebelled and the colonial officials used a large Baganda Protestant force, led by Kakungulu, to defeat them. After their defeat, he was put in charge of operations to prevent the Muslims still at large from linking up with the Sudanese soldiers stationed to the west of the country. The colonial officials also used Kakungulu in an expedition against Busoga, aimed mainly at safeguarding the route to the coast. He was also the commander of an army sent against the Buvuma islanders.

By this time, relations between Kakungulu and Apolo Kagwa, the chief minister of Buganda, were deteriorating; it soon became clear that Buganda could not accommodate both men. Simultaneously, the colonial officials were growing increasingly concerned about the situation in Bunyoro. Kabalega, the king of Bunyoro, was involved in conflicts with his neighbors, especially Toro. He was also joining with the Muslims who had fled to the area to threaten Buganda and the colonial officials. In 1893 the officials came to the conclusion that a full-scale invasion of Bunyoro and the subjugation of Kabarega was the only option open to them if order was to be restored in the area. Kakungulu commanded the Baganda troops, variously estimated to be between twenty and forty-three thousand strong. As a result of the role he played in the campaigns against Bunyoro, the British authorities rewarded him with a part of the Bunyoro territory, Bugerere. Kakungulu moved to Bugerere, where he established order and set up an efficient administrative system.

In 1897 Mwanga rebelled against British rule. After his defeat, he joined Kabalega in Lango, where the latter was taking refuge. The colonial administration decided to apprehend the two men, and Kakungulu was one of the principal commanders of the forces that captured both Kabalega and Mwanga. On his way back to Kampala, Kakungulu asked the British authorities for permission to expand his authority to Bukedi, and they agreed.

Bukedi refers to the area covering Pallisa, Bugwere, Budaka, and parts of Bugisu, Teso, and Tororo. It had become a place of refuge for those opposed to British control in Buganda. The British government was not willing to allot funds for the pacification of other areas of the protectorate; therefore, the protectorate government welcomed Kakungulu's offer. On his part, Kakungulu was looking for a kingdom where he would be kabaka, or king. In June 1899, he left for Bukedi accompanied by a small force. Kakungulu pacified the area and brought Budaka, Pallisa, parts of Bugisu, Teso, and Kumam within the protectorate. He set up his headquarters at Budaka, built roads, and established efficient administration using the Baganda chiefs. When Sir Harry Johnston came to negotiate the Uganda Agreement in 1900, he was so impressed by Kakungulu's achievement in Bukedi that he recommended he be considered for post of native assistant in charge of Bukedi and be paid a salary just like the chiefs in Buganda. However, in 1902 the protectorate officials took over Budaka from Kakungulu, on the pretext that he was mistreating the local people. He was sent to Mbale and given some land on which to settle.

In Mbale, too, Kakungulu worked hard to establish law and order even beyond the area he was officially allotted. He set up an administration using the Baganda chiefs. He and his followers established banana farms and constructed roads. Indian traders went to Mbale and started a brisk trade. In 1903 the new commissioner, James Sadler, met Kakungulu and was impressed by the way he handled the Africans and the respect they gave him, and he reinstated him as chief. In 1904 the headquarters of Bukedi was moved from Budaka to Mbale.

By 1906 the conflict between Kakungulu and the assistant collector at Mbale had made it difficult for the two to work together, so Kakungulu was removed. The protectorate administration feared to retire him at this point, due to his immense influence. He was therefore sent to Busoga in 1906, as the president of the Busoga Council. The post reduced him to a mere bureaucrat. Nonetheless, he succeeded in transforming the council into an effective organ. He also supervised the labor force that built the Kakindu Namasagali railway. In 1913 the colonial administration felt it was safe to discard Kakungulu, as his influence had diminished and he was no longer a threat. He was sent back to Mbale as a county chief.

Kakungulu assisted the colonial administration in Uganda in establishing rule in both Buganda and what became the Eastern Province of Uganda. Having built the foundations of an orderly administration, he was pushed aside by the colonizers, who used his work to their own advantage.

FILDA OJOK

See also: **Uganda: Colonization, Resistance, Uganda Agreement, 1890–1900.**

Further Reading

Gray, G. "Kakungulu in Bukedi." *Uganda Journal.* 27, no. 1 (1963).

Karugire, S. R. *A Political History of Uganda.* Nairobi and London: Heinemann Educational Books, 1980.

Kiwanuka, M. S. M. *A History of Buganda.* London: 1971.

Twaddle, M. "The Nine Lives of Semei Kakungulu." *History in Africa.* 12 (1985).

———. *Kakungulu and the Creation of Uganda: 1868–1928.* London: James Currey; Nairobi: E.A.E.P; Athens: Ohio University Press; and Kampala: Fountain Publishers, 1993.

Wright, M. *Buganda in the Heroic Age.* Nairobi: 1971.

Kalonga Masula: *See* Maravi: Kalonga Masula: Empire, Trade.

Kampala

Kampala has a population of over one million residents of whom at least 99 per cent are Africans. The current Kampala population projections for the next census in 2004 stand at 1.5 million.

Prior to the establishment of British rule in Uganda, Mmengo, the capital of the kingdom of Buganda, was the seat of political power in the Great Lakes region and the location of the palace of the king (*kabaka*) of Buganda. When, on December 18, 1890 Captain Frederick Lugard, acting on behalf of the British Imperial East African Company, established company rule over Uganda, he inevitably raised the company flag in the vicinity of Mmengo Palace.

The raising of the company flag and the Union Jack by Lugard on Kampala hill (now Old Kampala), marks the founding of Kampala City. In 1900 Sir Harry Johnston was appointed British special commissioner to Buganda and formally established British rule over Uganda, with his headquarters located at Lugards Fort at Old Kampala hill.

After formal establishment of British, the settlement grew rapidly both in size and activity, and in 1906 it was declared a township with a population of 30,000. Several Asian families, many of whom had initially worked as indentured laborers on the Kenya-Uganda railway, set up shops and homes. Kampala was quite crowded, which forced the colonial administration to move its offices to Entebbe, along the shores of Lake Victoria, where the governor's official residence was located. Entebbe then became the colonial administrative capital of Uganda Protectorate. The few remaining government offices were subsequently moved to Nakasero, an adjacent hill to the east of Kampala, but taking with them the name Kampala, effectively turning the original (Ka) Mpala hill into Old Kampala.

Business seems to have followed the government's move to Nakasero, as Asian traders set up their businesses there. Subsequently Nakasero was to become (and remain) the central commercial zone of Kampala. The Asian traders almost single-handedly controlled all commercial activity in the town, as they did in the rest of the country, until their expulsion by Amin in 1972.

Several shops of Indian Bazaar architectural style were set up and a few still remain as reflection of the city's early architectural history. Many of these historical buildings have sadly been pulled down to make space for new concrete high-rise skyscrapers. There are however several other landmarks of this early period of Kampala that still stand today. These include the Church Missionary Society hospital at Mmengo set up in 1897, the Roman Catholic cathedral at Rubaga, and the Anglican (Church of Uganda) cathedral on Namirembe hill. The British colonial administration set up Mulago hospital, which later became the Makerere College (University of London) teaching hospital in the early 1920s. Makerere College itself was founded in 1922 on land donated by the Buganda government.

The first Kampala town planning committee was set up as early as 1913 to plan and regulate the city's growth and development. By 1937 Kampala already had piped water and electricity from generators. Some major roads in the town had been paved and a drainage and central sewerage system was being developed. The residential neighborhoods experienced the prevalent colonial racially segregated residential pattern, as the European community moved to the top of Nakasero and the adjacent Kololo hills. The Asians occupied most of the lower western slopes of Nakasero, linking up with their old settlement on Old Kampala hill across the Nakivubo Channel. The Africans lived in the surrounding villages and rode into town on bicycles every morning. A few worked for Europeans or government while others delivered their home produce to the market for sale. It was not until 1950, when government started developing African quarters at Ntinda, Naguru, and Nakawa on the eastern fringes of Kampala, that the city got its first African residents. The only exception to this was the African suburb of Katwe, which became the hive of all African urban activity, both commercial and political, as well as labor organization and mobilization.

In 1946 the Uganda Broadcasting Service went on the air from Kampala as the country's first wireless broadcasting service. In 1949 Kampala attained municipal status with a population of 58,000, having increased from 35,000 in 1914. In 1959 Kampala got its first Ugandan African mayor, Serwano Kulubya. At independence in 1962, when Kampala was declared a city and officially became the capital of Uganda, its population had increased to 200,000.

These figures, however, should be read alongside the fact that the great majority of Africans on the city streets by day were, and still are, mainly nonresidents. In 1968, when Kampala incorporated the neighboring African villages of Kawempe (north); Nakulabye, Mmengo, and Natete (west); Makindye (south); and Nakawa, Luzira, Ntinda, and Kyambogo (east), the population of the resultant Greater Kampala swelled to 330,000. The 1994 comprehensive master plan of Kampala put its population at over one million, almost all African. This dramatic increase in Kampala's African population in the post-Amin years was partly due to the massive rural-urban migration to Kampala during the 1980–1985 civil war, during which Kampala was one of the few safe havens in the country. War refugees, especially from the Luwero triangle war zone, all flocked to Kampala for safety.

Kampala has had a number of firsts. The city hosted the first-ever papal visit to Africa, when Pope Paul VI visited in 1969. In 1975 Kampala was host to the Organization of African Unity (OAU) summit when Idi Amin was elected OAU chairman. In 1998 the city hosted U.S. President Bill Clinton when he visited the Great Lakes region and held a summit with nine African presidents from the region.

As the capital city of Uganda, and therefore the center of political power and seat of government, the city has suffered the brunt of most of the political turmoil and violence which the country has undergone since independence. The Battle of Mmengo, which ousted Sir Edward Mutesa and led to the abolition of Ugandan kingdoms, ushered in a culture of political violence, of which inhabitants of Kampala have been the main victims. The Amin regime subjected the country, and Kampala in particular, to violence and genocide. The overthrow of Amin in 1979 saw Kampala under siege; the city found itself engulfed in a war that nearly razed it to the ground. This was followed by five years of urban terrorism and cold-blooded massacre, the main proponents of which were based in Kampala. By 1986 when the National Resistance Movement stormed Kampala, it was almost a ghost town.

Since 1986 there has been a significant amount of rehabilitation of the city's basic infrastructure and services. The World Bank, the European Community, and other donors have given aid to rehabilitate the city. Today the post of mayor of Kampala is one of the most coveted elective offices in the country, perhaps only next to that of president of the Republic of Uganda. The Uganda Chamber of Commerce and the Uganda Manufacturers Association are both based in Kampala. The main railway head, as well as the only inland port, Port Bell, on the shores of Lake Victoria, are in Kampala.

David Kiyaga-Mulindwa

See also: **Uganda.**

Further Reading

Buwembo, J. "The Birth of a City: Lugards Fort Becomes a City." *Sunday Vision.* (June 1999): 11.

City Council of Kampala. *The City of Kampala One Hundred Years 1890–1990.* Kampala: Crane Publishers, 1991.

May, E. *Report on the Kampala Extension Scheme.* Entebbe: Kololo-Naguru Government Printer, 1947.

Kanem: Origins and Growth (Sixth–Tenth Centuries)

The Kanem Empire occupied a large area that includes parts of the republics of Niger, Chad, Cameroons, and Nigeria. The limits of the empire correspond approximately with the boundaries of the Chad Basin, an area of more than 300,000 square miles. The present lake is a shrunken version of a much larger area, which scholars now refer to as Mega-Chad. The drying-up of the Sahara after 8,000BCE resulted in the gradual diminution of the area known as Mega-Chad.

To be sure, the origins of Kanem can be traced to the settlement of the fertile areas of the lakes of Mega-Chad. The historical evidence suggests that in the first century BCE, there were probably two lakes. The two lakes were connected with each other through an area that is now known as the Jurab Depression. The configuration of the two lakes lasted until about 250 years ago when the Bahr al-Ghazal opening of Lake Chad became congested with residue, and water stopped running. The fertile soil of the lake must have provided copious amounts of food to hunters and gatherers who had created a culture that was changing from Middle Stone Age to New Stone Age.

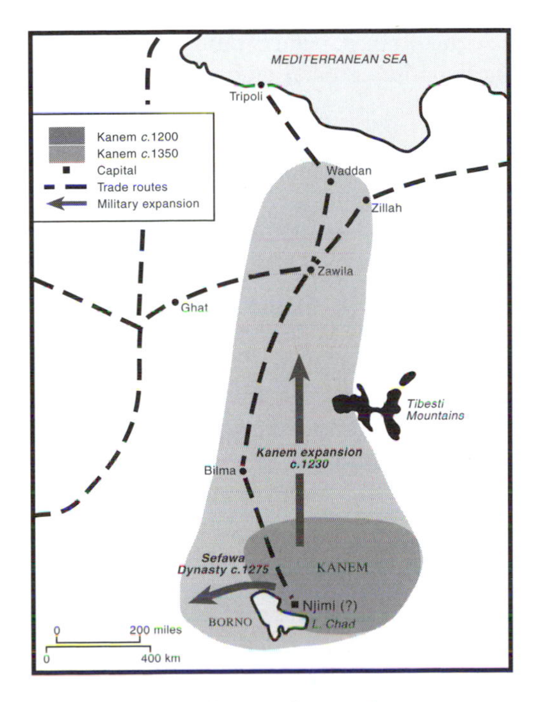

Kanem, eleventh–fourteenth centuries.

Between 2,000 and 1,000BCE, groups of Stone Age people moved into the area southwest of Lake Chad. Initially, they came to the area periodically, but later they began to settle the low hills that were adjacent to the flood plain. They made improvements on their dwellings over time as they further elevated their islands above the flood plains by amassing clay on the initial plane. They domesticated cattle and also hunted. The pottery of this people suggests that before 1,000BCE a food-producing culture had emerged in this area. In fact, the cultivation of *masakwa*, a sorghum, is believed to have been fairly widespread in these lands. The historical evidence would suggest that the inhabitants of this region were Chadic speakers.

The early history of the settlements in this region provides a background for understanding the beginning of the process of state formation in the Lake Chad region. One early interpretation explains the emergence of states in terms of the Hamitic hypothesis. The Hamitic hypothesis contends that the Lake Chad area was peopled by undeveloped Negroid peoples who were conquered and organized into politically centralized states by Semitic peoples from the north. Another interpretation, however, suggests that the rise of states in the Lake Chad region was not a result of conquest by a culturally superior external agency but through a process of interaction and reworking of the culture of the northern dwellers with that of the original inhabitants of the region.

The Lake Chad region is bounded in the north by the Fezzan, which in ancient times was dominated by the Garamantes. The Garamantes had succeeded in establishing a centralized state in the Fezzan by the fifth century. This state presided over trade relations with the towns of Mediterranean. The scope of their association with the interior is unclear, but the evidence suggests that they organized occasional raids to the south. To the south of the Fezzan were the Zaghawa. The Zaghawa appear in the documents of Muslim scholars in the ninth century. Al-Yaqubi was the first to mention that they lived in a land called Kanem. Also in this area could be found the Hawdin, Mallel, and al-Qaqu. It would seem that certain aspects of the political system of Kanem were a mixture of Mallel and Zaghawa political traditions. For example, the kings of Kanem became known as *mais,* which was the title held by the rulers of Mallel. By the tenth century the ruler of Kanem had extended his authority over the economically important Kawar oases.

By that time, a loosely organized centralized state had emerged in the region east of Lake Chad. It had arisen from a coalescing of a number of small rival states probably under the aegis of the Zaghawa. The development of trade and the ancillary needs of security and transport had facilitated the growth of these states. Also, by the tenth century the emergent state had taken control of the strategically placed Kawar oases, which further enhanced long distance commerce. The oral traditions of the people suggest that after a period of intense rivalry among the ruling families of the Zaghawa, the Saifawa dynasty imposed its overlordship over the others and ruled Kanem for a thousand years. The traditions suggest that Sayf b. Dhi Yazan was the founder of this dynasty.

After bringing together the disparate groups in the area, the Saifawa dynasty created a state east of Lake Chad with a capital at Njimi and began a process of imperial expansion. Although the Saifawa dynasty lasted for such a long time, it was by no means a dictatorship. The *mais* ruled through a royal council. Further, the empire was divided into provinces, with important administrative and commercial centers. The *mais* mother, elder sister, and first wife enjoyed great privileges, and for the most part, the royal family remained in control of the political process and ensured the longevity of the dynasty. In the eleventh century, the ruling class in Kanem embraced Islam.

EZEKIEL WALKER

See also: **Religion: Islam, Growth of: Western Africa.**

Further Reading

Barkindo, B. "The Early States of the Central Sudan: Kanem, Borno and Some of Their Neighbors to c. 1500 AD." In J. F. Ade Ajayi and M. Crowder, eds. *History of West Africa.* 3rd ed. Longman, 1985.

Hodgkin, T. *Nigerian Perspectives: An Historical Anthology.* London: Oxford University Press.

Levtzion, N., and J. F. F. Hopkins, eds. *Corpus of Early Arabic Sources for West African History.* Cambridge: Cambridge University Press, 1981.

Sykes, S. K. *Lake Chad.* London, 1972.

Usuamn, B., and B. Alkali, eds. *Studies in the History of Precolonial Borno.* Zaria, 1983.

Kanem: Slavery and Trans-Saharan Trade

The medieval empire of Kanem, to the east of Lake Chad, owed much of its economic fortune to its role as the southern terminus of the great trans-Saharan trade route from the Mediterranean sea coast of Tripolitania. That road via Fezzan and Kawar was possibly the oldest and certainly the most enduring and easiest Saharan crossing. It offered the shortest link between, on the one side, the entrepots of North Africa (with their direct access to southern Europe, Egypt, and the Levant) and on the other the Sub-Saharan markets for the raw produce drawn from deeper into tropical Africa. It brought economic and associated benefits to traders, rulers, and senior state officials on both sides of the desert, as well as to intermediate nomadic and oasis trading communities, while its role as a channel for north-south Islamic religious, cultural, intellectual, and technical influences had far-reaching implications for the development of Kanemi political, economic, and social institutions.

The road's earliest use at least four thousand years ago suggests that some sort of organized trading societies had long existed at its southern and northern end. The route exploited the natural amenities of the south-north Kawar oasis chain, about one-third of the way from Lake Chad to the Mediterranean, and the oases of Fezzan, about two-thirds of the way across. That the sea-borne Phoenicians recognized the road's potential about 500BCE suggests the existence of worthwhile trading opportunities with inner Africa, probably through the agency of the Garamantes people of Fezzan. But it is not really clear what was then traded across the Sahara, and in particular which produce of inner Africa was able to withstand the hazards, high costs, and mistreatment of desert transport to find ready markets as luxury goods in the Mediterranean world. Gold dust, animal skins, ivory, gemstones, perfumes, and some black slaves—the attested staples of the medieval export trade of inner Africa—are assumed also to have been carried across the desert in earlier times. But the regular trans-Saharan trade in black slaves supplied through markets in the Lake Chad region to end users in North Africa and the Middle East seems to have been established only after the rise of the Islamic caliphal empire in the seventh century. This was largely a replacement trade, since slaves in Islamic societies normally failed to maintain their own numbers by reproduction.

For the Islamic world, the largest and seemingly inexhaustible reservoirs of slaves were the inner regions of Sub-Saharan black Africa. Slavery was endemic there, and surplus or unwanted slaves were readily available for export. There is little doubt that Sudanese slavery, slave making, and trading all expanded under the stimulus of external Islamic demand. But the medieval empire of Kanem, as the prime supplier of slaves for the northbound trade to Fezzan and Tripoli, was itself an entrepot for peoples taken from the lands south of Lake Chad, and particularly from the Sara communities settled along the lower reaches of the Shari and Logone rivers. Kanemi raiders also exploited the country south of Baghirmi for slaves as the scale and scope of raiding expanded to keep pace with persistent North African demand. With the Islamization of Kanem occurring around the year 1100, jihad into pagan lands became an additional incentive and justification for slave raiding. The Islamic-pagan slaving frontier tended to shift deeper into tropical Africa in response to these pressures, although on the Shari-Logone flood plains it stabilized, leaving the same peoples and tribes vulnerable to Muslim Kanemi slave raiders for centuries.

About two-thirds of the black slaves exported northward from Kanem were women and young girls destined to meet the domestic and sexual demands of North African and Middle Eastern Islamic households. The trade seems to have developed a regular yearly pattern of one or two large slave caravans after the Ibadi Berber penetration of the central Sahara and the lands beyond it in the eighth century; the oasis of Zawila in eastern Fezzan became the trade's main Saharan entrepot. Numbers of slaves exported are hard to estimate, but on the basis of some reliable eighteenth- and nineteenth-century figures, an average traffic between Kanem and the Fezzan of around 2,500 slaves per year seems reasonable, with perhaps a quarter of those dying on the way, or being sold to final owners in the desert. Although some of Kanem's medieval rulers were famed for their wealth in gold, its export northward seems always to have had secondary importance to the slave trade (presumably the main source of state revenues), as also had the traffic in other raw products of inner Africa.

Northern imports into Kanem included textiles, arms, and other transportable manufactures of Europe, North Africa, Egypt, and the Levant. The main medium of exchange for exportable slaves seems, at least in the later Middle Ages, to have been the larger and heavier imported horses derived from the Barb breed of North Africa, with one horse buying fifteen to twenty slaves. Also from the north came the arms, stirrups, and other cavalry equipment that ensured the empire's military ascendancy, and particularly its large yearly booty in raided slaves for local use and export. Although Kanem also traded with Egypt and with Tunis, the central Saharan road was always so important to the empire's economic and political well-being that successive Kanemi rulers protected and controlled it at least as far north as the Kawar oases; similar concerns also no doubt prompted the brief annexation of Fezzan and the establishment of a new commercial capital at Traghen oasis in the thirteenth century. Under Kanem's successor state, Bornu, the central Saharan road to Tripoli continued as a channel for commercial and intellectual exchange until its ruin by European abolitionist and other pressures in the late nineteenth century.

John Wright

See also: **Slavery: Trans-Saharan Trade.**

Further Reading

Fisher, H. J. "The Eastern Maghrib and the Central Sudan." In *Cambridge History of Africa*, edited by R. Oliver. vol. 3. Cambridge: Cambridge University Press, 1977.

Martin, B. G. "Kanem, Bornu, and the Fazzan: Notes on the Political History of a Trade Route." *Journal of African History.* 10, no. 1 (1969): 15–27.

Thiry, J. *Le Sahara libyen dans l'Afrique du Nord médiévale* (The Libyan Sahara in Medieval North Africa). Leuven: Uitgeverij Peeters, 1995.

Urvoy, Y. *Histoire de l'Empire du Bornou.* Paris: Libraire Larose, 1949 Wright, John. *Libya, Chad, and the Central Sahara.* London: Hurst and Co., and Totowa, N.J.: Barnes and Noble, 1989.

Zeltner, J. C. *Pages d'histoire du Kanem, pays tchadien* (Pages of History of Kanem, a Chadien Land). Paris: L'Harmattan, 1980.

Kanem: Decline and Merge with Borno (*c.*1400)

An African state founded by the Kanuri, a mixture of people from south of the Sahara and the Berber from the north, Kanem lasted a thousand years from the ninth to the nineteenth century.

The Kanuri lived northeast of Lake Chad in Kanem (Kanuri for *anem*, south of the Sahara). During the first few hundred years of Kanem's existence, the Kanuri had been dominated by the Zaghawa nomads from the north until the eleventh century when a new dynasty, the Saifawa, named after the legendary hero from the Yemen, Saif ibn Dhi Yazan, was founded by Humai (*c.*1075–86) whose descendants continued to wield power in the Chad Basin until the nineteenth century. Perhaps of Berber origins, Humai established his capital at Djimi (Njimi) as the *mai* (king) and founder of the Saifawa dynasty. Kanem prospered from agriculture and livestock, but the power of the *mai* and his court was derived mainly from the trans-Saharan caravan trade. Merchants coming across the desert brought goods that enhanced the prestige and authority of the *mai*, Islam, and the literacy of Arabic.

By the eleventh century, Islam was the religion of the court, but the *mai* and his officials continued to recognize the rituals and festivals of the traditional beliefs throughout the long history of the state. The consolidation of the court enabled it to embark upon conquests and during the next two centuries Kanem expanded by military might and alliances with the Zaghawa nomads of the desert and Sahel as far west as the Niger river, east to Wadiai, and north to the Fezzan. The expansion of Kanem reached its zenith in the thirteenth century during the reign of *mai* Dunama Dabalemi ibn Salma (*c.*1210–1248) after which the power of the state began to decline, torn by a century of dynastic strife from within and the Bulala from without.

The introduction of collateral succession (one brother following another) rather than direct descent by primogeniture produced factions within the dynasty from the offspring of wives and concubines, short reigns, and instability that the Bulala exploited. The Bulala were nomads of the Nilo-Sahara language family living southeast of Lake Chad who invaded Kanem in the fourteenth century. They ravaged the eastern regions of Kanem, sacked Djimi, and between 1377 and 1389 killed seven successive *mais*, driving the Saifawa dynasty from the capital and their subjects west of Lake Chad into Bornu by the end of the century. The fraternal factionalism of the Saifawa dynasty continued throughout the fifteenth century until *mai* Ali Gaji ibn Dunama (*c.*1476–1503) asserted his authority over his rivals, consolidated his rule in Bornu, and defeated the Bulala who remained, however, a constant threat on his eastern frontier. He constructed a new, walled capital at Birni Gazargamu and, according to legend, was able to mobilize 40,000 cavalry in his army.

Throughout the sixteenth century Bornu expanded under a succession of able *mai*, the greatest of whom was Idris Alawma (*c.*1571–1603). He consolidated the internal administration of the state, expanded its empire and commerce, stabilized the Bulala frontier, and supported the propagation of Islam. Although a confirmed Muslim who supported the construction of mosques in Bornu, he did not make the *hajj* (pilgrimage) to Mecca and his subjects remained stubbornly committed to their traditional religions, which he respected. His successors in the seventeenth and eighteenth centuries continued these fundamental policies to defend the heartland of Bornu from incursions by the Kwararafe from the south, the Tuareg from the north, the growing power of the Hausa states to the west, and the resistance of the indigenous Mandara in Bornu.

These external threats were accompanied by the vicissitudes of climate that have historically determined life in the arid Sahel and parched savanna of the central Sudan. Drought was accompanied by famines, over which the *mai* had no control; all he could do was appeal to the spirits and Allah. The depression of the trans-Saharan trade during these centuries resulted in the loss of a constant supply of firearms, which was dramatically changing the balance of power in the *Bilad al-Sudan*.

More disturbing was the immigration of the Fulbe (Fulani) from Hausaland in the west. These pastoral nomads from western Africa eroded the state. They were disliked and discriminated against in Bornu and demanded redress for their grievances against the *mai*, his government, and his people. Supported by Uthman Dan Fodio of Sokoto, the Bornu Fulani rebelled in 1805 and would have prevailed if the *mai* had not called upon Muhammad al-Amin al-Kanemi, a Kanembu cleric, for assistance.

Al-Kanemi was reared in the Quaranic tradition, traveled widely, and made the *hajj* (pilgrimage) to Mecca. In the 1790s he returned to Bornu as a *malam* (teacher). Responding to the *mai*, he carried on a famous correspondence with Uthman Dan Fodio over the religious reasons for his Fulbe jihad against fellow believers, the Muslims of Bornu. He rallied the forces of Bornu to defeat the Fulbe, and by 1820 he had become the virtual ruler of Bornu with a new capital at Kukawa built in 1814. Known as the *Shehu* he consolidated the sultanate of Bornu before his death in 1837.

Thereafter his successors, the *Shehus* of Kukawa, ruled Bornu killing the last *mai* to end the ancient Saifawa dynasty in 1846. The short-lived *Shehu* dynasty was soon overthrown by the freebooter, Rabih Zubayr. Born in Khartoum in 1845, Rabih Zubayr was a successful slaver in the Upper Nile and later in the 1880s a warlord in the Ubangi-Chari River valleys. He defeated a French expedition in 1891, occupied the kingdom of Baguirmi, and conquered Bornu in 1894. Supported by his *bazinqir* (slave troops), he dominated the Chad and Bornu until defeated and killed at Lakhta on April 22, 1900, by a French force under Emile Gentile. The kingdom of Kanem-Bornu was now a province of the French West African Empire.

ROBERT O. COLLINS

See also: **Borno, Sultanate of.**

Further Reading

Brenner, L. *The Shehus of Kukawa: A History of the Al-Kanemi Dynasty of Bornu.* Oxford: Clarendon Press, 1973.

Cohen, R. *The Kanouri of Bornu.* New York: Holt, Reinhardt and Winston, 1967.

———. "From Empire to Colony: Bornu in the Nineteenth and Twentieth Centuries." In *Colonialism in Africa, 1870–1960*, vol. 3., edited by V. Turner. Cambridge: Cambridge University Press, 1971.

Urvoy, Y. F. "Bornu Conquest and Empire." In *Africa from Early Times to 1800*, edited by P. J. McEwan. London: Oxford University Press, 1968.

Usman, B., and N. Alkali, eds. *Studies in the History of Precolonial Borno.* Zaria: Northern Nigeria Publishing Company, 1983.

Kanem-Borno: *See* Chad: Nineteenth Century: Kanem-Borno (Bornu) and Wadai.

Kano

Kano has a population of about 600,000. It has a major role in Nigeria as both a commercial and a leather-working center. Kano also has a thriving industrial sector, producing peanut flour and oil, cotton textiles, steel furniture, processed meat, concrete blocks, shoes, and soap. Its tanned goatskin hides, for centuries traded north across the Sahara, were once known as Moroccan leather.

Kano is one of the original seven Hausa states, with a written history going back to the year 999. At that time Kano was already a few hundred years old. For centuries Kano had been a center of culture and a leader in handicraft goods as well as a commercial center. These attributes led to extensive contacts in North and West Africa. These contacts increased its ethnic heterogeneity. At first Arabs and Kanuri came to Kano and many remained there. Soon other traders converged on the city. These traders came from Katsina, Nupe, and elsewhere.

At about this same time, during the latter part of the fifteenth century, Gao gained its independence from the declining Mandingo Empire. Gao was the Songhai center on the Niger River. Songhai capitalized on the decline of the Mandingo Empire and became the leading power on the Niger. Askia el Hajj led the Songhai Empire to its highest point and made Timbuktu the leading intellectual center of the area.

During this period the Hausa states received notice when the noted traveler and historian Leo Africanus visited the Hausa states of Gobir, Katsina, and Kano. Songhai had conquered these states, further reinforcing Islamic influence there. Many Islamic scholars settled in Kano bringing the latest developments in Islamic scholarship to the area.

During the rule of Mohammad Rumfa (1494–1520), a contemporary of Ibrahim Maji at Katsina, Kano was transformed politically. The chieftainship changed into a centralizing force with a great concentration of power. The reign of Rumfa is remembered in oral tradition at Kano as a time of Islamic revival throughout the Hausa states.

The Hausa states became commercial centers because trade moved east as changes such as the Moroccan conquest of the Niger area led to chaos in the Niger region. Subsequently, the Hausa states came into close commercial and political contact with North Africa, marking a turning point in the history of the Sudan. Arab traders began to develop the direct trans-Saharan route from Kano through Agades, Ghat, and Murzuk to Tripoli.

After the fall of the Songhai Empire, this route brought influences from all over Africa, including Ghadames, Tripoli, Murzuk, and Cairo. Merchants from these areas migrated to Kano. This trade resulted in a steady flow of Egyptian goods. Kano imported from Egypt such things as perfumes, incense, the more expensive inks, mirrors, and Maria Theresa dollars. These silver dollars were used in the famous Kano silver work.

Because of these influences, Kano's prominence in commercial activity, and the political stability it brought, Islam became the religion of the elite in the 1500s, reaching the zenith of its influence and power in the next two centuries.

In 1809 the Fulani under Usman dan Fodio conquered Kano during the Fulani jihad. However, Kano was able to reclaim its commercial leadership under their rule. Kano became the greatest commercial center of the Fulani Empire. Perhaps, its greatest fame came from the superb work of its weavers and dyers. The raw cloth came from Tripoli. After being dyed it went back to Tripoli for sale in its markets.

In 1824, Captain Hugh Clapperton, the British explorer, overcame his initial disappointment in Kano when he visited its market. The market regulations and variety especially impressed him. Similarly, the market impressed Henry Barth, another explorer. Barth said that Kano had around 30,000 foreigners living in the city, making it "the emporium of central Africa." A simple list of its imports in the mid-nineteenth century gives an idea of its commercial activity. Kano imported silk from Tripoli, cotton from Manchester, sword blades from Solingen, and paper, mirrors, and needles from Nuremberg. While importing these modern luxuries, it continued to be a center for the salt trade, importing scarce salt from the salt caravans of the Sahara. Kano was an exporter as well as an importer. It exported its famous dyed and woven cloth, of course. But it also sold grain from Hausa farms, kola nuts, natron from Lake Chad, and slaves. Kano remained a slave center until the British ended the slave trade and, eventually, slavery itself in the twentieth century.

In 1903 the British consolidated their rule of northern Nigeria through capturing Kano, further increasing its ethnic heterogeneity. During the colonial period, which ended in October 1960, the British brought British law and created the country of Nigeria, uniting areas that had never before been united. The southern part of Nigeria modernized more rapidly and thoroughly than the north. Kano has made attempts to keep up with the more developed south with its university, museums, and educated elite.

However, despite massive building projects and its many educated men and women, there is a sense of little real change in Kano. The market still retains its ancient qualities as if Clapperton could return and not be surprised by it. Modern items are found but there are still stalls in which millet, guinea corn, rice, and peanuts are for sale in mounds through which buyers can finger the product. Desert nomads still purchase saddles and bridles from men sitting cross-legged in huts. Dye pits with the royal indigo dye still exist.

Beneath the veneer of modern Kano with its thriving twenty-first century economy, there is still traditional

Kano, with its Islamic emir, shari'a law, cycle of prayers, white-robed *al-hajiya*. The future of Kano lies in its amalgamation of these past and present characteristics and its ability to attune them to the demands of Nigeria in the twenty-first century.

FRANK A. SALAMONE

See also: **Rumfa Muhammad.**

Further Reading

Falola, T. *The History of Nigeria.* Westport, Conn.: Greenwood Press, 1999.

Forrest, T. *Politics and Economic Development in Nigeria.* Boulder, Colo.: Westview Press, 1995.

Kilby, P. *Industrialization in an Open Economy: Nigeria, 1945–1966.* London: Cambridge University Press, 1969.

Maier, K. *This House Has Fallen: Midnight in Nigeria.* New York: Public Affairs, 2000.

Mitchison, L. *Nigeria: Newest Nation.* New York: Frederick A. Praeger, 1960.

Smith, M. G. *Government in Kano, 1350–1950.* Boulder, Colo.: Westview Press, 1997.

Karagwe: *See* Great Lakes Region: Karagwe, Nkore, and Buhaya.

Karanga States: *See* Mutapa State, 1450–1884.

Karimojong: *See* Nilotes, Eastern Africa: Eastern Nilotes: Ateker (Karimojong).

Kasai and Kuba: Chiefdoms and Kingdom

The peoples living in what is now the Kasai region of the Congo vary from loosely organized chiefdoms to highly centralized states. In the north, Mongo influence is evident, while in the west, south, and east, the respective impacts of Kongo, Mbundu, Lunda, and Luba cultures are more pronounced. Among the most important Kasai ethnic groups are the stateless Pende, Lele, and Salampasu in the west; the highly structured Kuba in the northwest; the loosely organized Tetela (Mongo-related) and Songye (Luba-related) in the northeast; the Kasai Luba living in separate chiefdoms in the center and east; and the stateless Kete and more centralized Kanyok in the south. Over many centuries, trade, migration, warfare, and cultural borrowing among these groups have all contributed to a social, economic, political, and genetic melange. Although under Belgian rule the Kasai region was organized into territories, chiefdoms, and sectors, such political and ethnic tidiness had not existed before the colonial era.

Flowing north and west, the rivers in the Kasai region are tributaries of the Kasai and Sankuru Rivers that in turn join together before emptying into the much larger Congo River. Although the land close to the waterways is relatively productive, the savannas between the rivers (especially in southern Kasai) are less suitable for farming. As a result, people living in southern Kasai tended to cluster in the river valleys and claim hunting rights over surrounding grasslands. In the northern part of Kasai nearer to the great equatorial forest, people have access to a more varied environment that includes rivers, woodlands, and open clearings. Although all the Kasai peoples developed distinct ethnic identities marked by common language and culture, very few of the people had centralized political institutions and even those who did formed them during or after the 1700s.

Over the years, all peoples of Kasai have been affected by a number of profound changes. Probably as long as humans have settled in the southern part of Kasai, periodic droughts have led to famines that forced people to migrate in search of food and safety. Even those who had managed to save or grow sufficient food were endangered by roving bandits whose own lack of resources led them to plunder others. After about 1600, the influences of the Atlantic trade complex brought other transformations. Cassava and maize replaced bananas in the north and pushed out millet and sorghum in the south. Because the New World crops were more resistant to drought, less demanding in terms of harvest scheduling, and more likely to produce higher yields, these crops enabled people to build up food surpluses that supported increased trade and specialization. These crops also tended to shift more of the labor to women. Later, especially in the late 1700s and early 1800s, trade in ivory and slaves brought new wealth and power in the form of cloth, metal ware, liquor, and guns. In addition to this east-west trade, commerce between the forest regions to the north (a source of raffia, fish, slaves) and the savannas to the south (suppliers of copper, salt, and meat) preceded the opening of overland and riverine travel to the coast. Although much of the north-south and east-west trade was indirect, by the 1800s long-distance merchants able to mobilize impressive quantities of capital and scores of porters had become permanent fixtures in Kasai.

By the mid-1800s, the Cokwe from Angola were among the most successful because their long experience as hunters and gatherers of bee's wax gave them a comparative advantage in trade. Renowned for their ability and willingness to carry out business over vast expanses of territory, their social organization allowed them to easily incorporate newcomers and expand their politico-economic network.

Already in the 1600s and 1700s, strong political leaders began to emerge in Kasai. Taking advantage both of the dangers and opportunities that presented themselves, men emerged to serve as protectors, leaders of raiding groups, arbiters of disputes, and champions of commerce. Some became powerful and wealthy, attracting numerous youthful followers, obtaining slaves and clients, acquiring many wives, and fathering several children. All across Kasai, society became marked by clear hierarchies and tensions. At the bottom of the social order, slaves and clients (many former refugees) were marginalized as people without kin support. Such people were dependent upon their more powerful owners or patrons. Paradoxically, while the majority of the population regarded themselves as the "original inhabitants" of the land, they retained a mythological memory of autochthonous pygmylike people linked to the elemental spiritual forces controlling productivity and fertility. Also paradoxically, most "original inhabitants" could not expect to hold the highest political offices. Such positions were reserved for the families of the chiefly class. The ruling men and women of that class, people whose ancestors most likely were no different from those of the "original inhabitants," claimed to be outsiders with heroic and exotic roots that set them apart from their less powerful neighbors and subjects.

Because of the somewhat unsettled nature of society and because of the evident rivalries and rifts, witchcraft was a constant reality. Jealously, the desire for power, suspicion, the need for revenge, and guilt all contributed to a climate in which both the disadvantaged and the advantaged used witchcraft and suspected others of resorting to such antisocial supernatural powers.

While many of Kasai's leaders never established permanent polities, the Kuba (a name given to them by the Luba) in the northwest and the Kanyok in the southeast built formidable states. The Kuba kingdom was a multiethnic confederation under a Bushoong aristocracy. Related to the Lele, the Bushoong were one of several Mongo-speaking groups who migrated south from the forest region. By about 1700 they had gained ascendancy over their kin and neighbors (notably the Lunda-related Kete) to develop the basis for a strongly centralized and highly stratified kingdom. Shyaam aMbul aNgoong (*c.*1625–40), a long-distance trader and the reputed founder of the kingdom, was regarded as a key player in this process. Supposedly he founded the capital, conquered all the neighboring chiefs, and wielded awesome magical power. Paralleling the loss of political power by regional chiefs, regional gods and spirits also suffered diminished authority and prestige. By the mid-1700s, King Kot aNce was able to claim the authority to exile or execute subordinate chiefs. Although able to act in an arbitrary manner since he was thought to be endowed with an innate sense of justice, a Kuba king's proposals were subject to veto by a set of titled councilors. As a result of royal coercion and the introduction of crops from America, the kings were able to double agricultural surplus in their region. The surplus wealth was used for trade and to support a class of bureaucrats, warriors, artisans, and artists who worked to promote the power and glory of the king.

In southeastern Kasai, the Kanyok, who claimed Luba origins, were culturally, economically, and politically oriented toward the east and south. By 1700 they had developed a series of powerful regional chiefdoms which in turn were consolidated into a single polity by about 1800. This was achieved by leaders such as Chibang a Ciband (*c.*1775–1795), who strengthened the institution of the Mwen a Kanyok (supreme chief), and Ilung a Chibang (*c.*1820–1820), who cut ties with the Luba Kingdom. Like their Bushoong counterparts, the Kanyok leaders claimed distant and exotic origins that separated them from their more humble subjects. Like the Bushoong, the Kanyok benefited from the marked intensification of the slave and ivory trade in the late 1700s and early 1800s. By the mid-1800s, the Kanyok had become feared slave raiders who multiplied state wealth at the expense of their less centralized neighbors.

South of the Bushoong and west of the Kanyok, Lele and Kete peoples resisted the tendencies leading to political, social, and religious centralization. Village authorities and elders retained more power, parochial religious shrines remained more significant, and local lineages mattered more. On the other hand, both the Lele and Kete regions prospered less because they had a less pronounced division of labor and a less productive agricultural system. Both groups found it difficult to withstand the incursions of their more aggressive and prosperous neighbors. The same was true of the Luba Kasai people, living in the east central regions of Kasai.

Bundjoko Banyata and John C. Yoder

Further Reading

Douglas, M. *The Lele of the Kasaï.* London: Oxford University Press, 1963.

Felix, M. L. *100 Peoples of the Zaïre and their Arts.* Brussels: Hund Books, 1987.

Keeberghen, J. van. *Origine des populations du Kasayi.* "Collection Ponts." No. 15, Kananga, 1990.

Vansina, J. *The Children of Woot: A History of the Kuba Peoples.* Madison: University of Wisconsin Press, 1983.

———. *The Kuba Kingdom: Kings of Africa.* Madison: University of Wisconsin Press, 1992.

Yoder, J. C. *The Kanyok of Zaire: An Institutional and Ideological History to 1895.* Cambridge, Cambridge University Press, 1992.

Kaunda, Kenneth (1924–)
President of Zambia

President of Zambia from 1964 to 1991, Kenneth David Kaunda stood out as one of the most humane and idealistic leaders in the postindependence age. He played a notable role as a leader of the Frontline States in the long confrontation between independent black Africa and the white-dominated south, which only came to an end in 1994 with the election of Nelson Mandela as president of South Africa. A consummate politician, he spent much of his time shuffling top party figures to balance ethnic groups and their claims to power sharing. He was a poor economist and his critics claimed that had he devoted as much attention to Zambia's problems as he did to those of "confrontation" with the south, his country would not have descended to the level of poverty it had reached by the end of the 1980s.

At independence, copper was booming and provided Zambians with a relatively high standard of living, but when the boom came to an end in 1973, Kaunda showed little capacity for dealing with the new economic problems the country faced. Zambia sunk into debt. Throughout the 1980s, steadily deteriorating economic conditions substantially reduced Zambian living conditions. Kaunda was simply too busy on the international stage to deal adequately with domestic problems.

Kaunda began his political career as secretary of the Young Men's Farming Association, which was a stepping stone to the Northern Rhodesia African National Congress (ANC). In 1948 he founded and became secretary general of the Lubwa ANC branch; in 1950 he was appointed organizing secretary of the ANC for all of Northern Rhodesia. He rose to become secretary general of the ANC and deputy to its leader, Harry Nkumbula. He was firmly opposed to the Central African Federation (CAF), which came into being in 1953.

In October 1958, with a number of other young radicals, Kaunda quit the ANC to form the Zambia African National Congress (ZANC) with himself as president. He opposed the new 1958 constitution and ordered the ZANC to boycott it. On March 12, 1959, he was arrested for holding an illegal meeting (by then he was seen as the main opponent of the CAF in the colony) and was sentenced to nine months in prison. While in prison he suffered a second serious bout of tuberculosis; he was released on January 9, 1960.

Kaunda promptly formed a new party, the United National Independence Party (UNIP); his aim was to take Northern Rhodesia out of the CAF and achieve immediate independence. He launched a massive campaign of civil disobedience. Under the 1962 constitution, which he had initially opposed, Kaunda and UNIP contested the October elections; the result was inconclusive and UNIP joined Nkumbula's ANC in a coalition to form the colony's first government with an African majority, in which Kaunda became minister of local government and social welfare. The CAF came to an end at midnight on December 31, 1963, and a new constitution for Northern Rhodesia provided for self-government. In January 1964 Kaunda led UNIP to obtain a landslide victory and on January 22, he became prime minister of Northern Rhodesia, the youngest in the Commonwealth.

On October 24, 1964, Northern Rhodesia became independent as Zambia, with Kaunda as its first president. He was then at the height of his popularity and prestige.

Events to the south of Zambia, meanwhile, were already building up to a crisis. Nationalist wars against the Portuguese had begun in both Angola and Mozambique, while in Southern Rhodesia the end of the CAF was merely the prelude to a unilateral declaration of independence (UDI) that was to come on in 1965. In South Africa, Hendrik Wervoerd was implementing the system of apartheid throughout his country; South Africa also controlled Zambia's southern neighbor Namibia. These developments were to have a profound impact upon the fortunes of Zambia over the next quarter century and upon the career of its president. Following UDI in Rhodesia, Kaunda declared a state of emergency in Zambia. He was to make many pleas to Britain to intervene in Rhodesia but they fell on deaf ears. At home, meanwhile, Kaunda became involved in a permanent balancing act between the different ethnic power groups that made up Zambia. He was reelected president in 1968.

In 1973 Kaunda won a third presidential term as the sole candidate. A turning point in the fortunes of both Zambia and Kaunda came with the fall of copper prices in 1973; it was the beginning of what turned into a permanent economic crisis. The country now became deeply indebted until; on a per capita basis, Zambians were among the most indebted people in the world. An attempted coup of 1980 emphasized Kaunda's growing unpopularity and isolation from those he governed. The decade that followed witnessed a steadily deteriorating economy, an ever widening circle of critics, and constantly falling living standards for ordinary Zambians.

Kaunda's reputation outside Zambia stood much higher than at home. His efforts to find solutions in Southern Africa were rewarded in 1979 when Lusaka was made the venue for the Commonwealth Heads of Government Meeting (CHOGM) of that year. Lusaka became the headquarters of the ANC and SWAPO, and in 1985 Kaunda succeeded Julius Nyerere of Tanzania as chairman of the Frontline States. Yet, despite his external activities, by 1990 Kaunda's reputation had sunk to an all-time low at home, where demands for a multiparty system now came from both the National Assembly and UNIP, with the newly formed Movement for Multi-party Democracy (MMD) holding nationwide rallies to demand change. After months of stalling as pressures mounted, Kaunda agreed to a new constitution in June 1991. Elections for the Assembly were held in October 1991 and resulted in a huge defeat for UNIP, which only held 25 seats to 125 for the MMD. In the separate presidential elections of November the trade unionist Frederick Chiluba obtained 972,753 votes to Kaunda's 310,761.

Kaunda was the first African president to be defeated at the polls and retire gracefully; to Chiluba he said, "My brother you have won convincingly and I accept the people's decision." Despite his shortcomings, Kaunda stands out as one of the finest African presidents of his generation.

GUY ARNOLD

See also: **Nkumbula, Harry Mwaanga; Zambia: First Republic, 1964–1972: Development and Politics; Zambia: Nationalism, Independence; Zambia: Second Republic, 1973–1991.**

Biography

Kenneth Kaunda was born in 1924. He was secretary of the Chinsali Young Men's Farming Association in 1947, and secretary general, Northern Rhodesia's African National Congress in 1953. He formed the Zambia African National Congress in 1958. He was minister of local government and social welfare for Northern Rhodesia from 1962 to 1964. Kaunda was named first president of Zambia in 1964. In 1991 his term ended when he lost the presidential election to Frederick Chiluba. He has continued activity in the political realm, acting as president of the Institute for Peace and Democracy (The Kaunda Foundation) from 1991 until the present.

Further Reading

Arnold, G. *The Last Bunker: A Report on White South Africa Today*. London: Quartet Books, 1976.
Brownrigg, P. *Kenneth Kaunda*. Lusaka: Kenneth Kaunda Foundation, 1989.
Kaunda, K. D. *"Some Personal Reflections." Africa's Freedom*. London, 1964.
Keatley, P. *The Politics of Partnership*. London: Harmondsworth; Penguin, 1963.
Temple, M., and J. Sokoni. *Kaunda of Zambia*. Lusaka, 1964.

Kazembe's Eastern Lunda

The Eastern Lunda are the faction of the Lunda state system most accessible in western libraries through the writings of British anthropologist Ian Cunnison, who was interested in political institutions and their historical justification. This group, under the *mwata kazembe*, lives in the rich fishing areas of the Luapula river in northeastern Zambia; it is the remnant of what was a much larger hegemony before the mid-nineteenth century. By the time Cecil Rhodes staked his claim to this area as part of northeastern Rhodesia, the *mwata kazembe*'s western lands had already been usurped by M'siri, a trader from modern Tanzania who had settled in Katanga to exploit its resources in slaves and copper. The British recognized the claims of the *citimukulu* as a paramount Bemba chief, although the Bemba had been a decentralized linguistic-cultural entity that included the largest portion of the subjects of *mwata kazembe* (whatever the proportion of the far-flung Bemba who owed political allegiance to *mwata kazembe* and his vassals). The Eastern Lunda clearly represented a conquest state, with an aristocracy tracing political titles through descent lines different from those used in civil matters and with praise poems in an obsolete language rather than the vernacular Bemba. During the colonial and postcolonial periods, the Eastern Lunda have been confined to the Luapula valley and adjoining eastern shores of Lake Mweru, for authorities in Congo discouraged cross-border relationships with a chief on the eastern side of the border.

The direct origins of the Eastern Lunda polity lay in southern Katanga among people who spoke neither Ruund nor Bemba. A transitory Lunda political entity was centered on the Mukulweji River west of modern Kolwezi in the late seventeenth century. According to oral tradition, a kinsman of the Ruund *mwant yav* (a lordship title) by the name of *kazemb* Mutand Chiyemb'yemb had been sent to subdue Ndembu-speaking and so-called Kosa peoples in the area. The title *kazemb* has a military connotation, and Mutand conquered as far as the salt marshes of the Kechila plain along the Lualaba north of Kolwezi. According to tradition, he sought to hide the new economic resource from his sovereign but was betrayed by Nfwembe Chinyanta, who naturally rose in the eyes of the *mwant yav* and was named captain of the area in place of Mutand. At the end of a conflict marked by assassination and intrigue, Mutand received partial reinstatement but withdrew to the Lukoji River well to the west among the northern Ndembu-speakers. Nfwembe's son Nfwidima Nganga Bilonda began moving his base of operations eastward but retained the Mukulweji as his ritual capital and was buried there. His brother Kanyembo conquered the Luapula valley and made it his permanent base.

The Mukulweji polity represents a zone of primary "Lundaization." Whether Mutand was biological kin of the reigning *mwant yav* or only a political dependent so described by the rules of Lunda perpetual kinship, the titles used came from the Ruund political homeland at the Nkalany, as did some of the proper names. Today the Mukulweji is a no-man's land, near the borders of groups speaking Ndembu, kiLuba (but with matrilineal social systems and without the Luba political culture better known from farther northeast), and Sanga (another Luba dialect), with pockets of Ruund. The *kazembe wa lukoji* and the *mwata kazembe* of the Luapula were not alone; other southern Lunda titles tracing their origins to the Mukulweji include another *kazembe* in the Kechila salt marshes, *kanongesha*, *musokantanda*, and *ishindi*.

The most ancient praise songs among the Luapula Lunda are composed in kiLuba; the title *mùsokantanda* literally means "he who burns the land" in the same language. On the other hand, Mutand, the original captain sent by the Lunda court to carve out provinces in the south, and his successors have praise name elements suggesting Kete origins from outside the area, consistent with the *mwant yav* harnessing an ambitious young leader on the northern marches of his domain by sending him to the far south with royal blessing. The Eastern Lunda dynasty does not claim royal blood as descendants of a *mwant yav* but from a nephew of Ruwej, consonant both with their former great power and wealth and with only a tenuous biological connection with the Nkalany. It speaks of Nfwembe's clan, non-existent among the Ruund, and of a clan name that exists among the southern Luba of the Congo copperbelt. While there was likely Ruund participation in the Mukulweji conquest, it is clear that Lundahood is here a political rather than ethnic reality.

The Lunda who then settled in the Luapula valley conquered the Shila ("indigenous fishermen") living there previously. Calling themselves baLunda or bakaLunda, the conquerors were themselves divided into three subgroups: "true Lunda" (including the royal family above), the Bena Lualaba (absorbed during residence at Kechila), and the Bena Nkumwimba who came later. Intermarrying with the indigenous peoples, the Eastern Lunda dynasty claimed authority over groups living from the Lualaba to the approaches to Lake Nyasa. Lunda titles were generally held by people inheriting eligibility through a male line, yet the same individuals could participate in matrilineal clan politics at one stage of life and "patrilineal" royalty at another. The kiLuba praise songs anchoring the dynasty to the west are not the only sign of their origins on the Lualaba; the chief who installs a new *mwata kazembe* represents a group from there rather than the indigenous Shila of the Luapula, as could be expected. Nonetheless, many major officials bore titles known from the Ruund, and royal insignia were derived from the Nkalany.

The Eastern Lunda state was flourishing in the early nineteenth century when visited by the Portuguese expedition of Gamitto, following Bisa trading routes. The capital was a substantial urban entity, court protocol was refined, and the chief's authority was widely recognized in principle. Certainly its authority over the Sanga peoples (matrilineal Luba) of the Congolese copperbelt was sufficient to produce a marked Lunda influence on their political institutions. The Eastern Lunda successor state retained the Lunda constitutional model that had been established at the Mukulweji, and its continued similarity shows their faithfulness to it once adopted. The Eastern Lunda state developed into a much more complex society than that which had existed at the Mukulweji and therefore shows greater innovation in court titles than the smaller *kazembe* courts at Kechila and the Lukoji, but the Eastern Lunda may have obtained some titles and insignia through later borrowing from the Ruund, for the two major courts kept up regular commercial and political contact. When the *pombeiros* (agents responsible for obtaining slaves) crossed the continent from Angola to Mozambique at the start of the nineteenth century, their route led them from the Nkalany through the Luapula.

JEFF HOOVER

See also: **Lunda.**

Further Reading

Cunnison, I. "History and Genealogies in a Conquest State." *American Anthropologist.* 59 (1957): 20–31.

———. "Kazembe and the Portuguese, 1798–1832." *Journal of African History.* 2 (1961): 61–76.

———. *The Luapula Peoples of Northern Rhodesia: Custom and History in Tribal Politics.* Manchester: Manchester University Press, 1959.

Gamitto, A. C. P. *King Kazembe and the Marave, Cheva, Bisa, Bemba, Lunda and Other Peoples of Southern Africa.* 2 vols. Translated and edited by I. Cunnison, *Estudos de Ciencias Políticas e Sociais* (1960).

Hoover, J. J. "The Seduction of Ruwej: The Nuclear Lunda (Zaïre, Angola, Zambia)." Ph.D. diss., Yale University, 1978 (published by University Microfilms, 1979).

Keita, Modibo: *See* Mali, Republic of: Keita, Modibo, Life and Era of.

Kenya: Nineteenth Century: Precolonial

At the beginning of the nineteenth century, the East African interior was still a very secluded region in comparison with other areas of Africa. With its focus on the Eastern trade, neither the Swahili Arabs nor the Portuguese ventured beyond the small stretch of land along the Indian Ocean. The latter had ruled from the fifteenth to the eighteenth century but by the early eighteenth century Arabs from Oman had taken over the coastal zone near the equator. They started slowly

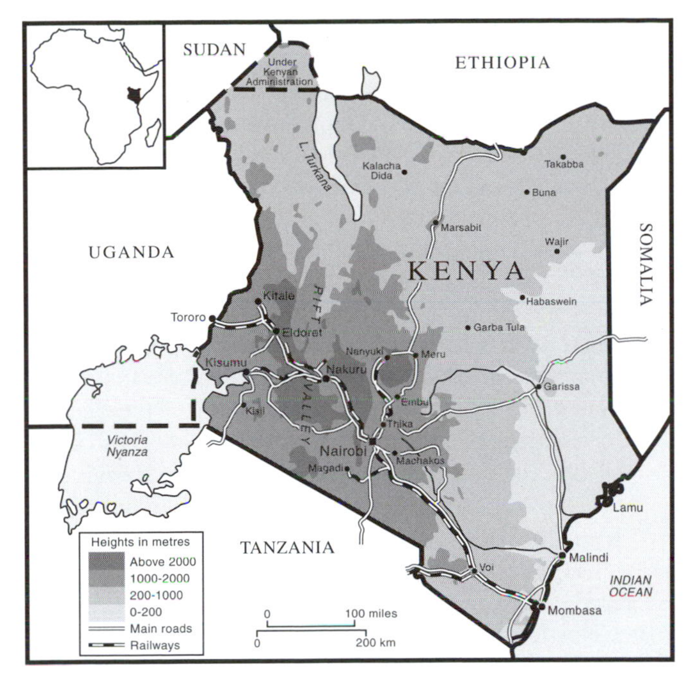

Kenya.

to penetrate the interior, moving toward the Buganda kingdom near Lake Victoria, albeit by a southern route. They mostly shunned the northern stretch of land that in the twentieth century would become known as Kenya.

During the nineteenth century, Kenya underwent tremendous changes and yet also retained a degree of continuity. While the period witnessed the end of the relative isolation of African societies in the interior, it marked the reduction of the relative significance of the cosmopolitan Islamic coast. Both areas experienced a process of evolution, expansion, and differentiation that facilitated the emergence of practices and institutions which would be interrupted by colonialism at the end of the nineteenth century. However, neither the interior nor the coast showed any reduced dependence on agriculture and trade as a means of survival and stimuli for change.

Several ethnic groups varying in size, internal organization, and language, such as the Bantus, Cushites, and Nilotes, constituted nineteenth century Kenya. Patterns of life among these groups demonstrated a strong relationship between the environment and internal evolution and extra-ethnic relations. Broadly, crop production and pastoralism shaped ethnic distribution, power, and influence. They determined not only group survival and expansion but also whether a community was sedentary or nomadic. Thus, land was to crop producers what pasture and water were to pastoralists, significant aspects of group life and class differentiation on the one hand, and sources of internal and external disputes on the other.

The Bantu-speaking groups monopolized crop production since they inhabited some of the richest agricultural lands in central and southwestern Kenya. With adequate rainfall and its loam fertile soils central Kenya nurtured one of the largest Bantu groups, the Kikuyu, who with their Mount Kenya neighbors, the Embu and Meru, were fairly self-sufficient in food production. All three groups grew beans, peas, sweet potatoes, sorghum, arrowroot, and millet besides taming goats, sheep, and cattle, albeit not on a similar scale to their pastoral neighbors, the Maasai.

Agriculture fundamentally influenced the internal evolution and external relations of the Mount Kenya Bantu throughout the nineteenth century. Internally, agriculture enhanced population increase and strengthened sedentary life, the two distinct features of farming communities as compared to pastoral ones in precolonial Kenya. Also, social organization, political leadership, religious rites, and technological innovation revolved around agriculture and land. Among the Kikuyu, for example, the "office" of the *Muthamaki* (the head of the extended family) evolved mainly to oversee land allocation, distribution, and arbitration over land disputes.

Externally, agriculture nurtured constant trade links between the Mount Kenya Bantu and their southern neighbors, the Bantu-speaking Akamba, and the Maasai due to the semiarid conditions and the overdependency on the cattle economy. The Akamba constantly imported food from the Mount Kenya areas. This led to the creation of strong regional networks of interdependency sustained mainly by the Akamba *Kuthuua* (food) traders. They exchanged beer, animal skins, honey, and beeswax for the Mount Kenya staples of beans, arrowroot, and yams. Indeed, for most of the nineteenth century the Akamba played a prominent role not only as regional traders but also as long-distance (especially ivory) traders. They were intermediaries between the coastal Mijikenda and the Kenyan hinterland. From the second half of the nineteenth century their position weakened when the Zanzibar traders became involved in direct commerce in the Lake Victoria region and northern regions such as Embu, as elephants had become depleted in the more central areas. They exchanged cloth and metal rings for ivory and occasionally for slaves.

In western Kenya the Nilotic Luo and Bantu-speaking Luyhia practiced mixed farming, rearing animals, and cultivating crops. The Luo were originally pastoralists but gradually changed to mixed farming as a result of their migration to the Lake Victoria region and its attendant effects on their predominantly cattle economy. During a significant part of the nineteenth century their social, economic, and political institutions, like those of the Mount Kenya people, revolved around the importance attached to land. Increased pressure on land and subsequent disputes orchestrated the evolution of *Pinje*, quasipolitical territorial units, among the Luo. The *Pinje* enhanced corporate identity besides protecting corporate land rights. External aggression toward their neighbors, particularly the Nilotic Nandi, Luyhia, and Gusii, added further impetus to the Luo identity in the nineteenth century. Kalenjin inhabitants (Sebei groups) of the Mount Elgon area were similarly involved in intensive intertribal warfare throughout the nineteenth century with neighboring groups, mostly Karamojong, Nandi, and Pokot pastoral groups. The Luyhia, like their Luo and Kalenjin counterparts in western Kenya, were also characterized by internal rivalry and external confrontation with neighbors over land and pasture. Among the major causes of the fighting were periodic droughts and famine; the latter occurring at least once every decade.

Some sections of the Luyhia, such as the Bukusu, kept animals while others such as the Kisa, Maragoli, Banyore, and Marama practiced farming. The less numerous and isolated Bantu-speaking Gusii further up the highlands of southwestern Kenya underwent similar economic changes to those of the Luo and Luyhia. Once avowed pastoralists when living on the Kano Plains of the Lake basin, they gradually lost their affinity with cattle with their migration to the present-day Gusii Highlands. They turned to crop production and reduced the numbers of animals they kept. Regional trade that involved the exchange of goods produced by different groups provided interethnic linkages and coexistence that mitigated against land-based conflicts among the various ethnic groups of western Kenya in the nineteenth century.

Providing an economic contrast to the Bantu-dominated agriculture were the Nilotic-speaking ethnic groups such as the Turkana, Nandi, and Maasai, who practiced pastoralism. They controlled large chunks of territories in nineteenth century Kenya partly because of the requirements of the nomadic pastoralism they practiced and their inherent militarism. Of all the pastoral groups in Kenya the Maasai were a power to be reckoned with. Their force had risen since the eighteenth century and culminated in a complex southward movement by Maa-speakers from the area to the west and south of Lake Turkana south to present-day Tanzania. By doing so they conquered, assimilated, and pushed aside other groups in the Rift valley.

However, unlike the Kikuyu who enjoyed increased prosperity and demographic increase, Maasai power declined tremendously during the nineteenth century in the face of climatic disasters that annihilated their predominantly cattle economy, internal strife that led to the partition of the Maasai into contending groups, and human and animal epidemics that reduced their population and cattle stocks. The Maasai were weakened by the succession disputes of the last years of the nineteenth century. At the dawn of colonialism they had been replaced by the Nandi who emerged as the dominant power in western Kenya and resisted European penetration. In the northeast a similar change of power occurred. Since the sixteenth century Galla pastoralists had aggressively expanded southward from southern Ethiopia and Somalia. They finally reached Mombasa and occupied the lowland areas behind the coastal strip. By the middle of the nineteenth century, however, the Galla, weakened by disease, had suffered several defeats at the hands of the Somali and gradually withdrew. Drought and rinderpest epidemics that swept through their cattle in the last decades of the century weakened them still further. This allowed the Mijikenda, although they suffered periodically from cattle raids by Maasai groups, to move slowly outward from the coastal zone in the latter half of the nineteenth century.

The Kenyan coast, unlike the interior, had experienced historical links with the outside world long before the nineteenth century. The Arabs dominated the area from the tenth century onward with an interlude of Portuguese rule and economic monopoly during the seventeenth and eighteenth centuries. With the ousting of the Portuguese, the nineteenth century saw the reestablishment of the Oman Arabs' rule that for economic and political reasons was consummated by the transfer of their headquarters from Muscat to Zanzibar in 1840.

The politically semiautonomous settlements and trading posts such as Mombasa, Malindi, Lamu, Pate, Faza, and Siu remained as much an enduring feature of the Kenya coast in the nineteenth century as it had been in the previous century. The towns had strong ties between themselves based on religious, linguistic, and economic homogeneity. Islam was the dominant religion in the same way that Swahili was the prevalent lingua franca. Agriculture and trade remained the backbone of the coastal economy. Mainly practiced by the rich Arab families, agriculture's economic significance continued apace with demands for agrarian produce in the Indian Ocean trade. Local trade between the hinterland and the coast was in the hands of interior middlemen and the coastal Bantu-speaking Mijikenda.

Despite the above developments, the resurgence of Zanzibar as the heart of commercial traffic and activity stimulated the gradual decline of the economic and political significance of Kenyan coastal towns. The dawn of colonialism in the 1890s added further impetus in that direction. The establishment of various colonial administrative posts in the interior, the building of the Uganda Railway (1896–1901) and the shifting of the colonial headquarters from Mombasa to Nairobi diverted attention from the coastal towns in the opening years of the twentieth century.

One of the most important discoveries that made the interior of Kenya known to the Northern hemisphere had been the confirmation of the existence of snow-capped Mount Kilimanjaro and Mount Kenya. A German missionary Johann Rebmann saw Mount Kilimanjaro in 1848. He had arrived in Kenya to assist Johann Krapf in Rabai Mpia, a small village to the northwest of Mombasa. Both worked for the Church Missionary Society (CMS) of London, a Protestant mission founded in 1799. The work of the CMS and other Christian missionaries was the main European activity in East Africa before partition.

Although Christian missionaries pioneered European entry into Kenya, they were not responsible for the establishment of European political control that came about mainly as a result of happenings outside East Africa. French-British rivalry, both in Europe where Napoleon's defeat transferred the Seychelles and Mauritius among others to Britain, and in Africa especially due to interests in Egypt, should be mentioned. This triggered a scramble for the East African interior, in particular to control the source of the river Nile. The rising power of Germany in the last quarter of the nineteenth century, resulting in claims for the Dar es Salaam region, forced Britain to act. British and German chartered companies divided mainland territories that formerly belonged to the sultan of Zanzibar. Soon Britain took over from the Imperial British East Africa Company and a boundary stretching from the coast to Lake Victoria was drawn between British and German East Africa in 1895. Thus, it took until the end of the nineteenth century for Kenya to be explored, evangelized, and finally conquered by Britain.

The arrival of European colonizers put an end to the dynamic spheres of influence and changing fortunes of the African groups. Settlers were encouraged to come to East Africa to recoup some of the costs incurred in the construction of the Uganda railway. Soon Kenya was to be transformed from a footpath a thousand kilometers long into a colonial administration that would redefine internal power.

Kenneth Samson Ombongi and Marcel Rutten

See also: **Kenya: East African Protectorate and the Uganda Railway; Religion, Colonial Africa: Missionaries; Rinderpest, and Smallpox: East and Southern Africa.**

Further Reading

Beachy, R. W. *A History of East Africa, 1592–1902.* London: Tauris, 1996.

Krapf, J. L. *Travels, Researches, and Missionary Labors during an Eighteen Years' Residence in Eastern Africa.* Boston: Ticknor and Fields, 1860.

Ochieng', W. R. *A History of Kenya*, London: Macmillan, 1985.

Ogot, B. A., ed. *Kenya before 1900.* Nairobi: East African Publishing House, 1976.

Oliver, R., and G. Mathew. *History of East Africa.* Oxford: Clarendon Press, 1963.

New, C. *Life, Wanderings, and Labours in Eastern Africa.* 3rd ed. London: Frank Cass and Co., 1971.

Salim, A. I. *Swahili-speaking Peoples of Kenya's Coast.* Nairobi: East African Publishing Bureau, 1973.

Willis, J. *Mombasa, the Swahili, and the Making of the Mijikenda.* Oxford: Clarendon Press, 1993.

Kenya: East African Protectorate and the Uganda Railway

The early history of the East African Protectorate (after 1920 the Colony and Protectorate of Kenya) was intimately linked with the construction of the Uganda railway. The completion of the railway had an immense impact on the protectorate.

The decision of the British government to formally annex Uganda as a British protectorate in 1894 necessitated the building of a railway to connect the area around Lake Victoria with the Indian Ocean coast. Nevertheless, it was not until July 1, 1895, that British authority was formally proclaimed over the territory stretching from the eastern boundary of Uganda, then approximately fifty miles west of present day Nairobi. It was called the East African Protectorate (EAP).

Having formally claimed this part of East Africa, the imperial government undertook to build the railway through the EAP for strategic and economic reasons. It was believed that a railway would help foster British trade in the interior as well as provide the means for maintaining British control over the source of the Nile. Politicians in Britain also justified the construction of the railway by arguing that it would help to wipe out the slave trade in the region. Construction of what became known as the Uganda railway began on Mombasa Island with the laying of the ceremonial first rail in May 1896. The British parliament approved a sum of £3 million for construction in August, though not without opposition from critics who claimed that the railway "started from nowhere" and "went nowhere."

Construction began on the mainland in August, and the railhead reached Nairobi, which became the railway headquarters, in 1899. The line reached Uganda in the following year and was completed to Port Florence (later Kisumu) on Lake Victoria in December 1901. From Mombasa to Kisumu, the railway was 582 miles in length. At £5,502,592, actual expenditure far exceeded the initial provision of funds by Parliament. The cost of the line was borne by the British taxpayer. The bulk of the labor used for construction, on the other hand, was provided by "coolies" recruited in British India. Slightly more than 20 per cent of these remained in Kenya following completion of the line; they formed a portion of the Asian (or Indian) population that took up residence in the EAP.

During the period of construction, railway building preoccupied colonial officials. Conquest of the peoples occupying the EAP was not as high a priority as the completion of the rail line. The colonial conquest was thus gradual and accomplished in piecemeal fashion, beginning in earnest only after the railway's completion. The Uganda railway facilitated military operations and was indeed the "iron back bone" of British conquest. By the end of 1908, most of the southern half of what is now Kenya had come under colonial control.

When completed, the Uganda railway passed through both the EAP and Uganda Protectorate. Imperial authorities quickly recognized potential difficulties in this situation. In order to place the railway under a single colonial jurisdiction, the Foreign Office, which was responsible for the EAP until 1905, transferred the then Eastern Province of Uganda to the EAP in April 1902. This brought the Rift valley highlands and the lake basin, what later became Nyanza, Rift valley, and Western provinces, into the EAP, doubling its size and population.

A substantial portion of Rift valley highlands was soon afterward opened to European settlement. Here also the construction of the Uganda railway played a significant part. The heavy cost of construction was compounded so far as the EAP and imperial governments were concerned by the fact that the railway initially operated at a loss and the EAP generated insufficient revenue to meet the cost of colonial administration. Thus the British government was forced to provide annual grants to balance the EAP's budget. In seeking to find the means to enhance the EAP's exports and revenues, its second commissioner, Sir Charles Eliot, turned to the encouragement of European settlement. From 1902 he drew European farmers to the protectorate by generous grants of land around Nairobi and along the railway line to the west with little thought to African land rights or needs. London authorities acquiesced in Eliot's advocacy of European settlement, which eventually led to the creation of what became known as the "White Highlands," where only Europeans could legally farm. It meant that land and issues relating to African labor played a huge part in colonial Kenya as European settlers played a significant role in its economic and political history.

Ironically, the advent of white settlers did little immediately to solve the EAP's budget deficits. Only in the 1912–13 financial year was the annual imperial grant-in-aid terminated. The EAP's improved revenues were mostly the result of increased African production for export via the Uganda railway. European settler-generated exports accounted for the bulk of those of the protectorate only after World War I.

It cannot be denied, however, that the Uganda railway played a huge part in the early history of the EAP, from paving the way for conquest of the southern portion of the protectorate to helping to determine its physical shape and the character of its population, in the form of its Asian and European minorities in particular.

Robert M. Maxon

See also: **Asians: East Africa.**

Further Reading

Hill, M. F. *Permanent Way: The Story of the Kenya and Uganda Railway.* 2nd ed. Nairobi: East African Railways and Harbours, 1961.

Lonsdale, J. "The Conquest State, 1895–1904." In *A Modern History of Kenya 1895–1980,* edited by William R. Ochieng'. Nairobi: Evans Brothers, 1989.

Lonsdale, J., and B. Berman. "Coping With the Contradictions: The Development of the Colonial State in Kenya, 1895–1914." *Journal of African History.* 20 (1979): 487–505.

Mungeam, G. H. *British Rule in Kenya, 1895–1912: The Establishment of Administration in the East Africa Protectorate.* Oxford: Clarendon Press, 1966.

Sorrenson, M. P. K. *Origins of European Settlement in Kenya.* Nairobi: Oxford University Press, 1968.

Kenya: Mekatilele and Giriama Resistance, 1900–1920

The Giriama (also spelled Giryama) were one of the most successful colonizing societies of nineteenth century East Africa. From a relatively small area around the ritual center called the *kaya*, inland from Mombasa, Giriama settlement spread during the nineteenth century to cover a great swath of the hinterland of Mombasa and Malindi, crossing the Sabaki River in the 1890s. It was a process of expansion driven by a conjuncture of circumstances. Long-standing tensions over resource control within Giriama society were accentuated by the new opportunities for accumulation created by the rapidly expanding coastal economy and the growing availability of servile labor, female, and male. The northward expansion took the form of a constant establishment of new homesteads by men who sought to accumulate new dependents of their own, and to assert a control over these dependents that could not be challenged by others—either their own kin, or the "gerontocracy" of other elders who claimed power through association with the *kaya*. The ambitions and the northward expansion of these pioneers were encouraged through engagement with coastal society. This was similarly undergoing a period of northward expansion, driven by the growth of a trade with the hinterland in ivory, aromatics, and other products, and by a growing regional demand for foodstuffs that encouraged the opening up of new areas of slave-based grain cultivation.

In the early years of British rule this expansion continued, and early administrators struck an accommodation with the most successful accumulators of the Giriama society that served the very limited needs of the early colonial state. But by the second decade of the twentieth century the demands of British rule had begun to conflict with the pattern of expansion and individual accumulation on which the nineteenth-century expansion had relied. The supply of slaves and runaway slaves from the coast had dried up after the abolition of slavery. British officials at the coast were increasingly concerned over the state of the coastal economy and sought to foster new plantation ventures, as well as supplying labor for the growing needs of Mombasa. Evidence taken for the Native Labor Commission in 1912–13 identified the Giriama as an important potential source of waged labor. In October 1912 a new administrator, Arthur Champion, was appointed to improve the supply of labor from among the Giriama, partly through the exercise of extralegal coercion and bullying, which was commonly used in early colonial states to "encourage" labor recruitment, and partly through the collection of taxes, which would force young men to seek waged work. Champion tried to work through elder Giriama men but demands for tax and for young men to go out to work struck directly at the pattern of accumulation on which these men relied: they sought to acquire dependents, not to send them away to work for others. British restrictions on the ivory trade were equally unwelcome. Champion found himself and his camp effectively boycotted.

The boycott was encouraged by the activities of a woman called Mekatilele (also spelled Mekatilili) who drew on an established tradition of female prophecy to speak out against the British and who encouraged many Giriama men and women to swear oaths against cooperation with the administration. This was a complex phenomenon, for it drew on an established accommodation between women's prophecy and the power of *kaya* elders, and exploited tensions between old and young and between *kaya* elders and the accumulators who pioneered the expansion to the north, as well as on resistance to colonial rule. Mekatilele was soon arrested and sent up-country; she escaped and returned to the coast but was rearrested and removed again. Meanwhile, in reprisal for the oaths and for some rather mild displays of hostility, the colonial administration first "closed" the *kaya* in December 1913 and then burned and dynamited it in August 1914. British officials were quick to understand Giriama resistance as inspired by oaths, prophecy, and the power of the *kaya*, but this probably reveals less about Giriama motivations than it does about colonial perceptions of male household authority as essentially good and stable, and magical or prophetic power as fundamentally subversive. In truth, Giriama resistance to British demands resulted from the disastrous impact of British policies and demands upon the authority of ambitious household heads.

The destruction of the *kaya* coincided with the outbreak of World War I, which immediately led to renewed efforts to conscript Giriama men, this time as porters for the armed forces. Giriama resentment was further inflamed by a British plan to evict Giriama who had settled north of the Sabaki, as a punishment for noncooperation and to deprive them of land and so force them into waged labor. In an act of routine colonial brutality, one of Champion's police, searching for young men, raped a woman and was himself killed in retaliation. Thrown into panic by the fear of a Giriama "rising," and finding themselves in possession of an unusually powerful coercive force, British officials launched a punitive assault on the Giriama, using two full companies of the King's African Rifles. As a result, 150 Giriama were killed, and hundreds of houses burned; officials found it difficult to bring the campaign to an end since there were no leaders with whom to deal and British policy had largely eroded the power of elder men. The campaign was finally called off in January 1915. There were no military fatalities. A continued armed police presence and the threat of further military reprisals ensured the clearance of the trans-Sabaki Giriama, the collection of a punitive fine, and the recruitment of a contingent of Giriama porters for the war.

Mekatilele returned to the area in 1919, and she and a group of elder men took up residence in the *kaya*. This continued to be a much-contested source of ritual power, but the idealized gerontocracy of early nineteenth century society was never reconstructed, and ritual and political power among the Giriama has remained diffuse. The trans-Sabaki was settled again in the 1920s, but Giriama society never regained the relative prosperity of the late nineteenth century.

JUSTIN WILLIS

See also: **Kenya: World War I, Carrier Corps.**

Further Reading

Brantley, C. *The Giriama and Colonial Resistance in Kenya, 1800–1920.* Berkeley: University of California Press, 1981.

Spear, T. *The Kaya Complex: A History of the Mijikenda Peoples of the Kenya Coast to 1900.* Nairobi: Kenya Literature Bureau, 1978.

Sperling, D. "The Frontiers of Prophecy: Healing, the Cosmos, and Islam on the East African Coast in the Nineteenth Century." In *Revealing Prophets: Prophecy in Eastern African History*, edited by D. Anderson and D. Johnson. James Currey: London, East African Educational Publishers: Nairobi, Fountain Publishers: Kampala, Ohio University Press: Athens.

Willis, J., and S. Miers. "Becoming a Child of the House: Incorporation, Authority and Resistance in Giryama Society." *Journal of African History.* 38 (1997): 479–495.

Kenya: World War I, Carrier Corps

Despite its strategic and commercial importance to the British Empire, the East Africa Protectorate (EAP, now Kenya) was unprepared for the outbreak of World War I. The King's African Rifles (KAR) were ill-prepared to sustain conventional military operations, as until that point it had been used largely as a military police force in semipacified areas. Moreover, the KAR possessed minimal field intelligence capabilities and knew very little about the strengths and weaknesses of the German forces in neighboring German East Africa (GEA, now Tanzania). Most importantly, the KAR lacked an adequate African carrier corps, upon which the movement of its units depended.

Hostilities began on August 8, 1914, when the Royal Navy shelled a German wireless station near Dar es Salaam. General Paul von Lettow-Vorbeck, commander of the *Schütztruppe*, which numbered only 218 Germans and 2,542 *askaris* organized into 14 companies, opposed the German governor, Heinrich Schnee, who hoped to remain neutral. Instead, Lettow-Vorbeck wanted to launch a guerrilla campaign against the British, which would pin down a large number of troops and force the British to divert soldiers destined for the western front and other theaters to East Africa.

On August 15, 1914, Lettow-Vorbeck defied Schnee and captured Taveta, a small settlement just inside the EAP border. Lettow-Vorbeck then launched a series of attacks against a 100-mile section of the Uganda Railway, the main transport link in EAP that ran almost parallel to the GEA border and about three days march from the German bases near Kilimanjaro. Relying largely on raids, hit and run tactics, and the skillful use of intelligence and internal lines of communication, Lettow-Vorbeck wreacked havoc upon the British by destroying bridges, blowing up trains, ambushing relief convoys, and capturing military equipment and other supplies. By using such tactics, Lettow-Vorbeck largely eluded British and allied forces for the first two years of the campaign.

Meanwhile, the British sought to resolve problems that plagued their operations in the early days of the war. A military buildup eventually resulted in the establishment of a force that numbered about 70,000 soldiers and included contingents from South Africa, Southern Rhodesia, (now Zimbabwe), and India. There also were Belgian and Portuguese units arrayed against the Germans. Captain Richard Meinertzhagen, who became chief of allied intelligence in December 1914, created an intelligence apparatus that quickly earned the reputation of being the best in the East African theater of operations.

In December 1915, the port of Mombasa received a great influx of military personnel and equipment such as artillery, armored vehicles, motor lorries, and transport animals. Many of the troops deployed to Voi, a staging area on the Uganda railway some sixty miles from the German border. General Jan Smuts, who became allied commander in February 1916, sought to launch an offensive from Voi against Kilimanjaro to "surround and annihilate" Lettow-Vorbek's forces. Rather than commit himself to a major battle, which would involve substantial casualties, Lettow-Vorbeck resorted to hit and run attacks while slowly retreating southward. During the 1916–1917 period, Smuts fought the *Schütztruppe* to a stalemate. In late 1917, General J. L. van Deventer assumed command of British forces in East Africa and eventually forced the Germans to retreat into Portuguese East Africa (now Mozambique). On September 28, 1918, Lettow-Vorbeck crossed back into GEA, but before he could launch a new offensive, the war ended.

Formed a few days after the outbreak of hostilities, the Carrier Corps, East African Transport Corps played a significant role throughout the East African campaign by supporting combat units in the EAP, GEA, and Portuguese East Africa. Its history began on September 11, 1914, when the Carrier Corps commander, Lieutenant Colonel Oscar Ferris Watkins, announced that he had recruited some 5,000 Africans organized into five 1,000-man units, which were subdivided into 100-man companies under the command of native headmen. Initially, enlistment in the Carrier Corps was voluntary. On June 21, 1915, however, growing manpower requirements forced the colonial authorities to pass legislation that authorized the forcible recruitment of men for the Carrier Corps.

In February 1916, the colonial government created the Military Labor Bureau to replace the Carrier Corps, East African Transport Corps. By late March 1916, this unit reported that more than 69,000 men had been recruited for service as porters. When the East African campaign moved to southern GEA at the end of that year, the demand for military porters again increased. On March 18, 1917 the colonial government appointed John Ainsworth, who had a reputation for fair dealing among the Africans, as military commissioner for labor to encourage greater enlistment. During the last two years of the war, his efforts helped the Military Labor Bureau recruit more than 112,000 men.

Apart from service in the EAP, the Carrier Corps accompanied British and allied forces into GEA and Portuguese East Africa, where they served in extremely trying circumstances. Chronic food shortages, inadequate medical care, pay problems, and harsh field conditions plagued all who participated in the East African campaign but Africans frequently suffered more than non-Africans. Agricultural production also declined because of labor shortages on European and African-owned farms.

Nearly 200,000 Africans served in the Carrier Corps; about 40,000 of them never returned. Thousands received medals or other awards for the courage with which they performed their duties. On a wider level, the Carrier Corps' contribution to the war effort was crucial to the allied victory in East Africa; indeed, without that unit's participation, the campaign never could have been fought. In the long run, many Carrier Corps veterans became important members of society. Some used the skills learned during wartime to become successful businessmen or community leaders. Others became politically active: Jonathan Okwirri, for example, served as a headman at the Military Labor Bureau's Mombasa Depot for eighteen months, then as president of the Young Kavirondo Association and as a senior chief. Thus, the Carrier Corps not only played a vital role in the East African campaign but also facilitated the emergence of a small but influential number of economically and politically active Africans.

THOMAS P. OFCANSKY

See also: **World War I: Survey.**

Further Reading

Greenstein, L. J. "The Impact of Military Service in World War I on Africans: The Nandi of Kenya." *Journal of Modern African History.* 16, no. 3 (1987): 495–507.

Hodges, G. W. P. "African Manpower Statistics for the British Forces in East Africa, 1914–1918." *Journal of African History.* 19, no. 1 (1978): 101–116.

———. *The Carrier Corps: Military Labor in the East African Campaign, 1914–1918.* Westport, Conn.: Greenwood Press, 1988.

Hornden, C. *Military Operations, East Africa.* Vol. 1. London: HMSO, 1941.

Miller, C. *Battle for the Bundu.* London: Macdonald and Jane's, 1974.

Moyse-Bartlett, H. *The King's African Rifles: A Study in Military History of East and Central Africa, 1890–1945.* Aldershot: Gale and Polden, 1956.

Savage, D. C., and J. Forbes Munro. "Carrier Corps Recruitment in the British East Africa Protectorate 1914–1918." *Journal of African History.* 7, no. 2 (1966): 313–342.

Kenya: Colonial Period: Economy, 1920s–1930s

Land, labor, and production were strongly contested arenas for the political economy of Kenya, firmly based in agriculture, during the 1920s and 1930s. The contestation revolved around the basic nature of Kenya's outward-looking economy: were its exports and revenue to be generated by European settlers or African peasants? The most important contestants were Kenya's European, Asian, and African populations, the colonial state in Kenya, and the Colonial Office in London.

Land was a bitterly contested issue in interwar Kenya as a result of the colonial state's decision to encourage European settlement in the highlands through the appropriation of large amounts of land. By the start of the 1920s, the colonial state and the metropolitan government had accepted the principle that the region known as the white highlands was reserved exclusively for European occupation. This segregated principle of landholding was challenged by Kenya Asians and Africans during the two decades. Kenya Africans not only protested against the reservation of the highlands for whites, they objected to the loss of African occupied land taken for settler use. They also complained about the land shortage in many of the African "reserves" created by the colonial state and expressed fears regarding the security of land in those reserves. Despite protests throughout the two decades, neither the colonial state nor the Colonial Office managed to appease African land grievances. The 1932 appointment of the Kenya Land Commission represented a major attempt to do so, but it failed. Its 1934 report endorsed the segregated system of land holding in Kenya, and this was enshrined in legislation by the end of the decade. It did little to reduce African land grievances. In fact, the contestation of the 1920s and 1930s made certain that land continued to be a volatile element in Kenya politics.

Labor was likewise an area of conflict as a result of the European settler demands for assistance from the colonial state in obtaining cheap African labor for their farms and estates. The state was all too willing to subsidize settler agriculture in this way, as through the provision of land. This reached a peak at the start of the 1920s, with the implementation of a decree in which the governor ordered state employees to direct Africans to work for settlers and the initiation of the *kipande* (labor certificate) system as a means of labor control. Protest, particularly in Britain, forced the alteration of this policy, called the Labor Circular, but the colonial state continued throughout the 1920s to encourage African men to work for settlers. This mainly took the form of short-term migrant labor or residence on European farms as squatters. However, the impact of the Great Depression altered Kenya's migrant labor system. With settler farmers hard hit by the impact of the depression, the demand for African labor was reduced and state pressure no longer required at past levels. Squatters, in particular, faced increasing settler pressure by the end of the 1930s aimed at removing them and their livestock from the white highlands.

Pressure from settlers formed a part of the broader struggle over production that marked the two decades. The end of World War I found European settler produce (especially coffee and sisal) holding pride of place among Kenya's exports. This caused the colonial state to direct substantial support to European settler production in the immediate postwar years in the form of tariff protection, subsidized railway rates, and provision of infrastructure and extension services in addition to land and labor for the settlers. The postwar depression exposed the folly of ignoring peasant production, as the Kenya economy could not prosper on the strength of settler production alone. Pressed by the Colonial Office, the colonial state turned to what was termed the Dual Policy, which aimed to provide state support and assistance to both settler and peasant production after 1922. Nevertheless, the Dual Policy was never implemented as settler production held pride of place for the remainder of the decade, particularly after the return of a favorable market for settler produce from 1924.

The Great Depression brought an end to the strength of settler production as most settlers and the colonial state itself faced bankruptcy by 1930. The colonial state sought to save settler agriculture by a variety of measures ranging from crop subsidies and a reduction in railway charges to the setting up of a Land Bank to provide loans to European farmers. At the same time, the colonial state sought to stimulate African production for domestic and external markets during the 1930s as a means of saving the colonial economy and the settlers, a course that enjoyed strong support from London. Thus the decade witnessed a greatly expanded role of the state in African agriculture from a determination of crops to be planted to attempts to control the market for African produce. The decade was characterized by the consolidation of the commercialization of peasant production in central and western Kenya in particular while settler farmers continued to pressure the state for protection of their privileged position (e.g., removal of squatter stock from their farms and directing the sale of African grown maize through the settler-controlled marketing cooperative). The state introduced coffee, previously a crop grown exclusively by whites, to African farmers, though on an admittedly minute scale. By 1939 the state's role in African production had expanded dramatically, but the contradiction between peasant and settler production had not been resolved. This and the contestation it provoked continued to characterize Kenya's political economy over the succeeding two decades, just as was the case with land and labor.

ROBERT M. MAXON

Further Reading

Brett, E. A. *Colonialism and Underdevelopment in East Africa*. London: Heinemann, 1973.

Kanogo, T. "Kenya and the Depression, 1929–1939." In *A Modern History of Kenya 1895–1980*, edited by W. R. Ochieng'. Nairobi: Evans Brothers, 1989.

Kitching, G. *Class and Economic Change in Kenya: The Making of an African Petite Bourgeoisie, 1905–1970*. New Haven: Yale University Press, 1980.

Maxon, R. "The Years of Revolutionary Advance, 1920–1929." In *A Modern History of Kenya 1895–1980*, edited by W. R. Ochieng'. Nairobi: Evans Brothers, 1989.

Stichter, S. *Migrant Labour in Kenya: Capitalism and African Response, 1895–1975*. London: Longman, 1982.

Talbott, I. D. "African Agriculture." In *An Economic History of Kenya*, edited by W. R. Ochieng' and R. M. Maxon. Nairobi: East African Educational Publishers, 1992.

Zeleza, T. "The Colonial Labour System in Kenya." In *An Economic History of Kenya*, edited by W. R. Ochieng' and R. M. Maxon. Nairobi: East African Educational Publishers, 1992.

Kenya: Colonial Period: Administration, Christianity, Education, and Protest to 1940

As in many other parts of Africa, the establishment of colonial administration formed the prelude for the spread of Christianity in Kenya. Christian missionaries, such as the Church Missionary Society (CMS), had enjoyed little success prior to the establishment of formal colonial control in 1895. It was only after the conquest and the establishment of a colonial administrative structure that Roman Catholic and Protestant missionary societies gained a foothold. Just as the process of establishing an administrative structure for the protectorate was gradual and incremental, so also was the introduction of Christianity. By the end of the first decade of the twentieth century, colonial control had been established over much of the southern half of Kenya, and missions had gained converts as well in the region under British rule. In those areas in particular, missionaries were pioneers in introducing Western-style education in Kenya. Christians who had experienced Western education became part of a new elite that gained salaried employment with the missions as teachers and pastors, or with the colonial state, as chiefs and clerks, and took the lead in economic innovation.

Moreover, Christians with Western educations played a significant part in the protest movements that emerged to challenge the policies and practices of the colonial state in Kenya prior to 1940 and to demand improved status for themselves within colonial society. Such protest movements, which did not seek an end to colonial rule, but rather reform within the system, came to the fore following the end of World War I and were most active in the areas where the missions had established the largest numbers of schools, namely central Kenya and the Lake Victoria basin. The war and its aftermath produced a number of hardships for Kenya's Africans, including higher taxes and greatly increased demands for labor from the colonial state and the colonial European settlers and for enhanced control over African workers, reduced market opportunities for African produce, and, in central Kenya in particular, heightened insecurity with regard to land. Many Kikuyu in that region had lost access to land as a result of European settlement, and in addition to a demand for the return of those lands, mission-educated men sought to pressure the colonial state so as to ensure their access to, and control over, land in the area reserved for Kikuyu occupation.

Protest emerged first in central Kenya with regard to the land issue. It was articulated by the Kikuyu Association (KA), formed in 1919 by Kikuyu colonial chiefs, and by the Young Kikuyu Association, quickly renamed the East African Association (EAA), formed in 1921 by Harry Thuku and other young Western-educated Kikuyu working in Nairobi, to protest against high taxes, measures initiated by the colonial state to force Africans into wage labor, reduction in wages for those employed, as well as land grievances. The EAA challenged the position of the KA and colonial chiefs as defenders of African interests. The organization had gained sufficient support by March 1922 for the colonial authorities to order Thuku's arrest. The latter produced serious disturbances in Nairobi and led to the banning of the EAA and the detention of Thuku for the remainder of the decade.

Nevertheless, another protest organization soon emerged in central Kenya to champion the interests of educated Christians and challenge the KA. This was the Kikuyu Central Association (KCA), formed in 1924. It was concerned with the land issue (e.g., shortage and insecurity of tenure), but the KCA also took the lead during the interwar decades in demanding a greater voice for its members in local affairs and demanding enhanced access to the means of modernization, including more schools and planting high value cash crops. In western Kenya also, the postwar period witnessed the emergence, during 1921, of a protest organization led by educated Christians in the form of the Young Kavirondo Association (YKA). It also articulated grievances such as increased taxation, low wages, and the oppressive labor policies of the colonial state. As with the KCA, leaders also advocated more schools and greater economic opportunities directly challenging the colonial chiefs as political and economic leaders in their home areas.

In addition to the forceful suppression of the EAA, the colonial administration responded to activities of these protest organizations by some concessions, such as the lowering of taxing and ending officially sanctioned forced labor for European settlers, by the introduction of Local Native Councils in 1924 where educated Africans might play a part, by making sure that such protests were confined to a single ethnic community, and by putting pressure on the missionaries to keep the political activities of their converts under control. In western Kenya, this led to recasting the YKA as the Kavirondo Taxpayers Welfare Association (KTWA) under the leadership of the CMS missionary William Owen, and the KTWA's focusing on welfare activities rather than political protest. The colonial state also co-opted some of the protest leaders; as a result some protest leaders of the 1920s became colonial chiefs by the 1930s.

Nevertheless, Western-educated men continued to take the lead in protest to 1940. As a result, some gained influence within the state structure as well as economic advantages, such as in trade licenses and crop innovation. Overall, however, these protest movements provided no real challenge to the colonial system itself. Such political and economic gains as resulted were limited. Despite consistent advocacy by the KCA, for example, little had been done by 1940 to address the increasingly serious Kikuyu land problem. Thus it is not surprising that after that date, many educated Africans turned to different forms of protest in an attempt to address African grievances and improve living conditions.

Robert M. Maxon

See also: **Thuku, Harry.**

Further Reading

Berman, B. *Control & Crisis in Colonial Kenya: The Dialectic of Domination.* London: James Currey; Nairobi: East African Educational Publishers; and Athens, Ohio: Ohio University Press, 1990.

Clough, M. S. *Fighting Two Sides: Kenyan Chiefs and Politicians, 1918–1940.* Niwot, Colorado: University Press of Colorado, 1990.

Kanogo, T. "Kenya and the Depression." In *A Modern History of Kenya 1895–1980*, edited by W. R. Ochieng.' London and Nairobi: Evans Brothers, 1989.

Maxon, R. M. "The Years of Revolutionary Advance, 1920–1929." In *A Modern History of Kenya 1895–1980*, edited by W. R. Ochieng.' London and Nairobi: Evans Brothers, 1989.

Strayer, R. W. *The Making of Mission Communities in East Africa: Anglicans and Africans in Colonial Kenya, 1875–1935.* London: Heinemann, 1978.

Kenya: Mau Mau Revolt

The Mau Mau peasant revolt in colonial Kenya remains one of the most complex revolutions in Africa. It was one of the first nationalist revolutions against modern European colonialism in Africa. Unlike other subsequent nationalist revolutions in Africa, the Mau Mau revolt was led almost entirely by peasants. The majority of its supporters were illiterate peasants who fought against the British military with courage and determination. Although the revolt was eventually defeated militarily by a combination of British and Loyalist (Home Guard) forces, its impact on the course of African history was significant. It signaled the beginning of the end of European power in Africa and accelerated the pace of the decolonization process.

The roots of the revolt lay in the colonial political economy. The colonization of Kenya by Britain led to the alienation of fertile land for white settlers from peasant farmers in Central Kenya, the home of the Kikuyu. This loss of land and the subsequent proclamation of "native reserves" sealed off possible areas of Kikuyu expansion. There arose a serious land shortage in Central Province that led to the migration of landless Kikuyu peasants to live and work on European settlers' farms as squatters in the Rift valley.

In the Kikuyu reserve, there were social tensions over land as corrupt chiefs and other landed gentry proceeded to acquire land at the expense of varieties of landless peasants. Some of these displaced peasants migrated to the expanding urban areas: Nairobi, Nakuru, and other townships in Central and Rift Valley provinces.

After World War II, there was widespread African unemployment in urban areas, especially in Nairobi. There was inflation and no adequate housing. A combination of these factors led to desperate economic circumstances for Africans who now longed for freedom, self-determination, land, and prosperity. The level of frustration and desperation was increased by the colonial government's refusal to grant political reforms or acknowledge the legitimacy of African nationalism. Even the moderate Kenya Africa Union (KAU) under Jomo Kenyatta failed to win any reforms from the colonial government.

From October 1952 until 1956, the Mau Mau guerillas, based in the forests of Mt. Kenya and the Aberdares and equipped with minimal modern weapons, fought the combined forces of the British military and the Home Guard. Relying on traditional symbols for politicization and recruitment, the Mau Mau guerillas increasingly came to rely on oaths to promote cohesion within their ranks and also to bind them to the noncombatant "passive wing" in the Kikuyu reserve. Throughout the war, the Mau Mau guerillas sought to neutralize "the effects of the betrayers." The guerillas relied heavily on the "passive wing" and hence could not tolerate real or potential resisters to their cause. In order to control the spread of Mau Mau influence, the British military and political authorities instituted an elaborate "villagization policy." Kikuyu peasants in the reserve were put into villages, under the control of the Home Guards. The aim was to deny the guerillas access to information, food, and support. The "villagization policy" led to corruption and brutality toward the ordinary civilian population by the Home Guard, whose actions were rarely challenged by the colonial government so long as they "hunted down Mau Mau." At the end of the war, the colonial government stated that 11,503 Mau Mau and 63 Europeans had been killed. These official figures are "silent on the question of thousands of civilians who were 'shot while attempting to escape' or those who perished at the hands of the Home Guards and other branches of the security forces." It had been a brutal bruising war that was destined to have long-term repercussions in Kenyan society.

The British government's response to the Mau Mau revolt aimed to strategically reinforce the power of the conservative Kikuyu landed gentry while, at the same time, proceeding to dismantle the political power of the resident white settlers. This was achieved through a combination of the rehabilitation process and a gradual accommodation of African political activities and initiatives. The overriding aim of the rehabilitation of former Mau Mau guerillas and sympathizers was to "remake Kenya" by defeating radicalism. Radical individuals detained during the period of the emergency had to renounce the Mau Mau and its aims. This was achieved through a complex and elaborate process of religious indoctrination and psychological manipulation of the detainees.

The Mau Mau revolt forced the British government to institute political and economic reforms in Kenya that allowed for the formation of African political parties after 1955. Most of the former guerillas were not in a position to influence the nature of these reforms nor to draw any substantial benefits from them. The conservative landed gentry who had formed the Home Guard had a significant influence on the post-emergency society. Since the start of counterinsurgency operations, these conservatives and their relatives had been recruited by the police, army, and the civil service. They were best placed to "inherit the state" from the British while the former guerillas and their sympathizers desperately struggled to adjust to the new social, economic, and political forces.

In postcolonial Kenya, the Mau Mau revolt has remained a controversial subject of study and discussion. The failure of the Mau Mau to achieve a military and political triumph has complicated discussions about its legacy. Former guerillas, without power and influence in the postcolonial society, have been unable to "steer the country in any direction that could come close to celebrating the 'glory of the revolt.'" There is controversy over the role that the Mau Mau played in the attainment of Kenya's political freedom. The ruling elite in Kenya have been careful to avoid portraying the revolt as a pivotal event in the struggle for independence. This has been done while continually making vague references to Mau Mau and the blood that was shed in the struggle for independence. Related to this is the emotive issue of the appropriate treatment (and even possible rewards) for former guerrillas.

The rising social and economic tensions in Kenya after 1963 have politicized the legacy of the Mau Mau revolt. Former guerillas have been drawn into the postcolonial struggles for power and preeminence by the ruling elite. The result has been a tendency by many of the former guerillas to adapt their positions to the current political situation. Both the governing conservative elite and the radical leftist opposition have invoked the memory of the revolt to bolster their positions.

WUNYABARI O. MALOBA

Further Reading

Barnett, D., and K. Njama. *Mau Mau From Within.* New York: Monthly Review Press, 1966.

Buijtenhuijs, R. *Essays on Mau Mau.* The Netherlands: African Studies Centre, 1982.

Clayton, A. *Counter Insurgency in Kenya.* Nairobi: Transafrica Publishers, 1976.

Furedi, F. "The Social Composition of the Mau Mau Movement in the White Highlands." *Journal of Peasant Studies.* 1, no. 4 (1974).

Gikoyo, G. G. *We Fought for Freedom.* Nairobi: East African Publishing House, 1979.

Kanogo, T. *Squatters and the Roots of Mau Mau.* London: James Currey; Nairobi: Heinemann Kenya; Athens: Ohio University Press, 1987.

Lonsdale, J., and B. Berman. *Unhappy Valley: Conflict in Kenya and Africa.* London: J. Currey; Narobi: Heinemann Kenya; Athens, Ohio: Ohio University Press, 1992.

Maloba, W. O. *Mau Mau and Kenya.* Bloomington: Indiana University Press, 1993.

Tarmakin, J. "Mau Mau in Nakuru." *Journal of African History.* 17, no. 1 (1976).

wa Thiong'o Ngugi. *Detained.* London: Heinemann, 1981.

Troup, D. W. *Economic and Social Origins of Mau Mau.* Athens, Ohio: Ohio University Press, 1988.

Wachanga, H. K. *The Swords of Kirinyaga.* Nairobi: Kenya Literature Bureau, 1975.

Kenya: Nationalism, Independence

In June 1955 the internal security situation in Kenya had improved sufficiently to enable the government to lift its ban on African political organizations. But colonywide parties remained illegal, and the Kikuyu of Central Province were excluded, except for a nominated Advisory Council of "loyalists." The government hoped that by fostering political participation among Kenya's other African ethnic groups progress would be made by nonviolent means, and some counterbalance to Kikuyu dominance of African politics would be achieved. Equally important, the possibility of "radical" African politics and violent protest being organized at a countrywide level was minimized.

By the end of 1956, as the withdrawal of the last British soldiers on counterinsurgency duty began, so too did registration of African voters for the first African elections to Kenya's Legislative Council (LegCo). Based on the Coutts Report of January 1956, the complicated qualified franchise, and the intricacies of electoral procedure meant that African elections did not take place until March 1957, six months after those for Europeans. The European candidates had been divided into two groups, six seats being won by those who approved of African political participation, against eight won by those who did not, led by settler politicians Michael Blundell and Group Captain Llewellyn Briggs, respectively. But they soon united to consolidate their numerical advantage over the eight newly arriving African Elected Members (AEMs).

Having unseated six of the government-appointed African members and thus assured of their mandate, the AEMs, led by Mboya, had different ideas. They rejected the Lyttelton Constitution as an irrelevancy imposed under emergency conditions, demanded fifteen more African seats, and refused to take ministerial office. The European members recognized that without African participation in government there would be little chance of future stability and agreed that they would accept an increase in African representation. Accordingly, in October, Alan Lennox-Boyd, the secretary of state for colonial affairs, accepted the resignations of the Asian and European ministers. This enabled him to present a new constitution: the AEMs would gain an extra ministry and six more elected seats, giving them parity with the Europeans.

The Africans, including those elected in March 1958, rejected what they saw as the disproportionate influence that the provisions for the elections to special seats left in European hands. Following the largely unsuccessful prosecution of Mboya's group for denouncing as "traitors" the eight Africans who did stand for election to the special seats, in June 1958 Odinga sought to shift the political focus by referring to Kenyatta and others as "leaders respected by the African people" in debate in LegCo. Not to be outdone in associating themselves with this important nationalist talisman, the other African politicians soon followed suit. Thus began the "cult of Kenyatta."

Keen to emulate political advances in recently independent Ghana, the African leaders pressed for a constitutional conference to implement their demands for an African majority in LegCo. Lennox-Boyd refused to increase communal representation, insisting that the Council of Ministers needed more time to prove itself. In January 1959, as the colonial secretary and the East African governors met in England to formulate a "gradualist" timetable for independence (Kenya's date being "penciled in" as 1975) the AEMs announced a boycott of LegCo. With the prospect that the two Asian members of the government would join the AEMs, undermining the veneer of multiracialism, Governor Baring demanded a statement of Britain's ultimate intentions for Kenya. Lennox-Boyd responded in April, announcing that there should be a conference before the next Kenya general election in 1960.

But in order for the conference to take place (scheduled for January 1960) with African participation, the state of emergency had to be lifted. By the time this occurred, on January 12, 1960, the Kenya government had enacted a preservation of public security bill that, beside enabling the continued detention and restriction of the Mau Mau "residue," and measures to preempt subversion, deal with public meetings, and seditious publications, also empowered the governor to exercise controls over colonywide political associations in accordance with his "judgement of the needs of law and order." This was not simply a political expedient. The defeat of Mau Mau led the Kenya government's Internal Security Working Committee to conclude in February 1958 that future challenges to stability would take the form of "strikes, civil disobedience, sabotage, and the dislocation of transport and supplies rather than armed insurrection." An Economic Priorites Committee "to study supply problems in such an eventuality" had been set up in April 1957; that same year saw some 4,000-plus strikes of varying intensity, and Mboya made frequent threats that if African demands for increased representation were not met, "the results would be far worse than anything Mau Mau produced."

Kiama Kia Muingi (KKM), or "Council/Society of the People," which emerged from the Mau Mau "passive wing" in March 1955, became so widespread, and too closely resembled Mau Mau, that it was proscribed in January 1958. Only political solutions to Africans' grievances were to be allowed. But, by December 1958, Special Branch had discovered contacts between KKM and Mboya's Nairobi Peoples' Convention Party. Only by the end of 1959, following a concerted campaign of repression, did the "KKM crisis" appear to be resolved. As a precaution, however, Britain took the unprecedented step of resuming War Office control of the East African Land Forces, thereby removing the military from "local political interference." The measure was announced at the constitutional conference and presented as a means of freeing up local revenue for development projects.

At the January 1960 Lancaster House Conference, the African delegates presented a united front, the result of collaboration since November. Again, the Africans pressed, unsuccessfully, for Kenyatta' s release. The outcome of the conference and subsequent negotiations was the concession by Iain Macleod of an effective African majority in LegCo, plus an increase in the number of Africans with ministerial responsibility. But the fissures in the African front resurfaced over the issue of whether to accept office, Mboya rejecting the constitution as "already out of date." By June 1960 the two major pre-independence political parties had been formed: the Kenya African National Union (KANU), principally Kikuyu, Luo, Embu, Meru, Kamba, and Kisii orientated, which boycotted the government, and the Kenya African Democratic Union (KADU), representing an alliance of the Kalenjin, Maasai, and Coast peoples.

In the February 1961 general election KANU won 67 per cent of the vote but refused to take its place in the government without Kenyatta's release, leaving KADU to form a coalition with Blundell's New Kenya Party and the Kenya Indian Congress. But the expansion of yet another Kikuyu subversive movement, the Kenya Land Freedom Army (KLFA)—many members of which also carried KANU membership cards—led the governor, Sir Patrick Renison, to press Macleod to reverse his decision on Kenyatta. It would be better, Special Branch advised, to release Kenyatta and gauge the impact of his return to Kenyan politics on the security situation while Britain was still "in control."

Although the African politicians had used "land hunger" and the presence (since 1958) of a British military base as political sticks with which to beat the colonial authorities over the issue of "sovereignty," a further constitutional conference in September 1961 broke down over access to the "White Highlands" because KADU rejected KANU's proposals for a strong central government, favoring instead a *majimbo* (regional) constitution. The "framework constitution," settled in London in February 1962, provided in principle for regional assemblies, and appeared to ameliorate tensions. But the coalition government, formed in April 1962, served as a thin veil over KADU-KANU ethnic tensions. The KLFA had spread: its oaths became increasingly violent; "military drills" were reported; over 200 precision weapons and homemade guns had been seized; and civil war seemed imminent.

It was no mere coincidence that, within weeks of KANU's June 1, 1963, electoral victory, and Kenyatta becoming prime minister and appointing an ethnically mixed government, the British Cabinet agreed to December 12, 1963, as the date for Kenya's independence. The apparent desire of the three East African governments to form a federation meant that to maintain its goodwill, and for procedural reasons, Britain could no longer prohibit Kenya's independence.

But the prospects for a federation soon collapsed and civil war seemed likely. At the final constitutional conference in September, Sandys therefore backed KANU's proposed amendments to the constitution, making it easier to reverse regionalism at a later date, as the best means to prevent chaos.

Nevertheless, on October 18, 1963, Britain began to make preparations to introduce troops into Kenya for internal security operations and the evacuation of Europeans. The victory of the "moderates" in the KADU parliamentary group and the defection of four KADU members to KANU a week later seem, on the face of it, to have been enough to ensure a peaceful transition to independence.

DAVID A. PERCOX

See also: **Kenya: Kenyatta, Jomo: Life and Government of.**

Further Reading

Kyle, K. *The Politics of the Independence of Kenya.* London: Macmillan, and New York: St. Martin's Press, 1999.

Percox, D. A. "Internal Security and Decolonization in Kenya, 1956–1963." *Journal of Imperial and Commonwealth History* [forthcoming].

———. "British Counter-Insurgency in Kenya, 1952–56: Extension of Internal Security Policy or Prelude to Decolonisation?" *Small Wars and Insurgencies.* 9, no. 3 (Winter. 1998): 46–101.

Tignor, R. L. *Capitalism and Nationalism at the End of Empire: State and Business in Decolonizing Egypt, Nigeria, and Kenya, 1945–1963.* Princeton: Princeton University Press, and Chichester, 1998.

Kenya: Kenyatta, Jomo: Life and Government of

Jomo Kenyatta (*c.*1894–1978) was born in Gatundu, Kiambu district, probably in 1894. His childhood was quite difficult due to the death of his parents. Early on, he moved to Muthiga where his grandfather lived.

Muthiga was close to the Church of Scotland's Thogoto mission. Missionaries preached in the village and when Kamau (Kenyatta's original name) became sick, he was treated in the mission hospital. Mesmerized by people who could read, he enrolled in the mission school. He accepted Christianity and was baptized Johnstone.

Leaving Thogoto in 1922, he was employed by the Municipal Council of Nairobi as a stores clerk and meter reader. The job gave him ample opportunity to travel extensively within the municipality. The allowed him to interact with his African peers, as well as Indians and Europeans. With his motorcycle, a novelty at the time, and wearing a beaded belt (*kinyata*) and big hats, he became a familiar figure in the municipality. Moreover, he established a grocery shop at Dagoretti, which became a meeting place for the young African elite.

Becoming acutely aware of the plight of Africans, he decided to throw his lot with the Kikuyu Central Association (KCA). He became its secretary general at the beginning of 1928 and editor of its newspaper, *Muiguithania* (The Reconciler). The future of Kenya was also being hotly debated in the 1920s, with Indians being pitted against the settler community. European settlers demanded responsible government, restriction of Indian immigration into Kenya, upholding of racial discrimination, and the creation of a federation of the East and Central African British colonies. Under these circumstances, the African voice needed to be heard. KCA decided to send an emissary to England for this purpose. Kamau became their choice due to his charisma, eloquence, and education. By then, he had assumed the name Jomo Kenyatta.

Kenyatta went to England in 1929–1930 and made presentations to the Colonial Office and other interested parties. The British government appointed the Carter Land Commission to investigate the land problem that had become the bane of Kenya's political life. Again KCA dispatched Kenyatta to London in 1931, where he remained until 1946.

Life in London provided Kenyatta with many opportunities for self-improvement. He enrolled at the London School of Economics to study anthropology. He traveled widely across Europe. He met with the African diaspora in Britain, gave public lectures, and wrote to newspapers about the inequities of the colonial system. He also found the time to write his major work on the Kikuyu, *Facing Mount Kenya* (published 1938).

The peak event of his time in Britain was probably his participation in the Pan-African Congress in Manchester in 1945. The participants committed themselves to fighting for the independence of their respective countries.

Upon returning to Kenya in 1946, he immediately became president of the Kenya African Union (KAU), which had been formed in the same year. His return initiated a new era in Kenyan politics. Here was a man who had lived in Britain for fifteen years and married a white woman, Edna Clarke. To many Kenyans, Kenyatta knew the white man's secrets and would use this knowledge to liberate them from the colonial yoke. His tour of the rural areas to popularize KAU attracted huge crowds.

As the clamor for *uhuru* (independence) gained momentum, two camps emerged within KAU. Kenyatta was a constitutionalist, while a faction of younger, more radically minded members, advocated for armed struggle. They began to prepare for a war of liberation by recruiting others into their movement, called the Land and Freedom Army, although it soon acquired the name Mau Mau. Initially, recruitment was through persuasion but increasingly it was carried out by force. Hence, violence escalated, and the colonial government declared a state of emergency on October 20, 1952, after the murder of Chief Waruhiu Kungu in broad daylight. Kenyatta, together with ninety-seven KAU leaders, were arrested. KAU leadership was accused of managing Mau Mau, a terrorist organization. Kenyatta was convicted, in what turned out to be a rigged trial, and jailed for seven years. He was interned in Lodwar and Lokitaung, in the remotest corners of Kenya. His release came only in 1961, after a swell of national and international outcry against his detention.

By 1956 the British and local military forces, supported by Kikuyu Guards, had contained Mau Mau. Nevertheless, Britain was forced to assess its role in Kenya and begin to meet some of the African demands. A series of constitutional changes were mounted and African representation in the Legislative Council gradually increased. Furthermore, the ban on political parties was lifted from 1955, albeit at the district level. These amalgamated in 1960 into the Kenya African National Union (KANU) and the Kenya African Democratic Union (KADU). The former was predominantly supported by the Kikuyu and Luo, while the latter attracted the smaller tribes, such as the Kalenjin and the coastal peoples.

Upon his release, Kenyatta unsuccessfully tried to reconcile the leaders of the two parties. He eventually joined KANU, becoming its president. KANU and KADU engaged in protracted constitutional negotiations centered on whether Kenya should be a federal or centralized state. Eventually KADU, which espoused federalism, was victorious. A semifederal system, *majimbo*, was accepted. In 1963 general elections were held which KANU won, ushering Kenya into independence on December 12, 1963, under Kenyatta's leadership (he was named president in 1964).

Kenyatta's government faced enormous problems. The formation of KANU and KADU was a glaring manifestation of tribalism, which threatened to tear Kenya apart as had happened to Congo. The economy was under the control of expatriates. It was also in shambles due to the flight of capital. There was rampant unemployment aggravated by landlessness. There were few well-trained and experienced indigenous Kenyans to man the civil service.

From the outset, Kenyatta preached the gospel of reconciliation and urged all Kenyans, irrespective of tribe, race, or color, to join together to work for the collective good. Thus he coined the national motto, *Harambbee* (pull together). In this regard, he encouraged KADU to disband, which it did in 1964, its supporters joining KANU. This reduced tribal tensions but produced an unexpected development. There emerged ideological divisions within KANU: a pro-Western wing that believed in capitalism, and a pro-Eastern cohort that sought to align Kenya with socialist countries. The former was led by Kenyattta and T. J. Mboya while the latter was led by Oginga Odinga, the vice president. This culminated in the ousting of Odinga as vice president in 1966. He then formed his own party, the Kenya Peoples Union, which was predominantly supported by the Luo.

To consolidate his position, Kenyatta embarked on a series of constitutional changes. He scrapped the *majimbo* constitution and increased the power of the presidency, including the power to commit individuals to detention without trial. He also increasingly relied on the provincial administration for managing government affairs and this led to the decline of KANU and parliament. So long as his authority and power were not challenged, he tolerated some measure of criticism and debate.

He eschewed the socialist policies that were in vogue in much of Africa. He vigorously wooed investors and courted the Western world. His policies paid dividends in that the economy grew by more than 6 per cent during his time in office. In late 1970s, this rate of growth contracted due to the vagaries of the world economy, such as the oil crisis of 1973–1974. Equally, he made efforts to indigenize the economy by establishing bodies that offered assistance to Kenyans. These include the Industrial and Commercial Development Corporation, Kenya National Trading Corporation, and Kenya Industrial Estates, among others. This assistance has a produced a class of local entrepreneurs that is playing a significant role in the Kenyan economy.

Critical to the survival of Kenya was the problem of squatters and ex-Mau Mau. In order to gain their support, the government settled them and the squatters in former settler-owned farms. In the first ten years, 259,000 hectares of land were bought and distributed to 150,000 landless people, who were also provided with development loans and infrastructure.

Kenyatta's government abolished racial discrimination in schools, introduced curricula and exams in secondary schools to prepare children for university entrance, and made efforts to increase the number of Kenyans in universities, both local and overseas. For example, between early 1960s and late 1970s university and secondary students increased from 1,900 to 8,000 and 30,000 to 490,000 respectively. And adult literacy jumped from 20 per cent to 50 per cent in the same period.

Kenyatta died on August 22, 1978. By then, he had provided Kenya with peace and stability for fifteen years. In a continent ravaged by war and coups, this was no small achievement. But one should not ignore the fact that corruption started to show its ugly face during his term. He relied heavily on his kinsmen, a factor that fuelled tribalism. He had fought very hard for freedom and yet became an autocrat, albeit a benign one. Few can deny that he laid a firm foundation for Kenya. He is thus referred to as *mzee* (respected elder) or Father of the Nation. In short, he was an exceptionally formidable and complex man.

GODFREY MURIUKI

Biography

Born Gatundu, Kiambu district, about 1894. Named secretary general of the Kikuyu Central Association (KCA), and editor of its newspaper, *Muiguithania* (The Reconciler), 1928. Goes to England, 1929–30. Returns the following year. Publishes *Facing Mount Kenya*, 1938. Participates in the Pan-African Congress in Manchester, 1945. Returns to Kenya, named president of the Kenya African Union, 1946. Convicted for the murder of Chief Waruhiu Kungu, 1952. Released due to national and international pressures, 1961. Named first president of Kenya, 1964. Died on August 22, 1978.

Further Reading

Barkan, J. D. "The Rise and Fall of a Governance Realm in Kenya." In *Governance and Politics in Africa*, edited by G. Hyden and M. Bratton. Boulder, Colo.: Lynne Rienner Publishers, 1992.

Kenyatta, J. *Suffering Without Bitterness*. Nairobi: Government Printer, 1968.

Murray-Brown, J. *Kenyatta*. London: Allen and Unwin, 1972.

Widner, J. A. *The Rise of a Party-State in Kenya: From 'Harambee' to 'Nyayo'*. Berkeley: University of California Press, 1992.

Kenya: Independence to the Present

At the attainment of independence in 1963, Kenya inherited an economy that was symptomatic of most African colonial economies: a predominantly agricultural economy, a manufacturing sector whose cornerstone was import-substitution financed by foreign capital, and a transport infrastructure that was insensitive to the internal economic needs of the majority of the population. In the social arena, literacy levels were fairly low and disease patrolled the majority of households.

The government of Kenya under the first head of state, Jomo Kenyatta (1963–1978), cogently identified and declared war on the three major enemies of economic development in postindependence Kenya: illiteracy, disease, and poverty. Sessional Paper No. 10 of 1965, titled "African Socialism and Its Application to Planning in Kenya," was promulgated as the government's blueprint for eradicating poverty, raising literacy levels, and providing health care services to the citizenry. But Sessional Paper No. 10 was more than just an economic document. It had the political taint of the Cold War era, when socialism and capitalism were struggling for economic and political space in the countries that were emerging from the womb of colonialism. Thus, besides its economic agenda, the document was also meant to appease both the radical and moderate wings of the ruling party, Kenya African National Union (KANU), by emphasizing private and government investment, the provision of free primary education as well as health care services.

Between 1963 and 1973 Kenya witnessed the smooth expansion of African-owned businesses as well as the growth of smallholder peasant agriculture, particularly in foreign exchange earning crops such as coffee and tea. Since 1967 smallholder production has invariably made up more than 50 per cent of Kenya's coffee output. While in 1964–1965 there were 22,343 growers of coffee with a total 5,133 hectares (12,684 acres); by 1987–1988 the number of growers had increased to 151,860 with the number of hectares having jumped to 57,688 (142,550 acres). This marked growth of smallholder peasant agriculture was evident in other crops such as sugar, cotton, and tobacco as well. Out of these developments in the agricultural sector, the cooperative movement became a significant instrument in handling the processing and marketing of cash crops. In sum, the GDP growth rate in the 1964–1974 period stood at an average of 6.60 per cent. But this economic growth was also a function of the political and economic developments in the region of eastern Africa.

Kenya benefited from flawed economic policies of the neighboring countries: Tanzania and Uganda. In Tanzania mass nationalization of private companies and banks scared away foreign investors. The policy of "villagization" in the rural areas also adversely affected the development of agriculture in Tanzania. Uganda, particularly under Idi Amin Dada, instituted the policy of indigenization that led to confiscation of Asian property. Amin's rule resulted in the breakdown of law and order in Uganda. These regional economic and political developments left Kenya as the only premier nation in the eastern African region with a sound economic policy as well as political stability to attract foreign investment.

However, the Kenya of the 1990s was quite a different political and economic terrain from that of the 1963 to 1974 period. After the economic prosperity of the first decade, Kenya faced a number of political and economic challenges, both from within and outside, that resulted in widespread poverty in a country that at the time of independence had the most developed economic infrastructure in the eastern African region and one of the most often cited as a showcase of economic success. With a population of about 30 million, the 1997–2001 Kenya National Development Plan put the level of absolute poverty in rural areas at 46.4 per cent, while the rate in the urban areas was estimated at 29.3 per cent. These official figures show that 75 per cent of the Kenyan population live in poverty. The GDP growth rate has been on the decline since 1974. While in the subsequent two decades, the GDP was at an average of 5.20 and 4.10 per cent, respectively, between 1994 and 1999 the country has witnessed an average growth rate of 2.50 per cent.

The causes of this decline are many, varied, and complex. The quadrupling of oil price in 1973; inflation in the developed countries and the accompanying high interest; the heavy borrowing of the 1970s; the unfavorable terms of trade; widespread corruption; internal political instability, particularly the ethnic conflicts that coincided with political multipartyism in the early 1990s which adversely affected the tourist industry; and the World Bank and IMF policies, particularly the structural adjustment programs, have in one way or another contributed to the current state of economic decline. The economic challenges of the 1990s are closely tied to the developmental as well as political policies that have been pursued since independence.

In industry and manufacturing, for example, the government used high tariffs and import licensing to encourage investment in the import-substitution industries. While this strategy yielded some success, it denied export promotion a viable economic space and stifled competition through protectionist policies. By the mid-1970s, all was not well in sections of the tariff-protected import substitution industries because they used more foreign exchange than they generated. As the pressure from the World Bank and International Monetary Fund intensified in the 1980s with the Kenyan leadership being advised to warm up to a competitiveness in the manufacturing sector and exit the industrial protectionist strategy, the industries began to feel the pinch brought on by the more open import liberalization regime. Company closures, retrenchment, and the state's forced retreat from subsidizing social programs such as education, and health care services have coalesced to force many people into the poverty trap.

The repayment of the national debt against the economic backdrop of the structural adjustment programs has been a painful experience. Due to widespread corruption, which started during the Kenyatta presidency and reached its apogee in the Moi era, international loans were spent on programs that did not benefit the poor. The loans were directed to private projects benefiting government officials and a small elite. By the late 1980s, the repayment of the debt was a burden borne by poor people, who did not have a voice in contracting the debt, but who bore the consequences of repaying it. The problem is not so much the size of the debt as the huge share of a country's income it takes to service it. In this regard, Kenya's case mirrors that of many other countries in Africa grappling with the challenges of economic growth, indebtedness, and the search for economic and political stability in the wake of structural adjustment programs and the resurgence of political pluralism. Of the forty heavily indebted poor countries identified by the World Bank and the International Monetary Fund (IMF) in 1996, thirty-two are located in Sub-Saharan Africa.

But the problem of economic development is also a function of politics and governance. Although Kenya's economy under the presidency of Jomo Kenyatta was quite healthy, it was deeply enmeshed in the cobweb of ethnicity, nepotism, and regional preferences. Nowhere is this manifested as in the case of land settlement schemes in the immediate postindependence era. Land has been a critical factor in Kenya's politics as well as economic development dating back to the onset of colonial governance. It was at the very heart of the Mau Mau revolt. In the post-independence period, it has been one of the major divisive issues whose repercussion has on occasions been expressed in bitter ethnic conflicts leading to death of thousands and displacement of many more over the last decade.

With funds provided by Great Britain at independence, the government of Kenya bought out European planters and then subdivided the land into relatively smaller portions, which were then sold to an emergent African elite who were provided with loans at low rates of interest, or turned to settlement schemes for the landless. On the positive side, the government's handling of land ensured smooth transition from the era of large-scale planters to the epoch of a majority small peasant holdings. It is this smooth transition that partly explains the expansion and economic vibrancy of the small-scale peasant holdings in Kenya. Through settlement schemes, hundreds of thousands of landless people were settled in various parts of the country, particularly in the Rift Valley, Central, Coast, and to some extent parts of Nyanza and Western provinces.

While the Jomo Kenyatta regime sought to distribute land, it became quite evident that the distribution of land to the landless Africans was not based on need alone. In fact, ethnicity was a major determinant. The "Africanization" of the former European settled areas was, by and large, reduced to the "Kikuyunization" of those lands with the members of the Kikuyu ethnic group being given large chunks of land in the Rift valley, with the tacit approval of the then vice president Daniel Arap Moi, a Kalenjin, and much to the chagrin of the local communities. Kenyatta, a Kikuyu, also appointed members of his ethnic group to key positions in the government, as well as parastatals. These policies that accorded ethnicity and patronage a pride of place in the allocation of resources resulted in the marginalization of most ethnic groups, regions and those who questioned the economic and political iniquities of the Kenyatta regime.

Kenyatta, while allowing regular presidential and National Assembly elections, was quite reluctant to allow competitive multiparty politics. In his last few years in office, he nurtured authoritarian tendencies that saw critics of his regime detained without trial. Under Kenyatta, Kenya became a de facto one-party state after the banning of the Kenya People's Union in 1969. Moi's first few years in office after his accession to power in 1978 was quite promising. He released all political detainees and prisoners, focused on an all-inclusive government, and exhibited populist policies that endeared him to the majority of the population, at least in the short run.

But behind these official exhibitions of compassion, openness, politics of inclusion, and populism, Moi, like his predecessor, Kenyatta, silently embarked on empowering his Kalenjin ethnic group. Internal dissent intensified leading to the 1982 abortive coup attempt by a section of the armed forces. Within a decade of his accession to power, Moi had presided over the making of Kenya a de jure one-party state, compromising of the independence of the judiciary and the legislature, unprecedented corruption, and decline of the economy. As the decade ending 1989 wore on, Moi was under intense political and economic pressure, both from within and outside, to allow multipartyism and embrace economic reforms on the pain of losing economic aid. Moi reluctantly succumbed to the pressure and presided over the repeal of the de jure one-party clause in the constitution and allowed multipartyism much to the chagrin of his close political and economic cohorts.

On the eve of the multiparty elections of 1992, ethnic clashes erupted in the Rift Valley, Nyanza, and Coast provinces aimed at the so-called non-indigenous people who would tilt the election in favor of a candidate from one of the major ethnic groups. Moi had presented himself as the only viable candidate who would protect the interests of the minority ethnic groups. In fact, the strategies of divide and rule and scare tactics have been the most portent and indispensable weapons of Moi's presidency and political survival. A parliamentary commission of inquiry into the clashes implicated the government. In the two multiparty elections conducted in 1992 and 1997, Moi emerged the victor because of a divided opposition. Although Moi was reelected in 1997 to serve his last term as the president of Kenya, he had to contend with two major challenges: economic stagnation and agitation for constitutional reform. Most international creditors remained reluctant to release aid because of the massive corruption in the country. The government's poverty eradication schemes failed to yield meaningful results. As a result, the unemployment rate spiraled and poverty continued to afflict the majority of the population.

In the midst of the foregoing economic problems, agitation for constitutional reform intensified with the civil society calling for drastic changes aimed at strengthening institutions as well as devolving powers from the office of the president. Moi reluctantly acceded to the demands, and after lengthy negotiations, a constitutional review commission was established under the leadership of Y. P. Ghai. Meanwhile, Moi proceeded to reorganize the ruling party, both with a view to identifying a potential successor as well as ensuring that the KANU emerged victorious in the 2002 general election. To further these two objectives Moi's KANU merged with National Development Party (NDP) led by a leading opposition politician, Raila Amolo Odinga in early 2002. KANU was transformed into a formidable political party destined to win the general election. But that was not to be. Moi's open and active support for Uhuru Kenyatta, son of the first president of Kenya, to be the KANU's nominee as the party's presidential candidate split the party.

Raila Odinga and other leading party officials, including Joseph Kamotho, Kalonzo Musyoka, and George Saitoti led those who disagreed with Moi, over the undemocratic way he settled on Uhuru Kenyatta as the preferred party's candidate, to decamp from KANU. They joined the Liberal Democratic Party (LDP), which Raila Odinga transformed into a major political party within a relatively short period of time. On the eve of the 2002 general election, LDP forged an alliance with the National Alliance of Kenya (NAK) led by Mwai Kibaki, Michael Kijana Wamalwa, and Charity Ngilu. The two parties formed the National Rainbow Coalition (NARC) and signed a memorandum of understanding (MOU) in which they agreed on a power-sharing formula as well as common election platform, which included completing the constitutional review within the first one hundred days in office, providing free primary education, eradicating corruption, stimulating economic growth, creating jobs, and enhancing national unity. To show unity of purpose, NARC leadership nominated Mwai Kibaki as its presidential candidate. NARC emerged victorious in the 2002 election, with LDP faction bringing in more votes and members of parliament than NAK, thereby ending nearly four decades of KANU rule. Moi handed over power peacefully to Mwai Kibaki.

NARC's victory under the leadership of Kibaki ushered in an era of optimism and expectation. International creditors expressed willingness to provide aid. The implementation of free primary education by the new NARC government convinced the people that the government was committed to its pre-election pledges. However, the hope, expectation, and goodwill that NARC victory brought began to wane barely after six months of Kibaki's presidency. The unwillingness on the part of the leadership to implement some of the election promises such as completing the constitutional review exercise within the promised time period, slow pace at which anticorruption campaign was being waged, use of ethnicity as a basis of appointing people to key positions in the civil service and reluctance to honor the MOU combined to dim the hope and expectation of Kenyans. Internal squabbles gained momentum with the LDP wing of NARC led by Raila Odinga demanding radical changes in governmental structure, immediate completion of the constitutional review and creation of the office of prime minister, full implementation of the MOU, and an aggressive anticorruption campaign. In contrast, the NAK faction insisted on effecting minimal reforms and suspending the radical reorganization of governmental structure until after the next general election scheduled for 2007. The postelection intracoalition conflict bedeviling NARC is instructive of the dilemma African leaders face in forging viable and working political coalitions based on clear and defined ideology of governance, the absence of which encourages nepotism, ethnicity, and regionalism.

GEORGE ODUOR NDEGE

See also: **Mboya, Tom J.**

Further Reading

Anyang', P. Nyong'o, and P. Coughlin, eds. *Industrialization at Bay: African Experiences.* Nairobi: African Academy of Sciences, 1991.

Anyang', P. Nyong'o, ed. *30 Years of Independence in Africa: The Lost Decades*? Nairobi: Academy Science Publishers, 1992

Haugerud, A. *The Culture of Politics in Modern Kenya.* New York: Cambridge University Press, 1996.

Human Rights Watch/Africa. *Divide and Rule: State Sponsored Ethnic Violence in Kenya.* New York: Human Rights Watch, 1993.

Maxon, R. M., and P. Ndege. "The Economics of Structural Adjustment." In *Decolonization and Independence in Kenya, 1940–1993*, edited by B. A. Ogot and W. R. Ochieng' Athens, Ohio: Ohio University Press, 1995, London: James Currey, 1995

Ochieng', W. R. "Independent Kenya, 1963–1986." In *A Modern History of Kenya*, edited by W. R. Ochieng'. Nairobi: Evans Brothers, 1989.

Odhiambo, E. S. A. "Reconditioning the Terms of Fact: Ethnicity, Nationalism, and Democracy as Political Vectors." In *Ethnicity, Nationalism and Democracy in Africa*, edited by B. A. Ogot. Maseno, Kenya, IRPS, 1997.

Ogot, B. A. "Transition from Single-Party to Multiparty System, 1989–1993." In *Decolonization and Independence in Kenya, 1940–1993,* edited by B. A. Ogot and W. R. Ochieng'. Athens, Ohio: Ohio University Press, 1995; London: James Currey, 1995.

Van Der Hoeven, R., and F. Van Der Kraal, eds. *Structural Adjustment and Beyond in Sub-Saharan Africa.* London: James Currey, 1994.

Kenya: Islam

The story of Islam in Kenya is venerable one. The islands of the Lamu archipelago appear to have harbored some of the earliest discovered Muslim communities in Sub-Saharan Africa. Furthermore, Islamic scholarship, both in Arabic and Swahili, reached notably high levels at Pate and Lamu, and it was from there that a new, more literate, brand of coastal Islam radiated southward during the seventeenth–nineteenth centuries. Immigrant Arab ulama (Muslim scholars) from southern Arabia largely were transmitters of this new scholarship.

Coastal Kenya met with fresh external influences in the nineteenth century. Scholars from Barawa introduced new methods at Siyu in the 1840s and trained a new generation of local Swahili shaykhs able to compete successfully with dynasties of Arab ulama who had monopolized scholarship until then. In addition, Somali shaykhs helped popularize Islamic teaching through the Qadiriyya brotherhood. Due to opposition from the influential Mazrui shaykhs, however, the Qadiriyya largely skipped Pate, Lamu, and Mombasa and experienced more success in Zanzibar and along the Tanzanian and Mozambique coasts.

The nineteenth century also witnessed significant penetration of Islam inland for the first time, though this success was notably less decided in Kenya than farther south due to the relative failure of the brotherhoods there. Rather, other developments accounted for this in the case of Kenya. By the 1840s and 1850s, coastal Muslims were brought into more frequent and intense contact with non-Muslims of the immediate coastal hinterland. The general cause was the expanding economy of East Africa, but the immediate reasons included growing agricultural production and expanded trade. New farming areas, including some slave plantations, were opened around the Shimoni Peninsula, Gasi, Mombasa, Takaungu, Malindi, and the Pokomo Valley. Muslim trading posts appeared among the Mijikenda by mid-century and later. The result of these expanded contacts by the third quarter of the century has been termed "rural Islamization." As Muslims advanced inland among traditionally non-Muslim peoples, conversions occurred individually and for a wide variety of reasons. However, much of this had to do with the growing presence of Muslim teachers who proselytized and taught useful new literary skills.

By the 1860s and 1870s, caravan trade for ivory became a more crucial factor linking coastal Muslims and peoples of the farther interior. Two major routes developed in Kenya. One was up the Pokomo Valley. The second went inland from Mombasa to Mt. Kilimanjaro or Kamba country; from thence it traversed the Rift Valley to the region east and north of Lake Victoria. Slowly, settlements of Muslims appeared along these routes. The most important was at Mumia's in northwestern Kenya, but others appeared at locations like Machakos, Kitui, Baringo, and Eldama Ravine.

The absence of an official policy toward Islam during the colonial era initially fostered its continued success upcountry. In the early days of colonial rule, Muslims were favored for posts as government agents. Early administrators like Arthur Hardinge thought coastal "Arabs" to be more "civilized" than other Kenyans, so many (especially Sudanese) were employed as soldiers in the "pacification" of inland areas. Afterward, others were employed at administrative centers as policemen, clerks, translators, surveyors, tax collectors, and headmen. The prestige attached to these positions in the eyes of local peoples provided fertile soil for proselytization by the individuals who filled them.

By the twentieth century, however, Islamization in Kenya lost its earlier momentum. The causes of this were the greater prestige attached to Christianity as the religion of the colonial masters and the specific role played by missionary Christianity. As most Kenyans quickly realized, the key to advancement in the new order was education, and the Christian missions largely were the providers of that key. In many cases, a pre-requisite to admission to schools was conversion, but even where it was not, Muslims, fearing conversion of their children, refused to send them to these schools. Inevitably, Muslims were left behind and were replaced in most positions by mission-trained Africans.

Such marginalization has continued in the postindependence era. The wealthiest and most influential members of Kenya's elite are those who have benefited most from Western-style educations. Generally, this has meant those who are Christians. At times, ethnicity and regionalism have been factors weighing against Muslim advancement, particularly coastal Muslims. The Kenyatta regime favored Kikuyus, most of whom were Christian and educated. President Moi has downplayed ethnicity, but until 1992 all members of his cabinet were Christians with Western-style educations.

Over the years, Kenyan Muslims themselves have been splintered in responding to these challenges. Some, like Shaykhs al-Amin Ali Mazrui, Abdallah Saleh Farsy, and, more recently, Nasoro Khamisi, have tried to reconcile Islamic teaching with the requirements of modern life. Their efforts against saint veneration, costly burial rites, and other innovations have aroused opposition from the Jamal al-Layl shaykhs of Lamu's Riyadha Institute. The coastal ulama also have experienced increased challenges of leadership from upcountry, non-Swahili shaykhs in the past two decades. This appears to have been due partly to efforts by the government to divide the Muslims of Kenya.

Since the late twentieth century, there has been a growing radicalization of Muslims all over East Africa. Some local shaykhs have received training in Saudi universities and have returned exhibiting a greater awareness of international Islam and its dilemmas. Some have expressed open sympathy with the Iranian revolution. Preaching by such individuals has helped galvanize Kenyan Muslims into greater political awareness, especially over issues of concern to the entire community (such as the reaction that followed passage of the Law of Succession). Widespread opposition to KANU and the return to multiparty politics in 1992 allowed the creation of the Islamic Party of Kenya to give a voice to community concerns in national politics for the first time. The government countered, however, by refusing to recognize the IPK and to support a rival party, the United Muslims of Africa. Relations between Kenyan Muslims and the government have continued deteriorating in the aftermath of the bombing of the United States Embassy by Islamic terrorists in August 1998.

RANDALL L. POUWELS

See also: **Religion, Postcolonial Africa: Islam.**

Further Reading

Anderson, J. N. D. *Islamic Law in Africa*. London: Cass, 1970.

Chande, A. "Radicalism and Reform in Modern East Africa." In *The History of Islam in Africa*, edited by N. Levtzion and R. L. Pouwels. Athens, Ohio University Press, forthcoming.

Sperling, D. "The East African Hinterland and Interior." In *The History of Islam in Africa*, edited by N. Levtzion and R. L. Pouwels. Athens, Ohio University Press, forthcoming.

Strobel, M. *Muslim Women in Mombasa, 1890–1975*. New Haven: Yale University Press, 1979.

Kérékou, Mathieu: *See* Benin, Republic of (Dahomey): Kérékou, Mathieu.

Kerma and Egyptian Nubia

The roots of the Kerma culture extend back into the late Predynastic period in Upper Nubia at least north of the Debba Bend, contemporaneous with the later (Classic and Terminal) phases of A-Group culture in Lower Nubia. Little evidence for its continuity has yet been found, but what there is indicates a social and political development of fewer but larger "statelets" and small "kingdoms." Egyptian control over Lower Nubia during the Old Kingdom (which effectively erased all traces of the A-Group) allowed it to trade directly with the "Pre-Kerma" peoples who controlled the Upper Nubian Nile corridor. At the type site and probable capital of Kerma itself, just south of the Third Cataract, a major and densely populated "Pre-Kerma" settlement with circular houses up to 5 meters in diameter was revealed directly beneath the Middle Kerma period cemetery.

In the absence of written Kerma texts and with only a few Egyptian records, four developmental phases of the Kerma culture are recognized archaeologically through ceramic typology. The Early, Middle, Classic, and Late (or Post-) Kerma periods correspond roughly in Egypt to the late Old Kingdom and First Intermediate period, the Middle Kingdom, the Second Intermediate period, and finally the brief final phase in early Dynasty XVIII. The history of Kerma still must be viewed in relation to Egyptian history: power and control alternated between the two and was dominated by their need to control the river traffic in trade goods, and the gold mines of the Wadi Allaqi in the eastern desert were exploited first by Egypt in the Old Kingdom. The Nile was still, at this time, much farther east than today.

By the end of the Old Kingdom, a recognizable "Early Kerma" culture is visible archaeologically from the Batn el-Hajar at least as far south as the Debba Bend. It is distinct from other contemporaneous cultures nearby, the "C-Group," which appears to be the successor of the A-Group in Lower Nubia and the nomadic pastoralist "Pan-Grave" peoples, mostly in Nubia's Eastern desert. Even further south, and possibly in some form of trading relationship with Early Kerma although not (directly) with Egypt, are the nomadic herders of the Western Butana (identified at the site of Shaqadud) and, even farther, the "Gash Group" ("Middle Kassala") of the Southern Atbai. Other areas are insufficiently understood for comment, although cattle-keepers occupied the Wadi el-Howar.

Tall pottery vessel. Predynastic. Egyptain Museum, Cario. © Wener Forman/Art Resource, New York.

"Kerma" is an entirely modern identification for this civilization, taken from the major city and its adjacent cemetery excavated in 1913–1916 by G. A. Reisner and until the 1950s virtually the only Kerma site known. The ancient Egyptian name for the Kerma territory appears to have changed over time. It probably was (at least in part) "Yam" in the late Old Kingdom, and perhaps later "Irem." The designation "Kush," usually cited in pejorative terms, begins to appear in the Egyptian records in Dynasty XII, and most likely this is the Egyptian name corresponding to the powerful and centralized Upper Nubian "Kerma" state by that time. Two Middle Kerma kings, Awa'a and Utatrerses, are named on these texts, and those of other Kushite rulers also are attested.

During the Old Kingdom, Egypt controlled access along the Lower Nubian Nile as far as the Second Cataract but, at its end, was forced to retreat down to Aswan. Late Old Kingdom traders such as Harkhuf had traveled beyond the Second Cataract to conduct their business with the emerging Kerma state, but such expeditions are not evident later. The power vacuum thus created was filled by Kerma cultural and political expansion northward almost to Aswan throughout the Early Kerma/First Intermediate period in Egypt. The pastoralist C-Group peoples also became culturally distinct in Lower Nubia, but their relationship to the Kerma intruders is as yet not entirely clear. The increased power and importance of Kerma (both city and state) by the early Middle Kingdom may have been the reason why its Dynasty XI founder, Nebhepetre Montuhotep II, initiated a military campaign to regain control of Lower Nubia.

Eventually, the powerful Dynasty XII kings constructed a series of massive mud-brick military fortresses at strategic points along the Lower Nubian Nile, which controlled all access north of the Second Cataract by the time of Senwosret I. The other known major Kerma settlement and cemetery guarded this main Upper Nubian/Kerma frontier at Sai Island just south of the Batn el-Hajar, which Egypt did not breach until Dynasty XVIII. The Egyptian army recruited entire contingents of Nubian mercenaries, most famously archers, who seem to have been mainly Pan-Grave and known as the "Medjay." Its success, bypassing the C-Group population, is indicated in part by the much increased quantity of Egyptian goods from Early to Middle Kerma graves. Other features (including hieroglyphic writing and much iconographical adoption) suggest some overlying Egyptian acculturation, with Egyptian traders, craftsmen, and advisers resident at Kerma itself. Nontheless, the unique character of the Kerma culture was retained.

The decline of the Middle Kingdom in Egypt followed the pattern at the end of the Old Kingdom, with Egypt withdrawing to Aswan and Kerma again wresting control of all Lower Nubia at the beginning of the Second Intermediate Period/Classic Kerma phase. The Egyptian fortresses continued to be manned by both Egyptian and Nubian soldiers, but they now served the king of Kush, not of Egypt. This is the apogée of Kerma civilization, during which the largest of the royal burial tumuli were constructed, the capital expanded considerably and massive quantities of exotic imported Egyptian goods (mostly originating in Upper Egypt and often heirloom pieces) are found throughout Kerma. The kingdom also expanded southward beyond the Debba Bend at least to the Fourth Cataract at Napata. It was as powerful at this time as Egypt had been in the Middle Kingdom. In Egypt, Kamose (the last king of Dynasty XVII) at Thebes complained he sat "between an Asiatic (the Hyksos king at Avaris) and a Nubian (the Kushite king)" who were politically allied against him. He and his Dynasty XVIII successors successfully campaigned in both directions for the next century, expelling both the Hyksos and the Kushites and regaining territorial control. This time they followed an entirely different policy, penetrating into the Near East as far as the Euphrates River and, in the relatively brief late or post-Kerma phase, into Upper Nubia itself.

JACKE PHILLIPS

See also: **Egypt, Ancient: New Kingdom and the Colonization of Nubia; Kush; Meroe: Meroitic Culture and Economy; Napata and Meroe.**

Further Reading

Bonnet, C. "C-Group," and "The Kingdom of Kerma." In *Sudan: Ancient Kingdoms of the Nile*, edited by D. Wildung. Paris and New York: Flammarion, 1997.

Davies, W. V., ed. *Egypt and Africa: Nubia from Prehistory to Islam.* London: British Museum Press and Egypt Exploration Society, 1991.

Kendall, T. *Kerma and the Kingdom of Kush 2500–1500 B.C.* Seattle: University of Washington Press, 1997.

Lacovara, P. "The Internal Chronology of Kerma." *Beitrage zur Sudanforschung.* 2 (1987): 51–74.

O'Connor, D. *Ancient Nubia, Egypt's Rival in Africa.* Philadelphia: The University Museum, 1993.

Khama III (*c.*1835–1923)

Botswana King

Boikanyo Khama, otherwise popularly known as Khama III, Khama "the Good," or Khama "the Great," was born in 1835 at Mosu near the Makgadikgadi Salt Pans, not very far from the Boteti River in the Central District of Botswana. He was the son of Kgosi Sekgoma I, credited for having reorganized the Bangwato Batswana, one of the major ethnic groups of the Central District of Botswana, into a formidable kingdom.

Khama III grew up in Shoshong. Like most Batswana youths, he looked after goats and calves before he graduated to herd cattle as an adolescent. He was exposed to Christian teachings by a Botswana evangelist known as Kgobati. In 1860 Khama III and his brother Khamane were baptized by Heinrich Schulenburg of the German Hermannsburg Missionary Society, who had been among the Bangwato at Shoshong since 1859. Two years later, Khama married Elizabeta, a convert and daughter of Tshukudu, a prominent member of the Ngwato royalty. Khama III became a staunch, almost fanatical, Christian. Adhering to Christian ideals, he refused to marry other wives as demanded by local tradition. As a result, Khama III and his brother fell out with their father, who saw his sons as shunning the traditions of their own people.

The London Missionary Society (LMS), which replaced the Hermannsburg in 1862, supported the actions of the two heirs against their father. Successive LMS agents (the Reverends John Mackenzie, Roger Price, and James Hepburn) saw Sekgoma as a villain bent on halting Christian progress. The Bangwato town of Shoshong became divided into two factions, Christian and pagan. The two factions entered a civil war in 1866 that culminated in the defeat, albeit temporarily, of the Christians.

Meanwhile, an uncle, Macheng, supposedly the legitimate heir apparent, became the Kgosi (chief) twice before he was ousted by Khama III in favor of his father, Sekgoma I. In 1875 Khama III, with the backing of the Christian community, ousted his father and became the Kgosi of the Bangwato until his death in 1923.

Khama became Kgosi at a time when white traders, travelers, and missionaries from the south were entering his country. Shoshong, his capital, became an important link to the interior where ivory and ostrich feathers, important commodities of the time, could be obtained and exchanged for money and manufactured goods.

Khama III reformed his kingdom along Christian ideals. From 1876 he banned initiation ceremonies, all

Bangwato were to observe Sunday as the Sabbath and no wagons were allowed to pass through Shoshong on that day. Christianity became the official religion of Bangwato. Polygamy was prohibited, and payment of *bogadi* (bride price) was ended. He allowed daughters to be entitled to inheritance, a practice hitherto unheard of in the Bangwato society. He abolished payment of tribute by conquered peoples and allowed them to use their cattle and land the way they saw fit. He opened *kgotla* (traditional assembly) meetings with prayer and above all banned both European liquor and traditional beer. Some of these reforms caused dissension as some members of the Bangwato were banished for criticizing the Kgosi for banning traditional brew, and being too stern in implementing these reforms. Raditladi, Mphoeng, the Kgosi's own son Sekgoma II, and their respective followers were exiled for opposing the Kgosi and his reforms.

From 1876 Khama III was plagued by white encroachment into his country. The Boers of the Transvaal in South Africa, notorious for their practice of land domination, were threatening to take Khama III's land. With the advice of missionaries who became his secretaries and advisers in foreign matters, he appealed for British protection against the Boers.

The British protectorate over Botswana, which was welcomed by Khama III, came in 1885 through a British soldier known as Charles Warren and Rev. Mackenzie, former missionary in his country. The British were intent on securing "the road to the north" to prevent Batswana country from being taken over by the Boers and Germans in South West Africa (Namibia). This arrangement suited Batswana, and Khama III pledged to be always a British ally.

In 1893–1894, Khama ensured his loyalty to the British by supporting Cecil John Rhodes's British South Africa Company's (BSA) invasion of Matebeleland. A year later Khama was shocked to learn that the British government was to hand over Batswana country to be annexed to Rhodes's newly founded colony of Rhodesia.

With the help of the LMS missionary W. C. Willoughby and two other chiefs, Sebele of Bakwena and Bathoeng of Bangwaketse, the three leaders journeyed to England in 1895 to protest against being handed over to company rule. Colonial Secretary Joseph Chamberlain was at first unwilling to listen to their pleas but changed his mind when they had mustered enough support from religious movements in Britain to sway British opinion in their favor. The protectorate would not be handed over to the BSA Company, and the chiefs would continue to rule their people as before.

From 1900 until his death, Khama III continually clashed with the protectorate administration and the missionaries. The latter wanted to buy land, while the former invented laws for the protectorate without consultation. He suspected the protectorate administration of trying to hand over the Batswana country to the Union of South Africa, which was formed in 1910. Khama III died of pneumonia in 1923 and was succeeded by his son, Sekgoma II, father of the first president of Botswana.

P. T. MGADLA

See also: **Botswana.**

Further Reading

Dachs, A. *Khama of Botswana.* London: Heinemann, Educational Books, 1971.

Hepburn, J. D. *Twenty Years in Khama's Country.* C. H. Lyall (ed.) 3rd ed. London: Frank Cass and Co., 1970.

Parsons, Q. N. "The 'Image' of Khama the Great 1865–1970." In *Botswana Notes and Records.* Vol. 13. 1971.

Parsons, N. *King Khama Emperor Joe and the Great White Queen: Victorian Britain Through African Eyes.* Chicago and London: University of Chicago Press, 1998.

Tlou, T. "Khama III: Great Reformer and Innovator." In *Botswana Notes and Records.* Vol. 2. 1969.

Khartoum

Located at the confluence of the Blue and White Niles, Khartoum was originally a small fishing village. When the Turco-Egyptian forces of Muhammad Ali Pasha, the viceroy of Egypt, invaded the Sudan in 1821, it became a small outpost of the army. In 1824 the military governor, Uthman Bey, a Circassian, realized the strategic importance of Khartoum. He constructed a fort garrisoned by a full regiment, but the headquarters for the Turco-Egyptian administration in the Sudan remained at Sennar until 1825 when Mahu Bey, a Kurd, was appointed in command of the province of Sennar.

Camel racing in Khartoum, Sudan, 1960s. © SVT Bild/Das Fotoarchiv.

He resided, however, at Khartoum rather than Sennar and stationed his troops across the Blue Nile at Qubbat Khujali.

In 1826 Ali Khurshid Agha was appointed "governor of Sennar" but moved the administrative capital to Khartoum, which he devoted much energy to developing. Settlers were given land grants. The original mosque built in 1829 was demolished in 1837 and one that could accommodate the faithful was built in its place. Barracks, a military storehouse, and a dockyard were constructed by the Nile. Townspeople were encouraged to replace their tents with houses of brick and mortar. The market (*suq*) prospered, the trade routes were protected, and the population increased.

After the opening of the White Nile through the Sudd to the verdant and populous lands of the upper Nile a small but influential community of European traders settled in Khartoum. Led by the Savoyard, Antoine Brun-Rollet, they traded in ivory and supported the Roman Catholic mission to Central Africa that established its headquarters in the capital. In 1854 the new viceroy, Muhammad Sa'id (1854–1863) under pressure from European governments and bankers, closed the profitable public slave market in Khartoum and appointed the first Christian governor of the Sudan, Arakil Bey. His tenure (1856–1858) was cut short by his death in 1858.

During the reign of the khedive Isma'il (1863–1879), Khartoum expanded to accommodate his imperial ambitions in the Upper Nile and northeast Africa. Muslim merchant princes now organized large expeditions in Khartoum to proceed up the White Nile, through the Sudd, to the fertile grasslands and forests of the Bahr al-Ghazal and Equatoria. Isma'il employed the services of Sir Samuel Baker in 1869 to expand his khedivial empire from Khartoum to the great lakes of equatorial Africa. The administrative offices, military barracks, and the dockyard were expanded to accommodate the need for troops and steamers.

In 1881 Muhammad Ahmad al-Mahdi revolted against the Turco-Egyptian government in the Sudan, rallying the Sudanese in a jihad that swept all before them to besiege Khartoum and the new governor general, Major General Charles George Gordon sent by the British government to resolve the Sudan question and the revolt of the Mahdi. Gordon had previously served in the Sudan as governor of Equatoria under the khedive Isma'il. He arrived in Khartoum on February 18, 1884, realizing that there could be no accommodation with Muhammad al-Mahdi whose Ansar besieged the capital in September. The Mahdi arrived before Khartoum in October, and Gordon, a military engineer, organized the long siege of the city behind its walls. By the new year 1885 the garrison and public, despite Gordon's efforts, could no longer sustain themselves.

Upon the approach of a British relief expedition, the Mahdi ordered the assault on January 26, 1885, during the month of low Nile. The exhausted garrison was overwhelmed, Gordon was killed, the populace massacred or enslaved, and the city reduced to ruin and deserted. The capital of the Mahdists state was removed across the confluence of the White and Blue Niles to Omdruman.

Upon the reconquest of the Sudan by the Anglo-Egyptian forces under the command of General Horatio Herbert Kitchener in 1898, Khartoum became the capital of the Anglo-Egyptian Sudan. Like Gordon, Kitchener was a military engineer who took personal command in its reconstruction, laying out its grid, according to legend, in the form of the British flag but with broad boulevards presumably that could be easily enfiladed by the machine guns of the conquerors.

During the Anglo-Egyptian Condominium, Khartoum gradually evolved into a modern city dominated by the government buildings and the Gordon Memorial College, which became the University of Khartoum in 1956. There was light manufacturing, printing, food processing, technical schools, and the Sudan National Museum and the Ethnographical Museum. Upon independence its population was 476,218.

ROBERT COLLINS

See also: **Sudan.**

Further Reading

Arkell, A. J. *A History of the Sudan from the Earliest Times to 1821.* Westport: Greenwood Press, 1974.

Holt, P. M. *A Modern History of the Sudan: From the Funj Sultanate to the Present Day.* London: Wiedenfeld and Nicolson, 1967.

Holt, P. M., and M. W. Daly. *A History of the Sudan from the Coming of Islam to the Present Day.* 5th ed. London: Longmans, 2000.

Stevenson, R. C. "Old Khartoum, 1821–1885." *Sudan Notes and Records.* Vol. 47. 1966.

Khayr al-Din: ***See*** **Tunisia: Khayr al-Din and Constitutional and Administrative Reform, 1855–1878.**

Khoi-Dutch Wars: ***See*** **Cape Colony: Khoi-Dutch Wars.**

Khoisan Resistance: ***See*** **Cape Colony: Khoi-Dutch Wars.**

Kibiro: ***See*** **Great Lakes Region: Ntusi, Kibiro, and Bigo.**

Kilimanjaro: ***See*** **Upare, Usambara, and Kilimanjaro.**

Kimbangu, Simon, and Kimbanguism

Simon Kimbangu was born on September 24, 1889, at Nkamba, near Thysville (now Mbanza-Ngugu), in the Lower Congo. Kimbangu, which literally means in the Kikongo language "the one who reveals what is hidden," was the member of a group, the Bakongo, that had long experienced Christianity and Christian revivalist movements. Due to the Christian heritage of the Lower Congo, colonial missions, including the British Missionary Society (BMS), established their first centers there. Kimbangu was brought up within the religious realm of the BMS. He became a Christian as a young man. In July 1915, after being thoroughly instructed by the missionaries, he was baptized along with his wife, Marie Mwilu. For a short period he was a teacher at the mission school in Mgombe Lutete where he further familiarized himself with the Bible of which he gained a strong command. He also ministered as an evangelist at Nkamba and enjoyed a particularly favorable reputation among the white missionaries who described the young Kimbangu as a good and thoughtful man who read his Bible and performed his tasks conscientiously.

Kimbangu received his first call to "tend Christ's flock" one night in 1918. After declining the call he finally sought refuge in Kinshasa where he worked at various menial jobs without ever finding peace of mind, for even in Kinshasa the voice that called him to minister for the Gospel reached him. He returned to Nkamba and, on the morning of April 6, 1921, performed his first healing by laying his hands in the name of Jesus Christ on a critically ill woman. The second miracle was the raising to life of a dead child, and many more followed from healings of sick people to prophecies. At first, people thought Kimbangu was using charms but he eventually managed to convince people by insisting, "It is Christ who has performed these miracles through me. I have no power to do these myself." From then on, pilgrims started flocking to Nkamba to seek healing and instruction.

Kimbangu's message summoned people to renounce their non-Christian ways. It combated polygamy, profane dances, and fetishes. Kimbangu and the movement he initiated represented a Christian African reaction against colonization and colonial evangelization, although, it is worth noting, Kimbangu never opposed the authorities but championed obedience to the powers to be, which in the case of the Lower Congo also meant for the people to yield to forced labor and continue to pay a burdensome poll tax.

Faced with a staggering desertion of workers and servants who flocked to Nkamba, the colonial administration branded Kimbangu an *illuminé* (visionary) who was seeking popularity that later might coalesce into an organized rebellion in a region particularly prone to such outbursts. A state of emergency in the districts of Mbanza-Ngugu and Luozi was declared and Kimbangu, after hiding for a few months, gave himself up and was arrested in September 1921, after only less than six months in the ministry. A military court charged him with sedition and civil disobedience, and he was sentenced to death in what seemed to be a legal travesty, but the sentence was soon commuted by King Albert to life imprisonment. Kimbangu was transferred to Elisabethville (Lubumbashi) where he spent thirty years in solitary confinement.

In the absence of the leader and in the face of a relentless colonial repression that took the form of destruction of places of worship (Nkamba was totally destroyed by the Belgians) and massive deportations, the movement went underground and, not surprisingly, branched out into various independent splinter groups, such as Nguzism, Mpadism, and Kakism. It later and quickly spread into French Congo and Gabon.

In 1959, after several decades of concealed activities, Kimbanguism was finally recognized by the Belgian colonial administration and placed on the same footing as the Catholic and Protestant churches. Under the leadership of Joseph Diangienda, Kimbangu's second son who claimed his father's mantle, the movement organized itself into an official church known as the Church of Jesus Christ on Earth through the Prophet Simon Kimbangu (*Église de Jésus-Christ sur Terre par le Prophète Simon Kimbangu*, EJCSK). EJCSK represents an attempt at forging a typically African Christian church against the backdrop of the "colonial mission" and the postcolonial dictatorship.

During the long reign of the dictator Mobutu Sese Seko, the Kimbanguist movement became one of the regime's clients and its most fervent defender. The church went from an explicit policy of no interference with politics to safeguarding Mobutu's regime and promoting *Mobutisme*. In return, when in December 1971 Mobutu decided to ban all the "sects" in the country, EJCSK was not only granted a privileged status but also benefited from the repression of dissident religious groups that were forced either to disband or join EJCSK. Mobutu's regime guaranteed the church's financial prosperity and political protection as well.

Today, EJCSK enjoys a status as the third largest organized religious denomination in the Democratic

Republic of Congo (DRC). It has become a powerful financial institution with hundreds of Kimbanguist schools and temples across the country, an imposing *Institut pédagogique et théologique* (Institute of Education and Theology) in Kinshasa, and a mausoleum in Nkamba, called the New Jerusalem (where Kimbangu's remains had been transferred), which attracts tens of thousands of pilgrims every year. In addition, EJCSK has extensive social services in agriculture, youth work (including several boy scouts troops), and cooperatives.

Since the promotion of EJCSK under Mobutu, one important feature in the social life of the church has been the leading role played by Kimbangu's three sons, especially Joseph Diangienda. Until his death, which occurred in 1992, he was considered a *zimvwala*, a title that confers prophetic and royal authority within the church. He was also called *tata mfumu'a nlongo* (sacred head). Diangienda's veneration by Kimbanguists reached such heights that after his burial a few devoted followers spread the word that he would resurrect within three days as Christ did. To the the disappointment of many followers, Diangienda never rose from the dead and his confirmed death, mirroring that of Mobutu a few years later, intensified doctrinal as well as political divisions within the Kimbanguist church that threaten the church's destiny.

CHARLES DIDIER GONDOLA

See also: **Congo (Kinshasa), Democratic Republic of/Zaire: Mobutu, Zaire, and Mobutuism.**

Further Reading

Anderson, E. *Messianic Popular Movements in the Lower-Congo.* Upsala: Studia Ethnographica Upsaliensia, 1958.

Martin, M.-L. *Kimbangu: An African Prophet and His Church.* Translated by D. M. Moore. Grand Rapids, Michigan: Eerdmans Publishing Company, 1976.

Kimberley, Diamond Fields and

The year 1870 is widely regarded as a turning point in South African history, for it marks the beginning of the mineral revolution upon which South Africa's industrial transformation was to be based. On the eve of this mineral revolution, the territory that constitutes the modern state of South Africa consisted of a mixture of British colonies, Boer (Afrikaner) republics, and independent African states. Economically, the region was largely based upon pastoralism, hunting, and subsistence agriculture. The rapid expansion of white settlement, characteristic of earlier decades, had slowed as Africans became better armed with guns and better organized so as to resist further encroachment. The political balance of power between black and white in South Africa, however, was about to be transformed by the impact of mineral discoveries at Kimberley.

The first diamond was picked up north of the Cape Colony near the confluence of the Vaal and Orange Rivers in 1867 and sold to a trader from the Cape. Over the next two years, increasing numbers of diamonds were found and traded by local Batlhaping (Tswana), Griqua, and Kora along the lower reaches of the Vaal. Large numbers of black and white speculators, adventurers, and traders converged upon the spot, eager to find the source, and during 1870 diamond "mines" were found both at "river diggings" on the Vaal and at "dry diggings" further south. Politically, the territory was disputed between Waterboer's Griqua, Batlhaping, Orange Free State, and South African Republic (Transvaal). The British government at the Cape put the matter to arbitration at Bloemhof and, despite evidence to the contrary, decided territorial claims in favor of Waterboer, who by then had been persuaded to seek British "protection." Thus, by the end of 1871, the British, who had started the year with no claims to the region at all, had annexed the whole of the diamond fields as the Crown Colony of Griqualand West. By then the "dry diggings" had been shown to contain the largest and richest mine of all, "New Rush," which was renamed Kimberley after the British secretary of state for the colonies. Griqualand West remained a separate Crown Colony until 1880 when it was appended to the Cape Colony.

In the early days of the diamond fields, black and white alike had staked claims and dug and traded for diamonds alongside and in direct competition with each other, both employing black laborers to do the actual digging. But when the flood of diamonds onto the world market led to falling prices, white claim-holders organized themselves into "mutual protection" associations and enforced racist exclusivity over the right to hold diamond claims. Claim-holders were the only ones legally allowed to sell diamonds to the merchants who had set up shop at Kimberley. Part of the white claim-holders' paranoia was due to the belief that black laborers were the most likely people to conceal diamonds found at the bottom of the shafts and they were most likely to sell those stolen gems through black claim-holders. In practice, all claim-holders were equally likely to trade in stolen gems, but competition was fierce and, in the politics of a colonial society, the white claim-holders pressured the British authorities to impose tighter restrictions on the movement and activities of Africans on the diamond fields. Thus emerged the notorious "pass" system in early South African industrial society—a remnant of Cape slavery from the early nineteenth century.

As the diamond mines were dug more deeply, industrial machinery was required for haulage and for pumping out floodwater, and the individual claim-holdings gave way to capitalized companies. Competition between companies, however, still stimulated overproduction and unstable prices. The logic was amalgamation and, eventually, monopoly, an objective achieved by Cecil Rhodes's De Beers Consolidated Mining Company in 1888–1889. Then production and labor was cut, the market was stabilized, and capital investment and long-term profitability was secured. By then the African role in diamond mining had become restricted to that of unskilled migrant laborer, mostly on short-term contract, during which they were confined, controlled, and searched in fenced company compounds.

Beyond the confines of the Kimberley mines, the impact of the mineral revolution was profound. In a hitherto lightly populated dry part of the southern African interior, there grew up, almost overnight, a city of some 30,000 people. Besides the loss of political control by the various claimants to the diamond fields, the initial impact was mostly one of opportunity. Kimberley needed food and fuel, and local farmers, African and Afrikaner, responded with enthusiasm to the openings of production for market rather than for subsistence. Local Batlhaping cattle-owners sold surplus milk and cattle and bought ploughs and wagons with the proceeds, while Afrikaners from the Transvaal and Orange Free State, and Basotho from Basutoland (Lesotho), found a market for greater grain production. The most profitable marketable item through the1870s and early 1880s was firewood to fuel the mines' steam-driven pumps, crushers, and haulage gear. "Wood riding" only declined as a profitable activity after 1885 when the extension of the railway from the Cape enabled the importation of cheap Welsh coal to the diamond fields.

The widest-felt impact of the diamond mines, however, was as a market for migrant labor. Africans came from as far away as Mozambique and the northern Transvaal to work on short-term contracts at the diamond fields. Competition between claim-holders meant that initially wages were relatively attractive: pay for one month's work could purchase a muzzle-loading gun, or several suits of second-hand clothing and domestic pots and pans. Although migrant labor later became a means of survival for the dispossessed, initially it was an opportunity to purchase firearms for hunting and defense of land.

The collective impact of all these factors was greater competition for access to land and labor, and its potential resources. Combined with a greater proliferation of firearms, this resulted in heightened potential for armed conflict. It is no coincidence that the late 1870s and early 1880s was a period when southern Africa experienced greatly increased level of warfare—wars of rebellion, resistance, and conquest.

KEVIN SHILLINGTON

See also: **Labor, Migrant; Rhodes, Cecil J.; South Africa: Confederation, Disarmament and the First Anglo-Boer War, 1871–1881**

Further Reading

Marks, S., and R. Rathbone, eds. *Industrialisation and Social Change in South Africa: African Class Formation, Culture, and Consciousness, 1870–1930.* London: Longman, 1982.
Mathews, J. W. *Incwadi Yami.* London, 1887.
Roberts, B. *Kimberley: Turbulent City.* Cape Town, 1976.
Shillington, K. *The Colonisation of the Southern Tswana, 1870–1900.* Johannesburg: Ravan Press, 1985.
Trollope, A. *South Africa.* 2 vols. London, 1878.
Turrell, R. "The 1875 Black Flag Revolt on the Kimberley Diamond Fields." *Journal of Southern African Studies.* 7, no. 2 (April 1981): 194–235.
———. *Capital and Labour on the Kimberley Diamond Fields, 1871–1890.* Cambridge, Cambridge University Press, 1987.
Worger, W. *South Africa's City of Diamonds: Mine Workers and Monopoly—Capitalism in Kimberley, 1867–1895.* New Haven, Conn.: Yale University Press, 1987.

Kinshasa

In 1881 the American explorer Henry Morton Stanley, acting on behalf of King Leopold of Belgium, founded what was to become the city of Leopoldville on the banks of the Congo River. Geography determined the location. Leopoldville was established at the downstream end of an extensive network of river transportation in the Congo Basin, dominated by the thousand-mile stretch of the Congo River navigable up to what is now Kisangani, and just before an extensive series of rapids (the Cataractes) renders the river nonnavigable as it heads to its mouth at the Atlantic Ocean.

A remote outpost for most of its first twenty years, Leopoldville was connected to the Atlantic and

Leopoldville (Kinshasa), 1955; the capital of the Belgian Congo with 400,000 inhabitants. © Lode van Gent/Das Fotoarchiv.

ultimately to the rest of the world in 1898, when the railway linking it to the inland seaport of Matadi was completed. Establishment of the railway allowed Leopoldville to develop as a commercial center, in particular as a transit point for rubber and other products from the interior of the Congo bound for Europe, and for goods imported from Europe and headed for the interior. Thus, for example, between 1910 and 1930 the volume of goods passing through the river port of Leopoldville each year grew from 19,000 tons to nearly 275,000 tons, representing almost a doubling every five years.

In 1923 Leopoldville became the capital of the Belgian Congo, and by the end of the 1920s the city had become an important administrative center. The growth of the city was rapid. Like many other emerging cities in Sub-Saharan Africa, Leopoldville was not located where human resources were plentiful, and hence it was necessary to import workers to meet the growing demand for labor. Recruitment of workers in rural areas served to attract Congolese men to employment in the emerging modern economic sector. The Great Depression of the 1930s slowed the city's growth briefly: 6,000 men were sent back to their rural areas of origin in 1930 and 7,000 more were sent back in 1932 in response to the corresponding sharp decline in demand for labor. This incident reflected the considerable control over labor and unemployment exercised by the colonial authorities, and it also emphasized the sensitivity to external events of this new urban center in Sub-Saharan Africa.

The importance of external events was further highlighted with the onset of World War II. Supplies to Leopoldville were cut off, and as a consequence the city was obliged to develop rapidly its industrial base so as to become more self-sufficient. Labor recruitment, as before, was focused on finding men to work in the city's growing modern economy, and the colonial government strictly controlled migration to Leopoldville. Hence, the city was characterized by relatively small proportions of women and children. The addition of considerable industrial activity to the city's existing commercial, transportation, administrative, and industrial activities resulted not only in substantial diversification of the city's economy but also in a doubling of the population between 1940 and 1945 and a doubling again between 1945 and 1950.

By 1960 Leopoldville had a population of roughly 400,000. When the Belgian Congo became independent in mid-1960, the controls on migration were effectively eliminated, and, fueled by the internal political strife of the early 1960s, the city began another period of rapid growth. This growth was accompanied by a variety of economic and social changes, including rapid expansion of the informal or unstructured sector of the economy, and continuation of the substantial extension of schooling to women that had just begun near the end of the colonial period.

From 1965, when General Joseph Désiré Mobutu seized power in a coup d'état, until the mid-1970s the city (now named Kinshasa, after one of the villages that existed near the site where Stanley first established Leopoldville) and the country experienced a period of political stability and economic growth. In the early 1970s, on the heels of this political and economic success, President Mobutu announced a policy to promote "Authenticity." To further "Authenticity," the President required citizens to abandon their European names in favor of African ones, he changed the names of many other cities throughout the country from their colonial designations to African names, and he changed the name of the country from Congo to Zaire. However, following the implementation in 1973 and 1974 of ill-conceived policies of "Zairianization" and radicalization (which essentially expropriated most businesses owned by foreigners and typically turned them over to unqualified Zairians, with very harmful and long-lasting adverse consequences), and the sharp decline in world copper prices that took place at roughly the same time (copper was the main source of export earnings and government revenue), the economy entered a period of protracted crisis from which it has not yet emerged.

The chronic crisis that began in the mid-1970s was accompanied by stagnation in the modern sector of employment and continued growth of the informal sector. Despite these problems, the population of the city continued to grow rapidly throughout the 1970s and 1980s. Economic growth and development were further hindered by a notoriously corrupt and poorly functioning public sector (some political scientists described the governance system as one of "kleptocracy"). During the 1980s, the country's government attempted, with assistance from the International Monetary Fund and the World Bank, to implement a series of structural adjustment programs aimed at improving efficiency of operation of the public sector and encouraging the growth and development of the private sector. A number of economic reforms were adopted, but political support for structural adjustment was unsteady and had an "on-again, off-again" character.

Beginning in the latter half of 1990, the chronic economic crisis became acute. After a number of years during which inflation had averaged 40 to 50 per cent per year and real incomes declined substantially, suddenly very rapid inflation of 2,000 to 3,000 per cent per year emerged, as the monetary authorities effectively abandoned any efforts to adhere to the structural adjustment program. The ensuing economic crisis, occurring in the midst of a political crisis characterized by increasingly vocal calls for democracy and the ouster of President

Mobutu, came to a head in late September 1991. Initiated by soldiers who had seen the real value of their salaries shrink to almost nothing, rioting, looting, and generalized civil disorder broke out in Kinshasa and then spread to other urban centers throughout the country. This resulted in the withdrawal of foreign donors and in a considerable shrinkage of the Congo's and Kinshasa's fragile modern sector. A second round of looting and pillaging, this time solely by the military, took place at the end of January 1993.

Inflation continued at an accelerated pace after late 1991, reaching as high as 500 per cent in one month in Kinshasa at the end of 1993 and averaging 10,000 per cent and more on an annual basis for much of 1993 and 1994. In 1995 and during the first half of 1996, inflation slowed to less than 20 per cent per month, corresponding to well under 1,000 per cent per year.

By 1997 Kinshasa's economy was in shambles. Manufacturing activity nationally, which is heavily concentrated in Kinshasa, was cut in half from 1990 to 1993–1994. There was slight improvement in 1995 and early 1996, but by mid-1996 industrial production was at only 50 to 60 per cent of its 1990 levels. Transportation from the countryside to the cities became increasingly difficult, food prices skyrocketed, and malnutrition became increasingly prevalent.

In brief, the chronic crisis that characterized the Congo's and Kinshasa's economy since "Zairianization" in the mid-1970s became an acute crisis in the early 1990s. The political situation remained deadlocked until May 1997, when a rebellion begun in late 1996 with assistance from neighboring countries and led by Laurent Désiré Kabila succeeded in taking power from President Mobutu.

Not long after declaring himself president, Mr. Kabila changed the name of the country back to Democratic Republic of Congo. While his government showed early success in slowing inflation, changing the economy so as to replicate the relative prosperity of the early 1970s will be a far more difficult task. President Kabila now presides over a country rich in mineral wealth and with substantial agricultural potential but one also with a badly deteriorated transportation and production infrastructure, ruined by years of neglect, governmental corruption, and more recently, extreme economic instability and civil war.

Exacerbating the difficulties confronting the Kabila government is the fact that a rebellion broke out in eastern Congo in early August 1998. For a brief period, there was fighting in Kinshasa and elsewhere in the western part of the country. With considerable assistance from several other Sub-Saharan nations, the Kabila government was able to defeat the rebels in Kinshasa and western Congo, but the rebels have succeeded in capturing a significant share of eastern Congo. At present, Kinshasa is the second-largest city in Sub-Saharan Africa, with a population estimated at six million in 2003. However, in view of the country's ongoing political difficulties, its capital city faces an uncertain future.

DAVID SHAPIRO

See also: **Congo, Democratic Republic of/Zaire.**

Further Reading

Baeck, L. "Léopoldville, phénomène urbain africain." *Zaïre*. 10, no. 6 (1956): 613–636.

Capelle, E. *La Cité Indigène de Léopoldville*. Elisabethville: Centre d'Etude des Problèmes Sociaux Indigènes, 1947.

Denis, J. "Léopoldville: Etude de géographie urbaine et sociale." *Zaïre* 10, no. 6 (1956): 563–611.

Houyoux, J., and K. Niwembo. *Etude démographique de Kinshasa*, 1977; reprinted in 1986 as *Kinshasa 1975*. Kinshasa: Bureau d'Etudes, d'Aménagement et d'Urbanisme and Brussels: ICHEC.

Maton, J. and A. Van Bauwel. "Zaïre 1996: Analyse des chiffres mensuels et trimestriels: La politique macro-économique au premier semestre 1996." Ghent: Ghent University, 1996.

Shapiro, D. "From Leopoldville to Kinshasa." In *Women's Education, Employment, and Fertility in Kinshasa, Congo, 1955–1990: A Descriptive Overview*. Unpublished monograph. University Park, Pa.: Department of Economics, The Pennsylvania State University, 1997.

Whyms, *Léopoldville, 1881–1956*. Brussels: Office de Publicité, S. A., 1956.

Kitara: *See* Great Lakes Region: Kitara and the Chwezi Dynasty.

Kongo, Teke (Tio), and Loango: History to 1483

Archaeological evidence of material culture and linguistics combine to suggest that west-central Africa was settled by farming populations after about 1,000BCE. At present, the archaeological work is scattered and sketchy, and new work, especially in areas like Angola where very little systematic work has been done, is likely to modify any conclusions. The early settlers probably spoke languages of the western Bantu family and formed a part of the Bantu migration that originated a millennium earlier in Cameroon. Within five hundred years, knowledge of ironworking had also spread to the region, so that by 200BCE the region was making iron and steel tools.

At present the earliest evidence of complex society comes from Kayes and Madingo-Kayes, located in modern Congo-Brazzaville, where two large settlements located only approximately two miles apart seem to form the center of an interacting group of sites covering a larger area. Such a complex corresponds quite well with the polity that was called a *wene* in seventeenth-century Kongo, whose rulers bore the title *mwene*, derived from a personal form of the noun, though the archaeological evidence could not confirm such a pattern of authority.

A finely made and uniform pottery over a larger area suggest the presence of a trading network, and perhaps some consolidation of political authority, which flourished in the period 100–350. Unfortunately, there is little evidence of what activity took place in the following period, and most of these early sites were abandoned after 400.

The kingdoms that covered the region north of the Kwanza and east of the Kwango, and extending northward along the Zaire River and the coast up to Gabon when the first Portuguese arrived in the area in 1483, can be correlated with an archaeological culture known as the Mbafu group, whose earliest manifestation seems to be around 1400. Unfortunately, the absence of systematic investigation of the main settlements of this culture and any preceding culture makes it unlikely that archaeology can add much more to our understanding of the region at the present time.

Oral traditions, written down in the sixteenth century, help fill in the gaps between the archaeology and the earliest eyewitness written documents. Kongo traditions of the origin of the country, which have been periodically written down since the late sixteenth century, were constitutional documents intended to establish the basis for government by anchoring political customs of the time of writing in allegedly ancient precedent. The stories of origin have changed over the years as the constitution of the country changed, so that the foundation tale of the seventeenth century reflects the specifics of Kongo in that period, while the traditions of the nineteenth century and today relate to yet another constitutional arrangement. For this reason, it is best to focus specifically on the earliest traditions for understanding the earliest periods, while recognizing that even these might distort events of earlier periods for purposes of constitutional precedent.

The earliest traditions describe the origins of the kingdom of Kongo as a federation of several earlier and smaller polities such as Nsundi, Mpangu, and Mbata in the valley of the Inkisi River, or Soyo along the coast south of the Zaire River. Genealogies written in the seventeenth century point to a foundation around 1390 and credit one Nimi a Lukeni with it. Kongo probably was one of several federations of smaller polities at the time, such as the "Seven Kingdoms of Kongo dia Nlaza," a rival confederacy situated between the Inkisi and Kwango Rivers south of the Tio Kingdom that fell under Kongo's control in the late sixteenth and early seventeenth century.

In sixteenth-century versions of Kongo tradition, the original state seems to have allowed for an elected monarchy within a royal family by the hereditary rulers of the relatively independent provinces of the federation, especially Mbata, which had a special relationship with the king. However, Kongo's constitution was changing by the time the first Europeans arrived, and in particular, early sixteenth century Kongo had a number of royal provinces (Mbamba to the south, for example, or Nsundi to the northeast) in which independent rulers had been defeated and were replaced by appointees of the king.

In addition to allowing for the appointment for limited terms of rulers of some provinces by the king, the provinces of both the federation and its subordinate sections were expanding, particularly Mbamba in the southwest, Nsundi in the northeast, Soyo on the north coast, and Mbata on the east, and incorporated other smaller entities into them. The kings of Kongo further strengthened their own position by concentrating population in or around their royal city of Mbanza Kongo, which was described by the earliest visitors as already being as large as the Portuguese city of Évora (10,000–15,000 inhabitants). The concentration of demographic and economic resources around his capital allowed the king of Kongo to overshadow the provinces and increase his authority. This had thus led to the consolidation of a kingdom of considerable centralization, and had already laid the groundwork for further centralization of authority by the early sixteenth-century kings.

The Tio Kingdom probably was just as old as Kongo, although we have no traditions before the nineteenth century that can trace its origin and hence no details concerning its early government. It is mentioned in early sixteenth century documents around the Maleba Pool region. North of Kongo the emerging kingdom of Loango is not mentioned at all by the earliest visitors to the coast, and only appears in the later sixteenth century. Traditions set down in the seventeenth century relate its origin to Kongo, although these probably only reflect the southern kingdom's prestige and not a real relationship of origin and authority. Loango was not mentioned, for example, in royal titles of the sixteenth-century kings of Kongo, though some states north of the Zaire, like Vungu (mentioned only in the seventeenth century, but then as the origin of Kongo itself) probably predated Kongo.

JOHN K. THORNTON

Further Reading

Hilton, H. *The Kingdom of Kongo*. Oxford, 1985.

Thornton, J. "The Kingdom of Kongo, ca. 1390–1678: History of an African Social Formation." *Cahiers d'études Africaines*. 22 (1982): 325–342.

Vansina, J. *Paths in the Rainforest: Toward a History of Political Tradition in Equatorial Africa.* Madison, 1990.

Kongo Kingdom: Afonso I, Christianity, and Kingship

The arrival of the Portuguese navigator Diogo Cão at the mouth of the Zaire in 1483 took the Kongolese by surprise. Although it was a large, growing, and powerful kingdom, Kongo had no contacts with the world beyond its immediate neighbors and the extent of its regional trade routes before the Portuguese arrived. Nevertheless, Kongo rapidly accepted the newcomers and quickly moved to integrate itself into the Atlantic and European world. Kongo's earliest relationship with Portugal is studied with the intention of understanding a pristine encounter between African and European, akin to the meeting of the Tainos with Columbus less than a decade later.

The initial contact involved an exchange of hostages, and then the decision by Kongo's ruler, Nzinga a Nkuwu, to enter into formal relations with Portugal and to accept baptism. In 1491 King João II of Portugal sent a small fleet to Kongo to accomplish this purpose. The atmosphere was charged as the Portuguese and Kongolese jointly celebrated the baptism first of the *mwene* (ruler) of Soyo, the coastal authority of Kongo, and then the king himself, who was baptized on May 3, 1491, with the name João I in honor of the king of Portugal.

This first expedition of Portuguese to Kongo, and several others that followed in the next twenty years, were conceived as an exercise in cultural change. In addition to the spiritual help in guiding the new Christians, Portuguese colonists, including farmers and crafts people, also came to Kongo to teach new ways of doing things and living.

Only a few days after the baptism of João I, Portuguese armed forces left with the royal army to assist in the suppression of the rebellion of a small province located near the Zaire River. The campaign was a success, and the combined forces returned to Kongo's capital of Mbanza Kongo in triumph before the Portuguese leaders left for Portugal.

There are almost no historical records of the next fifteen years, during which time João I died and was succeeded by his son, Afonso Mvemba a Nzinga, sometime between 1506 and 1509. A very large portion of the next period of Kongo history, up until the middle of the sixteenth century, is known to historians almost entirely through the letters of Afonso to the kings of Portugal, Manuel I and João III. Thus, this critical period in Kongo history is illustrated primarily by sources of African authorship, which elucidate the relationship with Portugal and Portuguese resident in Kongo, and also political structures in the early Kongolese state.

Afonso's correspondence, and some collaborating evidence, reveal him to be literate, fervently Christian, and anxious to learn as much as possible about Portugal and Europe. Afonso claimed that he took power in a succession struggle with a pagan half-brother, Mpanzu a Kitima, in a cataclysmic battle that Afonso won with the help of an apparition of Saint James. He established the Roman Catholic Church in Kongo, provided for its funding, and moreover, studied the religion carefully himself and along with his own advisers and those from Portugal. He sent numerous children to Portugal and Europe to study, including his son Henrique Kinu a Mvemba, who was made a bishop in 1518 and returned to Kongo in 1521. Afonso also created an educational system that made the upper classes literate in Portuguese.

The end result was the development of a uniquely Kongolese form of syncretic Christianity, revealed in the vocabulary of early catechisms, and the observations of priests, such as the Jesuits who came to Kongo shortly after Afonso's death. It combined Kongo's older religious norms, with their emphasis on territorial spirits and ancestors, with the cult of the saints in such a way that Kongolese religion was enhanced rather than replaced. This work was so effective that it remained the Kongolese faith until the twentieth century.

Afonso was also anxious to acquire Portuguese skills, and encouraged Portuguese carpenters, stonemasons, and other craftsmen to live in Kongo. He constructed a palace, a city wall, and numerous churches of stone and developed a corps of Kongolese craftsmen who had mastered this craft. Other Portuguese techniques, like agriculture and making of bread were less successful in Kongo.

Afonso's relations with Portugal and the resident Portuguese have often been studied through his correspondence, especially letters of complaint issued in 1514 and 1526, and occasionally at other times. In these Afonso complained that the Portuguese in his service were immoral, lazy, and sometimes incompetent, at other times that some Portuguese conspired with his subjects to destabilize the kingdom or promote the slave trade. He was particularly concerned that Portuguese, especially those resident in the island of São Tomé (in the Gulf of Guinea), traded with his neighbors without his permission or control. These neighbors included Mpanzulumbu, located near the mouth of the Zaire, Kiangala on the coast north of Luanda, and probably also the kingdom of Ndongo to his south. In all these areas, Kongo had limited control in precontact times, and the growing Portuguese trade represented both assertions of independence on the part of the African partners and tax evasion on the part of the Portuguese. At one point, in 1526, Afonso proposed stopping all trade with Portugal because he claimed that his own subjects, including members of the nobility had been seized.

Whatever the specific events he alluded to, there is little evidence that Kongo's sovereignty was substantially undermined, or that Afonso's reign was a noble failure to transform the country, as some scholars have contended. When Afonso died in 1542, he passed on a country that was stable, expanding its influence and authority, and committed to continuing the Christian faith. It would be over a century before the debilitating civil war that actually did destroy the country would begin.

JOHN K. THORNTON

Further Reading

Hilton, A. *The Kingdom of Kongo.* Oxford, 1985.

Thornton, J. "The Kingdom of Kongo, ca. 1390–1678: History of an African Social Formation." *Cahiers d'études africaines.* 22 (1982): 325–342.

———. "Early Kongo-Portuguese Relations, 1483–1575: A New Interpretation." *History in Africa.* 8 (1981): 183–204.

Vansina, J. (with T. Obenga). "The Kongo Kingdom and Its Neighbours." In B. A. Ogot (ed.). *General History of Africa.* Edited by B. A. Ogot.Vol. 5. UNESCO, 1981.

Kongo Kingdom, 1542–1568

When King Afonso I (1509–1542) died at an age of over eighty, he left a multigenerational set of successors behind him to struggle over the throne. His son Pedro I Nkanga a Mvemba ruled briefly, before being forced to take refuge in a church by Afonso's half brother, Francisco I Nkumbi a Mpudi, whose equally brief reign ended in 1545 when Afonso's grandson Diogo I Mpudi a Nzinga overthrew him. In 1550 Diogo put Pedro on trial for plotting treason against him; the legal process of this trial is an important source for understanding how succession was undertaken in Kongo in the mid-sixteenth century.

The nature of this struggle reveals how far the country had moved toward centralization of authority since the early sixteenth century. When Afonso came to the throne, the kingship was effectively elective, probably through an original constitution of Kongo that called for the selection of the ruler by the powerful independent nobility of Kongo's original loose federation. Afonso owed his own power, he wrote in 1514, to the good offices of the Mwene (ruler of) Mbata, the most powerful member of the federation. Later, shortly before 1529, Afonso had written to Portugal explaining that he could not name a successor without the consent of the Mwene Mbata. Yet if Mbata, or Soyo, probably another early member of the federation played a role in selecting kings earlier, they played no apparent role in the mid-sixteenth century.

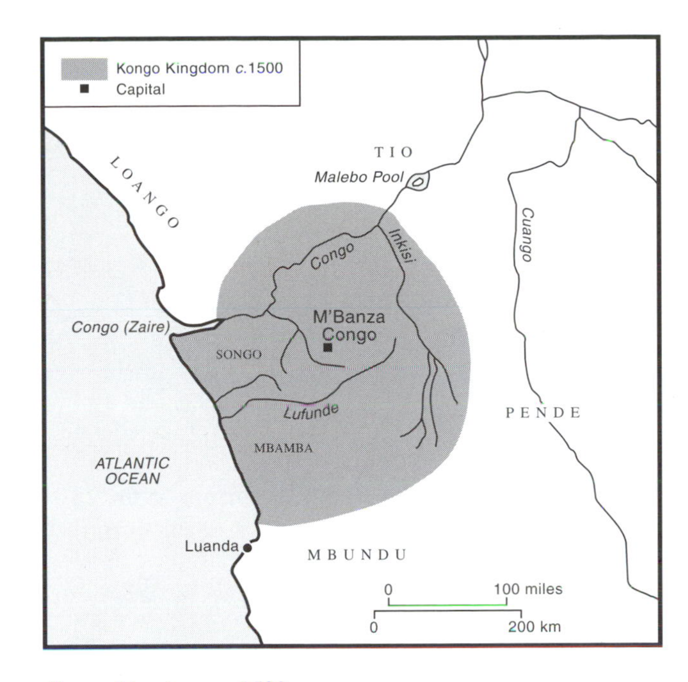

Kongo kingdom, *c.* 1500.

Instead, Diogo relied largely on his ability to appoint officials to those provinces of the kingdom that were in his power: Vunda, Mpemba, Nsundi, Mpangu, and other smaller ones. Yet it was not always easy to make the appointments that were technically in his gift, for he moved very slowly to replace his predecessors' appointed officials and even five years after ascending the throne had not completely filled these positions with his supporters. Pedro's plot, in fact, revolved around getting one or another of these appointed officials to rebel against Diogo in his favor. In the end, however, Diogo managed to force all to swear that they would never support anyone of Pedro's *geração*, a Portuguese term that probably translated the Kikongo word *kanda*, which in turn referred to a large and complex faction united by kinship, clientage, and other bonds for political means.

By the mid-1550s, however, Diogo was firmly in control of Kongo and its establishment. He had steered the church out of the hands of Jesuits, whose mission between 1548 and 1555 had sought to place both the church and the Portuguese resident community under their (and the Portuguese crown's) control. In 1553 he won the right to appoint a captain of the Portuguese against rights of the Portuguese throne. He was troubled, as was Afonso, with growing Portuguese trade with Ndongo, but he expanded the country. Southward he consolidated control over Kiangala along the coast, and under his guidance Kongo gained control all along the south border of the country and into the east as well.

When Diogo died in 1561 there was a brief succession dispute between two of his sons. One son, named Afonso II, ruled before being overthrown by his brother Bernardo I (1561–1567). During Bernardo's reign, members of rival *kandas*, perhaps connected to Afonso II, plotted against him, and he faced one open rebellion led by a discontented nobleman who started out in Mpangu and also seized Nsundi. Some of the Portuguese community also joined in this rebellion but were slaughtered and their property seized. Not all the Portuguese joined in, and those who remained loyal were still secure.

Bernardo took an interest in expansion to the east, for early seventeenth-century tradition maintained that he died fighting the "Jagas," who seem to have resided in the region of the Kwango. The fact that his successor, his uncle and Diogo's son, Henrique I, also died in the east (fighting against the Tio kingdom) the very next year, 1568, clearly suggests a strong movement towards the Kwango, and equally strong opposition.

Henrique's death appears to have set off a succession dispute of great significance. Henrique left the capital and civil government of Kongo in the hands of Alvaro Nimi a Lukeni lua Mvemba, the son of his wife by a previous husband when he went to the east. After Henrique's death, Álvaro managed to be proclaimed king Álvaro I, on the basis that Henrique left no issue of his own. At this point, the "Jagas" invaded Kongo.

The origin and nature of the Jagas is a disputed point in Kongo historiography. The most detailed account places their origin along the Kwango, though historians have posited other locations. They were described as rootless cannibals who stormed the country through Mbata, sacking Mbanza Kongo and driving Alvaro to an island in the Zaire River. Some historians have taken this story literally and maintain that they were from the Kwango region, displaced by fighting there. Others see a local revolt behind the Jaga movement, perhaps in support of the Mwene Mbata, who had a claim to Kongo's throne should the royal dynasty ever die out. Since contemporary documents suggest that Álvaro's succession to the throne represented the end of one dynasty and the start of another, a rebellion from Mbata is not out of the question.

Whatever the cause, Álvaro's desperate plight inspired him to seek Portuguese help to restore him to the throne, help that came from São Tomé under the guidance of Francisco de Gouveia Sottomaior in 1571. He and his force of six hundred men did eventually place Álvaro back on the throne, but at a price. The price was, among other things, permitting Portugal control of the mines of precious metal (none was found), to colonize Luanda island, and probably to collect tribute from the shell money (*nzimbu*) mines there, and the submission of the Portuguese residents in Kongo to an official appointed by the king of Portugal. Álvaro apparently also swore a symbolic vassalage to the Portuguese crown, though this carried very little significance.

John K. Thornton

See also: **Kongo, Teke (Tio), and Loango: History to 1483; Kongo Kingdom: Jaga Invasion to 1665; Kongo Kingdom: Afonso I, Christianity, and Kingship; Portugal: Exploration and Trade in the Fifteenth Century.**

Further Reading

Hilton, A. *The Kingdom of Kongo*. Oxford, 1985.

Thornton, J. "The Kingdom of Kongo, ca. 1390–1678: History of an African Social Formation." *Cahiers d'Etudes Africaines*. 22 (1982): 325–342.

Vansina, J. (with T. Obenga). "The Kongo Kingdom and Its Neighbours." In *General History of Africa*, edited by B. A. Ogot. Vol. 5. UNESCO, 1981–1992.

Kongo Kingdom: Jaga Invasion to 1665

Kongo's King Álvaro I Nimi a Lukeni lua Mvemba (1568–1587) took power under irregular circumstances upon the unexpected death of his predecessor. He was not descended directly from Henrique, being the son of his wife by a previous husband. Later, apologetic genealogists made him a descendant of Afonso I's (1509–1542) second daughter, Isabel Lukeni lua Mvemba, when the issue of the first daughter, Nzinga a Mvemba, had finished, an approach that oversimplifies the real descent of the kings after Afonso. Challenges to his claim may have lay behind the Jaga invasion, which temporarily drove him from the throne and forced him to ask Portugal for assistance.

What Alvaro's success really illustrates, however, is the degree to which the electoral system had been bypassed by kings who could more or less choose their successors from either children or clients. Kongo's administrative centralization had increased, especially now that the appointment and dismissal of the governors of the major provinces was primarily in the hands of the kings and drawn from his clients and family (together making up his *kanda*). Once the Jaga threat was removed, and the Portuguese expedition of Francisco Gouveia de Sottomaior had been withdrawn in 1576, Álvaro consolidated his control over the country.

When Paulo Dias de Novais arrived to colonize Angola for Portugal in 1575, Álvaro had had to accept this as the price of Portuguese support, and in fact sent some forces to assist the Portuguese governor. When Dias de Novais's small force was nearly destroyed in

Ndongo in 1579, Álvaro dispatched an army to help. While unsuccessful, the attempt effectively removed claims that Portugal might have had over Kongo.

Álvaro extended Kongo eastward, and in the 1580s began a campaign to have his capital, which he renamed São Salvador after its principal church, designated as an episcopal see. He died before he saw these projects to their conclusion, but his son, Álvaro II Mpanzu a Nimi (1587–1614) continued them.

Álvaro II's succession was contested by his brother and by members of the *kanda* his father had displaced, and it was at least five years before he was secure against revolts. Once secure, however, he began moving, through strategic marriages and appointments, to bring the hereditary ruling elites of Soyo and Mbata, the traditional electors of Kongo, more fully under his control. The process he initiated would be a long one, successfully completed in Mbata but strongly resisted in Soyo, which thanks to its participation in international trade boasted a large urban capital, Mbanza Soyo, and ready access to the wealth of the Atlantic.

Álvaro II continued making conquests in the east, bringing Kongo to its fullest extent by around 1610. In 1596 he won the right from Rome to have his own bishop, but Portugal claimed the right to name the bishop. The Portuguese bishops favored Angolan interests over Kongolese ones and sought to extend church control beyond what Álvaro considered acceptable bonds.

The process of centralizing the powers of the king that had taken place during the reigns of Álvaro I and II, while it had changed Kongo's constitution, created new problems. The powerful provincial nobility could support rival claimants to the throne and might rebel when the victor sought to remove them. Álvaro III Nimi a Mpanzu (1614–1622), who won the crown over a rival shortly after Alvaro II's death, faced constant rebellion from his predecessors' appointees, who refused to yield their places to his own appointees. When he died in 1622, they forced the election of a compromise king, Pedro II Nkanga a Mvika, from a client lineage (said to be descended from Afonso's third daughter, Ana Zumba a Mvemba).

The compromise only complicated matters, for Pedro's son Garcia I Mvemba a Nkanga (1624–1626) tried unsuccessfully to force his own appointees into these offices, and was overthrown by one of them, Manuel Jordão, duke of Nsundi in favor of Ambrósio Nimi a Nkanga (1626–1631), one of Álvaro II's descendants.

After short reigns by several kings unable to consolidate their control, various provinces were held by members of two *kandas*, one, the Kinkanga a Mvika established by Pedro II, and the other, the Kimpanzu from the descendants of Alvaro II. Soyo was also involved, for its rulers not only resisted integration into Kongo, but thanks to interlocking marriages with both *kandas*, provided a refuge for losing *kandas*.

The Kimpanzu king Álvaro IV Nzinga a Nkuwu took over from Ambrósio in 1631. In 1633 when he sought to remove Daniel da Silva, related to Soyo's ruling house, as duke of Mbamba, he was strongly resisted, eventually calling on two brothers from a client family (later called the Kinlaza) Álvaro Nimi a Lukeni and Garcia Nkanga a Lukeni. When Álvaro IV died in 1636, and his Kimpanzu successor Álvaro V sought to remove them, they rebelled and took over the kingship, first as Alvaro VI (1636–1641) and then as Garcia II (1641–1661).

Garcia's reign was marked, first by the suppression of all Kimpanzu officeholders, and then by the elimination of those from the Kinkanga a Mvika, completed by 1657. He was less successful in several sustained military efforts against Soyo, the last holdout against consolidation of royal control. Not only did Soyo resist and defeat Garcia's armies, but the Kimpanzu managed to take refuge there to continue to nourish their hopes of returning to power. Despite this failure, though, Garcia was in other ways Kongo's strongest king, presiding over a powerfully centralized kingdom at the height of its territorial extent.

When Garcia died in 1661, his son António Vita a Nkanga easily succeeded him to the throne and quickly eliminated potential rivals. António, however, was drawn into a border dispute with Portuguese Angola over control of the small state of Mbwila. In the Battle of Mbwila (or Ulanga as it was known in Kongo) in 1665, Kongo's army was defeated, leaving António dead on the battlefield and no clear-cut successor. The stage was set for a disastrous civil war.

JOHN K. THORNTON

Further Reading

Hilton, A. *The Kingdom of Kongo*. Oxford: 1985.

Thornton, J. "The Kingdom of Kongo, ca. 1390–1678: History of an African Social Formation." *Cahiers d'Etudes Africaines*. 22 (1982): 325–342.

———. *The Kingdom of Kongo: Civil War and Transition, 1641–1718*, Madison: 1983.

Vansina, J. (with T. Obenga). "The Kongo Kingdom and Its Neighbours." In *General History of Africa*, edited by B. A. Ogot. Vol. 5., UNESCO, 1981–1992.

Kongo Kingdom: Seventeenth and Eighteenth Centuries

When King António I Vita a Nkanga died at the Battle of Mbwila-Ulanga (1665) a succession struggle ensued, with both Kinlaza and Kimpanzu *kanda's* candidates. Fighting was as much Kongo against Soyo as between rival branches, Soyo supporting Kimpanzu kings and nobles of Kongo supporting Kinlaza ones. The Kinlaza Álvaro VII Mpanzu a Mpandu (1665–1666) was ousted by the Kimpanzu Álvaro VIII Mvemba a Mpanzu (1666–1668), who in turn was overthrown by the Kinlaza, Pedro III Nkanga a Mpanzu (1668–1670). Pedro, in turn, was driven out by Kimpanzu Álvaro IX Mpanzu a Ndbwila (1669–1970), and fled with his followers to the mountainous region of Mbula, south of the Zaire, to build a rival capital at Lemba, where he remained until his death in 1683.

Meanwhile, another Kinlaza contender, Rafael I Nzinga a Nkanga, sought the aid of Portuguese Angola, not only to place himself on the throne but to conquer Soyo. Rafael's gambit threatened Kongo's sovereignty, but the Portuguese army sent to assist him was decisively defeated by Soyo's forces at the Battle of Kitombo (October 18, 1670). Rafael reoccupied São Salvador, and the Kimpanzu, rebuffed, set up a dynasty in exile at Luvota, in southern Soyo, where a line of short-lived kings, including Afonso II and III, ruled under the tutelage of the elderly Dona Suzanna da Nóbrega, effective head of the Kimpanzu *kanda*. Daniel I retook São Salvador for the Kimpanzu in 1674 but was driven out by the Kinlaza forces of Pedro III in 1678. Pedro III did not reoccupy the city, but sacked and abandoned it, leaving the once proud capital depopulated, too vulnerable to be defended or reoccupied.

A series of regional powers had now emerged, each headed by someone with a claim to the throne established through a *kanda*. The Kimpanzu continued in Luvota with Soyo's support, while Kinlaza contenders were found in Lemba, headed by Pedro III, and his son João II (1683–after 1716) after his death. Another Kinlaza branch ruled in the southwest at Nkondo headed by Dona Ana Afonso de Leão and her nephews. Yet another *kanda*, composed of people of mixed Kimpanzu-Kinlaza descent occupied the mountain of Kibangu in the east with would-be kings André I (1689), Manuel I (1690), Álvaro X Agua Rosada (1690–1695), and his brother Pedro IV Agua Rosada (1695–1718) as their claimants. The province of Nsundi to the north, meanwhile, fell under the control of Kimpanzus appointed in the 1660s and remained under their hereditary control, maintaining a nominal loyalty to Kongo, but no longer a participant in its politics.

The politics of the late seventeenth century revolved around attempts to reoccupy São Salvador, the spiritual capital of the country, first by Manuel in 1690, and then briefly by both João II and Pedro IV in 1696. No one could hope to restore the country without occupying the capital, and yet no one was prepared to risk the occupation without forces more sizable than could be mustered by any of the pretenders. At the same time, missionaries of the Capuchin order, who had worked in Kongo since 1645 and were much respected, attempted to broker a negotiated restoration.

Pedro IV achieved this restoration by persuading his rivals that he could be king while respecting their rights to hereditary control in their respective areas. After winning nominal recognition from Ana Afonso de Leão's faction, Pedro moved to reoccupy the capital in 1701.

The reoccupation and repopulation of the capital was slowed by two factors. First, the head of the colonizing expedition, Pedro Constantinho da Silva, who had interests in Soyo as well as at Kibangu, rebelled. Second, a popular antiwar movement, headed by Beatriz Kimpa Vita, temporarily disturbed the process. Beatriz, who claimed to be possessed by Saint Anthony, spoke to the desire of the common people for an end to the wars and a restoration of the capital. When political leaders rebuffed her, she founded a mass movement and became the first to reoccupy the capital. Constantinho da Silva joined the movement to occupy the capital in his own name and allied with the Kimpanzu of Luvota, whose candidate Manuel joined him and supported the Antonians.

Pedro IV and Ana Afonso de Leão countered by managing to capture, try, and burn Beatriz as a heretic. In 1709 Pedro stormed São Salvador, later beating off an attack from João II. Pedro's restoration rested on allowing the regional rulers to retain hereditary control in their own realms in exchange for promises that their lines rotate as king.

When Pedro IV died in 1718, he was succeeded by Manuel II, from the Kimpanzu of Luvota. As unpublished documents in Rio de Janeiro reveal, Manuel's long reign helped to stabilize Pedro's peace. He faced challenges from Kinlaza of Nkondo, with fighting in 1733–1734. When Manuel died in 1743, he passed the crown on to Garcia IV (1743–1752) of the Kinlaza of Mbula (now in Matari) in accordance with Pedro's compromise.

Garcia met with opposition from those who did not wish to honor the compromise. Manuel's widowed queen, who returned to Luvota, fostered the ambitions of that faction while fearing Garcia. Garcia was succeeded by Nicolau I (1752–post 1758), probably from the Kimpanzu faction of Luvota, and he was succeeded by Sebastião I from the Kinlaza of Matari. In 1763 or 1764, Pedro V, of the Luvota faction became king but was forced to withdraw to Luvota by Álvaro XI (1764–1779), a Kinlaza from Matari.

When Álvaro died a new struggle developed, between his heirs, Pedro V's from Luvota, and the Kinlaza of Nkondo, who had not had a chance to rule since Pedro IV's compromise. José I, from Nkondo, emerged the victor in 1781 and passed power on to his brother Afonso V when he died in 1785, putting Pedro

IV's settlement in full disarray. The Agua Rosadas of Kibangu, Pedro IV's descendants, established a regency to determine the succession. Although several kings (Álvaro XII, Aleixo I, Joaquim I) were elected, the regency became a new constitution involving participation of both Kinlaza factions and the Agua Rosadas. Henrique I (1794–1803) emerged from the regency, but when he sought to end it, he was overthrown by Garcia V Agua Rosada, whose long rule (1803–1830) established a new system.

John K. Thornton

Further Reading

Broadhead, S. "Beyond Decline: The Kingdom of Kongo in the Eighteenth and Nineteenth Centuries." *International Journal of African Historical Studies*. 12 (1979): 615–650.

Hilton, A. *The Kingdom of Kongo*. Oxford: 1985.

Thornton, J. *The Kongolese Saint Anthony: Dona Beatriz Kimpa Vita and the Antonian Movement, 1684–1706*. Cambridge and New York: 1998.

———. *The Kingdom of Kongo: Civil War and Transition, 1641–1718*. Madison: 1983.

Vansina, J. (with T. Obenga). "The Kongo Kingdom and Its Neighbours." In *General History of Africa*, edited by B. A. Ogot. Vol. 5 of 8. UNESCO, 1981–1992.

Kouyate, Tiémoko Garan (1902–1940?)

Teacher, Journalist, Political Activist

A nearly forgotten pioneer of African nationalism, Tiémoko Garan Kouyate was prominent in the small left-wing anticolonial movements in France in the 1920s and 1930s. These movements had for a time a close but troubled relationship with the Communist International and the French Communist Party, the only powerful force totally opposed to Western colonialism in that period (1920–1935), and Kouyate was one of the first African communists. He came from the first generation of Western-educated Africans in French Soudan (now Mali), where he was born on April 27, 1902, at Segou. He went to the Ecole Normale William Ponty, a celebrated teacher training college founded by the French at Goree in Senegal, and worked as a teacher in Côte d'Ivoire from 1921 to 1923.

He was awarded a scholarship for further studies in France (something very rare then) and went to the Ecole Normale at Aix en Provence. He soon ceased his advanced teacher training there, possibly being expelled, and went to join in the radical political movements started by a few people from the French colonies living in France: Algerians, West Indians, Vietnamese, and some Africans. Some organizations and newspapers were founded by those "colonials" in the 1920s with help from the French Communist Party (PCF), but with both radical and more "reformist" individuals sometimes working together, as in the Ligue Universelle de la Défense de la Race Noire (LUDRN) and the companion journal *Les Continents* in 1924. Later a more radical Comité de Défense de la Race Nègre (CDRN) was set up on July 4, 1926. The dominant figure in this was Lamine Senghor from Senegal (1889–1927), a communist who sought to keep his organization an independent one for black people. Senghor (no relation of Léopold Senghor, Senegal's first president) attended the Brussels Congress of 1927, which led to foundation of the League Against Imperialism (LAI) by communist and other anti–colonial campaigners. Soon afterwards the CDRN spilt up, and in May 1927 the more militant Black anti-imperialists formed the new and radical Ligue de Défense de la Race Nègre (LDRN), again headed by Senghor until his early death a few months later. Kouyate became the leading figure in this anticolonial group, whose ideas were spread particularly through its newspaper *La Race Nègre*.

Kouyate told the famous African American leader W. E. B. Du Bois (on April 29, 1929) that the LDRN's aim was "the political, economic, moral, and intellectual emancipation of the whole of the Negro race. It is a matter of winning back, by all honorable means, the national independence of the Negro peoples in the colonial territories of France, England, Belgium, Italy, Spain, Portugal . . . and of setting up in Black Africa a great Negro state." The French colonial authorities regarded the LDRN as a dangerous subversive organization and banned *La Race Nègre* in the colonies. Meetings were reported by police spies and the alleged proceedings were described in regular circulars on "revolutionary activity" sent to colonial governors.

The communist connection added to the colonial rulers' concern. It was always there, but for a time Kouyate rejected communist subsidies and control, maintaining contact with noncommunist black personalities. However, after 1928 the Comintern and PCF exerted closer control, all the more easily as the LDRN had no other source of funds than the communists. After Kouyate spent four months in Moscow in 1930 he called for fuller submission to Comintern direction. The Africans and West Indians in the LDRN had resented communist control and now a split occurred in 1930–1931. Emile Faure, a half-Senegalese activist, took control of the LDRN under that name, and asserted independence of the communists. Kouyate and his followers stuck with the communist paymasters and created a new organization in 1932, the Union des Travailleurs Nègres (UTN), a name reflecting Kouyate's energetic work to organize black workers, especially seamen, in France; in 1932 he attended the Altona (Hamburg) conference of the International of Seamen and Harbor Workers, organized by George Padmore, secretary of the communist-sponsored International Trade Union Committee of Negro Workers (ITUC-NW). Kouyate and the Trinidadian activist Padmore were prominent in radical black organizations linked to the Comintern and Moscow for some years.

The Kouyate group's newspaper in Paris was renamed *Le Cri des Nègres* and was subsidized by communist funds. But Kouyate still resisted complete communist control, and he was expelled from the PCF in October 1933 and from the UTN the following month.

Remaining in Paris, Kouyate helped organize protests among black people and others against the Italian invasion of Ethiopia in 1935. In December 1935 he started a monthly magazine, *Africa*, initially with help from the LDRN, still active, and the North Africans' party in France, the Etoile Nord Africaine (ENA). Apart from fierce attacks on Italy, the magazine's tone was far from Kouyate's earlier militancy; like many other anticolonial campaigners, and like the PCF after 1935, Kouyate now concentrated on calling for reforms for Africans' benefit. After the Popular Front government came to power in France in 1936, Kouyate tried to start a "federation of African youth" based in Dakar and in 1937 wrote to the governor general of French West Africa proposing a federal-style association of France and its colonies. But the tamed radical had no further influence with the colonial authorities who had once feared him as a firebrand. For a time in the late 1930s he received money from the French ministry of the colonies.

Tiémoko Garan Kouyate met a mysterious death during the Nazi occupation of France. According to one story he was entrusted by the Germans with money for propaganda and was executed for pocketing the money; but this has not been confirmed. It is likely that Kouyate had always been ready to take money from any source available, while simultaneously trying to maintain his independence from external influences. He was clearly wrong if he thought he could try this with the Gestapo; but earlier he had, despite compromises, been able to maintain campaigning activity on behalf of Africa for years, as one of the few active campaigners against imperialism in Africa in the interwar period.

JONATHAN DERRICK

See also: **Mali (Republic of): Nationalism, Federation, Independence; World War II: French West Africa, Equatorial Africa.**

Biography

Born in French Soudan (now Mali) on April 27, 1902, at Segou. Attended the Ecole Normale William Ponty in Senegal, and worked as a teacher in Côte d'Ivoire from 1921 to 1923. Awarded a scholarship for further studies at the Ecole Normale at Aix en Provence. Became involved in radical politics. In 1927 became head of the radical Ligue de Défense de la Race Nègre (LDRN). Spent four months in Moscow in 1930, thereafter encouraged further loyalty to the Communist Party abroad. In 1932 formed a new organization, the Union des Travailleurs Nègres (UTN). Organized protests against the Italian invasion of Ethiopia in 1935. Started a magazine, *Africa,* in December 1935. Died under uncertain circumstances during the Nazi occupation of France.

Further Reading

Dewitte, P. *Les mouvements nègres en France 1919–1939* (Black Movements in France, 1919–1939. Paris: Harmattan, 1985.

Langley, J. A. *Pan-Africanism and Nationalism in West Africa 1900–1945.* Oxford: Oxford University Press, 1973.

Kruger, Paul (1825–1904)

South African Statesman

Stephanus Johannes Paulus ("Paul") Kruger was born at Bulhoek, Eastern Cape, on October 10, 1825, the descendant of a German soldier employed by the Dutch East India Company. At the age of ten, he and his family took part in the Potgieter trek to the Transvaal. Like many of his peers he married early, in 1842, and again, on the death of his first wife, to her cousin Gezina du Plessis, by whom he had sixteen children. His bush skills, physical prowess, and leadership qualities were early recognized: in 1852, he was appointed deputy commandant for the expedition against Sechele, and after a period in which he successfully negotiated his way around and through the internecine squabbles that characterized the infant Transvaal republic, he was elected commandant general (in effect, the second highest office of state) in May 1864.

The final step on the political ladder beckoned in 1871, when Marthinus Pretorius resigned, following the Keate Award against the Transvaal. However, maintaining that he lacked the education required, he declined to stand, and the Cape Afrikaner Thomas Burgers took office instead. Relations between the two men soon deteriorated, the extreme Calvinist Kruger suspecting Burgers of religious unorthodoxy.

In May 1873 Kruger stood down and his post was immediately abolished. After a short period of withdrawal, he returned to active political life but pointedly turned down Burgers' offer to head the punitive expedition against Sekhukhune in 1876, declaring that it lacked God's blessing. Meanwhile, the Transvaal was rapidly drifting toward political and financial bankruptcy. Burgers attempted to mend fences by appointing Kruger vice president in March 1877, but within weeks, Theophilus Shepstone had annexed the republic on behalf of Britain, claiming that he had the support of the majority of Transvaal Boers. Kruger immediately challenged this assumption, thereby staking his claim to future leadership. He headed a deputation to London later that year requesting a plebiscite; when this was refused, he organized an independent referendum that came out strongly in favor of independence, which was again refused when he returned to London in 1878. Mass protest meetings were then held, culminating in the Paardekraal (later, Krugersdorp) gathering in December 1880, at which independence was proclaimed on December 16. A short conflict then ensued (the First Boer War) marked by a British military reverse at Majuba Hill (February 1881). Fearing a wider confrontation with the Boers, comprising a majority of whites in South Africa as a whole, William Gladstone conceded a limited independence, which included an assertion of British suzerainty over the new state (Pretoria Convention, August 1881).

Kruger was inaugurated president in 1883, after an easy electoral victory over his main rival Piet Joubert. His first term of office saw success with Britain's removal of some of the restrictions of the Pretoria Convention, including the deletion of the suzerainty claim in the revised London Convention (February 1884). But the principal event of his first presidency was the discovery of gold in the Witwatersrand in 1886, which in a decade transformed the republic and increased its revenue twenty-fold, making it the primary economic power in South Africa.

During Kruger's second term of office (to 1892), a large, mainly British immigrant population (the "Uitlanders") established itself on the goldfields. Kruger sought to protect the Boers' and his political position by imposing a fourteen-year residence period for the franchise, building a railway to Delagoa Bay (completed in 1894) to lessen his dependence on Great Britain, and boosting his state revenues by granting monopolies over such vital commodities as dynamite, actions that imposed further burdens on the mining industry. Kruger's growing obduracy on this issue (and the narrowness of his victory over Joubert in the 1892 presidential election) was instrumental in inspiring the notion of a coup against his administration, supported by military assistance from outside. This was set in motion by Cecil Rhodes, who used the pretext of Kruger's oppression of the Uitlander community to organize the disastrous Jameson Raid in December 1895. The raid represented the high point of Kruger's career, winning him widespread international sympathy, enhanced by his shrewd decision to return Jameson and his men to the British authorities for punishment.

Thereafter, Kruger's status within the republic was unassailable: he was returned with a large majority over Joubert's "Progressive" platform in 1898, a victory that considerably strengthened his hand in his dealings with Alfred Milner, the South African high commissioner. The Uitlander franchise was again the main point at issue between the two sides, with the British claim to suzerainty being revived by Milner when Kruger was persuaded by his advisers to compromise on the franchise issue. Kruger's eventual decision to initiate war in October 1899 was based on the expectation that a quick Boer military victory would induce Britain to negotiate a settlement, as in 1881.

The South African War instead became a prolonged conflict in which Britain sought to regain its prestige as the leading imperial power, and the Boers reverted to traditional commando methods of fighting after the loss of Pretoria in mid-1900. Kruger himself left for Europe in September 1900 to rally support for the Boer cause. However, widespread public sympathy failed to translate into anything material. Disappointed, Kruger sought sanctuary in Holland, and died in the Swiss town of Mentone on July 14, 1904.

Kruger's reputation has suffered at the hands of both hagiographers and vilifiers. To older Afrikaner historians he was the God-fearing, incorruptible, and legendary folk hero; to many British observers, he was an ignorant, corrupt, obstinate, bigoted, and essentially hypocritical figure. Both of these views are essentially propagandist. Kruger seems to have encouraged the spread of probably mythical stories about his hunting adventures, and like many elderly statesmen who have enjoyed long periods of office, behaved in an increasingly autocratic and idiosyncratic fashion. On the other hand, despite his firmly Calvinist beliefs, he had good personal relations with non-Calvinists, and indeed, people with no religious faith. His "illiteracy" (certainly exaggerated) was moderated by a phenomenal memory that gave him obvious advantages in negotiation. And in the aftermath of the Jameson Raid, he embarked upon the modernization and reform of his administration, appointing among others the future South African leader, Jan Smuts, as state attorney in 1898. His personal attitude to the black majority was at least marked by an honesty often lacking in the practice of individuals such as his main rival, Cecil Rhodes.

MURRAY STEELE

See also: **Afrikaans and Afrikaner Nationalism, Nineteenth Century; Boer Expansion: Interior of South Africa; Jameson Raid, Origins of South African War: 1895–1899; Rhodes, Cecil J.; South Africa: Confederation, Disarmament and the First Anglo-Boer War, 1871–1881; South Africa: Gold on the Witwatersrand, 1886–1899; South African War, 1899–1902.**

Biography

Born Stephanus Johannes Paulus Kruger at Bulhoek, Eastern Cape, on October 10, 1825. Took part, with his family, in the Potgieter trek to the Transvaal in 1835. Married in 1842. Later remarried upon death of his first wife; had sixteen children with his second wife. Appointed deputy commandant for the expedition against Sechele in 1852. Elected commandant general in 1864. Stood down in 1873. Appointed vice president in 1877. Inaugurated as president in 1883. Died in Mentone, Holland, on July 14, 1904.

Further Reading

Davenport, T., and C. Saunders. *South Africa: A Modern History.* Basingstoke: Macmillan, and New York: St. Martin's Press, 2000.

Fisher, J. *Paul Kruger: His Life and Times.* London: Secker and Warburg, 1974.

Marais, J. *The Fall of Kruger's Republic.* Oxford: Clarendon Press, 1962.

Meintjes, J. *President Paul Kruger: A Biography.* London: Cassell, 1974.

Nasson, B. *The South African War, 1899–1902.* London: Arnold, and New York: Oxford University Press, 1999.

Kuba: *See* Kasai and Kuba: Chiefdoms and Kingdom.

Kumasi

Kumasi is the capital of Asante in the Republic of Ghana in West Africa. Today, Kumasi is the second most important city in Ghana and covers a total area of fifty-seven square miles with a population of about one million. Kumasi has tremendous importance as a political, cultural, and commercial center. Much has been written about this historic city based on both oral and literary sources. The origin of this city is traced to the activities of the descendants of Ankyewa Nyame, the great ancestress of the royal *Oyoko* clan that has ruled Kumasi and presided over Asante since approximately the seventeenth century. Through a series of migrations, Ankyewa Nyame and her descendants settled first at Asantemanso then moved to Kokofu, all in the southwestern part of the present day Ashanti Region. One of her descendants, Oti Akenten, allegedly moved and settled at Asaman in the Kwaman forest. According to oral traditions, the newcomers from Kokofu purchased the land from the original settlers in the Asaman area. This position is contrary to popular notions about traditional land acquisition and ownership among the Asante. It was this site that evolved into the modern day Kumasi.

Significantly too, before the Oyoko migrants from Kokofu moved into the present area of Kumasi, there were several independent settlements each with its own head. Among them were Amakom, Kaase, Suntreso, and Tafo. At this stage, the main significance of the Kwaman area of which Kumasi became a part was based on its commercial role. From the end of the seventeenth century, it assumed increasing political significance when Osei Tutu succeeded Obiri Yeboa as ruler of Kwaman. Through a series of shrewd moves involving dynastic marriages and political alliances, Osei Tutu, with the advice of his close friend and spiritual guide, *Okomfo* Anokye, was able to forge a strong political-cum-military union involving independent neighboring states like Mampon, Nsuta, and Bekwai. Osei Tutu headed this union that became known as Asante. With it the Asante in 1701 defeated Denkyira, their traditional enemy and overlord. Afterward, Osei Tutu ceased to be merely ruler of Kumasi (*Kumasihene*) but became that of Asante (*Asantehene*). Consequently, Kumasi began its meteoric rise to cultural and political eminence. Under Kumasi leadership, Asante had virtually conquered the entire region that came to constitute the British Colony of the Gold Coast (later renamed Ghana) by the beginning of the nineteenth century.

As the traditional political capital, Kumasi was the residence of the *Asantehene*. All important Kumasi officeholders and functionaries who performed services associated with the Kumasi court and their families were also resident there. The court had the responsibility of maintaining political order and expanding Asante territory. The national assembly met in Kumasi. Thus, all important officeholders throughout Asante also had temporary residence there, or at least visited occasionally to attend to official business. From the time of the *Asantehene,* Osei Tutu, Kumasi became the cultural capital. In this capacity, it was the venue for such important national festivals like the annual *Odwira,* which was an occasion for affirmation and renewal of personal allegiance to the *Asantehene* by officeholders.

In the precolonial period, the core of Kumasi population was made up of the *Oyoko* royals, their spouses, officeholders, and functionaries. There was also a small, carefully controlled settler community of "strangers," mainly coastal Fante and Muslim clerics from the northern Savanna region. They were usually involved in the commercial life of the city. Kumasi was at the center of trade routes radiating to the north, south, east, and west that linked the Gold Coast to the outside world via the Western Sudan and the Atlantic coast. Kumasi residents themselves often did not engage in direct agricultural production. Rather they depended on producers from the outlying villages for their food supplies. The main economic activity in

Kumasi involved the production and distribution of goods like imported commodities, gold ornaments, and services in the court that ensured the maintenance of the sociopolitical order.

Asante desire to participate in and control the maritime trade in the Gold Coast frequently led to confrontations with her southern neighbors and indirectly with the British, who by the nineteenth century had emerged as the most important European power there. It was as part of this saga that British forces invaded Asante in 1873–1874, burned the city, and unilaterally imposed the debilitating Treaty of Fomena on Asante. Between 1874 and 1883 there was relative peace and attempts were made to rebuild Kumasi. In 1883 there was a disputed succession that degenerated into a civil war (1883–1888). In 1888 Kwaku Dua III, later Agyeman Prempe I, was installed *Asantehene*. He renewed efforts to regenerate Kumasi. By 1896 the British had developed more fully their imperial strategy known as "the forward policy." Under it the British attempted to undermine the integrity of Asante by abducting Agyeman Prempe I and sending him, together with his principal advisers and close relatives, into exile in the Seychelles, and imposing British hegemony on Asante.

From this period, the modernization of Kumasi began. The British continued to use it as their administrative headquarters for their new political creation of "Ashanti." In this new capacity, modern buildings were constructed to house government offices. A Western judicial system was introduced along with Western concepts of local government. In 1925, the Kumasi Public Health Board was established as the basis of a modern local government. By 1989, it had evolved into the Kumasi Metropolitan Assembly.

The communication system was also modernized with the construction of motor roads, railway, postal, and telegraphic systems. Christian organizations, like the Basel and the Wesleyan Methodist Missions, moved in to proselytize. At the same time they began to establish schools and to construct church buildings and dwelling houses for themselves that were emulated by their converts. European firms also established branches there. The genesis of the modern banking system was also in this era. Competitive house building in Kumasi was a characteristic of this period, as house ownership was a means of asserting wealth and status in modern Kumasi society.

Despite attempts at innovation, the hallmark of Kumasi continues to be the coexistence of modernity and tradition that is likely to persist well into the twenty-first century.

Wilhelmina Joseline Donkoh

See also: **Asante Kingdom: Osei Tutu and Founding of; Ghana, Republic of.**

Further Reading

Abloh, F. A. *Growth of Towns in Ghana: A Historical Study of the Social and Physical Growth of Towns in Ghana*. Kumasi: Department of Housing and Planning Research, Faculty of Architecture, University of Science and Technology, 1967; rev. 1972.

Arhin, K., and K. Afari-Gyan, eds. *The City of Kumasi Handbook: Past, Present and Future.* Cambridge: Faxbooks/Hart-Talbort Printers, 1992.

Brown, J. W. *Kumasi 1896–1923: Urban Africa During the Early Colonial Period.* Ph.D. diss., University of Wisconsin, 1972.

Donkoh, W. J., *N.V. Asare's History of Asante in Tshi with Introduction*, Birmingham: M Soc Sc Dissertation, University of Birmingham, 1990.

Garlick, P. C. *African Traders in Kumasi.* Accra: Economic Research Division, University College of Ghana, 1959.

McCaskie, T. C. *State and Society in Pre-colonial Asante*, Cambridge: Cambridge University Press, 1995.

Schildkrout, E., ed. *The Golden Stool: Studies of the Asante Centre and Periphery.* New York: Anthropological Papers, American Museum of Natural History, 1987.

Tipple, A. G. *The Development of Housing Policy in Kumasi, Ghana, 1901 to 1981: With an Analysis of the Current Housing Stock.* Newcastle: Centre for Architectural and Development Overseas, University of Newcastle upon Tyne, 1987.

Wilks, I. *Forests of Gold: Essays on the Akan Kingdom of Asante*. Athens: Ohio University Press, 1993.

Kumbi Saleh: *See* Ghana, Empire of: History of.

Kush

The term "Kush" was used by ancient Egyptians to designate one of the states to the south of their frontier at the First Cataract. Modern scholars have equated the Kingdom of Kush with the culture based at the town of Kerma in northern Sudan. This Kingdom of Kush coexisted with the Egyptian Old Kingdom, and during the Second Intermediate Period rivaled it in power. The beginning of the New Kingdom saw a resurgence of Egyptian power allied with an aggressive foreign policy which led, around 1500BCE, to the conquest of the Kingdom of Kush and the occupation of its territory. Egyptian control of this area waned during the eleventh century BCE, and into the resulting power vacuum arose another polity, also called the Kingdom of Kush, but frequently referred to today as the kingdoms of Napata and Meroe.

There is much debate as to the origins of this second Kingdom of Kush centered on the question of whether there was continuity from the New Kingdom into the early Kushite period, or whether there was a complete break of several centuries. Most of the evidence hinges on the necropolis at el-Kurru, located slightly downstream of the Fourth Cataract. The el-Kurru cemetery was excavated by George A. Reisner in 1918 and 1919. He was able to document a developmental sequence in the burials, from simple pit graves covered by small tumuli, to rock-cut tombs decorated with painted wall plaster, entered by descending a stepped dromos and covered by pyramids. He believed that the earliest of these burials was of the first ruler of Kush; the nature of the grave and the date assigned to it, in the ninth century BCE, indicate that there was discontinuity between the Egyptian New Kingdom and the rise of the Kushites. Excavations at the nearby site of Hillat el Arab, where contemporary, but richer, graves to the early graves at el-Kurru have been found, open a whole new debate that has yet to be developed.

By the mid-eighth century BCE, the Kushites were already a major power. Their kings had adopted Amun as their state god, and they were in a position to interfere in Egyptian affairs as champions of that god. Kashta was the first Kushite king to enter Egypt, but it was his successor Piye who conquered the whole country and ruled over an empire stretching from central Sudan as far north as the Mediterranean. Although Kushite control of Egypt lapsed as a result of conflicts with the Assyrians in the mid-seventh century BCE, the Kingdom of Kush survived for another thousand years.

The main religious center of the Kushites was at Jebel Barkal, which they called the "Pure Mountain" and believed to be the dwelling place of Amun. Barkal was one of a number of important sites at Napata that included a large complex of temples and palaces at the foot of the mountain, a temple, palace, massive storerooms, and cemetery at Sanam Abu Dom across the river, and the royal burial grounds at el-Kurru slightly downstream and Nuri slightly upstream. The political capital was probably moved regularly, the king progressing annually from his palace at Meroe far to the south to the major temples of Amun at Napata, Krtn, Gematon (Kawa), and Pnubs (Tabo or Kerma).

At the end of the fourth century BCE, the royal cemetery at Nuri was abandoned and, after a brief return to the ancestral cemetery at el-Kurru, thereafter almost all royal burials were at Meroe. In funerary culture, as in many other aspects of Kushite civilization, the influence of pharaonic Egypt was considerable, although the Kushites did not slavishly borrow from their northern neighbor. Rather, the Kushites selectively adopted religious ideology and artistic and architectural styles, and modified them to suit their own needs. In the architectural field, the pyramid is one of the most distinctive borrowings from Egypt (although the Kushite pyramid is derived from the nonroyal pyramids of the New Kingdom, which were a feature of Egyptian sites south of Aswan, rather than from the royal pyramids of the Old and Middle Kingdoms). Temples of the state god, Amun, were also of Egyptian type, although temples of local gods were distinctively Kushite.

The early Kushites used Egyptian as their written language but probably spoke an entirely unrelated language known as Meroitic. There is evidence that, early in the second century BCE, this language was committed to writing using two alphabetic scripts, one with characters borrowed from Egyptian hieroglyphs, the other a "cursive" script with some characters derived from Egyptian demotic. Almost all later inscriptions are written in one or another form of Meroitic, a language that remains untranslated at this time.

The withdrawal from Egypt does not seem to have had any serious repercussions for the Kingdom of Kush although the retention by the kings of the title "King of Upper and Lower Egypt" brought them into conflict with their northern neighbor on more than one occasion. In 593 BCE, Psammetik II invaded Kush and may have sacked Napata. Relations thereafter, with the latest Egyptian pharaohs and the Ptolemies, were largely peaceful or confined to small-scale military activities in the frontier zone. The arrival of the Romans in Egypt brought a renewed bout of fighting which may have culminated once again in the sack of Napata, although the frontier was drawn far to the north at Maharraqa.

There was much mutual benefit for Kush and Egypt from peaceful coexistence. Kush stood athwart one of the main trade routes from central Africa to the Mediterranean world and profited handsomely from its position as a middleman in that trade. The trade was probably entirely in the hands of the monarchy, and the wealth generated from it was of fundamental importance for the coherence of the state, it being used as patronage by the ruler to guarantee the support of the regional elites. The loss of the monopoly over this trade, which shifted eastward to the Red Sea, coupled with the increasing impoverishment of the later Roman Empire, may have been one of the causes of the dissolution and collapse of the Kushite state in the fourth century.

DEREK WELSBY

See also: **Kerma and Egyptian Nubia; Napata and Meroe.**

Further Reading

Adams, W. Y. *Nubia: Corridor to Africa.* London and Princeton: Allen Lane, 1977.

Shinnie, P. L. *Meroe: A Civilization of the Sudan.* London: Thames and Hudson, 1967.

Török, L. *The Kingdom of Kush: Handbook of the Napatan-Meroitic Civilization.* Leiden: Brill, 1997.

Welsby, D. A. *The Kingdom of Kush: The Napatan and Meroitic Empires.* London: British Museum Press, 1996.

Kwarafa: *See* Benue Valley Peoples: Jukun and Kwarafa.

L

Labor: Cooperative Work

Cooperative labor, in the form of work parties or other forms of voluntary collaboration, is historically widespread in Africa, and continues to play an important role in many areas. Two basic types of work group have been identified, though the distinction between them is blurred and many work groups had (and have) elements of both. The first is exchange labor or the "reciprocal work group," a small group of households that worked for each other regularly and in rotation, usually performing agricultural tasks. These were often relatively permanent groups, with fixed leaders and membership, though changes in the composition of the group could occur. Typically, the organizer provided everyday food and drink for the workers but the occasion was not associated with any kind of festivity. The second and larger type is referred to as the "festive" work group; food and drink were prepared and people came along on an appointed day to work, on the basis of either a public or private invitation. The work was concluded by the festive consumption of beer or other alcoholic drink. Reciprocity was not as strictly defined as in the former type, since these were ad hoc groups, disbanding after the task has been completed.

The basis of recruitment into work parties varied widely and could use ties of kinship, political unit, or locality, though in practice it was usually neighbors or people from the same territorial unit who collaborated. The morality involved was almost universally based on notions of reciprocity and mutual helpfulness, and the pool of potential workers was large. Those who contributed labor did so on the basis of close relationship, mutual interest, friendship, reciprocal obligation, or some other kind of preexisting link. In some areas, such as parts of Malawi and Zambia, extradomestic forms of labor cooperation were historically rare. In other cases cooperative labor was an aspect of formal, villagewide associations. Among the Wolof, for example, these associations were organized partly on an age and gender basis and were called *kompin,* after the French *compagnie*. They had established leaders, cut across kinship and class lines, and had a variety of functions aside from cooperative agricultural work, much like an age-set organization.

Although the homestead was the basic unit of production in most African societies, relying primarily on its own members, larger labor combinations were necessary for certain heavy or time-consuming tasks. Work parties were in demand at crucial points in the agricultural cycle that affected everybody (ploughing, sowing, weeding, and harvesting) but fields were not all ready for a particular task at precisely the same time, allowing collective labor inputs to be staggered. There were considerable benefits accruing from this if it enabled land to be planted, hoed, or harvested at the optimum time. Apart from breaking labor bottlenecks, cooperative work groups had another advantage in that they were not specialized. They could be called upon to perform a wide variety of tasks and reciprocity was usually reckoned in terms of labor time spent rather than the task performed.

Some writers maintain that it would have been economically more efficient for people to do the work themselves rather than expending energy and other resources on brewing beer for a work group. Others estimate the amount of labor devoted to beer brewing as being about half of the labor gain from a work party. Economic surveys in East and West Africa showed that there was little reliance on indigenous forms of cooperative work among "progressive" farmers, and it seems that work parties were in fact not suited to the constraints of more modern, cooperative production instigated by an external agency, whether of a capitalist nature or in terms of an ideology such as *ujamaa*.

Many commentators feel that festive labor was undertaken by poorer people, to the benefit of wealthier households or political leaders, and that exchange labor was found mainly among households of relatively equal economic status. However, the evidence on this is not conclusive, due to the many different forms of cooperative labor, the uncertain nature of the distinctions between them, and the variable conditions under which work parties operated in different parts of the continent. Many work groups operated under a general assumption of reciprocity and mutual helpfulness, in that people helped each other without expectation of immediate return, but in the knowledge that the receiver could be asked to provide labor, grain, or something else, in the future. The sanction for nonparticipation confirmed the principle of reciprocity, with those not working as expected being refused assistance when they themselves needed help. It has also been claimed that cooperative work was a means of redistributing wealth from richer to poorer households and that without it the latter would not have been able to manage certain vital tasks.

A number of writers have pointed out that cooperative work groups cannot be seen simply as indigenous or traditional responses to the need for collaborative effort, as something persisting from an unchanging past, and different from more modern forms of work. Instead, work parties are often responses to particular historical situations where labor was scarce, where poverty created a shortage of resources such as draught animals or agricultural implements, and where cash or hired labor were in short supply. Cooperative labor often survived, facilitated, or developed in reaction to, radical economic and cultural change. For example, in some cases cooperative work of the large, festive type may have arisen where labor shortages resulting from slavery coincided with the introduction of commercial export crops. Cooperative work may therefore be quite recent in some places, and one cannot make assumptions about its lineal development from, or into, other forms of work, including wage labor. In some of the documented cases work parties arose or intensified as a result of the introduction of cash cropping; in other cases similar circumstances led to the development of wage labor and a decline of cooperative forms.

Where homesteads became smaller due to factors such as population decline, a lower incidence of polygyny, missionary influence, growing individualism, and the independence of younger people, labor combinations sometimes became more widespread as a means of ensuring production. Urbanization and the absence of migrant workers exacerbated rural labor shortages in many places and work parties were a way of overcoming this problem. Changes in the nature of rural production, and the introduction of new technologies such as the plough, were also important, because they created new labor demands. Where production became more intensive due to the adoption of new crops or the introduction of cash crops, or where production was expanded due to new technology, cooperative work was sometimes one of the innovative responses that facilitated this.

PATRICK MCALLISTER

Further Reading

Donham, D. L. *Work and Power in Maale, Ethiopia*. Ann Arbor: UMI Research Press, 1985.

Englund, H. "The Self in Self-Interest: Land, Labour and Temporalities in Malawi's Agrarian Change." *Africa*. 69, no.1(1999): 139–159.

Erasmus, G. J. "Culture, Structure and Process: The Occurrence and Disappearance of Reciprocal Farm Labour." *South Western Journal of Anthropology*. 12, no. 4 (1956): 444–469.

Geschiere, P. "Working Groups or Wage Labour? Cash-Crops, Reciprocity and Money Among the Maka of Southeastern Cameroon." *Development and Change*. 26, no. 3 (1995): 503–523.

Moore, M. P. "Co-operative Labour in Peasant Agriculture." *Journal of Peasant Studies*. 1, no. 3 (1975): 270–291.

Saul, M. "Work Parties, Wages, and Accumulation in a Voltaic Village." *American Ethnologist*. 10, no. 1 (1983): 77–96.

Worby, E. "What Does Agrarian Wage Labour Signify? Cotton, Commoditisation and Social Form in Gokwe, Zimbabwe." *The Journal of Peasant Studies*. 23, no. 1 (1995): 1–29.

Labor: Decline in Traditional Forms of Exploitation

While some assert that colonialism was accompanied by systematic abuse of African labor, European colonial rule in Africa ultimately produced major changes in the traditional labor regime as it launched an attack on slavery and pawning and, consequently, on chiefs' rights in these areas.

Slavery in Africa, as elsewhere, was essentially an economic system although it was also justified on religious and social grounds. The nineteenth century witnessed a tremendous increase in slavery in Africa. Attempts to build new states or reform existing ones formed the basis for the increase in slavery. Abolition of external slave trade and the attempt to develop a "legitimate trade" in African raw materials stimulated slavery's growth across the continent, particularly in coastal societies and their hinterland. Zanzibar's emergence as an entrepôt and major clove producer stimulated slavery's growth in East Africa. In the savanna regions victorious Islamic jihad movements promoted increased production and trade that were both heavily dependent on slave labor. Thus, the Sokoto caliphate in northern Nigeria emerged as Africa's largest slave society by the end of the nineteenth century. Traditional forms of exploitation fell heavily on women.

Women dominated the slave and pawn populations in Africa as they were highly regarded for their productive and reproductive functions.

Closely interwoven with pawning and slavery was the issue of chiefs' rights. Chiefs could, and did, call on labor assistance for community projects (such as clearing paths and streams) and for work on royal properties, but as chiefs also became active slave masters, this brought the question of forced labor to the attention of European colonizers. European interest in nineteenth-century Africa was heavily influenced by economic and humanitarian concerns. Europeans professed an antislavery ideology for much of the nineteenth century, and their conquest of Africa was justified on this ground. Merchants and Christian missionaries called for the abolition of slavery (although for different reasons) that had increased as a concomitant of the state-building revolution which swept across Africa. Yet European colonial administrators found that immediate abolition of slavery was against their own interests. They needed the support of the chiefs, who were major slave-owners, to install the colonial system, and this made them less inclined to abolish slavery. Initially, therefore, it was something of a paradox that the erection of colonial rule witnessed the continuation of pawning and slavery, and the strengthening of the power of chiefs.

Opposition to slavery was dictated by colonial economic considerations. Surpluses from slave labor would not accrue to European capitalists, and this was contrary to the expectations of colonialism. Slaves were not consumers, and the prevailing doctrine held that slave labor was unproductive; consequently, both would adversely affect European industry. Simultaneously, colonialism made huge demands on labor and aimed to develop a wage-labor market in Africa. These could only be accomplished by an attack on slavery. Further, slavery was a moral wrong that would be righted by abolition. Generally, Europeans thought that slavery had to be abolished as part of the process of establishing European political control. Initially, however, European administrators (Belgian, British, French, German, and Portuguese) were reluctant to abolish slavery immediately for fear of undermining the chiefs and inducing economic dislocation. Yet the establishment of European rule and the economics of colonialism did produce an assault on the traditional labor regime and on the rights of chiefs therein.

Slavery was abolished by a combination of economic, administrative, and legal measures effected by Europeans as well as by a flight from the estates on the part of the slaves themselves. African slaves abolished slavery and broke the power of the chiefs when they deserted their masters in large numbers, often in the wake of the European military conquest. The conquest and subsequent *pax Europeana* ended the numerous wars that had stimulated the supply of slaves in places like Yorubaland where warfare had been endemic throughout the nineteenth century. Conquest undermined the basis of political power of some chiefs by reducing their ability to acquire slaves and utilize them as followers or dependents. Europeans, however, emphasized the prevention of new slavery. This was a consequence of the 1890 Brussels Conference, which concluded that cessation of the slave raid and slave trade were priorities in the antislavery campaign. If there was no new slavery, ran the argument, slavery would die a natural death.

European officials introduced various moderate antislavery devices. The French freed the slaves of their enemies but allowed their allies to retain their slave population; while the British tended to abolish the legal status of slavery in British courts but not in the Native Courts that were based on Islamic law or "native law and custom" and dominated by the slave owners. Colonial administrations passed laws abolishing slavery. In French West Africa a judicial code introduced in 1903 gave no sanction to slavery, and two years later new enslavement and slave trade were outlawed there while the Portuguese outlawed slavery in 1910. Germany and Britain passed laws to abolish slavery in their colonies by the turn of the twentieth century and began to enforce these laws a decade later. However, slavery continued to operate in Ethiopia and elsewhere where abolition was circumscribed by various devices. Thus, for example, all slaves in southern Nigeria were freed on March 31, 1901, but in northern Nigeria only those persons born or brought there after this date were free. Reform of the traditional labor regime was a slow process. Administrative reluctance apart, the demand for slaves did not disappear overnight and slave markets continued to operate. In addition, pawning remained prevalent during the adverse economic conditions of the 1930s.

The decline in traditional forms of exploitation stemmed partly from international pressure, particularly from League of Nation agencies. The League focused on slavery across Africa including Ethiopia and Liberia, which were independent states and members of the League. It set up a Temporary Slavery Commission that produced a Slavery Convention (September 25, 1926) which outlawed pawning, slavery, and slave raiding but which also recognized the existence of "voluntary slavery." In the 1930s the League appointed an Advisory Committee of Experts on Slavery, which examined the extent to which pawning and slavery were declining and strongly opposed continued "voluntary slavery." It is best remembered for pushing Britain into finally abolishing slavery in northern Nigeria (1936).

However, the League's general examination of global labor conditions also helped to undermine

African traditional labor practices. Investigations by the International Labor Organization (ILO), particularly in the realm of forced labor, intertwined with the antislavery campaign. ILO observations frequently questioned, even challenged, the rights of African chiefs to utilize labor and called for reforms to limit their powers. Indeed, the 1926 Slavery Convention banned the use of forced labor except for paid labor on public works, and in 1930 the ILO Convention on Forced Labor prohibited the use of forced labor "except for limited public purposes." Across Africa forced labor ordinances or similar measures were implemented to define and regulate the duties and rights of chiefs under colonial rule.

Pawning, slave trade, and slavery continue to exist in Africa. It represents the last vestiges of a complex system of labor exploitation that developed significantly in the nineteenth century but was undermined by European colonial control in the twentieth century.

RICHARD A. GOODRIDGE

Further Reading

Austen, R. A. *African Economic History: Internal Development and External Dependency.* London: Currey, and Portsmouth, N.H.: Heinemann, 1987.

Cooper, F. *From Slaves to Squatters: Plantation Labor and Agriculture in Zanzibar and Coastal Kenya, 1890–1925.* London: Heinemann, 1997.

Lovejoy, P., and J. Hogendorn. *Slow Death for Slavery: The Course of Abolition in Northern Nigeria, 1897–1936.* Cambridge: Cambridge University Press, 1993.

Manning, P. *Slavery and African Life: Occidental, Oriental, and African Slave Trades.* Cambridge: Cambridge University Press, 1990.

Miers, S., and M. Klein, eds. "Slavery and Colonial Rule in Africa." Special issue of *Slavery and Abolition.* 19, no. 2 (August 1998).

Labor, Migrant

The expansion of European capitalism and the process of colonization in the late nineteenth and early twentieth centuries resulted in a complex interaction between preexisting social formations and the emergent colonial order. The colonial system was characterized by a new administration that revolved around the colonial state. The system also brought new economic changes, which included monetization of the economy, taxation, and the development of wage labor. Migrant labor in colonial Africa was a distinct system of wage labor that entailed the migration of the worker to and from the workplace, often for a defined period of time, which was usually outside the rural area from where the worker was recruited and to which he returned after the expiry of the contract.

Migrant labor emerged as an integral part of the colonial economy. It was a brought on by the interaction between the preexisting African social formations and the newly instituted colonial economic system. In order to construct roads to facilitate colonial administration, work in the mines or settler plantations, and other colonial establishments the state required the supply of cheap labor. The demand for labor became intense during the formative years of colonial governance in Africa because many people were unwilling to leave their homes to go and work hundreds of miles away in colonial establishments. The demand became even more acute in the settler colonies, such as South Africa, Zimbabwe, and Kenya, where Europeans established huge plantations. Because of the labor-intensive nature of colonial plantation agriculture, demand often exceeded supply. As a result the colonial governments often resorted to a variety of methods ranging from outright force to legislation in order to procure labor for colonial establishments as well as private European plantation owners.

During the initial stages of colonial rule, the mobilization of labor was done through government-appointed chiefs, who were accountable to the local European administrator. Usually the chiefs were given wide-ranging powers including punishing those who evaded work in colonial establishments. The delegated authority was often used arbitrarily.

Demand for work among Africans was also created by the introduction of the poll tax, which had to be paid in cash. This made some Africans work for the purpose of getting money for the poll tax. As a result, once they had got enough money to meet their tax needs these workers would return home. In a sense they kept on moving to and from the workplace depending on their basic needs as well as tax obligation. However, some peasants could avoid going out to work so long as they could grow cash crops and raise money for their taxes. This was acceptable in the nonsettler colonies such as Uganda and Ghana where a vibrant African peasant sector was crucial in sustaining the colonial economy. However, in the settler colonies peasants were discouraged from growing cash crops on the grounds that it would lead to competition for labor between Africans and European planters. Thus as the colonial period wore on, the poll tax as a method of producing workers was found to be not entirely effective in producing the workers.

Besides the poll tax, therefore, the colonial governments often resorted to legislation. Able-bodied men were compelled by law to work for a certain number of months in one year. They were free to return home after discharging their responsibility as required by law. However, the migrant worker had to carry a work pass as a testimony of having fulfilled the required obligation.

The colonial state cherished the notion of migrant labor because it was fairly cheap to maintain. The workers did not have strong attachment to the workplace.

They were there for brief periods of time. Also, in most cases their families did not accompany them to the workplace. Hence housing projects for African migrant laborers were developed to cater for only the worker and not his entire family. Migrant laborers had few, if any, medical and retirement benefits. Low wages, economic security, and harsh working conditions made workplace as well as colonial labor establishments unfriendly environments. Workers tried to create a conducive environment where they had temporarily migrated, especially in the cities, to provide for their economic and social comfort. They formed social welfare associations, usually along ethnic and regional lines, which helped members of the group during times of need.

In some cases migrant labor had to contend with reprimands, flogging, and beating. Indeed, brutality was sometimes carried to the extreme in some countries, particularly in Belgian Congo where worker rights violation were not uncommon. Sadistic punishment, including dismemberment and murder, was widespread much to the chagrin of the citizenry and civilized world.

However, the workers often fought back in a variety of ways. Go-slows, defections, demonstrations, and violent confrontations were employed to force the colonial state as well as private employers to accede to worker's demands. While many colonial governments established a number of commissions of inquiry into the question of labor and attendant benefits as well as workplace safety, there was hardly any major improvement in the condition of the workers until after World War II. It is against this backdrop that for the migrant laborer, the workplace was not considered "home." The comforts of home were rare in the workplace. Home was where they were recruited from and to which they returned after the expiry of their contracts. It was at home where they lived in dignity and enjoyed the support of the immediate as well as extended family.

The inability of the colonial state to provide for the welfare of labor made the worker's allegiance to rural residential home an obvious necessity. This loyalty to the rural home delayed the development of the urban working class. The worker split his active working life between the city and other colonial establishments on the one hand, and rural home on the other. Sometimes proceeds saved from the workplace were invested in rural areas by establishing retail businesses or purchasing and accumulating livestock. Migrant laborers also fostered social change. In the way they dressed, few items they bought in towns and cities, and general topical conversations about the colonizer, the migrant laborers were instrumental in the movement of ideas from urban to rural areas and vice versa. They constituted a major link between the two geographical locations and, in some cases, countries. In the context of southern Africa, the Mozambican workers traveled to and from South Africa to work in the mines. Migrant labor was therefore mobile and expansive in geographical setting.

The departure of the migrant laborers (who were invariably men) from rural areas to the colonial workplace impacted rural household division of labor as well as production patterns. African women farmers took over responsibilities that were hitherto held by the migrant male laborers. The result was increased roles for women in the management of the household economy and the rise of female-headed households. As a result, the intensification of women's labor led to the generation of wealth through small-scale agriculture and local trade in rural households where men had left for work in the colonial establishments. Since the colonial state hardly encouraged women's participation in the economy as migrant laborers, those women who made their way into the towns were not readily absorbed into the mainstream economy. Instead, they engaged in petty trade, selling agricultural produce such as vegetables, corn, and potatoes to the workers and other urban dwellers. Furthermore, the emergence of sex commercial workers during the colonial period has been partly attributed to the colonial state's encouragement of male migrant labor and the inability to provide work for the females who migrated to the colonial townships.

While the history of labor unrest in Africa predates the 1930s, strikes and violent protests increased in number and intensity after that period. Indeed, it was not until the 1930s and 1940s that migrant labor began to stabilize with increased numbers beginning to identify with the townships and the workplace. The number of workers increased substantially outstripping demand. Coercion and legislation were no longer enforced vigorously. This shift can be explained by a number of factors. First, the monetization of the economy had stabilized and cash had become an important aspect of daily transactions. Hence the need to get money had become a necessity that could not be easily wished away. Also, the development of Western education particularly at the pre–high school levels was producing enough literate workers for colonial establishments. Third, the Depression of the early 1930s and near collapse of the colonial economy left many people jobless. Also, after World War II the urban population increased in numbers. Although the colonial powers made a major shift in their investment policy by establishing import-substitution industries, the demand for jobs far outstripped the available opportunities.

The post–World War II period constitutes a major divide in the history of labor activism. Although there was massive investment of capital and social reform in Africa undertaken by the colonial powers, there was a gap between expectation and achievement. Throughout the continent the strikes not only became more widespread, but they increased in intensity as well. Besides strikes by workers in private companies, there were strikes by public employees such as railway workers, dockers, telegraphists, and postal workers. Contemporaneous with the unrest was the decolonization wave that began to gain momentum in the 1940s and peaked in the 1950s. The long record of colonial state's reluctance to effectively address labor issues was quickly turned into a commentary on the undesirability of colonial governance. Nationalism and labor activism coalesced and led to the demand for independence.

GEORGE ODUOR NDEGE

Further Reading

Cooper, F. *Decolonization and African Society: The Labor Question in French and British Africa.* Cambridge: Cambridge University Press, 1996.

Harries, P. *Work, Culture, and Identity: Migrant Laborers in Mozambique and South Africa, 1860–1910.* Portsmouth, N.H.: Heinemann, 1994.

Hotchschild, A. *King Leopold's Ghost.* New York: Houghton Mifflin, 1999.

Robertson, C. *Trouble Showed the Way: Women, Men, and Trade in the Nairobi Area, 1890–1990.* Bloomington: Indiana University Press, 1977.

Stichter, S. *Migrant Labor in Kenya: Capitalism and African Response, 1895–1975.* London: Longman Group, 1982.

White, L. *The Comforts of Home: Prostitution in Colonial Nairobi.* Chicago: Chicago University Press, 1990.

Labotsibeni (*c.*1858–1925)

Queen Mother of Swaziland, 1890–1899; Queen Regent of Swaziland, 1899–1921

Queen Labotsibeni was born about 1858 at Luhlekweni homestead in the Hhohho region in northern Swaziland. She was born when her father, Matsanjana Mdluli, was part of a Swazi regiment fighting a Pedi chief named Tsibeni near the present day town of Barberton in South Africa. Despite the circumstances of her birth, she lived a life dedicated to avoiding war.

Gwamile, her popular name, was a name of honor meaning the "indomitable one." This accolade was given to her by her Swazi subjects; it was also recognized by the British colonial administration. The name was bestowed in recognition of Gwamile's ability to contain colonial encroachment and to protect Swazi sovereignty and culture. Labotsibeni restored most of the country's political and economic power between 1902 and 1921. Subsequent Swazi generations have acknowledged Labotsibeni's greatness. Economic, social, and political stability in Swaziland during the precolonial era were an enduring legacy of Queen Mother Labotsibeni's moral stature, radical anticolonialism, and political shrewdness. A measure of her popularity among the Swazi is that she is acknowledged as one of the greatest rulers and queen mothers or queen regents in Swazi history. She transcended the status generally assigned to women in Swazi society.

Labotsibeni came from a distinguished family and clan. The Mdluli are divided into two branches and both have played an important role in the evolution of modern Swaziland since the eighteenth century. She came from the northern Mdluli clan, which was distinguished by its expertise in skills for military intelligence. The southern branch of the Mdluli's were trusted with the responsibility of producing an *insila,* a fictional blood brother to Swazi rulers. The Mdluli's are regarded as right-hand office bearers in Swazi society. Her lineage may have destined her to political fame, but it was more her personality—brave and assertive—that made her a distinguished Swazi ruler.

She was courted by Prince Mbandzeni, whom she initially rejected. A few years later, when he became king in 1875, Labotsibeni became his wife. She bore three sons, Bhunu, Malunge, and Lomvazi, and a daughter, Tongotongo.

Swazi succession law states that a king should not be succeeded by blood siblings. Therefore, none of Labotsibeni's children could be king. Yet another Swazi tradition provides that a king is king by the blood of his father through his mother. This conflict in traditions and principles of succession could have caused unusual turmoil. Labotsibeni had the knowledge and experience, based on her background, to justify and account for her manipulation of these traditions.

Following the death of King Mbandzeni on October 7, 1889, Labotsibeni was designated *Indlovukati* (Queen Mother) on September 3, 1890, when Bhunu was selected as the future king. Bhunu's reign was the shortest in Swazi history. When Bhunu died in December 1899, he left behind six widows, each with a single child, and one widow was pregnant. Three of the children were easily disqualified from competing for the kingship because they were female, and Swazi tradition only allows male succession to that rank. Although guided by succession principles, the elders failed to find an heir acceptable to all royal factions. One interpretation of this event was that this was an expression of deference to Labotsibeni; they sought her involvement by creating the impression that they had failed to reach a decision because the problem was so difficult that it could only be resolved by someone of Labotsibeni's stature. Her choice was Nkhotfotjeni, son of Lomawa Ndwandwe. The boy was only about three months old, yet the decision was welcomed with great acclaim. Labotsibeni became queen regent until Nkhotfotjeni's coronation as Sobhuza II on December 22, 1921.

Many of her contemporaries acknowledge that she was a shrewd and clever politician. T. R. Coryndon as resident commissioner, with a wide colonial experience in southern Africa remarked in 1907 that as "woman of extraordinary diplomatic ability and strength of character, an experienced and capable opposition which it (the colonial administration) was for some time incapable of dealing with" (Jones, p.402).

Chris Youé (1985) explained how the local colonial administration, led by Coryndon from 1905 to 1917, plotted but failed to dethrone Labotsibeni. She challenged Coryndon's approach to the land question in Swaziland. Her husband had parceled away virtually the whole country through a complicated system of assigning land, grazing pasture, and mining rights. The whole arrangement had the potential that the Swazi king would control resource rights and adjudicate in any subsequent conflicts. Through the Concession Proclamation of 1909, Corydon granted freehold title in land and gave Swazis on settler land five years in which to move to land set aside exclusively for them. Labotsibeni accepted this capitalist dispensation but challenged it by mobilizing her people donating cattle in order to buy back the land the Swazis had lost. This approach was modified to in-value the colonial administration in 1913 and has remained the operational policy in postcolonial Swaziland when addressing landlessness.

In the context of the Swazi power structure, Labotsibeni faced major challenges. First, she had to contain power struggles and to unite the Swazi nation during the rule of the young crown prince, Nkhotfotjeni. In terms of Swazi tradition, the youngest son who has no blood brothers or sisters is the one usually chosen to succeed his father. There was a feeling that Nkhotfotjeni's appointment as crown prince was rushed, because LaMavimbela was pregnant at the time of Bhunu's death. Selection should have waited for her to give birth. As it transpired, LaMavimbela delivered a son, Makhosikhosi, whose candidature was as good as, and probably better than, that of Nkhotfotjeni. However, the clan status of LaMavimbela attracted more questions than could explain the clan's contribution to the long history of the Swazi monarchy. On consultation, Labotsibeni recommended Nkhotfotjeni, because of his mother's background. The anti-Mona factions considered Labotsibeni's decision as calculated to prolong her reign or as designed to install her favorite son, Malunge.

At the turn of the century, the Swazi population increased its hostility toward Labotsibeni because of frequent droughts between 1902 and 1907. Tradition assigned the queen mother the power to make rain and the Swazis were angry at the frequency of droughts. The droughts at the turn of the century led the Swazi to believe that it was wrong for Labotsibeni to be queen mother when her grandson was designated as the future king. People felt that her capability to make rain was undermined because she defied and defiled tradition. Meetings of the Liqoqo, the inner council or cabinet, became irregular, and in 1904 Labotsibeni had to fine her subjects to compel them to attend national ceremonies.

The local British officials also helped LaMdluli's cause. The Swazi rallied behind Labotsibeni because the British had systematically alienated most of the land to white settlers. This was finally consolidated in the Land Partition Proclamation of 1909 that left the Swazis in control of only about one-third of their country.

Labotsibeni acknowledged that she could not get back the land militarily and that land had become a commodity to bought or sold in an open market. She subsequently set up a Lifa Fund to which her people contributed money for buying back the land from the colonial government and white settlers. Although discontinued in 1915, Sobhuza revived it in the late 1940s resulting in Swaziland repossessing about 60 per cent of the country at the end of the 1960s. Labotsibeni had ensured support from her people. In the presence of 2,000 Swazis armed with traditional weapons, Labotsibeni condemned the British land policy.

Labotsibeni's distinguished political and economic achievements acquire further significance when related to Labotsibeni's contribution in the field of education. Labotsibeni insisted that her grandson, crown prince Nkhotfotjeni, should receive a modern education. There was strong opposition from the Swazi chiefs and royalty. Labotsibeni strongly believed that the power of white people lay in "books and money" (Matsebula, 1987), and the Swazi could appropriate some of that power for themselves by appropriating the tools of white people, and using those tools to empower themselves. Labotsibeni recognized the importance of literacy for a twentieth-century head of state. Over the opposition of the elders and aristocracy, she arranged that a school be established at Zombodze, where Sobhuza completed early education. He later moved to Lovedale in South Africa for more education. Thus, due to Gwamile's insight, Swaziland had a monarch in 1921 who had received more formal education than several African heads of state at the end of the colonial era in the 1960s.

Labotsibeni played a critical role in the making of the Swazi nation. Clearly, the role of individuals in the making of a nation is a complex one; but there is no doubt that Labotsibeni provided much needed leadership to the Swazi nation and that the British colonial officials met their fair match in her. She died December 5, 1925, at Embekelweni, then the Swazi national capital.

ACKSON M. KANDUZA

See also: **Swaziland.**

Further Reading

Crush, J. *The Struggle for Swazi Labour, 1890–1920.* Kingston: McGill-Queens University Press, 1987.

Jones, H. W. *Biographical Register of Swaziland.* Durban, University of Natal Press, 1993.

Kanduza, A. M. "Ambiguities in Women History: The Case of Swaziland." *Eastern Africa Social Science Research Review.* 12, no. 1 (1996).

Matsebula, J. S. M. *A History of Swaziland.* 3rd ed. Cape Town: Longman, 1987.

Youé, C. P. *Robert Thorne Corydon: Proconsular Imperialism in Southern and Eastern Africa, 1897–1925.* Buckingham Shire: Colin Symithe, 1986.

Lagos

For most of the twentieth century, Lagos was the capital of Nigeria, and it remains the major hub of economic activities, as well as the home of the country's principal harbor, roads and rail terminal, the international airport, a large population, and a high number of schools and colleges. A new educated elite emerged here during the nineteenth century, which dominated politics until 1960, when Nigeria obtained independence. Demands for major reforms and anticolonial resistance occurred in Lagos, thus making the city a center of administration, politics, and media. The tradition of protest continues, either in violent street demonstrations or in a peaceful manner, daily reported in the newspapers and magazines that are concentrated here.

With an annual population growth rate close to 15 per cent, Lagos grows at a pace faster than most African cities and is always receiving a large number of permanent settlers and floating migrants. From the 1870s to 1963, the administrative territory of Lagos expanded from 4 square kilometers to 65 square kilometers, while the population increased from 28,500 to almost a million.

Lagos retains all the attractions and dynamism of a modern city, including the presence of leading hotels, nightclubs, and criminal syndicates. A crowded population of over three million people lives in the Lagos Island, a small area, with the mainland connected to it by three bridges.

Lagos is part of the Nigerian coastal belt that separates the mainland from the Atlantic Ocean. Due to the maze of swamps, lagoons, river estuaries and creeks, settlement patterns are fragmented. Heavy rainfall, low topography, and bad drainage conditions limit farming activities and impose constraints on city planning. Although it has a small land area, it is one of the most densely populated cities in Africa.

The city's historical origins lie in a very distant past. Originally settled by the Aware, the people interacted with their neighbors and became connected with the economic network of the Yoruba, Bini, and Egun regions in what are now the southern parts of modern Nigeria and the Republic of Benin. As could be expected, the sea, river, and lagoons served as waterways, while an economy based on fishing and salt making also developed. The ecology was peculiar, and Lagos was able to manipulate this to its advantage in trade relations with its neighbors, although the need to control the waterways generated warfare and intense competition for power. When Euro-African relations began developing in the fifteenth century, places located along the sea, such as Lagos, became centers of commerce and European gateways to Africa. Lagos became a major slave port: its kings, chiefs, and merchants profited by playing the role of middlemen, obtaining goods from Europeans in exchange for slaves from the Yoruba hinterland.

Following the abolition of the slave trade in the first half of the nineteenth century, many liberated slaves, known as Saro and Amoro, migrated to Lagos from such places as Liberia and Sierra Leone and the West Indies. A new cosmopolitan culture emerged, reflecting ideas from Brazil, the United States and England. As Lagos became more important to British trade and strategic interests, it was occupied in 1851 and governed as a consulate for ten years. It is from Lagos that the British encroached on the hinterland to establish a Protectorate later incorporated into the modern country of Nigeria. Lagos remained a dominant seat of British rule throughout the first half of the nineteenth century.

In 1967 the status of Lagos was further enhanced by the creation of Lagos State, with its headquarters in the mainland area of Ikeja. In the 1970s Nigeria witnessed an oil boom, which brought a phenomenal increase in the number of private cars (far more than the available roads could carry), a massive expansion in personal and business buildings, and rapid economic development. In 1976 Lagos lost its federal capital status to Abuja, although it took another 15 years for actual relocation to begin. However, the establishment of a new federal capital has not diminished the status of Lagos. Many federal businesses and diplomatic offices are still located there. A coastal location continues to ensure a dominant role in the manufacturing sector. As the commercial capital with an international airport, it is still the center of finance, industry, and commerce.

Suburban development continues to the north and west of Lagos Island at a pace faster than the supply of water, telephone, electricity, and the expansion of the road network. Due to traffic congestion and overpopulation, Lagos continues to experience enormous planning and social problems. The majority of those who depend on the social services of Lagos or for their jobs live far away in the mainland. Daily journeys to work are long and unpleasant, as commuters rely on small buses and the city has no mass transport system. As vehicles compete for space on the congested roads, a journey of five miles can take two hours.

The social structure reflects a gross imbalance between rich and poor, especially in housing conditions and living standards. Housing is often substandard: many people crowd into small places, while others are forced to sleep in open spaces without toilet facilities. Excessive population growth means that public expenditures on housing and social services have very limited impact. As transportation and housing costs soar on a regular basis, many continue to live far below the poverty level, while the city remains the largest slum in the country.

Urban planning started too late and has remained haphazard, with a great deal of damage already done to virtually all sectors of city life. Due to a flat and low-lying terrain, the city is flooded after heavy rains and areas close to the sea are under threat of being submerged. There is also the problem of gross mismanagement by city officials. To compound both is the lack of solutions for slum clearance and traffic congestion as well as inadequate housing, and social facilities. In spite of all these problems, the people are friendly and optimistic, and as Fela Anikulapo-Kuti said in a famous song, they are noted for "suffering and smiling."

TOYIN FALOLA

See also: **Lagos Colony and Oil Rivers Protectorate; Nigeria.**

Further Reading

Adefuye, A., B. Agiri, and J. Osuntokun, eds. *History of the Peoples of Lagos State.* Lagos: Lantern Books, 1987.

Aderibigbe, A. B., ed. *Lagos: The Development of an African City.* Lagos: Longman, 1975.

Barbour, K. M., J. S. Oguntoyinbo, J. O. C. Onyemelukwe, and J. C. Nwafor. *Nigeria in Maps.* London: Hodder and Stoughton, 1982.

Barnes, S. T. *Patrons and Power: Creating a Political Community in Metropolitan Lagos.* Manchester: Manchester University Press, 1986.

Falola, T. "The Cities." In *Nigeria Since Independence: The Society*, edited by Y. B. Usman. Ibadan: Heinemann, 1989.

Folami, T. *A History of Lagos: Nigeria.* New York: Exposition Press, 1982.

Smith, R. S. *The Lagos Consulate, 1851–1861.* London and Lagos: Macmillan and the University of Lagos Press, 1978.

Lagos Colony and Oil Rivers Protectorate

In the middle decades of the nineteenth century, Lagos was a trading post actively involved in the illegal slave trade, following the British Abolition Act of 1807, and the subsequent British naval patrolling along the West African coast. Although Britain's formal, colonial presence started only in 1861 in the town, the immediate events leading to the formation of the Lagos colony date back to 1851, when British marines led by Consul John Beecroft attacked Lagos to disrupt the slave trade carried out by local African kings, working closely with Dahomean and Portuguese slave traders. In 1852 a consul was appointed at the town that represented Britain's first consular authority on the coast in the region. This form of diplomatic presence was the emblematic representation of Britain's informal empire in Africa, and in many other parts of the world around this time.

In West Africa in the bights of Biafra and Benin, consular authority reached back to 1849 when Beecroft was appointed as the British consul at the island of Fernando Po. Earlier the British navy had used this island as a naval base against slaving ships between 1827 and 1834, when Britain considered purchasing it but the amount Spain required was estimated to be too high. Changes in technology also furthered British presence, namely the introduction of steamships. Although regular mail service between West Africa and the home country was started in 1852, the flow of communication up the introduction of telegraph was still slow. This resulted in a high level of autonomy of individual consular actions. The political activities of Consul Campbell between 1853 and 1859, and Consul Foote's military expedition in Porto Novo in 1860 all point toward the *fait acompli*, which was so characteristic of the period's British policy toward the region. It was often the case that the London government faced a situation where significant actions had already been taken, making it more difficult to retreat than to follow the initial lines of events. Also, with the consular presence at Lagos, Britain engulfed itself in local affairs, especially in the troubled relations between different Yoruba states, supported by or opposed to the strong neighboring Dahomey. The continuous diplomatic turmoil with local African chiefs, especially with Kosoko, the former ruler of Lagos finally led to the decision in London to annex Lagos and create yet another coastal colonial urban enclave in West Africa.

After Lagos was created as a colony in 1862, the amount of problems only increased. The affairs of the small colony necessarily became linked to the events of Abeokuta, Dahomey, and Egbaland that extended behind the colony. The town under British administration was becoming an increasingly important trading post on the coast, an enclave that could not be avoided by any trading party. Governor Glover implemented an active policy, based on signing treaties, but London was not interested in furthering its actual sphere of interest. A series of wars raged after 1864 where the

British never took part actively, although traders supplied weapons, thus giving support to some warring parties.

Another element of colonial Lagos was the extremely high European mortality that gave rise to the name of "White Man's Grave" at least since 1822, applied to the entire region of West Africa. It had some elements of truth that Lagos was a place that required three governors, one in a coffin on his way home, one dying in the town and one on its way to replace him. An estimated 30 per cent annual mortality was relatively frequent up to the 1860s. With regular use of quinine, this mortality began to decline but the region retained its former image as the "deadliest spot of the Empire" at least up to the early 1900s. This notion of imperial periphery could be recognized in the almost total disregard for material development of the town. Apart from the construction works carried out at the harbor, the most important buildings that were erected were those built by the Creole community. The state of public health and hygiene, a very characteristic element of British policy in parts of urban India for example, was neglected almost totally. The town's total population was around 20,000 in the 1860s, to double by 1900. Of these, there were very few Europeans, their number hardly exceeding 20 to 30 people, including colonial officials and traders.

The most important economic factor of Lagos, and of the Niger Delta, was the increasing demand in Britain for palm oil, which was used for soap making but especially as a lubricant for fine machinery. Britain's most important palm-oil exporting region was the Niger Delta and the immediate surroundings of Lagos. The introduction of steam ships secured a more profitable trade since while the number of actual voyages decreased, the total tonnage increased by four times between 1850 and 1890. At the same time however, from the late 1850s onward the price of the palm oil fell, complicating the trade further especially for the participating African merchants. The Niger Delta was probably one of the most important economic positions Britain held in the region since over half of its palm oil import, worth over $1 million originated from there.

Britain's presence in the Niger Delta region was based on a combination of the consular authority (from 1849) and the works of the Courts of Equity, up to the mid-1880s. These institutions, in short were created to regulate trade and to provide some legal forms, based on written treaties between African and European merchants. Although initially these courts had no legal power over British subjects, this changed from the 1860s. Over the decades from 1849 to the late 1870s these institutions were responsible for introducing Western concepts of property, contract or punishment to the Delta. In 1872 consular authority was defined within legal frameworks, providing the opportunity for authorized interference into commercial and, indirectly political affairs.

The events in the decade of the 1870s gained an additional element in the form of European economic and, eventually, political rivalry. In 1877 Gorge Goldie Taubman arrived to the Niger to find a pressing commercial competition between French and British companies. He soon realized that Britain's only option was to exclude other European rivals, an aim that he achieved shortly after the foundation of the amalgamated merchant organization, the United Africa Company in 1879. This already pointed toward the problems of the 1890s since the French companies were already receiving state subsidies while the British were not. The strengthened British traders in the Oil Rivers now only had to deal with local African merchants, of whom Jaja of Opobo was probably the most famous who, stepping out of his middlemen status, started to organize palm-oil shipments to Britain on his own. The European merchants, together with the British consul could not allow this, and in 1887, Jaja was trapped in a meeting and deported to Teneriffe. The next event was the formation of the Royal Niger Company, Britain's chartered company that played an increasingly important role in the region that in the 1890s was inserted between French and German spheres of interest in Dahomey and in the Cameroons.

LÁSZLÓ MÁTHÉ-SHIRES

See also: **Delta States, Nineteenth Century; Igboland, Nineteenth Century; Nigeria: British Colonization to 1914; Royal Niger Company, 1886–1898.**

Further Reading

Brown, S. H. "Public Health in Lagos, 1850–1900: Perceptions, Patterns and Perspectives." In *The International Journal of African Historical Studies.* 25, no. 2 (1992): 337–360.

Burns, Sir Alan. *History of Nigeria.* London: George Allen and Unwin, 1969.

Crowder, M. *The Story of Nigeria.* London and Boston: Faber and Faber, 1978.

Dike, O. K. *Trade and Politics in the Niger Delta 1830–1885.* Oxford: Clarendon Press, 1966.

Kubicek, R. V. "The Colonial Steamer and the Occupation of West Africa by the Victorian State, 1840–1900." *Journal of Imperial and Commonwealth History.* 18, no. 1 (1990): 9–32.

———. "British Policy, Trade and Informal Empire in the Mid-Nineteenth Century." In *The Oxford History of The British Empire.* Vol. 3, *The Nineteenth Century,* edited by A. Porter and A. Low. Oxford: Oxford University Press, 1999.

Lynn, M. "Law and Imperial Expansion: The Niger Delta Courts of Equity, c. 1850–1885." *Journal of Imperial and Commonwealth History.* 23, no. 1 (1994): 54–76.

Máthé–Shires, L. "Imperial Nightmares: The British Image of 'The Deadly Climate' of West Africa, c. 1840–1874." *European*

Review of History/Revue européenne d'Historie. 8, no. 2 (2001): 137–156.
Smith, R. S. *The Lagos Consulate 1851–1861.* Berkeley and Los Angeles: University of California Press, 1979.

Lalibela and Ethiopian Christianity

King Lalibela (ruled *c.*1200–1250) was the most famous king of the short-lived Zagwe dynasty (dynasty of the Agaw) that came after the demise of the Aksum kingdom. The Zagwe period runs from about 1137 to 1270, and the Agaw are one of the oldest indigenous people of Ethiopia. They originally occupied a large part of northern Ethiopia, extending from Bogos in Eritrea to Agawmeder Gojjam. The Balaw people in Eritrea are descendants of the Agaw. The Agaw also lived in Lasta, the center of their Zagwe kingdom. Nowadays most Agaw people live in the Agawmeder region of northwestern Gojjam. The Agaw language is classified as Cushitic. The Agaw had converted to Christianity during the Aksumite kingdom.

Of all the tremendous cultural achievements of the Zagwe dynasty, the rock-hewn churches that bear Lalibela's name stand out the most. The eleven churches carved out of rock made Lalibela's name immortal. So famous is he in the history of Ethiopian Christianity that Lalibela was canonized by the Ethiopian Church.

Remarkable as the achievements of Lalibela were, there is hardly any historical record detailing his life or reign. Partly due to the notion that the Zagwe were usurpers of power from the legitimate "Solomonid dynasty," this period of Ethiopian history is a neglected field of inquiry. The life and times of King Lalibela are shrouded in mystery, while the churches he built are given miraculous explanations, such as the assertion that the rock-hewn churches at Lalibela were built by angels. Whatever the hagiographical tradition says, Lalibela built in all eleven rock-hewn churches of which ten were built in a group of two, one consisting of six, and another of four churches. The eleventh one was built separately, for unknown reasons. This church attempts to duplicate Jerusalem; the small stream that runs through the churches is called Yordanos, after the River Jordan in Jerusalem.

King Lalibela strengthened the foundations of Ethiopian Christianity. The Zagwe kings before and after him maintained strong relations with the outside Christian world, including the age-old relations with the Egyptian Church. Interestingly, the famous twelfth-century Egyptian ruler Salah al-Din, who expelled Europeans from Jerusalem, gave Ethiopians a number of churches in the Holy Land, which in turn increased the number of Ethiopian pilgrims to Jerusalem. The Zagwe kings expanded the frontiers of the Christian kingdom.

By the time of King Lalibela, Christianity in Ethiopia had taken firm roots. Eight centuries earlier, King Ezana of Aksum had converted to Christianity. From that time onward, biblical and other ecclesiastical works were translated into Ge'ez, the Aksumite script. The fundamental tenets of Ethiopian Christianity derive mainly from Coptic Egypt. Among the uniquely Ethiopian traits of Christianity is the particularly strong presence of Old Testament–based ritual, which helps give Ethiopian Christianity its syncretic character.

Judaic elements in Ethiopian Christianity include the observance of the Sabbath on Saturday as well as Sunday. Christian Ethiopians follow the dietary laws laid down in Leviticus, in the Old Testament, by avoiding pork and other "unclean" foods. Following Judaic law, male babies are circumcised eight days after birth, while they are baptized forty days after birth. The structure of churches is similar to Jewish temples, while the dance of the *dabtara* with their drums and sistrum resembles the dance of Levites in front of the Ark.

Of all the Judaic elements, the most profound in distinguishing Ethiopian Christianity is reverence for the Ark of the Covenant, the *tabot*. Christian Ethiopia believes that the original Ark of the Covenant is in Ethiopia, kept in the safety of Aksum Tseyon (Zion) Church. As custodians of the Ark, Ethiopians believe that they have replaced Jews as God's chosen people. Some historians argue that this belief was introduced and popularized during Lalibela's reign.

The allegation that the Zagwe were usurpers from the "legitimate" Solomonid dynasty led to many rebellions by those intent upon returning power to the Solomonid rulers. The Zagwe kings patronized Dabra Libanos monastery in Eritrea, while neglecting traditional church centers like Aksum and Dabra Damo. This created resentment against the Zagwe. Amhara was one of the regions under Zagwe rule, and it was the Amhara chieftain Yekuno-Amlak who overthrew the Zagwe kingdom and brought about the so-called Solomonid restoration in 1270. Throughout the Aksumite, Zagwe, and Solomonid periods, Christian Ethiopia's fundamental social structure, religious life, and patterns of external relations remained essentially unchanged.

TESHALE TIBEBU

See also: **Ethiopia: Aksumite Inheritance, *c.*850–1150; Ethiopia: Solomonid Dynasty, 1270–1550.**

Further Reading

Isaac, E. *The Ethiopian Church.* Boston: H. N. Sawyer Co., 1967.
Selassie, S. H. *Ancient and Medieval Ethiopian History to 1270.* Addis Ababa: United Printers, 1972.

Tamrat, T. *Church and State in Ethiopia, 1270–1527*. Oxford: Clarendon, 1972.

———. "Ethiopia, the Red Sea and the Horn." In *The Cambridge History of Africa*. Vol. 3, *From c.1050 to c.1600*, edited by R. Oliver. Cambridge: 1977.

Ullendorff, E. *Ethiopia and the Bible*. London: Oxford University Press, 1968.

Lancaster House: *See* Zimbabwe: Zimbabwe-Rhodesia, Lancaster House and Independence, 1978–1980.

Land and "Reserves," Colonial

The idea of a "reserve" for the exclusive occupation of Africans was first mooted by the Dutch East India Company in 1774 to prevent frontier conflict between Cape settlers and the San in South Africa. The idea, however, was never translated into practice. It was not until much later in the colonial period, during the late nineteenth and early twentieth centuries, that reserves became a commonplace in regions of white settlement. Reserves were inextricably linked to the great debate among Europeans on the solution to the so-called native problem. Were Africans to live separately from whites, under traditional forms of land tenure, or were they to be assimilated into an integrated European-dominated society? Were reserves to be the repositories of tribalism, so that Africans could, in the parlance of the 1920s and afterward, "develop along their own lines," or were they temporary places of refuge that would, with the spread of capitalist farming, disappear with the passage of time? These debates, however, only became significant after reserves had been established. Much of the legislation of the twentieth century, including the South African Natives Land Act of 1913 (often seen as the true beginning of a systematic reserves policy) was constrained by existing patterns of land settlement. In other words, the advance of white settlement, by treaty with, or conquest over, African societies, determined where Africans should live. Reserves emerged in an ad hoc fashion in accordance with the political and economic circumstances of white-black conflict.

The earliest laws setting up reserves (then called locations) can be traced to mid-nineteenth century South Africa. In the South African Republic (Transvaal), the government endeavored to control Africans by pass laws, disarmament decrees and setting up small reserves, under the charge of military personnel, which were meant to provide labor for the white farmers who had expropriated the best land. While the reserves were predominantly labor reservoirs, they were also, following the Natal model, a way of preserving peace and security by "divide and rule." Historians have pointed out that the weakness of the republican state meant that African locations were not surveyed or demarcated. Yet, similar circumstances prevailed later in other white settler territories. In Kenya, for instance, while many reserves were established by the "pacification" campaigns that preceded World War I, these reserves were administrative constructs. It was not until 1926 that most of these reserves were formalized (or "gazetted"), and even by 1929 less than half of them had had their boundaries demarcated by trenches or cairns of stones. In southern Rhodesia (Zimbabwe) the position was just as unclear. More than 100 reserves were established between 1897 and 1902, but the Native Department officials who created them did so in an haphazard fashion, with no procedural directives, no maps, little or no knowledge of the terrain, and without establishing any criterion for land suitability or potential. As Angela Cheater (1990) notes: "the early origins of the reserves [in Zimbabwe] are obscured by conflicting dates and apparently non-existent statutes." A key problem facing those charged with land apportionment during and after World War I, when the debate on reserves policy was in full flourish, was finding out where the reserves actually were.

Reserves, then, often constituted "remaindered" land, land not taken up by European farmers and concession companies. Reserve boundaries often became dependent on the boundaries of European farms, and as many of the latter were "unoccupied," or rather occupied by African tenants or squatters, and themselves were not clearly fenced off, the distinction between "black" and "white" land was blurred. As John Overton tells us, in the case of Kenya, the black-white frontier "was at first a concept, an economic interface, not a physical border." Nor did the appropriation of prime land and its privatization mean that all Africans were shunted off to the reserves. The 1903–1905 Lagden Commission in South Africa estimated that 1,398,787 Africans lived on white farms, more than half the number (2,458,281) that inhabited the reserves. These figures even exaggerate the reserve population given the fluid movement of migrant labor to the towns and private land. While most Africans who lived outside the reserves lived as sharecroppers ("Kaffir farmers") and labor tenants, a few were landlords in their own right. It was this phenomenon—black occupation of white land—that triggered the drive to segregation in the twentieth century. Indeed, the main thrust of the 1913 Natives Land Act and the Land Apportionment Act (1930) in Rhodesia was to deny Africans the right to purchase land in the white area.

The appropriation of black land was, from the beginning, linked to the desire to control African labor. The "Native Wuestion" in Africa, as many have pointed out, is hard to divorce from the labor question (throughout the entire colonial period). The attempts to "civilize" Africans were tied up with the drive to proletarianize them. Some settlers, like the witnesses before the Transvaal Labour Commission (1904) and the members of the 1919 Economic Commission in Kenya, wanted to abolish reserves altogether. The 1915 Land Commission in Rhodesia, appointed by the British government to ensure sufficient reserve land for the Ndebele and Shona, actually recommended an overall reduction in reserve acreage. This would, according to the chairman, Robert Coryndon, help end "tribalism" and ensure a more sufficient labor supply. The bases for these recommendations were that Europeans were best able to develop agricultural land, and that the prime task of Africans was to supply labor to white farms. This was not segregation, though; Coryndon regarded segregation as a "dangerous tendency" (Youé, 1986); and while his commission may have tampered with the reserves, they were not abolished. In fact, Rhodesian reserves were rendered untouchable in the 1923 constitution of self-governing colony.

The myriad attempts to finalize or formalize the white-black division of land between the two world wars meant that reserves continued while reserve policy changed. There are many reasons for this. The failure of European regimes to civilize, or proletarianize, Africans, was in part due to the enterprise of African farmers, in both the reserves and on private land. Reserve land was not universally poor land (although most of it was); Beinart points out that much of the reserve land in South Africa "was largely within the higher rainfall zone. Some of it may have become very poor, but initially it was not the worst land" (1994). Indeed, a government development plan promulgated in independent Kenya (1966) reckoned that 80 per cent of the country's fertile land was located in African areas. Proponents of segregation, as well as radical scholars, have pointed to this as a deliberate objective of reserve policy: to ensure the social reproduction of a work force and social security for the unemployed, the old, and infirm. However, the tremendous variation in reserve conditions (the Ndebele referred to their first two reserves as "cemeteries not homes") should warn against such generalizations. The initial allocation of land had much more to do with the expedients of conquest than the theories of the conquerors (or their historians). Also, the reserves were centers of political power; chiefs were essential allies in colonial collaboration. White supremacist states were restricted in their action by ground-level power relations; tampering with reserves was almost as dangerous as meddling with white property rights.

It is not surprising that, despite all the legislative acts and commissions of enquiry, land settlement patterns in southern and eastern Africa remained a seemingly anarchic tapestry of white farms, forest areas, unassigned land, and reserves. The latter were rarely contiguous wholes, or host to a homogeneous ethnic or "tribal" group, something that makes a mockery of the apartheid state's attempt to set up independent homelands or Bantustans in South Africa from the 1950s.

One of the key factors in the drive to segregation was the success of African farmers living on white land. Land legislation in the twentieth century was primarily devoted to abolishing Africans rights to acquire title in the European farm areas. Concern with depreciating land values, lack of labor, economic competition (often portrayed as "racial friction"), and the possibility of Africans assuming political rights motivated settler regimes not so much to consolidate reserves but to extinguish African rights in European areas. Nonetheless, this was not followed up immediately with forced removals, although many Africans were caught in the squeeze. White farmers were still dependent on squatter labor, and the political economy of the reserves prevented a wholesale repatriation. Almost 25 years after the critical Natives Land Act, the South African Native Affairs Commission (1936) lamented its nonimplementation. By this time it had become a commonplace in settler societies to add land to reserves (variously called release areas, native purchase areas, or native leasehold areas) to accommodate "progressive" African farmers and relieve the pressure on reserve land. These extended reserves were part and parcel of the segregationist project; reserves increasingly became tribal homelands where Africans could develop on their own lines, politically and economically.

From their beginnings as leftover land in the era of conquest, reserves eventually became the cornerstone of segregation policies throughout southern and eastern Africa. Initially, reserves were primarily the outcome of the military and economic pressures of colonial contact; later they became potential homelands, embraced, if somewhat reluctantly, by Africans and liberal whites as the only hope for black survival and development. Attempts to develop a reserve policy was as much predicated on African intrusions into designated white territory as it was on the actual developments in the reserves. The outcome was not an easily-identifiable colonial grid pattern (what John Harris of the Anti-Slavery Society once referred to erroneously as "black and white squares"), nor one in which the legislation provides a reliable guide. The making of African reserves in white settler territories actually preceded segregation, reserve policy, and notions of trusteeship. Controlling Africans on the land proved to be a lengthy and politically charged process.

Chris Youé

Further Reading

Beinart, W. *Twentieth-Century South Africa.* Oxford, Oxford University Press, 1994.

Cheater, A. "The Ideology of 'Communal' Land Tenure in Zimbabwe: Mythogenesis Enacted?" *Africa.* 60, no. 2 (1990): 188–206.

Keegan, T. *Rural Transformations in Industrializing South Africa: The Southern Highveld to 1914.* Braamfontein, Ravan Press, 1986.

Overton, J. "The Origins of the Kikuyu Land Problem: Land Alienation and Land Use in Kiambu, Kenya, 1895–1920." *African Studies Review.* 31, no. 2 (1988): 109–126.

Palmer, R. *Land and Racial Domination in Rhodesia.* London, Heinemann, 1977.

Plaatje, S. *Native Life in South Africa.* Johannesburg: Ravan Press, 1982.

Sorrenson, M. P. K. *Land Reform in Kikuyu Country: A Study in Government Policy.* Nairobi, Oxford University Press, 1968.

Welsh, D. *The Roots of Segregation: Native Policy in Natal, 1845–1910.* Cape Town: Oxford University Press, 1971.

Wilson, M, and L. Thompson, eds. *Oxford History of South Africa.* Vol. 2, *South Africa 1870–1966.* Oxford, Clarendon Press, 1971.

Wolpe, H. "Capitalism and Cheap Labour Power in South Africa: From Segregation to Apartheid." *Economy and Society.* 1 (1972): 425–426.

Youé, C., and R. T. Coryndon. *Proconsular Imperialism in Southern and Eastern Africa, 1897–1925.* Waterloo, Canada: Wilfrid Laurier Press, 1986.

Language Classification

There are approximately 2,000 African languages, an estimated one-third of the world's total, spoken by some 750 million speakers (Grimes, 1996; Heine and Nurse, 2000). (See Table 1 for numbers of speakers and locations of selected major languages.) The history of African language classification has at times been highly contentious, and a valid and comprehensive genetic classification was not worked out until the second half of the twentieth century. Following Greenberg's (1963) seminal and now widely accepted classification, African languages group into four distinct phyla- or superfamilies: Afroasiatic, Niger-Congo, Nilo-Saharan, and Khoisan.

The Afroasiatic phylum contains almost 400 languages spoken across the northern third of Africa in addition to southwest Asia. There are six primary branches: Ancient Egyptian (extinct), Semitic, Berber, Chadic, Cushitic, and Omotic. All Afroasiatic languages except Semitic are spoken on the African continent. Prominent languages include Amharic, Arabic, Hausa, Hebrew, Oromo, Somali, Tamazight, Tigrinya, and Wolaytta.

The vast Niger-Congo phylum contains close to 1,500 languages (more than any other phylum in the

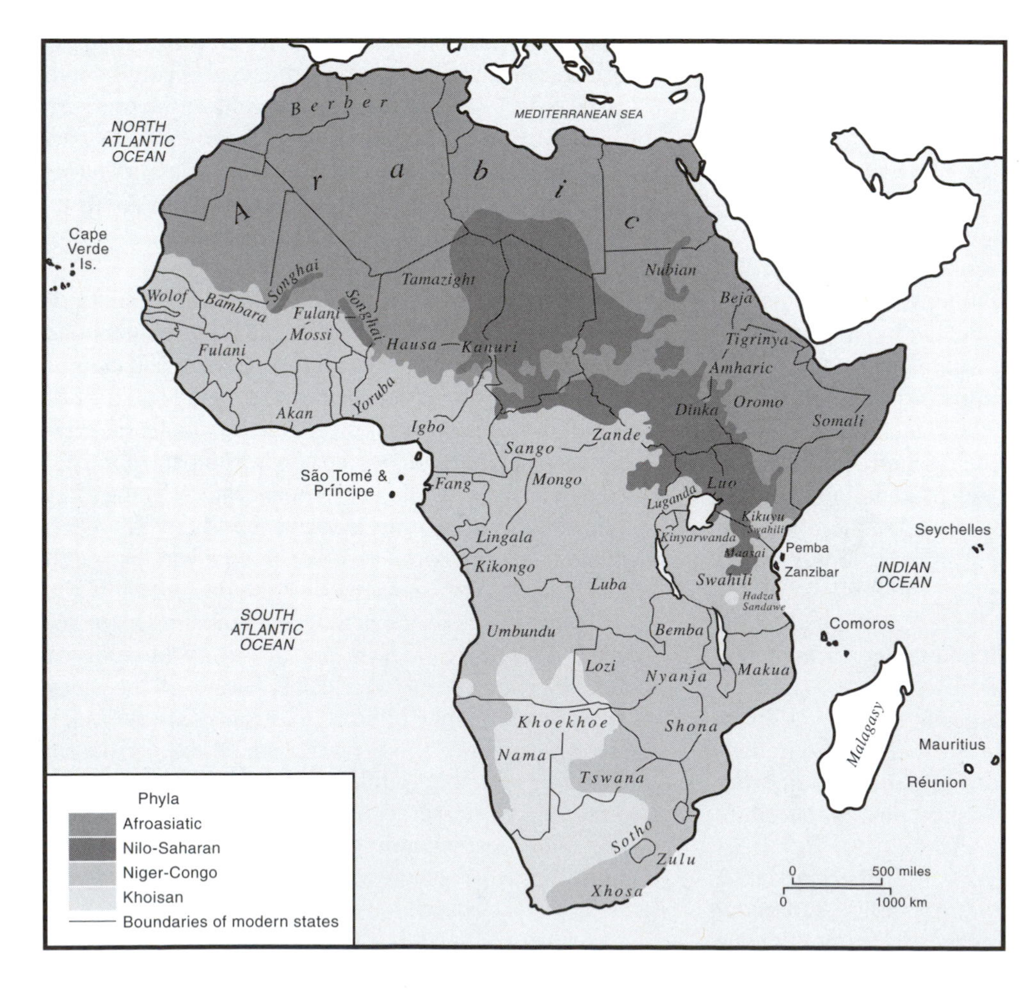

Languages of Africa.

world) and the Bantu subfamily alone covers much of the southern two-thirds of the continent. Niger-Congo includes Kordofanian, a family of languages spoken in the Nuba hills of the Kordofan area in the Republic of Sudan, in addition to most of the languages of western, central, and southern Africa, belonging to families such as West Atlantic, Mande, Gur (Voltaic), Kru, Kwa, Benue-Congo, and Adamawa-Ubangi. Revisions of Greenberg's (1963) subgrouping reassigned Kwa and Benue-Congo to the same south central group of Niger-Congo, and the position of the Mande languages within Niger-Congo is in dispute. Some of the larger Niger-Congo languages include Akan, Fulani-Fulfulde, Igbo, Kikongo, Kikuyu, Kinyarwanda, Lingala, Manding-Mandinka (including Bambara), Sango, Shona, Swahili, Wolof, Xhosa, Yoruba, and Zulu.

The nearly 200 languages in the heterogeneous Nilo-Saharan phylum are spoken mainly in central and east-central Africa, and they display such considerable diversity that their genetic unity is contested by some linguists. Proposed coordinate branches include: Saharan, Maban, Fur, Songhai, East Sudanic, and Central Sudanic (the latter two are essentially a regrouping of Greenberg's "Chari-Nile" branch). Songhai, together with Fur, is an isolate and its phylogenetic affiliation is controversial, with some linguists placing it in the Mande group of Niger-Congo. Other major Nilo-Saharan languages are Dinka, Kanuri, Luo, Maasai, and Nubian.

Khoisan languages are found mainly in the southern and southwestern region of Africa, especially Botswana and Namibia, as well as in Angola, South Africa, Zimbabwe, and Zambia, and include the languages of the San ("Bushmen") and Khoekhoe ("Hottentot"). As a result of the expansion of Bantu-speaking peoples from the northwest and the European occupation of the region, many Khoisan languages are extinct or on the brink of extinction, and only about thirty to thirty-five remain with a mere 200,000 or so speakers (120,000 of whom speak Khoekhoe). The phylum divides into two primary groupings: (1) South African Khoisan, including Khoekhoe (Nama); and (2) two East African ("click language") isolates spoken in northern Tanzania, Sandawe, and Hadza. The genetic unity of the Khoisan family remains controversial, however, due in part to the paucity of language data.

Malagasy, a language belonging to the Western group of the Austronesian (Malayo-Polynesian) family, is spoken on the island of Madagascar. Although it has some loanwords from South African languages as Arabic and Swahili, Malagasy falls outside the African language phyla.

Serious descriptive work on African languages did not begin until the seventeeth century, when several major grammars were published, for example, Kongo (1659) and Amharic (1698), in addition to some dictionaries, for example, Coptic (1636) and Nubian (1638), often written by European missionary scholars. After a period of relative stagnation, the late eighteenth and nineteenth century saw the publication of some important word lists, for example, Koelle (1854). A number of major works on linguistic classification also appeared, with the result that by the middle of the nineteenth century three African language families were generally recognized: Bantu, Nama-Bushman, and Hamito-Semitic—although there were still many disparate languages that did not fall into these families.

From the second half of the eighteenth century, African linguistics was dominated by German-speaking scholars. Two significant classifications were proposed by Lepsius and Müller, with initial versions published in the 1860s (Sebeok, 1971; Ruhlen, 1987). Both recognized Hamitic, Semitic, Bantu, Negro/Mid-African, and Bushman, with Bantu and Semitic reasonably unified and well defined. However, there were differences as to how the groupings related to each other, and how languages such as Fulani (Niger-Congo phylum), Hausa (Afroasiatic), Maasai (Nilo-Saharan), and Hottenot (Nama [Khoisan]) fit into the overall picture.

In the early part of the twentieth century, Meinhof (1912, 1915) emerged as the most influential African linguist of his generation. He classified the languages of the continent into five independent phyla: Sudanic, Bantu, Hamitic, Semitic, and Bushman. Some of Meinhof's classifications (supported in part by another prominent linguist, Westermann) were, however, erroneously based on nongenetic typological and racial criteria. West African Sudanic languages, for example, were defined as those lacking the diagnostic Bantu "noun class systems." In addition, Meinhof followed Lepsius in lumping together Hausa and Hottentot (Nama) into his proposed Hamitic family (adding Fulani and Maasai), the assumption being that the Hamitic languages were related primarily because they had grammatical gender. In classifying Hamitic, Meinhof also resorted to irrelevant cultural and racial (as well as racist) factors. Speakers of Hamitic languages became largely coterminous with cattle-herding peoples with essentially Caucasian origins, intrinsically different from, and superior to, the "Negroes of Africa," and the putative Hamitic family ended up encompassing languages from every phylum on the continent.

Meinhof's retrograde views held sway until Greenberg's intervention. Greenberg's comprehensive reclassification of African languages (developed in the 1950s and expanded and definitively revised in 1963) was a breakthrough of seismic proportions. Although it met with some hostility initially, not to say outraged rejection from some Bantuists, his overall classification has stood the test of time and has come to represent the standard, universal frame of reference (Newman 1995). Greenberg combined West Sudanic and Bantu into a phylum he called "Niger-Congo" (including Fulani) and relegated Bantu to a relatively low-level node on the family tree as a minor subgroup of a subgroup of the Benue-Congo branch of Niger-Congo. (Westermann [1927] and others had already noted common features between West Sudanic and Bantu languages, implicitly

Table 1. Selected Languages by Phylum

Language	Estimated numbers of speakers (millions)	Countries/regions where mainly spoken
Afroasiatic		
Amharic	20m	Ethiopia
Arabic	160m	Middle East, north/northeast Africa, Sudan, western Sahara
Hausa	35m	Northern Nigeria, southern Niger
Hebrew	4/5m	Israel
Oromo	14m	Ethiopia, Kenya
Somali	8m	Somalia, Djibouti, Ethiopia, Kenya
Tamazight	3m	Morocco, Algeria
Tigrinya	6m	Ethiopia, Eritrea
Wolaytta	2m	Ethiopia
Niger-Congo		
Akan	7m	Ghana
Bambara	3m	Mali
Fulani	8m	West Africa, Sudan
Ganda	3m	Uganda
Igbo	17m	Nigeria
Kikuyu	5m	Kenya
Kinyarwanda	9m	Rwanda
Kongo	3m	Congo, Angola, DR Congo (Zaïre)
Lingala	8m	Congo, DR Congo (Zaïre)
Luba-Kasai	6m	DR Congo (Zaïre)
Sango	5m	Central African Republic
Shona	7m	Zimbabwe
Swahili	5m (but used by more than 30m as a *lingua franca*)	Tanzania, Kenya and east Africa
Wolof	2m	Senegambia
Xhosa	6m	South Africa
Yoruba	20m	Nigeria, Benin
Zulu	9m	South Africa
Nilo-Saharan		
Dinka	1/2m	Sudan
Kanuri	4m	Nigeria
Luo	3/4m	Kenya
Maasai	1m	Kenya, Tanzania
Nubian	1m	Sudan
Songhai	3m	Mali, Niger, Burkina Faso
Khoisan		
Khoekhoe	120,000	Namibia, Botswana
Sandawe	10,000	Tanzania

Figures based on Grimes (1996) and Heine and Nurse (2000).

pointing to a valid historical-phylogenetic relationship.) Greenberg also reassigned the Kordofanian languages to Niger-Congo to form the Niger-Kordofanian superfamily and combined a number of smaller groups and languages (including Maasai) into a new "Nilo-Saharan" phylum. Nama was placed within the Khoisan phylum; previous classifications of Khoisan languages had also been partially based on extralinguistic cultural and typological features. He also dismantled the fallacious Hamitic family and long-established Hamito-Semitic dichotomy, replacing them with five main branches—Ancient Egyptian, Berber, Chadic (including Hausa), Cushitic, and Semitic—and renamed the phylum "Afroasiatic." (Omotic was subsequently taken out of Cushitic and set up as an independent sixth branch within Afroasiatic.)

Greenberg's heuristic approach was based on the method of "mass comparison" or "multilateral comparison." This discovery procedure involved closely comparing sound-meaning resemblances—in basic vocabulary as well as grammatical morphemes—across a large number of languages at the same time. Another crucial principle underpinning Greenberg's historical-genetic classification was that it was based exclusively on linguistic evidence, not on the specious presence or absence of vague typological or areal features, or extraneous ethno-anthropological traits.

Since 1963 there have been differences of opinion concerning the internal composition of each of Greenberg's four African phyla in addition to the boundaries between them, all of which have undergone subsequent elaboration and refinement. The essence of his continent-wide classification, however, has stood up to detailed examination and analysis.

PHILIP J. JAGGAR

See also: **Johnston, Harry H.**

Further Reading

Greenberg, J. H. *The Languages of Africa.* Bloomington: Indiana University, 1963. Reprinted with minor corrections, The Hague: Mouton, 1966.

Grimes, B. F., ed. *Ethnologue: Languages of the World.* 13th ed. Dallas: Summer Institute of Linguistics and the University of Texas at Arlington, 1996.

Heine, B., and D. Nurse, eds. *African Languages: An Introduction.* Cambridge: Cambridge University Press, 2000.

Meinhof, C. *An Introduction to the Study of African Languages.* London: J. M. Dent and Sons, 1915.

Newman, P. *The Classification of Chadic within Afroasiatic.* Leiden: Universitaire Pers, 1980.

———. *On Being Right: Greenberg's African Linguistic Classification and the Methodological Principles Which Underlie It.* Bloomington: Institute for the Study of Nigerian Languages and Cultures and African Studies Program, Indiana University, 1995.

Ruhlen, M. *A Guide to the World's Languages.* Vol. 1, *Classification.* Stanford: Stanford University Press, 1987.

Sebeok, T. A., ed. *Current Trends in Linguistics.* Vol. 7, *Linguistics in Sub-Saharan Africa.* The Hague: Mouton, 1971.

Language, Colonial State and

During the colonial period in Africa, the various European powers pursued policies designed to most effectively ensure peak efficiency and productivity within their colonies. Colonial authorities rarely implemented such policies with the interests of indigenous peoples in mind. Rather, they generally viewed the African population as a labor pool that could provide maximum output at minimum cost. Colonial policies, especially as they affected Africans, encompassed every imaginable function in the colonial apparatus, including taxation, policing, agricultural and mining production, administration, and transportation.

In addition to these areas, colonial powers sought to create language policies, usually under the rubric of educational policies, that would both complement their colonial ideologies and enhance the mechanisms by which they ruled over large and diverse African populations. Although their approaches to the question of language were quite different, they nevertheless all had one thing in common: their policies served colonial interests but rarely included consideration of their African subjects' needs and desires.

European aims in devising colonial language policy can generally be distilled into two major goals. The first was to create an elite group of educated Africans who could either speak the language of the European colonial power or a suitable *lingua franca*. These privileged people would then serve as administrators in the colonial government, thus reducing the need to relocate, at great expense, European administrators. The second goal was to promote a single language for the conduct of everyday functions within the colony.

Although each power was quite successful in the first endeavor, they were less successful in the second. While it was fairly simple to identify which few black students would receive further education, and thus, further language instruction, it was much more difficult to ensure that the entire population of the colony would also receive even minimal exposure to language instruction, given the colonies' financial shortfalls. In order to achieve the second goal, European colonial rulers also had to somehow overcome Africa's tremendous linguistic diversity, a task of immense proportions, and one that colonial structures could not very well accommodate.

Thus in most colonial states in Africa, a small Western-educated African elite emerged to fill mid-level roles essential to the colonial enterprise, primarily as civil servants and teachers. A rare few even allowed to attend European universities. Ironically, these elites also became the leaders of African independence movements in the 1950s. But the vast majority of Africans living under colonial rule continued speaking their local languages and perhaps took on the language of administration, education, and power as necessary for the conduct of daily business.

The French were the most successful in making their language and culture an integral part of the indigenous peoples' lives. Under the idealistic French doctrine of "assimilation," and in conjunction with the governing principle of direct rule, colonial subjects were to become participants in French culture, if not full citizens. To make this process more than rhetorical, however, the French needed to devote more extensive resources to the colonial educational structure and to make opportunities available for every African to assimilate into French culture. They took neither of these measures.

In order to become a "French citizen of African origin," Africans had to fill several requirements, including passing a test in French language proficiency. Despite the fact that much lip service was paid to the "civilizing mission" and the goal of assimilation, by 1936 less than 1 per cent of the entire population of French West Africa could claim the status of "French citizen of African origin." Although French was the language of instruction in colonial schools, only a tiny percentage of Africans actually attended school. While men like Senegalese president Leopold Senghor ultimately gained prominence in postcolonial politics through their successful assimilation into French culture, his example was more the exception than the rule. For the vast majority of peoples living under French colonial rule, the ideal of assimilation was out of reach, simply because the French did not provide the tools necessary to bring it within the reach of ordinary Africans.

Similarly, Britain, Belgium, Germany, and Portugal pursued the goal of European language instruction halfheartedly at best. Each successfully built a functional colonial administration based on the presence of a relative few Western-educated Africans who spoke the language of administration. Each followed its own particular model of colonial rule, with the British system of indirect rule usually considered more liberal and far less paternalistic than the Belgian and Portuguese direct rule patterns. Opportunities available to Africans for advancement within the colonial governments were, as in the French colonies, limited at best. Correspondingly, only a few Africans received full instruction in European languages.

In some cases, Europeans chose to advocate certain African languages as their language of administration. For example, Kiswahili became the most widely spoken indigenous language on the African continent in part because of German efforts to increase the language's efficacy as a *lingua franca,* so as to spare the expense of extensive education in the German language. The British similarly encouraged Hausa as a *lingua franca* in West Africa. Both of these had long histories as languages of trade, and each thus served in a very practical manner as a *lingua franca* connecting many different peoples in trade, colonial administration, and military forces. As for other, more localized African languages, most Europeans considered them suitable only for primary school instruction, and certainly not worthy of further development for use within the colonial structure.

Since the end of the colonial period, much debate has occurred in literary circles concerning the continued influence of European languages on African educational systems and literature produced by African writers. As Kikuyu writer Ngugi wa Thiong'o argues in his landmark 1986 treatise *Decolonising the Mind,* "in the twentieth century Europe is stealing the treasures of the mind to enrich their languages and cultures. Africa needs back its economy, its politics, its culture, its languages, and all its patriotic writers."

Yet most African writers continue to write for publication in European languages, and this trend appears to be well entrenched. According to the *UNESCO General History of Africa*, there has been no sustained effort on the part of African governments to develop comprehensive language policies to promote the growth of African languages or integrate these languages into the increasingly global economic and political structure.

This is a challenge that Africa will continue to face throughout the twenty-first century. European colonial rulers inserted European languages into the African landscape and encouraged small numbers of Africans to aspire to full literacy in those languages, thus producing the elite group of Western-educated Africans who later led their nations to independence. It remains to be seen how contemporary Africans will resolve the tension between wanting to break with their colonial past by promoting their own languages yet wanting also to participate fully in the global economic and political structure, an undertaking that presently requires command of European languages.

MICHELLE MOYD

See also: **Colonialism: Impact on African Societies.**

Further Reading

Fabian, J. *Language and Colonial Power.* Berkeley: University of California Press, and Cambridge: Cambridge University Press, 1986.

Ngugi wa Thiong'o. *Decolonising the Mind.* Oxford: James Currey, and Portsmouth, N.H.: Heinemann, 1986.

Owomoyela, O., ed. *A History of Twentieth-Century African Literatures.* Lincoln: University of Nebraska Press, 1993.

Sow, A. I., and M. H. Abdulaziz. "Language and Social Change." In *UNESCO General History of Africa.* Vol. 8, *Africa Since 1935*, edited by A. A. Mazrui and C. Wondji. Berkeley: University of California Press, and Oxford: Heinemann Educational, 1993.

Law, Islamic: Postcolonial Africa

The role of Islamic law (shari'a) in postcolonial Africa has varied from country to country as a result of the relative size of Muslim communities, the institutional traditions of legal systems, and historical contexts. In North African states with overwhelming Muslim majorities, Islamic law during the colonial period had come to be limited to personal matters: marriage, divorce, and inheritance. Muslim courts had been integrated to centralized judicial systems. Colonial authorities often maintained recognition of different legal traditions within Sunni Islam (Maliki, Hanafi, and Shafi'i), and, in the Maghrib, the legal tradition of Ibadi Islam.

With the establishment of independent national states, starting in the 1950s, there were numerous efforts to codify law, necessarily eliminating recognition of variant traditions that had been rationalized in religious terms but were incompatible with the unitary emphasis of nationalist ideology. Codification also brought to the fore debates over women's legal rights. Through the 1970s the trend was, in varying degrees, toward greater protection of women's rights, notably in Tunisia. One of the best known of such reforms was that passed in Egypt in 1979, which restricted a husband's right to take an additional wife without his first wife's permission. This was dubbed "Jehan's law" in reference to the wife of then-President Anwar Sadat.

However, in some cases, notably Egypt and Algeria, there has been a trend toward more conservative interpretations of Islamic law since the 1970s, aptly symbolized by the repeal of "Jehan's law" in Egypt in 1980. This trend can be attributed to authoritarian regimes seeking to placate increasingly strong Islamic political movements through concessions on social issues, and to the popular perception that legal reforms were associated with a small, privileged, westernized elite.

In eastern and southern Africa, Islam had long been primarily a coastal phenomenon, and Islamic law only achieved official recognition from colonial authorities in Zanzibar and the coastal cities of Kenya. Where Muslim communities existed in the interior, Islamic law was applied only on an informal basis, without governmentally appointed judges.

Postcolonial Tanzania had the largest proportion of Muslims in its population, but its government had a strong commitment to separate national politics from religion. In the elaboration of a national code of family law in the 1970s, the government consulted religious leaders and added flexible provisions to assuage the sensibilities of different communities.

In Kenya, where separate Islamic courts had survived in coastal cities, there have been repeated conflicts stemming from the national government's efforts to impose common legal norms in matters such as inheritance. The Muslim courts have been marginalized and are increasingly identified as "women's courts." The frequency with which women risk of making family disputes public by resorting to these courts is a product of deteriorating economic conditions and the weakening of kinship networks.

National governments throughout Sub-Saharan Africa have often set up national Islamic councils composed of prominent religious authorities. Their purpose is to mediate between Muslim communities and the national government, and to establish a consensus as to the solution of religious questions, especially in matters of ritual, such as the correct manner of prayer or appropriate behavior at funerals. Such disputes were connected with the growing influence of the puritanical Wahhabi movement, especially among members of younger generations who have had some formal Islamic education.

Most states of West Africa and the Sudan belt conform to the observations made for eastern and southern Africa, but there are two crucial exceptions, Nigeria and the Sudan. It is in these two countries that Islamic law poses the most difficult issues on the African continent.

During the colonial period in Northern Nigeria, the British had given formal recognition to Islamic law, administered both in the *alkali's* (Muslim judge's) courts, and in the courts of the region's traditional rulers. It was applied not only in matters of personal law but, with some modifications, in homicide, injury, and theft cases as well. But in southern Nigeria the British recognized only local ethnic legal traditions.

As Nigeria headed toward independence in the 1950s, the harmonization of legal systems became a matter of fundamental importance. A system of regional courts provided some insulation for Islamic law in the north when independence arrived in 1960. But with the end of the regional system in 1966, the emir's courts lost formal recognition and the *alkali's* courts were more strictly subordinated to the national system. Since then there have been periodic campaigns to establish a separate Islamic court of appeal at the national level. The most important of these was that of 1978–79 during the framing of the Second Republic's constitution. In the end, conservative but pragmatic northern politicians such as Shehu Shagari preferred compromise on this issue to imperiling national unity.

The Sudan inherited from the colonial period a centralized Islamic judicial system and a corps of well-trained judges with a forward looking reputation. Indeed the British promoted the Sudan as a model for modernization of Islamic law in northern Nigeria. However, the most striking and original legal ideas came not from a jurist, but from the engineer Mahmoud Mohamed Taha, founder of the Republican Brothers. He formulated a theoretical basis for the reform of Islamic law in *The Second Message of Islam*, first published in 1967.

But with the growing influence of the Islamic revival in the early 1980s there was a push toward adapting Islamic law as the basis of national law for all Sudanese, regardless of religion. President Jafar Nimeiry, his popularity in decline, exploited this issue by announcing in May 1983 that Islamic law should be the basis of the Sudan's national law in all domains. In 1985 he sanctioned the execution for apostasy of Mahmoud Mohamed Taha, whose ideas sharply challenged such a conservative and intolerant interpretation of Islam.

After the National Islamic Front came to power in Sudan in 1989, its leader, Dr. Hasan Turabi, followed two directions in Islamic legal policy. One was to give greater prominence to the application of Islamic legal principles in the socioeconomic domain, for instance by promoting interest-free Islamic banking. The other was to search for a means to balance respect for the rights and identities of non-Muslims with insistence on maintaining the Islamic character of the state. Nevertheless, a power struggle developed between Turabi and President Umar al-Bashir, culminating in Turabi's arrest in 2001, on the charge of undermining the state.

Allan Christelow

See also: **Islam in Eastern Africa; Religion, Postcolonial Africa: Islam; Sudan: Turabi's Revolution, Islam, Power.**

Further Reading

Anderson, J. N. D. *Islamic Law in Africa.* London: Frank Cass, 1955.

Brenner, L., ed. *Muslim Identities and Social Change in Sub-Saharan Africa.* Bloomington: Indiana University Press, 1993.

Christelow, A. "Islamic Law in Africa." In *History of Islam in Africa*, edited N. Levzion and R. Pouwels. Ohio University Press, Athens:Ohio University Press, 1999.

Hill, E. *Mahkama! Studies in the Egyption Legal System.* London: Ithaca Press, 1978.

Kukah, M. H. *Religion, Politics and Power in Northern Nigeria.* Ibadan: Spectrum, 1993.

Taha, M. M. *The Second Message of Islam.* Translated and introduced by A. Ahmed an-Na'im, Syracuse, N. Y.: Syracuse University Press, 1987.

Law and the Legal System: Postcolonial Africa

Postcolonial African nation-states are grappling with the problem of integrating the "consequential reception of laws derived from colonial imposition" and their own indigenous common law and Islamic legal heritage. How these plural legal traditions address the legalities of modern politics, commercial development, criminal law, and family law is the great issue of postcolonial law.

In South Africa the struggle against apartheid contoured the constitutional considerations during the liberation negotiations. The *Freedom Charter* adopted by the African National Congress became the driving force behind the 1991 Congress for a Democratic South Africa (CODESA). At CODESA, sixteen of the nineteen attending political parties signed a constitutional declaration that supported a "multiparty democracy, universal adult suffrage, and an independent judiciary." The ANC also pushed for the constitutional inclusion that "the land shall be shared amongst those who work it." For the ANC, land redistribution, as well as other bill of rights guarantees, is the basis for social justice.

However, in Kenya, land law changes in the postcolonial period continued the colonial practice of using British common law, which emphasizes individual freehold tenure because it appeared to be more adaptable to modern commercial development. In contrast, Ghana maintained and balanced the spirit of African communal land holding with its British legal heritage. At independence, both countries advocated their own particular views of "African Socialism" as the basis of national integration, while simultaneously confronting the legalities of tribal land tenure that fragmented and inhibited the formation of a national consciousness.

Criminal law within the postcolonial period has to contend with African traditional justice, behavior, and thinking. In the rural areas where homogeneous ethnic groups exist, traditional justice, faced with adversarial controversy, has sought to restore harmony with all litigious parties by an equitable restoration of the original rights and obligations of these individuals vis-à-vis the community. However, in urban areas, with their multiple ethnicities, the legacy of an Anglophone- or Francophone-style criminal proceeding dominates depending on circumstance. Individuals will seek out either the indigenous or European legal system depending on the controversy and how they perceive the prospects of a particular system rendering a judgment in favor of their interests.

The dynamic and oscillating political terrain in the postcolonial period prompted dramatic legal changes. Ghana's first president, Kwame Nkrumah, used the legal device "The Presidential Command" to veto legislative threats. Nkrumah's legal vision for Ghana was disrupted with his overthrow in 1966. The new National Liberation Council suspended the 1960 Republican Constitution. With the rise in coups d'etat and military authority in the early postcolonial period, the law's legitimacy was in constant flux.

Islamic law heritage was influenced by similar political winds of change. In the Sudan, the influence of colonially imposed law and thinking contoured "Mohammadan Sacred Law." The colonial system permitted the authority of sheikhs' courts only in the areas of personal or domestic law. By 1968 the postcolonial, revolutionary Sudan state defined itself as a "democratic, socialist Republic based on the guidance of Islam." With the Nimeiri coup in 1969, a new civil code was adopted which, because of antagonistic political dynamics, was modified in 1976 and later modified once again according to "Islamic Law, justice, equity and good conscience." One political dynamic that created legal issues was that the majority of Muslims in the Sudan belonged to the Maliki legal tradition while the secular politics and the legal training of their jurists led the Sudanese state to adopt the Egyptian legal ideas of the Hanafia school. In the Sudan most legalists were trained in Cairo and took advanced degrees in England. They favor legal eclecticism but usually lean toward English common law tradition. What the supreme law of Islam, shari'a, will eventually become in postcolonial Africa, as witnessed in the Sudan, will be determined by the ebb and flow of modernity.

Western-trained African jurists influenced the restatement of indigenous law in many postcolonial legal codes. Various African nations called together representatives of traditional district councils who with the aid of these Western-trained African jurists, sat down to integrate and unify the varied legal systems. One can imagine the legal problems to overcome in this process, when many African nations have multiple Islamic legal traditions, as well as both patrilineal and matrilineal legal relationships. The influence, in the juridical system or in the legislature, of Western-trained legalists ensured that Western legal ethics and structure would prevail in the procedural codification and the resolution of legal conflict in this period. Western common law principles of "individualism, equity, liberty, and justice" would make any customary law repugnant that transgressed the Western interpretation of these legal ideas.

Family law or personal law has also contoured by Western legal tradition. Supreme courts of Namibia, Nigeria, and Zimbabwe have ruled on domestic issues in keeping with the United Nations Convention on the Rights of the Child, which sought to equalize the status of girls with boys. The 1990 African Charter on the Rights and Welfare of the Child further sought to address the rights of children. An example of this protection was the Zimbabwe case of Mdutshana Dube. In this case, an administrative court found a forty-year-old man guilty of rape via a forced marriage with a sixteen-year-old girl. This was a "Western" adjustment to customary law that considers a girl past puberty to be ready for marriage and sexual relations and, therefore, an adult.

The influence of the Western legal tradition has caused difficulty in developing a unified code of family law. Parties in disputes reveal the problematic between particular customary law and, for example, English common law. The S. M. Otieno case in Kenya, involving a mixed marriage between a deceased Luo man and his Kikuyu widow who sought to have him buried on the family farm, is a classic example. Her reasoning was that they were married under the colonial Marriage Act of 1902, which, according to legal experts, gave her Christian authority over the final resting place of her husband. However, elders of the Luo clan insisted that Mr. Otieno be buried on ancestral Luo land as required by customary law. Both Kenya's High Court and the Appeals Court ruled in favor of the Luo clan leaders, leading to the accusations that such a decision was antimodern, anti-individual rights, and, according to the National Council of Women of Kenya, antiwomen.

The future of law in postcolonial Africa will continue to involve the complexities, difficulties, and the procedural modulations of integrating Western legal heritage with the indigenous and Islamic traditions. Postcolonial laws will also be redefined by the exigencies of politics, economics, and social trajectories.

MALIK SIMBA

See also: **Colonialism, Inheritance of: Postcolonial Africa; Kenya: Independence to the Present; Law, Islamic: Postcolonial Africa; Nkrumah, Kwame; Socialism in Postcolonial Africa; South Africa: 1994 to the Present.**

Further Reading

Abun-Nasr, J., U. Spellenberg, U. Wanitzek, eds. *Law, Society, and National Identity in Africa*. Hamburg: Herlmut Buske Verlag, 1990.

Albertyn, C. *Achieving Equality for Women: The Limits of a Bill of Rights*. Johannesburg: Centre for Applied Legal Studies, 1992.

Anderson, J. N. D. *Islamic Law in Africa*. London: Frank Cass and Co., 1970.

Brillon, Y. "Juridical Acculturation in Black Africa and its Effects on the Administration of Criminal Justice." *International Annals of Criminology*. 16, no. 1 and 2 (1977): 193–232.

Darian-Smith, E., and P. Fitzpatrick, eds. *Laws of the Postcolonial.* Ann Arbor: University of Michigan Press, 1999.
Hutchison, T., ed. *African and Law: Developing Legal Systems in African Commonwealth Nations.* Madison: University of Wisconsin Press, 1968.
Ncube, W., ed. *Law, Culture, Tradition, and Children's Rights in Eastern and Southern Africa.* Darmouth, England, Ashgate: USA, 1998.
Steytler, N., ed. *The Freedom Charter and Beyond: Founding Principles for a Democratic South African Legal Order.* Cape Town: Wyvern, 1991.
Woodman, G., and A. O. Obilade, eds. *African Law and Legal Theory.* New York: New York University Press, 1995.

League of Nations: *See* Mandates: League of Nations and United Nations; Namibia (Southwest Africa): League of Nations, United Nations Mandate.

"Legitimate Commerce" and the Export Trade in the Nineteenth Century

Europeans did not initially arrive in Africa looking for slaves. They were more interested in gold, spices, and routes to the Indies, only to quickly realize that slaves offered the quickest profits. By the eighteenth century, Europe's trade with Africa was primarily in slaves. Nevertheless, trade in gold, ivory, dyewoods, and gum arabic remained important. By the late eighteenth century, shipping had grown more efficient, which meant that bulk commodities could be profitably traded. In addition, the industrial revolution was creating markets in Europe for different African goods. Machines needed lubrication, which was provided by vegetable oils. The nineteenth century saw increasing attention to personal cleanliness, especially in Britain, which created a demand for soap, also produced from vegetable oils. In addition, ivory was used for billiard balls and piano keys and gum for cloth dying and medicines.

When Britain abolished the slave trade in 1807 and pressured the rest of Europe to follow its example, these new items came to be called "legitimate commerce." The slave trade was, however, only illegitimate in Europe and North America. African slave-trading states had an interest in continuing the slave trade and often resented the sudden change in European policy. For some, like Asante, the sudden end of the trade left them with the problem of how to use the many slaves flowing into market centers. The new trade differed from the old in that it was in commodities rather than persons. Where African states were able to continue the slave trade, they did so. In areas easily controlled by European ships, slave exports declined quickly. In others, like northeast Africa or Mozambique, exports increased. The Egyptian conquest of the Sudan opened up a new slaving frontier. African merchants in both East and West Africa combined trade in persons and commodities, using income from one to purchase the other. Slave exports, which reached a peak of about 80,000 a year in the 1780s, were still above 40,000 a year up to 1850. Furthermore, the internal slave trade actually increased as slaves poured into areas where their labor could be used to produce commodities.

Palm oil exports to Britain rose to 1,000 tons in 1810 and then rose to over 40,000 tons in 1855. The French consumer was not willing to buy the cheap yellow soap the British were using, but French industrialists learned to produce an attractive soap from processed peanut oil. As a result, British interests developed most dramatically in palm oil-growing areas and the French in peanut-growing areas. The innovators in West Africa were the cultivators and the merchants. In East Africa the state played a key role. From 1818 Sayyid Said, the sultan of Oman and Zanzibar encouraged his Arab countrymen to plant cloves. By 1840 Zanzibar was the world's largest clove producer. Said also encouraged Indian financiers to settle in the East African ports and provide capital for traders who were going into the interior to buy ivory and the slaves. Slave exports from East Africa were a by-product of efforts to provide slaves for the clove plantations. In South Africa, white Africans, who migrated into the interior to escape British control, began exporting wool.

In the period from 1820 to 1850, the demand for African exports was fueled by increasingly favorable terms of trade. The demand for African products and the prices Europe was willing to pay were increasing, while European industrialization was reducing the cost of exports, particularly of cotton textiles. This pattern changed in the second half of the century, though exports continued to grow. New uses were found for vegetable oils even as petroleum replaced them as an industrial lubricant. Cotton was exported from Egypt and West Africa and coffee from Angola. First Sao Thomé and Fernando Po exported cocoa, then the Gold Coast and Cameroon. By 1910 the Gold Coast was the world's largest cocoa producer. East Coast plantations produced sesame, copra, and grain. The tapping of wild rubber trees developed from the 1870s and expanded dramatically to satisfy the market for tires and rubber raingear. The rubber boom lasted until after plantation rubber came on stream in 1908 and underwrote the creation of colonial infrastructure in colonies as diverse as Guinea, Gabon, and the two Congos. In South Africa, significant quantities of diamonds were discovered in 1870 and gold in 1886.

This growth in trade was taking place when prices for African products were declining and the terms of trade growing worse. Wherever production was expanding, there was a demand that could rarely be met by free labor. For African rulers and state builders, slaving remained the most profitable business available and the only way to acquire the new breech-loading rifles necessary for political survival. The last quarter of the century was probably the bloodiest period in African history. For European economic interests, the insecurity engendered by these conflicts was increasingly seen as a barrier to economic growth. Until the 1870s these economic interests in Africa were primarily commercial. They invested neither in production nor in transport. They provided credit for African merchants who brought goods to coastal ports.

The economic side of the "Scramble for Africa" was the increasing importance of investment. The most important investments were in railroads. The largest system was in South Africa, where diamonds and then gold provided the basis for a network, which transformed South Africa into a modern industrial society. By 1910 the network extended north across Rhodesia to the copper-rich southern Congo and to ports in Angola and Mozambique. In the 1870s the French began work on a system draining the Senegalese peanut basin and connecting it to the Niger. In the 1890s railroads also began to be extended into the interior in Nigeria, the Gold Coast, Guinea, Sierra Leone, Togo, Dahomey, and Kenya. For areas dependent on human labor for transport, the cost of this transport dropped to a minute fraction of what it had been. Money was also invested in modern ports, in steamboats, and in roads. All of these investments required protection.

MARTIN A. KLEIN

See also: **Slavery, Colonial Rule and.**

Further Reading

Austen, R. *African Economic History: Internal Development and External Dependency*. Portsmouth, N.H.: Heinemann, 1987.

Cooper, F. *Plantation Slavery on the East African Coast*. New Haven: Yale University Press, 1977.

Dike, K. O. *Trade and Politics in the Niger Delta*. Oxford: Clarendon Press, 1956.

Eltis, D. *Economic Growth and the Ending of the Transatlantic Slave Trade*. Oxford: Oxford University Press, 1987.

Hopkins, A. G. *An Economic History of West Africa*. New York: Columbia University Press, 1973.

Marks, S., and A. Atmore, eds. *Economy and Society in Pre-Industrial South Africa*. London: Longman, 1980.

Sheriff, A. *Slaves, Spices and Ivory in Zanzibar*. London: James Currey, 1987.

Lenshina, Alice (*c.*1920–1978)

Religious Leader and Prophet, Founder of the Lumpa Church

Alice Lenshina Mulenga Mubisha was born in the early 1920s in Chinsali District. She married Petros Chitankwa Mulenga, a carpenter at the Lubwa mission of the United Free Church of Scotland (UFCS). She was a baptismal candidate at the church. The couple and their children lived in Kasomo village, a few miles from Lubwa.

In 1953 she had a traumatic religious experience that changed her life forever. After falling seriously ill, Lenshina died four times. Each time she revived after her relatives had already gone into mourning. Jesus, she claimed, had called her to a river where he told his people to send her back, as her time had not yet come. He taught her hymns and showed her the Book of Life, which he had laid on her head kerchief, where it left a yellow mark. Jesus also instructed her to visit "the people of whiteness/the pure ones" (*Abena kubuta*), who would have a message for her.

On September 18, 1953, a still very sick Lenshina told Reverend Fergus McPherson at Lubwa Mission her story. McPherson instructed her to thank God for her recovery and dedicate herself to serving him. In November she was baptized and named Alice by the Bemba minister at Lubwa, Reverend Paul Mushindo.

Despite being only a congregant of the UFCS, Alice Lenshina attracted a following among the Bemba villagers, who listened to her preach and sing her the hymns given to her by Jesus. The songs that Jesus taught her were a powerful means of getting her message across to the people because Alice Lenshina sang in the local Bemba musical tradition, unlike the missionaries.

The crowds that flocked to Kasomo village to hear her included both Protestants from Lubwa and Catholics from the White Fathers' Ilondola Mission. Alice Lenshina's congregation at Kasomo continued to grow, and as her power increased, the church at Lubwa tried to rein her in. Charging that monies collected at Kasomo had not been surrendered to the church but kept by Alice Lenshina and her husband, the couple was suspended. In addition, both the White Fathers and the Scottish mission declared Alice Lenshina a heretic.

Lenshina set up her own church and appointed her own ministers. Attempts by the Lubwa missionaries to reclaim her followers were not successful; only 400 out of the 3,000 who left to follow her returned to the fold. Lenshina's church came to be known as Lumpa, Bemba for "the foremost church."

Like any independent African church, Lenshina's Lumpa sought to indigenize Christianity. Whereas most male-led churches promoted polygamy, Lenshina outlawed polygyny and widow inheritance, a decree Zambian feminists are still battling against today. She also preached against alcohol and witchcraft, using the medium of song more than the spoken sermon. The ethnomusicologist Mwesa Mapoma has noted that music and song are the means by which the Bemba communicate with God, as regular speech is considered profane.

By 1957 the Lumpa Church had spread to neighboring districts and was known throughout the Central African Federation. The church structure was more formalized and its rules codified. During this time, the nationalist struggle for independence was gaining momentum. The Lumpa Church was heading for a confrontation with the nationalist politicians, because Lenshina's followers were forbidden from participating in political activities.

In order to escape harassment by the United National Independence Party (UNIP) youth brigade members who were out to recruit more members to the nationalist cause, Lumpa followers set up their own independent villages. They saw themselves as Zionists leaving Babylon so as not to mix with infidels, whereas the UNIP members regarded Lenshina's followers as a stumbling block to independence.

Lenshina's power was spiritual first and political second. As a healer, she clearly had both political and religious authority. As a lawmaker, she did not merely repeat the Christian commandments of the missionaries but made them relevant to the lives of villagers. As a Bemba woman from a polygynous household in a matrilineal society, her Christianity could not but be feminist. Lumpa rules subverted many powerful interests in colonial society, and she was not without enemies, but the transitional UNIP government of Kenneth Kaunda was especially unhappy with Lenshina. It has been said that members of Kaunda's family in Chinsali were close to the Lumpa Church, but Kaunda himself was convinced that Lumpa members had become antisociety, and thus a threat to his government. Kaunda argued that "no clean-living and thinking man can accept the Lenshina passports to Heaven as anything more than worthless pieces of paper—a usurping by an imposter of the majesty of God Almighty. Such teaching cannot be allowed to corrupt our people and cannot and would not be tolerated by any responsible government" (van Binsbergen, 1981).

There were several fights between Lumpa and UNIP supporters in Chinsali villages. As the confrontations grew, they came to involve the police and army units. Many of Lenshina's followers were killed in riots and battles.

Alice Lenshina did not lead the uprising against UNIP. Her followers' disastrous confrontation with the Territorial Army on the eve of Zambian independence was blamed on her, but the men in her inner circle, including her husband, prevented her from giving herself in until the governor had guaranteed their safety. When she was detained and her followers sent to rehabilitation centers to begin the process of reintegration into a society that regarded them as savages, the defeat of the Lumpa Church was complete.

When Alice Lenshina died in December 1978 she had rejoined the UFCS, which had by then been incorporated into the United Church of Zambia. Lumpa, however, did not merge with the Scottish church or die with Lenshina. Some of Lenshina's followers are still active in the New Jerusalem Church, and others have openly called for the ban on Lumpa to be lifted. Their continued faith in the Lumpa message proves that Lenshina succeeded in establishing a new church, albeit one that has yet to win official recognition and acceptance.

OWEN SICHONE

See also: **Religion, Colonial Africa: Independent, Millenarian/Syncretic Churches; Religion, Colonial Africa: Prophetic Movements; Zambia: Religious Movements.**

Biography

Born in the early 1920s in Chinsali District. Married Petros Chitankwa Mulenga. Undergoes her religious, near-death experiences in 1953. Baptized into the United Free Church of Scotland that same year. Charged with extortion and declared a heretic by church leaders in 1955. Sets up the Lumba Church, which spreads to neighboring villages by 1957. Attacked by the United National Independence Party (UNIP) and Kenneth Kaunda. In several confrontations, many of her followers were killed. Died December 1978.

Further Reading

Binsbergen, W. J. van. *Religious Change in Zambia: Exploratory Studies.* London: Kegan Paul, 1981.

Bond, G. C. "A Prophecy that Failed—The Lumpa Church of Uyombe, Zambia" In G. Bond, W. Johnson, and S. S. Walker, eds. *African Christianity: Patterns of Religious Continuity.* London and New York: Academic Press, 1979.

Makasa, K. *Zambia's March to Political Freedom.* Nairobi: Heinemann, 1985.

Roberts, A. D. *The Lumpa Church of Alice Lenshina.* Lusaka: Oxford University Press, 1972.

Leopard's Kopje: *See* Iron Age (Later): Southern Africa: Leopard's Kopje, Bambandyanalo, and Mapungubwe.

Leopold II: *See* Stanley, Leopold II, "Scramble."

Lesotho: Treaties and Conflict on the Highveld, 1843–1868

The modern nation of Lesotho was almost single-handedly created by Moshoeshoe I in the mid-nineteenth century. At the same time, the territorial boundaries of

Lesotho.

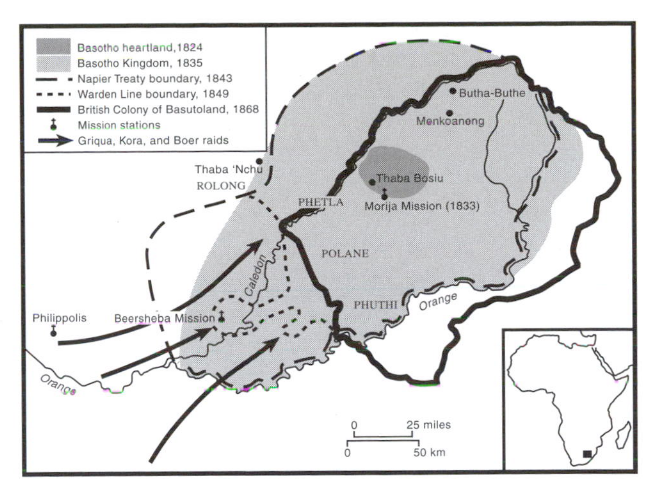

Lesotho, 1824–1868.

the state were gradually fixed in a long process of diplomacy and conflict.

The arrival of Voortrekker immigrants in the Caledon Valley after 1836 complicated an already complex configuration of political authority. Sekonyela's Tlokwa and Moshoeshoe's BaSotho were the strongest military forces, perpetually at odds with each other. Since 1834 a community of several thousand Rolong under the Tswana chief Moroka had been growing up at Thaba Nchu. Other newcomers included groups of Kora, Griqua, and so-called Bastards, all of them in possession of horses and guns. The Boer settlers opportunistically played these forces off against each other. In the absence of any agreed authority to regulate land titles, overlapping claims to sovereignty abounded, constantly threatening to provoke open warfare. The parties to these disputes were able to defend their claims in writing because a large number of Protestant missionaries had settled in the Caledon Valley. Agents of the Paris Evangelical Missionary Society had decided that Moshoeshoe offered them the best chances of future success and therefore stood ready to back up his claims. Agents of the Wesleyan Methodist Missionary Society had led the Rolong trek to Thaba Nchu and established stations with a number of other groups whose land claims they were prepared to defend when called upon. The Boers, of course, had their own literate spokesmen who maintained continuous correspondence with relatives and well-wishers in the Cape Colony. These parties vigorously lobbied British authorities in the hope of securing support for their various causes.

From the commencement of the Great Trek, the Cape government had maintained that the Voortrekkers continued to be British subjects, potentially accountable for any crimes they might commit beyond the borders of the colony. On the other hand, they did nothing to enforce their claimed authority until 1842, when they sent an expeditionary force to Natal. In 1843 they announced the annexation of that territory. This gave them a more direct interest in the Caledon Valley, which lay along the overland routes of trade and communication linking Natal to the Cape. A tentative move toward regularizing political authority in the Caledon was made by Governor Napier, who concluded a treaty with Moshoeshoe in 1843 that recognized the Orange River as the southern boundary of the kingdom and the Drakensberg escarpment as the northeastern border with Natal. In addition, a sizeable territory on the northern side of the Caledon River extending nearly to the Rolong stronghold of Thaba Nchu and as far up river almost to the mission station of Mpharane in Sekonyela's territory was acknowledged as belonging to Moshoeshoe.

Unfortunately, this did nothing to curb disputes over land. As a further aid to pacification, the Cape appointed a British resident with headquarters at Bloemfontein. Henry Warden, resident from 1846, bungled from crisis to crisis until in 1848, the political landscape was transformed by the appearance of a new British governor, Sir Harry Smith. Within months of taking office, Smith attempted to untie the Gordian knot of highveld problems by annexing the entire area between the Orange and Vaal Rivers as the Orange River Sovereignty. A Voortrekker force that attempted to challenge the new dispensation was defeated at Boomplaats in 1848. However, in the wake of this victory, Smith and Warden, who remained resident, pursued policies favoring white settlers and Moshoeshoe's rivals, Sekonyela and Moroko. Warden laid down new boundaries that deprived the BaSotho of nearly all their lands north of the Caledon River. He followed this up with a rash attempt to crush the allied forces of Moshoeshoe and his ally Moletsane. Warden's ragtag army of British, Griqua, Boer, Kora, and Rolong forces was defeated at the battle of Viervoet mountain, in June 1851.

Disillusioned by the never-ending conflicts, the British colonial secretary, Earl Grey, initiated a policy of withdrawal, beginning with the Sand River Convention of 1852, which dropped all claims to territory north of the Vaal River, and agreed to release Boers in those regions from their status as British subjects. Next, Sir George Cathcart, who succeeded the discredited Harry Smith in 1852, agreed that the Orange River Sovereignty should be abandoned. However, he determined to make one final show of force on the highveld. Backed by a force of 2,000 men, he delivered an ultimatum to Moshoeshoe, demanding 10,000 cattle and 1,000 horses as reparations for alleged thefts perpetrated by the BaSotho and the Taung. When these were not delivered, he attacked in December 1852. To his astonishment, the BaSotho cavalry put up an impressive defense and the British suffered heavy losses. Moshoeshoe, realizing that he could not prevail in the long run, now agreed to Cathcart's terms. A few months later he decisively defeated his old rival Sekonyela. Hopes that this might finally settle border problems were dashed by the Bloemfontein Convention of 1854, which transferred sovereignty to a Boer government without specifying a boundary between the new Orange River Free State and the BaSotho kingdom.

An agreement of 1855 fixed the boundary at the old "Warden Line" but failed to end conflict. President Boshof of the Free State declared war on the BaSotho in March 1858 but was defeated in a short campaign, which led to the transfer of some land back to the Sotho in an agreement of September 1858. Despite this victory, time was against Moshoeshoe. With each passing year the Free State became more populous and prosperous. In a second war lasting intermittently from 1865 to 1868, the BaSotho forces were outnumbered, outgunned, and plagued by internal divisions. At length the British high commissioner, Sir Philip Wodehouse, decided to intervene. Believing that victory for Free State would weaken Britain's strategic position at the Cape, and moved by the suffering of the BaSotho, he first cut off ammunition supplies to the Free State and then, on March 12, 1868, annexed Moshoeshoe's kingdom as the Crown Colony of Basutoland.

NORMAN A. ETHERINGTON

See also: **Boer Expansion: Interior of South Africa; Difaqane on the Highveld; Moshoeshoe I and the Founding of the Basotho Kingdom.**

Further Reading

Davenport, T. R. *South Africa: A Modern History.* Basingstoke: Macmillan, 1991.

Harington, A. L. *Sir Harry Smith: Bungling Hero.* Cape Town: Tafelberg, 1980.

Keegan, T. J. *Colonial South Africa and the Origins of the Racial Order.* Cape Town: David Philip, 1996.

Lye, W. F., and C. Murray. *Transformations on the Highveld: The Tswana and Southern Sotho.* Cape Town: David Philip, 1980.

Thompson, L. M. *Survival in Two Worlds: Moshoeshoe of Lesotho 1786–1870.* Oxford: Clarendon Press, 1975.

Wilson, M., and L. Thompson, eds., *The Oxford History of South Africa.* Vol. I, *South Africa to 1870.* Oxford: Clarendon Press, 1969.

Lesotho (Basutoland): Colonization and Cape Rule, 1868–1884

At the height of the 1865–1867 war between Basotho and the Free State Boers, Sir Philip Wodehouse (British high commissioner to South Africa and governor of the Cape Colony, 1862–1870) persuaded the British government to allow him to declare Moshoeshoe I's territory British territory. By this time Moshoeshoe's pleas for a relationship with the British government, which dated back to the early 1840s, had become earnest; whereas earlier he had sought to influence the character of that relationship, he now wanted a relationship on any terms that the British might wish. On March 12, 1868, Wodehouse declared Moshoeshoe's kingdom British territory, and Basotho British subjects.

But this marked only the beginning of Moshoeshoe and Wodehouse's troubled partnership as they attempted to secure British protection for Basotho. The period between March 1868 and February 1869 was a time of much correspondence and political intrigues. Wodehouse's March 12 declaration had not been unequivocally authorized by the Colonial Office. In part, the British government's failure to give Wodehouse clear signals was due to its program of reducing personnel costs and other expenditure related to colonization; the assumption of responsibility over Basotho was not in keeping with this plan. The Cape parliament was dominated by interests sympathetic to the Free State Boers and hostile to the establishment of good relations between Moshoeshoe and the Cape or the British government. Wodehouse not only found himself dealing with intrigues engineered by those who did not agree with his actions in Natal and elsewhere, he also found that in many instances, these groups and individuals were encouraged by the very man whom he was assisting to secure British protection: namely, Moshoeshoe. The procrastination of the British government in authorizing Wodehouse to extend British rule over Basotho forced Moshoeshoe to pursue, behind Wodehouse's back, the alternative of his territory's annexation to Natal. The Natal colony welcomed his overtures and made very strong moves to have Lesotho annexed to that colony. On February 12, 1869, Wodehouse managed to sign, with the Free State's delegation, the Aliwal North Treaty establishing the boundaries between Basotho's and the Free State Boers' territory. While the treaty was being considered for ratification by the British government, in 1869 Moshoeshoe encouraged and funded a mission to England to secure its repudiation.

On the basis of Moshoeshoe's overtures to Natal and the keenness of that colony to annex Lesotho, the Colonial Office supported a union between Lesotho and Natal. However, Wodehouse was opposed to it, fearing Basotho would soon rebel against Natal's colonial policies (which he considered unsuited to Basotho) leading to more instability. Instead, he favored Lesotho's annexation to the Cape Colony, an option opposed by the Cape parliament. In the end, Wodehouse successfully persuaded the Colonial Office to let him assume personal responsibility over Lesotho while he prepared the political ground in Lesotho and the Cape parliament for an eventual annexation of Lesotho to the Cape. This finally came about in 1871 after three years of uncertainty and confusion about who actually exercised power in Lesotho, and whether the administration of the country was based on colonial or customary law.

To prepare Basotho for annexation to the Cape Colony, Wodehouse had contemplated a gradual process of introducing colonial law and institutions to avoid the abrupt removal and replacement of indigenous law and political structures. However, his successors did not share his patience and tact. The men who succeeded Wodehouse and the officials they sent to Lesotho adopted a program of rapidly introducing colonial law into the country; and they had very little regard for the sensitivities of the groups who felt that such rapid change threatened their interests. The most critical of these were the chiefs who felt that their power over the people was being deliberately eroded, and the men who were opposed to the partnership that colonial law formed with the church to fight polygamy and advocate a more liberal status for women. Thus, although political stability returned after Lesotho's colonization, making economic recovery and prosperity possible from the early 1870s, there was simmering discontent among key political figures.

From the mid-1870s southern Africa as a whole became a battleground, as African chiefdoms took up arms against colonial rule and its destruction of their political systems and ways of life. The Basotho were no exception. In 1879 chief Moorosi protested the attempts by a young colonial magistrate to encroach on his power by assuming the responsibility to allocate land in the chief's territory, and taking the side of a widow who showed preference for colonial law over customary conventions in the way she wanted to conduct herself. The uncompromising attitude of both sides (the chief believed colonial policies were stripping him of all his power, while the Cape Colony government sought to end opposition to their policies and used Moorosi as an example to other chiefs) led to a full-scale war between Chief Moorosi and the colonial forces supported by Moshoeshoe I's successor, Chief Letsie.

Soon after the war ended with Moorosi's defeat early in 1880, Lesotho as a whole was at war with the Cape Colony. This time the issue was guns, and the conflict has come to be referred to as the "Gun War." Faced with several uprisings in its colonies in the region, the British government decided to disarm African chiefdoms. For Lesotho the policy was implemented by its immediate overseer, the Cape Colony government. Basotho refused to hand over their, guns arguing that they posed no threat to colonial rule. Once again the two sides were not prepared to compromise and war broke out in September 1880. It soon became clear that the war was at a stalemate—Cape forces had the advantage of better arms, but Basotho knew the terrain better and could count on the cooperation of the villagers. Furthermore, the war put an economic strain on the Cape Colony, which spent approximately $5 million on the conflict. In view of these factors, a ceasefire was agreed and the war was brought to a close in April 1881. Over the course of the next three years, the Cape Colony government attempted to reassert its authority over Lesotho, but Cape rule had become so unpopular that the government's various schemes (including a proposition that the chiefs take over all internal affairs and leave external affairs to the Cape) were rejected by Basotho. Consequently, in 1883 the Cape government negotiated with the Colonial Office for Lesotho to be handed over to Britain. In March 1884 Britain passed a law un-annexing Lesotho from the Cape Colony; from that date to 1966 Lesotho was ruled directly by Britain.

MOTLATSI THABANE

See also: **Cape Colony: Origins, Settlement, Trade; Moshoeshoe I and the Founding of the Basotho Kingdom.**

Further Reading

Atmore, A. "The Moorosi Rebellion: Lesotho 1879." In *Protest and Power in Black Africa*, edited by R. I. Rotberg and A. A. Mazrui, eds. New York: Oxford University Press, 1970.

Burman, S. B. *Chiefdom Politics and Alien Law: Basutoland Under Cape Rule, 1871–1884.* London: Macmillan, 1981.

Gill, S. J. *A Short History of Lesotho, From the Late Stone Age Until the 1993 Elections.* Morija: Morija Museum and Archives, 1993.

Theal, George McCall. *Basutoland Records.* Vols. 4, 5, and 6. Unpublished manuscripts.

Thompson, L. *Survival in Two Worlds: Moshoeshoe of Lesotho, 1786–1818.* 70. Oxford: Oxford University Press, 1975.

Lesotho (Basutoland): Peasantry, Rise of

The Kingdom of Lesotho was forged out of the destructive wars of the 1820s, when the Koena clan, under the celebrated leadership of Moshoeshoe, was able to bring together a disparate group of displaced people under its protection. Using the promise of protection, land, and cattle (often raided from neighboring peoples), Moshoeshoe was able to gradually draw together a large number of followers, who became known as the Basotho, and consequently extend his power to become the dominant leader in the southern high veld.

While cattle formed the basis of the kingdom's early wealth and power, by the middle decades of the nineteenth century Lesotho became the region's major producer of grains. By the 1870s Basotho peasant farmers were producing bumper harvests of grain, in particular maize, from the soils of the Calendon valley and exported their crops to as far away as the Eastern Cape and especially to the newly opened diamond fields around Kimberley. Peasant production in Lesotho remained high throughout the final three decades of the nineteenth century, but during the early twentieth century it gradually declined, in the face of competition from cheap imported grain, the development of capitalist agriculture elsewhere in South Africa, restrictive colonial policies (in order to secure labor for the mines) and, arguably, environmental decline.

The rise of peasant production in Lesotho was intimately linked to the expansion of the colonial frontier and the spread of new goods and techniques beyond the frontier. The arrival of the Paris Evangelical Missionary Society (PEMS) missionaries in 1833 was welcomed by Moshoeshoe, who wished to learn more about the Europeans and their new technologies, which had been made known to the Basotho by migrants returning from the eastern Cape. The PEMS missionaries brought with them European goods including, crucially, the iron plough. This new technology allowed Basotho farmers to plough and plant large areas under maize. Another technology that the Basotho were particularly keen to acquire was that of firearms.

While Moshoeshoe had managed to defeat or enter into alliances with many of his neighboring clans, he still had a number of powerful rivals, including the Griqua, a group of outcasts and miscellaneous adventurers from the Cape Colony who had formed a new polity beyond the colonial frontier. From the 1840s on, a new threat arrived within the Basotho's realm, as Vooretrekkers from the Cape began to settle the southern high veld. Frequent cattle raiding and pillaging led to periodic disruptions of the developing farming system. On the other hand the new settlers were not self-sufficient grain farmers, concentrating their activities on livestock production, hunting, and cattle raiding, and were therefore reliant upon Basotho farmers to meet their day-to-day food requirements.

During this early period it was often the ruling lineages that led the way in increased production. Using tribute labor, the chiefs were able to plough large areas, and they benefited greatly from increased maize exports. However, the arrival of the Voortrekkers (Afrikaans-speaking settlers from the Cape Colony) meant that over the next few decades the Basotho chiefs increasingly lost control of some of their best arable lands to the north and west of the Calendon River. In a series of battles the Basotho gradually lost control of these areas and eventually sought the protection of the British colonial authorities to prevent further territorial losses to the Voortrekkers. This support was eventually gained in 1868, but at the cost of the majority of their best farming lands.

This did not mean, however, that Basotho ceased to farm the "conquered territories" (as the area came to be known in Lesotho). In fact, many Basotho entered into various forms of rental agreements, including sharecropping, with the Voortrekkers, and they continued to expand their agricultural production. With the onset of relative peace following the declaration of British protection, peasant production boomed in Lesotho during the 1870s. While chiefs and commoners closely associated with the missions had dominated the maize export market in earlier decades, it was now the turn of the ordinary Basotho to transform themselves into independent peasant producers.

Using cattle-drawn ploughs Basotho peasant farmers planted more land under maize and reaped impressive harvests. Previously food production had been primarily the responsibility of women, while men had concentrated on livestock rearing, but the use of cattle-drawn ploughs meant that men began to play a greater role in agriculture.

The growth of the colonial economy also led to increased opportunities for Basotho to access European goods through wage labor. During the late nineteenth century, Basotho migrants often took short-term contracts to work on the new mines in Kimberley and later on the Rand or on the farms of the eastern Cape or the Orange Free State. Wages earned from these short-term contracts tended to be reinvested in peasant agricultural production, by the purchase of ploughs, livestock, or horses. As in earlier decades, guns remained a desirable investment as the Basotho saw these as being crucial to their ability to protect their land from further encroachment. When the Cape colonial authorities, whom the British had put in charge of the territory's administration, tried to disarm the Basotho in 1880, it led to the onset of the Gun War, which resulted in the British resuming direct administration of Lesotho.

Despite the disruptions of the Gun War, Basotho peasant farmers continued to increase their output. This growing peasant sector presented both a threat and an opportunity to the chiefs. Independent agricultural production meant that commoners were no longer as reliant upon the chiefs, and the gradual growth of a wealthy farming class, often strongly associated with one of the churches, provided a clear political threat. Nevertheless the chiefs were able to benefit politically from their control over the allocation of land, and they benefited materially from the institution of tribute labor and from demanding a proportion of returning migrants' earnings.

While South Africa's mineral revolution provided the impetus for the rise of the Basotho peasantry in the late nineteenth century, the development of mines also contained the seeds for its subsequent decline. The arrival of railways from the Cape meant that Basotho peasant farmers had to now compete with cheap imports from North America, while the capital produced by the mines was available for investment, often at subsidies rates, into white agriculture. Furthermore, the British colonial authorities responded to the demands of mine owners and actively discouraged peasant production in order to ensure the increased outflow of migrant labor. During the early twentieth century, Lesotho gradually slipped from being the breadbasket of the region to reliance upon remittances from migrant workers and on imported maize. Some Basotho peasant farmers, both inside Lesotho and in the conquered territories, continued to be successful into the middle of the twentieth century, but for most the transition from granary to labor reserve was completed by the 1930s.

THACKWRAY DRIVER

Further Reading

Eldredge, E. A. *A South African Kingdom: The Pursuit of Security in Nineteenth Century Lesotho*. Cambridge: Cambridge University Press, 1993.

Kimble, J. "Clinging to the Chiefs: Some Contradictions of Colonial Rule in Basutoland, c. 1890–1930." In *Contradictions of Accumulation in Africa: Studies in Economy and State*, edited by H. Bernstein and B. K. Campbell. London: Sage, 1985.

———. "Labour Migrancy in Basutoland, 1870–1885." In *Industrialisation and Social Change in South Africa: African Class Formation, Culture, and Consciousness, 1870–1930*, edited by S. Marks and R. Rathbone. London: Longman, 1982.

Murray, C. "From Granary to Labour Reserve: An Economic History of Lesotho." *South African Labour Bulletin*. 6, no. 4 (1980): 3–20.

Lesotho (Basutoland): Colonial Period

British colonial rule of Lesotho (or Basutoland, as it was known to the colonial authorities) has often been portrayed as a rule characterized by neglect. With the exception of a brief initial period when the territory was administered by the Cape Colony (1871–1884), the colonial administration's primary objective was to maintain the status quo. The major political issue for the colonial authorities was the persistent South African demand that the territory be transferred to South African control. Facing opposition to this transfer from groups such as the Anti-Slavery Society and the Fabian Colonial Bureau in the United Kingdom and from African opinion in Lesotho, the colonial authorities resisted these calls for transfer and were happiest when they could simply avoid discussing the issue. The colonial administration allowed the chiefs to exercise a large degree of control, so long as they did not challenge British political or economic objectives, primarily the continued outflow of migrant labor to the South African mines.

The peasant agricultural sector in Lesotho was vibrant in the last three decades of the nineteenth century, but during the early twentieth century it entered a period of terminal decline. Given the fact that a major aim of British colonial policy was to encourage the outflow of labor to the mines, the British were not, at first, concerned by this decrease in domestic production and, arguably, even introduced policies that hastened the demise of the peasant sector.

By the 1920s, however, the colonial authorities had become increasingly concerned about the state of Lesotho's agricultural sector; therefore, from the late 1920s they began to introduce agricultural development policies and projects. Of particular importance to the territory were policies aimed at the control of soil erosion, one of the major causes of the decline in the eyes of colonial officials, though this view has been challenged by some recent scholarship. These new interventions had very little impact and the 1930s were a particularly difficult decade. The global recession meant that there was a declining market for Lesotho's remaining agricultural exports, such as mohair and wool, while wage-earning opportunities for migrant laborers also decreased. Furthermore, the early 1930s saw a series of devastating droughts, resulting in poor harvests and a massive decrease in livestock populations. Despite repeated efforts at agricultural development projects in the post–World War II era, the economy of Lesotho continued to suffer throughout the colonial period. A few wealthier farmers, often chiefs, did manage to make significant income from agriculture, especially in the mohair industry, which recovered and flourished in the mountain areas from the late 1940s onward. The vast majority of households, however, were unable to meet even their subsistence needs from agriculture. The lack of other exploitable natural resources mean that colonial Lesotho was forced to rely on the export of its labor resources simply to survive.

Migrant labor existed in Lesotho even before the advent of colonial rule but increased with the development of the diamond and then gold mines in South Africa. During the early colonial period migrant labor was characterized by short contracts that were undertaken to earn funds to buy specific European goods, such as guns, ploughs, and blankets. From the early twentieth century, however, the destruction of independent peasant production in Lesotho meant that most households came to rely upon remittances from migrant labor for the majority of their subsistence needs. Labor recruiters worked with the colonial authorities, and often with the chiefs, to ensure that a constant stream of cheap labor was available from Lesotho to service the needs of South Africa's mines. Young men tended to leave Lesotho on repeated labor contracts over a number of years, returning to Lesotho only for short breaks between contracts. Other Basotho left to find opportunities in the informal sector that arose to service the needs of the new urban labor forces. While men continued to dominate the migrant labor system, increasing numbers of women also migrated, both temporarily and permanently, to Johannesburg and other large cities especially during the 1930s and 1940s. The last decades of colonial rule saw a decrease in the number of Basotho leaving Lesotho for informal sector jobs, as South African influx controls increased under the apartheid regime. Large numbers of men continued to leave Lesotho on mining contracts, but these were formalized and strictly controlled.

In general the colonial authorities were keen to support the power of chiefs, though they also intervened to make sure that apparently loyal chiefs gained the most powerful positions. During the early colonial period the territory was officially ruled through two parallel administrative structures, one headed by the colonial resident commissioner, with a number of supporting departments (such as agriculture and education) and a series of district commissioners. The other administrative structure, known as the Native Authority, was headed by a paramount chief, who was advised by a national council of senior chiefs representing individual wards (the Basutoland National Council). Ward chiefs, in turn, had a number of lesser chiefs and headmen under their control. Chiefs could either directly inherit chieftainships or they could be "placed" in charge of an area by a superior chief. The system of "placing" was used by senior chiefs to ensure that subordinate chiefs were under the control of a loyal follower. This system led to frequent disputes among chiefs and the proliferation of chieftainships.

In an effort to rationalize the Native Authority, the colonial government introduced a series of "reforms" designed to bring the system increasingly under the colonial authority's control and to administer the country through a system of indirect rule similar to that adopted in other British colonial territories. These reforms were opposed by many of the chiefs but were eventually accepted by the Basutoland National Council in 1938. The colonial authorities took an increasingly interventionist role in the chiefly affairs and, crucially, became the arbitrators in a dispute about the succession to the position of paramount chief. This effort by the colonial authorities to rationalize the system of Native Authority did not result in the hoped for decrease in conflict between chiefs. The late 1940s and early 1950s saw a whole series of so-called medicine murders, closely associated with power rivalries between senior chiefs, in particular between the British colonial authorities chosen candidate for paramount chief, the regent Mantsebo, and her brother-in-law and rival, Chief Bereng.

The spate of "medicine murders" fueled calls from a small but vocal African educated class, who lobbied the colonial authorities to be included in the running of the territories affairs. The colonial authorities were also under attack from a more radical grass roots movement, called Lekhotla la Bafo, who combined calls for a return to rule by "traditional Chiefly administration" with strong ties to the growing African nationalist movement in South Africa. With the development of an apartheid ideology, South African pressure for the transfer of Lesotho to its control decreased, as the policy was now to organize the African population into autonomous ethnically based states, and the British gradually moved toward granting Lesotho Independence. The Basutoland National Council was first expanded to include commoners representing certain interest groups (such as traders) and subsequently to include directly elected representatives. Lesotho was eventually granted full independence in 1966.

THACKWRAY DRIVER

See also: **Colonialism: Impact on African Societies.**

Further Reading

Coplan, D., and T. Quinlan. "A Chief by the People: Nation versus State in Lesotho." *Africa.* 67, no. 1 (1997): 25–59.

Epprecht, M. "Women's 'Conservatism' and the Politics of Gender in Late Colonial Lesotho." *Journal of African History.* 36, no. 1 (1995): 25–56.

Jones, G. I. *Basutoland Medicine Murder: A Report on the Recent Outbreak of "Liretlo" Murders in Basutoland.* London: HMSO (Cmd 4907), 1951.

Machobane, L. B. B. J. *Government and Change in Lesotho, 1800–1966: A Study of Political Institutions.* Basingstoke: MacMillan, 1990.

Maloka, T. "Khomo Lia Oela: Canteens, Brothels and Labour Migrancy in Colonial Lesotho, 1900–1940." *Journal of African History.* 38, no. 1 (1997): 101–122.

Pim, A. W. *Financial and Economic Position of Basutoland: Report of the Commission Appointed by the Secretary of State for Dominion Affairs*. London: HMSO (Cmd 4907), 1935.

Lesotho: Independence to the Present

Lesotho gained its independence from Britain on October 4, 1966. Throughout the colonial period, the government did very little to develop the country's economy. Although Basotho were said to depend on agriculture for their livelihood, they mainly practiced subsistence agriculture; most families depended on earnings of relatives working in the South African mines and other sectors of that country's economy. Due to a lack of industrialization, very little urbanization had taken place during the colonial era, and today Lesotho's rural population still constitutes more than 80 per cent of the total population, which is currently estimated at 1.8 million, growing at the rate of 1.5 per cent annually.

Until January 1986, when Chief Leabua's government was overthrown by the army, the central policy of the government's economic strategy was the establishment of parastatal agencies to assist private sector investment. Between 1967 and 1975, the government established three such agencies, the Lesotho National Development Corporation (LNDC, 1967), the Lesotho National Development Savings Bank (Lesotho Bank, 1971), and the Basotho Enterprise Development Corporation (BEDCO, 1975). The LNDC was meant to attract foreign entrepreneurs to invest in Lesotho's industrial development. Lesotho Bank was a means by which the government sought to mobilize small deposits from the nation, turn them into capital, and avail them to investors. BEDCO's mission was to assist small- to medium-scale local entrepreneurs with business skills and finance. Although of colonial origins, Co-op Lesotho was also supported as a facility to assist farmers and other cooperative associations with seeds and related requirements. However, this strategy made very little impact on Lesotho's employment opportunities and economic development. LNDC's concessions to foreign investors included a five-year tax holiday and allowing them to repatriate their profits. Investors took advantage of these conditions and shut their operations at the end of the five-year tax holiday. Clients of Lesotho Bank and BEDCO were mainly middle-class elements from the civil service. The loans they secured from these institutions ended up in investments such as housing and very few went toward investment in successful commercial activities.

Foreign companies continuing to do business in Lesotho are mainly Taiwanese textile manufacturers. They employ a sizeable but extremely poorly paid, largely female labor force. For their part, government-sponsored credit institutions have found it difficult to force ministers and high-ranking government officials to repay their loans. The consequent high default rate has led to the collapse of institutions such as Co-op Lesotho and, more recently, Lesotho Bank and serious financial problems for others like BEDCO.

Lesotho's agricultural productivity began to deteriorate in the late 1920s and never recovered after the 1930s depression. At the heart of this deterioration was a combination of factors including decline in soil fertility, lack of resources to develop and change farming practices, soil erosion caused by overcrowding, overstocking, and Lesotho's topography. The failure of agriculture increased Basotho's dependence for jobs and earnings on the mines and other sectors of the South African economy. However, the numbers of Basotho able to find jobs in South Africa mines began to fall in the late 1980s. This trend continues and unemployment in Lesotho stands at more than 40 per cent, while the labor force increases at a rate of 25 per cent annually.

Lesotho's 1966 constitution provided for a constitutional monarchy in which executive power was exercised by a cabinet made up of a prime minister and his ministers and answerable to the parliament; the king acted on the advice of the prime minister and could delay but not veto, government and parliament action. From the late 1950s to the mid-1960s, when politicians negotiated Lesotho's independence constitution with Britain, King Moshoeshoe II and his supporters attempted, but failed, to secure a political dispensation that would give him power. This issue became a source of political instability in Lesotho in the immediate postindependence period, as the king and his supporters joined groups that were attempting to unseat the postindependence government, which had gained only a slender majority in parliament in the preindependence elections of 1965.

The first postindependence elections were held in January 1970. Chief Leabua of the ruling Basutoland National Party (BNP) lost but refused to hand over power to Ntsu Mokhehle's Basutoland Congress Party (BCP) and suspended the constitution. Leabua proceeded to reign in all those who opposed him. By the end of that year he had successfully subdued the king.

In an attempt to force Leabua to reinstate constitutional rule, the donor community on whom the government depended greatly for financing development projects suspended or threatened to suspend aid.

Leabua reacted by establishing an interim parliament in 1973 and forming a government of national unity and reconciliation in 1975, after forcing Mokhehle into exile in 1974. Although significant opposition leaders boycotted these moves, some members from opposition parties participated in them. The resulting fragmentation of parties and the flight of Mokhehle weakened opposition to Leabua's dictatorial rule.

The international community continued to pressure the government to reinstate constitutional rule. In response, and taking advantage of developments in South Africa, the government adopted a progressive foreign policy while tightening its grip on power and intensifying repression inside the country. From the mid-1970s Leabua joined the international anti-apartheid and pro-liberation movement chorus. By the time he was overthrown by the army in 1986, he had established diplomatic relations with Cuba, the USSR, the People's Republic of Korea (PRK), the People's Republic of China (PRC) and a number of socialist governments in Eastern Europe.

The military regime that assumed leadership in 1986 made an alliance with the palace in an attempt to secure legitimacy. According to the arrangement, King Moshoeshoe II was the head of state; below him was a Military Council made up of five colonels and headed by Major General Metsing Lekhanya, who was also head of government. The next tier was made up of a civilian, mainly technocratic, Council of Ministers. This government established more cordial relations with South Africa, forced ANC and other refugees to find alternative asylum, expelled PRC and PRK emissaries, and reestablished ties with Taiwan.

Although the first order passed by the junta declared that executive power was vested in the king, in practice it was exercised by Lekhanya and the Military Council. This caused tensions between the major general and the king who found support within the Military Council of two cousins who were members of that body. Taking advantage of Lekhanya's fatal shooting of a student in 1988, the king and his cousins attempted but failed to oust Lekhanya. The state, no doubt at Lekhanya's prodding, began legal proceedings against one of the king's cousins who had been implicated in the murder of two former ministers in 1986. The king declined Lekhanya's request to suspend his cousins from the Military Council. The tension that had existed between the two men became a public falling-out, and Lekhanya forced the king into exile and installed Crown Prince Mohato as King Letsie III in 1990. In 1991 Lekhanya was overthrown by junior officers who installed one of the members of the Military Council, Colonel Phisoane Ramaema, as head of government.

Under increasing pressure from the post–Cold War international community and local civil society, elections were held in 1993 and won by the BCP, the leaders of which had returned from exile in 1988. King Letsie III put pressure on the democratically elected government to reinstate his father as king, but the government responded by pointing out that his father was not deposed by them. Under further pressure, the government appointed a commission to investigate the circumstances under which Moshoeshoe II had been dethroned. Persons appointed to this commission were either members of the ruling party, whose reluctance to reinstate the king's father was evident, or individuals whose antimonarchical inclinations were well known. Regarding this as a farce intended to keep his father out of power, the king gained the support of the army which was still suspicious of Mokhehle and staged a coup d'état on August 17, 1994. Local, regional, and international pressure was exerted on the king, and Mokhehle's government was reinstated in September 1994, under an agreement that forced the government to reinstate Moshoeshoe II in January 1995. A year later, he died in a car accident and was succeeded by Letsie III.

In 1998 Lesotho's third parliament was elected and the Lesotho Congress for Democracy (LCD) won 79 of the 80 seats. This result sparked off protests by supporters of opposition parties from May until September 1998, which paralyzed the already weak government that had assumed power after the elections. The king, security forces, and other public institutions were sympathetic to opposition parties and abetted or turned a blind eye to antigovernment protests. On September 22 the government secured the assistance of Botswana and South African security forces to restore order. An investigation by a regional task team discovered that there had been irregularities in the administration of the elections but contended that these could not have affected the outcome. The government and opposition parties accepted the recommendation of the investigation team that the elections be annulled, and the Interim Political Authority (IPA), consisting of members of all parties that participated in the 1998 elections, was set up to review Lesotho's electoral system. Elections were held in 2002 under the new system, with the approval of foreign election observers, in which the LCD won a majority and Prime Minister Bethuel Pakalitha Mosisili was elected to another five-year term.

MOTLATSI THABANE

See also: **Jonathan, Chief Joseph Leabua; Mokhehle, Ntsu.**

Further Reading

Bardill, J. E., and J. H. Cobbe. *Lesotho: Dilemmas of Dependence in Southern Africa.* Colorado: Westview Press, and London: Gower, 1985.

Baylies, C., and C. Wright. "Female Labour in the Textile and Clothing Industry of Lesotho." *African Affairs.* 92 (1993): 577– 591.

Macartney, W. J. A. "The Lesotho General Election of 1970." *Government and Opposition. 4* (1973): 473–494.

Mothibe, T. H. "The Rise and Fall of the Military-Monarchy Power-Sharing, 1986–1990." *Africa Insight.* 20, no. 40 (1990): 242–246.

Weisfelder, R. F. "Early Voices of Protest in Basutoland: The Progressive Association and Lekhotla la Bafo." *African Studies Review.* 17, no. 2 (1974): 397–410.

Lesotho: Nationalism and Independence

The emergence of nationalist movements in Lesotho dates back to the formation of the Basutoland Progressive Association (BPA) and Lekgotla la Bafo (LLB), the Commoners' League, in 1907 and 1919, respectively. The BPA was a moderate organization that drew its membership from Lesotho's educated elite, who advocated modernization. They resented the partnership that the colonial regime had established with the chiefs and saw themselves as the natural allies of the colonial regime in its program of modernizing Basotho. They regarded chieftainship as an anachronistic institution and wished to abolish chiefly privileges. They did not demand independence but sought a political dispensation that accorded them a more prominent role at the expense of the chiefs. For some time, the organization's pleas for a more meaningful representation in the chief-dominated Basutoland National Council (BNC) failed, and the colonial regime successfully used the petitions of the BPA as a way to keep the chiefs compliant.

Lekgotla la Bafo was a radical conservative grassroots organization that campaigned against what it regarded as Britain's failure to adhere to the terms of its colonization of Lesotho and the undermining of precolonial institutions, particularly chieftainship. According to the organization, Lesotho was a protectorate and not a colony; this status required that Britain only protect Lesotho while leaving Basotho to govern themselves with their institutions without any colonial interference. The LLB established relations with left-wing organizations such as the Communist Party of South Africa and sometimes took positions that were at odds with its conservative nature. Like the BPA, LLB put pressure on the colonial authorities for representation of the commoners in the BNC. However, this pressure benefited not the LLB but the moderate BPA. Unable to ignore the persistence of the BNC, but fearing the inclusion of militant members of that organization in the council, colonial authorities began appointing members of the BPA to the BNC. LLB's petitions for representation in the council were met with the response that the commoners were adequately represented by members of the BPA.

The two organizations proved unable to keep up with the content and nature of the political consciousness that came with the end of World War II. The BPA was too civil and polite and its strategy of petitioning the colonial regime had proved largely ineffective. Contrary to the LLB's political stance, the majority of people in Lesotho wanted to be ruled and represented in government institutions by individuals or groups they elected and not by precolonial institutions and the chiefs, as the organization demanded. By the 1950s the appeal of both organizations waned and their place was taken by political parties that emerged at the time; the membership of the BPA scattered throughout the ranks of various political parties, mainly the Basutoland Congress Party (BCP), formed in 1952, and the Marematlou Freedom Party (MFP), an alliance formed in 1962 made up of Basutoland Freedom Party, BFP, which broke away from the BCP in 1961, and the royalist Marema-Tlou Party formed in 1958. The majority of the members of the LLB joined the BCP. The Basutoland National Party (BNP) formed in 1959 benefited mainly from a conservative membership that had been instilled with respect for authority, and which had therefore never joined the BPA or LLB.

As the first party to be formed and a successor to the LLB, which had had a troubled relationship with the colonial authorities, the BCP drew more distrust from the colonial regime than the other two parties. Because it had started agitating for independence at a time Britain's decolonization agenda was in its infancy, the BCP had seemed the most militant, adopting the strategy of petitioning the United Nations and mobilizing the sympathy of other international bodies against colonial rule in Lesotho.

From the mid-1950s, the BNC and these parties pressed for constitutional reforms. In 1958 a delegation of the BNC convinced the British government to transform that body into a legislative council with powers to make laws on internal affairs. This changed status of the council enabled its members to participate in the various steps toward Lesotho's decolonization, including the drafting and negotiation of the country's postindependence constitution. In 1960 District Council elections were held with a view, among others, to elect individuals to the Legislative Council. The BCP won thirty of the 40 seats but could not really exercise any power, which remained firmly in the hands of the colonial officials and a body, the Executive Council, established to run various ministries. However, being elected members of the Legislative Council gave BCP members a platform from which to call for Lesotho's independence. By 1962 the Legislative Council established a commission to make proposals for self-rule. In 1963 the commission toured the country soliciting views on the role of the monarchy in Lesotho politics;

the result of this consultation was that the king should be a constitutional monarch, a view which was strongly canvassed by the BCP.

The proposals resulting from the work of the commission in 1962 and 1963 formed the basis of constitutional negotiations between the British government and the delegation of the Legislative Council that were completed in 1964. During these talks, the king and some of the members of the delegation tried to secure an executive role for him but failed. In April 1965 the preindependence general elections were held to determine the first postindependence government. Of the 60 seats that were contested, the BNP won 31, the BCP 25, and the MFP 4. Because Chief Lebua, the leader of the BNP, had lost the contest in his constituency, it was his deputy, Chief Sekhonyana 'Maseribane, who became Lesotho's first prime minister. However by July 1965, Chief Leabua had won a by-election and assumed leadership of the party and the government.

The fact that Britain had accepted the need to free its colonies and had embarked on implementing its decolonization plan meant that the struggle for Lesotho's independence was a peaceful one characterized by negotiations rather than force. Because they dominated the Legislative Council and formed the majority in the delegations which that body entrusted with the negotiations for Lesotho's independence, members of political parties were able to secure a constitution that took power away from the traditional elite and gave it to elected representatives.

MOTLATSI THABANE

See also: **Jonathan, Chief Joseph Leabua.**

Further Reading

Edgar, R., *Prophets with Honour: A Documentary History of Lekhotla la Bafo*. Johannesburg: Ravan Press, n.d.

Gill, S. J. *A Brief History of Lesotho: From the Late Stone Age Until the 1993 Elections*. Morija: Morij a Museum and Archives, 1993.

Laurence, P. "Basutoland: 1945–1960: A Study of Emergent African Nationalism." Master's thesis, University of Natal, n.d.

Mapetla, P. "The Role of the Basutoland Progressive Association (BPA) in the Formation of the Modern Political Parties in Lesotho." A paper submitted in fulfilment of the BA degree, National University of Lesotho, April 1985.

Weisfelder, R. F. "Early Voices of Protest in Basutoland: The Progressive Association and Lekhotla la Bafo." *African Studies Review*. 17, no. 2 (1974): 397–410.

Lewanika I, the Lozi, and the BSA Company

In its quest for empire "on the cheap" in the late nineteenth century, the British government was not averse to using commercial companies to exact concessions from African leaders. This is what happened during the 1890s, when Cecil Rhodes's newly chartered British South Africa Company (BSAC) made agreements with Lewanika, the powerful monarch of the central African kingdom of Bulozi. The king, or *litunga* ("owner of the earth"), anxious to preempt the threat of invasion from the Ndebele, eager to secure British protection as a modernizing force, and mindful of rival factions within his own regime, took the initiative in pressing for BSAC intervention.

At first, though, company interest in the region, primarily floodplain on the upper Zambesi, was fleeting and fitful. Rhodes was concerned with forestalling the Belgian advance on mineral-rich Katanga, and the Lozi kingdom was en route. By the time the BSAC's brash agent had reached the Lozi capital of Lealui, Katanga had been lost. Frank Lochner, however, stayed to negotiate, in mid-1890, one of the many concessions that Lewanika signed with the BSAC over the next twenty years.

The Lochner concession gave the company the perpetual right to mine, trade, and build railways in the Lozi Empire (but not within the central kingdom) in return for British protection, the appointment of a British resident, and an annual salary for Lewanika. The concession was allowed to lapse, in part because the BSAC became embroiled in conflict with the Ndebele, but it illuminates two significant themes in Lozi-Company relations. First, the BSAC acknowledged Lewanika's authority, whether real or fictitious, over a wide swathe of what later became northwestern Rhodesia (the Lozi Empire, termed Barotseland by the imperialists, was incorporated into northern Rhodesia in 1911 and is nowadays the western province of Zambia), something which would reinforce company claims to possible mineral-bearing areas. Second, the company took a laissez-faire approach to the Lozi kingdom (Bulozi) itself, because the exchange economy of the floodplain offered little prospect for profit and because it was considered imprudent to disturb the internal power structure.

The Lochner concession was followed by seven years of company neglect, despite the repeated protestations of Lewanika's French missionary ally at Lealui, Francois Coillard, and despite the concerns of the Foreign Office of a Portuguese threat. It was not until late 1897 that Rhodes sent one of his younger associates, Robert Coryndon, to take up the position of resident. Coryndon and four others, representing mighty Albion, were met by hundreds of Lozi, many in ceremonial dress, at Lealui on October 20, 1897. For the subsequent ten years, it is perhaps more appropriate to talk of Coryndon-Lewanika relations, as the BSAC was concerned only with establishing a nominal presence in Barotseland. A minimal white presence in a militarily powerful central African state offers little guide to power relations, however; most historians see Lewanika's participation in the Scramble as a fateful ploy that reduced his empire, undermined Lozi sovereignty, and eventually decimated the floodplain economy.

The concessions signed in 1898 (the Lawley concession) and 1900 (Lewanika concession) are a matter of some contention. Lewanika and his senior *indunas* (as well as Coillard and a high-ranking member of the Barotse police) charged the company with deceit and intimidation. Even so, Lewanika managed to maintain control of his inner kingdom (company headquarters were far from Lealui) and garner support for his rule (Coryndon despatched a patrol to the royal capital in 1905 to forestall a coup). The company's actions were also circumscribed by Colonial Office overrule, at least in a legalistic sense, once the 1899 Order in Council incorporated Barotseland into northwestern Rhodesia. The concessions (another followed in 1906) were also significant in sorting out the technical arrangements of rule between the BSAC and the British government.

Mainga (1973) argues that it was not so much the early administrative concessions that tore the kingdom apart but the end of slavery and tribute labor. The advent of a cash economy has always placed severe strains on indigenous societies; the company certainly saw the formal abolition of slavery (accomplished by decree in 1906) and the imposition of a hut tax as a means of mobilizing labor for the white economy, something which would erode the foundation of the Lozi power. Lewanika was, however, well aware of the meaning of British rule from his missionary contacts and friendship with Khama of the Ngwato. In the phase of company neglect (1890–1897), he had engaged on a number of slave raids, for the first time among the Luvale in the west, and into Ila and Toka country, to gather slaves surplus to his requirements and, perhaps more importantly, to claim political authority where it was only tenuous before. Lewanika was an African imperialist whose *modus operandi* was little different from the BSAC itself. When tribute was superseded by the hut tax in 1902–06, Lewanika not only secured 10 per cent of the receipts but the installation of *indunas* in outlying districts. For Lewanika such symbolic acts legitimized his authority and were no doubt linked to a well–thought out scheme to entrench the power of the Lozi ruling elites.

Lewanika was also alert to the potentially damaging effects of colonial capitalism, but this he could not control. During his lifetime (he died in 1916), labor migration from Barotseland (especially to the South African mines) was just a steady trickle, but when an outbreak of bovine pleuro-pneumonia and subsequent embargo on cattle sales (1915) ended an era of prosperity, labor migration increased substantially. By the interwar years, Barotseland was one of the poorest regions of northern Rhodesia.

Lewanika often complained that the BSAC did not live up to its agreements to modernize his kingdom, to build schools, promote infrastructural development, and ensure the financial security of the Lozi aristocracy. British "protection" did not live up to its early, or even written, promises. The BSAC, as an imperialist and capitalist corporation, made severe inroads on Lozi independence. This should not obscure the fact that Lewanika secured the best terms of collaboration than any central African leader, as well as the continuation of a separate Lozi identity in colonial and independent Zambia.

CHRIS YOUÉ

See also: **Lozi Kingdom and the Kololo; Rhodes, Cecil J.; Zambia (Northern Rhodesia): British Occupation, Resistance: 1890s.**

Further Reading

Caplan, G. *The Elites of Barotseland 1878–1969: A Political History of Zambia's Western Province*. London: C. Hurst and Co., 1970.

Clarence-Smith, W. G. "Slaves, Commoners, and Landlords in Bulozi, c.1875–1906." *Journal of African History*. 20, no. 2: 219–234.

Mainga, M. *Bulozi under the Luyana Kings: Political Evolution and State Formation in Pre–colonial Zambia*. London: Longman, 1973.

Roberts, A. *A History of Zambia*. London: Heinemann, 1976.

Stokes, E. "Barotseland: The Survival of an African State." In *The Zambesian Past: Studies in Central African History*, edited by E. Stokes and R. Brown. Manchester: Manchester University Press, 1966.

Youé, C. P. "The Politics of Collaboration in Bulozi, 1890–1914." *Journal of Imperial and Commonwealth History*, 13, no. 2 (1985): 139–156.

Liberia, Nineteenth Century: Origins and Foundations

Liberia emerged out of a context of conflicting dreams, expectations, and plans. For several hundred years before 1800, the Grain Coast of West Africa had been a source of slaves, palm oil, and malgretta peppers for ships coming from Europe and America. The trade was controlled by coastal chiefs—mainly Dei, Bassa, Vai, and Kru—while the interior peoples such as the Gola, Grebo, Kpelle, and Loma provided many of the products. For their part, the Mandingos were important merchants linking regions of the interior with the large Mande-speaking world to the north. Although several large multiethnic confederations emerged along the main trade routes to the coast, most people lived in relatively small-scale communities led not only by political chiefs but by the religious and cultural heads of the so-called secret societies that included all adult males and females. It was here that the Liberian nation was established.

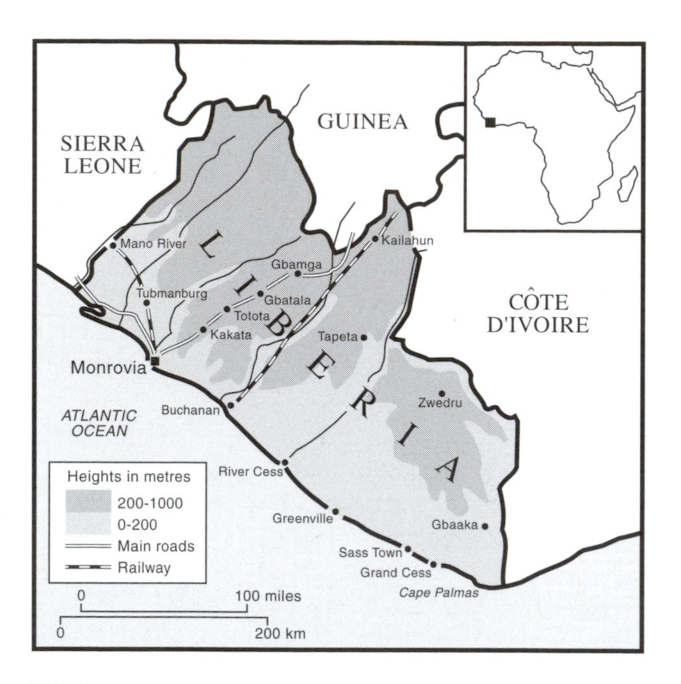

Liberia.

Liberia began as a project of the American Colonization Society (ACS), an alliance of southern slave holders, northern abolitionists, and religious optimists. In the south, as cotton gained importance and the value of slaves increased around 1800, the fear of slave revolts intensified. The catalyst for such uprising, it was feared, would be the growing population of free blacks living in the urban areas. In the north, especially, the sentiments unleashed by progressive religious and social movements called the institution of slavery itself into question. Because few Americans—even the more liberal—entertained the notion of a multiethnic society, many thought the best solution was to rid the United States of blacks by transporting them to Africa. Thus, was born the American Colonization Society. Leading Americans such as Robert Finley, Elias Caldwell, Bushrod Washington, Henry Clay, Daniel Webster, and Andrew Jackson attended the founding meeting in 1816. Their goal was to solicit financial and political backing of the U.S. government. Very early on, the ACS lost the support of northern blacks and the leaders in the abolitionist movement. For example, Paul Cuffee, a wealthy black sea captain who had gone to West Africa as early as 1811 to search for land to resettle black people, distanced himself from the ACS because he feared its goal was deporting blacks from America rather than civilizing, Christianizing, and developing Africa. William Lloyd Garrison turned against the ACS when he realized it was not supported by northern black religious leaders who saw the organization as a tool of southern slave owners. Congress did appropriate $100,000 for the ACS but refused to approve the resettlement of blacks from America. Instead, the money was authorized for a settlement of recaptive Africans taken from illegal slave operations. Thus, when the ship the *Elizabeth* sailed from New York on January 31, 1820, the 86 settlers were officially regarded as carpenters, seamstresses, nurses, and cooks sent to prepare for the recaptives who would be taken from interdicted slave ships.

In April and December 1821, while the settlers remained in Sierra Leone, several white ACS agents contacted the local Dei chiefs in the area of modern-day Monrovia and persuaded them to "cede" land for a settlement. In March 1822, the first settlers, wards of the ACS, arrived to begin a new life in Africa.

From the beginning the small settlement struggled. By November 1822, the settlers experienced their first armed clash with their local African hosts. Hostilities continued for several more decades. During these years the settlers were greatly outnumbered by the indigenous peoples. In the first 12 years of its existence, fewer than 3,000 people emigrated from the United States. Not only did these first emigrants experience high mortality rates, a significant number returned to America or Sierra Leone. And, although some like Rev. Daniel Coker, Rev. Lott Carey, and J. J. Roberts were educated free blacks, most were manumitted slaves. Although the ACS envisioned the emigrants would take up agriculture and become self-sufficient farmers, many of them turned to commerce.

The first few years of settlement were marked by autocratic ACS control. Soon, the settlers chafed at the insufficient rations and the rigid rule of the ACS. In 1823 the conflict actually escalated into an armed attack against an ACS warehouse. In response, the white clergyman Ralph Gurley was sent to investigate the complaints and a new "Plan of Government" was adopted in 1825. The plan retained power in the hands of the ACS, but a settler was now designated as vice agent.

In addition to internal discontent, the colony was plagued by the intrusions and threats of European imperial powers. Claiming that neither the settlers nor the ACS had the right to regulate commerce along the coast, British, French, and Spanish captains engaged in trade the settlers considered smuggling. Furthermore, both Britain and France laid claim to large amounts of territory considered part of the ACS domain. Since the United States refused to recognize the colony and because European powers claimed only governments, not societies, could assert sovereignty over land, Liberia's future was bleak.

In response to these serious threats, the ACS and the settlers began to contemplate independence as the best way to preserve Liberia. In 1839 the ACS established a commonwealth, an organization designed to join Liberia (the Monrovia area) with ACS-linked settlements

(Bassa and Sinoe) down the coast. When Governor Buchanan died in 1841, he was succeeded by Joseph Jenkins Roberts, the first settler to serve as Liberia's chief executive. An April 1845 incident proved to be the catalyst that led to actual independence. When the commonwealth government seized the *Little Ben*, an English schooner attempting to evade Liberian tariffs, the British responded by seizing a Liberian vessel and imposing a substantial fine on its owner Stephen Benson. Shortly after this incident, the ACS passed a resolution offering self government to the Commonwealth. In July 1847 delegates from Montserrado (Monrovia region), Bassa, and Sinoe (then called Mississippi) met in Monrovia to declare independence and prepare a constitution. Because of the paternalistic outlook of the participants, because of concerns about defending themselves against hostile indigenous peoples, and because of their overwhelming fear of European nations, the framers of the constitution vested great power in the hands of the president. After adopting the constitution, the settler community elected J. J. Roberts as the first president of Liberia. In 1857, Maryland in Africa, another settler state located in the extreme southeast, joined the new Republic of Liberia.

JOHN C. YODER

Further Reading

Beyan, A. "The American Colonization Society and the Origin of Undemocratic Institutions in Liberia in Historical Perspective." *Liberian Studies Journal.* 14, no. 2 (1989): 140–151.

Gurley, R. *Life of Jehudi Ashmun, Late Colonial Agent in Liberia with an Index Containing Extracts from His Journal and Other Writings: With a Brief Sketch of the Life of the Rev. Lott Cary.* Washington: J. C. Dunn, 1835.

Guannu, J. S. *Liberian History up to 1847.* Smithtown, N.Y.: Exposition Press, 1983.

Holsoe, S. "A Study of Relations between Settlers and Indigenous Peoples in Western Liberia, 1821–1847." *African Historical Studies.* 4, no. 2 (1971): 331–362.

Miller, R. *"Dear Master": Letters of a Slave Family.* Ithaca: Cornell University Press, 1978.

Sawyer, A. *The Emergence of Autocracy in Liberia: Tragedy and Challenge.* San Francisco: Institute for Contemporary Studies, 1992.

Shick, T. *Behold the Promised Land: A History of the Afro-American Settlers in Nineteenth-Century Liberia.* Baltimore: The Johns Hopkins University Press, 1977.

Liberia, Nineteenth Century: Politics, Society, and Economics

On the surface, Liberian society in the nineteenth century exhibited a high degree of division and discord. The most obvious fault line pitted African Americans against the indigenous peoples. The settlers who first came in 1822 regarded themselves as emissaries of a superior Western civilization marked by distinctive dress, diet, religion, governance system, and moral values. Even within the settler community there were clear distinctions between the lighter-skinned mulattos, who often had arrived in Liberia with more education and possessions, and the lower-status, darker-skinned immigrants, who often had been newly emancipated as part of a bargain leading to their expatriation.

In addition to the emigrants from America, from 1846 to 1867, the American government deposited approximately 5,700 people taken from slave ships captured on the high seas. These "recaptives" represented a diverse mixture of people drawn from the Congo-Angola region or from Nigeria (Ibo and Yoruba especially). The indigenous African communities were also divided into more than a dozen distinct language groups and hundreds of political entities of various sizes and government systems.

In spite of their obvious differences, peoples living in Liberia displayed numerous similarities, reflecting their common status as Africans. The settlers and the indigenous peoples believed political, social, and religious leadership rightly belonged to an elite minority. For the settlers this role fell to the Monrovia merchant class, which dominated government, church, fraternal orders, business, and the military. Indigenous society, for its part, was controlled by elders who regulated the community's affairs from the seemingly impenetrable inner circles of secret societies.

The recaptives, who came in large groups (756 people in 1846 and 4,701 in 1860) and were incorporated into settler society, served as a powerful social bridge between settler and indigenous culture. Although settler propaganda claimed the recaptives were completely integrated, more candid assessments indicated that even at the century's end many recaptives, known as Congoes, retained obvious elements of their ancestral culture that would have influenced their settler patrons. By the later decades of the nineteenth century, churches and schools served as vehicles of cultural exchange among the settlers, indigenous peoples, and recaptives. By then, Liberia College (opened in 1862) and Cuttington Collegiate and Theological School (founded in 1869) enrolled students from both settler and indigenous backgrounds. In addition, the educator Edward Blyden (1832–1912) advocated the integration of all Liberians.

Although people in all segments of society relied on subsistence farming (rice in northwest, tubers in the southeast) and fishing, trade was the preferred occupation for ambitious individuals. Mandingos (Mande-speakers claiming descent from prestigious northern war leaders), powerful coastal chiefs, and the settler merchant elite competed to control this source of wealth. Although slavery ended in the 1850s, domestic servitude continued. For example, the highly stratified

Vai society used slave labor for farms. And, to some extent, the slave trade was replaced by the export of contract labor. Local chiefs, settler politicians, and British, French, and Spanish labor recruiters all participated in these arrangements. Thus, Liberian workers (all of indigenous extraction) labored on coffee, cocoa, tea, and cotton plantations in places such as Gabon, Cameroon, or Fernando Po.

However, by the 1880s the economy had decayed. The great merchants, unable to compete with steam ships, became mere agents of the more efficient and more highly capitalized European firms. Thus, by the end of the 1800s, the great German banking and trading houses such as A. Woermann dominated Liberian trade and finances. Furthermore, lower prices, synthetic dyes, agricultural competition from French and British colonies, and New World substitutes for African products hurt Liberian exports. The government, having exhausted its resources in pacification campaigns against indigenous peoples, resorted to ruinous borrowing from the foreign firms and banks. By the end of the 1800s, about half of Liberia's budget was devoted to debt service while the other half went to paying salaries and rent for official buildings the government leased but did not own.

Politics was dominated by concerns about relations with indigenous peoples, tensions between the Monrovia elite and the upriver settlers, fiscal solvency, and protecting Liberia's borders against the encroachments of the British and French. Although most interior people eventually submitted to Monrovia by the end of the century, in the 1850s, 60s, and 70s conflicts with the Kru and Grebo strained the government's resources. Long accustomed to dealing with the outside world directly, the Kru and Grebo resisted Monrovia's efforts to collect tariffs, control trade, and appropriate land. A particularly fierce battle in 1875 (the Grebo mobilized between 5,000 and 7,000 men) was resolved only with the assistance of the U.S. Navy. Although "victorious," the Liberian government recognized that it would need to negotiate and accommodate rather than impose its will. Increasingly, Monrovia developed alliances with supportive or compliant indigenous leaders. Even so, by 1870, government control rarely extended more than 40 miles inland from the sea.

Internally, tensions between the mulatto merchant elite based in Monrovia and their darker-skinned competitors from the upriver settlements resulted in the formation of a new political party to challenge the Monrovia-centered Republican Party. The True Whig Party, founded in Clay Ashland, elected Edward J. Roye as president in 1869. However, the mulattos, led by former President J. J. Roberts, bitterly attacked Roye for the unfavorable terms of a foreign loan he negotiated. Consequently, Roye was arrested in October of 1871 and in February 1872 he was sentenced to be hanged for treason. The upriver settlements contemplated secession but the crisis ended when Roye drowned while attempting to escape from prison. Hillary R. W. Johnson, a Monrovia Republican turned True Whig, emerged as the dominant figure in Liberian politics. President from 1884 to 1892, Johnson was the major player behind the scenes for the last quarter of the nineteenth century. Although unable to resolve the fundamental economic, ethnic, and social problems, Liberia's leaders did manage to preserve the nation's precarious independence.

JOHN C. YODER

Further Reading

Anderson, B. J. K. *Narrative of a Journey to Musardu: The Capital of the Western Mandingoes, Together with Narrative of the Expedition Despatched to Masahdu in 1874*. London: Frank Cass, 1971.

Dunn, D. E., and S. Holsoe. *Historical Dictionary of Liberia*. Metuchen, N. J.: Scarecrow Press, 1985.

Liebnow, J. G. *Liberia: The Quest for Democracy*. Bloomington: Indiana University Press, 1987.

Sawyer, A. *The Emergence of Autocracy in Liberia: Tragedy and Challenge*. San Francisco: Institute for Contemporary Studies, 1992.

Shick, T. *Behold the Promised Land: A History of the Afro-American Settlers in Nineteenth-Century Liberia*. Baltimore: The Johns Hopkins University Press, 1977.

Liberia: Firestone

For most of the twentieth century, Liberia was an impoverished country controlled by an Americo-Liberian elite who regarded the indigenous population as little more than a resource to be exploited. Until World War II, Liberia's major export was labor. Americo-Liberian politicians used the Liberian Frontier Force to coerce government-appointed chiefs into supplying men for the trade, mainly to the cocoa plantation on Spanish Fernando Po and the Congo.

The government was chronically short of revenue, with expenditure regularly exceeding income. Facing mounting debts, the Liberian government borrowed $500,000 from Sir Harry Johnston's Liberian Development Corporation in 1906. While $150,000 went to foreign creditors, most of the money disappeared with the Liberian Development Corporation. When the Liberian government sought to renegotiate the loan in 1908, the British government insisted on taking control of the customs department and Frontier Force. Liberia turned to the United States. In 1912 the United States organized a new loan of $1.7 million at 5 per cent interest and took over the customs department, loan repayments having first call on customs revenue.

In 1910, in an attempt to raise noncustoms revenue, the government granted land to the British Mount Barclay Company to develop plantation rubber. The venture failed to generate anticipated revenue and collapsed. World War I further eroded the national economy with the collapse of exports to Germany. Falling producer income sparked uprisings by the Kru, crushed by the Frontier Force with American military aid.

In desperation, President Charles King (1920–1930) sought financial support from Marcus Garvey's "Back to Africa" movement. The scheme soon collapsed under the political threat of an African-American influx, disillusion with promised investments, and pressure from neighboring colonial governments. Unexpected assistance, however, materialized in the person of American tire magnate Harvey Firestone.

In 1922 Britain instituted the "Stevenson Plan" to force up rubber prices through a 75 per cent restriction on production, thereby securing a means to repay its wartime indebtedness through sales to the United States, the world's largest rubber consumer. Harvey Firestone countered by offering a $5,000,000 loan to Liberia in returned for a 99-year lease on a million acres, as well as Liberian government support in labor recruitment. The Liberian government initially rejected the Firestone proposal, hoping for direct American financial support. Firestone lobbied the U.S. State Department, campaigning for a source of rubber under "American control." Under pressure from the American government, Liberia signed an agreement with Firestone in 1925. In return for a $5,000,000 loan at 7 per cent interest, financed through Firestone's Finance Corporation of America, Firestone was granted a 99-year lease on the Mount Barclay rubber plantation and options on the 99-year lease of an additional million acres. Firestone promised to construct and maintain a harbor at Monrovia, subsequently scuttled on the grounds of expense.

The Liberian Labour Bureau was to supply 50,000 workers annually for the new venture. However, the anticipated rubber-export revenue failed to materialize. Dutch Indonesian rubber production undermined the Stevenson Plan and world rubber prices collapsed. The Liberian politicians and the Liberian Frontier Force intensified the trade in contract labor Spanish Fernando Po.

In 1928 Harvard Professor Raymond Buell published *The Native Problem in Africa*, criticizing American economic imperialism in Liberia and the labor trade. The U.S. government sought to distance itself from the scandal by lodging a diplomatic protest with Liberia, sparking in turn a League of Nations' commission of inquiry. The appalling labor conditions on Fernando Po were glossed over, but the Liberian government was accused of trafficking in Kru and Grebo tribesmen. The inquiry recommended an end to the export of labor, reform of Liberian native administration, encouragement of African American immigration and an "Open Door" policy to foreign investment. As a result, President King and Vice President Yancy were forced to resign in 1930.

The United States wanted to maintain its political and economic hegemony but resisted pressure for direct intervention in Liberia. President Edwin Barclay (1930–1944) proved adept at avoiding fundamental reforms, while effectively neutralizing various European schemes for an external takeover of Liberia by diplomatic procrastination.

As the impact of the depression was felt by the Liberian economy, the national debt mushroomed. In 1932 the Liberian government suspended repayments of the Firestone loan and the following year abrogated American control of customs revenue. Firestone unsuccessfully lobbied for American military intervention. In 1936, under pressures of British and Dutch rubber restrictions and rising prices, Firestone agreed to renegotiate the loan, with reduced interest and other concessions, in return for renewed payments and mining rights within his leasehold.

Dramatic economic recovery in Liberia only came with World War II. When Japan conquered the British and Dutch East Indian rubber colonies in 1942, Liberian rubber took on international economic and strategic significance. In the rush to expand rubber production at lowest costs, Firestone exploitation of Liberian labor was ignored.

President William Tubman (1944–1971) instituted an "open door" policy to private foreign investment and enjoyed unqualified American government support. While increasing his own political domination, Tubman forged alliances with indigenous leaders, drawing them into the ruling True Wing Party and American–Liberian establishment, as partners in the exploitation of the peasantry. Increased investment and diversification into mining and infrastructure after the war lessened dependence on rubber and fuelled economic growth, if not more equitable distribution. The Cold War and African decolonization resulted in continuing American strategic investments in Liberia, but low wages and lax labor regulation remained the major attraction for private foreign investors.

Increasing revenue facilitated improved education and health facilities, but corruption, nepotism and widening socioeconomic disparities persisted under Tubman and President William Tolbert (1971–1980). The Korean War led to heightened demand for rubber and, in 1959, Firestone agreed to new increased taxes based on profits. But the fall in world rubber prices with the development of synthetic rubber in the 1960s exerted further pressure for real reduction in labor costs. Adverse terms of trade through the 1970s eroded living standards. The bloody coup led by Sgt. Samuel Doe in 1980, ending American-Liberian rule, did little to alter the exploitation of ordinary Liberians and set the stage for decades of political instability and civil war.

David Dorward

See also: **Liberia: Tubman, William V. S., Life and Era of.**

Further Reading

Buell, R. L. *The Native Problem in Africa.* Vol 2, 704–888. New York: Macmillan, 1928.

Chalk, F. "The Anatomy of an Investment: Firestone's 1927 Loan to Liberia." *Canadian Journal of African Studies.* I, no. 1 (1967): 12–32.

Johnson, C. S. *Bitter Canaan: The Story of the Negro Republic.* New Brunswick and Oxford: Transaction Books, 1987.

Saha, S. C. *A History of Agriculture in Liberia, 1822–1970: Transference of American Values.* Lewiston, Edwin Mellen Press, 1990.

Saigbe-Boley, G. E. *Liberia: The Rise and Fall of the First Republic.* London: Macmillan, 1983.

Schmokel, W. W. "The United States and the Crisis of Liberian Independence, 1929–1934." *Boston University Papers on Africa. Vol. 2*, pp.303–337. 1966.

Sisay, H. B. *Big Powers and Small Nations: A Case Study of United States-Liberian Relations.* Lanham: University Press of America, 1985.

Sundiata, I. K. *Black Scandal: America and the Liberian Labour Crisis, 1929–1936.* Philadelphia: Institute for the Study of Human Issues, 1980.

Liberia: Tubman, William V. S., Life and Era of

President of Liberia

William Vacanarat Shadrach Tubman (1895–1971) was Liberia's seventeenth president. Tubman enacted many reforms, including property and voting rights for women, and the creation of a national public school system. He was the first Americo-Liberian president of Liberia to sponsor development for the indigenous Africans of Liberia. Tubman called this his "national unification policy." He supported indigenous African laws that were "humane and reasonable" and encouraged immigration of blacks from the United States, the Caribbean, British West Africa, and Latin America. Throughout the Cold War, Tubman headed the conservative, pro-American, "Monrovia Group," which opposed Kwame Nkrumah's radical "Casablanca Group." Despite this, he was anticolonial and an advocate of African independence, like his nemesis Nkrumah of Ghana. The Tubman era lasted a quarter of a century. Liberia enjoyed social peace and economic development while he ruled the land.

In 1914 William was ordained as a Methodist minister and he taught at the seminary, while studying law. In 1917 he passed his bar exam and became county attorney. He gave free legal advice to anyone who needed it, regardless of ability to pay. This made him popular with the masses and boosted his political career. Elected to the Liberian Senate in 1923, he represented the ruling True Whig Party. At age twenty-eight, he became the youngest senator in Liberian history. Voters elected him for a second term in 1929. Tubman won his first presidential election in 1944. He served seven consecutive terms as president of Liberia, the longest of any Liberian president.

His first act as president was to declare war on Germany and Japan. He offered Allied Forces supplies, ports, airports, and staging areas for the war effort. President Franklin D. Roosevelt invited him to the White House, and he became the first black guest to spend the night there.

Tubman launched his "Open Door Policy," which invited foreign investment and trade as well as the exploitation of Liberia's natural resources. The result was rapid economic growth. The Firestone company developed extended rubber plantations it owned since 1890. Liberia's iron ore industry expanded. Tax revenues from rubber and iron paid for new roads, schools, bridges, markets, and hospitals. The capital, Monrovia, grew from 12,000 people in 1939 to 134,000 in 1970. Critics use this era to illustrate the limitations of "growth without development." The core dominated the periphery and leading government officials became the leading business people. Skewed distribution of benefits caused unrest.

The political base supporting Tubman included lower echelon Americo-Liberians and indigenous Africans. He also had supporters in the elite inner circle of the True Whig Party and the Masonic Order, of which he was an officer. Generous patronage secured the loyalty of his followers. His greatest problem was that many members of the elite whom he depended upon to implement his policies feared that including indigenous Africans in the opportunity structure would deny them their "birthright" and undermine their standard of living. To get around this problem Tubman appointed many members of his family to important positions. He also depended heavily upon foreign advisers and technicians, not involved in party machinations, to modernize Liberia.

The assimilation policy was supposed to be a one-way street. Indigenous Africans would assume Christian names, join the cash economy, and become part of the Americo-Liberian community. In reality, many assimilated Africans restored their African names and made it acceptable to wear African clothing in public. Tubman became formal head of the Poro secret society. African culture, once viewed as "barbaric" and "uncivilized," was embraced. By 1963 the True Whig Party included a platform plank urging, "a national cultural awakening to develop the essential African and Liberian culture." African nationalism was awakening pride in the African heritage. The term "Americo-Liberian" fell into official disfavor. Tubman had released the genie from the bottle and no one could return it.

The unification program was useless without the "Open Door Policy," which preserved the high Americo-Liberian standard of living using foreign investment to supply indigenous Africans with higher living standards and social services, such as health care and education, without imposing either austerity measures or higher taxes on wealthy Americo-Liberians. It worked, and Liberia attracted twenty-five large firms who invested in Liberia, where formerly only one—Firestone—had invested there. Republic Steel Corporation of the United States and the Liberian-Swedish Minerals Company (LAMCO) developed Liberia's iron ore. Foreign investments created thousands of jobs for Liberians bringing many into the cash economy for the first time. Low levels of education condemned most Liberians to low paying nontechnical jobs while expatriates secured most of the high-income jobs. This created dissatisfaction and criticism of Tubman. Lebanese merchants took advantage of the "Open Door Policy" to dominate the wholesale and retail sectors of the economy. By 1960 Lebanese merchants controlled half of all middle level economic activities in Liberia. Liberians resented this. The richer they grew, the more political discontent increased in both the indigenous and Americo-Liberian communities.

Tubman firmly suppressed opposition. Protection of direct foreign investment involved quashing worker unrest in foreign concessions. Suppression of antigovernment protest at the University of Liberia became commonplace. Discontent within Liberia's Armed Forces (LAF) led to rumors of coup plots. Suspected of plotting to assassinate Tubman and overthrow the government, indigenous military officers belonging to the Aborigine Liberation Movement were spied upon. Opposition was poorly organized and uncoordinated. Henry Bioma Fahnbulleh, a distinguished Liberian diplomat, was arrested after serving as ambassador to Nairobi. Accused of plotting to overthrow the government, Liberia sentenced him to 20 years imprisonment. Discontent was growing.

Tubman's legacy is mixed. He was tenacious, shrewd, and artful as a politician. He created economic prosperity amid growing political unrest. He gave the vote to both men and women, rural and urban populations, and he promoted national unity. Social services, school, hospital, and road construction grew under his leadership. Despite this, Tubman was paternalistic and intolerant of opposition. He believed in Americo-Liberian rule and kept power in their hands, even while trying to lessen the gap between rulers and subjects. Tubman created greater opportunities for indigenous Liberians. Transforming government from an Americo-Liberian monolith into a mosaic, which included indigenous Liberians, he expanded the institutions of government and made them more inclusive. He strengthened the office of the president at the expense of the legislative and judicial branches; nevertheless, Tubman brought Liberia into the modern age and maintained stability amid turmoil. However, a growing debt problem, falling commodity prices, reduced government spending, unpaid public salaries, few incentives for new foreign investors, and a small domestic market spelled trouble for Liberia's future. Absent peaceful means to change, Liberians turned toward violent solutions. Tubman survived several assassination attempts and died peacefully in his sleep in 1971.

DALLAS L. BROWNE

Biography

Born on November 29, 1895, at Harper, Liberia. His parents were from Georgia in the United States, but they raised him among the Grebo. Entered the Harper elementary school in 1903. Attended Cape Palmas Seminary and Cuttington College and Divinity School. Served in the Liberian military, rising to the rank of colonel. Elected to the Liberian Senate in 1923. Elected for a second term in 1929. Won his first presidential election in 1944. Served seven consecutive terms as president, the longest of any Liberian president. Died in 1971.

Further Reading

Anderson, R. E. *Liberia, America's African Friend.* Westport, Conn.: Greenwood Press, 1952.

Banks, D. A. *A Biography of President William V. S. Tubman.* London: Macmillan, 1967.

Dunn, D. E., and S. B. Tarr. *Liberia: A National Policy in Transition.* Metuchen, N. J.: Scarecrow Press, 1988.

———. *Liberia: The Evolution of Privilege.* Ithaca, N. Y. Cornell University Press, 1969.

Liebenow, J. G. *Liberia: The Quest for Democracy.* Bloomington: Indiana University Press, 1987.

Lowenkopf, M. *Politics in Liberia: The Conservative Road to Development.* Stanford, Calif.: Hoover Institution Press, 1976.

Smith, R. *William V. S. Tubman.* Amsterdam: Van Ditmar, 1967.

Townsend, R. E., ed. *President Tubman of Liberia Speaks.* Monrovia, Liberia: Consolidated Publications, 1959.

———. *The Official Papers of William V. S. Tubman, President of the Republic of Liberia.* London: Longman. 1968.

Wreh, T. *The Love of Liberty: The Rule of President William V. S. Tubman of Liberia.* London: C. Hurst, 1976.

Liberia: Tolbert, William Richard, Life and Era of

President of Liberia

William Richard Tolbert (1913–1980) became the eighteenth president of Liberia in January 1972, the last of the old succession of Americo-Liberian presidents.

On April 12, 1980, a military coup d'étât, led by Master Sergeant Samuel Kanyon Doe, overthrew Tolbert, executing him and several members of his cabinet, on Monrovia Beach in front of television cameras.

Devoted to Christianity, Tolbert was an ordained minister in the Baptist Church. Between 1965 and 1970 he served as president of the Baptist World Alliance. Tolbert later became chief adviser for the All-African Missionaries Evangelistic Union in 1973.

Government attracted Tolbert and he took a position as a typist for the national treasury in 1934. Tolbert was promoted to disbursement officer for the government in 1936. In 1943 he won election to the National House of Representatives on the True Whig Party ticket. Tolbert became the youngest man to be elected vice president (serving under President William V. S. Tubman) in Liberian history in May 1951.

When Tubman died in 1971, Tolbert assumed power. He no longer wanted other Africans to view Liberia as a vassal or "colony" of the United States. Tolbert openly negotiated with South Africa, at a time when it embraced apartheid or legal racism, which made it repugnant and a pariah among nations. He aggressively established diplomatic relations with the USSR and Czechoslovakia. Tolbert also cultivated improved relations with radical Guinea. These actions improved relations with neighboring states and culminated in the formation of the Economic Community of West African States. In 1979 Liberia hosted the Organization of African Unity, which elected Tolbert president.

Reform-minded, Tolbert fired corrupt cabinet ministers, revamped Liberia's national security system, freed political prisoners, encouraged greater freedom of the press, and lowered the voting age to eighteen. The presidential yacht cost $250,000 a year to maintain, so he sold it. Liberia's presidents drove state-owned Cadillacs; he sold his and bought a Volkswagen. Making surprise raids in early morning hours, he tried to ensure that civil servants actually earned their pay. Appalled that civil servants had to give the True Whig Party one-month's salary every year to support the party, Tolbert abolished this custom, winning him new supporters among the civil servants. Lowering and subsidizing the price of rice improved his popularity among the urban poor.

Liberia became the world's leading maritime power, despite owning only two merchant ships, by allowing foreign ship owners to register their vessels under Liberia's "flag of convenience." The Firestone Rubber Company continued to flourish as its 90,000-acre rubber plantation thrived under Tolbert's "open door policy." By 1973 Liberia ranked as the world's third-largest iron ore producer. Pressuring foreign companies to hire more Africans, Tolbert also raised taxes levied on company profits. Tolbert insisted on a greater role for Liberians in foreign-owned companies. Liberia, however, did not have enough trained local manpower to absorb the new opportunities thus created. Consequently, foreign managers and technicians continued to benefit from the creation of high paying skilled work.

As more and more Liberians were drawn into the cash economy, a new problem emerged: "back street boys." These were urban drifters unable to find employment who engaged in urban crime waves. They lived in squalid neighborhoods of Monrovia and were a potential source of unrest. Poor sanitation and inadequate housing made them susceptible to demagogues. In an economic climate of falling export prices and dwindling opportunities, even for university graduates, Liberia was a source of potentially explosive unrest throughout the 1970s.

Africanization of an economy long controlled by foreign interest became one of Tolbert's goals and his means of dealing with frustration that was boiling over into anger. Calling for greater self-sufficiency, Tolbert tried to promote a new subsidy on rice. The opposition opposed this since his family was among Liberia's largest rice growers. Gabriel Baccus Matthews, an admirer of Julius Nyerere of Tanzania, and leader of the Progressive Alliance of Liberians (PAL), organized a peaceful demonstration in Monrovia. An estimated 10,000 "back street boys" joined PAL's 2,000 activists. The back street boys soon rioted, looting retail stores and rice warehouses.

Tolbert ordered the militia to restore order. They had orders to "shoot to kill" and they fired on demonstrators, killing 74. He proceeded to jail political opponents on charges of sedition. In January 1980, the PAL officially registered as an opposition party under the name People's Progressive Party (PPP). In March the PPP, with backing from elements within the Liberian Armed Forces, launched a general strike, and called for Tolbert's removal. It was in this highly charged environment that on April 12, 1980, Sergeant Doe murdered Tolbert and seized control of Liberia.

DALLAS L. BROWNE

Biography

William Tolbert was born on May 13, 1913, in Bensonville, Liberia. Attended Bensonville Elementary School. Studied at Crummell Hall Episcopalian High School. Graduated *summa cum laude* in 1934 from the University of Liberia. Married Charlotte A. Hoff. Elected vice president under President William V. S. Tubman in May 1951. Assumed presidency upon Tubman's death in 1971. On April 12, 1980, a military coup d'étât, led by Master Sergeant Samuel Kanyon Doe, overthrew Tolbert, executing him and several members of his cabinet, on Monrovia Beach.

Further Reading

Boley, G. E. S. *Liberia: The Rise and Fall of the First Republic.* New York: St. Martin's Press, 1984.

Brown, D. "On the Category 'Civilized' in Liberia and Elsewhere." *Journal of Modern African Studies.* 20, no. 2 (June 1982): 287–303.

Cordor, S. H. *Facing the Realities of the Liberian Nation.* Philadelphia: Institute for Liberian Studies, 1980.

Gray, B. A., and A. Batiste. *Liberia During the Tolbert Era.* Washington, D.C.: Library of Congress, 1983.

Guannu, J. S. *An Introduction to Liberian Government: The First Republic and the People Redemption Council.* Smithtown, N. Y.: Exposition Press, 1981.

Hlophe, S. S. *Class, Ethnicity, and Politics in Liberia: A Class Analysis of Power Struggles in the Tubman and Tolbert Administrations from 1944–1975.* Washington, D.C.: University Press of America, 1979.

Sankawulo, W. *Tolbert of Liberia.* London: Ardon Press, 1979.

Shick, T. W. *Behold the Promised Land: A History of Afro-American Settler Society in Nineteenth-Century Liberia.* Baltimore: Johns Hopkins University Press, 1980.

Sundiata, I. *Black Scandal: America and the Liberian Labor Crisis, 1929–1936.* Philadelphia: The Institute for the Study of Human Issues, 1980.

Liberia: Doe, Samuel K., Life and Era of

President of Liberia

Samuel Doe (1951–1990) ruled Liberia in the 1980s. The corruption and brutality of his rule made the civil war of the 1990s all but inevitable. Doe seized power by means of a bloody coup, and during his ten years in power he steadily created enemies for himself while providing the justifications for an eventual uprising against him.

Doe, who was a member of the Krahn, was born on May 6, 1951, and in 1969, aged 18, he enlisted as a soldier in the Liberian army. He was enrolled in the Radio Communications School of the Ministry of Defense in Monrovia, where he completed his training by 1971. In 1979 Doe was chosen for further training at a camp run by U.S. Special Forces and was then promoted to master sergeant.

On April 12, 1980, accompanied by 17 soldiers, Doe carried out the coup that brought him to power. They broke into the executive mansion (the head of state's residence) in Monrovia where Doe and his men killed the president, William R. Tolbert, as well as about 30 officials and guards. Doe promoted himself to commander in chief of the armed forces and also made himself chairman of the People's Redemption Council. He promised he would return the country to civilian rule, although no date was set for this development. Notoriously, he had 13 of Tolbert's senior ministers and associates publicly executed on Monrovian Beach; pictures of this brutal spectacle provided a lasting image of his methods and set the tone for his ten-year tenure of office.

In an attempt to legitimize his rule, Doe advanced himself as a candidate in elections for the presidency that were held in 1985, and although these elections were widely seen to have been rigged, Doe only won by a narrow margin. What popularity he had declined steadily thereafter and Doe was obliged to maintain his position by increasing levels of oppression.

By the end of the 1980s, Liberia was ready to erupt against Doe's depredations, and a civil war to oust him was launched by two separate dissident groups at the end of 1989. The original uprising, which was an unplanned explosion of anger against the Doe regime, began in Nimba county near the border with Côte d'Ivoire over the Christmas period of 1989. After ten days of fighting, an estimated 10,000 people had fled across the border into Côte d'Ivoire to escape the violence. At this point the majority of the rebels were Gio people, the principal tribe of Nimba county, who directed their anger and attacks upon the Krahn.

There were two rebel leaders: Charles Taylor, leader of the main rebel group the National Patriotic Front, who later became president of Liberia; and Prince Yormie Johnson. Both men found no difficulty in gathering dissident soldiers to launch a series of attacks upon government targets. In the event they proved every bit as brutal and indiscriminate as Doe and the regime they wanted to oust from power; they were responsible for massacres of women and children and their forces ravaged the country, reducing Liberia to a state of chaos and fear. During the early stages of the war, few soldiers on either side were killed; most of the casualties were among the civilian population. At the same time, an ethnic pattern of killing emerged, with the Gio supporters of Taylor attacking Krahn civilians, and the Krahn retaliating against the Gio.

By the end of January 1990 an estimated 50,000 people were hiding in the bush of Nimba county in an effort to evade retaliation by government forces, and for a time it appeared that Doe's supporters might regain control. In April 1990, Doe claimed "there is no inch of this nation not under the control of the government." However, by the end of that month, the United States was advising its 5,000 citizens then in Liberia to leave, while British Airways was offering special flights to airlift out Commonwealth citizens. Taylor's army was then reported to be 3,000 strong as against 7,000 troops supposed to be loyal to Doe. Meanwhile, the numbers of refugees fleeing the increasingly savage fighting had risen to 300,000. By June the two rebel groups had seized control of the greater part of Monrovia, while Doe had fortified the executive mansion as his headquarters.

Taylor had fled Liberia in 1984 facing corruption charges and had taken $900,000 with him to the United States. As he advanced so his forces increased and by the end of May when he captured Buchanan, the country's second port, he had an estimated 10,000 followers. Then he captured Roberstfield, Monrovia's international airport.

The month of June spelled the end of Doe's rule, although he held on until September. The government forces began to disintegrate, turning upon each other on inter-ethnic lines, and by the end of the month some 750,000 people (half the population of Monrovia) had fled the capital as the rebel forces closed in. By that time, U.S. and British warships lay off Monrovia, ready to evacuate their citizens. Doe announced that he would welcome an international peacekeeping force if this could be arranged at the conference on the future of Liberia then being held in Sierra Leone. By this time discipline among government troops was nonexistent. Summary executions had become common, while army morale had collapsed. Demonstrators in Monrovia called on Doe to resign. By July no more than 1,000 of his troops remained in Monrovia, which had become a ghost city; they were routed whenever they confronted the rebels.

Liberia's neighbors, led by Nigeria, worked through the Economic Community of West African States (ECOWAS) to create a peacekeeping force (ECOMOG) that was ready to intervene at the beginning of September when it established its headquarters in Monrovia. It was commanded by Ghana's Lieutenant General Arnold Qainoo and included troops from Gambia, Ghana, Guinea, Nigeria, and Sierra Leone.

On September 9, 1990, Doe, accompanied by a bodyguard of sixty Krahn soldiers, left the executive mansion to visit the ECOMOG headquarters in order to negotiate his escape from Monrovia. However, he was intercepted en route by Yormie Johnson's soldiers. He was tortured, mutilated, and then killed on September 10.

Doe's inglorious end was the prelude to a long, drawn-out power struggle for the presidency between Charles Taylor, Prince Yormie Johnson, David Nimbley (Doe's former minister of defense), and Amos Sawyer, a former politician backed by ECOWAS. Only after years of strife and political maneuvering were elections finally held in May 1997, which brought Charles Taylor and his National Patriotic Party to power with 49 out of 64 seats in the House of Representatives and 21 out of 26 seats in the Senate.

GUY ARNOLD

Further Reading

Asibey, A. O. "Liberia: Political Economy of Underdevelopment and Military 'Revolution Continuity of Change.'" *Canadian Journal of Development Studies.* 2, no. 2 (1981): 386–407.

Barret, L. "The Siege of Monrovia." *West Africa.* (23–29 November 1992): 816–818.

Brehun, L. *Liberia: The War of Horror.* Accra: Adwinsa Publications, 1991.

Clapham, C. *Liberia.* Basingstoke: Macmillan Press, 1994.

Okolo, J. E. "Liberia: The Military Coup and Its Aftermath." *The World Today.* 37, no. 4 (April 1981): 149–157.

Reno, W. "Foreign Firms and the Financing of Charles Taylor's NPFL." *Liberation Studies Journal.* 18, no. 2 (1993): 175–187.

Ruiz, H. A. *Liberia: Destruction and Reconstruction.* Washington, D. C.: U.S. Committee for Refugees, 1992.

Liberia: Civil War, ECOMOG, and the Return to Civilian Rule

On Christmas Eve 1989, an armed group under the leadership of the National Patriotic Front of Liberia (NPFL) infiltrated Liberia's Nimba County from Côte d' Ivoire. Its stated aim was to overthrow the regime of Samuel Doe, which had been in power since April 1980. In the aftermath of the incursion, the Liberian government responded with counterinsurgency forces under the direction of the Armed Forces of Liberia (AFL), which repulsed the threat posed to the regime's authority. Corruption and ineffectiveness eventually undermined the AFL's capacity to provide credible resistance to the NPFL. As a result, within four months of launching the rebellion, the NPFL laid claim to over 90 per cent of Liberian territory. It maintained *de facto* control over these territories, with the exception of the capital Monrovia and its immediate environs.

Two important incidents occurred in May 1990 to interfere with what could have been a swift NPFL victory. First, the inception of diverse faction groups that became a characteristic feature of the civil war began when a breakaway faction, the Independent National Patriotic Front of Liberia (INPFL), was formed to challenge the monolithic NPFL. Eventually, by the time the civil war ended in July 1997, seven other factions had been formed. Second, the Economic Community of West African States (ECOWAS), the subregional organization that represented the interests of member-states, discussed the Liberian civil war at its ordinary summit of heads of state and government in Banjul, Gambia.

ECOWAS's discussion of the civil war coincided with the initiation of several conflict resolution processes. These contained two critical central components. One was political and the other military. The most decisive political decision was the establishment of a standing mediation committee (SMC) comprising of Ghana, Gambia, Mali, Nigeria, and Togo. Its mandate was to resolve conflicts among ECOWAS member states in a harmonious manner. Between May and early August 1990, several diplomatic and negotiation processes were initiated by the SMC to resolve the civil war. These involved meetings with the incumbent president, the leadership of the NPFL, and several other identifiable Liberian groups. None of these efforts, however, resolved the conflict. Eventually, the impact of the war in terms of refugee outflows, the deteriorating human rights circumstances in Liberia, and the condition of entrapped foreign nationals worsened and began to influence not only the contiguous states but other ECOWAS states much further afield. Second, as an ancillary to controlling the engulfing crisis, the SMC established an ECOWAS cease-fire monitoring group (ECOMOG) to intervene and resolve the crisis. ECOMOG was also mandated to demilitarize and demobilize combatants as enshrined under different peace accords. ECOMOG's establishment was made feasible by the earlier promulgation of three separate security-related protocols. These were the 1976 Protocol on Non Recourse to Violence, the 1978 Non-Aggression Protocol, and the 1981 Protocol on Mutual Assistance and Defense, which became operational in 1986.

The political decision to deploy ECOMOG in Liberia was made on August 6 and 7, and the troops were eventually deployed on August 24, 1990. This made ECOMOG, which comprised forces from Gambia, Ghana, Guinea, Nigeria, and Sierra Leone, the most rapidly deployed peacekeeping force in history. Its mandate was to secure Monrovia and reinstate democracy. As the war escalated and new alliances and cross-alliances were formed, ECOMOG's mandates were constantly changed and expanded from peacekeeping to peace enforcement and peace support operations. Simultaneously, its troop capacity was increased by including non-West African troops from Tanzania, Uganda, and Zimbabwe. Due to the nature of Liberia's civil war and ECOMOG's inexperience in dealing with such crises, the United Nations established the United Nations Observer Mission to Liberia (UNOMIL) in September 1993. Its mandate was to monitor and verify the demilitarization and demobilization components of diverse peace accords which ECOMOG was to enforce. UNOMIL thus became the first peacekeeping mission undertaken by the UN in cooperation with a peacekeeping mission already set up by another organization. Operationally, ECOMOG's collaboration with UNOMIL sought to arrange a rational division of labor and authority between the two organizations, while concurrently mounting a humanitarian and security mission in a country without any definitive form of authoritative government. Through this collaborative venture, ECOMOG and UNOMIL managed to demilitarize and demobilize almost a third of the estimated 33,000 armed combatants.

While ECOMOG formed the military component of ECOWAS' two-pronged strategy to resolve the civil war, different political endeavors were also initiated to end the war. These resulted in thirteen major peace accords that were signed during the three different phases of the political search for a resolution. The first was the SMC period from May 1990 to June 1991. This was followed by the Committee of Five period, which was an adjunct to the SMC phase from June 1991 to June 1992. It comprised Côte d'Ivoire, Gambia, Guinea-Bissau, Senegal, and Togo. Finally, the Committee of Nine (C9), which was inaugurated on November 7, 1992, included Benin, Burkina Faso, Côte d'Ivoire, Ghana, Guinea, Nigeria, Togo, Gambia, and Senegal. The most important accords were the Banjul Accord of 1990; Lomé Accord, 1991; Yamossoukro I–IV Process, 1991–993; the Cotonou Accord, 1993; Accra and Akosombo Accords, 1994–1995; Abuja I Accord, 1995; and Abuja II Accord, 1996.

After several years of often tortuous attempts at peace, the Abuja II Accord introduced several concurrent processes that paved the way for a transitional government, disarmament, demobilization, and the 1997 special elections. The most innovative contribution of Abuja II to the peace process was the introduction of a stringent sanctions regime. This targeted faction groups in cases of noncompliance with diverse components of the accord. The processes for the return to civilian rule was closely tied to the military components of peace accords. As a result, the original schedule was for electoral processes to commence after demilitarization and demobilization was completed. Under Abuja II, these two processes were to be completed by January 31, 1997, whereupon elections would be held on May 30, 1997. Consequently, an Independent Election Committee (IECOM) was established to conduct the elections. Several difficulties arose in organizing the elections. Some were related to the registration and demobilization of combatants. Not only that, most of the factions that had fought in the war and had converted their military groups into political parties argued that the logistics for the elections had not been properly worked out. Closely related to these problems were IECOM's financial problems and lack of qualified manpower and institutional incapacity to organize the elections. ECOWAS considered these complaints and as a result, the elections were postponed until July 19, 1997. Paradoxically, but not surprisingly, Charles Taylor won the elections by gaining 75 per cent of the vote, which was declared free and fair by an international observation corps. Liberia's twenty-first president was inducted into office on August 2, 1997, thus ending seven years of brutal civil war.

Emmanuel Kwesi Aning

See also: **Taylor, Charles**

Further Reading

Adeleke, A. "The Politics and Diplomacy of Peacekeeping in West Africa: The ECOWAS Operation in Liberia." *Journal of Modern African Studies*. 33, no. 4 (1996).

Adibe, C. E. "The Liberian Conflict and the ECOWAS-UN Partnership." *Third World Quarterly.* 18, no. 3 (1997).
Alao, A. *The Burden of Collective Goodwill: The International Involvement in the Liberian Civil War.* Aldershot: Ashgate Publishers, 1998.
Alao, A., J. Mackinlay, and F. Olonisakin. *Peacekeepers, Politicians, and Warlords: The Liberian Peace Process.* New York: UN University, 1998.
Aning, K. E. "Eliciting Compliance from Warlords: An Analysis of ECOWAS's Liberia Experience, 1990–1997." *Review of African Political Economy.* 81 (December 1999).
Hubband, M. *The Liberian Civil War.* London: Frank Cass, 1998.
Levitt, J. "Humanitarian Intervention by Regional Actors in Internal Conflicts: The Case of ECOWAS in Liberia and Sierra Leone." *Temple International and Comparative Law.* 12, no. 2 (1998): 333–375.
Official Journal of ECOWAS. "*ECOWAS Decisions on the Liberian Crisis—Special Supplement of the Official Journal.*" 21 (1992).

Libreville

Libreville (Freetown), the capital of Gabon, is named after a village of freed slaves built in the Comptoir du Gabon in 1849. This *comptoir* (cartel), created by the French in 1843, was established in the Gabon estuary by the French Navy to combat the slave trade in the west coast of Africa. This French establishment had its origin when Bouet-Willaumez obtained a piece of land in the left bank of the estuary from "King" Denis Rapontchombo in 1839. In 1842 the post was moved to the right bank of the estuary with the agreement of the rulers of the villages of Dowe, Glass, Quaben, and Louis. It is from this position that France extended its influence over the Gabon region by signing alliance treaties with local chiefs between 1843 and 1846. In 1849 fifty "receptive" slaves from the ship *Elizia* or *Ilizia* were brought to the Gabon estuary after a three-year sojourn in Senegal. They were resettled in the village "Libreville."

The name was given to this village by Bouet-Willaumez in remembrance of Freetown in Sierra Leone, where liberated blacks were also being settled by the British. The fifty recaptive slaves were given a house and a piece of land, and in 1850 a decision was made by French naval officers to transfer the Fort d'Aumale from its previous position near the seashore to a new site on top of the Okolo plateau near Libreville. Catholic missionaries occupied the old buildings of the French post. The village Glass, which was the main trading center at the time of the French installation, was experiencing competition from French factories, which established themselves near the post between 1850 and 1854. These economic dynamics were accompanied by constructions that were to constitute the future city of Libreville. In 1865 houses in concrete built on the plateau announced the French *comptoir* with the administrative building, the hospital, a military housing compound, and the Church of the Immaculate Conception. In addition to these constructions, there were the old Mpongwe villages of Glass, Louis, Quaben, Denis, and the American missionaries at Baraka.

At the time of these urban transformations, the French establishment was already the starting point for the exploration of interior regions. These explorations, carried out throughout the second half of the nineteenth century by explorers, made the Gabon *comptoir* a strategic location. When the French Congo was created in 1888, the name "Libreville" was given to the whole French establishment, including the Mpongwe villages, and Libreville became the capital of this new political entity. De Brazza, the French commissioner, resided in Libreville in 1882 and 1883. The lieutenant governor, who replaced the high commissioner after the creation of the Afrique Equatoriale Française (AEF) in 1910, also resided in Libreville. These political changes were accompanied by the development of new administrative services, a colonial military, and the growing European population.

At the end of the nineteenth century, Libreville was still the only city in the Congo basin. But Brazzaville, created in 1881, was named capital of the AEF in 1910. Despite the loss of that position, Libreville found compensation in its role as capital of the Gabon colony. The real colonization of Gabon began in the twentieth century with the effective occupation of the country. New infrastructures were established which dynamized administrative functions of Libreville. At the beginning of the twentieth century, traditional factories and concessionary companies existed side by side and aggressively exploited local populations. This concessionary regime did not meet the expectations of the French colonial authorities, and the concession system was reorganized in 1910. It is only with the rise of industry centered on *Okoumé* trees that the Gabonese economy experienced a real boom before World War I, leading to a massive increase of the budget of the Gabonese colony. This economic boom went along with the emergence of a consumer market. The economy of Gabon passed therefore from a subsistence economy to an exchange economy, a direct consequence of the Okoumé industry.

This sudden development of a local consumer market at the beginning of the twentieth century gave Libreville a territorial radiation, which was lacking in the previous century. Libreville benefited from this, because factories and concession companies had their headquarters in Libreville. These headquarters established themselves near administrative services. The city also experienced an increase in office buildings and a steady flow of employees. Libreville received new equipment and developments, such as ports, and public sanitation. In 1940 modern engines were used to build two roads linking Libreville to Owendo and Libreville to Kango and Lambaréné. In 1946 factories for the transformation of timber were also built in Libreville.

After World War II, Libreville was not only the capital of the Gabonese colony but also *chef lieu de region*, and *chef lieu de district,* further enhancing Libreville's stature. Libreville was also the "spiritual center" of the colony. Missionaries opened schools and libraries and other reading rooms. Around that time, between 2,500 and 3,000 individuals, victims of the economic crisis that affected the timber industry in the 1930s, found refuge in Libreville. This floating population came to live side by side or intermingle with other people from central and west Africa and the old Mpongwe stock.

Rural exodus was also another factor explaining the presence of rural populations. Migrants hoped to find abundant and well-paying jobs, and inexpensive merchandise, in Librevile. They usually settled in such quarters as Nombakele, Derrière la prison, or Derrière l'hopital. The Fang mainly established themselves in Lalala. These new quarters were different from the old Mpongwe villages of Louis, Glass, and others, as their characteristics were established before this demographic overflow. After independence, the rural exodus intensified with the oil boom of the 1970s, and new quarters and neighborhoods, mainly slums, emerged. In preparation for the 1977 Organization of African Unity (OAU) summit, new roads and buildings were constructed, giving Libreville a more modern appearance.

François Ngolet

See also: **Gabon; Resettlement of Recaptives: Freetown, Libreville, Liberia, Freretown, Zanzibar.**

Further Reading

Bucher, H. "Liberty and Labor: The Origins of Libreville Reconsidered." *Bulletins de l'Institut Fondamental d'Afrique Noire.* Series B, 41 (1979): 478–496.

Fyfe, C. "Freed Slave Colonies in West Africa." In *Cambridge History of Africa.*Vol. 5, *1790–1870.* London. Cambridge University Press, 1976.

Lasserre, G. *Libreville: La ville et sa région.* Paris: Armand Colin, 1958.

M'bokolo, E. *Noirs et Blancs en Afrique Equatoriale.* Paris-La-Haye: Mouton, 1981.

Patterson, K. D. *The Northern Gabon Coast to 1875.* Oxford: Clarendon, 1975.

Schnapper, B. *La politique et le commerce français dans le Golfe de Guinée de 1838 à 1871.* Paris-La Haye: Mouton, 1961.

Libya: Yusuf Pasha Karamanli and the Ottoman Reoccupation, 1795–1835

Yusuf Pasha Karamanli (1795–1832) was the last great ruler of the semi-independent Karamanli dynasty that ruled the nominally Ottoman regency of Tripoli

Libya.

(approximately modern Libya) from 1711 to 1835. Under Yusuf's predecessor, Ali Pasha (1754–1795), the regency had suffered political, economic, and social decline, worsened by tribal revolt, drought, and epidemics. By the early 1790s the country was in disarray and the aged pasha was unable to restrain the rivalries of his three sons. The youngest, Yusuf, eventually usurped the throne, first by murdering his elder brother, Hassan, and then, after Ali Pasha's fall from power and a period of political chaos, by forcing his second brother, Ahmed, into exile and poverty. Yusuf Pasha was a cruel, ruthless, calculating, and unprincipled tyrant, a man of great personal charm, whose main failure was to come to terms with the changing conditions of the age, and whose soaring ambitions for his little country were unfulfilled.

It took him almost ten years (1795–1805) to consolidate his rule at the center of power in Tripoli, restore some financial and economic confidence, build up the military force needed to extend his undisputed, centralizing power inland, and build up the naval strength intended to revive Tripoli's role as a corsairing state. These Saharan and Mediterranean ambitions were driven by the pasha's urgent need for more revenues than the primitive local farming and herding economies could provide, or the nomadic and seminomadic tribes of the interior could be persuaded to pay. State revenues were levied on the parasitic activities of the Tripoli corsairs in the Mediterranean and the trans-Saharan traders in black slaves; both sources were irregular and unpredictable but both, Yusuf Pasha believed, could be made to yield more.

The Napoleonic Wars and the Anglo-French struggle for domination of the Mediterranean enabled the pasha to regain a certain local supremacy for his corsair fleet, initially expressed in a pro-French policy. His ability to levy safe-passage tribute from maritime powers was, however, challenged by the newest such power, the United States. In 1801 Tripolitanian corsairs seized several American ships, but American freedom of the seas was asserted in the subsequent war. In the meantime, Britain's growing Mediterranean ascendancy, and in particular the implications of the Battle of the Nile (1798), which stranded Napoleon's punitive expedition in Egypt, the capture and occupation of nearby Malta (1800), and the Battle of Trafalgar (1805) were not lost on the pasha.

The British bombardment of the leading corsair base, Algiers, in 1816 finally persuaded Yusuf Pasha that the Mediterranean was no longer a safe or reliable source of corsair revenue. He promoted his Saharan policies accordingly, seeking to impose his recognized and centralizing policy over the few towns, trading oases, and scattered tribes of his regency. He thus pacified much of what is now modern Libya, bringing its eastern province, Cyrenaica (Barqa) under tighter rule and almost eliminating the large and rebellious Awlad Slaiman tribe of the Sirtica that had disrupted trans-Saharan trade for many years. In 1810 he sent troops to Ghadames oasis to secure the nearest stages of the southwest trade route to the Niger Bend and the Hausa states. In 1813 he overthrew the Awlad Mohammad dynasty that had ruled the southern province of Fezzan for the past 300 years. He thus achieved his objectives of closer control over and further stimulation of Fezzan's trans-Saharan traffic in black slaves and gold that had always underpinned the province's rule as a semi-independent but tribute-paying fief of Tripoli.

To speed the flow of black slaves into Fezzan and Tripoli, he mounted slaving raids deep into the southern Sahara and beyond. By 1817 he was ready to project the regency's power, influence, and lust for slaves into Sub-Saharan Africa. This imperial ambition coincided with British plans to explore inner Africa by the shortest Saharan routes from Tripoli. Such projects were prompted and nurtured by the remarkable British consul general, Colonel Hanmer Warrington, who held the post from 1814 to 1846 and who up to the mid-1820s wielded extraordinary power and influence over the pasha. While Britain took advantage of the close relationship with Yusuf Pasha and his claims to protect travelers right across the Sahara to send three important exploratory missions into the interior from Tripoli (1819–1925), the pasha's own trans-Saharan ventures were not a success. By the mid-1820s his relations with Consul Warrington had been undermined by the issue of the missing papers of the murdered British explorer, Major Alexander Gordon Laing; Tripoli's mounting debts to Britain; and a clear revival of local French interests.

The pasha's serious international debt crisis, with resultant diplomatic and naval pressure from Britain and France, combined with tribal revolt in the interior, disruption of Saharan trade, and an outbreak of dynastic and civil strife, forced his abdication in August 1832 in favor of his son, Ali. But the succession was disputed (with the British and French consuls supporting opposing claimants) and was still unsettled when the Ottoman fleet intervened in May 1835. Ali Pasha was arrested, Karamanli rule was ended and, after 120 years of effective independence, the regency of Tripoli again came under the direct rule of Constantinople, which lasted until the Italian invasion of 1911. Constantinople had intervened to secure at least one North African possession following Egypt's effective independence under Mohammad Ali, the French conquest of Algiers, and the growing and dangerous local rivalry of Britain and France.

Yusuf Pasha had managed to sustain Tripoli's independence for nearly forty years against all the pretensions of outside powers. But in the long run he was unable to come to terms with the more complex and pressing political and economic realities of the post-Napoleonic world. As the Ottoman Turks after him were to find, the country's economic base was unable to provide realistic alternatives to such unacceptable activities as Mediterranean corsairing and the trans-Saharan slave trade.

JOHN WRIGHT

See also: **Tripoli.**

Further Reading

Bergna, P. C. *I Caramanli.* Tripoli: Plinio Maggi, 1953.
Dearden, S. *A Nest of Corsairs: The Fighting Karamanlis of the Barbary Coast.* London: John Murray, 1976.
Folayan, K. *Tripoli during the Reign of Yusuf Pasha Karamanli.* Ife-Ife: University of Ife Press, 1979.
Micacchi, R. *La Tripolitania sotto il dominio dei Caramanli.* Verbania: A. Airoldi, 1936.
Morsy, M. *North Africa 1800–1900: A Survey from the Nile Valley to the Atlantic.* London and New York: Longman, 1984.
Narrative of a Ten Years' Residence at Tripoli in Africa. London: Henry Colburn, 1817.
Rossi, E. *Storia di Tripoli e della Tripolitania dalla conquista araba al 1911.* Rome: Istituto per l'Oriente, 1968.

Libya: Muhammad Al-Sanusi (*c.*1787–1859) and the Sanusiyya

Religious Leader; Founder of a Sufi Brotherhood

Born at al-Wasita near Mustaghanim in western Algeria in 1787, Muhammad al-Sanusi was the founder of a Sufi brotherhood, which provided the framework for later state development in Libya, although it was also influential in what is currently Chad. Although the Sanusiyya is often portrayed as a politico-military organization, al-Sanusi originally established his brotherhood as a strictly religious order, characterized by teachings and devotional practices aimed at strengthening the faith of the Sufi initiate and inculcating within him a spirit of moral purity. Only in the late nineteenth and early twentieth centuries, when French, Italian, and British colonialism in Saharan Africa was at its peak, did the Sanusiyya adopt a position inclined toward military struggle.

As a young man, Muhammad al-Sanusi left his home in Algeria to pursue his studies at the thriving Moroccan cultural center of Fez, where he studied law and tradition and was initiated into several Sufi orders, including the Nasiriyya branch of the Shadhiliyya. His natural restlessness and desire for learning prompted him eventually to leave Fez for the scholarly centers of the Islamic East. In 1823 he arrived in Cairo, at that time under the rule of Muhammad Ali, and took up studies at the great mosque-university of the Azhar. In 1826 he made the Hajj to Mecca, where he came into contact with the influential Moroccan sufi master Ahmad ibn Idris (1749?–1837) and joined his circle of disciples. Following Ibn Idris's departure from Mecca in 1828, al-Sanusi, as the most senior and accomplished of his disciples, was placed in charge of the former's students. When Ibn Idris died in 1837, many of these students recognized al-Sanusi as a Sufi master in his own right. Opposed by Mecca's conservative religious establishment, al-Sanusi led his band of followers from the Hijaz to the more hospitable environment of North Africa and, after a period of fruitless wandering, eventually settled in the relatively remote region of Cyrenaica, in northeastern Libya. The establishment in Cyrenaica of the group's first *zawiya*, or Sufi lodge, at al-Bayda in 1842 marks the beginnings of a distinct Sanusiyya brotherhood, as opposed to what had been up to that point a loose community of scholars inspired by the teachings of Ahmad ibn Idris.

Driven by a strong missionary impulse, Muhammad al-Sanusi made it his mission to reform what he considered to be the heavily corrupted religious beliefs and practices of Cyrenaica's mostly Bedouin population. To this end, he was instrumental in establishing throughout Cyrenaica and the Fezzan a hierarchically directed network of *zawiyyas* that functioned not only as centers of religious instruction but also as social and economic centers designed to introduce the local populations to the sedentary values associated with normative, scripturalist Islam. In terms of administration, al-Sanusi appointed for each *zawiyya* a shaykh, who held spiritual authority and was responsible for teaching and the distribution of *zakat*, and a *wakil*, or deputy, who was in charge of the lodge's economic upkeep. The establishment of *zawiyyas* at the territorial junctures of two or more competing tribes enabled the shaykhs to function as "holy outsiders" who, through their alleged possession of *baraka* (divine favor), were equipped to arbitrate tribal disputes and thus encourage an environment of regional peace and mutual cooperation. The creation of disciplined communities organized around an ethic of pious endeavor was an important factor in the development of a lucrative trans-Saharan trade route that, under Sanusi auspices, came to link the Mediterranean littoral with Waddai in the south.

Muhammad al-Sanusi's message, the substance of which he inherited from Ahmad ibn Idris, was common to the moderate reformist trend which characterized much of the Sufism of the eighteenth and nineteenth centuries. He rejected the ecstatic and extravagant aspects of the Sufi tradition and advocated instead a path which looked to the pious example of the prophet Muhammad. The brotherhood's *dhikr,* or ritual remembrance of God, consisted of the phrase *Allah al-Azim* ("God is the Most Great"). Muhammad al-Sanusi left behind a written corpus of some 44 titles, which included works dealing with Maliki law, *ijtihad* (independent legal reasoning based upon the Quran and the example of the Prophet), and the *dhikr* requirements of forty other Sufi orders. These latter, he claimed, were all now superceded by the "Muhammadan Way" of the Sanusiyya.

Upon his death in 1859, Muhammad al-Sanusi was capably succeeded by his son, Muhammad al-Mahdi (1844–1902), who transferred the headquarters of the brotherhood from Jaghbub to Kufra, a cluster of oases some 1,000 kilometers from the Mediterranean. The brotherhood's move south has been explained as an attempt by its leadership to escape the political authority of the Ottoman Sultan Abdul Hamid II, but more likely it was done in order to be closer to the vibrant trading economy of Wadai. Whatever the reason, the Sanusiyya's southward orientation brought it into conflict with the French, who at that very moment were penetrating the region of Lake Chad. Hostilities between the French and the Sanusiyya broke out in 1901 at Bir Alali and continued sporadically until the fall of the *zawiyya* at Ayn Galakka, south of Gouro, in 1913.

A second conflict arose with Italy, which invaded Libya in 1911 during the leadership of the third Master of the brotherhood, Ahmad al-Sharif (1872–1933), who had succeeded his uncle Muhammad al-Mahdi in 1902. As a defensive measure, Ahmad al-Sharif enhanced his relations with the Ottomans and, in order to mobilize his followers, proclaimed the jihad. When World War I broke out, the Sanusiyya allied itself with the Central Powers and in 1915 unsuccessfully attacked Italy's British ally in Egypt. Defeated on all fronts, al-Sharif handed the affairs of the brotherhood to his cousin, Muhammad Idris and in 1918 fled to Istanbul on a German submarine. Idris signed agreements with the Italians, who provided the Sanusiyya with a semblance of autonomy, but with the rise of fascism in Italy in the 1920s hostilities recommenced. In this final and conclusive struggle, noted for the fierce resistance mounted by Umar al-Mukhtar, one of the brotherhood's leaders, the Italians managed by 1932 to destroy the Sanusiyya's organization of *zawiyyas* and thus its influence in the countryside. The war is widely recognized as having been one of the most brutal colonial wars of the twentieth century.

The leadership of the brotherhood, however, survived the war with Italy, and when Libya was granted its independence on December 24, 1951, Muhammad Idris, who had spent the war years in exile in Egypt, was proclaimed king. Under his rule, the Sanusiyya displayed signs of revival but was unable to recover anything approaching its former prestige. In 1969 the Free Unionist officers under the leadership of Colonel Qadhdhafi removed King Idris from power and proclaimed a republic. Qadhdhafi's regime has not tolerated the Sanusiyya and has done its best to excise its role in Libya from the historical record.

JOHN CALVERT

Biography

Muhammad al-Sanusi was born at al-Wasita near Mustaghanim in western Algeria in 1787. He left Algeria to pursue law studies in Fez. He was initiated into several Sufi orders. In 1823 he went to Cairo to study at the mosque-university of the Azhar. In 1826 he made the Hajj to Mecca, met Ahmad ibn Idris, and joined his circle of disciples. When Ibn Idris died in 1837, al-Sanusi was recognized as a Sufi master and the logical heir to Idris's leadership role. Al-Sanusi and his followers moved frequently, eventually settling in Cyrenaica, in northeastern Libya. In 1842 the groups' first *zawiya*, or Sufi lodge, was established at Cyrenaica. Al-Sanusi died in 1859.

Further Reading

Evans-Pritchard, E. E. *The Sanusi of Cyrenaica.* London: Oxford University Press, 1949.

Le Gall, M. "The Ottoman Government and the Sanusiyya: A Reappraisal." *International Journal of Middle East Studies* 21 (1989): pp.91–106.

Martin, B. G. *Muslim Brotherhoods in 19th-Century Africa.* Cambridge: Cambridge University Press, 1976.

Vikor, K. *Sufi and Scholar on the Desert Edge: Muhammad b. 'Ali al-Sanusi, 1787–1859,* London: Hurst and Co., 1995.

Ziadeh, N. *Sanusiyya: A Study of a Revivalist Movement in Islam.* Leiden: E. J. Brill, 1958, rev. 1983.

Libya: Italian Invasion and Resistance, 1911–1931

By 1900 Turkish Tripolitania and Cyrenaica (approximately, modern Libya) were among the last African territories not under European claim. Italy, a latecomer to the European "scramble" for African possessions, had gained Eritrea and Somalia but failed disastrously in 1896 to annex Ethiopia. It thus looked to Tripoli for compensation for imperial designs frustrated elsewhere. A persuasive nationalist lobby argued that possession of Tripoli would confirm Italy's great power status, while ensuring domination of the central Mediterranean. Tripoli, it was claimed, was the gateway to the supposed wealth and rich trade of Sub-Saharan Africa. It was also promoted as an agricultural settler colony for surplus and landless Italians, half a million of whom were then emigrating every year. From 1907 a policy of "peaceful penetration" of Turkish North Africa had little success, but local hostility to Italian ambitions offered the necessary cause for war. In late September 1911 an ultimatum to Constantinople, declaring Rome's intention to occupy Tripolitania and Cyrenaica, was followed by a massive sea-borne invasion in early October, and the ports of Tripoli, Benghazi, Derna, Homs, and Tobruk were occupied. Yet, despite overwhelming Italian superiority in men, arms, and modern equipment (including aircraft, motor transport, and wireless), conquest was not the expected "military parade." For the Libyans, rather than hail the invaders as liberators from oppression, as had been expected, reinforced the small Turkish regular forces with thousands of their own volunteer fighters in a display of popular Islamic solidarity.

While the Italians could not be driven from coastal bridgeheads covered by their heavy naval guns, they made little progress inland. In November 1911 a royal decree placed Tripolitania and Cyrenaica under the Italian Crown. But by early 1912 the war had reached stalemate. Secret diplomatic contacts led in October to the Treaty of Ouchy: while leaving Italy in nominal control of Tripolitania and Cyrenaica, it also recognized the local spiritual authority of the ultan-caliph, thus encouraging continuing Libyan resistance (particularly the resistance of the Sanusi confraternity in Cyrenaica) to a perceived infidel invasion.

Between 1912 and 1914 Italy conquered an arc of territory in northern Cyrenaica, but the Sanusi still controlled most of the country. Tripolitania was more easily overrun because local leadership was divided and demoralized and the terrain less easily defended. The southern Saharan province of Fezzan was invaded in 1913 (partly to inhibit further French advance northward through neighboring Chad), but Italian control was insecure. By the end of 1914 a Libyan counterattack had forced the invaders back to Tripolitania. Except for small heavily defended enclaves at Tripoli and three other ports, Tripolitania was abandoned even before Italy's entry into the European war in May 1915. Local leaders then took advantage of the resultant power vacuum to declare an independent republic at Misurata supported by Italy's wartime enemies, Turkey, Germany, and Austria. Also with Turco-German encouragement, the Sanusi in Cyrenaica attacked British positions in Egypt in 1915–1916; but peace was brokered in 1917. Despite their apparently common interests, Tripolitanians and Cyrenaicans failed to work together at this opportune time, revealing a fatal weakness in Libyan resistance to long-term Italian ambitions.

Lacking the political and military will to start a war of colonial reconquest after World War I, Italy instead sought compromises with the Sanusi in Cyrenaica and the Tripolitanian Republic. Each province was given a parliament and governing and local councils through which Rome hoped to exercise light-handed control: in Cyrenaica, the Sanusi leader, Sayyid Idris, was recognized as hereditary emir. But little came of these good intentions: the Tripolitanian Republic collapsed in tribal anarchy, and in Cyrenaica Italo-Sanusi cooperation broke down in late 1921. The perceived dangers to Italian interests in Tripolitanian leaders' belated acceptance of Sayyid Idris as emir of all Libya in November 1922 had already been contained by the new governor of Tripolitania, Count Giuseppe Volpi, who had earlier that year started the military reconquest of the province, declaring martial law and rejecting all constitutional arrangements with the Libyans. As Benito Mussolini came to power in October 1922, northern Tripolitania was being reoccupied, Volpi having in effect anticipated by some months the fascist colonial policy of military reconquest soon to be applied to all Libya. Fascist Italy's new colonial war lasted nine years, with small numbers involved in petty engagements over vast areas. Like other European forces elsewhere in contemporary North Africa, the Italian military found no easy way of defeating local nomads' pugnacious guerrilla tactics.

By mid-1924, the Italians controlled the most useful and populous parts of northern Tripolitania. Over the following four years the wilder country to the south was slowly penetrated and the tribes "pacified" and disarmed: in 1928 the Sirtica desert was occupied. By early 1930 Colonel (later General) Rodolfo Graziani had completed the conquest of southern Tripolitania and Fezzan. In Cyrenaica, by contrast, the terrain was harder and Sanusi-inspired resistance more effective. Guerrillas led by the aged Sanusi Shaikh Umar al-Mukhtar were particularly active in the wooded highlands of the Gebel Akhdar. The Sanusi center at Giarabub oasis was occupied in 1926 and that at the remote Kufra oases in 1931, but tribal resistance was only overcome with draconian measures, including the detention of most of the nomadic population in large concentration camps in order to deny the guerrillas supplies and recruits. Only the capture and execution of Shaikh Umar al-Mukhtar in late 1931 effectively ended Cyrenaican resistance. Rather than accept Italian rule, up to 100,000 Libyans sought exile in neighboring French African territories or in Egypt.

Costing many thousands of Libyan lives, the twenty years of wars of conquest provided an invaluable and undeniable basis for Libyan claims to an internationally brokered independence after World War II and were to be depicted by both royalist and republican postindependence regimes as a popular nationalist resistance.

JOHN WRIGHT

Further Reading

Bandini, F. *Gli Italiani in Africa: Storia delle guerre coloniali (1882–1943)* [The Italians in Africa: History of the Colonial Wars (1882–1943)]. Milan: Arnoldo Mondadori, 1980.

Boswell, R. J. B. *Italy, the Least of the Great Powers: Italian Foreign Policy before the First World War.* Cambridge: Cambridge University Press, 1979.

Del Boca, A. *Gli italiani in Libia.* Vol. 1, *Tripoli bel suol d'amore, 1860–1922.* Vol. 2, *Dal fascismo a Gheddafi* [The Italians in Libya. Vol. 1, Tripoli "Beautiful Land of Love," 1860–1922. Vol. 2, From Fascism to Gheddafi]. Rome-Bari: editori Laterza, 1986 and 1988.

Evans-Pritchard, E. E. *The Sanusi of Cyrenaica.* Oxford: Oxford University Press, 1949.

Malgeri, F. *La guerra libica (1911–1912).* Rome: Edizioni di Storia e Letteratura, 1970.

Wright, J. *Libya.* London: Ernest Benn, and New York: Praeger, 1969.

Libya: World War II and the Kingdom of Libya, 1942–1969

Following the British victory at El Alamein (October 1942), Italian Cyrenaica was occupied by the Eighth Army for the third and final time. In January 1943, Tripoli—the elusive objective of two and a half years of fighting in North Africa—fell to the British. Free French forces advancing across the Sahara from Chad occupied the southern province, Fezzan. British military administrations were set up in Cyrenaica and Tripolitania, with a similar French administration in Fezzan. Under the terms of the 1907 Hague Convention, they governed Libya as occupied enemy territory on a "care and maintenance" basis.

The question of Libya's future was postponed until after the war. But in return for support for the British war effort by the Cyrenaican Sanusi leader, Sayyid Mohammad Idris, and his followers, Britain had in January 1942 given a public pledge that Cyrenaica would never again fall under Italian rule. The postwar debate about Libya's future lasted many years, reflecting the emerging rifts of the Cold War and the strategic interests of the occupying powers. While Britain believed Cyrenaica could become an alternative military base to the Suez Canal Zone in Egypt, France saw Fezzan as a strategic buffer, protecting French African possessions from outside infiltration. The strategic importance of the U.S. Wheelus air base near Tripoli grew as the Cold War developed. In Libya itself, interests were divided between Cyrenaica, apparently centerd around the prestigious Sanusi leadership and ready to become a semi-independent emirate under British protection, and Tripolitania, economically and socially more "advanced" but torn by republican infighting and the interests of a large and vocal Italian settler community. Although the country was considered too poor and quite unprepared for independence (Italy having renounced all claims) the impasse was broken by the decision of September 1948 to refer its future to the United Nations. The General Assembly voted in November 1949 for Libya's full independence by the end of 1951, federating Cyrenaica, Tripolitania, and Fezzan in a united kingdom under a Sanusi monarch, Sayyid Idris.

The Kingdom of Libya, an apparently fragile product of bargains and compromises between domestic and foreign interests, lasted nearly eighteen years (1951–1969). In its early years, King Idris (age 61 on accession and a wily constitutional monarch) acted as the centralizing link between the centrifugal powers of the three provinces (each with governments of their own) and the relatively weaker central administration. There were no political parties or any organized sources of opposition, and the democratic parliamentary system that the UN had provided before independence was dominated by tribal and oligarchic family interests. This led to frequent government changes as ministers jockeyed for the "rewards" of office.

The kingdom's greatest early drawbacks were extreme poverty (per capita income in 1951 was an estimated $35 per year) and lack of economic opportunities and trained personnel. Libya was obliged to "live on its geography," its main source of income coming from military base-leasing agreements with the United States and Britain. Necessary gestures to Arab solidarity such as joining the Arab League in 1953 did little to alleviate growing hostility from the Arab World (and especially from Nasserite Egypt) to inevitably close ties to the West, including reliance on Western defense and foreign aid.

A secure economic lifeline came with the start of lavish spending by foreign companies on oil exploration in the mid-1950s and then with the start of oil exports in 1961. No country exploited its oil reserves so quickly: revenues rose from a mere $3 million in 1961 to $1,175 million in the kingdom's last year, 1969. The fact that most oil was found in one province, Cyrenaica, prompted the abolition of the potentially separatist federal system and the proclamation of the unitary kingdom of Libya in 1963.

By then, a country of under two million people was exposed to all the pressures and excesses of a typical Third World oil boom. While there were few financial constraints on state spending on economic and social development, it took time for the benefits of oil wealth to filter down to people with newly aroused expectations. If many of the royalist regime's development projects only began to show results after the 1969 revolution (which inevitably took the credit), it did fail to curb the conspicuous corruption, wealth-getting, and consumption of many of its leading political figures and entrepreneurs. Nasser-led Egypt, which had large economic and social influence, also caused trouble by criticizing the Kingdom for hosting foreign military bases when there was no financial necessity to continue doing so.

As the elderly king Idris had no convincing heir, the succession remained uncertain. There was no obvious single source of opposition to a regime able to buy the acquiescence of disgruntled individuals or cliques. But there were strong demonstrations of undefined and largely uncoordinated public hostility in 1964 over the foreign bases issue and in 1967 over the Arab-Israeli war. Public corruption and the king's over-reliance on the Shalhi family for advice were further sources of discontent, checked by well-armed provincial police forces. By 1969 several disparate groups were apparently preparing coups that would end the uncertainty over the succession and the future of the valuable prize that Libya had become, among them the small group of junior Force officers led by Captain Moammar Gadafi.

The Kingdom of Libya was at best a fragile creation, always vulnerable during its 18 years of existence to internal divisions and external pressures. Western notions of monarchy were alien to the Arabs, and kingdoms in the turbulent 1950s and 1960s were prime targets for Arab nationalists. King Idris, although generally respected as a scholar, was both an inadequate custodian of Libya's new-found wealth and a cause of likely turmoil on his death or abdication. Yet the kingdom survived during two of the Arab world's most troubled modern decades. It showed a certain dogged resilience in the face of its many crises and it began the exploitation of the oil wealth that was in the 1970s to give Libyans the highest standards of living and social welfare in Africa. These were no slight achievements for this benign and unassuming despotism.

JOHN WRIGHT

See also: **World War II: North Africa.**

Further Reading

Assan, G. *La Libia e il mondo arabo* [Rome and the Arab World]. Rome: Editori Riuniti, 1959.

Bodyanski, V. L., and V. E. Shagal. *Sovremyennaya Liviya (Spravochnik)* [Modern Libya: A Guide]. Moscow: Izdatyelstvo Nuaka, 1965.

Farley, R. *Planning for Development in Libya. The Exceptional Economy in the Developing World.* New York: Praeger, 1971.

Khadduri, M. *Modern Libya: A Study in Political Development.* Baltimore: John Hopkins Press, 1963.

Norman, J. *Labor & Politics in Libya and Arab Africa.* New York: Bookman Associates, 1965.

Pelt, A. *Libyan Independence and the United Nations: A Case of Planned Decolonisation.* New Haven: Yale University Press, 1970.

Villard, H. S. *Libya, the New Arab Kingdom of North Africa.* Ithaca: Cornell University Press, 1956.

Wright, J. *Libya: A Modern History.* London and Canberra: Croom Helm, and Baltimore: John Hopkins University Press, 1982.

Libya: Gaddafi (Qadhdhafi) and Jamahiriyya (Libyan Revolution)

Libya's revolutionary republican regime came to power on September 1, 1969, with the overthrow of the pro-Western Sanusi monarchy, which had ruled the country since independence in December 1951. The new Libyan Arab Republic was led by a revolution command council of twelve junior army officers; Captain Muammar Gaddafi promoted himself to colonel on seizing power. Although clearly radical, pan-Arab, and Nasserist in outlook and intent, these new leaders for some time lacked the practical experience to implement their more revolutionary ideals. Nevertheless, their first year in power was marked by some striking achievements, including the evacuation of remaining British and American military bases, expulsion of the small but influential Italian and Jewish communities, the suppression of all political parties, the start of the far-reaching price and ownership confrontation with the international oil companies, and the promise of the full commitment of Libyan oil wealth to the cause of Arab unity and the liberation of Palestine.

For over 18 months after seizing power, the new regime promoted Colonel Gaddafi's emerging socialist ideology through ad hoc popular rallies. But the decision of April 1971 to unite with Egypt and Syria obliged the leadership to provide a working political structure, with the Egyptian Arab Socialist Union taken as a model for the republic's sole political organization. The first Arab Socialist Union (ASU) national congress in March and April 1972 seemed to encourage open public debate and a popular decision-making process based on traditional tribal gatherings seeking consensus rather than majority decisions.

Since coming to power, Gaddafi had always sought legitimacy in his claim to represent the popular will. He had no difficulty in basing his ideology on Islam, for he saw no contradiction between religious consciousness and political decision-making. Gaddafi believed that Islam would again bring the Libyans in particular, but also Arabs and Muslims everywhere, to spiritual and political regeneration. This belief inspired the so-called third international theory that emerged in late 1972. It proposed a middle way between the failed ideologies of atheistic communism and materialistic capitalism by harnessing the two main forces of human history: religion and nationalism.

Socialist in character and purportedly to be universal in its appeal, the theory became the official philosophy of the 1973 "cultural revolution." By early that year, it was clear that the ASU and other means of mass mobilization had failed to rouse the politically apathetic Libyan people to "tumultuous popular revolution." Thus Gaddafi himself became a political agitator, launching the "cultural revolution" in April 1973 with a five-point program, including suspension of all existing laws, purging the "politically sick" (including Marxists, communists, atheists, and Muslim Brothers), arming the people to protect the revolution, an administrative revolution to destroy bureaucracy and the bourgeoisie, and a "cultural revolution" to "refute and destroy" everything contrary to the Holy Quran. The people were urged to "run the government and assume the responsibilities of power" through "popular committees" intended to involve them directly in political processes and to control the revolution from below. The resultant "Quranic socialism," as practiced in Libya up to the late 1970s, was a moderate type of redistributive socialism on the Swedish model, underpinned by the massive oil revenues that financed a model welfare state. Economic conditions became more difficult in the 1980s under the impact of Gaddafi's even more egalitarian notions and a fall in oil revenues.

In response to growing domestic and external opposition, Gaddafi began a new phase of political evolution in 1975. Based on his ideas of popular democracy, policies were to be debated and approved in Basic People's Congresses and other popular committees and gatherings before being passed to a General People's Congress, whose 1,000 members were to coordinate them for implementation. Gaddafi set out his new ideas in three brief and artless political, economic, and social essays, which appeared as *The Green Book* in 1975–1976. Then, in March 1977, "the establishment of people's power" and the "end of any form of conventional institution of government" were proclaimed. At the same time, the country's name was changed to Socialist People's Libyan Arab Jamahiriyya, Gaddafi's neologism "Jamahiriyya" being generally translated as "state of the masses."

In theory, direct people's power was not unsuited to Libyans' social traditions and temperament and to a small and politically docile population unused to dissent, which was protected from the excesses and failures of such experiments by its oil wealth. But in practice the exercise of popular democracy, at least in the more complex areas of government, was constrained by the need for guidance and informed decision-making from a leadership that remained effectively in power, even if titles and functions had changed. The policies and actions of the Libyan revolution continued to bear the stamp of Gaddafi's unique thought and personality long after he had officially ceased to lead it.

Revolutionary foreign policy similarly reflected Gaddafi's own ideas and prejudices, often put into effect by the lavish deployment of oil revenues. Through its "sacred duty to all revolutions," especially in Asia, Africa, and Latin America, the regime for many years gave largely unquestioning and ill-informed financial aid to so-called liberation movements and organized malcontents the world over struggling against "oppressive regimes." It is not at all clear that accounts of such spending have ever been kept, either as a financial record or as a political one. Gaddafi's personal obsession with Arab unity as a means to Arab revival and the liberation of Palestine led Libya into many abortive attempts to unite with neighboring states (Egypt, Sudan, Tunisia) and more distant ones, with failure leading to Gaddafi's increasing hostility towards Arab regimes and leaders. Unsuccessful Arab policies prompted his deeper involvements in the later 1970s in the seemingly less daunting affairs of Sub-Saharan Africa in the name of "revolutionary and Islamic solidarity." Intervention in the complex civil war in neighboring Chad led to prolonged Libyan military occupation of the northern third of that country, only ended by ignominious defeat by Chadian forces in 1987.

Militarism was one of the most striking features of the Libyan Jamahiriyya by the early 1980s, characterized by the purchase of a formidable arsenal, a near tripling of armed manpower since the 1970s, and general military training through conscription and "popular militias." First France and then the Soviet Union were the main suppliers of aircraft, tanks, and other equipment, bought for cash, and in far greater quantities than the Libyans could themselves use. If neighboring states looked askance at this military buildup, the United States in particular became increasingly concerned about Tripoli's foreign policies, and especially the elimination of exiled Libyan dissidents, and the regime's perceived support for "international terrorism." Following the Libyan-inspired oil price and ownership revolutions of the early 1970s, most U.S. companies left the country. Relations with Washington worsened, particularly during the Reagan administration, with U.S. aircraft bombing Tripoli and Benghazi in 1986. Strong suspicions about the Gaddafi regime's involvement in the sabotage of an American airliner over Lockerbie, Scotland, in 1988, and the later sabotage of a French airliner over the Sahara, led to Libya's further international isolation and years of United Nations sanctions, lifted only when the two Libyan Lockerbie sabotage suspects were handed over for trial in the West in 1999.

The extraordinary phenomenon of revolutionary Libya very largely reflected the ideas, prejudices, and ambitions of it leader, Colonel Gaddafi. By the end of the twentieth century, when he had been in power for 30 years, most Libyans in a young society knew no other leader or system. Gaddafi, as their country's first truly Libyan leader, still had a special relationship with fellow Libyans, even if in the 1990s there was evidence of growing and violent domestic opposition to his regime and to the prospect of succession by one or both of his sons. His ability to act as he did at home and abroad were always fueled by the oil revenues that for years allowed lavish and apparently unaccounted spending on domestic projects and foreign ventures. These were often of questionable use or value to a nation whose finite oil reserves represented the greatest single source of wealth it was ever likely to own.

JOHN WRIGHT

See also: **Chad: Libya, Aozou Strip, Civil War; Libya: Foreign Policy under Qaddafi; Libya: Oil, Politics, and OPEC; Oil.**

Further Reading

Allan, J. A. *Libya: The Experience of Oil.* London and Canberra: Croom Helm, 1981.

Bearman, J. *Qadhafi's Libya.* London, Zed Books, 1986.

Davis, J. *Libyan Politics: Tribe and Revolution, An Account of the Zuwaya and their Government.* London, I. B. Tauris, 1987.

El Fathaly, O., and M. Palmer. *Political Development and Social Change in Libya.* Lexington, Mass.: Lexington Books, 1980.

El Shahat, M. *Libya Begins the Era of the Jamahiriyat.* Rome: International Publishing House, 1978.

First, R. *Libya: The Elusive Revolution.* Harmondsworth, England: Penguin, 1974.

Qathafti, M. al-. *The Green Book: Parts One, Two, and Three.* Tripoli: Public Establishment for Publishing, Advertising and Distribution, n.d.

Wright, J. *Libya: A Modern History.* London and Canberra: Croom Helm, Baltimore: John Hopkins University Press, 1982.

Libya: Oil, Politics, and OPEC

No country has developed and exploited new-found oil reserves faster than did the Libyan kingdom in the 1960s. On the eve of the 1969 revolution, only eight years after the start of commercial production, it overtook Kuwait as the world's fifth oil exporter and was challenging Iran's position. But in the early 1970s, revolutionary Libya curbed output and briefly became the engine of far-reaching oil pricing and ownership changes.

Foreign oil companies, both the seven "majors" and the so-called independents, were first drawn to Libya by the promising terms of the first (1955) petroleum law. The kingdom offered potential diversity for Middle Eastern oil, apparent political stability, reliance on Western patronage and military protection, plus unrestricted sea-borne access to expanding Southern and Western European oil markets. High-quality commercial crude oil was first found in 1959; exports started in 1961 and by 1969 nearly a dozen foreign companies or consortia of companies were exporting crude from five Mediterranean terminals. Output peaked at 3.7 million barrels per day (b/d) in April 1970.

From the start of oil production, the Libyan kingdom made various and partly successful attempts to increase its share of the new wealth. In 1962 it joined the Organization of Petroleum Exporting Countries (OPEC) set up by five exporters in 1960 to counter falling world oil prices. Between 1961 and 1969 the state's share of receipts per barrel exported rose from 50 U.S. cents to $1.05—by then well above the OPEC average. But the new revolutionary regime was not satisfied with such revenues, which would have been higher but for the large tax-deductible discounts allowed to "independent" companies as "marketing expenses." Taking advantage of oil supply blockage in the Middle East (including the continued post-1967 war closure of the Suez Canal) and ordering companies to cut output, it put irresistible pressure on the "independents" without alternative means of supply to agree to modest price rises that other companies, "majors" included, were then obliged to accept. Libya's strength was its new-found role as West Europe's largest single oil source: neither companies nor governments wanted confrontation over demands reflecting an acknowledged political agenda as well as an economic one.

The 1970 settlement was the first big rise in crude oil prices depressed since the late 1950s and a tacit acceptance of Libyan oil's special values. Fellow members of OPEC then quickly followed the Libyan lead, taking advantage of continuing supply difficulties to achieve the Tehran Agreement of February 1971. This saw companies settling for tax and price rises that gave six Gulf producers roughly equal terms with Libya. But as Libya was at a renewed disadvantage, companies were again pressured into accepting further tax and price rises (the so-called Tripoli Agreement of April 1971), which confirmed the continuing underlying strength of Tripoli's bargaining position and the value of Libyan oil.

Libya earned higher annual oil revenues from lower exports: $1 billion from 945 million barrels exported in 1968, compared with $22 billion from 622 million barrels in 1980. The Tehran and Tripoli Agreements were the direct outcome of revolutionary Libya's brief, politically and economically motivated confrontation with the oil companies. For a time, they transferred control of oil prices to OPEC; the resultant spiral in world oil prices was given further twists by the 1973 Middle East war and, after renewed price weakness in the mid-1970s, by the Iranian crisis of 1979–1980. But market forces reasserted themselves later in the 1980s as industrial countries cut reliance on OPEC oil. Libya's actual revenues from stagnant prices and output were much lower than expected: exports fell from over two million b/d in 1979 to barely one million in 1982.

In the meantime, revolutionary Libya had started the progressive nationalization of foreign company interests. Some such moves were avowedly political (such as the outright seizure of British Petroleum's [BP's] substantial interests in October 1971 as a direct result of British action in the Gulf); but some companies kept part-interests in producing fields in cooperation with the state National Oil Corporation. Others entered production-sharing agreements with the state. Again, other OPEC members followed the Libyan lead, bringing about radical changes in company-government relations that were to be more enduring than the ephemeral price and tax agreements of the early 1970s.

Within a few years of the 1969 revolution, foreign companies had almost stopped new oil exploration and development in Libya and later did the least needed to safeguard their remaining positions. Exploration has been relatively sluggish since 1970, compared with the 1950s and 1960s, although some important new oilfields were found and developed in the west and south and offshore in the Mediterranean. In the 1970s the country began to put greater emphasis on enhancing the value of its oil by increasing participation in such "downstream" operations as refining, petrochemicals, and marketing.

All these activities were greatly hampered by deteriorating relations with the United States during the Carter and Reagan administrations over Tripoli's perceived support for "international terrorism." Libya not only lost the United States as its leading crude oil customer but found itself increasingly cut off from superlative American oil industry technology and expertise, an isolation made even deeper in the 1990s by United Nations embargoes over the Lockerbie airplane bombing controversy.

Oil (and considerable volumes of commercially under-exploited natural gas) represent the greatest source of wealth Libya has known. Its high quality and closeness to large European consumers made it eminently marketable. In the early 1970s the new radical regime led the way in temporarily remedying years of crude oil under pricing and revised the traditional relationship between oil companies and producer governments. But its extremist politics and reputation undoubtedly inhibited the development of Libya's full potential as an oil state in the 1980s and 1990s.

JOHN WRIGHT

See also: **Libya: Foreign Policy under Qaddafi; Oil.**

Further Reading

Ghanem, S. M. *The Pricing of Libyan Crude Oil.* Valletta: Adams Publishing House, 1975.

Gurney, J. *Libya: The Political Economy of Energy.* Oxford: Oxford University Press, 1996.

Khader, B., and B. El-Wifati, (eds.), *The Economic Development of Libya.* London and Sydney: Croom Helm, 1987.

Waddams, F. C. *The Libyan Oil Industry.* London and Canberra: Croom Helm, 1980.

Wright, J. *Libya: A Modern History.* London and Canberra: Croom Helm; Baltimore: John Hopkins University Press, 1982.

Libya: Foreign Policy under Qaddafi

Over the course of more than 30 years as president of Libya, Muammar al-Qaddafi (there are several variant spellings) has earned a reputation for a penchant for encouraging and exporting revolutionary and terrorist movements.

Almost as soon as he came to power in 1969, Qaddafi tackled the oil companies, determined to bring them under control either by nationalization or by taking a majority shareholding in them. His successful takeover of the oil companies lent new strength to the Organization of Petroleum Exporting Countries (OPEC), allowing it to become a formidable cartel able to challenge Western economic power in the Middle East. Qaddafi came to power when Libya's oil output was peaking, which gave him two advantages: he could implement reforms in Libya without imposing taxes, and he could use the surplus derived from oil wealth to finance a highly independent foreign policy.

Qaddafi's first concern was Arab unity, for which he insistently called during his early years in power. In a controversial speech delivered in July 1972, Qaddafi said, "The sacred mission of all true (Muslim) believers today is to fight Great Britain and the United States. And if these countries think of fighting us in the Middle East, we will fight them on their own territories."

Qaddafi was also a firm opponent of Israel. In 1973 the year of the Yom Kippur War and OPEC's increased power, Qaddafi played a leading role in creating poor relations between Israel and Africa; he claimed, with some justification, that he had persuaded Chad, Congo, Niger, and Mali to end relations with Israel. In April 1973 he adopted an anti-Israel stance in the Organization of African Unity (OAU), demanding that Ethiopia (which housed the OAU headquarters in Addis Ababa) sever relations with Israel, or that the OAU be moved elsewhere. Eventually, in October of that year, Ethiopia did break off relations with Israel. Qaddafi was persistent in his demand that black Africa should demonstrate solidarity with the Arab states against Israel. He made many efforts to drum up greater support for the Palestinians.

Qaddafi cast his net wide in Africa. Libyan interventions in the civil war in neighboring Chad were less a matter of exporting revolution than deciding which side to back in an unstable situation where Libya could reap advantages in terms of *realpoliti*; in 1976 Libya claimed 52,000 square miles of Chad (the Aozou Strip) which had rich uranium deposits. Here, however, Qaddafi found himself opposed to both France, which intervened a number of times in support of the Chad government, and the United States, which supported France in order to block Qaddafi's ambitions.

Elsewhere in Africa, Qaddafi's interventions were more quixotic. He supported the Eritrean rebels against the government of Haile Selassie, then switched his support to the government once Haile Mariam Mengistu had seized power. He supported the Polisario rebels of Western Sahara against Morocco until, for a brief period, there seemed to be a chance of a union between Morocco and Libya. He supported the "Christian" SPLA in southern Sudan against the Muslim north, despite his wish to spread Islam, because he was quarrelling with President Nimeiri. By the early 1970s Qaddafi was supplying arms and money and providing training for liberation movements in Eritrea, Rhodesia, Guinea Bissau, Norocco, and Chad, and aid for Togo and Uganda. Following the closure of the Zambia-Rhodesia border in January 1973 he provided financial aid for Zambia, as well as support for the ZANU and ZAPU guerrillas. His support for Idi Amin in Uganda in 1972 when the latter was expelling Asian foreigners to Britain did not endear him to London; he also sent four hundred troops to Kampala that year in support of Amin when pro-Obote forces first invaded Uganda from Tanzania.

At the very least, Qaddafi showed poor judgment in his support for such brutal figures as Amin and Bokassa. African leaders were becoming increasingly disturbed by his foreign interventions.

The West might have been less antagonistic toward Qaddafi had he confined his interventions to the Arab world and Africa, but he insisted upon his right to intervene in areas the Western powers regarded as their own back yards, so to speak. In 1972 he supported the Black Muslim mosque in the United States. He sided with the prime minister of Malta, Dom Mintoff, in his quarrel with Britain over finances for British base facilities. He warned President Marcos of the Philippines that he would support the Muslim revolt in that country and, generally, was always ready to support small and often obscure nationalist movements. In 1976 Qaddafi proclaimed his support for the Movement for Self-Determination and the Independence of the Canaries Archipelago, as well as the Sardinian, Corsican, and Basque nationalists. He made overtures to the Welsh, Scottish, and Irish nationalists, and later provided arms for the Irish Republican Army (IRA).

His support for the Muslim Moro National Liberation Front (MNLF) in the Philippines was sufficiently aggravating to that country to persuade Imelda Marcos to attend talks in Tripoli, where she agreed to some form of Moro autonomy; although this agreement came to nothing, the fact that the talks were held at all is testimony to Qaddafi's influence at the time. In the mid-1970s Qaddafi behaved as though he was on a par with the United States and Europe in terms of world power and influence. In 1977 he entertained Fidel Castro on an official visit, which infuriated Washington.

Despite deep-seated Arab and African suspicions of Qaddafi, he retained a measure of popularity because of his willingness to stand up to the United States and Europe. As soon as he came to power in 1969, he insisted that Britain an the United States remove their military bases from Libya.

He made an enemy of the United States early on, due to his antagonism to Israel, his success in nationalizing oil, and, at least according to Washington, in his support of terrorist groups. In 1981 Washington accused Qaddafi of orchestrating an assassination attempt on President Ronald Reagan. In 1983 the U.S. State Department produced a report on "The Libya Problem" in which it accused Qaddafi of supporting leftists in Venezuela, Colombia, Chile, Costa Rica, and Honduras, while also offering paramilitary training in Libya to left-wing groups from South and Central America. The United States increased its pressures upon Libya, which culminated in the air raid of April 14–15, 1986, which resulted in 130 casualties, including Qaddafi's adopted daughter. The core of the U.S. case against Qaddafi was that he supported terrorism and terrorist movements around the world.

In the case of Britain, the two outstanding events that soured relations were the killing of Police Constable Yvonne Fletcher outside the Libyan Embassy in London in 1984 and the Lockerbie airplane bombing of 1988. In 1999, after 16 years, Britain resumed diplomatic relations with Libya when it accepted responsibility for the death of Fletcher and agreed that the two Libyans suspected of the Lockerbie attack should be tried under Scottish law (although the trial would be held in Holland).

Any assessment of Qaddafi while still living and president of Libya must be provisional. He has provoked angry reactions in the West, which in real terms in this case means in Britain and the United States. While several of his policies and actions have been questionable or reprehensible, it seems likely that special condemnation has been reserved for him simply because of he has dared to stand up to the great Western powers.

GUY ARNOLD

Further Reading

Arnold, G. *The Maverick State: Qaddafi and the New World Order.* London and New York: Cassell, 1996.

Blundy, D., and A. Lycett. *Qadhafi and the Libyan Revolution.* London: Corgi Books, 1988.

Davis, B. L. *Qaddafi, Terrorism, and the Origins of the U.S. Attack on Libya.* New York: Praeger, 1990.

Lemarchand, R. *The Green and the Black: Qadhaffi's Policies in Africa.* Bloomington: Indiana University Press, 1988.

"The Libyan Problem." *Department of State Bulletin.* Washington, D.C. (October 1983): 71–78.

Simons, G. *Libya: The Struggle for Survival.* Basingstoke: Macmillan, 1993.

Literacy and Indigenous Scripts: Precolonial Western Africa

The extent of literacy in precolonial Africa has been greatly underestimated and little studied. While some communities of precolonial West Africa may have made no use of writing, in others, a significant minority or even a majority of persons could read one or more languages. Some West African societies produced a significant body of writing in Arabic and/or in African languages rendered in modified Arabic script, while many more developed conventional systems of graphic signs, conveying a wide range of meanings and information.

The oldest Arabic documents from West Africa consist in eleventh century stone inscriptions from southern Mauritania (then associated with the Soninke people) and eastern Mali (still associated with the Songhay people). Several thousand Arabic manuscripts have been cataloged so far, including well over a thousand original titles. These comprise chronicles, devotional and mystical poetry, legal and theological treatises (including commentaries on standard, medieval Middle Eastern and North African works), and biographical dictionaries. Knowledge of the sixteenth- to nineteenth-century history of the savanna areas depends largely on the chronicles composed there. Several legal works composed by West African authors have been widely studied in the Muslim world. West African calligraphic styles are derived from North African ones. A very small number of manuscripts were illustrated, mainly in the Soninke- and Moorish-speaking areas of southern Mauritania.

The oldest extant Kanuri, Hausa, and Fulfulde manuscripts, written in modified Arabic script, date from the eighteenth century; diacritics were added, and a few letters altered, in order to represent sounds not found in Arabic. Hausa and Fulfulde works include religious and legal ones designed for a lay audience, and a wide range of poetry, including elegies of political and religious leaders. The Arabic meters were employed in both Fulfulde and Hausa, since all three languages share an opposition between long and short vowels and many opportunities for rhyme. In the Futa Jalon in present-day Guinea, where a majority of persons may have been able to read their native Fulfulde in Arabic script, folktales and humorous stories were also committed to writing. Manding- and Soninke-speaking scholars have always preferred to write in Arabic, but Manding transcribed in Arabic characters was used for correspondence, especially in the Gambia.

Major centers of learning in which Arabic was the exclusive or primary vehicle of written expression include the cities of Jenne and Timbuktu in present-day Mali, and those of the nomadic Moors (who speak an Arabic dialect as their native language) in present-day Mauritania and northern Mali. The Futa Jalon was a major center of Fulfulde composition, while both Fulfulde and Hausa were widely employed in the Sokoto caliphate (founded in the opening years of the nineteenth century in what is now northern Nigeria). Knowledge of both Arabic and Arabic-derived scripts was acquired in the Quranic schools, as these have been misleadingly called. While the first phase of the curriculum was largely restricted to reading, reciting, and copying the Quran, the second phase, which emphasized comprehension, consisted in in-depth study of Arabic works, representative of several branches of Islamic learning, through oral translation and explanation in the pupils' native languages, thus providing a significant example of the complex interrelationships among oral and written media in West Africa.

Use of *tifinagh* for transcribing Tamachek, the language of the Tuareg (themselves a branch of the Berber-speaking peoples, primarily localized in North Africa) goes back even further. This alphabet is derived from the Libyan ones attested since Carthaginian times and is known primarily from rock inscriptions but was also used for record-keeping and correspondence. It has not, however, been traditionally used for extended compositions, Arabic being preferred for this role. As with many of the alphabets of antiquity, its clearly separated letters could be written in any direction (vertically, from right to left or vice versa), without any spaces between words. There is some regional and dialectal variation as to the number, form, and phonetic values of the letters.

A considerable number of West African peoples have conventional systems of graphic signs. Very elaborate ones are found among the Manding, Dogon, and Bozo peoples of present-day Mali, and it has been hypothesized that these developed in part in emulation of Arabic writing. However, such systems are also found in areas where Muslim influence has been less strong, or is unlikely. Thus, among the Ashanti and other Akan-speaking peoples of Ghana and Côte d'Ivoire, where gold was of great political, economic, and symbolic significance, many goldweights bore signs that indicated their precise ponderal value; other signs corresponded to proverbs, while yet others represented concepts (for example, certain aspects of the Supreme Being). The *nsibidi* system of the Ekoi, Igbo, and Ibibio peoples of the Cross River area of present-day Nigeria used over a thousand signs to represent a considerable number of concepts as well as some sounds. *Nsibidi* was used to record court cases and convey complex messages, including warnings in wartime, and for summarizing folktales and personal narratives; its pictograms thus constituted a true writing system. As with the Malian systems of graphic signs, knowledge of *nsibidi* was often acquired within the initiation societies; but unlike the Malian ones, the *nsibidi* signs were often tattooed on the body or dramatically enacted through gesture. Rulers and leading personalities among the Yoruba of what is now southwestern Nigeria sent symbolic objects, consisting primarily of carefully arranged cowries, seeds, and other plant substances, to convey important messages. Although certain shell and plant configurations had conventional meanings, the symbolic objects were usually presented by one or more persons who also delivered an oral message.

The period immediately preceding the establishment of effective Western rule was characterized by the invention of at least one syllabary (system in which each symbol corresponds to a syllable rather than to a vowel or consonant), as well as at least one quasi-alphabetic form of writing. About 1833 a young man of the Vai people of present-day Liberia and Sierra Leone developed a syllabary for this Northern Mande language, after a celestial book was revealed to him in a dream. He may also have been inspired by the graphic signs in use among the Vai, as well as the syllabary—invented about a decade earlier—of the Cherokee Indians of North America, knowledge of which could have been conveyed to him by Christian missionaries. About 1896 King Njoya of the Bamum people of present-day Cameroon invented a pictographic system, following a dream, and elaborated it further with the help of his people. He revised this system several times, developing a number of calligraphic styles and progressively moving toward a syllabic and, ultimately, a nearly alphabetic system. Both Momolu Duwalu Bukele of the Vai and King Njoya of the Bamum were aware of Arabic and European writing, and both attempted to teach their inventions to children and adults in schools established for this purpose. The Vai syllabary was used primarily for correspondence. The Bamum system was used to compose a history of the kingdom, a law code, and a religious treatise, and in correspondence through the 1930s.

There is some measure of continuity between the precolonial writing systems and the ones used in West Africa today. New attempts to adapt the Arabic alphabet to African languages continue to be made in Muslim areas, sometimes with the backing of foreign-based or international organizations. *Tifinagh* has been computerized and has become a vehicle of literary revival in Berber-speaking areas of the Maghreb as well as among the Tuareg of the Saharan and Sudanic areas. The modified Latin scripts introduced by the British administration in order to transcribe Fulfulde and Hausa in northern Nigeria were based upon the adapted Arabic ones, still used concurrently with the now-dominant Latin-derived scripts. The Vai syllabary remained in extensive use at least through the 1970s and inspired or foreshadowed the invention of several syllabaries and alphabets by speakers of other West African languages in the 1920s to 1960s. Not only are many traditional symbolic systems still in use in rural areas, but they have inspired contemporary artists, catering to popular, elite, and international audiences, as well as industrial—especially textile—design.

TAL TAMARI

See also: **Futa Jalon; Songhay Empire.**

Further Reading

Dalby, D. *Africa and the Written Word*. Lagos: Afprint Nigeria, 1986.

Goody, J. "Restricted Literacy in Northern Ghana." In *Literacy in Traditional Societies,* edited by J. Goody. Cambridge: Cambridge University Press, 1968.

Griaule, M., and G. Dieterlen. *Signes graphiques soudanais* [Sudanese Graphic Signs]. Paris: Hermann, 1951.

Hiskett, M. *A History of Hausa Islamic Verse*. London: School of Oriental and African Studies, 1975.

Hunwick, J. O., et al. *Arabic Literature of Africa*. Vol. 2, *The Writings of Central Sudanic Africa*. Leiden: E. J. Brill, 1995.

Niangoran-Bouah, G. *The Akan World of Gold Weights*. 3 vols. Abidjan: Les Nouvelles éditions africaines, 1984, 1985, 1987.

Ould, E., S. Amar, and J. Johansen. *Handlist of Manuscripts in the Centre de Documentation et de Recherches Historiques Ahmed Baba, Timbuktu*. Vol. 1. London: Al-Furqan Islamic Heritage Foundation, 1995.

Wilks, I., "The Transmission of Islamic Learning in the Western Sudan." In *Literacy in Traditional Societies,* edited by J. Goody. Cambridge: Cambridge University Press, 1968.

Literacy: Vehicle for Cultural Change

Literacy was not new to Africa in the twentieth century. Several North African peoples, such as the peoples of ancient Egypt along the Nile River valley, the Nubians of the Eastern Sudan, and the Axumites of the Ethiopian highlands had their own forms of writing. In the case of Egypt, hieroglyphics were in use by 3300BCE. In Nubia and Ethiopia, the Meroitic and Ge'ez script were employed by the beginning of the Christian era.

The next major literary influence on the African continent was the Arabic language introduced with Islam in North Africa in the seventh century. Islam and the Arabic language spread to West Africa from the eleventh century, but Arabic only became a major influence on the East African coast after the eighteenth century. European languages next spread on the African continent. From the fifteenth century, as coastal-dwelling Africans came into more frequent contact with European traders, a few learned to read and write in such languages as French, Portuguese, and English. Olaudah Equiano and Ottabah Cugoano, for example, were slaves from West Africa who learned to read and write as slaves. They both gained their freedom in the late eighteenth century and wrote books condemning the Atlantic slave trade.

Many of the changes and possibilities literacy brought to Africa in these earlier times were echoed in the twentieth century as well: the creation of a literary elite, increased efficiency of state systems and tax collection, a universalistic legal system, and creation and adoption of state or regional religions. In most societies where literacy existed before the twentieth century, it was a skill possessed by relatively few. In Muslim Africa, for example, only a small number of boys attended Quranic school and advanced religious classes. It was not until the twentieth century that the majority of Africans lived in societies where literacy provided the foundation of their governments, religions, and long distance communication.

The agents who brought literacy to Africa in the precolonial and colonial century were missionaries, greatly aided by their African auxiliaries: teachers and catechists. The majority of Africans educated in the late nineteenth and early twentieth centuries were youth and young adults, mostly male. From their first days in Africa, missionaries began schools in order to teach Africans to read the Bible or the catechism. Frequently, they taught in the local language (except in French and Portuguese colonies) in order to facilitate pupils' learning to read and write. The products of these schools first became teachers, catechists, and low-level government employees. They earned a small salary paid in cash by the government or the mission that enabled them to acquire items costly in traditional African economies, such as cloth, salt, and sugar.

One of the factors that distinguished literacy education of the twentieth century from that of previous centuries was that, rather than pursuing religious education, many sought to learn to read and write for other reasons. Literacy began to be important for economic survival. Africans who wanted to read and have access to some of the power and knowledge possessed by their European masters needed to be literate. Africans often pushed missionaries to offer more education than they were currently providing and in some cases, like in Kikuyuland in Kenya in the 1930s, they established their own schools to meet the growing African demand for education.

Literacy brought several important changes to African societies. Educated Africans were in a position to negotiate and succeed in the emerging colonial order with its numerous regulations and new communication and transportation systems. Africans skilled in reading and writing became part of an emerging educated elite. The same education also brought conflict to African families. Because youth were educated far more often than their elders were, they were better equipped for the new economy. This heralded an alteration of power relations within gerontocratic African cultures. Finally, a school-going child's time and energy were now divided between school and family. Families had to cope with fewer young laborers and children were taught to expect a different adult life than that of their parents.

One of the consequences of writing and literacy was that written materials introduced foreign and irrelevant elements. In an oral society, what is spoken of, remembered, and transmitted is that which is relevant to the particular society. As Goody writes, "Oral cultures are highly localized" (1998: 168). But the training in reading and writing African students received paid little attention to the pupils' social context. Both the implicit and explicit curriculum of these schools introduced Africans to a new lifestyle that involved time schedules, strict discipline, uniforms, and an emphasis on individual achievement. In addition, the subject matter that was taught emphasized Western ideals such as Christianity and monogamous marriage. The stories that Africans read about in the Bible and in books on church and saints' history introduced them to worlds beyond their own. Little effort was made to teach aspects of indigenous cultures, so educated people were at once wise in the ways of the West and often ignorant of many of their own cultural traditions. The missionary and colonial emphasis on educating boys, often supported by African parents, created a significant gap between African men and women and the opportunities available to them in the colonial order. Men could be employed, women were expected to be farmers and to raise families. This education gap is still a problem for many African women.

With written expression comes the ability to look back on documents of the past and to observe changes through time, as well as the ability to critique records of the past. In colonial Africa, the very education offered by missionaries, and later colonial governments, became a tool in the hands of educated African men and women. Some, able to read the Bible for themselves, found discrepancies between the Holy Book and the actions and words of the missionaries, or found Christian mission spirituality lacking and founded their own churches. The Aladura church among the Yoruba of Nigeria and the Kimbanguist church of the Belgian Congo are two examples of African churches initiated by mission-educated men. In addition, educated African men organized trade unions and political organizations aimed at reforming the colonial system. Later in the colonial period, Africans used their knowledge of Western history and philosophy to fight for their own rights and freedoms. The French revolution, Marxist philosophy, and other historical traditions influenced African intellectuals. Freedom fighters in apartheid South Africa such as Nelson Mandela were influenced by events in Russia and communist ideas. John Africanus Horton, an educated West African, argued that just as the great kingdom of Rome was the result of a long historical process, the same achievements were possible in Africa. Introduction of literacy by Europeans thus enabled Africans to use European intellectual traditions to fight for religious and political equality.

Despite the many changes brought about by literacy, it is important to realize that literacy was but one of many forces introduced during the colonial period that instigated social change. Furthermore, literacy is still not universal and orality remains an important part of most African cultures. Oral historical traditions are still maintained, though now often influenced by written histories. Education, whether Koranic or state, also relies heavily on oral instruction. Literacy changed African families, religions, and governments, but it also continues to be mediated by long-standing cultural traditions of oral discourse.

KATHLEEN R. SMYTHE

See also: **Education; Religion, Colonial Africa: Missionaries.**

Further Reading

Burns, A. *The Power of the Written Word: The Role of Literacy in the History of Western Civilization.* New York: P. Lang, 1989.

Goody, J., ed. *Literacy in Traditional Societies*. Cambridge: Cambridge University Press, 1968.

Goody, J. "Literacy and the Diffusion of Knowledge across Cultures and Times." In *Creation and Transfer of Knowledge: Institutions and Incentives*, edited by G. B. Navaretti et al. Berlin: Springer-Verlag, 1998.

Graff, H. J. *Literacy in History: An Interdisciplinary Research Bibliography.* New York: Garland Published, 1981.

———. *The Labyrinths of Literacy: Reflections on Literacy Past and Present*, New York: Falmer Press, 1987.

Guy, J. "Making Words Visible: Aspects of Orality, Literacy, Illiteracy, and History in Southern Africa." *South African Historical Journal*. 31 (1994): 3–27.

Masemann, V. "The 'Hidden Curriculum' of a West African Girls' Boarding School." *Canadian Journal of African Studies*. 8, no. 3 (1974): 479–494.

Twaddle, M. "On Ganda Historiography." *History in Africa*. 1 (1974): 85–100.

Literature, Western: Africa in

Parataxis as a Narrative of Otherness

In European thought, Africa has remained the strange other, the resource, and, now, the market and experimental laboratory of European technology. Africa has been a textual, narrative, representational subject or "object-being" in European writing since antiquity. For Greco-Roman writers such as Herodotus, Diodorus, Philostratus, Pliny, and Aeschylus, Africa was both an expression, a symbol of physical, natural apartness, and the sign of difference itself. Herodotus was probably the first classical writer of substance to configure Africa within the rhetoric of parataxis, that is, within the tradition of placing things side by side. For Herodotus, the Africans of the Sahara were different from the Greeks because, unlike the Greeks, they had "wooly hair" and "their eyes in their breasts," and thus were "wild men and . . . wild women" (*The History*, Book II, chap. 191).

The same framing device was deployed by Diodorus Sicululs in whose works the Africans—the blacks, who lived in the hidden interior—were a savage folk, who had, Diodorus wrote, "flat noses and woolly hair . . . [were] extremely savage and display[ed] the nature of wild beast . . . [were] far removed as possible from human kindness . . . they present[ed] a striking contrast when considered in the light of our [Greek] customs" (*Works*, Book III, chap. 8).

These and other examples demonstrate the fact that it was in writing that Herodotus and Diodorus exercised a noncorporal power over Africa, and it was writing that endowed European thought with the power to name Africa, along with its material, spiritual, and cultural contents. Thus, Herodotus and Diodorus became speaking or writing subjects who transformed Africa into an object of writing, a construct of thought. The works in reference contain a considerable degree of desperation, inspired perhaps by the impatience of Herodotus and Diodorus with the distance of Africa, the farness of those Africans hidden in the interior, concealed from the observing, inspecting, probing, and inscribing gaze of the writers. The signification of Africa as the other enabled Herodotus and Diodorus to idealize Greek culture, to in fact elevate it over African culture. Invariably, writing allowed or enabled the two Greek writers to demarcate identity and difference, to impose a binary opposition between Greek and African essences, a dichotomy in which the Greeks were civilized, were as Diodorus puts it, "the light of our [Greek] customs" and the Africans were savages, "entirely savage and display the nature of a wild beast."

The Medieval Context: Framing the Heathen

The classical conception of Africa as "alien" and "wild" continued well into the medieval period. European cultural identity was discursively and ideologically sustained and dominated by theology, by Christian and Islamic thought specifically. Hence, much medieval writing about Africa took the form of what Mudimbe (1985) calls "missionary discourse." In this postulation, Africans were encoded as depraved pagans and infidels.

Missionary discourse required a stable convention of representation. Consequently, it made its object, the African, exist outside civil society and established normative values. It made him something other than man in the theological sense. In this way, "conversion" is coterminous with "representation"; mission is equated with technique. Inevitably, all Christian missionaries to Africa had first to write the "pagan" before "converting" his or her mind and space. This conception formed the nucleus of the ideology of civilizing or converting the native, and the root of slavery, imperialism, and colonization.

The Renaissance: Inscribing the Terra Nulla

The European Renaissance developed new observations and consolidated existing ones about Africa through the combined activities of travel writers, missionaries, and poets. From Vasco da Gama's 1415 voyage around the western coast of Africa, a new generation of writers (represented primarily by Antoine

Malfante and Alvise da Cadamosto) began to frame Africa as an exotic land, and its inhabitants and cultures as savage, alien, and malformed. Africa was also depicted as a source of great wealth that its natives had neglected to use for their own benefit.

The development of these conceptions coincided with a search for new sources of wealth and trade by the emerging European powers. It also coincided with the rise of a literate, urban-based reading public all over Western Europe. This reading public demanded to be entertained with sensational stories of strange and remote lands.

It was in the Renaissance literature of travel, as typified by the writings of Eannes de Azurara, Father Jerome Merolla de Sorrento, John Ogilby, and William Smith, that a distinctively modern European discourse of cultural identity and difference was born. With those writers, Africa was wild and unhistorical, and the dark skin of the "native" epitomized a universal antiaesthetic. Azurara, for example, wrote that it was legitimate to imprison and enslave Africans because they were not Christians, and had, unlike Europeans, no knowledge of bread and wine (84–85).

Yet such accounts of Africa in the early phase of modernity coexisted, rather contradictorily, with a romantic narrative of Africa's fabulous wealth, immense commercial and industrial potential, and, not infrequently, with fantastic details about African kings and nobility, who were inscribed as possessing great wealth, vast harems, powerful armies, and prestigious courts.

The Enlightenment: Encoding the Other

By the late eighteenth century, the height of the Enlightenment, Africa had become the sign of inherent, biologically given, racial inferiority. The experiences of colonial-plantation slavery, the slave trade, and formal colonialism were sustained and justified ideologically by pseudoscientific racism. Long, Linnaeus, Buffon, Hume, Locke, Cuvier, Blumenbach, Kant, and Hegel justified the degradation of black people on essentially racial grounds. These thinkers and writers also argued that blacks were fit only for manual (slave) labor. Racist ideology was the paradigmatic basis of the ideology of Europe's civilizing mission to the rest of the world.

The Enlightenment bequeathed to European writers on Africa a contradictory and contradicting discourse of reason, rational mastery of nature, a Promethean ideal of self-affirmation, "scientific" racism, racialist comparative anatomy, racial aesthetics, imperialist ideology, the rhetoric of progress and of the civilizing mission. This would be modified and mediated by Romantic ideology to produce what has variously been called "colonial discourse," "rhetoric of empire," and "imperialist ideology."

The Postenlightenment Heritage

The entrenchment of Enlightenment and Romantic discourses in, for example, Joseph Cornrad's *Heart of Darkness* (1899) and Andre Gide's *Travels in the Congo* (1929), meant the "fabrication" of a style of symbolizing Africa in which the enormous complexities of the continent are reduced to simple conventions or rhetorics of representation, such as "oddity," "savagery," or "darkness. Within this textual practice of representing Africa, the continent as a whole is rendered as a story, a narrative, a writable spatial and metaphysical configuration. But such writing was not only a mapping of territory preliminary to colonial mastery of it, but also the production of what Pratt calls "Europe's differentiated conceptions of itself in relation to something it became possible to call 'the rest of the world'" (1992, p.5).

Thus, "Africa" has been, since the fifteenth century at least, the "Other" against which "Europe" had had to define itself. As Conrad's Marlow shows, the European or Western writer could only think of Africans authoritatively or positively by silencing and negating the other identity; that is, could only think within the binary of civilized/savage, white/black, or Europe/Africa.

This, then, is the secret of Western representations of Africa: to dispel its own cultural anxieties (the threatening other), and to rationalize its own deep desire for order, Europe or the West needs a savage and exotic Africa to affirm its own identity; hence the Western writer's construction or framing of Africa as chaos, disorder, excess, and wildness. To this extent, the African represented in Western writing is only a code or a metaphor—in short a myth, a mere representational object, more the effect of poetic ordering than reality.

Postcolonial Trends

The rhetorics and discourses of "African" representation have survived African decolonization. In this context, it is useful to discuss briefly four European and American texts written within the tradition of Western literary representation of Africa, even after independence.

In his *Africa: A Biography of the Continent* (London: Hamish Hamilton, 1997), J. Reader encodes Africa as a mirror that reflects humankind's troubled "rites of passage." According to Reader, Africa is not only the ancestral home of humankind but also the center of today's tensions, civil wars, dislocations, and genocides. Reader's central texts are Conrad's *Heart of Darkness* and V. S. Naipaul's *A Bend in the River* (1980).

For Dervla Murphy, whose *South from the Limpopo: Travels through South Africa* (London: John Murray, 1998), was written after her 6,000-mile bicycle journey south of the Limpopo River, modern South Africa defies the binaries of white-black that had formed apartheid's metaphysics. Murphy herself shows great anxiety over the new South Africa. She even devotes a large space, for example, to demonstrating the capacity of the blacks for forgiveness in spite of the wrongs of apartheid.

In Western writing, the debasement of the other affirms the Western writer's mastery of form. A recent travel text by W. Langwiesche (*Sahara Unveiled: A Journey Across the Desert,* Pantheon Books, 1996) is written within this rhetorical frame. The book is an account of Timbuktu, an ancient city in the present day Republic of Mali. The author, an American, records his journey to Timbuktu, which he calls, with rhetorical verve, a city "long famous for being far away." For Langwiesche, the real, and perhaps the fictional Timbuktu is a "sleepy, sandy inglorious place, with only the faint traces of history to recommend it." Also, Timbuktu is, despite its function as an aesthetic metaphor of the exotic, a locale of roguish and unfaithful thieving natives, not worth the visit. Langwiesche is clearly retracing the footsteps of Mungo Park (1795–1797), Gordon Laing (who perished in the city in 1822), and Rene Caillie, who survived the journey and wrote a sensational account of it in 1830.

Langwiesche's narrative is a modernist version of Park's and Caillie's narrative of Timbuktu. In Langwiesche's text, the desert locale is harsh, forlorn, and politically hopeless. He restores order to it, as the literary critic might say, however, by fashioning, for the Western reader, an entertaining and edifying tale about the city itself. This is called superscription: the blanketing of the real object of writing all over it. The reader is told that Timbuktu was, or is, nothing but sooty-dark natives and crumbling walls. Much of the text registers its author's disappointment at not finding the fabled Timbuktu of the sixteenth century, where, says Langwiesche, "the ruling classes ate on plates of gold."

In 1988 Alex Shoumatoff, an American journalist, published *African Madness* (New York: Knopf), a collection of his journalism. One of the stories revolves around the author's search for the source of the HIV virus that causes AIDS. Shoumatoff journeys to the Ituri rain forest in the Congo, the setting for Stanley's *In Darkest Africa* (1890), Speke's *Journal of the Discovery of the Nile* (1863), Conrad's *Heart of Darkness* (1899), and Naipaul's *A Bend in the River* (1980). For Shoumatoff, Africa is the *locus classicus* of the apocalypse: hunger, disease, war, and death while for Stanley, Speke, Conrad and Naipaul, the African landscape is exotic, primal, and vegetative. As Shoumatoff nears the so-called AIDS epicenter, he finds whole villages devastated by AIDS; he sees poverty, hopelessness, and fear on the face of the country.

While Speke and Stanley walked in the African jungle, Shoumatoff mainly reports the cities, for he hears only "shrieks of madness and alienation" and nothing else in scores of Central African cities. Indeed Shoumatoff's is an updated version of Conrad's account of the Congo (1899).

Resistance

Although there is, as Achebe has argued, a "dominant image of Africa" in Western writing, dominant ideas or ideologies always bear an uncertainty: they are never monolithic, but crisis-ridden, marked by contradiction, ambiguity, and anxiety.

This only goes to show that there could be no integrated or unified vision of an alien culture or reality; that writing is multivalent and contradictory, for not only is signification itself racked by difference but also traversed by conflict, doubt, fissures, and indecision. Thus colonial discourse, imperialist ideology, or hegemonic representation is, as authority, incomplete.

However, "resistance" should not be seen as the automatic function of shifting signifiers: Western representations of Africa mask the silent inscription of the native informant or native presence. Representation is, and can only be, transitive. It is about something ontologically distinct, in spite of appearances to the contrary. In Western discourse, "knowledge" or "representation" could only be produced through interaction or negotiation with native informants or guides. Even in the so-called fictional texts, such as Conrad's *Heart of Darkness* or H. Rider Haggard's *King Solomon's Mines* (1885), "representation" amounts to no more than appropriating or configuring native ideas and presences as, and into, a story, a narrative/narrativized object.

However, the emergence of a postcolonial African literature written by Africans signifies the coming into being of an African perspective. Despite this ontological fact however, there are more question than answers: What form should African writing take? Should the African writer aspire to be the writing subject? Should African writing be a metaphor for Africa? Resistance is equally structured around ambiguities and as an ontological essence, Africa is yet to provide its own processes of self-regeneration distinguishable from Europe.

TANIMU ABUBAKAR

See also: **Achebe, Chinua; Colonialism Inheritance of: Postcolonial Africa; Colonialism: Impact on African Societies.**

Further Reading

Achebe, C. "An Image of Africa: Racism in Conrad's *Heart of Darkness.*" *Massachusetts Review.* 18, no. 4 (1977): 782–794. Reprinted in C. Achebe, *Hopes and Impediments.* London: Heinemann, 1988.

Azurara, *The Chronicle of the Discovery and Conquest of Guinea*. London, Hakluyt Society, 1896.
Eze, E. *Racism and the Enlightenment*. London: Routledge, 1997.
Forbes, V. S. *Pioneer Travelers of South Africa: A Geographical Commentary Upon Routes, Records, Observations, and Opinions of Travelers at the Cape, 1750–1800*. Cape Town: A. A. Boekemn, 1965.
Hammond, D., and A. Jablow. *The Africa That Never Was: Four Centuries of British Writing About Africa*. New York: Twayne Publishes, 1970.
Kenneh, K. "Africa and Cultural Translation: Reading Difference." In *Cultural Readings of Imperialism*, edited by K. Ansell-Pearson et al. New York: St. Martin's Press, 1997.
Loomba, A. *Colonialism/Post-Colonialism*. (esp. pp.57–193). London: Routledge, 1998.
Msiska, M., and P. Hyland, eds. *Writing and Africa*. London: Longman, 1997.
Parek, B. "The West and its Others." In *Cultural Readings of Imperialism*, edited by K. Ansell-Pearson, B. Parry, and J. Squires. New York: St. Martin's Press, 1997.
Park, M. *Travels into the Interior of Africa*. 1799.
Pratt, M. L. *Imperial Eyes: Travel Writing and Transculturation*, London: Routledge, 1992.
Said, E. *Culture and Imperialism*. New York: Vintage, 1993.
———. *Orientalism*. London: Routledge and Kegan Paul, 1978. (See the Second Edition with an Afterword by Said. New York: Vintage, 1995).
Snowden, F. M. *Blacks in Antiquity: Ethiopians in Greco-Roman Experience*. Cambridge, Mass.: Harvard University Press, 1970.
Spurr, D. *The Rhetoric of Empire: Colonial Discourse in Journalism, Travel Writing and Imperial Administration*. Durham, N. C.: Duke University Press, 1996.
Street, B. V. *The Savage in Literature: Representations of Primitive Society in English Fiction, 1858–1920*. London: Routledge and Kegan Paul, 1975.
Tiffin, C., and A. Lawson. *De-Scribing Empire*. (esp. pp.1–11; 230–235). London: Routledge, 1994.

Livingstone, David (1813–1873)

Scottish Missionary, Explorer, and Antislavery Propagandist

David Livingstone combined a deep Christian faith with a passionate interest in science. This passion, together with his faith, lasted all his life; his notebook kept in his last dying days contains passages of deep devotion together with careful drawings and notes of local plants and fish, as well as of the local language ciBemba.

In 1839 he was accepted by the London Missionary Society (LMS) and was given by them some basic theological training. In 1840 he was ordained as a minister and sailed to South Africa. He was stationed initially at Kuruman, the home of Robert Moffat, translator of the Bible into seTswana. He married Moffat's daughter Mary in 1845. While there, Livingstone deliberately spent months in the bush without European companions so as to learn seTswana thoroughly. In those early months, he became convinced that only Africans themselves could effectively propagate Christianity in Africa, an opinion not held by Moffat. Two other things became clear to him as he settled into mundane mission station work at Mabotsa, Chonuane, and then Kolobeng. The first was that he was not cut out for such work. The second was that he was called to open the way into the interior for Christianity and commerce, the twin influences that he believed would bring Africa into "the corporate body of Nations" (*Missionary Travels*, p.28). The route from the Cape was too difficult for regular communications, so a new route had to be found. Having been bitterly criticized for taking his family with him on his earlier treks to the north, which had earned him some fame as a cartographer, he felt that it would be best for them now to go back to Scotland.

In 1851 while in Cape Town to see the family off, he wrote several attacks on British policy in the Cape, defending the Xhosa and the so-called Hottentot rebels in their war with the Cape Colony, an episode ignored or passed over by his many biographers. Meanwhile his African friend Sechele and his bKwena at Kolobeng had been attacked by the Transvaalers, and Livingstone's house and property had been destroyed. Undaunted he set off for the north and reached Linyanti, the maKololo capital in modern Barotseland, in October 1853, where he was well received. It was with subsidies of men and supplies from the maKololo that he set off on his *Viagem contra Costa* (march from coast to coast). He and his maKololo arrived at Loanda on May 31, 1854. Portuguese slaving rendered this route unacceptable, so they marched back to Linyanti and on down to Quelimane on the East Coast, arriving on May 20, 1856. He was the first European to see *Mosi oa Tunya*, the immense falls on the Zambesi that he named after Queen Victoria. Livingstone was convinced the Zambesi was to

David Livingstone. © Das Fotoarchiv.

be the Mississippi of central Africa. He left his companions, with Portuguese consent, at Quelimane, promising to return and go back with them to Linyanti; he then sailed for the England where he was received as a hero.

In Britain he published his *Missionary Travels and Researches,* which sold seventy-thousand copies, thus ensuring financial security for him and his family. His many lectures produced a new public interest in Africa but only one practical outcome, the creation of the Universities Mission to Central Africa (UMCA).

In 1858 he accepted an appointment from the British government to head an expedition to the Zambesi valley to map the area and open it up to international trade. He discovered the Cabora Bassa rapids, which he had unwittingly bypassed on his first journey. He turned to the Shire valley, and what is now Malawi, as the area of potential for Christianity and commerce. The massive increase in both Swahili and Portuguese slaving in the area made his plans seemingly impossible, however, and caused the UMCA to withdraw and the government to close the expedition. Poor relations between Livingstone and most of the European staff, and the deaths of Bishop Mackenzie, the UMCA leader, and Mary Livingstone added to the disaster.

From 1864 through 1865 he was in Britain, campaigning tirelessly to provoke international action to end the East African slave trade. Some influential people still trusted his judgment enough to support his return to Africa to seek the headwaters of the Congo and the Nile and to report on the slave trade, his obsessive concern until his death. From January 1866 Livingstone was back in Africa, where he wandered over northern Mozambique, Malawi, eastern Zambia, western Tanzania, and the eastern Congo. At times he had paid African porters and, as with the European staff of the Zambesi expedition, his relations with them broke down. During these years he became the focus of intense interest in America and Europe, particularly when H. M. Stanley's well-publicized expedition "found" him in 1871. A small group of African friends were loyal to him to the end. When he died, they buried his heart on May 1, 1873, and carried his eviscerated body to the coast.

After his state funeral in Westminster Abbey, a great number of books and pamphlets published over the course of the next forty years transformed Livingstone into the patron saint of the European conquest of Africa, a position far removed from his original stance as one who hoped to bring Africa into "the corporate body of Nations."

ANDREW C. ROSS

See also: **Europe: Explorers, Adventurers, Traders; Missionary Enterprise: Precolonial.**

Biography

David Livingstone was born on March 19, 1813, in Blantyre, Lanarkshire, into a Gaelic-speaking family that had moved to the Lowlands only one generation before. While working in the local mill he completed his school education to university entrance, which allowed him to enter what is now Strathclyde University in 1836 to study both science and medicine, continuing to work in the mill for four months of the year. He and his family were members of an Independent chapel. In 1839 he was accepted by the London Missionary Society. He continued his medical training in London, returning to Scotland to qualify as a physician through the Faculty of Physicians and Surgeons of Glasgow in 1840. In 1840 he was ordained as a minister and sailed to South Africa. He married Mary Moffat in 1845. In 1871 he was "found" by Stanley's expedition. He died in 1873.

Further Reading

Holmes, T. *Journey to Livingston: Exploration of an Imperial Myth.* Edinburgh: Canongate Press, 1993.
Jeal, T. *Livingstone,* London: Heinemann, 1973.
Livingstone, D. *Missionary Travels and Researches in South Africa.* London: John Murray, 1857.
Livingstone, D., and C. Livingstone. *Narrative of an Expedition to the Zambesi and Its Tributaries.* London: John Murray, 1865.
Parsons, J. W. *The Livingstones at Kolobeng 1847–1852.* Gaberone: Botswana Society and Pula Press, 1997.
Seaver, G. *David Livingstone: His Life and Letters.* London: Lutterworth Press, 1957.
Shepperson, G. "Livingstone and the Years of Preparation 1813–1857." In *Livingstone: Man of Africa,* edited by B. Pachai. London: Longman, 1973.

Loango: Slave Trade

The coast and immediate inland areas north of the Zaire River were occupied by fishers and then by farming people during the first millennium BCE. Iron working made its appearance in the region by 400BCE and quickly replaced the use of stone tools at many sites. The archaeological complex of Kayes and Madingo-Kayes, dating from around 100CE to 400CE, can be seen as an early complex society, with settlements of varying size and complexity, regional exchanges, and uniform material culture.

However, it is not until the twelfth or thirteenth century that the pottery styles typical of historic periods appeared, and there is a significant gap in our limited knowledge of the development of the population.

The people of the northern region probably spoke dialects of the Kikongo language, which was also spoken further south in the large and powerful kingdom of Kongo. The northern people had possibly spoken them for centuries before the arrival of the Europeans in the late fifteenth century.

The earliest travelers to the region made no mention of the kingdom of Loango, although its two southern neighbors, Kakongo and Ngoyo, are mentioned in Kongo documents of 1535. It was not until the 1570s that Portuguese documents from Angola mention a kingdom of Loango, after which date a regular trade emerged between the newly established Portuguese colony and the northern kingdom, initially mostly in copper and ivory, though in the 1620s occasionally there were also slaves among the exports of Loango. Although the earliest account says that the king of Loango was once a vassal of Kongo, by 1580 he was simply a "friend," Kongo documents do not claim lordship over the country at any point in the sixteenth century.

Modern traditions trace large population movements into the region without offering chronological specificity, and some historians have seen in these an origin in the fourteenth century, about the same time as Kongo, with Loango being an initially subordinate part of a large Kongo federation. But the documentary records suggest that the kingdom was of later date. A seventeenth-century description and account of history does not suggest great antiquity and describes the many wars and battles required to bring the various provinces, many of which were formerly independent, into a single rule.

The earliest descriptions of the kingdom in the early seventeenth century divide it into several central districts, ruled by members of the royal family, and outlying conquests that were ruled by older, well-established local dynasties. Loango also seems to have dominated the old coastal states of Ngoyo and Kakongo, although never quite reducing their sovereignty. There was, in addition, a royally appointed set of officials in all areas performing bureaucratic and administrative functions. In the 1610s and 1620s the royal provinces were ruled by close kinsmen—brothers and sisters' children—who were to succeed the king and rotate their provinces. The king who died in 1624 was in fact succeeded by the ruler of the district of Kaye, in accordance with these arrangements. If the kingdom was founded primarily by conquest originating, according to a seventeenth century account, from the small state of Nzari on the river Zaire, and if the king of 1624 had really ruled sixty years, as an account written of his death indicate, it is quite possible he was the founder of Loango. Even allowing for a longer development, the rotation system might have been this king's own expedient.

In any case, the king ruling in 1663 decided to become a Christian (baptized as Afonso) and had to head off a rebellion from a "cousin" because of it. He was killed in rebellion, although the throne passed, perhaps irregularly to another ruler of the royal family, though not without a lengthy civil war. The king who died about 1700 was not immediately succeeded by anyone, but instead a long regency ensued, led by his "queen mother"—not a biological mother, but a woman chosen by the king during his reign to be a coregent with special powers to govern succession. Earlier sources mention the queen mother as an honored member of the administration.

These alterations of central government may have allowed some of the officials to gain both hereditary control of their offices and to accumulate personal wealth. Loango became a much bigger exporter of slaves during the late seventeenth century, and it is likely that some of the wealth of this trade was taken in by wealthy officials, especially if royal power was slackened by succession struggles and interregna. Shipping records and fragmentary accounts suggest the emergence of a powerful class of people who owed their status more to commercial wealth and less to the state.

Some of these people were heads of merchant organizations involved in long distance trade. Loango merchants developed the custom of traveling long distances to reach markets first pioneered in the copper trade. The main mines were in the Niari valley and surrounding areas, located across the mountains of Mayombe in area not under Loango sovereignty. The practices and organization of the copper trade made Loango well conditioned to participate in the long distance slave trade. Much of Loango's slave trade came not from within its territory or even its neighbors but from more distant inland kingdoms such as the Mpumbo region and especially Kongo and the Angola region. Merchants from Loango, known outside their country as "Mubilis," traveled in caravans and established bases in these distant places, and delivered slaves from those areas to Dutch, English, and then French merchants established at Loango, and its two southern neighbors, Ngoyo and Kakongo. These two latter states seem to have gained considerable independence as Loango became weaker.

By the end of the eighteenth century the central power of Loango was much compromised by the emergence of wealthy brokers and officials who purchased their offices and enjoyed considerable independence, though the powers of the king were still quite strong. Kings seem to have still retained power over their administration, in spite of their greater independence.

JOHN K. THORNTON

See also: **Kongo, Teke (Tio), and Loango: History to 1483; Kongo Kingdom.**

Further Reading

Martin, P. *The External Trade of the Loango Coast, 1576–1870: The Effects of Changing Commerical Relations on the Vili Kingdom of Loango.* Oxford,1972.

Vansina, J. (with T. Obenga). "The Kongo Kingdom and Its Neighbours." In *General History of Africa,* edited by B. A. Ogot. Vol. 5 of 8 vols. UNESCO, 1981–1992.

Lomé

Lomé is not the oldest town in Togo, but today it is the most important urban center, as much for its political, administrative, and economic functions as for its cultural functions. It is one of the sea gates of Africa, with a deepwater port that has made it a transit point for Togo's landlocked neighbors in the Sahel. According to the most recent estimates, as of the year 2000 Lomé and its periphery together had around 1 million inhabitants.

Lomé's singularity stems from the fact that, unlike the majority of the capital cities of African countries, it is neither a city of strictly colonial origin nor an ancient, precolonial city. It is one of the few capital cities in the world that are located on a border with a neighboring country, in this case Ghana; and it has been marked by three successive waves of colonization: German, British, and then French.

In effect, it has been founded twice. To begin with, there were two traditional villages, Bè and Amoutivé, which had their origins in the seventeenth century, with the dispersal of the Ewe from their original city, Notsé, around 100 kilometers from the coast. Today, the Ewe are spread across three countries: Togo, Ghana, and Benin. The Bè and the Amoutivé, the traditional landowners of Lomé, contented themselves with their small village on the littoral of a lagoon (part of a Quaternary formation extending along a large part of the coast of West Africa, from Côte d'Ivoire to Nigeria, with some zones of interruption and some very large areas that effectively constitute lakes). The inhabitants of Lomé turned their backs on the sea, making their living from fishing in the lagoon and from cultivating the soil of the sandbar, known as Tokoin, that lies to the north of the lagoon.

The second and more decisive foundation of Lomé was due to the arrival of more migrants. Some belonged to the Anlo, another branch of the Ewe that had previously been settled farther to the west; some were Guin from Aného; and others were of diverse origins, notably a group from Sierra Leone descended from Afro-Brazilians who had returned to the African coast at the start of the nineteenth century. The special feature of this second wave of occupants of the site of Lomé was that it essentially comprised African merchants who participated in both the Atlantic trade and the trade among Africans themselves. They were thus intermediaries between the coast and the lands of the interior, to which they sent products unloaded from seagoing vessels. At a later stage, around the beginning of the 1880s, these merchants came from the west to the site of "Bey beach" (as the Bè littoral is called on old maps). Their migration followed the decisive victory of the British over the Ashanti kingdom in 1874 and the gradual extension of British colonization to the east. One of the consequences of these events was that the British became determined to control the coastal trade by levying taxes on the Anlo, and other merchants, in Kéta and their other dependencies. Thus it was that the merchants came to be established, first at Denu and Aflawu, and then at Lomé.

However, the name "Lomé" derives from the tradition of the first inhabitants, who settled at a site where the presence of shrubs known as *alo* gave rise to the name *alo-mé* ("among the *alo*"), and this became Lomé. Despite the later development of the city, the inhabitants of the old Bè villages retained their traditions. For them, the most important place was still the sacred forest of Bè, the sanctuary of the god Nyigblin, a factor in the religious unity of most of the Ewe on this section of the coast (see Etou, 2001).

It is undeniable that the development and the attractiveness of Lomé arose from its function as a cosmopolitan city, where tradition and modernity cohabited in harmony. The development of trade after 1881 compelled the German colonial authorities to make the city into the capital of their colony of Togo in 1897. Since then, the construction of an administrative district covering 150 hectares, alongside the old merchant districts, the epicenter of the city, where several commercial firms of diverse national origins became established.The gradual extension of the urban periphery, above all in the aftermath of World War II, led to the birth of the megalopolis of Lomé, which now covers around 15 square kilometers.

Its function as a capital city has made Lomé the most important economic center in the country, as well as the site of numerous challenges to the political order. It was in Lomé that, in January 1933, a riot by women set the pattern for the opposition to the French colonial order, in particular over the issue of taxation. This tradition of opposition was also maintained throughout the course of the long struggle for the independence of Togo, which was proclaimed on April 27, 1960. On October 5, 1990, Lomé was also the locale for violent demonstrations against the government, which was accused of violating human rights.

Lomé's principal advantages remain its infrastructure of hotels; its port; its rich and colorful culture; and its very diverse architectural heritage, ranging from the traditional to the modern and taking in a mixed historical legacy that includes Gothic (the Catholic cathedral, built during the era of German rule), "tropicalized" Classical, and Afro-Brazilian. The warmth of Lomé's welcome begins with the permanent smile of the Togolese, and the charm of the women selling goods in the great markets of Lomé, which today have been left by the famous "Nana-Benz" to the "Nanettes." Private houses, usually surrounded by walls that are made of painted cinder blocks in varied colors, and are often relatively low, can be seen everywhere in the city, except in the old commercial districts, which are being reconstructed. Given the mode of individual ownership of land, allied with both traditional and modern practices, there is practically no spatial discrimination within each district.

Despite political problems, and the partial degradation of infrastructure, since the 1990s, the city of Lomé has not lost its charm, and its people still recall the city's history, symbolized by the many vestiges of the past in its everyday life. Lomé, a city at a crossroads, has lent its name to the series of four "Lomé conventions," the agreements between the European Union and the group of African, Caribbean, and Pacific (ACP) countries, which were all signed there.

N. Adovi Goeh-Akue

Further Reading

Gayibor, N. L., ed. *Histoire des Togolais.* Lomé: Presses de l'UB, 1997.

Lomé Conventions, The

The Treaty of Rome (March 25, 1957) contained in its fourth part specific clauses for the "association" of the newly created European Community with overseas territories, which at that time were mainly French colonies. These clauses aimed at endorsing their trade capabilities and promoting their development. They envisaged trade agreements (privileged access to the European market for overseas products) and financial help (through the European Development Fund). Specific points were defined in a convention that was attached to the treaty and was supposed to last for five years (1958–1963). During that period, most of the countries concerned became independent. However, they agreed to renew the convention on a contractual basis.

This convention was signed in Yaoundé in July 1963 between the six states of the European Community and eighteen states from Africa and Madagascar, for a duration of five years (and was renewed for an other five years in July 1969: Yaoundé II). Former clauses were preserved, but joint institutions were set up to allow the newly independent countries to take part in the administration of the association.

With the enlargement of the European Community in 1972, and especially with Great Britain joining, new countries (former British colonies) came to be part of the association. A new convention was signed in Lomé in February 1975 between nine European states and forty-six African, Caribbean, and Pacific (ACP) states. The number of countries affiliated with the convention has increased since then; seventy-two Third World countries are now associated. The convention has been renewed in 1979 (Lomé II), 1984 (Lomé III), 1989 (Lomé IV), and 1995 (Lomé IV). During that time new organizations and sources of assistance have been devised, and old ones have been improved.

The European Development Fund has become one of the most important of these sources and has maintained its specificity compared to other international sources of funding. It gives donations rather than loans. Projects have to be prepared and proposed by the associated countries themselves and then adopted by the fund, which finances and controls their implementation. The fields it covers have been extended. The first fund, which was set up in 1959, was mainly concerned with investments in social and economic infrastructures (especially communication routes). The priorities of the second fund (1963) were extended to include rural development. Technical assistance was also added to help the ACP states prepare and implement their projects. Since 1975 more emphasis has been put on industrial development.

The Lomé conventions (I and II) attempted to strike a balance between financial aid and the needs of the ACP states given their varied degree of development. This was made possible through a diversification in the kinds of financial aid granted. More attention was focused on the less developed countries. At the same time, these conventions asked the ACP states to assume greater responsibility in the implementation of projects, which led to an increased decentralization in the administration of the Fund. In 1975 new schemes and tools were set up, such as compensatory financing schemes including the Stabex, a system meant to stabilise the export incomes of the ACP states. It protects states against possible loss in their export incomes due to natural disaster or price collapse. Lomé II introduced another system, the Sysmin, which focused specifically on mined products. Through a similar scheme of financial aid, it allows the ACP states to keep their mines working when the incomes from these mines are and threatening production.

All such plans have made the European development scheme quite unique. However, its efficiency has remained inconsistent, and opinions vary on the matter. The last Lomé conventions (Lomé III and IV) envisaged new mechanisms for control in order to increase efficiency. They proposed improved coordination between European actions and the policies followed by each ACP state, more consideration for local cultures when devising or considering proposals, and for the preservation of the global environment. They encouraged the ACP states to set up a more secure institutional environment for attracting private investments.

Since Lomé IV, democratization has been considered as a condition for further aid. Previously, the conventions worked under the premise of giving aid regardless of the political regime and status of the ACP state in question. Lomé II only referred to the respect due to "human dignity." Lomé III mentioned "human rights" but without providing further precision. Lomé IV clearly meant human rights as defined by the United Nations (including political rights). It placed the matter in the chapter titled "Aims and Principles of Cooperation." This emphasizes a new focus on the connections between aid, political development, and economic efficiency.

VÉRONIQUE DIMIER

Further Reading

Edye, D., and V. Lintner. *The Lomé IV Convention: New Dawn or Neo-colonialism.* London: University of North London Press, 1992.

Long, F. *The Political Economy of ECC Relations with Africa, Caribbean and Pacific States: Contribution to the Understanding of the Lomé Convention on North/South Relations.* Oxford: Pergamon, 1980.

Ravenshill, J. *Collective Clientism: The Lomé Convention and North/South Relations.* New York: Columbia University Press, 1985.

Stevens, C., ed. *EEC and the Third World: A Survey: Renegotiating Lomé.* London: Medder and Stoughton, 1984.

Lozi Kingdom and the Kololo

The origins of the Luyi or Aluyana, as the Lozi people were originally called, are carefully concealed in myths designed to maintain the prestige and selectiveness of the ruling dynasty. "Luyi" or "Aluyana" means "people of the river." According to myth, the Lozi came from Nyambe (the Lozi name for God). This myth of origin implies that they were indigenous, not immigrants, to the western province of Zambia. The Lozi myth is believed to have expressed an important truth because in the Lozi society, where the dynasty originated from mattered less than the nature of the land they colonized. However, historical evidence suggests that the Lozi came from the Lunda Empire. Consequently, the Lozi kingdom developed an imperial structure similar to other kingdoms that had a similar background. The kingdom was favored by a relatively prosperous valley environment that facilitated dense settlement of the people.

Once the kingdom had been founded, it had a special economic base that consisted of fertile plains of about hundred miles long which were flooded by the Zambezi River every year. The kingdom, also generally known as Barotseland, accommodated peoples of clear distinct origin and history as opposed to the true Lozi who occupied the flood plain. These peoples lived in the surrounding woodland.

The Lozi kingdom was founded in seventh century by people believed to have come from the Lunda Empire to the north. It is also believed that the newcomers introduced intensive cultivation of the flood plain. By 1800 various peoples to the west were brought under Lozi rule while to those to the east and west paid tribute in form of labor. The flood plain was mainly administered by relatives of the king in the early days of the dynasty. Later some kind of royal bureaucracy—an unusual development anywhere in Africa—replaced the earlier system. This was possible because of the plain, which made demand for control a matter of political control as well. As guardian of the land, the king built up a following of loyal officials who he allocated states on the plain. The system enabled Lozi kings to make political appointments on the basis of personal merit instead of birth. As such any such appointees could lose both office and land allotted to them if they fell out of favor. Trade also developed between the various peoples in the region.

Trade in fish, grain, and basket work for the iron work, woodwork, and barkcloth made Barotseland fairly self-sufficient. The Lozi also raided the Tonga and the Ila for cattle and slaves. However, the Lozi did not participate in the slave trade because they needed to retain slaves themselves to perform manual labor in the kingdom. The control of trade made the Litunga more powerful in his kingdom. Through his *Indunas*, the Litunga was able to have almost total control of the economy of the Lozi kingdom.

Following the Mfecane (a series of migrants set in motion by Shaka Zulu's empire in South Africa), the Kololo were forced to move north to the Zambezi River. In 1845 the Kololo leader Sebitwane found the Lozi kingdom split by succession dispute following the death of the tenth Litunga Mulambwa in 1830. The succession dispute resulted into a civil that split the Lozi kingdom into three groups. Sebitwanes warriors quickly overrun the Lozi kingdom. The Kololo imposed their language on the Lozi, although their conquest was hardly disruptive. As a small group of nomad warriors who had turned into herders and not cultivators, they found the Lozi to have been well established. Their language became a unifying influence in the kingdom. Soon Kololo kingship became far more popular in style than that offered by the Lozi. Unlike his predecessor, the Kololo king was more of a war-captain and was freely accessible to his fellow warriors. This was unlike the Lozi Litunga who was surrounded by rituals and taboos, and hence kept secluded. Because of this, Kololo kings were liked and easily accepted by most Lozi subjects. Sebitwane won the loyalty of his subject people by giving them cattle, taking wives from various groups and even giving leaders conquered people important positions of responsibility. He treated both the Kololo and Lozi generously.

However, despite this apparent popularity, the Kololo kings failed to come to terms with the special circumstances of Barotseland. They therefore made their capitals to the south of the central plain, among marshes that they considered secure from their traditional adversaries, the Ndebele, to their south.

The kololo did not disrupt the economic system of the Lozi, which was based on mounds and canals of the flood plain. However, the political system of the Kololo was very different from that of the Lozi. In the Kololo political system, men who were of the same age as the king were made territorial governors. Initially, this ensured that the flow of tribute to the king's court. The system did not, however, guarantee the continued operating system of the flood plain.

The Lozi kingdom was prone to malaria and had eventually developed an immunity to the disease. The Kololo, however, were not immune, and were often afflicted with the disease. This greatly undermined the Kololo ability to resist the Lozi when the latter rose against their conquerors. The various Lozi princes who had escaped and fled from Kololo invasion had taken refuge to the north. Among them was Sepopa.

Following the death of Sebitwane in 1851, he was succeeded by weak rulers. His son Sekeletu was not as able a ruler as his father. He died in 1863 after which Kololo rule declined completely. The Lozi and the Toka-Leya, who had also been under Kololo rule, rose against the Kololo and declared themselves independent. The Kololo did not put up any serious resistance because they were terribly divided.

In 1864 Sepopa raised a Lozi army that took advantage of malaria-afflicted Kololo and successfully defeated it. Sepopa revived the Lozi institutions, but the problem of royal succession resurfaced, and it remained a source of weakness for the revived Lozi kingdom. Consequently, Sepopa was overthrown in 1878. For two years instability reigned until 1878 when Lewanika became king of the Lozi as Litunga. He too continued to have difficulties retaining his position as king. He was constantly under threat of attack from the Ndebele in the south. This relationship with the Ndebele forced Lewanika to take a friendly attitude toward European visitors to his kingdom.

BIZECK J. PHIRI

See also: **Difaqane on the Highveld; Lewanika I, the Lozi and the BSA Company; Tonga, Ila, and Cattle.**

Further Reading

Flint, E. "Trade and Politics in Barotseland During the Kololo Period." *Journal of African History.* 2, no. 1 (1970): 72–86.

Langworthy, H. W. *Zambia Before 1890: Aspects of Precolonial History.* London: Longman, 1972.

Mainga, M. "The Lozi Kingdom." In *A Short History of Zambia*, edited by B. M. Fagan. 2nd ed. Nairobi: Longman, 1968.

Muuka, L. S. "The Colonisation of Barotseland in the 17th Century." In *The Zambesian Past*, edited by E. Stokes and R. Brown. Manchester: Manchester University Press, 1966.

Roberts, A. *A History of Zambia.* London: Heinemann, 1976.

Smith, E. W. "Sebetwane and the Makololo." *African Studies.* 15, no. 2 (1956): 49–74.

Luanda

The capital city of Angola is situated in the northwest of the country on the coast, where a natural deepwater port is its primary economic *raison d'être*. The harbor has approximately four square miles suitable for ships to berth.

The Portuguese explorer Paulo Dias de Novais (grandson of the famous navigator Bartholmeu Dias) founded the city in 1575, becoming its first governor. Local Mbundu peoples inhabited the area before the arrival of the Portuguese settlers who established a permanent presence on the coast. The Ndongo kingdom was located inland from Luanda island, which protected the bay. Its king was called Ngola, from which the name Angola was derived. The area was originally under the influence of the Kingdom of Kongo. Tax was paid to the king in cowrie shells and the city's name originates from the local word for "tax," which was *loanda*. It later became known as Sao Paulo de Luanda. The Ngola withdrew his influence from the Kingdom of the Kongo, forming a temporary alliance with the Portuguese. Portugal's presence was reinforced when the imposing Sao Miguel fortress was built on a hill next to Luanda island, which is now an isthmus following twentieth century construction work. The fortress remains a dominant feature of the city and was turned into a museum of the revolution soon after independence, while still retaining a security function. After the Portuguese military base was established, a century of warfare followed before the Ndongo kingdom was subjugated.

Luanda acted as a refueling and restocking station for Portuguese and other merchant fleets, but the main economic impetus for its growth came from the slave trade, which lasted for almost four centuries. As early as 1627, the settlement became the center of the Portuguese colonial administration and a base from which missionary expansion could take place. The Portuguese colony of Brazil provided a heavy demand for Angolan slaves. The Portuguese Crown received a tax for every slave exported and successive governors had an effective license to enrich themselves as long as they delivered the tax to Lisbon.

Tensions frequently existed between colonists and the governor and would occasionally erupt over the relative distribution of the rewards of the slave trade. Hence, in 1666 the new governor arrived from Brazil, only to depart again soon thereafter on the same ship, when the colonists revolted. Given the prevailing slave trade links, Angola was more a colony of Brazil than of Portugal. Indeed, immediately following the 1822 revolt of the Brazilian colonists against the Portuguese crown, there was a mutiny of troops in Luanda. Strong cultural links to Brazil remain to the present, with Luanda's elite more influenced by Europe and the Americas rather than by Southern African neighbors.

The Portuguese settlers in Luanda were essentially traders and soldiers. Many were convicted criminals deported to the colonies, and they were commonly known as *degradados*. By the mid-nineteenth century, 1,466 whites out of an overall white presence in the colony of 1,832 were located in Luanda. There were only 156 white women and a growing group of "mixtos," or mixed race people, numbering 5,759. The remainder of the population of the colony was black slaves (86,000) and free blacks (300,000).

Luanda was to develop a profound Creole culture, which remains apparent to the present day. Essentially this was a blend of Mbundu, Portuguese, and Brazilian influences. This Creole culture of the elite tended to create a sense of superiority toward the predominantly "Bantu" interior. It has fuelled discontent in the provinces, a factor heightened by the civil war that took place in the final quarter of the twentieth century between the MPLA government based in Luanda and the UNITA opposition. Luanda is seen as being privileged, while the provinces feel a sense of neglect.

The massive growth of Luanda only occurred in the twentieth century, especially in the final decades. It became the jewel in the Portuguese colonial African crown by the middle of that century. The enormous natural resource wealth of Angola was primarily channeled for export from the port of Luanda with some of the trading wealth accruing to the city. The Luanda railway, the oldest in the country, first became operational in 1901 and expanded thereafter, along with road transportation routes to the interior. In the colonial era these developments facilitated coffee, cotton, diamond, and salt production, which became the principal exports replacing the slave trade. What was to transform Luanda profoundly was the discovery of petroleum in 1955. A major oil refinery was built in the northern part of the bay of Luanda. A massive cement factory was also constructed. Other industries developed, primarily to meet the needs of the white settler population, which greatly expanded in the third quarter of the twentieth century. After a slow start, by the mid-1970s oil replaced coffee as the principal export revenue generator.

After independence the Luandan government became overwhelmingly dependent on oil revenues as domestic agricultural and industrial production collapsed. From the country being a food exporter prior to independence, Luanda now became heavily dependent upon food imports. This increased the relative isolation of Luanda from the rest of the country, as it became financially dependent not on its trade links to the interior, but on off-shore oil revenues.

By the beginning of the twenty-first century, Luanda was a vast sprawling city, home to approximately one-third or more of the country's population. The city has grown literally out of control in terms of residential development. A key feature of the city is the principal informal market place, arguably the largest in Africa, north of the city and named after a popular Brazilian soap opera watched avidly in the early years of Angolan television. The downtown port area retains some magnificent colonial architecture, notably the Central Bank along with a ribbon of modern high-rise offices, including the university, as well as residential apartments. Immediately inland and climbing up the hillside are commercial, administrative, and relatively affluent housing and then there spreads out an enormous mass of makeshift housing, built from cement blocks, with zinc roofs, in various states of disrepair which the poor inhabit.

The overriding impression of Luanda is of urban services entirely swamped by uncontrolled population expansion. Hundreds of thousands of internally displaced persons, because of the war, flooded into the relative safety of the capital, swelling the already high natural urban population increase. The massive exodus of whites at independence represented a huge drain of management and technical expertise. Black education had been sorely neglected and service provision began to deteriorate, although new opportunities opened up for access to health and education services previously denied to the black population. Water, sanitation, and refuse collection is vastly overloaded. Markets are unsanitary, health and education facilities are stretched to breaking point other than those provided for the small, wealthy political and business elite which is interconnected. The greatest problems facing the city are providing clean water and effective sanitation and waste disposal services. All of the city's problems come together in the Bay of Luanda, which is dangerously polluted. Much of the city's waste is eventually deposited there, ships in the port discharge oil and other pollutants. Since the island of Luanda became connected to the mainland, this interrupted the tidal flow that helped in the past to flush out the pollution from the bay, albeit not entirely effectively.

BARRY MUNSLOW

See also: **Angola.**

Further Reading

Bender, G. *Angola Under the Portuguese: The Myth and the Reality*. London: Heinemann, 1978.
Birmingham, D. *Trade and Conflict in Angola: The Mbundu and their Neighbours under the Influence of the Portuguese 1483–1790*. Oxford: Clarendon Press, 1966.
Clarence-Smith, W. *The Third Portuguese Empire*. Manchester: Manchester University Press, 1985.
Davidson, B. *In the Eye of the Storm: Angola's People*. London: Longman, 1972.
de Andrade, H. D. P. Women, Poverty, and the Informal Sector in Luanda's Peri-Urban Areas. Luanda: Development Workshop, 1994.
Duffy, J. *Portugal in Africa*. London and Baltimore: Penguin Books, 1961.
Heimer, F. W. *Social Change in Angola*. Munich: Weltforum Verlag, 1973.
Marcum, J. *The Angolan Revolution*. 2 vols. Cambridge: MIT Press, 1969–1978.
Newitt, M. *Portugal in Africa: The Last Hundred Years*. London, 1981.
Wheeler, D. L., and R. Pélissier. *Angola*. London: Pall Mall Press, 1971.

Luba: Origins and Growth

Speaking of the Luba state is not a simple matter, for earlier studies have contributed to the idea of a centralized sociopolitical complex and have exaggerated the prestige of the imperial house of Kalala Ilunga as the central theme of Luba history. This focus has produced a skewed view, requiring newer efforts to give a more balanced view that is closer to the historical realities.

The origins of the state are controversial, in terms of localizing where political organization emerged. The earliest particularly Luba political forms are generally traced to the Kalundwe region of Chief Mutombo Mukulu; the territory between the Lomami and Lovidjo Rivers, and the northwestern region called Mongage. All these regions share a common founding hero, Kongolo Mwana or Kongolo Mwamba, although his origin is unclear. He would have settled among the "Bakolanga," an indigenous population who would adopt the name Baluba, and organized them politically around the *bumfumu*, the power of a chief called *mfumu*, a proto-Bantu term.

From this eventful period, tradition recalls the construction of a capital at Mwibela near Lake Boya, regrouping various previously scattered populations. A foreign hunter known as Ilunga Mbidi Kiluwe arrived here from the northeast; he married the two sisters of Kongolo Mwamba (Mwana), Bulanda, and Mabele. Discord developed between Kongolo and Mbidi Kiluwe, who left his brother-in-law for an unknown destination. Bulanda bore a son named Kalala Ilunga from the marriage, and he soon began to overshadow his uncle, making the latent conflict between them an open one. As the situation turned increasingly in his favor, *kalala* (a title meaning "commander," "general," "guide") Ilunga sized power from his uncle and cut off his head.

This first period is characterized by a sociopolitical organization based on the family, and in which the *mfumu* was the head of a village dominated by a single extended family. The mode of production was based equally on sharing and solidarity. The *mfumu* acted as leader and oversaw all the problems of the community, assisted by a council of elders who were, in effect, the senior family members. The *mfumu* was chosen by an electoral council or *kitango*, convoked once a vacancy was observed, generally by death, with the oldest members of the family initiating the succession. Often the brother of the deceased *mfumu* was elected; otherwise, a son or a nephew was chosen. The insignia of the *mfumu* include a *lukano* or *lwelo* (bracelet), *ngwele* (iron wire bracelets for both the wrists and ankles), the skin of the *nzuzi* (civet), and the *nsala* (tuft of parrot feathers).

The second period centers around Kalala Ilunga, whose reign initiated an expansionary period for the Luba. He introduced into the area a new kind of political power, *bulopwe*. Luba society became patrilineal, and the political structure becomes more complex. *Bumfumu* was related to the self-sufficient economy, with power often held by women in the group; *bumfumu* as a type of political power is often described as the "wife" of *bulopwe*. The *bulopwe*, a sacred dignity or political power by initiation, eventually diffused throughout central Africa and contributed to the expansion of Luba culture. It also created centrifugal forces to the extent that the area of Luba culture is a mosaic of autonomous states. In its essence, *balopwe* is an autonomous power and thus someone who holds it cannot, in theory, be subordinated to another. The only relationship that can exist between two *balopwe* is one of senior and junior within the same family. There was thus a swarming of *balopwe* through the area, creating stable and independent sociopolitical, economic, and cultural communities, even if acknowledging a common source of their power.

Tradition tells us little of the end of the reign of Kalala Ilunga, for that was of little interest to contemporary historians compared with the accomplishments of his reign. We know that there was a series of *balopwe* but with an uncertain line of succession. However, there is relative agreement on the most powerful line of *balopwe* from Nday Mwine N'kombe to the separation of the brothers Kasongo Nyembo and

Kabongo Nkumwimba, that is, from the end of the seventeenth century to the beginning of the twentieth century.

Historical developments after the reign of Kalala Ilunga were limited, for the attempts of several *balopwe* of the Lomami-Luvidjo area to bring other *balopwe* under their control seem to have failed in the long term. Cultural expansion was not synonymous with the expansion of political control.

JOHN C. YODER

Further Reading

Reefe, T. Q. *The Rainbow and the Kings: A History of the Luba Empire to 1891.* Berkeley and Los Angeles: University of California Press, 1981.

Van d der Noot, A. "Histoire de l'Empire Luba." *Bulletin des Juridictions Indigènes et du Droit Coutumier.* 2 (1953–1955): 1–5.

Vansina, J. *Kingdoms of the Savanna.* Madison: University of Wisconsin Press, 1966.

Luba: Seventeenth and Eighteenth Centuries

Although the Luba kingdom was one of the most celebrated states of Central Africa's eastern savanna, historians are reduced to conjecture regarding its genesis. The earliest explicit reference to the kingdom was written in 1832 and no archeological research yet has been conducted in the region of the ancient capitals. Therefore, the only available sources for early Luba history are linguistic data and oral traditions. Linguistic records demonstrate that, for centuries, the Luba and Lunda shared political terminology. Oral traditions, transmitted in Luba royal and provincial courts as well as in the *mbudye* secret society, an institution closely associated with kingship, also shed light on the Luba past.

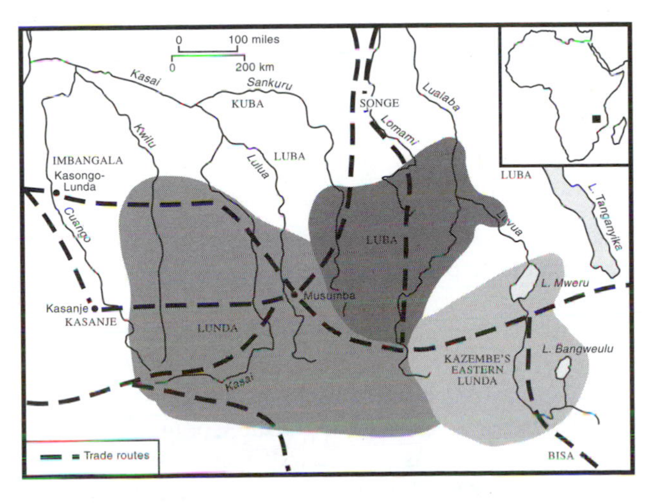

The Luba and Lunda empires, seventeenth–eighteenth centuries.

Relying on his own field research and on written sources, Thomas Q. Reefe wrote *The Rainbow and the Kings* (1981), the first critical monograph on Luba history. Rejecting earlier literalistic approaches, Reefe interpreted accounts about the kingdom's foundation as mythical tales or as political charters. Thus, the historical existence of the first kings (Ilunga Mbidi Kiluwe, Nkongolo Mwamba, Kalala Ilunga, Ilunga Mwila, and Kasongo Mwine Kibanza) was called into question. And, after these founding heroes, oral tradition consisted only of lists of kings. Not only did these lists lack details about the leaders, the lists' order differed depending on the source. This inconsistent genealogical segment included Kasongo Bonswe, Kasongo Kabundulu, Ngoye Sanza, and Kumwimbe Mputu.

It should be noted, however, that an oral tradition devoid of mythical elements is associated with one or more of the following ancient kings: Ilunga Mwila, Kasongo Mwine Kibanza, or Kasongo Bonswe. That tradition recalls a war against chief Madya who lived near the source of the Luguvu River. This clearly ancient tale suggests that the early Luba kingdom emerged very near that region.

Beginning with Ndaye Mwine Nkombe, there is a general consensus regarding the Luba royal genealogy. Furthermore, the reigns are associated with precise and plausible events. Estimating each generation at about thirty years in length and working backward from known events in the nineteenth century, Reefe proposed the following chronology, noting that the earlier dates are increasingly approximate:

Ilunga Kabale: *c.*1840–*c.*1870
Kumwimba Ngombe: *c.*1810–*c.*1840
Ilunga Nsungu: *c.*1780–*c.*1810
Kumwimba Kaumbu and Miketo (Ilunga Nsungu's cousins who ruled *c.*1780)
Kekenya: *c.*1750–*c.*1780
Kadilo: *c.*1720–*c.*1750
Ndaye Mwine Nkombe: *c.*1690–*c.*1720

The location of the ancient capitals provides important information about the Luba state. When a king died, his successor had to relocate. The old capital then became an autonomous domain directed by a court of dignitaries associated with a female medium in whom the previous sovereign was incarnated. This institution, which preserved the ancient political centers as memorials, makes it possible to map the displacement of the political center of gravity over the course of several centuries. Until the end of the eighteenth century, the capitals were located in the basins of the Luguvu, the upper Luvidyo, and the upper Lusanza Rivers. This assured the Luba kings an important commercial position. There were rich deposits of iron in the upper

Luvidyo basin. And in the nineteenth century, between the Mwenze and Mwibay rivers to the southwest, great salt deposits attracted hundreds of workers and merchants during the dry season. West of the Lomami, very near the center of the kingdom, lived the Ilande. Deeply involved in long-distance trade, it is likely that already in the seventeenth and eighteenth centuries the Ilande played a critical role on the great north-south economic axis. This route linked the Maniema forest, eastern Kasai, western Katanga, and the Copperbelt. The Luba heartland, with its iron, salt, and other products flowing to the royal court in the form of tribute to the king, became an important stage in this trading network.

The Luba kings certainly would have profited from their enviable economic situation. But they also proved to be good diplomats, employing a political strategy based on marriage alliances, and they were excellent cultural entrepreneurs. Attachment to the Luba court was—and still is—synonymous with legitimacy in many political entities, sometimes even those far from the Luba heartland. The Luba court was a ritual center without equal in a very large region. Provincial chiefs came here to obtain their emblems of power (sculpted objects, royal fire, white chalk, etc). The Luba installation rituals that made the Luba prince a true sacred king capable of mediating with the world of the spirits were paradigmatic models serving as a touchstone for most dignitaries and kings in the eastern savanna.

The process by which the Luba kingdom expanded is known only through sketchy evidence. For example, nothing tells us when the region directly south of the historical heartland (the Lovoy River basin) came into the kingdom's orbit. We do know that Kadilo (*c.*1720–*c.*1750) undertook campaigns into Songye country far to the northwest of the kingdom. His successor Kekenya (*c.*1750–*c.*1780) seems to have directed his military efforts toward the banks of the Lualaba River. Kumwimba Kaumbu (*c.*1780) died soon after fighting the Songye. The next ruler, Ilunga Nsungu (*c.*1780–*c.*1810) moved his capital south, nearer the Mashyo salt pans that were a major source of commercial and tribute wealth. Ilunga Nsungu's two successors also established their courts in the Mashyo area. That region is actually called Buluba (Luba country), perhaps because this was the location for the capitals of the conquering leaders who transformed the kingdom into a true empire.

During the reign of Ilunga Nsungu, the Luba experienced setbacks on their western frontiers. They failed to subdue the kingdom of Mutombo Mukulu. And the Kanyok, whose small chiefdoms had remained within the Luba political and ideological orbit throughout the eighteenth century, were united into a strong state that proved capable of rejecting the designs of their powerful neighbor. In contrast, the Luba successfully penetrated far beyond the eastern banks of the Lualaba River. They pursued a politic of conquest in the entire Luvua-Lukuga corridor (as far as Kalemie on Lake Tanganyika). So long as the local chiefs agreed to become loyal clients, they could remain in office (for example the celebrated Kyombo Mkubwa). Elsewhere, the conquerors set up Luba dynasties. The *mbudye* secret society seems to have played an important role in propagating Luba ideology and mythology throughout the region. Ilunga Nsungu's successors continued this aggressive policy for another half century after his death in about 1810. This political and military effort was halted only by the arrival of slave and ivory traders whose superior arms brutally ended Luba expansion.

PIERRE PETIT

Further Reading

Burton, W. F. P. *Luba Religion and Magic in Custom and Belief.* Musee royale d'Afrique centrale, Sciences humaines 35 (Tervuren, 1961).

D'Orjo de Marchovelette, E. "Notes sure les funérailles des chefs Ilunga Kabale et Kabongo Kumwimba: historique de la chefferie Kabongo: histoire de la chefferie Kongolo [Notes regarding the funerals of chiefs Ilunga Kabale and Kabongo Kumwimba: A chronology of the Kabongo chiefdom: A history of the Kongolo chiefdom.] *Bulletin des juridictions indigènes du droit coutumier congolais.* 18, no. 12 (1950): 350–368; 19, no. 1 (1951): 1–13.

Petit, P. "'Les charmes du roi sont les esprits des morts.' Les fondements de la royauté sacrée chez les Luba du Zaïre." [The King's Charms Are the Spirits of the Dead: Foundations of the Luba of Zaire's Sacred Kingship]. *Africa (Journal of the International African Institute).* 66 (1996): 349–366.

———. *Les sauniers de la savane orientale. Approche ethnographique de l'industrie du sel chez les Luba, Bemba et populations apparentées (Congo, Zambie)* [Salt Makers of the Eastern Savanna. . . .]. Académie Royale des Sciences d'Outre-Mer, Bruxelles (2000).

Reefe, T. Q. *The Rainbow and the Kings: A History of the Luba Empire to 1891.* University of California Press, Berkeley, 1981.

Van der Noot, A. "Quelques éléments historiques sure l'empire luba, son organisation et sa direction." *Bulletin des juridictions indigènes du droit coutumier congolais.* 4, no. 7 (1936): 141–149.

Womersley, H. *In the Glow of the Log Fire.* London: Peniel Press, 1975.

Lubumbashi

Capital of Katanga Province and second city of the Democratic Republic of Congo, it owes its name to a small river.

When the railroad from Cape Town through Rhodesia approached the Belgian Congo, the colonial government wished to avoid an influx of British colonists from the south. Thus in 1908 the seat of the Comité Spécial du Katanga (CSK) was transferred from Lukonzolwa on Lake Moeru toward the southern border. Cdts Tanneau and Émile Wangermée set up camp on the Kafubu

River. In 1910 a permanent government post was established on its tributary, the Lubumbashi.

In contrast, Union Minière du Haut-Katanga, which had begun exploratory drilling at Kambove, was thrilled to find the railhead reaching Ndola near the Rhodesian-Congolese border in 1908. It therefore decided to begin work with the Congo Star mine near the Kafubu, as it would be first to have rail links, facilitating ore and metal transport.

Circumstances thus favored the creation of Elisabethville, now Lubumbashi. Wangermée, representative of the CSK, was named vice governor-general for Katanga on July 29, 1910. He refused to move to Kambove, chosen by the government of the Belgian Congo as capital of Katanga. By then construction of the city had already begun, as the copper refinery required a water supply; the railroad, at the Sakania border in 1909, reached Elisabethville September 27 and the Congo Star mine on October 1. On September 1, the government had named Elisabethville Katanga's capital in place of Kambove, and on November 9 Wangermée signed documents giving it the status of "urban district." The name honored Queen Elisabeth of Belgium, who had accompanied Albert I to the Belgian Congo before his accession to the throne, visiting the Congo Star mine.

Elisabethville served as capital of Katanga province from 1910, as headquarters of the district of the Upper Luapula (later Upper Katanga) from 1912 to 1929 and from 1932 to 1961, as headquarters of the territory of the same name from 1912 to 1956, and an urban district from 1929 to 1932 and 1956 to 1957. It received the status of city in 1941, modified by law in 1957. The city seal, bearing the words *Ex imis ad culmina* (from the depths to the heights) was registered in 1954.

Lubumbashi had been laid out by South African advisers on a site chosen by Wangermée, aided by the Swiss engineer Itten on the peneplain east of the Lubumbashi River. Thus there were two separate cities, one white (today's commune of Lubumbashi plus Bel-Air) and the other the native quarter. The region between the two cities was reserved for public buildings, churches, hospital, schools, and a prison operated by whites for Africans. The white quarter was reserved for Belgians and those assimilated to them, with darker-skinned foreigners (Arabs, Indians, Sephardic Jews, Greeks, Italians) living in peripheral areas such as Bakoa and Ndjandja. During the colonial period, racial segregation extended to two adjoining cemeteries.

Reserved for blacks and created by ordinance in 1912, the native city was moved away from the white section during the depression and transformed into an incorporated *centre extra-coutumier* in 1932. It eventually grew into four townships: Albert I (now Kamalondo, begun 1921), Kenya (1941), Katuba (1950), and Ruashi (1954), plus the rural satellite town of Karavia. In 1957 the city was divided into five communes, one for Europeans and the four for Africans. The inhabitants of each elected a council that chose the mayor; no Katangese was selected among the four African townships, with most of the mayors Kasaians.

The Katangese reacted by creating CONAKAT (Confederation of Katangese Tribal Associations) under the presidency of Godefoid Munongo of the Yeke royal family. In the 1960 elections most of those who were to become leaders of the secessionist Katanga government were initially elected as CONAKAT provincial deputies from Elisabethville districts including Tshombe, Munongo, and Kibwe.

In 1970 the Mobutu government renamed the capitals of Congo and its provinces during Mobutu's "Authenticity" campaign, and Elisabethville retook the name of the original government post by the stream.

As in other African cities, most of the city's growth has come during the last forty years, after Congo's independence. In 1970 the commune of Kampemba was separated from that of Lubumbashi (ex-Elisabeth), and in 1977 the outlying Commune Annexe was created. Particularly during the Second Republic, numerous shanty towns appeared around the city, including: Cinq-Ans/Kasungami, Zaïre, Kigoma, Madame Jeanne/Masangoshi/Quartier Six, Kawama, Zambia, Naviundu, Bongonga, Kinkalabwamba, Tabacongo, Kalebuka, CampAssistants, Kimbwambwa, Kalubwe, Foire, Katuba Mbujimayi, Katuba Gbadolite, and Katuba Kisanga.

From its inception, the city of Lubumbashi has played a variety of roles. It was both an industrial town, based on the copper smelter using ores from mines outside the city, and a political nexus as the administrative center of the wealthiest province in the country. The rail and road border crossings from Rhodesia remained rural outposts, ensuring that Lubumbashi was the customs and distribution pole for the southeastern third of Congo, with which it had rail links. Since 1956, with the opening of the Université Officielle du Congo et du Ruanda-Urundi (now the Université de Lubumbashi), it has been an academic center, with several other institutions of higher education also present. It has an international airport, opened in 1958, the site originally having been an overnight stop on flights between Europe and South Africa in the days of propeller planes and visual navigation.

The city had a population of 754 Europeans in December 1910; 1,200 in 1912; 2,483 in 1925; and 20,000 in 1960. The African population stood at 8,000 in 1912; 13,990 in 1923; 32,637 in 1929; and 161,000 in 1960. The population in 2000 was approximately two million.

The best-known symbols of the city are the tall refinery chimney and the pyramid of slag towering over the city. Major architectural landmarks include Governor's Residence and Imara and Twendelee schools (1910s), Saints Peter and Paul Cathedral, Makutano Club, Jerusalem United Methodist Church, and the Jewish synagogue (1920s), the courthouse and Mazembe stadium (1930s), the post office, former CSK headquarters, the theater, St. Mary's Basilica, and the railway headquarters (1950s), Gécamines tower and the two hospitals (1960s), and Hotel Karavia and Mobutu Stadium (1970s).

MICHEL LWAMBA BILONDA

Further Reading

Fetter, B. S. "African Associations in Elisabethville: Their Origins and Development." *Études d'Histoire Africaine.* 6 (1974): 205–223.

———. *The Creation of Elisabethville, 1910–1940.* Stanford: Hoover Institution, 1976.

Lugard: *See* Nigeria: Lugard, Administration, and "Indirect Rule."

Lumumba, Patrice (1925–1961)

First and Only Elected Prime Minister of Congo

A recognized African leader on the international stage for little more than two years before he was murdered, Lumumba nonetheless became an icon for newly independent Africa, all the more so because of the belief that the West had played a role in his death.

Lumumba founded the Mouvement National Congolais (MNC) in October 1958; it was Congo's first nationwide political party. In December 1958 Lumumba attended the first All-Africa People's Conference in Accra, Ghana, and subsequently returned to the Congo a far more militant nationalist. Following the violent suppression of two days of rioting in Léopoldville in January 1959, the Belgian government announced a program to lead the Congo to independence over five years. More radical nationalists denounced this as too slow and called for the boycott of the proposed municipal and rural elections. Belgian repression followed and on October 30, 1959, the forcible dispersal of an MNC rally in Stanleyville led to thirty deaths. Lumumba was imprisoned on a charge of incitement to riot. The MNC subsequently changed its tactics and entered the elections to win 90 per cent of the votes in Stanleyville.

Belgium then felt obliged to hasten the process of independence and convened a conference of all political parties to meet in Brussels in January 1960. The MNC refused to take part without Lumumba, who was released from prison so that he could attend the conference.

Prime Minister Patrice Lumumba (second from left) of the Republic of the Congo, photographed with an aide, Capt. Mawoso (second from right), as he arrived in New York to establish direct contact with the United Nations secretary general in order to find a speedy solution to the problems facing his country. July 24, 1960. © SVT Bild/Das Fotoarchiv.

Patrice Lumumba's political party, the MNC, won a majority of seats in the May 1960 elections one month before the Congo became independent on June 30, 1960. The country was, by any standard, ill-prepared for independence. Moreover, prior to the handover of government authority, the Belgians had produced a new constitution that assigned to six provincial governments the same competencies as those of the central government, an arrangement that was an invitation for an immediate power struggle between the provinces and the center. Such a power struggle duly erupted within days of the country's independence. Lumumba, who favored a strong, centralized, truly national government, had been made prime minister while his political rival, Joseph Kasavubu, who preferred a loose federal structure and the creation of a BaKongo state, became president. The first signs of breakdown came with riots followed by a mutiny of the Force Publique for better pay and conditions. These disturbances led to an exodus of Europeans.

The great mineral wealth of the Congo meant that a number of Western nations (the excolonial power Belgium, Britain, and France as well as the United States, with a principal motive of Cold War strategy) were not prepared to see these resources lost to the West. A political struggle developed between Lumumba, who was accused of "selling" the country to the Soviet Union, and the charismatic political leader of the mineral rich Katanga province, Moise Tshombe, whose sympathies were pro-Western, while he also enjoyed close ties with Western business interests.

On Independence Day, attended by the King of the Belgians, the new prime minister considered himself and the Congolese people slighted when he was not scheduled to speak at the formal ceremony handing over power on June 29, 1960. Following a paternalistic speech by King Baudouin, which praised Belgium's great "civilizing mission" in the Congo, Lumumba defied protocol and made a radical speech in reply, in which he castigated the brutality and injustice of Belgian rule in the Congo. In doing so, the prime minister merely confirmed the suspicions of the Belgian government: that Lumumba was an implacable enemy of Belgian interests in the region.

On July 11, 1960, Tshombe announced that Katanga was to secede from the Congo. On the following day Lumumba appealed to the United Nations to help restore order and maintain the integrity of the Congo by preventing Katanga's secession. The United Nations faced a formidable task, and although Secretary General Dag Hammarskjold acted swiftly, the United Nations was unable to prevent the immediate secession of Katanga. Government forces did manage to take control of Kasai Province and prevent a second secession there. Belgium, which had significant economic stakes in the mineral wealth of Katanga, assisted Tshombe with mercenaries and other political support in his attempted breakaway, with the result that the province was not to be brought back under central control for three years.

After Lumumba's dismissal by Kasavubu in September (the West by then saw him as "too independent") the UN recognized the new Kasavubu government set up in October; this split African opinion, dividing continental opinion between radicals who supported Lumumba and moderates who supported Kasavubu. Lumumba had been given UN protection while he was in Leopoldville, but when he attempted to travel to Stanleyville, which was the center of his support he was captured by Kasavubu forces on December second. On January 17, 1961, he was handed over to Tshombe in Katanga, where he was first tortured and then killed.

Following his death Lumumba became a national and African hero. While the failure of the United Nations to protect him did the world organization great harm, his death also damaged Tshombe's reputation. Lumumba's importance lay more in his symbolism than any actual political achievements, although he was the first Congolese politician to create a national rather than a regional party. He was seen as the victim of Western manipulation of a fragile new state whose potential wealth ensured that it would not be left to its own devices.

The release of documents in Belgium in 1999 provided evidence of primary Belgian complicity in Lumumba's death, and on December 9, 1999, the Belgian parliament decided to set up a commission of inquiry into Lumumba's death and Belgium's responsibility for it.

GUY ARNOLD

Biography

Born July 2, 1925, at Onalua in Kasai. Granted full Belgian citizenship. Obtained a job as a postal clerk in Léopoldville (Kinshasa) and later in Stanleyville (Kisangani). In 1955 became president of a Congolese trade union of government employees and also an active member of the Belgian Liberal Party in the Congo. Wrote *Congo My Country,* published posthumously in 1963. In 1956 went on a tour to Belgium; on his return to the Congo, arrested and imprisoned for one year on a charge of embezzling post office funds. Named prime minister in 1960. Murdered in 1961.

Further Reading

Abi-Saab, G. *The United Nations Operation in the Congo, 1960–1964.* London: Oxford University Press, 1978.

Arnold, G. *Historical Dictionary of Civil Wars in Africa.* Lanham, Maryland: Scarecrow Press, 1999.

Bob, F. S. *Historical Dictionary of Zaire.* Metuchen, N. J.: Scarecrow Press, 1989.

Chakravarty, B. *The Congo Operation, 1960–1963.* Delhi: Historical Section, Ministry of Defence, Government of India, 1976.

Epstein, H. M., ed. *Revolt in the Congo, 1960–64.* New York: Facts on File, 1965.

Grip. *Congo-Zaire: La Colonisation: L'Independence, Le Regime Mobutu—et Demain?* Brussels: Groupe de Recherche et de l'Information sur la Paix (GRIP), 1989.

Kanza, T. *Conflict in the Congo: The Rise and Fall of Lumumba.* London: Harmondsworth, Penguin, 1972.

Legum, C. *Congo Disaster.* Baltimore: Penguin Books, 1961.

Lumumba, P. *Congo My Country.* London: Praeger, 1963.

Merriam, A. P. *Congo: Background of Conflict.* Evanston, Ill.: Northwestern University Press, 1961.

New African. "History will one day have its say." *New African.* 382. (2000): 18–30.

Lunda: Mwaant Yaav (Mwata Yamvo) and Origins

The Ruund (nuclear Lunda) inhabit northwestern Katanga Province of the Democratic Republic of Congo and adjoining areas in Kasai Province and Angola. At least, such is the modern ethnic group with its specific language (uRuund), political system (acknowledging the *mwant yav*), ethnic consciousness, and bilateral kinship system relatively rare in Africa. By such a definition, the aRuund are a half to one million at the beginning of the twenty-first century. In more restrictive earlier use, the name referred only to the inhabitants of the Nkalany valley (the upper Mbuji-Mayi). In its largest sense, peoples from northeastern Zambia to southwestern Congo, including a broad swath of Congo, northwestern Zambia, and eastern Angola, are identified and/or identify themselves by the generic term "Lunda."

Lunda/Ruund/Ruwund; Mwant Yav/Mwaant Yaav/ Mwata Yamvo/Mwatiamvwa: spellings vary because of the many languages sharing this political legacy and due to their filtering into print through various European languages over 150 years. Spellings used here approximate Ruund usage, without final vowels and with certain sounds in neighboring Bantu languages replaced by others; the orthography distinguishes between long vowels (*mwant yav*) and double vowels (Ruund).

The far-flung Lunda political tradition associated with the *mwant yav* kingship developed in the seventeenth and eighteenth centuries. It was perhaps the largest precolonial state in Central Africa, although in disorder by the time Leopold II sent agents to claim the area for his Congo Independent State.

According to the "Lunda Love Story" of oral tradition, it began as a simple village community along the Nkalany. Nkond, the presiding elder, left his emblems (particularly an iron bracelet wound with human flesh, the *rukan*) to his daughter Ruwej rather than to disrespectful sons. As chief, Ruwej was brought a handsome intruder from the east captured by her villagers: Chibind ("hunter") Yirung. Smitten, she made him her consort. The variants of the tradition, given by the Ruund and their neighbors, suggest little reaction; as a man, a woman chief has the right to choose her partner(s); he is, however, a "consort" and not a "husband." The crisis came later. As menstrual blood causes ritual impurity, women must "go to the edge," leaving the village temporarily. Ruwej began entrusting the insignia to Yirung, and not all the community could accept an outsider holding the emblems of sacred power. Some departed.

Versions of the story collected since the nineteenth century name among them the famous founder-heroes of Angolan states and ethnic groups, but linguistic analysis shows the names to be foreign loanwords from Angola. For the aRuund with their use of perpetual kinship, adding these names to the core tradition is like musical improvisation on an older theme, adapting it to the political and economic realities of the 19th century savannah. Traditions vary as to whether Yirung was killed, driven out, or tolerated by those who remained with Ruwej.

Traditions agree that the dynasty began not with Chibind Yirung but with his son, Yav a Yirung. The childless Ruwej was the sociological mother; a maidservant the birth mother. In the Lunda central court, Ruwej is perpetuated by the *nswan murund* ("heir of the friendship") and the birth mother by the *rukonkish*. Both positions have played major political roles in recent centuries, with the *rukonkish* usually a close biological relative of the *mwant yav*. The *nswan murund* derives her authority through her own line and exercises a veto during the election process for a new *mwant yav*. Yav a Yirung thus embodied not only the earth rights of the first occupants but also the high chiefly culture of a more sophisticated state than the original Nkalany community, a political legitimacy symbolized by the direction of the rising sun.

Little evidence suggests that the Luba state center of northern Katanga was in close contact with the Lunda court until the eighteenth or nineteenth century. Colonial authors often link Chibind Yirung with the historic Luba state of the *mulopwe* centered northwest of the Upemba depression, but nineteenth century transcriptions of the tradition give his origins in small states closer to the Nkalany though always to the east.

There is nonetheless abundant linguistic evidence of cultural cross-fertilization along that border. The aRuund are on the northeastern edge of one group of savannah Bantu languages, the Luba languages and dialects being their neighbors to the east and north. Further north, evidence suggests that patrilineal Luba-Kasai immigrants absorbed Ruund-like communities having simple pre-*mwant yav* political organization.

The Lunda political model that developed at the Nkalany includes a sovereign chosen from among a hereditary group, but among the bilateral aRuund, any descendant by male or female line is eligible; and with chiefly polygamy this ensures a wide field of candidates. Among peripheral Lunda, this often shows up in ethnology as a distinct inheritance system for chiefs: for example, "patrilineal" among the matrilineal Bemba-speakers of the Mwata Kazembe subsidiary state. Typically, there are political titles reserved for women and the optional election of women to other titles; this, of course, was not absent among other matrilineal peoples to their south. Chiefs are typically nominated by groups of specified political stakeholders, often pass a veto of a woman titleholder, and are installed by land chiefs representing the original occupants. The royal court was intricately organized, with spatial residence corresponding to political functions and state geography. Titles were also linked by the metaphor of perpetual kinship, with each titleholder succeeding to the identity as well as the position of the chiefly founder.

Lunda political insignia included the *rukan* (reserved for those claiming sovereignty), wound copper bracelets on wrists and ankles (with relative numbers on right and left sides indicating paternal or maternal ties to the title), and animal skins. Since at least the nineteenth century the most visible are elaborate beaded crowns and full cloth skirts with contrasting borders.

JEFF HOOVER

Further Reading

Cunnison, I. "Perpetual Kinship: A Political Institution of the Luapula Peoples." *Rhodes-Livingstone Journal.* 20 (1956): 28–48.

Duysters, L. "Histoire des Aluunda." *Problèmes d'Afrique Centrale.* 38 (1958): 75–98.

Hoover, J. J. "The Seduction of Ruwej: The Nuclear Lunda (Zaïre, Angola, Zambia)." Ph.D. diss., Yale University, 1978 (published by University Microfilms, 1979).

Palmeirim, M. "Of Alien Kings and Ancestral Chiefs: Essays on the Ideology of Kingship among the Aruwund (Lunda)." Ph.D. diss. University of London, 1994.

———. "The Sterile Mother: Aspects of Court Symbolism among the Lunda of Mwant Yaav (Aruund)." M. Phil. thesis, London School of Economics, 1986.

Turner, V. "A Lunda Love Story and Its Consequences: Selected Texts from Traditions Collected by Henrique Dias de Carvalho at the Court of the Muatianvua in 1887." *Rhodes-Livingstone Journal.* 19 (1955): 1–26.

Vansina, J. *Kingdoms of the Savanna.* Madison: University of Wisconsin Press, 1966.

Lunda: Kingdoms, Seventeenth and Eighteenth Centuries

The Lunda Empire was perhaps the largest precolonial state in central Africa, with major outlying centers along the Kwango in the west and in northeastern Zambia along the Luapula to the east, each a thousand kilometers from the heartland along the Nkalany (upper MbujiMayi) valley. Cultural influence of the Lunda political model reached even further.

The caveat is that African states before the colonial period were very different from modern concepts of state. They typically were more interested in annexing people than land, thus in a sparsely populated subcontinent with agricultural systems based on shifting cultivation of leached tropical soils they had only vague borders. Concepts of sovereignty and authority could be very different from such in Europe, for example, where the medieval feudal state was also very different from modern bureaucratic governments.

The social system of the Ruund, at the heartland of the Lunda Empire is interrelated with political development. The Ruund lie along the northern edge of the "matrilineal belt" across Africa in the savanna lands south of the forests among agricultural peoples not heavily involved in cattle-raising. Far from molding human relationships by fixed vagaries of birth, Ruund kinship is lived out as political choice. Ethnic groups to the north and east tend to be strongly patrilineal; groups to the south are matrilineal. Ruund has a Hawaiian kinship vocabulary, calling aunts and uncles on both maternal and paternal sides "mother" and "father," and cousins "siblings." (Separate gender neutral terms exist for older and younger sibling of same sex but only one for a sibling of opposite sex.) A special term exists for the maternal uncle, also called "mother without breasts"; the paternal aunt is called either "mother" or "female father." Marriage exchanges were limited to mutual hospitality and material tokens, and either spouse could initiate divorce. The web of kin soon extends throughout the community, with any two individuals likely tracing common kinship in a variety of ways. Which ties are operative at a given time depends much on circumstances and interests.

As with other societies having bilateral kinship, there is no defined lineage or clan able to practice social solidarity. The basic family unit is the *dijikw* "hearthfire," composed of more than one *divumw* ("belly"). A larger unit is the *divar*, "family party," which is neither exclusive (one can exploit membership in several) nor ascriptive (it can be ignored since not exclusive). The extended family is thus incapable of resolving routine social conflicts to the degree normal in most Central African societies, and recourse to state institutions becomes more attractive. Likewise, where conflict between obligations to kin and state ideals of impartiality typically weaken African states, weakened ascriptive kinship among the Ruund favors stronger state structures.

In a reciprocal to the weak political role of Ruund kinship, Lunda political networks are couched in a kinship metaphor. Relationships among chiefs are identified as to whether a titleholder is a "child of Ruwej," a "child of the *mwant yav,*" and so forth. The relationship may be generic: one title is considered a child of another. In other cases, the oral traditions would appear to give much more biographical data: a specific titleholder was the son of a specific *mwant yav* (a lordship title).

Taking such traditions at face value is naive, for they may speak only of political relationships. Traditions recorded in the nineteenth and twentieth centuries generally name three brothers of Ruwej, the heroic mother of the Lunda State; Kinguri and Chinyama are universally cited by name and as the founders of the Imbangala slave-trading state on the upper Kwango and of the Luvale/Lwena people who expanded into southwestern Katanga and western Zambia in the nineteenth century. Early traditions may have spoken of Ruwej's disrespectful brothers, but the names now cited are modern grafts; none reflects the sound shifts that have taken place within the Ruund language after the period of Ruwej.

The Ruund political model offered a flexible and evocative structure for a far-flung political and economic network from 1700 to 1860. Long-distance trade was carried out in the guise of gift exchange, making it difficult to interpret the reports of nineteenth century Portuguese travelers such as Graça, for each recipient could interpret the gift received as recognition of authority by the donor. It is difficult to evaluate which gift was of superior value (and thus who might be seen as truly tributary) in a situation where one donor was often far more involved in the world economy than the other. In other cases, gifts were symbolic rather than economic (lion or leopard skins, reeds filled with salt, scarlet parrot feathers, etc.). Recognition of a chief as a "child of Ruwej" acknowledged ancient status and a right to some autonomy within the Lunda State. Recognizing Chokwe elephant-hunters and raiders as followers of Ndondj, one of the purported disrespectful brothers of Ruwej, established a fictive bond favoring cooperation but also explained the conflicted relationships that led the Chokwe to depose more than one *mwant yav,* even occupying the Ruund heartland and imposing a decade-long interregnum in the late nineteenth century.

The widespread system of Lunda states was created both by spawning governors who operated with the blessing of the *mwant yav*'s court and by assimilating consenting local authorities. An example of the latter are local land chiefs who often remain the ritual investors (*atubung*) of Lunda territorial lords. The franchising of ambitious titleholders is exemplified by the Yaka *kiamfu* on the Kwango River far to the west and the *mwata kazembe* on the Luapula to the east. Both were kiLuba-speakers who set up Lunda states outside their home areas. Similarly, ambitious Kete from Kasai province were sent to the matrilineal Lunda-Ndembu to impose Lunda rule. Such chiefs as the *kanongesha* in northwestern Zambia or the *mwata kazembe* in northeastern Zambia continued to recognize the *mwant yav*'s sovereignty, yet little economic revenue could have been derived by the *mwant yav* from such distant subordinates. Restive governors could be nudged back to order by sending an *iyikej* overseer as resident ambassador. Particularly within economically important areas (slave sources either closer to the trading centers of Angola or more densely populated as in southern Kasai), armed bands of "catchers," *atukwat,* acted as enforcers. Nonetheless, much of the longevity of Lunda states derived from the ingenious flexibility of the political system rather than simply from brute military force. Subchiefs obtained ideological justification and prestige from belonging to the larger network; the central court obtained more imported luxury goods (beads, cloth, etc.). The kinship metaphor allowed the system to stretch and bend with changing political and economic realities until the rising scale of trade in the nineteenth century required a more rational economic model than gift exchange.

JEFF HOOVER

Further Reading

Hoover, J. J. "The Seduction of Ruwej: The Nuclear Lunda (Zaïre, Angola, Zambia)." Ph.D. diss., Yale University, 1978 (published by University Microfilms, 1979).

Thornton, J. "The Chronology and Causes of Lunda Expansion to the West, *c.*1700–1852." *Zambia Journal of History.* 1 (1981): 1–13.

Lunda: Titles

The Lunda Empire extended in a swath from west of the Kwango to east of the Luapula, not because of some demographic flowering in what is a relatively sparsely populated area, but because of the political utility of the state model developed along the Nkalany (upper Mbuji-Mayi) River by the Ruund in the seventeenth century and due to larger economic factors impinging on central Africa.

Population pressure is often posited in the rise of the Luba kingdom of the *mulopwe* to the east, due to abundant protein from the fish of the Upemba depression coupled with agriculture on the plateau and varied mineral resources. However, Kapanga territory is today the least populated area in western Katanga, and the most densely populated nearby areas (Luiza territory in Kasai) represent ethnic groups who fought tenaciously to escape Lunda incorporation. While the *musumb* (capital) of the *mwant yav* appeared an impressively large agglomeration for nineteenth- century central Africa to Portuguese visitors, the gravitational pull of the Lunda headquarters is responsible, for travelers crossed large empty areas to reach it. The empty lands reflect in part a century of slave trade but also poor Kalahari sand soils and limited or inconveniently located permanent water sources.

Elements of the Lunda title system likely developed during the seventeenth century, and by the late seventeenth century the current title of *mwant yav* ("Lord Yav") had emerged with Yav a Yirung and his successors. Oral traditions recall considerable conflict during the preceding generation, with dissidents going into exile. Yav's father Yirung was a wandering hunter who had happened upon the community with Ruwej as its chieftainess, and she made him consort. Yav's mother was a maidservant, for Ruwej was sterile. This tradition has been interpreted by Western academics as a euphemism for Luba conquest (although no kiLuba loanwords witness to a forced occupation), or a cosmological myth. If the interpretation based on a conquest by the historical Luba *mulopwe* state is unlikely, the "love story" clearly does represent a syncretic cultural process.

At the Nkalany and to the immediate east, Ruund- and kiLuba-speaking populations intermingled along their linguistic border. Certain titles are based on kiLuba rather than Ruund linguistic roots yet are clearly not borrowed from the Luba political tradition. The widespread title *nswan mulapw*, "vice chief," is composed of Ruund *nswan*, "heir," and Luba *mulopwe* "lord." The Luba loanword is not used in other Lunda contexts, whether for God or for political authorities, so its spread is a marker of the Lunda political model. Luba-speaking groups such as the Sanga and the Luapula Bemba to the southeast, who belonged to the Lunda political system rather than that of the *mulopwe,* have distinct verbs: *-swana*, "to inherit a chiefly title," and *-piana,* "to inherit from a parent." Other Lunda titles are not widespread among the large Luba states, but exist in Kanyok or Kalundwe bordering the Aruund, with possible etymologies in their Luban speech forms, and thus seem to have been borrowed by the Ruundd from their immediate kiLuba-speaking neighbors.

Other titles belong to an older heritage among the most closely related Bantu languages. *Mwant yav* is based on the generic term for "chief" or "lord," replacing the proto-Bantu *mfumu* in these languages, plus the name of the dynasty's founder. Many titles found across the Lunda world seem to have been coined among the aRuund during the development of the Lunda state model. They were then borrowed and imposed as parts of the overall architecture of a Lunda chieftainship.

Lunda expansion took place along an east-west axis, and to a lesser degree toward the south. In part, this reflects the easier communications across the savanna than in the rain forest to the north. This deep cultural sharing across the grasslands is also reflected in the older shift in Bantu languages from seven to five vowels as various groups pushed south into the savanna. The slave trade on the Atlantic coast (and perhaps, to a much lesser degree, the Indian Ocean trade in copper, slaves, and cloth) was a magnet directing expansion laterally toward the coast.

The Ruund did not expand significantly toward the more densely populated north among the Kete and Kanyok, The loosely-organized Kete appear to have been the closest linguistic and cultural kin of the Nkalany Ruund, but they resisted assimilation energetically enough to have been placed in Kasai province when the Belgians drew and redrew lines during the 1900s and 1930s, putting the Lunda who acknowledged the *mwant yav* in Kapanga territory and thus eventually in Katanga. Relationships were largely of slave raiding by the *mwant yav* and of resistance by the Kete. The Kanyok had a state tradition of their own, sharing a few titles and concepts with the Ruund but much more with their kiLuba-speaking kin to the southeast and tshiLuba-speakers to their northwest. Kanyok and Ruund remember military campaigns between them as well as alliances against others, showing both conflict and cooperation among these neighboring states.

Before the 1750s Lunda captains were operating in both the Kwango valley of the modern Yaka and in north central Angola among those who became the Shinje Lunda and had already established themselves. Likewise, the *mwata kazembe* governorship on the Luapula River in northeastern Zambia (see further) began about 1740. Western expansion was documented by the Portuguese. By 1807 the *mwant yav* was sending embassies directly to the Portuguese in Luanda.

The Kanyok language of the Luba group shares the lack of final vowels with Ruund, a phonological fashion that appears to have begun far to the northwest, extended east along the lower Kasai River, and peters out with them. This and what appears to be pioneering Lunda adoption of manioc cultivation in the far center of Africa suggests a possible earlier western trading network toward the Congo River that predated the eighteenth century Imbangala slave-cloth trade and its nineteenth century Chokwe-Ovimbundu replacement.

Political expansion was largely by "franchising." The founder of the *kiamfu* state among the Yaka was kiLuba-speaking, as were the *mwata kazembe* and other Lunda captains spun out by an ephemeral expansion polity on the Mukulweji river in southern Katanga. The Luapula Lunda speak of a cowskin belt given as a token of naturalization as a Lunda chief. The ideology of perpetual kinship and a chiefly system somewhat separated from kinship groups was a flexible political cement, holding heterogenous groups together under the umbrella of the *want yav*, "the power of Yav," and of an often fictive *kwol kwetw*, "our home village."

JEFF HOOVER

Further Reading

Hoover, J. J. "The Seduction of Ruwej: The Nuclear Lunda (Zaïre, Angola, Zambia)." Ph.D. diss., Yale University, 1978 (published by University Microfilms, 1979).

Kodi M. W. "A Pre-colonial History of the Pende People (Republic of Zaire) from 1620 to 1900." 2 vols. Ph.D. diss., Northwestern University, 1976 (published by University Microfilms, 1977).

Miller, J. C. *Kings and Kinsmen: The Imbangala Impact on the Mbundu of Angola*. Oxford: Clarendon, 1976.

Ndua S. K. "Histoire ancienne des populations Luba et Lunda du plateau du Haut-Lubilashi: Des Origines au début du XXe siècle (Bena Nsamba, Inimpimin et Tuwadi)." Doctoral thesis, Université Nationale du Zaïre, Lubumbashi, 1978.

Papstein, R. "The Upper Zambezi: A History of the Luvale People, 1000–1900." Ph.D. diss., University of California-Los Angeles, 1978 (published by University Microfilms, 1979).

Schecter, R. "History and Historiography on a Frontier of Lunda Expansion: The Origin and Development of Kanongesha." Ph.D. diss., University of Wisconsin, 1976 (published by University Microfilms, 1977).

Thornton, J. "The Chronology and Causes of Lunda Expansion to the West, *c.*1700–1852." *Zambia Journal of History.* 1 (1981): 1–13.

Lundu: *See* Maravi: Phiri Clan, Lundu and Undi Dynasties.

Luo: *See* Nilotes, Eastern Africa: Western Nilotes: Luo.

Lusaka

Lusaka, the capital of Zambia, was not initially founded as the administrative center of the country. The origin of the city, which was founded in 1905, was related to the extension of the railway line from South Africa through southern Rhodesia to the Broken Hill (Kabwe) mine. During the construction of the railway line, it was decided that sidings would be established at twenty-mile intervals. This process determined the location of Lusaka.

Initially Lusaka was located in the Chilanga subdistrict of the Luangwa district, the headquarters since 1905. The headquarters remained at Chilanga until 1931, when it moved to Lusaka.

In 1913 a village management board for Lusaka was established. During World War I, the area under the jurisdiction of the Village Management Board was extended northward to include areas where considerable suburban development had taken place. The increase in European settlement in the Lusaka area necessitated the enactment of the Lusaka Township Regulations in 1922. Further extension of the administrative area was done in 1928 to the east, where another considerable white settlement had developed.

Europeans were attracted to the area because of cheap land sold by the Northern Copper Company, which did not find any minerals in the area. The township began with a farm settlement by G. B. Marrapodi, an Italian contractor who was granted extensive farm land to the north and northeast of the siding. The Dutch Reformed Church was established on one of Marrapodi's farms. In 1912 a hotel, which became the Lusaka Hotel, was opened. The growing European and African population necessitated the establishment of an administrative body for Lusaka. By 1931 there were 1,961 Africans and 433 Europeans in Lusaka.

The economy of Lusaka was originally agriculturally based. Lusaka developed into a commercial center for the farming population of the area. Lusaka was emerging as a commercial center, as opposed to an administrative center, for the country.

The status of the region changed in July 1931 when the colonial government decided to build a new capital city in Lusaka, which was chosen for its centrality in the country following the amalgamation of northeastern and northwestern Rhodesia in 1911. Lusaka was subsequently transformed into the country's capital. The governor and other government departments and officials relocated to Lusaka from Livingstone in 1935.

Because of the outbreak of World War II in 1939, very little was done to implement plans for the new capital in line with Professor S. D. Adshead's report, which had been submitted in April 1931. However, after the war, Lusaka experienced an influx of European settlers. Lusaka also experienced a growing demand for industrial plots of land. These developments changed the character of Lusaka from a retail commercial center into an industrial town. The Village Management Board was replaced by the Lusaka Management Board, which undertook the expansion of Lusaka in response to the increasing European and African population.

By 1963 it was evident that Lusaka was not a settler city like cities in the south. During the federal period (1953–1963), the African population of Lusaka grew rapidly, forcing the administration to address this increase in development. Lusaka had emerged as a major employment center because of the shift of the seat of the colonial government. After the war, Lusaka had developed heavy industries and bulk storage sites.

When the federation was dissolved in 1963 and Zambia gained its independence in October 1964, Lusaka assumed a new and more powerful status, becoming the capital of Zambia. In anticipation of the coming independence in 1964, Lusaka's infrastructure was further developed through the construction of the University of Zambia (the first phase was completed in 1965), Lusaka International Airport (completed in 1967), a new national assembly, and the Mulungushi House complex on Independence Avenue to house government departments and ministries. In addition new hotels were built to provide accommodation for the many visitors to the country whose entry port was Lusaka, especially those arriving by air. The University Teaching Hospital, the main referral hospital in the country, is located in Lusaka.

Lusaka was planned as a garden city, to facilitate agricultural activities within the city limits and in the residential areas. However, this concept was increasingly ignored or disregarded by development projects. Areas that were previously left for greenery were built up as pressure for real estate grew in the city, especially during the Second Republic. By the 1990s, Lusaka had lost much of its earlier beauty because of unplanned developments in the city.

Lusaka has hosted several important regional and world conferences. In April 1969 Lusaka hosted the East and Central Africa Summit Conference, which led to the signing of the Lusaka Manifesto on relations with Portugal, Rhodesia, and South Africa. In 1970 Lusaka hosted the Non-Aligned Conference of heads of state and government. The hosting of that conference necessitated the building of the Mulungushi International Conference Center near the National Assembly. In 1995 Lusaka hosted the peace talks between the Angolan government and UNITA, generally referred to as the Lusaka Protocol. In July 1999 Lusaka hosted peace talks between the Democratic Republic of Congo and rebel forces, which culminated in the signing of a ceasefire agreement. These significant events have earned Lusaka the moniker of Africa's "City of Peace." In September 1999 Lusaka hosted the eleventh ICASA world conference of AIDS.

Lusaka has grown to a vibrant city of 2 million people. The infrastructure of Lusaka continues to grow and a new shopping complex, the Manda Hill Shopping Mall, was built in 1998–1999. Because of the increase in commercial activities in the city, the business district has expanded, with some companies operating from previously exclusively residential areas.

The growth of Lusaka led to the development of Kafue Township some thirty miles to the south, which operates as Lusaka's heavy industrial area. Kafue is home to the Kafue Nitrogen Chemicals Company and the Kafue Textiles Company.

BIZECK J. PHIRI

See also: **Zambia.**

Further Reading

Bradley, K. "Lusaka: The New Capital of Northern Rhodesia." *Sutu.* 36 (1981).

Collins, J. *The Myth of the Garden City.* Lusaka: UNZA, Institute for Social Research (Zambian Urban Studies No.2), 1969.

Muyangwa, P. M. "The Planning and Growth of Lusaka, 1900–1970." In N. R. Hawkesworth, ed. *Local Government in Zambia.* Lusaka: Lusaka City Council, 1974.

Sampson, R. *So This Was Lusaakas.* Lusaka: Multimedia Publications, 1971.

William, G. J. *The Peugeot Guide to Lusaka.* Lusaka: Zambia Geographical Association, 1984.

Williams, G. J., ed., *Lusaka and Its Environs: A Geographical Study of a Planned Capital City in Tropical Africa.* Lusaka: Zambia Geographical Association, 1986.

Luthuli, Albert John Mavumbi (1898–1967)

Antiapartheid Politician

Winner of a Nobel Peace Prize in 1960, Albert Luthuli was a politician and a leading figure in the struggle for the liberation of South Africa from the apartheid system.

Luthuli was a product of Christian Mission Schools at both the primary and secondary levels. He served, at various times within South Africa, as chairman of the Congregational Churches of the American Board; president of the Natal Mission Conference; and the executive director of the Christian Council of South Africa. In addition, he attended religious conferences in Madras, India, in 1938, and in the United States of America in 1948. Luthuli's belief in the teaching of Christianity was to be reflected in his political outlook, in which passive, nonviolent resistance to injustice was regarded not only as the correct opposition tactic but also a spiritual force in itself.

In 1935 Albert Luthuli was made the chief of the Abasemakloweni Zulu and this warranted his relocation to his home town, Groutville, to administer justice. After a few years of service on various race–relations committees in South Africa, Luthuli joined the African National Congress (ANC) in 1945, rising rapidly through the ranks to the presidency of the Natal province branch in 1951. As a traditional ruler, Luthuli threw his influence behind the struggle against the apartheid government in South Africa. In 1952, for instance, when, in protest against the government's discriminatory policy, a defiance campaign in which race laws were deliberately violated was jointly launched by the ANC and South African Indian Congress, Luthuli openly supported the campaign and encouraged his people to participate in it. This open involvement in nationalist politics was opposed by the government. Consequently, in October 1952 the government ordered him to choose between his membership of the ANC and his chieftainship; but he refused to do either. The government reacted by deposing him of his chieftaincy in November, restricting him to his village. Barely a month after, Luthuli was elected president general of the ANC while the restriction order was till in force. He remained the ANC president until his death.

Meanwhile, following the lifting of the restriction order in 1954, Luthuli flew to Johannesburg to protest a scheme in which Africans were deprived of their remaining land rights in Johannesburg and were ordered to leave the suburb of Sophiatown and resettle in the new location of Meadowlands. He was not only prevented from speaking but served a further two-year ban by the government. He was arrested in December 1956 along with 145 other leaders of ANC and charged for high treason but released a year later with 66 others.

In May 1959, after addressing mass meetings of nonwhites and whites in western Cape Province, Luthuli was again placed under house arrest in his village and banned from all gatherings under the Suppression of Communism Act, a broad statute employed indiscriminately against all opponents of apartheid. In March 1960 the restriction order was relaxed to enable him to attend his trail for treason. On his way to Johannesburg on March 26 to give evidence at the trial, Luthuli publicly burned the pass that he, like all Africans, was required to carry, as a protest against the massacre of hundreds of Africans on March 21 that year during a peaceful demonstration at Sharpeville. He also called for a national day of mourning on March 28 in honor of those killed by the police during the Sharpeville incident.

With Luthuli at the head of the ANC of various levels from 1945 to 1967, the organization completed its transformation from an assembly of notables into a popular nationalist movement. Admittedly, Luthuli was unable to play an assertive part in ANC campaign, due to his frequent imprisonment or the government's constant banning orders that confined him, most of the time to Groutville. Nonetheless, his resilience in spite of all the rigid restrictions, coupled with his strong advocacy for moderation and nonviolence in his struggle for full political, economic, and social rights for the oppressed Africans made him a national hero and earned him international respect and support. Not surprisingly, therefore, in 1960 Luthuli won the Nobel Peace Prize, which was awarded to him the following year in Norway. While accepting the award, he remarked unequivocally that the prize was a tribute not only to himself but to all democrats of all races, particularly the Africans, who had endured and suffered for so long in seeking a peaceful resolution to the problem of race relations in South Africa.

Luthuli's 1962 book, *Let My People Go*, which was partly his autobiography and partly a history of the ANC, further enhanced his reputation for its contents and scholarly presentation. The ban on the ANC was still in force when Albert Luthuli died in Durbanon July 21, 1967, in what appears to many as a premeditated murder.

S. Ademola Ajayi

See also: **South Africa: Defiance Campaign, Freedom Charter, Treason Trials: 1952–1960.**

Biography

Born in 1899 in Salisbury (now Harare) in Southern Phodesia (now Zimbabwe), Luthuli grew up in Groutiville in the Natal Province of South Africa. Son of a Congregationalist Mission interpreter and preacher, young Luthuli attended Mission Primary School, Adams College, a Mission secondary school in Natal, where his academic brilliance shone forth and was rewarded with a scholarship to Fort Hare University. However, he turned down the offer in order to work and earn money to support his family. Luthuli became an instructor of Zulu history and literature at Adams College from 1921 to 1936 when he was made a chief by his people, the Abasemaklolweni Zulu. Consequently, Luthuli relocated to Groutville. Luthuli entered politics in 1945 as a member of the ANC. In 1952 he was deposed from his chieftancy and elected ANC president, a position in which he served until his death in 1967. He was awarded the Nobel Peace for 1960. In 1962 Luthuli was elected rector of the University of Glasgow but was not allowed to travel to Britain for his installation. Luthuli died in Durban, South African on July 21, 1967.

Further Reading

Callan, E. *Albert John Luthuli and the South African Race Conflict*. Kalamazoo, Mich., 1965.

Gordimer, N. "Chief Luthuli." *Atlantic Monthly*. 203, no. 4 (1959): 34–39.

Luthuli, A. *Let My People Go*. New York, 1962.

Pillay, G. J. *Voices of Liberation* .Vol. 1, Albert Luthuli. Pretoria, 1993.

Luwum, Janani (1922–1977)

Archbishop of Uganda

Janani Luwum was born in 1922 in Mucwini, a village in northern Uganda. He belonged to the Acholi ethnic group. His father, Eliya Okello, was one of the early converts to Christianity in the area and a teacher. Janani Luwum did not start primary school until age ten, but he performed very well and joined Gulu High School, some eighty miles away. After high school, Janani joined Boroboro Teacher Training College in Lira, run by the Church Missionary Society. By this time, Janani was a nominal Christian. He completed his teacher training in 1942 and was posted to teach in Puranga Primary School in his home district.

The turning point in Janani's life came on January 6, 1948, when, during a Christian convention, he became a "born again" Christian, and a member of the *balokole* group. The *balokole*, a Luganda word meaning "saved ones," was an East African revival movement that started in the 1930s. At his conversion, Janani declared that he had become a leader in Christ's army and was prepared to die for Jesus Christ, should that be God's will. Janani became a fiery and demanding evangelist. He decried smoking and drinking and urged others to repent and turn to Christ. He decided to leave teaching in order to go into full-time ministry with the church of Uganda.

In January 1949, Janani joined Buwalasi Theological College. At the end of his course, he was posted to St. Philip's Church in Gulu as a lay reader. The bishop was so happy with his work that he sent him back to Buwalasi in 1953 for an ordination course, and he was ordained a deacon in December 1955. Keith Russell, the new bishop of northern Uganda, wanted to prepare a new generation of church leader who would take over from the missionaries. It was through his influence that Janani obtained sponsorship for a course at St. Angustine's College in Canterbury, England.

Upon his return in 1959, the bishop posted him to what he considered the toughest parish in his diocese, Lira Palwo. The parish had twenty-four churches, communication was poor, church offerings were few, and there was little devotion to the church in the region. As this was the eve of political independence, political parties and political activity diverted people's attention from the church. Luwum worked hard but met with little success. In 1962 he was appointed vice principal of Buwalasi Theological College, but soon afterward he returned to England to study at the London College of Divinity. He returned in 1965 and was made the principal of Buwalasi Theological College.

In 1966 Luwum became the provincial secretary of the church of Uganda and he moved to Kampala. This was a difficult time in the country as well as in the church. In 1966 Uganda experienced its first political crisis, which forced the Kabaka (king) into exile. Archbishop Leslie Brown was succeeded by Sabiti, a non-Baganda. These developments angered the Baganda, and Luwum, as provincial secretary, had to deal with the ensuing difficulties. In 1968 he was appointed bishop of the newly created diocese of northern Uganda. He was consecrated in January 1969 in a colorful ceremony attended by high-ranking politicians, and security officers including Idi Amin, who was then chief of the Uganda Army.

Luwum took on the weakest diocese in the province. The church congregation had dwindled, the buildings were in a state of disrepair, some clergy had resigned, and donations to the church were extremely low. Janani worked hard to improve the situation but met with little success. The situation worsened after the coup d' étât led by Idi Amin on January 25, 1971. Thousands of soldiers originating from Acholi were killed. There was intense suffering, bitterness, and fear, and Luwum worked hard to bring God's comfort to the people.

In 1974 Luwum became the archbishop of Uganda, Rwanda, Burundi, and Boga-Zaire. All Asians had been expelled from the country in 1972, the economy was collapsing, prices were rocketing, and people were dying. Relations between the church and state continued to deteriorate as the church leaders condemned the government's brutality and unjust treatment of the people. Meanwhile, opposition to the government was growing, and President Amin began to see the church as an enemy of the government. On January 30, 1977, Amin met with his advisers to discuss the situation and they drew up a plan to eliminate all opposition, with Luwum high on their list of suspected dissidents.

On February 5, 1977, armed men raided the archbishop's house, searching for weapons. The following week, the Protestant bishops met to discuss, among other things, the raid on Luwum's house. They drafted a strong and frank memorandum to the president expressing their disapproval of the government. The president refused to meet with the bishops. On February 14, he summoned Luwum and accused him of plotting to overthrow the government. Amin called a meeting of all government officials, members of the armed forces, ambassadors, and religious leaders. The vice president chaired the meeting and publicly accused the archbishop of plotting with the former president Milton Obote to overthrow the government. Luwum was arrested, together with two cabinet ministers. The next morning, newspaper headlines informed the country that they died in a car accident while trying to escape, although it was widely accepted that they had, in fact, been murdered by Amin's regime. Janani Luwum was proclaimed the first martyr of the church of Uganda's second century, in a memorial service.

Filda Ojok

See also: **Uganda: Amin Dada, Idi: Coup and Regime, 1971–1979.**

Biography

Born in 1922 in Mucwini, a village in northern Uganda. Attended Gulu High School and Boroboro Teacher Training College. Completed his teacher training in 1942 and was posted to teach in Puranga Primary School. Became a "born again" Christian, January 6, 1948. Named archbishop of Uganda, Rwanda, Burundi, and Boga-Zaire in 1974. Died February 17, 1977.

Further Reading

Ford, M. *Janani: The Making of a Martyr.* Lakeland, Marshall, Morgan and Scott, 1978.

Sentamu, J. "Tribalism, Religion and Despotism in Uganda." In *The Terrible Alternative: Christian Martyrdom in the Twentieth Century*, edited by A. Chandler. London: Cassell, 1998.

Mary, C. *Candles in the Dark: Six Modern Martyr of the Church of Uganda.* Kampala, 1984.

Henry Okullu, Kodwo E. Enkrah, Akiki Bomera Mujaju, and John Mbiti. *Archbishop Janani Luwum Memorial Lectures: A Twentieth Century Christian Martyr of the Church of Uganda.* Kampala: Centenary Publishing House, 1999.

Festo Kivengere. *I love Idi Amin Marshal.* London: Morgan and Scott, 1977.

Lyautey, General Hubert: *See* Morocco: Lyautey, General Hubert, and Evolution of French Protectorate, 1912–1950.

M

Ma' al-'Aynayn (1830–1910)

Shaykh, Religious Scholar, and Political Leader

Ma'al-'Aynayn is the more familiar nickname of the Sufi shaykh, religious scholar, and political leader Sidi al-Mustafa Wuld Muhammad Fadil. Ma'al-'Aynayn's father was Muhammad Fadil Wuld Mamin (d.–1868) whose Sufi teachings he helped to disseminate throughout the western Sahara and Morocco in the second half of the nineteenth century.

A member of the pastoral nomadic Ahl Jih al-Mukhtar, Ma'al-'Aynayn was a prodigious student said to shun all distractions in order to pursue his studies. He completed his early education with various members of the Ahl Jih al-Mukhtar before passing under his father's tutelage. Roughly a decade later, Muhammad Fadil acknowledged Ma'al-'Aynayn's mastery of the esoteric and exoteric religious sciences by bestowing on him the ceremonial turban of a shaykh that authorized him to transmit his teachings to others.

Ma'al-'Aynayn left the Hodh in 1857 en route to the Muslim holy cities of Mecca and Medina in order to complete the *hajj*. In Marrakech he gained an audience with the Moroccan sultan's heir apparent Sidi Muhammad and followed this meeting by a visit with Sultan 'Abd al-Rahman in Meknes. Impressed by his guest and perhaps aware of Muhammad Fadil's reputation, 'Abd al-Rahman arranged for Ma'al-'Aynayn to accompany members of the Sultan's family who were departing for Arabia by steamer. This auspicious introduction began a lifelong association between the shaykh and the Moroccan ruling family.

Upon returning from the *hajj*, Ma'al-'Aynayn settled briefly in the town of Tinduf on the desert's northern edge where he married among the Tajakant, whose organization of caravans between Moroccan and Algerian cities in the north, and southern Saharan towns such as Timbuktu and Arawan, revived Tinduf in the latter half of the nineteenth century. Ma'al-'Aynayn next embarked on a several year period during which he traveled widely in the western Saharan regions of Saqiyat al-Hamra', Tiris, and the Adrar, in many cases contracting marriages among the people with whom he came into contact, and in the process gaining a following drawn to him by his growing reputation as a mystic, mediator, and miracle worker. The social bonds symbolized in these marriage contracts endured beyond the actual marriages, most of which quickly ended in divorce, and reputedly, the shaykh married 116 times without exceeding the Quranic proscription of four concurrent wives. By the time Ma'al-'Aynayn returned to his father's camp in the Hodh in 1862, he remained just long enough to receive his shaykh's blessing to return permanently to that region of the northwestern Sahara, where he had already established himself as an important religious and political figure.

Ma'al-'Aynayn's standing with the 'Alawi rulers of Morocco continued to grow throughout the second half of the nineteenth century, aided by highly placed followers in the royal court. Moroccan Sultan Hassan's head of the imperial guard Idris b. Ya'ish and more importantly, his royal chamberlain Ahmad b. Musa, better known as Ba Ahmad were both Ma'al-'Aynayn's disciples. The Sultan in turn sought to use the shaykh's influence in the Saqiyat al-Hamra' as a means of extending Moroccan hegemony there and shoring up his southern defenses against increasing European incursions. From the mid-1880s, Hassan recognized Ma'al-'Aynayn as his *khalifa* or official representative over the lands between Tarfaya and Dakhla on the Atlantic coast.

Ma'al-'Aynayn had continued to live a predominantly nomadic existence until the late 1890s. Then, with financial and logistical support from the new sultan, the adolescent 'Abd al-Aziz, whose grand vizier and now de facto ruler was the disciple Ba Ahmad, Ma'al-'Aynayn undertook the construction of a large walled compound at a site known as Smara in the Saqiyat al-Hamra'. A visitor to Smara at the turn of the century testified to the tremendous attraction this structure in the desert had on the region's nomadic inhabitants. Ahmad al-Shinqiti states that no less than 10,000 people were living in tents around Smara, all cared for by the caravans that arrived daily bringing supplies. Smara's importance as a trade entrepot had increased greatly at that time due to a protracted struggle between the Tajakant and their rivals the Tekna that decimated Tinduf and diverted most of the trade westward to Smara. News of a more aggressive French colonial expansion emanating from their post at Saint Louis on the Senegal River also arrived with the caravans. Ba Ahmad and Ma'al-'Aynayn attempted to counter French expansion along the desert's southern edge by sending emissaries along the caravan routes offering the Sultan's backing in resisting the French.

The murder in 1905 of Mauritania's first colonial commissioner General Xavier Coppolani hastened the military conquest northward toward Smara. French colonial sources implicated Ma'al-'Aynayn in Coppolani's death, although there is no conclusive evidence that he played a direct role in the attack carried out in the central Mauritanian town of Tijikja. However, Ma'al-'Aynayn was actively engaged in resistance efforts, calling for a jihad against the French and using his influence with the Sultan to secure arms and ammunition, while several of his sons directly engaged French forces in battle. By 1909 the French had advanced as far as the Adrar, forcing Ma'al-'Aynayn, his family, and followers to evacuate Smara for Tiznit in Morocco's Sus region. From Tiznit, Ma'al-'Aynayn set out for Fez where, some historians assert, he intended to seize power from Sultan 'Abd al-Hafiz, whose overthrow of 'Abd al-Aziz the shaykh had initially supported after 'Abd al-Aziz signed the Act of Algeciras in 1906. Forced to turn back before reaching Fez by a large French military presence, Ma'al-'Aynayn returned to Tiznit where he died on October 28, 1910.

Ma'al-'Aynayn left a substantial written legacy dominated by works on Sufism and Islamic jurisprudence that also covered a wide and eclectic range of topics. Popularly ascribed authorship of over 400 works, less than 100 can be identified with verifiable titles. Forty-three of his writings, or approximately one-fourth of all book titles published in Morocco between 1891 and 1900, were lithographed in Fez largely with Ba Ahmad's financial backing.

Glen W. McLaughlin

See also: **Western Sahara: Nineteenth Century to the Present.**

Biography

Born in approximately 1831 in the Hodh region of southeastern Mauritania. After being educated by the Ahl Jih al-Mukhtar and his father, Ma'al-'Aynayn left the Hodh in 1857 for Mecca and Medina in order to complete the *hajj.* Settled briefly in Tinduf. Traveled for several years in the western Saharan regions of Saqiyat al-Hamra', Tiris, and the Adrar. Returned to the Hodh in 1862. Nomadic up until the late 1890s, when he undertook construction of the compound at Smara. Engaged in anticolonial resistance efforts. Called for a jihad against the French. Evacuated Smara for Tiznit in Morocco. Died in Tiznit on October 28, 1910.

Further Reading

Caro Baroja, J. *Estudios Saharianos.* Madrid: Instituto de Estudios Africanos, 1955.
Desire-Vuillemin, G. *Histoire de la Mauritanie.* Paris: Editions Karthala, 1997.
Harmon, S. A. "Shaykh Ma' al-'Aynayn: Armed Resistance and French Policy in Northwest Africa, 1900–1910." *Jusur.* 8 (1992): 1–22.
Martin, B. G. *Muslim Brotherhoods in Nineteenth Century Africa.* Cambridge: Cambridge University Press, 1976.
Marty, P. "Les Fadelia." *Revue du Monde Musulman.* 31 (1915–1916): 139–220.
al-Shinqiti, Ahmad b. al-Amin. *al-Wasit fi tarajim udaba' Shinqit.* Nouakchott: Mu'assassa Munir, 1989.

Maasai: *See* Nilotes, Eastern Africa: Eastern Nilotes: Maasai.

Macaulay, Herbert (1864–1946)

Nigerian Politician and Nationalist Leader

From 1898 until his death in 1946, Herbert Macaulay, more than any other individual, dominated the politics of Lagos. Having grown up in a rigidly Victorian household, as assimilated and Europeanized as any African elite of his time, Macaulay was not opposed to British imperialism as such. He was neither a revolutionary nor a demagogue as the colonial officials and his enemies portrayed him. Liberalism was his creed. With an acute sense of history, he espoused a doctrine of democratic self-government for the colonies based on justice and equality, within the British commonwealth, all of which ran counter to the ideology of colonial government and white supremacy prevalent in his time. With characteristic passion and great vigor, he threw himself into every political controversy in Lagos, never for once looking back, conceding defeat, or compromising. A great pamphleteer and propagandist, a man of unusual intellectual and social talents, he directed his bitter, but biting and effective invectives against all policies and practices of the colonial administration that he considered objectionable and against the interests of the Nigerian peoples, as he perceived them.

In case after case, and with the aid of his newspaper, *The Lagos Daily News*, Macaulay became a tireless and outspoken critic of British imperialism. As early as 1905, he published a scathing attack on the British deportation and imprisonment of two leading chiefs of Ilesa and took special exception to the jaundiced reporting of the case in the British Press, which described the victims as "nigger chiefs." His wars against what he repeatedly described as the British arbitrary use of power, ruthless disregard of common courtesy, and arrogant indifference to pledges and assurances, would bring him into many confrontations with the government, while making him a popular hero among the masses.

In 1908 Macaulay launched a campaign against a proposed water rate or tax and against the Hausa Land Ordinance, which gave the colonial government wide power to acquire any land in the country. In another pamphlet he exposed a scandal in the Nigerian Railway, which the colonial administration was trying to cover up. He was one of the leading figures in the White Colonial Church question, which demanded leadership positions for Africans in the church. Between 1912 and 1913, he was the spokesman of the Lagos Auxiliary of the Aborigines Protection Society and was appointed to lead a delegation of the society to London to testify against land acquisition before a British parliamentary committee. But on the eve of his departure, he was arrested, charged with perjury, and sentenced to five years imprisonment, even though the five assessors of the court had each returned a verdict of not guilty.

The crisis over land came to a head in the celebrated Chief Oluwa's Apapa Land case. Chief Oluwa, with the active support and advice of Macaulay, sued the Lagos government and demanded full compensation for the government acquisition of his family land at Apapa. When he lost the case in Nigeria, Chief Oluwa, accompanied by Macaulay, took the case to the Privy Council in London. The Privy Council upheld Chief Oluwa's appeal for full compensation. Thus instead of the 500 pounds offered by the government, Chief Oluwa in the end collected a check of 22,500 pounds. Apart from bringing Macaulay into the limelight, the Oluwa case was a landmark in Nigerian history. To the chagrin of the colonial administration, the case established the principle of compensation for the chiefs as absolute owners of the land. Hardly had the dust of this case settled, when Macaulay again became embroiled in another case involving the *Eleko* or ruler of Lagos, Esugbayi. The trouble began with certain press interviews that Macaulay granted in London speaking about the plight of the *Eleko* and sharply criticizing the colonial administration. The Lagos government demanded that the *Eleko* publicly denounce Macaulay. When the *Eleko* refused, he was suspended, then deposed, and later deported. Macaulay launched a tenacious campaign in Nigeria as well as in England to have the *Eleko* reinstated. Eleven years later in 1931, and with the ascension of a new governor, the *Eleko* was restored back to his throne.

Macaulay's popularity transcended the confines of Lagos. Leaders of the Itsekiri and Urhobo invited him to represent them in their struggle against British oppression. The chiefs of Benin wrote him to express their appreciation of his kindness to Benin people resident in Lagos. In 1937 the Igbo people of Ogidi in eastern Nigeria, got him to write a petition to the government requiring a council for them. His involvement in organized politics led him to found the first political party in Nigeria, the Nigerian National Democratic Party (NNDP). Though he could not contest election, because of his earlier convictions, he remained the principal force behind the party that dominated and won every election held in Nigeria between 1923 and 1938, when the more radical Nigerian Youth Movement seized the initiatives. In 1944, two years before his death at the age of eighty-two, he became the first president of the first modern political party in Nigeria, the National Council of Nigeria and the Cameroun, a party largely organized by Nnamdi Azikwe, who became its first general secretary.

Macaulay was admired by many in his lifetime and memorialized, decades after his death, on the Nigerian currency as the "Father of Nigerian Nationalism" and thus of modern Nigeria. However, he also had many enemies, by whom he was criticized as self-centered, egocentric, vindictive, and of suspicious motives. While whatever might be said of Macaulay's motives and flamboyant styles, no one would deny his personal charm, his dignified bearing, his generosity to the less fortunate, and his genuine sympathy for indigenous cultures and institutions. Equally impressive was his ability to identify with, connect to, and inspire the populace. In the defense of their interests he deployed his power of erudition, his indefatigable skill as a journalist and bibliophile.

FUNSO AFOLAYAN

See also: **Nigeria: Colonial Period: Intelligentsia, Nationalism, Independence.**

Biography

Born in Lagos in November 1864. Started elementary school in 1869 and attended CMS Grammar School, Lagos, 1877–1880. Joined the Lagos Civil Service as a clerk in 1881. Left for England in July 1890. Studied surveying and civil engineering at Plymouth and music and piano tuning in London. Returned to Lagos in September 1893 and was appointed Surveyor of Crown's Land, a position he occupied till 1898, when he resigned and obtained a license for private practice.

That same year, he married Caroline Pratt, who died a year later. From 1908 onward, he became involved in several cases and issues that repeatedly brought him into conflicts with the colonial administration. Notable among these were his pamphlet on the Railways (1908), his involvement in the Apapa Land Case (1920–1921), the Gunpowder Plot Rumor Case (1928), and the deposition and reinstatement of Eleko Esugbayi (1920–1931). Was imprisoned twice by the colonial administration. Founded the NNDP in 1923 and became the president of the NCNC in 1944. Became sick in the course of a national NCNC political tour and was brought back home to Lagos, where he died on May 7, 1946.

Further Reading

Cole, P. *Modern and Traditional Elites in the Politics of Lagos.* London: Cambridge University Press, 1975.

July, R. *The Origins of Modern African Political Thought: Its Development in West Africa During the Nineteenth and Twentieth Centuries.* New York: Frederick A. Praeger, 1967, and London: Faber and Faber, 1968.

Kopytoff, J. H. *A Preface to Modern Nigeria: The "Sierra Leonians" in Yoruba, 1830–1890.* Madison: University of Wisconsin Press, 1965.

Sobande, O. A. *Notes and Comments on the Life of Mr. Herbert Macaulay.* Ebute Metta: Moonlight Printing Works, 1948.

Tamuno, T. M. *Herbert Macaulay, Nigerian Patriot.* London: Heinemann Educational Books, 1975.

Thomas, I. B. *Life History of Herbert Macaulay.* Lagos: Tika-Tore Press, 1947.

Machel: *See* Mozambique: Machel and the Frelimo Revolution, 1975–1986.

Madagascar: Prehistory and Developments to *c.*1500

Madagascar, the fourth largest island in the world (area 587,000 square km), lies in the southwest Indian Ocean, separated from Mozambique on mainland Africa by some 230 kilometres. It, like India, separated from the vast continent of Gondwanaland some 200 million years ago, before the evolution of the larger mammals, and remained isolated from human contact until a relatively modern era.

The origins of the Malagasy are one of the great remaining historical mysteries. The issue is significant both in terms of the history of Madagascar and because of what it reveals about pre-Islamic, trans-Indian Ocean trade networks. Since at least the sixteenth century, visitors to the island observed two main physiognomic types, "Negroid" and "Malay-Indonesian." The majority view until the 1970s was based on Grandidier, who held

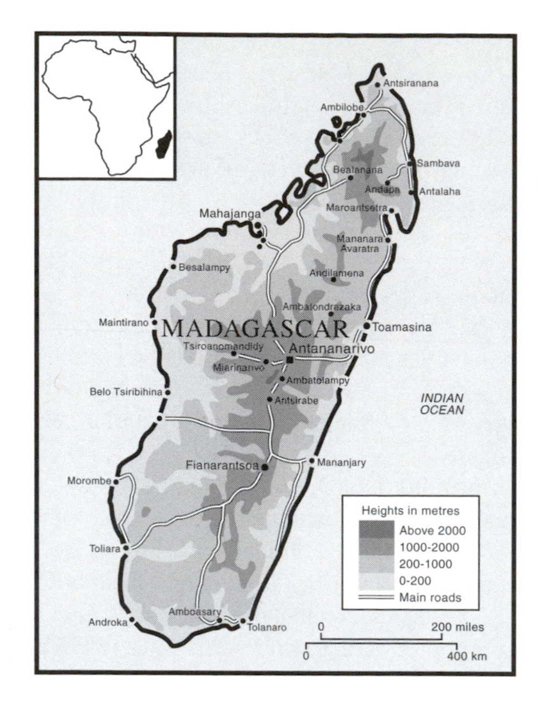

Madagascar.

that Austronesians were the first to settle Madagascar. Impelled by a sense of adventure, they left their Indonesia-Pacific homelands and sailed directly across the Indian Ocean in successive fleets of outrigger canoes. Kon-Tiki-style expeditions have since confirmed that such voyages are possible. Since the 1970s, most scholars have followed Ferrand, a contemporary of Grandidier, in proposing an Indonesian migratory route that followed the old maritime network along the northern rim of the Indian Ocean, from Indonesia to Sri Lanka and India, and from there to East Africa via the Persian Gulf and Arabia.

There exist some traditions of autonomous African migrations to Madagascar, but, in the absence of African oceanic sailing technology, it is more likely that Africans either intermarried with Austronesians prior to their settlement of Madagascar, or accompanied the latter, whether voluntarily or involuntarily. Slavery was introduced into Madagascar by outsiders as a consequence of prior involvement in a long-distance maritime slave trade. Genetic studies support the view that the forefathers of most present-day Malagasy originated from Bantu-speaking East Africa and from the Austronesian world.

The issue of timing is also contentious. Grandidier speculated that migrations to the island started during the last millennia BCE and continued through to the early centuries CE. Dahl, on the basis of the scarcity of Sanskrit terms in the Malagasy language, argued for a departure from Indonesia in the first centuries CE. Evidence of Indonesian cultural influence in East Africa, but a lack of tangible evidence of Indonesian settlement there has led most historians to argue that the island was settled prior to the expansion of Islam, at the latest by the middle of the first millennium. However, archaeologists have to date found no firm evidence of human settlement in Madagascar prior to the eighth century. Thus, the evidence to date supports the view that the human species, which arguably first developed in Africa, probably did not colonize the largest African island until the eighth or ninth century, and that although some groups were African, others were wholly or predominantly Austronesian, thus constituting the most western outreach of this family of peoples.

From the seventh century, Muslims dominated the main trading routes of the Indian Ocean, and in the east African region an Islamic-Swahili economy flourished from the thirteenth to fifteenth centuries. Coastal entrepôts of importance were established not only along the east African coast but also on the northwest and northeast coasts of Madagascar, controlled by "Arab" groups (the *Antalaotra*) from the Swahili coast, Arabia and the Persian Gulf, and Indians (the *Karany*). However, in 1223 a Malagasy force temporarily seized Aden, a key entrepôt in east-west maritime trade, while direct commercial contact between Indonesia and Madagascar continued, at least intermittently, until the thirteenth century and possibly until the start of the sixteenth century, when tradition has it that the Merina, the most "Austronesian" looking, and from about 1800, the economically and politically dominant people of the island, first reached Madagascar.

The settlement pattern was largely dictated by geographic and climatic factors. The island possesses a high central plateau that, running on a north-south axis almost the entire length of the island, divides the narrow eastern littoral from the western plains. The east coast has a tropical climate and was covered with thick forests; the inland region is mountainous, infertile, and largely temperate. The western plains, covered variously with forests, bushes, and grass, has a varied climate; the north being semitropical and the south largely desert. The ease of coastal navigation and the physical barriers to travel into the interior meant that settlement extended from the northwest southward down the western littoral and along the northern and eastern coasts. Significant colonization of the high plateau interior occurred probably only in the second millennium. The size, topography, climate, relative isolation, and "virgin" nature of Madagascar ensured that such colonization was a slow process, resulting in small dispersed and largely self-sufficient settlements whose affairs were governed by chiefs guided by a group of elders.

The mixture of Indonesian, African, and Arabic was reflected in the material culture of the Malagasy. The original settlers brought aspects of Indonesian material culture, notably riziculture, banana cultivation, rectangular house construction, and outrigger canoes. By origin a maritime people, they also took readily to fishing. African influence was also strong. Large groups of Bantu speakers existed on the west coast of Madagascar as late as the start of the seventeenth century and the raising of zebu, cattle originally imported from East Africa, became one of the principle economic activities in western and southern Madagascar. However, only communities on the northwest and northeast coasts remained in constant contact with the Muslim-dominated commercial network of the Indian Ocean, which exported natural products like tortoiseshell, beeswax, and honey. In return, it absorbed some of the commodities shipped from the east African hinterland, and commodities shipped from other regions of the long distance maritime trade network, including Indian glass beads, silk, and Chinese porcelain. Such commerce was facilitated by the regularization of direct voyages (using the monsoon) between western India and East Africa, and including Madagascar, and the gradual expansion of human settlement into the interior of the island.

GWYN R. CAMPBELL

Further Reading

Brown, M. *A History of Madagascar.* Ipswich: Damien Tunnacliffe, 1995.

Campbell, G. "Theories Concerning the Origins of the Malagasy." In *Australes*, edited by M. Michel and Y. Paillard, Paris: l'Harmattan, 1996.

Deschamps, H. *Histoire de Madagascar.* Paris: Berger-Levrault, 1972.

Vérin, P. *The History of Civilization in North Madagascar.* Rotterdam and Boston: A. A. Balkema, 1986.

———. *Madagascar.* Paris: Kathala, 1990.

Madagascar: Malagasy Kingdoms, Evolution of

The evolution of kingdoms in Madagascar was closely linked to economic developments and to Muslim ideology. Madagascar was first settled sometime during the first millennium by a proto-Malagasy people of mixed Austronesian-African genetic heritage. Originally seafaring traders, they first colonized the coasts of Madagascar. Settlements were initially small and scattered, relatively concentrated populations developing only in ports on the northwest and northeast coasts linked to the Indian Ocean maritime network and in fertile valleys, notably in the northwest and in the southeast where rice was cultivated. Not until the mid-second millennium did communities of any size develop in the sterile plateau.

By the close of the first millennium, the main ports were dominated by the Silamo, Islamized trading groups of Arabic (Antalaotra) and Indian (Karany) origin. They imported an ideology of royalty that, of limited scope in the scattered coastal trading communities, proved extremely valuable in controlling the inputs of land and labor vital to agricultural production in the hinterland. The ideology of kingship became particularly pronounced in the comparatively densely populated valleys of southeast Madagascar from the fourteenth century with the establishment of Antalaotra dynasties claiming to have come from Mecca. The east coast of Madagascar was until the seventeenth century marginal to the maritime trading network and denied constant contact with their Antalaotra colleagues on the northwest coast, the ruling elites in the southeast of the island adopted the Malagasy language and most Malagasy customs. They nevertheless retained the ideology of kingship, buttressed by the possession of the sorabe, sacred writings in Arabic characters, knowledge of which was closely guarded by a small group with sacerdotal influence called the ombiasy.

Under Antalaotra influence a number of petty kingdoms developed in the southeast; they may have influenced the principalities that emerged in the southern part of the central plateau (Betsileo). However, there is debate over the origins of the first large and relatively centralized Malagasy kingdoms that emerged among the Sakalava of west Madagascar during the seventeenth century and the Merina of the high central plateau from the close of the eighteenth century. Some scholars hold that ombiasy carried the ideology of kingship across southern Madagascar to Menabe, thus stimulating the rise of the first large Sakalava kingdom, and that that ideology spread progressively northward up the west coast, promoting the creating of the Ambongo and Iboina kingdoms. Kent rather holds that the kingdom of Menabe was the creation of migrants of mixed Austronesian-African origin from Great Zimbabwe. Whatever the case, the magical and divinatory powers of the ombiasy were certainly much appreciated by ruling elites and were officially employed by the first sovereigns of the united Merina kingdom at the end of the eighteenth century and start of the nineteenth century. Nevertheless, the basis upon which both the Sakalava and Merina kingdoms were built was economic rather than ideological.

Madagascar long lay on the periphery of the Indian Ocean trading system which linked the regions bordering the northern part of the Indian Ocean. Critical to this commercial network were the monsoons, a particularly stable system of winds and currents that facilitated maritime sail. Only the north and northwest of Madagascar were connected to this system, most of the island lying beyond its reach, isolated from sizeable markets. This changed from the sixteenth century with the arrival in the Indian Ocean of rival European nations, for Madagascar lay on their route to the East, which passed the Cape of Good Hope. In consequence, both southwest and east Madagascar became incorporated into Indian Ocean trade. Various attempts to found European colonies in the island failed, largely due to a hostile disease environment, but trading posts were maintained and Madagascar became a significant reprovisioning base and supplier of slaves to service European trading entrepôts, notably at the Cape and Batavia.

The impact of this was first felt most strongly in western Madagascar, which, unlike most of the east coast, possessed many protected anchorages, large tracts of agriculturally productive land (rice, maize, and cattle) and large rivers (e.g., the Mangoky, Tsiribihina, and Betsiboka) navigable far into the interior. It also possessed in the Silamo, a well-organized body of middlemen fully integrated into the Muslim dominated trade network of the northern Indian Ocean. Silamo leaders became the commercial advisers of Sakalava kings who were often sufficiently influenced to adopt Islam and marry their daughters to prominent Antalaotra. Benefiting from burgeoning foreign trade, the Sakalava reduced most of northern and central Madagascar to tutelage.

In the late seventeenth century, European pirates hounded by the British and French navies from the West Indies maritime trade in the Indian Ocean, were also attracted to Madagascar where they established bases along the west and northern coasts of Madagascar. In the northeast, where they married into the families of the local Malagasy elite, their offspring formed the basis of the Betsimisaraka dynasty that came to rule over most of the eastern littoral. However, the rise of the Betsimisaraka dynasty owed little to traditional maritime trade. Rather, it was based upon the stimulus to the regional economy given by the rise of a plantation economy on the Mascarene Islands of Réunion and Mauritius from the mid-eighteenth century that swung the balance of commercial power from the west to the east coast of Madagascar. The Mascarenes specialized in labor-intensive cash crops for export, becoming heavily dependent upon imports of food and servile labor. Although some provisions and slaves were shipped from the coasts of East Africa and west Madagascar, east Madagascar constituted the closest and cheapest source of supply for the Mascarenes. In its turn, Mascarene demand stimulated the production of agricultural produce and export of slaves from eastern Madagascar. In part the latter was met by the coastal population, but the main source of slaves by the late eighteenth century was the plateau interior, where the adoption of drainage schemes and highly successful hydraulic rice cultivation had facilitated rapid growth in, and concentration of, population. The struggle to control the slave export trade, and the return trade in armaments, was similarly a decisive factor in the emergence of the Merina kingdom in the late eighteenth century.

GWYN R. CAMPBELL

Further Reading

Brown, M. *A History of Madagascar.* Ipswich: Damien Tunnacliffe, 1995.

Deschamps, H. *Histoire de Madagascar.* Paris: Berger-Levrault, 1972.

Kent, R. K. *Early Kingdoms in Madagascar 1500–1700.* New York: Holt, Rinehart and Winston, 1970.

Lombard, J. *La royauté Sakalava: Formation, développement et effondrement du XVIIe au XXe siècle.* [The Sakalava Kingdom: Its Establishment, Development and Fall, from the 17th century to the 20th century]. Tananarive, 1973.

Madagascar: Merina Kingdom, Nineteenth Century

In the mid-eighteenth century, Imerina, a small landlocked region in the largely sterile high central plateau of Madagascar, was plagued by famine and wracked by civil wars. By the 1890s it was politically united, economically self-sufficient and had become the trade center of the entire island. There were two main reasons for the political ascendance of the Merina. First, the Merina crown expanded agricultural production to the extent that it supported a sharp rise in population and the emergence of a significant specialist artisan sector. Second, from the mid-eighteenth century a plantation economy developed on the Mascarene islands of Réunion and Mauritius whose planters looked chiefly to Madagascar for provisions and slaves. The Merina crown, profiting from its ability to meet the demand for slaves, by the early nineteenth century emerged as the most powerful state in the island. It subsequently launched a program of imperial expansion, in an attempt to subject the entire island to Merina rule, which was halted by French colonial conquest in 1895.

The traditional historical interpretation is that the Merina unified all peoples of the island under a humane and modernizing monarchy, forging for the first time a Malagasy nationality. As a result of the 1820 British alliance, the Merina banned the slave export trade, received missionaries who founded a Western education system, artisans who helped construct the basis for one of the earliest attempted industrial revolutions in the world, and soldiers to create a well-equipped standing army. From the mid-nineteenth century, they introduced a constitutional monarchy, adopted Christianity as the official religion, and were among the first countries in the world to make schooling compulsory. Despite this, the French conquered Madagascar in 1895 under the banner of their "civilizing mission." The reaction was immediate and from 1895 to 1897 the island was wracked by the Menalamba uprising, one of the earliest nationalist revolts in African history.

The reality was different. In the mid-1820s, the Merina rejected the British alliance and adopted self-sufficient policies, central to which was the conquest of the entire island and the exploitation of its human and natural resources to promote the imperial Merina economy. *Fanompoana* (nonremunerated forced labor for the state) became the organizing principle of the imperial economy. As the state enjoyed monopoly control of everything of value, this labor tax for the free population included everything from military service and public works to industrial and agricultural labor.

The history of industrial *fanompoana* in the munitions factories from 1830 to 1857 is unique in precolonial Africa. At its height, the central Mantasoa complex comprised five factories with water-driven machines that produced a wide range of products but which specialized in the manufacture of muskets and cannon. It was constructed with a *fanompoana* force of 20,000, equivalent to about 5 per cent of adult males registered for *fanompoana* in Imerina, and was maintained with a permanent workforce of 5,000. *Fanompoana* was supplemented by slave labor: captives from imperial campaigns and imported African slaves.

From the mid-nineteenth century, the imperialist momentum slowed, but a general stagnation of trade from the late 1870s and the intensification of military conflict with the French precipitated the imperial Merina regime into bankruptcy. In consequence, it dramatically enlarged the scope and intensity of *fanompoana*, created largely through the state church (founded in 1869), which further supplied the ideology of empire; Christianity in subjugated regions became totally identified with Merina imperialism. Military conscription was applied to the Betsileo, and industrial forced labor was extended to include women and children. By the 1890s *fanompoana* reaching crisis proportions. In Imerina and Betsileo, which practiced finely balanced hydraulic cultivation of rice, even a few weeks absence during critical agricultural periods could bring economic ruin to a rural household.

Moreover, far from forging a common national identity, Merina imperial oppression and exploitation exacerbated ethnic tension and created an antipathy amongst non-Merina peoples toward the Merina that hindered the emergence of a "Malagasy" identity. Indeed, it could be argued that common antipathy toward the Merina forged a "national" consciousness amongst the Sakalava who, in the eighteenth century, had possessed a formidable empire to which the Merina had paid tribute, and who considered that the latter were a race apart; not of the original Malagasy stock, they possessed lighter complexions than other peoples of the island, spoke a different dialect, and willingly cooperated with foreigners. Indeed, in some quarters an ideology of resistance developed that identified the Merina as a foreign imperial power.

From the 1880s *fanompoana* extended via the schools to children alienated Merina subjects who deserted both industrial projects and the land, resulting in the collapse of the industrial experiment and in an increasing incidence of harvest failure, famine, and disease. At the same time, incessant ethnic conflict frustrated the Merina vision of empire and limited their effective rule to, at maximum, one-third of the land surface of the island, comprising in the main the central plateau and most of the east coast. Moreover, as Merina military power started to wane from the 1850s, the Sakalava and Bara launched ever-increasing raids against the plateau heart of the Merina empire. Persecuted by the state and by the Sakalava and Bara warriors, ordinary subjects fled, often to form brigand groups whose depredations accentuated the plight of those who remained. By the late 1880s entire tracts of the plateau were deserted and famine and disease—malaria, smallpox, typhoid—increased, the latter often reaching epidemic proportions. When the French troops took the Merina capital in 1895, they were largely unopposed.

The majority view is that the *Menalamba* revolt of 1895–1897 was fueled by a patriotic desire to oppose unjustified French colonial pretensions and restore a united Malagasy kingdom. The revisionist view is that the French decision to impose a protectorate and rule through the existing Merina administrative structure ignited the anger of those—both Merina and non-Merina—who wished to see the swift demise of a corrupt and oppressive Merina regime. It is significant that the chief targets of the rebels were not the French, but rather the institutions and personnel, both indigenous and foreign, of the state church and schools—the primary means of recruitment of forced labor.

GWYN R. CAMPBELL

See also: **Madagascar: Colonial Period: French Rule; Madagascar: Malagasy Kingdoms, Evolution of.**

Further Reading

Campbell, G. "Slavery and *Fanompoana*: The Structure of Forced Labour in Imerina Madagascar, 1790–1861." *Journal of African History.* 29 (1988): 463–486.

———. "The Menalamba Revolt and Brigandry in Imperial Madagascar, 1820–1897." *International Journal of African Historical Studies.* 24, no. 2 (1991): 259–291.

———. "The History of Nineteenth Century Madagascar: 'le royaume' or 'l'empire?" *Omaly sy Anio.* (1994): 331–379.

Kent, R., ed. *Madagascar in History.* Berkeley: Foundation for Malagasy Studies, 1979.

Raison-Jourde, F., ed. *Les souverains de Madagascar*—[The Monarchs of Madagascar]. Paris: Khartala, 1983.

Madagascar: French Conquest, Colonization

For most of the eighteenth century, the British and French competed bitterly for ascendancy in the Indian Ocean, but victory in the Napoleonic Wars (1793–1815) gave predominance in the region to Britain. In the western Indian Ocean, Britain deprived France of its trading posts in Madagascar and of Mauritius and Réunion, returning only the latter to France in the postwar settlement. Stung by the loss of Mauritius, France continued to fight for influence over Madagascar, where it possessed considerable historical claims, based upon former settlements at Fort Dauphin (Taolanaro) (1642–1674), and subsequent trading posts, notably at Fort Dauphin and Antongil Bay. An 1818–1819 French expedition seized Nosy Boraha, an island off the east coast of Madagascar, and Tintingue and Fort Dauphin (Taolanaro) on the mainland. However, malaria decimated colonists, and the fall of Portal from government in Paris in 1821 resulted in the abandonment of a systematic colonial policy and the curtailment of imperial expansion on financial grounds.

Moreover, the British-trained Merina army seized the reoccupied French trading posts in Madagascar. Autarkic policies adopted from the mid–1820s led the Merina to reject both British and French influence in the island and to ban foreign access to Malagasy labor. This was anathema to Réunionnais planters who

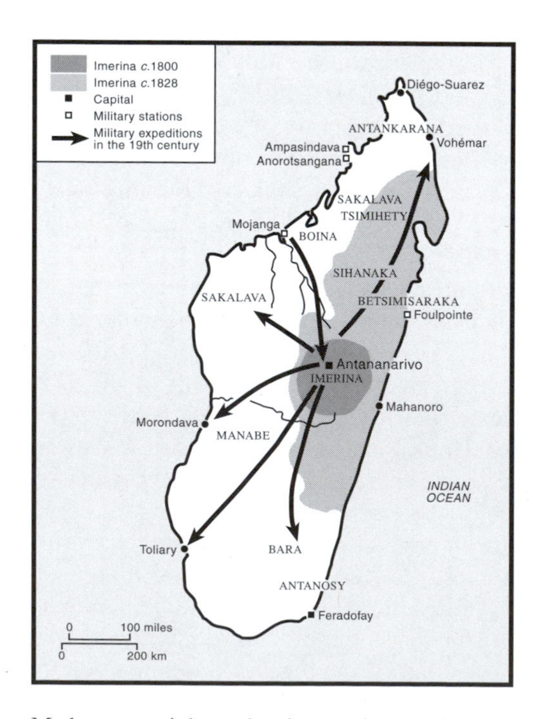

Madagascar, eighteenth–nineteenth centuries.

depended on imports of cheap labor and provisions, of which Madagascar was the closest supplier. Their pleas for colonizing Madagascar were supported by the French Navy (and ultra-Royalists), which presented the island as the potential equivalent to France of Australia to Britain. In 1829 the government of Charles X briefly revived the imperial momentum: French forces backed a Betsimisaraka revolt on the east coast, where they attacked the main ports of Toamasina and Mahavelona. However, following the July 1830 Revolution, Louis Philippe (ruled 1830–1848) sought to appease British sentiment and in July 1831 French troops were withdrawn from mainland Madagascar, leaving as their sole Malagasy "dependency" the malarial island of Nosy Boraha. For the next half-century, French governments proved unwilling to engage in colonial ventures that might either offend Britain, the dominant global power, or burden the French treasury. Hence, while in 1841 ratifying treaties negotiated by the French Navy establishing protectorates over the neighboring islands of Mayotta and Nosy Be, the French government failed to heed calls for intervention in mainland Madagascar. This was the case even following the 1845 Merina ban on European trade and the 1848 emancipation measure that plunged Réunion into a prolonged economic crisis for which planters presented the colonization of Madagascar as a panacea. Indeed, from 1845 a *modus vivendi* was reached whereby France tacitly recognized British predominance in East Africa.

Thus, when in the early 1850s a group led by Rakoto Radama, heir apparent to the Merina throne, called for the French to intervene and establish a protectorate, Napoleon III refused. The latter desired imperial glory but was influenced less by the Saint-Simon school that stressed indirect rule and Catholic missionary activity more than direct rule. Indeed, in line with British policy, France in 1861, abolished colonial monopolies and adopted free trade—a policy even endorsed by the French Navy. Within this framework France in 1862 signed a treaty of "eternal friendship" with Radama II of Madagascar. The 1868 Franco-Merina treaty, while permitting freedom of access, movement, settlement, and trade to foreigners, as well as religious liberty, thus satisfying the bulk of the "open door" demands of Western powers, nevertheless recognized the Merina ban on both the freehold sale of land and the emigration of Malagasy labor.

From the late 1870s France's attitude changed in favor of colonial expansion although not until the 1882 Egyptian affair was there a convergence of metropolitan and regional interests in favor of a forward movement in Madagascar: In 1883, de Mahy, the Réunion deputy and leader of a stop gap administration in France, started a conflict with the Merina that in December 1885 ended in the cession to France of the port of Antsiranana (Diego-Suarez), an indemnity of 10 million francs and an ill-defined protectorate over the island. In 1886 France also declared a protectorate over all the neighboring Comoro islands.

The main pretext for intervention in Madagascar centered on the factors of French historic rights and its "civilizing mission." The real motivation was the desire to preserve international status following military defeat by Germany in 1870–1871. The French feared that if they failed to react to what they perceived as British attempts to claim a monopoly in Africa from the mid-1870s, their national status would be further eroded. In Africa, Britain concentrated upon those regions deemed essential to its wider imperial interests; notably Egypt, South Africa, and Zanzibar. Thus Protestant missionary calls to support the Merina were ignored by the British government, which in 1890 signed a treaty recognizing French hegemony in Madagascar in return for French acceptance of British paramountcy in Zanzibar.

The French colonial cause was boosted by hopes of economic gain. The 1880s depression created a domestic audience receptive to arguments that colonies were a necessity for the employment of surplus domestic capital and industrial manufactures. These ideas converged with those of planters and traders on Réunion, suffering from depressed sugar prices following the conversion of France to sugar beet production, who viewed Madagascar as a potential field of settlement for its surplus and impoverished population. Madagascar not only possessed valuable tropical resources (forest products and plantations of coffee, cocoa, and spices), it also possessed gold the exploitation of which induced gold rushes to the island in 1891 and 1895.

However, forces within Madagascar that precipitated a crisis of the indigenous Merina aristocracy also played a major role in the French takeover of the island. Policies centered on self-reliance not only failed to stimulate an industrial revolution, but excessive exploitation of *fanompoana* (nonremunerated forced labor) undermined the traditional economy. The emphasis on *fanompoana* resulted in the flight of ordinary farmers from the land and created an increasingly vicious circle of social protest, famine, and disease. French pressure aggravated the situation, notably the imposition by France in 1885 of a $2 million war indemnity. The Merina court reacted by increasing domestic taxation and *fanompoana*. By the early 1890s the cumulative effects of this had so critically undermined the economy that it precipitated a crisis. Merina subjects fled civil *fanompoana* and soldiers deserted the imperial army *en masse*, so that when Senegalese troops finally relieved the malaria-stricken French expeditionary force of 1894, their passage to the Merina capital was virtually unopposed.

A widespread insurrection followed the French protectorate imposed in 1895. Traditionally interpreted as a nationalist revolt against the French, the uprising was primarily directed against the maintenance under the French protectorate of a Merina administration universally detested for its corruption and highly exploitative forced labor regime. Hence, the chief victims of the rebels were not the French, but the property and agents of the Merina state church, the institution through which *fanompoana* and other taxes were levied. The reaction of the French was, in the central provinces to replace Merina with French colonial administration, and in certain other regions, notably in Sakalava land, where there existed a strong tradition of independence, to grant a certain degree of indirect rule.

GWYN R. CAMPBELL

Further Reading

Brunschwig, H. "Anglophobia and French African Policy." In *France and Britain in African Imperial Rivalry and Colonial Rule,* edited by P. Gifford and W. Roger Louis. New Haven, 1971.

Campbell, G. "Missionaries, Fanompoana and the Menalamba Revolt in Late Nineteenth Century Madagascar." *Journal of Southern African Studies.* 15, no. 19 (1988), 54–73.

———. "Crisis of Faith and Colonial Conquest: The Impact of Famine and Disease in Late Nineteenth-Century Madagascar." *Cahiers d'Études Africaines.* 32 (1992), 409–453.

Kent, R. K. "How France Acquired Madagascar." *Tarikh.* 2, no. 4 (1969).

———, (ed.) *Madagascar in History: Essays from the 1970s.* Berkeley: Foundation for Malagasy Studies, 1979.

Wastell, R. E. P. "British Imperial Policy in relation to Madagascar, 1810–1896." Ph.D. diss., London University, 1944.

Madagascar: Colonial Period: French Rule

It has traditionally been considered that colonization had a greater, mostly negative, impact upon colonized peoples than any other factor in history, except possibly the slave export trade. Subject to the dictates of the colonial administration, the Malagasy alongside other colonized peoples were exploited, and their economy distorted, for the benefit of the colonizing power.

In reality, French colonial aspirations in Madagascar were severely restrained by external and domestic forces, the major one of which was the fluctuations in the international economy. Thus the establishment of colonial rule in Madagascar was facilitated by the recovery in the international economy in the decade prior World War I and by high European demand for tropical produce during and immediately after the conflict. Prices remained relatively buoyant until the depression, when the colonial administration introduced

The port of Toamasina (Tamatave), eastern Madagascar, about 1930. © SVT Bild/Das Fotoarchiv.

protectionist measures designed to assist European settlers and companies.

A second external constraint was the climate. A cyclone strong enough to destroy 50 per cent to 80 per cent of plantation trees and cause considerable damage to the transport and ports infrastructure hits the east coast of Madagascar on average once every ten years. From 1939 to 1959, the region was visited by forty-nine cyclones, of which twenty-nine were of medium to severe velocity at over 100 miles an hour. Such natural factors, that accentuated the difficulties and thus cost of transport in an island of rugged terrain, isolated from most sizeable foreign markets, caused considerable year to year variations in the total value of trade.

The lack of labor constituted the major domestic hindrance to the French. Governor General Gallieni (1896–1905) envisaged the formation of a "Franco-Malagasy" race, but metropolitan French settlers were deterred by malaria and the generally infertile soils of Madagascar; the island attracted a mere handful of large French companies that survived only by diversifying: from commerce to plantation production and vice versa; and within agriculture by adopting a variety of cash crops. Thus the major "European" presence in Madagascar was impoverished Mascarene créole planters who depended on access to cheap Malagasy labor. Slavery was abolished in 1896, but many of the 500,000 liberated slaves remained in their former master's homes as servants. Moreover, the population and population density was low, while the quality of labor was poor due to malnutrition, disease, and alcoholism. Only from the late 1930s did colonial health policies succeeded in accelerating the birth rate and lowering the death rate, with the result that the population expanded.

Moreover, the Malagasy were notoriously averse to contract labor. After initial attempts to recruit Indian and Chinese immigrant labor failed (the last immigrant workers were repatriated in 1907), the French administration, like the precolonial Merina regime, imposed forced labor, but their demand for labor for public works conflicted with the labor demands of private European concerns. Pressure from the latter resulted in private European access to SMOTIG, a public works scheme founded in 1926 using Malagasy military conscripts. Because of abuses, forced labor measures were periodically suppressed—including SMOTIG, which was banned in 1936. They also caused immense economic hardship for the Malagasy who did all in their power to evade them. As a result, they failed to relieve labor shortages, and European planters increasingly recruited Antandroy, Antaisaka, and Antaimoro contract labor from the more densely populated valleys of southeast Madagascar.

The traditional approach also underestimates the dynamic role under colonial rule of ordinary Malagasy. There was initially little difference between the immediate precolonial and colonial era for most Malagasy, some 90 per cent of whom continued to be employed in subsistence agriculture. However, in the 1920s the rise in the world price of tropical commodities led growing numbers of small farmers to grow successfully, alongside subsistence crops, export crops such as coffee, cocoa, vanilla, and sisal, the profits from which could be used to pay the taxes that released the producer from forced labor. Moreover, lower overheads and use of family labor enabled Malagasy producers to survive climatic and other vicissitudes better than poor créole producers.

During the 1930s depression, the colonial administration decided to favor coffee over other cash crops and introduced incentives to that effect. These measures had the inadvertent effect of persuading large numbers of small Malagasy producers to grow coffee. From 1932 both indigenous and European producers had access to agricultural credit at a maximum of 3 per cent interest, and by 1935 there existed 21 European and 292 Malagasy Agricultural Credit associations comprising over 8,000 members. At the same time, the cooperative movement took off, cooperatives playing an essential role in World War II, stockpiling products, notably coffee, which could no longer be shipped to France, and furnishing credit to producers. By 1945 there existed twenty-four Malagasy cooperatives (with 13,373 members) and by 1952, forty. Indigenous producers also appear to have gained substantially more than créole planters from technical assistance offered by the agricultural section of the administration.

By the time of the post–World War II boom in tropical products, the Malagasy farmer dominated the production of coffee, which was responsible for roughly one-third of exports by value. This applied both to high quality *Arabica* coffee, produced in comparatively small quantities mainly in the central highlands, and to lower quality varieties (*Kouliou* on the east coast and *Robusta* in the northwest), produced in far greater quantity in the lowlands. It is in this context that the 1947 revolt may be viewed. In 1946–1947 the administration, responding to European planter pressure, ignored the decision to ban forced labor in the French Union, and imposed it in the coffee producing regions of the east coast. The local Malagasy interpreted the measure as an attempt to stifle their own, more efficient production of coffee and rose in revolt. The rebels gained virtually no support from nationalist groups in Imerina and were brutally suppressed with the loss of probably between 90,000 and 100,000 Malagasy lives, one of the single bloodiest episodes in colonial history.

The damage inflicted by the revolt and its suppression effectively squeezed the créole planter out of production of coffee (which by 1952 accounted for 44 per cent of total exports) which, even on larger European plantations, was mostly in Malagasy hands. The créoles mostly entered the retail trade in urban areas but failed to displace the established position there of Indian or Chinese middlemen. The 1947 revolt also helped boost the nationalist cause, which had advanced rapidly in the aftermath of World War II when French prestige had suffered due to defeat by Germany, followed in 1942 by a British and South African invasion force that toppled the Vichy French administration in Madagascar. Rising nationalism, combined with the anticolonial stance of the United States, which through the Marshall Plan was largely responsible for resuscitating the war-devastated French economy, led to a change of colonial policy, and in 1960 France granted Madagascar political independence.

GWYN R. CAMPBELL

Further Reading

Brown, M. *A History of Madagascar.* Ipswich: Damien Tunnacliffe, 1995.

Campbell, G. "The Cocoa Frontier in Madagascar, the Comoro Islands and Réunion, c.1820–1970." In *Cocoa Pioneer Fronts since 1800*, edited by W. G. Clarence-Smith. London: Macmillan, 1996.

———. "The Origins and Development of Coffee Production in Réunion and Madagascar." In *Coffee Pioneer Fronts, 1800–1970*, edited by W. G. Clarence-Smith. London: Macmillan, forthcoming.

Deschamps, H. *Histoire de Madagascar.* Paris: Berger-Levrault, 1972.

Vérin, P. *Madagascar.* Paris: Kathala, 1990.

Madagascar: Great Rebellion, 1947–1948

The Malagasy rebellion of 1947–1948 is designated by several terms: "troubles," "war," "insurrection," and "flight." Each name conveys different aspects of what is certainly one of the most important, complex events in Madagascar's history. The rebellion started the night of March 29, 1947, when an extensive network of groups affiliated with the Democratic Movement for Malagasy Reform (MDRM), a Malagasy political party whose leaders were in the process of legally negotiating independence within the confines of the French political system, launched an insurrection. The revolt erupted simultaneously at a number of different points on the east coast, as rebel bands armed with spears and the occasional gun attacked military garrisons, administrative centers, and Malagasy sympathizers with the colonial regime, burning buildings and killing a number of French administrators and settlers. The French administration responded with force, leading a terrifying campaign of military repression that was matched by the brutality of rebel soldiers, who often forced civilians to join their cause. By the time the rebellion was declared officially over in December of 1948, 550 French were dead, and 100,000 Malagasy had been executed, tortured, starved, or driven into the forest. Over 11,000 appear to have been killed as a direct result of French military action.

The rebellion of 1947 was both an independence war and a popular revolt against state structures that came into being during and just after World War II. In 1940 the colonial administration aligned itself with Vichy France, which in turn sparked off a British invasion of Madagascar. The British handed the island over to a non-Vichy-aligned French government, which proceeded to use Madagascar as a reservoir of men and raw materials. The administration increased forced labor to intolerable proportions and seized peasant landholdings for the war effort. In 1943–1944 a famine broke out in the south of the island. In order to prevent starvation, the administration set up a "Rice Office" to control requisitions. The office was extremely unpopular because it created a huge black market in rice. Throughout Madagascar, villagers bore the brunt of the requisitions and were left without rice for their own consumption. At the same time, educated Malagasy were aware of independence struggles in other French colonial territories like Indochina, as well as the French humiliation at the hands of the Germans during World War II. This wider political context, in tandem with the growth of an organized independence movement whose claims were augmented by rumors that spread throughout the countryside, appears to have created an ambiance favorable to revolt.

A number of different theories have been advanced to try and explain the exact timing and organization of the rebellion. When the rebellion broke out French colonial officials blamed the leaders of the MDRM, which had enjoyed a substantial electoral victory in the provincial elections held in February 1947, and whose leaders were in the process of negotiating a peaceful independence. Circumstantial evidence was readily available. Rebels that had attacked the military garrison at Moramanga wore MDRM insignia and military expeditions aimed at destroying rebel camps found numerous documents bearing military orders in the name of the MDRM. The French further argued that because the MDRM was comprised largely of Merina (eight-tenths of MDRM organizers were Merina), the most powerful ethnic group in Madagascar, that the Merina had provoked the rebellion. French insistence on blaming the leaders of the MDRM and the Merina allowed the colonial government to destroy indigenous political development in the country, thereby reinforcing the French presence.

However, the colonial thesis of an MDRM and Merina led rebellion oversimplifies the case. When the rebellion broke out, the MDRM leaders were in the process of trying to obtain autonomy for Madagascar within the framework of existing political processes. While certain sections of the MDRM undoubtedly participated in the rebellion, the party leaders sought to distance themselves from the events, condemning the rebels and their actions. Characterizing the rebellion as a Merina plot is equally problematic. When French control over the island was relatively loose early in World War II and a seizure of power possible, the Merina remained friendly to the French. Moreover, those Merina who did advocate change did so within the limits imposed by the colonial system. Further, most of the fighting took place on the east coast, outside of the area traditionally occupied by the Merina. Merina were clearly key in organizing the growth of the MDRM, but members of the Betsimisaraka, Bezanozano, and Tanala ethnic groups from the east coast occupied many of the key military positions in the rebel army.

A more plausible explanation of the rebellion lies in the nature of the MDRM and its political affiliations. The MDRM was not a hierarchical structure, but rather a loose coalition of different organizations and personal networks, including two secret societies, the National Malagasy Party (PANAMA) formed in 1941, and the National Malagasy Youth (JINY) founded in 1943, whose members were ready to obtain independence by violent means. Initially supportive of the deputies' efforts, the secret societies eventually grew impatient with the slow legal process and demanded violent, and immediate, action. Propagandists, some of whom were members of the MDRM, circulated through the countryside, declaring that, "the authority of the deputies has replaced that of France" and advised people, under threat of force, to stop working on colonial concessions. They also announced that Madagascar belonged to the Malagasy and that all Europeans would soon die. Some members of the MDRM advocated independence by legal means, but others were involved with the secret societies and eventually decided to follow a more radical policy by setting off the rebellion.

The crushing defeat suffered by the Malagasy, and the atrocities that were committed both by the French against Malagasy and among Malagasy, has made the place of the rebellion in Malagasy historical memory highly problematic. During the First Republic (1960–1972), the violence of the rebellion was largely ignored in favor of President Tsiranana's policy of reconciliation. During the Second Republic (1975–1992) President Ratsiraka tried to resuscitate the memory of the rebellion as part of a long series of nationalist struggles culminating in his rule. However, many rural participants who perceived the rebellion as the result of their foolish engagement in state politics do not accept the nationalist interpretation of the rebellion; their experience has left them deeply mistrustful of the postcolonial state.

JENNIFER COLE

Further Reading

Cole, J. "The Uses of Defeat": Memory and Political Morality in East Madagascar." In *Memory and the Postcolony*, edited by R. Werbern. London: Zed Books, 1998.

Randrianja, S. *Le Parti Communiste (SFIC) de la Région de Madagascar (1936–1939).* [*The Communist Part in the Region of Madagascar*] *(1936–1939).*

Tronchon, J. *L'Insurrection Malgache de 1947: Essai d'Interprétation Historique* [*The Madagascan Revolt of 1947: An Essay of Historical Interpretation*]. Paris: Karthala, 1986.

Madagascar: Reconciliation, Reform, and Independence, 1948–1960

The period immediately after the Great Rebellion was marked by general repression: specifically, restrictions upon the press, and an increasing French influence in the economic and cultural domains. The autochthonous people remained without many rights and privileges enjoyed by citizens. In accordance with the idea of having the economy of the metropolis and its overseas territories working complementarily, France remained attached to protectionism and thus encouraged exportation, although it invested little into industries. The trade companies (Marseillaise, Lyonnaise, and the Industrial and Commercial Company of Emyrne) were the biggest beneficiaries of this policy. Some agroindustrial companies also profited, such as the Sugar Company of Mahavavy in the northwest. Big settlers also made profits, while small settlements continued to collapse, and only a minority of the Malagasy population did well under these new economic circumstances.

Between 1947 and 1952, during the implementation of the economic and social development plan, priority was given to infrastructure, specifically, roads. Subsequent four-year plans accentuated the modernization of agriculture through development schemes. During the 1950s there was an increase in agricultural production, but any related gains affected less than 10 per cent of the peasant population. This period was also marked by a strong demographic growth, thanks to a better health care system (specifically, mobile hygiene groups). Finally, the decade that began with educational reforms in 1951 witnessed a remarkable increase in schooling and the opening of European-style secondary schools for Malagasy students. The implementation of quotas that reserved a certain number of spots in rural schools and the Myre of Vilers (the school for civil servants in Antananarivo) for indigenous residents enabled the development of a non-Merina elite.

A series of different questions—amnesty of political prisoners, municipal reform, the stakes in elections at different levels, the road to emancipation—fostered debates in the press between moderate and intransigent nationalists. Even though newspapers reached only a minority of citizens effectively, the press had efficiently served the committees that mobilized in favor of those who had been imprisoned. The church, too, played a key role in these committees. Catholic ecclesiastics, particularly Father Jean de Puybaudet, contributed to the establishment of trade unions, to counterbalance the communist influence. In a letter of 1953, the Catholic hierarchy affirmed the legitimacy of the aspiration for independence. The combined action of the different pressure groups resulted in the granting of a partial amnesty for prisoners in 1954–1955.

After 1956 the political atmosphere became increasingly charged. The year began with legislative elections. For this occasion, the nationalists, who presented themselves as heirs of the Mouvement Democratique de la Renovation Malagache (MDRM), set up an electoral committee, which was eventually transformed into a party, the Union of the Malagasy People. However, its principal opponent, the Parti des déshérités de Madagascar (PADESM), won the election for the third consecutive time since 1951—a rather mixed victory due to internal divisions. With the announcement of the *loi cadre* (enabling law) in June 1956, and the elections for the provincial assemblies—the first stage of the installment of the new institutions (Representative Assembly, then Council of Government)—the country fell into a state of turmoil.

Political divisions occurred at a rapid rate. France continued to play a role in the political situation. Its attitude during the restructuring of the PADESM at the end of 1946 was very significant and influential. France favored Deputy Philibert Tsiranana over Senator Norbert Zafimahova, who had formed the Union of Social Democrats of Madagascar with the conservative wing of the PADESM, which was predominantly strong in the East and South. With the encouragement of the socialist high commissioner André Soucadaux, the Tsimihety teacher Philibert Tsiranana, elected Deputy in January 1956, founded the Social Democratic Party (PSD). Tsiranana, who since 1954 had spoken in favor of a progressive independence, skillfully established a dialogue with the moderate nationalists. With the support of the administration, he was propelled to the head of the Council of Government.

Before the ascent of the PSD, a dozen hostile organizations of the *loi cadre,* along with proponents of independence, defined a combined strategy during an assembly held in Tamatave in May 1958. After the referendum of September 1958, before which the PSD had campaigned in favor of the maintenance of a Malagasy state within the French, several of these organizations established the *Antokon'ny Kongresin'ny Fahaleovantenan'I Madagasikara* (Congress Party for the Independence of Madagascar, AKFM) under the direction of the young pastor Richard Andriamanjato, successor of Ravelojaona, one of the primary nationalist figures in the capital. Throughout this time, the process of decolonization was occurring gradually. On October 14, 1958, the Congress of Provincial Assemblies officially proclaimed the Republic of Madagascar. The new state presented itself with a flag, a national anthem, and finally a constitution (April 29, 1959). Tsiranana was elected as the new nation's first president. On June 26, 1960, Madagascar officially obtained its independence.

FARANIRINA RAJAONAH

Further Reading

Anonymous. "Comment on devient président . . ." ["How to Become President . . ."] *Réalités malgaches* [*Malagasy Realities*]. 17 (1972): 31–38.

Brown, M. *Madagascar Rediscovered: A History from Early Times to Independence.* London: Damien Tunnacliffe, 1978; as *A History of Madagascar.* London: Damien Tunnacliffe, 1995.

Hardyman, J. *Madagascar on the Move.* London: Livingston Press, 1950.

Lupo, P. *Église et decolonization à Madagascar.* [*Church and Decolonization in Madagascar.*] Fianarantsoa: Ambozontany, 1973.

Maron, C. *L'hebdomadaire Lumière de Madagascar (1935 à 1972)* [*The Weekly Light of Madagascar (1935 to 1972)*]. Aix-en-Provence: Presses Universitaire d'Aix-Marseille [University Press of Aix-Marseille], 1977.

Rabearimanana, L. *La presse d'opinion à Madagascar de 1947 à 1956. Contribution à l'histoire du nationalism malgache de l'Insurrection à la veille de la Loi-Cadre. [The Opinion Press in Madagascar from 1947 to 1956. Contribution to the History of Malagasy Nationalism from Insurrection to the Eve of the "Loi-Cadre."]* Tananarive: Librarie Mixte [Mixed Bookstores], 1980.

———. *La vie rurale à Madagascar de la crise de 1930 à la veille de l'Indépendance (1930–1958) [Rural Life in Madagascar from the Crisis of 1930 to the Eve of Independence (1930–1958).]* Thèse pour le doctorat d'État. [Dissertation for the D.Litt]. Paris 7, 1994–1995.

Rajaonah, F. "Hymne pour un État malgache (19ème-20ème siècles)" ["Hymn for a Malagasy State (19th-20th Centuries)"]. *Annuaire des Pays de l'océan Indien.* [*Yearbook of the Countries of the Indian Ocean.*] 15 (1997–1998): 15–34.

Randriamaro, J.-R. *PADESM et luttes politiques à Madagascar. De la fin de la Deuxième Guerre mondiale à la naissance du PSD.* [*The PADESM and Political Struggles in Madagascar. From the End of WWII to the Birth of the PSD.*] Paris: Karthala, 1997.

Robequain, C. *Madagascar et les bases disperses de l'Union Française. [Madagascar and the Dispersed Bases of the French Union.]* Paris: PUF, 1958.

Spacensky, A. *Madagascar. Cinquante ans de vie politique de Ralaimongo à Tsiranana. [Madagascar. Fifty Years of Political Life from Ralaimongo to Tsiranana.]* Paris: Nouvelles Éditions Latines [New Latin Editions], 1970.

Madagascar: Independence to 1972

Once euphoria after the advent of independence had died away—happening under the sign of reconciliation with a general amnesty of political prisoners and the return of exiled MDRM representatives—the opposition renewed its criticism with regard to the regime that it qualified as neocolonial. But none of its principal adversaries was in the position of acting as counterweight to the Parti Social Démocrate (PSD): neither the Parti du Congrès pour l'Indépendance de Madagascar (AKFM), party of managers mostly established in the capital, nor the MONIMA (National Movement for the Independence of Madagascar) of the old nationalist militant, Monja Jaona, a predominantly peasant party with a stronghold in the south. In fact, at the prompting of the secretary general, the minister of the interior, André Resampa, the PSD—a solidly structured mass party with a section per subprefecture, women's associations, and youth movements—rapidly became a dominant party.

In 1960 the PSD took 61 per cent of the votes cast for the legislative elections and 75 per cent for the general councils of the provinces. Five years later, these proportions changed to 88 per cent and 96 per cent, respectively. It is true that the PSD benefited from the weakness of the opposition, but its triumph in mobilizing the rank and file was also due to the capacity of its leaders, shaped by sister parties: the French SFIO, the German SPD, and the Israeli Mapaï. In addition, the PSD had control over the administration, which suggested a PSD state that had taken over the place of the French by opening up the National School of Administration. If in 1960 the great majority of senior officers who started their career in the French army were Merina, now the "Malagasyization" of the officer corps started, from 1966 onward, at the Military Academy of Antsirabe, with some worries regarding the equilibrium between regions. But, in accordance with the cooperation agreements, France maintained a strong presence in the military realm (technical assistance and military bases) and retained its status as privileged partner of a state turned resolutely toward the East. However, due to events, the government acted pragmatically in its foreign relations as it was forced to find a socialist Malagasy way: a difficult quest between the rejection of communism, foreign pressure, state interventionism, and a concern with preserving its perceived position as authentically Malagasy.

Madagascar needed help, and international organizations, particularly in Europe, were very generous in giving it, but this increased the small nation's dependence on outside sources. Madgascar had its own money (the Franc FMG); even though it might have been advantageous to belong to the Franc Zone, it is true that belonging to that Zone would limit Madagascar's maneuvering space on the other hand. If France—which in 1960 drained two-thirds of all exports—was a client for only one-fourth of exports in 1970, it nevertheless supplied two-thirds of Madagascar's importations, mainly in facilities and raw materials for substitution industries almost entirely in foreign hands, mostly French companies and some Indo-Pakistanis (*Karana*). In addition, the *Karana* in the west and the Chinese in the east still dominated commerce and served as intermediaries for the old trading companies or the new French companies that represented finance capitalism. In short, foreign planters supplied three-fourths of the value of fixed exports almost exclusively by revenue cultures encouraged in detriment of food crops. In this way, even though foreigners were a minority (1.5 per cent of 7,000,000 inhabitants according to the 1970 census), they were preponderant to a degree that the national bourgeoisie, which had inherited fortunes founded on commerce or had benefited from state interventionism, could not compete.

In a country where 85 per cent of the population lives in the countryside, the state intervened essentially in the rural sector, in view of what it called "politics of the stomach," especially after the rice-growing crisis of 1965. This became obvious in the creation of public establishments like the state farm *Ny Omby* (The Oxen), under the responsibility of managing directors or societies of mixed economies in charge of "rural valuing." Next to these capitalist ventures, other experiences appeared to be of a more socializing and participative nature, but state interventionism did not favor their success. This was the case with the development project that was based upon *fokonolona* (communal collectivities). In the end, state interventionism, which expressed itself also through the Civic Service and the Commissariat of Rural Animation, did not prevent the pauperization of the countryside, disadvantaged with regards to the cities due to the maintenance of agricultural prices at extremely low levels. One can therefore understand that the divide between the powerful and the peasantry increased. The revolt of the south, the germ of the movement that eventually brought down the regime, was one of the most obvious proofs.

In a region struck by famine and a severe livestock disease in 1970, the zeal of the tax collectors in gathering the head and oxen taxed exasperated the population. Following the call of the MONIMA, in the night of April 12, 1971, villagers equipped with arms besieged the prison, the police station, and the administrative offices in several small towns. A severe repression followed an uprising that, far from being a simple peasant revolt, should have become a generalized insurrection, which was seen as premature by the intellectuals of the MONIMA in the capital. In Antananarivo, however, while the dissent at the core of the PSD ended toward the end of May 1971 in the dismissal of Resampa, the strongman of the regime (who was favorable to the revision of the cooperation agreement and was the presumed heir of a physically diminished president), latent discontent breaks out among the young. The young, threatened by unemployment, mobilized against an undemocratic instruction. Acculturation was particularly strong at the universities. The situation of the young, who underwent social and cultural dispossession, made for a potentially revolutionary group. The announcement of educational reforms did not stop the strike started in January 1972 by medical students and supported by the Federation of Student Associations of Madagascar.

While the movement was growing stronger, Tsirana—the only presidential candidate and presented by his supporters as chosen by God and the ancestors to lead the country—was reelected for the third time. He retained the status quo, despite his promises to the contrary, and dissatisfaction permeated the capital. The population responded to the decision of the government to resort to violence—arrests and deportations of 400 students in May and firing into the population assembled before City Hall by the paramilitary police of the Republican Security Forces on May 13—with the announcement of a general strike. On May 18, 1972, Tsiranana handed over full powers to Gabriel Ramanantsoa, chief general of the armed forces, nominated prime minister.

FARANIRINA RAJAONAH

Further Reading

Adloff, R. and V. Thompson. *The Malagasy Republic: Madagascar Today.* London: Stanford, 1965.

Anonymous. "Madagascar 1971." *Christianisme Social [Social Christianity].* 56 (1971): 275–322.

———. "Jeunesse malgache. Une nouvelle classe?" ["Malagasy Youth. A New Class?"] *Réalités malgaches. [Malagasy Realities.]* 21/1972: 19–20.
Brown, M. *Madagascar Rediscovered. A History from Early Times to Independence.* London: Damien Tunnacliffe, 1978; as *A History of Madagascar.* London: Damien Tunnacliffe, 1995.
Cadoux, C. *La République Malgache. [The Malagasy Republic.]* Paris: Berger-Levrault, 1969.
Delval, R. "La formation des cadres de la République malgache à l'institut des Hautes Études d'Outre-Mer (1958–1966)." ["The Formation of Executives of the Malagasy Republic at the Institute of Higher Studies of Overseas Territories (1958–1966)." In *L'Afrique Noire française à l'heure des Indépendances."* [In *French Black Africa at the Time of the Independences.*] edited by C.-R. Ageron and M. Michel, Paris: CNRS, 1992.
Gendarme, R. *L'économie de Madagascar: Diagnostic et perspectives de développement.* [*The Economy of Madagascar: Diagnostic and Perspectives of Development.*] Paris: Cujas, 1963.
Hugon, P. *Économie et enseignement à Madagascar.* [*Economy and Instruction in Madagascar.*] Paris: International Institute of Educational Planning (UNESCO), 1976.
———. *La République Malgache.* [*The Malagasy Republic.*] Paris: Berger-Levrault, 1965.
Rabenoro, C. *Les relations extérieures de Madagascar de 1960 à 1972.* [*Malagasy Foreign Relations from 1960 to 1972.*] Paris: L'Harmattan and Aix-en-Provence: Presses Universitaires d'Aix-Marseille [University Press of Aix-Marseille], 1986.
Serre, G. *Données politiques et institutionnelles des changements de régime à Madagascar.* [*Political and Institutional Data on Regime Changes in Madagascar.*] Mémoire de l' Institut d'Études Politiques [Thesis for the Institute of Political Studies]. Paris, 1975.

Madagascar: Reform and Revolution, 1972–1989

After the fall of the Parti Social Démocrate (PSD) regime, speech became freer, and newspapers and leaflets flourished. For months, the seminars coordinated by the strike committee offered discussion spaces, with their eyes on the National Congress of September 1972. The insurrection favored the emergence of a proletarian party, the MFM (*Mitolona ho an'ny Fanjakan'ny Madinika* [They who struggle for the power of the small]), under the leadership of the academic Manandafy Rakotonirina, former member of the MONIMA, which ostensibly located its support among the peasantry and the working class, but whose clientele, then strictly urban, was essentially made up of young scholars and ZOAM (*Zatovo Orz Asa Malagasy* [Young Malagasy without work]). By guaranteeing a legitimacy to General Ramanantsoa, the plebiscite of October 8, 1972 permitted him to have his way vis-à-vis the radical wing of the movement, leading to the marginalization of the strike committee and the eviction of Tsiranana.

The constitutional law of November 7 installed a transitional regime charged with renewing Malagasy society in five years. Ramanantsoa formed a government of a national union of civil and military technicians, supported by the AKFM and popular with the rural masses after the suppression of the head and oxen tax. The revision of the cooperation agreements (April 1973), followed by the withdrawal from the Franc Zone, reinforced the reputation of frigate captain Didier Ratsiraka, minister of foreign affairs. The state augmented its participation in the banks and created societies of national interest for import-export, and the collection and distribution of agricultural products. The popular development master's program, which rested on the rehabilitation of *fokonolona* village communities, transformed into base cells of a pyramidal state structure until they reach the national level, contributed to the popularity of Colonel Ratsimandrava, minister of the interior. In the "Malagasyization" of education, the government showed great prudence before the reluctance, or even the hostility, of provincial peripheries due to historical reasons. In fact, this apolitical way did not stop the activism of the parties, like the Malagasy Socialist Party, which emerged from the rapprochement between the PSD and the Malagasy Socialist Union of André Resampa. What is more, governmental factions were facing fundamental choices, for example between communitarian and state capitalism. Finally, in 1974, when financial scandals compromised the regime, the country went through a severe economic crisis (a consequence of the paralysis of the activities in 1972, the retreat from the Franc Zone, and the world economic crisis), and the tensions in the army exploded into an open conflict. Even though averted, the coup d'étât led by Colonel Bréchard Rajaonarison, originally from the southeast, led Ramanantsoa to hand over the power to the minister of the interior. One week later—the day after Ratsimandrava, who by crisscrossing the country had established a real dialogue with the peasants, was assassinated under circumstances that have not yet been elucidated—a military directorate took power with Andriamahazo, military governor of Antananarivo in May 1972, as its leader.

Ratsiraka distinguished himself from among the leadership of this institution through a program that he described as inspired by the movement of 1972, and he managed to gain a majority. Knowing that he could count on the provinces, he enlarged his political base to include students and the ZOAM of the capital, thus preparing his ascension, to which he acceded as president of the Supreme Council of the Revolution (CSR) when the directorate was dissolved in June 1975.

During the second part of 1975, Madagascar entered a period of disruptions, which, following the program traced by Ratsiraka in the *Charter of the Socialist Revolution* (the Red Book of the regime), was supposed to result in the establishment of a new state based on the model of popular democracies. Through the referendum of December 21, which called for one answer to three questions—approve the Charter or not, of a constitutional project, and of the choice of Ratsiraka as president—Ratsiraka obtained a plebiscitary legitimization (95 per cent of the vote). The promulgation of the constitution on December 31 officially founded the Democratic Republic of Madagascar, whose policy, defined by the CSR, was implemented by the government. The regime favored relations with the countries of the East, particularly North Korea. Political expression passed exclusively through the channel of progressive organizations, members of the National Front for the Defense of the Revolution (FNDR). Different parties stuck to it, but the AREMA (Avant-garde of the Malagasy Socialist Revolution), the party of the president, acquired in less than a year an ultradominant, if not crushing, position. The revolution implied the nationalization of vital sectors of the economy, and the army took part in this process. Contrary to Ratsimandrava's project, the socialist *fokonolona* received orders from above as decentralized collectivities, in accordance with democratic centralism. Decentralization manifested itself in the cultural realm through the opening of regional universities that never operated well or smoothly.

The accelerated "Malagasyization" of primary education—without adequate support material or a coordination with other educational levels, and with a lack of experienced teachers—provoked strong criticism. Public schools lost some of their prestige in relation to the private establishments loyal to the French, which, starting in 1983, progressively regained importance as relations with France improved. In addition, while demographic growth remained strong, the country looked on as the state-controlled economy collapsed. Low agricultural prices did not encourage productivity. In the industrial domain, the excessive investment policy launched in 1979 revealed itself to be a setback. The chronic shortage of current consumption products accompanied the disorganization of markets in a country where the communication infrastructure was deteriorating. Financial bankruptcy compelled the state, put under pressure by the IMF and World Bank, to institute liberalization policies. As a result, there was a drop of 25 per cent of the average revenue per capita between 1980 and 1987, and the gap between rich and poor widened.

Even though some notables benefited from liberalization and privatization, the state was in a state of full socioeconomic decomposition and was threatened by great political instability. The universities were centers of permanent protest. Insecurity raged across the country. Oxen were stolen again with renewed zeal; in the capital, gangs of young unemployed people provoked clashes. The religious forces represented by the FFKM (Fikambanan'ny Fiangonana Kristiana Malagasy), the council of Christian Churches formed in 1980, which in 1982 had already denounced the regime for some of its practices (electoral fraud, repression, resort to the political police), reiterated its warnings in 1985. Within the FNDR, the preponderance of AREMA was questioned. The rupture finally occurred the day after the presidential elections of 1989, which see the reelection of Ratsiraka for a third mandate but only with a majority of 60 per cent—a result that announced another revolution.

FARANIRINA RAJAONAH

Further Reading

Archer, R. Madagascar depuis 1972. La marche d'une revolution. [Madagascar since 1972. The Course of a Revolution.] Paris: L'Harmattan, 1976.

Bouillon, A. "Le MFM malgache." ["The Malagasy MFM."] Revue française d'études politiques africaines. [French Revue of African Politics.] 95 (1973): 46–71.

Brown, M. *Madagascar Rediscovered. A History from Early Times to Independence*. London: Damien Tunnacliffe, 1978; as *A History of Madagascar*. London: Damien Tunnacliffe, 1995.

Chaigneau, P. "Le système des parties à Madagascar." ["The Party System in Madagascar."] Penant. 781–782 (1983): 306–347.

———. Rivalités politiques et socialisme à Madagascar. [Political Rivalries and Socialism in Madagascar.] Paris: Centre des Hautes Études sur l'Afrique et l'Asie Modernes [Center for Higher Studies on Modern Africa and Asia]. 1985.

Clignet, R. and B. E. L'école à Madagascar. [School in Madagascar.] Paris: Karthala, 1995.

Hugon, P. "La crise économique à Madagascar." ["Economic Crisis in Madagascar."] *Afrique Contemporaine*. [*Contemporary Africa*.] 144 (1987): 3–22.

La Deuxième République Malgache (Extraits de l'Annuaire des Pays de l'Océan Indien). [The Second Madgascan Republic (Extracts from the Yearbook of the Countries of the Indian Ocean.)] Aix-en-Provence: Presses Universitaires d'Aix-Marseille [University Press of Aix-Marseille], 1989.

Leymarie, P. "L'AKFM malgache." ["The Malagasy AKFM."] Revue française d'études politiques. [French Revue of Political Sciences.] 107 (1974): 41–61.

Rasamoelina, H. "Le vol des boeufs en pays betsileo." ["Theft of Oxen in Betsileo Country."] *Politique Africaine*. [*African Politics*.] 52 (1993): 22–30.

Madagascar: Democracy and Development, 1990s to the Present

Since President Didier Ratsiraka rejected all challenges of the 1989 elections, the small improvement in daily life toward the end of the 1980s opened up the opportunity for the opposition to react. As the only participants in the two national consultations of 1990 that committed Madagascar to the transition to democracy, they boasted the title of civil and political society's

Lively Forces. The initiative for organizing these meetings, suggested by the national Committee for election observations, returned to the Fikambanan'ny Fiangonana Kristiana Malagasy (FFKM), the council of Christian churches formed in 1980, which enjoyed moral authority, due to the relative importance of the Christian community (45 per cent of Malagasy), the action of confessional organizations in the realm of health and education, and the role of the churches in the history of nationalism.

The leaders of the FFKM mobilized the participants of the consultations by picking up the biblical parallel of God freeing the Israelites from the pharaoh. They invite their compatriots to work for the liberation of the country, by following the example of Moses, who received the order from God to "make his people walk up" to the Promised Land. This exhortation became the slogan of Lively Forces, whose leader was the surgeon Albert Zafy, who had served in the Ramanantsoa government; its message of hope motivated the opposition. Starting in May 1991, when the social demands at Antananarivo turned into a vast political protest, the mass of students, mothers, civil servants, and managers—different from that of May 1972—listened religiously to the message.

The FFKM's failure at mediation led the Lively Forces to organize a counterweight and to better structure the movement that also reached provincial capitals. Playing upon ethnoregional rivalries, Ratsiraka tried to substantiate the idea of a protest that was exclusive to Antananarivo, and therefore to the Merina. The late nomination of the mayor of Antananarivo, Guy Razanamasy, as prime minister did not stop the opposition, which demanded the departure of Ratsiraka by organizing a peaceful march on the Presidential Palace on August 10, 1991. The impressive demonstration became highly dramatic and controversial. Officially, several dozen protesters fell, shot by the presidential guard. The generalization of the strike, the coexistence of two governments, and the proclamation of federal states by provincial notables, who counted on traditional authorities to defend the socialist regime, created great confusion until the political parties, including the FFKM, reached an accord on the establishment of a transitional regime on October 31, 1991. The functioning of the government was maintained, but a high state authority was led by Albert Zafy who supervised governmental activities. The difficulties of coordinating the institutions and respect toward the consensus between the different political tendencies limited efficacy. The essential event during this transitory period was the adoption by referendum, on August 19, 1992, of a constitution created as part of a national forum.

The constitution of the Third Republic affirmed in its preamble the superiority of the state of law and instituted a parliamentary system that submitted the investiture of the prime minister, designated by the resident, to the National Assembly. The voting system, based on proportional representation, was favorable to small parties, and excluded any possibility for the chief of the government to have a parliamentary majority available. Also, after Zafy's victory over Ratsiraka, who was not eliminated from the presidential race for the sake of democracy, and after the relative success of Zafy's sphere of influence during general elections, the conflicts within the executive branch, as well as pressures brought by those opposing the Assembly, threw the country into chronic instability and led to a detrimental immobility in the nation.

In fact, the successive devaluations of the Franc FMG, inflation, excessive debt, and a deficit all contributed to the deterioration of the economy. In 1996, close to three-fourths of the population lived below the poverty line. The political class hoped for a revival of the economy after the finalization of an accord with the Bretton Woods institutions. The question of negotiations with the IMF and World Bank took center stage in political debates. Zafy adopted a revision of the constitution via a referendum on September 17, 1995, which was supposed to encourage economic recovery by guaranteeing political stability. The high rate of abstention illustrated the population's cynical disinterest. But despite the reinforcement of the president's powers, the parliamentary group of the opposition neutralized Zafy and his followers in a few weeks through successive schemes: a motion of censure against the government, a boycott, and finally the motion of impeachment against the president.

The anticipated presidential elections (which mobilized only 50 per cent of voters) of January 1997 resulted in ratifying Ratsiraka's return "by default." The president, who had been toppled by a popular movement, benefited partly from the disenchantment of his compatriots and partly from the errors and slowness of the leaders of the increasingly divided Lively Forces.

In 1999 Marc Ravalomanana, the mayor of Antananarivo, gained notice on the national political scene after building up a large and devoted following in the city. He ran against Ratsiraka in the bitterly contested 2001 presidential election, which was followed by a six-month-long power struggle. The United States and France recognized Ravalomanana as the victor and legitimate president, and Ratsiraka decamped to France. Although Ravalomanana has vowed to fight poverty and unemployment, he faced a daunting task, given the weak economy and political violence that has marked Madagascar.

Faranirina Rajaonah

Further Reading

Déléris, F., ed., *Madagascar. Le Marais [Madagascar. The Swamp]*. Paris: L'Harmattan, 1996.

"Les îles de l'océan Indien" ["The Islands of the Indian Ocean."] *Le Moniteur du Commerce International. [The Monitor of International Commerce.]* 1263 (1996): 20–33.

"Madagascar." Dossier thématique établi par Françoise Raison-Jourde. [Thematic Dossier established by Françoise Raison-Jourde]. *Politique Africaine [African Politics]*. 52 (1993): 3–101.

"Madagascar," *Vivant Univers [Lively Universe]*. 435 (1998).

"Madagascar. Dossier politique." ["Madagascar. Political Dossier."], *Afrique Contemporaine [Contemporary Africa]*. 181 (1997): 39–70.

"Madagascar. La constitution du 19 août 1992" ["Madagascar. The Constitution of August 19, 1992"]. *Afrique Contemporaine [Contemporary Africa]*. 166 (1993): 56–80.

Manassé et Gaëtan Feltz. (eds.). *Démocratie et développement. Mirage ou espoir raisonnable? [Democracy and Development: Miracle or Reasonable Hope?]* Paris: Karthala, 1995.

Raison-Jourde, F., "The Madagascar Churches in the Political Arena and their Contribution to the Change of Regime 1990–1993" in *The Christian Churches and the Democratisation of Africa,* edited by P. Gifford. Leiden, New York, Köln: E. J. Brill, 1995.

Ravaloson, J., "Madagascar: la révolution tranquille" ["Madagascar: The Quiet Revolution"], *Revue Africaine de Politique Internationale [African Revue of International Politics]*. 15 (1993): 139–154.

Ravaloson, J., *Transition démocratique à Madagascar [The Transition to Democracy in Madagascar]*, Paris: L'Harmattan, 1994.

Ravelojaona, B. "Madagascar: la logique de crise" ["Madagascar: The Logic of the Crisis"]. *Année Africaine [African Year]*. (1990–1991): 301–325.

Razafintsalama, H., "Madagascar: le handicap de l'absence d'accord avec le FMI et la Banque mondiale" ["Madagascar: The Handicap of the Absence of an Agreement with the IMF and the World Bank"]. *Marchés tropicaux et méditerranéens [Tropical and Mediterranean Markets]*, hors série 1 [Special serie 1] (1994): 29–35.

Verseils, P., "Madagascar: une Eglise forte dans un pays en crise" ["Madagascar: A Strong Church in a Country in Crisis"]. *Mission*. 1 (1990): 5–6.

Madikizela-Mandela, Winnie (1934–)
Antiapartheid Activist

Winifred Zanyiwe Nomzamo Madikizela was twenty-three when she met Nelson Mandela, who was then nearly forty, a father of three, and had been separated from his first wife for a year. The highly charismatic couple married in June 1958, when Mandela was on trial for treason. She admired his intellect and self-discipline; he introduced her to a wider world, which included active political involvement. The banned activist Helen Joseph became her mentor. One of those arrested for protesting against the pass laws in October 1958, she was as a result dismissed from her job at Baragwanath hospital.

From 1960 with the African National Congress (ANC) a proscribed organization, her husband began to work underground, and she saw even less of him. He was then arrested and sentenced, first to five years and then to life imprisonment. She was allowed only occasional visits to Robben Island, and was constantly harassed by the police. In May 1969 she was detained and treated in appalling fashion in jail before being charged with taking part in the activities of the banned ANC. The charges were dropped, but she was redetained and recharged, under the Terrorism Act. Her lawyer Sydney Kentridge was, however, able to show that the new charges were no different from the previous ones, so she was released in October 1970. Her spell in jail hardened her; some claim she never recovered from the way she was treated.

She continued to be hounded by the police and had great difficulty finding work. Her banning order lapsed in September 1975 and was not reimposed, perhaps because of the sympathies she showed at this time with the Black Consciousness movement. With the Soweto uprising, however, she was detained in August 1976 and spent five months in the Fort Prison, before in May 1977 being banished to Brandfort in the Orange Free State (present-day Free State). There she had to live in a three-room shack in the black township, under highly restrictive conditions. When her second daughter, Zinzi, who had accompanied her, had to be sent back to Johannesburg, she was even more isolated. But she remained active, studying for a University of South Africa social work degree, and opening a day care center for children and a library in the township. As the Release Mandela campaign gained support worldwide in the early 1980s, her fame grew as the symbol of antiapartheid resistance. Her autobiography, *Part of My Soul*, published in 1984, sold well, and she became a heroic figure, especially in the African American community. She was often called "Mother of the Nation."

In 1985 when her Brandfort house was bombed, and on one of her visits to Johannesburg, she refused to return to Brandfort and remained in Soweto, in her Orlando West house, although she soon began building a much larger house in what was known as Beverley Hills. In November 1985 flying to Cape Town to see her husband, who had been taken to a hospital, she met the minister of justice, Kobie Coetsee. Her banning order was then relaxed, and she addressed some public meetings.

She formed her own personal vigilante gang, the Mandela United Football Club, in 1986. Stories spread of her involvement with Umkhonto we Sizwe, the military wing of the ANC, and of acts of brutality and terror committed by members of the Football Club. It was at this time that she became known as "The Lady," for people in Soweto were afraid to say her name. Both the United Democratic Front and her husband counseled her to disband the club, but she refused. In late December 1988 the fourteen-year old Stompie Seipei was taken to her house, interrogated, and later found brutally murdered. Soon afterward, her close friend and medical doctor, Abubaker Asvat, was shot and killed.

On February 11, 1990, Winnie Mandela walked beside her husband as he left Victor Verster prison. For a time she could glory in her new role, but her husband was busy and remote, and his dreams of a return to a romantic relationship began to fade. She was more bitter than he, and remained wedded to revolutionary ideas. In February 1991 she was brought to trial for kidnapping and being an accessory to assault, found guilty, and sentenced to an effective five years in jail. In the trial, she claimed that she had been in Brandfort at the time of Seipei's death. On appeal, the sentence was reduced to two years, which was suspended, and a fine. When she openly went abroad with a new lover, Dali Mpofu, her husband moved out, then announced that he and his wife were separating. In March 1996 they were divorced, and she announced that she wished to be known as Madikizela-Mandela. Further allegations against her surfaced, including misappropriation of funds in the welfare department of the ANC.

Winnie Madikizela-Mandela was a powerful speaker who expressed populist and Africanist views, and when she visited squatter camps she usually set aside her fancy clothes and put on camouflage fatigues. As a vote-getter and person of influence, the ANC decided that, despite being a convicted criminal, she should be placed high on its list for the election, and was duly elected to parliament in April 1994. She was made deputy minister for arts and culture but did not take her official duties seriously, and was dropped from office in 1996. Her antipathy to Cyril Ramaphosa, one of those who had been critical of her in the late 1980s, is thought to have helped lead to his marginalization. She was too important a person to be forced out of the movement, and was retained on the ANC list and reelected to parliament in 1999. She retained her position as head of the ANC Women's League, and was nominated deputy president of the ANC at the Mafeking conference in December 1997.

In November 1997, after she had refused to apply for amnesty, she was subpoenaed to appear before the Truth and Reconciliation Commission. Those who gave evidence against her included Katiza Chebekhulu, a member of her Football Club who had gone into hiding for years and now claimed that he had seen Winnie murder Seipei. Others charged that she had been involved in other disappearances and in the murder of Asvat. The proposition of bringing new formal charges against her was entertained, but ultimately discarded. It was widely recognized that this imperious woman had displayed exceptional courage in fighting apartheid and had played an important role in mobilizing anti-apartheid resistance while her husband had been in jail, but had herself become one of the tragic victims of apartheid.

CHRISTOPHER SAUNDERS

See also: **Mandela, Nelson; South Africa: Antiapartheid Struggle: Townships, the 1980s.**

Biography

Born in the Bizana district of Transkei, the daughter of an Mpondo schoolteacher. Brought up a Methodist and educated at local schools, including Shawbury High School. Went to Johannesburg to train as a social worker at the Jan Hofmeyr School. Married Nelson Mandela, 1958. Divorced 1996.

Further Reading

Gilbey, E. *The Lady: The Life and Times of Winnie Mandela.* London: Vintage, 1994.
Harrison, N. *Winnie Mandela: Mother of a Nation.* London: Gollancz, 1985.
Mandela, W. *Part of My Soul Went with Him*, edited by A. Benjamin. Harmondsworth: Penguin, 1985.
Sampson, A. *Mandela.* London: HarperCollins, 1999.
Tutu, D. *No Future Without Forgiveness.* London: Rider, 1999.

Al-Maghili (*c.*1425–1504)
Muslim Jurist and Reformer

Muhammad ibn abd al-Karim al-Maghili was born in Tlemcen, western Algeria. Al-Maghili fought against the privileged status of the Jewish community in Tuwat in the Sahara Desert. He also fought against the Jewish community's establishment of a synagogue. When the local African community opposed his position, he appealed to authorities in North Africa, who supported him.

al-Maghili embarked on a series of travels, which spread his influence throughout the western Sudan. He held particular influence over Mohammed Rumfa of Kano. For a time al-Maghili was the gray eminence behind the throne, directing Rumfa in his plan to make Kano an authentic Islamic state. al-Maghili corresponded with Rumfa throughout his life and wrote his influential *The Obligation of Princes* as a handbook for him.

After leaving Kano, al-Maghili went to Gao and instructed Askia Mohammed in Islamic law. So strong was his influence that Askia Mohammed asked him to answer a questionnaire for him on Islamic practice.

al-Maghili is also famous for founding one of the major Islamic brotherhoods, the Qadiriyya. Fellowship spread throughout West Africa and became a major factor in its Islamization.

al-Maghili's fame continued to grow after his death. His book became a text for rulers wishing to apply the shari'a (Islamic law) in a situation of initial Islamic centralization. The Fulani under Usman dan Fodio, for example, used *The Obligation of Princes* as a guide to reforming the Hausa states they conquered and establishing their version of an authentic Muslim state.

FRANK A. SALAMONE

See also: **Hausa Polities.**

Further Reading

Hodgkin, T. *Nigerian Perspectives.* London: Oxford University Press, 1975.

Paden, J. *Religion and Political Culture in Kano.* Berkeley: University of California Press, 1974.

Maghrib: Arab Conquest of, 650–715

The Maghrib, which from ancient times was the home of many different Berber tribes, existed under a series of foreign invaders. Of all the foreign rulers, the Arabs who conquered the region in the mid-seventh century made the most profound impact on the people. The Arab invasions swept away the last vestige of the Byzantines who had been in control in most parts of North Africa, including the Maghrib, from the beginning of the sixth century.

The Arab penetration of the Maghrib began in earnest following the completion of their conquest of Egypt with the fall of Alexandria in September 642. Initially undertaken as a means of gaining greater military prestige and wealth for the Arab soldiers on one hand, coupled with a religious zeal for extending Islam's influence on the other, by the mid-660s expansion into the Maghrib was viewed within the wider context of the religio-imperial confrontation of the Umayyad state with the Byzantine forces. However, the Arab advance into the Maghrib was by no means an easy task. Used to deploying forces rapidly across the desert or semidesert, they had to contend with the formidable naval fleets of the Byzantines along the coastal flank. Worse still for the Arabs, the Byzantine forces in North Africa received constant reinforcement through their naval base at Carthage. Until the development of their own naval power, therefore, it was difficult for the invading Arab forces to secure permanent control of the Maghrib area.

There were other major obstacles blocking Arab advancement into the Maghrib. The northern fringes of the Sahara from Tripoli westward was the home of a warlike group of Berbers, the Zenata, who were well versed in the use of camels in mobile warfare and who posed a great threat to the Arabic incursion. Besides, beyond the Aures Mountains was Numidia, a complex of valleys and mountains in western Tunisia and eastern Algeria, where some Berber chieftains had erected considerable kingdoms that had for centuries been accustomed to resisting foreign conquests. Consequently, early Arab incursion took the form of raids rather than systematic conquest and even then, for over two decades between 643 and 667, the Arab forces that raided the Maghrib avoided the Byzantine positions. As a result of the precarious position in which they found themselves, the Arabs never succeeded in venturing very far nor in dominating the Maghrib until the second half of the seventh century.

Meanwhile, at the beginning of the second half of the seventh century, a veteran Arab army commander, Sidi Ugba ibn Nafi, began the long series of campaigns that culminated in the eventual Arab conquest of the Maghrib. He swept across the western desert through Libya into modern day Tunisia and Algeria. In 670, he established a new city in Tunisia called Qairawan, which became a strategic military base for further conquest as well as a center for spreading Islam among the Berber inhabitants of North Africa. Ugha ibn Nafi's first major military venture beyond Qairawan to Morocco ended in disaster in 683 when, on his return toward his base in Qairawan, his army was trapped and subdued by the forces of a Numidian coalition under their king, Kussaila. However, the division between the Numidian and their Zenata Berber kinsmen, and the inability to cooperate in a common cause against their Arab opponents eventually paved the way for the latter to recover, after which they defeated the Berber groups in quick succession. The Numidians were the first to be suppressed. Thereafter, with the advent of Arab naval power, the Byzantine control over Carthage was dismantled. And eventually, in 702, the Arab forces defeated the combined forces of Zenata tribes led by a queen, al-Kahina (the priestess). With al-Kahina's death the last serious Berber attempt to resist the Arabs during the era of conquest came to an end. The succession of victories paved way for the Arabs to March further westwards.

By 715 a belt of land, about 200 miles wide, had been brought under Arab control in the Maghrib, stretching from the borders of Egypt to the Atlantic coast and extending southward into the Fezzan and into the Sus region of southern Morocco. At the same time, a band of Berbers, who had welcomed the Arabs as their deliverers from Byzantine oppression, teamed up with their new overlords to form a mixed Arab-Berber army that embarked on further conquests across the Strait of Gibraltar.

Following these successful conquests, most parts of the Maghrib were officially placed under Arab governors resident at Qairawan. Repeated attempts were made to bring the whole area under unified political control together with Muslim Spain, and repeatedly they broke down, giving rise to kingdoms roughly corresponding to the present division into Morocco, Algeria, Tunisia, and Libya. In the early years of Arab rule, the city life of the Roman era continued to flourish and the Maghrib enjoyed a high level of cultural development. Similarly, trade increased considerably in the Maghrib, as in other parts of North Africa. From Morocco horses, camels, and olives were exported to the Near East. Most important was that the Arabs gained access to the gold of the western Sudan. Slaves were also brought across the desert.

The Arab regime, however, brought with it a major revolution through the introduction of Islam, which steadily replaced Christianity that had hitherto been the dominant religion in most of the Maghrib, since the incorporation of North Africa into the Roman Empire in about 146BCE. A mixed Arab-Berber Muslim society, similar to that in neighboring Egypt, developed. Under Islam, the Maghrib went through a long series of changes influencing every aspect of the people's existence. The administrative and legal systems, family life, education, philosophy, and the general worldview of the people were all profoundly influenced by Islam. In due course the urban and agricultural Berbers became assimilated into this civilization. This, together with the fact that Arabic became the everyday language of most of the people (except in mountainous areas such as the Atlas range in Morocco and the Kabylie mountains of Algeria, where the Berbers maintained their old language and culture together with a fierce spirit of independence), and the considerable admixture of Arab blood through intermarriage, accounts for the fact that Islam is still a considerable force in the region and that Algeria, Libya, Morocco, and Tunisia to this day regard themselves as Arab states, with ties to the Middle East as much as to Africa.

S. Ademola Ajayi

See also: **Ibn Khaldun: History of the Berbers; Maghrib: Muslim Brotherhoods.**

Further Reading

Abun-Nasr, J. M. *A History of the Maghrib.* Cambridge, 1975.

Gellner, E., and C. Micaud, eds. *Arabs and Berbers: From Tribe to Nations in North Africa.* London, 1973.

Levtzion, N. "The Sahara and the Sudan from the Sudan from the Arab Conquest to the Rise of the Almoravids." In *Cambridge History of Africa.* Vol. 2, *From c. 500 B.C. to AD 1050.* Cambridge, 1978.

Lewis, B. *The Arabs in History.* London, 1950.

Yusuf, F. H. *The Arabs and the Sudan from the Seventh to the Early Sixteenth Century.* Edinburgh, 1967.

Maghrib: Marinids, Ziyanids, and Hafsids, 1235–1359

The unification of the Maghrib by the Almohads was followed by a period of political fragmentation under the Marinids, Ziyanids, and Hafsids. The successors of the Almohads in Morocco and Algeria, the Marinids and Ziyanids, were Zanata Berbers. However, while the Marinids were distinguished by their independence, the Ziyanids had become vassals of the Almhoads, who rewarded them with a fiefdom in Tlemcen. After the Almohad Empire was weakened by a defeat at the hands of a combined force of Castilians and Arogonese at Las Navas de Tolosa in 1212, the Marinids invaded northern Morocco from the Sahara. Likewise, in 1235, the Ziyanid leader Yaghmorasan conquered local Zanata lineage groups and established Ziyanid independence in western Algeria. On a campaign to restore Almohad authority, the Almohad caliph al-Sa'id was killed in battle by Yaghmorasan in 1248. The defeated Almohad army was annihilated in the same year by Marinid forces, led by Abu Yahya, who established the Marinid capital in the northern Moroccan city of Fez. From there, the Marinids advanced on the Almohad capital of Marrakech, which fell in 1269. At the same time, the Ziyanids set up an independent sultanate at Tlemcen.

The caliphal title to spiritual and political authority across the empire was, however, inherited neither by the Marinids or Ziyanids, but by the Hafsids. By the time the last Almohad caliph fell to the Zanata usurpers, the Hafsids had established themselves as the guardians of the doctrines of the Almohad religious movement and thus legitimate heirs to their spiritual and political authority. The Hafsid ruler, Abu Zakariya, assumed the caliphal title of commander of the faithful (*amir al-muminin*) after 1235 and extended his sway over Tripoli and Algeria. Hafsid forces took Tlemcen in 1242. In exchange for the recognition of Hafsid supremacy, the Ziyanids were allowed to regain their territory in Algeria. During the reign of Abu Zakariyya's successor, al-Mustanisr (1249–1277), the Marinids recognized Hafsid suzerainty, while the crusade of Louis IX of France was repulsed by the Hafsids in 1270. Ibn Khaldun recorded that al-Mustanisir's reign was a period of economic prosperity and cultural florescence. Afterward, however, the Hafsid state split between rival contenders to the throne, which enabled a Hafsid minister, the Vizier Ibn al-Lihyani, to usurp the throne in 1311. The Hafsid restoration under Abu Bakr in 1318 did not resolve conflicts among the nobles in the cities and the increasing autonomy of the Arab lineages in the countryside, before Hafsid supremacy was challenged from the west.

In 1323 the Ziyanid sultan, Abu Tashfin, invaded Hafsid domains in eastern Algeria, but he was defeated by an alliance of Hafsids and Marinids. The Marinid sultan, Abu al-Hasan then sought to claim the mantle of the Almohad caliphs by reuniting North Africa into a single political community. First, the Marinids attacked the Castilians at Gibraltar and then occupied western Algeria. Abu Tashfin died defending Tlemcen against the Marinids in 1337. While the expulsion of the Marinids from Spain in 1344 indicated that the glory of the Almohad Empire would not be revived, Abu al-Hasan's conquest of Tunis in 1347 did briefly reunite North Africa as a single political community. Marinid rule in Tunis was cut short, after the Hafsids reestablished their influence over the unruly Arab lineages that had, alongside the Hafsid viziers (high Muslim officials), instigated the Marinid occupation. Nevertheless, the Marinid sultan Abu al-'Inan resumed the Marinid bid for supremacy, when he assumed the title of commander of the faithful and conquered Tunis in 1357. As the last Marinid to unite North Africa under one rule, he was also the last Marinid not controlled by his viziers. In 1357 he withdrew to Fez, and although his army campaigned in Tlemcen in 1358, Abu 'Inan was assassinated by one of his viziers before his imperial ambitions could be renewed. Ziyanid independence was thus restored in 1359.

Political fragmentation marks the era of the Marinids, Ziyanids, and Hafsids. Yet, these dynasties established kingdoms centered on the strategic commercial cities of Fez, Tlemcen, and Tunis, which had prospered under Almohad patronage. The cities continued to supply West African gold, ivory, and slaves, to the Middle East and to Europe, as well as being the center of regional commercial networks. Nevertheless, North Africa's "golden age" had passed. To account for this decline, many have seen the influx of Arab pastoral tribes from the eleventh century as a determining factor in political fragmentation and agrarian degradation, which had an impact on economic development. However, the contraction of the cultivated area had begun much earlier, with the collapse of the Roman Empire. Therefore, the devastation of agrarian society memorialized in the great historical works of Ibn Khaldun cannot be attributed to the Arab lineage groups solely. Perhaps the picture of political, cultural, and economic decline depicted by Ibn Khaldun is overdrawn, given that his era coincided with the ravages of the plague in the middle of the fourteenth century, which devastated the population.

Ibn Khaldun's theory of the cyclical rise and decline of kingdoms was undoubtedly influenced by the battle for supremacy waged by the Marinids, Ziyanids, and Hafsids. While the dynasties claimed political legitimacy by reference to the Islamic, political language and symbols established by the Almoravids and Almohads, their authority rested upon dynastic, military power. To compensate for the loss of the Islamic political leadership, North African, Islamic society turned to the leaders of the Sufi religious brotherhoods, the marabout. In the thirteenth century, the Sufi movement flowered under the disciples of the twelfth century mystic, Abu Madyan (Boumedienne). To share in religious legitimacy, the dynasties patronized the Sufis, as well as the Malikite law school, which resulted in the foundation of religious universities (*madrasas*) and mosques, as well as state patronage for religious festivals. Although many have interpreted this as medieval religious decadence, it enabled the process of Islamization of North African society to continue.

The struggle for supremacy in the thirteenth and fourteenth centuries resulted in stalemate, but the contest consolidated the frontiers of an indelible state system. And while the dynasties continued to rely on the Almohad practice of recruiting Berber and Arab lineages for military service, the states were more than tribal confederacies. Rather than rely solely on the tribe, the ruling dynasties remade society by building an urban and rural nobility. Arab and Berber lineage groups with tax-collecting privileges dominated the rural hinterland, while in the cities the ruling dynasties engendered the formation of a ruling nobility of viziers, as well as a secretarial class composed of Islamic scholars (*'ulama*) and those who claimed descent from the Prophet (*shurafa*). Ibn Khaldun was one of those scholars trained in Islamic law and philosophy who attained high political rank in the royal courts, as well as living amongst the Berber tribes, where he was sent to raise military recruits. His itinerant career indicates the interrelationship between court, city, and countryside. It also illustrates that, while neither the Marinids, Ziyanids, or Hafsids could reestablish the Islamic Empire of their predecessors, the imperial legacy afforded them a common political culture.

James Whidden

See also: **'Abd al-Mu'min: Almohad Empire, 1140–1269; Berbers: Ancient North Africa; Ibn Tumart, Almohad Community and.**

Further Reading

Abun-Nasr, J. M. *A History of the Maghrib.* London: Cambridge University Press, 1971.

Brett, M. "Arabs, Berbers, and Holy Men in Southern Ifriqiya, 650–750/1250–1350 AD." *Les Cahiers de Tunisie.* 29, no. 118, 533–559.

Ibn K. *Histoire des Berberes et des dynasties musulmanes de l'Afrique septentrionale* [History of the Berbers and the

Seven Centuries of Muslim Dynasties in Africa], translated by B. de Slane and edited by P. Casanova. Paris: P. Geuthner, 1925–1956.

Julien, C. *History of North Africa: From the Arab Conquest to 1830*, translated by J. Petrie and edited by C. C. Stewart. New York: Praeger Publishers, 1970.

Laroui, A. *The History of the Maghrib.* Princeton: Princeton University Press, 1970.

Shatz-Miller, M. *L'historiographie merinide: Ibn Khaldun et ses contemporains* [Marinid Historiography: Ibn Khaldun and His Contemporaries]. Leiden: E. J. Brill, 1982.

Maghrib: European Expansion into, 1250–1550

Two points should be kept in mind when considering European expansion into the Maghrib from the mid-thirteenth century onward. First, contact with Europe generally involved one of the emerging naval powers at that time, that is, Portugal and Spain. Second, this expansion took place concomitant with a reversal of fortune for Islam in the same area, precipitated by the collapse of the Almohads. For the three hundred years that followed, the European presence in North Africa began to make itself felt, slowly and not always surely, but felt nonetheless. And while Islam may have been banished from Spain and Portugal at this time, this was not the case in North Africa. In fact, during this period there was little significant political change in the region, in spite of Islam's wider regional decline. Of greater importance was the "return of the Christians" to North Africa after an absence that began with the Islamic conquests of the seventh century.

Significant European expansion in the Maghrib was not possible while Europe itself was under the control of forces from North Africa. It was Dom Afonso who provided significant victories to this end for the Portuguese. He took Faro from the Moors in 1249 and Silves the next year, so that by 1250 Portugal could claim to be territorially complete and free of Moorish forces. Afonso followed these successes with several North African expeditions, earning him the sobriquet "the African." The Spanish too, by 1252, had reduced Islamic dominance to Granada. It was not until 1492 that the forces of Isabella of Aragon and Ferdinand of Castile took Granada from the Moors, ending nearly 800 years of Moorish influence in Iberia. Although they did not wait until then to begin their foreign adventures, the fall of Granada did embolden them sufficiently to give an extra push to a war in Africa. (One result of the victory in Granada was that, as an act of thanks, Queen Isabella gave funds to Columbus so that he could look for a sea route to the Indies.) An agreement signed between England and Portugal in 1303 allowed the latter's ships into English ports, as well as guaranteeing they would not be harried at sea. This led to the growth of the Portuguese fleet and, after winning the Battle of Aljubarrota (1385), they were also free from the threat of Spanish interference. Guarantees of this were bolstered in 1411 when the peace between Castile, Aragon, and Portugal was formally settled, allowing their foreign adventures to begin in earnest. Just how quickly was seen by the action of the Portuguese at Ceuta (1415) when a force of 200 ships and 20,000 troops took the port with little resistance. For the next century, Ceuta was central to all of Portugal's exploits in the Maghrib, in spite of the fact that they never held the hinterland, forcing them into the costly position of having to supply the town entirely by sea.

The Portuguese, under Henry the Navigator, tried to take Tangier in 1437, with disastrous results. The Muslim forces only allowed them to return to their ships and leave if Ceuta was surrendered. The Portuguese force agreed, leaving the king's youngest brother as a hostage, while the Portuguese *Cortes*, or parliament, refused, thus leaving Prince Fernando to die in captivity. In spite of this, the North African expansion continued with the conquests of Al Qasr Kabir (1458), Arzila and Tangiers in a subsequent attempt in 1471, Safim (1508), Azamor (1513), and Mazagao (1514). Although the Portuguese did raid as far as Marrakech, this was uncharacteristic and they were largely confined to their coastal possessions. This last marked the extent of the Portuguese expansion in the region.

The successful Portuguese attack against Tangier was followed by the sack of the city and the massacre and enslavement of its inhabitants. In addition, it was carried out despite a declaration by the pope that war against a nonaggressive nation was not justified. To avoid upsetting Rome, the Portuguese employed the services of privateers to do the job. Privateers worked from privately owned and operated armed vessels that were commissioned by governments to act on their behalf, thereby allowing a government to avoid declaring any attack a national action. They were not pirates, whatever their brutal methods might suggest, as they acted within an accepted legal framework, and they eventually became indispensable to states on both sides of the Mediterranean.

Spanish efforts to carve out a Maghrib empire began in earnest in 1509 when Spanish forces captured Oran. By 1535 they were sufficiently emboldened to undertake an expedition against Tunis and in 1541 a failed attempt against Algiers when their fleet was destroyed by a storm. On the whole the Spanish experience was disappointing to them, when compared to the maritime dominance displayed by their Portuguese neighbors. Portugal led the way in this European movement in part because of its position on both the Atlantic and the Mediterranean. It was also united earlier than its neighbors and compact, led by a military aristocracy with nowhere else to go but abroad. Also important was the religious element, and the desire not only to rid Europe of Muslims, but to take Christianity to the Islamic world and beyond.

The Europeans presence in North Africa during this period was always going to prove difficult, especially when, as with Ceuta, entire garrisons had to be supplied exclusively from home and by sea. A series of defeats, coupled with the mounting drain on domestic budgets, persuaded the Portuguese to gradually withdraw from a number of their Maghrib possessions. The weakness of the ruling Watassi in Morocco was another cause for concern for the Portuguese as it led directly to the Saadi, who were originally from Saudi Arabia, to attack and capture Agadir in 1541. At this time the Saadi had declared jihad against the infidel invaders and they swiftly took control of the majority of the country, defeating both Moroccan and Portuguese forces. By 1550 the dream of empire in the Maghrib was essentially finished as Portugal fell back from all of its bases except Ceuta, Tangier, and Mazagan.

EAMONN GEARON

See also: **'Abd al-Mu'min: Almohad Empire, 1140–1269; Portugal: Exploration and Trade in the Fifteenth Century.**

Further Reading

Abun-Nasr, J. M. *A History of the Maghrib.* Cambridge: Cambridge University Press, 1975.

Barbour, N. *A Survey of North West Africa.* London and New York: Oxford University Press, 1962.

Ehret, C. *The Civilizations of Africa: A History to 1800.* Charlottesville: University Press of Virginia, 2002.

Hiskett, M. *The Course of Islam in Africa.* Edinburgh: Edinburgh University Press, 1994.

Le Gall, M., and K. Perkins, eds. *The Maghrib in Question.* Austin: University of Texas Press, 1997.

Martin, P. M., and P. O'Meara, eds. *Africa.* Bloomington: Indiana University Press, 1986.

Murphy, E. J. *History of African Civilization.* New York: Thomas Y. Crowell Company, 1972.

Maghrib: Ottoman Conquest of Algiers, Tripoli, and Tunis

The conquest of Istanbul in 1453 established the Ottoman Empire as the preeminent Islamic state, as well as placing it at the center of a maritime, commercial empire. Eastern Mediterranean trade was largely in the hands of Venetians and Genoese, who were rivaled only by the Muslim corsairs (*ra'is*), while in the western Mediterranean the Iberian states of Portugal and Spain had established frontier posts on the North African coast from the early fifteenth century. At the same time, the Marinid kingdom of Morocco collapsed in 1465 and Hafsid power in Tunis disintegrated after the death of 'Uthman in 1488, which left North African ports prey to the Spanish and Portuguese. The crisis created by the Christian threat in the west was doubled after the fall of Granada to the Castilians in 1492, after which thousands of Andalusians, or Moriscos (Muslim exiles from the Iberian peninsula), poured into the North African ports. The Ottoman response was motivated by a combination of religious zeal and commercial interest, which launched the Ottomans into the western Mediterranean to block Iberian expansion.

The Iberian states, Castile and Aragorn, having waged the *reconquista* for centuries, were the historical enemies of the Muslim states of North Africa. When the Ottomans took up the Muslim cause in the west, corsairs recruited by the Ottomans in the Aegean set out to the western frontier, and from North African ports staged raids on the Spanish coast. In response, Spain seized the port of Mars al-Kabir and Oran in 1505, Bougie in 1509, and Tripoli in 1510. A Muslim corsair in the service of the Hafsids of Tunisia, 'Urudj Babarossa, responded to Algerian appeals against Spanish aggression in 1516. He established himself as the ruler of Algiers, which was already a base for the holy war, having a large population of Andalusians, who supported the war against Spain. Algiers was relatively isolated, on the periphery of the Marinid, Ziyanid, and Hafsid realms therefore it provided a secure base for expansion into the North African interior. After conquering the hinterland of Algiers, 'Urudj defeated the Ziyanids at Tlemcen but died in combat after he was besieged by their Spanish allies in 1518. In 1520, 'Urudj's brother, Khayr al-Din Barbarossa sought the assistance of the Ottoman sultan Selim, who sent him 2,000 janissaries and artillery. Although Algiers was lost after Hafsid and Marinid assaults between 1520 and 1525, in 1529 Khayr al-Din retook Algiers and the Ottoman sultan, Sulayman, appointed him *beylerbey* (*bey* of *beys*) of North Africa.

In 1533 Khayr al-Din was appointed *kapudan-pasha* (admiral) and rebuilt the Ottoman fleet in Istanbul and then, alongside Sinan Rais, engaged Spanish forces across the western Mediterranean, briefly occupying Tunis in 1534. However, the Spanish restored the Hafsid caliph in that year and thus made Tunisia the forward bastion of the Spanish Empire in the Mediterranean. The Ottoman counterattack was swift, with Khayr al-Din's occupation of Minorca. After his death in 1546, Darghut Rais led the offensive, taking Tripoli in 1551 and defeating a Spanish fleet off the Tunisian island of Djerba in 1560. In Algiers, Khayr al-Din's son and successor, Hasan Barbarossa, took Tlemcen from the Spanish in 1553 and established Ottoman control over eastern Algeria while his successor,

'Ulj 'Ali, launched an unsuccessful invasion of Tunisia from Algiers in 1569.

The struggle for mastery of the Mediterranean was decided at Lepanto two years later, when the Ottoman navy was defeated by a league of papal, Spanish, and Venetian forces. This, together with the capture of Tunis by 'Ulj 'Ali and Sinan Rais in 1574, established a Mediterranean frontier that divided Christian Europe from Muslim North Africa. While the truce of 1580 between Philip II of Spain and the Ottoman sultan Murad III indicated the withdrawal of the great powers, this did not bring a general peace to the region. Instead, North African and European states became part of a complicated intercontinental system that vacillated between war and peace, evident in the intrigues of Algiers and France to undermine the accord between the Spanish and the Ottomans after 1580.

A reorganization of the Ottoman territories in North Africa was undertaken after the death of 'Ulj 'Ali in 1587. Murad III incorporated Algiers, Tripoli, and Tunis into the imperial administration as provinces or regencies, ruled by governors (*wali*) with the rank of *pasha*. Effective occupation meant control over the surrounding Arab and Berber lineages, which was enabled by Ottoman gunpowder weapons in the hands of the janissary troops, led by Ottoman officers, the *deys* and *beys*. In Tripoli, local notables were brought together in a council (*diwan*), presided over by the *deys* and the Ottoman *pasha*. Appointed triennially, the *pashas* of Tripoli established Tripoli as a commercial center for seafaring and trans-Saharan trade. To ensure the African trade, the Fezzan was invaded in 1576–1577 and the local sultan was forced to recognize Ottoman suzerainty, which extended Ottoman influence to the frontiers of the West African kingdom of Bornu.

Algiers, like Tripoli, was an Ottoman bastion in a landscape defined by tribal politics, divided between lowland Arab tribes and highland Berbers. But Ottoman political ideology was uniquely suited to conquer and rule under such conditions, because it clearly distinguished between the state and society, the *khassa* and the *ra'iya*, with the latter ideally viewed as a mosaic of religious and national communities. While the *pasha* was the appointed representative of the sultan, real power was held by the corsairs, organized in a corporation (*ta'ifa*), and the military (*ojaq*), led by deys. The corsairs made Algiers the leading North African port, meanwhile, the military advanced into the interior, conquering the neighboring lineage groups, who were then made allies of the Ottomans in still further expeditions. The Berber allies of the Ottomans were known as *zouaves*, while the Arab allies were referred to as the *makhzen* tribes, signaling their alliance with the Ottoman state. The new political landscape was thus divided between an Ottoman oligarchy in Algiers, the *makhzen* tribes, and the subjects. Intermarriage, however, blurred the distinction between the Ottoman state and North African society, by creating a class referred to as the *kulughlis*, an indigenous political class whose Ottoman culture did not prevent them from identifying with the territorial state they had helped to carve out in Algeria.

In Tunisia, as in Algeria, a class of indigenous origins emerged alongside the Ottomans; however, the integration of the Ottoman officials and indigenous society went further. Initially government was divided between a *pasha*, appointed by the Ottoman sultan, and the *bey*, who was responsible for local administration, such as tax collection, which led him to control provincial politics. In 1590 the janissaries, led by their officers, the *deys*, wrested control of Tunis from the *pasha* and his council, and placed it in the hands of the leading *dey*. 'Uthman Dey (1590–1610) was primarily concerned with internal order, suppressing revolts amongst the Arab lineages of Tunisia. So, while the conquest of North Africa by the Ottomans was driven by a Christian threat to the Muslim community, it resulted in the emergence of new political units in North Africa.

James Whidden

See also: **Barbary Corsairs and the Ottoman Provinces: Algiers, Tunis, and Tripoli in the Seventeenth Century; Maghrib: Algiers, Tunis and Tripoli under the Deys, Husaynids, and Karamanlis in the Eighteenth Century.**

Further Reading

Abun-Nasr, J. M. *A History of the Maghreb.* London: Cambridge University Press, 1971.

Fischer, G. *The Barbary Legend: War, Trade, and Piracy in North Africa 1415–1830.* Oxford: Clarendon Press, 1957.

Hess, A. C. *The Forgotten Frontier: A History of the Sixteenth-Century Ibero-African Frontier.* Chicago: Chicago University Press, 1978.

Julien, C. *History of North Africa: From the Arab Conquest to 1830,* translated by J. Petrie and edited by C. C. Stewart. New York: Praeger Publishers, 1970.

Shuval, T. "The Ottoman Algerian Elite and its Ideology." *International Journal of Middle Eastern Studies.* 32, no. 2 (2000): 323–344.

Maghrib: Algiers, Tunis, and Tripoli under the Deys, Husaynids, and Qaramanlis in the Eighteenth Century

The prosperity of the cities of Algiers, Tunis, and Tripoli declined after the seventeenth century, particularly profits from seafaring, yet, at the same time the ruling elites of these cities consolidated their autonomy within the Ottoman Empire. In Tunisia and

Tripolitania, hereditary dynasties were founded early in the eighteenth century. Meanwhile, in Algiers, the ruler, or *dey*, was chosen from amongst the Ottoman militias, or *ojak*, which had become a semi-indigenous oligarchic class. While the cases of Tunis and Tripolitania were comparable, the case of Algiers was distinct in so far as the ruling oligarchy continued to identify with the imperial system, rather than the local society, which had an impact upon the structure of Algiers society.

In Tripoli, the *kulughlis*, those of mixed Ottoman and Libyan origin, represented an indigenous class who rivaled the power of the Ottoman *pasha* and janissaries. One of them, Ahmad Qaramanli, led a revolt against the Tripoli government in 1711, with the support of *kulughlis* and an Arab lineage group. As the *bey* of Tripolitania, Ahmad Qaramanli rebuilt the navy and army, concluding treaties with Holland and Genoa for the necessary European technological improvements and armaments. Subsequent attempts by the Ottomans to restore their authority were unsuccessful, as a result, Ahmad Qaramanli was recognized as the hereditary *pasha* of Tripolitania in 1722. Under ‘Ali Qaramanli (1754–1793) Tripoli prospered by a contradictory policy of naval warfare against European shipping and good relations with Christian and Jewish merchants in the port of Tripoli. However, the outbreak of the plague in the 1780s, which cost Tripolitania half of its population, had a particularly severe impact upon the Christian and Jewish populations because of their concentration in urban quarters. Nevertheless, Tripoli in the eighteenth century was a typically cosmopolitan Mediterranean city. Its prosperity continued through the Napoleonic era, as a result of Yusuf Qaramanli's (1796–1832) policy of capitalizing on the rivalry of Britain and France in the Mediterranean.

In Tunis the Husyanid dynasty secured its hereditary title to the office of *bey* in 1710, with the support of the bourgeois class of Tunis. Wealth in Tunis was distributed between the ruling family and the bourgeoisie, which dominated the central area of the city. To this degree, Tunis corresponds to the typical Islamic city of the Middle East. The *madina* of Tunis was the political and religious heart of the city, consisting of the central market (*suq*), mosque, and the *qasba*, or citadel. The Zaytuna Mosque was one of the foremost in the Islamic world, founded in 745, it acted as a symbol of the Islamic identity of the city and of the country. In the eighteenth century, the Husaynid beys added to the complex, founding schools (*madrasas*), where the founders built their tombs as well as public fountains. The founder of the Husaynid dynasty, Husayn Ibn ‘Ali (1705–1735), accentuated the Islamic character of his dynasty by constructing mosques and schools, as well as convening a *diwan* (council) that included members of the local, Tunisian religious class. During the reign of Hammuda ibn ‘Ali (1782–1814), rural landholders were also absorbed into the political system, alongside the religious and merchant classes of Tunis, beginning a process of administrative reform that would continue into the nineteenth century.

Whereas in Tunisia and Tripoli the ruling dynasties integrated important social groups into the political system, the *deys* of Algiers remained a distinct group. Intermarriage between the military elite and local Algerians did occur, but the *kulughlis* were increasingly excluded from access to political positions. Likewise, the wealthy quarters of Algiers were almost exclusively of either Turkish or Algerian composition. The *deys* resided in the center of the city, in a vast complex of palaces. The complex included administrative and judicial offices, while the janissaries were housed nearby, alongside the port, as well as in the *qasba* on the western wall of the city. The residences of the Algerian commercial and religious elite, on the other hand, were mostly in the southern quarter of the city, segregated from the Turkish ruling elite. Likewise, ethnic divisions were apparent in the system of urban government of Algiers, which placed each ethnic group under a headman (*amin*) responsible for policing and answerable to the mayor (*shaykh al-balad*). The clearest line of social cleavage was that between the Turkish-speaking oligarchy and the remainder of society, Berber, Arab, Andalusian, and Jewish. Exclusivity was the consequence of a political system beset with factional struggles, which forced the ruling *deys* to isolate themselves from society. Their political history is thus obscure, with twenty-eight *deys* succeeding each other between 1671 and 1830, many of whom died by assassination. The alienation of the ruling oligarchy within the capital city was reflected in the relative isolation of the capital from provincial Algeria, which was predominately rural. Perhaps 10 per cent of Algeria's population was urban. The population of Algiers, at 50,000, was less than half that of Tunis at the end of the eighteenth century.

Tunisia had an advanced, industrial economy in the eighteenth century. The manufacture of the fez or *shashiya*, as well as fine clothing and textiles, was comparable to the most complex capitalist industries in Europe. The artisans of Tunis produced commodities for markets in all the provinces of the Ottoman Empire. Tunis, Tripoli, and Algiers were also important outlets for Sub-Saharan products, trading local and European manufactured goods for African slaves, gold, ivory, gum, feathers, and spices. The vibrancy of the ports is reflected in their response to the stimuli of the Napoleonic wars, when Algiers' dominance of corsair seafaring was rivaled by Tunis and Tripoli. Whereas in the seventeenth century Algiers had launched as much as 75 ships, the number had been reduced to twenty or less after the decline of the eighteenth century. However, there was a dramatic revival in the last decade of the century. Algiers constructed its first modern frigate in 1791, under the direction of a Spaniard, while Tunis relied upon its merchant capitalists to provision a fleet of fifteen to thirty ships, which equaled the number at the peak of corsair activity in the seventeenth century.

Other factors, however, contributed to the relative decline of North African commerce from the seventeenth century, such as political disorders in West Africa, which disrupted the trans-Saharan routes in the late eighteenth century, as well as the plague, which represented a demographic and economic catastrophe. Carried by Ottoman troops from Istanbul, the plague made its first appearance in Tripoli in 1701 and spread to Tunis in 1705. It reappeared in Tunis again in the 1730s and in Algiers by 1740. The greatest epidemic occurred in the 1780s, when Tunis lost 18,000 inhabitants between 1784 and 1785 and Algiers 16,000 between 1786 and 1787. The impact of the plague upon Tripoli was perhaps even more profound. Yet, the reorganization of the political and commercial system in Tunisia under Hammuda, like the revivification of seafaring under Yusuf Qaramanli, represented something of a revival. While the relative isolation of Algiers in relation to Algerian society, together with the long-lasting impact of the plague and the European policy of economic exclusion after 1814, weakened North African societies on the eve of European imperial expansion into Northern Africa.

James Whidden

Further Reading

Le Tourneau, R. *Les Villes musulmanes de l'Afrique du Nord* [The Muslim Cities of North Africa]. Algiers: Maisons des livres, 1967.

Morsy, M. *North Africa 1800–1900: A Survey from the Nile Valley to the Atlantic.* New York and London: Longman, 1984.

Panzac, D. *Les Corsaires barbaresques: La Fin d'une Epoquee 1800–1820* [Barbary Corsairs: The End of an Era 1800–1900]. Paris: CNRS Editions, 1999.

Raymond, A. *The Great Arab Cities in the 16th–18th Centuries.* New York: New York University Press, 1984.

Valensi, L. "Esclaves chretiens et esclaves noir a Tunis au XVIII siecle" [Christian and African slaves in 18th century Tunis]. *Annales Economies Societes Civilisations*, 22, no. 6 (1967): 1267–1288.

———. "Calamites demographiques en Tunisie et en Mediterranee orientale aux XVIII et XIX siecles" [Demographic calamities in Tunisia and the eastern Mediterranean from the 18th to 19th centuries]. *Annales Economies Societes Civilisations.* 24, no. 6 (1969): 1540–1561.

———. *On the Eve of Colonialism: North Africa Before the French Conquest*, translated by K. J. Perkins. New York: African Publishing Co., 1977.

Maghrib: Muslim Brotherhoods

Earliest evidence for the presence of Sufism (Islamic mysticism) in the Maghrib dates to the early eleventh century, nearly a quarter millennium later than its appearance in the Islamic East. The first Sufi brotherhoods in the region grew up around rural mosques and instruction centers known as *ribats* built on the frontier between lands under Muslim rule and those outside of Muslim authority. The *ribats* served in some cases as defensive outposts against threatening non-Muslim neighbors, but primarily as bases from which to carry Islam, strongly influenced by the Maliki school of law, to the region's non-Muslim or nominally Muslim inhabitants. One such *ribat* was built on the Atlantic coast of Morocco at the site known as Tit-n-Fitr near a community of Sanhaja Berbers. Over time those associated with the *ribat* evolved into the *Ta'ifa al-Sanhajiyya* Sufi brotherhood. As its name implies, the *Ta'ifa al-Sanhajiyya* remained ethnically oriented toward Sanhaja Berbers even as it extended its influence more widely throughout the Maghrib. Similar ethnically or tribally based Sufi brotherhoods arose out of the establishment of *ribats* elsewhere in the region, such as the Masmuda based *Ribat Shakir*, originally built in the foothills of the Atlas Mountains to defend against attacks by the heterodox Barghawata Berber confederation.

The most influential figure in the transition of Maghribi Sufism from such parochial beginnings into more multiregional, multiethnic forms of Sufi brotherhood was the Andalusian Abu Madyan Shu'ayb (d.1198). Abu Madyan received his education in the esoteric sciences from a diverse group of Maghribi masters but most notably the Arab Ibn Hirzihim in Fez, and the illiterate Masmuda Berber ascetic Abu Yi'zza. Scholars disagree about the veracity of claims that Abu Madyan also completed the pilgrimage to Mecca and met the Iranian jurist and Sufi preacher 'Abd al-Qadir al-Jilani (d.1165). From his prayer center in the Algerian city Bijaya (Fr. Bougie), Abu Madyan attracted a considerable enough following to be perceived as a threat by the Almohad caliph Ya'qub al-Mansur. Forced to appear before the caliph, the aged shaykh died on his way to the capital Marrakech. Abu Madyan's teaching of a "middle path" balancing worldly and spiritual concerns influenced the development of Sufism throughout the Muslim world, while his prominence in the initiatic chain (*silsila*) of so many later Maghribi Sufis earned him the honorific title "Shaykh of Shaykhs."

The two most prominent Sufi brotherhoods in the premodern Maghrib were the Shadhiliyya, named after its Moroccan founder Abu'l-Hasan al-Shadhili (d.1258) and the Qadiriyya, which takes its name from 'Abd al-Qadir al-Jilani. Al-Shadhili came into contact with the Iraqi Rifa'iyya brotherhood first in Egypt through Abu'l Fath al-Wasiti (d.1245), and upon returning to Morocco, under the tutelage of 'Abd al-Salam b. Mashish (d.1228). The Rifa'iyya possessed a more developed institutional character and al-Shadhili incorporated a similar organizational structure into the Shadhiliyya. The Qadiriyya brotherhood first entered the Maghrib from Andalusia in the sixteenth century through the efforts of 'Abd al-Qadir al-Jilani's descendants and spiritual successors living there. Although al-Jilani did not personally found the brotherhood that bears his name, his written legacy on rules governing the behavior of disciples indicates an institutional dimension akin to that associated with the Shadhiliyya. Despite the structural changes effected by the Qadiriyya and Shadhiliyya orders, affiliation to a particular brotherhood continued to signify foremost an association with a Sufi master's teachings while connoting no formal, much less exclusive allegiance to that master or his brotherhood.

The eighteenth and early nineteenth centuries was a period of reform and renewal throughout the Muslim world, and the Sufi order became in many cases the center for much of the reformist activity. The increased ease by which Muslim pilgrims worldwide were able to travel to the holy cities of Mecca and Medina further internationalized Sufi brotherhoods and aided in the circulation of reformist ideas. The period also saw the creation of several new Sufi orders arising out of the traditional Sufi networks but possessing qualities that suggest a signal change from their predecessors. Although significant differences existed among these new reformist brotherhoods, generally they shared the following traits: a central, hierarchical organization; a greater missionary emphasis, particularly focused on Islam's peripheries; a pietistic emphasis on correct practice; the use of vernacular languages religious texts; and a predilection for communal rather than individual performance of invocations accomplished to achieve heightened spiritual states.

One of the most influential figures during this period was the Moroccan Ahmad ibn Idris (d.1837). Born near the port city of al-'Ara'ish, Ibn Idris moved to Fez where he studied at the famous Qarawiyyin mosque school and also studied with a number of Sufi shaykhs all of whom were associated with the Shadhiliyya. Later, Ibn Idris distanced himself from his Shadhili masters asserting that the legendary figure al-Khadir had taught him while in the Prophet Muhammad's presence the prayers and litanies that he in turn taught to his own disciples. Ibn Idris traveled to Mecca in 1799 and remained in the East the rest of his life, living at different times in Mecca, Egypt, and the Yemen. While he does not seem to have aspired to create a new brotherhood, Ibn Idris is indirectly responsible for the creation of the Sanusiyya in Cyrenaica, the Mirghaniyya and Majdhubiyya in the Sudan, and the Rashidiyya in Egypt, which were all founded by his closest followers.

Like Ibn Idris, the Algerian Ahmad al-Tijani (d.1815) journeyed to Mecca after several years in Fez where he was initiated into the Qadiriyya, Nasiriyya, and Tayyibiyya brotherhoods. En route to Mecca, al-Tijani was initiated into the Khalwatiyya while in Cairo. He too relinquished his ties with past masters after receiving instructions directly from the Prophet Muhammad to do so. Unlike Ibn Idris, al-Tijani consciously sought to create a new brotherhood under his authority and he eventually forbade his followers from having affiliations with other brotherhoods besides the Tijaniyya. The Tijaniyya found its greatest success in Saharan and Sub-Saharan West Africa beginning in the mid-nineteenth century.

GLEN W. MCLAUGHLIN

See also: **Abu Madian, al-Shadhili, and the Spread of Sufism in the Maghrib.**

Further Reading

Abun-Nasr, J. M. *A History of the Maghrib in the Islamic Period.* Cambridge: Cambridge University Press, 1987.

———. *The Tijaniyya: A Sufi Order in the Modern World.* London: Oxford University Press, 1965.

Cornell, V. J. *Realm of the Saint: Power and Authority in Moroccan Sufism.* Austin: University of Texas Press, 1998.

Khushaim, A. F. *Zarruq the Sufi: A Guide in the Way and a Leader to the Truth.* Tripoli: General Company for Publication, 1976.

Levtzion, N. "Eighteenth Century Sufi Brotherhoods: Structural, Organisational and Ritual Changes" in *Islam: Essays on Scripture, Thought and Society: A Festschrift in Honor of Anthony H. Johns*, edited by P. G. Riddell and T. Street. Leiden: E. J. Brill, 1997.

O'Fahey, R. S. *Enigmatic Saint: Ahmad Ibn Idris and the Idrisi Tradition.* London: C. Hurst and Co., and Evanston: Northwestern University Press, 1990.

O'Fahey, R. S. and B. Radtke. "Neo-Sufism Reconsidered." *Der Islam.* 70/1 (1993): 52–87.

Popovic, A. and G. Veinstein (eds.). *Les Voies d'Allah: Les ordres mystiques dans l'islam des origines a aujourd'hui*, Paris: Librairie Artheme Fayard, 1996.

Radtke, B. "Sufism in the 18th Century: An Attempt at a Provisional Appraisal." *Die Welt des Islams.* 36/3 (1996): 326–364.

Schimmel, A. *Mystical Dimensions of Islam.* Chapel Hill: University of North Carolina Press, 1975.

Maghrib Unity, European Union and

Until the independence of Algeria in 1962, the concept of Maghrib unity was, for the most part, confined to a solidarity of action against a common colonial power and a united struggle for the liberation of each country in the region. At independence, the attachment and commitment to this ideal of unity remained an irreversible aspiration, and was even embedded in the earliest constitutions of Tunisia (1959), Morocco (1962), and Algeria (1962). The continuing belief in the necessary unity of the Maghrib, by excluding any form of political union, was to be underlined on economic grounds as emphasized in the conclusions of the Maghrib foreign ministers' meeting in Rabat in February 1963. Regional unity or integration was perceived as a potentially effective medium not only for helping rapid economic development in the region but also for harmonizing policy toward other groupings, particularly the European Union (EU).

The first postcolonial attempt at regional integration goes back to the early 1960s. Factors that helped set this process into motion included, among others, the partial settlement of border disputes that emerged following independence, and the Organization of African Unity's suggestion regarding the common development of mineral resources in those disputed areas. Another driving force was the UN Economic Commission for Africa's assessment that, in a report tabled after a visit to the region in 1963, drew the attention of the Maghrib countries to coordinated projects that could benefit more than one country and urged consultation to avoid duplicating industrial investments. All these factors prompted the first Conference of Maghrib Economic Ministers in Tunis in 1964, which launched the Maghrib Permanent Consultative Committee to coordinate and harmonize economic policies among the partner countries.

Agreements signed in Tunis and Tangier in 1964 provided for the coordination and harmonization of development plans, including those for industries and services, as well as intraregional trade and relations with the EU (European Economic Community at that time). A Maghrib Center for Industrial Studies was established in 1968 in Tripoli, with financial and technical assistance from the United Nations Development Program, to promote joint projects. However, cooperation broke down because each country's industrial policy ignored those of its partners, resulting in the proliferation of rival industries, such as steel and fertilizer manufacture.

In relation to Europe, the EU, in its wish to conclude association agreements with the Maghrib countries, favored joint negotiations toward a single free-trade area for all these countries. They neither harmonized their attitudes nor coordinated their positions, and each country individually negotiated its own deal, leading to separate association accords in 1969 with Morocco and Tunisia, and cooperation agreements in 1976, with Algeria included this time.

The chief impediments to any tangible achievement were each country's embarking upon different economic policies, and their subordinating of the regional construct to individual political and economic choices. In addition, the frequency of inter-state frictions, particularly in the 1970s, was not conducive to dialogue and negotiation between partner countries. Tunisia's disengagement from the abortive declaration of union in 1974 with Libya worsened relations between the two countries for several years. More serious was the Algerian-Moroccan disagreement over the Western Sahara from 1975 onward, which decisively halted all progress on the regional front for more than a decade, during which period the Maghrib region was to witness the development of alliances (Tunis axis and Oujda axis) instigated by Algeria and Morocco, arguably more for political than economic considerations.

Improved interstate relations (resumption of diplomatic relations between Algeria and Morocco in May 1988 and normalization of diplomatic ties between Tunisia and Libya later) paved the way for a renewed interest in regional integration. This culminated in the establishment of the Arab Maghrib Union (AMU) in February 1989, which became a matter of survival in light of the global trend toward the formation of regional trading blocs, and more important, the southern enlargement of the EU and the imminent completion of the European internal market.

Among the central objectives of the AMU was the strengthening of links between partner countries in order to ensure stability and enhance policy coordination, both regionally and with the outside world. A common development strategy was adopted in 1991, outlining four steps for integration with fixed deadlines for establishing a free trade area by the end of 1992, a customs union by the end of 1995, a common market by the end of 2000, and at a later stage with no specified date, an economic and monetary union. Up to April 1994, the AMU partner countries had signed several agreements related to diverse economic, environmental, and sociocultural areas. However, very few of these agreements had been translated into action.

The still-unresolved Western Sahara issue, the domestic problems in Algeria, and the repercussions of UN sanctions on Libya over the years raised serious obstacles to the necessary development of the group. After Libya's refusal to take over the AMU chairmanship from Algeria in January 1995, the activities of the organization were frozen and its fate became uncertain. The AMU's prospects for developing a relationship with the EU that would substitute for bilateral arrangements, and thus enable its founders to bargain collectively, also faded. Again, and within the framework of the Euro-Mediterranean partnership policy launched in 1995, each country negotiated on a bilateral basis, and both Morocco and Tunisia already concluded new agreements.

The postindependence attempts at integration in the Maghrib, while favored by a propitious environment, at least in terms of geographical proximity and common historical and cultural backgrounds, have proven unsuccessful as they have been overridden by the national constraining realities of a political and economic nature. Evidently this lack of progress adversely affected the degree of coordination of their external relations, especially vis-à-vis their major trading partner, the EU. It remains to be seen whether recent developments in the region (the easing of sanctions on Libya, the relative improvement of the domestic situation in Algeria, and the new leadership in Morocco) can provide a spur to the regional process of integration.

AHMED AGHROUT

See also: **Algeria: International Relations, 1962–Present; Algeria: War of Independence, 1954–1962; Libya: Foreign Policy under Qaddafi; Polisario and the Western Sahara; Tunisia: Modern International Relations.**

Further Reading

Aghrout, A. "The Maghrib: Regional Integration and Relations with Europe." *International Politics.* 34, no. 1 (March 1997): 97–102.

Aghrout, A., and M. Alexander. "The Euro-Mediterranean New Strategy and the Maghrib Countries." *European Foreign Affairs Review.* 2, no. 3 (Autumn 1997): 307–328.

Aghrout, A., and A. Geddes. "The Maghrib and the European Union: From Development Cooperation to Partnership?" *International Politics.* 33, no. 3 (September 1996): 227–243.

Aghrout, A., and K. Sutton. "Regional Economic Union in the Maghrib." *The Journal of Modern African Studies.* 28, no. 1 (March 1990): 115–139.

Daoud, Z. "*La création de l'UMA*" [The creation of the AMU]. *Monde Arab-Maghrib-Machrek.* 124 (April–June 1989): 120–138.

Oualalou, F. *Après Barcelona . . . Le Maghrib est nécessaire* [After Barcelona . . . The Maghrib is necessary]. Casablanca: Toukbal Publications, 1996.

Robana, A. *The Prospects of an Enlarged Economic Community in North Africa—Managing Economic Integration in the Maghrib.* New York: Praeger Publishers, 1973.

Mahdist State: *See* Sudan: Mahdist State, 1881–1898.

Mai Dunama Dibalami (1210–1248)

Mai Dunama Dibalami was arguably the most prominent ruler of the Kanem Empire. The Kanem Empire emerged in the central Sudan in the region that runs from the Sahel into the Sahara northeast of Lake Chad. Kanem began as a southern Saharan confederation of nomadic groups, under the leadership of the Zaghawah. By the ninth century, the Zaghawah had settled in Kanem, whereupon they began a campaign of military expansion during the thirteenth century. Mai Dunama Dibalami was a central figure in the expansion of Kanem during this period.

Dibalami is credited with extending the territorial limits of the kingdom from the Niger to the Nile. He exerted control over the Fezzan and brought stability to long-distance trade between North Africa and Kanem. He also organized military expeditions to the west of Lake Chad, where in 1252 he campaigned against the Mabina, Kalkin, and Afuno. The expansion of Kanem under Dibalami facilitated control of two major routes of the trans-Saharan trade: the north-south trade from Tripoli to Kanem and the east-west routes from Egypt to Ghana-Mali-Songhai.

The major exports from Kanem were slaves, elephant tusks, ostrich feathers, and live animals. In exchange, Kanem imported horses, which were central to the creation of the Kanem cavalry. The evidence suggests that the cavalry of Dibalami was composed of 41,000 horses. In addition, Kanem also imported garments, fabrics, and iron weapons from the north. For example, the Islamic sources state that during the tenure of Dibalami garments were shipped from the Tunisian capital into Kanem. The prosperity of the trans-Saharan trade depended on the stability provided by the different powers that were situated in the different parts of the network of trade routes. In the north, the kingdom of Fezzan was the bulwark of the trade. The Berber chiefs of Kawar dominated the central region. In the south, Kanem provided security for the trade routes.

In the thirteenth century, however, under Dunama Dibalami, the historical evidence suggests that Kanem had supplanted the Berber chiefs of Kawar and the Berber dynasty of Banu Khattad as the dominant force in the trans-Saharan trade. Apart from dominating both ends of the north–south trade, it was also important for the Kanem kings to prevent the diversion of trade to alternate routes. To this end, the king of Kanem gained control over the western town of Takedda and also extended his control over Dadjo and Zaghawa to the east.

The Kanem under Dunama Dibalami was by no means a huge empire with a strong centralized organization. In fact, historical sources are imprecise as to the actual power the king of Kanem wielded over the Fezzan. Further, Kanem control of the eastern parts was tenuous. It is doubtful whether Dibalami extended his empire as far as Darfur. Although Dibalami fought a protracted war against the Tubu of Bahr-al-Ghazal, he did not succeed in imposing his rule over them. Nor did he succeed in subjugating the peoples living around the Lake Chad and on the islands. What this suggests is that the expansion of Kanem under Dibalami was concentrated on the northern region. Kanem relations with the southern region were based on economic interest. The southern region was the main source of slaves for the trans-Saharan trade, as they were non-Muslim peoples. It was therefore not in Kanem's economic interest to extend the frontiers of Islam to this important source of slaves.

Nevertheless, the evidence suggests that Dibalami was a remarkable Muslim reformer, and during his reign Islam flourished. Dibalami used Islam to legitimize his rule. It also provided a justification for expansion through or holy war against unbelievers. He is credited with having founded a *madrasa* in Cairo for the states under the control of Kanem. Dunama also imposed Islam on the Berbers of the central Sudan.

It would appear that as Kanem expanded under Dunama Dibalami so did Islam spread. Islam brought a number of advantages to Kanem. It facilitated the spread of writing and scholarship. Further, the use of Muslim jurists aided the king of Kanem in consolidating its control by applying Islamic law to traditional customs. A contingent of judges was created in all the major towns with a high court in the capital. Further, because of the central location of Kanem, it became a center for the dissemination of Islamic thought and culture. It also became a nucleus for the cross-fertilization of ideas between the Mediterranean cities, the Middle East, and the central Sudan. There were also significant economic advantages to the spread of Islam into Kanem. Islam facilitated diplomatic relations with the states of North Africa and Arabia. The evidence suggests that as these diplomatic ties were strengthened, trade was also enhanced. The economic ties from Kanem did extend to Tunisia in the north and Egypt and Arabia in the east.

In spite of the great success of Dunama Dibalami, Kanem had begun to show signs of internal crumbling before his death. The eastern frontier was wracked by revolts, especially by the Bulala. This was compounded by internal squabbling among the ruling families. Nevertheless, there was up to a century of stability after the death of Dibalami, before Kanem entered a period of decline.

EZEKIEL WALKER

See also: **Kanem.**

Further Reading

Bawuro, B. "Early States of the Central Sudan: Kanem, Borno, and Some of their Neighbors to c. 1500 AD." In *History of West Africa*, edited by J. F. A. Ajoyi and M. Crowder. 3rd. ed. Vol. I. London: Longman, 1985.

Hodgkin, T. *Nigerian Perspectives: An Historical Anthology.* Oxford University Press.

Law, R. *The Horse in West African History.* Oxford: Oxford University Press, 1980.

Levtzion, N., and J. F. F. Hopkins, eds. *Corpus of Early Arabic Sources for West African History.* Cambridge: Cambridge University Press, 1981.

Smith, A. "The Early States of the Central Sudan." In *History of West Africa*, edited by J. F. A. Ajayi and M. Crowder. London: Longman, 1971.

Makeke, Charlotte Makhanye

Advocate for Women's Rights

Charlotte Manye Maxeke (1874–1939) was an important figure in African religious and political circles of the early twentieth century and was a prominent advocate of women's rights. She was born in 1874 near Fort Beaufort. Her father was a Sotho from the Transvaal who migrated to the eastern Cape for work. Instead of returning to his homeland, he married a Christian Mfengu woman, converted to Christianity, and became a preacher. Charlotte was the eldest of the six children. The parents were committed to providing education for their children, and Charlotte Manye studied at mission schools in Uitenhage and Port Elizabeth.

By 1890 the Manye family moved to Kimberley, where Charlotte Manye worked as a teacher, one of the few professions open to educated African women. Charlotte and her sister Kate gained local renown for their singing. The vibrant African elite community of Kimberley was much influenced by the tour of the African American singing troupe, Orpheus McAdoo's Virginia Jubilee Singers, which toured South Africa from 1890 to 1898. This troupe provided the African elite with a model of black achievement. Inspired by the example of the Virginia Jubilee Singers, two British impresarios formed a sixteen-member choir to tour Great Britain. The choir was intended to raise money for an African college in South Africa. Charlotte and Kate Manye were part of this troupe, which toured from 1891 to 1892, and sang before Queen Victoria. Although the tour created a sensation, the group had financial and management problems and was almost stranded in Britain.

Charlotte Manye signed up for a second choir tour of North America in 1893. She hoped to use this tour as a way to gain access to higher education opportunities that were unavailable in South Africa. This tour also foundered and the choir was abandoned in Ohio. The group fortuitously met Reverend R. Ransom, a minister of the African Methodist Episcopal (AME) Church. The AME Church was the oldest black denomination in the United States. With Ransom's help, six members of the choir, including Charlotte Manye, enrolled at AME Church's Wilberforce University in Ohio. A local branch of the AME's Woman's Parent Mite Missionary Society befriended Charlotte Manye and gave her financial and emotional support. While in Ohio, Charlotte Manye frequently lectured on South Africa.

Charlotte Manye wrote her sister Kate, who was then living in Johannesburg, about her experiences and the AME Church. Kate was acquainted with Ethiopianists, African Christians who broke away from mission churches and formed independent, black-led, churches. One prominent Ethiopianist, Reverend M. Mokone, acted on the basis of Charlotte's letter, and initiated contact with the AME Church. This contact eventually led to the establishment of the AME Church in South Africa.

Charlotte Manye earned a Bachelor of Science degree from Wilberforce University and returned to South Africa in 1901, intending to work as an AME missionary and teacher. She was the first black South African woman to earn a university degree. Due to the South African war, Manye was unable to proceed to her mission field in the Transvaal and worked in Cape Town. After it was safe to proceed, Charlotte Manye moved to Pietersburg and established a school and other mission work. A fellow South African graduate of Wilberforce University, Marshall Maxeke, soon joined Charlotte Manye and became head of the mission. Charlotte and Marshall married, had a son, and continued their mission work as a team. Among the many schools in the Transvaal that the Maxekes established was the Wilberforce Institute, near Johannesburg. At the invitation of a chief in the Transkei, they began work among the Thembu people. Around the end of World War I, Charlotte and her husband moved to the Johannesburg area, ending the most active phase of her mission work.

Charlotte Maxeke and her husband were involved in the African politics of the early twentieth century. Marshall Maxeke joined the South African Native National Congress, later the African National Congress, at its founding. Charlotte Maxeke was influenced by the massive passive resistance campaign of women in Bloemfontein, who in 1913 protested extending passes to women. Charlotte Maxeke helped found the Bantu Women's League, which was formed, in part, to represent women who were excluded from full membership of the South African Native National Congress. She served as its president in 1918 and was part of a group that met with Prime Minister Louis Botha to protest the passes for women.

Through the 1920s Charlotte Maxeke continued her public involvement. She was a popular speaker and broadened her concerns to include the urban issues affecting African women and children. She and her husband were involved in the Johannesburg Joint Council Movement, an interracial group of liberal whites and moderate Africans dedicated to discussing and improving interracial relations. Charlotte Maxeke testified before many government commissions in order to ensure that African perspectives were represented. She continued her mission activity by visiting African women in prison. While Charlotte maintained her public life in politics and the church, she also provided for her extended family. Her husband was increasingly incapacitated by heart disease and died in 1928. Charlotte Maxeke worked variously as a probation officer, a "native welfare" officer, and briefly operated a domestic service bureau. In the late 1920s Charlotte returned to the United States for a meeting of the AME Church. Through the 1930s Charlotte Maxeke continued her political and religious work. She was one of the organizers of the National Council of African Women, a successor to the Bantu Women's League, and she served as its first president. Charlotte Manye Maxeke died in 1939.

MODUPE G. LABODE

Biography

Charlotte Manye Maxeke was born in 1874 near Fort Beaufort. She earned a bachelor of science degree from Wilberforce University in Ohio, United States, and returned to South Africa in 1901. She married Marshall Maxeke and had a son. She helped found the Bantu Women's League, serving as its president in 1918. She died in 1939.

Further Reading

Campbell, J. *Songs of Zion.* Chapel Hill: University of North Carolina Press, 1998.

Erlmann, V. *African Stars: Studies in Black South African Performance.* Chicago: University of Chicago Press, 1991.

———. "Africa Civilised, Africa Uncivilised: Local Culture, World System and South African Music." *Journal of Southern African Studies;* 20, no. 2 (June 1994): 165–180.

Karis, T., and G. M. Carter (eds.). *From Protest to Challenge: A Documentary History of African Politics in South Africa, 1822–1964.* Vol. I. Stanford: Hoover Institution Press, 1979.

McCord, M. *The Calling of Katie Makanya: A Memoir of South Africa.* New York: John Wiley and Sons, and Cape Town: David Philip Publishers, 1995.

Page, C. A. "Charlotte Manye Maxeke." In *Women in New Worlds: Historical Perspectives on the Wesleyan Tradition,* edited by H. F. Thomas, R. Skinner Kell, and L. Queen. Nashville: Abingdon, 1982.

Skota, T. D. M. (ed.). *The African Yearly Register.* Johannesburg, 1931.

Xuma, A. B. *What an Educated African Girl Can Do.* Nashville: The Women's Parent Mite Missionary Society of the AME Church, 1930.

Makenye Kalemba (1835?–1899)

Collaborator and Resister in Kasai, 1880–1900

Makenye Kalemba was one of the African leaders of the last quarter of the nineteenth century who undertook reform of their society, managing to come to a degree of understanding with the Europeans but finally resorting to armed struggle to preserve independence.

Makenye Kalemba was born between 1830 and 1835 into a chiefly family in the clan of Bena Kashiya among the Luba people in the valley of the central Lulua River around the present-day city of Kananga in the western Kasai region. His father, Tunsele-Twa-Ilunga, chose him as his successor probably because of his leadership qualities. Makenye made a number of business trips to Angola, and his village, Kempe, developed into a prosperous commercial center that attracted Chokwe traders and became the point of departure of caravans of ivory, wax, and slaves to Angola. The triumph of his clan over its rivals resulted from the accumulation of wealth and firearms in the framework of long-distance trade and from the acquisition of ritual powers, the *Nkwembie* (spirit of force). By 1865 Makenye had the economic, social, and symbolic capital to contribute to the political integration in the valley of the central Luluwa.

Makenye adopted various political strategies to extend his power, including gift-giving, feasting, the use of force, and the control of trade with the Chokwe. With the accumulated capital, Makenye was able to institutionalize his power by introducing new principles of legitimacy. His nickname, Kalemba, became a dynastic name. His son Tshisungu took the name of Kalemba Mwana (Kalemba Junior). Makenye Kalemba adopted the Chokwe title of "Mwanangana" ("landowner") and instituted a rigorous hierarchy at his court. From that time on Makenye was invariably referred to as the "King of Bena Moyo" (king of people who greet each other by *moyo,* or life) mostly by his people, and "King of Bashilange" by the Chokwe.

Religious rituals contributed to fostering unity and social cohesion. However, the extent of political centralization—that is, the number of people over whom he exercised power and from whom he could collect taxes—was still limited to a few clans and clients. There were other clan leaders who did not share Makenye's religious enthusiasm and political goals. Thus, his main challenge for the two decades after 1865 remained the integration of his rivals, as well as new groups, into the emerging state of Bena Moyo.

On October 30, 1881 Mwananganga Makenye Kalemba welcomed Dr. Paul Pogge and Lt. Herman Wissmann, German explorers sent to participate in what was later known as the "Scramble" for Africa, to Kempe. Their meeting provoked a great cultural misunderstanding. The Germans had a colonial project; they understood their mission to be a scientific expedition with a political agenda, namely, the exploration of the Kasai River basin, and the installation of a German post in the region. Lt. H. Wissmann even reported that Makenye Kalemba and his Luba "nation" constituted an appropriate target for evangelization. Kalemba and his subjects, however, believed the newcomers were their ancestors (*bajangi*) coming back to life in the form of white men to recreate a paradisiacal world where there would be no sickness, aging, or death. Makenye seized control of this cultural capital to further the process of political centralization. With the help of Makenye Kalemba, Pogge and Wissmann explored the central Kasai basin between December 1881 and April 1882.

The arrival of the Germans created tension between Makenye Kalemba and Muamba Mputu, the latter accusing the first of appropriating his *bajangi.* But Makenye was preoccupied with deeper existential dilemmas: the behavior and the activities of his *bajangi* did not conform to prevailing cultural categories. He started the painful task of redefining them.

In 1884 King Leopold II of Belgium hired Wissmann to complete his geographic discoveries and to collect data on the natural and human resources in the Kasai basin. Makenye Kalemba gave Wissmann a piece of land on the banks of the Lulua River, where they built a German station called "Luluabourg," that the Angolan porters named "Malandji" in memory of Malange, their native city in Angola. The king also helped Wissmann build canoes for the exploration of the Kasai river.

Makenye Kalemba expressed his hope of establishing a meaningful partnership with the Europeans. He made a blood pact (*ndondo*) with Wissmann, with the understanding that they would become "brothers" who would provide each other with assistance in all circumstances and refrain from acts of hostility. Thus, indirectly, Makenye became an ally of King Leopold II. One provision of this (verbal) pact stipulated that a breach of the agreement would result either in the death of the traitor and his family members, in the worse case scenario, or in the removal of his power. The war against Katende, one of Makenye's rivals, that followed thereafter tested the solidity of the pact. The conquered chief spent four months in Luluabourg's prison.

In 1885 Makenye Kalemba accompanied Wissmann in his exploration of the Kasai River. Their expedition clarified the relationship between the Kasai and Congo Rivers. The trip to Nshasa and Leopoldville was an important learning experience for Makenye and his subjects. It highlighted the difference between the Luba values and those represented by the Congo Free State (CFS) and its agents. He came back convinced that his recent religious experience was an illusion, for there were more *bajangi* beyond his territory than he had imagined. Furthermore, the *bajangi* were mortals and were unable to protect their "descendants" from violence and suffering.

With the return of Wissmann and other CFS agents (the Belgians de Macar and Le Marinel) to Luluabourg in April 1886, the center of trade in wax and ivory shifted from Kempe to Luluabourg, now perceived as the "Paradise of Congo." Through various hegemonic processes, the CFS administrators transformed Luluabourg into a center of political power and positioned themselves as arbiters between Makenye Kalemba and the other chiefs. But Makenye Kalemba did not see these attempts at centralization as an encroachment upon his sphere of influence. Actually, he mobilized the firepower of the Europeans to promote his own interests. The attack against Muamba Mputu that took place in 1887, with the help of de Macar and Le Marinel, is a good case in point. Muamba Mputu was defeated after two fierce battles and, according to tradition, he escaped from the battlefield only thanks to his magical powers.

In 1887 Makenye Kalemba was at the peak of his power in a prosperous land. Despite an increasing number of CFS agents, merchants, and missionaries in Luluabourg, the relationship with Kalemba was cordial. The region had abundant natural resources, and there was little competition for resources.

This political peace slowly broke down under the pressure of merchant capitalism and the CFS. The competition between the European trading companies and the local population for resources sharply increased and provoked tension between them. Makenye Kalemba now faced a serious challenge to his political and economic power from the CFS and its agents, who openly questioned his "independence" and the activities of Chokwe and Bihe traders in Kempe. The *entente cordiale* gave way to a "hostile attitude" on the part of Makenye and his subjects.

The tension erupted into open conflict when CFS agents ordered Makenye to transfer the collection of tributary taxes to the CFS. The conflict started in early 1891 and continued after the death of King Makenye from pneumonia in 1899. Resistance to colonial rule persisted until 1924, when the Belgian colonial administration recognized Kalemba Muana as chief of the Bena Kashiya clan, not the king of the Luba-Lulua.

KALALA NGALAMULUME

See also: **Congo (Kinshasa), Democratic Republic of Zaire: Nineteenth Century: Precolonial; Congo (Kinshasa), Democratic Republic of Zaire: Belgian Congo: Administration and Society, 1908–1960.**

Further Reading

Ntambwe, L. "Les Luluwa et le Commerce Luso-Africain." *Etudes d'Histoire Africaine.* 6 (1974): 55–104.

Wissmann, H. *Im Innern Afrikas.* Leipzig: F. A. Brochamn, 1888.

———. *Unter Deutsche Flagge Quer Durch Africa, von West nach Ost.* Berlin: Globus Veslog, 1888.

Zandijcke, van. *Pages d'Histoire du Kasayi.* Namur: 1953.

Makhzen: *See* Morocco: Mawlay Hasan and the Makhzen.

Makurra: *See* Nobadia, Makurra and 'Alwa.

Malagasy Kingdoms: *See* Madagascar: Malagasy Kingdoms, Evolution of.

Malaria: *See* Epidemics: Malaria, AIDS, Other Disease: Postcolonial Africa.

Malawi: Ngoni Incursions from the South, Nineteenth Century

The Ngoni incursions into the regions west and east of Lake Malawi are part of a broader historical phenomenon which is commonly known as *Mfecane*. It comprises a whole series of Bantu migrations, which proceeded northward from southern Africa as far as Lake Victoria. The Ngoni were a cattle-rearing Bantu people, ethnically and linguistically very closely related to the Swazi, Zulu, and Xhosa.

The reasons for the northbound migrations of the Ngoni from their original home in Natal have to do primarily with the long drought there at the end of the eighteenth century, which led to the decimation of cattle stocks and a famine that lasted several years.

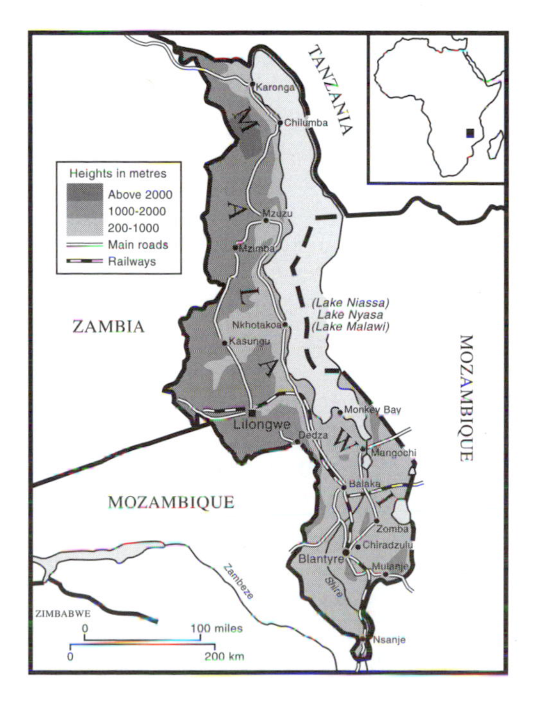

Malawi.

In consequence, different chiefdoms made war on each other over scarce water and forage resources. In the course of these conflicts, age-sets were transformed into military reserves. Not only could a standing army thereby be maintained, it was also possible to more easily integrate defeated peoples into such a military unit, because within such a transformed age-set a strong feeling of solidarity arose from the experience of common military service.

According to the dominant oral traditions, it was Chief (*Inkosi*) Zwide who initially emerged victorious in these campaigns, after taking captive his last opponent Dingiswayo in 1818, who died a few days later. Thereupon Shaka, one of Dingiswayo's client chiefs, took up the fight against Zwide, and already in 1818 (some sources say 1821 or 1822) defeated Zwide and killed him. Zwide's surviving followers fled northward, beginning the Ngoni migrations.

According to other sources, however, the migrations had been triggered earlier, in 1817, by Zwide's assault on Matiwane's Ngwane at Mzinyathi River, some time before the Zulu under Shaka became independent. Regardless of which of these scenarios is correct, the losers of the conflicts fled northward in three main groups. One settled in southern Mozambique, while the two other sections under Zwangendaba and Shongonane invaded the region of present-day Zimbabwe. In 1823 Zwangendaba subjugated the Tonga and incorporated them into his military units. He then continued on to the valley of the Limpopo River, where Shongonane refused him obedience. Zwangendaba crossed the Limpopo, further integrating defeated tribes into his military units. Some traditions report, however, that this policy of assimilating peaceful tribes, who had not undergone the intensive military training like the Ngoni, actually reduced the military effectiveness of Zwangendaba's troops.

In 1835 Zwangendaba crossed the Zambezi. However, his rearguard under Mputa Maseko, with the main body of the cattle, failed to make the crossing. Zwangendaba, for unclear reasons, did not wait for them. Without his cattle and his rearguard, Zwangendaba settled for five years among the Nsenga, many of whom were integrated into the Ngoni forces. The losses of livestock were balanced by Zwangendaba through the systematic confiscation of cattle owned by neighboring peoples. In 1840 or 1841 he invaded the Chewa dominion of Mzimba on the Lundazi River and settled among the Tumbuka and their Chewa masters.

While the Tumbuka were forced to work in the fields for their new Ngoni overlords, several Chewa chiefdoms were conquered and devastated, such as Chulu and Gebisa. Zwangendaba then marched through the region of Kasungu, migrated further northwards in 1842 and 1843, and settled among the Sukuma, east of the southern tip of Lake Tanganyika. He died in the village of Mapupu sometime between 1845 and 1848. Meanwhile Mputa Maseko's fraction of the Ngoni had settled in the Songea region, in the southeastern part of present-day Tanzania.

After Zwangendaba's death, violent disputes over the succession broke out, which had lasting and partially destructive effects on the areas concerned. Zwangendaba had designated his favorite son Mbelwa as his heir, but he had not yet reached puberty. Mbelwa's claim to the throne was soon challenged by two major factions. The first was led by Zwangendaba's brother Ntabeni Jele, who was striving for the throne on behalf of his oldest son Mtutu. The second faction, supported by most of the army, was commanded by Zwangendaba's cousin, Mgayi Jele. Ntabeni died shortly afterward, his armed forces retreating to the southwest in the face of the approaching Mgayi. Some of the fleeing units fell upon the Nyamwezi, who were settled on the southwestern side of Lake Tanganyika. Other Ngoni units fled to Lake Victoria, where Stanley heard in 1871 that they lived in permanent conflict with neighboring peoples. Mgayi died shortly after his campaign against Ntabeni and left no successor.

Several Ngoni groups invaded Ufipa; another group settled near Songea. This last branch under Zulu Jama, a royal adviser (*Induna*) acting in his own interest came to blows with Mputa Maseko, who was already settled there. Mputa was killed, and his successor Chikuse was forced to retreat southward with his people along their original northward route until they reached an area southwest of Lake Malawi, where they still live. Meanwhile Mtutu crossed the Luangwa to the east, avoiding armed Bemba units. Around 1865 he attacked the Chewa Chief Mbang'ombe, besieging him for years in his hill fortress until Mbang'ombe surrendered.

Mtutu then settled in the Nsenga country and adopted their language. In the meantime, Mtutu's brothers had reached Nkamanga in Malawi about 1855, where they installed Mbelwa as their chief.

The military power of the Ngoni in Malawi, already considerably eroded from decades of fighting and subsequent fragmentation, dwindled further with the installation of a British protectorate in Nyasaland in 1891.

The Ngoni incursions had, and continue to have, a lasting influence on the peoples involved. These campaigns claimed many lives in nearly all the regions surrounding Lake Malawi; along with this went the deliberate and systematic devastation of settlements and economic resources. Originally unwarlike peoples were integrated into the Ngoni military structures and, thus trained, attacked other ethnic groups. Even groups not integrated by the Ngoni, such as Bena, Hehe, or Sangu, adopted Ngoni military tactics. A partial collapse of the economic infrastructure occurred: crops rotted on the stalks, the fields could no longer be tilled, and local and regional trade experienced severe disruption. Victims of the Ngoni campaigns invited Europeans, notably missionaries, to come to Malawi (Nyasaland) as their protectors, with far-reaching consequences.

REINHARD KLEIN-ARENDT

See also: **Difaqane on the Highveld; Mfecane; Mozambique: Nguni Ngoni Incursions from the South; Tanganyika (Tanzania): Ngoni Incursion from the South; Zambia: Ngoni Incursion from the South; Zimbabwe: Incursions from the South, Ngoni and Ndebele.**

Further Reading

Barnes, J. A. *Politics in a Changing Society: A Political History of the Fort Jameson Ngoni.* Manchester, Eng.: Manchester University Press, 1967.

Cobbing, J. "The Mfecane as Alibi: Thoughts on Dithakong and Mbolompo." *Journal of African History.* 29 (1988): 487–519.

Eldredge, E. A. "Sources of Conflict in Southern Africa, c.1800–1830: The 'Mfecane' Reconsidered." *Journal of African History.* 33 (1992): 1–35.

Rangeley, W. H. J. "The Angoni." *The Society of Malawi Journal.* 19, no. 2 (1966): pp.62–86.

Read, M. *Children of Their Fathers: Growing up Among the Ngoni of Nyasaland.* London: Methuen, 1959.

Redmond, P. M. "Some Results on Military Contacts Between the Ngoni and Their Neighbours in 19th Century Southern East Africa." *Transafrican Journal of History.* 5, no. 1 (1976): 75–97.

Malawi: Long-Distance Trade, Nineteenth Century

The long-distance trade in both ivory and slaves in the region of present-day Malawi was frequently the business of the same political and ethnic groups as in precolonial times; indeed, the same trade routes were used.

Elephant hunting and the trade in ivory have always been a major concern of the local Yao and Makua peoples of Malawi and Mozambique. Trade relations between coastal settlements and Yao ivory traders probably began to develop in the sixteenth century, and by the end of the seventeenth century represented a well-organized system. Until the end of the eighteenth century, the ivory routes ran from the areas north and south of the Zambezi to the Portuguese-controlled Mozambique island, with the ivory probably following the routes of the older gold trade. At the beginning of the nineteenth century, however, the town of Kilwa became practically the sole export harbor for ivory because of the ruinous Portuguese taxation policy in Mozambique, which had made it prohibitively expensive to trade ivory there. Kilwa had extended its economic hinterland as far as Lake Malawi during the slave trade with the French possessions in the Indian Ocean in the second half of the eighteenth century.

The ivory was brought by Yao and Makua from the areas between the Zambezi and the northern tip of Lake Malawi to Kilwa or Mozambique island; from there the goods were shipped by Arabs, Swahili, or Indians to coastal settlements like Zanzibar and Mombasa, which maintained trading relations with customers in India, China, Europe, and North America. The ivory trade experienced a boom around the 1840s, when more and more vessels from the United States and Europe began anchoring at Zanzibar; the Industrial Revolution in the United States and Western Europe had brought about a fashion revolution, and an interest in luxury goods. Ivory was needed for products such as billiard balls and decorative carvings.

In the eighteenth century and at the beginning of the nineteenth century, the trade routes from Zambezia and Malawi to the coast came increasingly to be exploited for slave trading. Until 1820 the Arabs and Swahili at the coast had been content with their role of providing markets for slave caravans from the interior, which were largely organized by Makua, Yao, or Nyamwezi. But soon the demand for slaves grew precipitously, first through the expanding plantation economy on the French island possessions and Madagascar in the second half of the eighteenth century, then through the development of a plantation economy at Zanzibar and Pemba in the first half of the nineteenth century. Madagascar remained an important customer for slaves throughout the nineteenth century; from about 1860 on, however, the French increasingly covered their need for workers through the importation of cheap labor from India. The profit margin in the slave trade to Zanzibar and Madagascar, however, became so considerable that Arabs and Swahili started to explore the long-distance trade routes themselves.

In Malawi and neighboring territories, primarily Yao, Bisa, Ngindo, and Nsenga, fell victim to the slave trade, as prisoners of war or as repayment for debts; children were exchanged by their families for food during famines. Portuguese from Zambezia, as well as Arabs, Makua, and particularly Yao, were involved in slave raiding, acquisition and transport. The Yao, originally hunters themselves, could survive only by committing themselves to the hunting and selling of slaves. The Yao controlled the ivory and slave trade at the Shire and Zambezi Rivers until the late 1880s. They withstood threats by Bisa and Ngoni, not least because they had been supplied with firearms by the Portuguese and the Arabs. In the 1880s most of the Yao chiefs in Malawi were involved in slave hunting, particularly east of the M'lela River, in the territory of the Lomwe and later around Lake Malawi, mainly in Jumbe, Angoni, Magwangwara, Makanjile, and Mpenda.

Although the trading partners of the Yao were mostly Arabs and Swahili, the slave trade was financed initially by Europeans, subsequently by Arabian and Indian merchants at the coast. Relatively rarely, however, would Arabs or Indians enter the slave-hunting grounds themselves. Rather, they concentrated on a few trading posts, where their Yao, Makua, or Bemba representatives exchanged captured slaves for guns. The Arabs then brought the slaves to Lake Malawi, and across to Lindi, Kilwa, and Mikindani. A significant share of the slave trade can be ascribed to the Ngoni, who would sell prisoners of war when necessary.

During the 1880s the role of the British in these regions became increasingly pervasive. At Zanzibar the British antislavery campaigns produced considerable results, but in the south the more remote slaving routes through Malawi and Mozambique remained intact and supplied a whole chain of smaller slave-exporting harbors between Kilwa and Sofala. From there, the slaves were smuggled to more northern coastal trading centers. As late as 1875, some 2,000 to 4,000 slaves were presumably exported in this way. Pressure upon the slave hunters and traders grew through British trading companies and missionaries, who were settling in Malawi (Nyasaland) in increasing numbers; reservations for runaway slaves were set up in the course of the antislavery campaigns. Between 1887 and 1889 serious fighting erupted between agents of the British Line Company and Arab or Yao traders, which interrupted the slave trade. Threats by influential antislavery lobbyists in Britain to urge the annexation of the coastal hinterland of Mozambique persuaded the Portuguese authorities, starting in the middle of the 1880s, to take military action against the slave trade.

In 1892 the Portuguese opened Zambezia to international capital, which encouraged the penetration of the traditional slave-hunting grounds by Europeans. Concurrently the British were increasing their influence in Malawi, and the Germans pushed forward their frontiers in Tanganyika. Thus the slave trade was suppressed, although the resistance of Arab slave traders continued at least until 1899.

The slave raids resulted in a depopulation of the area west of Lake Malawi and in serious disturbances of economic activities like agriculture and trade. Reports of contemporary European eyewitnesses regarding the number of slaves involved were probably exaggerated and should be seen in the context of propaganda moves by missions and trading companies interested in an intensified European penetration of Malawi. For the years around 1850, for example, modern estimates reckon that about 10,000 to 12,000 slaves were exported annually from Kilwa.

REINHARD KLEIN-ARENDT

Further Reading

Alpers, E. A. *Ivory & Slaves in East Central Africa: Changing Patterns of International Trade to the Later Nineteenth Century.* London, Nairobi, Ibadan, and Lusaka: Heinemann, 1975.

Brown, B. "Muslim Influence on Trade and Politics in the Lake Tanganyika Region." *International Journal of African Historical Studies.* 4, no. 3 (1971): 617–629.

Hanna, A. J. *The Beginnings of Nyasaland and North-Eastern Rhodesia 1859–1895.* Oxford: Clarendon Press, 1969.

Sheriff, A. "Ivory and Economic Expansion in East Africa in the Nineteenth Century." In *Figuring African Trade,* edited by G. Liesegang, H. Pasch, and A. Jones. Berlin: Dietrich Reimer, 1986.

———. *Slaves, Spices & Ivory in Zanzibar: Integration of an East African Commercial Empire into the World Economy, 1770–1873.* Athens: Ohio University Press, 1987.

Malawi: Missionaries and Christianity, Nineteenth Century

Although Jesuit missionaries operated in the Zambesi valley in the seventeenth century, they do not appear to have gone up the Shire into Malawi. The first missionary to enter Malawi was David Livingstone when, in his capacity as leader of the government sponsored Zambesi Expedition, he entered southern Malawi in January 1859. In April 1861 the first formal missionary party arrived in the Shire Highlands. They were missionaries of the Universities Mission to Central Africa (UMCA), a mission created in response to Livingstone's famous appeal in his Cambridge lectures of 1857. Bishop C. F. Mackenzie was the leader of the expedition. Unfortunately the antislavery fervor of the mission led to conflict with local Yao chiefs involved in slave trading. After Mackenzie's death and that of other members of the mission from malaria, the new bishop, Tozer, withdrew the mission to Zanzibar in December 1863 despite bitter protests from Livingstone.

The return of Livingstone's body to Britain in 1874 and his funeral in Westminster Abbey triggered new interest in Malawi, particularly in Scotland. The Free Church of Scotland as well as the Church of Scotland decided to send missions to Malawi in honor of Livingstone. The Free Church Mission, which arrived in 1875, was called the Livingstonia Mission, the Church of Scotland Mission, which arrived in 1876, called its first station Blantyre, round which the modern city of Blantyre later grew up. The Livingstonia party soon to be headed by Robert Laws, who held the post until 1927, included four Xhosa missionaries from Lovedale in the Cape, among whom the longest serving was William Koyi.

The Livingstonia Mission was established first at Cape Maclear at the south end of Lake Malawi, but in 1880 they moved to Bandawe in what is now the Northern Province and began their long association with the north where Robert Laws built in the 1890s at Khondowe mountain, a medical, educational, and evangelistic institution similar to Lovedale in South Africa. This rapidly became the center of a network of schools across the province and what is now northeastern Zambia, where David Kaunda (the father of President Kenneth Kaunda) was one of the pioneer Livingstonia missionaries. The institution trained Africans in the skills required for the modern economy reserved in Rhodesia and South Africa for whites as well as teachers and ministers.

The initial party of missionaries at Blantyre made a disastrous beginning and a number of them were dismissed, leaving David Clement Scott, who arrived in 1880, to rebuild relations with the local chiefs. This he did very effectively aided by a number of African colleagues, notably Joseph Bismarck. He also rapidly built up a cadre of young African leaders for the church; among the most notable were Harry Kwambili Matecheta, Mungo Chisuse, Thomas Mpeni, and John Gray Kufa, who was hanged by the British in 1915 for his support of John Chilembwe.

Scott was so effective in his attempts to enter into African culture that he produced in 1890 his *Cyclopaedic Dictionary of the Chimang'anja Language*, a volume that still lies behind all subsequent attempts to produce a dictionary of the language variously called Nyanja or Chewa. His radically pro-African stance, for example he wrote articles criticizing Rhodes and the British South Africa Company's conquest of Zimbabwe, led to his being forced to retire from Malawi in 1898.

It was the lobbying of the British government by the Scottish missions and their supporters that led to British intervention in the area. The Scots' campaign started in 1889 when they feared that Malawi would soon be divided between the Portuguese and the Swahili traders from Zanzibar. However, when British support appeared as if it would take the form of rule by Rhodes's British South Africa Company the Scottish missions campaigned against this successfully and again in 1893 when it appeared that Rhodes might still get control of Malawi.

In 1901 the Livingstonia Mission became a mission of the United Free Church of Scotland but more significantly African church leaders from Blantyre and Livingstonia met and sought with missionary support the creation of one Presbyterian Church in Malawi. At another conference in 1904 this was agreed though complicated negotiations in Malawi and Scotland and problems of geographical distance delayed the formal legal institution of the autonomous Church of Central Africa Presbyterian (CCAP) until 1914.

Meanwhile, in 1886 the UMCA returned to the area establishing its headquarters on Likoma island. Then in 1888 the Cape Synod of the Dutch Reformed Church (DRC) began work in the area between the Blantyre and Livingstonia areas. Despite very different attitudes to education from the Scottish missions, the church produced by this mission did join the CCAP in 1924.

A quite different group of missions entered Malawi after it became a British Protectorate in 1891. The first was Joseph Booth's Zambesi Industrial Mission founded close to Blantyre in 1892 soon to be followed by the Nyasa Industrial Mission. These and several other missions that sought to support themselves by commercial agriculture tended to settle in the Shire Highland where there was some commercial development and the beginnings of international trade. It is important to notice that the DRC, the UMCA, and these new missions all shared a very limited vision of the education appropriate to Africans in contrast with Blantyre and Livingstonia. Their attitude was that the creation of literacy in the vernacular was all that was necessary; in contrast the Scots placed great emphasis on advancing education in English to as high a level as they could afford to organize.

Sometime in 1900, the Reverend John Chilembwe, a Malawian converted under the influence of Joseph Booth and trained in the United States, began the Providence Industrial Mission in Chiradzulu. In 1901 his mission was reinforced by two African-American missionaries, the Reverend N. L. Cheek and Miss Emma Delaney. The American missionaries left in 1906 leaving Chilembwe alone.

Also in 1901 an African American missionary, Thomas Branch, and his family founded the Seventh Day Adventist Mission, though afterward the expatriate staff of this church were predominantly white. There were also a number of small but lively Christian independent churches begun in Malawi, notably by Elliot Kamwana, Charles Chinula, and Charles Domingo.

Roman Catholic missions entered Malawi only in 1901. The White Fathers had been in the Mangoche district briefly in 1890–1891 but only in 1901 did they begin effective work in what is now the central and northern Provinces. The southern province was assigned to the Montfort Marist Fathers and the sisters of the Society of the Daughters of Wisdom. By the late twentieth century, approximately half of the population of Malawi belonged to either the Roman Catholic Church or the CCAP.

One notable feature of Malawian Christianity was that, before 1914, it had produced an indigenous Malawi hymnody. These hymns, set to traditional tunes, were created by a number of independent pastors and Livingstonia CCAP church leaders, principally Charles Chinula, Mawelero Tembo, Jonathan Chirwa, and Peter Thole (known as "the sweet singer of the Ngoni"). This is in stark contrast to mission Christianity elsewhere in Africa at that time, in which translations of European hymns set to European tunes were the rule.

ANDREW C. ROSS

See also: **Livingstone, David; Religion, Colonial Africa: Conversion to World Religions; Religion, Colonial Africa: Missionaries.**

Further Reading

Langworthy, H. *"Africa for the Africans": The Life of Joseph Booth.* Blantyre: CLAIM, 1996.

Linden, I. *Catholics, Peasants, and Chewa Resistance*. London: Heinemann, 1974.

Reijnaerts, H., A. Nielsen, and M. Schoffeleers. *Montfortians in Malawi: Their Spirituality and Pastoral Approach.* Blantyre: CLAIM, 1997.

Ross, A. C. *Blantyre Mission and the Making of Modern Malawi.* Blantyre: CLAIM, 1996.

Ross, K. R., ed. *Christianity in Malawi: A Source Book.* Gweru: Mambo Press, 1996.

Shepperson, G., and T. Price. *Independent African: John Chilembwe and the Origins, Setting and Significance of Nyasaland Native Rising of 1915.* Edinburgh: EUP, 1958.

Malawi: Colonization and Wars of Resistance, 1889–1904

The hasty decision by Britain in 1889 to declare a British protectorate in Malawi was precipitated in a large part by a Portuguese expedition led by Lieutenant António Maria Cardoso to the area of Lake Malawi in 1888. The expedition sought to establish a mission and expand Portuguese influence in the area of central Africa claimed by Portugal between Angola and Mozambique. Cardoso's expedition posed a direct threat to the interests of the chain of Scottish missions in the region and to British hopes of securing a land corridor between its colonies in eastern and southern Africa. In 1889 Britain therefore appointed Harry Hamilton Johnston as the new British consul to Mozambique and the interior.

Johnston's first task was to negotiate a treaty with the Portuguese. It was proposed that the Portuguese should extend their territories into Malawi as far as the Bua River, in return for a strip of land west of the Luangwa River that would link British interests in southern and eastern Africa. In essence, the offer was to swap southern and central Malawi for southern, central, and northern Zambia. While these terms satisfied the wishes of the British government, they offered the Portuguese large tracts of land formerly under the control of Scottish missionaries. The church was furious, and more than 11,000 Scottish church ministers and elders signed a memorandum protesting against the draft agreement. The British government was persuaded to reject the deal.

In May 1889 Johnston departed from London with two thousand pounds that Cecil John Rhodes had given him to pay for new treaties with the rulers of Malawi. Using a British gunboat, he forced his way through the Chinde entrance of the Zambezi to the Shire River. This was a direct challenge to the Portuguese and an assertion of British rights to free navigation along the Zambezi. At same time a second Portuguese expedition, led by Serpa Pinto, was marching up the Shire River signing treaties with chiefs. From the boat, Johnston authorized John Buchanan, a missionary coffee farmer and acting consul, to write to Pinto stating that the Kololo country and the Shire Highlands north of the Ruo River had been placed under British protection. The Kololo enjoyed special status, as they had been brought to the area some decades before by David Livingstone. South of Chiromo, Johnston met with Pinto and told him that proceeding north could result in war with Britain. Pinto returned to the coast to consult with his superiors. He left Lieutenant Coutinho in charge of the force. Coutinho defied Johnston and, continuing north, attacked a stockaded Kololo village.

A war of words erupted between the British and Portuguese governments. On September 21, 1889, Buchanan raised the British flag in front of his Zomba residence and wrote to Coutinho informing him that the British had declared a protectorate over the "Makololo, Yao, and Machinga Countries." The protectorate was known as the Nyasaland Districts. From September to December 1889 Johnston traveled widely and concluded treaties with rulers on the lower Shire, the Shire Highlands, the western shores of Lake Malawi, and southern Tanzania before returning to London. On January 10, 1890, the British minister in Lisbon presented an ultimatum to Portuguese, demanding that the governor of Mozambique withdraw all Portuguese troops on the Shire, in Kololo country, or in Mashonaland. The Portuguese acquiesced, and all troops were moved south of the Ruo.

The years 1890 and 1891 saw a series of agreements that laid out the boundaries of present day Malawi. In July 1890 an Anglo-German convention defined the northern border of the Protectorate at the Songwe River and the northern lakeshore. The Germans ceded a large area in Malawi that they had previously claimed in return for Heligoland in the North Sea. In August it was agreed with the Portuguese that the eastern border of the protectorate would be as it is today. The southern border was defined as a line from Chiromo to a point on the Zambezi midway between Tete and

Kebrassa. This was adjusted in a final Anglo-Portuguese Convention on June 11, 1891. In this agreement the Portuguese ceded land south of the Zambezi in return for some areas north of the Zambezi that had previously part of the protectorate. The confluence of the Ruo and Shire Rivers was the new and final dividing line. The western border of the protectorate was fixed in the same month by an agreement between the Foreign Office, the British South Africa Company, and the African Lakes Company.

Johnston returned to Malawi in July 1891 to take up his new appointment as commissioner for the Nyasaland Districts and consul general to those territories under British influence north of the Zambezi. Alfred Sharpe was appointed vice consul and Captain Cecil Maguire was put in charge the Nyasaland armed forces. Maguire came from the Indian army and brought with him forty Sikh infantry and thirty Muslim cavalrymen. This force was increased by a further two hundred Indian recruits in 1893. The British Treasury paid the salaries of the British officials. The rest of the funds needed had to be raised, the bulk coming from Cecil Rhodes.

A priority of Johnston's administration was the eradication of the slave trade. This led to military conflict with the Yao. Two days after arriving in Malawi, Johnston sent a force of Sikhs against the slave-trading chief Chikumbu, who had attacked a mission and some coffee planters at Mulanje. Other similar strikes upon the Yao followed. Of particular strategic importance was an attack on Mponda of the Machinga Yao in October 1891. Mponda's village was at a strategic crossing point on the Shire River just south of the lake. This location had allowed his father to control the ivory and slave trade in the region and so gain great prominence and wealth. Although Mponda's position was somewhat unstable because of an armed struggle against his brother, Chingarungwaru, he was a key figure in the slave trade network of the southern lake region. On October 19, the British shelled Mponda's village and eight days later Mponda signed a treaty. Fort Johnston was built across the river from Mponda to maintain the peace.

Not all of the early attacks on the Yao were this successful. In 1891 a British assault on Zarafi was repulsed and an attack on Kawinga failed to dislodge him from his stronghold on Chikala Mountain near Zomba. Two campaigns were also waged against Makanjira during 1891 in an attempt to end slave trading on the eastern lake shore. In the second one Maguire was killed. It was not until a third campaign in 1893 that Makanjira was defeated and forced into Portuguese territory. Fort Maguire was established to watch over the site of Makanjira's old headquarters.

On February 22, 1893, the Nyasaland Districts were given the new title of "British Central Africa." By this time, roughly one-fifth of the land belonged to planters, traders, and missionaries, one-fifth to Rhodes' British South Africa Company, one-fifth to the British Crown, and two-fifths to Africans. Johnston was concerned that some of non-African owned land had not been justly and honestly acquired from African rulers. He spent two years reviewing all claims, and reduced some in size and rejected others. All those accepted gained title deeds in which it was stated that existing villages and field could not be disturbed or removed without government permission. All existing villagers could live on their land freely without paying rent, but new villages could only be established if the landowner approved and tenants of them had to pay rent. This led to the hated and abused *Thangata* system, whereby people were forced to work on plantations for no pay in lieu of rent.

Johnston focused his attentions in 1894 on the Ngoni. In central Malawi two brothers of the Maseko Ngoni, Gomani and Kachindamoto, had been fighting for paramountcy since 1891. Two wars are remembered: the Mwala wa Nkhondo and the Mlomo wa Nkuku. These wars were ended in November 1894 when a force under Captain Edwards intervened and made the two chiefs declare peace. With the south and center pacified, Johnston turned his attention to northern Malawi. The areas around Nkhotakota had been one of the major African slave trading stations since the 1840s ruled by a series of Arab traders called Jumbe. After the signing of a treaty, relations between Jumbe III and Johnston had been amicable. But, when Jumbe IV was charged, and convicted of murder in December of 1894, the Jumbe's were banished to Zanzibar and Nkhotakota fell under direct British rule. With the Jumbe's gone the last slaving stronghold was that of an Arab trader named Mlozi who lived in the far north at Karonga. But, in February 1895, before an attack could be organized, the Yao chiefs Makanjira, Zarafi, Kawinga, and Matapwiri launched a four pronged attach to oust the British from the Shire Highlands. The attack lacked co-ordination and was repulsed. In September Johnston launched a massive counterattack in which Zarafi was ejected from his stronghold, Matapwiri was forced to surrender and Makanjira was forced permanently across the border. The Yao lands were finally cleared of both slave traders and guns.

The assault against Mlozi, and his allies Msalemu and Kopa Kopa, came in December 1895. Mlozi was captured by a Tonga soldier, Sergeant Major Bandawe, tried by Ngonde chiefs and hanged. His death marked the end the slave trade in Malawi. Soon after this attack Johnston was crippled by illness and was forced to leave Africa. He handed over power to Sharpe who concluded BCA military operations within six months of taking office. The final campaigns were launched against the Yao chiefs Tambala and Mpemba as well as the Chewa chief Mwase Kasungu. The Ngoni chief Gomani was also arrested after harassing the mission at Dombole and was executed for "seditious behaviour." By 1897 the only significant region not under direct colonial rule was northern Ngoniland. The rest of the country had been divided into twelve districts, each with a collector who collected customs duties and hut taxes and acted as a policeman and magistrate. Northern Ngoniland, the area between the South Rukuru River and Hora mountain, remained autonomous and paid no taxes until a serious outbreak of rinderpest disease in 1903. This killed the large herds of Ngoni cattle and ended the Ngoni ability to retain independence. On September 2, 1904, the northern Ngoni signed an agreement with the British and when, a month later, the British flag was hoisted over Hora Mountain by Hector MacDonald, the last section of Malawi submitted to colonial rule.

BENJAMIN SMITH

See also: **Johnston, Harry H.; Livingstone, David; Rhodes, Cecil J.**

Further Reading

Baker, C. A. *Johnston's Administration: A History of the British Central Africa Administration 1891–1897.* Zomba: Government Press, 1970.

Boeder, R. B. *Alfred Sharpe of Nyasaland: Builder of Empire.* Blantyre: Montford Press, 1981.

Pachai, B., (ed.) *The Early History of Malawi.* London: Longman, 1972.

———. *Malawi: The History of the Nation.* London: Longman, 1973.

Pike, J. G. *Malawi: A Political and Economic History.* London: Pall Mall Press, 1968.

Malawi (Nyasaland): Colonial Period: Land, Labor, and Taxation

As was the case in most British colonies, the shapers of colonial land, labor, and taxation policies in the Nyasaland Protectorate (modern Malawi) faced the difficult task of balancing their obligation to African welfare with the necessity of developing the protectorate along capitalist lines. In the 1890s the British government allowed private companies and individuals to acquire vast tracts of land in the territory as a low-cost way to establish their claim to central Africa. Since Nyasaland lacked exploitable mineral reserves, these concerns relied on low cost African labor to produce cash crops for export. Although the Nyasaland government often doubted the wisdom of supporting the European planters, it believed commercial agriculture had to be the basis of the protectorate's economy and therefore sought ways to encourage Africans to produce crops for the world market. Conversely, British missionaries, who had lobbied for the annexation of Nyasaland to put an end to slave trading, were committed to preserving the humanitarian ideals that provided the moral justification for British rule. While they believed in the "civilizing" power of work, they were not willing to tolerate exploitation of the African work force. Colonial authorities in Nyasaland therefore faced the difficult task of transforming local patterns of subsistence and generating labor for European estates without provoking humanitarian criticism or African unrest.

The Nyasaland government sought to accomplish these goals through taxation and land alienation. In the last decades of the nineteenth century, foreign economic concerns acquired title to roughly 15 per cent of the arable land in Nyasaland. In return for calico, copper wire, and other trinkets they pressured African rulers into signing away their people's claims to enormous tracts of land. John Buchanon, a former member of the Church of Scotland Mission, acquired one million acres in the southern half of the protectorate, while Cecil Rhodes's British South Africa Company claimed almost three million acres in the north. Sir Harry Johnston blocked further land alienation when the territory became a protectorate in 1891 but left most of the remaining estates intact. In the first decades of the colonial era, territory in Nyasaland was divided into three main categories: land held by European planters, land leased from the Crown, and Crown land. Technically, all African land fell into the last category until 1936, when the government reserved all unsold land exclusively for African use as Native Trust land. This land included the holdings of the British South Africa Company, which surrendered its claims in the north in exchange for exclusive mineral rights to the region.

The main European agricultural estates were concentrated in the Shire Highlands of Nyasaland's southern province. The planters hoped that the cool climate of the highlands would be ideal for producing coffee, cotton, and tobacco for export, but they had difficulty turning a profit due to poor weather, fluctuating prices on the world market, high transportation costs and, most importantly, difficulties in attracting and retaining African labor. The estate owners therefore used their political influence to lobby the government to stimulate the flow of wage labor through taxation. Faced with a hut tax ranging from three to six shillings, Africans had to either grow cash crops or work for the planters to earn the money to pay their taxes. The government forced defaulters to spend a month working for private employers and granted tax rebates to Africans who worked voluntarily for Europeans. Yet these measures failed to solve the labor shortage in the southern province because most local Africans worked just long enough to pay their taxes.

As a result, the planters turned to immigrants from Mozambique, known as the Lomwe, to supply the bulk of their labor needs. As immigrants, the Lomwe earned the right to settle on the estates in return for supplying the planters with labor. This arrangement became codified under an existing system of labor obligations known as *thangata*, under which Africans had provided tributary labor to their rulers in precolonial times. As the primary landholders in colonial Nyasaland, the planters turned this obligation into a form of rent, and required their tenants to work for up to six months per year in return for access to land. The original inhabitants of the estates were technically excused from *thangata*, but the distinction between native and immigrant gradually blurred as Lomwe immigration increased. Estate owners often extracted extra labor from their tenants through intentionally poor record keeping and abusive African overseers, and in 1915 John Chilembwe led a violent uprising against the system that forced the government to pay more attention to conditions on the estates. After World War I, African tenants received the right to pay their rent in currency, cash crops, or labor but still faced eviction if they left the estates to look for work.

Yet even *thangata* could not make the estates sufficiently profitable enough to be the sole basis of Nyasaland's economy. Although colonial officials had initially hoped the planters would become the economic backbone of the protectorate, they eventually realized that individual African growers could produce cash crops like cotton and tobacco more efficiently and profitably than the planters. To encourage African production, the British Cotton Growing Association established ginning factories and buying centers in the Shire valley in 1910. The protectorate tapped this production by stationing collectors at the markets to ensure the farmers paid their taxes. In 1923 the association acquired the sole right to purchase cotton from African growers by promising the colonial government half its profits. Many African farmers became quite prosperous and successfully outbid the planters for the available supplies of African labor. Moreover, the creation of sufficiently lucrative markets for tobacco and cotton allowed Africans to pay their taxes and escape the pressures that drove poorer workers to the European estates.

Commercial agriculture never took hold in Nyasaland's northern province during the colonial era. The necessity of using steamers on Lake Malawi to transport produce to the southern railhead made it too expensive to export the north's agricultural commodities for the world market. Although the region was blessed with a favorable climate and fertile soil, most African farmers in the province grew food for local consumption. Moreover, the British South Africa Company, the main landowner in the region until 1936, worried that developing the north's agricultural capacity would reduce the number of Africans who worked in the Rhodesias as migrant laborers. While taxation in the south created inexpensive wage labor for the estates, northerners left for better paying jobs on farms and mines in South Africa and northern and southern Rhodesia. Nyasaland's numerous mission schools produced a large, well-educated class of Africans who worked as clerks and artisans in the south, and the northern province's Livingstonia Mission was the primary supplier of educated labor migrants. By 1937 the government estimated that 90,087 Nyasalanders were working abroad, which amounted to approximately 18 per cent of all able-bodied males in the protectorate.

The Nyasaland government originally tried to restrict this flow of African labor because the journey south was often dangerous and employers in Rhodesia and South Africa had a reputation for exploiting African migrants. Labor migration also reduced agricultural production, increased divorce rates, and contributed to the spread of venereal disease when the young men returned home. Yet during the depression the colonial government had no choice but to encourage labor migration to raise revenue and decrease unemployment. The money that migrants sent home to their families became an important source of revenue for the protectorate, and by the early 1950s Nyasaland's remittances from abroad totaled almost £700,000 ($1,099,400).

Faced with these pressures, colonial officials allowed South Africa's Witwatersrand Native Labour Association and southern Rhodesian farmers to hire laborers directly in the north, but in the southern province the planters used their political influence to ban all foreign labor recruiters.

These patterns of southern agricultural production and northern labor migration held throughout most of the colonial era, but by the end of World War II the inequities of the colonial economy began to generate significant African opposition. In the south the estates became increasingly overcrowded, with population densities approaching four hundred people per square mile. The planters still resisted successfully government attempts to regulate relations with their tenants and the *thangata* system continued to generate considerable discontent. A widespread and dangerous famine in 1949 brought on by drought and the shift from food to cash crop production further increased tensions. The Nyasaland African Congress spoke for most farmers when it called for the redistribution of land. Its pressure for tenant rights, coupled with anger over Nyasaland's incorporation into the Central African Federation, led to a rural uprising in 1953 that forced the protectorate government to call out the army.

Colonial officials tried to address these grievances through an ambitious program of labor reforms, resettlement, and soil reconditioning. To reduce tensions over the *thangata*, they allowed tenants to pay their rent in cash if they chose to leave the estates to work. They sought to address growing African land hunger through ambitious hydrological projects intended to reclaim flood land and purchased failing estates from struggling planters. The most ambitious of these development schemes was the £8 million Shire Valley Project that was intended to relieve pressure on the most overcrowded southern districts. Yet many African farmers rejected the project because the protectorate government tried to enforce unpopular agricultural policies including a ban on planting on hillsides and riverbanks, replacing small-mound planting with contour ridging, and adherence to a mandatory planting schedule. Moreover, much of the new land was poorly watered and infested with dangerous wild animals. Faced with mounting African opposition and an inability to raise enough money to fund even a fraction of the projects, the Nyasaland government abandoned its most invasive and unpopular agricultural policies to avoid provoking political unrest in the years leading up to independence. Its attempts to balance the humanitarian responsibilities of colonial rule with the economic necessities of making the protectorate pay had proved impossible.

TIMOTHY PARSONS

See also: **Colonial Federations: British Central Africa.**

Further Reading

Baker, C. *Seeds of Trouble: Government Policy and Land Rights in Nyasaland, 1946–1964.* London: British Academic Press, 1993.

Mandala, E. *Work and Control in a Peasant Economy: A History of the Lower Tchiri Valley in Malawi, 1859–1960.* Madison: University of Wisconsin Press, 1990.

Vaughan, M. *The Story of an African Famine: Gender and Famine in Twentieth-Century Malawi.* Cambridge: Cambridge University Press, 1987.

Malawi (Nyasaland): Colonial Period: Chilembwe Rising, 1915

The Chilembwe Rising of 1915 was a relatively small-scale outbreak, involving not more than 900 people, who were mostly immigrants from Portuguese territory, with a leadership of "Westernized" Malawians headed by the Yao preacher John Chilembwe (*c.*1871–1915). Their first target was the Bruce Estates at Magomero, notorious for its brutal and exploitative labor conditions, where three white supervisors were killed on the evening of January 23, 1915. Early the next morning, another party failed to obtain more than a handful of weapons in a bungled raid on a Blantyre store. Thereafter, the rising quickly lost its focus. Prior to an imminent attack by government troops, Chilembwe's forces evacuated their stronghold at the preacher's village, Mbombwe (near Chiradzulu), and their leader was killed a few days later near the Portuguese border.

Although the rising was, in military terms, little more than a series of skirmishes, it has become a landmark event in the history of Malawian, and indeed, African nationalism, as evidenced in the issue of stamps commemorating the fiftieth anniversary of the rising, and the appearance of Chilembwe on the current K200 Malawi banknote. Also, it has become the subject of an intense historical debate, involving consideration of factors such as Chilembwe's personality and apparent quest for martyrdom, the impact of the prewar colonial system (labor, taxation, race discrimination) on Chilembwe and his followers, the relative influence of the radical missionary Joseph Booth, and African American political thought (Chilembwe studied in the United States at the end of the 1890s), the millennial teachings of Watch Tower and other chiliastic groups, and the involvement of Malawians in white men's wars, including World War I. There is the further complication (noted in Shepperson and Price's classic account, 1987) that much of the direct evidence has disappeared: documents seized from the "rebels" in January 1915 were destroyed in the conflict at the central secretariat in February 1919.

The depiction of Chilembwe as political martyr, who died for his oppressed people, is based on George Simeon Mwase's account of the rising (*c.*1931–1932), which draws on the reminiscences of some of its survivors, and points to a parallel with John Brown's antislavery stand at Harper's Ferry, prior to the American Civil War, and familiar to the preacher from his time in the American South. Mwase's editor, R. I. Rotberg, subsequently made a psychiatric study, focusing on Chilembwe's asthma, failing eyesight, and indebtedness as sources of unbearable strain, turning the hitherto "model" Westernized African into an advocate of anticolonial violence. The failure of the rebels to capitalize on their "gesture" at the Bruce Estates is adduced as evidence that Chilembwe never expected victory; his aim was simply to expose the failure of the government to "help the underdog," as he put it in his (unpublished) letter to the *Nyasaland Times* of November 26, 1914.

However, the martyr thesis has received some justified criticism. Why did Chilembwe wait until nearly the end of January to launch his revolt, some time after his letter was dispatched, and even longer after the Battle of Karonga (September 1914), referred to in his letter, in which black Malawians had sustained casualties?

Pachai has credibly suggested that Chilembwe's decision was actually taken at the last moment, following a tip-off that the authorities were going to arrest him for sedition. The nature of such a last-minute, preemptive action, would certainly account for what appears to have been a general lack of preparation, and also explain his hesitation after the failure of the Blantyre arms raid, which could have been founded on a feeling of uncertainty about what to do next.

Enquiries into the ideological character of the rising raise further material issues. Shepperson and Price have emphasized the Baptist, and generally nonmillennial, genesis and development of Chilembwe's Providence Industrial Mission, quite distinct from Elliott Kamwana's Watchtower (Kitawala) movement that flourished further north. However, Jane and Ian Linden have noted the strong millennial currents flowing through the various churches in the territory as a whole before 1914, the product of the social malaise affecting African society generally during the early colonial period, but given a focus by Watchtower's prediction of a "Second Coming" in October 1914. Against this background of fear and uncertainty, Chilembwe and his followers apparently saw the outbreak of hostilities in August 1914 as the fulfillment of the grim predictions of war made in the Old Testament Book of Daniel. While there is scant direct evidence about Chilembwe's thoughts in his final days, this explanation may go some way toward explaining his apparently desperate behavior in January 1915.

Similar debate has occurred about the "nationalist" character of the rising. Noting that the *Nyasaland Times* letter was written "in [sic] behalf of his countrymen," Mwase (and Rotberg) see it as nationalist. At the other extreme, Leroy Vail regards it merely as a local revolt of exploited immigrants from Portuguese East Africa, coordinated by a handful of "educated" men like Chilembwe. Pachai terms it a half-way stage in the development of modern nationalism, while in a detailed analysis of its composition, Shepperson and Price point out that it failed to win wider support as the majority of Malawians were still "tribesmen," oriented toward their traditional political and social structures, and thus unresponsive to "marginal men" like Chilembwe who had tried, with little success, to be truly accepted in the white man's world. While noting his importance as a symbol and inspiration for later Malawian nationalists, this interpretation seems the most credible of those currently on offer.

MURRAY STEELE

Further Reading

Linden, J., and I. Linden. "John Chilembwe and the New Jerusalem." *Journal of African History.* 12, no. 4 (1971): 629–651.

Pachai, B. "An Assessment of the Events Leading up to the Nyasaland Rising of 1915." In *Malawi: Past and Present*, edited by B. Pachai, G. Smith, and R. Tangri, Blantyre [Malawi]: CLAIM, 1971.

Rotberg, R. "Psychological Stress and the Question of Identity: Chilembwe's Revolt Reconsidered." In *Rebellion in Black Africa*, edited by R. Rotberg. London and New York: Oxford University Press, 1971.

Rotberg, R. (ed.) *Strike a Blow and Die: A Narrative of Race Relations in Colonial Africa by George Simeon Mwase*. 2nd ed. London: Heinemann, 1975.

Shepperson, G., and T. Price. *Independent African: John Chilembwe and the Origins, Setting and Significance of the Nyasaland Native Rising of 1915.* 2nd ed. Edinburgh: Edinburgh University Press, 1987.

Malawi (Nyasaland): Colonial Period: Federation

After World War I the administration of the Nyasaland Protectorate moved toward a policy of "indirect rule" somewhat modified because of the small but influential settler community. The traditional chiefs and headmen were given increasingly important roles and they responded by becoming the government's loyal servants. The only critical response from Africans to the administration came from a movement that was developed primarily by those men (in this period it was only men) educated before the war by the Livingstonia and Blantyre missions. The movement began when, in 1912, the North Nyasa Native Association and the West Nyasa Native Association were formed with the encouragement of Dr. Robert Laws.

After the war other associations were formed in the northern and southern provinces but none in the entral province where, except in Ntcheu District, neither the Blantyre nor Livingstonia Missions had any influence. In the 1930s Lilongwe produced a Native Association but it was founded by Blantyre and Livingstonia alumni who were resident there. (This lacuna has significance for the subsequent history of Malawi.) These groups were explicitly antitribal, they kept in touch with each other, and their closeness is seen in the way that they each adopted what were in effect the same set of rules. The movement, loosely organized though it was, became by the 1930s a national pressure group whose leaders had each received the informal but effective forms of post primary education that both Scottish missions had developed before the war. However, it should be noted that Livingstonia and Blantyre both began to change in the 1920s. They came into line with the other missions and the wishes of the government and settlers and concentrated on primary education.

Beginning in 1930, members of the administration tried to prevent the associations having direct access to the governor. The officials insisted that Native Association minutes, letters, and petitions should only reach the secretariat if approved by the district councils dominated by chiefs and headmen. However, this move eventually failed, as it was decided that the communications of the associations could be sent directly to the secretariat.

The administration faced a number of massive problems between the wars for which it produced no solutions: First, there was the encouragement of cash crop production by African farmers versus the demands of the planters. Another problem was the attraction of high wages in South Africa and Rhodesia that was making the protectorate a labor reserve for the south, versus the planters' veto on any increase in local wages in the public or private sectors. Finally, the serious pressure on land in the southern province due to significant immigration from Mozambique was a concern.

The Native Associations pressed for higher wages in the protectorate, a more just tax collecting system, and the development of secondary and higher education. Twice their activities produced very hostile reactions from the settlers and the administration. The first instance was when, in 1930, they opposed the legislation that made it a criminal act for an African man to have sexual relations with a European woman. They attacked the measure specifically as discriminatory because it did nothing to protect African women. The second was in 1937 when they pressed for African membership of the Legislative Council with educated Africans electing half the council's membership.

However the greatest threat to the welfare of the people was the continuance of the pressure from the south for the absorption of Nyasaland into a settler-ruled Greater Rhodesia. This was a continuation of Rhodes's attempt to takeover Nyasaland frustrated by Scottish pressure groups that gained the ear of Lord Salisbury in 1892–1893.

In 1927 the Hilton Young Commission was set up by the British government to investigate the question of the closer union of the British East and central African possessions. Hilton Young himself recommended a form of amalgamation of the central African territories but the other members opposed him. They confessed to have been influenced by the evidence of the Native Associations representative Levi Mumba and of the missionaries of the Livingstonia and Blantyre Missions about the unanimity of African opposition to closer contacts with the south. The settlers in all three territories did not give up. The British government set up in 1938 a royal commission under Lord Bledisloe in response to their pressure. It reported in 1939 and all members were agreed on the intensity of African opposition to amalgamation in Nyasaland that had been expressed by the chiefs as well as by the associations and the missions. Indeed, at the request of Nyasa Christians the General Assembly of the Church of Scotland formally petitioned the government opposing amalgamation in May 1939.

The outbreak of World War II did not distract the politicians of southern Rhodesia from continuing to press their case. Meanwhile in Nyasaland the associations had come together in 1944 under the leadership of Levi Mumba and James D. Sangala to create the Nyasaland African Congress (NAC). The new movement continued the old policy of seeking more power for Africans within the British colonial system that they saw as tolerable and markedly different from what went on south of the Zambesi.

All was to change after the end of the war, in which thousands of Malawi soldiers served with distinction. First, the Labour government and then, in 1951, the new Tory leadership in Britain listened to the Rhodesian case and deliberately discounted the warnings of the same groups that had opposed amalgamation in 1939. The only concession to the opposition, which was particularly strong in Scotland, was for the government to stop short of amalgamation and set up a federation of the three territories, with the local administration of the northern territories remaining under the Colonial Service. This was an arrangement that pleased no one and which had massive inbuilt administrative problems.

The NAC mounted a massive campaign of civil disorder that was put down quickly and firmly and the federation came into being in September 1953. This marked a massive change in Malawi history for the people's trust in Britain was decisively damaged by what they saw as betrayal.

Some African leaders and white liberals like Andrew Doig felt they should try to make the best of a bad situation and help make the federation work as a genuine experiment in multiracialism. By 1957 they were convinced this was impossible and resigned their positions. Moreover they feared that the federal government was about to get the Dominion status it sought in order to entrench white supremacy. In this crisis a new group of very young leaders, most of them graduates, came to the fore in the congress. They sought withdrawal from the federation and also, as soon as possible, independence from Britain whose good intentions could no longer be trusted. H. M. Chipembere, M. W. K. Chiume, Orton Chirwa, the Chisiza brothers, and others gave the congress a new dynamism and growing popular support. They were aware of the uneasiness of traditional village people about their youth, and to meet this problem they made the fateful decision to invite back to Malawi the respected senior, almost legendary figure of H. Kamuzu Banda.

Andrew C. Ross

See also: **Banda, Dr. Hastings Kamuzu; Zambia (Northern Rhodesia): Federation, 1953–1963; Zimbabwe (Southern Rhodesia): Federation.**

Further Reading

Chanock, M. L. "Ambiguities in the Malawian Political Tradition." *African Affairs*. 74 (1975): 326–346.

Gray, R. *The Two Nations*. Oxford: Oxford University Press, 1960.

Jones, G. *Britain and Nyasaland*. London: George Allen and Unwin, 1964.

McCracken, J. *Politics and Christianity in Malawi, 1875–1940*. Cambridge: Cambridge University Press, 1977.

Macdonald, R. J., ed. *From Nyasaland to Malawi: Studies in Colonial History*. Nairobi: East African Publishing House, 1976.

Van Velsen, J. "Some Early Pressure Groups in Malawi." In *The Zambesian Past*, edited by E. Stokes and R. Brown. Manchester, Eng.: Manchester University Press, 1965.

Malawi: Nationalism, Independence

Although the story of Malawian nationalism has tended to start with the formation of the Nyasaland African Congress in 1944, its development goes back to the interwar years when welfare, or native, associations were established in various parts of the colony. Among such organizations were the North Nyasa Native Association (1912), the Mombera Native Association (1920), the Chiradzulu Native Assocation (1929), and Zomba Native Association, also in the 1920s. Generally cautious, and happy to work within the colonial framework, the associations were concerned predominantly with issues that concerned their localities. Such matters included health, education, labor migration, and its effects on families, markets and marketing, communications, and the numerous licenses that were introduced by the government (an example being dog licenses, regarded by Africans as unnecessary and a major nuisance).

On the whole, the leadership of the associations was Western-educated, and consisted mostly of teachers, clergymen, and civil servants, all of whom viewed themselves as qualified to represent the majority in their areas. As early as the mid-1920s, umbrella associations had been created to discuss, and advocate on, matters concerning wider areas. For example, there was the Southern Province Native Association, formed in Zomba, and there was the Representative Committee of the Northern Province Native Associations, also established in Zomba.

By the early 1940s it became clear to leaders such as Lewis Mataka Bandawe, senior clerk in Blantyre, and James Sangala, also a government clerk in that town, and member of the Blantyre and Zomba Native Association and of the Southern Province Native Association, that matters of concern to Africans were territorial in nature. Only through a united representation would they achieve meaningful political and socioeconomic gains. Many Western-educated Malawians in Blantyre and other centers thought likewise, including James Ralph Chinyama, a Lilongwe-based businessman and activist, and Levi Mumba, a respected senior clerk, founder of the North Nyasa Native Association and president of the Representative Committee of the Northern Province Associations.

In 1943 the Nyasaland African Council was formed in Blantyre and, in the following year, changed its name to the Nyasaland African Congress (NAC). Mumba was its first president general, and Charles Matinga, the secretary general. This was the first nationalist political association in the colony, in the sense that its membership extended to all regions of Nyasaland, crossed ethnic boundaries and acted as the main mouthpiece of African opinion. It should also be noted that the leadership was basically the same as that of the pre–World War II native associations, elitist and moderate; nor was the agenda a radical departure from the interwar situation. Among NAC's main preoccupations were African representation on the legislative council, greater government involvement in African education, improvement of teachers salaries, removal of the color bar, more European respect for Africans, and continued African opposition to any form of federation of the Rhodesias and Nyasaland. The relationship between the leadership and the rural communities was minimal, primarily because those in the upper echelons of the NAC assumed that they knew and understood the needs of the masses. This attitude, the organization's poor financial situation, its initial resistance to employ a full-time organizer, and the government's tendency to disregard it, made the NAC a particularly ineffective organization throughout the 1940s.

The NAC, and African politics in general, went through a particularly difficult time in the period of 1949 to 1956. Charles Matinga, who had become president general of the party in 1946, had to resign in 1950 on grounds of financial mismanagement, favoritism, and weak leadership. His successor James Chinyama did not fare much better and was forced to resign in 1954. A major problem was the gulf between those at the top and those they were supposed to speak for; this was especially evident in the events of 1953.

In 1953, there were riots in the Shire Highlands, mainly in Thyolo, Mulanje, and Zomba, primarily connected with land problems that had plagued the area since European settler farms were established at the end of the nineteenth century. There were also major incidents in Ntcheu, leading to the arrest of the traditional ruler, Inkosi Philip Gomani. The events in the latter place and, to an extent, those in the Shire region, were a reaction to the imposition in October 1953 of the Federation of the Rhodesias and Nyasaland, a union that was unpopular among Africans. The establishment of the federation coincided with new agricultural and conservation measures that were disliked by

Africans. For most rural producers, these regulations and the federation were inseparable evils, directly associated with colonialism. The riots and other forms of resistance which occurred in other parts of the country did so largely independent of the national leadership of the NAC which had opposed violence, and was divided on the matter of the federation.

In 1955 changes in the constitution enabled the election, a year later, of five Africans to the Legislative Council. For the first time the NAC, which won all five seats, had a voice in the corridors of power. Of the new members, Henry Chipembere and Kanyama Chiume belonged to a new generation of nationalists who wanted immediate constitutional changes leading to majority rule; they also realized that new and effective leadership was required, and, on their recommendation, Dr. H. Kamuzu Banda was recalled from Ghana to lead the NAC.

Banda, who all along had supported the NAC morally and financially and had acted as its main external spokesman, returned to Nyasaland in July 1958 and reorganized the NAC. For the first time, there was truly a common language between the central executive of the NAC and the people. He was now openly and strongly challenging the government on issues that concerned them most: agriculture and conservation, health, education, bicycle taxes, and, for those in the Shire Highlands, *thangata* (labor tenancy). By February 1959 the political atmosphere throughout the country was highly charged, and violent incidents began to occur in some districts. Convinced that the NAC was about to organize a general rebellion, the governor, Sir Robert Armitage, declared a state of emergency on March 3, resulting in the banning of the NAC and detention without trial of Banda and hundreds of NAC people.

A British Commission of Inquiry, led by Justice Patrick Devlin, determined that the governor had overreacted. Banda was released in April 1960 and appointed to lead the Malawi Congress Party (MCP), which since September 1959 had effectively replaced the NAC. In July constitutional talks took place in London, leading to the first general elections in August 1961, which the MCP won overwhelmingly. Most of the positions on the Executive Council (EC) went to the party, with Banda becoming minister of natural resources and local government. Further constitutional talks in London in 1962 led to internal self government status in 1963; the EC was replaced by a cabinet, and Dr. Banda became prime minister. In September more constitutional discussions, presided over by R. A. Butler, minister for central African affairs, determined that Nyasaland would become independent on July 6, 1964, after general elections in April of that year. All MCP candidates went to parliament unopposed; in July Banda became prime minster of independent Malawi, the name adapted from that of the ancient Maravi Empire.

Owen J. M. Kalinga

See also: **Banda, Dr. Hastings Kamuzu; Malawi: Independence to the Present.**

Further Reading

Baker, C. *State of Emergency: Crisis in Central Africa, Nyasaland 1959–1960.* London: I. B.Tauris Publishers, 1997.

———. *Retreat From Empire: Sir Robert Armitage in Africa and Cyprus.* London: I. B. Tauris Publishers, 1998.

Chiume, M. W. Kanyama. *Kwacha.* Nairobi: East African Publishing House, 1975.

Macdonald, R. J. (ed.) *From Nyasaland to Malawi: Studies in Colonial History.* Nairobi: East African Publishing House, 1976.

Pachai, B. *Malawi: The History of the Nation.* London: Longman, 1973.

Sanger, C. *Central African Emergency.* London: Heineman, 1960.

Short, P. *Banda.* London: Routlege and Kegan Paul, 1974.

Rotberg, R. I. *The Rise of Nationalism in Central Africa: the Making of Malawi and Zambia, 1873–1964.* Cambridge, Mass.: Harvard University Press, 1965.

Williams, T. D. *Malawi: Politics of Despair.* Ithaca, N.Y.: Cornell University Press, 1978.

Malawi: Independence to the Present

At independence on July 6, 1964, Malawi's economic prospects were so poor that many in the international community did not have much hope for its survival as a viable nation state. It had no minerals of economic worth, and African agriculture was mainly subsistence. The principal exports, tea and tobacco, were dominated by European settler farmers. The transport infrastructure was inadequate, as was the educational system.

The supremacy of the Malawi Congress Party (MCP) and the power of Dr. Hastings Kamuzu Banda were consolidated following a major crisis parliament in August 1964, which resulted in the dismissal of the six ministers who had opposed the new prime minister on major policy issues. Malawi was deprived of able politicians and, from then onward, Banda's team consisted of diehard party loyalists who rarely challenged him. The policies of the MCP and the government became indistinguishable, and parliament lost its effectiveness. People suspected of disagreeing with Banda or the party were detained without trial, some for more than twenty years. In 1971, Banda, president since Malawi's attainment of republic status in 1966, was declared Life President; dictatorship and abuse of human rights were to continue throughout the 1970s and 1980s.

Throughout the 1960s, Malawi sought to wean itself from British budgetary aid and to improve the socioeconomic welfare of the citizenry. The strategy was to promote cash crop production as a foreign exchange earner while also encouraging food self-sufficiency but, realizing that the ability to move produce from rural areas to local and international markets was crucial for economic development, the government also embarked on a major expansion of this sector of the economy. By 1990 there were 8,000 miles of bituminized roads up from 242 miles at independence; there were also extensions to the railway system in the 1970s and 1980s. With road and railway extensions underway, government sought the assistance of the World Bank and other aid agencies to plan and execute rural development projects, especially those relating to smallholder agriculture. From 1965 to 1978 there were major projects in Lilongwe, Karonga, and the Lower Shire where, although food production was advocated, the stress was also on cash crops such as cotton, tobacco, and groundnuts. This approach was revised in 1978 because results fell short of expectations, giving way to the National Rural Development Project (NRDP), which covered wider areas and gave farmers more access to extension and credit facilities. By the 1980s it was clear that there was no real growth in smallholder production; certainly yield did not match the increase in population at the rate of 0.3 per cent per year. Only in the estate sector (mainly tea, tobacco, and sugar) did real growth take place.

Significant in this regard were the Agricultural Development and Marketing Corporation (ADMARC), and Press Holdings, both with large agricultural interests. ADMARC also had a virtual monopoly on the marketing of smallholder produce, an arrangement that was much to the disadvantage of the producers. The two organizations also embarked on major joint ventures and, in this way, Banda controlled critical aspects of the country's economy.

By the mid-1980s Malawi's economy was not healthy, partly because of internal factors—including expensive projects such as the new Lilongwe airport and the Kamuzu Academy—and partly because of external factors such as the cost of fuel imports and commodity prices at international markets. As a result, the World Bank and the International Monetary Fund (IMF) introduced structural adjustments that had to be accepted as a precondition for financial relief. Subsidies on items such as fuel and fertilizer were affected, raising their prices. Peasant production and self-sufficiency were negatively affected, as unemployment rose.

Malawi achieved a more noteworthy success in education for, while the development plans of the 1960s and 1970s emphasized agriculture and transport, they also recognized the role of education, including raising the level of literacy, in attaining the goals of the government. Primary school education expanded threefold: in 1964, 350,000 pupils were enrolled, rising to 481,500 in 1973, increasing further to 1.3 million in 1990, and by a further 50 per cent five years later. The same applied to teacher and vocational training and secondary school education. Although this development did not meet the demand, it was a major improvement on the pre-independence situation. In the meantime, the University of Malawi opened in 1965 and, in the next two years, it incorporated the Polytechnic in Blantyre, the Soche Hill College in Limbe, and the Bunda College of Agriculture in Lilongwe. In 1974 Soche Hill College and the Institute of Public Administration at Mpemba became part of Chancellor College at its new campus in Zomba.

In late 1978 the Kamuzu College of Nursing was founded, followed, ten years later, by the new College of Medicine. The latter was expected to solve the problem of the shortage of doctors as many of those sent to study abroad did not return, mainly because of poor facilities and low pay. Since the 1960s many more nurses and clinical workers have been trained, but doctor shortages have remained critical. Health education and primary health care both suffered as a result. With AIDS becoming a major factor since the mid-1980s, the pressure on health facilities increased throughout the 1990s.

Dr. Banda's dictatorship had been ignored by Western powers because of his strong anticommunist views and his support for the West. With the dissolution of the Soviet Union and the end of the Cold War, Banda's Western allies insisted on political reform, which they now linked with aid.

Malawian exiles had always called for change and, within the country, clandestine groups were organizing opposition. On March 8, 1992, a letter from the Roman Catholic bishops was read in all their churches detailing, among other things, the effects of human rights abuses and poverty on family life and social relationships. Soon afterward, Chakufwa Chihana, head of a regional trade union organization, openly challenged the government, which then arrested him. More internal and external pressure upon Banda led to a June 1993 referendun that displayed overwhelming support for multiparty democracy. In the general elections of May the following year, Banda lost to Bakili Muluzi of the United Democratic Front, which won the majority of seats in parliament.

Besides fostering the young democratic culture, the new government had to contend with economic problems that had worsened during the withdrawal of aid in 1991–1992. Inflation went up by over 40 per cent and, between 1997 and 1999, the Malawi kwacha was devalued by over 60 per cent, leading to a dramatic rise in the cost of consumer goods, fuel, fertilizer, and maize; medical supplies in hospitals became scarce. At the behest of the IMF and the World Bank, liberalization and privatization of the numerous parastatal organizations, including ADMARC, went into full force. Although free primary school education was introduced in 1994, the teacher: student ratio widened, and the need for classrooms also increased tremendously.

In June 1999 Muluzi was reelected. Charged with a tepid response to reports of corruption in his government, he reorganized his cabinet in 2000. In 2002 a proposed constitutional amendment, which would have allowed Muluzi to run for a third five-year turn, was rejected by parliament. In January 2003 demonstrations were held to protest Muluzi's further attempts to amend the constitution in his favor. In the face of this pressure, the proposed amendment was retracted.

OWEN J. M. KALINGA

See also: **Banda, Dr. Hastings Kamuzu; Malawi: Nationalism, Independence; World Bank, International Monetary Fund, and Structural Adjustment.**

Further Reading

Centre of African Studies. *Malawi: An Alternatative Pattern of Development.* Seminar Preceedings No. 25. Centre of African Studies, University of Edinburgh, 1984.

Lwanda, J. L. *Kamuzu Banda of Malawi: A Study of Promise, Power, and Paralysis.* Glasgow: Dudu Nsomba Publications, 1993.

———. *Promises, Power Politics, and Poverty: Democratic Transition in Malawi 1961–1993.* Glasgow: Dudu Nsomba Publications, 1996.

Nzunda, M. S., and K. R. Ross, (eds.). *Church, Law, and Political Transition in Malawi 1992–1994.* Harare: Mambo Press, 1995.

Phiri, K. M., and K. R. Ross (eds.). *Democratization in Malawi: A Stocktaking.* Blantyre: CLAIM, 1998.

Sahn, D. E., J. Arulpragasam, and L. Merid. *Policy Reform and Poverty in Malawi: A Survey of a Decade of Experience.* Cornell Food and Nutrition Policy Program. Monograph 7 (December 1990).

Williams, T. D. *Malawi: The Politics of Despair.* Ithaca, N. Y.: Cornell University Press, 1978.

Mali Empire, Sundiata and Origins of

The late Guinean historian Souleyman Kanté (1922–1987), writing in the Maninka script known as N'ko, which he invented, shared the belief of many that the Mali Empire dates from the first half of the thirteenth century, possibly about 1235–1236. Basing his dates on oral tradition and Arabic sources, Kanté estimated that Sundiata was born about 1205, ruled Mali for about twenty years, and died about 1255. More than a century after the time of Sundiata, he was known to the eminent Arab historian Ibn Khaldun (1332–1406), who refers to him by one of several names that are still heard in recitations by the Maninka bards of northeastern Guinea: "Their greatest king, he who overcame the Susu, conquered their country, and seized the power from their hands, was named Mari Jata." Khaldun's sources claimed that Sundiata ruled for twenty-five years.

When official oral traditionists (*jeliw*) of the West African Mande peoples recount episodes of events that led to the founding of the Mali Empire, they name Sundiata as the early thirteenth-century charismatic leader responsible for unifying the formerly autonomous chiefdoms of the Mande territories into what was to become one of the great empires of the Middle Ages. Consistent with Mande belief that charismatic leaders receive their power from their mothers, Mande epic tradition emphasizes the roles of key women in addition to recalling the exploits of male heroes.

The oral tradition, which we must rely on in the absence of written documentation, focuses on kinship themes and spiritual power sources that are essential components of the Mande worldview. The story begins with Sundiata's future father, the *mansa* (chief, king) of Konfara (the town is often identified as Niani, although it was of a later era), whose courtiers include his chief bard *(jelikuntigi)* Nyankurnan Dugha Kouyaté and the influential Muslim adviser Tombonon Manjan Bè. The *mansa* consulted his diviner to determine which son would best serve as his successor and learned that he has not yet found the wife who will deliver the greatest of his offspring. Meanwhile, in the mysterious land of Do and Kri, the powerful sorceress Do Kamissa, the "Buffalo Woman," assumed her animal form and embarked on a deadly rampage, because her brother the *mansa* of that land, refused to share the family legacy with her. The Buffalo Woman eventually surrendered the secret of her mortality to two adventurous young hunters from a distant land, the brothers Danmansa Wulanba and Danmansa Wulanni. Kamissa divulged the secret of how she could be killed, on the condition that when offered the reward of a young bride, the hunters refuse all others in favor of the ugly, physically deformed Sogolon Wulen Conffi, who is destined to give birth to Sundiata. After killing the rogue buffalo, selecting Sogolon, and being rejected by her as suitors, the brothers delivered her for marriage to the predestined father of the hero.

Sogolon's subsequent pregnancy was cursed by her jealous co-wives, especially Sansurna Bèretè, mother of the father's eldest son Dankaran Tuman. Sundiata was born crippled but eventually walked and achieved the reputation of a great hunter. After long suffering at the hands of her rivals, Sogolon retreated into exile with Sundiata and his siblings, eventually finding refuge with Faran Tunkara at his town of Kuntinya in Mema, on the desert frontier (Souleyman Kanté estimates that the period of exile commenced *c.*1226).

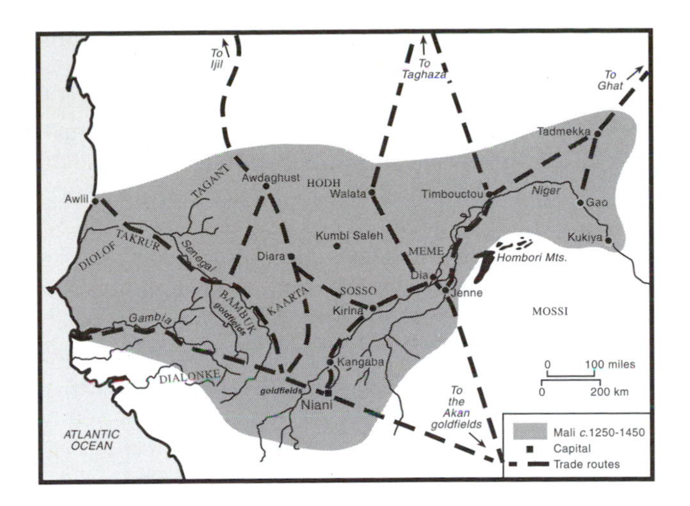

Mali, *c.*1250–1450.

Back in Mande, Dankaran Tuman became *mansa* upon his father's death but was unable to defend his lands against Susu conquest and eventually fled south to the land of the Kissi in the forest region. Desperate for effective leadership after years of Susu domination, the Mande people sent a delegation to search for the exiled Sogolon and Sundiata. Once the exiles were found in Mema by the delegation, the aged Sogolon died there, and Sundiata returned to Mande where he accepted the kingship (*mansaya*) and prepared to lead his people against their Susu oppressors.

During the period leading up to the final battles with Susu, a potentially divisive conflict of interest had to be resolved by one of Sundiata's most powerful supporters, Fakoli Koroma. Fakoli was the son of Mansa Yèrèlènko of the powerful iron-producing territory of Nègèbòriya, which lay in northern Mande near the Susu frontier. A junior wife of Mansa Yèrèlènko was Kosiya Kanté, sister of Sustis ruler Sumanguru (or Sumaworo), and she was Fakoli's natural mother. Tradition indicates that Kosiya died young and that Fakoli was raised by Yèrèlènko's senior wife Ma Tènènba, the third of three famous Condé ancestral women of Do and Kri, along with Do Kamissa and Sundiata's mother Sogolon. Thus Fakoli owed allegiance to both Mande and Susu, and as the general leader of several powerful, weapons-producing blacksmith clans, his decision of which side to fight on could sway the outcome of the war. Fakoli initially sided with his uncle Surnangurti, but for reasons that are not entirely clear (political intrigue seems to have been a factor), Fakoli reversed his decision and marched into Mande in time to place his formidable troops at Sundiata's service in the war with Susu.

Among Sundiata's other powerful supporters were his brother Manden Bori, who had endured the years of exile with him, as well as the leaders of the Kamara and Traoré (or Tarawèlè) lineages. The mountainous Kamara stronghold of Sibi and Tabon, like Nègèbòriya, commanded a northern zone near the frontier with Susu. Tradition indicates that Sibi under its mansa Tabon Wana Faran Kamara was the most influential of the pre-imperial autonomous states of Mande, and the most knowledgeable Maninka bards believe that Sundiata's sister Kolonkan married into the Kamara ruling lineage after returning from exile with her brothers. Tiramakan (or Turamaghan) Traoré is particularly recalled as distinguishing himself after the war with Susu by leading a successful expedition against the Jolof in what is now Senegal, thereby expanding Mali's western frontier.

The final great battle in which Mande defeated Susu is recalled as taking place in a region near the Niger River. The defeated Sumanguru is said to have been last seen downstream near the mountain of Kulikoro, in which his spirit is still believed to dwell. Modern demographic evidence supports oral traditional claims that in subsequent years a majority of the Susu population migrated out of their former territories southward toward the Atlantic Ocean, in what later came to be known as the Guinea coast.

Souleyman Kanté dates the actual founding of the Mali Empire from the time of a great council meeting after the defeat of Susu, at a place called Kurukanfuga (*c.*1236). It was in that open space, near today's Kangaba, that Sundiata assembled his subjects and introduced the laws and political system of the great western Sudanic state that would reach its apogee a century later under Mansa Musa (1312–1337) and flourish until the early fifteenth century, when the Songhay Empire replaced Mali as the preeminent western Sudanic state.

David C. Conrad

See also: **Songhay Empire.**

Further Reading

Abu Zayd 'Abd al-Rahman ibn Khaldun. "Kitab al-ibar wa-diwan al-mubtadawa- 'l-khabarfi ayyam al-'arabwa-' l-'ajamwa- 'l-barbar." In *Corpus of Early Arabic Sources for West African History*, edited by N. Levtzion and J. F. P. Hopkins. 333. Cambridge: Cambridge University Press, 1981.

Austen, R. (ed.). *In Search of Sundiata: The Mande Epic as History, Literature and Performance*. Bloomington: Indiana University Press, 1999.

Conrad, D. C. "Searching for History in the Sundiata Epic: The Case of Fakoli." *History in Africa* 19 (1992): pp.147–200.

Conrad, D.C. (ed.). *Epic Ancestors of the Sundiata Era: Oral Tradition from the Maninka of Guinea*. Madison: University of Wisconsin African Studies Program, 1999.

Innes, G. (ed.). *Sundiata: Three Mandinka Versions*. London: School of Oriental and African Studies, 1974.

Johnson, J. W. (ed.). *The Epic of Son-Jara: A West African Tradition*. Bloomington: Indiana University Press, 1986.

Levtzion, N. *Ancient Ghana and Mali*. London: Methuen and Co., 1973.

Niane, D. T. *Sundiata: An Epic of Old Mali*. London: Longmans, 1965.

Mali Empire: Economy

Mali was the cradle of one of the greatest empires in precolonial Africa. It was built on gold and flourished during the Middle Ages of Europe. This great state, which evolved in the savanna zone, originated from a Mande (Mandingo) cultural core, from where it extended its sway over a large number of states and societies. Mali arose as a successor state to the Old Ghana Empire, which had collapsed in 1235 after the onslaught of the ruthless Susu king, Sumanguru. His power was challenged by the Keita, a Mande group. This group, originally traders, had endeavored to develop political control over a number of kingdoms in the adjacent territories. After prolonged warfare, the Keita group produced a king, Sundiata (1230–1255), who overthrew Sumanguru and went on to capture the capital of Ghana. From the remnants of Ghana he laid the foundations for the new Mande empire, which from 1240 became the major political and commercial power for the whole of western Sudan.

Mali was the product of a southerly Mande group. They possessed fertile land, which afforded better conditions for agriculture and gave them more direct control over the alluvial gold fields. The group aimed to control the whole Sudan, as far as the Niger bend, where the new southern termini for the trans-Saharan trade, Timbuktu and Gao, were situated.

In this, Sundiata and his successors achieved remarkable feats. By the fourteenth century, they controlled an empire that reached some 1250 miles from the Atlantic in the west to the borders of northern Nigeria in the east, from the southern Saharan caravan centers of Audaghost, Walata, and Tadmakka in the north, to the borders of the Guinea forests in the southwest.

The expansion of the Mande from the thirteenth century, however, often had important political and economic consequences. The victory of Mali over the Susu opened the way for expansion northward, which enabled the empire to gain control over the end destinations of the trans-Saharan trails. Its controls extended over the Sahara desert, which included the valuable salt mines of Taghaza and the copper mines of Takedda. The movements of Mali westward over the upper valley of the Senegal and toward (present day) Gambia enabled it to hold sway over all the internal trade routes. The pattern of their movement to the east and southeast appears to have been determined to some extent by the existence of largely agricultural communities. This no doubt enhanced the vitality of Mali, as by the fifteenth century there was a considerable trade in millet, rice, cotton, and livestock within the empire. Mali had created an empire whose main artery was the river Niger and the commercial cities of the Niger bend.

The gold deposits in Mali made the empire great. The extent of the wealth of the empire was brought into bold relief by the famous pilgrimage of Mansa Musa (1312–1337) the ruler of Mali to Mecca in 1324. His splendid passage through Cairo, according to Al-Omari (an Arab scholar), had an unsettling effect on exchange rates: "the people of Cairo earned incalculable sums from him whether by buying and selling or by gifts. So much gold was current in Cairo that it ruined the value of money. . . ." Such profligacy nearly ruined Mansa Musa, who experienced serious political troubles on his return to West Africa. Nevertheless, the visit succeeded in advertising the wealth of the empire, thus attracting more traders and Muslim scholars who contributed immensely to the economic and cultural development of the empire. Apart from his visit to Mecca, Mansa Musa also strengthened the links of his empire with the Muslim community in the outside world. He initiated diplomatic relations with the sultans of Morocco. Mansa Musa's contact with North Africa brought important development in architecture. On his return from Mecca, he was accompanied by an Andalusian architect, Es-Saheli, who went on to build an impressive palace in Timbuktu and Gao. The materials and architectural style were new to Mali, since he adopted the flat roof of north Africa, the pyramidal minaret, and burnt bricks.

Mali at its peak was not only a center of civilization, scholarship, and custodian of an orderly system of law and government but a remarkable economic success. The whole atmosphere of the empire was one of peace and prosperity. Law and order was maintained so well that people laden with goods could travel the length and breadth of the empire without fear of harassment. The semidivine status of the king of Mali projected the aura of a ruler of a very wealthy state. For instance, Ibn Battuta, a Berber of Tangier who visited Mali in 1532, was immensely impressed by the majesty that surrounded the king. He marveled at his exalted status and the wealth at his disposal. Whenever the king gave a public address, he did so on a three-tiered dais covered with silks and cushions and with a ceiling supported by elephant tusks. Before the king advanced a throng of dancers, praise-singers, and slaves, and behind him were his three hundred bodyguards.

The glittering courts of Mali were, however, maintained at a considerable cost to human lives. Both by inheritance and conquest, the king acquired a number of slave villages. The peoples of these villages were forced to provide the king with annual fixed quantities of produce or service so that all the needs of his court were satisfied. Another set of slave villagers, the *arbi*, acted as domestic servants, personal bodyguards, and royal messengers to the king.

The regeneration of the empire was ensured by a succession of dynamic rulers until the end of the fourteenth century, when it disintegrated due to dynastic struggles, several weak rulers, revolts, and secessions in the outlying provinces.

OLUTAYO ADESINA

Further Reading

Ajayi, J. F. A., and I. Espie. *A Thousand Years of West African History.* Ibadan and Surrey: Ibadan University Press and Nelson, 1965.

Davidson, B. *The African Past.* Harmondsworth: 1966.

Fage, J. D. *A History of West Africa: An Introductory Survey.* Cambridge: University Press, 1969.

Levtzion, N. *Ancient Ghana and Mali.* 1973.

Stride, G. T., and C. Ifeka. *Peoples and Empires of West Africa: West Africa in History 1000–1800.* Middlesex and Nairobi: Thomas Nelson and Sons, 1971.

Mali Empire: Decline, Fifteenth Century

The empire of Mali, founded by the Mande (or Mandingo) conqueror Sundiata Keita in the thirteenth century, stretched from the coast of what is now Gambia in the West to the city of Gao on the river Niger in the East, and from the Teghazza saltmarshes of the Sahara in the north to the edges of the forests of modern Guinea and Côte d'Ivoire in the south. It was the largest and most powerful of the political formations in West Africa in the Middle Ages, reaching its peak under Mansa (Emperor) Musa, who reigned from 1307 to 1332. In the fifteenth century, however, it began to decline, and it disappeared from the political map of Africa around the beginning of the seventeenth century. The heart of the empire was composed of the commercial centers of Djenn, Timbuktu, and Gao, which lay along the middle loop of the Niger and maintained relations with the Arab countries to the north. After Mali lost this crucial region to the Songhay kingdom, the Mansas turned their attention to the west, where the Portuguese had just started their commercial ventures along the Atlantic coast of Senegambia. The appearance of these European mariners on the shores of Africa seemed to offer a lifeline to the Juula, the Mandingo merchant caste, who now directed their caravans westward.

From the beginning of the fifteenth century onward, Mali also became the target of military campaigns launched from the Sahel by two nomadic peoples, the Moors and the Tuaregs. It was at around the same time that the Songhay kings, who were vassals of the Mansas, threw off the Mande yoke. Both these developments were made possible by the increasing weakness of the central government, which in turn owed much to the succession crisis within the ruling family at the end of the fourteenth century. The descendants of Sundiata, the senior branch of the dynasty, had rebelled in an attempt to retrieve the supreme power from the junior branch, descended from one of Sundiata's brothers, which had monopolized the throne ever since the accession of Mansa Musa, and the empire had been weakened by assassinations and palace intrigues. The Tuaregs, Saharan nomads who had earned the respect of the Malian forces from the thirteenth century onward, took advantage of the succession crisis to rise up and drive the Mande garrison out of Timbuktu in 1433. The Mansas also lost control of Walata, Nema, and the whole of the Sahel region that they had once ruled. As a result, they lost control of the trails across the Sahara that had linked their empire with the commercial centers of the Maghrib and Egypt.

However, the decisive blow was struck against the Malian empire with the rise to power of Sonni Ali, a prince of Gao who displayed unrivaled energy and ambition. It was Sonni Ali who drove the Tuaregs away and then made himself master of the whole of the loop of the Niger as far as Djenn, the most important of the commercial centers. Having lost the cities of the Sahel and the rich territories of the inland delta of the Niger, Mali was effectively pushed back into the West. Its Senegambian provinces, heavily populated by Mande, rapidly acquired greater economic importance following the arrival of the Portuguese mariners, whose desire to open trading relations with Mali stemmed from its reputation for being rich in gold, a reputation that had haunted the imaginations of Europeans since the days of Mansa Musa. The Juula willingly sent their caravans to the ports at which the Europeans' ships had just arrived, which are now in Gambia and Guinea but were then also ruled by the Mansas. The Wanga and Juula merchants bought black and blue cotton fabrics, Indian textiles, and embroidered clothing from the Portuguese, although it frequently happened that the Juula brought so much gold with them that the caravels (the Portuguese ships) could not carry enough merchandise to exchange for it.

The Portuguese duly recognized and valued the commercial skills of the Juula, and from the mid-fifteenth century began to ask them for slaves: trading relations between Africans and Europeans were about to be transformed, at a very rapid pace and to the advantage of the Europeans. The Malian trade along the coast continued up to the end of the sixteenth century, but the main effect of these contacts between the Portuguese and the local rulers, who were vassals of the Malian Empire, was that these rulers tended to become ever more independent of the authority of the Mansas.

Among the non-Mandingo subjects of the Mansas, the Fulani, a pastoral people of the Sahel, were among the first to break away from their rule. Ever since the thirteenth century, the Fulani had been moving far to the south in search of pasture and watering holes and had thus established a strong presence in Futa-Toro, on the banks of the river Senegal, in Macina, in the inland delta of the Niger, in Futa-Jallon, in the grassy valleys, and in the Bondu savanna. For a long time they submitted to the laws imposed on them by the farmers, but from the fifteenth century onward they rose up, throughout the region, and became the masters of the sedentary population in their turn, going on to create their own powerful states. The uprising of the Fulani was led by their tribal chief Tenguella, and it was in order to combat him that in 1490 the Mansa of Mali sought military aid, or at least a supply of firearms, from the Portuguese. They responded by sending an impressive delegation to Niani, but although these envoys came laden with gifts, they did not supply any weapons to the emperor.

Tenguella then gathered a powerful army and organized an effective cavalry, so that the Fulani were able to cause devastation wherever they went. Their campaign against both the Songhay and the Mande lasted from 1480 to 1512, under both Tenguella and his son, Koly Tenguella, who proved to be a strong leader of men like his father. Having built a major fortress in Futa Jalon, and having left his son in charge of it, Tenguella led a campaign to the East against the Songhay, who had been trying to move westward in the footsteps of the Mande, seeking control of the gold mines of Bambuk. The Fulani and the Songhay clashed at Diarra in 1512: Tenguella was defeated and killed by Amar Kondjago, a brother of the Askia (ruler) of Gao, Mohammed.

Tenguella carried on the war, recruiting a large army of Baga, Kokoli, Badiaranke, and Mande mountain warriors and leading it out from the fortress. He adopted the Mandingo title of "Silatigi" ("trail head" or "guide"), although the Portuguese came to known him simply as the Grand Fulani. He then drove the Malian forces back towards what is now Gambia, conquered the kingdoms of the Wolof and Futa Toro, and imposed his rule over the numerous local dynasties in the West, setting up his capital at Anyam-Godo in Futa Toro. The Mande, expelled from Futa Jalon and Futa Toro, were left with no more than a narrow corridor of land along the river Gambia, linking them to the Atlantic.

The Mansas still hoped to establish a stable relationship with the Portuguese, who did not hesitate, however, to sign commercial contracts directly with the local rulers who were vassals of Mali. Even so, on two occasions, in 1481 and 1495, King John II of Portugal sent envoys to Niani, where Mansa Mahmud II received them with pomp, only to have his repeated requests for firearms rejected. In 1534 his grandson Mansa Mahmud III also received envoys from Portugal at Niani, this time led by the King's representative at the fortress of El Mina. Yet while the Mansas committed themselves to favoring Portuguese trade on the River Gambia, the King of Portugal secretly gave aid to many of the provincial governors, rulers, and chiefs, helping them to free themselves from central control and thus undermining the authority of the Mansas. As a result, Saalum and other kingdoms and principalities, as well as the Mande provinces of Gabu and Gambia, became independent of the Mansas. Niani, being located more than 1,500 kilometers (930 miles) from the coast, could not cope with all these rebellions.

At the end of the sixteenth century Mansa Mahmud IV attempted to take advantage of the weakness of the pasha of Morocco, following the disruptions caused by the Moroccan conquest of the lands of the Songhai, by recruiting a large army and launching a campaign to reconquer Djenn. He relied on the complicity, or at least the neutrality, of a number of the local rulers, and his army made a deep impression on the Moroccans. However, the Moroccans used firearms to repel the Mansa, and neither he nor his successors ever again attempted to regain control of Djenn. In any case, after the death of Mahmud IV his five sons divided what was left of the empire between them, and in the seventeenth century the empire of Mali vanished from the political map of Africa.

DJIBRIL TAMSIR NIANE

See also: **Mali Empire, Sundiata and Origins of; Songhay Empire: Sonni Ali and Founding of an Empire.**

Further Reading

Manny, R. *Tableau géographique de l'ouest africain au Moyen Age—Mémoires Dakar* [Geographical Picture of West Africa in the Middle Ages, Dakar Remebrances]. IFAN, 1961.

Niane, D. T. *Recherches sur l'Empire du Mali* [In Search of the Mali Empire]. Paris: Présence Africaine, 1975.

Person, Y. "Le Moyen Niger au Xve siècle d'après les sources européennes." In *Histoire Générale de l'Afrique* [Niger in the Fifteenth Century, From European Sources], edited by D. T. Niane. Vol. 4. UNESCO, 1985.

Mali (Republic of): Economy and Society, Nineteenth Century

Most of the territory of the present-day Republic of Mali had not been occupied by colonial forces until late in the nineteenth century, when the French penetrated the area and occupied Kita, Bamako, and Segou. Subjugation of the thinly populated northern area, where Tuareg nomads lived, took place only in the first decades of the twentieth century. The economy was mainly agricultural, and cattle herding Fulbe lived mainly in the Niger valley.

The most important infrastructural determinant for the economy was the river Niger. Caravan routes were also of great importance, in particular the routes that connected Mali with the north. Westward the most well-known trade route was the Mandesira, which connected the relatively green and fertile area south of Bamako (where gold was found), with the area dominated by the Senegal River. Southward, various smaller trade routes connected the area with the Guinean coast. The landscape of this area is quite flat, which facilitates transport; in the south of present-day Mali, however, during the rainy season river tributaries tend to overflow; they were serious impediments to any form of mobility (trade or warfare).

Political power along the Niger was not centralized, although the authority of certain rulers could cover immense areas. Such rulers levied taxes in semiautonomous polities and in adjoining polities that they dominated. At the periphery of their area of influence, which was contested by another ruler from a polity even farther away, income was produced from pillaging. These so-called warrior states, as Roberts (1987) has described, were led by a ruler who closely collaborated with an elite of warriors that lived from a surplus of production they took by taxing or violence. These warriors and rulers were not involved in products that stimulated and increased production, such as irrigation. The rulers of polities that paid taxes to "the center" in turn levied taxes from the agriculturists and passing traders, whose safety they guaranteed.

The relationships between warrior states were fickle; a former center of political power could quickly become the periphery of another polity. Some polities seem to have been able to avoid this fate, such as the great state of Segou, but still these polities suffered from rapid changes within the ruling elite as well as regarding the size of their area of influence.

Kinship relations were important, and relations in general were often expressed in terms of kinship; a ruling group or segment that was accepted and represented as the "younger brother" of adjoining "older brother" ruling families was actually the army leader in times of communal warfare or defense. After the war, the "younger brother" group had to distribute the pillaged gains. After the communal effort, collaboration stopped, and often internal conflict arose. On a more local level, relations were in terms of host versus guest/stranger. These relations were often clearer in task division and more stable in hierarchy and role than those in terms of kinship.

A majority of the population belonged to ethnic groups that are today classified as Mande cultures.

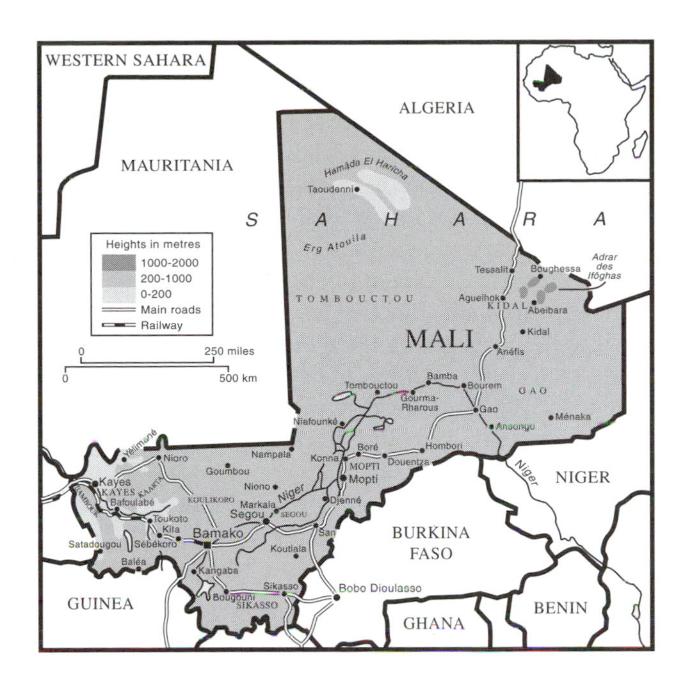

Mali.

They all had a patrilineal descent system, shared similar institutions (secret societies, mask associations), and spoke related languages. Mande groups were organized in three status categories: freemen, artisans, and slaves. Slaves often were former freemen who were captives from warfare or house slaves (who were descendants from captives). Within a few generations, house slaves were often able to marry into their "host" family, thus becoming a freeman with a "guest" status. The category of artisans, which made up 5 per cent of the population, was endogamous. In theory (but often not in practice), artisans were not directly involved in warfare; they were griots (bards), blacksmiths, leatherworkers, or weavers.

In the nineteenth century, jihads swept through this area, but these seem not to have changed fundamentally the organization of the polities and the attitude of the people: as Hanson (1996) described. The soldiers of Umar Tal left the Futanke region (present day Senegal) to conquer Karta, but soon lost their religious zeal after victory and preferred to settle as agriculturists instead of pursuing their jihad further eastward.

In the south, Samori Touré organized an empire in the period 1865–1898, the year he was captured by the French. Samori's deeds are vividly remembered, often in a positive way, although Samori actually destroyed many towns and villages with his scorched-earth tactics. At the end of the nineteenth century, Tieba Traore established a powerful polity with Sikasso at its center. Clashes between Tieba and Samori weakened their armies, thus facilitating the French conquest of the Sudan after the Berlin Conference.

The nineteenth century was characterized by increased construction of so-called *tata*, or walled fortifications. Changes in warfare strategies and the jihads that raged in the area stimulated the construction of *tatas*. However, recent excavations in Dya, north of Djenne, demonstrate that walled towns already existed before the jihad era. *Tatas* varied greatly in size (height 2 to 5 meters) and material (dried mud, dried mud with pebbles). The main function of *tatas* was defense. If possible the local populations made use of geographical characteristics to organize defense; those who lived close to a river built a shed at the other side of the river, while those who lived close to cliffs or rocks, prepared a hiding place from which they could throw stones at invaders. In oral tradition, people state that agriculture was also dangerous in times of peace; unguarded workers were said to fall easily victim to slave-raiders.

The French took the small polities as the territorial bases for the canton and *cercle* structure they introduced at the end of the nineteenth century and reorganized during World War I. In present-day oral traditions, the canton structure of the end of the nineteenth century is often imagined as representing the "traditional kingdoms." This has resulted in contrasting claims by villages that aimed to establish "communes" to meet the government's request for decentralization: some focused on the canton structure, while others had the "traditional kingdom" in mind.

JAN JANSEN

See also: **Mali, Republic of: Traoré, Moussa, Life and Era of.**

Further Reading

Hanson, J. H. *Migration, Jihad, and Muslim Authority in West Africa—The Futanke Colonies in Karta*. Bloomington: Indiana University Press, 1996.

Jansen, J. "The Younger Brother and the Stranger—In Search of a Status Discourse for Mande." *Cahiers d'Etudes Africaines*. 144 (1996): 659–688.

Person, Y. *Samori—Une révolution Dyula*. 3 vols. Dakar: Mémoire IFAN, 1968–1975.

Roberts, R. *Warriors, Merchants, and Slaves: The State and the Economy in the Middle Niger Valley, 1700–1914*. Stanford: Stanford University Press, 1987.

Robinson, D. *The Holy War of Umar Tall*. Oxford: Oxford University Press.

Mali (Republic of): Alliances and Wars

Numerous changes, driven mainly by Islamic jihads and the French invasions, occurred in the nineteenth century on the territory that constitutes present-day Mali. Social and economic development accelerated, sometimes fueling rebellions. Animist traditions and Islamic rule had difficulties coexisting. Evolving trade patterns steadily undermined the caravan trade, which had been the mainstay of power and wealth in the region for centuries.

The earliest major event was Ahmadu Lobo's creation of the Hamdallahi caliphate in Macina (1818). Successful though his undertaking had been during his lifetime, rivalries arose under the reign of his heirs and came to a head under his grandson Ahmadu III (1852–1862) when the Tukulor Empire, created by the jihad of al-Hajj Umar, threatened the neighboring Bamana kingdom of Segu. What happened then was symptomatic of the depth of the intra-African enmities that facilitated European conquest. Umar attempted to forge an alliance with fellow Muslim Ahmadu against the Animist Bambara, but Ahmadu refused, mistrusting Umar, member of a Muslim brotherhood different from his own. He saw the Tukulor invading his sphere of influence and believed they would attack him after having defeated the Bamana. Indeed, Umar conquered both the kingdom of Segu and Macina, and then he moved on to Timbuktu. His actions triggered another fratricidal war. An alliance of dispossessed northern Tuareg and Macina Fulani destroyed his armies and killed him (1864).

During his lifetime Umar had also faced crises due to the other major cause of upheavals at the time, European imperialism. He had early (1848) offered the French collaboration. He foresaw little conflict, believing that the French merely wanted trade, while he wanted to build an empire. The French ignored his proposal and instead moved inland in Senegal and hence into Mali, building a fort at Medina (1855). In 1860 it finally suited Louis Faidherbe, governor of Senegal, to agree to a treaty accepting the Senegal River as common boundary. Umar was free to continue his conquests, but his son Ahmadu inherited both the internal problems of a shaky empire and the external threat of French colonialism. He continued negotiations with the French and assumed a friendly attitude. He did not take advantage of their weakened position when their garrisons were depleted during the Franco-Prussian War (1870), yet the French tacitly continued to support his enemies.

During the last twenty years of the century the tempo of change accelerated. The French formulated their policy to reach the Niger so as to obtain uninterrupted communications between their holdings in the Sudan and their increasingly important territories in Côte d'Ivoire. After 1885 occupation became essential for them in view of the stipulation approved at the Berlin Conference, namely that claims on African colonies had to be based on actual occupation.

The French undertook railway construction from Senegal to the Niger to improve communication lines.

In 1881 Simon-Joseph Gallieni negotiated the Treaty of Nango with Ahmadu to forestall Tukulor opposition. Ahmadu doubted Gallieni's offer of friendship but was internally too weak to oppose him. The French soon broke the treaty, penetrated the Tukulor Empire, took Bamako and then Kita. Again, Ahmadu's reaction was temperate.

Meanwhile, near Bamako, the French encountered a formidable enemy about whom they knew little, Samori Touré. Samori, a Malinke, had started out as a trader and soldier. He was an outstanding tactician and administrator, who visualized building an empire in the area that had long been the base of Mande commercial expansion and settlement. Though born in an animist family, he had in 1868 proclaimed himself a religious Islamic leader. Intent on equipping a powerful army and building an empire, he in turn had given the French no thought until they occupied Bamako where he attacked them, but failed to dislodge them.

Actually, the French were more vulnerable than they appeared in 1885. Their lines of communication were overextended, and they were forced to combat a new enemy on the border between Guinea and Mali, Marabout Mahmadou Lamine. Yet, African leaders did not move. Ahmadu was unwilling to support Lamine, who proclaimed himself the spiritual heir of his father, Umar Samori sought to profit from the distraction by accepting a compromise agreement which left him free to tend to his empire. By 1888, Ahmadu and Samori had signed similar treaties with Gallieni, both nominally accepting French protection in exchange for recognition of their authority and the sale of modern weapons.

Treaties, however, meant little. The new French commander, Louis Archinard, captured Segu in 1890. Ahmadu was forced to fight. He made conquest difficult for the French, but they persisted. In 1891 he made one last stand in Macina. Archinard had to stop to restore order in Segu, but in 1892 he conquered Macina. The defeat of the Tukulor empire was complete.

Meanwhile, the French also routed Samori. In 1891 they invaded his capital, Bissandugu, but they found a desert; Samori had followed a scorched-earth policy. By 1894 he was in present-day Côte d'Ivoire, again in the way of communication between French possessions. In vain he sought an alliance with the British, who also saw him as a threat. Pursued and captured he died in exile.

The French proceeded to take Timbuktu. They now had control of all of modern-day Mali, and incorporated it, with Senegal, into what they called the French Sudan. In 1895 they united all their territories in West Africa into one administrative unit named French West Africa. (Mali would reacquire the name of its ancient empire when it gained independence in 1960.)

Besides the firearms gap, nothing had helped the French colonize Mali more than disunity between Africans, who saw the Europeans as less dangerous than their African rivals. They were familiar with the goals of the Africans, while they could not quite evaluate what French rule might mean. Surrounded by traditional enemies, they concentrated on treaties by which they hoped to gain access to the French superior firepower. And so, in most of their campaigns in Mali, the French had African allies. Moreover, the so-called French forces, while commanded by French officers, were made up of African soldiers.

NATALIE SANDOMIRSKY

See also: **Touré, Samori (*c.* 1830–1900) and His Empire.**

Further Reading

Ajayi, J. F. A., and M. Crowder, eds. *History of West Africa.* Vol. 2. Burnt Mill, Essex: Longman, 1987.

Djata, A. *The Bamana Empire by the Niger, Kingdom, Jihad, and Colonization 1712–1920.* Princeton: Markus Wiener, 1997.

Forde, D., and P. M. Kaberry, eds. *West African Kingdoms in the Nineteenth Century.* London: Oxford University Press, 1967.

Hargreaves, J. D. *West Africa Partitioned.* 2 vols. London: Macmillan, 1974, 1985.

Kanya-Forstner, A. S. *Conquest of the Western Sudan: A Study in French Military Imperialism.* Cambridge: Cambridge University Press, 1969.

Robinson, David. *The Holy War of al-Hajj Umar Tal.* Oxford: Clarendon, 1985.

Mali (Republic of): Colonial Soudan Français

Once the conquest of the Niger valley was complete, the French sought to integrate the regional economy into their own while placing as few demands as possible on metropolitan taxpayers. In order to convince private enterprise to participate, the government had to provide security for French lives and investments. In the short run, that required a convincing display of military force. In the long run, it meant convincing Africans to adopt French culture.

The French organized the society of French Soudan (colonial Mali) into a strict hierarchy with Europeans at the highest levels of authority, Africans at the lowest levels, and a few "evolved" Africans admitted to the middle rungs to serve as intermediaries. To train the first intermediaries, the French opened the "School for Hostages" (later "School for the Sons of Chiefs") in Kayes in 1886 to teach the French language. Although the French succeeded in establishing some useful relationships, like that with Abdul Lahi ben Ahmadou, the grandson of El Hadj Umar, many chiefs were hesitant and instead sent the sons of their subjects. As a result, the first group of evolved Africans included a mixture of men who were recognized as leaders by the local

Inauguration of the Sotuba Channel, Mali (Soudan), by the french minister of the colonies, M. Maginot, in the 1930s. © SVT Bild/Das Fotoarchiv.

population, and men who were viewed as pawns in a power struggle between local leaders and the French.

The French began to draft Africans for military service in 1912, and a disproportionate number came from the French Soudan, the Bambara population which was viewed by the French as strong, docile, and particularly immune to suffering. Following World War I, African veterans enjoyed special access to jobs in the expanding colonial bureaucracy, and many obtained positions of responsibility under the French to which they could never have aspired under traditional rulers. They were joined in the 1930s by the first graduates of colonial schools like the École Primaire Supèrieure et d'Apprentissage in Bamako and the École William Ponty near Dakar. After World War II a mixture of union members, teachers, postal workers, and war veterans provided personal contacts between the French and Africans in the urban areas around Segou and along the railway west of Bamako. However, the concentration of French personnel along the major axis of transportation meant that most Soudanese had only sporadic contact with French culture.

To finance their plans, the French tried to develop the export economy. The possibilities were limited because the colony was landlocked, but the western portion was accessible to ocean-going ships in late August of each year via the Senegal River. In the first two decades of colonial rule, the French encouraged Africans to exchange gum arabic and rubber at forts along the Senegal River. Once the Colonial Marines began to build a railway from the Senegal to the Niger River in 1881, European merchants shifted their operations to Kayes at the railway's western terminus.

After the Kayes-Niger railway opened in 1904, European merchants moved their operations to Bamako at the railway's eastern terminus. Bamako became the colonial capital and nearly doubled in size between 1902 and 1912, then doubled again to 15,000 inhabitants by 1920. As steamship transportation became more reliable, European merchants established new trading posts downstream to buy wool and animal skins, and by 1907, they traveled as far east as Gao, 1,300 kilometers from Bamako.

After World War I the French encouraged Soudanese farmers to produce peanuts, which already enjoyed considerable success in coastal Senegal. The government also promoted the production for export of traditional crops like cotton and rice, plus animal products from pastoralists who lived in the region. The largest project, the Office du Niger, joined several cotton and rice-growing projects in 1925 to form a semipublic corporation based in Segou. During the depression, the French encouraged men to migrate to Senegal to grow peanuts and to Côte d'Ivoire to work on the cocoa plantations.

Since the main colonial transportation route ran east-west to the coast, it received little business from local trade, which followed routes that ran north and south between the Saharan salt mines and the Ivorian forest. The cost of transportation to the coast made Soudanese exports relatively expensive in world markets, so except for periods of high world prices, the revenue from the export economy never matched French expectations. The French tried to augment their revenues by collecting a cash "head tax" beginning in 1905. The French institutionalized the use of forced labor with the 1912 military conscription law, and Soudanese draftees were assigned to work on roads in the colony or projects near the coast. After World War I thousands of Soudanese were forced to work on the railway to Senegal as well as and canal and dam projects of the Office du Niger.

Forced labor, taxation, and military conscription provoked resistance, and local institutions remained strong in the absence of a larger European administrative contingent. The French were forced to rely on good relations with influential local leaders to get co-operation from the Soudanese. The French rarely challenged local religious authorities and even went so far as to discourage Christian missionaries from entering the area. Although Roman Catholic missions were eventually founded as far north as Timbuktu, they won few converts outside of the capital at Bamako, the administrative town of Segou, and a few other locations along the railway and in the Niger valley.

The French actively cultivated the support of leaders from the two main Muslim brotherhoods, the Qadirriyya and the Tidjianiyya. Colonial officials in the 1920s saw Islam as an antidote to "communist influence" and viewed with suspicion the development of rival brotherhoods like that which followed

Mohammed al Tashiti Hamallah of Nioro du Sahel. Collaboration of the mainstream brotherhoods with the French was also an issue in the rise of the Wahabiya, who sought to reunite local Muslims with international Sunni Islam after World War II. However, neither of these movements ever became dominant, and in 1957, many Wahabi merchants became the targets of urban violence in Bamako.

Many more Soudanese resisted by deserting from forced labor camps and migrating to the English colonies to avoid taxes and conscription. By the 1930s they began to remind French authorities of their legal obligations to prevent the worst abuses, and following World War II, the Soudanese mounted sophisticated legal challenges to the French system. In particular, Soudanese railway workers proved especially militant during the strike that lasted from October 1947 to March 1948. European workers at the *Office du Niger* staged their own strike on February 1, 1950, and other African workers struck the steamship service in 1954 and the electric company in 1955, while African consumers staged a boycott to protest against a French tax on dried fish in 1956.

The elections to create the French Fourth Republic triggered the formation of political parties led by African civil servants and traditional leaders. Fily Dabo Sissoko, a teacher and descendant of traditional chiefs, won the 1946 election with French backing, but Mahmadou Konaté, another teacher, gained the support of a younger generation of teachers and civil servants. In October 1946 Konaté and other members of the Union Soudanaise (US) hosted delegates from all of the French African colonies at the Congress of Bamako where they united in the Rassemblement Démocratique Africaine (RDA). Konaté died in May 1956, but his sucessor, another teacher named Modibo Keita, successfully rallied the party members, and in 1959, the US-RDA absorbed its main rival, Fily Dabo Sissoko's Parti Progressiste Soudanais. At the elections for the Mali Federation in 1960, Keita was unopposed and he became the first president of Mali.

During the 1950s the French attempted to neutralize local discontent by increasing their investment in economic development. The Office du Niger completed the Sansanding Dam on the Niger River in 1947 and added more canals and irrigated land throughout the 1950s. Bamako received sewage lines, drinking water, a maternity hospital, and other government buildings, as well as a bridge over the Niger River and regularly scheduled flights to Dakar and Paris. Towns like Kayes, Gao, Mopti, Segou, and Timbuktu all received airports and other improvements, while in 1954, a bus service started operations from Bamako to Mopti.

The investments in infrastructure were not matched by investments in social programs. In part because of an acute shortage of teachers, only 836 Soudanese completed secondary or vocational school between 1905 and 1947. Although the French began building new schools and replacing mud-brick buildings with concrete block structures after the war, the teacher shortage persisted and by 1950, the colony served barely 23,000 students out of an estimated school-age population of over half a million. Additional medical facilities were constructed in Bamako, and the largest private companies were required to provide clinics for their workforces, but most Soudanese saw no change before independence.

James A. Jones

See also: **Mali, Republic of: Keita, Modibo, Life and Era of; Mali (Republic of): Nationalism, Federation, Independence.**

Further Reading

Maharaux, A. *L'Industrie au Mali.* Paris: L'Harmattan et CNRS, 1986.

Meillassoux, C. "A class analysis of the bureaucratic process in Mali." *Journal of Development Studies.* 6 (January 1970): 97–110.

———. "The Social Structure of Modern Bamako." *Africa.* 35, no. 2 (April 1965): 125–142.

Roberts, R. L. *Warriors, Merchants, and Slaves: The State and the Economy in the Middle Niger Valley, 1700–1914.* Pala Alto, Calif.: Stanford University Press, 1987.

Snyder, F. G. *One Party Government in Mali: Transition Towards Control.* New Haven, Conn.: Yale University Press, 1965.

Mali, Republic of: Nationalism, Federation, Independence

In Mali, which was known as Soudan français (French Sudan) during the colonial era, anticolonial demands began with the arrival of the French and continued to be expressed as long as they remained in the territory. Such demands took various forms, ranging from resistance to the census, taxation, and schooling, to open revolts. However, they did not take on a more nationalistic tone, in favor of independence, until World War II, when the recruitment of infantrymen, and the rising burdens of taxation and forced labor induced by the war effort, led to increasing discontent. The Brazzaville conference of February 8, 1944, which recommended better representation of the colonies in the future but refused to grant them self-government, did nothing to reduce this discontent.

After the war the new international context, notably the weakening of the French colonial system and the confrontation between the major blocs, reinforced desires for emancipation among the Sudanese. The *évolués* ("the developed" or "progressive"), as African intellectuals were then known, established numerous associations, such as the Foyer du Soudan (Sudan the

Homeland), led by Mamadou Konaté, or Art et travail (Art and Labor), led by Modibo Keita. The first political expression of the Sudanese people occurred on October 21, 1945, when just 3,500 of them were authorized to elect a single representative to the Assemblée nationale constituante française (French National Constituent Assembly). This exercise in consultation led to the victory of Fily Dabo Sissoko, who was also reelected on June 21, 1946, when the second Assemblée constituante (Constituent Assembly) was chosen, at the expense of Mamadou Konaté, the Secretary General of the Sudanese section of the Confédération générale du travail (CGT, General Confederation of Labour).

Meanwhile, the first political parties had begun to be recognized from the beginning of 1946: the Parti démocratique soudanais (PDS, Sudanese Democratic Party), which was close to the Parti communiste français (PCF) (French Communist Party); the Bloc soudanais (Sudanese Bloc), which was close to the Section française de l'Internationale ouvrière (SFIO, French Section of the Workers International, or Socialist Party); and, finally, the Parti soudanais progressiste (PSP, Sudanese Progressive Party), led by Fily Dabo Sissoko, which was favored by the French administration. Opposition crystallized around the issue of the Congress of Bamako, in October 1946, which saw the creation of the Rassemblement démocratique africain (RDA, African Democratic Rally). The Union soudanaise (US, Sudanese Union), of which Modibo Keita was Secretary General, became the RDA's section for the French Sudan, through a merger between Mamadou Konaté's Bloc soudanais and Modibo Keita's PDS, but Fily Dabo Sissoko rejected the RDA's connections with the PCF and refused to join it.

In the elections held on November 10, 1946, for the three Sudanese seats in the National Assembly, the PSP and the US-RDA began a struggle that was to last until 1958. The PSP was victorious up to 1956. Thus, in 1946 it sent two deputies, Fily Dabo Sissoko and Jean Silvandre, to the Assemblée nationale, while the US-RDA was represented by Mamadou Konaté alone. The outcome was the same on June 17, 1951, when their mandates had to be renewed. Similarly, in the elections for the newly created territorial assemblies the PSP won twenty-seven seats, as against thirteen for the US-RDA.

Things started to change in January 1956, when the French Sudan was to elect four deputies. The US-RDA obtained a majority and won two seats, for Konaté and Keita. In the territorial elections, which were crucial because they were to put in place the institutions established under the Framework Law of June 23, 1956, there was a veritable electoral landslide in favor of the US-RDA, which won fifty-seven seats, as against six for the PSP. As a result, it was the US-RDA that formed the first council of ministers for the French Sudan, on May 21, 1957. The executive was headed by Jean-Marie Koné because Modibo Keita had in the meantime become, first, a deputy speaker of the National Assembly, and then secretary of state for France d'outre-mer (the French Overseas Territories). Over the course of succeeding years, Fily Dabo Sissoko and other members of the PSP joined the US-RDA, which had no opposition by 1959.

Another rupture had begun, however; this time between those who opposed the existing federations and those who favored them. This rupture became obvious in September 1957 at the RDA congress. The majority of delegates there supported the retention of the federations, as advocated by the Senegalese leader Léopold Sedar Senghor, so that the redistribution of resources between the territories could continue. However, the president of the RDA, Félix Houphouët-Boigny, rejected the idea. This conflict became all-important after the referendum of September 28, 1958, in which a large majority voted "Yes" to the new constitution of the Fifth Republic.

The two camps proved to have taken up entrenched positions at the federal congress, held in Bamako in December 1958, at which the "federalist" delegations from Senegal, the French Sudan, Upper Volta, and Dahomey decided that their territories should unite as "Mali," in memory of the historic empire of that name. At Dakar on January 14,1959, these delegations established a federal constituent assembly and elected Modibo Keita as its speaker. However, when the time came to ratify the constitution drafted by this assembly, only the French Sudan and Senegal adopted it, as of January 22, 1959. The Federation of Mali therefore brought only two territories together when it was officially launched on April 4, 1959, with Léopold S. Senghor leading the Federal Assembly and Modibo Keita as chief executive. Negotiations with France began in January 1960, and on June 20 France recognized the independence of the Federation of Mali.

The federation was to have a brief existence of precisely three months, as dissension grew rapidly between the Senegalese, who feared Sudanese domination, and the Sudanese, who preferred to reinforce the integration of the new state. Political confrontations, disagreements over federal structures, and the personal rivalry between Senghor and Keita led to crisis. The elections to various responsible posts, held in Dakar on August 20, 1960, became the pretext for the split. Sudanese politicians were arrested by Senegalese troops and sent back to Sudan by train under military arrest, while the National Assembly of Senegal unilaterally proclaimed their country independent. On September 11, France ratified this proclamation; it then sponsored Senegal's application for membership in the United Nations. Having lost all hope of restoring the federation, the former French Sudan in turn proclaimed its independence on September 22, retaining the name Mali. Modibo Keita was to continue to preside over its destiny until he was overthrown in a coup d'étât on November 19, 1968.

This ephemeral and isolated attempt to unite former colonies within a larger federation, which would have greater economic and financial viability, had misfired. The "Balkanization" of the former French West Africa became irreversible: the desire for the unity of Africa had given way to nationalisms.

PIERRE BOILLEY

See also: **Mali Empire, Sundiata and Origins of; Mali, Republic of: Keita, Modibo, Life and Era of.**

Further Reading

Ageron, C. R. *La décolonisation française.* Paris: Armand Colin, 1991.

Ansprenger, F. *The Dissolution of the Colonial Empires.* London: Routledge, 1989.

Benoist, J. R. de. *Le Mali.* 2nd ed. Paris: L'Harmattan, 1998.

Crowder, M., ed. *Cambridge History of Africa.* Vol. 8, *1940–1975.* Cambridge: Cambridge University Press, 1984.

Diarrah, C. O. *Le Mali de Modibo Keita.* Paris: L'Harmattan, 1986.

Foltz, W. J. *From French West Africa to the Mali Federation.* New Haven, Conn.: Yale University Press, 1965.

Holland, R. *European Decolonization, 1918–1981: An Introduction Survey.* London: Macmillan, 1985.

Mali, Republic of: Keita, Modibo, Life and Era of

President of Mali

Modibo Keita (1915–1977) stood in the elections for the Assemblée constituante française (French Constituent Assembly) on October 21, 1945, but lost to Fily Dabo Sissoko. He then became involved in the Parti Démocratique soudanais (PDS, Sudanese Democratic Party), which was close to the Parti communiste français (PCF, French Communist Party). Next, he joined the Bloc soudanais (Sudanese Bloc), in opposition to Fily Dabo Sissoko's Parti soudanais progressiste (PSP, Sudanese Progressive Party), which was supported by the colonial administration. The PSP was victorious once again in the elections for the second Constituent Assembly, on June 2, 1946.

At the Congress of Bamako (October 18–21, 1946), Modibo Keita was a delegate from French Sudan and took part in the creation of the Rassemblement démocratique africain (RDA, African Democratic Rally). Its section in French Sudan took the name of the Union soudanaise (US, Sudanese Union), and in January 1947 Keita became its general secretary. After he had denounced the "slave-master regime" of the French administrator in a speech at Sikasso, he was arrested on February 21, 1947, and transported to the Santé prison in Paris, but he was freed two months later. This allowed him to play an active role in the major railway workers' strike at the end of 1947.

In 1948 Keita was elected to the Territorial Assembly of French Sudan, and then, in 1953, he became an adviser to the French Union. In the legislative elections of January 1956, he was elected as a deputy to the French National Assembly, and he became its deputy speaker in October that year. Finally, in November, he was elected mayor of Bamako. This high standing in the political world led to his appointment in 1957 as secretary of state for France d'outre-mer (the French Overseas Territories). During the constitutional referendum campaign of 1958, Modibo Keita adopted a decidedly federalist position and called for a "Yes" vote.

After the proclamation of the République soudanaise (Sudanese Republic) in November 1958, Keita became the presiding officer of its Great Council, but he did not give up his preference for unification. However, the opponents of unification, notably Félix Houphouët-Boigny, ensured that the Fédération du Mali (Federation of Mali), established in April 1959, brought together only Senegal and the former French Sudan. Modibo Keita was appointed head of the federal government, while Léopold Sedar Senghor became the speaker of its Assembly. The Federation became independent on June 20, 1960, but rivalries within the government and political divergences led to its collapse soon afterward. Modibo Keita and the other representatives of the former French Sudan were expelled and sent to Bamako in August 1960, and Senegal unilaterally declared independence. On September 22, 1960, Mali, reduced to the former French Sudan alone, declared independence in its turn, with Modibo Keita as its president.

Keita's activities as leader of Mali, which he sought to lead in the direction of socialism, had uneven effects. He undoubtedly had some success in external relations. He never ceased to agitate for African unity, starting out by joining the Casablanca Group, and then taking part in the conference that established the Organization of African Unity in May 1963. He also committed Mali to the movement of nonaligned countries, which selected him to represent them in talks with U.S. President John F. Kennedy in 1961. Mali also undeniably derived significant international recognition from the relations that Keita maintained with the Eastern Bloc, and from his international travels, not only to the Soviet Union and China, but also to many other countries in Africa, Asia, and the Middle East. In addition, he successfully oversaw the orderly ending of French colonization, bringing about the departure of the last French soldiers in September 1961 and, in 1962, signing the first agreements with France on economic and cultural cooperation.

Keita's domestic policies were not as successful. Hoping to secure economic independence for Mali, he started a currency reform in July 1962: the country left the Franc Zone and the Malian franc was introduced instead. This initiative failed, however. The economic difficulties that arose from agricultural underproduction, low productivity, and the decline in the balance of trade were aggravated by the weakness of the Malian currency. In 1967 Mali was forced to rejoin the Franc Zone, and its currency was devalued by 50 per cent in the process.

The realization of the original currency reform had also revealed President Keita's authoritarian conception of government. When opposition by the merchants led to riots, the government put the former leaders of the independence movement, Fily Dabo Sissoko and Hamadoun Dicko, on trial, and had them condemned to death. Their sentences were commuted to life imprisonment, but both prisoners met their deaths in 1964, in circumstances that remain unclear but do not reflect well on Modibo Keita. In 1963 a rebellion broke out among the Tuaregs of the Saharan massif of Adrar des Ifoghas, in the north of the country, who opposed the Malian government and its "socialist" reforms. Modibo Keita, anxious about the unity of the country, once again chose to adopt a policy of repression, and hundreds were killed. The revolt was crushed in 1964, but the lasting distrust that resulted from these events was to undermine relations between the nomads and the settled population for some time to come.

Excessive tendencies toward socialism and bureaucracy in society and the economy produced other forms of discontent. In particular, peasants objected to the granting of monopolies over the commercial sale of produce to state companies and a network of cooperatives, as well as to the creation of "collective fields" in every village. In June 1968 an uprising at Ouolossébougou was met with harsh repression, which helped to deepen existing tensions. Keita tried to reassert his grip on politics by creating a "Comité national de défense de la Révolution" (National Committee for the Defence of the Revolution) and, on January 22, 1968, replacing the National Assembly, which he had dissolved, with a legislative body of twenty-eight people. On November 19, 1968, he was overthrown by a group of army officers and placed in detention, first at Kati, and then at the prison in Kidal, where he remained until his death in May 1977. Nevertheless, Keita retains a significant positive reputation in Mali, where a center dedicated to his memory was recently opened.

PIERRE BOILLEY

See also: **Mali, Republic of: Nationalism, Federation, Independence.**

Biography

Born in Bamako in 1915. Elementary school 1925–1931, higher elementary school 1931–1934, école normale William Ponty (William Ponty teacher-training school) 1934–1936. Elementary school teacher in Bamako and Sikasso. General secretary of the US-RDA from January 1947 onward. Arrested in February 1947 and released two months later. Elected to the Territorial Assembly of French Sudan. Adviser to the French Union in 1953. Elected as a deputy to the French National Assembly in January 1956; became its deputy speaker in October. Elected mayor of Bamako in November 1956. Twice appointed a secretary of state, 1957–1958 (in the governments of Bourgès-Maunoury and Gaillard). Elected president of the Great Council of the Fédération de l'Afrique Occidentale (AOF, West African Federation) in January 1959 and head of the government of the Federation of Mali in April. President of Mali from the declaration of independence onward. Received the Lenin Prize for Peace in May 1963. Arrested by a group of army officers on November 19, 1968 and interned in the prison at Kidal, in northern Mali, until his death. Funeral in Bamako on May 17, 1977.

Further Reading

Ajayi, J. F. A., and Crowder, M. *History of West Africa.* London: Longman, 1974.

Diagouraga, M. *Modibo Keita, un destin* [*Modibo Keita, A Fate*]. Paris: LivreSud, 1992.

Diarrah, C. O. *Le Mali de Modibo Keita.* Paris: L'Harmattan, 1986.

Hazard, J. N. "Marxian Socialism in Africa: The Case of Mali." *Comparative Politics.* (October 1969): 1–16.

Snachter-Morgenthau, R. *Political Parties in French-speaking West Africa.* New York: Oxford University Press, 1964.

Snyder, F. G. "The Political Thought of Modibo Keita." *Journal of Modern African Studies.* 5 (1967): 79–106.

Mali, Republic of: Traoré, Moussa, Life and Era of

Head of State of the Republic of Mali, 1968–1991

Moussa Traoré (1936–) was a young lieutenant when he participated in the 1968 military coup that overthrew Modibo Keita, the first president of independent Mali. Senior officers, who engineered the coup, feared that African leaders, such as Sekou Touré (Guinea), Félix Houphouët-Boigny (Côte d'Ivoire), or Léopold Sédar Senghor (Senegal), might come to Keita's defense. Consequently they readily agreed to have Traoré head the Comité Militaire de Liberation Nationale (Military Committee of National Liberation, or CMLN) they formed, which was to govern Mali for ten years.

His preparation for the position was scant: officer training at the Military College of Fréjus (France) and seven years in the Malian army, mostly as military instructor at Kati. At first his job was facilitated by support from the Malian population, tired of the economic deprivations caused by Keita's failed socialist experiment. The CMLN proclaimed a new order and promised reforms and a return to civilian government. In 1974 it held a referendum on a new constitution that was favorably received by Malians, and in 1979 it sponsored presidential elections. Moussa Traoré, by then a general, was elected to preside over a civilian government, but democratization was only a slogan. Traoré had already ruthlessly eliminated all opposition and potential rivals, and institutionalized a one-party system. Through his party, the Union Démocratique du Peuple Malien, he controlled all aspects of Malian life. He was reelected in 1985.

Within the parameters of his dictatorship, Traoré did endeavor to improve conditions in poverty-stricken Mali and to gain international respect and support for his country. He made progress in unifying a nation made up of numerous diverse ethnic groups speaking multiple languages. He attempted to increase the yield of subsistence farming and to introduce new agricultural techniques for the cultivation of the main cash crops, peanuts, and cotton. He gained international recognition as president of the Organization of African Unity (OAU) and favorable press for his 1987 Bamako Initiative to enhance the availability of medicinal products in Africa, and for co-chairing the UN World Summit for Children, held in New York in September 1990.

Traoré was pragmatic. He did not abruptly reverse Keita's popular socialist policies; instead, he supported existing programs with resumed financial aid from France and other Western donors. However, severe droughts repeatedly exacerbated poverty in essentially agricultural Mali. In order to receive aid and attract foreign investments, Traoré had to comply with the austerity programs demanded by the International Monetary Fund (IMF) and the World Bank. He had to cut government spending, liberalize the economy, and privatize state-owned businesses. He found himself in a bind: the changes caused widespread unemployment and economic hardship, which triggered massive protests by government employees, workers, and students in 1987. To pacify them, Traoré implemented several reforms. He dismissed some corrupt public officials, gave civilians partial access to government through periodic local and National Assembly elections and appointment to the Council of Ministers, and made minor economic concessions. These, however, were insufficient to prevent the IMF from suspending aid. The government found itself unable to meet payrolls. Protests and strikes resumed.

Border disputes with neighboring countries and ethnic upheavals in northern Mali, moreover, required destabilizing military expenditures. In 1985 Traoré fought brief wars with Burkina Faso over a narrow strip of desert in the Agacher region. Fortunately, the International Tribunal in The Hague was able to work out a compromise acceptable to all; however, no such solution was available regarding Touareg rebellions.

The national borders created by colonization and confirmed at independence had disrupted the nomadic Tuareg's patterns of transhumance and transformed about 300,000 Tuareg into Malian citizens. Deprived of their traditional livelihood, they started rebelling in 1962. Droughts in the 1970s and 1980s deepened their plight. Rebellion spread, and Traoré sent the army to restore order. The heavy-handed repression provoked further, more serious uprisings. A relative peace was achieved only after Traoré's presidency had ended in 1991. At the start of the twenty-first century, the Tuaregs' survival is still not assured.

These problems, along with the ravages caused by droughts in the mid-1980s, and the fluctuations of world prices for the cash crops that were Mali's only export, undermined Traore's hold on the country. In 1988, as democratic movements gained momentum in Mali as in other African countries, voices demanding liberalization and a multiparty political system grew louder. Civil disobedience became the order of the day in January 1991. The National Workers Union of Mali declared an open-ended general strike, and daily unruly demonstrations took place in the capital, Bamako. Traoré refused all concessions and ordered the army to shoot into crowds.

The widespread opposition had organized new political parties. In March 1991, Moussa Traoré's regime was overthrown in a palace revolution led by lieutenant colonel Amadou Toumani Touré, former commander of the presidential guard, who became the head of the Conseil National de Reconciliation (National Council of Reconciliation). The council removed all existing governmental institutions, sought civilian participation, and declared its intention to move rapidly toward democratization. Indeed, by April 1991 a transitional government made up of both military and civilians was in place. Alpha Oumar Konaré was elected president in free elections in 1992.

Moussa Traoré was tried as a murderous dictator in 1993 and sentenced to death. The sentence was never carried out, and in 1997 Konaré commuted it to life imprisonment. The former president was tried again in late 1998, this time for financial misdeeds. Again he was sentenced to die, although estimates of the seriousness of his economic crimes vary. In 1999 Konaré commuted this second sentence in a spirit of national reconciliation. In 2002, just before leaving office, Konaré announced an official pardon, which Traoré reportedly refused.

NATALIE SANDOMIRSKY

See also: **Mali (Republic of).**

Further Reading

Bingen, J., et al. (eds.) *Democracy and Development in Mali.* Lansing: Michigan State University Press, 2000.
Djime, H. *L'Aube des Démocraties: la Chute de Moussa Traoré* [The Dawn of Democracies: the Fall of Moussa Traoré]. Bamako: L'imprimerie G. Mounkoro, 1997.
Konaté, H. *Le procès crimes de sang* [The Blood Crimes Trial]. Bamako: Editions Jamana, 1993.
Stamm, A. L. *Mali.* Santa Barbara, Calif.: ABC-CLIO, 1998.

Mali, Republic of: Politics, Economics: 1990s

During the 1990s there was a veritable transformation of Mali, which undoubtedly changed more in those ten years than in the three decades that preceded them. The first upheaval that Mali underwent was its transition to democracy. Ever since independence, the political life of the country had been shaped by single-party regimes: that of Modibo Keita's Union soudanaise-Rassemblement démocratique africain (US-RDA, Sudanese Union-African Democratic Rally) from 1960 to 1968, then that of Moussa Traoré's Union démocratique du peuple malien (UDPM, Malian People's Democratic Union) until 1991. In addition, the circumstances were not exactly favorable, since there was a rebellion by the Tuaregs and the Moors in the north of the country, and the economy was in a disastrous state. Nevertheless, Mali has been able to handle these difficulties in a positive way.

In June 1990 the first offensives by the Tuareg Mouvement populaire de l'Azawad (MPA, Azawad People's Movement) and the Moorish Front islamique et arabe de l'Azawad (FIAA, Azawad Islamic and Arab Front) were harshly suppressed by the Malian army: the north of the country became a zone of slaughter, and large numbers of nomads fled from the region to take refuge in Algeria or Mauritania. However, in December 1990 the government and the rebels signed the Tamanrasset Accords.

In the south, meanwhile, democratic forces organized "associations"—since parties were banned—such as the Association des élèves et étudiants maliens (AEEM, Association of Malian Schoolchildren and Students), the Association pour la démocratie au Mali (ADEMA, Association for Democracy in Mali), and the Congrès national d'initiative démocratique (CNID, National Congress for the Democratic Initiative). These provided frameworks for the discontent that had been exacerbated by the dictatorial character of Moussa Traoré's government, its deplorable management of the economy, and its nepotism. Popular demonstrations, and strikes by schoolchildren and students, led to riots in Bamako from March 22 to March 25, 1991, which resulted in death for scores of people and injuries for many others. The Malian army then took power, under the leadership of Amadou Toumani Touré, and on March 31, 1991, it established the Comité transitoire de salut public (CTSP, Transitional Committee of Public Safety).

The new regime accepted a multiparty system and organized a national conference over the following months. Moussa Traoré was imprisoned along with his wife, Mariam: he was twice condemned to death by the Bamako Criminal Court, in 1994 for his crimes of violence, and in 1998 for his economic crimes. While the rebels launched new offensives in the North, the CTSP entered into lengthy negotiations, accepted mediation by France, Algeria, and Mauritania, and, on April 11, 1992, succeeded in signing a national pact with the Mouvements et fronts Unifiés de l'Azawad (MFUA, Unified Azawad Movements and Fronts), providing for the integration of the rebel fighters and greater involvement of the northern regions in the political and economic life of Mali.

In 1992 there was a series of exercises in democracy: the referendum on the new constitution (January 12), and elections for municipal authorities (January 19), the legislature (March 8), and the presidency (April 12 and 26). The ADEMA won two-thirds of the seats in the National Assembly, and its founder, Alpha Omar Konaré, became the first democratically elected president of Mali. Amadou Toumani Touré gave up power, as he had promised he would, and returned to his military duties.

However, President Konaré, who was reelected on May 11, 1997, for a second and final five-year term, had to face some difficult challenges. On the political plane, he had to deal with the rise of a radical opposition, concentrated in the Collectif des partis politiques d'opposition (COPPO, Collective of Opposition Political Parties), which had decided on a total boycott of the referendum and the elections. The disturbances that arose from its intransigence did not end until 1999, when the COPPO finally disintegrated. In the North, there were delays in the implementation of the National Pact, confrontations between the army and the rebel movements, which had not been disarmed, and rivalries between the nomads and the Songhay fighters of the Mouvement patriotique Ganda Koy (MPGK, Ganda Koy Patriotic Movement), which gave rise to fears of new outbursts. However, the region gradually returned to a state of calm normality, symbolized by the ceremony of the "Flame of Peace," in Timbuktu on March 27, 1996, when thousands of weapons were burned and all the different rebel movements formally dissolved themselves.

The improvement in the situation in the north allowed the Tuareg refugees to return home in stages, in a process that ended in May 1997 for those who had taken refuge in Mauritania, and in October for those returning from Burkina Faso. Finally, the special status envisaged in the National Pact exclusively for the northern regions was transformed into a measure of large-scale decentralization that was extended to all the regions of Mali. The lengthy process of preparing technical resources and personnel for this decentralization culminated in the communal consultations of May 2 and June 6, 1999, which completed the process of creating 682 new communes (communities) intended to bring government closer to local populations.

On the economic plane, the successive governments of democratic Mali succeeded in redressing the catastrophic conditions that prevailed at the beginning of the 1990s. On September 15, 1993, Abdoulaye Sékou Sow submitted proposals aimed at reducing the budget deficit, which was the main requirement of the IMF, and Ibrahim Boubacar Keita, who became prime minister since February 1994, succeeded in convincing both the IMF and the World Bank to grant Mali financial assistance amounting to 1.2 million French francs. Mali also received aid from its main partners, most notably France and the European Union. A little while earlier, Mali, along with the other countries in the Franc Zone, had felt the effects of the 50 per cent devaluation of the CFA franc initiated by France and the IMF. This devaluation created significant problems for large sections of the population, but it also allowed Mali to stabilize its international trade by reviving its exports, notably of its main product, cotton, of which it is the second largest producer in Africa after Egypt, but also of agricultural produce and gold. Following the success of the Structural Adjustment Plan for 1992–1995, negotiations were reopened in February 1996, and in 1997 the plan was extended for a further three years.

Mali has succeeded in restructuring its public sector, while maintaining a high priority for education, and in improving its balance of trade. For several years it has enjoyed a series of bumper cereal harvests as well as exceptional cotton harvests. The inflation rate, which exceeded 30 per cent at the beginning of the 1990s, has been brought under control: by 1999 it had fallen to 4.2 per cent. The economy has been revived, with growth rates being held steady at between 4 and 6 per cent a year. Numerous problems remain, including a low endowment of energy sources, an underdeveloped industrial sector, and difficulties with tax receipts, in a country where most of the population live below the threshold of poverty. Nevertheless, there has been real political and economic progress during the 1990s.

PIERRE BOILLEY

Further Reading

Ag Youssouf, I., and R. E. Poulton. *A Peace of Timbuktu: Democratic Governance, Development, and African Peacemaking.* New York and Geneva: UNIDIR, 1998.

Boilley, P. "Aux origines des conflits dans les zones touarègues et maures." *Relations internationales et stratégiques.* IRIS/Université Paris-Nord. 14, (1996): 100–107.

———. "La démocratisation au Mali: un processus exemplaire." *Relations internationales et stratégiques.* IRIS/Université Paris-Nord. 14 (1994): 119–121.

Cerdes. *Le processus démocratique malien de 1960 à nos jours.* Bamako: Editions Donniya, 1997.

Diarrah, C. O. *Le défi démocratique malien.* Paris: L'Harmattan, 1996.

———. *Vers la IIIe République du Mali.* Paris: L'Harmattan, 1991.

Lode, K. *Synthèse du Processus des Rencontres Intercommunautaires du Nord Mali (août 1995 à mars 1996).* Stavanger: Impress-AEN, 1996.

Programme de Décentralisation. *Rapport de synthèse des rencontres régionales sur le découpage territorial (avril à juillet 1995).* Bamako: Mission de décentralisation de la République du Mali, 1995.

Ronnfeldt, C., and R. Andersen. *Options for Preventative Action: Multilateral Development Organisations' Impact on the Conflicts in Mali and Rwanda.* Fridtjof Nansen Institute (September 1998).

Mamluk Beylicate: *See* Egypt: Ottoman, 1517–1798: Mamluk Beylicate.

Mamluk Dynasty: *See* Egypt: Mamluk Dynasty (1250–1517): Army and Iqta' System; Egypt.

Mamluk Dynasty: *See* Egypt: Mamluk Dynasty (1250–1517): Plague; Literature, Western: Africa in.

Mandates: League of Nations and United Nations

The movement for the protection of colonial subjects began to form in the sixteenth century when Spanish social reformers urged Emperor Charles V to end forced labor in Spain's American colonies, set up free and independent labor communities, and use cash incentives instead of slave labor to encourage agricultural production. The goal was to halt human exploitation and the decline of the native American population. In the eighteenth century, British political leaders asserted that at the core of the concept of trusteeship was the humane treatment of colonial subjects, and that colonies were "a sacred trust" of imperial powers. In India, for example, Edmund Burke believed that British colonial authorities should not only promote British imperial interests but also protect Indian life, culture, and property against the depredations of over-zealous colonial officials. By the beginning of the nineteenth century, the doctrine of trusteeship had received widespread support from theologians, philosophers, moralists, social reformers, and politicians, all of whom advocated a policy of fairer treatment of the native populations in far-flung colonial territories.

The outbreak of World War I in 1914 accelerated the quest for the creation of an international organization capable of mediating international disputes and promoting the welfare of colonial peoples. In an address to a joint session of Congress on January 8, 1918, U.S. President Woodrow Wilson laid out Fourteen Points upon which peace could be maintained in the postwar years. In the Fifth Point, Wilson envisaged an "absolutely impartial adjustment of all colonial claims" based on the interests of the people. The realization of that goal proved problematic at the 1919 Paris Peace Conference. Through secret treaties Britain, France, and their war-time allies (with the exception of the United States, an associated power) resolved to maintain their respective colonial empires while agreeing not to relinquish control over enemy colonies they had captured during the war. The justification was that these colonies posed a threat to world peace and international commerce. In the end, the idea of an international trusteeship as a first step toward the protection of colonial populations and the eradication of colonial rule applied only to the German and Turkish colonies in the Middle East, Africa, and the Pacific Ocean.

Article 22 of the Covenant of the League of Nations created the mandate system that encapsulated the principles enunciated by the various social and political reformers by the dawn of the twentieth century. The allied and associated powers divided the former German and Turkish colonies into three classes of mandates. In descending order, each class of mandates reflected a degree or two of readiness for independence. The class A mandates, administered by Britain and France, were colonies that formerly belonged to the Turkish Empire in the Middle East (Trans-Jordan, Lebanon, Syria, Palestine, and Iraq). The peace conferees considered these to have attained a level of political development such that they could be granted provisional recognition as independent states with their own self-governing institutions. The primary responsibility of the "advanced nation" to which they were entrusted was to provide administrative advice and assistance until they achieved full independence. The class B mandates, adjudged by the powers to be politically less advanced than those in the Middle East, were located in Africa. They included Tanganyika, Togoland, the Cameroons, and Ruanda-Urundi; they were administered by Britain, France, and Belgium.

These mandatory powers undertook to nurture freedom of conscience and religion, suppress the slave trade and the traffic in arms and liquor, maintain the open door, and prevent the establishment of military fortifications and the training of the local populations for offensive military purposes. The remaining former German colonies in Africa and the Pacific Ocean were categorized as class C mandates. These included southwest Africa, New Guinea, Nauru, Western Samoa, and the Caroline, Mariana, and Marshall Islands. Since the allied and associated powers considered these territories to be politically the least advanced of Germany's former colonies, they were administered "as integral portions" of the mandatory powers and in accordance with their existing laws. In many other respects, the C mandates were similar to the B mandates in Africa to the extent that they lacked self-governing institutions or local autonomy. To ensure compliance with Article 22, each mandatory power was required to submit annual reports to the Permanent Mandates Commission (PMC). Further, the terms of the individual mandates could not be altered without the consent of the Council of the League of Nations.

Thus, Article 22 of the covenant formalized the idea that the well-being and development of colonial subjects was "a sacred trust of civilization" to be monitored by the League of Nations. However, the division of former enemy colonies into three classes of mandates concluded a chapter in the secret territorial arrangements of the Great War. It represented a compromise between the principles of self-determination enunciated by President Woodrow Wilson and the allies' insistence upon the outright annexation of the former German and Turkish colonies as the prize of victory. In theory the mandate system placed these colonies under the "tutelage" of the "advanced nations" and admonished them to further their well-being and development toward independence. In practice the mandates were governed as colonies of the mandatory powers. In the A and B mandates, local leaders were excluded from the central administration of their respective territories. For example, in Tanganyika the first two Africans to serve on the Legislative Council were appointed in 1945; the number was increased to four by the end of the decade. The Executive Council remained a preserve of British colonial officials until the 1950s, when the first two Africans were appointed to it.

World War II not only hastened the decline of Europe's colonial empires but also rendered obsolete the entire machinery of the League of Nations, which formally ceased to exist on April 18, 1946. The postwar era began with the establishment of the United Nations Organization (UNO) in 1945 and the adoption of a wide-ranging resolution on mandates by the General Assembly. The resolution reiterated the purposes of Article 22 of the Covenant of the League of Nations. Apart from noting with satisfaction the manner in which the League of Nations had performed its supervisory functions over the mandates, the General Assembly also commended the PMC for its success in guiding Iraq, Syria, Lebanon, and Jordan toward independence between 1932 and 1946. Palestine remained problematic, Jews and Arabs fought for control before and following the creation of Israel in 1948.

With the demise of the League of Nations, the UNO assumed responsibility for the administration of the mandates. Under Chapter XI, Article 73 of the United Nations Charter (adopted at San Francisco on June 26, 1945), the A and B mandates were renamed "non-self-governing" trust territories under the supervision of the same mandatory powers that had administered them since 1919. Chapters XII and XIII provided for the establishment of an international trusteeship system to replace the mandate system. The Trusteeship Council succeeded the PMC. Its functions included the examination of annual reports and petitions and the conduct of tours of inspection of the various trust territories.

While reaffirming the principles entailed in Article 22 of the Covenant of the League of Nations, the new UN Charter took a positive step further by recognizing the growing demand for self-rule in the trust territories especially since the adoption of the Atlantic Charter by the United States of America and Britain in 1941. Among other things, the UN Charter urged the administering powers to respect the culture of the people, promote their economic, social, and educational advancement, treat them justly, and protect them against abuses of all kinds. In a welcome departure from past practices, the charter also called upon Britain, France and the other powers to take account of the political aspirations of the people as they develop free political institutions for eventual self-government. With the exception of Southwest Africa (Namibia), which became independent in 1990 after a protracted national liberation war against South Africa, the administering state, all of the African trust territories achieved independent statehood between 1960 and 1962. Apart from Palau (part of the Caroline Islands) and the Mariana Islands, which are still U.S. territories, the Pacific trust territories won their independence between 1962 and 1986.

World War II marked a significant turning point in the history of colonial rule and the trusteeship system. Contrasted with the previous mandate system of the League of Nations, the UN trusteeship system recognized the right of self-determination of colonial peoples as an essential element in the maintenance of peace in the post-war world. By recognizing that right, the UN Charter ended a quarter century of political uncertainty for the world's colonial peoples and territories. The keys to understanding the change of direction were the nationalist frustrations engendered by the failure of the 1919 Peace Conference to take a resolute stand in favor of self-determination, the inability of the League of Nations to prevent World War II, the Atlantic Charter's enunciation of the right to national self-determination in the colonies, and the nationalist ferment of the wartime and postwar years. After centuries of political agitation by social reformers, politicians, theologians, and other concerned groups and individuals, the UN trusteeship system finally ushered in a new era of decolonization in Africa and the Pacific Ocean.

PETER A. DUMBUYA

See also: **Colonialism: Impact on African Societies; World War I: Survey; World War I: North and Saharan Africa; World War II: French West Africa, Equatorial Africa; World War II: North Africa; World War II: Sub-Saharan Africa: Economic Impact.**

Further Reading

Albertini, R. Von. *Decolonization: The Administration and Future of the Colonies, 1919–1960*, Garden City, N.Y.: Doubleday, 1971.

Ambrosius, L. E. *Wilsonian Statecraft: Theory and Practice of Liberal Internationalism During World War I.* Wilmington, Del.: Scholarly Resources, 1991.

Baker, R. S. *Woodrow Wilson and World Settlement*, 3 vols., Garden City, N.Y.: Doubleday, 1922.

Chowdhuri, R. N. *International Mandates and Trusteeship Systems: A Comparative Study*. The Hague: Martinus Nijhoff, 1955.

Digre, B. *Imperialism's New Clothes: The Repartition of Tropical Africa, 1914–1919*. New York: Peter Lang, 1990.

Dumbuya, P. A. *Tanganyika Under International Mandate, 1919–1946*. Lanham, N.Y., and London: University Press of America, 1995.

George, D. L. *Memoirs of the Peace Conference*. 2 vols., New Haven: Yale University Press, 1939.

Hall, H. D. *Mandates, Dependencies, and Trusteeship*. New York: Kraus Reprint Company, 1972.

Knock, T. J. *To End All Wars: Woodrow Wilson and the Quest for a New World Order*. New York and Oxford: Oxford University Press, 1992.

Northedge, F. S. *The League of Nations: Its Life and Times, 1920–1946*. New York: Holmes and Meier, 1986.

Walters, F. P. *A History of the League of Nations*, London: Oxford University Press, 1969.

Mandela, Nelson (1918–)

President of South Africa, Antiapartheid Activist

Nelson Rolihlahla Mandela was born on July 18, 1918, in the small village of Mvezo in the Eastern Cape. Following the death of his father, Mandela was "adopted" by the egent of the Tembus, Chief Jongintaba Dalindyebo. With the intention of preparing the boy for a career as a councillor to the Tembu king, the regent sent him to be educated at the Clarkebury Institute, Healdtown College, and the University of Fort Hare.

In 1941 Mandela was expelled from Fort Hare and, faced with an arranged marriage, he fled to Johannesburg. His first job was as a night watchman with Crown Mines. Among his new friends was Walter Sisulu, who would become a lifelong political colleague. Sisulu introduced Mandela to a liberal law firm who employed him as an articled clerk. By 1944 Mandela was an active member of the African National Congress (ANC) Youth League. In the same year he married a young nurse, Evelyn Mase.

As a member of the Youth League, Mandela adopted a position of African nationalism, strongly opposed to the influence of the Communist Party of South Africa. During 1951 Mandela began to accept the importance of a strategic alliance between the ANC and the Communists. In 1952 he played an important organizing role in the Defiance Campaign. In the same year Mandela established the first African law firm in South Africa in partnership with his political colleague, Oliver Tambo.

Throughout most of the 1950s, Mandela was either "banned" or on trial. At the same time he wrote a number of essays and speeches. In 1953, for example, he developed the M-plan, a secret cell-structure for the ANC. In 1956 he contributed an article to *Liberation* on his interpretation of the Freedom Charter. He noted that when the Freedom Charter was instituted "the non-European bourgeoisie will have the opportunity to own in their own name and right mills and factories, and trade and private enterprise will boom and flourish as never before." This sentence would attain great importance in the decades that followed as Mandela had to defend himself against the accusation that he was a secret member of the Communist Party. In the mid-1950s, Mandela's first marriage broke down and he married Winnie Nomzamo Madikizela in 1958.

Mandela had been arrested in 1956 and charged with treason along with 155 other political leaders. Five years later, the treason trial ended and Mandela and his co-accused were found to be innocent of the charges leveled against them. In the wake of the Sharpeville massacre and the banning of the ANC (1960), Mandela decided to go underground and rapidly entered South African popular mythology as the "Black Pimpernel." In the same year he assumed the leadership of Umkhonto we Sizwe (MK), the military wing of the ANC. After extensive travels through Africa and a brief visit to London, Mandela was captured in Natal. In October 1962 he was sentenced to five years imprisonment. Less than a year later, this sentence was overtaken by fresh charges related to the capture of the MK high command at Rivonia in July 1963. Following the Rivonia trial, Mandela was sentenced to life imprisonment in 1964.

Mandela's years in prison steeled and hardened him for the negotiations that lay ahead. He rapidly emerged as the leader of the ANC group of political prisoners on Robben Island. Conditions were grim during the 1960s and visits by relatives were infrequent. However, by the mid-1970s, hard labor was phased out and prisoners were allowed to take part in organized sports and academic study. With the arrival of black consciousness activists following the Soweto uprising, Robben Island became something of a university of revolution. For Mandela, this was the ultimate test of his political skill. Faced with radical youngsters imbued with militant passion, he successfully argued the case for nonracialism and collective discipline. In 1978, to note his sixtieth birthday, the first Free Mandela campaign was launched by the ANC and the antiapartheid movement in London. The Mandela campaigns would grow in magnitude throughout the 1980s.

In 1982 Mandela and a handful of his senior colleagues were transferred from Robben Island to Pollsmoor Prison. Secret talks with representatives of the government began in the mid-1980s, although Mandela engaged in these talks without the authorization of the exiled ANC. In December 1988 he was moved to Victor Verster Prison. In February 1990 President F. W. de Klerk announced Mandela's release and lifted the ban on various liberation organizations. Mandela had served twenty-seven years in prison.

The transition period in South Africa between 1990 and 1994 was tortuous. As the leader of the ANC, in practice, if not to begin with in name, Mandela tended to stand apart from the negotiations, only intervening in moments of crisis. He traveled throughout the world raising funds for the ANC and was greeted with almost universal acclaim, in the process finding himself acknowledged as one of the great iconic figures of the twentieth century. In 1993 Mandela shared the Nobel Peace Prize with F. W. de Klerk although their relationship was marked by resentment. In the same year, following the murder of Chris Hani, Mandela appeared on television to calm the anger of the people. It was apparent that fundamental power had already shifted in South Africa. This was confirmed by South Africa's election in April 1994 during which the ANC won a resounding victory.

As president of South Africa from 1994 to 1999, Mandela devoted his time in office to reconciliation with his former enemies. Although the "Rainbow Nation" suffered economic crisis and burgeoning crime, he was not a hands-on politician; rather, as president Mandela was something of a monarchical figure. In 1998 he married for the third time, to Graca Machel. Mandela retired in 1999, having guided South Africa through its first period of majority rule. Mandela's retirement set something of a precedent in Africa by demonstrating that a great leader can willingly hand over the reins of power.

JAMES SANDERS

See also: **Luthuli, Albert John Mavumbi; Madikizela-Mandela, Winnie; South Africa: Antiapartheid Struggle, International; South Africa: Defiance Campaign, Freedom Charter, Treason Trials: 1952–1960; South Africa: 1994 to the Present; South Africa: Transition, 1990–1994.**

Biography

Born on July 18, 1918, in the small village of Mvezo in the Eastern Cape. Expelled from the University of Fort Hare and moves to Johannesburg to avoid an arranged marriage in 1941. Becomes active in the ANC Youth League. Marries Evelyn Mase in 1944. Established the first African law firm in South Africa with his political colleague Oliver Tambo in 1952. Divorces and marries, to Winnie Nomzamo Madikizela, in 1958. Arrested and charged with treason in 1956. The ANC banned, and Mandela goes "underground," in 1960. Captured in Natal, and sentenced to life imprisonment in 1964. Released February 11, 1990. Shared the Nobel Peace Prize with F. W. de Klerk in 1993. Served as President of South Africa from 1994 to 1999. Married for the third time, to Graca Machel, in 1998. Retired in 1999.

Further Reading

Benson, M. *Nelson Mandela: The Man and the Movement*. London: Penguin, 1994.
Mandela, N. *Long Walk to Freedom*. Rev. ed. London: Abacus, 1995.
———. *Nelson Mandela Speaks: Forging a Democratic, Nonracial South Africa*.
Sampson, A. *Mandela: The Authorised Biography*. London: HarperCollins, 1999.

Mandinka States of Gambia

The Mandinka, a major ethnic group in Gambia, trace their origin to the earliest group of human beings that occupied the Sudanese Belt in the Stone and Iron Ages. These early human beings were hunters and made and used stone and iron weapons such as knives, axes, scrapers, hammers, and needles. Later they made weapons like spears, harpoons, clubs, shields, blowguns, bows, and arrows.

The black population that inhabited the Sudanese Belt occupied a small portion of the area prior to the year 700. They continued to practice agriculture and were able to develop larger and more dense populations than those whose preoccupation was cattle rearing. They eventually colonized the forest areas of West Africa.

During the early Islamic contact period, from 700BCE onward, long distance trade played an increasingly important role in influencing the economic, social, and political patterns of western Sudan. The trade brought wealth to some parts of West Africa, which laid the foundation for social stratification and state formation. When the empire of Ghana emerged, the Mandinkas formed part of the Mande-speaking peoples of the Soninke Clan. The Mande people were also known as Manden, Malinke, Mndinka, or Mandingo.

After the fall of the empire of Ghana in 1076, all the former tributary states that made up the empire regained their independence. It was not until 1235 that a small Mandinka kingdom emerged. The kingdom was ruled by a Mandinka king, Sundiata Keita, who was credited with laying the foundation of the powerful Mali Empire. In fact, according to oral tradition, the Mandinka expansion into Gambia commenced during the rule of Sundiata in the thirteenth century.

Mandinka immigration was carried out through both peaceful means and military expansion. Some Mandinka moved to the Senegambia region prior to the establishment of the Mali Empire. The early migrants traveled south and west in search of better farmland, food, and shelter. Some traders and hunters moved with these people into the well-watered land area in the Senegambia. When they settled, they engaged in agriculture and intermarried with the indigenous ethnic groups of the region.

The military expeditions were carried out at the request of Sundiata. He sent one of his generals, Tiramang Traore, west to conquer Cassamance and Guinea Bissau in the thirteenth century. Consequently, Tiramang defeated the local population easily and laid the foundation of the Kaabu Empire, which eventually stretched as far as Gambia. Kaabu became the center of Mandinka culture. Its capital was located at Kansala. Tiramang also conducted expeditions against the neighboring Jollof Empire on behalf of Sundiata.

The immigration of the Mandinka's from Mali to Gambia resulted in the formation of many Mandinka families as a result of intermarriage. Tiramang was married into the Sanneh family. Mandinka families like Sanyang, Bojang, Conteh, and Jassey trace their ancestry to the inhabitants of the Mali Empire.

Toward the end of the thirteenth century, the Mandinka controlled a land area that stretched from Gambia to Futa Jallon. Several Mandinka states made up the Mandinka Empire of Kaabu: Kantora,Tumaana, Jimara, Wurapina, Nyamina, Jarra, Kiang, Foni, and Kombo. Kombo, a former Jolla state, had been forcefully conquered by the Mandinka. The kingdoms of Baddibu and Barra were overcome by Amari Sonko, another general of Sundiata Keita. Amari established the Sonko dynasty in both kingdoms.

The Mandinka states had a centralized system of government under the *mansas,* or chiefs. The local government was staffed by village heads who were also known as *al-cadi*. They were members of the nobility whose chief function was to distribute land and enforce judicial measures. They presided over minor cases and collected taxes.

From the fourteenth century, trade settlements were established in the Mandinka states. The villages where trade was conducted were large and populous. The impact of the Atlantic trade was felt in Gambia; it played a decisive role in the economic, political, and social evolution of the states in particular and the people in general. From the fifteenth century, success in trade, military expertise, and strong government made it possible for the Kaabu Empire to reach its zenith in the sixteenth century.

The fifteenth century also witnessed the Portuguese exploration of West Africa. The Portuguese conducted a very profitable business with the Mandinka at the time. In 1491 Rodrigo Bebello, a Portuguese, and seven members of his group met with Mandimansa, the Mandinka ruler of Kantora state. They established friendly relations that subsequently led to the development of a regular trading system. The Mandinka traded in gold, slaves, ivory, and beeswax. The commodities were brought from the interior and exchanged with crystal beads, iron bars, brass pans, fire arms and ammunitions, liquors, tobacco, caps, and iron. All the items of trade were measured in bars of iron, which gave them equal quantities of all goods that were exchanged.

The trade in the Mandinka states also attracted the Berbers and the Moors who had settled in Gambia earlier in the eleventh century. The Berbers and Moors who were Muslims opened small Koranic schools where boys were taught to read and write in Arabic. The Mandinka kings enrolled their children in the schools and employed the Muslim teachers, or *marabouts*, to pray and make charms for them.

The *marabouts* also intermarried with local Mandinka women, thus creating Muslim families. Some of the Mandinka who practiced African traditional religions also converted to Islam.

The Mandinka merchants traveled in trade caravans that comprised 40, 50, or 100 people. They used the river valleys to buy and sell. Some local Mandinka traders joined the groups in the river valley. The women and slaves carried the loads on their heads. Donkeys were also used to carry the loads. The women led the journey while the men followed in the rear. On arrival at a village, the women cooked the food for the party to eat. Items that were available for exchange were woven cloth, ivory, beeswax, hides, gold, civet cats, green parrots, perfumes, corn, shea butter, salt, fish, and iron. The traders paid taxes to the caravan leaders.

As the various peoples of the Senegambia established their settlements, the Mandinka also built settlements and villages and developed their own unique culture. The cultural development was accompanied by customs like naming ceremonies, initiation, marriages, and funeral rites.

Between the sixteenth and seventeenth centuries, the Mandinka Empire of Kaabu was the most important empire of the Senegambia region. The success of the theocratic revolution in Futa Jallon at the beginning of the eighteenth century, however, affected the end of the expansion of the Kaabu Empire.

MICHAEL J. JUSU

Further Reading

Gray, J. M. *A History of the Gambia.* London: Frank Cass, 1966.

Hrbek, I. *General History of Africa III, From the Seventh to the Eleventh Century.* Abridged ed. Paris: UNESCO Series, 1992.

Niane, D. T. *General History of Africa.* Vol. 4, *Africa from the Twelfth to the Sixteenth Century.* Paris: UNESCO Series, 1984.

O Got, B. A. *General History of Africa V, Africa from the Sixteenth to the Eighteenth Century.* Paris: UNESCO Series, 1992.

Sonko-Godwin, P. *Ethnic Groups of Senegambia Gambia.* Sunrise Publishers, 1994.

Mane: Migrations, Sixteenth Century, History of

The era between 1545 and 1606 is considered to be significant in the social history of the West African region that became part of modern Sierra Leone, Liberia, Gambia, Guinea, Côte d'Ivoire, and Ghana, because it was during this period that the Africans whom the Portuguese called the Mane came into contact with African ethnic groups like the Bakwe, Grebo, Kru, Gola, Vai, Kpelle, Loma, Kissi, Mende, Kono, Temne, Bulom, Lokos Fula, Susu, and the Europeans who were arriving in the area about this time. The simultaneous arrival of the Mane and Europeans, together with the impact they and the Africans of the region had on each other, have added to the confusion regarding the origins and ethnic backgrounds of the Mane. Indeed, scholars have paid more attention to the origins, migrations, and invasions of the Mane than the roles they played in the development of West African social, economic, and political orders, especially from 1545 to 1800.

Nearly all treatments of Sierra Leone in the fifteenth and sixteenth centuries by European observers portrayed the Mane as invaders who conquered the early inhabitants of the area and those of what became known as Liberia in 1822. There is little consensus, however, on the beginning of their migration or their specific date of arrival in Sierra Leone. Alvares de Almada, a Cape Verdean Afro-Portuguese, wrote in his 1594 book that the Mane had been waging wars on the early inhabitants of Sierra Leone for a hundred years and added that they were in fact Mende. De Almada based his latter assessment on the fact that the Mane spoke, dressed, and used the same weapons as the Mende. He noted that the Mane had arrived in Sierra Leone through what became Guinea. He later speculated that their empire expanded from the coastal area between the Gold Coast (Ghana) and Gambia. Captain R. Avelot, in his study of Sierra Leone, considered the Mane as Temne, and dated their arrival as about 1550. Anthropologist Northcote Thomas maintained in his 1919 publication that the Mane were not Temne, and added that the former arrived in Sierra Leone in the early 1500s. John Hawkins, an English enslaver on the West African coast in the 1560s, maintained that the Mane, whom he described as Sumbose, arrived in Sierra Leone in 1561. He failed, however, to address the origins of their migrations.

While the above-mentioned studies are characterized by contradictions, Walter Rodney's 1970 study of the Upper Guinea illustrates that not all their arguments are misleading. Basing his analysis on published and unpublished records together with Mende oral traditions, Rodney traced the origins of the Mane migrations to the southern end of ancient Mali; and noted that they were to move to the interior of Côte d'Ivoire, and then to the Gold Coast, where they had minor conflicts with Portuguese traders. He maintained that the Mane, under their female leader Macarico, were expelled from Mandimansa in 1505 for unknown reasons. This was followed by their migrations in two directions: one toward the east coast, and the other, which constituted the bulk of the migrants, toward the coastal area of what became Liberia. It was during their westward movement that the Mane are said to have come into contact with the Bakwe, Kru, Grebo, Vai, Kissi, Loma, Mende, Bulom, Temne, and others. Indeed, the impact of the Mane in the pre-Liberian area was illustrated by their establishment of the kingdom of Quoba in the vicinity of Cape Mount, several miles from the southeastern end of Sierra Leone. Macarico's son was reportedly killed in the Mane War against the Bulom, whose influence was felt in Cape Mount. This event was followed by the death of Macarico in 1545.

The advent of Mane was reinforced in the coastal area of Upper Guinea through military means, and by collaborating with Europeans or pitting one African group against another. The Mane had worked with the Kru and Europeans against the Vai to promote their political, military, and material objectives in the Cape Mount region. The Mane also employed such strategy in the establishment of the kingdom of Boure in Sierra Leone.

Mane migrations had several effects in the area of Sierra Leone and what would become Liberia. Mende, Kissi, Bulom, Kru, Temne, Loma, and others who were recruited into the Mane army not only used Mane weapons; they were also indoctrinated to be loyal to the new Mane leadership. Reciprocally, the Mane new army used the Mende who had migrated from the north to the area earlier as informants. It has been demonstrated that the language the Mane and their recruits spoke took the form of the Mande language. The social attributes of the Bulom, Kissi, Loko, and Gbande reflected Mane characteristics. However, the Mane were socially and culturally absorbed over time by these other ethnic groups.

The Mane stengthened the transatlantic slave trade on the coastal area of Sierra Leone and the region that was to become Liberia. They collaborated with Europeans and other Africans to enslave a large number of Kono, Mende, Sape, Bulom, Gola, Vai, Loma, Gbande, and Kpelle for the Americas. More than 300,000 Africans were enslaved from the coastal area of the future Liberia alone. The Mane army was essentially a slave capturing-organization, especially in the early eighteenth century.

The Mane have been credited with introducing new military weapons and strategies, a large centralized political system, and techniques of weaving cotton, making iron and medicine in Sierra Leone and in the future Liberia. They helped spread the Mande language in West Africa.

AMOS J. BEYAN

See also: **Sierra Leone: Temne, Mende, and the Colony; Slavery: Atlantic Trade: Effects in Africa and the Americas.**

Further Reading

Beyan, A. J. "The Transatlantic Trade and the Coastal Area of Pre-Liberia." *The Historian.* 57, no. 4 (summer 1995): 757–768.

Davis, R. W. *Ethnohistorical Studies on the Kru Coast.* Newark, Del.: Pencader Publisher, 1976.

Fyfe, C. *A History of the Sierra Leone.* London: Oxford University Press, 1962.

Kup, A. P. *A History of Sierra Leone, 1400–1787.* Cambridge: Cambridge University Press, 1960.

Rodney, W. *A History of the Upper Guinea Coast, 1545–1800.* London: Oxford University Press, 1970.

Mansa Musa, Mali Empire and

The Mali Empire occupied its greatest level of achievement during the period extending through Mansa Musa's reign (1312–1337) and that of his brother Sulayman (1341–1360). During this time of its greatest expansion, Mali's territory is believed to have extended from the headwaters of the river Niger and from where the Gambia and Senegal Rivers reach the Atlantic coast, to the southern fringes of the Sahara and the Niger Bend country beyond Timbuktu. The prosperity of Mali's rulers (*mansaw*) was based on its control of commercial centers and routes to the goldfields. Highly valued imports such as copper and salt were heavily taxed, and the *mansaw* accumulated vast quantities of gold by exacting tribute from the producers. Mali's citizens included many intermingled groups who spoke each others' languages. These included speakers of Mande dialects such as Maninka, Bamana, and Soninke, in addition to neighboring groups such as the Fula and Dogon. While trade was extremely important, the majority of the population were engaged in agriculture, cattle-raising, and fishing, with specialized artisan groups such as blacksmiths, leatherworkers, and potters.

Much of the information about Mansa Musa that was recorded during his own time comes from the Arabic writings of al-'Umari (1301–1349), who interviewed eyewitness informants in Cairo, Ibn Battuta (1304–1368) who visited Mali in 1352–1353, and the famous Arab historian Ibn Khaldun (1332–406) who recorded oral historical traditions from Malian scholars. The combined descriptions of al-'Umari and Ibn Battilta evoke a royal court in which the *mansa* occupied a lofty pavilion and sat on a dais decorated with ivory and silk under a dome adorned with an image of a golden bird the size of a falcon. On ceremonial occasions the *mansa* was dressed in a gold turban and crimson gown. He carried a quiver and bow as part of the royal insignia and was escorted by hundreds of musicians and armed slaves. When Mansa Musa rode on horseback, the large flag that signaled his presence was yellow on a red background. In Mande society it was customary for the ruler to speak through an intermediary, or *jeli*, and the leading spokesperson of the Malian court that was visited by Ibn Battuta (in the time of Mansa Sulayman) was flitted with fine garments of silk brocade, a sword with a golden sheath, and boots with spurs. Ibn Battuta reported that any ordinary citizen called into the sovereign's presence had to go in ragged clothes to express his humility, and that when the visitor was addressed by the *mansa*, he must strip to the waist and sprinkle dust on his own head and back.

Mansa Musa was reputed to be a pious Muslim, and he became famous outside of the Mali Empire owing to circumstances of his pilgrimage to Mecca in 1324. Before leaving Mali on a journey that would take at least a year, in keeping with local custom Mansa Musa consulted a diviner to learn the most auspicious date for his departure. He waited nine months for the appropriate date, during which time provisions for the journey were collected from all corners of the realm. When the *mansa* departed there were thousands of people in his retinue including members of the court, baggage carriers, and bodyguards. According to the *Ta'rikh al-Fattash*, which was written more than three centuries after the event (*c.*1665), Mansa Musa was also accompanied by his senior wife, Inari Kanuté with five hundred of her own servants.

The royal caravan from Mali reached Egypt after suffering months of hardship crossing the Sahara Desert, emerging near the pyramids at Cairo. Both al-'Umari and Ibn Khaldun heard from their informants that Mansa Musa left Mali with somewhere between 80 and 100 loads of gold, and his extravagant spending throughout the journey, and especially in Cairo, made his pilgrimage a sensational event. According to al-'Umari's informant, Mansa Musa's arrival gift to Sultan al-Nasir included 50,000 dinars, and he was similarly generous to many others. The Malian emperor flooded Cairo with such wealth that it depressed the value of gold for more than a decade following his visit.

Witnesses in Cairo were impressed with Mansa Musa's piety and with the dignified manners of his well-dressed companions. The emperor was repeatedly interviewed, and asked about his kingdom and the circumstances by which he became *mansa.* Sultan al-Nasir presented Mansa Musa and his courtiers with richly ornamented robes of honor, saddled and bridled horses, the use of a palace for the duration of their visit, and pack animals and provisions for their onward journey to Mecca. After about three months in Cairo, the Malian caravan continued to Mecca in the company of Egyptian pilgrims.

While in Mecca, Mansa Musa succeeded in recruiting four *shurafa* (descendants from the Prophet Muhammed's family) to accompany him back to Mali with their families. Ibn Khaldlin reported that returning to Cairo from Mecca, the Malians narrowly averted disaster when they became separated from the larger Arab caravan and had to make their way to Suez where they survived on fish until they were rescued. By the time the pilgrims returned to Cairo, the gold Mansa Musa had brought with him had run out, and he found it necessary to borrow money from the city's merchants, which he later repaid at an exorbitant rate of interest. In addition to the *shurafa* from Mecca who returned to Mali with Mansa Musa, there was Abu- Ishiq al-Sahili, a poet and architect from Andalusia. Al-Sahili created an elegant, domed palace in Mansa Musa's capital and later settled in Timbuktu where, it is believed, he built one of the mosques.

Mansa Musa is credited with establishing Mali's reputation of greatness far beyond his imperial territories by means other than his extravagant expenditures during the famous pilgrimage. He encouraged Islamic scholarship by sending students to study in Fez and initiated diplomatic relations between himself and the king of Morocco. For this purpose, high-ranking dignitaries from each kingdom were exchanged as ambassadors. The mutually beneficial relations continued with the successors of these monarchs, until late in the fourteenth century, when both Mali and Morocco fell prey to dynastic rivalries.

Before departing on his famous pilgrimage, Mansa Musa had appointed his son Magha to rule in his place. Upon Mansa Musa's death in 1337, Magha again assumed control. His succession deprived Musa's brother Sulayman of the power which customarily belonged to the eldest male in the family. However, Magha died within four years and Sulayman became mansa at that time. Though described by Ibn Khaldun as a wicked, tyrannical ruler, Mansa Sulayman successfully maintained the empire that had enjoyed its golden era under the benign and able rule of Mansa Musa.

DAVID C. CONRAD

See also: **Ibn Khaldun; Mali Empire.**

Further Reading

Conrad, D. C. "A Town Called Dakajalan: The Sunjata Tradition and the Question of Ancient Mali's Capital." *Journal of African History. 35* (1994): 355–377.

Hunwick, J. O. "The Mid-Fourteenth Century Capital of Mali." *Journal of African History. 14* (1973): 195–206.

Levtzion, N. *Ancient Ghana and Mali.* London: Methuen and Co., 1973.

Levtzion, N., and J. F. P. Hopkins (eds.). *Corpus of Early Arabic Sources for West African History.* Cambridge: Cambridge University Press, 1981.

Manyika of Eastern Zimbabwe

The Manyika, whose country is known by the same name, are eastern Karanga who lived in the Eastern Highlands, in an area defined by the Odzi, Rebvuwe, Pungwe, and Gairezi Rivers. This is a cool, well-watered high plateau, 5,000 to 6,000 feet above sea level. The Portuguese first referred to the Manyika in 1513, when Antonio Fernandes traveled from Sofala to the Mutapa State. Fernandes reported that they were well organized politically and traded gold with Sofala. From 1573 onward, written sources refer to Manyika rulers as Chikanga.

Traditions dating from the mid-sixteenth century locate Manyika origins in the Mutapa State. Karanga language gradually spread toward the Indian Ocean. Traditions relate that some Zimbabwe Culture stone buildings appeared there at the same time. Late sixteenth-century Portuguese accounts record that Teve, Manyika, and Danda were once ruled by Mutapa's sons, but nineteenth-century traditions suggest they broke away from the state as a result of poor relations with Changamire, king of the Rozvi.

The Chikanga dynasty ruled Manyika from the second half of the sixteenth century, taking over from an earlier dynasty, linked to Barwe. The new dynasty claimed origins from Mbire, in the Mutapa State. It seems that Mutapa, who ruled up to 1694, was expelled from the state and went into an alliance with Changamire Dombo, who conquered Manyika in 1693–1695. In the mid-nineteenth century, the Chikanga title was changed to Mutasa, excluding rival houses to the throne.

Like the rest of the Karanga, the smallest socioeconomic unit in Manyika was the household, which was part of a village, followed by a ward and then country (*nyika*). *Nyika* represented the largest administrative unit, encompassing several wards. Highly respected women functioning as royal magistrates headed some wards. This institution of women governors helped maintain centralized control of the state. Several *nyika* constituted the state, controlled by the king who in turn enjoyed absolute powers, but in practice ruled with the consent of his subjects. The king lived at *guta*, the royal court. The most important Manyika ceremony was the election and installation of the king. To avoid civil war the election of kings was conducted secretly, and only publicized at coronation. Contesting houses to the throne usually rejected this.

Rozvi kings recognized Manyika rulers through envoys sent to present the king-elect with emblems of kingship (crown, conus shell, and battle-axe) and other symbols of authority. For their tasks envoys were paid in cattle. The Rozvi practiced this only at the beginning of their reign as an exercise in political integration. This, however, did not prevent succession conflicts.

The Manyika had no standing army except about 200 men who defended the capital. When invaded by the Portuguese in the late sixteenth century, they recruited approximately 2,000 men to defend their territory. Lack of a standing army put the Manyika at a disadvantage, especially during civil wars.

The basis of Manyika economy was agriculture. Crops grown included millet, sorghum, groundnuts, cowpeas, bananas, and maize. Cultivation, harvesting, and processing of crops was done communally. Some harvested grain was stored in granaries for drought relief, or for special ceremonies. Cattle were an important part of Manyika society. They were acquired through inheritance, court fines, tribute, bride-price, and trade. They were used as insurance following bad harvest, exchanged for grain, redistributed following the death of their owner, or presented as payment for a bride.

A variety of animals were hunted for food. The king organized communal hunting parties. Elephants were killed mainly for ivory, which was traded at Sofala, especially during the sixteenth century. Ivory trade flourished until the nineteenth century.

The Manyika were also involved in industrial activities and workshop trades. Pottery-making produced a variety of domestic utensils. Bark string was woven into cloth. Iron was smelted to produce hoes, an integral part of the agricultural system. These hoes could be exchanged for wives. Copper was used to produce bangles and bracelets.

Gold attracted Swahili and Portuguese traders from the Indian Ocean coast. It was gold that brought the Portuguese into Manyika in the late sixteenth century and resulted in the *feira* (market) of Masekesa. We do not know how much gold was exported but it was probably second to ivory as a source of Manyika wealth. Its production to meet the demands of external traders disrupted agriculture during the sixteenth and seventeenth centuries.

Although some Portuguese managed to visit Manyika gold mines in 1514–1515, direct contact intensified after 1569. Before this, coastal and hinterland rulers fought for the control of trade with the coast. This forced the Portuguese to abandon Sofala for the Zambezi, where they settled at Sena and Tete in 1531. They defeated the Swahili traders in order to monopolize trade. Between 1559 and 1575 the Portuguese had attempted to invade the Mutapa State, first through Francisco Barreto, who tried to penetrate the hinterland using the Zambezi but was halted by disease, and then Vasco Fernandes Homem, who in 1573 came through Sofala. This brought the Portuguese into Manyika, but the expedition failed to locate gold mines. The invasion resulted in the development of *feiras* in Manyika that included Masekesa, Matuca, and Vumba. They were part of a wider network of trading places, established in Manyika, Mukaranga, Teve, Madanda, and Barwe during the seventeenth century. Masekesa lasted until the nineteenth century.

The gold trade was disrupted by Portuguese aggressive tendencies during the seventeenth century, when they interfered in the politics of Manyika, Mutapa, and Torwa. Between 1632 and 1695 the Portuguese reigned chaos in southern Zambezia, virtually taking over control of trade, relegating local rulers into puppets. *Feira* activity increased. In 1675 the Manyika resisted Portuguese invasion. The Rozvi, who in 1684 took control of Masekesa, halted the Portuguese.

Rozvi domination of Manyika started with the 1693–1695 war, which resulted in the attack on *feiras* of Massapa, Dambarare, and Masekesa. Masekesa was reopened for trade in the 1720s. Before that trade seems to have shifted to Teve. Between 1720 and 1730 the Portuguese tried to make peace with the Rozvi. The Manyika paid tribute annually to the Rozvi in the form of cloth, cattle, and gold. This sustained Rozvi political domination on the Manyika, which, however, slowly waned as the eighteenth century progressed.

Meanwhile, the Portuguese tried to negotiate with the Rozvi for increased access to Manyika. This was, however, complicated by Manyika succession disputes, (*c.*1795–1833). The Rozvi only managed to intervene twice. This was unfavorable to the Portuguese, who suffered increased difficulties in their trade with the Manyika. By the end of the eighteenth century, Rozvi influence was on the decline. Apart from the succession disputes dominating Manyika politics from about 1795, Nguni invasions during the first half of the nineteenth century also weakened both the Rozvi and Manyika.

INNOCENT PIKIRAYI

See also: **Sena, Tete, Portuguese, and Prazos.**

Further Reading

Beach, D. N. "Archaeology and History in Nyanga, Zimbabwe: An Overview." In *Aspects of African Archaeology: Papers from the 10th Pan-African Association for Prehistory and Related Studies*, edited by G. Pwiti and R. Soper. Harare: University of Zimbabwe Publications (1996): 715–718.

———. *The Shona and Zimbabwe, 900–1850: An Outline of Shona History*. Gweru: Mambo Press, 1980.

Bhila, H. H. K. "Trade and Survival of the African Policy: The External Relations of Manyika from the Sixteenth to the Nineteenth Century." *Rhodesian History*. 3 (1972): 11–28.

Bhila, H. H. K. *Trade and Politics in a Shona Kingdom: The Manyika and their African and Portuguese Neighbours, 1575–1902*. Burnt Mill, Harlow, Essex, and Harare: Longman Group, 1982.

Soper, R. C. "The Nyanga Terrace Complex of Eastern Zimbabwe: New Investigations." *Azania*. 31 (1996): 1–35.

Mapungubwe: *See* Iron Age (Later): Southern Africa: Leopard's Kopje, Bambandyanalo, and Mapungubwe.

Maputo

Maputo provides the best natural harbor on the coast of East Africa, as the island of Inhaca helps partly to enclose and protect the bay. The inland area of the southern coast of Mozambique is dry and has poor soil with the exception of the river valleys, where intensive agricultural production is possible.

Portugal's earliest presence along the southeast African coast centered on the northern part of Mozambique, beginning in the fifteenth century. The main areas of activity and settlement were Mozambique Island down to Sofala and inland along the Zambezi River. Only very much later did Delagoa Bay in the extreme south become important and Lourenço Marques (after independence renamed Maputo) become the capital of this Portuguese colony.

Diamond and gold discoveries in the 1870s and 1880s in South Africa, along with the attendant massive development of Johannesburg and the Transvaal were to have enormous implications for Lourenço Marques, as this was the closest natural harbor to serve the import and export needs of the South African mines. In the early nineteenth century, the Nguni invasions from South Africa brought most of the area from the Limpopo River in the south to the Koniati under the control of the Gaza kingdom, restricting Portuguese influence. Portuguese rights to Delagoa Bay were recognized internationally in 1875, and with the economic development of the region fuelled by the burgeoning gold mines of the Rand, in 1888 Lourenço Marques was officially designated the capital of the territory and the conquest of the African peoples was finally consolidated. A railway line linking the Transvaal to the port of Lourenço Marques begun in the 1880s, was completed in 1894. Alongside of the railway, road links to South Africa were created and these became the arteries for the export of South Africa's mineral resources and trade imports. They were also the means by which tens of thousands of Mozambicans traveled every year to work on the South African mines. Total tonnage handled in the port increased rapidly from a quarter of a million tons at the turn of the twentieth century to one million tons by 1914 (half of which was coal).

Lourenço Marques was assured of a continuing and growing economic base under a series of conventions signed between the Portuguese colonial government and South Africa, which linked use of the port by South Africa with Mozambique's provision of migrant laborers to the mines of the Rand. This was extremely lucrative for the Portuguese colonial regime. The flow of migrants was regularized, with the colonial government receiving a fee for every miner hired. Under the terms of an agreement made in 1909, the port of Lourenço Marques was guaranteed 50 per cent of the Transvaal trade, with fees paid for the use of the railway in exchange for supplying mine labor. A new rail line linking southern Rhodesia to the port was also constructed, increasing the importance of transit trade earnings to the economy from neighboring interior states.

South Africa exerted a powerful influence over Lourenço Marques, such that in January 1929, it was able to oblige the Portuguese government to nationalize the port and railway, in an effort to improve the functioning and efficiency of the system. Much of the stevedoring and freight handling, however, was undertaken by private South African companies. At this time, only 11 per cent of Mozambique's exports were going to Portugal, while 34 per cent were destined for South Africa. In the 1930s new refrigeration plants were built to cope with the increase in South African food exports.

From the 1930s, following Salazar's takeover in Portugal and his subsequent nationalistic dictatorship, increasing white settlement was encouraged in Mozambique. Lourenço Marques began to expand, developing a significant number of industries to meet the settler's needs. The city took on distinct characteristics. The so-called cement city was occupied by the whites predominantly, surrounded on two sides by the ocean. Outside of this area were the shanty towns, or "canico" areas, named after the local reed used to construct the huts. There was a stark contrast among the services, facilities, and standards of living available in the two areas.

The beginning of the independence struggles in Portugal's African colonies from the 1960s led the colonial power to reverse its earlier economic nationalist stance encouraging foreign investment, and the economy of the city boomed. Once again, South Africa was the major player and by the 1970s, Mozambique derived over 40 per cent of its gross national product and between 50 and 60 per cent of its foreign exchange earnings from that country. Lourenço Marques became a major tourist destination for South Africans. Apartheid policies preventing interracial sexual relations led to a huge growth in the prostitution industry, with an estimated 50,000 prostitutes in the city by independence.

With independence in 1875, the city underwent drastic changes. A large emigration of whites led to a massive influx of blacks from the "canico" shantytowns into the "cement" city. The city deteriorated initially; property was nationalized while maintenance and rehabilitation projects were suspended. A major social benefit was the increased availability of services and facilities (water, sanitation, health, and education) to the black population. South African destabilization and an expansion of the armed Renamo opposition movement's activities created a further massive population expansion, swamping service providers as people sought the safety of the capital city. Maputo became the prime focus of government activity, appropriating the majority of development aid, which accounted for 70 per cent of the GDP from the mid- to late-1980s until the early 1990s.

From the late 1980s the government increasingly opened up the economy to foreign investment (after an early postindependence experiment with socialism).

The city became revitalized by the end of the twentieth century following an end to the civil war and the holding of democratic elections. There was substantial investment in an aluminum smelting plant and a major initiative to revitalize the port and transit facilities to the interior in cooperation with the South African government and the private sector. Privatization of the economy and of housing led to a renewal of the city, and tourism increased. Maputo became the main beneficiary of one of the highest economic growth rates in Africa at the end of the twentieth century. The government's strict adherence to the International Monetary Fund and World Bank structural adjustment program led to a major program of debt relief, clearing the way for continuing economic development.

BARRY MUNSLOW

See also: **Mozambique.**

Further Reading

Grest, J. "Urban Management, Local Government Reform and the Democratisation Process in Mozambique: Maputo City 1975–1990." *Journal of Southern African Studies.* 21, no. 1 (1995).

Isaacman, A., and B. Isaacman. *Mozambique: From Colonialism to Revolution, 1900–1982.* Boulder, Colo: Westview, 1983.

Katzenellenbogen, S. *South Africa and Southern Mozambique.* Manchester, England: Manchester University Press, 1982.

Mondlane, E. *The Struggle for Mozambique.* Harmondsworth: Penguin African Library, 1970.

Munslow, B. *Mozambique: The Revolution and Its Origins.* London and New York: Longman, 1983.

Newitt, M. *A History of Mozambique.* London: C. Hurst, 1995.

Maraboutic Crisis: *See* Morocco: Maraboutic Crisis, Founding of the 'Alawite Dynasty.

Maravi: Phiri Clan, Lundu and Undi Dynasties

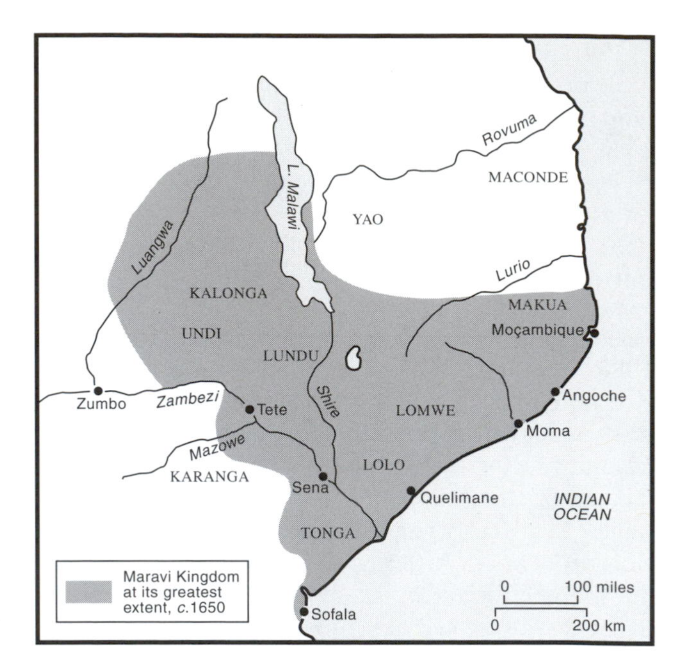

Maravi Kingdom, seventeenth century.

The present-day Chewa are descendants of a number of local groups who had resided in the region between the southern tip of Lake Malawi and the lower Zambezi since early in the first millenium invading groups established a number of chiefdoms over the various Chewa groups sometime between the fifteenth and the seventeenth centuries. Soon after their arrival these invaders called themselves "Maravi," which means "fire flames." Among the most renowned Maravi chiefdoms were Undi, Lundu, and Kalonga. These names derive from those of their rulers and were also bestowed upon succeeding rulers as titles. The Maravi rulers were of the Phiri clan, whose remote origins may have been in the Luba territory. The immediate origins of Undi and Lundu lie in the early period of Kalonga in the sixteenth century. Oral sources state that disputes over succession led members of the Phiri clan, among whom were Lundu and Undi, to leave Kalonga and to form their own Maravi chiefdoms.

These traditions recount that Undi, the brother of the deceased Kalonga, failed to gain the support of the councilors, who appointed the chiefs, although he had the support of most of the royal lineage. Undi soon departed, apparently taking with him all female members of the royal lineage and a large number of other supporters. For a long time thereafter successors to the Kalongaship had to be sought from Undi, who controlled the royal lineage. Undi's departure from Kalonga can be dated from Portuguese records to before the last half of the sixteenth century. Undi went farther west to establish his capital in the Mano area between the Kapoche and Liuye Rivers in Mozambique. In 1614 a Portuguese source mentions trade with a chief "Bundy" in the area north of the Zambezi-Liuye confluence. By about the same date, and certainly by 1640, Undi's Mano chiefdom had begun to expand to the north and northwest into the Nsenga territory, which lies in present-day Zambia. These areas were far from Portuguese trade centers and evidently did not benefit from long-distance trade until after they were accepted into Undi's chiefdom. In return for the tribute from the ivory-rich Nsenga areas Undi reciprocated by providing a redistribution of imported trade goods.

The degree of Undi's authority was limited as his chiefdom was decentralized. When there was a crisis needing military action Undi had to rely on the support of his subordinate authorities. The powers of chiefs, tributary chiefs, and of Undi himself were based on the reciprocity of goods and services. The chiefs, as owners of the land, distributed land to headmen for peasants to use. To ensure the well-being of his people, the chief performed ritual duties, apart from those performed by rain-callers and keepers of spirit shrines, and settled legal disputes. For these services the chief received tribute of both goods, including ivory, and labor force.

Evidently due to the heightened Portuguese involvement in the ivory trade in Undi's chiefdom, increasingly more traders were employed by the Portuguese traveling to Undi's capital. One result of this development was that, by 1750, a number of gold mines were discovered and opened by the Portuguese. Portuguese individuals received Undi's permission to work the mines with slave labor. In return, Undi received revenues from the profits made. The Portuguese, however, had preferred to negotiate directly with Undi's subchiefs and not with Undi himself, and thus undermined Undi's authority. Moreover, the Portuguese in the Zambezi valley sent professional hunters, the so-called *Chikunda*, equipped with firearms for hunting elephants to Undi's territory. These hunters did not have permission to hunt from Undi and paid tax solely to the local subordinate chiefs, who were increasingly reluctant to send revenues to Undi. Undi, in turn, could not redistribute the wealth. The Portuguese, and later the Yao and Bisa, acting as agents to Arab merchants, encouraged this decentralization of trade that resulted in a decentralization of authority and finally in secession. When the chiefdom was largely fragmented, the Ngoni arrived and struck the final blow to the Undi chiefdom in approximately 1835.

Less is known about the Lundu chiefdom. Lundu had founded his chiefdom in the lower Shire valley probably in the second half of the sixteenth century. The power of Lundu was based on two factors. First, he controlled the river route into the Shire Highlands and had his stronghold opposite Sena and Tete. Second, the chiefdom had an extraordinary agricultural potential due to a combination of wet-land and dry-land cultivation that in times of drought gave it a decisive advantage over much of lower Zambezia. Thus the valley also became important to the Portuguese settlers along the Zambezi as a granary in times of drought and scarcity. The first mention of Lundu in a Portuguese document refers to the year 1614 that has led to the alternative hypothesis that Lundu did not develop until around this time.

Unlike Undi, Lundu had absolute supremacy in ritual matters, even in respect to the rain ceremonies which were normally performed by ritual specialists who were independent of the rulers. The hypothesis is that Lundu, with the help of the Zimba armed forces, initiated a repressive system to obtain total control not only of ritual matters but also of production and trade in and around the lower Shire valley. The expansionist wars waged by Lundu in the closing decade of the sixteenth century probably coincided internally with a massive attempt at centralization of political power. With his Zimba allies Lundu could defeat the Portuguese in 1592 and 1593. Sometime after this he became a powerful ally of the Portuguese of Tete. In 1622, however, he was defeated by his rival, the Maravi chief Muzura, who at that time had made a deal with the Portuguese. Why Lundu had become an enemy of the Portuguese remains unclear.

Even so, the Lundu paramountcy survived until modern times and remained an important factor in the Mbona rain cult. By the 1860s the Lundu paramountcy had nearly collapsed due to the slave trade and was only saved by allying to the British. It was officially restored after Malawi independence and formed one focus of modern Chewa nationalism.

REINHARD KLEIN-ARENDT

Further Reading

Langworthy, H. W. "A History of Undi's Kingdom to 1890: Aspects of Chewa History in East Central Africa." Ph.D. diss., Boston University, 1969.

———. "Conflict Among Rulers in the History of Undi's Chewa Kingdom." *Transafrican Journal of History.* 1 (1971): 1–24.

Schoffeleers, J. M. "The Meaning and Use of the Name Malawin Oral Traditions and Precolonial Documents." In *The Early History of Malawi*, edited by B. Pachai. London: Longman, 1972.

———. *River of Blood: The Genesis of a Martyr Cult in Southern Malawi, c. A.D. 1600.* Madison: The University of Wisconsin Press, 1992.

Maravi: Zimba "Invasions"

Knowledge about the Zimba and their role in the history of Zambezia derives mainly from several contemporary Portuguese documents and from African oral tradition. The Zimba were apparently Bantu-speaking invaders, who dwelt in the lower Zambezi region and managed to expand their influence to a large part of Makualand by about 1590. The sources frequently refer to them as cannibals. There is no direct documentary evidence providing information on the origin of the Zimba and their motivation for invading northern Zambesia. A popular hypothesis in regard to their geographical origin describes the Zimba as refugees from the south bank of the Zambezi. Two arguments in favor of this hypothesis can be put forward. First, over the course of the twentieth century, the Shire valley witnessed immigration from the east and from the west, but only immigrants coming from the south, especially from the hinterland of Sena, have been associated with the name "Zimba." Thus, there must have been some kind of preexisting tradition linking the name "Zimba" to these peoples. The second argument derives from evidence related to ritual practices. *Tundu* (or *Tondo*) was the name of a legendary Zimba leader of the 1590s. During the following centuries this figure was transformed by the peoples of the lower Shire valley into a male spirit responsible for all kinds of natural disasters and plagues. Traditions and rituals concerning *Tundu* consistently associate him with the south.

Several hypotheses exist as to the motivation of the Zimba invasions. The most influential one was developed primarily on the basis of oral tradition, and suggests that the Zimba operated as a mercenary force under Lundu, the ruler of the Maravi state of the same name. Lundu himself may have given his consent to the formation of the Zimba army, or he was able to use the already existing Zimba army for his own purposes. Lundu did not have an army worth mentioning at his disposal and was dependent on armed assistance from outside. This suggests that it was the Zimba who provided Lundu with the offensive fighting power he required to reach his goal. Thus, the Zimba were in alliance with the Lundu of that time and the latter used them to consolidate his power in the Shire valley and beyond. In this respect, the Zimba raids can probably be seen in connection with Lundu's striving for ritual supremacy, particularly in regard to rain-making cults. This supremacy was unknown to the other Maravi states, where rain ceremonies were performed only by ritual specialists, who were in principle independent of the secular rulers. The ritual supremacy of the secular ruler could apparently be achieved only by force. Circumstantial evidence indicates that Lundu exercised extreme repression to obtain total control not only of ritual power but also of production and trade in and around the lower Shire valley. In sum, it can be concluded that the expansionist wars waged by Lundu in the last decade of the sixteenth century coincided internally with a massive attempt to centralize political power by forcing a large segment of the population into total subjection and by fundamentally restructuring the system of economic production and distribution. This points to the fact that the Lundu state, together with the rival Maravi state of Muzura, was already well established in the second half of the sixteenth century, if not earlier.

According to Portuguese sources, prior to 1590 the Zimba's main stronghold lay opposite Sena, one of the most important Portuguese entrepôts within the Monomotapa kingdom in the lower Zambezi region. Apparently Muslim Swahili, Portuguese, and African groups traded luxury goods there. Chiefs with whom the Portuguese maintained good relations were frequently threatened by Zimba raids, probably initiated by Lundu. In 1592 the Portuguese captains of Sena and Tete, de Santiago and de Chaves, put together an army to rid themselves of this threat. However, when they reached the fortified village of the Zimba near Sena they were ambushed by them, several hundred Portuguese including both captains as well as African allies were killed. Since the Zimba had become too overconfident in their power and increasingly bellicose, the captain of Mozambique, de Sousa, assembled an army in 1593, equipped it with artillery, and marched toward the fortified settlement of the Zimba. Despite their artillery and a massive assault, the Portuguese failed to conquer the fort and after two months they decided to return to Sena. However, the Zimba overpowered those Portuguese forces that were still in the camp, killed some of them, and seized a considerable amount of equipment and artillery. Soon afterward the Portuguese and the Zimba made peace and the traffic on the river was opened again. In 1597 there was renewed fighting, after which the Zimba leader Tundu offered peace to the Portuguese of Sena in approximately 1599. Nevertheless, the new captain of Mozambique, de Ataide, sought leave for a punitive campaign against the Zimba, who by that time were in control not only of the north bank of the Zambezi but also of much of the coastal area and the nearby regions.

A second hypothesis that attempts to explain the motive behind the Zimba raids maintains that the states of Lundu and Muzura did not exist as formal systems until the first quarter of the seventeenth century. In this view the overall situation just before and after 1600 was rather one in which powerful groups of invaders, including the Zimba, forming one of several groups of Maravi invaders, were in search of a suitable environment in which to set up a feudalistic state system. Defeated by the Portuguese and thus unable to settle south of the Zambezi, the Maravi chiefs changed direction and invaded the Mozambique lowlands. It may have been one of these incursions during the 1580s that gave rise to the legend of the marauding, cannibalistic Zimba. Portuguese sources recall an episode from 1589, when a Zimba war party reached the East African coast, attacked Kilwa, pillaged Mombasa, and proceeded to Malindi, where they were annihilated by armed forces of the local Segeju people. However, there are scholars who argue that the Zimba raids on the East African coast have been misinterpreted and should better be understood in terms of frictions in local political relations. Some even go so far as to suggest that the entire existence of the Zimba was a delusion of the Portuguese.

Contemporary Portuguese sources explain the Zimba raids on the East African coast with reference to an ambitious minor Zimba chief, who emigrated from his homeland with an armed force in order to conquer foreign territories and attain fame and notoriety.

During the following centuries certain groups of professional elephant and hippopotamus hunters were called "Zimba." Today, groups exist in the Shire valley who call themselves Zimba, but who are probably descendants of nineteenth-century immigrants.

REINHARD KLEIN-ARENDT

Further Reading

Alpers, E. A. "North of the Zambezi." In *The Middle Age of African History*, edited by R. Oliver. London: Oxford University Press, 1967.

Newitt, M. D. D. "The Early History of the Maravi." *Journal of African History.* 23 (1982): 145–162.

Phiri, K. G. M. *Chewa History in Central Malawi and the Use of Oral Tradition, 1600–1920.* Ph.D. diss., University of Wisconsin, 1975.

Schoffeleers, J. M. *River of Blood. The Genesis of a Martyr Cult in Southern Malawi, c. A.D. 1600.* Madison: The University of Wisconsin Press, 1992.

———. "The Zimba and the Lundu State in the Late Sixteenth and Early Seventeenth Centuries." *Journal of African History.* 28 (1987): 337–355.

Maravi: Kalonga Masula: Empire, Trade

The sources on early Maravi history—contemporary Portuguese written documents and African oral tradition—are scarce and often contradictory. Thus, modern historiography relying on these sources often bears the character of mere speculation.

Sometime between the fifteenth and the seventeenth centuries, invaders established a number of chiefdoms over the various Chewa groups settled in the region between the southern tip of Lake Malawi and the lower Zambezi. These invading rulers were of the Phiri clan and are said to have originally come from the Luba region. According to oral tradition they called themselves "Maravi," probably soon after their arrival. This term means "fire flames," since the land shimmered like flames in the sunshine when it was first seen by the newcomers.

Among the most renowned Maravi chiefdoms were Undi, Lundu, and Kalonga. These names derive from their founding rulers and were also bestowed upon succeeding chiefs as title. Kalonga's chiefdom probably expanded slowly and did not reach its peak of power until the early 1600s, partly as a result of the stimulation of trade in ivory and cloth with the Portuguese. Kalonga exploited the Zambezi trade and controlled movement along the Shire from his center of power which lay near the south-west corner of Lake Malawi. Oral traditions reveal that at some point, probably in the late 1500s, there was a dispute over succession which seems to have had disastrous effects on Kalonga's central authority. Undi, the brother of the deceased Kalonga, was passed over as successor, whereupon he left Kalonga, taking with him all the female members of Kalonga's part of the royal Phiri lineage. This meant that Kalonga had no means of ensuring his own succession. Since he did not have a mother or sisters to produce brothers and nephews, he could not rely on the continuing support of close royal kin in his capital. Instead he was burdened with the restrictions of the councillors who were recruited from the Banda clan. For a long time thereafter successors to the Kalongaship had to be sought from Undi who controlled the royal lineage. An important element in the decline of Kalonga's central authority could also have been the influence of external Muslim and Portuguese traders.

In the early seventeenth century, chief Muzura established a powerful state on the southern border of Kalonga, controlling most of northern Zambezia. This state is first mentioned in Portuguese records in 1608 and last mentioned in about 1635. Many writers have assumed that this Muzura was the paramount chief of the Maravi and holder of the title of Kalonga. There is, however, no documentary evidence at all to show that Muzura was a Kalonga and no tradition recorded by the Maravi remembers a Kalonga of that name. The very meager evidence suggests that the state founded by Muzura north of the Zambezi later became known as the "empire of the Maravi," and that the paramountcy which he established later assumed the title of Kalonga.

In 1616 the term Maravi is used for the first time to describe Muzura's capital. Muzura's expansive ambitions were fostered by his military alliance with the Portuguese, who helped him to defeat Lundu in 1622. It is likely that these military activities were of some importance in the expansion of "Kalonga" Muzura's chiefdom in the 1600s. This is remembered in the oral traditions of Undi, Mkanda, and others. After the defeat of Lundu, political dominance in the region was taken over by Muzura. This is the first time that the term Kalonga is mentioned in Portuguese documents. In 1631 Muzura shifted his allegiance in favour of an alliance against the Portuguese. This alliance had been forged by Kaparidze of the Karanga, who had been ousted by the Portuguese as a rival claimant to the throne of the Monomotapa, and by the Manyika. The uprising failed and the Portuguese maintained power in Karangaland and probably south of the Zambezi, while the north bank of the Zambezi continued to be controlled by Muzura and his successors. By 1667 the area north of the river is generally referred to by Portuguese sources as being the empire of Maravi, ruled by Kalonga. Most Maravi chiefs could maintain their authority until the nineteenth century, particularly their monopoly over trade, even in the face of the decentralizing tendencies within their chiefdoms. Occasionally Portuguese references before 1800 give the impression that a trade monopoly was also being maintained by Kalonga. It is mentioned that he restricted trade, especially in ivory, to himself and two other rulers at the end of the seventeenth century.

However, in comparison to other Maravi states, decentralization took place in Kalonga at a relatively early stage. The weakness at the center was probably due to an ill-suited successor and the lack of relatives to support Kalonga about 1750. A weakness at the center could easily be taken advantage of by subordinates who either felt that they were receiving insufficient services or desired to control tribute and external trade to their own benefit. As the eastern and southern parts of Kalonga's chiefdom had probably seceded in the mid- or late seventeenth century, and as Undi had established himself independently, it would appear that Kalonga's economic position was greatly weakened. Since the chief was the ultimate owner of the land he had the right to collect tribute, but he also had certain responsibilities, both to the land and to the welfare of the people living on it.

The Maravi chiefs received ivory hunted in their country and other raw materials such as skins. The export of ivory and other tribute goods by the chiefs was important in terms of the maintenance of their central authority as the imported goods were redistributed to the chief's subordinates. This redistribution secured the economic dependence of these subordinates. The chief virtually had a monopoly over the collection of ivory tribute and its sale to external traders. The breaking of this monopoly and the decentralization of the chief's control over tribute and trade finally led to the general decline of the central powers not only of Kalonga, but sooner or later of all Maravi chiefs. The role of the Portuguese in this process is not yet clear. The Portuguese may have undermined Kalonga's central authority, since they tended to negotiate with local subordinate rulers.

REINHARD KLEIN-ARENDT

Further Reading

Alpers, E. A. *Ivory & Slaves in East Central Africa.* London: Heinemann, 1975.

Newitt, M. D. D. "The Early History of the Maravi." *Journal of African History.* 23 (1982): 145–162.

Schoffeleers, J. M. *River of Blood: The Genesis of a Martyr Cult in Southern Malawi, c. A.D. 1600.* Madison: The University of Wisconsin Press, 1992.

———. "The Zimba and the Lundu State in the Late Sixteenth and Early Seventeenth Centuries." *Journal of African History.* 28 (1987): 337–355.

Margai, Sir Milton: *See* Sierra Leone: Margai, Sir Milton: Independence, Government of.

Marinids: *See* Maghrib: Marinids, Ziyanids, and Hafsids, 1235–1359.

Marrakech

Marrakech (sometimes written as Marrakesh) is the capital of southern Morocco, a city of 745,541 (1994), the fourth largest in Morocco after Casablanca, Rabat-Salé, and Fez. The spoken Arabic *Mer-r‹ksh* provides Western languages with the name of the country, Morocco, Maroc, Marueccos, and so forth. The word is undoubtedly of Berber origin, but its meaning is unknown.

Marrakech is today composed of three parts: the older city, the Medina; Guéliz, which is the former European town, planned as a separate modern city with its own central business district and suburbs; and numerous extensions of the city, some planned, some mere *bidonvilles* (shantytowns) that have grown up to the north and west of the Medina mostly since the 1960s. The Medina is effectively Marrakech as it was before the arrival of the French and the establishment of Guéliz, which was drafted as a whole plan in 1919 and represents one of the more successful French urban designs, intended as a method of retaining the architectural integrity of the old city as well as providing a segregated atmosphere for colonial life. The Medina is entirely walled, has numerous massive gates, and contains many distinctive neighborhoods and quarters. It is flanked on two sides by massive royal gardens (Agdal and Menara), themselves walled and part of the urban matrix. The city is focused on the Djemma al-Fna, a vast and chopped-up open square, devoted to cookshops at night and story tellers, acrobats, and other entertainment and services by day. Aside the square lies the dominating minaret of the Koutoubia ("booksellers") Mosque, which dates from the Almohad era of Sultan Yaqub al-Mansour (*r.*1184–1199) and is the stylistic older twin to the Giralda of Seville. Vast markets (*suqs*) penetrate the Medina, purveying textiles, brass, and leather goods to the legions of tourists who make Marrakech Morocco's top tourist destination.

Marrakech, the "Red City"—so named for the color of the sun-dried earth (adobe) that composes the basic urban building material—is an Islamic city, founded by the Almoravid (al-Mur‹bitun) movement as it swept out of the western Sahara and established itself in Morocco in the mid-1000s. While the date of the founding of Marrakech is debatable, most scholars have settled on its construction begun in 1070 on orders of Abu Bakr ibn 'Umar, which were carried out by Yussef Ibn Ben Tashfin, the Almoravid conqueror of Morocco and Spain.

Marrakech supplanted an earlier city, Aghmat, located some distance away at the mouth of the Ourika valley in the High Atlas. A Berber capital, Aghmat was probably founded about 704 as part of the Kharijite revolt that swept Morocco's early Islamic history but had become firmly welded to the political fabric of Morocco, largely dependent on power from Fez. The Almoravids first built a *qsar* (fort), which was excavated and revealed to be intact during the colonial era. As Marrakech grew, Aghmat withered, and so Fez and Sijilmasa, the greatest cities of Morocco to this time, had a new rival, strategically located to rule, as did 'Ali Ben Yussef, Yussef's heir (*r.* 1106–1143), from Algiers to the Atlantic and from the Sahara to the Ebro. It was in 'Ali's reign that Marrakech began to flourish as a kind of western Baghdad, and savants such as the philosopher Avenpace of Zaragossa and doctors Avenzor of Seville and Avenzoar congregated at the court. 'Ali was no cosmopolite, however, and the intellectuals of Marrakech found themselves in jail from time to time.

In the High Atlas south of Marrakech, Berbers, organized as a new religious movement, the Almohad (al-Muwahidin, "Unitarians"), saw the Almoravids, initially the bearers of a fundamentalist strain of Islam, as corrupt and venal. In 1147 Marrakech was attacked by the Almohad 'Abd al-Mu'min (*r.* until 1163), who conquered the city, sacked and destroyed many Almoravid structures, and resanctified others for his use. Almohads invaded Spain and succeeded in reformulating effectively the same imperial domain as their predecessors had. An example of the rise and fall of Islamic dynasties later outlined by Ibn Khaldun, the Almohads rose to greatness over their first three sovereigns, and in particular, the third, Yaqub al-Mansur, created many of the main lines of Marrakechi urbanity traceable to today. Long-distance trade soared as new souks, notably a cloth bazaar (*qaysariya*) for sale of Italian and eastern fabrics; the booksellers of the Koutoubia and the Koutoubia itself; and numerous *fonduqs* (caravanserais) were established. Intellectual life of the Almohad court exceeded that of the Almoravids: Averroes wrote his *Essay on the Substance of the Universe* in Marrakech; Avenzoar lived to return to the Almohad court.

In symmetry to their rise, the Almohads declined over several generations and fell into in-fighting in which Marrakech suffered great destruction in the 1220s and until 1232. In the breach, Merinids, Berber warriors from western Algeria, took control of Morocco. Marrakech, which had been reduced to a regional kingdom, was taken in 1269 and for most of the succeeding 230 years of the Merinid dynasty, Marrakech was ruled through a series of semiautonomous princes dependent on central authority in Fez. One prince, Yusuf ben Abi Iyad, was inspired to rebellion in 1308; after being defeated by imperial troops along the banks of the Oued Oum er-Rbia north of Marrakech, he spirited back to the city, plundering along his way, and sought refuge with a *shaykh* in the Atlas, who turned him in. He was killed and the heads of 600 of his followers were rammed on stakes along the city ramparts. Princely Merinid rule continued through the 1300s, and at some unknown point in the 1400s, which is very poorly known in Moroccan history, local leaders, the Hintata, came to play a dominant role and were identified as the "kings" of Marrakech when the Portuguese conquered the coastal town of Safi in 1508.

Threat of the Portuguese conquest of all southern Morocco, including Marrakech, led to the emergence of the Saadians, powerful *sharifs* (descendants of the Prophet Muhammad) from the Draa valley, who leveraged their holiness and military acumen to defeat the Christians, itself a struggle that lasted most of the sixteenth century, and establish a new Moroccan dynasty at Marrakech. The Portuguese, at last defeated in what F. Braudel called the "last Crusade of Mediterranean Christendom" at the Battle of Three Kings or Oued al-Makhazine (1578) in northern Morocco, the victorious Saadians turned their attention to the embellishment of Marrakech under the reign of Moulay Ahmad al-Mansur, the "Golden" (*r.* 1578–1603). Most elaborate of all buildings built by Mansur was the Badi ("incomparable") Palace, decorated with Carrara marble paid for by cane sugar grown in the Sus valley (southwestern Morocco).

Under the Saadians, but especially Mansur, Morocco pursued a policy of Saharan conquest, and took Touat, Gourara, and then the empire of Songhay, focused on Timbuktu, in 1590–1591. This aggressive policy withered following Mansur's death, as did the Saadian state, but its impact on the Ottomans and European powers was great; harboring a prestige for Morocco that far outlasted Morocco's actual strengths.

With the rise of Morocco's present dynasty, the Alawites, in the seventeenth century, the seat of government left Marrakech for all time, moving to Fez, Meknès, and eventually Rabat. Moulay Ismail (*r.* 1672–1727) destroyed the Badi Palace and removed the marble to his newly remade capital at Meknès. From time to time (down to the present), an Alawite sultan sojourned in Marrakech and important building projects completed, but the center of power moved elsewhere. At the beginning of the twentieth century, the young sultan Moulay Abdel Aziz (*r.* 1894–1908) spent six years in Marrakech, the result of which was the Bahia ("splendid") Palace. Antiforeign sentiment grew in these years, and the murder of the French doctor Mauchamp in Marrakech in 1907 only heightened xenophobia in Morocco and the crisis atmosphere that accompanied European, and especially French, policies toward Morocco. His brother and successor, Moulay Hafid, abdicated in June 1912, at a time of extreme popular unrest following the signing of the Treaty of Fez (March 14, 1912), which established the protectorate over Morocco.

In Marrakech a shaykh, Ahmad al-Hiba, emerged as the head of (self-declared) Islamic resistance against the French and proclaimed himself sultan in August 1912. Having taken the city, al-Hiba proceeded to arrest selected French residents of Marrakech, including the vice consul. General Lyautey then speeded up the French conquest of Marrakech, which was accomplished swiftly under the direction of General Mangin. In September 2,000 holy fighters died at Sidi Bou Othmane, just north of Marrakech. General Mangin occupied Marrakech the next day. He was accompanied by Thami al-Glaoui, leader of the Atlas "grands caids" who threw in their lot with the French early after a generation of serving as rural tax collectors for the sultans. Al-Hiba escaped, his movement collapsed, and he died in obscurity in 1919. Thami Glaoui played a key role in the protectorate and became virtual lord of Marrakech and the Atlas in the 1930s and 1940s.

James A. Miller

See also: **Maghrib; Morocco.**

Further Reading

de Cenival, P. "Marrakush." In *The Encyclopedia of Islam.* Vol. 6. New ed. Leiden: E. J. Brill, 1991.

Deverdun, G. *Marrakesh des origines à 1912.* Rabat: Editions Technique Nord-Africaines, 1959.

Rogerson, B. *Morocco.* London: Cadogan Books, 1997.

Martial Races

Imperial states often recruited their military force from supposedly "martial" groups from the margins or outside the empire altogether. Sometimes armies of this kind, as for example the Mamluks in Egypt became self-perpetuating, and politically dominant. In colonial Africa, soldiers were recruited mainly from particular ethnic groups. Such forces sustained the colonial system, but in many cases the ethnically unbalanced composition of the armed forces constituted a problematic legacy for succeeding independent African states.

Where the process of conquest was particularly lengthy and brutal, as in Algeria and South Africa early in the nineteenth century, or later in Angola and in German South West Africa, units of the metropolitan army and locally recruited white settlers were used. In Egypt and the Sudan, Britain took over the Khedive's army, extended the practice of recruiting Africans from the south and, for major expeditions, used metropolitan troops. Sudanese mercenaries trained in Egypt took part in the British conquest of Uganda and in German expansion in East Africa. German forces in Kamerun were recruited elsewhere in West Africa. The first soldiers of the Force Publique in the Congo Free State were recruited from Zanzibar and from West Africa.

Elsewhere, local Africans were crucial both to the process of conquest and to the maintenance of colonial control. In British Africa, particularly in East Africa, allies crucial to the conquest such as Ganda and Maasai played little part in the later colonial armies. In French Africa, continuity between the army of conquest and the army of colonial occupation was much greater. Everywhere the pattern of recruitment to the colonial armed forces was the product of a mixture of expediency and imperial theory, in particular the notion of "martial races." British thinking about "martial races" derived from experience in India. There it owed much to the belief that in the Great Rebellion of 1857 the Raj had been betrayed by high caste soldiers of the Bengal army and rescued by troops recruited in the Punjab. The theory of "martial races" was elaborated after 1880, when, faced with a threat from Russia, General Roberts restructured the Indian army.

Arguments from military need combined with a range of sometimes-contradictory notions derived from the current thinking about race, masculinity, and the impact of climate and geography. The ideal recruit, who would display courage, loyalty, and a ready obedience, was thought to be an illiterate peasant of Aryan descent, and possibly of Islamic religious adherence, from a remote northern mountainous region. Officials with Indian experience imported the notion of the "martial races" into British Africa as part of the mélange of ideas about race that underpinned colonial rule throughout Africa. In Africa as in India two possible objectives were differently emphasized in different contexts. On the one hand it was necessary to guard against the danger of rebellion. That objective was best secured, Lord Lugard argued in the *Dual Mandate in Tropical Africa* (1922), by recruiting troops from the geographical and social margins of local society rather than from locally dominant groups. On the other hand Africa might serve, as India had done, as a source of military manpower that could be deployed elsewhere in the tropics or even in Europe, in which case recruitment might need to draw more generally from the whole population.

In British Africa military forces were comparatively small and recruited mainly from rural, inland, savanna regions. Thus in Gold Coast recruitment concentrated on the northern territories, and French territories beyond, rather than the Gold Coast Colony and Asante. Within the north some groups, in particular the Frafra, increasingly predominated. In a sense Frafra ethnic identity was a product of their close involvement with the military; they became a "martial tribe" as a consequence of being recruited in such numbers. In Nigeria too recruitment concentrated on the north. Hausa remained the language of command, but the rank and file were increasingly recruited from the non-Hausa regions of the middle belt. In East Africa recruitment was highly differential. In Uganda, in addition to the original Sudanese, transmuted into Nubi, recruitment concentrated on northern groups, particularly Acholi. In Kenya, Kamba and Kalenjin predominated. British military thinkers were sceptical of using African troops outside Africa. But in both world wars British African forces were substantially expanded, with a necessary broadening of the range of recruitment, including the recruitment of educated southerners in West Africa. In the Burma campaign the West African Frontier Force's light armament and use of carriers rather than mechanised transport was deployed to good effect.

In French Africa, particularly in North Africa, the metropolitan French army played an important role. In tropical Africa forces recruited locally from subjects rather than citizens increasingly replaced French troops. The first recruits to the Tirailleurs Sénégalais, founded in 1857, were largely slaves, and former slaves continued to contribute substantially well into the twentieth century, although high-status Africans, served in the French forces. Recruitment concentrated on the Sudan and Upper Volta, and Bambara became the linqua-franca of the Tirrailleurs. That preference was justified in part by the use of "martial race" arguments, in particular the notion that peoples from the forest zone were unsuited to military combat. In *La Force Noire* (1910), Charles Mangin, who had served under Archinard and who had strong right-wing sympathies, developed French thinking about "martial races" in a more expansive form. He believed that the human resources of French Africa were a vital part of France's defense against potential German threat, in part on the grounds that for cultural and biological reasons Africans were particularly well suited to war. Mangin's views were not universally accepted, but the necessities of the conquest of Morocco and even more dramatically of World War I entailed a large expansion of France's African armies. Expansion on that scale could only be achieved by a form of conscription first introduced in 1912 and consolidated in 1919. In the Belgian Congo the size of the Force Publique, though employed mainly in internal security, necessitated the use of compulsion. Here too, however, certain areas contributed more recruits than others and the use of Lingala as a *lingua franca* contributed to the development of Bangala ethnic identity.

The idea of "martial races" was part of the highly racialized worldview of the colonial period that found expression in may ways, for example in the Kiplingesque notion of a possible affinity between brave men across racial divides. The idea of "martial races" did affect recruitment, particularly in British Africa, but even there it was secondary to the imperatives of "divide and rule" and the demands of major international conflict.

JOHN DAVIDSON

See also: **Egypt: Mamluk Dynasty (1250–1517): Army, Iqta' System; Nigeria: Lugard, Administration and "Indirect Rule."**

Further Reading

Adekson, J. 'B. "Ethnicity and Army Recruitment in Colonial Plural Societies." *Ethnic and Racial Studies.* 2, no. 2 (1979): 151–165.

Echenberg, M. *Colonial Conscripts: The Tirailleurs Sénégalais in French West Africa, 1857–1960.* London: Heinemann and James Currey, 1991.

Kirk-Greene, A. H. M. "'Damnosa Heritas': Ethnic Ranking and the Martial Races Imperative in Africa." *Ethnic and Racial Studies.* 3, no. 4 (1980): 393–414.

Killingray, D. "The Idea of a British Imperial Army." *Journal of African History.* 20, no. 3 (1979): 421–436.

———. "Imagined Martial Communities: Recruiting for the Military and Police in Colonial Ghana, 1860–1960." In *Ethnicity in Ghana: The Limits of Invention*, edited by C. Lenz and P. Nugent. Basingstoke: Macmillan, 2000.

Killingray, D., and D. Omissi (eds.). *Guardians of Empire: The Armed Forces of the Colonial Powers c.1700–1964.* Manchester: Manchester University Press, 1999.

Omissi, D. *The Sepoy and the Raj: The Politics of the Indian Army, 1860–1940.* Basingstoke: Macmillan, 1994.

Parsons, T. H. *The African Rank-and-File: Social Implications of Colonial Military Service in the King's African Rifles 1902–1964.* Oxford: Heinemann and James Currey, 2000.

Mascarene Islands Prior to the French

The Mascarene Islands, composed of the islands of Mauritius, Réunion and Rodrigues, were uninhabited prior to European settlement. The Portuguese are credited with having discovered the islands, although it has been contended that Arabs, Phoenicians, and Dravidians also visited the islands, although no documentary evidence exists to prove this claim. Wax tablets bearing "Arabic-looking" inscriptions were found on the shore of Mauritius by Jolinck, the first Dutch sailor to have toured the island and recorded his observations, but no research has been carried out on them.

The "Arab sounding" names of Cantino and al-Idrisi found on Portuguese maps (dating to 1502 and 1165, respectively) have led some historians to conclude that Arabs first visited the island. However, this view has been contested by several scholars, based on several observations. There are no existing maps of Mauritius of non-European origin. Idrisi was a cartographer for King Roger I of Sicily. The names, rather than deriving from Arabic, may be Sanskrit words.

It is not clear who first set foot upon Rodrigues Island. Some believe that it was Diego Fernandez Pereira, who was a navigator in the expedition of Pedro Mascarenhas. Others suggest that it was Diego Rodriguez, a Portuguese captain, who discovered Rodrigues between 1534 and 1536. Pingré, writing in 1761, mentions yet another name, that of Vincent Rodrigue de Lagos, whose name appears on a map found in the Linschot papers of 1611.

Whatever the truth may be about the discovery, the island only became settled in 1691 by François Leguat and seven companions. Leguat was a French Protestant refugee from Holland and had been sent to the Mascarenes to found a colony on Rodrigues. He was forgotten there, and lived there with his companions until 1693, when they decided to leave the island. They built a boat and returned to Mauritius, which was still under Dutch occupation. He wrote extremely detailed diaries, and it would seem that the island did not receive a single visitor during his stay there, although he observed Portuguese names engraved on the trunks. After 1693 Rodrigues remained uninhabited until 1725, when it was occupied by the French.

The first navigator to arrive in Mauritius was believed to be Pedro Mascarenhas, sometime between 1500 and 1530. On Portuguese maps, Mauritius was known under several names: "Santa Apolonia," "Mascarenhas," "Diego Roiz," and "Cirne." The Portuguese did not settle there; rather, they seem to have used the island to obtain fresh water and fruit. However, they did introduce or set loose monkeys, pigs, goats, and rats upon the island, which wreaked havoc upon the ecological balance of the island.

The island was also visited by pirates, and both British and French ships, but no one established themselves there until 1598, when the Dutch took possession of the island and began a settlement in 1638. It is claimed that the Dutch used the island as a port of call on their way to and back from the East Indies. Fewer ships came to Mauritius after 1611, when the Dutch governor general of the East Indies suffered a shipwreck off the west coast. Nevertheless, the island was expected to produce some revenue, and governors were encouraged to exhort colonists to engage in agriculture, and search for ebony and ambergris, which were sold at high prices in Europe. The colonists however, were reluctant to sell everything they found to the Dutch East India Company, especially as there was a more lucrative trade being carried on privately with passing pirate ships. Supplies did not come regularly from Europe, and the colonists were often on the verge of starvation.

The establishment of a port of call at the Cape of Good Hope sealed the fate of Mauritius as a potential Dutch settlement; interest in Mauritius dwindled. The settlers asked to be repatriated to the Cape, and the last batch of settlers left the island in 1710. The coastal forests had been decimated and it is during Dutch occupation that the Dodo bird was last seen. Numerous other species also disappeared during that time.

The failure of the Dutch settlement can be attributed to their unwillingness to import more labor. The Dutch East India Company did not want for the number of slaves to exceed the free population. Although a slave trade was started by Adrian Van der Stel and later by Hugo, very few of these slaves were brought to Mauritius. Those who were did not adapt to the conditions in Mauritius and suffered a high mortality rate.

VIJAYA TEELOCK

Massassi and the Kaarta State

In the seventeenth century, the Massassi dynasty of Bambara chiefs and kings (*faama)* was founded by Kaladian Kulibali (1652–1682) at Segu, on the south bank of the Niger River. In the eighteenth century, the kingdom was consolidated by Mamari Kulibali (*c.*1712–1755) who used the traditional age-set organization of the Bambara. He recruited slave solders, the *tonjon*, to expand the state while driving out rival Bambara clans including the Massassi. He assumed the title of *faama* (king) until his assassination by the *tonjon* in 1755. The Massassi fled across the Niger to establish their authority north of the Baoute River in the Sahel and savanna of Kaarta, which was a terminus of the trans-Saharan caravan trade and a center for the east-west trade routes between the Niger and Senegal Rivers.

The Massassi, known as the Kulibali, asserted their control over the Jawara Soninke, Mandinka, Bambara, and Fulbe by 1800 to establish the kingdom of Kaarta. It derived its wealth from the export of slaves and

The Tomb of Biton Koulibali. Segu, Mali, 1976. Photograph © David C. Conrad.

horses in return for Saharan salt from the north and gold and kola nuts from the south. Cloth was the principal currency. The Massassi relied on *tonjon* to establish their authority, for the Kulibali were divided into six lineages that produced internecine disputes and rival candidates for the throne. They made little attempt to include the indigenous chiefs in their courts, but the *faama* observed traditional Bambara rituals, led by a priesthood that maintained the court temple with altars and objects called *bori* to ensure the fertility of women and the land. Muslim clerics, most of whom were Soninke and involved in the caravan trade, were tolerated but not permitted to interfere in the enslavement of Muslims and their sale or other Bambara customs repugnant to Islam.

Massassi rule in Kaarta was unpopular but uncontested until the 1840s. The Kulibali kept firm control of the fertile Kolombine region and the caravan routes to the Upper Senegal and its rich gum and cloth trade that had hitherto been the monopoly of the state of Khasso. In the 1820s the Kulibali had expanded to the east at the expense of their former rulers in Segu, until checked in the 1840s by the Muslim regime in Masina. They never successfully subdued the Awlad Mbark Berbers to the north, whose mobile camels and cavalry eluded the more pedestrian forces of the Massassi and their *tonjon*. The Jawara Soninke of Kaarta never reconciled themselves to Massassi Kulibali rule and revolted in the 1840s. Although defeated, they continued their insurgency, which weakened the resources of the state.

In the mid-nineteenth century, the tenth *faama*, Mamadi Kanja (*c.*1844–1855), moved the capital from Yelimane in the Kolombine to Koghe and then to Nioro in order to have greater control of the caravan routes from the north and to suppress the Jawara insurgency. His unreliable cousins remained in central Kaarta, in its scattered garrisons, to face the jihad of Al-Hajj Umar Ibn Said Tal and his Tucolor army from the upper Senegal. Tal was determined to impose Islam on the Bambara Massassi of Kaarta. The walled towns of the Kulibali, Yelimane and Koghe, fell to Al-Hajj Umar and his Jawara allies. He occupied the Massassi capital of Nioro on April 11, 1855. Mamdi Kanja submitted and converted to Islam. Bambara shrines were destroyed and mosques were built.

This was the formal end to the Massassi dynasty of the Kulibali, but in defeat the Massassi demonstrated a remarkable unity to regain their privileged position in Kaarta. Violent Bambara Massassi revolts against Al-Hajj Umar broke out in 1855 and 1856 that were ruthlessly suppressed, but at great cost to the invaders. Thereafter the successors of Al-Hajj Umar colonized Kaarta with Fulbe from the Senegambia, while maintaining commercial relations with the Berber traders for salt in return for gold, kola, and slaves. The Massassi staged an abortive revolt in the 1870s but were defeated and driven into exile by the successor to Al-Hajj Umar, Amadu Sheku Tal in 1874.

Kaarta recovered from these years of violence. The Massassi returned in 1879 and there was a brief period of peace. Threatened by the loss of their slaves from the French policy of abolition, thousands of Fulbe in the Senegambia migrated to Kaarta, where they played a leading role in the resistance to French expansion. The Fulbe colonists found in Kaarta land, slaves, minimal government, mosques, and Quranic schools. They supported Amadu, who sought to create at Nioro in Kaarta the Islamic society of his father. In the autumn of 1890, Captain Louis Archinard led 200 French officers and men and 1,500 African *tirailleurs* to defeat Amadu and destroy the last vestiges of Tucolor authority in Kaarta. After a brief skirmish outside Nioro on January 1, 1891, Amadu abandoned the capital and fled eastward to Masina to make the last stand against the advancing French forces. The Massassi and the Bambara of Kaarta were to become reluctant subjects of the French empire in west Africa, where revolts against French authority were ruthlessly suppressed. At the beginning of the twentieth century, Kaarta was still a divided region. In the north and west the population was approximately 150,000; slaves made up one-third of that population. In southern Kaarta, the Bambara descendants of the Massassi remained to control the trade and the land as in the past.

ROBERT O. COLLINS

Further Reading

Montiel, C. *Les Bambara de Ségou et du Kaarta*. Paris: Larose, 1924.

Pollet, E., and G. Winter. *La société soninke*. Bruxelles: Institu de sociologe, Université libre de Bruxelles, 1971.

Raffenel, A. *Nouveau voyage dans le pays des nègres* [*New Travel in the Country of the Blacks*]. Paris: Impr. et Libraire Centrales des Chemins de Fer, 1856.

Robinson, D. *The Holy War of Umar Tal*. Oxford: Clarendon Press, 1985.

Tauxier, L. *Histoire des Bambara*. Paris: P. Geuthner, 1942.

Massawa, Ethiopia, and the Ottoman Empire

Since the Aksumite period, the Red Sea and its ports were the main outlet for Ethiopia's contacts, for trade and other purposes, with the outside world. For this reason, Ethiopian rulers have always sought to exercise hegemony over the Red Sea ports or, at least, to have unrestricted access to the Red Sea coast. For similar commercial reasons control of the ports in particular, and the Red Sea basin in general, was a matter of crucial importance to all other powers with interest in the Red Sea trade. This was especially true of Egypt, the

Ottoman (Turkish) Empire, which conquered Egypt in 1517, and Portugal, which had by 1502 established a sea route to India via the Cape of Good Hope and sought to protect it through control of the Red Sea ports. Given the circumstances, conflict between these various powers with interest in the Red Sea could hardly be avoided in the sixteenth and seventeenth centuries.

From at least the tenth century, the port of Massawa, situated on an offshore island, and its twin port of Arkiko, situated on the mainland opposite the island, became the principal Red Sea ports for Ethiopia's external trade. The twin ports therefore became the main targets for control in the struggle over the Red Sea coast at this period.

By the beginning of the sixteenth century, Ethiopia exercised hegemony over the twin ports. They remained under Ethiopian control until 1557, when they were seized by the Ottoman Turks operating from Egypt.

With the revival of trade in the Red Sea, the Arabian peninsula, and the Persian Gulf from the late fifteenth century, the expanding Ottoman Empire turned its attention to these areas, conquering Egypt in 1517 and Aden in 1538. From about 1520 to about 1566 the Ottoman Turks struggled unsuccessfully with the Portuguese for control of the trade route to India and the Far East. Their failure against the Portuguese led the Ottomans to settle for dominating the Red Sea coast.

To this end, the Turks occupied the port of Massawa in 1557 and thereafter sought to establish their hegemony over Ethiopia's coastal province. Conflict between the Ottoman Turks and Christian Ethiopia over Massawa and its hinterland became a regular feature of the history of the area.

In their effort to create a hinterland for Massawa, Ottoman troops seized and fortified Arkiko on the mainland, advanced inland onto the plateau and occupied Debarwa, the capital of Ethiopia's coastal province (*Bahr midr*), fifty-seven miles from the coast. A wall was constructed around Debarwa and a mosque built there. An *eyalet* of Habesh, or Ottoman province of Ethiopia, was created with its headquarters at Massawa. Turkish-Ethiopian conflicts had thus began.

In 1559 Ethiopians expelled the Ottomans from Debarwa, but up to the end of the seventeenth century, the Ottoman Turks not only made periodic incursions into Debarwa but also meddled in the internal politics of Ethiopia. Ethiopia's relations with the Ottoman authorities in Massawa were marked by uneasy coexistence. Several incidents reflect their tense relations. In 1561–1562, Uthman Pasha, the Ottoman governor of Massawa, made peace with Bahr Nagash Yishaq and sent troops to support the latter in his revolt against emperor Minas (1559–1563). Like many other provincial governors, Yishaq resisted the centralizing policy of the emperor. During the sixteenth and seventeenth centuries, a number of the emperors of Ethiopia attempted reforms to centralize political military and administrative power in the hands of the imperial authority at the expense of the provincial governors; the governors, on their part, wanted to be independent of the central imperial authority and therefore invariably opposed the reforms by rebelling against the reforming monarch.

Bahr Nagash Yishaq and his Ottoman allies defeated Emperor Minas in battle in 1562 but Minas's successor Sarsa Dengel won back the allegiance of the Bahr Nagash by restoring Tigrean autonomy. As a result, the alliance fell apart.

In 1572 the Ottoman Turks attacked and captured Debarwa, but once again they were evicted in 1574 by their erstwhile ally, Bahr Nagash Yishaq. Three years later an alliance was made between the Ottoman Turkish governor of Habesh, Ahmad Pasha, and Bahr Nagash Yishaq, in disgrace at the time but as ambitious as ever. This alliance led to another clash between Ethiopia and the Turks. In the encounters that followed, the Ethiopian emperor defeated the allied forces in two successive battles, leaving both allied leaders dead on the battlefield at Addi Quro on December 17, 1578. In 1588 the Ottomans again occupied Debarwa, but this time the occupation was short-lived; thereafter, they restricted their activities to Massawa, which they occupied until the late nineteenth century.

Over the course of the seventeenth century, Ottoman power and interest in the Red Sea declined; the garrison at Massawa was reduced while Arkiko was handed over to a Beja family, which subsequently governed the mainland port on behalf of the Ottoman Turks. The Beja governor was given the title of Na'ib.

Despite the weakened position and interest of the Ottomans on the coast, the ever-shifting relationship between the Turks and Ethiopia continued during the seventeenth century. In the first quarter of the century there were tensions from time to time between the two over Turkish raids for cattle in Ethiopia's coastal province or confiscation of goods destined for Ethiopia from overseas or over imposition of high tariffs on such goods. Each time such a situation developed, Ethiopia was able to secure restitution or compliance from the Turks by stopping caravans from going to the coast.

In 1648, however, Ethiopia and the Ottomans in Massawa temporarily settled their differences and made an agreement that required the Ottoman governor of Massawa to prevent Europeans in general and Catholic missionaries, in particular, from entering Ethiopia via Massawa. This agreement followed up on Emperor Fasiladas's (1632–1667) expulsion in 1632 of the Jesuit missionaries who, starting from 1557, had attempted to convert Ethiopia to the Roman Catholic faith. The Jesuit missionary activity brought divisions not only within the church but also in the Ethiopian polity and resulted in a devastating civil war during the reign of Emperor Susneyos (1607–1632).

The uneasy coexistence between Ethiopia and the Ottoman Turks in Massawa continued for the rest of the seventeenth century and into the next century. Although Ethiopia was interested in controlling Massawa and was able to exercise influence there because the town depended on the mainland for water and other supplies, Ethiopia was not strong enough to militarily capture the port from Ottoman control. On the other hand, though dependent on the mainland for supplies, the Ottoman Turks were either not interested enough or too preoccupied in other areas to have wanted to conquer Ethiopia.

R. H. Kofi Darkwah

Further Reading

Abir, M. *Ethiopia and the Red Sea.* Totowa, N.J.: Frank Cass and Company, 1980.

Haggai, E. *Ethiopia and the Middle East.* London: Lynne Reinner Publishers, 1994.

Jones, A. H. M., and E. Monroe. *A History of Ethiopia.* Oxford: Clarendon Press, 1974.

Pankhurst, R. *The Ethiopians.* Oxford and Malden: Blackwell Publishers Limited, 1998.

———. *History of Ethiopian Towns from the Middle Ages to the Early Nineteenth Century.* Stuttgart: F. Steiner Verlag Wiesbaden, 1982.

Van Donzel, E. "Massawa." In *Encyclopedia of Islam*, edited by E. Van Donzel. Leiden, 1993.

Matthews, Z. K. (1901–1968)

South African Educationalist and Political Leader.

Zachariah Keodirelang (Z. K.) Matthews was a prominent leader of the African National Congress (ANC) in the 1940s and 1950s, and a pioneer African educationalist at a time when there were very few black academics in South Africa.

Matthews was strongly influenced by Christian, Cape liberal traditions that emphasized the power of education to resolve social inequalities and belief in a nonracial society. He had ties with white liberals, serving on the executive of the South African Institute of Race Relations. Yet he also believed that Africans should run their own lives and that their history should be written from an African point of view. His own family and Tswana oral traditions stressed the theft of his people's land by colonizers.

Throughout his career Matthews sought to combine academic and public life. In 1930 he was elected president of the Natal Bantu Teachers' Association and in 1941–1942 held office as president of the Federation of African Teachers' Associations. He served on the 1936–1937 Royal Commission into Higher Education in East Africa and the 1945 Union Advisory Board on Native Education, and also sat on the Ciskei Missionary Council.

Increasingly, opportunities for black advancement were blocked under segregationist and, after 1948, apartheid policies, driving members of the black elite such as Matthews into politics. He helped launch the All-African Convention in 1935 but then joined the ANC in 1940, being elected to its National Executive in 1943 and helping draw up *African Claims* (1943) and the *Program of Action* (1949), seminal statements of the ANC's transition to a more mass-based movement. Elected president of the Cape ANC in 1949, in the same year he declined nomination as national ANC president by Congress Youth League activists led by Nelson Mandela.

During the 1940s the ANC had an ambiguous policy toward state structures, which could at times be used to aid African interests. Hence Matthews, together with other ANC figures, was elected in 1942 to the Natives' Representative Council (NRC), a consultative body with no real power. In this forum he defended African rights and in 1946, on behalf of the NRC's African members, condemned the "wanton shooting" by police of striking African mineworkers. However, despite the urging of ANC radicals, it was not until 1950 that he resigned from the NRC in protest of apartheid policies.

Matthews remained active in politics in the 1950s. He was involved in preparations for the Defiance Campaign but did not take part in its actions, as from June 1952 to May 1953 he was a visiting professor at the Union Theological Seminary in New York City where, despite pressure by Pretoria, he also lobbied the United Nations. At the 1953 ANC annual conference, in response to questions about alternatives to apartheid, he proposed a Congress of the People to draw up a charter to embody the aspirations of all South Africans. This landmark Congress was held in 1955 and its product, the Freedom Charter, became a core policy document of the ANC for the next four decades. Matthews also served as ANC deputy president general under Chief Albert Lutuli, delivering the 1955 presidential address on his behalf. However, state repression increased and in December 1956 he and his son Joe, together with many other prominent ANC leaders, were detained for the treason trial. Matthews was acquitted only in April 1959 and was again detained during the 1960 emergency. Nevertheless, he continued to contribute to various unity initiatives, including the 1960 Cottesloe Consultation of the World Council of Churches in Johannesburg and briefly resumed the post of Cape ANC president.

Facing persecution, Z. K. left South Africa in 1961. In exile he focused on ecumenical work, spending five years as Africa director of the World Council of Churches in Geneva but also speaking out against apartheid. In 1966 he became Botswana's ambassador to the United States and permanent representative to the United Nations. He died in Washington, D.C. in 1968 and was buried in Botswana.

Matthews was a prolific writer and wrote numerous scholarly and press articles on South African politics and history, as well as works on Tswana history and culture, and a posthumously published autobiography.

Matthews was a moderate, and wary of radicals. Yet he also was influenced by African nationalist ideas prevailing in the post-1940 ANC, and his consistent advocacy of black rights and his elevated status as a pioneer African educator made him an important force for unity in the ANC. He came to see that the ANC had to become an effective mass movement, and his liberalism did not prevent him from acknowledging, in the early 1960s, that the ANC's turn to armed struggle took place only when all peaceful avenues had been closed. His legacy endures. In 1997 Thabo Mbeki told the South African Truth and Reconciliation Commission that Z. K. Matthews was "an outstanding leader of our people."

PETER LIMB

See also: **Mandela, Nelson; South Africa: Defiance Campaign, Freedom Charter, Treason Trials: (1952–1960).**

Biography

Zachariah Keodirelang (Z. K.) Matthews was born in Barkly West, Cape Colony, in 1901. Graduating from Lovedale Missionary Institution and the South African Native College (later University of Fort Hare) he was appointed in 1925 as the first African principal of Adams College, Amanzimtoti, Natal. Received an LLB degree (the first African to receive this honor from the University of South Africa) in 1930 and was admitted to the Johannesburg bar. In 1934 he was awarded an master's degree from Yale University and then was a research fellow at the International Institute of African Languages and Cultures at the London School of Economics under anthropologist Bronislaw Malinowski. Appointed Lecturer in social anthropology and Bantu law and administration at Fort Hare in 1936. Promoted to professor of African studies in 1945. In 1954 and 1956 he was acting principal and remained at Fort Hare until 1959 when he resigned over the apartheid government's discriminatory policy of "Bantu Education." Helped launch the All-African Convention in 1935 but then joined the ANC in 1940, being elected to its national executive in 1943. From June 1952 to May 1953 he was a visiting professor at the Union Theological Seminary in New York. In December 1956 he detained for the treason trial. Matthews was acquitted only in April 1959. Detained again during the 1960 emergency. Left South Africa in 1961. Named Botswana's ambassador to the United States and permanent representative to the United Nations in 1966. Died in Washington, D.C. in 1968.

Further Reading

Juckes, T. J. *Opposition in South Africa: The Leadership of Z. K. Matthews, Nelson Mandela, and Stephen Biko.* Westport, Conn: Praeger, 1995.

Karis, T., and G. Carter, eds. *From Protest to Challenge: A Documentary History of African Politics in South Africa, 1882–1964.* Vol. 4, Political Profiles 1882–1964, by G. Gerhart and T. Karis, 79–81. Stanford: Hoover Institution Press, 1997.

Kros, C. "'Deep Rumblings': Z. K. Matthews and African Education before 1955." *Perspectives in Education.* 12, no.1 (1990): 21–40.

Matthews, F. B. *Remembrances.* Bellville: Mayibuye Books, 1995.

Matthews, Z. K. *Freedom for My People: The Autobiography of Z. K. Matthews: Southern Africa 1901 to 1968*, with a Memoir by M. Wilson. London: Rex Collings, and Cape Town: David Philip, 1981.

Saayman, W. A. *A Man with a Shadow: The Life and Times of Professor Z. K. Matthews: A Missiological Interpretation In Context.* Pretoria: University of South Africa, 1996.

Verhoef, G. "Z. K. Matthews." In *New Dictionary of South African Biography*, edited by E. J. Verwey. Pretoria: HSRC, 1995.

White, T. R. G. "Verging on Treason: Z. K. Matthews and the Congress of the People Campaign." *Journal for Contemporary History.* 21, no. 1 (1996): 106–123.

Mau Mau Revolt: *See* Kenya: Mau Mau Revolt.

Mauritania: Colonial Period: Nineteenth Century

Nineteenth-century Mauritania remained a stateless society dominated by nomadic and semisedentary Arabo-Berber pastoralists (Moors), with Black Wolof and Tukolor sedentary cultivator communities located primarily along the Senegal River. Enslaved blacks and descendants of freed slaves bound by clientage to their former masters existed throughout Mauritanian society.

A process of cultural and linguistic Arabization among the Muslim Moors that had begun in the sixteenth century with the first influxes of small groups of Arab immigrants culminated in the nineteenth century. By the end of the century, the Berber Znaga dialect had largely given way to the Arabic dialect known as Hassaniyya, and patrilineal Arab genealogies had largely supplanted older matrilineal Berber genealogies as the basis for constructing social identity.

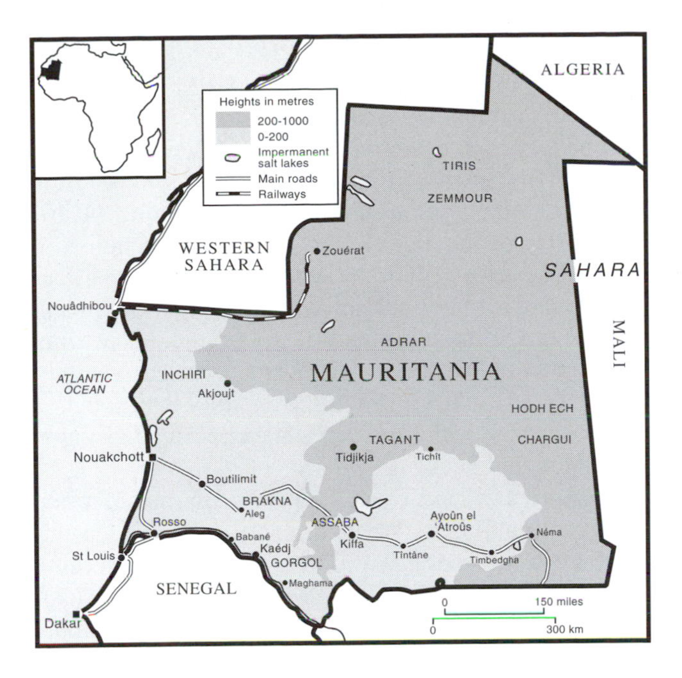

Mauritania.

Important sources from that period suggest a rigid social stratification dominated by Arab warriors called the *Banu Hassan* and Berber clerics known as the *Zawaya*. In fact, social identity, both genealogically and occupationally, was considerably more fluid. Groups periodically merged, disbanded or emigrated, acquiring or shedding aspects of their identity in the process. Similarly, groups once engaged in nomadic pastoralism occasionally became sedentary in the transition into trade or scholarly activity, while others adapted to a new pastoralist culture after moving from regions that supported camel husbandry to regions that were better suited to cattle. Warriors who based their livelihood on raiding and the collection of protection tribute were sometimes forced into tributary status themselves by more powerful groups, and in some cases relinquished their arms altogether under threat of punishment or under the influence of religious leaders. At other times, groups whose leaders were revered spiritual figures had recourse to take up arms against one another, as occurred between the Kunta and the Tajakant on numerous occasions throughout the century.

The gum arabic trade, transacted at trading ports established on the Senegal River's right bank in the southwestern Mauritanian region known as the *Gibla,* spurred growing European interest in Mauritania throughout the nineteenth century. Europeans used gum arabic, a resin found in the variety of acacia tree prevalent across southern Mauritania, in the production of textiles and pharmaceuticals. *Banu Hassan* groups initially dominated trade at the ports and required toll payments by Moorish and French traders (or their indigenous representatives) alike. A growing French military presence in Senegal gradually eroded *Hassani* authority, first by granting French protection to, then by establishing French authority over, agricultural communities formerly under *Banu Hassan* hegemony on both banks of the Senegal River. By mid-century, the governor of Senegal Louis Faidherbe was able to exact *Hassani* recognition of French sovereignty even over the right bank ports.

In 1899 the French colonial ministry successfully lobbied to expand French authority throughout West Africa, including Mauritania. Responding to a request by France's prime minister for a means of achieving this goal at minimal cost in men or materiel, an Algerian-born Corsican in the colonial administration named Xavier Coppolani proposed a method of "peaceful pacification" that was quickly embraced in the foreign office. Coppolani's plan entailed coopting Moorish religious leaders through promises of protection from the region's endemic raiding, thereby removing the major obstacle to their religious and commercial endeavors. Early on, Coppolani succeeded in gaining the cooperation of the most influential religious figures in the *Gibla*, Shaykhs Sidiyya Baba and Sa'd Bu.

Coppolani also attempted to play on rivalries among warrior groups in his efforts to gain a foothold in the region, although early success with this divide and conquer strategy proved ephemeral. Faced with stiffening resistance, Coppolani's initial strategy quickly gave way to overtly military means of conquest. Moors opposed to the growing French presence turned to Sa'd Bu's brother Ma' al-'Aynayn whose close relations with the Moroccan sultan and outspoken opposition to any foreign incursion drew the growing resistance movement to him. The French attributed Coppolani's assassination in 1905 to Ma' al-'Aynayn's machinations though largely on circumstantial evidence. From his compound at Smara, Ma' al-'Aynayn led the struggle to force the French out, until 1909 when he and his followers were driven from Smara in the face of an advancing French force and were forced to flee to Tiznit in southern Morocco.

The French government incorporated Mauritania into its wider colonial administration of Afrique Occidental Française (AOF). Organized to mirror other AOF civil territories, France divided Mauritania into administrative units known as *cercles* that remained largely intact even beyond independence. Mauritania was proclaimed a separate colony in 1920, although still under the auspices of the AOF's governor general. Notwithstanding these administrative changes, French "pacification" of the whole of Mauritania would not be complete until 1934. Even then, many of the colony's nomadic inhabitants remained either beyond the pale of French rule or subject to only nominal government control. In 1944 a decision to add the eastern region known as the Hodh to Mauritania from the adjoining territory the Soudan (modern Mali), created the borders that exist today.

Following the end of World War II, France responded to growing criticism both at home and abroad of its continued role as colonizer by initiating steps to grant its colonial subjects greater autonomy. In accordance with the 1946 constitution of the Fourth Republic, Mauritania formally became part of the French Union as an overseas territory. The election of Mauritania's first representative to the French National Assembly in 1946 underscored considerable political divisions among Mauritanians. The more progressive elements were predominantly socialist, avowedly nationalistic, and hostile to the region's traditional chieftaincies, while more conservative elements drawn primarily from the traditional power structure sought to maintain the status quo including retaining close ties with France. The progressives, with the backing of the French Socialist Party, carried the day, electing the young nationalist and political neophyte Horma Wuld Babana.

Wuld Babana ultimately alienated his core constituencies by remaining in Paris throughout his tenure as representative in order to pursue his own personal political ambitions, and when he launched a new political party in 1948, the Entente Mauritanienne, it failed to secure a solid base in Mauritania's developing political arena. A rival party formed that same year with the backing of the traditional chieftains, the *Union Progressiste Mauritanienne* (UPM), filled the political vacuum; its candidate, Sidi al-Mukhtar N'Diaye, succeeded in unseating Wuld Babana in his 1951 reelection bid. Wuld Babana remained a controversial figure on the Mauritanian political scene for several more years, but his support of Moroccan claims of a Greater Morocco that included Mauritania finally doomed his political future.

The following year the UPM won all but two of the twenty-four seats in the General Council, which France had established as a consultative body and a first stage in granting greater future legislative autonomy to the territory. Not long after its formation, leadership of the UPM passed to Mukhtar Wuld Daddah, a member of Sidiyya Baba's important Gibla tribe the Awlad Ibiri. Wuld Daddah attended school in Saint Louis, Senegal, before serving the colonial administration as an interpreter during World War II. After the war, he studied in France where he attained a law degree, becoming the first Mauritanian trained in French law. Despite the UPM's continued success under Wuld Daddah's guidance, the party failed to represent all segments of Mauritanian society's interests.

In the mid-1950s, a generational divide among party members resulted in the formation of the Association de la Jeunesse Mauritanienne (AJM) whose members were impatient with the older UPM leadership. The AJM sought to push harder for Mauritania's independence and democratization, but its pan-Arab inclinations alienated many non-Moors. The Bloc Democratique du Gorgol (BDG) arose among Mauritania's Halpulaar population largely in response to fears of closer ties with the Arab north, and in particular, of calls for political unity with newly independent Morocco. On the other end of the political spectrum, the Nahda al-Wataniyya al-Muritaniyya Party represented Moors in the north of the territory who sought a rapprochement with Morocco while opposing federation with Mali and Senegal.

In April 1957 the French government moved a step closer to granting its West African colonies independence by reorganizing the AOF into distinct governing councils. Wuld Daddah was selected to form a Mauritanian government, and in an effort to achieve national unity, he drew from opposition and allies alike to form a cabinet. In May 1958 Wuld Daddah formed a new party the Parti du Regroupement Mauritanien (PRM) that fused the UPM, remnants of Entente Mauritanienne, and moderates in the AJM. Nahda remained as the only opposition party capable of challenging the PRM until a corruption scandal and internal dissent destroyed its viability as a mainstream political force. In response to Nahda's increasingly militant posture, Wuld Daddah's government banned the party and arrested its leaders. This left the PRM unchallenged on the eve of Mauritanian independence.

France granted Mauritania autonomy as a member of the French Community in October 1958, and on March 2, 1959, the Islamic Republic of Mauritania adopted its first constitution. Over the course of the next eighteen months France transferred power to Wuld Daddah's government culminating on November 28, 1960, with a proclamation of Mauritanian independence.

GLEN W. MCLAUGHLIN

Further Reading

Cleaveland, T. "Islam and the Construction of Social Identity in the Nineteenth Century Sahara." *Journal of African History.* 39 (1998): 365–388.

Desire-Vuillemin, G. *Histoire de la Mauritanie: Des origines a l'Independance.* Paris: Editions Karthala, 1997.

Ould Cheikh, A. W. *Elements d'histoire de la Mauritanie.* Nouakchott: Centre Culturel Francais, 1988.

———. "Herders, Traders, and Clerics: The Impact of Trade, Religion and Warfare on the Evolution of Moorish Society." In *Herders, Warriors, and Traders: Pastoralism in Africa,* edited by J. G. Galaty and P. Bonter. Boulder, Colo.: Westview Press, 1991.

Taylor, R. M. "Warriors, Tributaries, Blood Money and Political Transformations in Nineteenth Century Mauritania." *Journal of African History.* (1995): 419–441.

Webb, J. L. A., Jr. *Desert Frontier: Ecological and Economic Change along the Western Sahel 1600–1850.* Madison: University of Wisconsin Press, 1995.

Mauritania: Independence and Western Sahara, 1960–1979

Mauritania achieved independence from France on November 8, 1960, establishing itself as the world's first Islamic republic. The president of the pre-independence Conseil, General Mukhtar Wuld Daddah, succeeded in unifying existing tribal, ethnic, and ideological divisions to become Mauritania's first prime minister. Morocco's Sultan Muhammad V (d.1961), and then his successor Hassan II, claimed Mauritania as part of a historical "Greater Morocco" and not only refused to recognize an independent Mauritania but used his influence to sway other Arab leaders to deny the state's legitimacy. Faced with this diplomatic affront, Wuld Daddah looked to his Sub-Saharan African neighbors for support while maintaining strong ties to France, including a French military presence that remained in Mauritania until 1966.

Throughout the early 1960s, Wuld Daddah moved Mauritania gradually toward single-party rule. A revised constitution passed in May 1961 by a National Assembly dominated by Wuld Daddah's Parti de Regroupement Mauritanien (PRM) centralized authority in the office of the president, and on August 20, 1961, Wuld Daddah handily won the country's first presidential election. Soon after, the PRM and certain of the other smaller political parties convened to create a new unified political party the Parti du Peuple Mauritanien (PPM) under Wuld Daddah's leadership, and in 1965 a constitutional amendment granted the PPM sole legal status as a political party.

By the mid-1960s, most Arab League member states had reversed their earlier positions and entered into diplomatic and economic relations with Mauritania. Bolstered by growing Arab support, Wuld Daddah embarked on a domestic policy of Arabization in 1966 whose centerpiece was the replacement of French as the official language in education and government with Arabic. This decision alienated many black Mauritanians for whom Arabic was not a principal language and ensuing protests led to repressive police actions that left several dead and dozens wounded, while numerous prominent black leaders were arrested.

Algerian President Boumédienne succeeded in initiating a dialogue between Wuld Daddah and Morocco's King Hassan II that led to a Moroccan renunciation of its claims to Mauritania in 1970 and the establishment of diplomatic relations between the two countries. No longer dependent on France's protection from Morocco and facing growing nationalist pressure within Mauritania, Wuld Daddah took steps to distance himself from France that increased further the country's dependence on his Arab allies. Mauritania issued a national currency, the ougiya, in 1973, replacing the French CFA (Communaute Financiere Africaine) used by other francophone West African countries. The following year Wuld Daddah nationalized MIFERMA, the French-owned iron ore consortium. By the mid-1970s, Wuld Daddah had achieved internal stability albeit at times through repressive measures, and stability vis-à-vis his regional neighbors through successfully balancing Mauritania's position in both African and Arab political spheres.

Events surrounding the decolonization of Spanish Sahara not only jeopardized this stability but ultimately brought Wuld Daddah's rule to an end. For as long as Spain retained its hold over the colony, Wuld Daddah was able to voice public support for its inhabitants' right to self-determination with the assurance that Spain's presence afforded as a buffer between Morocco and Mauritania's vast northern border. The rapprochement between Wuld Daddah and Hassan II altered Wuld Daddah's position, and in Madrid on November 14, 1975, he signed a secret tripartite agreement with Spain and Morocco that called for partitioning Spanish Sahara between the two countries following Spain's imminent departure.

Forced by Morocco's decision to carry out the Madrid agreement and annex its portion of the former colony in January 1976, Wuld Daddah dispatched troops to Rio de Oro, renaming the territory Tiris al-Gharbiya. The Polisario Front, the militant force of the movement for Western Saharan independence, immediately struck at Mauritania. The Polisario leaders rightly felt that Mauritania was far more vulnerable to attack than Morocco and less prepared to sustain an armed conflict over the annexed territory. Polisario waged a campaign that quickly crippled Mauritania's economy by significantly disrupting the transport of iron ore from the northern mining town of Zerouate to the port in Nouadhibou, as well as striking targets much deeper into Mauritania. The entire country suffered a severe psychological blow when, on two occasions, the Polisario forces reached the Mauritanian capital Nouakchott and attacked the presidential palace with mortar fire. Efforts to respond to this threat by more than quintupling the size of the Mauritanian army placed additional stress on the country's rapidly weakening economy, but did little to reverse its military fortunes.

In mid-1977 Wuld Daddah took the unprecedented step of signing a mutual defense pact with Morocco that, among other things, allowed Morocco to station nearly 9,000 soldiers on Mauritanian soil. In addition, the Mauritanian president turned to former colonizer

France for military aid and air support. These decisions were both unpopular and ultimately ineffectual in turning the tide of war. Finally, the cumulative effect of Wuld Daddah's efforts to sustain control of Tiris al-Gharbiya was more than his presidency could bear. A group of disaffected military officers under the leadership of Colonel Mustafa Wuld Salek staged a bloodless coup d'étât on July 10, 1978, arresting Wuld Daddah and several of his closest aides.

Competing agendas within the newly formed government known as the Comité Militaire de Redressement National (CMRN) impeded efforts toward a settlement despite the Polisario's unilateral cease-fire against Mauritania. In April 1979, a second bloodless coup led by Lieutenant Colonel Ahmad Wuld Busayf under the banner of the Comite Militaire de Salut National (CMSN) removed Wuld Salek from power and promised a more aggressive effort to reach a peace agreement. However, Wuld Busayf died in a plane crash on May 27, 1979, and Lieutenant Colonel Muhammad Khuna Wuld Haidallah succeeded him as prime minister. The Polisario responded to Wuld Haidallah's early cautious diplomacy by resuming attacks on Mauritanian targets in an effort to force Wuld Haidallah's hand. On August 5, 1979, the CMSN signed an agreement in Algiers relinquishing Mauritania's claim to Tiris al-Gharbiya and agreeing to hand its administration over to the Polisario, but before this could occur, Moroccan forces occupied Tiris al-Gharbiya.

GLEN W. MCLAUGHLIN

Further Reading

Gerteiny, A. G. *Mauritania.* New York: Frederick A. Praeger, Publishers, 1967.

Hodges, T. *Western Sahara: The Roots of a Desert War.* Westport: Lawrence Hill and Company, 1983.

Mercer, J. *Spanish Sahara.* London: George Allen and Unwin, 1976.

Thompson, V., and R. Adloff. *The Western Saharans.* London: Croom Helm, 1980.

Mauritania: Domestic and International Politics and Conflict, 1980s and 1990s

Mauritania's history in the last two decades of the twentieth century was infused with cataclysmic political upheavals at both the domestic and international levels. The ousting of the first elected government of President Moukhtar Ould Daddah, in a military coup in July 1978, and the establishment of the Military Committee for National Salvation (Comité Militaire de Salut National: CMSN) was to mark a critical turning point in the country's history. The first two years of military government, from 1978 to late 1979, witnessed a spate of changes: political parties were banned while the National Assembly was disbanded; existing government bodies were dissolved and the country's constitution was suspended, while within the military authority itself there were incessant counter-coups and cabinet reshuffles.

In January 1980 the governing Military Committee announced the dismissal of the then head of state, Lt. Col. Mahmoud Ould Louly, who had been in office since May 1979. He was replaced by Lt. Col. Mohamed Khouna Ould Haidalla, who had been prime minister and minister of defense under Louly's government. In April of that year, a group of exiled Mauritanian army officers then in asylum in Morocco allegedly plotted a countercoup, aimed at turning Mauritania toward a more active policy against the Polisario, the organization fighting for the independence of Western Sahara. Following this, several members of the military and former government ministers were arrested. A cabinet reshuffle took place thereafter, resulting in the dismissal of some top military officers, including the army chief of staff and the interior minister. In May, Haidalla accused the French of masterminding disturbances, resulting in the forced departure of all French troops. In June 1980 an opposition movement in Paris, known as the Mauritania Democratic Alliance, was formed in a bid to return ousted President Daddah (then exiled in Paris) to power. Prompted by the extent of Mauritania's socioeconomic crisis, the regime of Ould Haidalla began a process of initiating a few far-reaching changes. Slavery was made illegal on July 15, 1980, although it took some time before the full implementation of the abolition law was felt.

An experiment in civilian government was initiated on December 15, 1980, but ended abruptly less than five months thereafter, with the restoration of full military rule under Haidalla's control as supreme commander by the end of April 1981. However, Ould Haidalla began to restrict the fundamental rights of the people. The harsher provisions of the shari'a (Islamic legal code) were enforced, especially against perceived political dissenters. Similarly, he clamped down on his opponents through incessant harassment and/or imprisonment. However, Haidalla could not carry his military colleagues in the CMSN along in his policies and actions. He was accused of sanctioning a mode of government based on waste, corruption, and abuse of power. Specific allegations of economic impropriety were leveled against him in his dealings with fishing industry, the country's main foreign exchange earner, from which his family was accused of making huge profits to the detriment of the country.

In the realm of foreign relations, his colleagues in the military junta accused Haidalla of working too closely with the Polisario Front. Tension was further heightened by his unilateral decision to recognize the Saharawi Arab Democratic Republic (SADR) government-in-exile in February 1984, a move that incurred the wrath of Morocco. On December 12, 1984, Colonel Haidalla was overthrown in a bloodless coup led by Col. Moaouiya Ould Sid Ahmed Taya.

The new government of Ould Taya began a process of rapid economic and political transformation. Political prisoners were promptly released, while amnesty was granted to exiles. He instituted anticorruption measures and imposed austerity programs to cut down government expenditure, although these were later revised in 1986 as a result of incessant protests by the country's civil servants. Politically the Ould Taya's government, like its predecessor, granted official recognition to the SADR but kept itself apart from the activities of the Polisario Front. He initiated a process of gradual transition from military to civil rule beginning with the ministerial elections conducted in December 1986.

However, internal stability was short-lived, as the mid-1980s onward witnessed increasing political unrest to which the military head of state reacted by descending heavily on his opponents, both real and imagined. The period was characterized by unprecedented retirement of workers, arrests, detention without trial, and politically motivated assassinations. This incurred the indignation of the Amnesty International and allied organizations that repeatedly accused Ould Taya's government of human rights abuses. Among the groups that rose to challenge the status quo in Mauritania was the Forces de Liberation des Africains en Mauritanie (FLAM), which was established in 1983, with its operational base in Dakar, Senegal. Collaborating with other groups in the country, FLAM sought to unite black Mauritanians in a concerted struggle against the increasing Arabization of that country, while agitating for equal rights and privileges with the Moors, especially in matters of education and employment. The government accused the FLAM membership of undermining national unity and security especially through their distribution of an inflammatory "Manifesto of the Black African Mauritanian." Several activists were arrested and sentenced to prison terms ranging from two to five years. This development further heightened the existing racial tension in Mauritania.

The trend worsened when, in October 1987, Ould Taya's government claimed it had uncovered a coup plot, a development that led to mass arrests and detention of fifty-one Tukular senior military officers, three of whom were later executed while others were sentenced to various prison terms. Over five hundred other black Mauritanians from the rank and file of the army were dismissed from the armed forces.

By the late 1980s racial tensions within Mauritania and the concomitant widespread discontentment in the country had assumed an international dimension, spilling over into neighboring Senegal. The fear was aggravated by the news of the death of many black Mauritanians, especially Tene Youssouf Gueye, a renowned black writer. Many Mauritanians and Senegalese are of the same ethnic stock (i.e., Fulani, Soninke, or Tukulor), and there had been several years of close links between the two neighboring states and, as records indicate, citizens of the two states crossed their respective borders without hindrance to trade and work. By April 1989, however, media propaganda over the alleged prison deaths in Mauritania as well as the ill-treatment of black Mauritanians created tension in Senegal and contributed to the demise of the two nations' peaceful coexistence.

The tension came to a head in April 1989, when disagreements between Senegalese farmers and Mauritanian herdsmen over grazing rights in the Senegal River valley led to clashes, shootings, and looting on both sides. Rioting broke out first in Dakar where Senegalese embarked on massive killing of Mauritanians and the destruction of their property. A few days later, the Mauritanians retaliated, attacking Senegalese in Nouakchott and Nouadhibou. By August 1989, diplomatic relations between the two countries had been severed, leading them to the brink of war in 1989–1990.

While the conflict with Senegal was still raging, internal racial crises continued to engulf Mauritania. Apart from FLAM, whose members were unrelenting in their struggle for equality between the black Mauritanians and their Arab counterparts, a new black militant opposition movement, Front Uni pour la Resistance Armee en Mauritanie (FURAM) emerged on May 1, 1990. FURAM engaged in armed struggle to reject the continued Arabization of Mauritania and the marginalization of blacks. Its constant attack on government military positions, especially at Saboualla, near Kaedi, brought the Ould Taya government to accuse it of masterminding a coup in collaboration with some Senegalese.

Meanwhile, the 1990s witnessed two additional international crises for Mauritania. Civil disorder in neighboring Mali in 1990 had forced Tuaregs to seek refuge in Mauritania. The Malian government thereafter accused Mauritania of harboring Tuaregs who were using Mauritania as a military base for launching attacks on Mali. This created diplomatic tension between the two countries. The next international crisis emanated from the outbreak of the Persian Gulf War in 1990 during which Iraq, under Saddam Hussein, invaded Kuwait. Mauritania, believed to have had close relation with Iraq predating the Gulf War, declared open sympathy and support for that nation. This development aroused the indignation of Mauritania's numerous Arab allies who responded by imposing sanctions.

For much of the 1990s, the political waters of Mauritania remained murky. Tension was high and there were continued allegations of coup plots between 1990 and 1991 leading to mass arrests and executions. In 1992 political activities gathered momentum all over the country. Earlier in 1991, Ould Taya had announced preparations for the conduct of multiparty elections the following year. In the presidential election that followed in January 1992, Ould Taya was declared winner, on the platform of the Parti Republicain Democratique et Social (PRDS). The result was declared unacceptable by the combined group of opposition parties led by the Union des Forces Democratiques (UFD).

Despite these protests, the civilian government led by Ould Taya took control, initiating measures to address the myriad of problems it inherited. Economic problems persisted, generating domestic protests in major towns and cities in 1995 over mounting inflation, especially the rising price of bread. In the area of international politics, a degree of normalcy was restored as diplomatic relations were reestablished with Senegal, Mali, Kuwait, and other members of the Arab league. On the whole, up to the close of the 1990s, Mauritania's domestic and international politics still remained plagued by hope and frustration.

S. Ademola Ajayi

See also: **Mali, Republic of: Politics, Economics: 1990s; Senegal: Independence to the Present.**

Further Reading

Pazzanita, A. G. *Historical Dictionary of Mauritania.* 2nd ed. Lanham, Md. 1996.

Uweche, R. (ed.). *Africa Today*: 1017–1029. London: Africa Books, 1996.

Mauritania: Ethnicity, Conflict, Development, 1980s and 1990s

The Islamic Republic of Mauritania, composed of both the Arab Maghreb and Sahelian West Africa, is a multiethnic country consisting of an Arabic-speaking majority who refer to themselves as the Arabs, or Moors, and African minorities consisting of Tukolors, Wolof, Fulani, and Soninke. The country, with substantial deposits of iron ore, copper, and gypsum has a size of 400,000 square miles. It borders Morocco in the north, Algeria and Mali in the east, and Senegal in the south.

Mauritania had attained its independence from France in 1960. Ever since, the nation had been embroiled in mutual ethnic antagonism, suspicion, instability, and chaos. The government of Mauritania consciously contributed to the hostility that has become an enduring characteristic of this West African state.

The ruling Arab-Moors comprise approximately 80 per cent of the country's population. Immediately after independence, they attempted to "Arabize" the former French colony, without regard for the wishes of the African minorities. The imposition of compulsory Arabic instruction in secondary schools in 1966 led to major riots and deaths, especially in the Senegal valley.

The Arab-Moors continued to dominate politically and their commitment to the gradual implementation of Arabic as a national language did not weaken. This heightened the conflict between the different groups.

The late 1980s and early 1990s further witnessed the inability of the country to come to terms with its multiethnicity. In April 1989 a serious crisis erupted that pitched the Arab-Moors against the blacks. The immediate cause of this was traced to a minor border clash caused by the movement of the nomadic Arab-Berber herdsmen southward, in search of pastures for their cattle. While still on the Mauritanian side of the river Senegal, the herds destroyed the farms of the minority Fulani, Wolof, Soninke, and Bambara ethnic groups. The protest by the black population led to fighting, in which two Senegalese farmers were killed. The angry Senegalese retaliated by attacking Mauritanians in Dakar, the Senegalese capital. Anti-Senegalese clashes also erupted in Nouakchott, the Mauritanian capital. Hundreds of people were killed in the ethnic riots. The clash prompted an exodus of refugees in both directions.

But while the Senegalese government quelled the riots on its own side, the Mauritanian government, under the leadership of President Maaouya Ould Sid' Ahmed Taya (who had seized power in a bloodless military coup in December 1984), seized the opportunity to visit terror on the ethnic populations in the south. Within three months, more than a thousand minorities had been killed.

Mauritania's military government, dominated by the Arab-Moors, began expelling ethnic minorities after accusing them of fraudulently acquiring Mauritanian citizenships. It claimed that Mauritania was exclusively owned by Arabs, and that the ethnic minorities had been placed in the south by the French colonial administration. An official policy to rid Mauritania of its minority population was thus effected. Scores of dark-skinned people were thereafter deported to Senegal irrespective of age, status, and nationality. Mauritanian students in the University of Dakar were withdrawn from their courses of study.

In response, black Mauritanians launched a guerrilla movement from neighboring Senegal called the Mauritanian African Liberation Forces (FLAM). The mass expulsions and torture inflicted on Mauritanian blacks led to villagers in the south setting up so-called resistance committees along the 800-kilometer long border. A sizeable number of black soldiers in the Mauritanian army also deserted.

The violence in the country abated with the advent of multiparty democracy in 1991. A new multiparty constitution was drafted by the ruling Military Committee for National Salvation. (This document replaced one that had been suspended after a military coup in 1978.) Mauritania had been governed under one-party systems virtually since independence. A referendum was held in July 1991 to approve the new constitution, which allowed for an unlimited number of political parties. FLAM suspended its guerilla warfare when Mauritanians voted for a new multiparty constitution.

The military ruler, Sid' Ahmed Taya, ran on the platform of the Democratic and Social Republican Party (DSRP). He won the 1992 multiparty elections in the first round with over 62 per cent of the vote, defeating former political exile Ould Daddah, half-brother of the country's first president. The DSRP also won fifty-two of the seventy-nine seats in the parliamentary elections.

In the election, the Movement for Democracy and Unity (RDU) got one seat, while Independents took nine seats. Voting for the remaining seventeen seats proved inconclusive and went to a second round of voting on March 13, 1992. In the parliamentary elections, official results reported a national turnout of just under 39 per cent, compared with 48 per cent in the presidential elections of 1992. A boycott by six opposition parties, including the high-profile Union of Democratic Forces (UFD), reduced voter numbers in pro-opposition areas, particularly in the south, where black Mauritanians claimed they were oppressed by the Arab-led government.

President Taya's election was protested by the opposition. Five people were killed in a subsequent demonstration that greeted the election result, as security forces opened fire on people outside the headquarters of President Taya's main rival, Ould Daddah. After this episode, the guerillas of FLAM renewed their armed resistance to the government. A similar confusion attended the second presidential election of the democratic era. In 1997 the opposition criticized the government for creating an electoral commission that was not independent and which was established mainly to serve the interests of just one clan. The incumbent president won the election as he had done in 1992.

In spite of the country's tribulations, appreciable progress had been recorded in the socioeconomic spheres. In July 1980 the Mauritanian government officially abolished slavery in the country. A decree to this effect was issued by the then ruling Committee of National Redemption. The law put an end to the plight of Mauritania's black population, which under the cover of the "Islamic Dogmata" was deprived of its civil rights. The abolishing of this obnoxious practice was revolutionary as it would no doubt help speed up the social and economic development of one of the less-developed counties of Africa.

In 1993 Mauritania also adopted far-reaching economic reforms that yielded some positive results. According to an International Monetary Fund (IMF) survey, the country's average Gross Domestic Product (GDP) was sustained at an estimated rate of nearly 5 per cent between 1993 and 1995. The rate of inflation was also reduced to 9.3 per cent in 1993 and to 6.5 per cent in 1995. In 1996 the IMF approved a second yearly loan of $21 million for Mauritania under the Enhanced Structural Adjustment Facility, in support of the country's macroeconomic and structural adjustment program. In the same year, the Organization of African Unity (OAU) gave Mauritania a grant of $100,000 to finance projects in drought-affected areas.

OLUTAYO ADESINA

Further Reading

National Concord (Lagos), June 15, 1989.
National Concord (Lagos), April 30, 1991.
National Concord (Lagos), June 30, 1997.
Young, C. *The Politics of Cultural Pluralism*. Ibadan: Heinemann Educational Books (Nigeria) PLC, 1993.

Mauritius: Slavery and Slave Society to 1835

When slavery ended in Mauritius in 1838–1899, the blow to slave owners was both economic and psychological, as the white Creole ethos was that, by definition, the honorable man owned slaves. The British statutes against the slave trade were formally applied after the island capitulated in December 1810. So far as authority in London was concerned, Mauritius was supposed to survive, like the Caribbean colonies, on the natural increase of its existing slave population, in which women were heavily outnumbered and the mortality rate was high. If the slave trade from Madagascar and Mozambique continued into the early 1820s, as it did, this was due to the prevalence of established attitudes in colonial courts after the capitulation. Governor R. T.

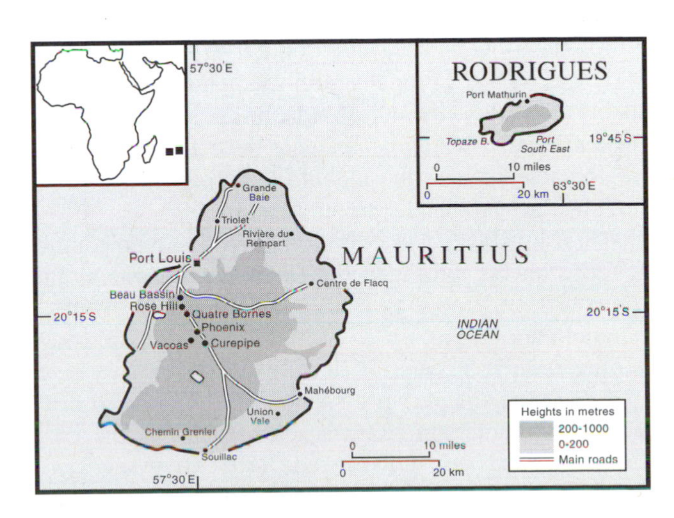

Mauritius.

Farquhar and his circle of British and white Creole officials thoroughly believed in slavery, expected revolt from slave owners if what they regarded as their rights were infringed upon, and feared the martial law that antislave-trade soldiers in the British garrison would willingly have imposed in order to bring the white population under firm control.

The economy depended on a steadily replenished supply of slaves. Between 1773 and 1810, 64,413 new slaves, mainly men, arrived from Mozambique ports and Zanzibar, with about a 25 per cent rate of mortality at sea, while another 12,979 embarked from Madagascar, with a 12 per cent mortality rate To set foot ashore at Port Louis was to be confronted by dockyard slaves with "their spines knotted like a pine tree, and their skins scaled and callous, with the flesh cracked into chasms, from which blood oozed out like gum" (Trelawney, p.187).

The records of slaves enfranchised for service showed how semiskilled urban roles that were once filled by whites had been taken over by slaves in the latter part of the eighteenth century; clearly they had often been hired out by their owners and allowed to keep part of their wages. Legal documents reveal slaves as owned by freed slaves, and the freed in their turn buying loved ones and relations out of slavery.

Just as this was never a self-supporting community of slaves (although there were approximately 14, 000 Creole slave children under the age of twelve in 1826), so it was not a static one either. Some 43,789 slaves changed hands between 1823 and 1830, when Sir Robert Farquhar was able to get the sugar duties changed in the island's favor. The high proportion of new slaves before, if not after, the capitulation hardly increased the security of the minority white, or even of the colored, population. Slaves were controlled directly by their masters, backed by white opinion and power, and only lightly mitigated in practice by theoretical protection offered to slaves by the Code Noire. By the 1740s slave-owners' rights extended so far as directing slave marriages. Compensation was paid to owners for their loss of slave capital. Roads, bridges, public buildings, and fresh-water canals were built and maintained by convicted slaves delinquent in serving their owners or considered a menace to public safety.

Theft by slaves was common. Arson and poisoning seem to have been much feared by slave-owners, but the courts generally showed an awareness of owners' paranoia about this, for an accusation of arson or poisoning against a slave did not always necessarily lead to conviction. There were special slave courts to deal with complaints and charges against slaves. The Port Louis bazaar saw slaves regularly flogged ("corrected," according to the official police records) and occasionally even burnt alive. A common punishment was condemnation to perpetual labor in chains, on public works.

British soldiers and seamen, in particular, found it intolerable that this system was regarded as so essential to the survival of colonial society by white slave-owners in Mauritius, that any relaxation of slave-owners' authority, under existing law or successive Orders in Council promulgated in London, was opposed and considered likely to bring on large-scale slave revolt. The fact was that Rassitatane's "revolt" in 1822 was the only outbreak to rise above the marauding of small bands for mere survival, and whatever may have been in the mind of this exiled, imprisoned, and escaping Madagascar noble, he had only about thirty men with him before his recapture and execution. This may be taken to show how effective the system was. Actually, rebellion was primarily carried out by white Creoles. To show that they were still Frenchmen, they took up arms against the abolition movement, forming an underground local government in the early 1830s. It planned attacks on the garrison but never achieved its goal of an independent island to fruition. Its members were duly acquitted of treason when tried before sympathetic local judges. Britain regarded this affair as a mere show of bravado and refused to implement an elected legislature as demanded by the group.

DERYCK SCARR

Further Reading

Bissoondoyal, U., and S. B. C. Servansing, eds. *Slavery in the South West Indian Ocean.* Moka-Mauritius: Mahatma Gandhi Institute, 1989.

Jeremie, J. *Recent Events in Mauritius.* London, 1836.

Scarr, D. *Slaving and Slavery in the Indian Ocean.* New York: St. Martin's Press, 1998.

Telfair, C. *Some Account of the State of Slavery at Mauritius.* Port Louis, 1830.

Trelawney, E. J. *Adventures of a Younger Son.* London: Oxford University Press, 1974.

Mauritius: Indentured Labor and Society, 1835–1935

Of all nations, Mauritius hosted the largest number of Indian indentured immigrants in the nineteenth century. Some 453,000 indentured laborers were brought to Mauritius, mainly from India, from 1834 to the 1920s. The sugar trade had begun to expand in 1815; this expansion continued at a more rapid pace from 1825. At the same time, a shortage of labor had begun to affect sugar planters, due to several factors: the abolition of the slave trade, the consequent ageing of the existing slave population, increased manumission, a high mortality rate, and a low birth rate. The recruitment of indentured labor from 1834 onward was thus a continuation of attempts to increase the labor supply. Most immigrants were embarked from the ports of Calcutta and Madras and to a lesser extent, Bombay. Mauritius became essentially one large sugar factory, with some 40,000 laborers arriving each year in the peak period.

One of the weaknesses of early indentured immigration had been the absence of women. The colonial government insisted that women form part of any ship carrying emigrants. Most women thus arrived as part of family or kin groups. Most of the women did not take up regular employment, but they did engage in household-based economic activities, such as cattle and poultry rearing and vegetable gardening. Some entered domestic service. A major difference with slavery was that families could be reconstituted. Planters themselves found wives for the laborers and hunted for wives who ran away. The dowry system as practiced in India became converted into a "bride price," with men paying for wives. The planters, contrary to what they had done under slavery, did not object to the formation of families; rather, they encouraged this development, so that they would be able to keep their labor force near or on the estate.

By the 1870s a process of labor stabilization had begun. If in 1860 only 33 per cent of the immigrants reindentured with the same employer, by 1870s, this had increased to 63 per cent. After their term of indenture, the control of immigrants thus became a prime concern for the authorities and the planters, and labor needed to be maintained near or on estates.

In Ordinance 16 of 1862, the concept of the "Old Immigrant" was introduced. In 1867 Ordinance 31 was passed imposing restrictions on the immigrant population that had not existed since the period of apprenticeship. This was the "pass" system, designed to keep track of the movements of laborers. Laborers were photographed and details of their employment were registered on a pass. Failure to carry a pass and produce it on demand led to arrest, imprisonment, and fines. "Old Immigrants" working on estates numbered some 54,383 in 1870 and were exempt from carrying passes. Children of "Old Immigrants" born in Mauritius were also exempt, although it was difficult for the authorities to distinguish between Indian-born and Mauritian-born. The law also did not apply to "Creoles of the Colony, the ex-slaves, and their descendants, the natives of Madagascar, or the African coast" (Report to the governor by Selby Smythe, Major-General, and others, April 4, 1872, RCE Appendix H, p.309).

Just as there were never any major slave revolts in Mauritius, so there were no revolts by indentured servants. Most protests related to work and living conditions and were carried out by small groups. There were also individual acts of violence and frequent desertion or complaints to the protector or magistrate. One significant event was the petition circulated by Adolphe de Plevitz and signed by over 900 laborers outlining their mistreatment in Mauritius. The petition led to the establishment of a Royal Commission of Enquiry. The report is one of the most comprehensive documents relating to the conditions of immigrants in Mauritius. The witnesses interviewed included magistrates, lawyers, accountants, and managers of estates, police, proprietors, and doctors (although no immigrants seem to have been formally interviewed).

After the expiration of their period of "industrial residence" on sugar estates, many indentured immigrants chose to live off the sugar estate. The mechanism by which this occurred and the ensuing transition from camp to village has yet to be analyzed by historians. The movement from camp to village also bore close resemblance to the ex-slaves' desire to leave the sugar estates after 1839, when the apprenticeship system was abolished. The transition for indentured laborers was a much smoother process because they were still able to retain their employment in and around the sugar estate. Both groups, however, faced the restrictions and control of plantation society. Despite these restrictions, villages sprang up in the shadow of the plantation. The movement from camp to village was not only an important historical event but a crucial one for former indentured laborers who began the process of recreating and rebuilding their society, somewhat shattered by the voyage, and period of stay in the camp. The "Indian village" was never recreated but there occurred the emergence of a hybrid culture, which also merits the attention of historians.

There had always been protests against the establishment of the indenture system, many seeing in it another form of "unfree" labor. Protests had come from India and England and even in the receiving colonies themselves. The British government had always seemed uneasy at the criticisms leveled against it but had shown little willingness to change the system. By the end of the 1870s, however, the peak of indentured immigration had passed, and in 1880 very few immigrants arrived. When Gandhi went to South Africa and witnessed firsthand the conditions there, he began a public campaign to have immigration banned. He also visited Mauritius and noted the total separation of wealthy urban Indians from the laborers. Manilall Doctor, a young Indian lawyer was sent to Mauritius and he defended laborers in court and campaigned for equal rights for immigrants. In Mauritius, there began to be protests at the continuation of indenture. Indentured immigration slowly came to a halt in the 1920s when the Sanderson Committee recommended that emigration be stopped.

Acquisition of land and increased access to education at the end of the nineteenth century led to the formation of a new social class among Indian immigrants and their descendants. The two processes brought social and economic mobility leading to a small but influential group made up of professionals and other educated Indo-Mauritians. They were to spearhead the anticolonial struggle and demand better conditions for workers and laborers on sugar estates. Their rise in economic and social status within "Mauritian" society was accompanied by a cultural renaissance leading to the commemoration of the centenary of the arrival of indentured laborers in Mauritius in 1935 and the founding of the Indian Cultural Review and the Indian Cultural Association.

VIJAYA TEELOCK

Further Reading

Bissoondoyal, U. (ed.). *Indian Labour Immigration.* International Conference of Indian Labour Immigration, October 1984. MGI Moka:1986.

Carter, M. *Indian Indentured Migration and the Forced Labour Debate' Itinerario.* 21, no. 1 (1997): 52–61.

———. *Lakshmi's Legacy, Testimonies of Indian Women in 19th Century Mauritius.* EOI, Rose-Hill: 1994.

———. *Servants, Sirdars, and Settlers: Indians in Mauritius 1834–1874.* Oxford: Oxford University Press, 1995.

Deerpalsing, S., and M. Carter. *Select Documents on Indian Immigration.* Vols. 1–3. MGI, Moka: 1994–1996.

Mauritius: Nationalism, Communalism, and Independence, 1935–1968

A movement toward independence only began in the 1950s, partly as a consequence of demands for increased mass political representation in the Legislative and Executive Councils, which had begun in the 1920s and 1930s. In 1951, the British classified Mauritius as a "class III" territory that needed a complex central government because of the unique difficulties caused by its simultaneous small size and complex, multifaceted population. The Colonial Office recommended the creation of a new category of territory, in which a system of self-government would address all concerns except defense and foreign policy, which would continue to be overseen by the British.

In 1942 Governor Mackenzie-Kennedy had made proposals for a new constitution. His proposals gave rise to great debate and two "Consultative Committees." Two camps emerged: the conservatives who did not want universal suffrage, and those who did. The Conservatives also asked for separate rolls for each "community." The question of adequate representation of minorities in a system of democratic elections based on universal suffrage came to the forefront. The underlying assumption was that people voted on a purely ethnic or religious basis, so that an elected candidate would only represent his own ethnic or religious group. Governor Mackenzie-Kennedy had a "distaste for Indian intellectuals" but was forced to implement British Labour policy giving "responsible government to local people."

Elections were held on August 10, 1948. Further elections brought further success to the Mauritius Labour Party (MLP). It strove to make people see that it represented all sections of the population. Today, many political observers see the movement toward independence as having been a struggle between the MLP (considered by some as representing the Indo-Mauritians), and the Parti Mauricien Social Democrate (PMSD) representing Afro-Mauritians and Franco-Mauritians.

The competition between different political parties and politicians to obtain the sympathy of the masses also changed the character of Mauritian politics. Politicians had now to appeal to the masses rather than to a select elite. Public speaking methods, the dimensions of meetings, and the nature and style of propaganda machine had to adapt. People like Seewoosagur Ramgoolam, Renganaden Seenneevassen, and other Western-educated intellectuals came to the forefront. Cr. Curé was replaced by Anquetil as president of the Labour Party; he was succeeded by the charismatic G. Rozemont. Curé and Ramgoolam had very different opinions on the methods to be used to achieve independence. Ramgoolam's training and familiarity with the British political system led him to adopt a parliamentary style of opposition. Curé, on the other hand, adopted a militant stand, confronting British authority directly. The other party to enter the political scene was that started by Sookdeo Bissoondoyal. His brother had started a campaign in 1939 among Hindu-Mauritians to encourage pride in Indian culture, and in 1958 Bissoondoyal founded the Independent Forward Bloc (IFB).

Proportional representation, as it came to be known, came to the forefront during 1955 when the Parti Mauricien began its campaign against what it called "Hindu hegemony." One attempt by Lennox Boyd, the secretary of state, to introduce proportional representation failed. In the MLP, it was the more radical elements that denounced proportional representation, seeing Mauritius as being composed of classes rather than ethnic groups.

In 1959 the principle of universal suffrage was accepted. In the elections that followed, the MLP won twenty-three out of forty seats. There was evidence that the principle of party loyalty was beginning to make headway and that people did not vote blindly for their own ethnic or religious group. The Labour Party, which obtained 41.4 per cent of the vote, received 57 per cent of the seats; the Parti Mauricien won 15 per cent of the votes and received 7.5 per cent of the seats. Ramgoolam was able to press for full independence, but the British wanted a counterweight to the Labour Party. They soon found one, in the form of the oligarchy, which became their perfect "opposition."

On March 12, 1964, a system of self-government was introduced to Mauritius. In 1965, Anthony Greenwood, secretary of state for colonies, visited Mauritius. He believed that further constitutional developments and changes would be acceptable to the majority of the population. In 1965, after the Labour Day demonstration, fighting broke out between gangs of various political parties. Despite this, the Colonial Office continued to press for constitutional progress. Independence was agreed to and the Barnwell Commission was appointed to recommend an electoral system. In 1966 the parliamentary under-secretary of state for colonies, John Stonehouse, visited Mauritius to review the Barnwell proposals. He agreed to establish a system of "best losers." In other words, seats were to be reserved for any ethnic group that was not represented. Although today this system is criticized for institutionalization of communalism, at that time, there was a concern to establish a system that would not exclude any group. Leaders of each political party accepted it, but whether this was believed to be a temporary solution or a permanent one is not known.

Elections were announced on August 7, 1967. There were 307,908 electors and once again the main election issue was over independence or continued association with Britain. The Labour Party, the Independent Forward Block (IFB), and the Comité d'Action Musulman (CAM) won 56 per cent of the vote (39 out of 62 seats).

The elections were clouded by the fact that riots broke out in January 1968. Twenty-five people were killed, a state of emergency was declared, and British troops were called in. Forty-four per cent of the island's electorate had voted against independence, a historic decision that indicated the divisions in the society.

At the first meeting of the Assembly, Dr. Ramgoolam once again presented a motion asking for full independence. This was approved, and on March 12, 1968, Mauritius became independent. The challenges facing the country were immense. Severe unemployment, high rates of illiteracy, poverty, and interethnic and religious tensions were some of the problems that the new government had to face.

VIJAYA TEELOCK

Mauritius: Ramgoolam, Seewoosagur, Government of

On March 12, 1968, Mauritius gained its independence as a state within the British Commonwealth. Sir Seewoosagur Ramgoolam (1900–1985), a British-educated Hindu doctor who for many years had enjoyed a broad base of popular support, became the country's first prime minister, heading a Labour-led coalition that found itself governing a country with deep-rooted economic problems.

During the 1960s, and to the detriment of economic reform, Mauritius had been preoccupied with the immediate objective of obtaining independence without provoking ethnic conflict or installing a Hindu-dominated government. Despite the recommendations of two 1961 reports, which noted the urgency of reducing population growth rates and encouraging economic diversification, little had been done to these ends: unemployment was high and rising, and the economy remained singularly dependent on sugar. The workforce was poorly trained, and the well-educated white-collar sector was emigrating, fearful for its future in an independent state. In 1970 Ramgoolam drew up a plan that called for sustained economic growth and established the basis for this growth, the Export Processing Zone (EPZ).

The EPZ aimed at attracting foreign and domestic capital for an industrialization program. It provided an attractive package, offering tax relief, government subsidies, and credit facilities, with promises of good infrastructure and the placing of no restrictions on capital transfer. The government promised a competent, cheap, and reliable labor supply, which the Mauritian public education system was able to supply, and from 1971 to 1975 the economy boomed.

Although the EPZ, based principally on textiles, was clearly a success, it was dependent upon the health of the sugar sector. During several years in the early 1970s while world sugar prices were extremely buoyant, Mauritius produced several bumper crops, and the resultant profits fuelled EPZ growth. Sugar profits also funded investment in the tourism sector, and in services, they also provided increased government revenue, thus permitting improvements to social services and infrastructure development.

Mauritius' continued status as a developing country attracted substantial development aid, particularly in view of its stable government and its potential as a development success story. In 1972 its close relationship with France led to the country being invited to join OCAM, the association of former French colonies in Africa. Aware that imminent British membership of the EEC would remove the privileges Mauritius enjoyed in the British market, Mauritius accepted OCAM's invitation and became the first Commonwealth state to obtain preferential access for its exports to the European Community, several years before the Lomé Convention.

Despite economic success, the Labour Party faced opposition. Poor economic conditions, high unemployment, and low wages in the late 1960s had led to the formation of the left-wing Mouvement Militant Mauricien (MMM) in 1969. Led by Paul Bérenger, a young radical who had spent 1968 in Paris, the MMM rapidly established itself as a force to be contended with. Appealing to the youth to renounce communalism and take up the class struggle, the MMM won a by-election in the strongly Hindu constituency of Triolet in 1970 and went on to further victories in the 1971 local elections.

In late 1971 the MMM backed striking workers and began preparing for the 1972 general election, but Ramgoolam invoked emergency powers under the Public Order Act, claiming the country could not risk social unrest. Political meetings were banned, trades union activity severely restricted, the MMM newspaper shut down, and a number of MMM leaders, including Bérenger himself, were arrested. The 1972 election was postponed until 1976, and although its leaders were released from prison, throughout the period Ramgoolam maintained restrictions on the MMM.

If Ramgoolam could justify his actions by pointing to the economic boom, it proved to be unsustainable. Rapid growth had fuelled inflation and a demand for imports; in the mid-1970s sugar prices collapsed and the rise in oil prices led to a worldwide economic downturn that did not spare Mauritius. Exports slumped and although the GDP continued to grow, the rate of growth had slowed, unemployment was increasing, and external debt was on the rise.

By the 1976 election, Ramgoolam realized that the MMM could no longer be ignored and all restrictions were lifted. Both Labour and the more conservative Parti Mauricien Social Démocrate (PMSD) attacked the MMM as Marxists, raising the specter of totalitarian rule, but the MMM had toned down its rhetoric and, in Aneerood Jugnauth, had found a candidate who would appeal to Hindus. The election was closely fought, and the Labour/PMSD coalition clung to a two seat majority, the remainder having been won by the MMM.

Throughout the late 1970s the economy continued to suffer and in 1979 the government was forced to appeal to the International Monetray Fund (IMF) for help. A structural adjustment program was put into place, including curbs on public sector spending and a devaluation of the rupee. It is to Ramgoolam's credit that the government maintained its commitment to social welfare policies, including free education and health care, during this period.

The IMF program eventually had the desired effect, but too late to save the government. The Labour Party was facing increasing criticism, particularly from within. A splinter group led by Harish Boodhoo launched accusations of corruption (two ministers were forced to resign in 1979), nepotism, and incompetence among the aging leadership, who were seen to be out of touch with the population. The MMM backed a general strike in mid-1979, while Boodhoo's insistent probing led to his expulsion from the Labour Party. He established the Parti Socialiste Mauricien (PSM), which formed an alliance with the MMM to fight the 1982 general election, thus guaranteeing the MMM the Hindu vote.

Both the Labour Party and the PMSD realized they had little chance of winning in 1982. The economy had yet to feel the effects of the structural adjustment program and serious cyclones from 1979 to 1981 had exacerbated the effects of a 21 per cent unemployment rate, falling foreign investment, unstable sugar prices, high inflation, and a 5 billion rupee foreign debt. The MMM presented a more moderate image than it had done in 1976; the alliance with the PSM reassured Hindus, while Bérenger went out of his way to court the private sector, especially the sugar estates. The election was a landslide victory for the MMM-PSM alliance, which won 62 per cent of the popular vote and all sixty available seats.

The 1982 election effectively marked the end of Ramgoolam's political career, and he was appointed governor general shortly thereafter. Despite the poor performance of the later years of his government, Sir Seewoosagur Ramgoolam is respected as the father of modern Mauritius. His role as a leader not only of Hindus but of all Mauritians, with his emphasis on dialogue and moderation and his perseverance in building a modern welfare state with a nonaligned foreign policy, won him friends and admirers both in Mauritius and abroad. It is without doubt due to his personal skills that Mauritius not only achieved not only independence but did so as a stable and harmonious democracy.

IAIN WALKER

See also: **Lomé Conventions, The; Mauritius: Nationalism, Communalism, and Independence, 1935–1968.**

Further Reading

Addison, J., and K. Hazareesingh. *A New History of Mauritius*. London: Macmillan, 1984.

Bowman, L. W. *Mauritius: Democracy and Development in the Indian Ocean*. Boulder, Colo.: Westview Press, and London: Dartmouth, 1991.

Dommen, E., and B. Dommen. *Mauritius: An Island of Success. A Retrospective Study 1960–1993*. Wellington: Pacific Press, and Oxford: James Currey, 1999.

Mannick, A. R. *Mauritius: The Development of a Plural Society*. Nottingham: Spokesman, 1979.

Mulloo, A. *Dr. S. Ramgoolam: His Life, His Work, His Ideas*. Port Louis, Mauritius: Swan, 1980.

Selwyn, P. "Mauritius, the Meade Report Twenty Years After" in *African Islands and Enclaves*, ed. Robin Cohen, Beverly Hills: Sage Publications, 1983.

Simmons, A. *Modern Mauritius: The Politics of Decolonization*. Bloomington: Indiana University Press, 1982.

Wellisz, S., and P. Lam Shin Saw. "Mauritius" in *Five Small Open Economies*, ed. R. Findlay and S. Wellisz. New York: Oxford University Press, 1993.

Mauritius: 1982 to the Present

Mauritius is one of the few African countries in which a multiparty system has been maintained since independence (1968), and where competitive elections have been held almost regularly. Over the last three decades, party politics have been influenced by interrelated ethnic and class conflicts, as well as by personal rivalries of party leaders, party breakaways, and tactical alliances. Over time, the latter have been indispensable to form parliamentary majorities.

While Mauritius is an intricately plural society, the country has managed to build a democratic consensus among rival politicians within a relatively stable political system. A key factor of Mauritius's politics is that successive governments have shown relative tolerance for opposition political rivals. As a result, while class and ethnic loyalties crisscross one another, the political system's relative consensus has helped prevent political competition from becoming a zero-sum game. In addition, over time political stability has also been underpinned by adoption of a "best loser" system. This has ensured the representation of ethnic minority interests on a partially proportional basis in Parliament. The key point is that both opposition and government leaders have shared an agreement to work together to politically marginalize any political forces perceived as antidemocrats. Moreover, the rival political leaders have agreed to regulate political competition along recognizably democratic lines, a state of affairs facilitated by the fact that there has not been much of a proliferation of new parties nor excessive instances of splits in the old ones.

Sugarcane fields in front of the Nicoliere Mountains, Mauritius, October 1, 2002. © Jochen Tack/Das Fotoarchiv.

The politically consensual trend began in 1982 when Sir Seewoosagur Ramgoolam, the founding father of independence, lost elections gracefully to the opposition. The results of the elections of that year brought a fundamental political change, as they showed a major swing toward the hitherto opposition Mouvement Militant Mauricien (MMM) and its small alliance partner the Parti Socialiste Mauricien (PSM), a breakaway from the ruling Mauritius Labour Party (MLP). Other than the two seats of the island of Rodrigues, won by the Rodriguan People's Organisation (OPR), the MMM/PSM won all sixty directly elected legislative seats. Candidates of the traditionally powerful parties—the MLP, the Muslim Action Committee (MAC), and the Parti Mauricien Social Democrate (PMSD)—which had, prior to the 1982 elections, dominated the Mauritian political scene were all but wiped out in elections.

The new coalition government, under the leadership of MMM president Sir Anerood Jugnauth as prime minister, turned out to be less radical than expected. This was not least because of the conditions for much-needed foreign loans set by the International Monetary Fund and the World Bank which strongly affected the government's economic and political agendas. Perhaps because of the enforced moderation, within a year the coalition had broken up due to the MMM fracturing. Paul Bérenger led his fraction of the MMM into opposition while Jugnauth, continuing as prime minister, founded the *Mouvement Socialiste Mauricien* (MSM) around his loyal MMM wing plus and PSM supporters. However, unable to command a parliamentary majority, Jugnauth called for new elections in 1983 and managed to continue as prime minister on the basis of an alliance formed by MSM, PMSD, and the MLP.

Helped by the electoral system, Jugnauth's alliance won comfortable legislative majorities in 1983 and 1987. Later, in 1991, when the MLP appeared to be negotiating an electoral pact with the MMM, Jugnauth managed to arrive at a new alliance between MSM and MMM. This resulted in a resounding victory for both Jugnauth and the MSM/MMM alliance and after the elections, Jugnauth retained his position as prime minister. However, as part of the alliance agreement, Mauritius became a republic by constitutional change in March 1992. Henceforward, a ceremonial president would replace the post of governor-general. The impact upon national politics was, however, minimal.

In 1993 the MMM split again. A breakaway faction, led by Paul Bérenger, joined the opposition. The loyal wing of the MMM stayed in the MSM-led coalition government and formed a new party, the Renouveau Militant Mauricien (RMM). Elections in 1995 were won overwhelmingly by the opposition Mauritian Labour Party and Bérenger's MMM. This marked the second peaceful transfer of power to the opposition via elections since independence. In June 1997 Bérenger was dismissed from the cabinet and most of the other MMM ministers resigned their posts in protest. The prime minister, Dr. Navin Ramgoolam, son of the former prime minister Sir Seewoosagur Ramgoolam, formed a new cabinet that included only MLP ministers except for one OPR member and one independent. Later, following further elections in September 2000, Anerood Jugnauth returned as prime minister with Paul Bérenger as deputy prime minister and finance minister. The 2000 elections were won on the back of an electoral pact between the MSM and the MMM, under which Jugnauth would take the premiership until 2003, when Bérenger, MMM leader, would take over the top job.

This transfer of power did not lead to a very different economic agenda. It is often noted that Mauritius' economic record under governments of different complexions has been more promising than in most other African countries. Since the early 1980s, Mauritius had had an average annual economic growth of more than 5 per cent, with unemployment in the region of 8 per cent. While in 2000 growth sank to 3.6 per cent, this was primarily due to a drought that affected the key sugar crop. Forecasts of improvements in 2001 and 2002 were eventually scaled down as a result of the depressed international economic situation. However, Jugnauth and Bérenger announced plans to build on encouraging aspects of the economy, notably the Export Processing Zone (EPZ). First introduced in 1970, EPZ manufacturing industries had increased rapidly during Jugnauth's first period in office in the 1980s and had steadily grown in importance since. Bérenger announced in 2001 that the aim for Mauritius was what he called a "quantum leap" to a "knowledge economy." This would involve the introduction of "cyber-cities" to further reduce the country's still heavy dependence on sugar and manufactured exports such as textiles.

JEFFREY HAYNES

See also: **Mauritius: Ramgoolam, Seewoosagur, Government of.**

Further Reading

Addison, J., and K. A. Hazareesingh. *New History of Mauritius.* Rev. ed. Stanley: Rose Hill, Mauritius: Editions de l'Océan Indien, 1993.

Brautigam, D. "Institutions, Economic Reform, and Democratic Consolidation in Mauritius." *Comparative Politics.* 30. no. 1 (1997): 45–62.

Caroll, B. W. "State and Ethnicity in Botswana and Mauritius: A Democratic Route to Development." *The Journal of Development Studies.* 33, no. 4 (1997): 464–486.

Mathur, H. *Parliament in Mauritius.* Stanley: Rose Hill, Mauritius: Editions de l'Océan Indien, 1991.

Selvon, S. *Ramgoolam.* Stanley: Rose Hill, Mauritius: Editions de l'Océan Indien, 1991.

Shillington, K. *Jugnauth, Prime Minister of Mauritius.* London and Basingstoke, Macmillan, 1991.

Mawlay 'Abd al-Rahman: *See* Morocco: Mawlay 'Abd al-Rahman, Life and Era of.

Mawlay Hasan: *See* Morocco: Mawlay Hasan and the Makhzen.

Mawlay Isma'il: *See* Morocco: Mawlay Isma'il and Empire of.

Mawlay Sulayman: *See* Morocco: Mawlay Sulayman, Life and Era of.

Mboya, Tom J. (*c.*1930–1969)

Kenyan Trade Unionist and Politician

Mboya was raised far away from his native Rusinga Island, in Lake Victoria in Luo Nyanza. Hence he developed a cosmopolitan personality from early childhood. He grew into a polyglot, speaking Dholuo, Kiswahili, English, Kikamba, and Kikuyu fairly fluently.

On joining the City Council, Mboya became the vice president of the Nairobi African Local Government Servants Association (NALGSA) and shortly transformed it into the Kenya Local Government Workers Union (KLGWU) where he became general secretary. He went on to become the general secretary of the Kenya Federation of Labor (KFL). Mboya argued that unions should concentrate on negotiating with the government to reap maximum benefits for the workers. He discouraged strikes as hampering economic growth. As minister for labor, Mboya presided over the establishment of the Industrial Relations Charter (IRC), forerunner of the Kenya Industrial Court (KIC).

Mboya became involved in the Pan-Africanist movement, to which he was introduced by Kwame Nkrumah of Ghana. The All African People's Conference (AAPC) of 1958 in Accra brought together five hundred leaders of parties and unions. Mboya was appointed the chairman of the conference.

Nkrumah and others such as Modibo Keita and Sekou Touré, espoused the idea of a political union for Africa from the start. Kenneth Kaunda, Julius Nyerere, Mboya, and others advocated piecemeal unity based on regional blocs. It was in this context that the question of international labor affiliation was posed: Should African labor affiliate to Euro-American organizations? Nkrumah opposed dependency on the West as a gimmick of neocolonialism. He viewed Mboya as being a lackey of the West. Mboya and the KFL had a long association with the International Confederation of Free Trade Unions (ICFTU). He reasoned that it was a partner in decolonization. In May 1961 Nkrumah's camp formed the All Africa Trade Union Federation (AATUF) in Casablanca. Mboya's camp walked out. In January 1962 they congregated in Monrovia, Liberia, to form the Africa Trade Union Confederation (ATUC).

Mboya's "American Connection" afforded him political mileage as well as resentment at home. Mboya played a crucial role in the decolonization process. He was first elected to the Legislative Council in 1957, and quickly set up the African Elected Members Organization (AEMO). He used the caucus to harmonize strategies for gaining independence. Mboya dominated the constitutional talks that resulted in the independence of Kenya. He was young, familiar with the Western press, ebullient, and a consummate schemer.

When the Kenya African National Union (KANU) was formed in 1960, Mboya became the general secretary and retained the position until his death. The party was formed and initially organized with the help of Nyerere's Tanganyika African National Union (TANU).

Mboya was appointed minister for justice and constitutional affairs in 1963, a position that involved formulating a new constitution. In this he worked closely with the attorney general, Charles Njonjo. The outcome was a republican constitution that made the opposition Kenya African Democratic Union (KADU), with its regionalist policies, difficult to operate. As a result of Mboya's persuasion and blackmail, KADU gradually diminished as its members joined KANU.

Mboya was appointed minister for economic planning and development in 1964. He held the position until his death in 1969. He thus became the architect of Kenya's development strategy, whereby he sought to create an African state and economy in harmony with African values. He recognized foreign aid and private investment as crucial components of economic growth. In 1967 in Lagos, Mboya called for a "Marshall Plan" for Africa while castigating the insensitivity of the West toward the continent. Mboya called for regional economic integration, which could result in a common market and currency for the continent. This dream was fulfilled in the 1990s with the formation of the various subregional economic blocs across the continent.

Mboya and Oginga Odinga were both Luo by ethnicity. Yet they remained political rivals. Jomo Kenyatta exploited this to get Mboya to undermine and destroy Odinga. This was accomplished in 1966 when Odinga, out of frustration, resigned from government to start an opposition that was never allowed to take root. What Mboya realized too late was that his brilliance, popularity, and capacity to organize turned the Kikuyu caucus in the government against him.

Mboya confided to his friends that his life was in danger. His mail was being tampered with, and on one occasion, his house guard had sprayed bullets into his empty vehicle. On July 5, 1969 after leaving his Treasury Building office, Mboya stopped at a chemist to pick up medicine. He was followed and gunned down by Isaal Njenga Njoroge. He was rushed to Nairobi Hospital, where he died on arrival.

The death of Mboya shook the nation and led to ethnic animosity, especially between the Kikuyu and the Luo. Cases of sporadic violence were witnessed in Nairobi and in Luo Nyanza. The mistrust between the ethnic groups lingers still and has contributed in no small measure to the subsequent history of Kenyan politics.

Mboya was buried according to Luo custom on Rusinga Island. Njenga was convicted of murder but insisted he had been carrying out orders from others. To this day, the identities of those who masterminded Mboya's demise remain unknown.

EDWIN GIMODE

See also: **Kenya: Independence to the Present: Kenya: Kenyatta, Jomo: Life and Government of.**

Biography

Thomas Joseph Odiambo Mboya was born August 15, 1930, on a sisal plantation estate in central Kenya. Attended the Jeans School, Kabete, where he trained as a sanitary inspector. Joined the Nairobi City Council in 1951. Attended Ruskin College at Cambridge University in 1955 where he studied industrial relations. Married Pamela Arwa in 1962. They had two sons and two daughters, in addition to Mboya's daughter from an earlier marriage. Appointed chairman of the All African People's Conference of 1958. Elected to the Legislative Council in 1957. Set up the African Elected Members Organization (AEMO). Named secretary general of the Kenya African National Union (KANU) in 1960. Appointed minister for economic planning and development in 1964. Died July 5, 1969.

Further Reading

Gimode, E. *Tom Mboya: A Biography.* Nairobi: East African Educational Publishers, 1996.

Goldsworthy, D. *Tom Mboya: The Man Kenya Wanted to Forget.* Nairobi: Heinemann 1982.

Mboya, T. *The Challenge of Nationhood: A Collection of Speeches and Writings.* Nairobi: Heinemann in association with Andre Deutsch, 1970.

———. "A Development Strategy for Africa: Problems and Proposals." (Chairman's Introductory Remarks, 8th General Session of the Economic Commission for Africa, Lagos, 13 February 1967).

———. *Freedom and After.* Nairobi: Heinemann, Kenyan Edition, 1986.

Rake, A. *Tom Mboya: Young Man of New Africa.* New York: Doubleday, 1962.

Media as Propaganda

Colonial authorities held inflated and often racist views of the subversive impact of African "exposure" to mass media, including radio, film, and print journalism. Such views arose from the propaganda legacy of World War II and were strengthened by the virulent anti-communist strains of the early Cold War years. The rise of serious African nationalist challenges to colonial domination after World War II set the stage for extensive, heavy-handed and generally unsuccessful late colonial information management policies. In South Africa and Namibia, these lasted well into the 1980s.

Colonial Britain was generally more credulous than France, Portugal, or Belgium, drawing from extensive wartime propaganda experience, to develop, use, and tightly control radio, newspapers, and film to fashion postwar information policies for its African territories.

Radio was first seen as a means for European settlers and colonial civil servants to keep in touch with African cities and the world outside Africa. It also served the needs of the small educated African elite. Britain and France introduced state radio services in West Africa during the 1930s. Kenya had radio as early as 1927, Rhodesia 1932, and South Africa 1924.

World War II, and the need to recruit and inform Africans, led to the first broadcasts in African languages. Britain used radio in pre-independence Ghana and Nigeria to explain the Second World War to Africans and to justify and promote their participation in it. France used colonial radio as a rallying point for Free French forces in West and Central Africa to counter pro-Vichy broadcasts from Dakar, Senegal.

Powerful transmitters installed for wartime propaganda purposes proved useful in postwar development of colonial radio. By 1945 the British Broadcasting Corporation (BBC) was recommending that national radio networks in English-speaking African territories be developed along lines similar to the model of a semipublic corporation in Great Britain. The French model for its African territories was more centralized and called for direct state control. African-language broadcasts did not begin in Francophone Africa until the late 1950s and early 1960s. As nationalist challenges mounted departments of information were set up in an effort to manage and regulate new official information sources, including territorial film units, radio services, and newspapers, while locking out contaminating foreign mass media.

Establishment of radio in many parts of colonial Africa coincided with a perceived need to set up government-run services as part of overall information management policies, while serving the news and entertainment needs of white settlers. The BBC was instrumental in bringing national services into operation in every Anglophone African territory by the end of World War II, providing financial and technical expertise and training.

Radio is the only true mass medium in Africa, reaching an estimated 85 per cent of Africans today, much more than any other medium. Although from its introduction in the 1920s radio was largely restricted to urban areas, the transister revolution, coinciding with the rise of African nationalism in the 1950s and 1960s, helped to spread it to even the most remote areas. Not only colonial government but liberation movements employed radio broadcasting to further political objectives, regime survival, or majority rule and independence.

Exiled political leaders were able to beam shortwave radio broadcasts into their home territories via Radio Cairo as early as 1953. As independence swept down the continent, from West to East, to southern Africa, additional foreign radio transmission facilities became available to liberation movements for transmitting programs in vernacular languages, much to the concern of colonial and white minority regimes.

In part to counteract this trend, South Africa started an external African service in 1958 and expanded its own domestic apartheid-style vernacular radio network, "Radio Bantu." The role of radio in the propaganda war remained firmly entrenched through the decades of African independence, into the late 1980s. South Africa maintained authoritarian control of radio and employed disinformation in broadcasts to maintain its hold on Namibia until 1989.

Use of mass media as propaganda tools for shaping or managing public opinion reached new lows in the information policies of white minority regimes in post-1948 South Africa and Southern Rhodesia from 1962 to 1979. Racist regimes in both states also used propaganda in attempts to burnish sagging images abroad. Between 1972 and 1977, the South African Department of Information undertook a multimillion dollar covert propaganda offensive to build a more favorable image of South Africa internationally by purchasing influence with U.S. and European newspapers.

Ownership and control were inherited by the new states following independence and, with the exception of a few religious radio services, it was not until the 1990s that commercial radio and deregulated, public service parastatal radio services appeared in Africa. African leaders have viewed radio as a powerful tool for national integration, development, and maintaining themselves in power. Highly centralized state broadcast monopolies could thereby be justified indefinitely.

Colonial authorities feared the subversive influences of foreign radio broadcasts from communist services, particularly Radio Moscow, although there is little evidence that more than a handful of Africans possessed the shortwave equipment or interest to listen. Far more listened to the postwar African services of the BBC, Radio France International, Radio RSA (South Africa), and other European services.

Similarly, and beginning in the 1920s, the forms that colonial film policy took were intimately linked with British, French, or Belgian efforts to build loyalty, if not legitimacy, for colonial rule. Colonial Film Units were set up and given the task of putting the best face possible on territorial administration, both for natives and for home populations. During the war years (1939–1945) colonial film served as a wartime propaganda tool. Following the end of the war, emphasis shifted to mass education and community development films aimed at strengthening the position of colonial governments. Africans still tended to be portrayed as inferior and dependent while Europeans were wise, powerful, and benevolent.

It was believed that film could enable illiterate people to understand and eventually participate in Western civilization and the modern world. At times, particularly in the case of film in British territories, the Colonial Office seemed to identify film as a partial panacea to solve major problems of communication and development in far-flung, illiterate territories of its African empire. Colonial administrators were initially fearful of exposing Africans to corrupting images of western life, or causing subjects to question colonial rule itself.

A desire to avoid contaminating commercial films led to a policy of providing noncommercial, government-produced documentaries and newsreels and tightly restricting import and distribution of foreign commercial films from Europe, America, or South Africa. Colonial censorship boards worked with local missionaries to cut scenes which might endanger the prestige of whites. Colonial film makers never trained Africans to make films. Frequency of exposure to films was limited, especially in contrast to radio, which came on strong in the 1950s.

Given the linguistic and cultural pluralism of African audiences in most territories and the limited number of mobile film vans, it was difficult to draw and keep large audiences. The ideology that underpinned many colonial films tended to sow more confusion than cultural guidance or education. The patronizing desire of colonial administrators to regulate cinema was intended to maintain a submissive, malleable population, capable of official guidance.

Perceived needs to "educate" Africans for citizenship and service and to create new consumers for European products also provided motivation for use of film. Films with religious themes made for African audiences in places like the Belgian Congo in the 1930s and 1940s used folktales and vernacular languages, as well as African actors, to advance missionary work of gaining and educating new converts. Cinema was a modern mass communication medium but easy to control by colonial authorities. Expansion of radio services led to the demise of Colonial Film Units by the mid-1950s.

JAMES J. ZAFFIRO

See also: **Drama, Film: Postcolonial; Journalism, African: Colonial Era; Press.**

Further Reading

Armour, C. "The BBC and the Development of Broadcasting in British Colonial Africa 1946–1956," *African Affairs*. 83/332, (July 1984): 359–402.

Head, S. (ed.). *Broadcasting in Africa*. Philadelphia: Temple University Press, 1974.

Huth, A. *Communications Media in Tropical Africa*. Washington, D.C., USIA, 1959.

Kerr, D. "The Best of Both Worlds? Colonial Film Policy and Practice in Northern Rhodesia and Nyasaland." *Critical Arts*, 7/2, (1993): 11–42.

Nwabughuogu, A. I. "The Role of Propaganda in the Development of Indirect Rule in Nigeria, 1890–1929," *International Journal of African Historical Studies*. 14/1, (1981): 65–92.

Nyamnjoh, F. B. "Broadcasting in Francophone Africa: Crusading for French Culture?" *Gazette*. 42/2, (1988): 81–92.

Pike, C. B. "Tales of Empire: The Colonial Film Unit in Africa, 1939–1950." *AfterImages*. 17/1. (June 1989): 8–9.

Riddle, C. "South African Attempts to Dominate Political Communication in Namibia Through Control of Radio, 1966–1989." *Gazette*. 52/1, (1993): 25–41.

Smyth, R. "The British Colonial Film Unit and Sub-Saharan Africa, 1939–1945." *Historical Journal of Film, Radio and Television*. 8/3, (1988): 285–298.

Smyth, R. "The Central African Film Unit's Image of Empire 1948–1963." *Historical Journal of Film, Radio and Television*. 3/2 (1983): 132–147.

Smyth, R. "The Development of British Colonial Film Policy 1927–1939." *Journal of African History*. 20/3, (1979): 437–450.

Smyth, R. "Movies and Mandarins: The Official Film and British Colonial Africa," in *British Cinema History* (edited by J. Curran, Totowa). N. J.: Barnes and Noble Books, 1983, 129–143.

Strebel, E. G., "Primitive Propaganda: The Boer War Films," *Sight and Sound*. 46/1, (December 1976): 45–47.

Windrich, E. *The Mass Media in the Struggle for Zimbabwe: Censorship and Propaganda Under Rhodesian Front Rule*. Gweru: Mambo Press, 1981.

Zaffiro, J. J. "Twin Births: African Nationalism and Government Information Management in the Bechuanaland Protectorate, 1957–1966." *International Journal of African Historical Studies*. 22/1 (1989): 51–78.

Zaffiro, J. J. *From Police Network to Station of the Nation: A Political History of Broadcasting in Botswana, 1927–1991*. Gaborone: The Botswana Society, 1991.

Medical Factor in Christian Conversion

The medical achievements of the second half of the nineteenth century coincided with the heyday of missionary enterprise in Africa. Thus, Protestant and Roman Catholic missions pioneered Western medicine in Africa. By all accounts, missionary medical work played a critical role in the conversion of Africans to Christianity. Reports drawn from various mission fields illuminate our understanding of the importance of missionary medical work in the conversion process. Among other things, it proved very effective in breaking down local prejudice and in winning the affection and confidence of the local people. The experiences of Protestant and Roman Catholic missionaries in various parts of Sub-Saharan Africa clearly illustrate the diplomatic importance of missionary medical work. In Nigeria, for instance, health care services rendered by missionaries of the British Church Missionary Society (CMS) fostered a dramatic change of relations, as in the Igbo town of Awka. According to the Rev. G. T. Basden, "During the disturbances at Awka, we were able to render assistance to some of the wounded," and, as a result, we won the confidence of our neighbors, and were thus able to establish ourselves in a place where, up to that date, our tenure had been . . . precarious . . . From being merely tolerated we were accepted as friends, and the relationship thus established has remained a cordial one ever since" (1966, p.204).

Similarly in Onitsha, Nigeria Roman Catholic medical work in 1890 had a dramatic effect. Not only did it provoke "a remarkable movement towards Roman Catholicism," it also led to the defection of CMS adherents to Roman Catholicism. Thus lamented the CMS station agent: "We are daily coming across cases of persons who used to belong to our church, but who now are Roman Catholics. In almost every case the means used to draw our people has been medicine" (Report of 1890). Sadly, plans to "fight the Romanists on their own grounds" failed, largely because of lack of medical supplies from headquarters.

In central and eastern Africa, as well, missionary medical work not only engendered "a speedy change in the attitude of the people" toward missionary propaganda, but missionary medicine proved to be "the bait to catch converts." Not surprisingly, the Rev. G. H. Wills of the Universities Mission to Central Africa triumphantly proclaimed missionary medical work as "one solid asset of the missionary work here." Initially, most religious agencies tended to deemphasize the value of medical work, believing, instead, that "faith alone" was sufficient to induce conversion. African realities, however, tempered religious orthodoxy, and hence the enthusiastic adoption of medical work as a necessary tool of Christian evangelism.

This commitment to missionary medical work was clearly reflected in the establishment of hospitals, dispensaries, clinics, and related facilities. These establishments became not merely centers of healing but powerful agents of religious indoctrination as well. As an illustration, patients who came for treatment at the medical facilities were often first given doses of religious instruction, and medical care afterward. Conversions often followed, thus demonstrating the "evangelistic efficiency of hospitals" and other health care facilities. Yet some missionaries have emphasized the humanitarian dimensions of missionary medical work: "If we saw no spiritual results; if we saw no converts brought out by medical missions . . . it would still be the burden duty of Christian people to do what they can with . . . western science which God has given, to alleviate misery, wretchedness, pain, and disease wherever it may be found" (*The Church Missionary Review*, 1921: p.23).

Available evidence suggests a close relationship between disease, Western medicine, and Christian conversion. In Africa, epidemics had a significant impact on conversion, as missionary response(s) to the pandemic influenza of 1918–1919 illustrates. Known popularly in Sub-Saharan Africa as the "Spanish" influenza, the epidemic spread rapidly throughout most of Sub-Saharan Africa, and wrought great havoc. Because of its novelty, there were no indigenous medical or magical remedies to deal with the disease. Thus, at the onset of the epidemic, missionaries provided medical care, and, in the process, expanded their missionary frontiers.

In Nigeria, the Roman Catholic missionaries were particularly active. In addition to providing medical relief to the suffering victims of disease, they reportedly baptized a large number, who were frightened into believing that, if they died without baptism, they would invariably suffer eternal damnation in hell. Christian eschatology thus contributed to conversions. Indeed, the growth of Roman Catholicism in parts of the present-day Imo state of Nigeria, at least as oral testimonies suggest, may be attributed partly to the Roman Catholic provision of health care during the pandemic influenza. In eastern, central, and southern Africa, too, studies show that missionary medical work, at this time of health crisis, resulted in conversions. African elders, for example, are said to have interpreted baptism as being synonymous with physical healing. Consequently, some patients opted for baptism, in the belief that it would restore good health. But missionaries were at pains to disabuse the Africans of this association. "Baptism," warned a Protestant missionary, "is [not] a charm for curing ills [illness]" (Ranger, p.275).

Clearly, African culture and cosmological ideas played a role in Christian conversion. African elders, for example, accepted Christianity with the impression that the new religion meant the addition of another deity (Jesus Christ) to the existing pantheon of gods. Besides, traditional African religion tends to gravitate toward pragmatism, meaning that Africans could switch allegiance from one deity/spirit to another, especially when, in times of social crisis, he/she appeared no longer powerful. Nevertheless, acceptance of Christianity did not imply abandonment of traditional ways of life. On the contrary, traditional values continued to exist after conversion.

FELIX K. EKECHI

See also: **Religion, Colonial Africa: Conversion to World Religions; Religion, Colonial Africa: Missionaries.**

Further Reading

Basden, G. T. Among the Ibos of Nigeria. 1966.

Boer, J. H. Missionary Messengers of Liberation in a Colonial Context: A Case Study of the Sudan United Mission. Amsterdam, The Netherlands: Rodopt, 1979.

Ekechi, F. K. "The Medical Factor in Christian Conversion in Africa: Observations from Southeastern Nigeria." *Missiology: An International Review.* 21, no. 3 (1993): 291–309.

Good, C. M. "Pioneer Medical Missions in Colonial Africa." *Social Science Medicine.* 32, no. 1 (1991): 1–10.

Ranger, T. O. "Godly Medicine: The Ambiguities of Medical Mission in Southeast Tanzania, 1900–1945." *Social Science Medicine.* 15B, no. 3 (1981): 261–277.

Ranger, T. O. "The Influenza Pandemic in Southern Rhodesia: A Crisis of Comprehension." In *Imperial Medicine and Indigenous Societies*, edited by D. Arnold. Manchester: Manchester University Press, 1988.

Medicine: *See* Health: Medicine and Disease: Postcolonial.

Mekatilele: *See* Kenya: Mekatilele and Giriama Resistance, 1900–1920.

Menelik II: *See* Ethiopia: Menelik II, Era of.

Merina: *See* Madagascar: Merina Kingdom, Nineteenth Century.

Meroe: Meroitic Culture and Economy

"Meroitic" is a modern term used to designate the later phases of the kingdom of Kush, known to the Greco-Roman world as the kingdom of the Aethiopians. The kingdom of Kush developed in the earlier part of the first millennium BCE and came to dominate most of the Nile valley from the First Cataract into central Sudan. Initially centered on the region called Napata at the downstream end of the Fourth Cataract, by as early as the later eighth century BCE a major community had developed at Meroe between the Sixth Cataract and the Nile-Atbara confluence. Until the fourth century BCE, all burials of the Kushite rulers were at Napata. However, early in the third century BCE the royal burial ground was transferred to Meroe where most subsequent rulers were buried. This is the date traditionally given to the transition from the Napatan to the Meroitic periods.

This was also a time of major cultural change. The Kushite state from very early in its history was heavily influenced by the culture of its usually more powerful northern neighbor, Egypt. Although from the later eighth into the mid-seventh centuries BCE, the Kushites succeeded in conquering Egypt, but this only served to reinforce the cultural dominance of pharaonic Egypt. During the fourth century BCE pharaonic control in Egypt, already disrupted by periods of Persian occupation, was replaced by the Macedonian regime of

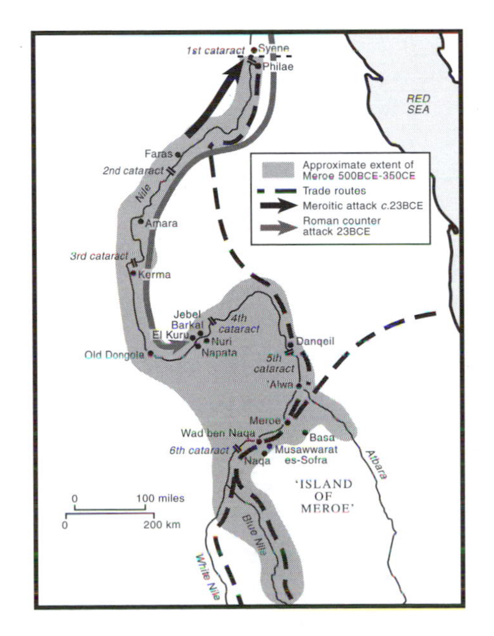

Meroe, 500BCE–350CE.

the Ptolemies after the conquests of Alexander. This ushered in a period of great cultural assimilation between the Greek and later the Greco-Roman worlds and pharaonic Egypt. The Kushites, in their turn, were heavily influenced by this new "Egyptian" culture. The distinction between the Napatan and Meroitic periods, therefore, is the result of a change in external stimuli, and the underlying continuity from one period to another must be stressed.

Meroitic culture was a dynamic mix of imported elements of Greco-Roman tradition grafted onto earlier imported elements of Pharaonic culture, all overlaid onto the culture of a basically African civilization. The Meroites did not slavishly adopt Egyptian cultural traits but, as in the Napatan period, were highly selective and modified where they considered necessary those traits so that Meroitic culture is a distinct entity in itself. The Meroites demonstrated their linguistic independence in retaining their own language, which was first committed to writing in the early second century BCE. Although the characters used were derived from Egyptian, the nature of the script was very different, being alphabetic rather than hieroglyphic. The structure of the language was also significantly different. Indeed, it is the unique nature of the Meroitic language, with no known close relations, which has frustrated all attempts to translate it.

Religion and funerary culture also demonstrate aspects of the unique Meroitic cultural identity. Although many of the state gods were of Egyptian origin, others were purely local deities. Chief among these was the lion god Apedemak, who was particularly popular in the region around Meroe. From the eighth century BCE the rulers adopted the pyramid as the funerary monument par excellence, to be appropriated by the elite. However, the indigenous tradition of burial under tumuli continued throughout the Napatan and Meroitic periods and on into the medieval period. Even in the royal burials, so Egyptianized in outward appearance, the discovery of human and animal sacrifices highlights the local cultural traits continuing from the Kerma period in the mid-second millennium BCE and extending into the post-Meroitic period in the fourth and fifth centuries.

One major cultural influence that was particularly strong in Egypt during the later phases of the Meroitic state was Christianity, but there is no evidence that this religion was accepted by the Meroites, who maintained their adherence to pharaonic religious practices long after they had been abandoned by most of the Egyptian population.

The subsistence economy of the Meroitic state was based on agriculture and animal husbandry. Manufacturing was on a large scale, particularly the production of pottery and perhaps of iron, but how these were integrated into the economy is unclear at the time of this writing. The Meroitic economy was nonmonetary, but whether it was a market economy or a redistributive economy is not documented. Pottery should furnish evidence for internal trade networks, but the study of this material as an indicator of trade is not yet well developed.

International trade may have largely been in the hands of the monarchy. The Meroitic state sat athwart the age-old trade route from Central Africa to the Mediterranean and Middle Eastern worlds, and was thus able to profit as a middleman in that trade. Trade in luxury goods, animal products, gold, and slaves may have been of fundamental importance for the coherence of the kingdom. The wealth generated by this activity could then be used by the ruler in the form of patronage to the regional elites to ensure the preeminence of the monarchy and the territorial cohesion of the state. The large amount of high status Greco-Roman objects found in the tombs of the rich are probably a physical manifestation of this patronage and do not furnish evidence for the involvement of a wide section of the populace in international trade. Many of these goods may have been obtained through gift exchange from the rulers of Egypt, and hence may themselves not be indicative of market trading. As early as the New Kingdom, the Egyptians had traded down the Red Sea with the Horn of Africa; this trade network was greatly expanded during the Greco-Roman period, probably with catastrophic results for the Meroitic elite. Robbed of control, or at least a significant share, of the lucrative African trade, this most likely led to a serious decline in the wealth and, therefore, in the prestige of the monarchy, and may have been a major factor in the fragmentation of the state in the fourth century.

DEREK WELSBY

See also: **Kush; Napata and Meroe.**

Further Reading

Adams, W. Y. *Nubia: Corridor To Africa*. Princeton, N.J.: Allen Lane, 1977.

Shinnie, P. L. *Meroe: A Civilization of the Sudan*. London. Thames and Hudson, 1967.

Török, L. *The Kingdom of Kush: Handbook of the Napatan-Meroitic Civilization*. Leiden: Brill, 1997.

Welsby, D. A. *The Kingdom of Kush: The Napatan and Meroitic Empires*. London: British Museum Press, 1996.

Metalworking: Origins of Ironworking

As a historical marker, the term "Iron Age" is both useful and misleading. It implies a sudden break with what preceded, and a revolutionary impact on all that followed.

In fact, the use of metals spread very gradually in Africa and overlapped the continued use of stone tools. Ultimately, however, the effect was revolutionary, encouraging greater economic productivity but also more deadly efficiency in warfare. The cultural impact of iron and other metals has been equally profound, if more diverse and harder to evaluate historically.

The history of metallurgy is better understood in Sub-Saharan than in North Africa. In the Sahel and lands to the south, we can say for certain that metals have been worked for more than two thousand years. Those who produced these metals and the objects they fashioned have played dominant roles in the history of the subcontinent. In many cultures, myths of origin refer to the introduction of metalworking as a signal event, while objects of iron, copper, and gold have long figured in political, economic, social, and religious life. So abundant were its deposits of gold that Africa was for centuries synonymous with the glittering metal, first to the Arab and Indian Ocean worlds, then to Europeans. However, in Africa itself iron has been the primary metal in all spheres of life, from utilitarian to ritual, and in many societies copper was traditionally more highly esteemed than gold.

Resources and History

The red soil typical of much of the Africa south of the Sahara is actually exposed lateritic crust, that is, low-grade iron. Metallurgists exploited primarily the richer deposits of oxides such as hematite, magnetite, and limonite. Gold, in both alluvial and reef form, also occurs much more widely throughout the continent than is generally realized but not all sources were utilized. Copper deposits, in contrast, are relatively scarce in West Africa, with the exception of areas of the southern Sahara in Mauritania and Niger and small deposits in eastern Nigeria but become more plentiful in regions of central and southern Africa. Lead occurs occasionally, especially associated with copper; tin was also exploited in a few areas, especially in southern Africa and possibly on the Bauchi plateau of Nigeria. Despite tenacious Portuguese beliefs to the contrary, there is little silver to be found in Africa, and use of that metal is recent except in the Sahara and Sahel.

During the period from about 500BCE to 500CE, the working of iron and copper spread over the entire continent, apparently in tandem; there is no evidence of a sequence from copper to arsenical copper or bronze and finally to iron as in the Middle East and Europe. The question of origins is still unsettled, in part because the chronology of metalworking is very uncertain in the regions from which it was earlier thought to have entered Africa. The lack of clear routes of diffusion has led some scholars to propose that metallurgy may have developed independently in Africa. Technically, this would have been difficult since iron smelting requires precise control of temperature and gases within the furnace, and it is hard to imagine how mastery of these factors would have been achieved without a long period of experimentation with metals that are easier to work such as copper and its alloys or without kiln firing of ceramics, which also demands high temperature pyrotechnology. Nevertheless, the possibility of independent invention has been newly strengthened by early dates associated with iron smelting in the Termit region of Niger. If these dates are substantiated, there is still a problem in explaining its irregular diffusion throughout West Africa.

The spread of metalworking throughout the Congo Basin, and into eastern and southern Africa was long held to be associated with the migration of Bantu agriculturists. More recent archeology and linguistic reconstructions have undermined this theory except in southern Africa. The technology seems to have spread in complex patterns, and at the same time stone-using hunter gatherers coexisted with iron-using farmers in many areas. Indeed, ironworkers themselves frequently continued to use stone tools for rough forging until very recently. Further, possession of iron technology is no longer considered the crucial element in Bantu expansion; conversely, non-Bantu speaking peoples are now believed to have been intimately involved in the evolution of iron technology even earlier than the Bantu.

Iron tools and weapons increased the efficiency of agriculture, hunting, fishing, and warfare, contributing to the evolution of complex societies characterized by production of surpluses, craft specialization, and social stratification. Iron, copper, and gold all entered circuits of trade. Raw iron and copper and forged objects were traded locally to peoples lacking resources or specialists. With the development of the trans-Saharan trade during the first and early second millennium CE. copper and brasswares became major imports into West Africa, often exchanged directly for gold. The opening up of maritime routes between Europe and West Africa in the second half of the fifteenth century led to an exponential increase in these imports and, for a brief period, in exports of gold. Eventually, too, iron bars also became a staple import from Europe. Africa's mineral wealth was a major catalyst for European conquest and colonialism.

Technology

As more and more sites are surveyed and excavated in Africa, the vast scale of precolonial iron smelting becomes apparent. While some industries produced only enough for local needs, others engaged in intensive production, often over long periods of time. The Middle Senegal valley, the Bassar region of western Togo, Kano and its environs in northern Nigeria, and the Ndop Main of Cameroon are thus far the best known of these proto-industrial centers, but areas of Futa Jallon and Yatenga may also have been major producers. Modern geological surveys have shown that virtually all copper deposits in Sub-Saharan Africa, with the exception of some of the deep ores in what became known as the Copperbelt (in Zambia), were identified and worked by indigenous metallurgists before the colonial period.

African smelters used an enormous variety of furnace types to produce bloomery iron or raw copper: open bowls, low shaft, high shaft, permanent, impermanent. So far it is impossible to tell whether furnace forms were dictated by the nature of local ores or even of the charcoals used almost universally for fuel. A peculiarly African innovation is the tall shaft furnace that relies on natural draft, drawing air into a number of holes around the base, rather than bellows; outside of Africa only a single example is known from Burma. While inefficient in its use of fuel, such a furnace avoids the intense labor inputs of bellows operators.

In some areas a single craftsman smelted and smithed iron and copper. In others there was a high degree of specialization among smelters and smiths and among those who forged tools and those who made ornaments of copper, brass, or gold. Further, these occupations were—and still are—often hereditary, especially in the western Sudan. Smiths and smelters were, however, invariably male, although women and children provided a great deal of the ancillary labor of mining, preparing ores, and making charcoal.

The art of lost-wax casting reached a remarkable level of perfection throughout West Africa as far south as the Cameroon Grassfields. This involves making a model of the object to be cast in wax, then enveloping it in clay. When the wax is melted, metal is run in to take its exact form. Finds from three small sites at Igbo Ukwu in southeastern Nigeria and dated to the eighth to tenth centuries CE include bronze pendants, staff heads, and vessels that illustrate the mastery of the technique as well as a virtuoso delight in replicating natural materials in metal. Although the method dates back to ancient Egypt, African brass casters have adapted their own refinements. Thus both Akan and Grassfields artists often attach crucible to mould to reduce the buildup of gases and enable the molten metal to flow more quickly and evenly. Although most lost-wax casting utilizes copper alloys such as bronze or brass because of their lower melting temperature and greater ductility without unwanted gases, some of the classic heads and figures from Ife were cast in pure copper, a technical feat of the first order.

Cultural Role of Metallurgists and Metals

While much of the literature emphasizes the "otherness" of the African smith, this is most characteristic of West African peoples such as the Mande, where smithing is limited to certain endogamous "castes," and of pastoral societies such as the Masai, where smiths are looked down on in part, at least, because they perform manual labor. Where the craft is not hereditary, aspirants must often pay costly apprenticeship and initiation fees, which tend to restrict access. Smiths may also function as sculptors, diviners, amulet makers, circumcisers, and morticians, and their wives, are often potters and excisers.

The complex and often ambivalent attitudes expressed toward smiths derive in large measure from the acknowledgment of their power. The rest of society, from farmer and hunter to king and priest, is dependent on their ability to transform inert matter into hoes, spears, emblems of authority and status, and symbols of the spirit-objects that are believed themselves to be endowed with agency. Because they literally "play with fire," metalworkers must acquire a great store of ritual knowledge. This is particularly true of smelting as the primary act of transformation: it usually takes place in isolation and involves invocations and offerings to the ancestors, strict observance of sexual and menstrual taboos, and ample use of medicines. Comparable rituals may attend the setting up of a new forge or manufacture of a new hammer or anvil.

Because of their evident access to supernatural power, smiths are often associated with kingship, especially in central Africa where they may play a major role in royal investiture and in manufacturing elements of regalia. Like chiefs, smiths are often feared as potential sorcerers or witches, since the power they wield can be beneficent or dangerous. Like chiefs too, smiths may have control over fertility, metaphorically—and even actually. Smelting rituals in particular frequently invoke the human model of gender and age to explain and insure transformative power.

EUGENIA W. HERBERT

Further Reading

Célis, G. *Eisenhütten in Afrika/Les Fonderies africaines du fer.* Frankfurt am Main: Museum für Völkerkunde 1991 [Iron Smelting in Africa].

Childs, S. T., and D. Killick, "Indigenous African Metallurgy: Nature and Culture." *Annual Review of Anthropology.* 22 (1993): 317–37.

Cline, W. *Mining and Metallurgy in Negro Africa.* Menasha, WI: George Banta, 1937.

Echard, N. (ed.). *Métallurgies Africaines.* Paris: Mémoires de la société des africanistes, 1983 [African Metallurgies].

Haaland, R. and P. Shinnie (eds.). *African Iron Working: Ancient and Traditional.* Oslo: Norwegian University Press, 1985.

Herbert, E. W. *Iron, Gender, and Power: Rituals of Transformation in African Societies*. Bloomington: Indiana University Press, 1993.

Herbert, E. W. *Red Gold of Africa: Copper in Precolonial History and Culture*. Madison: University of Wisconsin Press, 1984.

Maret, P. de "Ceux qui jouent avec le feu: la place du forgeron en Afrique centrale." *Africa*. *50* (1980): 24–79 [Those who play with fire: the place of the smith in Central Africa].

McNaughton, P. *The Mande Blacksmith in the Western Sudan*. Bloomington: Indiana University Press, 1988.

Schmidt, P. R. *Iron Technology in East Africa: Symbolism, Science, and Archaeology*. Bloomington: Indiana University Press, 1997.

Mfecane

Mfecane is a term widely used by historians from the late 1960s to the late 1980s to refer to a series of wars and population movements that took place over much of southern Africa from the 1810s to the 1830s. Before the 1960s, these upheavals had been known unproblematically in the relevant literature as "Shaka's wars" or "the Zulu wars," the implication being that they had originated under the explosive expansion of the Zulu kingdom during Shaka's reign. From the late 1980s, a small but growing number of historians began to challenge this notion. It was, they argued, primarily a product of colonial historiography, and, in the light of more recent research, could be seen as outdated and misleading. Far from being the cause of the upheavals, the expansion of Shaka's Zulu kingdom was in fact a product of them. The causes needed to be sought elsewhere.

When they were first aired in public, these revisionist views caused considerable controversy. By the later 1990s, however, as revisionist arguments became more nuanced, as well as more familiar, numbers of previously resistant historians were coming to accept that the long-established Zulu-centric explanations of the upheavals of the early nineteenth century needed to be comprehensively rethought. From being an unquestioned "fact" of history, the notion of the *mfecane* came to be seen as a particular interpretation of history which had outlived its usefulness.

The roots of the notion of "the wars of Shaka" go back to the *izibongo*, or praises, which were composed about the Zulu king by his official praise-singers during his lifetime. Versions of his praises recorded in writing in later times portray him, in terms that we can now see as highly exaggerated, as having been a great warrior and conqueror of other chiefs. After his assassination in 1828, such ideas fed into the overblown images of Shaka that were developed in books produced for European readerships by writers like Nathaniel Isaacs (*Travels and Adventures in Eastern Africa*, 2 vols., 1836). From the 1840s, fanciful descriptions of the might and despotism of Shaka spread widely in colonial travel writings and histories.

In the earlier literature with its strongly localized focus, Shaka's influence was not generally portrayed as having extended much beyond what is now the KwaZulu-Natal region. It was not until the 1880s that Shaka began to be cast more systematically as the originator of a chain reaction of violence and bloodshed that had spread through African societies across much of southern Africa. The main figure in the development of this idea, as in the development of so many other colonial stereotypes of South African history, was the well-known Cape historian George Theal.

In the first decades of the twentieth century, the notion of "Shaka's wars" was further elaborated by influential historians like D. F. Ellenberger (*A History of the Basuto, Ancient and Modern*, 1912), and Alfred Bryant (*Olden Times in Zululand and Natal*, 1929). From very different perspectives, black writers like Magema Fuze (*Abantu Abamnyama Lapa Bavela Ngakona* [*The Black People and Whence They Came*], 1922) and Rolfes Dhlomo (*Ushaka*, 1936) were also instrumental in purveying the notion of Shaka as a great conqueror. In the 1950s and 1960s, E. A. Ritter (*Shaka Zulu*, 1953) and Donald Morris (*The Washing of the Spears*, 1965) took advantage of an expanding Western interest in African history to produce best sellers that popularized ideas about Shaka as the founder of a mighty warrior nation.

An important shift in the packaging of this notion, though not in its basic assumptions, took place in the academic histories of Africa that began appearing in the 1960s. This was the period of decolonization, when new African nations were being formed and new views of Africa's past were being developed. In keeping with these ideas, historians in Western Europe, North America, and the newly independent countries of Africa were recasting Shaka as a "nation-builder," and the rise of the Zulu kingdom as the factor that had set in motion a process of nation-building among the early nineteenth-century black societies of southern Africa. The most influential work in this genre was John Omer-Cooper's *The Zulu Aftermath: A Nineteenth-Century Revolution in Bantu Africa* (1966), which was primarily responsible for introducing the term *mfecane* into the literature in place of "Shaka's wars." The word, which was derived from the Xhosa word *imfecane*, meaning something like "landless raiders," quickly became a widely accepted label for the upheavals of the 1820s and 1830s. Its meaning was also extended to cover a series of supposedly causative events stretching back into the later eighteenth century. By the early 1970s, inside and outside South Africa, the notion of the *mfecane* (or *difaqane*, in its seSotho form) was firmly entrenched in academic and popular histories and was making its way into school textbooks.

The consensus about the historical reality of the *mfecane* as a series of upheavals caused by the expansion of the Zulu kingdom was contested in 1988 by Rhodes University historian Julian Cobbing. In an article published in the *Journal of African History*, he forcefully argued that the upheavals of the early nineteenth century had been set in motion not by the expansion of the Zulu kingdom but by the expansion of the frontiers of European commerce and colonial settlement. The main destabilizing impact had come from slave-raiding and trading carried out by Dutch/Afrikaner and Griqua freebooters from the Cape frontier in the south and by Portuguese traders and their African allies from the Delagoa Bay region in the east. The convergence of waves of violence set in motion from these two epicenters had touched off chain reactions of conflicts among African societies on an unprecedented scale. The notion that it was Shaka and the Zulu who were to blame, Cobbing claimed, was an "alibi" made up by white colonial writers from the 1820s and 1830s onward to obscure the role played by white settlers and traders in establishing a traffic in slaves. The whole concept of the *mfecane* was too closely linked to simplistic Zulu-centric explanations to be salvageable: better, in his view, for historians to jettison not just the name but the very notion, and to reexamine the period afresh.

Cobbing's provocative arguments brought an immediate reaction from numbers of other historians. Critics asserted that he had greatly exaggerated the extent of the slave trade in southern Africa, that he had seriously distorted the available evidence to make his points, and that his arguments about the historiography of "Shaka's wars" were reductionist and simplistic. Sympathizers, on the other hand, found merit in Cobbing's thesis that the causes of the upheavals needed to be looked for primarily in the effects of colonial expansionism, though few were prepared to uncritically accept his arguments that the main cause had been an increase in European slave-raiding and trading.

The debates sparked off by Cobbing's intervention continue today. The main issue is not, as some commentators have thought, whether the upheavals of the early nineteenth century took place or not: it is about the nature of their causes, and the extent to which they can or cannot be seen as constituting a single historical event. Few, if any, historians would now defend the old idea that the upheavals were caused by the expansion of the Shaka's Zulu kingdom. Many, however, still want to hold on to the term *mfecane* as a useful label for them, whatever their causes. Others argue that to attach a single and misleading label to a long series of complex and widespread historical processes is an obstacle to understanding their causes, and that not simply the term but the general concept of the *mfecane* should be abandoned altogether.

JOHN WRIGHT

See also: **Boer Expansion: Interior of South Africa; Difaqane on the Highveld; Natal, Nineteenth Century; Shaka and the Zulu Kingdom, 1810–1840.**

Further Reading

Cobbing, J. "The Mfecane as Alibi: Thoughts on Dithakong and Mbolompo." *Journal of African History*. 29, no. 3 (1988): 487–519.

Hamilton, C. (ed.). *The Mfecane Aftermath: Reconstructive Debates in Southern African History*. Johannesburg: Witwatersrand University Press, and Pietermaritzburg: University of Natal Press, 1995.

Wright, J. "A. T. Bryant and 'the Wars of Shaka.'" *History in Africa*. 18 (1991): 409–425.

———. "Mfecane Debates." *Southern African Review of Books*, (September/October and November/December 1995): 18–19.

———. "Political Mythology and the Making of Natal's Mfecane." *Canadian Journal of African Studies*. 23, no. 2 (1989): 272–291.

Wylie, D. "A Dangerous Admiration: E. A. Ritter's Shaka Zulu." *South African Historical Journal*. 28 (1993): 98–118.

———. "Shaka and the Modern Zulu State." *History Today*. 44, no. 5 (1994): 8–11.

———. "Textual Incest: Nathaniel Isaacs and the Development of the Shaka Myth." *History in Africa*. 19 (1992): 411–433.

Middle Kingdom: *See* Egypt, Ancient: Middle Kingdom, Historical Outline.

Migration: *See* Gender and Migration: Southern Africa; Oromo: Migration and Expansion: Sixteenth and Seventeenth Centuries.

Military: Colonialism, Conquest, Resistance

In the last quarter of the nineteenth century, the European "Scramble" and subsequent partition of Africa was accomplished largely by military means. By 1900 fifty colonial territories had replaced some 1,000 African polities or states. The process of conquering African peoples continued well into the twentieth century, as primary resistance was replaced by secondary resistance. In Europe, colonial warfare was often referred to as composed of "savage" wars, compared to the supposedly "civilized" wars that went on between modern industrial states.

Until the mid-nineteenth century, the balance of weaponry and firepower of many African states was similar to that of European states. Both used single shot, muzzle-loading guns. However, Europe's industrial growth and the increased manufacture of new and more powerful weapons, rapidly widened the technological gap between African and European states. After

1850, European armies became better organized, and navies were increasingly equipped with larger, faster, steam-driven steel warships equipped with larger guns. The extending telegraph system could be used to call reinforcements and supplies. Soldiers were armed with breech-loading and then repeating rifles, and by the 1890s the quick-firing machine gun had become standard equipment in the modern army. The volume, range, and disciplined firepower of European forces was overwhelmingly greater than that of any African army.

Europeans learned more about tropical disease and its prevention, but this did not have any significant effect until most of Africa had been conquered. For example, over 6,000 French troops died of disease in the Madagascar campaign of 1895, and the majority of British casualties in the South African War (1899–1902), were due to disease rather than military combat.

Certain peoples in Africa were never effectively "pacified" by European colonial rulers. Some resistance was lengthy and only involved small armies, for example the struggle by the Somalis against the British and Italians. Other resistance wars resulted in long campaigns and large forces, for example the Rif war against the Spanish and French in Morocco in 1921–1925, and the Italian attempts to defeat the Senusi in Libya from 1912–1931. In these and other twentieth-century military operations, the European colonial powers deployed bomber and fighter aircraft, armored cars, and tanks against relatively poorly armed Africans.

At the time of the "Scramble," African states varied greatly in size. Some were large and relatively well-organized, such as Asante and Ethiopia, while others were small. Size and organization did not necessarily enable African states to resist foreign invasion; many large states collapsed following a major military defeat while small and seemingly less well-organized polities (the Nandi of Kenya for example) fought lengthy wars of resistance against the European invaders. Divisions within and rivalry between African states weakened their ability to resist foreign invasion and provided Europeans with African military allies. Some African states used diplomacy rather than war to secure better terms for themselves in the new colonial order (e.g., the Buganda Agreement, 1900). Ethiopia was the only African state to remain independent although eventually it was conquered by Italy in the brutal invasion of 1935–1936.

In the middle of the nineteenth century, some African states had access to firearms. These had to be imported, as Africa had no significant indigenous firearms industry. Local smiths could make and repair firearms, as did Samori Touré's *forgerons* in Guinea, although locally produced iron and steel tended to be of poor quality, as were the gunpowder and bullets produced within Africa. Muzzle-loading firearms, surplus to European requirements and superseded by new weaponry, continued to be imported into Africa where they were used for both hunting and warfare. By the Brussels Convention of 1890, the European colonial powers, determined to keep the balance of weaponry in their favor, placed an embargo on the import of modern precision weapons into Africa. A trickle of modern weapons continued to enter Africa, mainly in north and northeast Africa, to the benefit of Ethiopia. Thus, African soldiers went to war armed with a variety of weapons; some had guns but many carried spears, swords, clubs, or bows and arrows, all of which were inadequate to do battle with a well-equipped modern army.

Few African states had standing armies. Some South African societies, such as the Zulu, had well-trained armies organized by age groups, but in most states chiefs and vassals mobilized their men, who provided their own weapons, when hostilities threatened. During the 1880s the Asante state tried with little success to create a drilled and trained standing army. Women often accompanied African armies to provide food and comfort for the soldiers; in the army of Dahomey women also served as combatants. African soldiers mostly fought on foot. In some savanna and upland regions, for example Lesotho and the Sahel, horses were used in warfare. Mounted soldiers and horses, in cavalry states such as Sokoto, were protected by quilted armor.

In the early and mid-nineteenth century, mainly European (or West Indian) soldiers were used to fight African wars; this proved expensive of lives and money. European armies invariably required long and cumbersome supply lines which were vulnerable to attack and needed protection. In southern Africa, ox-wagons and horses moved supplies, but in tsetse fly-infected tropical areas, where draught animals could not be used, for even small campaigns thousands of human carriers had to be recruited, paid, fed, and forced to work.

From the 1870s onward small, locally recruited colonial armies were formed and increasingly became the mainstay of most military campaigns of conquest and "pacification." Many colonial soldiers were mercenaries who came from ethnic groups living in peripheral areas of a colony, or from neighboring colonies. Certain peoples from which soldiers were drawn, for example the Hausa, Kamba, and Bambara, soon became identified by European recruiters as "martial races." Most colonial armies numbered a few thousand infantry led by white officers. The Federal West African Frontier Force, created in 1898, consisted of fewer than 10,000 soldiers deployed in four colonies; the King's African Rifles in East Africa numbered a mere 2,440 soldiers in 1913. A larger army was the

Force Publique, which grew to 20,000 men in the Congo Free States; under its Belgian masters it earned a reputation for brutal behavior. African troops were usually raised for employment within the continent but the French increasingly used Tirailleurs Sénégalais, recruited in West Africa, in overseas campaigns. By 1912 the French, in order to compensate for their demographic weakness compared to Germany, had begun to recruit a large black African army for use in the event of a European war.

Most colonial forces were little more than lightly armed gendarmerie. They had several advantages over European troops: they were cheaper to employ, less susceptible to tropical diseases, could live off the countryside while on campaigns, and, despite one or two mutinies, proved to be generally loyal. Of the mutinies, the most serious was that by Sudanese troops employed by the British in western Kenya and Uganda.

In colonial wars African forces rarely stood much chance against the well-disciplined and superior fire of European-led armies. Occasionally, European forces were defeated because of poor leadership and overconfidence, by being outnumbered or taken by surprise. African armies could also take advantage of the terrain, for example the Asante used forest stockades from which to fight the British. European major defeats were few but had serious political repercussions in the metropoles. In 1879, a 1,250-strong British force was surprised and destroyed by the Zulu army at Isandlwana, although at a cost of some 3,000 Zulu lives. However, later that day a small garrison of 130 British troops, well armed and behind hastily erected defenses, successfully held off a Zulu force of 2,000 to 4,000 at Rorke's Drift. Established Zulu tactics of soldiers armed with spears advancing at speed like the horns of a cow to engulf the enemy from each side, revolutionary when used against rival African armies, were ineffective in the face of rapid and accurate rifle fire. The Zulu possessed guns but these were not their main weapons nor properly used. In 1896, at Adwa, the Ethiopians utterly defeated an Italian invading army that had divided into three columns; the victory helped secure Ethiopia's independence. And in 1921 a 10,000 strong Spanish army was defeated by the Rif in Morocco.

In most open battles against European armies, Africans were defeated and suffered high casualties. For example, in Sudan, at the Battle of Karari (Omdurman) in 1898, over 11,000 Mahdist soldiers, mainly armed with spears and swords, were killed by artillery and machine gun fire while the invading British and Egyptians lost a mere handful of men. African leaders had to change their military strategy if they wished to continue successful resistance. Guinea's Samori Touré, defeated in open battle by the French, resorted to guerrilla tactics and a scorched earth policy. Guerrilla warfare was the most successful form of African military resistance and made colonial "pacification" much more difficult, but also it often led to brutal action against civilians, as in the Nama-Herero rising in Namibia (1904–1907) and during the final stages of the South African War (1899–1902).

David Killingray

See also: **Colonial Armies, Africans in; Martial Races.**

Further Reading

Crowder, M. (ed.). *West African Resistance: The Military Response to Colonial Occupation*. London: Hutchinson, 1971.

Davidson, B. *The People's Cause: A History of Guerrillas in Africa*. Harlow: Longman, 1981.

Echenberg, M. *Colonial Conscripts: The Tirailleurs Sénégalais in French West Africa*, 1857–1960. Portsmouth, N.H.: Heinemann and London: James Currey, 1991.

Guy, J. J. "A Note on Firearms in the Zulu Kingdom with Special Reference to the Anglo-Zulu War, 1879." *Journal of African History XII*. 4 (1971). 557–570.

Ikime, O. *The Fall of Nigeria: The British Conquest*. London: Heinemann, 1977.

Journal of African History. XII, 2 (1971), special issue on "Firearms in Africa."

Killingray, D. and D. Omissi (eds.). *Guardians of Empire*. Manchester: Manchester University Press, 1999, chs. 1, 5, 8 and 11.

Lonsdale, J. "The Conquest State of Kenya, 1895–1905," and "The Politics of Conquest in Western Kenya, 1894–1908," in Berman.

Londsale, B. and J. Unhappy Valley: Conflict in Kenya and Africa. *Book One: State and Class*. London: James Currey, 1992.

Marjomaa, R. *War on the Savannah: The Military Collapse of the Sokoto Caliphate under the Invasion of the British Empire*. Tuusula: Finnish Academy of Science and Letters, 1998.

Morris, R. *The Washing of the Spears*. London: Jonathan Cape, 1966.

Smith, R. S. *Warfare and Diplomacy in Pre-Colonial West Africa*. London: Methuen, 1976.

Wilks, I. *Asante in the Nineteenth Century: The Structure and Evolution of a Political Order*. Cambridge: Cambridge University Press, 1975.

Woolman, D. S. *Rebels in the Rif*. Oxford: Oxford University Press, 1969.

Zulfo, 'I. H. *Karari: The Sudanese Account of the Battle of Omdurman*. London: Frederick Warne, 1980.

Military Rule: *See* Coup d'Étât and Military Rule: Postcolonial Africa.

Mining

Africa's mineral resources have excited European imaginations for centuries. Prester John's fabled wealth inspired the Portuguese in their early imperial travels, and the search for King Solomon's mines continued to figure in European thinking even in the twentieth century.

Workers in a uranium mine in Roessing, Namibia, 1996. © Charlotte Thege/Das Fotoarchiv.

Minerals were a major component of the "treasure-house myth" that convinced many nineteenth-century Europeans that penetrating the African interior would be highly profitable. The myth held some measure of reality, in that Arabs and the Portuguese had long been trading in African gold and copper when national rivalries, commercial interests, and military considerations led to European penetration of the interior. Where minerals, particularly gold, were found (or in some instances even just thought to exist) finance capital soon followed.

Europeans acquired rights to minerals by conquest, the expansion of colonial occupation and control, or by "negotiation." The Asante goldfields, for example, came under British control as part of the spoils of war, as did the copper mines of Katanga (Shaba) when King Leopold's claim to the territory was confirmed by killing the local ruler, Msiri. In the Transvaal, by the time gold was discovered on the Rand, European settler control was sufficiently entrenched that no formal acquisition of rights from Africans was considered necessary. Earlier, the Griqua had lost their claim to the Kimberley diamond area on the Cape in a dispute also involving the Orange Free State and the South African Republic. The concession in Mashonaland by Lobengula, the basis of the British South Africa Company's application for a charter to administer and exploit much of Central Africa, was obtained fraudulently; the two parties had very different ideas of what was granted. Similar concessions were negotiated elsewhere to justify mineral exploitation, ignoring the traditions that denied a chief the power to give away his people's land.

Railways were essential for maintaining viable mining operations, although a high proportion of lines were originally built for military and political purposes. Power for the railways, as well as for mining and smelting operations, was primarily supplied by coal. In the Transvaal, gold and coal mining were integrated, with further supplies from Natal. Wankie coal supplied the needs of southern Rhodesia and Katanga and later of the Copperbelt and Broken Hill (Kabwe). Nigerian coal was available for the Jos tin mines, and North African lines could rely on Algerian coal until steam engines were phased out in the 1950s.

In north and west Africa, labor demands were met by local populations or by migrant workers. Further south, the situation was different, due to the scale of operations and competition for labor from other economic activities (primarily agriculture) and because mineralized areas tended to be sparsely populated. Ethnically and geographically linked, and joined by the railway by 1911, Katanga's copper mines were more closely linked to neighboring northern Rhodesia than to other parts of the Congo.

As mining developed on the Copperbelt, northern Rhodesians were needed closer to home and permission to recruit for Katanga ended. In response the Belgians extended their own recruiting activities and adopted a system of stabilized labor, whereby men signed contracts for longer periods than earlier migrant workers, with accommodation, health and educational facilities being provided for wives and children. Copperbelt companies also adopted stabilized labor, taking advantage of a pool of experienced mineworkers. The Belgians did not adopt as restrictive a color bar as prevailed further south, although this was perhaps more noticeable on the railways, where many engine drivers came from west Africa.

Exploitation of the northern Rhodesian (Zambian) copper mines only became feasible during the interwar period when technological advances (developed in the United States and Chile) made it possible to treat their deep sulphide ores. In contrast, Katanga's oxide ores were closer to the surface, high grade, and relatively easily smelted. New technology also meant that the zinc and lead ores found at Broken Hill (Kabwe) that had previously proved financially disastrous for the British South Africa Company, could now be separated. Revenue from mining shifted the economic balance more toward northern Rhodesia, but southern Rhodesia, with its entrenched white settler population, continued to dominate the region politically.

Mines in southern Rhodesia, the Transvaal, and at Kimberley depended more heavily on migrant labor. Initially this was because African men and their communities were primarily interested in wage labor only as necessary to meet their needs or desires for cash and preferably at times when they were not required for agricultural work at home. At the same time, some people had developed almost a tradition of migrating into the Cape and elsewhere to find work. Mozambicans in particular formed a substantial part of the labor force in Kimberley and elsewhere. The Kimberley mines were able to meet their African labor requirements from people who came forward voluntarily, even after they stopped paying wages in guns and ammunition. Rand gold and coal mines required virtually continuous recruitment.

Large numbers of African workers were needed for the gold mines, partly because of initial reluctance to risk massive capital but also because labor was the only factor of production over which the companies could exercise cost control and thereby affect their profitability. Machinery and other essential materials were imported at prices and transport costs outside their control. Before 1899 the Kruger government imposed a dynamite monopoly—a factor in the Jameson Raid and South African (Boer) War—which forced the mining companies to pay a protective tariff on imported explosives. The companies could, as long as they cooperated with one another, pay Africans low wages. To succeed, this required a steady, large movement of Africans to work on the mines. The number of volunteers was insufficient, and many workers were provided by "touts," generally local traders who used debt to entrap Africans into agreeing to work on the mines for a wage considerably less than the "tout" received from the mining companies.

Many of these "touts" subsequently became licensed recruiting agents for the Chamber of Mines. The Chamber's Native Labor Department wanted to ensure a regular flow of labor to the mines and avoid a rising spiral of competitive wages. Restricted recruiting rights in the Transvaal pushed the search into neighboring colonies. The Rand (later Witwatersrand) Native Labor Association, formed expressly for the purpose in 1897 had its greatest success in Mozambique where the Portuguese were happy to allow men from the southern districts of Gaza and Inhambane to be recruited for the Rand in exchange for a capitation fee, guaranteed traffic for the railway line to Lourenco Marques (Maputo), and preferential access to Transvaal markets. Mozambicans had long migrated to other parts of southern Africa, one of their most important motives being to escape the harsh Portuguese labor regime. They contracted for longer periods, some remaining on the Rand for several years at a time, and for several decades constituted half or more of the Transvaal mine labor force.

Apart from the more glamorous and capital consuming mining of gold and gem diamonds, southern, central, west, and north Africa have a range of mineral resources that have contributed in varying degrees to the economies of many countries. Nonferrous metals are found in abundance, although some, notably copper, have declined in value with increased use of plastics. Phosphates and manganese are found in North Africa along with coal and iron. Uranium has also been significant, Katanga supplying the basis of early atomic experiments; and Namibia providing a substantial part of world supplies. A varied mineral resource base with substantial reserves of iron ore and limestone facilitated South Africa's industrialization and unsmelted iron ore became a major export from Mauretania. Also significant have been the industrial quality diamonds from Angola, Namibia, the Kasai region of Congo, Sierra Leone, and most countries of West Africa. The profitability of mining gem quality diamonds can only be maintained by the restrictive selling practices controlled by De Beers Consolidated's Central Selling Organization. Industrial diamonds, although not sold entirely without some regulation, have a more natural market in oil drilling and other industrial applications. Artificial diamonds threaten both.

It is not easy to determine the historic profitability of many mining companies. Apart from the lack of publicly available, accurate accounts, it is difficult to factor in to calculations the impact of direct and indirect transport subsidies, while the operations of international cartels also distort the picture. In South Africa gold mining was shown to be as profitable over the long-term as many other spheres of investment. Early fortunes tended to be made more from speculation in mining shares than from actual operations. Over time an increasing proportion of those profits were paid in South Africa rather than to foreign investors. Profits increased when the world's economies went off the gold standard between the wars and subsequently when the price of gold was allowed to float. However profitable mining remained highly speculative.

SIMON KATZENELLENBOGEN

Further Reading

Crush, J. *South Africa's Labor Empire: A History of Black Migrancy to the Gold Mines*. Boulder and Oxford, Westview Press, 1991 (African Modernization and Development series).

Duffy, J. A. *Question of Slavery: Labour Policies in Portuguese Africa and the British Protest*. Oxford: Oxford University Press, 1967.

Frankel, S. H. *Capital Investment in Africa: Its Course and Effects*. London: Oxford University Press, 1938.

Frankel, S. H. *Investment and the Return to Equity Capital in the South African Gold Mining Industry, 1887–1965: An International Comparison*. Oxford: Basil Blackwell, 1967.

Greenhalgh, P. *West African Diamonds 1919–1983: An Economic History*. Manchester: Manchester University Press, 1985.

Harries, P. *Work, Culture, and Identity: Migrant Laborers in Mozambique and South Africa*. Portsmouth, NH: Heinemann, and London: Currey, 1994.

Jeeves, A. H. *Migrant Labour in South Africa's Mining Economy: The Struggle for the Gold*. Kingston, Ont.: McGill-Queen's University Press, and Johannesburg: Witwatersrand University Press, 1985.

Johnstone, F. A. *Class, Race and Gold: A Study of Class Relations and Racial Discrimination*. London: Routledge and Kegan Paul, 1976 (International Library of Sociology).

Katzenellenbogen, S. "The miner's frontier, transport and general economic development." In P. Duignan and L. H. Gann, eds., *Colonialism in Africa 1870–1960: Volume Four, The Economics of Colonialism.* Cambridge and New York: Cambridge University Press for the Hoover Institution, 1975.

———. *Railways and the Copper Mines of Katanga.* Oxford, Oxford University Press, 197.

———. *South Africa and Southern Mozambique: Labour, Railways and Trade in the Making of a Relationship.* Manchester, Manchester University Press 1983.

Newbury, C. *The Diamond Ring: Business, Politics and Precious Stones in South Africa 1867–1957.* Oxford: Clarendon Press, 1989.

Mining, Multinationals, and Development

A major paradox of modern African development is that the continent is so richly endowed with mineral resources and yet remains the poorest in the world. This perception has fuelled considerable debate about both the colonial economic legacy and postcolonial impediments to effective linkages between the mining sector and broad-based economic progress. Discussion frequently focuses on negative aspects of investment by multinational corporations, but it remains necessary to recognize great spatial disparities in Africa's resource endowment and complexities in the historical pattern of mineral industry development.

A century of colonial exploration, prior to the 1960s, indicated widespread African mineralization, and this frequently led to the establishment of enclaves of capital-intensive mining, most notably on the Witwatersrand in South Africa. Insatiable demand for minerals during World War II and large-scale prospecting programs in the 1950s and 1960s confirmed Africa's vast but unevenly distributed mineral wealth. Southern Africa has been estimated to contain almost all the world's chromium reserves, Gabon and South Africa hold the world's largest manganese deposits, while Morocco and Tunisia have the largest phosphate resources. Massive deposits of gold, platinum, diamonds, copper, iron ore, bauxite, coal, and other minerals are also known. In general, the greatest concentration of mining is in southern Africa, with slightly lesser concentrations in the Maghrib, and a belt running through West Africa into the Congo basin.

Dependence on foreign mining companies, established in the colonial era, continued in many independent states, except where diminished by nationalization programs such as in Ghana (1961) and Zambia (1970), or in the unique case of South Africa, where large domestic mining corporations like Anglo-American and Gencor continued to dominate their own economy, as well as reaching out with mining investments in other parts of Africa. The increasingly capital-intensive and technologically-complex nature of mining projects frequently entailed a degree of reliance on foreign investment and personnel that encouraged charges of neocolonialism. The British multinational RTZ was particularly vulnerable in this regard, with large investments not only in Zimbabwe and Zambia, but also in Namibia where its half-stake in the Rössing uranium mine was highly politically sensitive before independence in 1990.

Criticism of foreign multinationals normally focuses on the enclave nature of mining developments, which underutilize local supplies and managerial talent, while exporting minerals in a semiprocessed state, suppressing spin-off industrial developments within the host nation. Most African copper, for example, is shipped as ingots to Europe or Japan, where it undergoes the far more profitable process of fabrication into wire and other end-products. Foreign mining companies also stand accused of reinforcing export dependency in host nations, and so their susceptibility to global economic crises. An excessive part of the profit from mining and mineral processing is often supposed to be siphoned out of Africa, leaving little capital for local social investment. In addition, mining multinationals have often been seen as corruptly influencing host political regimes, for example American, German, and Swedish iron-ore interests in Liberia, especially before 1980. In this context, multinationals appear to have considerable leverage in pressuring host nations, within unequal bargaining situations, into granting overgenerous mineral concessions. And, taking a longer-term view, it can be argued that foreign mining firms often lack concern for the environment, or the sustainability of communities based on mining and smelting projects.

Anxiety about such issues led many postcolonial African states to nationalize all or part of their mineral industries. In 1961, four years after independence, Ghana established the State Mining Corporation (SMC) to take over various gold and diamond mining interests, while in Zambia the state took over 51 per cent of the copper industry in 1970 (until then controlled by South African, British, and American interests). By the mid-1980s, nationalization was widespread: ranging from 100 per cent control of Zaire's copper industry by the state-owned Gecamines, and 100 per cent control of Moroccan phosphate production by OCP, to the 37 per cent state-owned Lamco that dominated Liberian iron-ore mining. However, state involvement in the minerals sector did not always resolve the fundamental problems involved in dealing with foreign markets and companies: leverage by the latter could still result in iniquitous agreements. A classic case arose when Ghana was pressurized into funding the expensive Volta River hydro-electric scheme during the 1960s, to provide the cheap electricity that would persuade the U.S.-based Kaiser Aluminium Corporation to build a large refinery in the country, which would then allow profitable mining of massive Ghanaian bauxite deposits, discovered before 1914. Once built, Kaiser controversially imported what it argued was cheaper Jamaican bauxite, despite protracted government pressure and anti-American demonstrations.

Nationalization also failed to protect mineral export-dependent nations like the Democratic Republic of Congo (Zaire) and Zambia from the world economic recessions of the 1970s and 1980s. Like most primary products, copper prices slumped (by 50% in real terms between 1970 and 1976 alone) and remained low in historic terms through to the late 1990s. The economic effects on Zaire and Zambia were severe, since copper exports for both had accounted for about a third of GDP in the late 1960s. Africa in general suffered profoundly from the deteriorating real value of its mineral exports throughout the last quarter of the century, a problem made worse by the apparent inability of African states to influence global commodity prices. The short-lived copper exporters' association, CIPEC (modeled on OPEC), of which Zambia and Zaire were leading members, failed in the 1970s to make any impression on price-setting mechanisms firmly rooted in centers like London and New York. Nationalization was, moreover, charged with crippling many of Africa's mining enterprises. The state-run Zambian Consolidated Copper Mines (ZCCM) was a prime example: political interference and poor management were reflected in badly deteriorating performance, with its share of world output slumping from 13.7 per cent in 1969 to 2.9 per cent in 1997.

South Africa's minerals sector requires some separate consideration, largely due to the country's distinctive historical development within the continent; generating an element of white capitalism—to a large degree independent of that in the European-American metropole—which has survived largely intact beyond the dismantling of apartheid. South Africa's mineral endowment is also one of the richest in the world: its mines since the late twentieth century have produced as much as two-thirds of the world's platinum, half its chromium and gold (although the latter declined to a fifth by 1997), and a fifth of its diamonds, as well as significant volumes of manganese, uranium, iron, coal, and copper. Political relations between government and the industry were close under apartheid, primarily through the medium of the Chamber of Mines (established 1889), dominated by the Johannesburg-based mining houses like Anglo-American and Gencor. Such corporations remain global operations of considerable stature: Anglo-American in particular is a huge multinational and by 1980 was estimated to control around 250 mining companies in twenty-two countries, as well as 73 manufacturing and financial concerns. Notwithstanding the considerable benefits accruing to the South African economy from the minerals sector, this has recently experienced deep recession, particularly in gold mining. Falling gold prices (from $613 an ounce in 1980 to $250 in 1999) resulted in massive lay-offs and mine closures: 40,000 were made redundant in 1990 alone, and a continued slide in profitability during 1999 led to threats that 80,000 could lose their jobs. The impact extends beyond the borders of South Africa, since thousands of migrants from countries like Mozambique and Lesotho have long relied on work in the Witwatersrand mines.

Africa in the 1990s witnessed indications of a reversal of the depression in the minerals sector of the previous two decades, with accelerating exploration programs throughout the continent both by African and foreign companies. The South African firm JCI prospected in Ghana, Tanzania, Ethiopia, and Swaziland, and in a reflection of shifting post-Cold War alignments, undertook a joint venture with the Mali government to reopen a gold mine last operated by the Russians in 1991. JCI has also been involved in the ongoing privatization of ZCCM, part of a wider program of denationalization by the Zambian government in the post-Kaunda era. More problematically, numerous multinationals have flocked to develop the mineral potential of Democratic Republic of Congo, during and after the civil war victory of Laurent Kabila. During the conflict, numerous firms scrambled for concessions from both sides: in 1997, for example, American Mineral Fields obtained a $1 billion concession from Kabila to rehabilitate the Kolwezi copper and cobalt project, near Lubumbashi, although President Mobutu and Gecamines dismissed the contract as illegal. After Mobutu's fall, foreign companies were joined by Zimbabwean, Namibian, and South African groups in the search for concessions. In November 1998 a Zimbabwean entrepreneur was appointed head of the reconstituted state enterprise, Gecamines.

The potential for future African mineral exploitation appears considerable, although the capacity for converting this into broader-based economic development will undoubtedly prove more difficult. It is also clear that with a continuing trend toward more capital-intensive mining and processing, the minerals sector will continue to need foreign capital and enterprise, even if more of this can be found in African-based firms like Anglo-American and JCI. But a key role for mining is clear, if only because the biggest challenge is faced by those African states such as Niger and Burkina Faso that have few identifiable economic mineral deposits and consistently rank among the world's poorest nations.

CHRISTOPHER SCHMITZ

See also: **Multinationals and the State; South Africa: Mining.**

Further Reading

Bosson, R. and B. Varon. *The Mining Industry and the Developing Countries*. New York: Oxford University Press, 1977.

Daniel, P. *Africanisation, Nationalisation and Inequality: Mining Labour and the Copperbelt in Zambian Development*. Cambridge: Cambridge University Press, 1979.

De Kun, N. *The Mineral Resources of Africa*. Amsterdam-London: Elsevier, 1965.

Fine, B. and Z. Rustomjee. *The Political Economy of South Africa: From Minerals-Energy Complex to Industrialisation*. London: Hurst, 1996.

Greenhalgh, P. *West African Diamonds 1919–1983: An Economic History*. Manchester: Manchester University Press, 1985.

Innes, D. *Anglo-American and the Rise of Modern South Africa*. London: Heinemann, 1984.

Lanning, G. and M. Mueller. *Africa Undermined: Mining Companies and the Underdevelopment of Africa*. Harmondsworth: Penguin, 1979.

Mikesell, R. F. and J. W. Whitney. *The World Mining Industry: Investment Strategy and Public Policy*. Boston-London: Allen & Unwin, 1987.

Seidman, A. W. and N. Seidman. *US Multinationals in Southern Africa*. Dar es Salaam: Tanzania Publishing House, 1977.

Widstrand, C. G. *Multinational Firms in Africa*. Dakar: African Institute for Economic Development and Planning, 1975.

Missionaries: *See* Angola: New Colonial Period: Christianity, Missionaries, Independent Churches; Religion, Colonial Africa: Missionaries.

Missionary Enterprise: Precolonial

Christianity flourished in Africa before it made its way to western and northern Europe. Preexisting beliefs in a single god existed in many parts of Africa and may have influenced the transition to monotheism in ancient Egypt. Much of Ethiopia, Nubia (the Sudan), and North Africa was Christianized by the fifth century. Nonetheless, from the fifteenth century onward, European Christian missionaries launched waves of evangelical agents into Africa.

Much of the fervor that fuelled Portugal's push down the Atlantic coast of Africa was a legacy of medieval Crusades to free the "Holy Lands" of the Middle East from Islamic domination. During the European Middle Ages, legends circulated about a mysterious Christian King, Prester John, who sought allies in the defense of his realm. Some speculated that that home was in Africa. When Portuguese navigators reached the Congo River in 1484, they encountered a powerful king who, if he was not Christian, was at least not Muslim. The missionary priests they dispatched in the

Livingstone's Zambesi expedition reaches Lake Malawi, September 1859. © Das Fotoarchiv.

hope of converting the Manicongo and his people to Christianity launched the first modern missions to Sub-Saharan Africa. As the Portuguese proceeded to seize strongholds in Angola and on the East African coast, Catholic missions followed. While the flame of Portuguese missionary enthusiasm subsequently waned, it never entirely died.

In the eighteenth century, Protestants turned their attention to Africa. Stimulated by movements in Central Europe which expected that Christ's second coming would be marked by the evangelization of the world, and sparked by the rise of Methodism in Britain which emphasized that salvation could be attained by individual effort, new missionary societies were formed to bring the Gospel to Africa. Moravian missionaries established a foothold in South Africa in the mid-eighteenth century. By the turn of the nineteenth century a host of British missionary societies had sprung up.

Some of the new enthusiasm for Africa derived from guilt about European participation in the Atlantic slave trade. First the Quakers, and then all the major Protestant denominations, denounced the trade as sinful. The British colony of Sierra Leone originated as settlement for freed slaves, led by Protestant evangelicals who hoped it might serve as a bridgehead for the conversion of Africa. The idea of substituting "legitimate trade" for the slave trade underpinned a number of early missions to West Africa, the most notable of which was the Church of England's push into Nigeria, led by an African bishop, Samuel Crowther.

The Cape of Good Hope with its less threatening climate and British government, proved to be a magnet for missionaries in the early nineteenth century. It also set the scene for what was to be a series of confrontations between white settlers and Christian evangelists.

Neither Dutch nor British settlers at the Cape cared much for the missionaries. They despised agents such as Johannes van der Kemp and James Read, who adopted African lifestyles. They feared agents such as John Philip, superintendent of the London Missionary Society in South Africa from 1822 to 1849, who advocated equal rights for Africans and championed the independence of African rulers. In 1854 John William Colenso was appointed as bishop of Natal and soon made himself an unpopular defender of African rights. By the 1870s American Congregationalists, French Calvinists, Scottish Presbyterians, German Lutherans, Roman Catholics, and Swedish and Norwegian missions had spread themselves along the South African coast and into the interior. The progress of their religion lagged behind the extension of their operations. Almost everywhere Africans seemed indifferent to their message. They made little headway among chiefs and the leaders of society. Their small congregations were drawn mostly from the poor, the outcast, and the alienated. In the face of such obstinacy, many missionaries openly prayed that the extension of European colonial rule might pave the way for the advance of their religion. On the eve of the Zulu War of 1879, for example, most missionaries in the region lined up on the side of the British invaders.

The double-edged character of nineteenth-century missions was exemplified by David Livingstone of the London Missionary Society. Initially employed as an assistant to the venerable Robert Moffat of Kuruman, Livingstone was discouraged by the agonizingly slow progress of his religion among the Tswana. Much more exciting was the discovery of new lands for the propagation of the faith. He was appalled by the white Afrikaner "Voortrekkers" who used force to seize African territory and steal African children. As he ventured out into unknown regions, he began to realize that Afrikaner slave trading was only a small part of the problem in East Africa. Like the West African missionaries before him, Livingstone advocated "Commerce and Christianity" as remedies for the slave trade. His expeditions to the Zambezi and the great lakes of East Africa were motivated by a desire to "open up" Africa to trade and missions. At the same time that he was exposing the evils of the slavers, he was paving the way for European colonization. His plea to the undergraduate students of Oxford and Cambridge in the 1850s inspired the Universities' Mission to Central Africa. When Africa seemed to have swallowed him up in the late 1860s, an international effort was launched to "find Livingstone." The explorer Henry Morton Stanley, whose embarrassed greeting, "Dr. Livingstone, I presume," confirmed his "rescue" of the lost missionary, went on to open the Congo River Basin to exploitation by the notorious regime of Leopold II's Congo River Free State. Commerce proved to be a dubious partner with Christianity.

Although European missionaries reaped the lion's share of publicity for the evangelical thrust into what they termed "the Dark Continent" (because, in their opinion, it had yet to be illuminated by "Christian truth") the basic work of conversion was done by Africans. Except in Uganda, mass conversions were rarely accomplished by European agency. Mission stations isolated themselves from the surrounding populations. African evangelists went out and met the people. A largely unsung army of African preachers made their continent the scene of Christianity's greatest modern triumphs.

Africa was also the scene of much religious innovation. Protestant missionaries, who stressed the importance of Scripture, worked hard at translating the Bible into African languages. This not only laid the basis for the today's grammars of those languages, it stimulated the workings of Africans' religious imaginations. The Old Testament spoke of ancient Hebrew people who allowed polygamy, people who aspired to live comfortably amid their flocks and fields, people who feared witches, who heard prophets, and who suffered under the yoke of foreign oppressors: in short, people who appeared to be like them. Wherever the Christian message was preached, it inspired Africans to craft their own interpretations of the Bible. It inspired some of them to prophetic utterance.

In the Congo, in the first decade of the eighteenth century, a young African woman announced that she had received direct messages from Saint Anthony and that she, Dona Beatrice Kimpa Vita, would shortly give birth to a child of divine fatherhood, who would correct the false interpretations of Scripture promulgated by the Catholic missionaries. As her Antonian Movement spread, authorities became alarmed and she was burned at the stake. In early nineteenth-century South Africa, a prophet, Ntsikana, arose among the Xhosa people with a message that combined African insights with the message lately promulgated in the region by missionaries. Luckier than Dona Beatrice, a hymn he composed is much loved and still sung in South African churches. Late in the nineteenth century, Protestant churches in southern Africa began to suffer defections from their congregations. One after another, a series of African Christians refused to conform any longer to the dictates of missionary authority and founded their own churches. By the end of the century there had been so many of these that not only missionaries but colonial authorities spoke of the "menace" of what was termed the "Ethiopian movement." In West Africa the growth of the new churches was termed the

Aladura movement. Some west and central African prophets acquired huge followings; among the most notable were the Prophet Harris of Côte d'Ivoire and Simon Kimbangu of the Congo.

Various scholarly interpretations of these movements have been put forward. Some hypothesize that they were reactions against the refusal of the European missionaries to treat their converts as equal and their hesitation to ordain them as ministers. Others, noting that the more authoritarian Roman Catholic missions suffered fewer defections, lean toward the opinion that Protestantism itself, with its emphasis on direct communication with the Holy Spirit and individual interpretation of the Scriptures, was responsible for fission in the churches. Still others see the prophetic Zionist and Ethiopian movements as veiled expressions of hostility to colonialism.

However, over the course of the twentieth century, many missionary organizations and mainstream churches made their peace with the secessionists. So did the state, for the realization grew that the Independent Churches (as they are generally called today) did not, for the most part, pose anything more than a symbolic threat to secular authorities. Today most of the Independent Churches are no longer condemned by missions as heretical but are accepted as a genuine and important aspect of the Christianization of Sub-Saharan Africa.

NORMAN A. ETHERINGTON

See also: **Religion, Colonial Africa: Independent, Millenarian/Syncretic Churches; Religion, Postcolonial Africa: Independence and Churches, Mission-Linked and Independent; Religion, History of.**

Further Reading

Barrett, D. B. *Schism and Renewal in Africa: An Analysis of Six Thousand Contemporary Religious Movements.* Nairobi: Oxford University Press, 1968.

Comaroff, J. and J. Comaroff. "*Of Reason and Revelation.*" Vol. 1, *Christianity, Colonialism, and Consciousness in South Africa.* Chicago: University of Chicago Press, 1991; Vol. 2, *Of Revelation and Revolution: The Dialectics of Modernity on a South African Frontier.* Chicago: University of Chicago Press, 1997.

Gray, R. *Black Christians and White Missionaries.* New Haven: Yale University Press, 1990.

Hastings, A. *The Church in Africa, 1450–1950.* Oxford: Oxford University Press, 1995.

———. *History of African Christianity, 1950–1975.* Cambridge, 1979.

Oliver, R. *The Missionary Factor in East Africa.* London: Longmans, 1952.

Porter, A. "Religion and Empire: British Expansion in the Long Nineteenth Century, 1780–1914." *Journal of Imperial and Commonwealth History.* 20 (1993): 370–390.

Sundkler, B. *Bantu Prophets in South Africa.* 2nd ed. London: Oxford University Press, 1961.

Mobutisim: *See* Congo (Kinshasa), Democratic Republic of Zaire: Mobutu, Zaire, and Mobutuism.

Mogadishu

Mogadishu is Somalia's largest city and its capital since independence. European writers and historians of the nineteenth and twentieth centuries routinely described it as having been founded in the tenth or eleventh century by Arab immigrants. We may perhaps never know the source word or words for Mogadishu, which may have come from some Bantu or Cushitic dialect. However, most certainly, in its early days, Mogadishu was a small fishing village like the many villages along the East African coast populated by Africans of Bantu descent; later it became part of the ancient network of trading towns that existed between Africa, Arabia, and India, as has been described in the *Periplus Maris Erythraie*, a Greek manual for seafaring merchants in the first century CE. At that time, Mogadishu was a seaport that exported tortoise shells, ivory, rhinoceros horn, and nautilus shells.

After the arrival of Islam, the city would become part of what was then the Swahili civilization, a series of Muslim city-states strung along the Indian Ocean, with Mogadishu being its most northern point. In its Swahili period, Mogadishu often became the adopted home of Asiatic travelers and seafarers; these immigrants contributed to the diversity of the city's population.

Some time after the tenth century, Mogadishu started a period of its history that might be the called Benadir period, distinct from the purely Swahili period. This later period marks the beginning of Mogadishu as a city ruled by Somalis who had migrated from the

The people of Mombasa line the streets for a British royal visit, 1956. © SVT Bild/Das Fotoarchiv.

north. This period is so named because the coast came to be known as the Benadir coast. The word "benadir" (cities; singular, "bendar"), is Persian and entered the Somali language through the northern ports, by way of sea merchants from the Arabian Peninsula and the Persian Gulf.

In 1331 Ibn Battatu, the Muslim traveler from what is now Morocco, visited the major coastal Somali cities; he described both the residents of Zeilah in the far north and those of Mogadishu as being of the same kind of people, namely black Berbers who spoke the Berber language ("Berber" was the medieval Arab term for Somalis and peoples closely related to them). He also mentioned that its merchants were wealthy and exported locally made textiles to Egypt and other places. Almost two centuries later, a Portuguese, Duarte Barbosa, described it in these words:

> It has a king over it, and is a place of great trade in merchandise. Ships come there from the kingdom of Cambay [India] and from Aden with stuffs of all kinds, and with spices. And they carry away from there much gold, ivory, beeswax, and other things upon which they make a profit. In this town there is plenty of meat, wheat, barley, and horses, and much fruit; it is a very rich place. (Hersi, p.196.)

Mogadishu's fortunes would change for the worse with the arrival, in the Indian Ocean region, of the Portuguese, the precursors of European enterprise, and domination in the Indian Ocean and Far East trade. In 1499 Mogadishu was bombarded by the Portuguese captain Vasco da Gama and was again attacked in 1518. The Portuguese were not able to take or keep the town under their domination; however, their raiding and piracy disrupted trade and thrust the coastal cities, including Mogadishu, into a deep decline.

In the seventeenth century the Abgal Yaquub, a Somali clan (located today in the north of Mogadishu) overthrew the Muzaffar dynasty and started the Abgal Yaquub dynasty. The Abgal instituted a system of governance in which the ruler was called an *imam* (the previous rulers of Mogadishu were either called sultans or shaykhs). Because of the new trade patterns established by Europeans in the Indian Ocean and Far East, the new dynasty was unable to restore Mogadishu's glory and prosperity. In the seventeenth, eighteenth, and nineteenth centuries the city drew inward and focused on its ties with the hinterland, especially in the Shabelle valley, which provided the city with produce.

In 1842 a power struggle developed between the heirs of the recently deceased imam: Ahmed Mohamed, the deceased imam's son, and a nephew, Ahmed Mohamud. As the succession conflict intensified, Mogadishu became a divided city, with a "no-man's land" separating its two halves of Shingani and Hamarweyne. With the conflict unresolved for a number of years and the city nearly ruined, elders from the Hamarweyne district sent a request to the Zanzibari ruler, who was of Omani origins, and had earlier manifested a desire to add Mogadishu to his new dominions in East Africa. In 1843, in response to that request, the Zanizabari ruler, Seyyid Said, appointed a Somali, one Ali Mohamed, as his governor. However, Zanzibari involvement remained nominal, and the Zanzibari ruler had to pay tribute to the powerful sultan of the Geledi, whose lands lay to the west of the city (Alpers).

Thus, Mogadishu's affairs remained in local hands. By the middle of nineteenth century, Mogadishu grew more prosperous by serving as an outlet to the increasingly productive farming communities of the Shabelle valley, which were producing grain, sesame oil, and Orchella weed for export (Cassanelli).

As the nineteenth century came to a close, another chapter of Mogadishu's history would start: the Italian period, which would last until 1960. In an age when major European powers were engaged in the "Scramble" for Africa, the Italians established their colony of Somalia, with its capital as Mogadishu. Today the Italian influence, whether in architecture or food, is still visible in the city, which had a large Italian population during the heyday of Italian colonialism in the region.

As the capital of the Somali Republic formed from British Somaliland and Italian Somalia, Mogadishu would see its importance increase phenomenally and would grow into the biggest Somali city. In the 1970s and 1980s, Muhammad Siad Barré's government would invest substantial amounts in renovating Mogadishu in an Italian style, marked by large government buildings, towering statues, and gardens. However, after Siad Barré was overthrown in 1991 in a bloody revolt, factional fighting reduced much of Mogadishu's public and commercial infrastructure into rubble. The city became divided into two zones, one held by Ali Mahdi, and the other by General Aidid. Later, more factional fighting created several smaller fiefdoms in Mogadishu, each governed by a warlord with his own militia. The city played a central role in the U.S.-led UN humanitarian international intervention dubbed "Operation Rescue Hope." In the aftermath of that failed mission, Mogadishu remains a divided city with no unified administration.

MOHAMED DIRIYE ABDULLAHI

See also: **Ibn Battuta, Mali Empire and; Somalia: Barré, Mohamed Siad, Life and Government of; Somalia: Nineteenth Century; Nomads to British and Italian Protectorates; Somalia: 1990 to the Present; Somalia: Pastoralism, Islam, Commerce, Expansion: To 1800.**

Further Reading

Alpers, E. "Toward a History of Nineteenth Century Mogadishu: A Report of Research in Progress." In Hussein, M. *Proceedings of the First International Congress of Somali Studies*, edited by H. M. Adam and C. L. Geshekter. 1992.

Cassanelli, L. V. *The Shaping of Somali Society: Reconstructing the History of a Pastoral People, 1600–1900*. Philadelphia: Pennsylvania University Press, 1982.

Diriye A. M. *Culture and Customs of Somalia*. Westport, Conn.: Greenwood Press, 2001.

Loughran, J., K. Loughran, J. Johnson, and S. S. Samatar, eds. *Somalia in Word and Image*. Washington: Foundation for Cross-Cultural Understanding, 1986.

Nurse, D., and T. Spear. *The Swahili: Reconstructing the History and Language of an African Society, 800–1500*. Philadelphia: University of Pennsylvania Press, 1985.

Mokhehle, Ntsu (1918–1998)

Prime Minister and Opposition Politician

The fifth of ten children, Ntsu Mokhehle grew up in his native village of Ha Mokhehle, in the Tejatejaneng district. After an irregular attendance of school punctuated by financial difficulties and illness, Ntsu finished his secondary education in the normal time of five years. In 1940 he went to Fort Hare on a government scholarship. His studies were marked by interruptions due to involvement in political activities.

While at Fort Hare, Ntsu met a group of individuals who would shape the political destinies of various countries in the region. His participation in activities aimed at addressing students' grievances and involvement in student politics in general at Fort Hare helped to widen and sharpen the political consciousness of a young man who had already shown his political awareness by joining Lekgotla la Bafo (LLB) in Lesotho in the mid-1930s. Ntsu also joined, led, or founded a number student organizations and teacher organizations. In their own way these organizations challenged colonialism and championed the nationalist cause, however narrowly.

Ntsu's involvement in wider, nationalist politics began with his membership in the LLB in Lesotho and the African National Congress (ANC) Youth League in South Africa.

After he returned to Lesotho in 1950, Ntsu suffered at the hands of the colonial regime, which blocked all his efforts to secure a job suitable for someone of his qualifications. This increased his determination to resist the colonial regime. In 1952 he formed the Basutoland African National Congress (BAC, the name was changed to Basutoland Congress Party, or BCP, in 1959). His membership in the LLB, combined with the blessing he received from the leadership of that ailing organization, gave him an almost ready-made following for his party.

Ntsu undertook a number of overseas trips in connection with Lesotho's advancement toward independence. He attended the All-African People's Convention in Ghana. In 1959 he visited Guinea Bissau and met President Sékou Touré. In 1962 he appeared before the United Nations' decolonization committee and petitioned that body to pressure Britain into granting Lesotho independence sooner. He was a member of the 1964 BNC delegation that finalized constitutional talks with Britain.

Although the BAC/BCP initially advocated a position similar to that espoused by the ANC, Ntsu himself had always subscribed to more militant Africanist and anticommunist views. Thus, when the Pan-Africanist Congress (PAC) broke away from the ANC in 1959, the BCP aligned with it. His ideological position notwithstanding, Ntsu was able to establish friendly relations with progressive organizations and individuals and, until the late 1970s, had cordial relations with a number of socialist countries.

His party won the 1970 general elections, but Chief Leabua refused to hand over power and incarcerated Ntsu and other opposition leaders. He was freed in 1970 after signing a document declaring that intimidation had marred the 1970 elections and that new elections would be arranged and held in due course. In 1974, frustrated by Chief Leabua's actions, Ntsu's supporters staged a poorly coordinated uprising which Leabua's forces easily crushed. Ntsu was forced to flee Lesotho and he lived in Botswana for a time before he was expelled and went to Zambia. Exiled and seeing no other means of overthrowing Leabua, Ntsu established a military wing of his party, the Lesotho Liberation Army (LLA), which began raiding Lesotho in 1979. At the same time, South Africa began its destabilization campaign against countries that it accused of harboring ANC and PAC: Lesotho was on that list. Soon South African operatives persuaded Ntsu that they had a common enemy and that they should work together. The LLA split and a faction led by Ntsu collaborated with South African agents.

Ntsu returned to Lesotho in 1988 and participated in processes leading to the restoration of constitutional rule in Lesotho. In 1993 his party won all sixty parliamentary seats, and he was named prime minister. However, his government was weak and suffered not only from lack of cooperation from state institutions filled with members of Leabua's party but also deep intraparty divisions. It was because of these divisions that, in 1997, Ntsu was forced to leave the BCP and form another party, the Lesotho Congress for Democracy (LCD). The majority of the parliament joined his party, and this new party formed a government. This caused a controversy that raged until the end of the term for Ntsu's government, in 1998. In the elections of that year, his party (now led by Pakalitha Mosisili) won in seventy-nine out of the eighty constituencies.

As a politician, Ntsu was known among his opponents as a man of no fixed principles; he took any political position that served his current interests. He had a keen lifelong interest in the history of Lesotho in general and in Moshoeshoe I in particular. Among his writings is a pamphlet in which he tried to synthesize Moshoeshoe I's ideas, sayings, and deeds into a systematic ideology.

Ntsu died in December 1998, shortly after his eightieth birthday.

MOTLATSI THABANE

See also: **Jonathan, Chief Joseph Leabua; Lesotho.**

Biography

Born in Ha Mokhehle, in the Tejatejaneng district, in 1918. Ntsu completed his primary education at a local Anglican primary school in 1933. In 1940 he went to Fort Hare on a government scholarship. He was expelled in 1941, the University readmitted him in 1942. He completed his degree in 1943. He taught and then rejoined Fort Hare in 1946 on a study grant from the South African Institute for Scientific Research. He completed the degree with distinction in 1947. Thereafter, he enrolled for a University Education Diploma, which he passed with distinction. In 1948 and 1949 he taught at South African schools before returning to Lesotho. In 1952 he formed the Basutoland African National Congress (BAC, the name was changed to Basutoland Congress Party, or BCP, in 1959). His party won the 1970 general elections, but Chief Leabua refused to hand over power and incarcerated Ntsu and other opposition leaders. He was freed in 1970 after signing a document declaring that intimidation had marred the 1970 elections and that new elections would be arranged and held in due course. In 1974, frustrated by Chief Leabua's actions, Ntsu's supporters staged a poorly coordinated uprising, which Leabua's forces easily crushed. He was forced to flee Lesotho and he lived in Botswana for a time before he was expelled and went to Zambia. Ntsu returned to Lesotho in 1988 and participated in processes leading to the restoration of constitutional rule in Lesotho. In 1997, he formed the Lesotho Congress for Democracy (LCD). He died in December 1998.

Further Reading

Khaketla, B. M. *Lesotho 1970: An Aftican Coup Under the Microscope.* Berkeley: University of California Press, 1972.

Leeman. *Lesotho and the Struggle for Azania.* 3 vols. University of Azania, 1985.

Macartney, W. J. A. "The Lesotho General Election of 1970." *Government and Opposition. 4* (1973): 473–494.

Mokhehle, N. (ed.). *Moshoeshoe I Profile, Se-Moshoeshoe.* Maseru: Mmoho Publications, 1990.

Moleleki, M. *Pale ea Bophelo ba Ntsu* [The Story of the Life of Ntsu]. Morija: Monyane Moleleki, 1994.

Momoh, Joseph Saidu: *See* Sierra Leone: Momoh, Joseph Saidu: Regime, 1986–1992.

Mondlane, Eduardo (1920–1969)
Politician, Leader of FRELIMO

Eduardo Chivambo Mondlane won one of the very few places for black students at the University of the Witwatersrand in Johannesburg, where he studied social sciences. Here, he encountered many new ideas, meeting with African students and discussing politics in the Diogenes Club, the Progressive Forum, and the Students Liberal Association. He mixed also in white circles and was exposed to many liberal ideas. Mondlane helped to establish the Nucleus of Mozambican Secondary Students (NESAM), predominantly involving Mozambican secondary school students in Lourenco Marques. It was organized by the few Mozambican students attending university in South Africa. A future president of Mozambique, Joaquim Chissano cut his political teeth through NESAM, later becoming its leader. As a result of these activities the Malan government in South Africa handed Mondlane over to the Portuguese authorities, where he was imprisoned and investigated by the PIDE state police.

He was later sent by the authorities to study in Portugal, as he was considered too dangerous if left in Mozambique.With the secret police continuing to keep him under surveillance, he decided to leave Portugal and continue his studies in the United States. After earning a doctorate, he became a university professor, then took up an appointment as a research officer in the United Nations Trusteeship department. This new post gave him some relative political immunity from persecution and he took leave to visit Mozambique for three months in 1961. As a guest of the Swiss Protestant Mission, he held numerous meetings with young people and built up support for the impending national independence struggle. Among those he met at that time was Samora Machel, the future president of Mozambique.

The dictatorship in Portugal forbade any African nationalist organizations inside the colonies. Mondlane kept some distance from the three protonationalist movements existing at that time, each of which had predominantly a regional base of support inside Mozambique but were obliged to have headquarters in neighboring countries. The National Democratic Union of Mozambique (UDENAMO) was based in

Southern Rhodesia, the National Union for Mozambican Independence (UNAMI) was based in Malawi and the Mozambique African National Union (MANU) was based in Tanganyika. In 1961 Mondlane met President Julius Nyerere of Tanzania, and it was agreed that Nyerere's country would provide a rear base. The following year, the Front for the Liberation of Mozambique (FRELIMO) was formed, joining together UDENAMO, UNAMI, and MANU under the presidency of Mondlane, with its external headquarters in Dar es Salaam.

Portugal, the colonizing power, was never likely to countenance African nationalist opposition in its colonies. FRELIMO, barred from legal and peaceful avenues of protest, launched an armed struggle in September 1964. Mondlane believed that to be effective, a guerrilla war would have to be waged in the countryside. He had absorbed the experiences of other successful armed struggles from around the world faced with a similar intransigent dictatorship and he applied the lessons of armed struggle creatively to Mozambique.

Mondlane had a rather turbulent time in the early years of FRELIMO, having to manage significant in-fighting, in addition to the main task of leading the anticolonial struggle. FRELIMO opened up war fronts in four provinces initially, but these were soon reduced to the two northernmost provinces of Mozambique, Niassa, and Cabo Delgado, bordering onto Tanzania. In 1968 a new front was opened up in Tete Province and support for FRELIMO grew. Unlike Angola, there were no substantial nationalist party rivals to FRELIMO, for which Mondlane can take much of the credit. He had a talent for identifying and coopting many able young men into the Central Committee of the party. He supported the young radicals in their battle with the old guard in the period surrounding FRELIMO's Second Congress held in 1968, notably Samora Machel, head of the army, Joaquim Chissano, and Armando Guebuza. In particular Mondlane stood firmly against those espousing racism, tribalism, and regionalism at that time. Mondlane inspired confidence in FRELIMO both internationally and among Mozambicans. As such, he was targeted by the Portuguese authorities and was assassinated in 1969, when he opened a parcel bomb.

Mondlane's avowed antiracism, inclusiveness, and opposition to tribalism and regionalism provided an important legacy for the FRELIMO party and for the politics of postindependence Mozambique. He is regarded as the father of Mozambican nationalism, even though he never lived to see the independence of his country.

BARRY MUNSLOW

See also: **Mozambique: Frelimo and the War of Liberation, 1962–1975; Mozambique: Machel and the Frelimo Revolution, 1975–1986.**

Biography

Born in the province of Gaza in southern Mozambique in 1920. Spent youth herding goats. Refused entry to secondary school inside Mozambique on the grounds of being too old, went to South Africa to continue his studies. Completed his secondary education in the 1940s at a school in northern Transvaal. Won a scholarship to the the University of the Witwatersrand in Johannesburg, where he studied social sciences. Sent to Portugal to study by the authorities, as he was considered too dangerous in Mozambique. Left Portugal to continue his studies in the United States, where he met his American wife, Janet Mondlane, with whom he had a son and two daughters. Studied sociology and anthropology, gaining a doctorate at Northwestern University. Became a professor, then took up an appointment as a research officer in the United Nations Trusteeship department. In 1962 FRELIMO was created and he assumed leadership. Assassinated 1969.

Further Reading

Christie, I. *Samora Machel: A Biography.* London: Pan Af, Zed Press, 1989.
Hawley, E. "Eduardo Chivambo Mondlane (1920–1969): A Personal Memoir." *Africa Today.* 26, no. 1 (1979): 19–24.
Henrikson, T. *Revolution and Counter-Revolution: Mozambique's War of Independence 1964–1974.* Westport, Conn.: Greenwood Press, 1983.
Isaacman, A. and B. Isaacman. *Mozambique: From Colonialism to Revolution, 1900–1982.* Boulder, Colo: Westview, 1983.
Mondlane, E. *The Struggle for Mozambique.* Harmondsworth: Penguin African Library, 1970.
Munslow, B. *Mozambique: The Revolution and its Origins.* London: Longman, 1983.
Newitt, M. *A History of Mozambique.* London: C. Hurst, 1995.
Pan A. *Eduardo Mondlane.* London: Pan Af, 1972.
Tobias, P. "A Little-Known Chapter in the Life of Eduardo Mondlane." *Génève-Afrique.* 16, no.1 (1977–1978): 119–124.

Monophysitism, Coptic Church, 379–640

The Christian church in Egypt (now known as the Coptic Orthodox Church) traces its beginnings to Saint Mark's evangelization in the year 41 and the Coptic Church calendar begins in 284. With the accession of Diocletian to the Roman throne, Mediterranean Africa was a vital player in Christianity during this period. In the first centuries of the Common Era, Egypt was the most significant see of the church, and the Catechical School of Alexandria was the center of Christian knowledge and philosophy.

In the late fourth- and fifth-century Roman world, Christianity was tied to political and economic power. After 392, when Emperor Theodosius consecrated Christianity as the state religion, the Christian church and its leadership became an integral part of the power structure of the Roman Empire. When Constantinople became the political capital of the Roman Empire, Alexandria became the third most significant Christian center (instead of second place) after Constantinople in the eyes of Eastern Christians in general. Yet, Alexandria remained a significant Christian center and had popular support from the tens of thousands of Egyptian monks. Alexandria also had support from time to time from Rome, as fear of Constantinople's authority threatened Roman pre-eminence.

Monasticism was another contribution that Egyptians made to the history of Christianity. The monastic practice became very popular in Egypt and was in many ways the soul of the Coptic Church in the fifth and sixth centuries. Monophysite theology, emphasizing only the divinity (as opposed to the humanity) of Christ, was in keeping with monastic ascetic practice that sought to deny human needs in order to obtain a higher spiritual existence.

By the fifth century, the bishops of Rome and Constantinople found the Egyptian leaders' preeminence threatening. Egyptians had maintained their own language and culture during Greek rule and resented imposition of foreign power and ideas. Theological disagreements, which reflected political schisms and power struggles, marked the fifth century Christian Mediterranean world. The difference in thinking between the Antiochene and Alexandrian schools of theology accounts for much of the debate that arose over Christ's nature and led to the rise of monophysitism. Antiochene theologians tended to be more concerned about rational interpretations of religious doctrine than mystical ones. They also laid greater emphasis on the full humanity of Christ and the distinction between human and divine natures, while Alexandrian theologians were much more mystical and emphasized the unity of the divine and human in one person.

In many ways, monophysite theology was a reaction to contemporary Nestorianism. Named for Nestorius (whose views are deemed heretical by the Roman Catholic and Orthodox Churches), this variant emphasized Christ's nature as distinctly dual, both divine and human. In 427 Nestorius, originally from Antioch, became bishop of Constantinople. His emphasis on the humanity of Christ attracted the attention of Alexandrian theologians. Cyril, the bishop of Alexandria (412–444), was one of the chief opponents of this belief, preaching what later monophysite believers looked upon as the foundations of their theology, that Christ was truly and only divine. While Cyril recognized the two natures of Christ, he claimed they had been joined by the hypostatic union to form one nature of the Incarnate Word. If there was a founder of monophysitism, it was Cyril.

Cyril's concerns were not simply theological. Like his predecessor, Theophilus, he wanted to reestablish the preeminence of the see of Alexandria. Emperer Theodosius II (*r.*408–450) called for a council at Ephesus (in western Asia Minor) in 431 to settle the dispute; Cyril presided as papal legate. Nestorius was condemned and deposed, and a new patriarch at Constantinople replaced him. Cyril's attack on Nestorius led Alexandria to new heights of power and influence in the Christian church.

Monophysite proponents were not only found in Egypt. Eutyches (378–457), archimandrite of a great monastery just outside the walls of Constantinople, took Cyril's orthodox statement in an extreme, heretical direction and proclaimed that Christ did not have the same nature as humans. (Monophysites today do not accept Eutyches' extreme interpretation of monophysite doctrine.) In Constantinople in 448, Bishop Flavian (patriarch of Constantinople) called a local synod during which Eutyches was deposed and excommunicated for his beliefs. Eutyches did not submit to his condemnation but instead sought support from the pope and Dioscor, the patriarch of Alexandria (444–451). Emperor Theodosius II was also sympathetic to Eutyches' position, as were many Egyptian theologians.

Dioscor, like Cyril, hoped to see the triumph of Alexandrian over Antiochene theology. A synod was held at Ephesus in 449 to resolve the dispute. Dioscor ensured his theological success with military assistance. The emperor also sent soldiers to protect Eutyches. The synod is remembered less for its dialogue than for its brutality. Soldiers rushed into the church on the first day, creating disorder and causing violence. Flavian was deposed and Eutyches was declared innocent. Those bishops reluctant to sign the sentences of deposition were compelled to do so by soldiers. This council was not regarded as a legitimate council in the West and was designated the Robber's Synod.

A new empress, Pulcheria, and her husband, Marcian (*r.*450–457), sympathetic to Flavian's antimonophysite position and more Western-oriented than Pulcheria's brother and predecessor (Theodosius II), called another synod at Chalcedon (across the Bosporus from Constantinople) in 451. Delegates presented evidence as to the violent methods employed by Dioscor at Ephesus. This time Dioscor lacked not only the emperor's support, but that of many in Alexandria, who felt he had mistreated Cyril's relatives. Dioscor and other monophysite theologians, such as Eutyches, were condemned and deposed. The dual, yet unified, nature of Christ was accepted as orthodox Christian belief. Monophysites and their belief that Christ's humanity was not of the same nature as humankind, and that Christ's one divine nature was to be emphasized above his dual nature, was deemed heretical by the Roman Catholic Church.

In Alexandria, the verdict of Chalcedon was met with anger. While some Egyptian Christian leaders accepted the new orthodoxy, most did not. Constantinople recognized the danger of Alexandria's volatility. The patriarch of Constantinople, Acacius (l471–489), with Emperor Zeno (*r.*474–491) addressed a letter of compromise (the *Henoticon*) to Peter Mongus. It accepted Cyril's theology, but rejected that of Nestorius and Eutyches. Mongus agreed with the compromise and thus led Alexandria from 477 to 490. This restored peaceful relations with Constantinople for a time and encouraged monophysite belief in the eastern portion of the empire. The Western church, however, rejected the *Henoticon* because it diminished the authority of the Council of Chalcedon.

By the sixth century, economic power in Egypt had passed to the monasteries and landowners. Egyptian monophysites were proselytizing in lands to the south, such as Nubia and Ethiopia. Most Nubians had converted to the monophysite variant of Christianity by the end of the sixth century. When Justin I acceded to power (*r.*518–527) in Rome, he challenged the Alexandria-Constantinople detente because he wanted to restore Constantinople-Rome relations. In 537 Emperor Justinian (*r.*527–565) chose Paul as the Christian patriarch in Alexandria. He was given military authority to enforce Chalcedon in Egypt. The Chalcedonian church that emerged was Greek-speaking and wealthy, although small in numbers. In contrast, the monks and peasants of the Nile valley, greater in numbers, remained monophysite, although their influence was limited.

Monophysite leaders began consecrating and ordaining themselves and developing a separate organization for their church in the mid-sixth century, while monophysite believers in Syria and Armenia established their own churches. The Muslim invasion of Egypt in 639CE led to the conversion of the majority of Christians to Islam over the course of the next several hundred years. The Coptic Church, although small, is the largest Christian church in modern-day Egypt, with 6 million members, out of a population of approximately 58 million.

KATHLEEN R. SMYTHE

Further Reading

Adeney, W. F. *The Greek and Eastern Churches.* Clifton, N.J.: Reference Book Publishers, 1965.

Atiya, A. S. *A History of Eastern Christianity.* Millwood, N.Y.: Kraus Reprints, 1980.

Bokenkotter, T. *A Concise History of the Catholic Church.* New York: Doubleday and Co., 1977.

Frend, W. H. C. "The Christian Period in Mediterranean Africa, c. AD 200 to 700." *The Cambridge History of Africa.* Vol. 2, *From c. 500 BC to AD 1050*, edited by J. D. Fage. Cambridge: Cambridge University Press, 1978.

Fortescue, A. *The Lesser Eastern Churches.* London: Catholic Truth Society, 1913.

Gonzalez, J. L. *A History of Christian Thought.* Vols. 1–2. Nashville: Abingdon Press, 1970.

Holmes, J. D., and B. W. Bickers. *A Short History of the Catholic Church.* New York: Paulist Press, 1984.

Wigram, W. A. *The Separation of the Monophysites.* London: The Faith Press, 1923.

Monrovia

Monrovia, located along the coast of West Africa at Cape Mesurado, has remained the capital of Liberia since it was founded in 1822. Its establishment was due to the initiative of the American Colonization Society, which was aimed at solving the then prevalent American problem of finding the best solution to the problems associated with freed black slaves. The society acquired land from the Dei rulers in 1822 for the resettlement of freed blacks who were willing to move to Africa.

Although Monrovia began with a small nucleus of returnee slaves from America, it was from here that what eventually became known as Liberia emerged. The Monrovia settlement grew in size and population over time, as more and more freed blacks arrived from the United States. With time, new settlements emerged inland, and so began what became the core and capital city of Liberia. The name "Monrovia" was derived from the name of the U.S. president who provided support for the establishment of the original settlement, James Monroe.

In its early years, the Monrovian population was comprised of the returnee freed slaves referred to as Americo-Liberians and the indigenous Dei and Bassa people who settled in the territory. The Americo-Liberians were, however, dominant in population as well as in the affairs of the state. Over time, the city grew increasingly cosmopolitan, with the Bassa, Kru, and Garebo kinspeople of the Dei swelling the indigenous population, as well as people from other West African states.

A remarkable feature of Monrovia is its deep water harbor, which makes it a key port in West Africa. It is therefore not only the seat of administration but also the commercial center of Liberia. Monrovia's port is the main outlet of Liberia's exports such as rubber, palm kernel, gold, and iron ore, as well as the main site where imports are received. The commercial activities of its inhabitants date back to the foundation of the city, for they have always been engaged in trade.

Monrovia is also the seat of the University of Liberia, which was founded in 1963, and where the Roberts Field International airport is located. The first constitutional conference in modern Africa was held in Monrovia in 1839. It is also the base of the first West Africa newspaper, the *Liberia Herald*, established in 1930.

Even though partly ravaged by the civil strife in Liberia, Monrovia was the only city that was not completely captured by the rebel forces throughout the duration of the 1989–1996 Liberian civil war. This is partly explained by the fact that it formed the military base of the ECOMOG peace initiative.

In 1999 President Charles Taylor was suspected of supporting antigovernment rebels in Ghana, Guinea, and Sierra Leon. The governments of these nations, in turn, lent support to anti-Taylor forces.

Fighting continued into 2003. In March of that year, the anti-Taylor forces, known as the LURD (Liberians United for Reconciliation and Democracy) marched toward Monrovia. Citizens in the capital were caught in warfare between the warring factions. In August, West African peacekeepers, ECOWAS (Economic Community of West African States), sent peacekeeping forces to Monrovia. Several hundred Monrovian citizens died in the crossfire. The starving populace was receiving food aid as of August and September 2003.

C. B. N. Ogbogbo

See also: **Liberia.**

Further Reading

Akpan, M. K. "The Return to Africa-Sierra Leone and Liberia." In *Tarikh: The African Diaspora*, edited A. I. Asiwaju and M. Crowder. 5, no. 4. London: Longman, 1980.

Jones, A. B. "The Republic of Liberia." In *History of West Africa*, edited by J. F. A. Ajayi and M. Growder. Vol. 2. London: Longman, 1973.

Webster, J. B., et al. *The Growth of Africa Civilization: The Revolutionary Years West Africa since 1800.* London: Longman, 1967.

West, R. *Back to Africa: A History of Sierra Leone and Liberia.* London: Jonathan Cape, 1970.

Morocco: Sa'dians

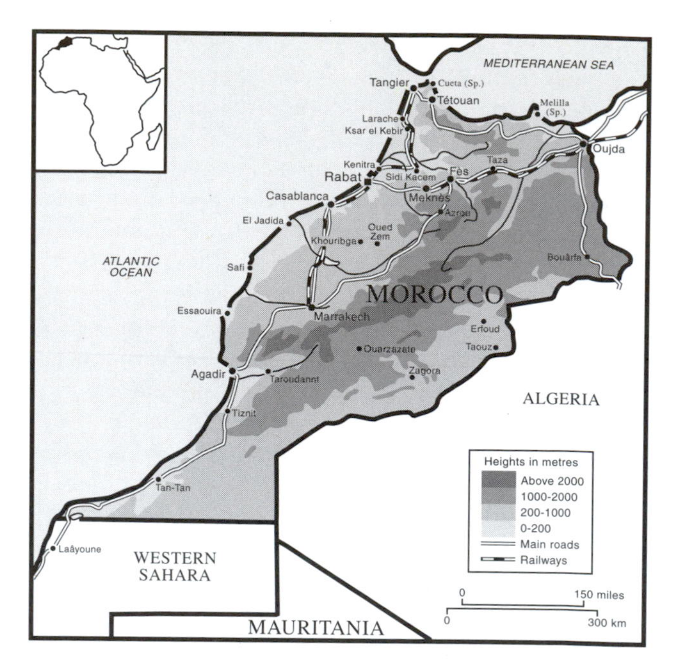

Morocco.

At the beginning of the sixteenth century, the opposite shores of the Mediterranean were characterized by contrasting political developments. Whereas Spain and Portugal had achieved some territorial integration and consolidation as dynastic states, the Maghrib was divided into competing "power states." According to Ibn Khaldun these were the Hafsids of Tunis (1229–1574), the Abd al-Wadids or Ziyanids of Tlemcen (1236–1550), and the Marinids/Wattasids of Fez (1269–1420; 1420–1540). They were the political offshoots of the defunct Almohad regime (1147–1269) that had exercised previously exercised unified political rule. The political fragmentation of the Maghrib rendered it vulnerable to its northern neighbors. The reaction to Portuguese imperialism in Morocco produced the Sa'dians, just as the opposition to Spanish imperialism in the rest of the Maghrib inaugurated the rule of the Ottomon Turks.

At various times in the fifteenth and sixteenth centuries, Portugal occupied a number of coastal towns on the Mediterranean and Atlantic coasts of Morocco: Ceuta (1415), al-Qasr al-Saghir (1458), Arzila and Tangier (1471), Safi (1481), Azemmour (1456), Massa (1497), Agadir (1505), Mogador (1506), Agouz (1507), and Mazagan (1514). The coastal towns became the base from which the Portuguese exercised a de facto protectorate over the immediate hinterland. Communities within this informal empire came under Portuguese supervision, prompted by security concerns, amounting to regimentation; those outside the imperial orbit were victims of periodic *razzias* by armed Portuguese bands. *Entradas*, as these *razzias* were called, were lucrative, if hazardous, ventures, procuring the booty, both human and material, which furnished much of the wealth of the Portuguese establishment in Morocco. The Portuguese occupation also entailed their control of Morocco's maritime trade. They instituted a monopolistic commercial regime on the seaboard, stifling indigenous enterprise

The humiliation of Portuguese domination called for an organized opposition, which the leadership in Morocco could not provide. The Sa'dians came to power in Morocco in answer to this need for a leader to champion the jihad against the Christian invader. The head of the family, who was also the shaykh of the *zawiya* of Tagmadart in the Dar'a, Abu 'Abdallah al-Qa'im, was elected for this purpose by the Sous community of southern Moroccon in 1511, with Agadir as the target of attack.

Agadir was, as it were, the Cinderella of the Portuguese possessions in Morocco. Its survival was always precarious. It never attracted sufficient financial and military support to guarantee its security in enemy territory, its

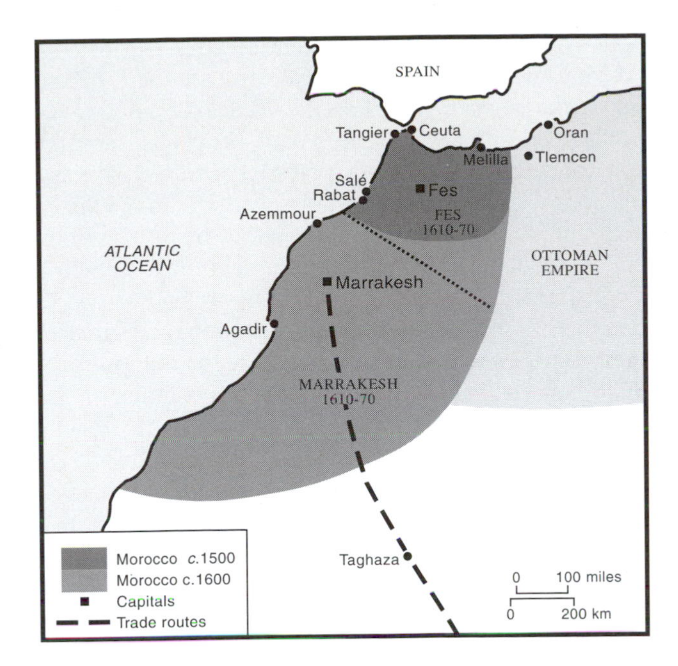

Morocco, sixteenth–seventeenth centuries.

garrison remained small and ill-provisioned, and its defenses were further weakened during the period of hostilities by the accidental explosion of a barrel of powder that opened a yawning breach in its walls, a disability the Muslims, occupying a hill that dominated Agadir, exploited to great advantage. In contrast to the adverse fortunes of Agadir, the Sa'dian movement enjoyed overwhelming superiority in numbers and benefited from the contraband traffic in arms and ammunition by European merchants, notably by the Genoese and the Castilians, but also by the French and the English. Agadir capitulated to the Muslim siege in 1541.

The fall of Agadir was crucial to the collapse of Portuguese power in Morocco. Agadir had served, if symbolically, as a front line against Sa'dian insurgence. Deprived of their advance protection, a number of Portuguese possessions north of Agadir fell to the onslaught of the Muslims: Safi and Azemmour (1541), and al-Qasr al-Saghir and Arzila (1550). These victories popularized the Sa'dian movement, generating the ground swell that swept from power (1549) the Wattasid sultan, Bu Hassun. He was temporarily reinstated in Fez in 1553, thanks to the Turks of Algiers, only to be killed in combat in September 1554 by Muhammad al-Shaikh, the leader of the Sa'dians. This marked the definitive establishment of the Sa'dian dynasty in Morocco. The maraboutic movement, provoked by Portuguese imperialism, was fundamental to the rise of the Sa'dians, whose legitimacy derived from the jihad to liberate the Muslim community from infidel domination.

The Sa'dians ruled Morocco as a unified entity for about half a century (1549–1603); the reign of Ahmad

Sqala de la Kashbah, an old Portuguese fort, Morocco. © Peter Schickert/Das Fotoarchiv.

al-Mansur, the conqueror of the Songhai empire in the western Sudan (1591), marked the peak of their power. Al-Mansur's political structure, typical of the power state, was held together by his personal authoritarianism rather than resting on institutional foundations. It collapsed immediately after his death in 1603. Multiple centers of power emerged in Morocco, presided over notably by the *murabitun* or marabouts. The last of the Sa'dians, Mawlay al-'Abbas, exercised a shadowy power in Marrakech until 1659, when he was ousted by a neighboring Berber group, the Shabana, under their leader, Abd al-Karim.

B. A. MOJUETAN

See also: **Morocco: Ahmad al-Mansur and the Invasion of Songhay.**

Further Reading

Abun Nasr, J. M. *A History of the Maghrib.* Cambridge: Cambridge University Press, 1971.

Braudel, F. *The Mediterranean and the Mediterranean World in the Age of Philip II.* 2 vols. New York: Harper and Row, 1976.

Cenival, P. de. *Chronique de Santa Cruz de Cap de Gué.* Paris: Publ de la section historique du Maroc, 1934.

Fishtali, A. (ed.). *Manahil al Safa fi Akhbar al-Muluk al-Shurafa,* Abdallah Ganun.

Julien, C. A. *History of North Africa: From the Arab Conquest to 1830.* Translated by J. Petrie and edited by C. C. Stewart. London: Routledge and Kegan Paul, 1970.

Laroui, A. *The History of the Maghrib: An Interpretive Essay.* Princeton: Princeton University Press, 1977.

Mojuetan, B. A. *History and Underdevelopment in Morocco: The Structural Roots of Conjuncture.* Hamburg: Lit Verlag, 1995.
———. "Ibn Khaldun and his Cycle of Fatalism." *Studia Islamica.* 53 (1981): 93–108.
Yahya, D. *Morocco in the Sixteenth Century: Problems and Patterns in African Foreign Policy.* London: Longman, 1981.

Morocco: Ahmad al-Mansur and the Invasion of Songhay

Ahmad al-Mansur (1578–1603) was the sixth ruler of the Sa'adian dynasty. Born in Fez in 1549, he was a son of the second Sa'adian sultan, Muhammad al Shaykh al Mahdi.

The Sa'adians were the first dynasty of *sharifs* (descendants of the clan of the Prophet) to rule in Morocco, having supplanted the Berber dynasty of the Banu Wattas earlier in the sixteenth century. Although they claimed origins in Arabia (specifically, Yambu in the Hejaz), and also claimed to be descended from the Prophet, the base from which they launched their conquest had been the valley of Dra'a. In 1510 Muhammad al Kaim bin Amr Allah, the first important head of the dynasty, had attacked the Portuguese at Agadir, and in 1524 his son Ahmad al Aaredj had taken Marrakech from the Wattassids and become the head of the new Sa'adian state. After a long struggle, he had had to give way to his brother Muhammad al-Shaykh, who was installed as leader at Fez in 1549.

Over the course of the following decades, there were further struggles within the family over who should succeed whom. Mulai Muhammad al-Maslükh mounted the throne in 1574, but his uncle Abd al-Malik, who had taken refuge in Istanbul, succeeded in taking power away from him, with the aid of the Ottoman pasha of Algiers, in 1576. However, Mulai Muhammad then succeeded in coming to terms with both Philip II of Spain and, more importantly, Sebastian I, the young king of Portugal. Sebastian set sail for Morocco in 1578 and joined his forces with those of Mulai Muhammad. On August fourth that year, these two allies came up against Abd al-Malik in what is known as the "Battle of the Three Kings" at al Ksar al-Kabir. Mulai Muhammad and Sebastian were both killed, while Abd al-Malik, already sick, died the same day. Victory went to Abd al-Malik's army nonetheless. His younger brother Mulai Ahmad, who had not even taken part in the battle, drew all the benefit from it, and triumphantly took up the reins of the sultanate under the name Ahmad al-Mansur, "the Victorious." His reign, which was to last for a quarter of a century, was one of the longest and most important in the history of Morocco.

The new sultan reorganized the country and the government. Under his authority, his guards, his court, and his administration (*makhzen*) took on an appearance resembling that of their Ottoman counterparts, notably through the appointment of beys and pashas. Al-Mansur was a great builder: he ordered the fortification of the cities of Taza, Fez, and Marrakech, and in the last-named city he had the palace of al-Kasr al Badi constructed. He also developed Morocco's diplomatic relations with the Ottoman empire, with Philip II's Spain, and, particularly after the destruction of the "invincible" Armada in 1588, with the England of Elizabeth I. English merchants obtained a monopoly on Morocco's commercial traffic through the privileges granted to their Barbary Company. Despite recurrent political disturbances, arising most notably from conspiracies by his nephews and his own son's claims to power, al-Mansur's reign was a relatively peaceful one. He died in Fez on August 25, 1603, in the midst of an epidemic, either of cholera or of the plague, that was then ravaging his country. His remains still lie in the mausoleum that he had had built for them in Marrakech.

Undoubtedly the single most important event in al-Mansur's reign was the conquest of western Sudan, which is described by all the historians of the Sa'adian dynasty and in the celebrated chronicles of Sudanese history, such as the *Tarikh al-Fattash* or the *Tarikh as-Sudan*. The motives for this Sa'adian expansionism included both a desire for greater power and a wish to enrich the country. The undertaking of the conquest can be best explained by reference to the desire for prestige, on the part of a ruler who regarded himself as a descendant of the caliphs of Islam, rivaling the Ottoman sultans; by the quest for black slaves for the sugarcane plantations of Sousse; but, above all, by the hope of controlling the important Saharan salt mines at Taghaza and Taodeni, and of gathering in the gold of Sudan.

There had been contact between Morocco and the Songhay people on the Middle Niger for several centuries—indeed since ancient times—but in launching his conquest, Ahmad al-Mansur took advantage of the decline of the empire of the Askias, which had been divided by internal struggles, been made the target of attacks by the Mansas of Mali, and fallen prey to famine. In 1578 the Askia ruler Daud acceded to Sultan Ahmad's demand that the exploitation of the salt mines be entrusted to Morocco, but this first extension of Moroccan influence over the Saharan salt industry proved to be insufficient. In 1581 the Moroccans occupied the oases of Tuat and Gorarin, the crossroads of the trade between the Mediterranean and the Sahel, and in 1584 they launched their first expedition in the direction of the Senegal River, although in the end this turned out to be no more than a raid, without any consequences.

In the autumn of 1590, however, an army of several thousand men (between 3,000 and 4,000 soldiers, accompanied by 8,000 dromedaries) set out from Marrakech under the command of Judar Pasha, a Spaniard who had been captured in Granada as a child. After advancing through Warzazat, the valley of the Dra'a, and Taghaza, the army reached the Niger on March 1, 1591, at Karabara, near Bamba. On March 12 it confronted the army of the Askia ruler Ishak II at Tondibi, around thirty-five miles from the city of Gao. Judar's troops, who were better organized and armed with cannons, crushed the Songhay army and pursued it as far as Gao. Ishak II then made peace offers that left Timbuktu open for the taking. Some months later, Mahmud ibn Zarqun replaced Judar Pasha, while the Askia Ishak was deposed by his brother Muhammad Gao, who was then captured by the Moroccans and executed in 1591. When the Moroccans conquered Jenne in 1592, the realm of the Askias collapsed. The whole of the Middle Niger fell under Moroccan domination, which lasted, in various forms, up to the early nineteenth century, under the control of the Arma, the successors of the Moroccan pashas.

Far from seeking the reconquest of Spain, Ahmad al-Mansur had succeeded in reorienting his foreign policy toward the south. He derived considerable financial benefits from doing so. Every year, a convoy of slaves and gold taken from Sudan arrived in Marrakech, and Sultan Ahmad acquired another epithet: Al-Dhahabi, "the Golden." However, the main result of the conquest was that Morocco gained control of three complementary zones of trans-Saharan trade: the Maghrib, now opened up to Europe and its products; the Sahara, with its rich endowment of salt mines; and the Sahel, with its gold and its slaves.

PIERRE BOILLEY

See also: **Sahara: Salt: Production, Trade; Songhay Empire: Moroccan Invasion, 1591.**

Further Reading

'Abd Al-Rahman Al-Sa'di. *Ta'rikh al-Sudan.* Paris: Maisonneuve, 1964.

Abitbol, M. *Tombouctou et les Arma.* Paris: Maisonneuve et Larose, 1979.

Ajay, J. F. A., and M. Crowder. *History of West Africa.* London: Longman, 1971.

Castries, H. de. *Une description du Maroc sous le règne de Moulay Ahmed el-Mansur.* Paris: Leroux, 1909.

Julien, C.-A. *Histoire de l'Afrique du Nord, des origines à 1830.* 1951. Reprint, Paris: Payot, 1994.

Kati, M. *Tarikh al-Fattash fi Akhbar al-Buldan wa-al-Djuyuṣh wa-Akabir al-Nas.* Paris: Maisonneuve, 1964.

La Veronne, C. de. *Histoire sommaire des Sa'diens au Maroc. La première dynastie chérifienne (1511–1659).* Paris: Geuthner, 1997.

Levi-Provençal, E. *Les historiens des Chorfas.* Paris: Larose, 1922.

Trimingham, J. S. *A History of Islam in West Africa.* New York: Oxford University Press, 1962.

Willan, T. S. *Studies in Elizabethan Foreign Trade.* Manchester, Eng.: Manchester University Press, 1959.

Morocco: Maraboutic Crisis, Founding of the 'Alawite Dynasty

The so-called maraboutic crisis in seventeenth century Morocco was a crisis of the state, the Sa'dian state, rather than a crisis of maraboutism. In so far as there was a crisis in regard to the *murabitun* or marabouts, this must be understood in political terms as a reference to their prominence in the politics of Morocco during the interregnum following the collapse of the state after the death of Ahmad al-Mansur. Their prominence obscured or overshadowed their hallowed religious and spiritual *raison d'être.* It was a crisis, as it were, of institutional identity arising from the prevailing political climate of anomie, which impelled the marabouts to a political vocation: the re-institution of the state as the means to political stabilization in Morocco. It was the competitive aspiration to the achievement of this end by various actors on the political scene that produced the Alawite dynasty.

No sooner had al-Mansur died (1603) than his three sons Zidan, Abu Faris, and Muhammad al-Shaikh engaged in a bloody and ruinous power struggle. The ensuing civil war (1603–1609) ended with the victory of Zidan, whose writ hardly extended beyond the southern capital city of Marrakech. The aftermath of the war was the demise of the state, and the dismemberment of the fragile political structure.

This "feudalization" or fragmentation of authority in Morocco was epitomized by the expansion of the jurisdictions of the marabouts to fill the political vacuum occasioned by the eclipse of the Sa'dian state. The *zawiya,* the center of activity of the marabouts, has been likened to the monastery in medieval Europe. Each *zawiya* is founded on a particular mystic or sufi doctrine, namely a corpus of ideas and rites constituting a theosophic system, a way (*tariqa*), as it were, to spiritual communion with the deity. Most *zawiya-s* in Morocco, from the sixteenth century onward, were organized on the basis of the Jazuliyya *tariqa.*

The most powerful of the *zawiya-s* during the interregnum was the *zawiya* of Dila, located strategically at the center of Morocco. Founded by Abu Bakr ibn Muhammad in the sixteenth century, the *zawiya* enjoyed reputation as a center of Islamic scholarship and a haven of hospitality, attributes which endeared it to the *talib* as well as the downtrodden. The political crisis of the seventeenth century provided the occasion for a political dimension to the activities of the *zawiya.* Under its energetic leader, Muhammad al-Hajj, the *zawiya* became the leading power in Morocco in the middle years of the seventeenth century (1641–1660).

It held sway in northern and central Morocco, including the northern Atlantic seaboard, together with the pirate republic of the Moriscos—Muslim refugees from Spain—and exercised power in Fez, without its leader, however, assuming the sovereign title of sultan, contended with being represented there by a lieutenant.

Second in political importance was the *zawiya* of Iligh, in the Tazarwalt region of the Sous. The *zawiya* was the dominant power in southern Morocco and the Saharan region, thanks to its leader Bu Hassun, controlling Sijilmasa, the northern terminus of the trans-Saharan trade, and the Atlantic ports of Agadir and Massa, important outlets to the commerce of Europe.

The most politically ambitious of the marabouts was Abu Mahalli. From his base in a *zawiya* located in the Sharan region of Morocco, he proclaimed himself the *Mahdi* to mobilize support for this political pretension, the occasion for which was provided by the cession of Larache (November 20, 1610) to Spain by Muhammad al-Shaikh to secure Spanish military assistance in the power struggle with his brothers. Abu Mahalli seized power in Marrakesh, assuming the title of sovereignty (May 20, 1612). Zidan was able to recover his throne only by pitting the forces of a rival marabout, Yahya ibn Abdallah, based in the High Atlas, against Abu Mahalli, who died in the encounter (November 30, 1613). Yahya, himself, died in March 1626 after two unsuccessful attempts to occupy Marrakech, his political ambition having been kindled by his restoration of Zidan.

Morocco in the second half of the seventeenth century presented the following configuration of power. Al-Ayyashi, a *condottiere* based in Salé and renowed as a holy warrior (*mujahid*), but now with the status of a warlord, had died in 1641 in his confrontation with the *zawiya* of Dila, the most formidable power in Morocco. albeit now in decline, as demonstrated by its defeat in 1660 by al-Khadir Ghailan, another warlord on the Atlantic coast thrown up by the political crisis, and also in the tradition of the *condottiere*. Operating from al-Kabir and Arzila, Ghailan was now unchallenged militarily and politically on the northern Atlantic seaboard. A Berber group, the Shabana, ruled in Marrakech, having usurped power from the last of the Sa'dians, Mawlay al-'Abbas, in 1659. The *zawiya* of Iligh continued to be dominant in the politics of southern Morocco.

Ironically, however, it was from a quarter much less known in Moroccan politics, namely the sharifan house of Sijilmasa in the Tafilalet, that a new dynasty was to emerge in Morocco to resolve the political impasse. Al-Rashid, after a period of preparation in which he built up a military organization to support his sovereign ambition, captured power in Fez and had himself proclaimed sultan (June 6, 1668). He then proceeded to eliminate the strongholds of power in Morocco: the *zawiya* of Dila (June 18, 1668); al-Kahdir Ghailan (July 1668); the Shabana of Marrakech (August 1668) and the *zawiya* of Iligh (July 19, 1670). Thus was established the Alawite dynasty after the prolonged interregnum following the death of al-Mansur in 1603. But al-Rashid died accidentally barely two years later (April 29, 1672), and it was left to his brother, Mawlay Isma'il, to consolidate the foundations of the new dynasty. The mythology of redemption from the political stranglehold of a legendary Jewish king provided the ideology of legitimation of the Alawite dynasty, in the way that the jihad of the sixteenth century that liberated the Muslim community from Portuguese domination served to legitimize Sa'dian rule.

B. A. MOJUETAN

Further Reading

Abun-Nasr, J. M. *A History of the Maghrib.* Cambridge: Cambridge University Press, 1971.

Laraoui, A. *The History of the Maghrib: An Interpretive Essay.* Princeton: Princeton University Press, 1977.

Mojuetan, B. A. *History and Underdevelopment in Morocco: The Structural Roots of Conjuncture.* Hamburg: Lit Verlag, 1995.

———. "Legitimacy in a Power State: Moroccan Politics in the Seventeenth Century during the Interregnum." *International Journal of Middle East Studies.* 13, no. 3 (1981): 347–360.

———. "Myth and Legend as Functional Instruments in Politics: The Establishment of the Alawi Dynasty in Morocco." *Journal of African History.* 15, no. 1 (1975): 17–27.

Morocco: Mawlay Isma'il and Empire of

Mawlay Isma'il (1672–1727) was the second sultan of the 'Alawi dynasty of *shurafa'* (descendants of the Prophet) from southeastern Morocco. The dynasty fought its way to power in the vacuum created by the collapse of the previous Sa'di dynasty early in the seventeenth century. When Mawlay Isma'il succeeded his brother, Mawlay al-Rashid, in 1672, 'Alawi control over Morocco was still tenuous, challenged by both domestic rivals and the existence of Spanish, Portuguese, and British enclaves on the coast. It was therefore Mawlay Isma'il's task to consolidate 'Alawi power. To achieve this end he adapted and synthesized elements from Morocco, the Ottoman Empire, and Sub-Saharan Africa with which he had a strong affinity as the son of Mawlay 'Ali al-Sharif and a black concubine. During his long reign Mawlay Isma'il constructed a tributary state, supported by a slave army and legitimized by reference to Islam, which achieved greater control over Morocco's towns and tribes than most regimes. He also recaptured several European enclaves and constructed a corsair fleet to assert Moroccan power in Atlantic and Mediterranean waters.

On becoming sultan, Mawlay Isma'il's had to defeat his domestic rivals for power, the most important of whom were al-Khidr Ghaylan, a northern warlord who had distinguished himself in action against the European coastal enclaves, and his cousin, Ahmad B. al-Mahriz, the governor of Marrakech, who set himself up as counter-sultan on his uncle's accession. Mawlay Isma'il defeated Ghaylan in battle, thereby securing the north, but Ahmad b. Mahriz remained a problem for fourteen years, during which he provided a figurehead for regular revolts in the south and east of the sultanate. He could not, however, challenge Mawlay Isma'il's control over the heartlands of Morocco. The second challenge faced by the new sultan was the construction of a viable system of government.

First he needed a reliable armed force to gather taxes and combat the centrifugal inclinations of the Moroccan tribes. He therefore founded a black slave army, the 'Abid al-Bukhari, modeled in part on the Ottoman Janissary corps and in part on the tribal forces of earlier Moroccan dynasties. Like the Janissaries, the 'Abid were a geographically marginal group transformed into a loyal military elite by palace training. Unlike the Janissaries, however, the 'Abid became a self-perpetuating servile kin-group, described as a "tribe" (*qabîla*) of the army. The tribal aspect was heightened by the corps' blood relations with the dynasty which resulted from sultanic use of 'Abid concubines. This gave it the character of a black sharifian super-tribe, a character shared by Mawlay Isma'il's other main corps, the Udaya, a cavalry corps recruited from southern Arab tribes and the central Saharan oasis of Tuat.

Mawlay Isma'il selected the small market town of Meknes as his capital and there constructed an enormous royal city, with architecture inspired by the Roman ruins at nearby Volubilis, the mud-brick complexes of Southern Morocco and West Africa, and the decorative styles of al-Andalus. This vast royal city functioned as the sultan's residence, the 'Abid training school and barracks, and a stage for 'Alawi court ceremonial. It was also the place where Mawlay Isma'il put the Europeans captured by his corsairs to work and received foreign delegations. From this imperial hub, he went on regular military progresses through his domains to extract taxes. During his constant peregrinations he employed the 'Abid to build and then occupy forts from the Rif mountains in the north to Tafilalt in the pre-Sahara. His fortifications gave provincial Morocco a more comprehensive governmental presence than ever before, and fortified its sensitive eastern frontier with Ottoman Algiers. Although the sultanate was a tributary state levying what it could from the country by deployment of its coercive powers, Mawlay Isma'il incorporated tribal notables into the governmental structure by appointing them governors (*qâ'id, quwwâd*), who enjoyed the prestige of their position in return for assisting the state in gathering taxes and maintaining law and order.

Formation of the 'Abid al-Bukhari and construction of a rural governmental network consolidated 'Alawi power but did not legitimize it. Many viewed the dynasty as alien and the elite of Fes deeply resented Mawlay Isma'il's raising of his servile black 'Abid above free Muslims. To legitimize the institutions he had created, he looked to Islam. In a society where many believed that the descendants of the Prophet held a special right to rule, he used his sharifian ancestry as a platform to transform himself from warlord to commander of the faithful (*amîr al-mu'minîn*), the religious and political head of the community of believers, the *umma*. He signaled his new position by leading the communal Friday prayer in Meknes, patronizing the religious establishment and dedicating the 'Abid al-Bukhari to the Islamic aim of expelling the 'infidel' Europeans from their coastal enclaves. During the 1680s, 'Abid forces secured the British evacuation from Tanger (1684), and expelled the Spanish from Laraish (1689) and Asila (1691), successes hailed as jihad victories which proved the legitimate right of the 'Alawi *shurafâ'* to rule. Devotion of state resources to the jihad also possessed the advantage of legitimizing tax collection as vital for the maintenance of Muslim unity and the financing of Islamic aims. Corsairing confirmed Mawlay Isma'il's reputation as a holy warrior and brought him considerable revenue which he supplemented by the high duties he levied on foreign trade.

In the 1680s and 1690s, Mawlay Isma'il began to expand southwards into the Sahara to revive the western trans-Saharan trade routes which had faltered due to political insecurity, and eastwards into the province of Algiers to consolidate his control over the eastern marches and capture the city of Tlemsen on the trade route east from Fes to Egypt. Although logical in terms of the close cultural and commercial relations between Fes and Tlemsen, Mawlay Isma'il's campaigns provoked an Ottoman counter-offensive from Algiers. The Ottoman forces easily defeated the 'Abid and the sultan was forced to terms in 1701. After this defeat, domestic politics became increasingly unstable as several of Mawlay Isma'il's sons challenged his rule. When he finally died in 1727, tensions between his many sons, between north and south, between town and tribe, quickly escalated into a civil war which lasted on and off for thirty years. During that time, however, the right to rule of the 'Alawi *shurafâ'* was not seriously questioned, suggesting the fundamental genius of Mawlay Isma'il. During his long reign he had created a durable framework for government, transformed the dynasty from warlords into sharifian commanders of the faithful, and secured the grudging recognition of the Ottoman Empire and several European states.

AMIRA K. BENNISON

See also: **Religion, History of; Sahara: Trans-Saharan Trade.**

Further Reading

Abun-Nasr, J. *A History of the Maghrib in the Islamic Period.* Cambridge: Cambridge University Press, 1987.

Blunt, W. *Black Sunrise: The Life and Times of Mulaï Ismaïl, Emperor of Morocco.* London: Methuen, 1951.

de Chenier, L. *The Present State of the Empire of Morocco.* London: G. and J. Robinson, 1788.

Mercer, P. "Palace and Jihad: The Early 'Alawi State in Morocco." *Journal of African History.* 18, no. 4 (1977): 531–553.

Nékrouf, Y. *Une Amitie Orageuse: Moulay Ismaïl et Louis XIV* [A Stormy Friendship: Mawlay Isma'il and Louis XIV]. Paris: Editions Michel Albin, 1987.

Pellow, T. *The History of the Long Captivity and Adventures of Thomas Pellow.* London, 1738.

Morocco: Sidi Muhammad and Foundations of Essawira

The founding of Essawira (as-Sawira in Arabic, Tassurt in Berber, and known as Mogador to Europeans) in 1764 by Sidi Muhammad bin Abdallah (1757–1790) was, according to the chroniclers of Moroccan dynastic history, among the most important achievements of the 'Alawid sultan's reign. Due west of the southern capital of Marrakech on the Atlantic coast, Essawira became a royal port, closely controlled by the sultan. The foundation of the new port was part of Sidi Muhammad's efforts, after three decades of political disorder and dynastic struggle following the death of Sultan Mawlay Isma'il in 1727, to consolidate control from the southern capital of Marrakech by gaining revenues from foreign trade. The central government frequently had difficulty controlling the trade along the southwestern coast, especially from the port of Agadir, where some of the commodities most sought after by Europeans were exported: olive oil, ostrich feathers, goat skins, and gum arabic. These goods were transported from the southern districts of Morocco or by the trans-Saharan caravans.

Sidi Muhammad hoped to concentrate all European trade and foreign merchants in one port where the central government administration (referred to as the Makhzan) could gain revenues from customs duties. The foundation of the port, however, was legitimized by the purpose of jihad. Ahmad al-Ghazzal, a courtier of Sidi Muhammad, states that the reason for the foundation of the port was that the estuary of Salé became blocked with sand for two months of the year, thus impeding the movement of the corsairs. Essawira provided a natural harbor that was partially sheltered by an island about 1,500 meters offshore. In reality, the activities of Moroccan corsairs were rapidly diminishing, and the real importance of Essawira was in conducting foreign trade. A few decades after its foundation, Essawira became the only maritime port where foreign trade was allowed, though this proved impractical in the long run and other ports also were used for trading certain commodities.

In ancient times, the offshore island was used by the Phoenicians for the production of a purple dye, and further archaeological evidence attests to Roman and Byzantine settlement on the island. The Portuguese established a short-lived fortress on the mainland in 1506. But at the time of Essawira's foundation in 1764, the only settlement in the area was the small village of Diabet to the immediate south of the port. Essawira was located in a relatively isolated region on the border between the Haha and Shiadma peoples. Without a fertile hinterland, food always had to be transported over some distance. The design of the town is attributed to a French engineer named Théodore Cournut, but according to tradition, Cournut was dismissed and the work was completed by Genoese renegades. Europeans often observed that the architecture and layout of the city appeared more orderly than those of other Moroccan cities, but as the city grew, it took on the shape of other cities in Morocco with its main thoroughfares in the commercial districts and port, and a more intricate web of narrow, windy streets in the Muslim quarters of the *madina* and the Jewish quarter (the *mellah,* as the Jewish quarters were called in Morocco).

The town was first peopled by soldier-settlers from the ranks of the Black soldiers, known as the *'abid,* and by a large number of families from Agadir, many of who were compelled to relocate to Essawira when Agadir was closed to commerce. Another group called the Bani 'Antar, who according to local tradition originated on the western flanks of the High Atlas Mountains, were among the early settlers, forming military units in the new town. Essawira was also inhabited by the local population of the Haha and Shiadma districts. Jewish merchants settled in large numbers, and Jewish peddlers and craftsmen soon followed. The Jewish population grew to about 30 per cent of the town's population.

Moroccan Jews became the crucial element in the town's foreign trade. According to Jewish tradition, representatives of ten of the most important Jewish families of Morocco from a variety of cities (Marrakech, Tetuan, Agadir, Safi, and Rabat) were chosen in 1766 and granted special privileges to conduct trade in the new town. Sidi Muhammad wished to attract all the principal merchants, European or Moroccan, to the new port. European, Muslim, and Jewish merchants built houses in Essawira, with promises that customs duties would be relaxed. Sidi Muhammad signed numerous commercial treaties with European states, encouraging foreign merchants to settle in Morocco. After a few decades, about thirty foreign merchant houses were located in Essawira: Italian, Spanish, French, English, Dutch, and Danish merchants settled there. The foreign merchants of Essawira formed a tribunal of commerce known as the *commercio*. The majority of the Moroccan merchants were Jews, with only a few prominent Muslim merchants. These merchants were known as *tujjar as-sultan* (or "merchants of the sultan"), and they were advanced sums of money by the Makhzan to conduct trade. The merchants were required to pay back their loans in monthly installments. Since taking interest was proscribed by Islamic law, the sultan expected to profit indirectly through customs duties. As official traders of the sultan, the merchants were granted houses in the casbah quarter, where government officials and the foreign merchants lived. Many of the Jewish merchants had representatives of their families in London, Amsterdam, and Livorno, cities with whom a major part of Essawira's trade was conducted.

Following the death of Sidi Muhammad bin 'Abdallah, and during the reign of Mawlay Sulayman, foreign trade dwindled, and few foreign merchants remained in Morocco. Most of the trade of Essawira remained in the hands of several prominent Moroccan Jewish merchant firms. Essawira's foreign trade grew again beginning in the 1830s, with increasing numbers of European merchants established in the town. Essaouria remained Morocco's most important seaport until the late nineteenth century.

DANIEL J. SCHROETER

Further Reading

Brignon, J., et al. *Histoire du Maroc.* Paris: Hatier, and Casablanca: Librairie Nationale, 1967.

Corcos, D. *Studies in the History of the Jews of Morocco.* Jerusalem: Rubin Mass, 1976.

El Mansour, M. *Morocco in the Reign of Mawlay Sulayman.* Wisbech, Cambridgeshire: MENAS Press, 1990.

Jackson, J. G. *An Account of the Empire of Marocco and the Districts of Suse and Tafilelt.* 3rd ed. London: William Bulmer and Co., 1814.

Le Tourneau, R. "Le Maroc sous le règne de Sidid Mohammed by Abd Allah (1757–1790)." *Revue de l'Occident Musulman et de la Méditerranée* 1 (1966): 113–133.

Schroeter, D. J. *Merchants of Essawira: Urban Society and Imperialism in Southwestern Morocco, 1844–1886.* Cambridge: Cambridge University Press, 1988. Translated into Arabic as *Tujjar al-Sawira: al-mujtama' al-hadariyya wa-l-imbiriyaliyya fi janub gharb al-Maghrib, 1844–1886*, by K. B. Srhir. Rabat: Mohamed V University, 1997.

———. "Royal Power and the Economy in Precolonial Morocco: Jews and the Legitimation of Foreign Trade." In *In the Shadow of the Sultan: Culture, Power and Politics in Morocco*," edited by R. Bourqia and S. G. Miller. Cambridge, Mass.: Harvard University Press, 1999.

Morocco: Mawlay Sulayman, Life and Era of

Mawlay Sulayman (1792–1822) was one of the sons of the sultan, Sidi Muhammad b. 'Abd Allah (1757–1790). He expected to spend his life as a religious scholar but the sudden death of his brother, the sultan Mawlay al-Yazid, in 1792 triggered a succession crisis that impelled him into the political arena. The two main contenders for power were Mawlay Salama, a northern candidate who represented the *mujahidin* (holy warriors) devoted to maintaining a military offensive against the Spanish enclaves of Ceuta and Melilla, and Mawlay Hisham in Marrakech, who represented the commercial interests of the south that had developed trade relations with European countries through southern Atlantic ports such as Essawira. The religious elite of Fes, or Fez, the most important city in the sultanate, however, doubted the viability of either candidate and called on Mawlay Sulayman to accept their oath of allegiance. Their choice almost certainly reflected their feeling that Mawlay Sulayman, as a religious scholar like themselves, would be sensitive to their wishes if he became sultan.

Mawlay Sulayman reluctantly accepted their oath of allegiance and quickly defeated Mawlay Salama to become sultan of the north. It took him seven years of war, however, to defeat Mawlay Hisham as a result of the competing commercial interests of Fes and Marrakech. The opening of the port of Essawira in 1764 had reoriented a significant proportion of the trans-Saharan trade from the eastern Tafilalt to Fes route, to routes from Tafilalt and the Wad Dar'a to Marrakech and Essawira. Thus while the south supported the development of Atlantic trade with Europe, the merchants of Fes denounced it as un-Islamic and sought to draw the trans-Saharan trade back to the eastern route. As long as the sultanate remained divided, both sultans competed to control Atlantic ports and their trade as essential sources of supplies and customs revenue, but Mawlay Sulayman's attitude changed after 1799 when Mawlay Hisham's death in a plague epidemic left him sole sultan of Morocco.

In the stable middle decades of his reign, Mawlay Sulayman responded to the wishes of the scholarly and mercantile elite of Fes and closed many coastal ports to European traders. He also shifted the tax burden from customs duties and market taxes (*mukus*), considered uncanonical by the *'ulama'*, to rural taxes sanctioned by the Shari'a (Islamic law). Other factors also influenced Mawlay Sulayman's attitude to foreign trade. Although the European consular community interpreted his actions as xenophobic, they in fact reflected pressures placed on the sultanate by the Napoleonic Wars. Since both the French and the British had threatened to bombard countries that supplied their opponent, trouble-free trade with Europe was virtually impossible. Mawlay Sulayman's decision to suspend trade enabled Morocco to maintain its neutrality. It also avoided domestic criticism of the sultan for allowing trade with the "infidel" at a time when popular fears of a Christian Europe offensive against the Islamic world were growing as a result of Napoleon's occupation of Egypt (1798–1801).

Internally, the most important effect of Mawlay Sulayman's commercial policy was his need to extend tax gathering among the mostly Berber-speaking tribes of the mountainous fringe of Morocco. In order to strengthen the military arm of the state, he sidelined several Berber communities that had served militarily during his father's reign and replaced them with Arabs from the south. He then dedicated his forces to campaigns into the Middle Atlas where several large Berber confederations challenged state power. His restructuring of the 'Alawi army and aggressive tax collecting coincided with the revival of rural religious brotherhoods. Religious revival dated to the reign of Sidi Muhammad who had tried to simplify the religious education offered by urban *madrasas* in order to educate a body of *'ulama'* capable of spreading simple urban orthodoxy in the countryside. The *'ulama'* largely rejected his initiative, but it struck a chord among Sufis, many of whom established new religious brotherhoods that promoted rural religious education through regional networks. The most important brotherhoods of this type were the Darqawa, which had supporters throughout the Rif and Middle Atlas into West Algeria, the Qadiriyya, which had adherents in West Algeria, the Rif and the eastern marches, and the Tijaniyya.

Mawlay Sulayman's relations with these brotherhoods, except the predominantly urban Tijaniyya, was tense. On the one hand, his tax-gathering policies created competition between the state and the brotherhoods for a share of tribal surpluses. On the other hand, they resented his critical attitude toward certain aspects of rural religiosity, including pilgrimage and offerings (*ziyara*) at the shrines of holy men and annual celebrations (*mawsim*, *mawlid*). The situation came to a head in 1819 when the sultan decided to march into the Middle Atlas to force the Berbers of the region to pay taxes. They resisted fiercely and lowland Berbers within the sultan's army promptly defected, creating a massive Berber coalition against the sultan, given integrity by the fact that the majority of the tribes involved were affiliated to the Darqawa brotherhood. Mawlay Sulayman's son and heir died on the field of battle while the Berbers captured the sultan and escorted him back to Meknes.

Mawlay Sulayman's humiliation at the hands of the Berbers triggered a widespread political breakdown that escalated into a revolt of Fes and the north against him. This revolt indicated a major crisis of confidence in the sultan in several areas of government. First, in addition to criticising popular Sufism, he had declared himself sympathetic to the Wahhabi movement in Arabia, breaking his long-standing alliance with the Fasi *'ulama'* who opposed Wahhabism. Second, he had reorganized government in the north and several Fasi families who had traditionally served the sultans felt sidelined. Third, his expensive and unsuccessful mountain campaigns brought his military credentials into question just as a European threat appeared to be developing. These grievances and doubts as to his abilities led to the revolt. Mawlay Sulayman spent the next years fighting his nephews Mawlay Ibrahim and Mawlay Sa'id for control of the north and then retreated to Marrakech to face further outbreaks of insurgency. He died in 1822 with the country still in a state of unrest and his ambitious plans to extend state control over the mountain fringe in tatters.

AMIRA K. BENNISON

See also: **Egypt, Ottoman, 1517–1798: Napoleon and the French in Egypt; Morocco: Economics and Social Change since Independence; Morocco: Mawlay 'Abd al-Rahman, Life and Era of.**

Biography

Mawlay Sulayman became sultan of the north in 1792, upon the death of his brother, the sultan Mawlay al-Yazid. In 1799 Mawlay Hisham's death in a plague epidemic left him sole sultan of Morocco. In 1819 he decided to march into the Middle Atlas to force the Berbers of the region to pay taxes. He was captured and escorted back to Meknes. Doubts concerning Mawlay Sulayman's leadership led to revolt. He spent the last few years before his death fighting his nephews Mawlay Ibrahim and Mawlay Sa'id for control of the north, eventually retreating to Marrakech. He died in 1822.

Further Reading

Abun-Nasr, J. *A History of the Maghrib in the Islamic Period.* Cambridge: Cambridge University Press, 1987.

Badia y Lieblich. *The Travels of Ali Bey in Morocco, Tripoli, Cyprus, Egypt, Arabia, Syria and Turkey between the Years 1803 and 1807.* London: Longman Hurst Rees Orme and Brown, 1816.

El Mansour, M. *Morocco in the Reign of Mawlay Sulayman.* Outwell, Wisbech: Middle East and North African Studies Press, 1990.

Jackson-Grey, J. *An Account of the Empire of Morocco*. London: Frank Cass, 1968.

Morocco: Mawlay ʻAbd al-Rahman, Life and Era of
Sultan of Morocco

The reign of Mawlay ʻAbd al-Rahman (1822–1859) marked Morocco's transition from the early modern to the colonial era. During his years as sultan, the balance of power in the Mediterranean shifted decisively in favor of industrial Britain and France, affecting all the North African states. The most dramatic event was the French capture of Algiers in 1830, which triggered resistance not only in the territories of the Turks of Algiers but also in Morocco, where it dominated political discourse for nearly twenty years. French colonialism pushed Morocco's rulers to initiate the process of military modernization already taking place in Tunis, Egypt, and the central Ottoman empire, a process resisted by the population. Less striking, but equally damaging to the sultanate in the long term, was European commercial penetration of the Atlantic seaboard, which began seriously in the 1840s and steadily disrupted state-society relations. Mawlay ʻAbd al-Rahman faced the task of steering the sultanate through this difficult period.

Mawlay ʻAbd al-Rahman became sultan in November 1822 after the death of his uncle, Mawlay Sulayman, who nominated him as heir on his deathbed. Mawlay Sulayman's choice of Mawlay ʻAbd al-Rahman over his own sons was unusual, indicating his belief that his nephew possessed the personal qualities needed by a sultan: the ability to mediate, to conciliate, and the warrior skills to prove himself on the field of battle.

He spent the first three years of his reign fighting to restore central power and authority, a task complicated by his lack of resources, the endemic disorder in the countryside, and opposition to his rule from the sons of Mawlay Sulayman and northern groups involved in the revolt. This period of unrest indicated a renegotiation of state-society relations, a regular occurrence in precolonial Morocco where a tension existed between the sultans, who aspired to create a centralized state, and their subjects, who accepted the principle of sultanic rule, but expected each sultan to prove himself fit for the task by guaranteeing prosperity, distributing largesse, and defending the faith.

Mawlay ʻAbd al-Rahman tackled the problems he faced by judicious diplomacy and regular military progresses to meet his tribal subjects, prove his power to them, and receive tokens of allegiance. When a major famine in 1825–1826 ended this troubled period, he tried to increase his prestige by reconstructing the ʻAlawi corsair fleet, which had fallen into disrepair during Mawlay Sulayman's reign, and using it to harass European shipping, a policy described as maritime jihad (*al-jihad al-bahriyya*). During the late 1820s his agents purchased several secondhand ships in Gibraltar that were refitted in Moroccan ports and then sent to sea in 1828. In order to preserve Morocco's foreign trade, Mawlay ʻAbd al-Rahman assured the European consuls in Tanger that his corsairs would not attack the shipping of countries which had treaties with the sultanate. The corsairs, however, paid scant attention to this proviso and their activities provoked a hostile response, which Mawlay ʻAbd al-Rahman had not expected. The British threatened to bombard Tanger, an Austrian squadron attacked the harbors of Laraish and Tetuan in retaliation for Moroccan capture of one of their vessels, and a number of disputes arose with Spain.

In 1830 the French capture of Algiers and the demise of the Turks sidelined the international disputes caused by Moroccan corsairing and put popular pressure on the sultan to launch a jihad against the infidel. Mawlay ʻAbd al-Rahman initially viewed the situation as an opportunity to expand his power eastward and incorporate the West Algerian city of Tlemsen into the sultanate. The ʻAlawi occupation of Tlemsen during the winter of 1830–1831 created tension between the inhabitants of the city and the ʻAlawi army, put a huge strain on resources, and triggered strident French protests. To save his reputation, Mawlay ʻAbd al-Rahman withdrew his troops but gave material and moral support to the emerging leader of resistance in West Algeria, ʻAbd al-Qadir. During the 1830s and early 1840s enormous quantities of arms and ammunition passed through Morocco to Algeria from Gibraltar, Tanger, Tetuan, and Fes, and volunteers from the Rif and eastern Morocco joined the Algerian resistance.

The intimate relationship between Mawlay ʻAbd al-Rahman and ʻAbd al-Qadir, however, led to continuous French protests and threats that culminated in the short 1844 Franco-Moroccan War. The French easily defeated the sultan's army and bombarded the ports of Tanger and Essawira, forcing Mawlay ʻAbd al-Rahman and his son, Sidi Muhammad, to set in train the modernization of the Moroccan military, using the example of Muhammad ʻAli in Egypt. Military modernization demanded an increase in state revenue, which the sultan hoped to gain through closer control of trade and the imposition of monopolies of the import and export of staple goods in the mid-1840s. The late 1840s also signaled the formation of *l'Algérie française*. In the last years of ter Algerian resistance, ʻAbd al-Qadir retreated to Morocco and endeavored to persuade Mawlay ʻAbd al-Rahman to go to war with France. When he refused, ʻAbd al-Qadir publicly accused him of reneging on his duties as an Islamic ruler creating a political crisis that was only resolved in 1847 when the sultan's armies finally forced 'Abd al-Qadir back into Algeria where he surrendered to the French.

Commercial issues dominated the last decade of Mawlay 'Abd al-Rahman's reign. His imposition of monopolies conflicted with the wishes of the sultanate's European trading partners, especially Britain, which exerted constant pressure for restrictions to be lifted. They were unsuccessful until the 1850s, when they gained general European support, and drew up an Anglo-Moroccan trade treaty (1856) that opened the sultanate to European manufactures and enabled Europeans to buy property in Morocco. This marked the beginning of serious European commercial penetration of Morocco that disrupted indigenous industry and frequently provoked hostile responses from the inhabitants of the sultanate. In the Rif the search for minerals by European speculators and Spanish extension of the enclaves of Ceuta and Melilla led to conflicts with local tribesmen that escalated into the Tetuan War of 1859–1860 between Spain and Morocco. During the war Mawlay 'Abd al-Rahman died, leaving his son Sidi Muhammad to continue the process of modernization and adaptation to Europe's growing stake in North Africa.

AMIRA K. BENNISON

See also: **Morocco: Economics and Social Change since Independence; Morocco: Mawlay Sulayman, Life and Era of; Northern Africa.**

Biography

Mawlay 'Abd al-Rahman was governor of Essawira. He commanded the army during the 1819–1821 revolt of the north. He was then appointed governor of Fez. He became sultan in November 1822, upon the death of his uncle. He died in 1859, during the Tetuan War between Spain and Morocco.

Further Reading

Abun-Nasr, J. *A History of the Maghrib in the Islamic Period.* Cambridge: Cambridge University Press, 1987.

Bennison, A. K. "The Dynamics of Rule and Opposition in 19th Century Morocco." *Journal of North African Studies.* 1, no. 1 (1996): 1–24.

Danziger, R. "Abd al-Qadir and Abd al-Rahman: Religious and Political Aspects of Their Confrontation, 1843–1847." *Maghreb Review.* 6, no. 1–2 (1981).

Kenbib, M. "The Impact of the French Conquest of Algiers on Morocco." In *The Moroccan State in Historical Perspective 1850–1985*, edited by A. Doumou. Dakar: Codesna, 1990.

Miller, S. *Disorienting Encounters: Travels of a Moroccan Scholar in France in 1845–1846.* Berkeley: University of California Press, 1992.

Schroeter, D. *Merchants of Essaouira: Urban Society and Imperialism in Southwestern Morocco 1844–1886.* Cambridge: Cambridge University Press, 1988.

Morocco: Economy and Society, Nineteenth Century

Peopled predominantly by a Berber-speaking population, Morocco in the nineteenth century was still largely a tribal society, defined as a society organized on the basis of kinship, which presupposes a society without the political superstructure of a state. In effect, Morocco was constituted by an aggregation of tribes, subordinated to an urban complex, the bureaucratic mechanism of the state.

Although the tribal world was largely outside the effective political orbit (territorial jurisdiction) of the sultan, it was, nonetheless, subject to his sovereignty (jurisdictional authority), symbolized by the mention of his name in the Friday sermon, or *khutba*. Here, then, is a concept of sovereignty that is not so much territorial as anthropological, which compels a revision of French historiography of Morocco. French historiography depicts it in terms of antagonistic jurisdictional bifurcation, the *bled el-makhzan* and the *bled es-siba*, the land subject to the control of government, and the land outside its control, a misconception or misinterpretation stemming from the perception of a totally dissimilar social reality in Western cognitive categories. Dissidence may amount merely to a renunciation of the burden of taxation, the index of political subjugation, which is not necessarily inconsistent with the

Dying the textiles for the traditional cloth of the Moroccans. After the cloth is pulled through the dye, the color is kneaded into the textile using feet. © SVT Bild/Das Fotoarchiv.

recognition of the sovereignty of the sultan as the imam of the community of the faithful. The dualistic picture of French historiography of Morocco may also have a "rationalizing" or ideological function: to present precolonial Morocco as ramshackle and incoherent in structure, and a prey to disorder, until French colonialism forged a unified political framework and a centralized administration, bringing the benefits of "law and order."

Morocco may be visualized, not in terms of a dichotomous but of a unified jurisdiction. Social anthropologists describe tribal societies in terms of the concept of "segmentarity," which captures the diffusion or the atomization of authority in these societies, although in Morocco some form of informal, trans-tribal or overarching jurisdiction was exercised by a ruling group of holy men or marabouts (*igurramen*).

Corresponding to the sociopolitical hierarchy of tribes, peasants, and the state was an economy at varying stages of evolution: a merchant capitalism of the state, coexisting with a "moral economy" of the tribes (in E. P. Thompson's economic anthropology), "instituted" or "embedded" in the routine of daily life, with "subsistence production and non-monetary circuits [predominating]" (Rodinson, 1978: pp.55–56).

The circumscribed ambience of the market economy and merchant capitalism was reflected in the foreign sector of the Moroccan economy, an "enclave economy," largely irrelevant to the vast majority of the population. "There was minimum recourse of the part of the fellah to the city or to foreign sources for the satisfaction of his needs" (Stewart, 1967: pp.16–17). The bulk of the population thus lived virtually in a closed economy, in which exchanges were, in the main, internal and geared largely to use value or the reproduction of the household, with beasts of burden as the means of transportation. There were no railways before 1911, the eve of colonialism, which introduced modern highways and motor transport to the Moroccan landscape.

The foreign sector was the prime mover of the market economy and merchant capitalism. The trans-Saharan trade continued the medieval commercial tradition, complementing maritime trade, and stimulated by the burgeoning industrial capitalism of Europe. In this way Morocco, together with other regions of the Third World, was incorporated into the global economy, serving capitalist reproduction through "unequal exchange" (Emmanuel, 1972).

Britain and France dominated Morocco's maritime trade, which recorded substantial expansion in the nineteenth century. Tangier and Casablanca were the leading ports, outstripping Essaouira in commercial importance. European merchandise, notably cotton goods (the principal item of British commerce), glassware, and hardware, as well as tea and sugar were exchanged, in the main, for wool, grain, hides and skins, gold, ivory, and ostrich feathers, the last three originating from the trans-Saharan trade.

External trade, both inland and maritime, was the realm of merchant capitalism. Its practitioners, mainly Jews, belonged to an aristocracy rather than a bourgeoisie. They were either connected with the court, trading on behalf of the sultan (*tajir-s al Sultan*), or in partnership with him. The state was, in fact, the merchant par excellence, epitomizing Karl Polanyi's concept of "administered trade," an *etatisme* inimical to the capitalist doctrine of *laissez-faire*, prompting the pressure by the European mercantile community for a liberal commercial dispensation on the coast. The result was the Anglo-Moroccan Treaty of 1856, which inaugurated as "open door" policy congenial to capitalist penetration of Morocco. The treaty introduced trade liberalization, abolishing erstwhile state monopolies and controls, and rationalizing a once arbitrary and chaotic customs regime. These gains were consolidated by two other commercial treaties. The first was the Spanish-Moroccan treaty of 1861, which ended the Spanish-Moroccan War (1859–1860), in which Spain was victorious. Morocco had to pay a war indemnity, necessitating her resort to a loan from the British capital market on the security of her customs receipts; and the second was the Franco-Moroccan treaty or the Beclard Convention of 1863.

The Beclard Convention revived the practice of "protection" in Morocco. French commercial agents in Morocco came under the regime of "protection" and thus lived in a "state of extra-territoriality" outside the jurisdiction of the Moroccan authorities. Other European merchants also claimed "protection" for their employees under the most-favored-nation clause.

European commercial pressure was to culminate in a crippling financial crisis in Morocco in the second half of the nineteenth century. The regime of "protection," through its abuse, covered a widening circle of the taxable population, severely reducing the fiscal revenue of the state. The standardization of the customs duties also reduced the revenue from customs, a major part of which had been committed to offset the loan secured to pay the war indemnity. Payment was in foreign currency or gold, which, together with the severe balance of payments deficits—Moroccan gold and silver coins as well as foreign specie were smuggled to Europe, and imports far exceeded exports—exhausted Morocco's reserves, with the concomitant of monetary devaluation. With devaluation, much less foreign exchange accrued to the treasury through foreign trade. The bankruptcy of the state, arising from its inability to generate revenue to meet its domestic and international commitments, impelled it to external loans, the prelude to colonialism.

The loans were secured principally from a consortium of French banks. By 1906 Moroccan debt stood at 206 million francs; the figure subsequently rose by 100 million francs, with Morocco's sources of public revenue pledged to its repayment. The stranglehold of French capital on Morocco had reduced it to a veritable French financial protectorate. Colonialism, signified by the protectorate treaty of March 30, 1912, was the political complement to the French financial protectorate.

B. A. MOJUETAN

Further Reading

Emmanuel, A. *Unequal Exchange: A Study in the Imperialism of Trade.* London: New Left Books, 1972.

Polanyi, K., et al. *Trade and Markets in the Early Empires.* Glencoa: The Free Press, 1957.

Rodinson, M. *Islam and Capitalism.* Austin: University of Texas Press, 1978.

Stewart, C. *The Economy of Morocco.* Cambridge, Mass.: Harvard University Press, 1967.

Wallerstein, I. *The Modern World-System: Capitalist Agriculture and the Origins of the European World Economy in the 16th Century.* New York: Academic Press, 1974.

Morocco: Hay, Edward and John Drummond, British Diplomatic Protection, 1829–1903

Edward Drummond Hay, a fluent Arabic speaker, was sent to Morocco by the British government in 1829, the year before France invaded Algeria on the pretext of avenging the dishonor done to its consul when the dey of Algiers slapped him in the face with a fly whisk. While perhaps not immediately apparent, the posting and incident in Algiers were to become of great importance to Great Britain. The French entry into Algeria became the first step in the formation of its North African Empire; the appointment of Hay as British consul put in Morocco one of the country's strongest advocates for continued Moroccan independence.

Hay worked to strengthen Anglo-Moroccan relations, and his language skills gave him greater credibility with the sultan. His focus as consul, though, had much to do with events in neighboring Algeria. He was at his post when the Treaty of Tafna was signed (1837), dividing Algeria into two spheres, one of French control, and one under the control of the Amir Abd al-Qadir. In 1843 these events became more imminent for Morocco, as Abd al-Qadir fled to the adjacent state, seeking protection and assistance from the sultan, Mawlay Abd al-Rahman. The sultan granted him haven in Morocco and agreed to provide military supplies for his movement, which predictably brought Morocco into direct conflict with France. In 1844 French forces commanded by General Bugeaud roundly defeated the sultan's army at the Battle of Isly. The defeat highlighted European military strength, and the resulting Treaty of Tangier forced Moroccan recognition of France's presence in Algeria and required the sultan to withdraw his backing of Abd al-Qadir and the anti-French movement in Algeria. The elder Hay helped negotiate the Treaty of Tangier but died suddenly in 1844. His son, John Drummond Hay, who had gone to Tangier as a temporary assistant for his father, stayed on, eventually replacing his father permanently as consul.

Like his father, the younger Hay was fluent in Arabic and had a vast knowledge of Morocco, unlike many other European diplomats in the country. Hay had joined the Foreign Office in 1840 and prior to his arrival in Tangier had served in Alexandria and Constantinople. In his post as British consul to Morocco, one of Hay's first tasks was to persuade the sultan to conclude an unfavorable boundary agreement with Spain at Ceuta. He also averted Swedish and Danish fleets from being sent to make war on Morocco by persuading the sultan to cease his demands for tribute from those two states.

In 1856 Hay's diplomatic skills achieved a substantial victory for Britain, when he began negotiations on a commercial treaty that would lower duties and abolish all monopolies. Hay presented it as a progressive treaty that would profit all parties and as something leaders around the world recognized as a beneficial means of exchange. Makhzen officials were not so easily convinced, though. They remained skeptical that changes in economic policy initiated by European countries would bring any real benefits to Morocco. In December 1856, a new treaty was signed; this treaty abolished monopolies, reduced import duties to 10 per cent, and fixed maximum amounts for export duties. In negotiating the treaty, Hay thus achieved some of Britain's primary economic goals in relation to Morocco. However, he also had to make some concessions to the Moroccan negotiators. Hay could not get the sultan to agree to allow foreigners to own land, and the sultan retained the right to reimpose export bans as he saw fit. Even so, the treaty was a substantial economic victory for Britain, essentially granting it most favored nation status in Morocco. While technically in force for a period of only five years, the agreement substantially reduced Moroccan control over its own trade policy.

The conclusion of the treaty did not stop Hay from demanding further concessions from the sultan. He continued to argue for more open markets and for land ownership rights for foreigners, and he was not hesitant to berate the makhzen for what he saw as violations of treaty arrangements; in 1864 he accused the sultan of selling a monopoly on fuller's earth to a makhzen official, thus violating the 1856 treaty. He was also a forceful advocate for the interests of individual Britons and for British companies. In 1864, when the Awlad Amran tribe refused to pay a British company located at Safi for the weapons they had received from the company, Hay held the makhzen responsible and forced it to pay the tribe's debts to the company. That same year, when a British traveler was killed en route to a religious ceremony, Hay forced the sultan to fire his local officials on the grounds that they had not ensured the safety of their areas.

Hay pushed for the further development of infrastructure in Morocco. His main goal in doing so was to make getting goods to ports and hence to Europe easier and faster, but Hay was skilled at presenting his plans to the sultan in ways that would make them think Britain was helping the sultan achieve his own goals. For instance, he persuaded Sidi Muhammad to develop his road system and ports so that, he said, the sultan could more quickly move his military around the country, thus giving the makhzen an advantage in subduing rebellious tribes. Sidi Muhammad was convinced and began a construction program of roads, merchants' quarters, and new port works.

Hay also served as a mediator between the makhzen and other European powers in Morocco. While Britain was officially neutral in Spain's war with Morocco in 1859–1860 the country, in the person of Hay and some Gibraltar navy officers, had given substantial technical aid to Moroccan forces. All this was for naught, as Spain won the conflict. But Britain remained involved, refusing to allow Spain to take Tangier and negotiating a treaty between the two parties. Britain got Spain to agree to withdraw from areas too close to the Straits of Gibraltar for British comfort by forcing the sultan to accept a treaty that clearly vastly favored Spain. The treaty included sizeable indemnity payments, Spanish seizures of territory around Ceuta, Melilla, and Ifni, as well as the sultan's permission for missionaries to build a church in Tetuan; it also laid groundwork for Spain and Morocco to negotiate a treaty like Morocco's 1856 treaty with Britain. This economic treaty, the Treaty of Madrid, was signed in 1861, and was followed by Belgian and French versions of treaty. The combined effect of these events was to bankrupt the makhzen, make the government look weak to its people (particularly for being forced to accept foreign religious institutions on its lands), and make it clear that Morocco's only European friends were the British—and even their friendship was limited.

John Drummond Hay retired in 1885 but continued to live in Morocco where he had spent so much of his life and career. He died in Tangier in 1893. Hay had been the dominant force in international diplomacy in Morocco for more than forty years, outlasting ten French consuls. While his connections via family and friends arguably made his job easier, his language skills helped him make close relationships with Moroccans. Hay frequently spent his leisure time hunting wild boars with prominent Moroccan officials. He also helped his Moroccan colleagues when he could, for instance by having British ships take children of the Moroccan elite to Mecca on pilgrimage and by getting medical treatment for the Moroccan elite from British military doctors in Gibraltar.

Despite his skill in diplomacy, his long tenure in Morocco, and his apparent enjoyment of his post and the country, Hay was not enthusiastic about the makhzen. In his memoirs, Hay called the Morocco's form of government "the worst in the world," noting that officials were not paid, extortion and bribery were commonplace, governors were greedy, as were ministers, and farmers suffered greatly. He wrote that Morocco had "no security for life, or property, no encouragement for industry, and it is only a matter of wonder that the whole country is not allowed to lie fallow."

While Britain remained France's main rival for influence in Morocco into the 1890s, with no other European country willing to take on Britain's role as the guarantor of independence yet not willing to see Britain withdraw from that role because of what that would mean for France and for the European balance of power, European power and influence in general in Morocco continued to grow into the early twentieth century. Land purchases by Europeans continued, the numbers of Moroccans under European consular protection expanded, and European press and diplomats vigorously publicized and protested what they viewed as the human rights abuses in the country. European hotels and beach resorts were built near Tangier, and tourism increased substantially. Leisure time activities began to be more closely regulated in order to organize them according to European tastes; the boar hunts Hay had so heartily enjoyed with his Moroccan colleagues were now illegal, as the Tangier Tent Club banned Moroccans from participating in the hunt, except as servants.

After Mawlay Hasan died in 1894, British-backed reforms picked up speed, backed by the new vizier and regent Ahmed Ibn Musa (Ba Ahmed). The reforms begun by Ba Ahmed and continued by the sultan Mawlay Abd al-Aziz after his formal ascension in 1900 were to strengthen Morocco against French pressures. But by 1903 significant rural protests against the reforms coupled with changes in European politics that demanded a reassessment of British and French policy combined to put France in the preeminent position in Morocco.

In 1901 the young sultan embarked upon a series of economic and administrative reforms to his provincial governments and asked Britain to support the moves. Given that the reforms would be costly and given that Britain was reluctant to alone bear their costs, the British advised the sultan to seek support from France as well, which meant solving thorny issues like the border question between Morocco and

French Algeria. While an agreement on this issue was reached, France was reluctant to endorse or fund the reform program.

Nevertheless, the sultan announced the new reform program at home, which included substantial spending on port works and the military, a new universal tax on agriculture and livestock to replace traditional *ushr* and *zakah* taxes, and elimination of old tax exemptions. The new projects drained the treasury.

At the same time that Morocco's economic problems were becoming quite dire, the country was losing the ardent support of Britain for its continued independence. By the early 1900s, British attention had been diverted further south, to South Africa and the ongoing war there. French economic interests in Morocco were substantial by this time. In addition, European events prodded Britain and France to agree to settle their disagreements over Egypt and Morocco, as well as Madagascar, Gambia, Siam, and Newfoundland. The secret Cambon-Lansdowne Agreement negotiated in 1903 and finalized the next year, gave France a free hand in Morocco in return for French renunciation of claims in Egypt. The British-French agreement was part of the formation of the British-French Entente, the first leg of the Triple Entente that preceded World War I. French involvement deepened in Morocco that year when a consortium of French banking, political, and business interests called the Comité du Maroc made a loan to the sultan in the staggering amount of 62.5 million francs—a loan to which substantial strings were attached. What was by that time all but a charade of independence continued until 1912 when France officially imposed its protectorate over Morocco.

AMY J. JOHNSON

See also: **Morocco: French and Spanish Protectorates, 1903–1914; Morocco: Mawlay Hasan and the Makhzen; Morocco: Spain in Morocco and the Sahara, 1900–1958.**

Further Reading

Burke, E. III. *Prelude to Protectorate in Morocco: Precolonial Protest and Resistance, 1860–1912*. Chicago and London: University of Chicago Press, 1976.

Cruickshank, E. F. *Morocco at the Parting of the Ways: The Story of Native Protection to 1885*. Philadelphia University of Pennsylvania Press, 1935.

Flournoy, F. R. *British Policy Towards Morocco in the Age of Palmerston (1830–1865)*. Westport, Conn.: Negro Universities Press, 1970.

Hay, J. D. *Journal of an Expedition to the Court of Marocco in the Year 1846*. 1848.

———. *A Memoir of Sir John Drummond Hay: Sometime Minister at the Court of Morocco: Based on his Journals and Correspondence*. London: Murray, 1896.

Parsons, F. V. *The Origins of the Morocco Question, 1880–1900*. London: Duckworth, 1976.

Pennell, C. R. *Morocco since 1830: A History*. New York: New York University Press, 2000.

Morocco: Mawlay Hasan and the Makhzen

The term "makhzen" (literally, "storehouse") in North African usage originally denoted the location where taxes were stored; gradually, it came to have the more specific meaning of local, decentralized places of tax revenue storage, similar to government treasuries. By the sixteenth century, this had become the generally used term for the Moroccan government. The makhzen, or government, was a formalization of submission of the tribes to the sultan. Included in this was the willingness of the tribes to defend the sultan and his rights. Broadly speaking, the makhzen's primary job was extracting taxes and maintaining a military to enforce taxation.

At the head of the makhzen was the sultan. The sultan had religious power; he held the title of *Amir al-Mu'minin* (Commander of the Faithful), he was seen as representative of Muhammad, and he was a *sharif* (descendant of the prophet Muhammad). As such, the sultan had inherited from his ancestors *baraka* (blessing, or power to do good). In theory, therefore, the sultan would not make errors. Yet while the sultan's religious stature was generally agreed upon, his political authority was not.

Mawlay Hasan (*r.*1873–1894), Sultan Hasan I, was the ninth ruler of the Alawi dynasty of Morocco that began with al-Rashid in 1664 and continues to govern the country today. While often considered one of Morocco's strongest rulers, even he had to create his own power base in accordance with this system. When his father died in 1873, Mawlay Hasan journeyed to several different places to receive the *bay'a* (oath of loyalty), fighting various factions along the way.

Despite his military skills, Mawlay Hasan was known primarily for the modernizing reforms that characterized his reign. As sultan, he tried to strengthen his state by adopting Western-style reforms. In his view, this policy of defensive modernization would gain for Morocco the reputation of a strong state whose sovereignty European nations should protect, and equally important, the reforms would allow the sultan to control the pace of social and economic change.

Mawlay Hasan's viewed the stabilization of currency and the creation of a more efficient tax collection system as the basis of his reforms, yet his program also included a number of significant military and administrative changes. Like other rulers in the nineteenth century, Mawlay Hasan recognized the superiority of European weapons and military training. The sultan began his reforms by continuing the expansion of the army begun by his father, Sidi Muhammad. He continued to increase the number of Moroccan troops; by the end of his reign, the sultan's army had approximately 16,000 infantry and 12,000 to 15,000 cavalry. While this was a substantial increase, it did not meet the sultan's ambitious goals. Moreover, it was rare that all troops were on active duty at any given time. Low and irregular pay posed further problems for Mawlay Hasan's military.

Mawlay Hasan also began a significant weapons purchase program. While the sultan bought most of his cannon and other weapons from Britain and France, agents from other countries frequently peddled their wares to the sultan of Morocco. In order to keep foreign influence balanced, and in order not to unduly offend any potential suppliers, the sultan arranged for weapons purchases from a variety of other countries as well, including Belgium, the United States, Germany, and Austria.

At the same time that he recognized the need to buy the latest weapons from Europe, the sultan also wanted Morocco eventually to be able to supply itself with modern weapons, eliminating its dependence on Europe. In keeping with these ideas, Mawlay Hasan built a cartridge factory from his father's gunpowder factory in Marrakech and built a new rifle factory to replace imports. Unfortunately, production in the new factory was slow, and its products were prohibitively expensive. These Moroccan-made rifles cost more than 3,000 francs apiece to produce, compared with the 50-franc price tag for an imported Martini-Henry rifle (the model they were to replace).

In addition to increasing the size of his army, procuring for the troops the latest weapons, and attempting import-substitution of military supplies, the sultan also saw the importance of modern training for his military. This training was accomplished in part by sending students abroad (primarily to Gibraltar and Royal Military Academy at Woolwich) and in part by importing instructors.

Sir Harry Maclean, a Briton, came to Morocco to train the army in 1876 and remained chief instructor of the infantry for thirty-two years. Other European countries objected to British preferential treatment and wanted a role in military training as well. Jules Erckman became France's chief military instructor of Moroccan troops. The two took different approaches that were indicative of their nations' policy toward Morocco, with the Briton Maclean stressing the need for training for Moroccan independence and the Frenchman Erckman stressing Moroccan dependence on France for guidance and training. Germany wanted a role as well, and it took over responsibility for the coastal artillery, with less than impressive results. (60-ton guns were supplied by Krupps; it took ten years to install them, and they were fired only twice before their cement emplacements cracked, rendering them useless.) Italy and Spain also wanted a role in the Moroccan military; the sultan agreed to allow the Italians to run the arms factory at Fez and to allow the Spanish to maintain one bridge. While undertaken in order to strengthen Morocco, these military reforms opened door to further European involvement, provided a stage for European rivalries to be played out, and resulted in huge expenses for the government. The makhzen's reforms were further weakened by tribal acquisitions of modern weapons after 1880. By this time, arms sales to the tribes in the interior had increased, often through smuggling. This served to make later sultans' attempts to form and solidify their tribal power base much more difficult.

Mawlay Hasan also recognized the need to alter the administrative apparatus. However, in doing so, his primary goal was not to fundamentally change the nature of Moroccan government. In this area, the sultan was primarily concerned about increasing his own power. In 1879 the sultan increased the power of the *wazir* (chief minister), making him responsible for overseeing the entire bureaucracy. To facilitate this, the Mawlay Hasan divided the country and its administration into three regions (from the Bou Regeg north to the Straits of Gibraltar; from the Bou Regeg south to the Sahara; and the Tafilalt) each with its own secretary and all under the jurisdiction of the *wazir*. He also appointed officials for daily palace operations. One official was in charge of order, military groups residing in the palace compound, and the presentation of people to the sultan. Subordinate to him were the master of the stables and the official in charge of the royal encampments. In the palace itself, one official was responsible for the domestic servants and there were several minor officials in charge of certain parts of domestic affairs.

One consequence of reform, however, was an increase in European influence in Morocco. This problem was evident to the sultan, as the conflict over the protégé system demonstrates. Protégés were Moroccans who provided services (such as translation and trading) for European governments and merchants. They were exempt from Moroccan law and were under the legal jurisdiction of a European consul. In practice, protégé status was hereditary and included not only the protégé but also all family members and retainers of the protégé. Europeans sometimes sold protégé status to the highest bidders. It was a system that lent itself to abuses and to the underreporting of actual protégés; in 1877, the European consuls general estimated there were 800 protégés, but there may have been three times that many.

In 1880 Mawlay Hasan requested British assistance in resolving the problems of the protégé system. The British government organized an international conference in Madrid to address the issue. The outcome of that conference was an agreement to limit protected status. According to its terms, protégés could not be government officials or criminals, their numbers had to be decreased, protégé status could not be hereditary, and foreigners and protégés had to pay gate and agricultural taxes. In return for these restrictions, foreigners were given rights to own land, and their native employees, if arrested, could not be acted against by the makhzen until their employers and their consul were informed. While the conference also agreed to preserve Morocco's territorial integrity, its benefits are debatable. The limitations of protégés were not widely enforced, Europeans gained some expanded rights, Tangier was turned into an internationally administered area, and the conference made Moroccan affairs an international issue, thus at least symbolically decreasing Moroccan sovereignty.

As a consequence of the reforms and the resultant increase in European presence in and influence on Morocco, the Mawlay Hasan had to face numerous calls for jihads directed against Europeans. However, he did not endorse these calls. In fact, the makhzen launched its own propaganda campaign against those who called for jihad, arguing that the Europeans would inevitably win in any conflict because of their military strength and that therefore, jihad against them was not permissible because the end result would be loss of Muslim territory.

The sultan died at Tadla on June 7, 1894. Before he died, Mawlay Hasan called his ministers together and had them sign a paper recognizing his fourteen-year-old son, Mawlay Abd al-Aziz, as Morocco's next ruler.

Verdicts on Mawlay Hasan vary from hailing him as a great leader and Morocco's last strong sultan to condemning him as the man who set the stage for the failure of the makhzen and the imposition of the protectorate. Mawlay Hasan's reforms were not meant to fundamentally restructure or change the system of government in Morocco. They were meant to make himself more powerful and his control firmer. Judged by these criteria, the reforms were a success; his control over Morocco was tighter at the end of his reign than at the beginning, partly thanks to modernizing his army and buying more and better weapons from Europe. The makhzen continued to function relatively well throughout his reign, dealing with issues like currency devaluation and continual European commercial pressure with some success.

Yet the reforms came with a price. Other groups in Morocco could use these same tactics to strengthen themselves as the makhzen had; they could trade with Europeans and buy arms from European sources as well. All of this meant increased European involvement in Morocco and a relative decrease in the power of the makhzen.

AMY J. JOHNSON

See also: **Morocco: Hay, Edward and John Drummond, British Diplomatic Protection, 1829–1903.**

Further Reading

Burke, E., III. *Prelude to Protectorate in Morocco: Precolonial Protest and Resistance, 1860–1912*. Chicago: University of Chicago Press, 1976.

Dunn, R. E. *Resistance in the Desert: Moroccan Responses to French Imperialism, 1881–1912*. Madison and London: University of Wisconsin Press and Croom Helm, 1977.

Parsons, F. V. *The Origins of the Morocco Question, 1880–1900*. London: Duckworth, 1976.

Pennell, C. R. *Morocco since 1830: A History*. New York: New York University Press, 2000.

Morocco: French and Spanish Protectorates, 1903–1914

The resignation of the renowned John Drummond Hay from his post as British consul and the failure and disgrace of Charles Euan Smith's reform proposals marked a gradual decline in British-Moroccan relations and a resultant weakening of both British power and British resolve to ensure Moroccan independence. Likewise, the 1894 death of the energetic reformist sultan Mawlay Hasan was a significant blow to the makhzen. The new sultan, Mawlay Abd al-Aziz, and his regent, Ba Ahmed (who governed the country until the sultan's official ascension in 1900) were determined to continue their predecessor's reforms. However, neither was able to do so as successfully as Mawlay Hasan had. Differences in the rulers' personalities and abilities coupled with a worsening economy, tribal revolts, and continually increasing European pressures on the country made early twentieth century Morocco a volatile place. Changes in European politics profoundly affected the country as well.

Unlike in earlier times, when Morocco successfully played off European interests against each other, the country now had few choices as to where to turn for aid. Britain was preoccupied with its South African war, and European political maneuvering had resulted in a secret 1903 agreement between Britain and France concerning Morocco. The so-called Cambon-Lansdowne Agreement, negotiated in 1903 and finalized the next year, resulted in Britain agreeing to not meddle in France's policies in Morocco in return for France renouncing its claims in Egypt. This agreement, part of a general settling of disputes over colonial territories by the European powers prior to World War I, meant that Morocco had lost the principal guarantor of its independence.

After the failure of the British-backed reform scheme, and given Morocco's need for financing, French foreign minister Theophile Delcassé saw France's opportunity to get leverage over the makhzen. He signified his approval of a new loan package for the country by the French banking consortium led by the Banque de Paris et des Pays-Bas. The loan agreement would include setting up a debt commission. The makhzen was not eager to assume a massive foreign debt. However, its attempts to avoid French loans were hampered in 1904 by the continuing rural tax crisis and by its need to spend significant amounts of funds on fighting Abu Himara, a pretender to the Moroccan throne who claimed he was Mawlay Muhammad (Sultan Mawlay Abd al-Aziz's brother) and his tribal allies.

Matters became complicated, however, when news of the impending deal spread to other officials and to tribal leaders in Morocco. In the spate of rumors that followed, the deal was said to be a manifestation of Britain's selling Morocco to France. The (accurate) idea that the loan package meant a massive increase in French control over Moroccan affairs appalled many in the makhzen and even forced the sultan to see the deal in a new light. A representative of the banking group arrived in Fez later that year to continue discussions. This aroused more opposition to the deal when it became evident that Morocco, in agreeing to the package, would be exchanging numerous small creditors with little enforcement power over loan repayment for one powerful creditor able to force repayment through its control of Moroccan customs. Makhzen officials began vocally protesting the loan.

In June the loan deal was finally negotiated and signed. Morocco received 62.5 million francs, with 60 per cent of its customs duties noted as collateral. To ensure security on its collateral, a debt commission (*Contrôle de la Dette*) was set up to oversee customs collection. The loan package also included public works programs, the foundations of a state bank for Morocco, and preferential treatment to the consortium banks in any future loans. The conclusion of the agreement meant France had achieved essentially unfettered control of the Moroccan government.

Border clashes with French Algeria continued as well, complicating French-Moroccan relations. In 1903 General Louis-Hubert-Gonzalves Lyautey had been sent to Morocco to secure the border areas. His refusal to remove his troops from the Ras el Ain oasis based on what he perceived as the need to protect French Algerians on the other side of the border caused a diplomatic stir and confirmed in the minds of many Moroccans that France did not have the interests of Morocco at heart.

In late 1904, Mawlay Abd al-Aziz, in an effort to resolve the differences among his officials and strengthen the antireform coalition, asked the ulama (religious scholars), the *ayan* (notables), and the *shurafa* (plural of *sharif*, a descendant of the prophet) to consult and make a recommendation to the makhzen on the proposed reforms. Not surprisingly, the recommendation was against the proposals. An accompanying *fatwa* on European advisers was issued by the ulama in Fez shortly thereafter, blaming Morocco's problems on the presence of foreigners in the country. Accordingly, the sultan informed the French minister in Fez that all Europeans employed by the Moroccan government were henceforth dismissed from their posts.

In 1905 the situation in Morocco was significantly altered by the visit of German Emperor Wilhelm II to Tangier. The German government proclaimed its support of Moroccan independence and of international treaties on Morocco (e.g., the Madrid Convention on protégés); France took umbrage and accused the Germans of meddling in affairs that were none of their concern. For Germany, Morocco provided an arena to challenge France indirectly. By proclaiming itself in favor of the status quo (independence) and supporting the indigenous antireform movement, Germany could help prevent the imposition of the protectorate (and hence further impede French colonial gains) without risking an outright conflict with its neighbor.

The German wrench thrown into the French works in Morocco resulted in the sultan formally declining the French reform program. It also resulted in the convening of the 1906 Conference of Algeciras, at which the European powers confirmed Moroccan independence and confirmed the economic equality of all European powers in Morocco. It also set up an international commission to deal with Moroccan reforms. While on its face these might appear to have been gains for Morocco, the reality was a bit different. The international commission on reforms was heavily dominated by France, and its extensive powers (including broad rights to intervene in politics and economics throughout the country) meant further erosion of Moroccan sovereignty. A state bank was formed to be the makhzen's lone financial agent. It had the power to issue currency and do whatever was necessary to stabilize the economy. This bank, like the reform commission, was French-controlled, with most of its officials coming from the Banque de Paris et des Pays-Bas. The sultan, who did not agree with the provisions stemming from the conference, was bullied into signing the agreement.

In signing the agreement, Mawlay Abd al-Aziz made himself the target of antireformers, who claimed he was weak and had submitted unnecessarily to European pressures. The agreement also galvanized opposition to continued European presence in Morocco. In 1907 this opposition resulted in attacks on Europeans in the city of Casablanca that led to France occupying the area. Across the border, French forces in Algeria entered Morocco and occupied another city, Oujda, as a response to border attacks launched from that area.

The country's fortunes did not improve the following year. In 1908 a civil war in Morocco pitted the sultan, Mawlay Abd al-Aziz, against his brother, Mawlay Abd al-Hafiz. Opposition to Abd al-Aziz as sultan had grown so strong following the 1906 agreement that he had little support to continue in his position, and the ulama formally deposed the sultan in favor of his brother. The following year, Mawlay Abd al-Hafiz was formally recognized by the European powers as the legitimate sultan of the Moroccan state. Yet all did not go smoothly for the new government. The new sultan still faced the ongoing Abu Himara rebellion and a rebellion by Abd al-Hayy Kittani, the head of the Kittani brotherhood. Both revolts were successfully put down.

In 1911 Morocco appeared to benefit from European rivalries once more, when a German gunboat appeared in Agadir, supposedly to protect German interests in the country. The arrival of the Germans was brought about by the occupation of Fez by French forces, following attacks on French citizens in that city. The sultan vociferously protested the French action, and Germany endorsed the sultan's position. The apparent German interest in Morocco was short-lived, however. The so-called Agadir Incident simply resulted in another European colonial tit-for-tat, with Germany recognizing French rights in Morocco in return for some territorial gains in the Congo.

The year 1912 dealt the final blow to Moroccan independence, which, by that time, was largely a fiction in any case. That year, the French forced the sultan to sign the Treaty of Fez, which formally established a French protectorate over southern Morocco. This agreement gave France permission to direct Moroccan foreign affairs and to oversee its domestic affairs. The same year, France and Spain agreed upon the establishment of a Spanish protectorate in the remaining areas of Morocco. While both regions were technically under the authority of the sultan, Moroccan independence was an illusion. After agreeing to the imposition of the protectorates, Sultan Mawlay Abd al-Hafiz abdicated and his more compliant brother Mawlay Yusuf took the helm of the now French and Spanish occupied Moroccan ship.

Lyautey was appointed the first resident general of Morocco and given almost total control of both the civilian and military branches of the administration. The first step for Lyautey's government in Morocco was to pacify the country. The Treaty of Fez had not been warmly accepted by the tribes. In May 1912, tribal allies attacked the city of Fez and its foreign institutions, with the support of a large number of the Moroccan residents of the city. The revolt was put down, but it did not signal the end of resistance to the protectorate. The rebellion of El Hiba, who had declared himself the leader of the *mujahidin* forces and dedicated himself and his supporters to expelling the French from the country, posed a more serious threat to the French occupation. He and his five thousand troops captured the city of Marrakech in 1912; the local ulama subsequently declared him the rightful sultan. While the government in Paris counseled restraint, Lyautey favored offensive action. An attack on Marrakech began and ended on September 5. The superior weaponry of the French forces turned the battle into a massacre, with more than two thousand Moroccans being killed versus four French dying in the battle.

In addition to pacifying the country, Lyautey also began an immediate reorganization of the apparatus of government. The central change was the division of the old makhzen into two sections, one whose officials would be Moroccan Muslims and another whose officials would be French. While the sultan remained the head of government, he was essentially a figurehead, and real power rested in the office of resident general.

Lyautey also initiated significant changes in property rights and land ownership. Land surveys were conducted, maps drawn, property rights commissions convened, and land registrations begun before French courts. Large amounts of land were expropriated by the new government in order to make land available for incoming French colonists and to make land available for the government to supply services (e.g., schools, security, medical facilities) for the new colonists.

The Spanish protectorate, centered in Tetouan, governed two sections of the country, one in the north and one in the far south. Here, the sultan theoretically governed through a chosen *khalifa*, who had subordinate officials, courts, and ministers. The *khalifa* was to be protected by the government of Spain, in the person of a high commissioner. The Spanish high commissioner was in charge of security, the maintenance of order, and the service ministries, such as health, commerce, industry, and communications. In other words, while the *khalifa* was supreme on paper, in reality, the high commissioner governed the Spanish zone in much the same way that the resident general was in charge of the French zone.

By 1914 the government of Morocco had been substantially changed. The new French protectorate had reorganized the government and taken control of most important government functions. Land seizures and increased immigration resulted in more Europeans entering the country than ever before and in the loss of much agricultural land by Moroccans. While the sultan continued to rule in name, he presided over a country that bore little resemblance to Morocco a mere twenty years earlier.

AMY J. JOHNSON

Further Reading

Burke, E., III. *Prelude to Protectorate in Morocco: Precolonial Protest and Resistance, 1860–1912*. Chicago and London: University of Chicago Press, 1976.

Dunn, R. E. *Resistance in the Desert: Moroccan Responses to French Imperialism, 1881–1912*. Madison: University of Wisconsin Press and Croom Helm, 1977.

Gershovich, M. *French Military Rule in Morocco: Colonialism and its Consequences*. Portland, Oregon: Frank Cass, 2000.

Hosington, W. A. *Lyautey and the French Conquest of Morocco*. New York: St. Martin's Press, 1995.

Morocco: Resistance and Collaboration, Bu Hmara to Abdelkrim (Ibn 'Abd El-Krim)

Before colonial occupation in the early twentieth century, Morocco was divided into an area under the control of the sultan's government, or Makhzen, the Blad al-Makhzen, and an area where his authority was nominally acknowledged but in fact slight, the Blad al-Siba. The Berber tribes of the mountainous regions, such as the High Atlas and the Rif were commonly in the Blad al-Siba, ruling themselves through local assemblies (*djemaa*). Actual rebellions by them and others were common in Moroccan history. Sultan Hassan I, who reigned from 1873 to 1894, tried to strengthen and modernize the central government, partly to help protect Morocco against European powers encroaching on the country, but had limited success. Under his pleasure-loving and spendthrift son Abdel Aziz, government authority steadily broke down.

Morocco borrowed heavily from European sources and mortgaged customs revenue for debt service. This helped European powers encroach further on Morocco; while others advanced their business interests and insisted on reforms in the Moroccan government, France was from 1900 out to assert its influence. In this situation local rebels and warlords arose, sometimes declaring opposition to the increasing influence of Westerners.

Jilali ben Idris al-Zarhuni al-Yusufi, alias Bu Hmara or Abu Himara, was a rebel who at first claimed to be the Sultan's disgraced elder brother Muhammad. From his first base at Oujda he razed the entire eastern border area and the Middle Atlas, and defeated the sultan's forces in December 1902 but was defeated in turn a month later, and in 1904, driven from his Taza base to the eastern Rif, near Melilla. He held out there for several years, claiming the title of sultan and granting "concessions" to foreign companies.

European powers' interest in Morocco led to the crisis between France and Germany in 1905 and the Act of Algeciras of 1906, which established virtual Franco-Spanish control of Morocco's finances and a port police force as well as a state bank under French control. The agreement was largely ineffective, and French troops occupied Oujda and landed at Casablanca in 1907. Then a powerful Berber chieftain in the High Atlas, Madani el Glaoui, induced Abdel Aziz' brother Abdel Hafiz to rise up against the sultan. After a few months they defeated Abdel Aziz (1907–1908) and Abdel Hafiz became Sultan. He ruled for four years and was able in September 1909 to defeat and capture Bu Hmara, who had tried unsuccessfully to extend the area under his control in the Rif; after capture he was brutally executed.

Some Moroccans hoped that Abdel Hafiz might be able to restore government authority and resist European encroachment, perhaps with outside help. He was influenced by pan-Islamist ideas developed in Ottoman Turkey and Egypt, and in 1909–1910 contacted Germany, Italy, and Turkey; a Turkish military mission was sent, financed by a Moroccan or Maghrebian organization in Cairo, al Ittihad al-Maghribi. At this time the Salafiyya school of Islamic thought was spreading in Morocco from the Middle East. It preached a return to the true original values of Islam and had the effect of encouraging Muslims to react against European colonialism. Its influence was to spread at the historic Qarawiyin University in Fez; Abdel Hafiz recalled from exile a prominent Salafi scholar, Abu Shu'ayb al-Dukkali (1878–1937).

This activity presaged the awakening of Moroccan, Arab and Muslim sentiment, partly through Middle Eastern influence, which was to challenge French domination. But from 1909 to 1912, these anti-French feelings had no tangible effect. France sent a new expedition in 1911 at the request of the sultan himself, when Fez was surrounded by rebels, and on March 30, 1912, France established a protectorate over most of Morocco. In effect, Morocco became a colony, although the monarchy and other traditional institutions were preserved. Marshal Lyautey, the first resident general, installed two administrations, one continuing the traditional government for certain limited purposes with Caids, Pashas, and Cadis, the other being the overriding French administration. Meanwhile Spain occupied a smaller northern area from 1909.

In the High Atlas, the French used the three major "Great Caids" of the Berbers, and especially the Glaoua, as instruments of their rule. The Glaoua were headed by Madani el Glaoui (1866–1918), who had been Abdel Hafiz's Grand Vizir after installing him on the throne, and then by his brother Thami el Glaoui (1879–1956), pasha of Marrakech. They ruled as semi-independent potentates, and Thami el Glaoui was for decades the leading collaborator of the French, apart from the sultan. In fact the sultan, while still respected by his people, was wholly subject to French orders; the decrees (*dahir*) issued nominally by him were in fact drawn up by the French resident general. After signing the protectorate treaty, Abdel Hafiz was deposed within a year and replaced by Sultan Youssef. The *khalifa* who represented the sultan in the Spanish Zone was equally subordinate to the colonial power.

Islam in Morocco was dominated by brotherhoods based on veneration of particular holy men; with the partial exception of the Tijaniyya of Tetuan, they backed colonial rule. But orthodox Muslims inspired by Salafiyya teaching opposed the brotherhoods both for that reason and on the grounds that their form of Islam was corrupt. This orthodox Islamic movement, based in Fez, led to the creation of "free schools," or modernized Muslim schools, from 1921, and later helped lay the ground for modern nationalism.

To the south of the Atlas there were uprisings by the "Blue Men," led by Ma el-Ainin who had recognized the sultan's rule in Mauritania a few years before, and who proclaimed himself sultan in 1910 but was defeated and then died later that year. The leadership was then assumed by his son Ahmed el Hiba in 1912. El Hiba revolted against the French occupation and proclaimed jihad at Tiznit. He took Marrakech in August 1912 but was then defeated, and steadily driven back in 1912–1913.

In World War I, the Glaoua helped Marshal Lyautey hold on to territory already occupied by France. Many areas, however, were not subdued, and German agents encouraged dissidence, operating mainly in Spanish Morocco (Spain being neutral in the war). Albert Bartels, the main German agent, worked against the French with Abdelmalek bin Muhyi al Din, a grandson of the famous Algerian resistance leader Abd el Kader; ex-Sultan Hafiz also worked with the Germans for a time, in Spain. In 1914–1918, after limited Spanish occupation (Tetuan was occupied in 1913), the Rifi Berbers remained effectively independent, some being ruled by the chieftain Raisuli, active since the early 1900s. He had at least 2,000 well-armed men, but although he was called "Sultan of the Jihad" he came to terms with the Spanish; for years he ran his fief based at Tazirut in the western Rif.

"Primary resistance" by Berbers was a constant worry to the colonial rulers but not a major threat. However, a new development occurred in Spanish Morocco when Muhammad ibn Abdel Krim al Khattabi, better known simply as Abd el Krim (1868–1963), united many of the Rifis in a concerted and well-organized war effort against the Spanish occupiers. Educated at Fez, he had been chief judge (*qadi*) in the old Spanish colony at Melilla, but he joined his father in organizing resistance when Spain began to extend its effective occupation in 1919. He led a confederation of Rif tribes to a crushing victory over the Spanish forces at Anual in July 1921. For four years much of the interior of Spanish Morocco was under Abd el Krim's control. He established a government based at Ajdir, with many modern features, breaking away from traditional Berber custom. There was an administrative system with *qadis* and *qaids*, and a miniature state called *al-dawla al-jumhuriya al-rifiya* (the state of the Rifian Republic). The government raised a large sum from ransoms for prisoners in 1923 and sought to acquire modern military equipment, besides establishing a telephone system and planning a new currency (never issued). There was a regular army (numbering approximately 2,000 to 3,000) besides troops recruited or conscripted all over the area under Abd el Krim's control; some European adventurers fought for him. He was celebrated in the Muslim world and appealed to Europeans' imagination.

He never won total support in the Rif but defeated Abd el Malek and then, in 1925, Raisuli. In that year, however, Abd el Krim attacked the French, and after initial successes he was defeated by the alliance of two European colonial powers. He had maybe 12,000 men at the end, against combined French and Spanish forces of 123,000 men and 150 aircraft. Abd el Krim surrendered to the French on May 25, 1926, and was sent into exile in Réunion.

JONATHAN DERRICK

See also: **Morocco: French and Spanish Protectorates, 1903–1914; Morocco: Lyautey, General Hubert, and Evolution of the French Protectorate, 1912–1950; Morocco: Spain in Morocco and the Sahara, 1900–1958.**

Further Reading

Abun-Nasr, J. M. *A History of the Maghrib*. 2nd ed. Cambridge University Press, 1975.

Burke, E., III. *Prelude to Protectorate in Morocco: Precolonial Protest and Resistance, 1860–1812*. University of Chicago Press, 1976.

Halstead, J. P. *Rebirth of a Nation: The Origins and Rise of Moroccan Nationalism, 1912–1944*. Harvard University Press, 1967.

Pennell, C. R. *A Country with a Government and a Flag: The Rif War in Morocco 1921–1926*, Cambridgeshire, Eng.: Menas Press, 1986.

Morocco: Lyautey, General Hubert, and Evolution of French Protectorate, 1912–1950

The name of General Hubert Lyautey (1854–1934), the first resident general of French Morocco, is synonymous with the concept of the protectorate. Lyautey was appointed in 1912 to oversee the creation of a new regime in Morocco and was charged with implementing the theory of protectorate. The sultan was to be maintained in position and respected, though authority ultimately belonged to the resident general, who was answerable to the Foreign Ministry in Paris.

Lyautey's first priority in 1912 was to complete the "pacification" of Morocco and consolidate the gains already made by French troops. However, with local resistance and geographical considerations making complete military victory unlikely, Lyautey decided to concentrate on achieving control of what he termed "useful" and "necessary" Morocco; that is, the areas of the country with some economic worth from agriculture or mining. Lyautey was keen to avoid the creation of an exploitative colonial regime in Morocco. He attempted to restrict European immigration so that the settler-native divide seen in Algeria would not be reproduced in Morocco, and to work with the settlers to avoid the excesses of colonialism.

This aim came into conflict, however, with his other main goal: rapid economic development of the protectorate. Foreign investment, principally from France, was welcomed; twenty-nine thousand settlers arrived in 1912 and 1913. A large-scale program of public works was undertaken, to construct roads, railways, and harbors. In addition to the immigration that this work attracted, a shift of population to the cities took place within Morocco; Casablanca's population rose from 12,000 in 1912 to 110,000 by 1921. During the World War I, agricultural exports to Europe brought a much-needed improvement in economic conditions. After the war, however, the problems posed by development became greater. Moroccans' living conditions in the cities saw little improvement, partly because Lyautey's insistence on respecting the local population meant that modern European cities had been constructed alongside the old and crowded *medinas*. In the countryside, meanwhile, Lyautey failed to prevent French settlers from seizing and exploiting large areas of land.

The military situation in the protectorate's early years was not a complete success either. Resistance to French "pacification" continued in the more remote areas and by the mid-1920s had found a leader in 'Abd al-Karim. He conducted a successful campaign in the Rif Mountains and achieved victories against depleted French forces in 1925. This episode, which underlined the limits of French success in winning popularity through economic and social development, coincided with Lyautey's resignation. By the time 'Abd al-Karim was defeated in 1926 by a combined French and Spanish force, Lyautey's Morocco resembled other colonies, with problems of inequality and exploitation already giving rise to nationalism.

Lyautey's successors as resident general, Steeg (1925–1929) and Saint (1929–1933), were more favorable to French immigration and colonization. European settlement progressed rapidly, and the character of immigrants changed; many were now Frenchmen of modest means, less receptive than earlier settlers to Lyautey's ideal of respect for indigenous society. During the depression of the 1930s, the settlers pressurized the French authorities to support them by relaxing labor laws, making it easier to employ poorly paid Moroccan casual labor while protecting the Europeans' investment in industry and agriculture. European living standards rose during the 1930s, while those of Moroccans dropped dramatically and unemployment became a serious problem in the still-expanding cities. Contact between the settlers and the Moroccans was minimal, and very few Moroccans were able to gain access to the modern economy or to posts in the protectorate administration.

The post-Lyautey era also saw little progress in the field of social and religious cohesion. French attempts to distinguish between Arabs and Berbers, the latter seen as easier to assimilate into the secular French state because of their supposedly weaker Muslim faith, had long been a feature of French rule in North Africa. In May 1930, the French authorities announced plans to regulate Berber law, with the intention of hastening the Berbers' assimilation and distancing them from Islam, which was considered to be the source of the Arabs' resistance to French rule. The Moroccan reaction was rapid, with protests against this separation of Arabs and Berbers, while the Sultan Sidi Mohammed, as spiritual leader, supported the protests in the name of Islam. Lyautey's aim of respecting Moroccan culture and belief appeared to have been forgotten by the authorities.

Social policy, too, revealed the failings of French rule. Despite a socialist government in France in 1936, Resident General Peyrouton (March–October 1936) refused to introduce progressive measures. Moroccan strikers were sacked or imprisoned while their European counterparts were able to negotiate with the authorities. Unrest among Moroccans increased in the face of growing inequalities, until General Noguès (October 1936–1943) was appointed as resident general to restore order. Noguès is generally seen as the only resident general to attempt to follow in Lyautey's footsteps. He attempted to prevent further growth of nationalism by raising the Moroccans' living standards, in particular by granting financial aid to the rural population and extending irrigation. The beginnings of Noguès' rule certainly encouraged nationalists and alarmed settlers, but the onset of World War II prevented the continuation of gradual reform.

Although Morocco fought in 1939–1940 as an ally of France, the subsequent defeat and division undermined France's prestige. The American influence during the war encouraged nationalists, and in 1944 the Atlantic Charter's guarantee of self-determination further threatened French authority. De Gaulle appointed a conservative, Puaux, as resident general in 1943 and riots in favor of independence were repressed, but popular support now rallied round the sultan as a symbol of independence, rather than merely hoping for reform of the protectorate regime. In 1946 the metropolitan government appointed the liberal, Labonne, as resident general, but though he was willing to anger the settlers by urging greater effort to move toward equality, his plan for an assembly with representation for both settlers and Moroccans was rejected by both sides. Furthermore, Labonne found that most of his administrative staff were staunchly conservative supporters of the settlers, undermining his plans for reform. Security forces violently repressed Muslim demonstrations; the sultan publicly criticized the French and turned to the United States and the Arab League. Labonne was replaced in 1947 by the conservative General Juin. Juin welcomed new settlers, heavily invested in the modern settler-controlled economy, and sought to oppose nationalism by encouraging any opposition to the sultan. His policies created the climate of bitter division and anti-French feeling that characterized the last years of French Morocco and further distanced the protectorate from Lyautey's legacy.

STEPHEN TYRE

Further Reading

Bidwell, R. L. *Morocco under Colonial Rule: French Administration of Tribal Areas, 1912–1956*. London: Cass, 1973.

Pennell, C. R. *Morocco since 1930: A History*. London: Hurst and Company, 2000.

Scham, A. *Lyautey in Morocco: Protectorate Administration, 1912–1925*. Berkeley: University of California Press, 1970.

Morocco: Spain in Morocco and the Sahara, 1900–1958

At the turn of the twentieth century, Spanish holdings in Morocco comprised the Mediterranean coastal *presidios*, or garrisons, at Melilla, Ceuta, and Alhucemas, as well as the Atlantic coastal enclave of Ifni, held by treaty since the fifteenth century, but which the Spanish had never successfully occupied. In 1884 a powerful Spanish commercial lobby pressing the government to compete with France in Northwest Africa's colonization had also succeeded in establishing a trade settlement at Villa Cisneros in the Western Sahara. The Spanish government signed a series of accords with France in 1900, 1904, and 1912 that further demarcated Spain's sphere of influence in Morocco to an area roughly one-twentieth the area under French control. Spanish Morocco included a strip of land that ran along the northern coast then turned southward into the Rif Mountains and a southern region from Rio de Oro in the Sahara to the Wadi Draa, as well as the area immediately surrounding Ifni.

Successive territorial agreements with the other European powers left the Moroccan Sultan 'Abd al-Aziz increasingly powerless to use international pressure to stem France and Spain's actions in Morocco. The 1906 Act of Algeciras to which 'Abd al-Aziz was a signatory gave the two countries virtual control over the country despite fictive recognition of the sultan's continued sovereignty. France first established a protectorate over Morocco in 1912 under the pretext of defending 'Abd al-Aziz's half-brother and usurper 'Abd al-Hafiz from a rebel force that was marching on Fez. Under the protectorate, both France and Spain began to expand control over their respective territories openly. For several years, the Spanish contended with a guerrilla war led by Ahmad al-Raisuli in the Jbala region around Tetuan and were even forced to recognize his de facto control over the area for a brief period. However, the far greater challenge to Spanish authority came from the Rifian leader Muhammad b. 'Abd al-Karim whose ideologically based opposition movement united the Rifian people in a self-proclaimed republic under his leadership. During the period from 1921 to 1926, 'Abd al-Karim's followers inflicted a series of heavy defeats on the Spanish, and the ease with which his forces defeated the Spaniards prompted him to expand his efforts into French controlled territory as well. This led ultimately to a combined Franco-Spanish force of nearly half a million men routing 'Abd al-Karim's force of sixty thousand and forcing his surrender in May 1926.

Faced with the struggle to assert Spanish supremacy in the Rif, successive Spanish governments made little effort to establish a presence beyond the coastal town of Villa Cisneros in the south. The region's military governor from 1903 to 1925, Francisco Bens Argandona, succeeded in nurturing positive relations with the region's inhabitants largely because the Spanish presence at that time posed no threat to local autonomy. In the absence of a Spanish military presence in the interior, the Spanish Saharan zone provided a place of refuge for Western Saharans involved in efforts to expel the French from the region, and became an ongoing source of diplomatic tension with France. Only in the early 1930s as France was on the verge of completing the subjugation of its Saharan territories after over two decades of fighting did Spain act to take control of its interior Saharan holdings.

Concerns about rising Moroccan nationalism following the founding of the *Istiqlal* (Independence) Party in French Morocco prompted the Spanish government to separate its Saharan territories administratively from its protectorate in Morocco. In 1946 they formed Africa Occidental Espanola (Spanish West Africa), which consisted of Spanish Sahara and Ifni.

Slow to recover from the damage to its economy caused by the Spanish Civil War, the Franco government invested little in the infrastructure of its colonies. Particularly in the Sahara, the lives of its nomadic inhabitants changed little under Spanish rule as administrators lacked the resources to control much less tax their subjects.

Spanish dictator General Francisco Franco sought to counter his country's political isolation in the years following World War II by courting diplomatic ties to the Arab Middle East. Franco recognized that his Moroccan colony could be a useful bargaining tool with Arab Muslim leaders. Toward this end, the Spanish government disavowed France's deposition of the nationalist Sultan Muhammad V in August 1953, while orchestrating public demonstrations in Spanish Morocco supporting Muhammad V, and granting amnesty or sentence reductions to prisoners. In late 1954 Spain delivered on promises of greater Moroccan participation in the governing of Spanish Morocco while stopping short of full Moroccan autonomy. A new government was formed that placed prominent nationalists in high-level ministerial positions, including the leader of nationalist efforts in Spanish Morocco 'Abd al-Khaliq Torres, who became minister of social affairs.

Spanish Morocco now became the nationalist movement's base of operations in its efforts to oust the French from Morocco, as the movement of smuggled arms and the carrying out of military training took place unimpeded, and perhaps aided by Spanish authorities. On March 2, 1956, both France and Spain recognized Morocco's independence as Muhammad V returned from exile in Madagascar to rule as king rather than sultan. Faced with relinquishing its holdings in Morocco, Spain refused to turn over control of its southern zone around Ifni, asserting that the area was in a state of anarchy and posed a threat to Spain's Western Saharan settlement. Villa Cisneros was not regarded as part of newly independent Morocco, despite nationalist protestations of a historical Greater Morocco claim to the region.

The conflict escalated throughout 1956 and 1957, from anti-Spanish public demonstrations in Ifni to politically motivated assassinations and sporadic fighting between the Moroccan Liberation Army and Spanish forces. Beginning in November 1957, the Liberation Army amassed a large enough force to drive the Spaniards from Ifni's hinterland. Faced with expulsion from the region altogether, Spain and France cooperated in unleashing a large-scale air and ground assault on several fronts that defeated the Liberation Army contingents in the first months of 1958. Despite its costly victory, Spanish administrators remained restricted to Ifni itself until its complete abandonment in 1969.

GLEN W. MCLAUGHLIN

See also: **Morocco: French and Spanish Protectorates, 1903–1914; Morocco: Immigration and Colonization, 1900–1950; Morocco: Lyautey, General Hubert, and Evolution of French Protectorate, 1912–1950; Morocco: Nationalism, Muhammad V, Independence, 1930–1961.**

Further Reading

Abun-Nasr, J. M. *A History of the Maghrib in the Islamic Period.* Cambridge: Cambridge University Press, 1987.

Driessen, H. *On the Spanish-Moroccan Frontier: A Study in Ritual, Power and Ethnicity.* Oxford: Berg Publishers, 1992.

El Mansour, M. "Moroccan Historiography since Independence." In *The Maghrib in Question: Essays in History & Historiography*, edited by M. Le Gall and K. Perkins. Austin: University of Texas Press, 1997.

Hodges, T. *Western Sahara: The Roots of a Desert War.* Westport: Lawrence Hill and Company, 1983.

Landau, R. *Moroccan Drama 1900–1955.* San Francisco: American Academy of Asian Studies, 1956.

Pennell, C. R. *A Country with a Government and a Flag: The Rif War in Morocco 1921–1926.* Boulder Colo.: Menas Press, 1986.

Morocco: Immigration and Colonization, 1900–1950

The year 1900 marked the official ascension of Sultan Mawlay Abd al-Aziz, for whom the regent Ba Ahmed had been governing the country since the death of the previous sultan, Mawlay Hasan, in 1894. Like his father, the new sultan was keenly interested in pursuing a program of modernizing reforms for his country. Unfortunately, economic pressures and continued European encroachment meant his reform programs were not as successful as those of his father had been. One form of increased European pressure on the Sherifan Empire was immigration. The number of foreigners resident in Morocco rose during the first half of the twentieth century, picking up significantly after the imposition of the French and Spanish protectorates in 1912.

The governmental changes begun by France's first resident general, Louis-Hubert-Gonzalves Lyautey, were designed to impose security and order in the country; they also made Morocco more attractive to French settlers. Lyautey's pacification program successfully put down several rebellions. His troops also spread throughout the country, establishing pacified areas where local economic activities began to flourish. French takeover of much of the apparatus of government coupled with the introduction of French courts with wide-ranging authority served, among other things, to encourage immigration. Even more significantly, large amounts of land were expropriated by the new government in order to make land available for incoming French colonists and to make land available for the provision of government services (e.g., schools, security apparatus, medical facilities) for the new colonists.

Yet Lyautey did not want settlement on the pattern of French settlement in Algeria. He had neither patience with nor respect for peasant settlers. Lyautey's view was that his government was to take care of the country and its native inhabitants—quite literally, to "protect" Morocco. Instead of encouraging small farmer immigration, Lyautey favored large-scale farming by major corporations, viewing this as a profitable and minimally disruptive type of agriculture. In his mind, land registrations and changes in property laws coupled with seizures of agricultural land and with expropriation of roads, rivers, beach areas, forests, land previous owned collectively by tribes would provide the basis for corporation agriculture in Morocco. Still, though, his reforms in the first year of the protectorate alone attracted some 29,000 new European (primarily French) settlers to Morocco. Most of these new immigrants settled in cities on the coast.

After World War I, the settler influx continued. Lyautey's successor, Theodore Steeg (resident general from 1925 to 1928), took a much different approach to the question of immigration and settlement. Unlike Lyautey, Steeg was a firm believer in the necessity of encouraging the immigration of small-scale, or peasant, farmers to Morocco. Lyautey had believed that so many small farmers could mismanage their lands and resources and become a burden to the state; he also realized that arable land in Morocco was limited and all settlement by French farmers would necessarily reduce the amount of arable land available to Moroccan farmers. The result would be that the untrained Moroccan farmers would move to the cities, where they would not be able to find jobs. Steeg however, believed the French small farmers would be a source of economic success. Time proved Lyautey correct, however, as many of the small farmers went under and required economic assistance from the protectorate—assistance that had come from taxes on native Moroccans. During the protectorate, 5,903 rural settlers farmed 1,017,000 hectares, 289,000 of which was expropriated by the government and then sold to the settlers, and the remaining 728,000 hectares of which had been acquired through private sale.

Urban immigrants who arrived in Morocco in the 1920s settled into a typically colonial lifestyle. They constructed and lived in European-style cities, much of whose architecture was explicitly modeled on that of Europe (in contrast to new buildings at the beginning of the protectorate, which were built with some concessions to local styles). They worked in European companies, socialized almost exclusively with other Europeans, rarely came into social contact with Moroccans, and took advantage of their access to the best goods and forms of travel. In other words, the immigrants were essentially segregated, by choice and economic position, from the Moroccan population.

In 1931 there were some 115,000 French settlers in Morocco, which represented a 42 per cent increase in only five years; some sources estimate the total foreign population at 200,000 by the mid-1930s. Not only had these settlers built and rebuilt Moroccan cities, but they had reinvigorated trade, built new towns in the interior, and reorganized agriculture along European lines. They also proved a powerful lobbying group, pressuring the French administration in Morocco for policies favorable to their interests and for political institutions wherein they could formally mobilize and influence French policy in the country.

In 1919 French settlers had successfully pushed for the formation of the Conseil du Gouvernement, which served as a debating and discussion body for the French population of Morocco. The organization of the settlers into a lobbying body allowed them to substantially influence policy decisions and the fates of the resident generals. Henri Ponsot, the resident general from 1933 to 1936, pushed for reforms and concessions to Moroccan nationalists and opposed a revision of the Algeciras Act of 1906 that would have altered tariffs for the benefit of the settlers. In response, the colonists demanded that the Conseil du Gouvernement be changed from a consultative group to one that would formally deliberate (and hence have more influence) on government policy. The conflict resulted in Paris recalling Ponsot, marking a major increase in the power of the settler population.

Immigration to Morocco began to decline after 1931, yet opposition to the settlers continued. In 1937 the diversion of water supplies by French settlers occasioned a large-scale riot in Meknes. The continued French presence, policy, and power in Morocco coupled with the privileged and segregated lifestyles of the settlers occasioned widespread discontent among most Moroccans. This discontent eventually led to the formation of several organized protest movements and parties. The *istiqlal* (independence) movement began before 1930 but became explicitly opposed to the continuation of the protectorate in 1930, after the government promulgated the Berber Dahir, which recognized Berber rights and promoted Berber separatism. The group, under the leadership of Muhammad al-Wazzani and Allal al-Fassi, drew up a program of reforms. Despite the split of the movement into two sections in 1937 (the same year al-Fassi was deported to Gabon for his nationalist activities), resistance continued.

World War II resulted in only minor demographic changes in Morocco. The 1939 German invasion of France prompted Muhammad V to send 20,000 of his troops to France to defend the country. When France was occupied by Nazi Germany in 1940, the resident general, Charles Noguès, sided with the new Vichy regime. Yet the sultan supported the Free French Movement, refusing to sign anti-Jewish decrees, and asserting that Moroccan Jews were his subjects like all the Moroccan people and he would defend their rights. This encouraged the resistance, as did American landings in Morocco in 1942 and the apparent support of U.S. President Franklin D. Roosevelt for Moroccan independence. While the French North African colonies became important sites of Free French organization, massive immigration to Morocco did not occur.

In 1944 the *istiqlal* group was formally made a party and appealed to the United States, USSR, France, and Britain to put an end to the protectorate. In 1947 the sultan, long in agreement with the group's aims, formally aligned himself with the party. By 1951 a new group called the National Front had been formed, incorporating several parties in both the French and Spanish zones. Despite mounting resistance and international pressure, France was not ready to abandon its position or its settlers in Morocco. In order to govern through a more tractable leader, France, in 1953, deported the independence-minded sultan to Madagascar and replaced him with an elderly uncle. Rather than solving the problem, this move galvanized the opposition, leading to two years of intensified attacks on French settlers, institutions, and property. In 1955 the Oued Zem massacre of ninety-five settlers prompted a French reconsideration of the issue. Shortly thereafter, negotiations to end the protectorate began. In 1955 both the French and the Spanish protectorates were ended, as was the international control of Tangier, and Morocco became once more an independent, sovereign state.

AMY J. JOHNSON

See also: **Morocco: Lyautey, General Hubert, and Evolution of French Protoctorate, 1912–1950; Morocco: Mawlay Hasan and the Makhzen.**

Further Reading

Bernard, S. *The Franco-Moroccan Conflict.* New Haven: Yale University Press, 1968.

Bidwell, R. *Morocco under Colonial Rule: French Administration of Tribal Areas, 1912–1956.* London: Frank Cass, 1973.

Dunn, R. E. *Resistance in the Desert: Moroccan Responses to French Imperialism, 1881–1912.* Madison: University of Wisconsin Press and Croom Helm, 1977.

Gershovich, M. *French Military Rule in Morocco: Colonialism and its Consequences.* Portland, Oregon: Frank Cass, 2000.

Halstead, J. P. *Rebirth of a Nation: The Origins and Rise of Moroccan Nationalism, 1912–1944.* Cambridge, Mass.: Center for Middle Eastern Studies of Harvard University, 1969.

Hosington, W. A. *Lyautey and the French Conquest of Morocco.* New York: St. Martin's Press, 1995.

Hosington, W. A. *The Casablanca Connection: French Colonial Policy, 1936–1943.* Chapel Hill: University of North Carolina Press, 1984.

Landau, R. *Moroccan Drama, 1900–1955.* San Francisco: The American Academy of Asian Studies, 1956.

Pennell, C. R. *Morocco since 1830: A History.* New York: New York University Press, 2000.

Stewart, C. F. *The Economy of Morocco, 1912–1962.* Cambridge, Mass.: Center for Middle Eastern Studies of Harvard University, 1964.

Woolman, D. S. *Rebels in the Rif: Abd El Krim and the Rif Rebellion.* Stanford, Calif.: Stanford University Press, 1968.

Morocco: Nationalism, Muhammad V, Independence, 1930–1961

After the death of Sultan Moulay Hassan in 1894, Morocco experienced a period of political turmoil characterized by contested successions and popular revolts. This contributed to the weakening of the country and thus paved the way for colonial domination. The Treaty of Fez, signed by the Sultan Mawlay Abdelhafid, established a French protectorate in March 1912. The treaty divided Morocco into three administrative zones: French Morocco, Spanish Morocco, and the international zone of Tangier. However, the "pacification" of the entire country proved extremely slow and difficult. Resistance from various tribes to European occupation, with the Rif War (1921–1926) led by Abd el-Krim being a prime example, lasted until the conquest was completed in 1934.

Morocco enjoyed the status of an independent country for centuries and thus foreign domination was vigorously opposed. Indeed, the crushing of the armed struggle had not brought an end to the resistance, for the opposition to occupation had only taken a different form which became political in nature and urban based. The movement had already started in the mid-1920s with two small groups of young nationalists in Fez and Rabat. Both Allal al-Fassi and Ahmed Balafrej were respectively acting as spokesmen for these two groups.

The Sultan Muhammad V, chosen by the French to succeed his father Mawlay Youssef in 1927, was still young (seventeen years old), without experience, and representing no threat to the existing alliance that developed between the sultanate and the French colonial administration during his father's reign. During the early years of his rule, he remained loyal to France, and on occasions showed certain sympathy with the nationalist movement. In addition to the effective French control exercised over the dynasty, he also found himself deprived of his actual powers as a monarch. In other words, he was essentially little more than a figurehead.

In 1930 the sultan signed the Berber Decree (*dahir*), a French-inspired legal instrument aimed at replacing Islamic law (Shari'a) by the customary tribal law in

Berber-dominated areas. Viewed as a "divide and rule" measure, it was met with wider protests both in Morocco and in other parts of the Muslim world. Inside the country it was a turning point, particularly for the nationalist movement, which is believed to have come fully to life as a consequence. Indeed, this led the nationalists to organize themselves into a movement called the National Action Bloc and make the sultan more aware of and sensitive to their aspirations, initially through the celebration from 1933 of the anniversary of his accession to the throne.

A detailed program of reforms was drawn up by the nationalists and presented to the sultan, the French government, and the residency in 1934. Although not disputing the protectorate treaty, this program addressed the failures and abuses stemming from direct colonial administration. It called for the strict application of the treaty terms and measures of political, economic, and social nature to promote the well-being of the indigenous Moroccan population. To the chagrin of the nationalists, these somewhat moderate demands were not given any consideration by the French government either immediately or later, in the form of "urgent demands," when the Front Popular assumed power in France in May 1936.

From 1937 the nationalists embarked on a campaign aimed at mobilizing the masses to support their cause. The demonstrations of solidarity by the population in many cities and parts of the country were met with brutal repression from the colonial administration. The nationalist leaders were arrested and some of them, such as Al-Fassi and Muhammad Ouazzani, were sent into exile afterward. As a result, the nationalist activity came to be severely restricted in the French zone. A situation that was quite different in the Spanish zone where the nationalist movement, represented by the Party of National Reforms and the Party of Moroccan Unity, was under less repressive conditions.

With the outbreak of World War II the sultan made a public statement in which he expressed Morocco's support to France and its Allies. The nationalists were also supportive of the sultan's declaration. In 1942 the Allied forces landed in Morocco and Algeria. And this was to herald a new era in the development of the nationalist movement and its relationship with the sultanate. In his meeting with the U.S. President Franklin D. Roosevelt a year later, the sultan was assured of the American support for Moroccan independence. During the same year the nationalists reconstituted their party, which became the Istiqlal (Independence) Party. Having taken matters into their hands, they presented the French residency and the sultan with a manifesto calling for the country's independence in 1944. The immediate reaction of the French was to arrest some prominent nationalist leaders, accused of intelligence with the Germans. This attitude only contributed to persuade the sultan that Moroccan aspirations could not be achieved under the protectorate system.

The visit made to Tangier in 1947 and the emphasis on Morocco's Arab ties marked a turning point in the sultan's commitment to the cause of independence. In view of his growing disapproval of the protectorate, the French government made some concessions, allowing the participation of Moroccans in the council of government. But these concessions were attacked because they meant the maintenance of the colonial rule in the form of a shared sovereignty. The sultan's refusal to sign decrees restricting his country's sovereignty made him emerge as a symbol of Moroccan unity and the nation's leader in the struggle for independence. His declaration demanding full sovereignty to Morocco in 1952, and subsequent maneuvers of French officials with the collaboration of certain Moroccan religious and Berber notables, led to his deposition and deportation to Madagascar. But his exile made him a living martyr and turned him into a national hero.

The pressure from the nationalist movement and the armed resistance that had just started to operate from the Spanish zone prompted the French government to reinstate him in 1955. A year later, agreements signed successively with France and Spain ended the colonial occupation and recognized the independence of Morocco. The sultan, adopting the title of king from 1957, skillfully managed not only to portray the monarchy as the exclusive embodiment of the country's unity but also to impose it as the dominant political institution. After his death in 1961, his son, Mawlay Hasan II, succeeded him (1961–1999).

AHMED AGHROUT

See also: **Morocco: Hassan II: Life and Government of; Morocco: Mawlay Hasan and the Makhzen.**

Further Reading

Al-Alami, M. *Mohammed V: Histoire de l'indépendence du Maroc.* Salé: Editions API, 1980.

Al-Fassi, A. *The Independence Movements in Arab North Africa*, translated from the Arabic by H. Z. Nuseibah. Washington, D.C.: American Council of Learned Societies, 1954.

Ashford, D. E. *Political Change in Morocco.* Princeton, N.J.: Princeton University Press, 1961.

Attilio, G. *Allal el-Fassi; ou l'histoire de l'Istiqlal.* Paris: Editions Alain Moreau, 1972.

Halstead, J. *Rebirth of a Nation: The Origins and Rise of Moroccan Nationalism 1912–1944.* Cambridge, Mass.: Harvard University Press, 1967.

Landau, R. *Moroccan Drama.* London: Hale, 1956.

———. *The Sultan of Morocco.* London: Hale, 1951.

Laroui, A. *The History of the Maghrib: An Interpretive Essay.* Princeton, N.J.: Princeton University Press, 1977.

Morocco: Hassan II, Life and Government of

King of Morocco

Hassan II (1924–1999) shared with all monarchs of his dynasty, the Alawites (French, Alaouite), the title "Commander of the Believers," which signifies a claim to the office of caliph (*khalifa*), or successor of the Prophet Muhammad and head of Islam. As such, Hassan was also head (imam) of Islam in Morocco and presented himself as the pious preserver of Muslim values on most public occasions, both sacred holidays and monarchic events. The annual presentation of fealty by the Moroccan elite on Throne Day (March 3), including the Islamic notables of the country (*'ulama*) in an act of allegiance (the *bay'a)*, was the most notable of these public acts merging monarchy with Islamic authority. Hassan controlled religious authorities tightly; any hierarchy of Moroccan Islamic figures culminated in Hassan himself. In other roles in the sphere of Islam, Hassan commemorated himself through the construction (finished 1993) of the world's second largest mosque (after Mecca's), the Hassan II Mosque on the Atlantic coast in the heart of Casablanca. Hassan was also head of the Jerusalem Committee of the Organization of the Islamic Conference, which struggled to protect the Islamic sites in Jerusalem in the 1980s and 1990s.

As king of Morocco, Hassan, like his father, Mohammed V (d. February 26, 1961), used the Arabic *malik* (king) rather than sultan (head authority) to describe his capacity, the use of which was an innovation following independence from France in 1956. As head of state of the kingdom of Morocco, Hassan was the head of the *makhzen* (treasury*)*, what Moroccans traditionally have called their government. In this sense, Hassan, like all Alawite monarchs, was head administrator of state. Ultimately all customs, laws, activities, and policies of the Moroccan state were dependent upon Hassan's will. He was a monarch in the complete sense of the word; his powers were effectively limited only by his interests. It was in his interest, he felt, and in the interests of his Alawite descendants whom he felt were forever destined to rule Morocco, to divest power in a limited and orderly fashion to the national parliament, the prime minister and his cabinet, the judiciary, and civil authorities. Hassan built a slowly emerging, occasionally revoked, but generally broadening constitutional monarchy in which he withheld the right to intervene at key points and retain ultimate power.

Hassan was sixteenth in the line of the Alawite dynasty that has ruled over the Atlantic, Saharan, Mediterranean, and Atlas mountain dominions that in some configuration have made up the Moroccan state since the time of Alawite sultans Rashid (*r.*1664–1672) and Moulay Ismail (*r.*1672–1727). Hassan emphasized Alawite connections to the Prophet Muhammad, underlining his large family's lineal descent from the founder of Islam, and identifying (as had Alawite leaders before) their special status as *sharifs* (descendants of the Prophet) as a way of continuing the legitimacy of Alawite rule in the modern world. Further, as *sharif*, Hassan was held by the Moroccan population, Muslim and Jewish alike, to have a quality of divine grace (*baraka*) far greater and more powerful than most humans.

Hassan represented deep traditional Islamic values in a modernizing state confronting the problems endemic to most countries in the Middle East and North Africa, as well as the wider developing world: rapid population growth, limited capital investment, and high unemployment coupled with rising economic and social aspirations. In Morocco, Hassan's long reign saw a thoroughly colonial society gain a strong sense of Moroccan identity and nationhood. Relations with independent Algeria, socialist and antiroyalist, were generally poor, suffering an early low point in October 1963 in a still unresolved territorial dispute known as the "War of the Sands" over the southeastern Moroccan boundary and the ownership of Tindouf. A long stretch of disharmony with Algeria followed the audacious Moroccan acquisition of the Spanish Sahara after Hassan's repudiation of the decision by the International Court of Justice in favor of self-determination for the Sahrawi people and the "Green March" of 350,000 Moroccan civilians directly into the disputed territory in November 1975. Algeria's subsequent championship of the Polisario (Western Saharan liberation fighters) and the long-term civil unrest in Algeria led to bad and often bitter relations with Morocco's eastern neighbor throughout most of Hassan's reign.

Relations with France remained generally strong throughout Hassan's reign. Exceptions reveal the tightly interwoven relationship between the ex-colonial power and Morocco: 1965–1969, in the aftermath of the the Ben Barka affair; 1973, following the unexpected nationalization of remaining French farms and shops; the mid-1980s, when Danielle Mitterand (wife of French President Francois Mitterand) infuriated Hassan with her support of the Polisario; and the aftermath of the publication of Gilles Perrault's *Notre ami le roi* (1990). The last was an anti-Hassan exposé, which reported Hassan's heavy hand regarding domestic dissent; his role in the murder of the Moroccan opposition politician, Mehdi Ben Barka, in France in 1965 (probably with the collusion of the French administration); and the active role played by Hassan and the Alaouite family in the French economy (owner of a chain of supermarkets; part owner of Hachette publishing, etc.). Hassan held respect in France for his superb control of the French language, as great as his mastery of Arabic. He was held to be one of the great orators of modern times. Hassan maintained friendly relations with powerful leaders worldwide; among the mighty whom Hassan sheltered when they fell from grace were Reza Pahlavi, shah of Iran (1979); and Mobutu, president of Zaïre (Democratic Republic of Congo, 1998).

Hassan's African strategies reflected his jealous safeguarding of Moroccan strategic policies. In 1984 Hassan signed a treaty of unity with Libya in a deal whereby Muammar Gaddafi withdrew his support for the Polisario for a Moroccan guarantee not to send troops to support the French in Chad. The treaty was repudiated by Gaddafi in July 1986, when Hassan became the second Arab leader (after Sadat) to talk with Israel in a meeting with Prime Minister Shimon Peres at the Moroccan vacation town of Ifrane. In 1976 and 1977, Hassan sent Moroccan troops to protect Mobutu's regime from rebels moving from Angola into Shaba region in operations known as Shaba I and Shaba II. Hassan's links with Mobutu can be traced to their efforts to maintain high prices for cobalt, of which the two nations were the major producers outside the Soviet Union in the Cold War era. As he gained confidence in his own leadership, Hassan maintained excellent relations with Washington, D.C. (although not during the presidency of Jimmy Carter, who questioned American military support of Morocco's Saharan adventure), often playing a behind-the-scenes role in the Cold War.

Hassan's contributions lie first in his long survival as ruler and his skill in leading Moroccans through the thirty-eight years of his reign toward a generally improved quality of life; in his efforts to bring Israelis to talk with Palestinians, rooted in his sense of patriarchy as an Arab-Islamic ruler of the nearly half million Moroccan Jews, nearly all expatriated; and in the acquisition of the Western Sahara, nearly doubling the land size of Morocco and increasing its territorial sea by an even larger amount. By the end of his reign, Hassan had weathered economic riots (especially, 1965, 1981, 1984, and 1994) and contained political opposition, while maintaining a firm grip on the Western Sahara.

Hassan survived two coup attempts on his life. At Hassan's birthday party at the Royal Palace at Skhirat (on the coast just south of Rabat) in July 1971, army officers led by Generals Oufkir and Medbouh failed in their attempt to kill him and take the government. In 1972 Hasan survived an attempt by his own air force to shoot his jet down as he was returning from France. Upon his death, the adulation of the Moroccan people for him and his family was clear; whether this was seated in the fear of the unknown or not is a question that has in many ways been answered by the early strong public support accorded his son and successor, Mohammed VI.

JAMES A. MILLER

See also: **Morocco: International Relations since Independence; Polisario and the Western Sahara.**

Biography

Born in the Royal Palace in Rabat on July 9, 1929, son of Mohammed V (*r.*1927–1961) and Lalla Abla. Schooled at the Royal Palace by French and Moroccan governesses and tutors. Imperial College founded 1942 for his secondary education and that of his siblings. Attended Casablanca Conference (Roosevelt, Churchill, de Gaulle, and Mohammed V), January 1943. Studied law at Bordeaux, receiving law degree in 1952. Accompanied father and family into exile in Corsica and Madagascar, 1953–1955. Named crown prince, July 1957. Chief of Staff of Royal Armed Forces, 1957. Named deputy premier by Mohammed V, May 1960. Married Lalla Latifa upon accession to the throne, March 3, 1961. Children: Meriem, 1962; Mohammed (*b.* September 6, 1963; now Mohammed VI); Asma, 1965; Hasna, 1967; Moulay Rachid, 1968. Died July 23, 1999.

Further Reading

Hassan II. *The Challenge: Memoirs of King Hassan II of Morocco*, translated by A. Rhodes. London: Macmillan, 1978.

Kahn, E. J., Jr. "A Reporter at Large: The King and His Children." *The New Yorker*. July 9, 1984, 45–59.

Leveau, R. *Le Fellah marocain, défenseur du trône [The Moroccan Peasant, Defender of the Throne]*. Paris: Presses de la fondation nationale des sciences politiques, 1985.

Miller, J. A. "Hassan II." In *Political Leaders of the Contemporary Middle East and North Africa*, edited by B. Reich. New York: Greenwood Press, 1990.

Waterbury, J. *The Commander of the Faithful: The Moroccan Political Elite—A Study in Segmented Politics*. New York: Columbia University Press, 1970.

Zartman, I. W. *Destiny of a Dynasty: The Search for Institutions in Morocco's Developing Society*. Columbia, S.C.: University of South Carolina Press, 1964.

———. "King Hassan's New Morocco." In *The Political Economy of Morocco*, edited by I. W. Zartman. New York: Praeger, 1987.

Morocco: Education since Independence

During the years preceding independence, the education system established in Morocco cultivated an educated Moroccan elite. Although it claimed to be open to the majority of the population, many were not able to take advantage of it. When independence was achieved in 1955–1956, it was estimated that only 18 per cent of school age children were actually attending school.

The first step taken after independence to further education was to create the Ministry of National Education (MOE). The MOE was responsible for providing facilities, designing curricula and formulating and implementing the country's education policies. The ministry had divided the country into regional school districts headed by an administrator who reported to the central administration in the country's capital of Rabat. Almost immediately, the MOE attempted to add Moroccan and Arabic elements to the educational system. The primary goal was to replace expatriate French faculty with Moroccans.

Unfortunately, for the first twenty years after independence, this policy was unsuccessful. It was not until the mid-1970s that Moroccans filled positions as teachers. As of that point, the MOE intended to complete "Moroccanization" on the secondary level by 1990, although it has not yet been entirely accomplished.

The process of introducing Arabic into the school system was commenced at independence. Total Arabization was not scheduled to be completed until the mid-1990s. The process, however, has not been as successful as the newly formed government originally anticipated.

Since independence, pre-primary education has been introduced throughout Morocco. The majority of pre-primary education is given through mosque-controlled schools called *kouttabs*. It is estimated that during the school year 1984–1985, about 667,000 children took advantage of these schools, even though education is not compulsory until the primary level, at age seven. Of this number, approximately 188,000 were female students.

Compulsory education, starting on the primary level, is a five-year program based on the French model. The program stresses mathematics and language skills, both in Arabic and, starting in the third year, French. Enrollment has steadily increased on the primary level since Morocco achieved independence. In 1975–1976, there was a total enrollment of 1,475,000, with 35 percent of those students female. This number increased to approximately 2,408,000 in 1985–1986. The percentage of female enrollment has stayed about the same. It is estimated that only 37 per cent of the total number of children enrolled in primary schools in 1985–1986 were female, showing only a slight improvement in the male-female ratio.

The secondary system is almost identical to that setup by the French during the protectorate years. Enrollment in secondary schools is not as high as it is at the primary school level. This is due to the fact that many parents in rural regions do not feel it is necessary for women to be educated past the elementary level.

However, in spite of the obstacles presented by tradition, there has been a steady increase in enrollment in secondary schools by both male and female students. By 1975–1976, for example, there were about 141,000 females enrolled in high schools, which represented approximately 30 per cent of the total secondary school enrollment. By 1983–1984, this figure had increased to 40 per cent of the total enrollment. In addition to public and private bilingual schools, there are also a limited number of schools that offer what is known as common education in preparation for entrance to higher education specializing in Islamic studies. In 1987–1988, there were more than 13,500 students enrolled in these types of schools.

Higher education has always been an integral part of Morocco, going back to the ninth century when the Karaouine Mosque was established. The mosque school, known today as Al Qayrawaniyan University, became part of the state university system in 1947. Up until 1989, it was part of six independent universities that made up Morocco's higher educational system. In 1989 university status was given to various other institutions that had previously been attached to the original six.

Besides the numerous universities, there is also another major area of higher education: technological and scientific institutions. These offer more vocational instruction in comparison to the academics that are found in the universities. All universities are technically supervised by the Ministry of National Education; however, they act independently, with each having its own administration and budget.

Enrollment has also increased at the university level. In 1963–1964 there were 7,310 Moroccans enrolled in higher educational programs. By 1987–1988, the number of students was estimated to be 157,484. This great expansion is due to the vast amounts of money that have been earmarked each year for the creation of advanced higher learning. All schools, except for those that are private, are funded entirely by the Moroccan government. According to one study, the MOE has received about 19 per cent of the state's national budget, which is about 6 per cent of the GDP.

One particular problem in the educational field that confronted Morocco was Berber education. The Berbers were the original and indigenous people of the Mahgreb region, and their influence was felt much more so in Morocco than in Tunisia. Sixty percent of the population spoke the Berber language in Morocco versus less than 1 per cent in Tunisia. Arabic, as well as French, was a foreign language to them, especially to those children in the rural regions. The policy under the French was to actually incorporate as many of the Berbers into their program of acculturation as possible. Education was to be extended to them; however, instruction would only be offered in French, as the new administration wanted to maintain a policy of separation between the Arabs and the Berbers.

In addition, the education of the Berbers was a sensitive political issue. The French regarded the Berbers as a group that needed "taming," which, they believed, could be accomplished initially through educating the children, who would in turn influence their parents. In 1930 the French issued the famous Berber Dahir, which was intended to isolate the Berber from the Moroccan

Arab. The idea behind this policy was to eventually create a group that would identify more with the French than with the Moroccan Arabs and Islam. Berber-only schools were opened, such as the Azrou. However, it was proved extremely difficult to deny entry to those that spoke Arabic. There were demands for Arab-speaking Bebers in many areas, especially the bureaucratic offices. The dream of a Franco-Berber education as envisioned by the French would never come to pass.

It was estimated that there were approximately 27,000 children in school out of a population of 900,000 school-aged children by 1940, approximately 3 per cent of the population. In 1946 a new resident general, Labonne, felt that these statistics were not satisfactory. He issued a mandate that, within two months, significant steps should be made toward opening more schools. The results were unprecedented: 383 schools were set up in the following two months, accommodating 19,000 children. An example of the push to create more schools and reach the indigenous population can be seen in the Benahmed region where there were only 160 children in 3 schools in 1940. Within a ten-year period, this figure rose to 1,575 children in 21 schools. This illustration was indicative of what happened throughout Morocco in the field of education.

BARBARA DEGORGE

Further Reading

Bidwell, R. *Morocco Under Colonial Rule, French Administration of Tribal Areas 1912–1956.* London: Frank Cass, 1973.

Davies, E. D., and A. Bentahila. "Morocco." In *Handbook of World Education: A Comparative Guide to Higher Education and Educational Systems of the World.* Houston: American Collegiate Service, 1991.

Ling, D. L. *Morocco and Tunisia: A Comparative History.* Washington, D.C.: University Press of America, 1979.

Massialas, P. "Morocco." In *World Education Encyclopedia,* edited by G. T. Kurian. New York: Facts on File Publications, 1988.

Morocco: Economics and Social Change since Independence

Unlike most countries in Africa, Morocco was not a colonial creation but rather a country with a long precolonial history and identity of its own to draw on. This was advantageous when it came to national and social unity, and the hoped for postindependence growth. Additionally, the effects of colonial rule on the country were less significant than on its neighbors due to the relative brevity of and limits to colonial rule: forty-five years as a French protectorate. On gaining independence in 1956, therefore, the country had to "rework" its social system, rather than having to create one. To the country's benefit, there was a solid economic infrastructure in place in 1956, including road and rail transport and port facilities. Casablanca alone was responsible for handling more than 80 per cent of Morocco's trade at that time. When King Muhammad V returned from exile, he immediately called for the constitution of an elected and representative government. However, there was no real system of government in place when independence was gained (palace aside) and so the king, who was extremely popular, became the de facto ruler with more power than had been possible when he had been Sultan.

Many Moroccans imagined that the end of the protectorate would mean that they would become wealthy overnight. They were soon disabused of this idea as the country's debt initially soared, primarily due to the fact that the country was now responsible for many expenses that the French had previously paid, such as defense, diplomacy, education, and public services. When French aid to Morocco was cut, the shortfall was made up by the United States who was paying 40 per cent of Morocco's development budget by the early 1960s.

Morocco's lack of significant natural resources has proved to be a hindrance to large-scale, postindependence economic development. The country's hydrocarbon reserves for example are tiny: 2,000 figures show the country managing to produce an average of less than 1,000 barrels of oil per day, compared to Algeria's 1,253,000 and Libya's 1,400,000. On the other hand, Morocco is estimated to hold approximately 75 per cent of the world's phosphate reserves, production of which even in the early 1950s amounted to 4 million tons per annum. Before independence, however, the wealth produced was controlled by a small number of Europeans and an even smaller number of Moroccans.

Agriculturally Morocco has always been fairly strong, with none of the water problems that affect other North Africa countries, due in part to the snow capped Atlas Mountains. In 1956, 70 per cent of the population relied on agriculture. A succession of three- and five-year plans were tried but frequently abandoned as the economy wasn't strong enough to sustain them for their full term. In 1973, when Morocco was the world's largest exporter of phosphates, the international price of phosphates tripled. The government spent the windfall on food subsidies for the cities and on enormous irrigation schemes that led to significant increases in cultivatable land, although without managing to make the country self-sufficient in foodstuffs as the majority of produce were exotic goods for export. Since 1960 Morocco has been a net importer of cereals. In 1974 phosphate prices collapsed and the economy disintegrated as inflation rose steeply. With growing trade deficits an IMF loan was secured in exchange for the promise of bringing the economy back under control.

Many workers left the country for Europe and better salaries (in excess of 1.3 million), sending a proportion of their earnings home. Those who did not make it as far as Europe swelled Morocco's urban centers, depleting the rural workforce so that agricultural production failed to keep up with increased demand due to population growth, or increases in the cost of living. This movement to the cities and a growing population led to health facilities falling behind growth on an annual basis, even though life expectancy has risen significantly since independence and is now at sixty-seven years of age. During the same period the rural population fell from 80 per cent to 45 per cent.

An Association Accord signed with the European Union in 1996 was aimed at promoting free trade, with Morocco gradually dismantling tariffs and customs duties on industrial imports from the EU over a twelve-year period, starting in 2000. The EU promised transitional aid to support economic modernization and agreed to maintain access for Morocco's traditional agricultural exports at their current levels. Morocco wanting full membership in the EU, first applied to join in 1987; in the meantime it is the largest recipient of EU financial aid.

The importance of education was realized immediately at independence, with the government espousing free and universal primary education. A program to make more places available in higher education was also put in place, especially for vocational training in everything from agriculture to the chemical industry in recognition of the country's two greatest economic possibilities. Great strides have been made but Morocco's literacy rate remains poor at under 50 per cent. Female illiteracy is still nearly double that of males and while urban school attendance figures were recently reported to be over 90 per cent, in rural areas they are as low as 63.

The role of women in Moroccan society is perhaps the most obvious change since independence. Women too fought for independence and the King encouraged a greater role for them in the new Morocco. The 1962 constitution states that men and women must have equal political rights and additionally that all citizens have equal rights to education and employment, although there is some resistance to the employment of women from Islamist conservatives and other traditionalists. However, there is no doubt that women have attained a prominence unimaginable forty years ago. Women have also been helped in this forward movement by the promotion of full literacy and the need across the country for more professionals.

One of the country's biggest challenges today is unemployment, which official figures put at more than 22 per cent and rising. The fear is that apart from the economic strain that this puts on the country there is always the chance that, if there is little hope for employment in the near future, those who feel disaffected and disenfranchised, especially the young, may turn to the Islamists and their promise of a better world. The May 2003 bombings in Casablanca are just the sort of incidents that support the government calls for greater assistance from the international community in their fight against terrorism.

EAMONN GEARON

See also: **Colonialism, Overthrow of: Women and the Nationalist Struggle; Morocco: Education since Independence; Morocco: Nationalism, Muhammad V, Independence, 1930–1961.**

Further Reading

Bourqia, R. and S. G. Miller (eds.). *In the Shadow of the Sultan: Culture, Power, and Politics in Morocco*. Cambridge: Harvard University Press, 1999.

Charrad, M. "State and Gender in the Maghrib." *Middle East Report.* (March–April 1990): 19–24.

Denoeuz, G. P. "Morocco's Economic Prospects: Daunting Challenges Ahead." *Middle East Policy.* 8, no. 2 (June 2001): 66–87.

Layachi, A. (ed.). *Economic Crisis and Political Change in North Africa.* Westport, Conn.: Praeger, 1998.

Pennell, C. R. *Morocco since 1830: A History.* New York: New York University Press, 2000.

Spencer, C. *The Maghreb in the 1990s: Political and Economic Developments in Algeria, Morocco, and Tunisia.* London: International Institute for Strategic Studies, 1993.

Morocco: International Relations since Independence

Independence did not mean that Morocco was economically independent of foreign (French) landowners, money, and assistance. Breaking diplomatic relations with France at the time of the Suez Crisis, for example, caused Morocco the loss of all financial aid from France—a not insubstantial sum. Franco-Moroccan relations were again strained during the Algerian war of independence, as the Algerian cause received broad support in Morocco. That said, Moroccan foreign policy since independence has tended to forge closer, though not trouble-free, relationships with other North African and European nations rather than with the Arab world or Africa.

In the last decade of the twentieth century links between Morocco and Europe grew steadily stronger, with the former being most voluble in its desire for ever-closer ties with the European Union. In 2002 more than 60 per cent of Morocco's exports went to Europe; the country was also the biggest recipient of EU development aid, and most cash remittances back into the country come from its nationals living and working across Europe. In 2002 Morocco began to implement an EU association accord that should establish tariff-free trade between Morocco and the EU by 2012. Morocco's head of state, King Muhammad VI, has even gone so far as to say that he would like future agreements to lead to complete freedom of movement for both labor and goods. One important concession the Moroccans have gained so far is a decision by Italy to cancel Morocco's debt to them, which was worth more than $100 million.

Relations between the United States and Morocco in the immediate postindependence period were somewhat strained due to the continued presence of a number of American airbases on Moroccan soil at a time when many in the country wished to forge closer links with the Middle East through the organization of the Arab League. Toward the end of 1959, frustrated by endless negotiations about their military presence, the United States announced that it would close all its bases (except the naval base at Kentira) within five years. Morocco lost financially as a result, but the nationalists claimed a victory against imperialism. During the Cold War, Morocco attempted to follow a path of nonalignment, straining relations at the national and international level in the process. When Morocco requested that U.S. supply aircraft with which to start a national air force, the Americans said no; the Moroccans swiftly found their order filled by the Soviet Union.

In 1991 Morocco sent 1,200 troops to Saudi Arabia in support of the war against Iraq, a decision that was not popular domestically and led to rioting in every major city. The strength of feeling surprised the regime but did not alter government policy. Since his accession in 1999, Muhammad VI has continued to place importance on closer relations with the United States, perhaps even more than his father did. A visit by the king to the United States in 2000, and strong condemnation of the September 11, 2001, attacks, helped bring the two countries closer together. The May 2003 bombings in Casablanca served to bring Morocco even closer to the United States and the undeclared war on Islamic fundamentalists.

Relations between Morocco and its neighbors have been most tense, and closer than ever, since independence. Most of this tension has come about as a result of Moroccan (and sometime Mauritanian) claims to what was Spanish (Western) Sahara. In 1973 the Polisario was formed in order (their manifesto stated) to establish an independent state there, a claim supported by the United Nations. Morocco took matters into its own hands in November 1975, when more than 500,000 civilians took part in the "Green March," and simply marched over the border and into the Saharan territory. The following year, the Polisario declared the independence of the Saharan Arab Democratic Republic and began a guerrilla war with Algerian support. Following a defeat by the Polisario, the Moroccan government took a new approach to the Western Sahara and, with Saudi backing, built a wall around the desert areas they claimed were theirs.

A UN-monitored ceasefire has been in effect, with countless incursions, since 1991, but the status of the territory is far from settled. Contracts allowing foreign oil companies to explore offshore Western Sahara, which Morocco sanctioned, are also on hold. In 2001 Muhammad VI went on a tour of Western Sahara, adopting the strong nationalist line that has over the years provided the monarchy with some of its strongest support. It was also as a result of support for an independent Western Sahara on the part of the Organization of African Unity (OAU) that Morocco resigned from the organization in 1982. Since coming to power, Muhammad VI has been following a path that retains all claims to the territory, while trying to move away from the referendum that was supposed to allow the local population to settle the issue once and for all.

Because of the Israeli-Palestinian issue, Morocco has at different times been in and out of favor across the region and the Arab world at large. Keen to maintain ties with oil-rich Saudi Arabia, Morocco sent troops to fight in the Six Day War (they did not arrive in time) and to the Golan Heights and Sinai in 1973. When claims to the Western Sahara seemed more important to the country, Morocco changed tack, attempting to gain favor for its territorial claims by sending a delegation of Moroccan Jews to America and by staging meetings between Israeli and Arab leaders in advance of Sadat's Jerusalem visit in 1977. Such actions certainly helped improve Moroccan-American relations, though not those with other Arab nations, although the old king never recognized Israel and always supported Palestinian claims. The importance of Hassan's role as mediator, however, was obvious by the attendance of both the Israeli president and prime minister at his funeral and the significant Jewish minority in Morocco may hope that Muhammad continues his father's example.

Morocco's immediate future would logically seem to involve closer ties with Europe, before world trade passes the country by. At the same time, it remains equally important that the country's Maghrebi cousins are not alienated; the 2003 Casablanca bombings might perhaps serve as a reminder to Morocco that such links with those of a similar background can help to foster greater security and strength in the region.

EAMONN GEARON

See also: **Polisario and the Western Sahara**

Further Reading

Brown, L. C. *Diplomacy in the Middle East: The International Relations of Regional and Outside Powers*. London and New York: I. B. Tauris, 2001.

Damis, J. *Conflict in Northwest Africa: The Western Sahara Dispute*. Stanford: Hoover Institution Press, 1983.
Hurewitz, J. C. (ed.). *The Middle East and North Africa in World Politics: A Documentary Record*. 2nd ed. New Haven: Yale University Press, 1975.
Morocco. London: Economist Intelligence Unit, 2003.
Mercer, J. *Spanish Sahara*. London: George Allen and Unwin, 1976.
Pazzanita, A. G., and T. Hodges. *Historical Dictionary of Western Sahara*. 2nd ed. Metuchen, N. J.: Scarecrow Press, 1994.
Pennell, C. R. *Morocco since 1830: A History*. New York: New York University Press, 2000.

Moshoeshoe I and the Founding of the Basotho Kingdom

Moshoeshoe (1786–1870) was the name taken by Lepoqo, son of Kholu and her husband Mokhachane, headman of the small village of Menkhoaneng in the valley of the Caledon River, which today forms the northern boundary between South Africa and Lesotho. While the year of his birth cannot be precisely fixed, 1786 is the date accepted by modern scholars. During his long life he laid the foundations of the Kingdom of Lesotho and died acknowledged as the father of his people, the man who defended their land against the encroachment of European settlers.

His family was not especially important, though a number of stories relate that he was marked out by the influential chief Mohlomi as a man destined for greatness. As a young man he acquired the nickname Moshoeshoe (pronounced "muh-shwee-shwee"), a word suggesting the sound made by the shaving of a sharp razor. This commemorated his skill as a cattle raider who could steal animals as swiftly and silently as a razor shaves hair. His opportunity to found a kingdom came when the Caledon River valley was convulsed in the 1820s by a series of wars which smashed existing political authorities—a period retrospectively named by historians the *lifaqane* or *difaqane*. From the west Kora and Griqua raiders with horses and guns penetrated the Caledon Valley, wreaking widespread havoc as they seized cattle and children. To the north of Moshoeshoe's village, the Tlokwa people, led by Queen Regent 'MaNtatisi and her son Sekonyela, became involved in wars with Hlubi and Ngwane chieftaincies from the neighboring KwaZulu-Natal region. These culminated in Hlubi and Ngwane invasions of the Caledon Valley in the early 1820s and a general reorientation of allegiances. Moshoeshoe emerged as an effective leader who gathered the remnants of many small groups together on the hilltop fortress of Botha-Bothe (sometimes Buthe-Buthe) in or about the year 1822. Here he successfully withstood a siege by Sekonyela's forces. In 1824 he moved his people to a more secure position, on the hilltop of Thaba Bosiu, which he defended against successive waves of attackers.

For the rest of the 1820s Moshoeshoe's primary concern was to restock his herds. Some he acquired by raiding south of the mountains into the territory of the Thembu and the Xhosa. Some he acquired by lending cows to his followers, who were allowed to milk them, while pledging that any calves that might be born would belong to the chief's herds. It was at this time that the name BaSotho (or Basuto) first began to be generally applied to Moshoeshoe's people. As his power grew, he formed new alliances, many of them cemented by marriages (his wives numbered more than 140 by the time of his death). The great accomplishment of this period was his displacement of his rival, Makhetha, who had a much better claim to inherited chieftainship. Makhetha perhaps unwisely allied himself to the Ngwane chief Matiwane and undertook a series of raids into Xhosa territory, where they were routed by a combined force of Xhosa, Thembu, and British forces. By the early 1830s Moshoeshoe had all but eliminated his rival.

The next period of Moshoeshoe's career is distinguished by the alliance he forged with Protestant missionaries of the Paris Evangelical Missionary Society whose first agents arrived in 1833. Well aware of the defeats inflicted on the Xhosa and other peoples on the eastern frontier of the Cape Colony, Moshoeshoe was pleased to have men at his capital who could communicate in writing with Cape authorities. He encouraged them to found mission stations throughout the territory he controlled. The missionaries welcomed his protection and wrote glowing tributes to his statesmanship, though they never converted him to their religion. They took his side in his wars against Sekonyela and other military rivals. During these years Moshoeshoe became increasingly powerful, partly because Sotho people who had fled to the Cape Colony during the wars of the 1820s now returned with cattle, horses, and guns they had bought with money earned working on farms. Moshoeshoe adopted a partially European lifestyle and set out consciously to modernize his kingdom by modifying many customs and traditions. He built a formidable military force armed with guns, whose centerpiece was a well-drilled cavalry.

A new chapter opened with the arrival of the first Voortrekkers (Afrikaans-speaking settlers from the Cape Colony) in 1836. Moshoeshoe took at face value their statement that they sought nothing more than safe passage through his territories. Soon, however, they began to settle near important sources of water, often claiming to have bought land from rival chiefs. In 1843, in a bid for British protection against the invaders, Moshoeshoe concluded a treaty with Governor Napier of the Cape Colony that he hoped would lay down firm boundaries. However, in 1848, a new Cape governor, Sir Harry Smith, annexed the entire region of "Transorangia." British Resident Henry Warden fixed a new boundary line that removed most BaSotho land north of the Caledon. This led directly to a war in which Moshoeshoe's forces decisively triumphed at the Battle of Viervoet Mountain in June 1851. Not long after, Britain decided to transfer the Orange River Sovereignty to an independent Boer government. General Sir George Cathcart determined to reassert British power by attacking Thaba Bosiu in December 1852, but it was Cathcart's forces who learned firsthand what a determined resistance could be mounted by the disciplined BaSotho cavalry.

After the British withdrawal, Moshoeshoe was left to his own devices in dealing with the government of the Orange Free State. He triumphed in the first war of 1858, but was facing defeat in the long second war (1865–1868) when Britain intervened to save the kingdom by annexing it as the Crown Colony of Basutoland. Not long after the annexation, Moshoeshoe died, on March 11, 1870, revered by friend and foe alike as one of Africa's greatest statesmen.

NORMAN A. ETHERINGTON

See also: **Boer Expansion: Interior of South Africa; Difaqane on the Highveld; Lesotho: Treaties and Conflict on the Highveld, 1843–1868.**

Further Reading

Eldredge, E. A. *A South African Kingdom: The Pursuit of Security in Nineteenth-Century Lesotho*. New York: Cambridge University Press, 1993.

Ellenberger, D. F. *History of the Basuto, Ancient and Modern*. London: Caxton, 1912.

Hamilton, C. (ed.). *The Mfecane Aftermath: Reconstructive Debates in Southern African History*. Johannesburg: Witwatersrand University Press, 1995.

Sanders, P. *Moshoeshoe: Chief of the Sotho*. London: Heinemann, 1975.

Thompson, L. M. *Survival in Two Worlds: Moshoeshoe of Lesotho 1786–1870*. Oxford: Clarendon Press, 1975.

Mosque, Sub-Saharan: Art and Architecture of

The aesthetic features of the Sub-Sahara mosque owe their origins to three primary religious, cultural, and historical interpretations. First, the institution of the Friday congregational prayer, a legal Islamic requirement for all men. Second, the efficacy of vernacular building traditions, especially in relation to the Muslim Mande, Fulani, and Hausa. These three ethnolingustic groups are among the dominant Muslim populations who inhabit Sub-Sahara West Africa; they were most influential and played an active role in the cultural web of interactions, trade, diaspora, and the early nineteenth-century jihad movements.

The third explanation is more closely related to the history of Sub-Saharan medieval dynasties, that is, the Ghana, Mali, Songhay dynasties, and the later nineteenth-century Sokoto and Tukulor Caliphates. Each dynasty played host to the formation of architectural traditions in Sub-Sahara Africa. During the reign of Mansa Musa, the fourteenth-century ruler of Mali best known for his pilgrimage (*hajj*) to Makkah, Arabia (1324–1325), religious and educational buildings were constructed at Gao and Timbuktu. Upon his return to Mali, Mansa Musa brought an entourage of scholars from the Muslim world, among whom was an Andalusian architect and poet, Ibn Ishaq as-Sahili (d.1346 in Mali). As-Sahili is reputed to have introduced a "Sudanese" style of architecture in West Africa through the commissions granted to him by Mansa Musa. Scholars have since expressed doubt as to whether the architectural works of as-Sahili were single-handedly achieved.

A number of indigenous factors have contributed to the formation of the Sub-Sahara mosque in general and the aesthetic nuances that we find in the Mande, Fulani, and Hausa mosques in particular.

The Mande Mosque

The Mande, and in particular the Dyula, carried Islam southward from the northern savannah to the forest verges in the late eleventh and early twelfth centuries. They also carried the basic forms of the hypo-style mosque that can be found at Timbuktu, Djenne, Mopti, and San (Mali); Bobo Dialasso (Upper Volta); Kong and Kawara (Côte d'Ivoire); and Larabanga (northern Ghana). These religious edifices are a particular style of rectangular clay building, hypo-style in plan, and uniquely idiomatic in their exterior character. Formal modifications occur in the features of the mosque as it travels from north to south, from Timbuktu to the Côte d'Ivoire and northern Ghana; these modifications pertain to size scale, structure, construction details, and variations in the plan.

Compacted earth construction is used consistently with lateral timber members to reinforce the exterior walls. Protruding timber members also act as scaffolding. The exterior walls are also strengthened by buttressing or with vertical ribs. The ribs also give the appearance of decorative crenellations, termite mounds, or ancestral pillars of varying size as they terminate at the parapet. Wider ribs on the exterior facade and in the center of the qibla-wall correspond to minarets. The flat roofs are reinforced with wooden joists; this is where the *muadhhin* stands to summon the faithful to prayer (*adhan*). The courtyard (*sahn*) is quite small or virtually nonexistent in Sub-Sahara mosques.

The Mande distinguish three functional types of mosques: (1) the *seritongo* used by individuals or small groups of Muslims for daily prayers, simply an area of ground marked off by stones; (2) the *misijidi* (*masjid*), *missiri*, or *buru* serves several households for their daily prayers or for Friday prayers; (3) the *jamiu*, *juma*, or *missiri-jamiu* used for Friday prayers, which serves the large community.

The Fulani Mosque at Dingueraye

Amid the fervor of the nineteenth-century jihad movement in the Futa Jalon, Guinea, a unique idiom and expression of mosque architecture was born. The Fulani mosque at Dingueraye is linked to Al Hajj Umar's (Umar ibn Uthman al-Futi al-Turi al Kidiwi, 1794–1864) stay at Dingueraye from 1849 to 1853 and served one of the principal functions of a *ribat*, a place from which the abode of Islam (*dar-al-Islam*) might expand.

The Fulani mosque at Dingueraye was the first instance in which the nomadic tent and the organization of nomadic space lent themselves with the greatest of ease to a new mode of spatial orientation. Two modes of spatial orientation are evident: The first is an ambulatory space that surrounds a cube building, the actual mosque. The outer layer of the spatial enclosure is very much like the Fulani sedentary hut enclosed by a palisade wall, which demarcates an edge. In the nomadic tradition this circular space is quite evident. According to local custom at Digueraye this outer layer is changed every seven years, at which time an elaborate ceremony is held for the occasion.

The second layer of space is the cube itself, which has heavy earthen walls and an earthen ceiling supported by rows of columns. A central post supports the exterior roof structure from within the cube, like a great big tree it radiates to its outer roof. But the central post, the perimeter columns, and the thatched roof dome are structurally separate from the earthen cube within.

The mosque at Mamou and Dabola, Guinea, also has central posts that support the roof of the cube. Its inner cube has singular openings in the perimeter wall very much like the openings in Umar's sketch. The position of the central post at Dingueraye and Mamou also approximates to the central element in Umar's diagram. These spatial patterns, the elements they employ, and the image they convey can be described simply as cultural metaphors. They are also concrete renditions of Fulani spatial concepts.

The Hausa Mosque at Zaria

The mosque at Zaria was built at the end of a period of puritanical fever (jihad) and reform, and during a period of religious formation wherein the Sokoto caliphate united the Hausa states under the leadership of Uthman ibn Fodio. In the post-jihad period the ascetic scholars mainly favored the building of mosques.

None of the earlier works of Babban Gwani, a great master builder, match the architectural vitality and structural vocabulary of the vault in the Zaria mosque. However, it is very unlikely that the Babban Gwani actually invented the Hausa vault, but there is no doubt that he made the greatest and boldest use of the vault. It is very likely that Katsina, being at the forefront of Hausa custom and civilization in the sixteenth and seventeenth centuries had developed the vault principles in reinforced earth technology. However, there are hardly any extant pre-jihad structures to support this hypothesis.

Professor Labelle Prussin argues that the vault is actually a synthesis of the Fulani tent armature, which was developed using Hausa skills in earth construction. The Hausa vault and dome are based on a completely different structural principle from the North African, Roman-derived stone domes. On the other hand, the Hausa domes incorporate, in nascent form, the same structural principles that govern reinforced concrete design. The bent armature in tension takes the horizontal thrust normally resisted by buttresses and tension rods and interacts with the compressive quality of earth. It was the development of this technology that permitted the transplantation of the symbolic imagery of Islam and in turn created a unique Fulani-derived architecture.

The increase in earth arch construction was particularly innovative in the post-jihad mosque at Zaria and the palaces of the period. The earth-reinforced pillars and the reinforced Hausa vaults are no commonplace construction. Very few pre-jihad buildings exhibit the structural solutions to an architectural problem of earth construction over such large spans. A more obvious solution can be found in the hypo-style mosques of Bauchi, or the Shehu mosque, Sokoto. Instead, given the program to provide a liturgical space, Babban Gwani in his organizing principle of geometry and structure derived a much more sophisticated and less formal plan than the hypo-style hall.

In determining the ceiling-type for a given building, the importance of the building, followed by the status of the patron, is brought together with the skill of the master mason. In context, a radical departure seems to have occurred from the simple trabeated type of construction which we find in the Shehu's mosque, the Kazuare mosque, and the Bauchi mosque, all built roughly in the same period (1820s) and the much later Zaria mosque (1836). The post and beam structure used to support short spans is quite commonly used in the earlier mosques, that is, Bauchi, and Shehu. They share a tradition with the Mande mosques of Mali and northern Ghana.

Akel Ismail Kahera

Further Reading

David, N. "The Fulani Compound and the Archaeologist." *World Archaeology*. 3, no. 2 (October 1971): 111–131.

Denyer, S. *African Traditional Architecture.* New York: Heineman, 1978.

Engestrom, T. "Origin of Pre-Islamic Architecture in West Africa." *Ethnos.* 24 (1959): 64–69.

Gardi, R. *Indigenous African Architecture.* New York: Van Nostrand Reinhold, 1973.

Leary, A. H. "A Decorated Palace in Kano." *AARP.* (December 1977): 11–17.

Moughtin, J. C. *Hausa Architecture.* London: Ethnographica, 1985.

Moughtin, J. C., and A. J. Leary. "Hausa Mud Mosque." *Architectural Review.* 137/818 (February 1965): 155–158.

Prussin, L. "The Architecture of Islam in West Africa." *African Arts.* 1, no. 2 (1968).

———. "Fulani-Hausa Architecture: Genesis of a Style." *African Arts.* 10, no. 1 (October 1976): 8–19; 97–98.

———. *Hatumere: Islamic Design in West Africa.* Berkeley: University of California Press, 1986.

———. "Islamic Architecture in West Africa: The Foulbe and Manding Models." *VIA.* 5 (1982): 52–69; 106–107.

Saad, H. T. "Between Myth and Reality: The Aesthetics of Traditional Architecture in Hausaland." Ph.D. diss., University of Michigan, 1981.

Moyen-Congo: *See* Congo (Brazzaville), Republic of: Colonial Period: Moyen-Congo.

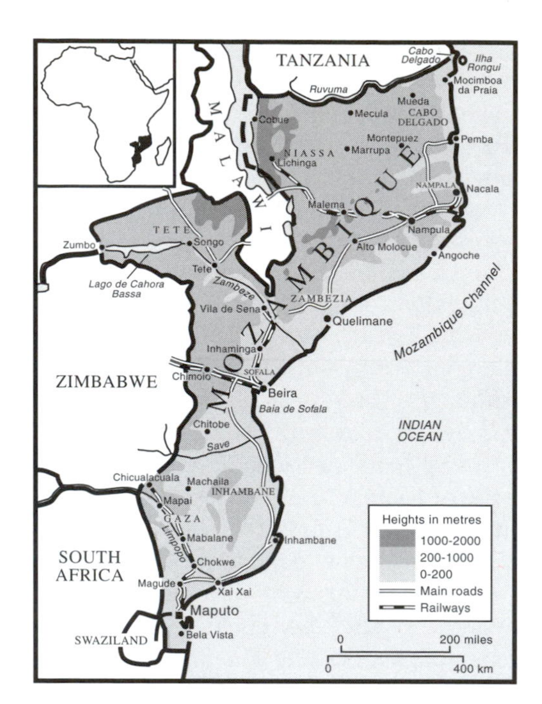

Mozambique.

Mozambique: Nineteenth Century, Early

Around 1800 most of the territory that was to be delimited as the Portuguese overseas province or colony of Mozambique later that century (mainly between 1869 and 1891) was the domain of independent African states. The Portuguese territory was a string of settlements with surrounding rural estates on the coast and on the Zambezi. Portugal maintained an administrative center on the island of Mozambique and garrisons at Ibo, Quelimane, Sofala, Inhambane, and Lourenço Marques (now Maputo) on the coast and Sena and Tete on the Zambezi. Intermittently the trade posts of Macequece (Manica) and Zumbo (now Feira, in present-day southeastern Zambia) also had garrisons until 1835, when they were withdrawn owing to threats of attacks and lack of funds to sustain them. Except around Lourenço Marques, which had only been occupied definitively in 1799 or 1800 and only counted military and civilian government servants until about 1815, the settlements were composed mainly of civil populations of local, Indian, and European origin. They were surrounded in 1800 by areas of estates where inhabitants of the Portuguese towns grew some of their food and maintained many of their slaves who seemed to have constituted up to two thirds of the permanent population of the settlements. Except for the fort of Lourenço Marques and the outposts of Macequece and Zumbo, the settlements had municipal status and the free citizens elected a municipal chamber, and a justice of peace, sometimes in conflict with the local military governor. Soldiers were mostly locally recruited and some literate youths held secretarial jobs and were trained as officers.

Regarding commerce and trade, imports of textiles and other trade goods where paid mainly from the sale of slaves and ivory. Ivory went mostly to western India, where most of the imported cotton textiles and some of the beads for trade were obtained. Slaves were exported mainly to Brazil and French possessions (Mascareignes and the Caribbean) and from about 1837 to Spanish colonies such a Cuba. Some food staples were imported from neighboring African mainland territories and the islands of Comoro and Madagscar.

Interruptions of the trade caused by Napoleonic Wars, a temporary Brazilian import ban on slavery (effective 1831 to *c.*1836), the general trade depression of 1831–1833, and interference with Portuguese Indian merchant vessels as parts of the activity of the British antislavery campaign around 1840–1845 caused crises in the activity of local Portuguese and Banian (*Vanya*) traders. Loss of capital around 1845, its emigration around 1831–1845 paved the way to trade capital from Bombay to take a lead in Mozambique in the 1850s and for new elephant hunters and traders from the metropolis and Goa.

In the interior, African chiefs consolidated lineage states. Examples are Cee Nyambe Mataka I in Niassa, who may have started around 1825–1830 Mwaliya near Montepuez in the 1790s, Ossiwa in Alto Molocue somewhere in nineteenth century, the Khosa, Dzovo Mondlane, and the Makwakwas in modern Gaza around

1810, Yingwane and Bila-nkulu near Inhambane possibly from 1780 onward. Those in the south were overtaken by the impact of the *mfecane* and foundation of new states like Gaza after 1821. Near the Zambezi, descendants of traders and military officers like the Caetano Pereiras and Cruz (Bonga) who had settled in African communities the hinterland of the Portuguese estate in the later eighteenth century area emerged around 1840 as local power holders, often at the cost of local dynasties like Undi. The successors to earlier states like the Mutapa, Barue, and Uteve states maintained their internal cleavages although some candidates occasionally managed to obtain a more prominent position.

The relatively extensive coverage of local events by sources permits us to trace some major droughts and famines as result of events related to the phenomenon of el Niño around 1745–1760, 1790, 1818–1833, 1844–1845, 1855–1862, in addition to Red Locust invasions mainly during the el Niño periods, as well as smallpox and measle epidemics. This and the effects of warfare during the *mfecane* are supposed to have had such an effect on the population that Gaza King Soshangane was said to have ordered in 1845 to stop the export of slave from his domains.

The independence of Brazil from Portugal in 1822 inspired a revolt of soldiers on December 16, 1822, in the island capital but had few other consequences. From the point of view of Portuguese administration the most significant event ending the period of absolutist rule in the shape of the populist dictatorship of D. Miguel (*c.*1826–1834) was the successful liberal revolution in Portugal of 1833–1834. It happened to take place during one of the trade crises toward the end of a long period of famines, when local revenues were down and no budget support came from Portugal. Local liberals deposed and substituted governors and imprisoned of some of the most able qualified representatives of the former government. The shortage of priests increased because the new regime also abolished religious orders, retaining the parish priests on the payroll of the crown. The effect of the trade crisis of 1831–1834 is highlighted by two events in the south. The governor of Lourenço Marques, Dionísio Ribeiro, had been executed at the orders of Zulu king Dingane in October 1833. He had been reluctant to meet the Zulu kings demands of tribute from his own stores and of a private trading company. There had been no trade and almost no government funds to sustain the garrison. A year later the governor Manuel da Costa of Inhambane was killed with most of the soldiers and able bodied men from Inhambane (apparently some 280 to 1,000 men) on a foray to recover impounded ivory at a distance of about 150 to 250 kilometers from Inhambane. The settlement itself was never approached by raiders, unlike Sofala, which was attacked by Nguni chief Nqaba in 1836. As a result attempts were made to build or repair fortifications around the main Portuguese settlements except Quelimane. (The governor of Sofala eventually shifted his administrative capital to the island of Chiloane.)

For the next decade and a half after the liberal revolution of 1834 the authority of the state institutions was very low and the attempts by military governors to reestablish their power (and possible use it for smuggling slaves) was countered by about eight isolated local revolts of the creole garrisons and settlers in the years 1840–1855, some of them apparently inspired by contemporary revolts in Portugal. Free trade policies and more direct control by the metropolis stabilized the administration after 1855. In 1834 control of movements of traders inside the colony was reduced and the establishment of Hindu and Muslim traders in the district capitals was no longer prohibited. They therefore started to spread out after 1838–1840.

GERHARD LIESEGANG

Further Reading

Clarence-Smith, G. *The Third Portuguese Empire, 1825–1975.* Manchester: UP, 1985.

Isaacman, A. *Mozambique: The Africanization of a European Institution, the Zambesi Prazos, 1750–1902.* Madison: University of Wisconsin Press, 1972.

Liesegang, G. "Dingane's Attack on Lourenco Marques." *Journal of African History.* 10 (1969): 565–579.

Mudenge, S. I. *A Political History of Munhumutapa.* Harare: Zimbabwe Publishing House, 1986.

Newitt, M. *A History of Mozambique*. London: Hurst and Co., 1995.

Mozambique: Nguni/Ngoni Incursions from the South

Between the ninth and twelfth centuries, the moister summer rain areas that were adequate for millet-based agriculture in modern South Africa had been occupied by Bantu populations almost to carrying capacity and a number of processes took place to accommodate the population pressure that was building up in the areas less affected by malaria. Increase of social differentiation and of age of marriage, armed competition over farming areas and pastures, emigration and conquests, and formation of larger states seem to have been social responses to these pressures in South Africa and possibly also southern Mozambique. During this period important nuclei the ethnolinguistic or cultural formations as we now know them—Karanga (Shona), northern, eastern, and southern Sotho, Nguni, Tsonga, Tonga—seem to have been formed in southor eastern Africa. Larger states developed in the Karanga area, which extended to south of the Limpopo. Disputes over sucession and land seem to have led to immigration both of Kalanga and Nguni groups to Mozambique south of the Save River. As far as migrations and especially the Nguni group are concerned in mid-sixteenth century the Portuguese encountered already in place a number of chiefdoms in southern Mozambique who according to traditions collected in the eighteenth and twentieth centuries had immigrated from the Nguni (or *Twa)* areas. In pottery traditions, this identity may not always have been visible and the immigrants were assimilated also linguistically to the Tsonga Chopi and BiTonga groups in southern Mozambique.

The seventeenth and eighteenth centuries saw further groups moving north who claimed origin in the south (modern Ngwane or Swaziland and the Middelburg Ndebele areas). Most prominent were the Dzivi and Nkumbe (Cumbana) groups in Inhambane. They rapidly assimilated to the northern Tsonga (Tswa) and Bitonga and were accompanied by other groups from the Limpopo and Nkomati valleys or further south. They include the Bila or Bilankulu (Vilanculos) who had already been moving north around 1720–1730. Their spears and shields and penis sheaths distinguished them from the older Tsonga-Chopi populations north of the Limpopo using bows.

After a period of another sixty years, which registers only local dynastic quarrels and fights for hegemony, a series of campaigns and destructive wars known as *mfecane* in South Africa spilled over into southern Mozambique. Unlike earlier periods of invasions the *mfecane* one was dominated by a sociopolitical system equipped with institutions functioning to incorporate individuals and existing political structures at different places and in overlapping institutions in a new sociopolitical system. The development of this system based on an older age-class system seems to have been the result of political competition in southeastern Africa around 1810–1821 that ended with the formation of the Zulu state, which incorporated the parent Mthethwa and remnants of the Ndwandwe state complexes and extended to Swazi and Ndebele. After a period of competition between the Ndwandwe and Mtetwa states—which may have lasted for a decade—decisive clashes had come in 1819–1821. The Mtetwa led by the military commander Shaka Zulu invaded the Ndandwe kingdom after a military victory and forced important groups of the royal lineage and a number of vassal chiefs ruling parts of the kingdom to move away to the north, where at least five almost independent nuclei attempted to survive from mid-1821 onward. The groups of refugees were headed by the exiled king Zwide (who may have died *c.*1822) and his sons, who chose to turn back until 1827, and autonomous leaders like Ngwana Maseko, Nqaba Msane, Sochangane Nqumayo, and Zwangendaba Jere, who chose to move on and become independent heads of state. Zwangendaba may have had the position of head *induna* or administrator of the house of Zwide.

Zwangendaba seems to have spearheaded the advance close to the present capital of Mozambique in 1821, passing Matola and later moving to Manhiça, where from 1821 to about 1825, when he moved to the Limpopo valley. Soshangane initiated attacks in Tembe in 1821 and operated in association with Zwangendaba Jere until 1826 or 1829. Nqaba had apparently moved to the area north of the Limpopo by 1823 and in 1826 crossed into the area north of the Savé, where he founded a state that existed for about ten years. He and his warriors, many of them locally recruited, were known as "Mataos," from which the present-day ethnic designation of Ndau is derived.

The emigration or flight of Zwangendaba from the Limpopo valley to the Venda and Zimbabwean Plateau in around 1827 or 1829, the defeat of Nqaba Msane by Soshangane around 1835–1836, the crossing of the Zambezi by Zwangendaba in 1835 and the Maseko in 1839 left the area between the Nkomati and the Zambezi to Gaza.

Parallel to the establishment of the Gaza state south of the Zambezi came the extension of Zulu rule to southernmost Mozambique from around 1824 to 1835 up to the Limpopo valley engulfing temporarily the Portuguese settlement of Lourenço Marques, which was also the aim of Swazi attacks in 1863 and 1864. The Nguni state of Swaziland exerted pressure east of the Libombos in the period 1840–1865 and maintained some presence there after the partition in 1886. Zulu military influence south of the Bay ended around 1878.

North of the Zambezi, the Nqabas group was defeated and destroyed in the upper Zambezi valley around 1840, but part of Zwangendabas followers and successors under his son Mpezeni and *induna* Zulu Gama managed to extend their power to Tete and Niassa provinces between 1870 and 1895. Remnants of a Maseko incursion to Niassa in around 1847/1860 stayed in present-day Niassa and Cabo Delgado provinces while the main group settled on the watershed on the present border between Tete province and Malawi, where the colonial conquest reached them around 1898/1900, after which the could go to war only as auxiliaries in colonial wars.

The new incorporative military and age-grade system of the Nguni after 1820 permitted to establish a more permanent domination and class society with some chances of promotion for the subject population. In contacts with their superiors the subjects used the language of the victors until the defeat of the systems by the colonial conquest.

GERHARD LIESEGANG

See also: **Difaqane on the Highveld; Malawi: Ngoni Incursions from the South, Nineteenth Century; Mfecane; Tanganyika (Tanzania): Ngoni Incursions from the South; Zambia: Ngoni Incursion from the South; Zimbabwe: Incursions from the South, Ngoni and Ndebele.**

Further Reading

Etherington, N. *The Great Treks: The Transformation of Southern Africa, 1815–1854.* London: Longman Pearson Eduction, 2001.

Hamilton, C. (ed.) *The Mfecane Aftermath: Reconstructive Debates in Southern African History.* Johannesburg: Witwatersrand University Press, 1995.

Liesegang, G. "Nguni Migrations between Delagoa Bay and the Zambesi, 1821–1839." *African Historical Studies.* 3 (1970): 317–337.

Newitt, M. *A History of Mozambique*. London: Hurst and Co.RITA-FERREIRA, A. 1974: Etnohistória de Cultura Tradicional do grupo Angune (Nguni). L. M. *Memórias do Instituto de Inv. Cient. de Moç.* II (247 pp.).

Mozambique: Colonial Period: Labor, Migration, Administration

Although Portugal established a presence in southern Africa long before any of the other European powers, it never had sufficient financial power or people to create a viable administration or to promote economic development. Even the establishment of effective occupation by reason of conquering the indigenous Africans was only completed in 1919. Early attempts to provide a foundation for that occupation and to promote some economic activity followed the Iberian pattern in the American colonies. Areas of northern Mozambique were granted to individuals in the form of *prazos,* within which the *prazeiros* had complete control; the right to exploit natural resources and people for their own profit, and in return for the payment of some taxes. The *prazos* were later replaced by three chartered companies, but Portugal's hold over Mozambique remained precarious, vulnerable to threats of takeover by Cecil Rhodes and Jan Smuts and to division between Germany and Britain. European diplomatic rivalries ensured that Portugal remained the nominal imperial overlord of Mozambique, but in economic terms the colony was dominated by the neighboring Boer republics and British colonies, subsequently the Union of South Africa and, to a lesser extent, Southern Rhodesia.

Partially to promote greater economic development, partly because of the ineffectiveness of the *prazo* system, the Portuguese created chartered companies which replaced it. The Companhia da Moçambique was given the right for fifty years to exploit and administer some 62,000 square miles north of the Savé River, including the major port of Beira. The company's financial backers were Belgian, French, and British; many heavily involved in the Transvaal and other parts of southern Africa and including, somewhat ironically, the British South Africa Company.

The Niassa Company and the Zambesia Company were also chartered by the Portuguese. They did not have the same degree of administrative responsibility as the Mozambique Company, and their authority was such that full administrative control was exercised by the Portuguese government virtually exclusively in southern Mozambique, south of the Savé River. This included the port of Lourenço Marques-Maputo on Delagoa Bay, one of the finest natural harbors on Africa's East Coast. That port was the starting point of the development of the economic links with the Transvaal and South Africa which were ultimately to a subimperial relationship in which Mozambique was the subordinate partner, South Africa the dominant.

In 1869, much to Britain's dismay, the Portuguese reached agreement with the Transvaal for the construction of a road linking the republic to Delagoa Bay, finally making a reality of a nonratified treaty of 1858. The road itself was easily built and completed in 1871. The Transvaal saw Delagoa Bay not only as the nearest port of entry and exit for its trade but also, and more important, as a means of access to the coast and world trade that was outside British control. For the Portuguese, the Transvaal represented Lourenço Marques' only hinterland of any potential value. To further cement the links between them, the 1869 Treaty also provided for free trade between the two countries.

In the course of negotiating this treaty, the idea of building a railway as well as a road was raised. A concession for the short stretch of line within Mozambique was granted to Edward McMurdo in 1884. For a variety of reasons, including fraud and shortage of money, the line's connection to the Witwatersrand's gold fields was delayed until 1895, the same year in which two other lines linking the Rand to the Cape ports and Durban were completed.

By 1895 the MacArthur-Forrest cyanide process for separating gold from its surrounding rock had ensured the long-term viability of the Rand goldfield, although not even the most optimistic of predictions could have justified building three rail links to the mines. Politics and the understandable desire of the different ports to reap whatever benefit they could from mine-related traffic played a great role in the decision-making process.

Although the mining industry had more lines than needed, it was seriously short of workers, for whom competition had been driving up wages beyond the ability of less profitable mines to pay. In 1896 the Transvaal Chamber of Mines, formed in 1889 primarily in an effort to control the wages spiral, and the Mozambique government agreed the terms on which Mozambicans would be recruited for work. The designated recruiting organization, was the Rand (later Witwatersrand) Native Labor Association (Wenela), set up that same year by the Chamber of Mines. Mozambicans had, from at least 1850, a history of migrating to various parts of southern Africa to seek work in agriculture, construction, and diamond mining. Attracted by higher wages than they could get in Mozambique, they also sought to escape social restrictions imposed on them and, more significant, the harshness of the Portuguese forced labor system. An approved, regularized system enabled the Portuguese not only to exert some control over population movements but also brought in revenue from the capitation fees levied on each recruit; all at virtually no cost to the Mozambique government.

Mozambicans rapidly became the most important single group of workers on the Rand. They also became especially experienced, as they frequently returned to the mines or simply renewed their contracts for extended periods. In 1901, even before the Anglo-Boer War ended, their value was recognized in a temporary agreement incorporating the continued right to recruit labor in exchange for a guarantee of traffic to the railway line to Lourenço Marques and the privileged right of entry of Mozambique goods and services to the Transvaal mining region. This right was reciprocal, and over the years the value of South Africa's exports to Mozambique greatly exceed that of its imports. Ultimately, Mozambique had only its male workers to use as a lever in negotiations with its more economically powerful neighbor. Despite pressure from Natal and elsewhere to end Mozambique's privileged position, that labor remained sufficiently important (some 50 per cent or more of the Transvaal mines labor force) for the arrangements to be incorporated into a formal convention in 1909.

Although the rail link from Lourenço Marques to the mines was shorter than any other, total shipping costs were not necessarily lower. It cost substantially more to ship goods between Lourenço Marques and Europe than was the case with the Cape ports and Durban; handling facilities at Lourenço Marques were not as good, and rates on South African lines were easily manipulated to attract traffic to them. Only the formal agreement ensured that the Mozambique line got any traffic at all, and what they did get attracted the lowest tariffs.

After World War I, efforts to renegotiate the convention failed. Cancellation had little practical effect and in 1928 it was renewed. To meet South African concerns about the working of the port at Lourenço Marques, the South African government secured a measure of control over it administration. South Africa's desire to limit the number of Mozambican recruit was met by restriction on the number of times workers simply renew their contracts without returning home. The interwar period also saw the introduction of deferred pay. A portion of workers' wages was withheld and paid through local authorities at home, ensuring the payment of taxes and generally the interjection into the local Mozambican economy of money that otherwise tended to be spent on the mines. When the price of gold was allowed to float on world markets, accumulated deferred pay was transferred in gold to the government of Mozambique at an artificially high rate of exchange. The Portuguese could then sell the gold at a profit. This arrangement continued until shortly after Mozambique became independent.

Mozambique could not necessarily rely on continuing high levels of demand for mine workers. The Rand mines only had a finite life, and the new mines opening up in the Orange Free State were not as labor intensive. Other sources of labor opened up in the 1930s with the removal of restrictions on bringing workers from tropical areas. Restrictions had been imposed because of the high susceptibility men from those areas had to illness, notably pneumonia, when they arrived on the Rand, with its relatively hostile climate. Nonetheless, Mozambicans continued to constitute a substantial portion of the Transvaal labor force.

As South Africa felt increasingly vulnerable to pressure from the spread of independence throughout Africa, allowing recruitment to continue was one way of supporting Mozambique as part of the *cordon sanitaire* around the apartheid state. Mozambique's independence meant that South Africa could and did restrict labor migration, more to Mozambique's detriment than South Africa's. During the antiapartheid struggle, Mozambique could not oppose apartheid too vehemently because of its vulnerability to reprisal and its continue economic subservience to South Africa.

SIMON KATZENELLENBOGEN

See also: **Rhodes, Cecil, J.; Smuts, Jan, C.; South Africa: Gold on the Witwatersrand, 1886–1899.**

Further Reading

Duffy, J. *Portuguese Africa.* Cambridge, Mass.: Harvard University Press, 1961.

Harries, P. *Work, Culture, and Identity: Migrant Labourers in Mozambique and South Africa.* Portsmouth, N.H.: Heinemann and London: Currey, 1994.

Henriksen, T. H. *Mozambique: A History.*

Katzenellenbogen, S. E. *South Africa and Southern Mozambique: Labour, Railways and Trade in the Making of a Relationship.* Manchester, Eng.: Manchester University Press, 1982.

Newitt, M. *A History of Mozambique.* London: C. Hurst, 1995.
———. *Portugal in Africa.* Harlow: Longman, 1981.

Mozambique: Colonial Period: Resistance and Rebellions

Mozambique was supposedly conquered by the Portuguese in the sixteenth century. However, it was not until the nineteenth century, during the "Scramble for Africa" that the Portuguese effectively colonized Mozambique. Landing at the port of Sofala on the coast of the Indian Ocean, in 1505, the Portuguese intended to exploit mineral deposits in the interior. The interior belonged to the Mwenemutapa Kingdom, rumored to have an abundance of gold deposits.

Portuguese traders and merchants were not the first foreign forces in the Mwenemutapa Kingdom. They found that Muslim traders had been trading in the area but the Portuguese used their military might and drove them away and established commercial and administrative centers at Sena, Tete, and Quelimane.

Portuguese presence in Mwenemutapa Kingdom, and indeed in the rest of Mozambique, was never accepted by Africans. In a bid to access mineral deposits, the Portuguese sent a religious mission in 1560 whose aim was to pacify and convert the king and his subjects to the Catholic religion. The mission failed and its leader was killed, as he was suspected of having nefarious intentions. Further attempts by the Portuguese to control Mwenemutapa Kingdom were futile, as they were repulsed. Resistance to Portuguese presence had begun.

During the seventeenth and eighteenth centuries, Portugal still had not effectively colonized Mozambique as the Portuguese officials entrusted with the colonizing venture were inefficient, being more interested in their own personal gain. To ensure some kind of loyalty and obligation, Portugal relied on individual settlers. These were given title deeds by the Portuguese king for lands they had coveted for themselves. From this system developed the *prazo,* or crown estate. The owner was known as *prazeiro.* These *prazeiros* acted as Portuguese imperial agents and were supposed to pacify the area and rule African kingdoms on behalf of Portugal. The *prazos* were notorious not only for land alienation but also for exploiting Africans as sources of labor and taxation.

In the seventeenth century, the Mwenemutapa was plagued by internal dissensions, which the Portuguese used to their advantage. They installed rulers of their own choice. It was this interference in the African political system, coupled with land alienation, and an oppressive and exploitative Portuguese system that sparked African resistances, rebellions, and oppositions. Even with Portuguese interference in the African political systems, Africans still resisted in order to assert their independence. Often Africans made alliances with their neighbors in a bid to oust Portuguese rule. Nhacumbiti of Mwenemutapa and Changamira of Rozwi made such an alliance in 1692, and subsequently the Portuguese were driven away. Sometimes Africans showed their resistance by attacking Portuguese commercial and administrative centers, including *prazos.*

The Portuguese tried to use the Catholic religion in a bid to control some of the African kingdoms. In the eighteenth century for instance, the Portuguese tried to control the Barue Kingdom in this manner. The Barue soldiers defended themselves by attacking *prazos* and Portuguese commercial centers. Other ethnic groups, notably Sena, Tonga, and Tawara, also resisted the Portuguese presence, protesting Portuguese interference in political and religious autonomy, and the notorious slave armies.

By the mid-nineteenth century, Afro-Portuguese *prazeiros* of the Zambezi valley were using their *Achikunda* slave armies to pursue their slave-trading activities, in defiance of Portuguese authority. By then British, French, and Boers of the Transvaal were showing increasing interest in the region of Mozambique, thus forcing the Portuguese to make strenuous efforts, during the 1860s, to bring the whole are more visibly under their control. They faced some of their strongest opposition from rebellious *prazeiros* who objected to this reassertion of Portuguese power. Nevertheless, a combination of military and diplomatic effort ensured that by 1875, the whole of the modern Mozambique coast was recognized by fellow Europeans as belonging to the Portuguese.

By the time of the "Scramble," the African kingdoms were not as well organized as they had been previously. They were replete with dissentions. Taking advantage of the situation, the Portuguese regrouped and remobilized, and from 1885 began to gain control of the Mozambique interior. Portugal then proceeded to establish its oppressive colonial system based mainly on forced labor and taxation, which the Africans resisted in various forms. Africans deliberately worked slowly, sometimes feigning illness, destroying agricultural implements or burning seeds so they would not grow. Some, like Mapondera, fled to areas that were not easily reached, from where and with the support of local societies, they attacked and destroyed symbols of Portuguese oppression. These kinds of resistances laid the foundation for national liberation movements of the 1960s such as the Front for the Liberation of Mozambique (FRELIMO). At other times, peasants simply revolted, destroying symbols of exploitation and Portuguese property and burning plantations. However, these revolts tended to be sporadic and uncoordinated, and therefore easily suppressed by the Portuguese.

One of the most common causes of resistance was taxation. Africans evaded paying tax, because they did not have the means to do so. They fled or hid before tax collectors arrived. Forced labor, or *chibalo*, also contributed to revolts. African peasants naturally preferred to expend their energies on their own lands, but the colonial system forced them to perform manual duties for the Portuguese. Often peasants staged small scale uncoordinated revolts, save for the 1893 rebellion in Tete, which temporarily united neighboring states in destroying symbols of oppression.

From about 1884 to the early twentieth century, Mozambique witnessed several rebellions aimed at driving out the Portuguese. The Massingire rebellion of 1884 was sparked by tax resistance. The 1897 Cambuenda-Sena-Tonga was the result of a 45 per cent increase in the hut tax. Makanga opposed the Portuguese demand of two thousand males for labor, Tawara wanted to assert the independence of the Mwenemutapa and the Shona in 1904 were against forced labor policies. The rebellions, significant as they were, were ultimately quelled because they were not united or well-organized.

Between 1900 and 1962, the Portuguese continued with their oppressive colonial system based on forced labor and taxation. Thousands of Africans were sent to South African mines and Southern Rhodesian plantations.

From the 1920s through the 1950s opposition to the Portuguese took various forms that included intellectual, rural, worker, church, and finally national opposition to Portuguese colonial system. Leading *assimilados* and mulattos of the 1920s started a newspaper, *O Africano* (The African), which spoke against the injustices of the Portuguese colonial system. In the 1950s writers and poets produced works condemning the atrocities of the Portuguese system. Workers also demanded better working conditions and wages and various independent churches expressed anticolonial sentiments. Meanwhile, the rural population continued with its sporadic and uncoordinated resistances.

It was not until the 1960s, when the ethnic and opposition groups united under FRELIMO, under the leadership of Eduardo Mondlane, that there was national resistance. Adopting guerilla tactics with the support of the rural peasants, FRELIMO resisted and fought the Portuguese until Mozambique achieved liberation in 1975.

P. T. MGADLA

Further Reading

Birmingham, D. *Frontline Nationalism in Angola and Mozambique.* London: James Curry, and Trenton, N.J.: Africa World Press, 1992.

Hanlon, J. *Mozambique: The Revolution Under Fire.* London: Zed Books, 1984.

Isaacman, A. and B. Isaacman. *Mozambique: From Colonialism To Revolution 1900–1982.* Boulder, Colo.: Westview Press, 1983.

Penvenne, J. *African Workers and Colonial Racism: Mozambican Strategies and Struggles in Lourenco Marques, 1877–1962.* Portsmouth, N.H.: Heinemann, 1995.

Vail, L., and L. White. *Capitalism and Colonialism in Mozambique: A Study of Quelimane District.* London: Heinemann, 1980.

Mozambique: Frelimo and the War of Liberation, 1962–1975

By the 1960s it was clear that the Portuguese government would not follow the precedent offered by its British and French colonial counterparts in negotiating, relatively peacefully, the terms of decolonization with the rising forces of nationalism in its African colonies, including Mozambique. Too economically underdeveloped to feel confident of retaining the neocolonial reins after its colonies' independence, Portugal's authoritarian political system at home was also one legitimized ideologically by the myth of empire and by ingrained practices of paternalism. Nationalists in Mozambique (but also in Angola and Guinea Bissau) would have to fight for their freedom against such a recalcitrant colonial power.

In the early 1960s, Tanzania became the central base for nationalists from throughout the southern African region who had come to similar conclusions about the imperatives of their own situations vis-à-vis white minority rule. In Dar es Salaam, encouraged toward unity by the Organization of African Unity (OAU) and certain continental leaders like Julius Nyerere and Kwame Nkrumah, a number of Mozambicans-in-exile came together, drawn from various of the quasi-nationalist movements then existent in territories neighboring Mozambique, from student and other organizations that had developed, up to a point, inside Mozambique itself, and from more distant exile (elsewhere in Africa, in Europe, and in North America). They moved to form, at a founding convention in September 1962, a more unified and effective organization to be named FRELIMO, the Front for the Liberation of Mozambique (soon referred to simply as "Frelimo"). Crucial to this development was Eduardo Mondlane who returned from a career of university teaching in the United States and employment with the United Nations to accept the position of first president of the new organization.

With the OAU Liberation Committee backing and by dint of a deft handling of relationships with other potential sponsors beyond Africa, both East and West, Frelimo soon outstripped rival claimants to nationalist primacy. Thus Frelimo was to prove far more skilled than other liberation movements in the region in drawing military assistance from both the Soviet bloc and China; its diplomatic efforts would also garner it an impressive degree of international acceptance, as well as considerable practical assistance for its "humanitarian" programs, from some Western governments (notably from the Scandinavian countries and Holland), churches and nongovernmental organizations (NGOs).

Frelimo's primacy in the eyes of the OAU and others was further consolidated by the movement's advances in military terms. After the training in Algeria of its first military cadres, including Samora Machel (soon to be head of the guerrilla army and later first president of independent Mozambique), the movement launched, in 1964, an armed struggle that would soon drive the Portuguese from large parts of both the Cabo Delgado and Niassa provinces, which bordered on Tanzania. Similar efforts were at first abortive in Tete, but from 1968 Frelimo reengaged more successfully in that province (via Zambia), pushing forward in the early 1970s to the Zambezi and ultimately, bypassing an inhospitable Malawi, into the middle of the country where it began to pose some threat to the Portuguese presence in Manica and Sofala provinces.

Such was the unifying logic exemplified by Frelimo, and the advantages reaped from the consolidation of its legitimacy within Africa and beyond, that only rather marginalized alternative voices were now heard within the broad camp of Mozambican nationalism. Much more apparent were tensions within Frelimo itself. The conventional political practices that had defined the brand of nationalism prevalent elsewhere in Africa seemed ill-suited to the requirements of the guerrilla warfare that was now deemed necessary. In consequence, one wing of the movement (influenced both by its own experience inside the country and by a sympathetic awareness, in those heady days of the 1960s, of the ideas of "people's war" associated with the Chinese and Vietnamese revolutions) began to advocate a more deeply grounded process of popular mobilization. The experience of these cadres also drew them towards an anti-imperialist critique of the nature of Portuguese colonialism and of the global capitalist system that framed it, another dimension of their radicalization.

Set against this increasingly leftist, even Marxist, tendency was a nationalist politics that instead emphasized a more exclusively racial reading of the imperatives of the anticolonial struggle and a more opportunist (elitist and entrepreneurial) practice of it. The contradictions within the movement that these differences produced may have helped trigger the 1968 assassination of Mondlane in Dar es Salaam, although the actual bomb that killed the Frelimo president was traceable to the Portuguese police.

Mondlane's death was no doubt a considerable loss to the movement in the long term, albeit one difficult to measure. Like the younger colleagues who would become his successors, Mondlane was certainly moving to the left, but his continuing presence at the heart of the movement might well have moderated the autocratic tendencies that Frelimo would eventually carry into government after 1975. More immediately, however, his death and the question of the succession merely brought into sharper focus an internal power struggle, one in which Samora Machel and the progressive group around him (with valuable support from Julius Nyerere, president of Tanzania where Frelimo was then primarily domiciled) prevailed over the more conservative Uriah Simango for the leadership. This elevation of Machel, a considerable military leader and a charismatic force, to the presidency meant a positive consolidation of the practices of armed struggle as well as a confirmation of the movement's leftward trajectory.

Some historians have questioned any such account of Frelimo's forging of effective and progressive purpose during this period. They have emphasized, for example, the importance of regional and racial factors to the movement's internal politics, viewing the group that emerged to power under Machel's leadership as being marked principally by their identity as "southerners" or "mulattos." Others have chosen to see them merely as constituting an arrogant elite-in-the-making in their own right, albeit one (some would add) self-righteously and uncritically wedded to a modernizing agenda. Such interpretations are almost certainly overstated, although, as regards the latter point, it is probably true that the very successes of the new leadership during this phase of their struggle helped blind them to certain complexities of the transformational project they would seek to realize for their country in the postliberation period.

Opinions also differ as to the extent to which Frelimo had actually rooted itself firmly in a popular base in its "liberated areas," even in those parts of the country where it had a palpable guerrilla presence. Nonetheless, the beginnings of a project of social transformation and popular empowerment (in terms of education, health, gender roles, even production) that the leadership felt it was witnessing in these areas helped further to radicalize its views as to what a liberated Mozambique could look like under the movement's leadership. It is also true that only a relatively small percentage of the population in the northern part of the country fell under the direct influence of Frelimo activity. Yet there can be little doubt that the movement had earned for itself a substantial credibility in the minds of a large proportion of the country's overall population by the time of the Portuguese coup in April 1974.

The precise reasons for the fall of Portuguese fascism are much debated. Nonetheless, the guerrilla challenge in Africa (and not least in Mozambique) to the regime's colonial project was an especially crucial factor in both draining the Portuguese army's morale and undermining the legitimacy of Marcelo Caetano's regime at home. Frelimo had been able to weather the combination of brutal intimidation (the massacre at Wiriyamu in 1972, for example), construction of strategic hamlets, and launching of "great [military] offensives" (such as the much trumpeted "Operation Gordian Knot") thrown at it in the early 70s. Then, even after the coup, Frelimo refused to be tempted by the neocolonial blandishments of General Spinola and instead kept the fighting alive until a more radical Portuguese government agreed both to transfer power to the movement and, as occurred in June 1975, to recognize the new nation's independence.

Fatefully, Frelimo had thus come to power with much popular support but without benefit of elections and indeed (so certain was it of its mission to further transform in socioeconomic terms the lives of its popular constituency) with a pronounced distaste for entertaining opposition to what it considered to be its noble purposes. The hierarchical tendencies implicit in its experience of the (necessary) militarization of its struggle but also imbibed from the authoritarian practices of even the most enlightened nationalist leaders elsewhere on the continent no doubt contributed to this predilection. But so too did the movement's heady pride in its victory, its self-confidence, and its unquestioning commitment to the progressive project, deemed to be at once socialist, modernizing, and developmental, that it had forged in the liberation struggle.

JOHN S. SAUL

See also: **Mondlane, Eduardo; Mozambique: Machel and the Frelimo, 1975–1986.**

Further Reading

Birmingham, D. *Frontline Nationalism in Angola and Mozambique.* London: James Currey, 1992.

Isaacman, A., and B. Isaacman. *Mozambique: From Colonialism to Revolution, 1900–1982.* Boulder, Colo.: Westview Press, 1983.

Mondlane, E. *The Struggle for Mozambique.* 2nd ed. London: Zed Books, 1983.

Munslow, B. *Mozambique: The Revolution and Its Origins.* London: Longman, 1983.

Newitt, M. *A History of Mozambique.* London: Hurst and Company, 1995.

Saul, J. S. (ed.). *A Difficult Road: The Transition to Socialism in Mozambique*. New York: Monthly Review Press, 1985.

Mozambique: Machel and the Frelimo Revolution, 1975–1986

After the overthrow of the Portuguese colonial presence in Mozambique, FRELIMO (soon, as a political party, simply "Frelimo") came to power in 1975 with

Cabora Bassa Dam, Mozambique. © Friedrich Stark/Das Fotoarchiv.

an ambitious agenda highlighting nationalist, developmental and socialist goals. Although he surrounded himself with a deeply committed and unified team, the key figure in this process was undoubtedly Frelimo's president, Samora Moises Machel. Born in southern Mozambique in 1933 and trained as a nurse, Machel left Mozambique in 1963 to join FRELIMO in Tanzania. After military training, he soon rose to be head of the army and, in the wake of Eduardo Mondlane's assassination and a subsequent struggle for primacy within the movement, to its presidency in 1969. In the liberation struggle he came to play an absolutely crucial role in sustaining and advancing FRELIMO's military challenge to Portuguese rule and consolidating the movement's leftward trajectory. He was a man of enormous charisma, if also one of rather overweening self-confidence, and something of an autodidact in matters of revolutionary theory. He was deeply concerned with transforming and modernizing his country and the condition of its peoples. There can be little doubt that Machel and key leaders of Frelimo, now in positions of governmental authority, thought that this transformation would occur along socialist lines: Machel's speeches were studded with statements regarding the evils of exploitation and the nature of the global imperialist system that allow of no other interpretation of the movement's intentions.

The realization of such intentions would prove to be more difficult. The departure at independence of most of the resident Portuguese (who also engaged in substantial sabotage on leaving) created chaotic conditions, while also underscoring just how vulnerable the inherited economy was, and just how few trained Mozambicans Portuguese colonialism had produced. In addition, Mozambique was to be struck by a range of natural disasters (droughts and floods) throughout Frelimo's early years in power. The new government was prepared to be quite pragmatic in certain respects (e.g., as regards its inherited linkages with South Africa), but the various crises of the transition probably encouraged Frelimo, which in any case was extremely ambitious, to embrace too many tasks at once. Moreover, there was limited room for maneuver for progressives in power in the then polarized world of the Cold War. In such a context, Frelimo's developmental agenda was also distorted by the impact of assistance from the Eastern bloc upon which it became overly, if almost inevitably, reliant.

In the event, the movement was drawn away from the peasant roots of its liberation struggle toward a model that, by fetishizing (with Eastern European encouragement) the twin themes of modern technology and "proletarianization," forced the pace and scale of change precipitously, both in terms of inappropriate industrial strategies and, in the rural areas, of highly mechanized state farms and (against the evidence of experience elsewhere in Africa) ambitious plans for the rapid "villagization" ("aldeias communais") of rural dwellers. Debate continues as to how (and indeed whether) a more expansive economic development strategy that effectively linked a more apposite program of industrialization to the expansion of peasant-based production might actually have been realized under Mozambican circumstances. Nonetheless, the failure to do so was to be a key material factor in placing in jeopardy Frelimo's parallel hopes of mobilizing popular energies and transforming consciousness.

Similarly, in the political realm, the authoritarianism of prevailing "socialist" practice elsewhere reinforced the pull of the movement's own experience of military hierarchy and of the autocratic methods conventionally associated with African nationalism to encourage a "vanguard party" model of politics, this being officially embraced at Frelimo's Third Congress in 1978. The simultaneous adoption of a particularly inflexible official version of "Marxism-Leninism" had a further deadening effect on the kind of creativity (both vis-à-vis the peasantry during the liberation struggle and as further exemplified in the transition period by the encouragement of grassroots "dynamizing groups" in urban areas) that the movement had previously evidenced. Such developments substantially contradicted any real drive toward popular empowerment, tending to turn the organizations of workers, women, and the like into mere transmission belts for the Frelimo Party. It is true that the kind of "left developmental dictatorship" now created by Frelimo witnessed successes in certain important spheres (health and education, for example) and advances in the principles (if not always the practice) of such projects as that of women's emancipation were impressive. Moreover, the regime took seriously the challenges to their emancipatory vision posed by the structures of institutionalized religion, by "tradition" and patriarchy, and by ethnic and regional sentiment. But the high-handed manner (at once moralizing and "modernizing") in which it approached such matters often betrayed an arrogance and a weakness in methods of political work that would render it more vulnerable to destructive oppositional activity than need otherwise have been the case.

The fact remains that the most important root of such "oppositional activity" lay in Frelimo's fateful decision to commit itself to the continuing struggle to liberate the rest of southern Africa, Rhodesia in the first instance but also South Africa, a point often downplayed by those observers who now choose to underestimate the high sense of moral purpose with which Frelimo assumed power in 1975. It was a choice for which the fledgling socialist state was to pay dearly, however. The cutting off of economic links with Rhodesia helped undermine the economy of Beira and its hinterland (especially when little of the promised international compensation for implementation of sanctions was forthcoming). And the support for ZANU guerrillas in advancing their own struggle prompted the Rhodesians to launch efforts to destabilize Mozambique, notably through the recruitment of renegade Mozambicans as mercenaries into a "Mozambique National Resistance" (the MNR, later Renamo) Then, after the fall of the Smith regime in 1979, the South African state itself chose to breathe fresh life into Renamo while intensifying the latter's cruel program of outright destabilization, characterized by its brutal targeting of Mozambican civilian populations, and its wilful destruction of social and economic infrastructures.

The conclusion carefully argued by Minter (1994: p.283) stands: that without such external orchestration, Mozambique's own internal contradictions would not have given rise to war. Once launched, however, the war did serve to magnify Frelimo's errors and to narrow its chances of learning from them. Indeed, such was the war's destructive impact on Mozambique's social fabric that what began as an external imposition slowly but surely took on some of the characteristics of a civil war. Given the nature of its own violent and authoritarian practices, Renamo could not easily pose as a champion of democracy (except in some ultraright circles in the West). Nonetheless, it had some success, over time, in fastening onto various grievances that sprang from the weaknesses in Frelimo's own project, Renamo seeking to fan the resentments of disgruntled peasants, disaffected regionalists, ambitious "traditionalists" (e.g., displaced chiefs). Meanwhile, under pressure, the Frelimo state itself buckled, its original sense of high purpose and undoubted integrity beginning to be lost. Thus, by the time open elections did finally occur in the 1990s as part of the peace process, Renamo had gained sufficient popular resonance to present a real challenge to Frelimo, albeit on a terrain of political competition reduced to the lowest kind of opportunistic calculation of regional, ethnic, and sectional advantage.

In the period covered in this entry such outcomes were not yet visible. And yet, by the early 1980s, Frelimo had begun to adapt its domestic policies in a less aggressively revolutionary, more market-sensitive direction. True, this was done (at its Fourth Congress in 1983, for example) in ways that could still be interpreted as realistic adjustments calculated primarily to ensure the long-term viability of quasi-socialist goals. In retrospect, however, they can also be seen as first steps in an effort to placate various Western actors, in particular the Reagan White House, which was now so aggressive in the region and a tacit supporter of South African strategies. By the 1990s such trends would witness a full-scale surrender by Frelimo to the globalizing logic of neoliberalism.

Just how far, had he lived, Samora Machel would himself have been prepared to travel down that road must remain a matter of speculation. Nonetheless, Machel had already presided over the movement's most humiliating capitulation, that to South Africa, as crystallized in the signing of 1984's Nkomati Accord. This pact found Frelimo trading abandonment of its support to the ANC for South Africa's promise to wind down its orchestration of Renamo's destabilizing activities. In fact, South Africa did no such thing, and Machel now proposed a (long overdue) housecleaning of state structures, in particular of the military. He was to perish, however, in October 1986, when his airplane crashed while returning from a meeting in Zambia (a crash which, some continue to claim, may have been engineered by the South Africans). Whatever the disarray and uncertainty that by now characterized Frelimo's overall project, the renowned unity of the movement's leadership core held firm. Joaquim Chissano, himself a veteran activist from the liberation struggle period, was elevated to the presidency.

John S. Saul

Further Reading

Christie, I. *Machel of Mozambique.* Harare: Zimbabwe Publishing House, 1988.

Hall, M., and T. Young. *Confronting Leviathan: Mozambique since Independence.* Athens: Ohio University Press, 1997.

Machel, S. *Samora Machel: An African Revolutionary/Selected Speeches and Writings,* edited by B. Munslow. London: Zed Books, 1985.

Minter, W. *Apartheid's Contras: An Inquiry into the Roots of War in Angola and Mozambique.* London: Zed Books, 1994.

Saul, J. S. (ed.). *A Difficult Road: The Transition to Socialism in Mozambique.* New York: Monthly Review Press, 1985.

———. *Recolonization and Resistance: Southern Africa in the 1990s.* Trenton: Africa World Press, 1993.

Mozambique: Renamo, Destabilization

South Africa's apartheid regime responded to independence and majority rule in neighboring states with a policy of destabilization, in which it covertly fomented war and created economic problems in those states. This had three purposes: to weaken those states and prevent them from supporting the South African liberation movements, to disrupt transport links and keep the countries dependent on South Africa (and thus disrupt the newly founded Southern African Development Coordination Conference, or SADCC), and to demonstrate to its own people and the wider world that black governments were incompetent and unfit to rule. From 1981 this policy received tacit support from the U.S. administration of President Ronald Reagan, which saw which South Africa as an anticommunist bastion standing up to black "communist" governments.

Resistencia Nacional Moçambicana (Mozambique National Resistance, or Renamo) was South Africa's agent in Mozambique, and during the 1981–1992 war, at least 1 million people died, 5 million were displaced or became refugees in neighboring countries, and damage exceeded $20 billion. Renamo was initially set up by the Rhodesian security services in 1976 when Mozambique imposed mandatory United Nations sanctions against Rhodesia (now Zimbabwe). Renamo's first members were Mozambicans who had been in particularly brutal Portuguese colonial units before independence, and who then fled to Rhodesia fearing punishment. Renamo made raids into central Mozambique, and built up recruits by raiding open prisons in rural areas. The main Renamo bases in Mozambique were captured in 1979 and 1980, and Renamo was largely defeated.

With independence in Zimbabwe in 1980, the remaining Renamo fighters were passed on to South African military intelligence, which set up special bases for them in northeast South Africa. Rhodesia had only used Renamo for harassment and intelligence, but South Africa built Renamo into a major fighting force with extensive training and supplies by boat and plane. South African commandos took an active part in key Renamo sabotage actions. Afonso Dhlakama was selected as the new commander. By mid-1981 Renamo was active in the two central provinces; by the end of

1983 it was disrupting travel and carrying out raids in six of the ten provinces; it required 3,000 Zimbabwean troops to protect the road, railway, and oil pipeline that linked the Mozambican port of Beira to Zimbabwe.

On March 16, 1984, Mozambique and South Africa signed the Nkomati Accord, under which South Africa agreed to stop supporting Renamo in exchange for Mozambique expelling African National Congress (ANC) members. Mozambique abided by the accord, but South Africa did not; support for Renamo was reduced but never stopped.

South Africa wanted to disrupt transport and commerce and destroy economic infrastructure in Mozambique, and it also wanted to destroy the image of the Front for the Liberation of Mozambique, popularly known as Frelimo. A central plank of its strategy was fear, and Renamo was molded into an effective terrorist force. Frelimo had gained its greatest popularity through its rapid expansion of health and education, so Renamo attacked schools and health posts and maimed, killed, or kidnapped nurses and patients, teachers, and pupils. The goal was to make people afraid to use health posts and send their children to school, and to make teachers and nurses afraid to work in rural areas, thus eliminating Frelimo's traditional sources of support. To disrupt commerce, shops were destroyed and there were brutal attacks on road and rail transport; wounded passengers were burned alive inside buses, but some were always left alive to tell what had happened, thus creating fear of travel. More than half of all rural primary schools, health posts, and shops were destroyed or forced to close.

In 1998 the United States deputy assistant secretary of state for African affairs, Roy Stacey, accused Renamo of carrying out "one of the most brutal holocausts against ordinary human beings since World War II." Renamo, he said, was "waging a systematic and brutal war of terror against innocent Mozambican civilians through forced labor, starvation, physical abuse, and wanton killing."

Renamo recruited largely by kidnapping large groups of young people. The Renamo members allowed the most determined of the kidnapped to escape. The rest were frightened into submission, forced to kill, and gradually molded into willing soldiers.

Travel and commerce became difficult in much of the country. By 1985, exports were only one-third of their 1981 levels, and GDP per capita was half of its 1981 level. By 1990, one-third of the population had fled to towns or neighboring countries, leaving rural areas depopulated. By 1992, the United Nations estimated that Renamo controlled 23 per cent of the territory of Mozambique, but only 6 per cent of the population.

Renamo had popular support in some areas, particularly in the center of the country. Peasants were critical of Frelimo for its opposition to "traditional leaders" and, in its rush to modernize the economy, for Frelimo's failure to adequately support the peasantry. The war and deteriorating economy turned many against Frelimo.

In 1992, after two years of negotiation in Rome, the government of Mozambique and Renamo signed a peace accord. Both sides were tired of war, and the ceasefire was quickly implemented. The peace accord implicitly accepted that there would be no truth commission, and thus no punishments would be meted out for atrocities committed during the war. Frelimo demobilized 66,000 soldiers; Renamo demobilized 24,000 adult soldiers and 12,000 child soldiers, according to the United Nations. The peace accord called for a new integrated army of 30,000 men, half from each side, but only 12,000 of the demobilized chose to join the army.

Renamo was recognized as a political party and received extensive donor support in the two years before the 1994 elections to convert it from a guerrilla force into a political party. Many people joined Renamo in that period, seeing it as the only viable opposition party.

Multiparty election on October 27–29, 1994, and December 3–5, 1999, were quite similar. Approximately two-thirds of all adults of voting age voted in each election. Both elections were declared free and fair by foreign observers who also praised the organization of the electoral process. Frelimo and its president Joaquim Chissano won both elections, but Renamo took a significant portion of the votes. Renamo boycotted the opening session of parliament after both elections, claiming fraud, but offering no evidence to support its claim.

In February 2000 southern Mozambique suffered the worst floods since 1895; 700 people died, 40,000 were saved by the Mozambique navy and South African air force, and 500,000 were displaced and assisted by the international community. Although Mozambique's per capita GDP continued to increase, the floods slowed growth in 2000, and the impact continued into 2001.

JOSEPH HANLON

See also: **Mozambique: Chissano and, 1986 to the Present; Mozambique: FRELIMO and the War of Liberation, 1962–1975; Mozambique: Machel and the Frelimo Revolution, 1975–1986; South Africa: Apartheid, 1948–1959.**

Further Reading

Hanlon, J. *Beggar Your Neighbours: Apartheid Power in Southern Africa*. Bloomington: Indiana University Press, 1986.

———. *Mozambique: Who Calls the Shots*. Bloomington: Indiana University Press, 1991.

———. *Peace Without Profit: How the IMF Blocks Rebuilding in Mozambique*. Portsmouth, N.H.: Heinemann, 1996.

Minter, W. *Apartheid's Contras: An Inquiry into the Roots of War in Angola and Mozambique.* Atlantic Highlands, N.J.: Zed Books, 1994.

United Nations Department of Public Information. *The United Nations and Mozambique: 1992–1995.* New York: United Nations, 1995.

Vines, A. *Renamo: From Terrorism to Democracy in Mozambique?* London: James Currey, 1996.

Mozambique: Chissano and, 1986 to the Present

Following the death of Samora Machel in 1986 in an airplane crash, Joaquim Chissano assumed both the presidency of Mozambique and of the ruling Frelimo party in a peaceful and uncontested transition. Chissano successfully led the transitional government to independence in 1974–1975 and was minister of foreign affairs in the postindependence government. Chissano came from the same area and ethnolinguistic group in the south of the country as Machel and his predecessor as leader of Frelimo, Eduardo Mondlane. All were Shanganas (named thus, after a famous Nguni leader) from Gaza province, yet none of the three leaders had a narrow "tribalist" outlook.

South Africa-backed destabilization, supporting the internal Renamo armed opposition, combined with failed radical socialist policies and an extended period of crippling drought, brought the country to its knees. The United Nations launched a series of unprecedented emergency humanitarian appeals for six successive years, beginning in 1987. Mozambique had become the poorest country in the world with a GDP per capita of less than $100. Under Chissano, the move toward the West and away from earlier Marxist-Leninist influence gathered pace. Mozambique joined the IMF and World Bank and attracted increasing levels of aid. By the early 1990s, 70 per cent or more of GDP was accounted for by aid, reflecting the ongoing emergency facing the country. Chissano's pragmatism was to help transform Mozambique into one of the few success stories in Africa, in terms of economic growth, in the final years of the twentieth century.

Chissano also presided over the complex transition from a single-party state to a multiparty electoral system. A new constitution in 1990 set up a multiparty state, along with the mechanisms for direct elections for the presidency and for members of parliament. Efforts were made throughout the 1990s to move away from the existing, extremely centralized, administrative model. Decentralization of state power only proceeded slowly, however, in a context of scarce resources and the prevailing political culture.

Transformation toward majority rule in South Africa reduced external support for Renamo. The war was recognized by both parties to the conflict as a stalemate, and under growing internal and international pressure, peace negotiations began between Frelimo and Renamo in 1990 in Rome. In October 1992, a General Peace Agreement was signed after a long and tortuous period of negotiations and compromise.

The peace process was successfully concluded, 92,000 rival troops were demobilized, and a small unified national army was created. Landmines were removed, and bridges and roads were repaired. A further task involved in the peace process was reintegrating the 2.1 million internally displaced persons and 1.7 million refugees. This was mainly undertaken between 1992 and 1994. Democratic elections were held in 1994. Frelimo won a majority of seats in parliament (129 compared with 112 for Renamo), and Chissano won the presidential vote quite convincingly. Yet Renamo received a clear majority of votes in the center of the country in its historical heartland. Frelimo won a majority in the south and in the north of the country, where its fundamental support lay. Over the remainder of the decade all evidence pointed to an effective transition from war to peace. Yet the need remained for a more even spread of the benefits of peace and economic development across the country if regional tensions were to be effectively managed.

Economic recovery was encouraged by the peace process and privatization. A considerable expansion of private investment took place, mainly in massive projects involving aluminum smelting and iron and steel production, offshore gas, heavy metal sands mining, hydroelectricity, and tourism initiatives. The major impediment to sustainable economic development remained the massive debt burden. A significant breakthrough occurred when Mozambique was chosen for the implementation of the highly indebted poor countries debt relief initiative enabling almost $3 billion of debt to be canceled. The government's strict adherence to the structural adjustment program had won it considerable international support for such a move. Gross domestic product was growing at 10 per cent per annum in the final years of the century. All of the primary schools destroyed by the war had also been restored. Effectively two decades of development were lost by the conflict. Inflation was also brought under control and the dire poverty of much of the population began to be tackled.

Mozambique benefited from active economic cooperation with its neighboring states, particularly South Africa. A major stimulus for economic renewal in the south of the country was the corridor initiative linking the South African industrial heartland of Gauteng with the port of Maputo. Other similar initiatives were planned with neighboring countries to the north. A good deal of the renewed economic well-being felt by the population resulted not only from peace and the opening up of access to the agricultural land of the interior, but also to the end of the decade of drought, which fortuitously coincided with the peace and the democratic elections. Access to land, security, and good rains kick-started the rural economy back to life. Subsistence food and commercialization circuits reopened and the free market policy framework promoted economic initiative.

BARRY MUNSLOW

See also: **Mozambique: Frelimo and the War of Liberation, 1962–1975; Mozambique: Machel and the Frelimo Revolution, 1975–1986; Mozambique: Renamo, Destabilization; Socialism in Postcolonial Africa.**

Further Reading

Abrahamsson, H., and A. Nilsson. *Mozambique: The Troubled Transition.* London: Zed Books, 1995.
Ferraz, B., and B. Munslow. *Sustainable Development in Mozambique.* Oxford: James Currey, 1999.
Hanlon, J. *Peace Without Profit: How Adjustment Blocks Rebuilding in Mozambique.* Oxford: James Currey, 1996.
Munslow, B. "Mozambique after Machel." *Third World Quarterly.* 10, no. 1 (1988): 23–36.
Newitt, M. *A History of Mozambique.* London: C. Hurst and Co., 1993.
Special Issue on Mozambique. *Journal of Southern African Studies.* 24, no.1 (1998).
Vines, A. *Renamo: From Terrorism to Democracy in Mozambique?* Oxford: James Currey, 1996.
Wuyts, M. "Foreign aid, structural adjustment and public management: the Mozambique experience." *Development and Change.* 27, no. 4 (1996).
Young, T., and M. Hall. *Mozambique since Independence: Confronting Leviathon.* London: C. Hurst and Co., 1997.

Mphahlele, Ezekiel (1919–)

South African Writer, Critic, and Teacher

Ezekiel (later, Es'kia) Mphahlele played a central role in the development of African literature and criticism in general, and literary opposition to apartheid in particular. His widely read autobiography, *Down Second Avenue*, is considered a classic of South African literature.

Born in Marabastad Township, Pretoria in 1919, Mphahlele spent part of his childhood with his extended family in the impoverished rural village of Maupaneng, northern Transvaal, before returning to Pretoria. Urban and rural experiences reflect and shape the ever-present themes of township life and African culture in his writings. Educated at St. Peter's Secondary School in Johannesburg (where schoolmates included novelist Peter Abrahams and PAC leader Zeph Mothopeng) and Adams Teaching Training College, Natal, he matriculated by correspondence in 1942 and worked as a clerk, typist, and instructor at the Enzenzeleni Blind Institute before taking up a teaching post at Orlando High School, Soweto, in 1945.

Mphahlele's first publication, *Man Must Live and Other Stories* (1946), was the first published collection of short stories in English by a black South African. Critics decried his "unsophisticated" style, but the stories captured the indomitable struggle for survival of poor urban blacks in the face of racial domination. He continued to teach, also gaining a bachelor of arts degree by correspondence from the University of South Africa in 1949. The increasing repression of the apartheid regime pushed him into action. Elected secretary of the Transvaal African Teachers' Association in 1950 he mobilized African teachers against the Bantu education bill that imposed a highly discriminatory and inferior state education system for blacks. His vocal opposition to "Bantu Education" led in 1952 to his dismissal and banning from teaching and his blacklisting in surrounding countries. He nevertheless obtained work as a teacher for a short time in 1954 in Lesotho and at St. Peter's. In 1955 he joined the African National Congress (ANC) and was briefly active in the organization, but was critical of its inattention to cultural and educational matters.

In 1955, as literary editor and reporter for the influential *Drum* magazine, he helped raise the visibility of young African writers and reported key events such as forced removals and bus boycotts but, ill at ease in journalism, and objecting to editorial censoring on the white-owned journal, he chose teaching and writing as his life's work. In 1956 he completed a master of arts thesis on black characters in South African fiction at the University of South Africa. Banned from teaching and in search of greater intellectual stimulation, he went into self-imposed exile the following year.

From 1957 to 1961, Mphahlele lived in Nigeria. He taught English and creative writing in the University of Ibadan Extra-Mural Department and interacted with important Nigerian writers such as Chinua Achebe and Wole Soyinka. In the 1960s, he traveled widely and helped establish cultural and literary centres, such as the Mbari Writers and Artists Club in Ibadan (1961) and the Chem-Chemi Cultural Center in Nairobi (1963). As an editor of the seminal literary journal Black Orpheus, he was instrumental in forging international visibility for black South African writers. He was part of an influential emerging group of writers, including Soyinka and Ngugi wa Thion'go, who challenged established literary mores. In 1961 he moved to Paris as director of the African section of the Congress for Cultural Freedom, an American-sponsored organization. He subsequently lived in Kenya, Zambia, and the United States. He taught and received a doctorate (1968) from the University of Denver and in 1974 became a professor at the University of Pennsylvania.

In exile Mphahlele published widely. *Down Second Avenue* (1959) met with great critical acclaim.

This autobiographical narrative vividly depicts his personal and community struggles against racism and captures the endemic poverty of black urban life and the oppression of white rule, but also the resilience of Africans. It also provides a glimpse of momentous events in South African history. In *The African Image* (1962), his first critical work and one of the earliest books of literary criticism by an African writer in English, he elaborated key themes in African literature, though critics pointed to his limited grasp of theory. In the sixties he also edited major anthologies of African literature (*African Writing Today* and *Modern African Stories*) as well as publishing his own short fiction (*The Living and Dead, and Other Stories* [1961] and *In Corner B* [1967]). Like his prose, his short stories convey the traumas of harsh urban life under apartheid and the little acts of resistance and desperation by ordinary Africans. His most successful stories include "He and the Cat," and "Mrs. Plum" (about patronizing whites). In the 1970s and 1980s, his literary criticism included *Voices in the Whirlwind and Other Essays* (1972). He published two novels, *The Wanderers* (1971), an autobiographical novel dealing with themes of exile, and *Chirundu* (1979), focusing on political corruption set in a thinly disguised Zambia. His also wrote a juvenile novella, *Father Come Home* (1984), set against a major event of South African history, the 1913 Natives' Land Act. However, his novels were not successful. *Afrika My Music* (1984), the sequel to his autobiography, described his exile and return to South Africa. A collection of his letters, *Bury Me at the Marketplace,* appeared in 1984.

After twenty years of exile he returned to South Africa in 1977 to teach at the University of the North in the Lebowa bantustan. His return soon after the bloodily repressed Soweto Revolt to a country still ruled by the apartheid system he had condemned proved controversial, and he was criticized by fellow exiles Dennis Brutus and Lewis Nkosi. This diminished his reputation as an unyielding antiapartheid writer but he stressed his need to seek literary inspiration in African culture and landscapes. The apartheid regime annulled his appointment and he was instead forced to work as a school inspector. He later secured a research position at the University of the Witwatersrand where in 1983 he was foundation professor of the Department of African Literature. After retiring in 1988 he continued to write but produced no major works.

Major themes of Mphahlele's creative work and life are alienation and the isolation of exile caused by apartheid and cultural colonization, and the antidote to this malaise, African humanism (or *ubuntu*), drawn from African culture. Like Ngugi, he sought to "decolonize the mind." While seeing literature as distinct from politics he found ways to incorporate into his fiction important political themes such as corruption. He also portrayed the strength of African women.

Mphahlele's work was crowned with literary achievements. He was nominated for the Nobel Prize and received numerous awards. But his major impact was on the development of a new approach to African writing. As a strong critic of the limitations of the *négritude* movement and ardent proponent of the self-assertion of African identity, he indirectly influenced the development of the Black Consciousness movement. An indication of his enduring influence is the continued presence of *Down Second Avenue* in South African school curricula.

PETER LIMB

Biography

Born in Marabastad Township, Pretoria in 1919. Matriculated at Adams Teaching Training College, Natal, by correspondence in 1942. Took up a teaching post at Orlando High School, Soweto, in 1945. Earned a B.A. degree by correspondence from the University of South Africa in 1949. Elected secretary of the Transvaal African Teachers' Association in 1950. Dismissed, banned from teaching, and blacklisted in surrounding countries in 1952. Completed an M.A. degree at the University of South Africa in 1956. Taught English and creative writing in the University of Ibadan. Moved to Paris to work as director of the African section of the Congress for Cultural Freedom in 1961. Taught and received a Ph.D. (1968) from the University of Denver in 1968. Appointed professor at the University of Pennsylvania in 1974. Appointed professor in the Department of African Literature at the University of the Witwatersrand in 1983. Retired 1988.

Further Reading

Manganyi, N. C. *Exiles and Homecomings: A Biography of Es'kia Mphahlele*. Johannesburg: Ravan Press, 1983.

Mphahlele, E. *The African Image*. Rev. ed. London: Faber and Faber, 1974.

———. *Afrika My Music: An Autobiography*. Johannesburg: Ravan Press, 1984.

———. *Down Second Avenue*. London: Faber and Faber, 1959.

———. *The Unbroken Song: Selected Writings*. Johannesburg: Ravan Press, 1981.

———. *Voices in the Whirlwind and Other Essays*. New York: Hill and Wang, 1972.

Obee, R. *Es'kia Mphahlele: Themes of Alienation and African Humanism*. Athens, Ohio: Ohio University Press, 1999.

MPLA: *See* Angola: MPLA, FNLA, UNITA, and the War of Liberation, 1961–1974.

Msiri: Yeke Kingdom

At the beginning of the nineteenth century, Swahili Arab merchants from Zanzibar extended their trading network deep into East and Central Africa. Although previously active in the hinterland of the Indian Ocean coast, they now moved inland in order to control the rapidly growing trade of slaves, ivory, and other products. Permanent trade centers emerged along the various routes leading to the interior. The most important routes led toward Lake Tanganyika and Lake Mwera where Swahili Arabs were present as early as the 1830s. The main link to Lake Tanganyika crossed the lands of the Nyamwezi and Sumbwa peoples south of Lake Victoria. The Swahili counted these people among their principal commercial partners. In fact, the Nyamwezi and Sumbwa were more than economic auxiliaries; they organized their own expeditions to the heart of the continent. For example, Sumbwa groups reached southern Katanga (Congo-DRC) in their quest for copper, ivory, and slaves. Under the impetus of the talented leader M'siri, whose own father had established friendship pacts with small Katanga chiefs, certain Sumbwa were permanently established in the region around 1850. In Katanga they became known as Yeke, a Sumbwa term for an elephant hunters' guild.

The region where the Yeke settled was far from the Luba, Lunda, and Kazembe kingdoms that were the great political centers of the time. From the start, the Yeke, who numbered no more than several hundred, had the foresight to establish good relations with their far more powerful neighbors. Relying on their guns and the sense of strategy they had developed in Tanzania, the Yeke gained control of the petty local Sanga chiefs. Unlike other slave trading groups that made no long-term plans, but relied only on force, the Yeke demonstrated a great capacity for integrating themselves into the political, social, and religious fabric of the region. They were especially skilled at utilizing the process of fictive kinship in order to bind themselves to their new allies. Cleverly manipulating kinship as a political tool, M'siri soon had himself proclaimed *mwami* (king).

During the 1880s, M'siri's Yeke kingdom reached its apogee. At that time the Yeke controlled southern and eastern Katanga where they managed to subdue a number of territories previously attached to the three great neighboring empires. Now, the Yeke state resembled a series of concentric bands. The Yeke exerted direct control over the immediate area around their capital, Bunkeya. Beyond that was a band of territories whose chiefs were obligated to pay tribute in exchange for regalia providing them with legitimacy. M'siri sometimes installed a Yeke resident ruler in these regions while at the same time bringing local princesses or chiefly heirs to be educated at the Yeke royal court. These policies led to the development of a pronounced Yeke presence within and influence upon the Katanga elite. Beyond this band was yet a third region that extended as far as Zambia. In this band, the Yeke sought not stable political centers, but merely commercial products such as slaves and ivory obtained through raids.

The Yeke were ideally situated on the line dividing the Indian Ocean commercial zone from that of the Atlantic zone. Thus, they could negotiate simultaneously with Luso-Angolan and Swahili-Arab merchants. Immense caravans containing hundreds, even thousands, of people regularly passed through the Yeke capital Bunkeya.

By the end of the 1880s, Leopold II, king of the Congo Free State, and Cecil Rhodes, whose operations were the vanguard of British colonialism, competed to gain control over M'siri. Both saw M'siri's capital as the gateway to a region reputed to contain great mineral wealth. Both Rhodes and Leopold organized expeditions, but Leopold was sucessful. In 1891 a fourth Belgian expedition reached Bunkeya. An argument broke out and M'siri died in the course of a shooting incident. M'siri's death coincided with the fall of the Yeke Kingdom. The state was undermined by rebellions led by local people who seized the occasion to emancipate themselves from Yeke control.

During the following years, the Yeke became the Congo Free State's principle allies in Katanga. This cooperation saved the Yeke from political obliteration and assured the establishment of a large colonial chiefdom ruled by the Yeke kings. Even today, Yeke influence far outweighs Yeke demographic importance (they number perhaps 20,000). M'siri's grandson, Godefroid Munongo, was the minister of interior in the secessionist Katanga government (1960–1963). Subsequently, Munongo occupied many ministerial posts in the government of Zaire. Munongo died in 1992 while participating in the National Conference in Kinshasa. The loss of such a powerful figure was damaging to the Yeke who since then have become the target of criticism. Other inhabitants of Katanga reproach them for not being original inhabitants of the region. The small groups of Yeke who were established outside of Bunkeya in the nineteenth century—mostly north of Lake Mwera and along the Luapula (including the Kitopi and Kashyobwe)—have been dispossessed of their rights to land they once held.

The Tanzania elements of Yeke culture such as their language (*kiyeke*, a Shisumbwa dialect now spoken only at the *mwami's* court) are now in decline. Nevertheless, the Yeke maintain their strong sense of identity. Recently, groups of young singers, dancers, and comedians have been established at Bunkeya in order to save and promote their culture. Each December 20, Yeke travel from all over Katanga to assemble at Bunkeya in order to celebrate the death of M'siri. This ceremony takes place at locations linked with the memory of that tragic event.

PIERRE PETIT

See also: **Rhodes, Cecil, J.; Stanley, Leopold II, "Scramble."**

Further Reading

Arnot, F. *Bihé and Garenganze: Or Four Years' Further Work and Travel in Central Africa*. London: James E. Hawkins, 1895.

Legros, H. *Une histoire du royaume yeke du Shaba (Zaïre)*. Brussels: Editions de l'Université Libre de Bruxelles, 1996.

Munongo, M. A. (ed.). *Pages d'histoire yeke*. Lubumbashi: Mémoires du CEPSI, 1967.

Verbeken, A. *Msiri, roi du Garenganze*. Brussels: Cuypers, 1956.

Mswati III: *See* Swaziland: Mswati III, Reign of.

Mugabe, Robert Gabriel (*c.*1924–)

Zimbabwean Politician and Former Guerrilla Leader

Head of government since independence from white minority rule in 1980, president of Zimbabwe, and leader of the ruling party, ZANU (PF) Robert Mugabe is a member of the Zezuru subgroup of the Shona ethnic cluster, which makes up roughly 80 per cent of the population today. He was born at the Kutanma Catholic mission near Zvimba in Makonde district, in what was then Southern Rhodesia.

Interested in a career as a teacher, he attending Catholic mission schools and worked as a primary school teacher at Kutanma until 1943, followed by stints at Empandeni and Hope Fountain missions until 1950. In that year he won a university scholarship to Fort Hare University in South Africa. Both his tertiary education and involvement with African nationalism began at Fort Hare. He received a B.A. degree in 1951. His education continued at the University of London. Over the next twenty years, partly in and out of prison, Mugabe earned four more university-level degrees in education, economics, law, and administration.

Returning in 1952, Mugabe continued teaching at mission schools, and in northern Rhodesia (Zambia) in 1955. In 1958 he moved to Accra in Ghana following its independence from British colonial rule to teach and experience African freedom personally. It was during this time that he met and married his first wife, Sally Hayfron. In May 1960 they returned to southern Rhodesia, where Robert became increasingly politically active in the executive body of the National Democratic Party (NDP), a newly formed nationalist movement. He served as secretary for publicity until the NDP was banned.

He served as deputy secretary general of the Zimbabwe African Peoples' Union (ZAPU) under Joshua Nkomo in the early 1960s. During this time, Mugabe was arrested frequently. While out on bail, he managed to flee to Dar es Salaam, ZAPU's exile headquarters. It was during this time, early in 1963, that Mugabe broke with Nkomo and joined the newly formed Zimbabwe African National Union (ZANU) under the Rev. Ndabaningi Sithole, serving as secretary general. Shortly after returning to Rhodesia, in mid-1963, he was rearrested and found himself in jail in 1964, when ZANU was banned. For the next ten years, Mugabe was held in prison or detention camps, until his release in 1974 as part of Ian Smith's general amnesty. Late in 1974, Sithole, still in detention, was suspended from ZANU by a vote of the executive committee and replaced as leader by Mugabe.

Following the 1975 assassination of Herbert Chitepo under suspicious circumstances at ZANU's operational headquarters in Lusaka, Mugabe, and Edgar Tekere moved to Mozambique in the wake of the end of Portuguese military occupation. From Maputo they reorganized ZANU and reactivated ZANLA, the military wing of the party. By 1977 Mugabe had become generally recognized as the uncontested leader of ZANU-ZANLA and a leading candidate in the eyes of African leaders for leadership of the still-divided national liberation movement. He was personally involved in both party affairs and military strategy, while traveling widely as key spokesperson in an international diplomatic campaign against the Smith-Muzorewa regime. By 1979 ZANLA had about 20,000 fighters under arms. Mugabe proclaimed himself a Marxist and was generally viewed as the most radical of all nationalist leaders.

In 1976, shortly before the beginning of unsuccessful negotiations with the Smith regime in Geneva, Mugabe and Nkomo had formed the Patriotic Front (PF). In 1978 both leaders participated in another round of peace talks in Malta, where they expressed support for independent elections in Zimbabwe. Terms of an internal settlement agreement, however, were denounced as a sellout by ZANU, which boycotted it. In 1979 Mugabe led the ZANU (PF) contingent to all-party talks at Lancaster House in London, which resulted in an agreement to hold elections.

Mugabe returned to Zimbabwe in January 1980 to stand in the upcoming elections as ZANU (PF) leader, after announcing that ZANU would contest the elections independently of the PF. Nkomo and ZAPU thereafter became a de-facto opposition party, representing the Ndebele speaking ethnic group which comprises roughly 20 per cent of the population. Mugabe stressed national reconciliation and support for all provisions of the Lancaster House agreement, including the twenty (out of 100) reserved parliamentary seats for whites. ZANU won fifty-seven seats, and Mugabe became prime minister, presiding over a coalition cabinet which included ZAPU and whites. Mugabe kept the defense portfolio for himself.

Mugabe proved pragmatic and cautious in honoring pledges for land redistribution so as not to alarm white commercial farmers, who were urged to stay. His policies angered some ZANU hard-liners, particularly former Mozambique comrade Edgar Tekere, who was dropped from the cabinet in 1981. Problems of internal security, fears of assassination, sabotage of military equipment, and South African espionage led to harsh military and police actions in Matabeleland province against alleged "dissidents." Nkomo, leader of the opposition, sharply criticized these attacks and was demoted in 1981.

Calls for socialist transformation of the economy and party approval of all major government policies intensified in 1982, as did calls to merge ZANU and ZAPU. The resulting political crisis came to a head in February 1982, following discovery of alleged ZAPU (ZIPRA) arms caches on farms owned by Nkomo, who was subsequently dismissed from cabinet. Near civil war conditions persisted in some parts of the country into 1984 and Nkomo fled the country at one point.

In 1984, at ZANU's second party congress, Mugabe increased his pressure for creation of a one-party state in advance of scheduled elections in 1985. ZANU won sixty-three seats, enabling it to amend the Lancaster Constitution. Pressures to merge ZANU and ZAPU continued into 1987 when a unity pact was signed and Nkomo became vice president. The ten-year provision of the Lancaster Constitution lapsed in 1990. White seats were abolished by amendment, an executive presidency was created, and Mugabe was inaugurated in December after he won reelection against weaker multiparty opposition, including Tekere's ZUM. A significant sign of increasing divisions within the ruling party was a vote to reject creation of a formal one-party state that same year. De-facto one-party rule was a given.

Mugabe stood for yet another term as president in 1995 elections, which witnessed a further erosion of formidable opposition party challengers. Economic problems had forced Mugabe to embrace IMF-World Bank structural adjustment policies and drop the socialist economic rhetoric by the early 1990s. Mugabe also began to step to greater prominence in regional and continental relations, serving as chair of OAU. Upon winning reelection, Mugabe made it clear he was not yet ready to consider setting a retirement date, although his health and general well-being were adversely affected by the death of his wife in 1992.

Growing civil society pressures for democratization combined with intensifying economic problems continue to cause major unrest, particularly in urban areas. Major strikes and demonstrations occurred in Harare in 1998 and 1999, leading some to predict the rise of a more serious political challenge to Mugabe, possibly from within the ranks of his divided party. Although he won the 2002 elections, they were decried as deeply flawed by both opponents and impartial foreign observers.

JAMES J. ZAFFIRO

See also: **Nkomo, Joshua; Zimbabwe: Since 1990; Zimbabwe: Conflict and Reconstruction, 1980s; Zimbabwe (Rhodesia): Unilateral Declaration of Independence and the Smith Regime, 1964–1979; Zimbabwe: Second Chimurenga, 1966–1979; Zimbabwe (Southern Rhodesia): Nationalist Politics, 1950 and 1960s; Zimbabwe: Zimbabwe-Rhodesia, Lancaster House and Independence, 1978–1980.**

Biography

Robert Gabriel Mugabe was born at the Kutanma Catholic mission near Zvimba in Makonde district, in what was then Southern Rhodesia. He attended Catholic mission schools and worked as a primary school teacher at Kutanma until 1943, followed by stints at Empandeni and Hope Fountain missions until 1950. In that year he won a university scholarship to Fort Hare University in South Africa. He received a B.A. degree in 1951. His education continued at UNISA and later the University of London. In 1958 he moved to Accra, Ghana. In May 1960, he returned to Southern Rhodesia, and joined the National Democratic Party (NDP). In 1963 he joined the Zimbabwe African National Union (ZANU). In 1974, named leader of the ZANU. First elected prime minister in 1980.

Further Reading

Astrow, A. *Zimbabwe: A Revolution That Lost Its Way?* London: Zed Books, 1983.

De Waal, V. *The Politics of Reconciliation: Zimbabwe's First Decade*. Capetown: David Philip, 1990.

Herbst, J. *State Politics in Zimbabwe*. Harare: University of Zimbabwe, 1990.

Kriger, N. "The Zimbabwean War of Liberation: Struggles Within the Struggle." *Journal of Southern African Studies*. 14/2 (1988): 304–322.

Mandaza, I., and L. Sachikonye (ed.). *The One-Party State and Democracy: The Zimbabwe Debate*. Harare: SAPES Books, 1991.

Martin, D., and P. Johnson. *The Struggle for Zimbabwe*. London: Faber and Faber, 1981.

Mitchell, D. *African Nationalist Leaders in Zimbabwe: Who's Who*. Salisbury, 1980.

Moyo, J. N. *Voting for Democracy: Electoral Politics in Zimbabwe*. Harare: University of Zimbabwe, 1992.

Mugabe, R. *Our War of Liberation: Speeches, Articles, Interviews*. Gweru: Mambo Press, 1983.

Ranger, T. O. "The Changing of the Old Guard: Robert Mugabe and the Revival of ZANU." *Journal of Southern African Studies*. 7/1 (1980): 71–90.
Sithole, M. "Ethnicity and Factionalism in Zimbabwe National Politics, 1957–79." *Ethnic and Racial Studies*. 3/1 (1980): 17–39.
Smiley, I. "Zimbabwe, Southern Africa and the Rise of Robert Mugabe." *Foreign Affairs*. 58/5 (Summer 1980): 1060–1083.
Smith, D., and C. Simpson with I. Davies. Mugabe, Harare: Pioneer Head, 1981.
Stoneman, C., and L. Cliffe. *Zimbabwe: Politics, Economics and Society*. London: Pinter, 1989.

Muhammad Abdile Hassan: *See* Somalia: Hassan, Muhammad Abdile and Resistance to Colonial Conquest.

Muhammad Ali: *See* Egypt: Muhammad Ali, 1805–1849: Imperial Expansion; Egypt: Muhammad Ali, 1805–1849: State and Economy.

Muhammad V: *See* Morocco: Nationalism, Muhammad V, Independence, 1930–1961.

Muhammad Al-Sanusi: *See* Libya: Muhammad Al-Sanusi (*c.* 1787–1859) and the Sanusiyya.

Muhammad Ture: *See* Songhay Empire: Ture, Muhammad and the Askiya Dynasty.

Muhammed bin Hamed: *See* Tippu Tip.

Multinationals and the State

Multinational corporations (MNCs), also called transnational corporations (TNCs), have increasingly engaged the attention of the international academic community for obvious reasons. Besides the fact that the MNCs were key agents in the shaping of the present world economic order, the continuing conflict between the MNCs and governments in the present age of economic globalization echoes the old debate over collective destiny, or common humanity, and national sovereignty. The crux of the matter has been how to achieve order and sustained good relations between the MNCs and the state. While the relationship between the home state and the MNCs forms part of the general matter under consideration, our primary concern here is the relationship between the host state and the MNCs.

As an international business enterprise with corporate headquarters in the home state and subsidiaries abroad, the MNCs were established with the motive of maximization of profits, that is, to serve the basic interests of the stockholders. As global business entities, they have the capacity to wield enormous financial muscle, advanced technology, and marketing skills to integrate production of goods and services on a worldwide scale.

Any discussion on the MNCs and the state in postcolonial Africa must necessarily commence with an acknowledgement of the continuity of the colonial practice of economic exploitation and domination of the host state in the immediate postindependence era. Since the relationship between the MNCs and the colonial state is outside the scope of this discussion, we can observe in passing that the MNCs and their cosmopolitan home governments were in an unholy alliance of economic domination of the African continent and thus got themselves enmeshed in the ocean created by the Machiavellis of this world. The continuity of the culture of domination in the postindependence period made the concept of neocolonialism gain currency in African discourse. As a new form of colonization, whereby the postcolonial states remained economically dominated by the former colonial masters and new external economic actors, the MNCs played roles which were more exploitative than anything else.

For the purpose of illustration, we shall take specific examples from North and Sub-Saharan Africa. The irksome economic domination of the state by the MNCs is evident in the example of Libya. There, King Idris, a conservative, allowed the operation of the MNCs on extremely generous terms, compared with those demanded elsewhere in the oil-producing world.

In Egypt the situation was no better. Before the ascendancy of Gamal Abdel Nasser to the Egyptian seat of authority, Egypt, for all intents and purposes, was a playground for European MNCs. In Liberia the MNC American Firestone stood like a colossus. At one point, Firestone set up its own security system, and technically became a state within a state.

The discoveries of gold, diamonds, and other minerals made South Africa a theater of multinational rivalry. The ascendancy of the American MNCs in South Africa was achieved through a complex interplay of the creation and manipulation of postwar multilateral donor institutions and trade agreements, adroit gold and dollar diplomacies, and the use of trade-related U.S. federal agencies like the Export-Import Bank. Indeed, by the 1950s, the U.S. MNCs had deeply ensconced themselves in nearly every sector of South Africa's economy.

With the rise of economic nationalism, African nation states rejected the status quo and did everything within their powers to reign in the multinationals. In Eygpt, President Nasser adopted radical leadership. His example appealed to many young African nationalists. In Libya a group of young officers led by Colonel Muammar Gaddafi deposed King Idris in 1969 while the latter was undergoing treatment in a Turkish spa. During May and June of 1970, Libya forced the oil companies operating on its soil to cut back production thus tightening the squeeze on Europe. In the negotiations that followed, Occidental Petroleum and other companies were compelled to yield to the demands of the Libyan government. By April 1971, through the instrumentality of increase in the posted price and share of the profit, Libya was receiving about 80 per cent more revenue than in the previous twelve months.

As the owners and patrons of the MNCs felt the effects of regulation, partial nationalization of MNCs, and the stringent measures placed on the operation environment of the MNCs by their African hosts, they realized that they could no longer play the game by the old rules of gun-boat diplomacy. Thus, they placed the matter on the global agenda. In this regard, the United Nations Economic and Social Council, in a resolution adopted on July 28, 1972, requested that the secretary general appoint a commission to carry out a study of the role of MNCs and their impact on the process of development as well as their affect on international relations. The group was also to formulate conclusions to be used by governments in making their sovereign decisions regarding national policy and to submit recommendations for appropriate international action.

In 1973 the UN organized a conference on the problems and prospects of the multinational corporations. Trends such as nationalization and expropriation, restrictive measures aimed at MNCs, the reservation of a substantial sector of the economic realm for nationals only, attempts by host countries to gain participation and control of policy making, production, and pricing of goods and services were addressed. Since that time, MNCs have taken steps to correct mistakes of the past and to negotiate directly with the their hosts for new arrangements. Consequently, the policies, guidelines, and priorities of the host countries have been largely implemented.

In the final analysis, it is pertinent to state that the relationship between the MNCs and their African hosts have ranged in character from hostility and resentment to willing or reluctant cooperation.

PAUL OBIYO MBANASO NJEMANZE

Further Reading

Behrman, J. N., and R. E. Grosse. *International Business and Governments: Issues and Institutions.* Columbia: University of South Carolina Press, 1990.

Caves, R. E. *Multinational Enterprise and Economic Analysis.* 2nd ed. New York: Cambridge University Press, 1996.

Choucri, N. "Multinational Corporations and the Global Environment." In *Global Accord: Environmental Challenges and International Responses*, edited by N. Choucri. Cambridge, Mass.: The MIT Press, 1993.

Hull, R. W. *American Enterprise in South Africa: Historical Dimensions of Engagement and Disengagement.* New York: New York University Press, 1990.

Versi, A. "Globalisation and Africa." *African Business.* 258 [October 2000]: 7.

Mummification: ***See*** **Egypt, Ancient: Funeral Practices and Mummification.**

Munhumutapa: ***See*** **Mutapa State, 1450–1884.**

Museums, History of: Postcolonial

Almost all African countries had a national museum at the time of independence. The majority of these museums were started by the various colonial administrations in these countries. This is not to say Africans had no interest in preserving their cultural heritage. There were indeed institutions, if only sometimes informal, that were responsible for this important task of propagating and preserving the cultural heritage. There were also individuals or groups of individuals who were responsible for the preservation of their societies' cultural heritage for posterity.

The national museums of the colonial era have continued to exist into the postcolonial period, but with very little or no development at all in some countries. There are exceptions, of course. Egypt has had museums from as early as 1863 and they have been multiplying ever since. South Africa has a number of regional museums. There are also several museums in every city and at least a museum in every sizable town in South Africa. There are also local history museums and in some areas, there are specialized museums like mine or military museums at various related locations. Countries like Kenya, Tanzania, and Nigeria also have made notable strides in their museum development. There are also countries like Botswana, which may not have multiplied the actual number of their museums but have nevertheless developed more programs at their existing museums. Botswana's mobile museum program, Pitse ya Naga, covers the entire country, visiting schools and local communities at given intervals.

Major museum development has, however, taken place in West Africa since independence. Many countries in West Africa have multiplied the number of their museums. Nigeria, for instance, now has at least forty-one museums. Ghana has twenty-one, Senegal fifteen, Côte d'Ivoire and Benin have twelve each. Mali has eight, while Guinea, Gambia, Liberia, and Burkina Faso have five museums each. The majority of these museums are museums of ethnography, or a combination of ethnography with history, archaeology, and/or natural history, but there are also many specialized museums, including military museums. Normally working against all odds, many African museums have successfully integrated more fully with the community they serve, instead of operating as foreign tourist attractions.

Many of the expatriate curators who initially ran national museums were replaced by indigenous African curators soon after independence. Although African curators were appointed to these posts and other museum positions, no funding was made available for them to do what they were supposed to do as museum professionals, apart from covering their recurrent expenditure, especially by way of salaries.

African museum professionals began creating regional and sometimes continentwide organizations to spearhead their professional concerns. Just before independence there was an organization for museologists in Africa, The Museums Association of Tropical Africa (AMATA/MATA), which survived until just after independence. Its last formal meeting was held in 1972 in Livingstone, Zambia. When UNESCO set up its Monuments and Museum Division, it came to the rescue of many African museums. UNESCO subsequently funded the establishment and administration of the Regional Conservation Center in Jos, Nigeria, for the training of African museum technicians, a field that badly lacked skilled personnel in many African museums after independence. The Jos Centre has trained quite a number of Africa's museum conservation technicians over the years.

In 1986 the southern African countries (except for South Africa, then run by the apartheid regime) set up the Southern African Coordination Conference Association of Museums and Monuments (SADCCAMM), bringing together museum professionals from at least seven southern African countries.

Similarly, West African museum personnel who had been quite active in the AMATA/MATA before its demise setup a new organization, the West African Museum Program (WAMP). WAMP has since been very active in bringing about regional collaboration and exchange of information and ideas between museum professional in Africa. Together with ICOM, WAMP published a directory of museum professionals in Africa, a very useful and handy sourcebook. Information on WAMP and its publications, and on a number of participating museums in its activities can now be accessed on the Internet.

Several other programs and projects have taken place in museums in Africa since the early 1980s. The Swedish African Museum Program (SAMP) is a training program between Swedish and African museums, which was launched in 1984. Its aim is to "develop a model for museums co-operation, by exchanging skills, information and sharing experience through solidarity across borders." The program has registered considerable success and many African and Swedish museums have benefited from this two-way training and exchange program.

The ICOM program, which used to conduct museum conservation courses in Italy, has since relocated these Prevention in the Museums of Africa (PREMA) courses to Africa and are now being hosted and conducted in different African countries annually. Several African museum professionals and museums are benefiting from these PREMA courses by training their personnel at technician level.

In 1991 the American Social Science Research Council also announced their competitive "African Archives and Museum Project: 1991–92" grants, for the preservation and documentation of archival and museum resources for scholarly use. This program attracted a total of ninety-five applications from African museums. Six museums from Zaïre, Cape Verde, Kenya, South Africa, Nigeria, and Zambia were awarded grants through this program.

Several regional workshops and conferences have been held and resolutions adopted mainly to draw African governments' attention to both the important role African museums can play in national development programs, cultural and national identity, as well as in fostering national unity and education. These professional gatherings have also highlighted the financial plight of the majority of African museums. However, because the situation on the ground is often that of a single national museum in many countries, it has been very difficult to enforce these resolutions on individual African governments. Several African national museums are usually under Home Office ministries such as community welfare, tourism, education, or home affairs, so they are always competing for funds with service-provider departments like prisons, police, or immigration. Since museums have nothing quantitative to put back into the national treasury, they have always come last in government spending priorities.

Museum professionals in Africa have now realized that they have to look elsewhere for funding if they are to carry out their mission. Thus, they are now targeting both regional and international programs that provide funding and grants. Organizations such as the European Union, SIDA, NORAD, the Ford Foundation, and Rockefeller Foundation supply funds for cultural institutions. A number of African museums have been able to obtain funds for research, documentation, and preservation of artifacts in their custody from such bodies.

Currently, there are a number of museum programs offering some form of professional assistance to African museums. These include Africa 2009, a ten-year program run jointly by UNESCO, ICCROM, and CRATerre-EAG concerned with conservation in Sub-Saharan Africa. There is also PREMA, ICOMOS, and AFRICOM. This last program grew out of a 1991 African museum professionals encounter in Lome, Togo, and later on in Addis Ababa in Ethiopia. AFRICOM works on a continentwide level to connect African museums with worldwide funding organizations. The program supports initiatives in training and education, exhibitions, fighting against illicit traffic of African cultural property, and supporting networks and future prospects in the field of museum development in Africa. It has the full support of the International Council of Museums (ICOM) and UNESCO.

DAVID KIYAGA-MULINDWA

Further Reading

Afigbo, A. E., and S. I. O Okita. *The Museum and Nation Building.* Oweri: News Africa Publishing Co., 1985.

Ardouin, C. D. (ed.). *Museums and Archaeology in West Africa.* Smithsonian Institution Press, 1997.

ICOM/SIDA/WAMP. *What Museums for Africa?: Heritage in the Future.* Rome: ICOM, 1992.

ICOM/WAMP. *Directory of Museum Professionals in Africa 1993/94.* Darkar: ICOM/WAMP, 1993.

Museveni, Yoweri Kaguta (*c.*1944–)

Political Scientist, Former Guerrilla Leader, and President of Uganda

Considered by many as a leading figure of the "new generation" of African leaders, Yoweri Museveni was born into a family of Hima cattle herders, a clan of the Ankole people of southwestern Uganda in about 1944. He was named Museveni in honor of the Abaseveni, those Ugandans who served in the Seventh Battalion of the King's African Rifles during World War II.

Early in Museveni's childhood his parents converted to Christianity, and from the age of seven he was sent to school. At Kyamate Primary School he met Martin Mwesiga and Eriya Kategaya, who were to become two close colleagues in the adult political struggles that lay ahead. In 1962, while at Ntare Senior Secondary School in Mbarara, Museveni became a born-again Christian, but in 1966 he broke with established Christianity over the missionaries' refusal to allow the Scripture Union to debate his motion condemning Ian Smith's Universal Declaration of Independence (UDI) in Rhodesia. For some time he had been unhappy with some of their biblical interpretations, and in particular he believed that their stand of evading "worldly" issues and condemning all violence, even as a means of liberation, was immoral. By this time Museveni had developed an interest in Ugandan politics. He and his student colleagues condemned the sectarian basis of much of Ugandan party politics: the DP (Democratic Party) and UPC (Uganda Peoples Congress), as they saw it, being primarily divided along a combination of religious and tribal sectarianism.

In 1967 Museveni went to the University of Dar es Salaam to study political science. He preferred Dar es Salaam to Uganda's own Makerere because he perceived it to be politically more radical and he saw Tanzania under Nyerere as the one African country that provided clear support for the liberation movements of southern Africa. Finding most of the university's staff not radical enough, Museveni founded the student discussion group, the University Students African Revolutionary Front. He made contact with the Mozambican liberation movement, FRELIMO, and met Eduardo Mondlane, Samora Machel and Joachim Chissano. In 1968 Museveni led a small group of students to visit the liberated zone in northern Mozambique. Contacts made at this time were to prove invaluable in the future when Museveni and his colleagues needed military training in guerrilla warfare.

Upon graduating in 1970 Museveni got employment in the President's Office in Kampala as a research assistant and he briefly joined UPC. Although professing to have distrusted Obote and the UPC since the mid-1960s, Museveni claims in his autobiography to have harbored a faint hope at this time of changing the UPC from within.

Within forty-eight hours of Idi Amin's coup d'état in January 1971, Museveni and four colleagues crossed into Tanzania intent on mustering support for a protracted liberation struggle. They made their way to Dar es Salaam, but Museveni at this time failed to gain Nyerere's support for any kind of struggle which did not entail the re-instatement of Obote as President of Uganda.

Through the 1970s Museveni was active in covertly recruiting sympathizers inside and outside Uganda, organizing military training, mostly in Mozambique, and infiltrating arms into the country. He took part in Obote's abortive raid into Uganda in September 1972, and in this and other clashes with Amin's men a number of his close friends were killed. When the Tanzanians finally invaded Uganda in 1979, Museveni accompanied them with a well-trained force of Ugandan exiles under his command.

Museveni served in the interim governments of Yusufu Lule and Godfrey Binaisa, but he was unhappy at the intrigues and lack of consensus then emerging. Ultimately, he supported the removal of both these interim presidents, but he was frustrated to find the old sectarian party politics of the 1960s revived. With Obote back in Uganda from May 1980, Museveni hurriedly formed his own party, the Uganda Patriotic Movement, to oppose him. After the deeply flawed election of December 1980 brought Obote back to power, Museveni declared the election "rigged" and took to the bush to fight his long-threatened liberation struggle.

The war was launched on February 6, 1981, with an attack on Kabamba barracks, to the west of Kampala. The attack by twenty-seven armed men failed to take the armory and Museveni led his men in some captured trucks by a circuitous route to the Luwero Triangle to the north of Kampala. Over the ensuing years of conflict and hardship, lessons were learned and under Museveni's leadership and training a well-disciplined National Resistance Army (NRA) was built from scratch. A National Resistance Movement (NRM) was formed under Museveni's chairmanship and a ten-point program was drawn up as the guiding principles for government once victory was achieved.

When Kenya's President Moi tried to broker a peace between the NRA and the Okello regime that had seized power from Obote in July 1985, Museveni used the Nairobi peace talks to stall for time while his men positioned themselves for the final assault on Kampala. The city fell to the NRA on January 27, 1986, and two days later Museveni was sworn in as president of Uganda.

On coming to power, Museveni placed a high priority on army discipline, national reconciliation, and economic reconstruction. The well-disciplined army soon gained wide respect among civilians, in marked contrast to the fear and contempt that greeted the sectarian and ill-disciplined armies of Amin, Obote, and Okello. Museveni instilled in the army a clear respect for human rights and for law as well as order.

On the economic front, financial discipline and economic liberalization were well established, and Museveni was instrumental in persuading parliament to approve the return to Ugandan Asians of assets seized by Amin in 1972. In his view, they were experienced businessmen with capital and a commitment to Uganda and thus an important part of his plans for the country's economic growth. Museveni's vision of the future entailed a large free trade area of eastern, central, and southern Africa as the only way to promote real African industrial and commercial development. To this end he was instrumental in the revival of the East African Community in Arusha, Tanzania, in January 2001.

National reconciliation and economic growth and reconstruction have proceeded well in the southern half of the country, but until the northern half, the home of Obote and Amin, is brought more fully into sharing the economic advantages of the south, Museveni's claims of national inclusivity remain somewhat hollow. Attacks in the north by dissident rebels who operate from bases in Sudan and eastern Congo have severely tested the Ugandan army which, ironically, Museveni himself had originally built out of small, mobile bands of guerrilla forces. Additional rebel attacks across the western border from the turbulent Democratic Republic of Congo (former Zaïre), prompted Museveni in 1998 to authorize the Ugandan Defense Force to cross into the Congo and pursue the rebels and their supporters there. In doing so Museveni embroiled Uganda in an ongoing civil war, which likewise involved the army of Rwanda. Whatever the strategic interests of Uganda in its neighbor's civil war, the Ugandan army's involvement in the Congo (until its withdrawal in 2003) has raised serious doubts about Museveni's much-vaunted judgment and integrity.

Politically, Museveni still holds out against multiparty politics as being likely to lead to sectarianism. The strategic and economic support that he continues to receive from Britain and America ensure that he is almost unique in Africa in not being pressured into accepting the multiparty prescription. His inclusive, nonparty "movement" system is, however, unlikely to survive his final five-year term, which began with his reelection as president in March 2001.

KEVIN SHILLINGTON

See also: **Obote, Milton; Uganda: Amin Dada, Idi: Coup and Regime, 1971–1979; Uganda: National Resistance Movement (NRM) and the Winning of Political Power; Uganda: Obote: Second Regime, 1980–1985; Uganda: Reconstruction: Politics, Economics; Uganda: Tanzanian Invasion, 1979–1980.**

Biography

Yoweri Kaguta Museveni was born into a clan of the Ankole people of southwestern Uganda in about 1944. Attended Kyamate Primary School from age seven. Attended Ntare Senior Secondary School in Mbarara. Became a born-again Christian in 1962. In 1966 broke with established Christianity. Began studies in political science at the University of Dar es Salaam in 1967. Graduated in 1970, took employment in the President's Office in Kampala as a research assistant. Sworn in as president of Uganda on January 29, 1986. Elected to his final, five-year term as president in March 2001.

Further Reading

Hansen, H. B., and M. Twaddle. *Changing Uganda*. London: James Curry, 1991.

———. *From Chaos to Order: The Politics of Constitution-Making in Uganda*. Kampala: Fountain Publishers, 1995.

———. *Uganda Now: Between Decay and Development*. London: James Currey, 1988.

Ingham, K. *Obote: A Political Biography*. New York: Routledge, 1994.

Museveni, Y. K. *Sowing the Mustard Seed: The Struggle for Freedom and Democracy in Uganda*, edited by E. Kanyogonya and K. Shillington. Basingstoke: Macmillan, 1997.

———. *What is Africa's Problem? Speeches and Writings on Africa.* Kampala: NRM Publications, 1992.

Music: Postcolonial Africa

In Africa today traditional, popular, and international music forms are found as accompaniments to a variety of activities. Traditional music transcends age, gender, and social class. It serves a formal function in various social and religious rites and is pervasive as an entertainment form. Popular music blends local and global influences and is most fashionable among urban youth. Popular music forms have been influenced by African American music such as rock 'n' roll, soul, rhythm and blues, reggae, and hip-hop, and by Caribbean music forms like calypso, rumba, and meringuemaringa. They are also characterized by the increased use of Western instruments, including electric guitars, horns, saxophones, and keyboards. Musicians integrate foreign sounds with indigenous styles to create new Africanized forms such as Congo jazz and *soukous*, burgher highlife, *juju*, Afro-beat, *mbalax*, *mbaqanga*, Afro-reggae, and African hip-hop.

In Central Africa, musicians living in and around Leopoldville and Brazzaville incorporated Afro-Cuban rhythms into their music and created Congo jazz, a popular music form that influenced new music styles throughout the continent. By the early 1960s, Congolese musicians such as Docteur Nico, Tabu Ley, and Manu Dibango began applying new guitar-playing techniques to the electric guitar and singing in the vernacular. In addition to the guitar, Congo music relied on an interplay of horns and percussion to create a sound that reflected new influences from abroad, including the American soul of James Brown and Aretha Franklin.

Bards (*jeliw*) of the Diabaté family playing ngoni. Kéla, Mali, 1976. Photograph © David C. Conrad.

Congo music quickly made inroads into the world music scene under the name *soukous*, one of its earlier dance forms. Spurred by the exodus of African musicians from the former French colonies to Europe, the popularity of *soukous* grew rapidly in the 1980s. One of the most popular musicians was Kanda Bongo Man, who moved to Paris in 1979 to escape the deteriorating economic conditions in Kinshasa. He worked to develop his own brand of *soukous*, increasing the pace of the music and reducing the size of the band by eliminating the horn section.

In West Africa, highlife music was the most popular music at the time of independence, especially in the former British colonies. By the mid-1960s, however, soul and rhythm and blues became more attractive to urban youth and popular music began to move in a new direction. Ghanaians resident in London formed the band Osibisa in 1969. They mixed highlife with rock 'n' roll and became famous within Africa and abroad. Later in the 1970s, Ghanaians living in Germany created another offshoot of highlife by adding synthesizers and electronic percussion instruments to earlier forms. They dubbed the new music "burger highlife" because they lived in the city of Hamburg.

In Nigeria, *juju* music also underwent major changes in the postindependence era. By the 1970s, Ebenezer Obey and King Sunny Ade, the most popular *juju* artists who gained fame through international tours, combined elements of traditional Yoruba music, Afro-Cuban rhythms, and American forms. The lyrics added social and religious commentary and the bands sometimes featured up to six or seven electric guitars linked together in a complex rhythmic pattern. No music from West Africa, however, can rival the status achieved by Fela Anikulapo Kuti and his Afro-beat during the 1970s and 1980s. Fela's music drew elements from African forms, particularly Congolese music and highlife, as well as African American soul and rhythm and blues. His bands were huge, consisting of horns, guitars and basses, keyboards, and percussionists, as well as a dozen singers and dancers. His lyrics, like the music, merged aspects of African and western cultures. Fela often sang in Pidgin and never hesitated to use his music to provide social and political criticism.

In the former French colonies of West Africa, Congolese styles dominated the popular music scene during the 1960s. In the following decade, however, *mbalax,* emerged in Senegal. It incorporated influences from calypso and Cuban music, African American soul and funk, as well as the previously dominant Congo forms. *Mbalax* utilizes local languages and instruments, including the *kora* (harp), the *balafon* (xylophone), and various percussion instruments. One of the most popular *mbalax* artist is Youssou N'Dour. Mali, Côte d'Ivoire, and Benin also saw a rising number of popular musicians in the late 1970s. The Malian, Salif Keita, blends elements of traditional *griot* music with West African, Cuban, and Spanish influences. He includes traditional instruments of Mali but also uses guitars, saxophones, and keyboards. Other popular artists achieved success as well. Combining local influences from Benin with rock 'n' roll, soul, and funk, Angelique Kidjo has become one of the most prominent female singers today. Her songs focus on important social issues and her African-inspired funk now attracts a large following.

South Africa, with the unique conditions imposed by the long history of apartheid, has produced unique music styles. Under apartheid, most blacks were forced to live in townships where new music forms emerged. These included *marabi*, a keyboard style originating in the 1920s. Another form, *mbaqanga*, has undergone many changes, but the various forms have all relied on a heavy bass and lead guitar to produce popular dance rhythms. During the 1970s, *mbaqanga* incorporated elements of rock music and was popularized by Juluka, a rare multiracial band that began with a Zulu guitarist, Sipho Mchunu, and an English-born musician, Johnny Clegg. Some of the most heralded musicians, realizing the impossibilities of working within apartheid-era South Africa, moved abroad. Miriam Makeba, known as the Empress of African song, left South Africa in 1959 and became one of the most famous female singers in the entire continent. She was a vocal critic of apartheid but, after its fall, was welcomed back to her home country. The trumpeter and vocalist, Hugh Masekela, also left South Africa and later toured with Fela and performed with Paul Simon on the *Graceland* tour.

The most popular forms of music in urban Africa at the turn of the millennium grew out of Jamaican reggae and western rap and hip-hop. During the early 1980s, reggae grew popular among urban youth, in part, because its lyrics proclaimed themes of mental and physical liberation for Africans everywhere. African musicians incorporated the ideologies of reggae but blended the rhythms with their own musical traditions to create a distinct musical idiom. Born in Côte d'Ivoire, Alpha Blondy has achieved success in African and international circles with his Afro-reggae. Others like Lucky Dube and Kojo Antwi blend reggae sounds with local influences to enhance the popularity of reggae among urban African youth.

In the 1990s African musicians began to fuse American rap and hip-hop with local rhythms and language to produce African variants that can be found in most every major city. One variant, South African *kwaito*, developed in the townships and mixes hip-hop, rhgthm and blues, and house music with local beats to give it more of a South African sound. Another variant, hiplife, contains undertones of highlife and has become immensely popular among Ghanaian youth. The vernacular lyrics of African rap and hip-hop express the identities of youth and relate to the conditions of everyday life in Africa. The influence of music from outside of Africa has had a profound influence on the development of African popular music forms. International styles, however, have not replaced traditional styles, but have rather fused with them to form new and unique popular styles that reflect the creativity of African musicians.

STEVEN J. SALM

Further Reading

Collins, J. *Highlife Time.* Accra: Anansesem Publications, 1996.

Coplan, D. *In Township Tonight: South Africa's Black City Music and Theatre.* Longman and Ravan, 1985.

Stewart, G. *Rumba on the River: A History of the Popular Music of the Two Congos.* New York: Verso, 2000.

Waterman, C. *Juju: A Social History and Ethnography of an African Popular Music.* Chicago: University of Chicago Press, 1990.

Wolfgang, B. *Sweet Mother: Modern African Music.* Chicago: University of Chicago Press, 1991.

Muslim Brotherhood: *See* Egypt: Salafiyya, Muslim Brotherhood.

Mutapa State, 1450–1884

The Mutapa state was established in the fifteenth century following the decline of Great Zimbabwe in the south. Swahili and Portuguese traders were in contact with it from the fifteenth and sixteenth centuries, respectively. Located in the northern part of the Zimbabwe Plateau, south of the Zambezi, its territorial limits have been exaggerated by earlier cartographers and chroniclers, who misled historians into thinking that it was an empire stretching from the Indian Ocean to the Kalahari Desert. From the early sixteenth century, the state controlled the northern limits of the Zimbabwe Plateau and the adjacent Zambezi lowlands. Kingdoms such as Manyika, Barwe, Uteve, and Danda are thought to have severed from the state. By the nineteenth century it was confined to Chidima, in the Zambezi.

Written evidence for the Mutapa state comes from the Portuguese, who entered the Zimbabwe Plateau at the beginning of the sixteenth century and compiled eyewitness as well as second-hand accounts of the state. The documents are inherently biased, as they focus mainly on trade and court politics. Oral traditions impart diverse information about the people once controlled by the state. Since the 1980s, archaeological work has been conducted in the northern Plateau and Dande, north of the Zambezi Escarpment, to identify the settlements connected with the state.

Oral traditions on the origins of the Mutapa state speak of migrations from Guruuswa, identified with the southern grasslands. The migrating parties were searching for salt deposits in the Dande area of the Zambezi. Its founders, according to traditions, conquered and subdued the Tonga and Tavara of the lower Zambezi, and the Manyika and Barwe to the east. Historical evidence suggests they initially settled in Mukaranga, the Ruya-Mazowe basin, before the sixteenth century, and conquered and integrated preexisting chiefdoms. This was necessitated by the need to control agricultural land and strategic resources, mainly gold and ivory, firmly placing the new state within the Indian Ocean trade network. Archaeological evidence links the rise of the Mutapa state with the demise of Great Zimbabwe in the fifteenth century. Since then stone buildings of the architecture similar to that used at Great Zimbabwe appeared in northern Zimbabwe. They represented major centers expressing a culture that spread from the south. These have been identified as royal courts. This was prompted by the increasing importance of the Zambezi River in the Indian Ocean trade initially channeled through Ingombe Illede. After 1500 there was a concentration of people in some areas such as Mount Fura and the adjacent Mukaradzi River to take advantage of incoming traders. Portuguese documents identify this area as Mukaranga, and its inhabitants as Karanga. They were part of the Mutapa state when the Portuguese arrived at the beginning of the sixteenth century.

Portuguese sources refer to Mutapa royal capitals as *zimbabwe*. These courts, although imprecisely located, are described as "big," and "of stone and clay." The Portuguese also observed numerous large towns and villages, some as big as three to five kilometers in circumference, with houses spaced within a stone throw of each other. The king lived in several houses separated by courtyards. These capitals had an approximate population of 4,000. Archaeological evidence locates most *zimbabwe* on the Plateau south of the Escarpment before the mid-seventeenth century.

Mutapa history from 1500 is dominated by Portuguese attempts to interfere with court politics, civil wars, conquests, and trade. The Tonga reacted to the Portuguese invasion of about 1570 with stiff resistance. This was followed by the Zimba invasions from Maravi, north of the Zambezi. From *about* 1600 to 1624, the Portuguese fought in civil wars involving Mutapa Gatsi Rusere, subduing the state, and from about 1629 to 1660s they turned its rulers into mere puppets.

Trading centers appeared since the late sixteenth century, where the Portuguese and Swahili middlemen exchanged with the locals Asian beads, glazed ceramics, and cloth with gold and ivory. Massapa, Luanze, and Dambarare seem to have been frequented most, compared to others found in the entire plateau area dominated by the state. Archaeological evidence from Baranda, which coincides with the Portuguese trading site of Massapa located in the Mukaradzi valley, show indigenous material culture similar to Great Zimbabwe, confirming a link between the Mutapa state and the former. Here the Portuguese maintained a permanent resident, tasked with negotiating terms of trade and monitoring Portuguese movement in the state.

Decline of trading activity in the state was due to Portuguese political interference, attempting to conquer the state. During the early seventeenth century civil war by rebels opposed to the ruling Mutapa and fuelled by the Portuguese seriously challenged central authority. The 1630s report lawlessness by some Portuguese *prazo* holders who raised private armies to rob or enslave people. Private fortifications are also reported.

Unstable conditions continued to up through the 1660s, seriously undermining trade in the eastern and central parts of the plateau, forcing traders to move further westward to open new markets. These too were abandoned subsequently. There was also loss of agricultural production, depopulation of the gold producing areas, and unregulated external trade. This undermined the authority of the rulers as it also encouraged revolts by peripheral groups that included the Portuguese *prazo* holders in the Zambezi. Fortifications arose in most parts of the state, and this is confirmed by archaeology. In the Ruya-Mazowe basin, more than 100 poorly coursed stone enclosures with loopholes (small, square openings probably used for peeping or as firing out points) are located on hill and mountaintops. These are probably the hill refuges used by rebels against Mutapa-Portuguese attacks. There are also reports of earthworks or wooden stockades (*chuambos*) built by the Portuguese. Toward the 1680s, conditions worsened, with disease decimating the human population in the area. The Portuguese were forced to leave the state. By the late seventeenth century the state had lost control of areas south of the Zambezi Escarpment.

The Mutapa state shifted toward Dande, north of the Zambezi Escarpment, during the early eighteenth century. The new state was limited in extend. To the eastern frontier, between Tete and the lower Mazowe, were the Portuguese *prazos* that it constantly attacked or occupied until the 1850s. Politically it was unstable as seen by quick successions and the civil wars fought between houses contending for the throne. Smaller, semi-independent polities controlled by some subrulers emerged in Dande and Chidima. Despite these, it survived because of its military strength, and ability to adapt well to new political circumstances. The Chikara religious cult of the Tavara was highly influential in regulating civil wars. Capitals were constantly mobile due to security considerations, severe droughts, and heat.

As a result they accommodated few people, only court officials, royal wives, and a garrison of about 500 fighters, except during times of war. During difficult periods, especially from around 1770 to 1830, it still managed to suppress revolts, fight *prazo* holders, and gain land.

In the nineteenth century, the Mutapa state survived the potentially destructive Ngoni invasions, serious droughts, and increased Portuguese attempts to reoccupy the lower Zambezi. However, after 1860, Portuguese *prazo* holders and their Chikunda armies began to assault the Mutapa state, invading it and forcing it to pay tribute. By 1884 the demise of the state seems to have been completed.

INNOCENT PIKIRAYI

See also: **Great Zimbabwe: Origins and Rise; Ingombe Ilede; Manyika of Eastern Zimbabwe; Nyanga Hills; Torwa, Changamire Dombo, and the Rovzi.**

Further Reading

Axelson, E. *The Portuguese in South Africa, 1600–1700.* Johannesburg: Witwatersrand University Press, 1964.
Beach, D. N. *The Shona and Zimbabwe, 900–1850: An Outline of Shona History.* New York: Heinemann, 1980.
———. *A Zimbabwean Past: Shona Dynastic Histories and Oral Traditions.* Gweru: Mambo Press, 1994.
Garlake, S. P. *Great Zimbabwe.* London: Thames and Hudson, 1973.
Mudenge, S. I. G. *A Political History of Munhumutapa.* Harare: Zimbabwe Publishing House, 1988.
Pikirayi, I. *The Archaeological Identity of the Mutapa State: Towards an Historical Archaeology of Northern Zimbabwe.* Uppsala: Societas Archaeologica Upsaliensis, 1993.
Pwiti, G. *Continuity and Change: An Archaeological Study of Farming Communities in Northern Zimbabwe, AD 500–1700.* Uppsala: Societas Archaeologica Upsaliensis, 1996.
Randles, W. G. L. *The Empire of the Monomotapa from the Fifteenth to the Nineteenth Century.* Gwelo: Mambo Press, 1975.
da Silva Rego, A., and T. W. Baxter, eds. *Documents on the Portuguese in Mozambique and Central Africa, 1497–1840.* Lisbon: Centro de Estudes Historicos Ultramarinos and the National Archives of Rhodesia and Nyasaland, 1962–1975.
Theal, G. M. *Records of South Eastern Africa.* Cape Town: C. Struik, 1898–1903.

Mutesa (Kabaka) (1856–1884)
Buganda Monarch

Mutesa epitomizes the traditional Buganda monarchy. However, his reign and person also marked the passing of old monarchism and the coming and embracing of enlightenment in Buganda, as the kingdom faced a new world.

Mutesa succeeded Kabaka Suuna as king in 1856, after a marvelously staged maneuvering and jostling for the throne by the elitist oligarchy at court. Being an insignificant prince, and therefore the least expected to contest the throne, the chiefs and promoters of other more eligible princes were caught unawares, only to finally accepted Mutesa as king.

Mutesa and his dignitaries. © Das Fotoarchiv.

By this time, there were already many Arab traders in Buganda. Mutesa wanted Buganda to be the terminus of all trade, rather than a thoroughfare. He coveted the monopoly to redistribute trade goods, especially firearms, to his neighbors.

Mutesa spoke both Kiswahili and Arabic and could read and write Arabic. At the time of his death he could converse with missionaries in English and translate to his courtiers in Luganda. He adopted Islam, outwardly observing all its rituals, but refused to undergo circumcision. In 1867 he decreed the Islamic calendar as official in Buganda and demanded the use of Islamic etiquette at court. The presence of Arab slave hunters from Khartoum in neighboring Bunyoro became a potential threat to Buganda and of great concern to Mutesa. He was persuaded to back a losing Bunyoro prince, but his forces were badly repulsed by Kabarega. By 1871 Mutesa had a minimum of a thousand armed troops.

Mutesa was suspicious of the activities and motives of Richard Gordon, who was openly working for the khedive of Egypt, intending to extend the Egyptian Empire into the Lake Region. Under these circumstances, therefore, political alliance with Sayyid Bargash, sultan of Zanzibar, made good political sense. In 1874 Cahille Long got Mutesa to sign a document, the contents of which he did not understand, but which amounted to ceding his kingdom to the khedive of Egypt. In April 1875 Mutesa tactfully jointly received both Gordon's agent, Ernest Linant, alias Abdul Aziz, and H. M. Stanley with the hope of playing them off one against another. In his dealings and discussion with both Stanley and Gordon's agents, Mutesa constantly demanded that Bunyoro remain as a buffer zone between Buganda and Egyptian territory to the north.

The famous 1875 Daily Telegraph letter by Mutesa calling for missionaries to come to Uganda was a result of these politicoreligious discussions with Stanley. However, evidence clearly shows that Mutesa's major concern was to have a group of European allies in his kingdom who would assist him when faced with the Egyptian (Gordon's) expansionist threat. His accommodating attitude to, and encouragement of, subsequent missionary enterprise in Buganda was part of his defense policy.

In 1877 the Egyptian threat became real when Nuehr Aga arrived with troops in the Buganda capital at Rubaga to claim the kingdom for the khedive, on Gordon's orders. Aga met very stiff resistance from Mutesa, and ended up as his captive. As a show of strength, Mutesa rounded up some seventy Muslims, who were executed publicly for Nuehr Agas benefit. However, Mutesa avoided open confrontation with Gordon who eventually sent Edward Schmitzler, alias Emin Pasha, to Rubaga to negotiate Nuehr Aga and his troops release by Mutesa.

The arrival of both the Church Missionary Society (CMS) and the Roman Catholic White Fathers missionaries in Buganda in 1879 provided a good opportunity for Mutesa to revive his long-term objective of getting both arms assistance and political alliance with a superior European power against threats of Egyptian encroachment from the north. Mutesa quickly noted the denominational and personal differences between the missionaries and exploited these to the fullest in achieving his personal aims. While he maintained relations with the Zanzibari Arabs, whose trade offered him the only sure supply of goods and arms, he also feigned conversion to Christianity to get maximum benefit from all foreigners in his country. Mutesa derived great satisfaction in staging impromptu theological and political discussions at his court between Muslims, Protestant missionaries, and Catholic missionaries.

Dr. Kirk, the British resident representative in Zanzibar, had promised Mutesa British intervention to ensure Buganda's independence in face of Egyptian aggression. Kirk's friendly gesture inspired Mutesa to try to enter direct negotiation with the British government; he decided to send an embassy to England. Three emissaries of Mutesa were escorted to England by CMS missionaries and were received by Queen Victoria in 1879. They returned to Buganda in 1881 with presents and messages of good will from Queen Victoria to Mutesa, but with no practical proposal of a political alliance between the two kingdoms, which was a great disappointment to Mutesa.

When, after the rise of Mahdism in Sudan in 1880, Gordon finally withdrew the southern garrisons in the Somerset Nile region, the Egyptian threat, which Mutesa had persistently felt, dissipated, leading to a sudden and dramatic change in his attitude toward the Christian missionaries who had refused his constant appeals to engage in trade. Christian missionaries henceforth suffered great hardships, including physical attacks on their persons.

One can only but guess what Uganda would have been like today if Mutesa was not the kabaka of Buganda and the person that he was at the time of the arrival of missionaries and subsequent European contact and colonization of Uganda. Mutesa's determined resistance to Egyptian domination saved Buganda from a possibly ravaging struggle for independence. Alternatively, Buganda could have become embroiled in the Mahdist upheavals with unpredictable consequence, as happened in the Sudan. Mutesa's decisions to ally with Britain, as opposed to France, may have determined the relatively liberal and unrestrictive relationship Britain had with Buganda, and subsequently with colonial Uganda.

Mutesa passed his kingdom on intact to Kabaka Mwanga, his son. The Mutesa I Foundation was started to commemorate Mutesa's achievements. The organization recognizes Ugandans who have made significant contributions to the development of their country.

David Kiyaga-Mulindwa

See also: **Uganda: Early Nineteenth Century; Uganda: Mwanga and Buganda, 1880s.**

Biography

Mutesa was born in 1856. He was one of the sons of Kabaka Suuna. Mutesa's mother was sold into slavery by Suuna. She entrusted her son to another king's wife, Muganzirwazza Nakkazi Muzimbo, who eventually became very dear to him. He was born as Mukabya, but later took on the names of Walugembe Mutesa. He took the throne in 1856. He died in 1884.

Further Reading

Ashe, R. P. *Two Kings of Uganda.* London: Frank Cass and Company, 1970.

Church Missionary Society. *The Victoria Nyanza Mission Chwa II.* Capt. H. H. D. Basekabaka Ababiri, W. M. Mutesa I ne D. Mwanga II Busega Mengo; G. W. Kabajeme 1922.

Grant, J. A. *A Walk Across Africa.* London: William Blackwood and Sons, 1878.

Gray, J. M. "Mutesa of Buganda." *The Uganda Journal.* 1, no. 1 (1934): 22–50.

Kiwanuka, M. S. M. *Mutesa of Uganda.* Nairobi: East African Literature Bureau, 1967.
Speke, J. H. *Journal of the Discovery of the Nile.* London: W. M. Blackwood and Sons, 1863.
Stanely, Sir H. M. *Through the Dark Continent.* London: Sampson Low, Saston, Scarcrow and Relivton, 1878.

Mwaant Yaav: *See* Lunda: Mwaant Yaav (Mwata Yamvo) and Origins.

Mwanga: *See* Uganda: Mwanga and Buganda, 1880s.

Mwata Yamvo: *See* Lunda: Mwaant Yaav (Mwata Yamvo) and Origins.

Mwenemutapa: *See* Mutapa State.

N

Nama: ***See*** **Namibia: Nama and Herero Risings.**

Namibia: Nineteenth Century to 1880

Southwestern Africa between the Kunene and the Okavango rivers in the north, the Orange River in the south, and the Kalahari to the west saw large-scale social restructuring and the final integration of its communities into the world market during the nineteenth century. The onset of missionary activity combined with the repercussions of Portuguese colonialism to the north and the advancing Cape colonial frontier, prior to more active German colonization after 1884. Induced by the nature of the area, the dominant modes of subsistence were foraging and pastoralism, with its concomitant social organization. Only in the north, where available rainfall allowed for agriculture, were sedentary forms of social organization possible.

The area to the north of Etosha was, by the 1800s, populated by different groups of agro-pastoral, Bantu-speaking Ovambo kingdoms, with considerable variation among them in terms of language and social custom and ranging from highly centralized kingdoms to rather loosely structured polities. Oral history, which is borne out by linguistic evidence, suggests that these communities were related to several groups of pastoral Herero, living in segmentary societies oft the partly mountainous area south of Etosha, between the Kalahari and Namib Deserts. This area was also known as Damaraland during the nineteenth century. Interspersed in economic and environmental niches were Khoisan-speaking Damara communities, whose mining and smithing skills provided them with a means of survival. Their history remains clouded, however. Khoisan communities, both larger pastro-foraging groups (Khoekhoe/Nama-speaking) as well as smaller groups of hunter-gatherers (San), peopled the southern stretches and exploited the least favorable environment of the area.

Since around the 1790s, groups of Oorlam raiders had crossed the Orange River from the south. On account of their long history in the colonial context of the Cape, these disenfranchised groups, who usually had originated from illicit master-slave sexual relations, brought with them not only the experience of colonialism but also important political, social, and religious institutions, which in the end would facilitate their suzerainty in southwestern Africa. Along with mother tongue variations of Khoisan, they spoke Cape Dutch, adhered to Christianity, had horses, arms, and wagons. Through all this, they provided the first link to the expanding world economy through the Cape nexus. This facilitated social change and provided lasting political influence in the encountered communities across the Orange River. Missionary activity, mainly by the German-based Rhenish Mission Society, was greatly facilitated by this development.

By the 1840s the Oorlam had established themselves in the south and, with a hegemonial position at present-day Windhoek in the center of the area, were ruled by the Afrikaner Oodam clan under their most important leader Jonker Afrikaner. Their economic base rested on yearly cattle raiding expeditions, of which the neighboring Herero communities around Windhoek and to the north bore the brunt, but which were organized as far as the northern Ovambo communities. This in turn sparked long-term social change, class differentiation, and political centralization among the Herero. As this process unfolded, mining interests, arms, ivory, and cattle trading made the establishment of Walvis Bay as an entrepot to the territory feasible. The bearers of this trade together with the missionaries, who by the 1850s were firmly established among the Herero as well, provided the Herero with weapons

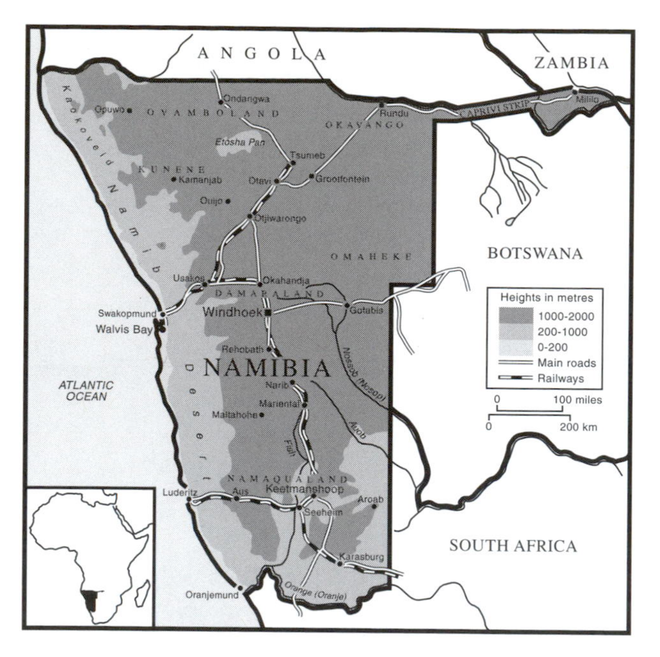

Namibia.

to such a degree that the Nama-Oorlam hegemony was effectively challenged and crumbled after 1860. Guns and the increasingly developing markets for cattle that could be provided from Hereroland in the wake of the mineral revolution in South Africa resulted in a distinct process of pastoralization of the Herero with the attendant development of separate, more centralized chiefdoms, one of which would over time be perceived to be paramount, the Maharero chiefs.

Ever-growing numbers of European traders and hunters operating in the area from the 1850s, particularly around Otjimbingwe and Omaruru, effected these developments as well. Sexual unions, but more often than not intermarriage and the establishment of families, left traces. The offspring of these families would very often be the most suitable agents of acculturation and negotiators of innovation and change in the economic, religious, and political spheres: translators, secretaries, and evangelists for the mission and the local rulers. During the latter half of the nineteenth century, Cape Dutch was used widely as a *lingua franca* in diplomacy, church, and trade.

The void created by the downfall of the Oorlam hegemony around Windhoek enabled the Baster, the last of such disenfranchised groups from the Cape, to move to the north and to settle at Rehoboth south of Windhoek in the early 1870s. This development, and the arrival of Boer trekkers from the Transvaal in search of yet more land led the Herero to invite colonial annexation by the British Cape Colony in an attempt to curb developments that were clearly perceived to be detrimental. The declaration of a protectorate over Walvis Bay and its surroundings in 1876 was a result of this.

In the 1870s and 1880s southern Nama groups reemerged on the political scene, again in their own fight. When Hendrik Witbooi, in a move inspired by divine intervention, tried to lead his community to a more northerly area, he was challenged by the by-now well-armed, rather wealthy, and organized Herero. This in turn often sparked decades of guerrilla warfare waged by the Witbooi Nama. It was in this situation, which again threatened the mission's endeavor after decades of only tenuous successes in their work, and given the background of heightened colonial awareness in Europe, that German missionaries started to agitate for colonial annexation. The German merchant Adolf Luderitz finally succeeded in concluding a treaty with a local ruler at Angra Pequena, which was known to be fraudulent. However, as the "Scramble for Africa" raised European political desires and anxieties, it was taken by Chancellor Bismarck as a stepping-stone to declaring the region a German protectorate. To fulfill the requirements of the Berlin Congo Conference of 1884, Germany started to erect a colonial administration from 1885 and to conclude treaties with a series of local rulers.

On account of their relative geographical inaccessibility, the Ovambo communities in the north were affected by the developments in the south far less, and only after the Finnish Mission Society started to make tenuous inroads in the 1870s. Processes of social stratification and large-scale pauperization led to a certain degree of feudalization, both of which were fully under way by the time of German annexation.

WOLFRAM HARTMANN

Further Reading

Dedering, T. *Hate the Old and Follow the New: Khoekhoe Missionaries in Early Nineteenth-Century Namibia.* Stuttgart: Franz Steiner Veflag, 1997.

Lau, B. *Namibia in Jonker Afrikaner's Time.* Windhoek, Namibia: Archeia, 1987.

Moorsom, R., and W. G. Clarence-Smith. "Underdevelopment and Class Formation in Ovamboland, 1845–1915." *Journal of African History.* 16, no. 3 (1975).

Williams, F.-N. *Precolonial Communities of Southwestern Africa: A History of Owambo Kingdoms, 1600–1920.* Windhoek: Archeia, 1991.

Namibia (Southwest Africa): German Colonization, 1893–1896

Germany's initially very limited colonial penetration of late nineteenth-century Namibia was made possible by Britain's lack of attention to it, and by the severe isolation of its various communities and the serious divisions and conflicts between them. German economic and political activities in Namibia began in the 1880s as the efforts of a Bremen tobacco merchant, Franz Adolf

The old German fort in the Etosha, about 1930. © Das Fotoarchiv.

Eduard Lüderitz, to acquire land and wealth through concessions from Nama leaders and the unexpected actions of the imperial chancellor, Otto von Bismarck, that led to the declaration of a formal German protectorate. German Protestant missionaries of the Rhenish Missionary Society entered Namibia much earlier, in the 1840s, and established stations and influence among the Herero and Nama, but not in the north.

Lüderitz sent his young business associate Heinrich Vogelsang to Cape Town and Angra Pequeña (an inferior harbor, transferred by Britain to the Cape Colony in 1884), where he arrived on Lüderitz' trading brig *Tilly* in April 1883. During the next months, Vogelsang persuaded the local chief of the Bethanie Nama, Josef Fredericks, to sign agreements transferring the land on the bay and then an extensive hinterland in exchange for money, rifles, and toys. With his agent raising the German flag at the renamed Lüderitzbucht and referring to the region inland as Lüderitzland, Lüderitz renewed a request he had made earlier to Bismarck for official recognition and protection.

In 1883 and 1884, Bismarck approached the British government cautiously over the status of Angra Pequeña, only to suddenly extend protection to Lüderitz' Namibian claims on April 24, 1884, an event that can be said to have inaugurated Germany's overseas colonial empire during the "Scramble for Africa." Bismarck soon extended this foothold into a larger Namibian colony. The crews of two naval vessels raised the German flag along the coast, at Angra Pequeña, Swakopmund, Cape Cross, and Cape Frio in August, enabling Germany to claim the entire coastline, except for Walvis Bay, from the mouth of the Orange River north to the Cunene River. To include the hinterland in the colony, Bismarck ordered his consul general for West Africa, the noted explorer Gustav Nachtigal, to secure protectorate treaties from the African chiefs.

In 1885 Lüderitz formed the Deutsche Kolonial-Gesellschaft für Südwest-Afrika but quickly lost control of it. His funds dwindled, causing him to sell off his concessionary rights to the company. He died in a boating mishap near the mouth of the Orange River in 1886. The company that eclipsed and survived him also obtained a number of mining and land concessions from the German government. Despite its recruitment of a small police force to safeguard gold operations near the Swakop River, the company was unable to locate significant mineral deposits or compel the Herero and Nama leaders to accept its control. Official representatives at first fared little better. Nachtigal's successor so far as Namibia was concerned, the first imperial commissioner of German South West Africa, Dr. Heinrich Göring, initially obtained agreements with African rulers, including Chief Maherero of the Herero. Angered by the inability of the Germans to prevent attacks from his Nama enemy, Hendrik Witbooi, and influenced by his Cape merchant ally, Robert Lewis, Maherero in 1888 renounced his agreement with Göring and forced the imperial commissioner to relocate his headquarters to the safety of the Walvis Bay enclave.

By 1889 German colonialism in Namibia was at a virtual standstill. Seeking to establish a degree of control in the center of its nominal protectorate, Germany sent out a small military contingent under Captain Curt von François, with orders to establish outposts but avoid fights with Africans. Landing at Swakopmund in January 1889, von François built a fort inland at Tsoabis. The following year he received reinforcements and built a second fort, known later as the Alte Feste, further inland, at Windhoek. In 1891, von François replaced Göring as imperial commissioner and transferred the colonial headquarters to Windhoek, which remained the capital of South West Africa during the German and South African occupation periods.

Relations with Namibians remained the key to German penetration of the territory. Maherero, the Herero ruler, renewed his recognition of the German protectorate and died in 1890. With his succession hotly contested, the Germans were able to adapt a strategy of divide-and-rule in Damaraland. Hendrik Witbooi, however, refused to submit to German overrule, and von François determined to destroy him. Additional reinforcements in early 1893 allowed the Germans to undertake a military campaign against the Witboois. von François attacked Hendrik Witbooi's camp at Hoornkranz on April 12, killing a number of his followers, mainly old men, women, and children. The Nama chief and most of his armed men survived the Hoornkranz massacre and fled to the Naukluft Mountains. Facing criticism in the Reichstag over von François' actions, Chancellor Leo von Caprivi sent out Major Theodor Leutwein, a military college instructor, as his special commissioner to investigate and possibly take control of the colony. Leutwein arrived at the start of 1894 and, with reinforcements, defeated Hendrik Witbooi. Witbooi signed a protectorate agreement with the Germans and served them as an ally for the next decade.

Leutwein took charge of the colony and turned his attention to the Herero, imposing a frontier for them that allowed German settlement in southern Damaraland. The succession to Maherero's chieftainship was contested between Nikodemus, his strongly independent nephew, and the younger and more pliable Samuel Maherero, his surviving son by a fourth wife. Unlike Nikodemus and many other Herero, Samuel accepted Leutwein's boundary, and the Germans supported the unpopular claim of Samuel to his father's chieftainship. Garrisoning Okahandja deep in Herero country, Leutwein during the brief "War of the Boundary" in May 1896 attacked and defeated Samuel's opponents, Nikodemus and his eastern Herero followers and the Mbanderu under Kahimeme. He then executed their leaders as rebels and confiscated their lands and herds as state property. An additional four hundred soldiers arrived in mid-1896 to ensure Germany's control of Namibia south of Ovamboland.

Alongside their divide-and-rule policy toward the Namibians, the colonial officials encouraged German and Afrikaner settlement in central and southern parts of the protectorate. In Berlin the Syndikat für Südwestafrikanische Siedlung recruited and sent the first twenty-five families to settle in the Windhoek region in 1892. A similar number arrived the following year. Military veterans began to receive tracts of land in return for their service. In 1896 the syndicate obtained an official grant of 20,000 square kilometers for German colonization in the districts of Windhoek, Gobabis, and Hoachanas. The severe rinderpest epidemic that arrived the following year further impoverished the pastoral peoples of the central and southern areas, facilitating land alienation and settler colonization in the years prior to the great uprisings of 1904–1905. By 1897, 2,628 Europeans, mainly German officials, soldiers, missionaries, and settlers, resided in Namibia.

LOUIS W. TRUSCHEL

See also: **Colonial European Administrations: Comparative Survey; Colonialism: Ideology of Empire: Supremacist, Paternalist; Colonialism: Impact on African Societies; Namibia: Nineteenth Century to 1880.**

Further Reading

Aydelotte, W. O. *Bismarck and British Colonial Policy: The Problem of South West Africa 1883–1885.* Philadelphia: University of Pennsylvania Press, 1937.

Bley, H. *South West Africa under German Rule.* Evanston: Northwestern University Press, 1971.

De Vries, J. L. *Mission and Colonialism in Namibia.* Johannesburg: Ravan Press, 1978.

Esterhuyse, J. H. *South West Africa 1880–1894: The Establishment of German Authority in South West Africa.* Cape Town: C. Struik, 1968.

Namibia (Southwest Africa): Nama and Herero Risings

The Nama and Herero risings against German colonial administration in German South West Africa turned out to be the most important historical event in the history of present-day Namibia. Though interrelated and of the same genocidal consequences for both Nama and Herero, they were two different wars of which only the Herero war has found its way into debates and publication. Both can only be understood in the context of the developing German colonial state in southwestern Africa, however.

Protocolonialist influence and European imperial influence had been at work in southwestern Africa for about one hundred years before formal, and later effective, German colonization. Germany, compelled by the dynamics of the "Scramble for Africa" declared southwestern Africa to be a German protectorate in 1884. Starting at Angra PequeMa and driven by the Bremen merchant Loderitz for the next decade, German officials, backed by a small military contingent and aided by missionaries and traders, set out to conclude nominal treaties of protection with local rulers and communities, which were either accepted, negotiated, or contested depending on local circumstance, political expediency, and historical experience. Both Hendrik Witbooi of the Nama and Samuel Maharero of the Herero exploited these developments and, assisted by the colonialist need for centralized political ruling structures, styled themselves paramount rulers. Windhoek, an existing settlement, was established as military and administrative headquarters in 1890.

In the 1890s the German-African treaties of protection were challenged in a number of insurrections, most notably so by Hendrik Witbooi with guerrilla warfare. Theodor Leutwein, who took over as the colony's first formal governor in 1893 ruthlessly established German colonial overlordship with military means and skillfully applied "divide and conquer" policies among the different communities. In 1894 Witbooi signed a peace treaty with Leutwein, starting a decade of German-Nama collaboration. Maharero's position as paramount chief of the Herero was consolidated. He effectively started the administration of the territory's central and southern areas with the installation of an executive and a judiciary. A closely-knit web of police stations for surveillance and control was established. The northern reaches of the territory remained largely untouched for much of the decade due to geographical inaccessibility and health reasons. Legislation was still largely effected in Germany. Active and planned colonization was embarked upon with the assistance of commercial and mining companies. Large tracts of lands, taken in the military campaigns of the 1890s and, declared as crown land, were used for settling German colonists. Ex-military personnel from the campaigns often chose to remain in the colony, married into local communities and either acquired land and stock through this or set themselves up on farms provided from confiscated, so-called crown land. The reverberations of the South African War (1899–1902) resulted in another wave of white settlers that were displaced by that conflict and chose to settle themselves in the southern parts of the territory.

During the 1890s and into the first years of the twentieth century processes of dispossession and indebtedness of African communities accelerated through exponentially growing trade and fraudulent credit practices between Germans and Africans. This was compounded by the Rinderpest pandemic of 1897–1898, with its ensuing effects of famine and subsequent droughts, and a general situation of lawlessness. Especially the sale of land by chiefs, in an attempt to retain political power and spurred by the pressures exerted by conspicuous consumption, helped to create a class of landless and impoverished, who in turn were desired by the growing, predominantly agrarian colonial economy.

Tensions between Herero and settlers grew and while the governor led a military campaign to quell a minor insurrection by the Boncleizwarts in the southern part of the territory, the Herero, led by Samuel Maharero, took up arms in January 1904. Sparing women, children, missionaries, and non-Germans, the Germans were surprised by this attack, and most male settlers were killed. Within two months the German forces had regained the military initiative with massive logistic and material reinforcements from Germany. When Leutwein was superseded by General Lothar von Trotha, because the former was blamed by settlers and colonial circles in Germany for leniency and the outbreak of the war, the situation had already calmed down. In this situation politicians were clamouring for a peaceful solution of the conflict to ensure that a steady supply of labor for the colony's economy was not annihilated, and missionaries started to argue for mercy, offering assistance to the colonial state in the pacification effort. von Trotha, however, enforced the Battle of Hamakari near Waterberg in August 1904, where a majority of the Herero had gathered. An already demoralized and exhausted enemy was thus forced to flee through the waterless Omaheke into the Kalahari Desert in an attempt to reach safer havens across the Bechuanaland border. Unknown but small numbers of refugees, including Samuel Maharero, reached Bechuanaland.

von Trotha's infamous Vernichtungsbefehl, or extermination order of October 1904, ordered the removal of the remaining survivors of the conflict from German territory. Every Herero found inside German borders, with or without arms and cattle, was to be killed, regardless of whether man, woman, or child. This order was in effect until December 1904 and repealed when it was realized how impractical and counterproductive it was, given the local circumstances and necessities. The remaining survivors in the colony were, with assistance of the missions, systematically collected and incarcerated in concentration camps, where another substantial number died due to unsanitary conditions and weakened health. An estimated 80 per cent of the Herero nation did not survive this conflict.

During the later stages of the Herero German war in October 1904, the Nama, under the leadership of Hendrik Witbooi, took up arms. The German forces could retaliate immediately in full force on account of the termination of the hostilities with the Herero and by early 1905 had succeeded in quelling this rising as well. The death of Hendrik Witbooi in military action left the Nama without their military and political leader. However, groups of Nama continued to keep German military forces at bay with guerrilla tactics until 1909, especially under the leadership of Jakob Morenga. Only an estimated 25 per cent of the Nama population survived this war. Scorched earth policies, concentration camps, and even the deportation of large numbers of Nama to other German colonies in Africa were responsible for this genocide.

A strict labor legislation was almost immediately enacted to permanently disenfranchise and dispossess the Herero and Nama and to counter the detrimental effect of the war on the labor market. Every individual above the age of eight had to wear a metal tag around her/his neck, which made rigid mobility controls thus possible. The Ovambo, among whom unknown numbers of Herero had found refuge during the war, were drawn into the colonial labor economy by more diplomatic means. On account of their military strength, due to their connectedness into the Portuguese economic networks, but by now also under attack in pacification campaigns waged by Lisbon, these were considered with respect by the German colonial administration. A series of treaties, concluded separately with different rulers regulated relations and the labor flow from Ovamboland to the colony.

A dependable labor flow became ever more important since the discovery of diamonds in 1908 in the south of the colony had started a phenomenal economic boom in the colony. This made German South West Africa the only German colony ever to realize a financial surplus. This growth of course happened on the background of an already burgeoning economy started by substantial numbers of ex-servicemen on land confiscated after the wars with large herds of confiscated cattle and cheap, conscripted labor. Still, substantial numbers of workers for the construction of railways and the diamond mining industry had to be acquired from the Cape Colony.

German colonialism came to an end in German South West Africa, when the Union of South Africa decided to join the war effort in 1914 and assist Great Britain against Germany. The Union Defence Force enforced a ceasefire in July 1915 near Khorab in the north of the territory, after which the territory was governed under military law until 1920. With the campaign against and final defeat of King Mandume of Oukwanyama in Ovamboland in early 1917 this northernmost part the territory was finally subjugated and brought under colonial domination. Processes of social and economic reorganization and restructuring among the Herero, and Nama, already under way during the last years of German influence, continued and received stimulus when South Africa, during its first years in GSWA, tried to present itself as a more benevolent colonizing force than the Germans. This served to underscore South Africa's attempt at being declared the mandatory guardian once the war was over. German colonial power was finally ended when South Africa was made the mandatory power "on behalf of his Britannic Majesty" under the terms of the Treaty of Versailles in early 1919.

WOLFRAM HARTMANN

See also: **Namibia (Southwest Africa): German Colonization, 1893–1896; World War I: Survey.**

Further Reading

Bley, H. *Kolonialherrschaft und Sozialstruktur in Deutsch-Südwestafrika, 1894 bis 1914.* 1968, Münster: Lit Verlag, 19?

Drechsler, H. *Südwestafrika unter deutscher Kolonialherrschaft. Der Kampf der Herero und Nama gegen den deutschen Impenalismus (1884–1915).* Berlin: Akademie Verlag, 1966.

Gewald, Jan-Bart. *Herero Heroes. A Socio-Political History of the Herero of Namibia, 1890–1923.* Oxford, James Currey, and Ohio University Press, 1998.

Katjavivi, R. *A History of Resistance in Namibia.* London: Currey, 1988.

Namibia (Southwest Africa): South African Rule

The Germans gave the name "South West Africa" to the protectorate they acquired in 1884. Their territory expanded until it included all of what is now Namibia, except for the port of Walvis Bay, which had been annexed by Britain in 1878 and brought under Cape, then South African rule from 1910. In 1915, during the World War I, South African troops conquered the territory from the Germans. The South Africans took over the name South West Africa and applied to it the entire country, including Walvis Bay. From the late 1960s an alternative name, Namibia (from the Namib desert), was adopted by the United Nations, and in the 1980s the South Africans came to accept the new name, though they used "South West Africa" as well, even after the decision to withdraw from the territory was made in 1988.

After five years of South African military rule, the territory was granted as a C-class mandate to South Africa by the League of Nations in 1920. South Africa continued many German practices, extended the system of reserves, and introduced more white settlers from the Union. Resistance by the Bondelswartz and other indigenous people was put down harshly. Though in terms of the mandate, South Africa was supposed to govern the territory in the interests of the inhabitants, South African rule was highly oppressive, and there was no effective check on what South Africa did in the territory.

When the League of Nations dissolved during World War II, the South African government of Jan Smuts hoped to be able to annex the territory, and formally applied to the newly formed United Nations (UN) in 1946 to do that, but its request was refused, largely on the grounds that the indigenous people had not been adequately consulted. The UN instead asked South Africa to place the territory under its trusteeship system, which provided for eventual independence for trust territories. When South Africa refused, a long-drawn-out legal battle began, in which the International Court of Justice at The Hague handed down a series of judgments on the status of South West Africa. In 1966 the Court decided that it had no legal standing in a case which turned on whether South Africa was governing the territory in the spirit of the mandate. The UN General Assembly then unilaterally terminated the mandate, a decision that was, a few years later, ratified by the Security Council. In 1971 that ratification was supported by an advisory opinion of the International Court of Justice, which ruled that South Africa's rule of the territory was illegal, and it should withdraw. In the same year a general strike of Namibian workers represented a new and massive example of resistance to one of the main pillars of South African rule, the contract labor system.

In the face of these developments, the South African government decided to abandon its policy of seeking to incorporate the territory to a greater and greater extent into its own administration, as a de facto fifth province, along with the creation of Bantustans there on the South African model. It decided instead that the territory should remain as one entity and be given a form of "independence" under South African auspices. An ethnically based advisory council was established, and in 1975 a conference of ethnic representatives was called together in the Turnhalle building in Windhoek. When it seemed that the Turnhalle might lead to the South African government granting "independence" to a local client group, a Western Contact Group was formed, consisting of the five Western countries then members of the UN–Security Council, to press for a form of independence that would mesh with the UN demand for a transfer of power to the people of the territory (UN–Security Council Resolution 385 of 1976). By April 1978 a formula had been worked out providing for joint UN–South African administration during a transition period in which the UN would provide a monitoring team and a force to keep the peace. The South African government accepted this plan in April 1978, probably without any serious intention of ever implementing it. Numerous reasons were advanced in the years following by South African government spokesmen to explain why the plan (embodied in UN Security Council Resolution 435) could not be implemented: the alleged partiality of the UN, the composition of the UN force to enter the territory during the transitional phase, the monitoring and location of the military bases of the People's Liberation Army of Namibia, the army of the South West African Peoples' Organizaation (SWAPO), and, from 1981, the presence of Cuban forces in Angola.

Operating from northern Namibia, South African military forces, and from 1980 South West African forces under South African command, launched raids against SWAPO bases in southern Angola. Brutal repression was used in northern Namibia to try to destroy SWAPO, while at the same time the Democratic Turnhalle Alliance (DTA) and other political groupings were built up in an attempt to form an anti-SWAPO alliance. Finally, as the result of an agreement signed in December 1988 between South Africa, Angola, and Cuba, providing for the withdrawal of the Cuban forces from Angola, the date for implementation was fixed for April 1989. From that month, the South African administrator general worked with the UN special representative in preparing the way for an election held in November, after which the remaining South African troops withdrew from the territory. The South African administration remained in place while a Constituent Assembly deliberated on a new constitution. With that agreed, Namibia became independent in March 1990 and the South African administration finally withdrew. The country's most important port, Walvis Bay, became part of Namibia by agreement with the South African government on March 1, 1994.

CHRISTOPHER SAUNDERS

Further Reading

Department of Information and Publicity, SWAPO of Namibia. *To be Born a Nation.* London: Zed Books, 1981.

Hayes, P., et al., eds. *Namibia under South African Rule: Mobility and Containment, 1915–1946.* Athens: Ohio University Press, 1998.

Leys, C. and J. Saul, eds. *Namibia's Liberation Struggle: The Two-Edged Sword.* Athens: Ohio University Press, 1995.

Vigne, R. *A Dwelling Place of Our Own: The Story of the Namibian Nation.* London: International Defence and Aid Fund, 1975.

Woode, B., ed. *Namibia 1884–1984: Readings in Namibia's History and Society.* London: Namibia Support Committee, 1988.

Namibia (Southwest Africa): League of Nations, United Nations Mandate

In December 1920, after five years of military administration, South Africa was granted the former German South West Africa as a C- class Mandate by the League of Nations, which meant that the territory was to be administered as if it were an integral part of the mandatory power. The new administration emphasized four policy aspects. First, it downscaled the administrative presence to about a quarter of what it was during the German heyday. At one stage the total civil service numbered just over two hundred. This lack of administrative capacity, while ostensibly cost-effective, meant that much of the draconian oppressive legislation it passed could not be implemented, suggesting that much of this legislation served to encourage interpersonal settler violence. Second, it changed the settler demographics. About half the German settler population were either deported or left voluntarily, at the same time "poor whites" from South Africa were encouraged to settle in the mandate.

After 1923 Germans were encouraged to become, in effect, "dual citizens" of both Germany and South Africa, and while the number of Germans rose, it did not do so as fast as the Afrikaner elements and this issue defined the tone of the settler-dominated "Legislative Assembly" inaugurated in 1925. The administration decision to encourage and to subsidize Angolan Afrikaners to resettle in Namibia not only threatened the German-speakers, but it also signaled the end of a balanced budget, since each new farmer was subsidized to the amount of approximately 2,500 pounds. Third, the administration pursued a policy of segregation based on the South African model. A "native reserve" was created in each magisterial district where idle and surplus blacks could be located and which would form a source of inexpensive labor. Fourth, transport and communications were expanded and incorporated into the South African system. Not only was the railway line expanded to Gobabis in the east of the territory, but more important, it was linked to the South African system; the operation of the railways and harbors was taken over by the South Africa Railways and Harbors Board, which had the effect of reorienting the territory in terms of trade and cultural domination away from Europe and toward South Africa.

These deployments were framed by an atmosphere of settler insecurity. Rumors enhanced the situation. Indigenous resistance, epitomized by the Bondelswarts Rebellion in 1922, the Rehoboth Rebellion in 1924, and the Ipumbu Affair in 1932 were suppressed using military aircraft especially brought in from South Africa for this purpose. Generally, however, the global economic depression coupled to drought and floods served to minimize capitalist development during the interwar years. Mining, fishing, and farming formed the major sectors of economic activity and, to service these, increasing use was made of contract migrant labor.

Fears of a possible Nazi incursion in 1939 led to a 300-strong South African Police contingent being sent to the territory and the incorporation of the police into the South African Police. Shortly thereafter the banking currency in the territory was also switched to South African.

World War II had relatively little direct impact on this region. About a thousand German males were interned and a small number of Africans did military service mostly as guards in South Africa. After the war there was a massive expansion in settler farming and "native administration" was incorporated directly into the South African equivalent. South Africa did not recognize the United Nations as the legal successor to the League of Nations and proposed to directly incorporate the territory. As part of this process it tried to implement most of the apartheid-like recommendations of the Odendaal Commission (1964) which greatly expanded the public service by creating twelve second-tier "ethnic administrations." Various rulings by the International Court of Justice were inconclusive until 1971, when it finally found that South Africa's presence there was illegal. This political uncertainty, in addition to hindering investment also had important ecological consequences as many speculators bought land and then overgrazed it in an effort to benefit from the South African meat market.

Resistance to South Africa's overrule became clear and increasingly well organized after World War II, spearheaded originally by Chief Hosea Kutako who, with the assistance of the Rev. Michael Scott, made petitioning the United Nations an effective tool. In the early 1960s political parties, like the South-West African Peoples' Organization (SWANU), were formed explicitly to promote independence, their importance underlined by the killing of people protesting removal from the Windhoek Old Location late in 1959. SWAPO commenced its armed struggle with a skirmish in 1966 and guerrilla and border war continued in increasing intensity up to independence.

In late 1971 Ovambo contract workers went on a massive and successful strike. This event created minor concessions but more important led directly to large numbers of refugees fleeing the country who provided many of the SWAPO cadres. In the face of increasing international pressure various internal political configurations were unsuccessfully offered by South Africa.

The international independence struggle was closely tied to the antiapartheid struggle, and as divestment and boycotts started affecting the economy of both South Africa and its major trading partners, the five Western permanent members of the UN Security Council (and major trading partners) served as mediators in trying to implement UN Resolution 435, which called for free elections in Namibia. Their efforts, abetted by a worsening economic crisis in South Africa and an unwinnable border war and coupled to the collapse of the "Second World" or Socialist Bloc eventually led to the arrival of the United Nations Transition Assistance Group (UNTAG) in April 1989. This transition is widely held up as one of the major successes of the UN system. The closely monitored elections were held in November 1989 and won by SWAPO, which took power when the country finally became independent at midnight on March 21, 1990.

ROBERT J. GORDON

Further Reading

First, R. *South West Africa.* Harmondsworth: Penguin, 1963.

Hayes, P., et al. (eds.). *Namibia under South African Rule.* Athens: Ohio University Press, 1998.

du Pisani, A. *SWA/Namibia: The Politics of Continuity and Change.* Johannesburg: Jonathan Ball, 1985.

Wellington, J. *South West Africa and its Human Issues.* Cape Town: Oxford University Press, 1967.

Wood, B. (ed.). *Namibia 1884–1984: Readings on Namibia's History and Society.* London: Namibia Support Committee, 1988.

Namibia: SWAPO and the Freedom Struggle

The struggle to free South West Africa (SWA) from South African rule was crucially framed by the internationalization of the question of the territory's future. SWA was originally ceded to South Africa as a League of Nations mandate, but in the 1940s the UN refused the territory's formal annexation by South Africa. Instead, after extensive negotiations, the General Assembly terminated the mandate (1966), declared South Africa's occupation illegal (a reading later [1971] endorsed by the International Court of Justice), and established a Council for Namibia to exercise formal trusteeship over the territory. In practice, South Africa would successfully defy the UN by continuing its occupation until 1990.

Under such circumstances, it was perhaps inevitable that Namibians, as they developed initiatives (a remarkable range of them for so small a population) to liberate their country, focused first and foremost on this international terrain: the Herero Chiefs Council played an important role in early Namibian initiatives at the UN, for example. Meanwhile, additional foci of opposition began to emerge in the late 1950s. A group of left-wing intellectuals crafted the South West African National Union (SWANU) from previously existing student organizations. But it was the South-West African Peoples' Organization (SWAPO) that would now place itself at the very center of the nationalist movement.

The roots of SWAPO's precursor, the Ovamboland Peoples' Organization (OPO), lay in the community of Ovambo migrant laborers working in South Africa and within SWA itself, but from 1960 OPO adopted a more inclusive nationalist strategy signaled by its new name. Confirming OPO president Sam Nujoma as SWAPO president, it began to relocate the center of gravity of its operations into exile in Tanzania. There, with the failure of unity efforts, SWAPO moved skillfully to gain exclusive international status for itself as voice of the new Namibia-in-the-making. SWAPO's courting of the OAU and its Liberation Committee, combined with its promise to launch military activity within SWA itself, led, in 1964, to SWAPO gaining OAU recognition as the "sole and authentic" representative of Namibia. Then, as pressure against South Africa's occupation of SWA mounted at the UN, SWAPO was granted, in 1973, the status of "authentic representative of the Namibian people" by the General Assembly.

Efforts to consolidate international support for Namibia were crucial, of course. South Africa was to try various schemes to legitimate its hold on Namibia, including the Odendaal Plan of the late 1960s for the "bantustanization" of Namibia, and the 1975 launching of the Turnhalle process designed to give the appearance of some devolution of power to Namibians themselves. Moreover, even though these various "reforms" failed, they were complemented by savage repression that was far more successful. True, some space was allowed for oppositional political activity in the southern and central "Police Zone" of the country, although SWAPO activists were harassed even there. In the north, the violence committed by the South African Defense Force and attendant locally based special forces (especially the notorious Koevoet) was even more extreme. This was particularly true of densely populated Ovamboland, which also provided the staging grounds for South Africa's many incursions into Angola against both the MPLA government and SWAPO (the massacre at SWAPO's Cassinga camp in 1978 producing as many as 900 casualties, for example). It is true that from the time of their first operation at Ongulumbashe in 1966, courageous guerrillas penetrated the country sufficiently often to earn the attention of the South Africans. Nonetheless, SWAPO was never able to mount a serious challenge to South Africa's military grip on Namibia.

From exile, the SWAPO leadership continued to strengthen its centrality within the emergent Namibian polity, its international status complementing its popular credibility internally. This helped sustain common cause against the apartheid state's presence in Namibia and its various schemes, albeit, some would argue, at the cost of permitting a damaging degree of control by the external SWAPO over strategic initiatives inside the territory. These costs were perhaps most visible in the late 1980s, when organizations of workers, students, women, and churchgoers who sought momentarily to broaden the terms of internal struggle and the autonomous empowerment of civil society along lines then being exemplified in South Africa were effectively discouraged from doing so by the exile leadership. Even more certain, however, were the costs of the leadership's ruthlessness in crushing tensions within its own ranks in exile. SWAPO members who questioned SWAPO's practices in exile were first imprisoned, with help from the Tanzanian authorities, in the 1960s, but the movement's internal crisis in Zambia (where SWAPO had shifted its base to in the 1970s) was much more serious.

Inside Namibia, the early 1970s had witnessed a vast popular upsurge (the dramatic strike of migrant workers in 1971–1972 and an impressive wave of youth-inspired resistance throughout the country). When this revolt was crushed by the South Africans, thousands of young Namibians went into exile to join the liberation movement. They soon discovered a SWAPO that many of them considered to be militarily ineffectual, undemocratic, and corrupt. In 1975 they called for a congress, as promised at SWAPO's previous 1969 Tanga congress, to discuss such matters. Nujoma instead persuaded the Zambian army to arrest some 2,000 of these new arrivals, while also having the putative leaders of this "coup" jailed in Tanzania with the connivance of his fellow presidents, Kenneth Kaunda and Julius Nyerere.

The SWAPO leadership largely whitewashed these events in a subsequent internal investigation while continuing with its pragmatic course of pursuing external backing. SWAPO had long since cornered Soviet support, for example, and was prepared to make various left-sounding pronouncements to seal this relationship, even as it complemented these with more moderate assertions aimed at other potential constituencies overseas. More difficult to finesse was the further playing out of the movement's authoritarian tendencies, which erupted, once SWAPO had shifted its center of operations to Angola in the 1980s, in a wave of often arbitrary incarcerations, torture, and even murder at its Lubango base of hundreds of alleged "spies" from within the movement. Set in a context of military frustration and considerable paranoia, these developments evidenced a security apparatus now almost completely out of control, its reign of terror manifesting ethnic, intraethnic, and regional tensions as well as the targeting of the more educated among SWAPO's cadres. As this deadly machine began to close in on even the most senior of the SWAPO leadership in the late 1980s, the movement was very close to the point of self-destruction.

Meanwhile, Namibia's broader fate had became hostage in the 1980s to the Cold War machinations of the United States. After 1977 a Security Council-based "contact group" of five Western powers largely took over the Namibia issue at the UN, rejecting further sanctions against South Africa but promising to facilitate resolution of the issue with the apartheid regime. This group in turn soon yielded to pressure from the United States to "link" Namibia's fate to the ending of Cuban support for the Angolan government (itself under siege from South Africa, with American backing) and thus helped stall international progress on Namibia. It was therefore fortunate that by the end of the 1980s the apartheid government, now facing (after its failed siege of Cuito Cuanavale) a costly military stalemate in Angola, was also seeing a need to reconsider its intransigent strategies closer to home. It now become party to negotiations over Namibia that (in a context which also registered the Soviet Union's own waning interest in southern Africa) finally realized the implementation of Security Council Resolution 385 of 1976, which called for UN supervision of free and fair elections in Namibia as a prelude to independence.

Significantly, SWAPO was largely excluded from these negotiations. Nonetheless, the movement had managed to so consolidate its political credentials within Namibia, and especially in the northern, more populous, Ovambo-speaking part of the country, as to be a near-certain winner once the complicated process of clearing the ground for elections was finally realized. In the event, SWAPO won forty-one of seventy-two seats in the UN-supervised elections of November 1989, permitting the new assembly to unanimously elect Sam Nujoma the first president of a liberated Namibia. Independence itself came on March 21, 1990.

Encouraged by new realities, both local and global, to abandon many of its more overtly authoritarian practices from exile as well as the socioeconomic radicalism that some of its earlier rhetoric implied, SWAPO now came to preside over a liberal-democratic constitutional system and a full-blown market economy. The darkest side of the movement's past practices seemed likely to reemerge only if any lack of success of that economic strategy were to polarize social contradictions dangerously and/or if a political opposition were to emerge credible enough to jeopardize SWAPO's electoral grip on power—which, among other things, would threaten SWAPO's military, security, and political elites with a reopening of questions regarding the movement's abuses of power in exile.

JOHN S. SAUL

See also: **Nujoma, Sam.**

Further Reading

Bauer, G. *Labor and Democracy in Namibia, 1971–1996.* Athens: James Currey Ohio University Press, 1998.
Becker, H. *Namibian Women's Movement, 1980 to 1992: From Anti-Colonial Resistance to Reconstruction.* Frankfurt: IKO, 1995.
Dobell, L. *Swapo's Struggle for Namibia, 1960–1991: War by Other Means.* Basel: P. Schlettwein Publishing, 1998.
Emmettt, T. *Popular Resistance and the Roots of Nationalism in Namibia, 1915–1966.* Basel: P. Schlettwein Publishing, 1999.
Heywood, A. *The Cassinga Event.* 2nd rev. ed.Windhoek: National Archives of Namibia, 1996.
Leys, C., and J. S. Saul. *Namibia's Liberation Struggle: The Two-Edged Sword.* Athens: Ohio University Press, 1995.

Namibia: Struggle for Independence, 1970–1990

There is a view (expressed in the work of Lauren Dobell [1998], for example) that the struggle for independence in Namibia was largely fought outside the country, chiefly by the diplomacy of the externally based South West African People's Organization (SWAPO) leadership. Within the country, certainly, SWAPO faced massive organizational problems, not only because of the way the population was dispersed across the land but also because the group's attempts to organize were met with harsh repression and violent reactions. Nevertheless, at certain moments the internal struggle played an important role in the process which eventually led to independence.

One of these moments came in 1971. After the International Court of Justice ruled that South Africa's rule of the territory was illegal, the two main Lutheran Church leaders wrote an open letter to the South African prime minister, John Vorster, which presented a stance of open support for independence; this was the first time that the churches had identified themselves with the movement for independence. Within months, from December 1971 to March 1972, a major strike took place that involved up to 13,000 contract workers, the backbone of the Namibian labor force. The external SWAPO leadership was taken by surprise by the scale of the strike, but quickly tried to capitalize on it. The new political consciousness born of the strike helped motivate the SWAPO Youth League to campaign against the imposition of the Bantustan policy in the north. The increasing resistance within the country to South African rule, and the threat of further mass action, undoubtedly played a part in the Vorster government's decision to shift ground and accept the idea of independence for the de facto colony. But South Africa wanted to control that process, to bring into office an independent Namibia—a government that would support, and not challenge, South African interests.

SWAPO was never banned in Namibia because of the international status of the territory, but its internal leadership suffered constant harassment at the hands of the South African authorities, and on a number of occasions its key officials were jailed; some of them were tortured and in September 1989 a top official was assassinated. As the increasingly vicious war in the north intensified, so repression elsewhere grew harsher. But in the mid-1980s, thanks to the reform program of the South African government, new space opened up for protest politics. The South African government knew that without international recognition of Namibian independence, the conflict with SWAPO would not end. It was not prepared to implement the Western plan for a transition to independence, accepted by the United Nations in September 1978, because it would almost certainly bring into office a SWAPO government, and it sought to create in the territory an anti-SWAPO front that could form an alternative to SWAPO. It therefore influenced a group of internal parties to form the Multi-Party Conference (MPC) in 1983, a wider grouping than merely the Democratic Turnhalle Alliance, which had won the internal election of December 1978. The MPC then pressed for the establishment of a Transitional Government of National Unity (TGNU), which came into office in June 1985. There was no new election, but to give the TGNU some legitimacy, more freedom of expression was allowed, and SWAPO began to organize as it had not been able to for over twenty years. It now again held mass rallies, and a new leadership, returned from imprisonment on Robben Island, organized the first effective trade unions. The Namibian Union of Mineworkers under Ben Ulenga formed the backbone of the National Union of Namibian Workers, and the SWAPO Youth League gained a new lease of life.

In the crucial year 1988, when South Africa at last began negotiating the implementation of the Western plan, there were widespread protests within the country, beginning in the north, where scholars at schools next to army bases protested against their proximity to the bases and called a school boycott. The school boycott spread throughout Ovamboland and into other areas, and workers began to give their support to the students. This growing internal crisis was one factor, argues Brian Wood, for the South African decision to go ahead with the implementation of the Western plan and to withdraw from Namibia.

After a delay of over a decade, implementation began on April 1, 1989, and a large United Nations presence entered the country to supervise the election that took place in the first week of November that year. SWAPO emerged victoriously, but with only 57.4 per cent of the vote, and not the two-thirds majority that would have enabled it to write the constitution for the new country on its own. By February 1990 the new constitution had been accepted, and the country became independent on March 21, 1990. Any account of the road to that independence must allow some space for internal resistance and mass protest in extremely difficult circumstances.

CHRISTOPHER SAUNDERS

See also: **Namibia (Southwest Africa): South African Rule; Namibia: Independence to the Present; Namibia: SWAPO and the Freedom Struggle; South Africa: Homelands and Bantustans.**

Further Reading

Cliffe, L. (ed.). *The Transition to Independence in Namibia*. Boulder, Colo.: Lynne Riener, 1994.

Dobell, L. *Swapo's Struggle for Namibia, 1960–1991: War by Other Means*. Basel: P. Schlettwein Publishing, 1998.

Leys, C., and J. Saul. *Namibia's Liberation Struggle*. London: James Currey, 1995.

Peltola, P. *The Last May Day*. Helsinki: Anthropological Society, 1996.

Soggott, D. *Namibia: The Violent Heritage*. London: Rex Collings, 1986.

Wood, B. "Preventing the Vacuum: Determinants of the Namibia Settlement." *Journal of Southern African Studies*. 17, no. 4 (1991).

Namibia: Independence to the Present

When Namibia became independent on March 21, 1990, numerous heads of state from around the world attended the celebrations held in the Windhoek stadium. But international attention soon dissipated, in part because nothing dramatic happened in Namibia. Some had feared that far-right-wing elements would try to destabilize the new government, but this did not occur. One of the main features of Namibia in its first decade since independence was its relative political stability.

The South West African People's Organization (SWAPO), the main liberation movement, that had gained less than two-thirds of the vote in the pre-independence election of November 1989, won over two-thirds in the next general election in December 1994, and retained its dominance in the December 1999 general election. The main opposition party, the Democratic Turnhalle Alliance, remained crippled by its association with South Africa and with Namibia's apartheid past, and steadily lost support. Mishake Muyongo, former vice president of SWAPO, took over as leader of the DTA from Dirk Mudge, but then left to take up the leadership of the separatist Caprivi Liberation Front. With some thousands of other Caprivians, he fled from Namibia to Botswana in late 1998, and was subsequently granted asylum in Denmark. A group of his supporters staged an armed attack on Katimo Mulilo, the chief regional center in Caprivi, in August 1999. This was the greatest threat to Namibian sovereignty since independence, but the attackers were quickly defeated. Allegations of human rights abuses by the Namibian security force against Caprivians then hurt Namibia's image, and tourists canceled visits in large numbers, but by September it seemed the threat was over.

Botswana's relations with Namibia remained cordial, despite the long drawn-out dispute between the two countries over the island of Katsikili/Sidudu on the Chobe River. When the two countries could not agree on the matter, it was referred by their governments to the International Court of Justice in The Hague for adjudication. Judgment in Botswana's favor in late 1999 was accepted by the Namibian government.

Another major development in 1998 was the establishment of a new political party, the Congress of Democrats (COD), under the leadership of Ben Ulenga, former trade unionist and long-time SWAPO member. He had been appointed Namibia's high commissioner in London but was unhappy when SWAPO approved the idea of changing the constitution to allow Sam Nujoma (the president) to serve a third term as president and was critical of Nujoma's decision to send Namibian troops to the Democratic Republic of Congo in support of Laurent Kabila, for no clear reason other than to add support to the intervention of Namibia's close partners in the Southern African Development Community, Angola, and Zimbabwe. The COD obtained the support of many intellectuals and members of the Windhoek elite.

Those disillusioned included some who pointed to creeping authoritarianism on Nujoma's part, and who disliked SWAPO's dominance of the political scene. Many former members of the SWAPO armed wing, the People's Liberation Army of Namibia, had returned to Ovamboland and not been able to find work. While some were absorbed into the police and the army, others claimed that the government had forgotten about them.

The continuing Angolan civil war meant that throughout its first decade of independence Namibia could never take the stability on its northern border for granted, but despite this, much economic development took place there, as ties between northern Namibia and southern Angola grew ever closer. It was on that border that the government planned a major hydroelectric scheme at the Epupa Falls, which not only threatened the lands on which some of the seminomadic Himba people lived, but was also much criticized by environmentalists. After the opening of the trans-Caprivi highway, which opened up the northeastern part of the country, the Kuwaiti government promised to fund the extension of the railway north from Otavi to the Angolan border. Nujoma himself had hopes of another port being built close to Ovamboland, but nothing more than a feasibility study was undertaken.

One objection to the Epupa scheme was that a new energy source had been discovered off the southern coast: the Kudu gas field, which could come on stream sooner, and send gas to Cape Town in South Africa for processing. Namibia remained highly dependent on its natural resources, and for some years in the mid-1990s its fishing industry fell on bad times, as the fish stocks declined. Although by the end of the decade they had recovered considerably, the falling price of uranium meant that production at the giant Rossing mine had to be cut back, and in 1998 the Tsumeb copper mine was closed, with the loss of thousands of jobs. Only diamonds retained their sparkle throughout the decade, in the middle of which the South African-based De Beers had made an agreement with the Namibian government for a partnership, creating a new company, Namdeb, in which the government held a 50 per cent stake. As this suggested, any idea of nationalizing the mines had disappeared after independence, as the country adopted orthodox capitalist policies. One of its successes was in creating economic enterprise zones, where tax was low and labor flexible. By the end of the 1990s, a number of such zones were in existence, at Walvis Bay and other places, providing the country with a small manufacturing sector, mostly producing export goods.

Most of Namibia's exports continued to go to South Africa. Relations with that country remained good, after the negotiating forum in South Africa had in 1993 agreed that Walvis Bay, Namibia's leading port, which the South African government had always claimed as its own territory, could be incorporated in Namibia. After some months of joint administration, the handover of Walvis Bay took place. When President Nelson Mandela came to office, he offered to take over the apartheid debt, which the Namibian government had inherited at independence. After long negotiations, this was done and over R700 million wiped off. The two countries worked together in the Southern African Development Community, and the two presidents paid a number of visits to each other's countries. One new threat they both had to face was the rapid spread of HIV/AIDS infections: by 1999 an estimated 15 per cent of all Namibians between the ages of fifteen and fifty were infected. By then, the total population was an estimated l.6 million.

Although the investment conference held in New York City in June 1990, shortly after independence, did not attract as much foreign investment as hoped, the government continued with investor-friendly policies and orthodox economic policies. The first SWAPO congress held on Namibian territory, which met in December 1991, did not challenge the leadership on central issues. A land conference held the previous June had begun to raise the tricky issue of land redistribution but in the years that followed very little was done to give effect to its recommendations. As it came to power, the SWAPO government had proclaimed national reconciliation as its policy. As the years passed, critics said that the only reconciliation they could see was with the small minority, at the cost of the black majority, most members of which still lived in poverty.

Namibia would not agree to participate in the South Africa's Truth and Reconciliation Commission, and the publication of Siegfried Groth's *Namibia: The Wall of Silence*, which told of the atrocities carried out in SWAPO's camps in Angola, provoked much controversy. Nujoma lashed out at the Beyond the Wall of Silence (BWS) organization, which had been established to campaign for the truth about what had happened in SWAPO's camps in Angola during the war to come out. Whites in particular were accused of undermining the government. While the media remained free, there was little probing of news or investigative journalism, and the government mostly remained tight-lipped about its policies. As Namibia entered the new millennium, it was clear that much time and effort would be needed to create a democratic culture.

CHRISTOPHER SAUNDERS

See also: **Mining, Multinationals, and Development; Namibia: SWAPO and the Freedom Struggle; Nujoma, Sam.**

Further Reading

Bauer, G. *Labor and Democracy in Namibia, 1971–1996.* Athens: Ohio University Press, 1998.

Economist Intelligence Unit, Country Surveys. *Namibia.* London: EIU, 1990–1998.

Groth, S. *Namibia: The Wall of Silence.* Cape Town: David Philip, 1995.

Leys, C., and J. Saul. *Namibia's Liberation Struggle.* London: James Currey, 1995.

Napata and Meroe

Napata and Meroe were the most important centers within the Kushite Empire, which flourished from the eighth century BCE to the fourth century CE. The exact meaning of the term Napata is unclear, but it probably designated a locality rather than a single site. Although there is some evidence for occupation in the Kerma Period, the earliest structural remains are those of a small temple, begun by the Egyptian Pharaohs Horemheb (1323–1295BCE) or Seti I (1294–1279BCE) and completed by Ramesses II (1279–1213BCE). Epigraphic evidence, however, records that a fortress with a shrine of Amun within it was constructed by Thutmose III (1479–1425BCE). Amenhotep II (1427–1400BCE) records that he sacrificed seven captive prisoners on his return from a successful campaign in southwest Asia and had the body of one of the victims hung on the walls of Napata.

Napata became a place of great religious significance to the Egyptians. On the right bank of the Nile stands Jebel Barkal, an isolated and prominent mountain with a sheer cliff-face over 100 meters high and a detached pinnacle 80 meters high. The Egyptians identified this mountain as the southern home of their state god Amun, calling it the "Pure Mountain."

Upon their adoption of the state god of Egypt, the Kushites held Jebel Barkal in equal veneration and began a building program at the foot of the mountain in the eighth century BCE, which developed into the largest religious complex in their extensive domains. The earliest Kushite temple may have been constructed by Alara (*c*.785–760BCE) or Kashta (*c*.760–747BCE). Piye (*c*.747–716BCE) was responsible for refurbishing and extending the New Kingdom temple of Amun, which on its completion was the largest in the realm. One of the most interesting temples, the Temple of Mut, was constructed, or reconstructed, by Taharqo (69–664BCE). The sanctuary chamber was hollowed out of the rock of the cliff face and decorated with reliefs one of which shows Taharqo making offerings to Amun who is depicted seated on a throne within the "Pure Mountain" itself.

Across the river and a few kilometers downstream, Sanam Abu Dom was the site of another large temple of Amun, with an adjacent palace and massive stores complex. The earliest Kushite rulers were interred at el-Kurru twelve kilometers downstream. Taharqo chose to be buried at Nuri, slightly upstream of Barkal but on the opposite bank, and most rulers from then on into the late fourth century BCE were interred there.

The earliest evidence for occupation at Meroe, which is on the left bank of the Nile and was reached by a direct route across the desert from Napata, is a number of circular timber huts dating to the tenth century BCE. The importance of Meroe was first documented at the time of the Kushite's invasion of Egypt two centuries later. An extensive cemetery, situated on a projecting spur of the plateau four kilometers to the east of the settlement, contained graves, many of which are clearly of wealthy and important individuals. The funerary customs and the artifacts buried with the deceased indicate that these people were subjects of the kings of Kush. By this date Meroe, although displaying a few regional characteristics, was an important and wealthy center of Kushite culture. From the later seventh century BCE Kushite rulers are attested in the city although they continued to be buried at Napata for several centuries thereafter.

During the mid-third and second centuries BCE, an area enclosed by a thick stone wall with projecting towers was constructed in the heart of the city. It was dubbed the Royal City by its excavator. Within were temples, palaces, and the so-called Roman baths, which functioned as a water sanctuary probably connected with festivals performed by the king on the occasion of the beginning of the annual inundation. A new Temple of Amun was erected on the east side of the Royal City. This was the second largest of the Amun temples in the kingdom after that at Napata and presumably was designed to replace the earlier temple of the god at Meroe which had stood on the site of the Royal City. At this time Meroe may have been on a island but, if so, the eastern channel ceased to flow by the beginning of the Christian era and thereafter a processional way flanked by temples was constructed leading up to the Amun temple. Elsewhere in the city most of the dwellings were of mud brick, one building succeeding another over the centuries until they formed a mound up to approximately ten meters in height. On the eastern side of the city there is extensive evidence for ironworking with large heaps of slag being a prominent feature of the landscape.

From the late fourth century BCE onward, most Kushite rulers were buried at Meroe; the pre-eminence of Meroe as an urban center was established. The reason for this move of the royal burial ground from Napata is unknown. It certainly does not represent an abandonment of the cult of Amun at Napata, which continued to flourish. Evidence for building activities at Napata continue for centuries and these include a large palace built by King Natakamani (*c.*1–20CE) who was also active in the Meroe region. At Napata, immediately to the west of Jebel Barkal, are two small pyramid cemeteries, one group dating to the period around 315–270BCE, the other to the period around 90–50BCE. Some of these are of Kushite rulers who certainly controlled the whole of the kingdom.

Napata may have been sacked by the armies of the Twenty-sixth Dynasty Egyptian ruler Psammetik II in 593BCE, and again by a Roman army under Petronius in 24BCE. The final abandonment of the site presumably occurred upon the collapse of the Kushite state in the fourth century. Meroe may have been occupied by the Aksumites from Ethiopia for a short period at that time. Like Napata, Meroe does not appear to have survived the collapse of the Kushite state, although burials of a slightly later date abound in the area.

DEREK WELSBY

See also: **Kerma and Egyptian Nubia; Kush; Meroe.**

Further Reading

Kendall, T. *A New Map of the Gebel Barkal Temples.* In *Études Nubiennes.* Vol. 2. edited by C. Bonnet, Geneva, 1994.

Shinnie, P. L., and R. J. Bradley. *The Capital Of Kush 1.* Berlin, Meroitica 4, Akademie-Verlag, 1980.

Török, L. *The Kingdom of Kush: Handbook of the Napatan-Meroitic Civilization.* Leiden: Brill, 1997.

———. *Meroe City, An Ancient African Capital: John Garstang's Excavations in the Sudan.* London: Egypt Exploration Society Occasional Publications 12, 1997.

Welsby, D. A. *The Kingdom of Kush: The Napatan and Meroitic Empires.* London: British Museum Press, 1996.

Napoleon: *See* Egypt, Ottoman, 1517–1798: Napoleon and the French in Egypt.

Natal, Nineteenth Century

A British colony from 1842 until 1910, this region of southeast Africa was so named because a Portuguese navigator, Bartholomew Dias, sighted its coast on Christmas Day (i.e., Christ's natal day) in 1497. For most of the nineteenth century, Natal was defined as the territory lying between the Drakensberg mountains and the sea between the Umzimvubu and the Thukela Rivers.

In the opening decades of the century, the district was caught up in tumultuous wars fought by a number of chieftaincies aspiring to assert hegemony over the region. By 1827 the Zulu kingdom forged by Shaka had emerged as the decisive victor. Some of the chiefs and communities formerly prominent in Natal moved away, but most accepted Zulu rule. The consolidation of power in the hands of a single government attracted the attention of a motley assortment of traders and hunters who were granted permission by Shaka to settle in the districts around Port Natal (modern Durban). Shaka commandeered their services as riflemen in his later wars and rewarded them with presents of cattle. By the time of Shaka's assassination in September 1828, the leading traders had married local women and acquired sizeable followings of servants and hangers-on.

Unscrupulously claiming to have been granted huge tracts of land, the traders attempted unsuccessfully to bring about a British annexation of Natal. Shaka was succeeded by his brother Dingane, who expelled most of the adventurers at Port Natal. During the early 1830s, however, he again allowed traders and hunters to move in.

The British colonial government of the Cape Colony now began to take a serious interest in the Zulu kingdom. Dr. Andrew Smith was sent as an emissary to Dingane in 1832, ostensibly to cement cordial relations. In his private communications, however, Smith argued that it would not be difficult to seize the king's domains. Some of Smith's party were farmers from the eastern districts of the Cape, who marveled at the open green pastures that stretched from the Port Natal up to the Drakensberg. Their reports asserted that the Zulu wars had cleared the land of people and that the territory was therefore ripe for settlement. These statements should not be taken at face value; twentieth century historians have comprehensively exposed them as self-interested propaganda. Nonetheless, the idea of lush cattle lands just waiting to be occupied made a powerful appeal to the imaginations of farmers whose expansion into the eastern districts of the Cape had been halted by the determined resistance of the Xhosa and Thembu people. When land hunger and dissatisfaction with British colonial administration provoked the mass emigration of farmers later known as the Great Trek, the intended destination of most of the so-called Voortrekkers was Natal. They were cheered on by colonial newspaper editors and property speculators who extolled their pioneering spirit and argued that the British government should extend its protection over them.

Dingane was understandably wary of an uninvited, audacious invasion of farmers in 1837. He told the Voortrekker leader, Piet Retief, that he had heard reliable reports that white men had been stealing Zulu cattle and other property. There could be no question of negotiating about grants of land until this property was returned. Retief claimed that the real culprit was the Tlokwa chief Sekonyela. In November 1837 he offered to lead an expedition to Sekonyela's headquarters in the Caledon River valley to reclaim the stolen goods. On his return he sent word to Dingane that Zulu property consisting of 700 head of cattle, 60 to 70 horses, and 30 guns had been retrieved and would shortly be returned to the king. When Retief and his party of seventy farmers and assorted servants arrived at Dingane's capital, they were received with apparent cordiality. The king, however, had determined to halt this invasion in its early stages and had prepared a calculated trap in the guise of a display of Zulu dancing on the third of February 1838. After Retief and his men had been persuaded to leave their horses and guns outside, the king gave the signal that the *amathakathi* (wizards or criminals) should be killed. The same day, regiments were dispatched to attack all the Voortrekker parties in Natal. They seized huge numbers of cattle and very nearly succeeded in exterminating the would-be colonists. After suffering heavy losses, the surviving Voortrekkers regrouped and determined to defend their de facto seizure of Natal by launching a counterattack on the Zulu king. They were assisted by the Port Natal traders who deserted Dingane and mobilized their small number of African servants and supporters for an assault in March 1838. Although these forces were resoundingly defeated, a better-armed expedition inflicted a catastrophic defeat on Dingane's forces at Blood River, where some 3,000 Zulu men died on December 16, 1838. A standoff ensued for several months. Despite their victory, the Voortrekkers had not succeeded in either of their principal aims, which had been to regain their lost cattle and to negotiate a cession of Natal.

Meanwhile, the British government at the Cape had become alarmed, fearing that the Voortrekkers had unleashed wars that would eventually threaten the stability of their own eastern frontier. A small force was sent to Port Natal in November 1838 for the purpose of arranging a settlement with the Zulu king. It was not their intervention, however, but the defection of Dingane's brother, Mpande, and 17,000 followers that proved decisive. Allying himself with the Voortrekkers, Mpande proclaimed himself king and defeated Dingane's forces in February 1840. The boundary between Zululand and Natal was now set at the Thukela River. A short-lived Voortrekker "Republic of Natalia" with its capital at Pietermaritzburg expired in 1842 when the British determined that for strategic reasons they must hold Port Natal; the Cape governor proclaimed the annexation on May 5, 1843.

The incoming government faced formidable problems. A population of a few thousand colonists was vastly outnumbered by an African population estimated to number 100,000. Under the secretary for native affairs, Theophilus Shepstone, lands known as Reserves were defined for exclusively African occupation and chiefs were made the principal instruments for the administration of justice and the collection of taxes in those areas. The success of this experiment in keeping the peace and defraying the cost of government caused it to be copied in other British colonies of southern, central, and eastern Africa. Shepstone's system also helped to lay the foundations of twentieth-century segregation and apartheid in South Africa by laying down separate legal systems for white and black citizens.

The colonial economy languished until the establishment of extensive sugar plantations in the coastal regions in the 1860s. A shortage of Africans willing to work on the extended contracts required by the sugar planters led to the importation of indentured laborers from South Asia who formed the nucleus of South Africa's Indian population. They were followed by free Indian settlers, including, in the 1890s, the young lawyer Mohandas K. Gandhi.

Africans responded positively to the opportunities presented by a market economy. They grew crops not only in the designated Reserves, but also on purchased or rented land. Others affiliated themselves to the many mission stations established in Natal. In the preeminent century of European evangelization, Natal's accessible location and large population made it a favorite destination for missionary organizations. Especially important were the missions established by English Methodists, American Congregationalists, Swedish, German and Norwegian Lutherans, and the Church of England. Under Anglican Bishop J. W. Colenso, Natal became the scene for influential innovations in missionary practice and theology. Although Colenso was convicted for heresy in 1864, he continued to be recognized by the British government as the official bishop of Natal, using his friendship with Theophilus Shepstone to advance his interests.

This alliance ended suddenly at the end of 1873, when Colenso objected to the harsh punishment Shepstone imposed on Hlubi Chief Langalibalele, who defied an order to account for unregistered rifles held by his people and attempted to flee over the Drakensberg into Lesotho.

The furor raised in Britain by Colenso's accounts of atrocities inflicted on the Hlubi led the Colonial Office in 1875 to suspend Natal's constitution of 1857 and to replace it with one less susceptible to the influence of white colonists. Three years later another crisis arose when the British attempted to federate the various colonies and republics of South Africa. The high commissioner, Sir Bartle Frere, who had been sent out to achieve this project, decided that the independence of the Zulu kingdom was a military menace and an obstacle to the economic success of the proposed federation. War was declared in January 1879 and despite unexpected early Zulu victories, eventually ended with the capture of the king Cetshwayo (who had succeed his father Mpande in 1873). An attempt to rule Zululand through thirteen separate chiefs plunged the region into a devastating civil war that ended in 1887 when the territory was officially annexed to Natal, thus extending the northern boundary to the border of Portuguese Mozambique.

In 1894 a concerted campaign by white settlers to achieve self-government was successful and the colony for the first time had an elected prime minister. African interests suffered greatly from the change, as the separate legal system established under Shepstone deprived them of the right to vote, unless they had been specifically exempted from "Native Law." Only a handful won exemption, ensuring the dominance of white interests. New laws curbed African rights to buy and own land, thus inhibiting the growth of the middle class. As the population grew the Reserves became overcrowded and degraded. By the end of the century people in the Reserves were already becoming dependent on the earnings of migrant workers.

The century ended spectacularly with the outbreak of the second Anglo-Boer War. Invading forces besieged the town of Ladysmith. Following British victory and the Peace of Vereeniging (1902), Natal saw its system of segregated reserves and dual legal system adopted by the entire Union of South Africa.

NORMAN A. ETHERINGTON

See also: **Anglo-Zulu War, (1879–1887) Boer Expansion: Interior of South Africa; Mfecane; Shaka and Zulu Kingdom, (1810–1840); South Africa: Confederation, Disarmament and the First Anglo-Boer War, 1871–1881.**

Further Reading

Duminy, A., and B. Guest (eds.). *Natal and Zululand from Earliest Times to 1910: A New History.* Pietermaritzburg: University of Natal Press, 1989.

Etherington, N. *Preachers, Peasants, and Politics in Southeast Africa.* London: Royal Historial Association, 1978.

Guest, B., and J M. Sellers. *Enterprise and Exploitation in a Victorian Colony: Aspects of the Economic and Social History of Colonial Natal.* Pietermaritzburg: University of Natal Press, 1985.

Laband, J, and P. Thompson. *Kingdom and Colony at War.* Pietermaritzburg: University of Natal Press, 1990.

Welsh, D. J. *The Roots of Segregation: Native Policy in Colonial Natal, 1845–1910.* New York: Oxford University Press, 1971.

National Party: *See* South Africa: Afrikaner Nationalism, Broederbond, and National Party, 1902–1948.

National Resistance Movement: *See* Uganda: National Resistance Movement (NRM) and the Winning of Political Power.

Nationalism: *See* Colonialism, Overthrow of: Nationalism and Anticolonialism.

Nationalism(s): Postcolonial Africa

The concept of nationalism has been defined as a sense of collective identity in which a people perceives itself as different from, and often superior to, other peoples.

Nationalism also implies the existence of a variety of shared characteristics, most notably a common language and culture, but also race and religion, as shown by the rise of Islamic revivalist movements in North Africa and other regions of the world with sizable Muslim populations.

The emergence of African nationalism and African demands for national self-determination (independence) from colonial rule followed a different pattern than its classic European counterparts of earlier centuries. The emergence of European "nations" (i.e., a cohesive group identity) generally preceded and contributed to the creation of European "states" (the structures of governance). The net result was the creation of viable nation-states that enjoyed the legitimacy of their peoples. This process was reversed in Africa. In most cases, the colonial state was created prior to the existence of any sense of nation. As a result, the creation and strengthening of a nationalist attachment to what in essence constituted artificially created African states became one of the supreme challenges of African leaders during the postcolonial era.

The emergence of African nationalism was also unique in terms of its inherently anticolonial character. African nationalist movements were sharply divided on political agendas, ideological orientation, and economic programs. Regardless of their differences, however, the leaders of these movements did agree on one point: the necessity and desirability of independence from foreign control. Anticolonial sentiment served as the rallying point of early African nationalist movements to such a degree that African nationalism was equivalent to African anticolonialism.

The emergence and strengthening of contemporary African nationalisms unfolded gradually in a series of waves beginning in the 1950s with groups of countries becoming independent during specific historical periods. The first wave emerged during the 1950s and was led by the heavily Arab-influenced North African countries of Libya (1951), Morocco (1956), Tunisia (1956), and the Sudan (1956). Two countries outside of North Africa also obtained independence during this period: the former British colony of the Gold Coast (Ghana) in 1957, followed by the former French colony of Guinea in 1958. This latter case was especially noteworthy in that Guinea was the only French colony to cast a negative vote against a 1958 referendum concerning the creation of a revised "French community of states." A "yes" vote would have confirmed continued French sovereignty while at the same time granting some degree of political autonomy to Guinea and the other French colonies. The response of the French government was to order the immediate withdrawal of all French aid and advisors from Guinea. Despite the acrimony involved in this latter case, the first wave of African nationalism was marked by a relatively peaceful transfer of power to African nationalists.

The second and largest nationalist wave emerged during the 1960s, when more than thirty African countries achieved independence. The majority of these countries were former British and French colonies in East, Central, and West Africa. All three Belgian colonies (Burundi, Rwanda, and Congo-Kinshasa) also acquired independence during this period, and were joined by the Republic of Somalia which represented a federation of the former British and Italian Somaliland territories. Aside from some noteworthy exceptions, most notably France's unsuccessful attempt to defeat a pro-independence guerrilla insurgency in Algeria and the emergence of the so-called Mau Mau guerrilla insurgency in Kenya, the nationalist movements of the 1960s were also largely peaceful in nature. The departing colonial powers had already accepted the inevitability of decolonization. Questions simply remained as to when and under what conditions.

A third wave of nationalism culminated in 1974. A military coup d'étât in Portugal led by junior military officers resulted in a declaration that the Portuguese government intended to grant immediate independence to the colonies in Africa. Coup plotters sought to end what they perceived as a series of African military quagmires that pitted poorly trained and unmotivated Portuguese military forces against highly motivated and increasingly adept African guerrilla insurgencies: the Frente de Libertacao de Mozambique (FRELIMO, Front for the Liberation of Mozambique) in Mozambique, the Partido Africano da Independencia da Guine e Cabo Verde (PAIGC, Independence African Party of Guinea and Cape Verde) in Guinea Bissau and Cape Verde; and three guerrilla groups in Angola—the Frente Nacional de Libertacao de Angola (FNLA, National Front for the Liberation of Angola), the Uniao Nacional para a Independencia Total de Angola (UNITA, National Union for the Total Independence of Angola), and the Movimento Popular de Libertacao de Angola (MPLA, Popular Movement for the Liberation of Angola). The violent path of nationalist movements in the former Portuguese colonies was further complicated in 1975 when Angolan guerrilla groups began an extended civil war over who would lead an independent Angola. The former French colonies of Comoros (1975), Seychelles (1976), and Djibouti (1977), however, achieved independence under largely peaceful terms.

A fourth wave of nationalism gathered strength during the 1980s and was directed against the minority white-ruled regimes in Southern Africa. Since 1948, South Africa was controlled by the descendants of white settlers known as Afrikaners. This minority elite established the apartheid (apartness) system in which blacks and other minorities (roughly 85 per cent of the population) were denied political rights. The apartheid system was eventually exported to the former German colony of Namibia after it became a South African mandate territory in the aftermath of World War I. Similarly, white settlers in Southern Rhodesia (Zimbabwe) led by Ian Smith in 1965 instituted a regional variation of apartheid after they announced their Unilateral Declaration of Independence (UDI) from British colonial rule.

The minority white-ruled regimes of southern Africa were confronted by nationalist guerrilla-led organizations that enjoyed regional and international support: the African National Congress (ANC) and the Pan-African Congress (PAC) in South Africa; the South West Africa People's Organization (SWAPO) in Namibia; and the Zimbabwe African Nationalist Union (ZANU), and the Zimbabwe African People's Union (ZAPU) in Zimbabwe. In all three cases, the military struggles were suspended after the white minority regimes agreed to negotiate transitions to black majority rule. Zimbabwe's transition in 1980 was followed by the creation of multiparty and multiracial democracies in Namibia in 1990 and South Africa in 1994.

The fourth wave of African nationalism culminated in South Africa's transition to democracy in 1994 and largely focused on the self-determination of individual colonial states. In the aftermath of the end of the Cold War, however, a series of nationalist movements have emerged that seek the self-determination of peoples within individual nation-states. The leaders of what potentially constitutes a fifth wave of nationalism often underscore the historic mistreatment of their peoples as part of their pursuit of two overriding objectives: the secession of their territories from existing African nation-states; and international recognition of their territories as independent nation-states within the international system.

The emergence of secessionist nationalist movements is neither unique to Africa nor simply a product of the post–Cold War era. The end of the Cold War has indeed fostered the reemergence of ethnically based nationalism on a global scale. The most notable outcome of this trend was the fragmentation of the former Soviet Union into fifteen independent republics. As demonstrated by the efforts of Nigeria's Igbo people to create an independent Republic of Biafra at the end of the 1960s, however, secessionist movements have existed in Africa since the beginning of the decolonization process. The post–Cold War era is nonetheless unique in that the demands for the self-determination of individual peoples appear to have increased in both scope and intensity, and the African and international communities appear increasingly willing to entertain secessionist demands. Achieving independence in 1993, Eritrea nonetheless serves as the only successful case of a secessionist nationalist movement during the postcolonial independence era.

The strength and long-term viability of similar secessionist nationalist movements, such as the internationally unrecognized claim to independence of the Somaliland republic, depends on a variety of factors, most notably the responses of the Organization of African Unity (OAU) and the international community. The OAU historically has opposed any attempts at secession because one of the hallmarks of the OAU Charter is the inviolability of frontiers inherited from the colonial era. Due to the multiethnic nature of most African nation-states, African leaders themselves remain fearful that changing even one boundary will open a Pandora's box of ethnically based secessionist movements and lead to the further Balkanization of the African continent into smaller and economically unviable political units.

PETER J. SCHRAEDER

See also: **Identity, Political.**

Further Reading

Carter, G. M., and P. O'Meara (eds.). *African Independence: The First Twenty-Five Years*. Bloomington: Indiana University Press, 1985.

MacQueen, N. *The Decolonization of Portuguese Africa: Metropolitan Revolution and the Dissolution of Empire*. London: Longman, 1997.

Neuberger, B. *National Self-Determination in Post-Colonial Africa*. Boulder, Colo.: Lynne Rienner, 1986.

Rimmer, D., et al. *Africa Thirty Years On: The Record and the Outlook After Thirty Years of Independence Examined for the Royal African Society*. London: James Currey, 1991.

Wilson, H. S. *African Decolonization*. London: Edward Arnold, 1994.

Nasser: *See* Egypt: Nasser: Foreign Policy: Suez Canal Crisis to Six Day War; 1952–1970; Egypt: Nasser: High Dam, Economic Development, 1952–1970.

Ndongo, Kingdom of

The Kingdom of Ndongo probably emerged as a consolidated realm in the highlands between the Kwanza and Lukala rivers in the late fifteenth and early sixteenth centuries. Sparse archaeological evidence can only tell us that agricultural populations probably occupied the area after 500BCE, and ironworking was practiced before the Common Era. It is possible that complex societies were already emerging in the early Iron Age, as they did further north.

Traditions of the later sixteenth century placed Ndongo's origins in Kongo, and Kongo royal titles include a "Kingdom of Angola" as early as 1535, but it is unlikely that Kongo played any substantial role in its origin or early development. Ngola Kiluanje, the king identified as the founder in tradition, was said to have expanded the kingdom westward, occupying much of the coastal lowlands on both banks of the Kwanza and coming near to the island of Luanda, which was under Kongo sovereignty in the early sixteenth century.

Shortly before 1520, the king sent an embassy to Portugal to establish relations similar to those of Kongo. The Portuguese sent an exploring party which established itself at Kabasa, Ndongo's capital, until they were forced out of the country for unknown reasons in 1526. Afonso I, king of Kongo arranged for their return to Kongo and then to Portugal.

Many Portuguese merchants, especially from the island of São Tomé, but also from Kongo, established themselves in Kabasa, illegally in the eyes of both the Portuguese crown and the kings of Kongo. By the mid-sixteenth century Ndongo had emerged as a major power in the area, and its armies were fighting against the king of Benguela in the central highlands of Angola, and the king of Songo to the east as its borders expanded. There were probably also border disputes and skirmishes with Kongo in the mountainous "Dembos" region between them, where sovereignty was hard for either monarch to establish.

In 1560 a new Portuguese mission came to Ndongo, led by Paulo Dias de Novais and including Jesuit missionaries. It was not successful either, and Jesuit priest Francisco de Gouveia was held prisoner when Dias de Novais left to return to Portugal in 1563.

In the mid-sixteenth century Ndongo was an extensively networked country. Local rulers, called *sobas* and descended from ancient families, controlled hundreds of small areas, grouped into several large provinces. The king controlled a large royal district directly next to the capital; several *sobas* in the area around Kabasa claimed descent directly from Ngola Kiluanji. Rulers also maintained villages populated by dependent peasants (*kijikos*) who supported the king, his family, military units of the royal army, and officials. There were also traditions of the king making grants of land and subjects to supporters and favorites.

Later traditions suggest that the office of king was hereditary in a single line founded by Ngola Kiluanje, but that succession might also have been by primogeniture, election by the *sobas* or election by the officials (*tendala* and *ngolambole* as well as others). The provinces were supervised by a group of roving officials. The *tendala* were in charge of administrative and judicial matters, while the *ngolambole* presided over military affairs.

In 1575 Paulo Dias de Novais returned to Ndongo with a royal grant from Portugal to create a colony on the coast, south of the Kwanza. He offered his services to Ndongo and fought for Ndongo in several campaigns against rebels. In 1579, however, factions in Kabasa allied with Portuguese merchants, who feared Dias de Novais, and perhaps a Kongo interest persuaded the king to massacre the Portuguese and expel them.

Thanks to help from Kongo, Dias de Novais was able to maintain some fortified positions, and he managed to conquer areas around Luanda and the north bank of the Kwanza through naval power and persuading *sobas* to join him against Ndongo. By the mid-1580s the Portuguese were strong enough to carry the war into the highlands from their base at Massangano. But Ndongo was sufficiently strong that they defeated the Portuguese forces decisively at the Lukala in late 1589. Dias de Novais, abandoned by many of his allied *sobas*, was driven back from the highlands. An impasse developed, finalized by a peace agreement around 1599 that fixed the border between the Portuguese colony and Ndongo.

During this crucial period, Ndongo was ruled by Mbandi a Ngola Kiluanji, who also worked to centralize his authority while fighting the Portuguese. Fifty years later, tradition represented him as favoring his wife and her brothers against nobles, but this was most likely part of a larger complaint against a policy of including them in decision making and office holding. He was killed in a revolt by being tricked into entering a fight against a rebel, only to be abandoned by his supporters. In any case, this hardly slowed the path of centralization pursued with equal vigor by his son and successor Ngola Mbandi.

On occasion, Portugal aided Ngola Mbandi against rebellious subjects, and a certain amount of competition between the two powers continued until the impasse was broken in 1617 by the Portuguese governor Luis Mendes de Vasconcellos. That year the Portuguese governor brought bands of Imbangala mercenaries from south of the Kwanza and led them with his own army in a series of devastating campaigns against Ndongo. The Imbangala were military groups who lived by rapine, capturing adolescent boys to replenish and augment their numbers; they were very effective soldiers. Between 1617 and 1620, much of the heartland of Ndongo was emptied of its population. Many of its inhabitants were sold to plantations in Brazil and Spanish America. Ngola Mbandi fled to islands in the Kwanza River and had to negotiate an unfavorable peace treaty in 1622. Despondent, he committed suicide in 1624, leaving behind a seven-year-old son, and leaving the country ripe for a bitter civil war that would bring Portugal deeper into the country and radically change the geography and politics of Ndongo.

John K. Thornton

See also: **Angola; Kongo.**

Bibliography

Birmingham, D. *Trade and Conflict in Angola: The Mbundu and Their Neighbours under the Influence of the Portuguese, 1483–1790.* Oxford, 1966.

Miller, J. C. *Kings and Kinsmen: Early Mbundu States in Angola.* Oxford, 1976.

Neo-Destour: *See* Tunisia: Neo-Destour and Independence, 1934–1956.

Négritude

The activist philosophy of *négritude* was at the origin of cultural nationalism in French-speaking Africa. The African poet and president of Senegal Léopold Sédar Senghor (1906–2001) and his friend Aimé Césaire, an avant-garde French West Indian poet from the island of Martinique, both first used the term in poems written in 1936, while they were university students in Paris. The development of *négritude* was later described by Senghor as a powerful "leavening agent" in the birth of a national sentiment among the peoples of Francophone Sub-Saharan Africa. Senghor stated that he was never so fraternal with Europeans in general, with Frenchmen in particular, as from the moment in which he discovered the value of *négritude*, which simultaneously had the effect of making him proud to be a black man.

Although Senghor has defined *négritude* as "Negro-African cultural values," this definition does not take into account the richness of this complex philosophy, which changes according to the period considered or the political inclinations of the individual espousing it. There are many *négritudes*: suffering *negritude,* which laments the abject conditions imposed on black people since the beginning of the slave trade, aggressive *negritude,* which clamors for recognition and primacy of African values and encourages literary, artistic, and scientific production by black people, conciliatory *negritude,* which advocates cultural miscegenation or cross-breeding between the newly rehabilitated African civilization and the other civilizations of the world, and an inventive *négritude* tending toward a new global or universal humanism which will be inspired by the eternal wisdom of Africa.

The historical approach is perhaps the best way to capture the meaning of *négritude*. Cheikh Anta Diop, the late Senegalese historian, wrote that *négritude* has a whole history of its own. Did it begin when the French West Indian poet Aimé Césaire invented the term sometime between 1932 and 1934? And should we, along with Senghor, recognize this authorship and "render unto Césaire that which is Césaire's?" Such an approach does not seem to be an entirely accurate way of describing the events leading to the development and popularity of *négritude*.

If it was Césaire who invented the term, it was Senghor who was most responsible for developing the underlying philosophy. They were, however, but two of the black men and women who launched the movement. It would indeed be difficult to understand *négritude* without mentioning the pioneering contributions of Paulette and Jane Nardal, university students in Paris from the French West Indian island of Martinique. In 1931 the Nardal sisters initiated the Parisian publication of *La Revue du Monde Noir* (Review of the Black World), a monthly magazine written in both French and English. Almost thirty years before independence movements swept through Africa, the *Revue* brought together such diverse young authors as the American leaders of the Harlem Renaissance Alain Locke; Claude MacKay; Countee Cullen; Langston Hughes; Nnamdi Azikiwe, future first president of Nigeria; Felix Eboue, future first black governor general of French Equatorial Africa; as well as future literary and political leaders Césaire and Senghor. The *Revue* studied the conditions facing black women and men and expressed faith in the future of the race and the necessity of creating a sentiment of solidarity among black peoples around the world. In addition, its editors hoped "to promote within the white race a mutual, complete, affectionate, and unprejudiced appreciation of the intelligentsia of all colored races." That appreciation was to be based on recognition of the scientific, literary, and artistic contributions of both past and present black leaders.

Soon after meeting with the editors of the *Revue,* Senghor tore up all the poems he had previously written on Western themes and started writing about the African experience he had suddenly been encouraged to value. Césaire, too, furiously railed against Western civilization's misdeeds toward Africa. A new black literary movement was launched and developed through the remaining years of the 1930s.

World War II brought about the fall of France to Nazi forces, but the "Free French" movement of Charles de Gaulle slowly gained headway in French colonial Africa. Thanks for the African efforts toward the liberation of France caused the post war government to incorporate Africans into the French parliament. Both Césaire and Senghor became members of the French political elite.

In 1947, with the encouragement of a host of famous French intellectuals as well Senghor and Césaire, a new journal, *Présence Africaine*, began publication in Paris under the direction of the younger Senegalese intellectual, Alioune Diop. In 1948 Jean-Paul Sartre wrote the preface to Senghor's *Anthologie de la Nouvelle Poésie Nègre et Malgache de Langue Francaise* (Anthology of New Black and Malagasy Poetry in the French Language). Sartre's analysis, titled *Black Orpheus,* made the term *négritude* one of the most discussed philosophical notions in French literary circles. Debates raged in the literary cafes and intellectual centers of Paris. Senghor and Césaire became heroes of that segment of the French intelligentsia who were profoundly attracted by the "exotic" literary outburst of these and other black writers.

From that moment on, black nationalists criticized *négritude* in quite different ways. Black communists called it a diversion with respect to the "class struggle." *Négritude's* emphasis on race undercut concentration on the class struggle. Those African nationalists who wished for independence in the 1950s objected to Senghor's attempts to incorporate Africans into a new French community, all the while insisting on Africans' uniqueness. Cultural crossbreeding was also anathema to those trumpeting Pan-Africanism. Throughout the 1940s and 1950s the new journal *Presence Africaine* continued the tradition begun by *Revue du Monde* Noir, providing a forum for the many intellectual currents developed by black intellectuals. It hosted two major international conferences bringing together black intellectuals from all over the world.

As the 1950s progressed, the literary and artistic *négritude* movement begun in the 1930s was rapidly incorporated as an aspect of the African rush to independence. What had begun as an effort by black intellectuals to instill race pride was overrun by the political changes in the colonial world demanded and achieved by those who followed the dictum of "Independence Now," as emphasized by third-world delegates at their ground breaking international conference held at Bandung, Indonesia, in 1955.

Thereafter, international recognition of people of African descent would come about because of their political, rather than merely their intellectual and artistic clout. The "culture first" of Senghor and the supporters of *négritude* was superseded by the "politics first" of Kwame Nkrumah, who won independence from British rule for the Gold Coast (Ghana) in 1957.

JACQUES LOUIS HYMANS

See also: **Senghor, Léopold Sédar.**

Further Reading

Jack, B. E. *Négritude and Literary Criticism: The History and Theory of "Negro-African" Literature in French.* Westport, Conn.: Greenwood Press, 1996.

James, A. A. *Modernism and Négritude: The Poetry and Poetics of Aimé Césaire.* Cambridge, Mass.: Harvard University Press, 1981.

Kesteloot, L. *Black Writers in French: A Literary History of Négritude.* Washington, D.C.: Howard University Press, 1991.

Neolithic North Africa

"Neolithic," or New Stone Age, is a term originally devised in Europe for that cultural period when polished stone artifacts appeared. It has subsequently been used in both Europe and the Near East to represent the time when domestication of plants and animals first began. Part of the "package" of the neolithic has come to include pottery, and although pre-pottery Neolithic is recognized in the Levant, when pottery appears, the domestication process is well under way. There is some question whether the term should be applied to Africa, as it would assume that using the name would mean the same processes have occurred in the two areas. In fact such assumptions have been made by French researchers (Camps, 1974), and also by Wendorf in the Western Desert of Egypt at Nabta Playa, where ceramics have been found dated to about 9300 years ago, and called Neolithic. Cattle bones associated with these ceramics are thus assumed to be domestic (Wendorf, 1994). This has been challenged, and opens up the possibility that ceramics may pre-date the earliest domesticated animals in North Africa.

Food production was well established and widespread throughout North Africa around 7,500 years ago. There are separate cultural areas that can be recognized archaeologically. The Nile valley, with its permanent water and predictable riparian forage, whose annually rejuvenated silts from the Nile flood, was later ideal for mixed farming of domestic grains and livestock, but in the early Holocene produced rich hunting and foraging (Wetterstrom, 1993). The central Sahara, with open grasslands, would have been subject to rainfall variation, including droughts, but permitted nomadic pastoralism. Cultural similarity exists over a wide area from the Nile valley in the Sudan to Mauretania (Smith, 1980), and suggests a similar spread of cultural contact that is exhibited by the nomadic Tuareg today, with a common language, but regional variation in dress, equipment, and other cultural signifiers. Another area is the Maghreb, divided into the southern Atlas Mountains and the open plains of the northern Sahara, known to Francophone archaeologists as the area of the "Neolithic of Caspian Tradition" (Camps, 1974); and the Mediterranean littoral, a winter rainfall area possibly in contact with the Near East, Iberian Peninsula, and the eastern Mediterranean Islands, where wheat and barley agriculture was practiced.

Contact between the Nile Valley and the eastern Sahara existed, with the Sahara perhaps being the main driving force behind domestication (Barich, 1998), and the Nile valley only catching up later as population increased, and pressure was brought to bear on the rich hunting that would have existed in the valley in the early Holocene.

By about 8,000 years ago, semipermanent villages were being created in the Western Desert, suggesting that wild resources were sufficient to keep people in one place for a period of the year. Shortly after this there are indications in the area of cattle burials that indicate ritual activities. These may well be the precursors of more elaborate cattle cults that dominated the beliefs of the states of the Nile valley during dynastic times.

By 7,500 years ago, small stock entered Africa from the Levant, and some would argue, so did the first domestic cattle. At this time, a gentler climate dominated the Sahara, offering an open grassland niche for the expansion of nomadic pastoralism with cattle (which are depicted on the rock walls of the Tassil n'Ajjer of southern Algeria [Lajoux, 1963; Kuper, 1978]). This rock art of the "bovidien" period is not homogeneous. There are two quite distinct styles and subject matter, but with domestic animals as the central theme. This would appear to reflect two racial groups, with one representing black African people, possibly precursors of the Fulani of West Africa today, and the other being of Mediterranean stock, showing individuals with light skin and long hair (Smith, 1993).

Intentional burial of cattle as part of ceremonies occurred in the Sahara before 6,000 years ago (Paris, 2000; Wendorf and Schild, 2001). Such "cattle-cults" predate anything similar in the Nile valley, so may be the precursor to what later becomes common in the valley. In the Nile valley, predynastic civilizations were appearing in upper and lower Egypt by 6,500 years ago. Lower Egypt, comprising the Nile Delta, most probably had strong affinities with the Levant. Much of the early cultural record, however, is obscured by the annual siltation of the delta by the Nile floods. The site of Merimbe beni Salame on the eastern edge of the delta has given the best record of early predynastic settlement in the northern sector. These were primarily traders who lived in small settlements. They buried their dead in individual graves, with few earthly goods placed within them. This is in marked contrast to the huge cemeteries of upper Egypt at Naqada and Abydos, where virtually every grave is filled with goods to ease the journey into the afterlife and the land of the dead. Not only is this an indication of strong religious beliefs, but the variation in quality of grave goods suggests that a hierarchy was already in place (Hoffman, 1980). This is an indication of a central authority that made possible the military conquest of lower Egypt, and the unification of the two areas 4,500 years ago.

ANDREW B. SMITH

See also: **Domestication, Plant and Animal, History of; Egypt, Ancient: Unification of Upper and Lower: Historical Outline; Stone Age (Later): Nile Valley; Stone Age (Later): Sahara and North Africa.**

Further Reading

Barich, B. E. *People, Water and Grain: The Beginnings of Domestication in the Sahara and the Nile Valley*. Rome: "L'Erma" di Bretschneider, 1998.

Hoffman, M. *Egypt before the Pharoahs*. London: Routledge and Kegan Paul, 1980.

Lajoux, J-D. *The Rock Paintings of Tassili*. London: Thames and Hudson, 1963.

Paris, F. "Livestock Remains from Saharan Mortuary Contexts." In *The Origins and Development of African Livestock: Archaeology, Genetics, Linguistics and Ethnography*, edited by R. M. Blench and K. C. MacDonald. London: University College London Press.

Smith, A. B. "The Neolithic Tradition in the Sahara." In *The Sahara and the Nile*, edited by M. A. J. Williams and H. Faure. Rotterdam: Balkema, 1980.

———. "New Approaches to Saharan Rock Art." In *L'Arte e l'Ambiente del Sahara Preistorico: Dati e Interpretazioni*, edited by G. Calegari. Memorie della Società Italiana di Scienze Naturali e del Museo Civico di Storia Naturale di Milano, 1993.

Wendorf, F. "Are the Early Holocene Cattle in the Eastern Sahara Domestic or Wild?" *Evolutionary Anthropology*. 3, no. 4 (1994): 118–128.

Wendorf, F., and R. Schild. *Holocene Settlement of the Egyptian Sahara*. Vol. 1: *The Archaeology of Nabta Playa*. New York: Kluwer, 2001.

Wetterstrom, W. "Foraging and Farming in Egypt: The Transition from Hunting and Gathering to Horticulture in the Nile Valley." In *The Archaeology of Africa: Food, Metals, and Towns*, edited by T. Shaw, et al. London: Routledge, 1993.

Neolithic, Pastoral: Eastern Africa

It is now abundantly clear that many regions of East Africa as far to the south as central Tanzania were formerly inhabited by stone-tool-using peoples who had no knowledge of metallurgy, but who had access to domestic animals. The archaeological remains of these peoples are most available in the highlands on either side of the Rift Valley in southern Kenya and northern Tanzania, although they are also indicated in the north Kenya plains east of Lake Turkana, in the Lake Victoria basin and, less certainly, in the coastal lowlands. They generally date between the second millennium BCE and the first millennium CE, although they appear to have been earlier in the north. They are conventionally known as Pastoral Neolithic (PN). Although widely adopted, the term is, unfortunately, misleading.

The term "Neolithic" has various connotations. Worldwide, it was originally used to distinguish, on the one hand, those later stone-tool-using peoples who made tools by grinding and polishing as well as by flaking and, on the other, their predecessors who relied exclusively on flaking. It was noted that ground-stone artifacts were often associated with pottery. Much later it was recognized in Europe that these typologically defined "Neolithic" communities had also been farmers: cultivators, herders, or both. Gradually, the presence of "food-production" in a pre–Iron Age context came to be regarded as the defining characteristic of the "Neolithic," at least among Anglophone archaeologists; many of their francophone colleagues continued to base their use of the term on purely typological considerations. Major problems arise when these Europe-based definitions are applied in African contexts.

In Africa some artifact types generally regarded as "Neolithic" are demonstrably earlier than either cultivation or herding. Pottery, for example, was made and used during the post–Pleistocene climatic optimum in what is now the southern Sahara at fishing settlements where there is no evidence for the practice of either cultivation or herding. Stone axes were ground and polished by stone-tool-using hunter/gatherers in the south-central African savanna as long as 18,000 years ago, long before such a technology was practiced in Europe.

Many archaeologists have concluded that it is inappropriate and confusing to use the term "Neolithic" in the context of Sub-Saharan Africa, but this proposal has met with some opposition, especially in East Africa. The confusion has there been compounded by its link with the word "pastoral." Pastoralism in anthropological usage denotes a society, often nomadic, that relies to a very large extent on domestic herds in ways that extend beyond subsistence. This is not demonstrable in the case of the PN. True pastoralists rarely cultivate, but it is only incomplete negative archaeological evidence which suggests that PN peoples did not also cultivate. Indeed, some archaeological indications are emerging which support the historical linguistic argument that cultivation was in fact practiced by some of these groups.

A further undesirable result of the use of the term "Pastoral Neolithic" is political. Modern nomadic pastoralists in East Africa face considerable pressure to abandon their traditional lifestyle, to settle, and to cultivate. The idea needs to be resisted that they are in some ways backward or even prehistoric peoples who are resisting progress. Pastoralism in the modern sense is probably not a particularly ancient lifestyle in East Africa, but one that has over the centuries become uniquely adapted to the environmental circumstances where it is practiced.

The defining features of PN are absence of metal and access to domestic animals. As noted above, such societies are attested archaeologically in many areas of East Africa. Their flaked stone artifacts were essentially of microlithic "Late Stone Age" type; their typology varies considerably along with the characteristics of the available raw materials which, in some areas most notably the Rift Valley highlands, included plentiful fine obsidian. The associated pottery likewise shows considerable variation, the significance of which is not properly understood. Faunal assemblages contain very variable proportions of domestic and wild species, both cattle and sheep/goat being included among the latter. Whilst it must be concluded that domestic animals were present in the region during this period, the manner in which they were exploited and by whom remain matters of uncertainty. It is by no means certain that all the peoples conventionally designated PN were themselves herders; they may have obtained stock by hunting or raiding from other sources. Floral remains, such as might demonstrate whether the PN peoples were cultivators have only very rarely been recovered or, for that matter, sought.

Both settlement and burial sites are known. The latter, including both inhumations and cremations, were often accompanied by characteristic stone bowls or platters, the function and significance of which remain unknown although they were sometimes paired with pestles. In several areas these burials were surmounted by stone cairns.

Several aspects of PN material culture appear to be rooted in earlier local traditions. This is particularly true of the flaked stone industries. On the other hand, the domestic animals were of species with no local wild ancestors: they must therefore have been introduced from elsewhere, presumably from a general northerly direction where they are attested archaeologically in earlier times. This gradual penetration from the north is supported by chronological evidence within East Africa, domestic animals being present for example at Dongodien near the northern end of Lake Turkana in the mid-third millennium BC, approximately a thousand years before there is convincing evidence for a PN presence in the Rift Valley highlands.

The distribution of PN sites extends through the East African highlands as far to the south as what is now central Tanzania. No convincing trace of them has yet been located in the south of Tanzania or beyond. It is noteworthy that this limit appears broadly to coincide with that which historical linguistic studies indicate for the former presence of Cushitic and Nilotic languages. Indeed there seems a strong likelihood that the PN people were speakers of such languages, study of which supports the view that some form of cultivation was practised at this time.

It is interesting to consider why this limit was established. The contemporary peoples further to the south appear to have been stone-tool-using hunter/gatherers who had no knowledge either of pottery or of metallurgy. They may have lacked any economic or other stimulus to adopt herding and the change of lifestyle that would accompany such adoption.

DAVID W. PHILLIPSON

See also: **Cushites: Northeastern Africa: Stone Age Origins to Iron Age.**

Further Reading

Ambrose, S. H. "The Introduction of Pastoral Adaptations to the Highlands of East Africa." In *From Hunters to Farmers: The Causes and Consequences of Food Production in Africa*, edited by J. D. Clark and S. A. Brandt. Berkeley, 1984.

Barthelme, J. W. *Fisher-Hunters and Neolithic Pastoralists of East Turkana, Kenya*. Oxford.
Bower, J. R. F. "The Pastoral Neolithic of East Africa." *Journal of World Prehistory*. 5, (1991): 49–82.
Leakey, M. D. and L. S. B. *Excavations at Njoro River Cave*. Oxford, 1950.
Phillipson, D. W. "Aspects of Early Food Production in Northern Kenya." In *Origin and Early Development of Food-Producing Cultures on North-East Africa*, edited by L. Krzyzaniak and M. Kobusiewicz. Poznan, 1984.

Neto, António Agostinho (1922–1979)

Poet and Activist

To the beautiful Angolan homeland
our land, our mother
we must return
We must return
to Angola liberated
Angola independent

This fragment of Agostinho Neto's poetry, written in prison in 1960, combines his exaltation of Mother Africa with combative tone previously unseen in his work. In a climate where direct political action was forbidden, the young Neto had become active in cultural organizations in the 1940s. His parents, Methodist teachers, had moved from the village Kaxikane to Luanda, where he finished secondary school. In 1944 he started working in the Angolan health services, but after 1947 he moved to Portugal to study medicine. Here he soon became involved in several cultural and political movements. In 1951 he was arrested and detained for several months as he was collecting signatures for the Stockholm Peace Appeal. After his release, he accepted the leadership of an Angolan student organization. In his speeches as well as in his poems, which appeared in several journals, he expressed the suffering of the Angolan people under Portuguese colonialism. His outspoken ideas were not appreciated by the Portuguese authorities and from February 1955 until June 1957 he was imprisoned again. Despite this, he was able to finish his medical studies in 1958 and in the same year married the Portuguese-born Maria Eugénia da Silva.

In 1959 he returned to Luanda, where he set up a medical practice and became one of the leaders of a movement called MPLA (Popular Movement for the Liberation of Angola), which had been founded in 1956. Yet, within a year after his return he was arrested again. This evoked protest and demonstrations in his home village, which were suppressed brutally: some thirty people were killed and the village was razed to the ground. Between June 1960 and August 1962 he spent time in Angolan, Cape Verdian, and Portuguese prisons. During this period, Neto's protest against colonialism had become more radical: he openly called for the need of armed struggle.

After he and his family managed to escape to Congo-Léopoldville (Kinshasa), Neto was elected president of the MPLA. It proved no easy task. His arrival led to rivalry within the MPLA leadership and a serious crisis ensued. Furthermore the balance between political ideology and practical guerrilla warfare turned out difficult to strike, the MPLA was hindered by its host country and its militants were attacked by rival FNLA fighters. Neto found himself leading a fractured movement with little support. In November 1963 Neto and other MPLA leaders were expelled from Congo-Léopoldville and moved across the river to Congo-Brazzaville. Here the movement was allowed to grow and slowly managed to gather some external assistance. For the MPLA president and his family this meant traveling to various countries: the Soviet Union, Ghana, Egypt, and Sudan. As MPLA activities were well-nigh impossible in the northern region because of FNLA rivalry, the MPLA shifted its attention to eastern Angola. Neto moved to Dar es Salaam in Tanzania and especially after Zambian independence in 1964 the MPLA set out to organize an "eastern front." The guerrilla war in east Angola brought new successes and new problems. Despite frequent visits to Angola, the MPLA leaders, based in Zambia and Tanzania, remained aloof of the daily life in guerrilla camps in the eastern Angolan bush. Mostly leftist intellectuals from Luanda, they devoted much time to ideological disputes and bureaucratic affairs—interests not shared by impatient military men on the ground. In 1973 matters came to a head: Neto, informed by the Russians, accused military commander Daniel Chipenda of assassination plans, Chipenda retorted with accusations of power abuse and absenteeism. Chipenda later seceded from MPLA.

Neto's leadership of MPLA, although subject to several internal crises and sometimes fiercely criticized, remained remarkably stable. In 1975 he became president of the independent republic of Angola. Again the task proved formidable. Even before independence, the long civil war in Angola had started. South African forces, in cooperation with UNITA and FNLA, were approaching Luanda and only by calling in Cuban support could the MPLA government prevent their advance. Apart from these external attacks, the government was plagued by internal difficulties as well. The war increased problems in the already fragile economy. Rhetoric of mass participation could not prevent the development of an elaborate and unfair state bureaucracy and many politicians remained out of touch with the people they were supposed to lead. Neto's character, modest and disciplined, but also reserved and distant did not help much to bridge the gap between leaders and the populace. In 1977 an attempt to stage a coup d'étât, including a plan to kidnap Neto, was suppressed by the government with Cuban support.

In 1979 Neto fell ill; he died shortly before his birthday in a Russian hospital. The day of Neto's death is a national holiday in Angola, a university was named after him, and statues have been erected in his honor in various countries; throughout Angola people tell legends about their former president. Yet, eighteen years after his death, Neto's widow complained that her late husband's remains, placed in an unfinished mausoleum, were treated with as much contempt as his ideals.

INGE BRINKMAN

See also: **Angola.**

Biography

Agostinho Neto was born September 17, 1922, in Kaxikane, Bengo province, Angola. He studied medicine in Portugal, where he became active in a range of cultural-political organisations. He was arrested after he returned to Angola in 1960 and detained for two years. After his escape in 1962, Neto became president of the MPLA. He and his family lived in various countries and traveled much to gather support for the MPLA movement. Upon independence in 1975, Neto became president of Angola. He died September 10, 1979, in a Russian hospital.

Further Reading

Birmingham, D. *Frontline Nationalism in Angola and Mozambique.* Trenton, N.J.: Africa World Press, 1992.
Burness, D. *Fire: Six Writers from Angola, Mozambique, and Cape Verde.* Washington, D.C.: Three Continents Press, 1977.
Davidson, B. *In the Eye of the Storm: Angola's People.* London: Longman, 1972.
"Father of Angola Rots in a Grey Mausoleum." *Electronic Mail and Guardian.* October 10, 1997.
Marcum, J. A. *The Angolan Revolution: Exile Politics and Guerrilla Warfare (1962–1976).* Cambridge, Mass.: MIT Press, 1978.
Neto, A. *Sacred Hope.* 1974.

New Kingdom: *See* Egypt, Ancient: New Kingdom and the Colonization of Nubia.

Ngugi wa Thiong'o (1938–)

Author, Playwright, and Professor

As a postgraduate student in England, Ngugi wa Thiong'o published his first novel, *Weep Not, Child* (1964), in the Heinemann's African Writers Series. The book was an immediate success, and is widely considered to be the first major novel in English by an East African writer.

Ngugi supported the ideas of the *négritude* movement and therefore emphasized African aesthetics and languages in his oeuvre. In addition, the ideas of Karl Marx and Frantz Fanon have played a key role in the development of Ngugi's thinking and writing. Fanon's work has sensitized Ngugi to the effect of colonial violence on the psyche of the colonized, and in particular to the consequences of cultural imperialism, such as a feeling of racial and cultural inferiority. Fanon's position on the use—even necessity—of violence as a legitimate means to overcome colonial rule reappears regularly in Ngugi's prose, a revolutionary element which also stems from his ideological proximity to Marx. He remains faithful to a Marxist critique of capitalism and the exploitation of the working classes (especially in the context of post-independence Kenya), as well as to the idea of a (pan-African) workers' revolution. While his early fiction addresses issues of decolonization in the context of British rule and the Mau Mau insurgency, his later fiction, for instance *Petals of Blood* (1977), criticizes the neocolonial exploitation of the Kenyan masses.

In 1981 Ngugi published *Detained*, both diary and memoir, as an account of and reaction to his first experience of politically motivated imprisonment, which resulted from the performance of the play *I Will Marry When I Want* (1982; co-written with Ngugi wa Mirii). The play offers a people's history of Kenya during and after the colonization and denounces the new rulers' exploitative dealings with workers. The government's drastic reaction can be explained in part by the fact that this particular text, being a play and originally written in Kikuyu, reached a different and much broader audience than did Ngugi's previous works.

Devil on the Cross (1982), written during Ngugi's first detention, blends novelistic forms with dramatic, cinematic, and oral story-telling elements. This work stands out as Ngugi's decisive turn towards a critical examination of a phenomenon that he described in great detail in *Decolonising the Mind* (1986), namely, the linguistic process of continued suppression of the colonized through the annihilation of indigenous language and thus culture. The celebration of these very languages and cultures has been at the center of Ngugi's work ever since. *Devil on the Cross*, accordingly, was written in Kikuyu (Ngugi's mother tongue and one of numerous Kenyan languages) and translated into English by Ngugi himself at a later date. Ngugi has continued to write plays, even after his forced exile in 1982. In order to reach a greater audience (one reason why Ngugi decided to write in his mother tongue), Ngugi started to get involved in film-making, seeing in this medium a better means for disseminating his ideas. His dedication to refamiliarize Kenyans with their own history and tradition also has lead to his writing a series of children's stories. Published in Kikuyu between 1982 and 1986, they tell of the adventures of the young character Njamba Nene.

In addition to his international reputation as a writer of fiction, Ngugi became famous as the most outspoken supporter for the use of African languages in both creative and scholarly writing, thereby fighting against the linguistic and, hence, also psychological aspect of (neo)colonization. Ngugi's contributions to writing in African languages are indeed manifold. In addition to his numerous plays and novels, Ngugi has edited the American-based scholarly journal *Mutiiri* in Kikuyu. Yet, in more recent publications Ngugi once again addresses his audience in English. *Penpoints, Gunpoints, and Dreams* (1998), a series of lectures first presented at Oxford University, and before that a revised edition of *Writers in Politics* (1997), seem aimed at a Western, even academic readership, thus apparently contradicting Ngugi's support of both the African and proletarian cause. However, both books conceptually continue the themes of earlier works. These are predominantly the role of literature, particularly performance, and the arts in postcolonial societies; governmental suppression and fear of critical artistic expression; similarities between African and Caribbean writing; the need for political struggle in the face of neocolonial exploitation; and finally a predominantly skeptical (Marxist) position on the future role of capitalism in African societies. Increasingly, however, Ngugi concerns himself with questions of exile and censorship, both of which are of immediate relevance to his own life. Even though most of Ngugi's recent scholarly writing is in English (a decision in part surely due to his continued exile in the United States), he remains highly critical of what he calls Europhonism, the exclusive use of European languages in African literature.

GERD BAYER

See also: **Kenya: Colonial Period: Mau Mau Revolt; *Négritude*.**

Biography

Born James Thiong'o Ngugi on January 5, 1938, in Limuru, Kenya. Attended local schools and entered Alliance High School in 1955. Received a B.A. in English at Makerere University College in Kampala (Uganda) in 1963. Worked as a journalist for a short period of time. Married in 1961. Left to attend graduate school at Leeds University (UK) in 1964. Changed name to Ngugi wa Thiong'o in 1977. At the end of that year, imprisoned in Mamiti Maximum Security Prison for a year, without trial, for involvement in a theatre. Left Kenya for London in 1982. In 1992, named professor of comparative literature and performance studies at New York University.

Further Reading

Cantalupo, C. (ed.). *Ngugi wa Thiong'o: Texts and Contexts.* Trenton, N.J.: Africa World Press, 1995.

Gikandi, S. *Ngugi wa Thiong'o.* Cambridge and N.Y.: Cambridge University Press, 2000.

Killam, G. D. (ed.). *Critical Perspectives on Ngugi wa Thiong'o.* Washington, D.C.: Three Continents Press, 1984.

Lovesey, O. *Ngugi wa Thiong'o.* N.Y. Twayne Publishers, 2000.

Ngugi wa Thiong'o. *Weep Not, Child.* London: Heinemann, 1964.

Ngugi wa Thiong'o. *A Grain of Wheat.* London: Heinemann, 1967.

Ngugi wa Thiong'o. *Homecoming: Essays on African and Caribbean Literature, Culture and Politics.* London: Heinemann, 1972 and N.Y.: Lawrence Hill, 1973.

Ngugi wa Thiong'o. *Petals of Blood.* London: Heinemann, 1977 and N. Y.: Dutton, 1978.

Ngugi wa Thiong'o. *Detained: A Writer's Prison Diary.* London, and Exeter, N. H.: Heinemann, 1981.

Ngugi wa Thiong'o. *Devil on the Cross.* London: Heinemann, 1982.

Ngugi wa Thiong'o. *Decolonising the Mind: The Politics of Language and African Literature.* London: James Currey, and Portsmouth, N. H.: Heinemann, 1986.

Ngugi wa Thiong'o. *Writers in Politics: A Re-engagement with Issues of Literature and Society.* 2nd rev. ed. Oxford: James Currey, and Portsmouth, N. H.: Heinemann, 1997.

Ngugi wa Thiong'o. *Penpoints, Gunpoints, and Dreams: Toward a Critical Theory of the Arts and the State in Africa.* Oxford: Clarendon and N. Y.: Oxford University Press, 1998.

Ngugi wa Thiong'o and Ngugi wa Mirii. *I Will Marry When I Want.* Oxford and Portsmouth, N. H.: Heinemann, 1982.

Ngwane Kingdom: *See* Swaziland: Sobhuza I, Foundation of Ngwane Kingdom.

Niger Delta And Its Hinterland: History to Sixteenth Century

The combined evidence of linguistics, archaeology, and oral traditions provides material for the discussion of early Niger Delta history up to the beginning of the transatlantic slave trade in the sixteenth century, from when written sources begin to appear.

The oral traditions of origin suggest that the Niger Delta peoples subsisted on the exploitation of local resources until population increases forced further migrations to other parts of the region. The different ecological zones of the delta provided numerous opportunities and resources for development and exchange. Most of the western and central delta was freshwater swampland where considerable farming along the seasonally flooded banks of rivers was possible. In the eastern delta mangrove, saltwater and swamp conditions dictated a subsistence economy based mainly on fishing.

The early populations of the Niger Delta carried out some iron and bronze work, and were prolific in the manufacture of household, industrial, and ritual pottery, as well as terra cotta figurines, masks, and smoking pipes. These activities already suggest contact with hinterland communities from whom at least the metal would have had to be imported. Fishing, hunting, and the manufacture of salt along the mangrove belt provided resources for subsistence and trade with the hinterland. However, plantains, bananas, water yams, and cocoa yams were farmed within the Niger Delta, supplementing products traded from the hinterland, especially yams and livestock. Cassava products, which became staple food sources in many parts of the Niger Delta, arrived much later, first in the western delta, from Brazil, in the wake of the Atlantic slave trade of the sixteenth century. Tobacco also arrived in this period, but the evidence of smoking pipes in excavations in the eastern delta suggest the earlier use of other materials for smoking.

Internal trade across the Niger Delta and into the hinterland in large canoes is reported in the oral traditions and confirmed by the linguistic evidence of the antiquity of the word for "canoe" in local languages. But the trade itself resulted in part from other changes triggered by migrations from the freshwater delta into the mangrove swamp regions of the eastern delta. These communities changed from reliance on farming and fishing, to depend on fishing and salt manufacture, and later, to trading to other ecological regions and the hinterland for food and livestock. These small fishing communities gradually changed into trading communities developing institutions for long distance trade. They became larger and more complex societies with the arrival of Europeans and the slave trade, from the incorporation of new members. In addition, the concentration of wealth and power in the hands of a few leaders was decisive in the creation of the "city-states" of Nembe, Kalabari, Bonny, and Okrika in the eastern delta. The internal trade expanded by the effects of the sixteenth century slave trade created the conditions for the creation of the well-know war-canoe "houses" or trading corporations of these city-states.

The Portuguese are reported to have made formal contact with the Oba of Benin in 1486 (Ryder, 1969). This suggests that they had begun to conduct business in the western delta on the Benin, Escravos, and Forcados Rivers before about 1480. There is evidence of such early trade in the eastern delta at Bonny and possibly at Elem Kalabari on the Bonny and New Calabar rivers,

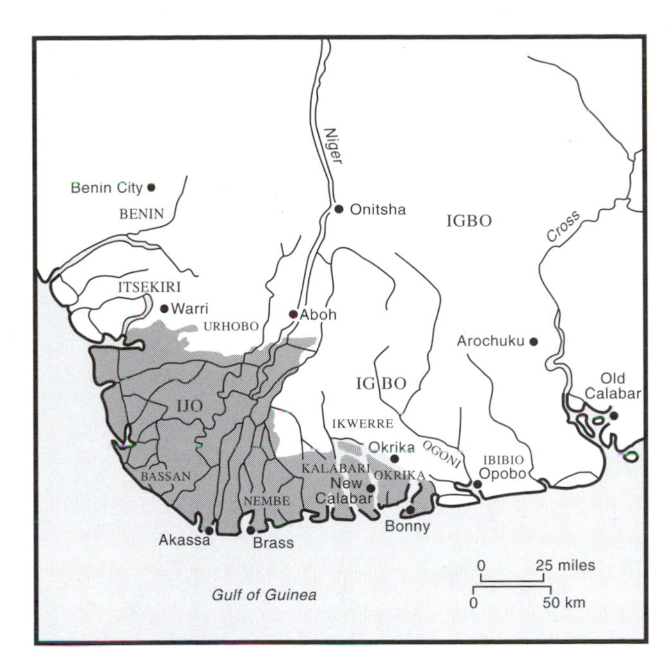

The Niger Delta and hinterland, sixteenth–eighteenth centuries.

the combined estuaries of which the Portuguese named Rio Real (Royal River). Indeed, the names of the rivers opening into the Atlantic provide obvious evidence of the early arrival of the Portuguese in the Niger Delta, where they even began missionaries activities at the western delta state of Ode Itshekiri. The oral traditions record their early impact identifying all subsequent white visitors by a name associated with the Portuguese.

The slave trade made the delta states the middlemen between the visitors on the coast and the hinterland communities. Accordingly, slaves representing virtually all ethnic communities of Nigeria passed through Niger Delta ports to the New World. The oral traditions record the impact of slaves incorporated into local communities, and some internal enslavement of even delta communities. But it has only recently come to light that some Niger delta peoples were also exported to the Americas. The evidence comes from the study of the Berbice Dutch Creole of Guyana, which incorporates words identifiable from many communities of the eastern Niger Delta, but predominantly from Kalabari, Ibani (Bonny) and Nembe (Smith, Robertson, and Williamson, 1987). This confirms the general reports in the oral traditions and in the accounts of visitors to the Niger Delta of piracy and other internal forms of violence, a great deal of which derived from domestic and overseas slave trading. These, indeed, were some of the conditions which promoted the formation of the trading and fighting corporations of the delta states, which themselves engaged in slavery, but also needed to enforce peace along their trade routes, the hinterland markets, and in their own communities. The food crops exchanges between the region and the Americas, and a few internal enduring institutions, constitute the legacy of the slave trade in the Niger Delta.

E. J. Alagoa

See also: **Portugal: Exploration and Trade in the Fifteenth Century; Slavery: Atlantic Trade: Effects in Africa and the Americas.**

Further Reading

Alagoa, E. J. "Long Distance Trade and States in the Niger Delta." *Journal of African History.* 11, no. 3 (1970): 319–329.

Alagoa, E. J., F. N. Anozie, and N. Nzewunwa, eds. *The Early History of the Niger Delta.* Hamburg: Buske, 1988.

Nzewunwa, N. *Niger Delta: Its Prehistoric Economy and Culture.* Oxford, 1980.

Ryder, A. *Benin and the Europeans.* London, 1969.

Smith, N. S. H., I. E. Robertson, and K. Williamson. "The Ijo Elements in Berbice Dutch." *Language and Society.* 16 (1987): 49–89.

Niger Delta and Its Hinterland: Peoples and States to 1800

The Niger Delta covers, at its maximum extent, territory extending from its northern apex on the Niger River, south of latitude six degrees north, to near latitude four degrees north at the coast. Along the coastline, it extends from close to longitude four degrees east and longitude eight degrees east. This triangle with a wide base is populated by peoples in the modern Nigerian states of Ondo on the west, where the delta merges into the Lagos lagoon, Delta state, Bayelsa state where the delta pushes farthest into the Atlantic ocean, and Rivers state in the east, where the delta merges into coastal creeks extending through Akwa lbom state in the Cross River valley. The Niger Delta has expanded and contracted in the past ten millennia through the transgression and regression of the Atlantic.

The Niger Delta is relatively diverse in its ethnic composition. It is settled by the related linguistic families of Ijoid, Yoruboid, Edoid, Igboid, and Delta Cross. The internally diverse Ijoid group covers all ecological zones of the Niger Delta from the coast from the eastern to the western periphery, and north to the apex. The Yoruboid group is located in the western delta adjoining the Lagos lagoon and the Yoruba mainland in southwestern Nigeria. The Edoid communities entered the Niger Delta from the northwest in the direction of Benin, the most common place of origin cited in the oral traditions of Niger Delta peoples. The Igboid communities occupy the regions east and west of the apex, and the Delta Cross group lies within the eastern delta periphery. Indeed, the Niger Delta became increasingly integrated in the course of the last millennium.

The Ijoid group is estimated to have separated from the Yoruboid, Edoid, and Igboid, and moved into the Niger Delta over seven thousand years ago, by apparently aquatic routes, down the Niger. The development of the group in relative isolation in the Niger Delta has resulted in its clear distinction from the others. It eventually subdivided into four major dialect clusters: Eastern Ijo (Kalabari, Ibani—comprising Bonny and Opobo—Okrika, and Nkoro), Nembe-Akassa, Izon (comprising scores of language communities in the western and central delta), and Inland Ijo (Biseni, Okordia, Oruma). The oral traditions of the more than forty ethnic/linguistic communities into which the Ijoid group has split over the past two millennia indicate movements outward from primary dispersal centers in the central Niger Delta. Thus, in the western delta, the Arogbo and Apoi Ijo communities live among Yoruboid communities in Ondo State, and the Olodiama, Furupagha, Egbema, and Ogbe Ijo live among Edoid and Yoruboid. Similarly, the Inland Ijo of the central Niger Delta live close to Delta Cross communities.

The Ilaje and lkale of Ondo State and the Itsekiri of Delta State constitute the major representatives of the Yoruboid group in the Niger Delta. They entered the western delta from the west less than two thousand years ago. Itsekiri traditions relate a more recent migration of Benin princes within the last millennium, resulting in the establishment of a Benin-type political state. The language of the Itsekiri has remained Yoruboid, and the people have had close enough relationships with the neighboring Urhobo and Ijo to have assimilated some of their cultural traditions.

Edoid communities of the Niger Delta comprise those classified as Southwest Edoid (Urhobo, Isoko, Eruwa, Okpe, and Uvbie/Effurum of Delta State), and Delta Edoid (Degema and Engenni of Rivers State, and Epie-Atissa of Bayelsa State). Oral traditions among some of these communities claiming migration from Ife, Igboid, and Ijoid areas must refer to relatively recent times or the entry of small numbers of immigrants. The majority of these groups have remained in the northern peripheries of the Niger Delta, but a few have penetrated deeper into the delta or moved across it into the central and even the eastern Niger Delta.

Igboid communities of the Niger Delta (Ika and Ukwuani of Delta State, Ndoni, Egbema, Ogba, Ikwerre, and Ekpeye of Rivers State) represent movements southward from more northerly locations. Claims among the Ogba and other Igboid communities to migration from Benin must refer to secondary movements of population. Test archaeological excavations at Ali-Ogba and neighboring sites suggest that the settlements in the northern Niger Delta hinterland took place over a thousand years ago.

The Delta Cross is made up of Central Delta (Ogbia, Abua, Odual, and others of Rivers State), the Ogoni (Khana, Gokana, Eleme, Ogoi, and Babbe of Rivers State), and Lower Cross (Obolo/Andoni of Rivers State, and the Ibeno, Ibibio, and Oron of Akwa Ibom State). These peoples of the Cross River valley moved into the eastern Niger Delta periphery in the last two thousand years. The Obolo tell of migration from as far east as the Cameroon republic.

Processes of integration among these diverse groups were assisted by environmental factors, since the goods and products of the Niger Delta complemented those of the hinterland. Thus, Niger Delta traders traveled as far north as the Niger-Benue confluence at Lokoja, exchanging dried fish and salt for the yams and other agricultural produce of the Igbo, Igala, Nupe, Hausa, and other groups. An external dimension was added to this dynamic situation with the arrival of European adventurers, traders, and missionaries from the end of the fifteenth through the nineteenth century. The Niger Delta peoples became middlemen in the transatlantic triangular trade between Africa, Europe, and the Americas, first in slaves, principally, and then in palm oil and kernels, from the late eighteenth century.

State formation in the Niger Delta was fueled by diffusion from such hinterland centers as Benin, Aboh, and possibly, the Igala polity of Idah, and from internal dynamics, assisted in the final stages by the impact of the overseas trade. The Itsekiri kingdom at Ode Itsekiri or Iwere served as the surrogate for the Benin Empire inside the western Niger Delta. The eastern Niger Delta city-states of Nembe (Brass), Elem Kalabari (New Calabar), Bonny, Okrika, and Opobo (from about 1870), provide examples of the development of state systems from internal Niger Delta factors.

E. J. Alagoa

See also: **Slavery: Atlantic Trade: Effects in Africa and the Americas.**

Further Reading

Abasiattai, M. B. (ed.). *A History of the Cross River Region of Nigeria.* Enugu and Calabar: University of Calabar Press, 1990.

Alagoa, E. J. "The Development of Institutions in the States of the Eastern Niger Delta." *Journal of African History.* 12, no. 2 (1971): 269–278.

———. *A History of the Niger Delta: A Historical Interpretation of Ijo Oral Tradition.* Ibadan: Ibadan University Press, 1972.

Bradbury, R. E., and P. C. Lloyd. *The Benin Kingdom and the Edo-speaking Peoples of South-western Nigeria.* London: International African Institute, 1970.

Horton, R. "From Fishing Village to City-state: A Social History of New Calabar." In *Man in Africa,* edited by M. Douglas and P. M. Kaberry. London, 1969.

Jones, G. I. *The Trading States of the Niger Delta.* London: International African Institute, 1963.

Niger: Nineteenth Century: Survey

Niger consists of two historically separate, though complementary, regions. The northern two-thirds, arid and hot, were inhabited by nomadic peoples, mostly Tuareg. The more fertile south was home to different peoples whose political center lay outside of Niger's borders. At the end of the nineteenth century, the French conquered the region in order to prevent the British from interfering with its trade with Côte d'Ivoire.

For most of the nineteenth century, the northern regions changed little. The Tuareg roamed freely, in harmony with the foraging needs of their herds, and benefiting from the preservation of their lucrative trans-Saharan trade routes, the easternmost of which ran northward from Lake Chad to Bilma (now in Niger) and through the Fezzan region to Tripoli. Their fiercely independent clans never formed a centralized government. The closest they came was creation of temporary loosely organized confederations, when they felt that their life style was endangered. Throughout the century the Tuareg continued expanding southward, probably driven by worsening droughts that destroyed oases between Lake Chad and Kawar. While they maintained Agadez as a key trade center, they also developed a commercial base in Niamey.

The southern and more fertile part of Niger traversed for a distance of about 350 miles by the Niger River in the west, and abutting on Lake Chad in the east, was populated by a variety of agriculturalist sedentary groups, either connected to states outside of Niger, or refugees from events which occurred beyond Niger's borders. The area was inhabited by Zerma in the west, mostly descendants of Songhai inhabitants of the Malian Empire, Kanuri in the east, which constituted an important province of the empire of Bornu in northeast Nigeria, and Hausa kingdoms in the center, either incorporating land on both sides of the border with Nigeria, or created by refugees from the south.

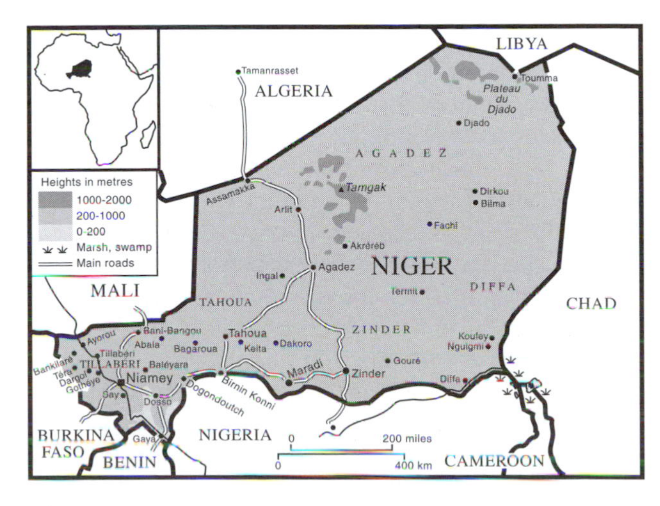

Niger.

Early in the nineteenth century, the Fulani jihad of Usuman dan Fodio, which developed in Hausa Sokoto in Nigeria, altered the status quo in all of southern Niger. Usuman's intransigent Islam was incompatible with the rule of the Hausa kings. By 1804 the situation was such that Usuman felt compelled to declare a jihad, with himself as an independent Muslim ruler.

The Hausa kings failed to organize a united front against the Islamic rebellion. Discontented Fulani and oppressed Hausa peasantry supported the jihadists. Within three years, almost all Hausa kings had been replaced by Fulani emirs, followers of Usuman. The core of the Sokoto caliphate consisted of the Hausa states of Katsina, Kano, and Zaria, together with the former smaller kingdom of Daura. Sokoto and Gwandu eventually emerged as the twin capitals of a new Fulani Empire.

Niger's population grew because of the influx of refugees. Hausa states were reborn in Niger. Thus, when after a bitter struggle Fulani led by Umaru Dallaji, overcame Hausa Katsina (1807) and Dallaji became emir, Hausa aristocrats fled northeast towards Damagaram (Zinder). Under the direction of Dan Kasawa, they settled near the boundary between Damagaram and Maradi.

This territory, then governed by Fulani Muslim officials as part of Katsina, had long been administered by Hausa under Hausa kings. A local Hausa administrator, Maradi Wagaza, had retained his post despite the Fulani conquest. Wagaza conspired with Kasawa to overthrow the Fulani. The Fulani were taken by surprise, the revolt spread rapidly and Kasawa moved to Maradi, where he proclaimed a renewed Hausa Katsina chiefdom.

Dallaji called for Bello's help against Kasawa who, supported by local Hausa and by Tuareg allies, counterattacked and freed a large section of northwest Fulani Katsina (1821). Maradi became a new Nigerian Hausa state, and with the support of adjacent states, continued to fight nearby Fulani dominions. For a long time neither side was strong enough to seize the other's capital and win a decisive victory, but they continued to raid each other's small towns. On the Nigerian side the British arrived at the turn of the century, just as the Hausa were about to overthrow the Fulani. The British instituted their policy of indirect rule, under which both Fulani and Hausa were supported equally. On the French side the colonizers concentrated on restoring order with their armed forces.

Meanwhile, at the eastern end of southern Niger, Sokoto forces had attacked the Kanuri empire of Bomu, the might of which was based on control of salt-producing sites and long-distance trade. The unforeseen consequence of the Fulani offensive was the creation of a new Hausa state in Niger. Peripheric Damagaram, initially a tributary of Bornu, was able to gain independence. Based in the city of Zinder, it took control of much of the trans-Saharan trade from there.

Bornu itself fought on. By1808 Fulani rebels and invaders had captured Birni Gazargamu, the capital, but the ancient royal family of Bornu founded a new Kanuri capital in Kukawa and restored Bornu's independence. Bornu had its own clerics. One of them, Muhammad al-Kanemi, challenged the Fulani's exclusivity on interpretation of Islamic law and inspired national resistance. By 1826 he was effectively master of a new Islamic state, though the traditional kings were maintained in office until 1846. When the king rebelled against al-Kanemi's son and successor, Umar, he was defeated and killed. Umar proclaimed himself the first sultan of Bornu. Gradually, on both sides of the border, Fulani and Hausa intermarried. Hausa, rather than Arabic, became the language of the region.

Two African conquerors brought their empire-building attempts to Nigerian soil in the late nineteenth century: Samori Touré and Rabih az-Zubayr. Both fought the invading French and lost. Neither left a durable imprint on Niger.

The French, who had first appeared on the scene in the late 1880s, concentrated their efforts on colonizing Niger. By 1903 they incorporated it into their Sudanic holdings and in 1922 declared it a separate colony.

NATALIE SANDOMIRSKY

See also: **Tuareg.**

Further Reading

Forde, D., and P. M. Kaberry (eds.). *West African Kingdoms in the Nineteenth Century.* London: Oxford University Press, 1967.
Fuglestad, F. *A History of Niger, 1850–1960.* New York: Cambridge University Press, 1983.
Obichere, B. I. *West African States and European Expansion: The Dahomey-Niger Hinterland, 1885–1898.* New Haven, Conn.: Yale University Press, 1971.
Salifou, A. *Histoire du Niger* [History of Niger]. Paris: Nathan, 1989.

Niger: French Occupation and Resistance

At the Conference of Berlin (1884–1885) the territory of Niger was placed within the French sphere of influence. The actual borders of the colony were decided by diplomatic negotiations in Paris and London as much as by military advances in the contested territories. Protracted discussions, centered on a demarcation line between modern Nigeria and Niger, finally led to an agreement to draw a line from Say, on the Niger River southeast of Niamey, to Barruwa, east of Lake Chad, and assign control north of this line to France and south to Britain (August 1890). However, the agreement could not be implemented, as neither France nor Britain had accurate knowledge of the area in dispute.

The French considered the presence of Britain in the region a threat to French colonies on the Atlantic, for if Britain gained control of the hinterland, trade would be diverted to British possessions on the coast. Therefore, it was imperative to conquer the hinterland as quickly as possible. This was the policy of Eugène Etienne, undersecretary of state for African colonies in Paris. He formulated the Chad Plan, based on the reports of Captain L. G. Binger's expedition (1887–1889) which proved that the Kong mountains, supposed obstacle to penetration, did not exist, and hence access from the Niger Bend to the Atlantic coast was possible. The new plan postulated a joining of Algeria and Tunisia with the Congo, and of French West African possessions with those on Lake Chad. It directly involved Nigerian territory.

Etienne organized an exploratory expedition. He sent Lieutenent P. L. Monteil to evaluate the extent of British presence in Sokoto, lay claim to unoccupied lands by concluding treaties with indigenous rulers who were not tied to any European power by prior treaties, and make recommendations regarding the actual course of the conjectural Say-Barruwa Line. Monteil reached Segu in October 1890, and then made his way across the Niger Bend region. In Say he concluded a treaty with the local ruler (1891). Hence he moved on to Sokoto, concluded a treaty with the sultan, and continued to the banks of Lake Chad. He returned to France in 1893, via Tripoli.

Both France and Britain began maneuvering under the principle that occupation was the key to possession. The French established military posts in South Niger in the late 1890s, and while they continued negotiating, they also became engaged in military actions in the Niger region. The most formidable resistance they faced in southern Niger came from self-made leaders whose conquests had led them to the region: Samori Touré and Rahib az-Zubayr.

Samori had established his military and political control over territories in adjoining Mali. He was a talented tactician who understood contemporary warfare. He procured as many modern weapons as possible; trained his men to use them, repair guns, and manufacture bullets. He avoided head-on confrontations and being cornered in vulnerable walled cities and resorted to guerilla tactics. He had, however, focused on his African rivals and failed to see that the French were after possession of the territory, not merely commercial development. When he realized his mistake and attempted to make alliances with other African leaders, it was too late. The French had to fight a number of campaigns against him; it took them until 1898, but they captured and exiled him.

In 1899 the French intensified their military efforts. Their offensive in Niger provoked determined resistance because of the comportment of the notorious expedition led by Captains Paul Voulet and Charles Chanoine, moving from Zinder to Lake Chad to join up with columns from north and equatorial Africa. Cruel and bloodthirsty, they seized food and supplies from drought-stricken populations, burned down everything in sight when met with resistance, and killed thousands. They conquered Damagaram and the city of Zinder, and plundered their way through Niger until they were finally killed by a mutiny of their own men. Under new leadership, the French column moved on to defeat Rabih.

Rahib az-Zubayr was a Muslim leader from the Nile Valley who had established a military empire in the districts immediately east of Lake Chad. By the early 1890s he had built a considerable force armed with light field artillery. He intended to move against the Fulani in Sokoto, but had to change his plans to stop a French column moving northward from the Congo. In 1900 his forces met the French on the Logone River, where his army was routed and he was killed.

This completed the French advance in West Africa. They had conquered a vast territory, and limited the expansion of Liberia and the British colonies. In 1900 Niger was made a military territory. It was then included in Senegambia and Niger (1903), which became Upper Senegal and Niger (1904), to be renamed the French Sudan in 1920.

While by the twentieth century the French controlled southern Niger, northern nomadic peoples, mostly Tuareg, resisted successfully for many more years. The Tuareg's unrestricted movements threatened French rule. The French sent a military mission into the Sahara to control and tax caravans. The Tuareg rebelled. French attempts to regulate them represented an attack on the existence they had led for centuries. They fought to maintain their right to roam freely in accordance with the needs of their herds, keep up their caravan trade, and safeguard their right to own slaves to cultivate their fields while they were engaged in their customary pursuits. Tuareg and French seized each other's animals, filled or poisoned wells, and destroyed crops. Due to the persistent Tuareg resistance, France did not occupy Agadez until 1904. There was one last serious Tuareg uprising in 1916–1917, a result of drought-caused famine, harsh taxes, and French recruitment of soldiers for World War I. The French had greater resources and help from Tuareg slaves. In the long run, the French were victorious. When defeated, many Tuareg fled to Nigeria. Civil authorities took over only in 1922, when Niger was made a separate colony within French West Africa.

NATALIE SANDOMIRSKY

Further Reading

Crowder, M. (ed.). *West African Resistance.* Evanston, Ill.: Northwestern University Press, 1968.

Hargreaves, J. D. *West Africa Partitioned.* 2 vols. London: Macmillan, 1974, 1985.

Isichei, E. *History of West Africa since 1800.* London and Basingstoke: Macmillan, 1977.

Kanya-Forstner, A. S. *Conquest of the Western Sudan: A Study in French Military Imperialism.* Cambridge: Cambridge University Press, 1969.

Niger: Colonial Period to Independence

It was for strategic reasons that France first established a presence in Niger, a country that borders on the Sahara, Lake Chad, and Nigeria. Foreign explorers had already penetrated the territory, the most famous being Heinrich Barth, and Niger had become a factor in the delineation of the French and British spheres of influence in the region. Their boundaries were first drawn along the Say-Baruwa line (August 5, 1890), but this was followed by a new delimitation (June 14, 1898) that favored the British. The signing of these two treaties was accompanied by marches into Chad by three major French expeditions, led respectively by Fourreau and Lamy, Voulet and Chanoine, and Gentil, and the first military posts were established from 1896. The occupation proceeded from west to east, then from south to north, and Niger came under military administration from 1901 to 1920. After numerous negotiations, France eventually obtained a more favorable rectification of the frontier under the convention of May 29, 1906, which was ratified in 1910.

The delineation of Niger's borders with the other French colonies went more smoothly. The border with Upper Volta dated from the creation of that colony, although in 1926 the districts outlined by Say were attached to Niger along with cantons in the Dori circuit. Thus, when the colony was dismembered (1932–1947), the districts of Dori and Fada N'Gourma remained attached to Niger until Upper Volta was reconstituted. By contrast, Niger's frontier with French Sudan remained imprecise, because of the problems surrounding pasturage and waterholes. The frontier with Chad had been fixed by the Franco-British convention of 1899, while the frontier with Algeria was fixed by the convention of Niamey (June 20, 1909), and that with Libya, first delineated in 1898, was modified in 1919.

Few Europeans settled in Niger, which was always inhospitable to them: there were only 513 there in 1926. This lack of personnel obliged the administration to secure a strong base among the traditional rulers. Despite the limited economic potential of the territory, the administration imposed taxes from 1906 and implemented a system of *prestations* (obligatory payments). Colonization induced profound disruption in a society that was already fragile because of the vagaries of the climate. Famine struck in 1900 and again, on a larger scale, in 1913–1914, and on the latter occasion it stimulated significant migration southward.

When World War I broke out in 1914, the conquest was still not complete. Military recruitment in the zones that had been "pacified" affected 3,948 men (0.33% of the population), although between 31 and 75 per cent of them were found to be unfit for service. The territory also provided produce for the French war effort and was compelled to take part in fund-raising. With the war, resistance to colonization, which had made its first appearance in 1899, became more widespread. There were two major uprisings: Firhun's and Kaocen's. Firhun declared a holy war and was supported by the Tuaregs: the repression that followed was brutal and intensive, reflecting the degree of disquiet that the uprising aroused. Firhun evaded the French but was killed in a clash between Tuareg groups on June 25, 1916. The uprising of the Kel Aïr took up where Firhun had left off but was also linked to the reoccupation of the Fezzan by the Ottoman Turks and to the activities of the Sanussiyya confraternity, which Kaocen, the rebel leader, had joined in 1909. A native of Damergou, he had gained the support of the sultan of Agadez. The major event in this second uprising was the siege of Agadez, which lasted for eighty-two days. Kaocen was taken prisoner by the Turks and hanged on January 5, 1919, while the sultan of Agadez, who was also taken prisoner, was strangled on the order of the Turks during the night of April 29–30, 1919. The Kel Aïr was devastated during these events.

On December 4, 1920, Niger was reorganized as a territory under civilian administration, and on July 1, 1922, it became a colony. The period from then until 1930 was marked by relative prosperity for an economy that continued to be centered on livestock, textiles, and foodstuffs. However, there was a major famine in the West in 1931, caused by the administration itself, which, according to official figures, led to the deaths of 28,867 people and the departure of 30,000 others. Meanwhile, education made very slow progress. There were only 1,892 children in schools in 1938. Medical services were also very limited. Niamey, which was not made the capital of the colony until 1931, acquired a hospital in 1926, and campaigns were launched against the main endemic and epidemic diseases, including smallpox, measles, meningitis, and trypanosomiasis. Niger once again passed into the hands of a military governor at the outbreak of World War II, because of its strategic location. In 1943 the levying of colonial taxes brought about another famine.

Significant transformations began in 1946 with investments by the Fonds d'Investissement pour le Développement Economique et Social (FIDES; Investment Funds for Economic and Social Development), while political activity underwent a remarkable expansion. The Parti progressiste nigérien (PPN; Progressive Party of Niger) became a section of the Rassemblement démocratique africain (RDA; African Democratic Rally), and during the 1950s three new parties appeared: the Union nigérienne des indépendants et sympathisants (UNIS; Niger Union of Independents and Sympathizers), le Bloc nigérien d'action (BNA; Niger Action Bloc), and the Union démocratique nigérienne (UDN; Niger Democratic Union). The UDN and the BNA then merged to form the Mouvement socialiste africain (MSA; African Socialist Movement), which joined in creating the Convention africaine [CAF; African Convention). Djibo Bakary led the CAF to victory over the PPN-RDA in the territorial elections of March 1957. The creation of the Parti du regroupement africain (PRA; African Consolidation Party) then entailed a change of name for the MSA, which became a section of the PRA under the name Sawaba ("liberty").

At the Congress of the PRA in Cotonou, a minority led by Djibo Bakary, who became general secretary, announced that it favored independence. It held to this position at the time when the Communauté française (French Community) was being formed, and accordingly campaigned for a rejection of the proposal. The French government, working with the colonial administration, the PRA's opponents, who had funds from the RDA, and the traditional chiefs, resisted this trend and succeeded in changing several people's minds, so that only 22 per cent of those voting on the proposed Communauté voted "No."

The referendum was followed by a major crisis. Djibo Bakary and his government were forced to resign, leaving the way open to the PPN-RDA under Hamani Diori. Boubou Hama became president of the Assemblée nationale (National Assembly) and commissioned Hamani Diori to form a government, which then promulgated the constitution of March 12, 1959. Shortly before, during February, the budget submitted by Djibo Bakary had been rejected and the municipal council of Niamey had been dissolved. Faced with these new developments, Djibo Bakary chose to go into exile. Niger took part in the establishment of the Conseil de l'Entente (Council of the Entente) in May 1959, and it was within this framework that it called for the transfer of powers and attained independence on August 3, 1960.

DANIELLE DOMERGUE-CLOAREC

See also: **Tuareg: Twentieth Century.**

Further Reading

Benoist, J. R. de. *L'Afrique Occidentale Française de 1944 à 1960*. Dakar: NEA, 1982.

Kimba, I. "Le Niger." In *L'Afrique Occidentale au Temps des Français, Colonisateurs et Colonisés 1860–1960*, edited by C. Coquery-Vidrovitch. Paris: La Découverte, 1992.

Olivier de Sardan, P. P. *Les Sociétés Songhay-Zarma (Mali-Niger)*. Paris: Karthala, 1984.

Niger: Independence to Present

Niger gained independence in 1960 by letting its membership in the French Community lapse. Since then, the country has been the victim of military coups, transitional governments, revisions of its constitution, poverty, social unrest, and civil war.

The contemporary turbulent history of the Republic of Niger results partly from the French colonizers' strategically motivated decision to make a territory with insufficient resources into a separate colony, and then draw its borders without regard to ethnic distribution or traditions.

The peoples of Niger have historically adopted very dissimilar lifestyles because its lands lie in different climatic zones. The northern two-thirds of the country lie in or adjacent to the Sahara desert, and are populated by nomads. The southern third, particularly along the Niger River basin and near Lake Chad in the southeast, is fertile and inhabited by sedentary farmers. Essentially, all that Niger's main ethnic groups—Hausa, Songhay-Zerma, Fulani, Kanuri, and Tuareg—had in common when the French arrived was Islam. At that, their Islamic faith was often nominal and adapted by each group to its own ancient beliefs. Populations of the area shared neither cosmology nor societal structure but rather identified with people of their own ethnic groups in what are now neighboring countries.

In precolonial times, pastoralists and agriculturalists were often quite peacefully interdependent. However, frontiers, modernization, urbanization, and French administrations that divided the population into two distinct groups, nomadic and sedentary, favoring the latter, accentuated tensions. Some feuds, like those caused by political jealousies between two southern groups, the Hausa and the Songhay-Zerma, were only periodically important. Other disputes grew into major lasting confrontations which interfered with development of the nation of Niger. The greatest difficulties arose between the government and the Tuareg.

From independence on, the Songhay-Zerma, the first group to be exposed to French education, dominated the regime and the army, and attempted to centralize power and subordinate the Tuareg, to the point where they even outlawed public use of Tamasheq, the Tuareg language. The Tuareg were accustomed to being independent traders and roaming freely across the desert, in accordance with the foraging needs of their cattle. When the creation of national borders made transhumance illegal, and the development of new trade patterns disrupted the activities of their desert caravans, they saw their way of life and their very identity in jeopardy. A proud and courageous people, hardened by survival under harsh conditions, they repeatedly took up arms against the government, disrupted life in Niger, and attracted international attention to their plight.

Independent Niger's first president was Hamani Diori, the Songhay-Zerma leader of the Nigerien Progressive Party (PPN), the local branch of the African Democratic Assembly (RDA), who consolidated his power and ran for president unopposed (1960). He favored traditional governmental structures and close ties with France. With help from a friendly French administration and favorable climatic conditions, he was able to rule over a period of relative political stability, notwithstanding a weak economy and ethnic conflicts. He was reelected in 1965 and 1970. In the early 1970s, however, severe droughts drastically affected crops, cattle died by the thousand, famine ensued, and dissatisfaction spread. The revelation that international emergency aid had been misappropriated by cabinet ministers accelerated the end of Diori's rule. The military overthrew and arrested him in 1974.

A Supreme Military Council (CMS) assumed power under the leadership of Lieutenant Colonel Senyi Kountché, who had engineered the coup. It suspended the constitution, replaced the legislature with a consultative National Development Council, and outlawed political parties. Kountché's first concern was to provide relief to the drought-stricken areas. He gave aid directly to collectivized farms he organized. The elite, which he had bypassed, undermined his programs, but then uranium mines were discovered in Niger. This unexpected windfall raised hopes for a better economic future; however only a few entrepreneurs made profits. Furthermore, soon global opposition to uranium mining depressed world markets. In the early 1980s, droughts returned and unrest resumed. Moreover the Tuareg, whom Kountché had alienated by ignoring their demands, had found a backer in Colonel Muammar Gaddafi. In 1985 the Tuareg, based in Libya, attacked Tchin-Tabarene. Kountché tried pacification and appointed a Tuareg secretary of state, but he fell ill in 1986 and died a year later, leaving problems unresolved.

Colonel Ali Saïbou, chief of staff of the armed forces, who had ruled during Kountché's illness, took over with promises of democracy and reform. He proclaimed a general amnesty for political prisoners, abolished the ban on political parties, and disbanded the CMS. However, he created a new ruling party and a new council to draft a constitution for the Second Republic. The constitution was approved by a popular referendum. Saïbou, the sole presidential candidate, was elected. Democracy was far from being a reality; the military still ruled. Problems with the Tuareg came to a head. Saïbou promised financial aid and preservation of Tuareg culture, but nothing changed. Rebel attacks and general lawlessness continued. In 1990 the Tuareg launched an all-out assault.

More threatening than Tuareg rebellions were economic problems. In order to qualify for international loans, Niger had to accept structural economic reforms. The budget cuts these required provoked student unrest and union strikes. In 1990, under international pressure and the threat of bankruptcy, Saibou tried liberalization; he announced that the constitution would be amended to allow political pluralism, promised less stringent austerity, and convened a conference, headed by noted Niger scholar André Salifou, to outline the country's political future. The turmoil persisted. The conference stripped Saïbou of his powers and elected Amadou Cheiffou, a civilian, caretaker of a transition government. Cheiffou obtained emergency loans from France and oversaw the drafting of a new constitution for the Third Republic, which established a multiparty system and direct presidential and legislative elections (1992).

Mohamane Ousmane became the first Hausa head of state by winning the presidency in free elections (1993). However, shortly thereafter, an opposition party won control of the legislature. This led to a prolonged stalemate and ultimately to Ousmane's downfall. Unrest resumed in the army and the unions. Social tensions were exacerbated by the devaluation of the CFA franc. In 1994–1995 Ousmane negotiated with Tuareg groups and reached a peace agreement that provided for autonomous regions for the Tuareg, their incorporation into security forces and civil service, an amnesty for all fighters, and a law to accelerate decentralization so as to ensure the development of all regions of Niger. This success did not suffice to bring about political stability.

In 1996 a military coup under the command of Ibrahim Baré Maïnassara, chief of staff of the armed forces, put an end to the long stand-off between Ousmane and prime minister Hama Amadou, which had paralyzed the government. Again the constitution was suspended, the national assembly dissolved, and a state of emergency proclaimed. A forum was convened to revise the constitution and electoral laws so as to ensure that the upcoming Fourth Republic would avoid repetition of past problems, The forum rapidly drew up a timetable for elections to appease international donors with whom Maïnassara needed to resume negotiations. Elected president in 1996, Maïnassara sought to improve the economic situation by developing regional cooperation and trade between African states. The country was comparatively quiet for a couple of years.

However, the political atmosphere deteriorated as Maïnassara solidified his hold on power. The legitimacy of governmental bodies was questioned. The army and civil servants held demonstrations demanding past pay due them; strikes proliferated. Further destabilization occurred when the president was assassinated by the palace guard and replaced by Major Daouda Maflam Wanke, the very man responsible for the assassination.

This unprincipled act alienated the international community, and in particular the French, who threatened to withdraw aid. As head of a fourteen-man National Reconciliation Commission, Wanke restored civilian rule. The draft constitution for the Fifth Republic envisaged a balance of power between president, government, and legislature. Peaceful elections took place in 1999. Mamadou Tandja, a retired army colonel originally from the southeastern region near Lake Chad, was elected. He promised to improve the conditions of workers and respect the principles of democracy. However, cabinet reshufflements and unstable relations with the Tuareg continued. Inhabitants still engaged mostly in subsistence farming. The few existing industries manufactured only consumer goods for local consumption. The transportation network remained inadequate, and the trade balance was in deficit.

But there are hopeful signs. Responsible administration has been able to secure debt reduction from foreign lenders. A 3 per cent inflation and a 4 per cent growth in Niger's GNP are foreseen for 2001. The government is improving sanitary conditions and attempting to raise the literacy rate, still around only 35 per cent. Tandja has joined leaders of neighboring nations to address problems regarding dramatic reductions of the Niger River's and Lake Chad's water level due to droughts and population growth, he has worked with the World Solar Commission hoping to harness solar energy to alleviate Niger's energy crisis. There are also signs of an awakening of national pride manifested by greater interest in preservation of the cultural and artistic heritage.

NATALIE SANDOMIRSKY

See also: **Libya: Foreign Policy under Qaddafi.**

Further Reading

Baier, S. *An Economic History of Central Niger.* Oxford: Clarendon Press, 1980.

Bernus, E. *Touaregs Nigériens: Unité Culturelle et Diversité Régionale d'un Peuple Pasteur* [Nigerien Tuareg: Cultural Unity and Regional Diversity of a Pastoral People]. Paris: Editions de l'Office de la recherche scientifique et technique outre-mer, 1981.

Carter, G. (ed.). *National Unity and Regionalism in Eight African States.* Itahca, N.Y.: Cornell University Press, 1966.

Decalo, S. *Historical Dictionary of Niger.* 2nd ed. Metuchen, N.J.: Scarecrow Press, 1989.

Grégoire, E. *Touaregs du Niger: le Destin d'un Mythe* [Tuareg of Niger: The Destiny of a Myth]. Paris: Karthala, 1999.

Miles W. F. S. *Hausaland Divided: Colonialism and Independence in Nigeria and Niger.* Ithaca, N.Y.: Cornell University Press, 1994.

Nicolaisen, J. *The Pastoral Tuareg: Ecology, Culture, and Society.* New York: Thames and Hudson, 1997.

Olivier de Sardan, J.-P. *Les Sociétés Songhay-Zerma, Niger-Mali* [Songhay-Zerma Societies, Niger-Mali]. Paris: Karthala, 1984.

Salifou, A. *Histoire du Niger*. Paris: Nathan, 1989.

———. *La Question touaregue au Niger* [The Tuareg Question in Niger]. Paris: Karthala, 1993.

Niger Mission: *See* Crowther, Reverend Samuel Ajayi and the Niger Mission.

Nigeria: British Colonization to 1914

The palm oil trade, which slowly replaced the slave trade by the 1850s, flourished and attracted more British merchants, mostly from Liverpool and Manchester. Although official presence was questioned when, in 1865, a parliamentary committee of the House of Commons suggested the slow withdrawal from the region, the formation of the United Africa Company (UAC) by Taubman Goldie, a former army officer, strengthened the informal empire of Great Britain in the region of the Niger delta. Lagos became a flourishing trading post on the coast, nearly reaching self-sufficiency by the 1870s, as desired by the metropolitan colonial government. At the same time, the earlier neglect of the town's infrastructure development would eventually result in a series of crises and require enormous sums of investment to enable Lagos to become the new colony's capital.

International events paved the way for an expansion into the interior, and a subsequent rivalry with other European colonial powers. In a series of events between 1882 and 1897, British forces of the UAC and the Lagos government marched against African forces in Yorubaland and the Niger delta. In 1897 the Benin punitive expedition put down the last remaining major opposing force in the south, although total subjugation of small enclaves was not completed until World War I. The northern war of conquest was led by Frederick Lugard, who had been actively involved in local affairs first as a commissioned leader of a treaty expedition in 1894 to Nikki, then later as the main organizer of the West African Frontier Force, Britain's regional colonial army. The hostilities against the states of the Sokoto Caliphate between 1900 and 1903 clearly demonstrated the European technical superiority in warfare. It proved again the truth of Hilaire Belloc's satirical rhyme: "Whatever happens, we have got, the Maxim gun, and they have not." The first hostilities

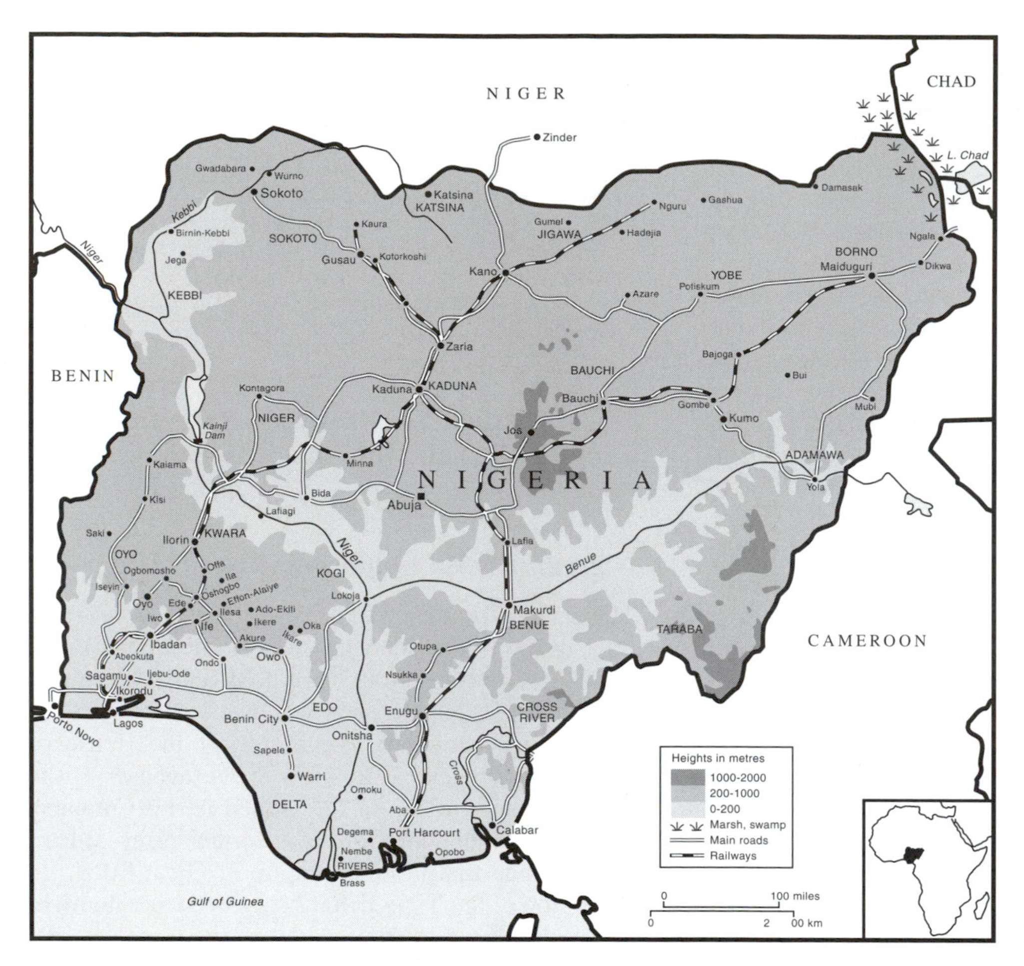

Nigeria.

between Europeans and a state of the Sokoto Caliphate broke out when, following a series of diplomatic infiltration, Nupe was conquered by troops of the Royal Niger Company (RNC), the successor of the UAC. In 1898 a British resident was sent to Sokoto itself, indicating a possible move toward diplomacy. This changed altogether when Lugard took command of the British forces and completed the brutal war in three years. The Battle of Burmi in 1903 is often seen as an unnecessarily brutal ending of the campaign that resulted in the death of over 600 people, most from the Fulani aristocracy.

Although the UAC received a royal charter and became the RNC in 1886, its rule lasted only until 1900, when the Protectorate of Southern Nigeria was formed. With the colony of Lagos and the Northern Nigerian Protectorate, the three Nigerias represented distinct administrations, problems, and approaches.

The oldest British settlement of Lagos, with a population of more than 40,000 people, presented a highly sensitive African intelligentsia with critical voices toward the administration. Additional problems of urban sanitation only caused further concerns that were not solved, despite the presence of governors like William MacGregor, who tried to address African needs and solve urgent issues of disease control and public sanitation, for example. His efforts and initiatives were often turned down by the Colonial Office as exaggerated, useless, and expensive. His only significant triumph was the building of the Lagos Canal and the draining of marshes around the town, which made further urban development possible.

The southern protectorate remained largely a trading enterprise. Many members of the company rule were accepted as administrators. Subjugation of resisting regions and peoples (especially the Tiv) presented a major problem for the southern protectorate. The different attitudes and composition of the administrative service could be traced through, for example, the neglect of African health issues prior to the amalgamation of Lagos and the eastern territories in 1906. For example, free quinine distribution for Africans against malaria was initiated as early as 1901 in Lagos, but it was an issue that surfaced in the east only after 1906. The most important figure after the 1906 amalgamation was Walter Egerton, who was the governor of the region up to 1912. His activities can be described as "anti-native" policy, especially against the Lagos intelligentsia, as he abandoned the earlier diplomacy and communication efforts, and took a more confrontational approach leading, for example to forced land expropriation in Lagos.

The north resembled a military occupation. Up to the eve of the amalgamation in 1914, the proportion of British officials remained the highest in comparison to traders or miners of the southern territories. The "empire's frontier" image attracted many young officials with upper-middle-class backgrounds who were among the first to enter the reformed colonial service, recruited on the initiatives of Ralph Furse from 1908. The region was a trial ground for the implementation of Lugard's policy of indirect rule (the practice of European colonial administration through retaining the members of the former ruling class of Fulani aristocracy). Although every effort was made by the administration to create a working system in the first years, the Satiru revolt in 1906 indicated that the British had to plan their rule more carefully. Following this event, the relationship between the local elite and the officials started to improve, and a balance of power was achieved.

Successful taxation on imports resulted in a large surplus of revenues in the south, a major reason for the amalgamation of the two southern regions in 1906 and later, with the return of Lugard in 1912, the north and south. By this time, the colony had developed into the most important tropical colony of Great Britain in Africa. Out of the 1,399 Europeans serving in the colonial service in Africa, 622 were employed by the government of Nigeria in 1914, a figure that was to rise in later years.

LÁSZLÓ MÁTHÉ-SHIRES

See also: **Benin Kingdom: British Conquest, 1897; Delta States, Nineteenth Century; Igboland, Nineteenth Century; Lagos Colony and Oil Rivers Protectorate; Royal Niger Company, 1886–1898; Yoruba States: Trade and Conflict, Nineteenth Century.**

Further Reading

Kirk-Green, A. *On Crown Service.* London: Tauris, 1999.

Lynn, M. "British Policy, Trade, and Informal Empire in the Mid-Nineteenth Century." In *The Oxford History of the British Empire.* Vol 3: *The Nineteenth Century*, edited by A. Porter and A. Low. Oxford: Oxford University Press, 1999.

Lovejoy, P. E., and J. S. Hogendorn. "Revolutionary Mahdism and Resistance to Colonial Rule in the Sokoto Caliphate, 1905–06." *Journal of African History.* 31(1991): 217–244.

McCaskie, T. M. "Cultural Encounters: Britain and Africa in the Nineteenth Century." In *the Oxford History of the British Empire.* Vol. 3: *The Nineteenth Century*, edited by A. Porter and A. Low. Oxford: Oxford University Press, 1999.

Philips, A. *The Enigma of Colonialism: British Policy in West Africa.* London: James Currey, 1989.

Nigeria: Lugard, Administration, and "Indirect Rule"

Although relations in the forms of treaties between the Sokoto Caliphate and the British National Africa Company reached back as far as 1885, the actual conquest of the Caliphate did not begin until 1897 when the troops of the Royal Niger Company (RNC) defeated southernmost parts of the caliphate, Nupe and Ilorin. While this was still not a formal conquest, as the RNC was a private commercial enterprise, in 1900 the West African Frontier Force (WAFF) marched against the caliphate. Hostilities lasted up to 1903 with the final battle of Burmi, where the troops of Sokoto were defeated.

The British troops, comprised mostly of recruited Hausa soldiers of the WAFF (with a handful of European officers) were led by Frederick Dealty Lugard. Born in India in 1858, he entered military service early, serving in the 1879 Afghan, the 1885 Sudan, and the 1886 Burma wars where he acquired some considerable military experience. He joined the service of chartered companies first in East Africa, then in 1894 in Nigeria. In 1897 Chamberlain commissioned him to organize the British imperial fighting force, the WAFF, in West Africa to withstand the growing challenge of other European powers and opposing African forces. By the time of the Sokoto war, Lugard had become known as the foremost figure of frontier wars and a successful organizer. He became the high commissioner for Northern Nigeria, where he remained until 1906. He returned there from his Hong Kong governorship in 1912 to amalgamate the south and the north, a task that was implemented by 1914. He retired in 1919 to serve various imperial positions in Britain, including the country's representative for the League of Nations' antislavery commission.

The form of rule initiated and implemented by Lugard in northern Nigeria is known as "indirect rule," a form of government recognized as the predominant political philosophy behind British colonial administration in the first half of the twentieth century. While in 1898 there were 156 British officials and only about 10 non-officials north of the Benue-Niger axis, in 1914, there were 543 officials present out of the total British population of 969 in the region. Following World War I, the number of officials in government service dropped to 399, while non-officials were well over 1,000 in 1,920. This relatively low number of administrators oversaw a region populated by an average of 54,000 Africans.

The mode of administration was based on the resident system, where African emirs and chiefs met with

British officers who acted as political advisors. The African leaders, who partially oversaw tax redistribution as well as legal affairs, retained a large amount of autonomy. Native treasuries, with British financial control, were responsible for local government fiscal policies and budgets. Autonomy applied to the British officers as well, although in a different sense. The image of Northern Nigerian service in the first two decades of the twentieth century typically presents a lonely officer, on tour most of the time, and responsible for various challenging duties, such as the suppression of slavery, road construction, and tax collection. Touring the administrative region was one of the most important ways of exercising colonial authority. The district officer was required to visit the villages of his district as a means of acquiring information about the state of the settlement. Lugard's blueprint for indirect rule, a book he wrote in 1922 (*The Dual Mandate*) describes this complex task.

The role of slavery has received some detailed analysis, suggesting that the initial British administration had an ambiguous role in maintaining some forms of it well after the onset of colonial rule. Following the official abolition of slavery in the caliphate, a mass slave exodus occurred across most of the territory where the British appeared. Since the caliphate's plantation economy was based on slave labor, these events precipitated a huge economic and social crisis. The issue of slave women was especially contentious, as some of them decided to remain in the service of their former masters, not opting for personal freedom. It as only the League of Nation's intervention that finally focused attention, and consequently a firm policy on the issue of slavery.

Another aspect of social change that occurred almost immediately in northern Nigeria was urbanization and growth of new metropolitan centers. Although initial selection for these places was "somewhat arbitrary," as Governor Bell remarked on Zungeru in 1910, by the early 1920s most of these colonial centers, especially Kaduna, functioned as commercial and railway junctions. Colonial town-planning also had aspects of paternalistic indirect rule; the applied principle was sanitary segregation that had its roots in a misconceived imperial medical idea of malaria prevention.

Urban-based economic circles had high expectations regarding the prospects of northern Nigeria. Cotton growing increased the region's economic viability, following the opening of the railway in 1911, due to a sudden boom in groundnut export, largely from small-scale farms. Colonial financial policy adopted the principle of direct taxation that had been widely used by the ruling Fulanis. Although it was a relatively successful policy, the large financial requirements resulted a continuous deficit. This was one of the main reasons why Lugard initiated the amalgamation of southern and northern Nigeria upon returning to West Africa in 1912, a task that was completed by early 1914.

LÁSZLÓ MÁTHÉ-SHIRES

Further Reading

Cell, J. W. "Colonial Rule." In *The Oxford History of the British Empire.*Vol. 4: *The Twentieth Century*, edited by J. M. Brown and W. R. Louis. Oxford: Oxford University Press, 1999.

Lovejoy, P. E., and J. S. Hogendorn. *Slow Death Foe Slavery: The Course of Abolition in Northern Nigeria, 1897–1936.* Cambridge: Cambridge University Press, 1993.

Lugard, F. D. *The Dual Mandate in British Tropical Africa.* London, 1922.

Philips, A. *The Enigma of Colonialism: British Policy in West Africa.* London: James Currey, 1989.

Tidrick, K. *Empire and the English Character.* London: I. B. Tauris and Co., 1990.

Nigeria: World War I

As a colony of Britain, Nigeria was drawn into World War I, forced to experience the anticipation of fear that came with it as well as the adjustment to the withdrawal of German commercial houses, the slump associated with the shortage of shipping, and the demand for resources to meet war necessities. The war did not last long enough for Nigerians to mobilize against the British, but the period witnessed a number of protests and the rise of an anti-imperialist ideology.

The country was loyal to the colonial administration headed by Lord Lugard, the first governor general, but not without some protests in the south. Even in the newly conquered areas in the north, opposition was rather subdued, in spite of attempts by the Ottoman caliph to rally all Muslims. The exploitative nature of colonial rule was still unfolding or yet unfelt in many places and therefore did not warrant widespread protest. The chiefs and kings saw no need to protest a system that was allowing them to consolidate and preserve their powers. Even the educated elite supported the war and were not yet in a position to build behind themselves a mass following. As far as the majority of the population was concerned, they knew too little about the war to raise much concern, although they did respond to changing economic fortunes.

Nigeria fulfilled three major war aims. First, it supplied much-needed raw materials. Second, it supplied manpower about 30,000 men from British West Africa. By and large, recruitment was done on a voluntary basis and was not large enough to create any population loss or social dislocation. The soldiers fought in the Cameroons and East Africa, and they returned home to put down local rebellions in Abeokuta. Third, colonies were expected to adjust their expenditure to ensure that Britain had adequate funds to prosecute the war.

Contributions, however small, were expected for the Prince of Wales' National Defense Fund.

While no battle took place in Nigeria, the country was not far away from volatile events in the German colonies of Togo to the west and Cameroons to the east, where wars were fought on African soil. The British and French took Togo and German Cameroons. The German community in Nigeria was interned, and its members later taken to England. Initially, the withdrawal of German firms in the cash crop export business created some hardships, but a rapid recovery followed as Britain and France increased the demand for wartime needs. Where a decline in cash crop exports was recorded, it did not devastate the economy, still largely dependent on food production.

The war was not, however, without its impact on the people and the course of future history. Of immediate consequence was the economic dislocation and disruption of trade. The trade with Germany, a primary importer of cash crops, had to be terminated. Germany was the biggest importer of palm kernels, in addition to large quantities of other items. Local trading elites preferred the Germans to the British, because credit terms were more generous. Alternative markets had to be found for groundnuts, cocoa, and palm products. Also, German imports had gained credibility among the people for their durability and quality, so substitutes, too, had to be found. For some periods, prices of exports fell while that of imports rose, fueling complaints in a number of quarters. However, as groundnuts and palm oil were of great importance as wartime needs, their prices actually increased, although the combines formed by British trading firms exploited the situation to their advantage. Among other economic consequences were the rivalry between foreign companies and local ones, unemployment, a halt to development projects, and inflation.

The major political impact of the war included security threats posed by Germany in Cameroons, the fear of insurrection, the possibility that a jihad could follow any support for Turkey, and the revolts that greeted the introduction of the system of indirect rule.

New ideas spread among the Nigerian troops who served in the British army. They acquired a better knowledge of Europeans and other places, thus broadening their minds. For a number of the soldiers and elite, the war cry of the principle of self-determination, that is, the right of different peoples to determine their affairs, was both appealing and attractive. Many naturally asked why this principle was not applied to them. The British feared that the failure to rehabilitate the discharged soldiers might create problems, since many of them had become accustomed to better living conditions. Lugard feared that Africans exposed to the use of guns and bombs and other knowledge might choose to use them against the British at a future time.

The transfer of ex-German colonies of Togo and Cameroons to the League of Nations, which then gave them to Britain and France in a mandate system, created a so-called theory of imperial responsibility: the preparation of Africans for eventual self-government and the idea that Africa should supply its raw materials in exchange for "civilization."

There were rebellions, some a direct result of the war, some against the introduction of indirect rule to the south, and others in the form of anticolonial resistance. Other causes of protests included the depleted British administration that lacked the resources to maintain security as well as economic recession, unemployment, and a number of war-time high-handed policies. In the Niger delta, a religious leader, Prophet Elijah II, was able to rally hundreds of people against the British. A decline in palm-oil exports and the hardship that followed drew to Elijah followers who expected that a German victory in the Cameroons would bring independence and prosperity to them. As the palm-oil trade revived, so too did Elijah see a decline in his popularity and the eventual collapse of his rebellion. In the east, parts of which were yet to be effectively occupied, revolts expressed resistance against the imposition of British rule. Among the Yoruba in the west, the introduction of indirect rule, which gave more power to the chiefs, created complaints and protests. Having been implemented in the north, Lugard extended the principle of local administration through the chiefs all over the country, in spite of different political and cultural systems. In the north, princes who had been denied access to power, Islamic religious leaders who resented the British, and the poor who were displeased with heavy taxation created their own revolts.

A protest of a different nature emerged from the educated elite, who had expected their loyalty for the British to be compensated by reforms and greater participation in a postwar government. A main voice during the period, the National Congress of British West Africa, had fully identified with British war aims, expecting the reform of the system of indirect rule, which had marginalized the educated elite. The disappointment instigated an agitation-based politics that gained momentum in future years.

TOYIN FALOLA

See also: **Nigeria: Lugard, Administration, "Indirect Rule"; World War I: Survey.**

Further Reading

Downes, Captain W. D. *With the Nigerians in German East Africa.* London: Methuen and Co., 1919.

Falola, T. *Politics and Economy in Ibadan, 1893–1945.* Lagos: Modelor, 1989.

Osuntokun, A. *Nigeria in the First World War.* London: Longman, 1979.
Perham, M. *Lugard, The Years of Authority, 1898–1945: The Maker of Modern Nigeria.* London: Collins, 1960.
Tamuno, T. N. *The Evolution of the Nigerian State: The Southern Phase, 1898–1914.* London: Longman, 1972.

Nigeria: Colonial Period: Railways, Mining, and Market Production

Although contact between the Nigerian area and Britain dates back to the sixteenth century, it was not until the mid-nineteenth century that Britain finally decided formally to colonize Nigeria. Throughout the precolonial and colonial periods, trade was the most important determinant of Anglo-Nigerian relations. In promoting her economic interest, Britain used both force and diplomacy in gradually bringing the different parts of Nigeria under its rule between 1861 and 1903.

The colonial era undoubtedly marks an important epoch in the modern history of Nigeria. Perhaps nowhere was the transformation of the country so dramatic than in the introduction of up-to-date means of transportation. Though not approaching its spectacular role in the industrial take-off of other countries such as Britain, Germany, and the United States, the railway system played a very significant part in opening up Nigeria to modern commerce. The British realized that the huge untapped or under-utilized natural and human resources of the country could only be exploited maximally through the provision of a relatively cheap, fast, and reliable means of transportation, which they found in the railway system. Railways stimulated mining and export crop production along their routes. Indeed, export expansion became the most obvious result of railway construction and a common justification for it as the twentieth century advanced.

Unlike other African colonies blessed with huge mineral deposits, such as Angola, Belgian Congo, Rhodesia, and South Africa, mining played a small role in the overall colonial economy of Nigeria. Apart from tin, the role of the other minerals like coal, columbite, and gold in the export sector was marginal. Tin was the first mineral deposit to attract any commercial interest in Nigeria. However, given the poor state of transportation until the extension of the railway to the mining areas of Bauchi in 1911, the Nigerian tin mining industry had very little hope of survival. Thus, just as in the case of cash crop production, the railway acted as a catalyst for the expansion of tin mining, especially on the Bauchi plateau. The export figures for the following years indicate an impressive increase in volume and value. In 1907, 212 tons valued at £25,265 ($41,428) were exported. The volume and value rose to 12,069 tons and £1,373,466 ($2,252,132) in 1930, respectively. By 1945 the volume and value had risen to 15,166 tons and £3,129,265 ($5,131,194), respectively. Destined to be a leading producer of crude oil, the production of the commodity by Nigeria only started toward the end of the colonial period.

Railways proved effective in transporting bulky export products down to the coast and in supplying imported goods to the people of the interior. This development witnessed an unprecedented expansion of trade, in terms of both exports and imports. Given the improved state of transportation, Nigerian producers responded to the growing external demand for commodities such as palm products, cocoa, groundnuts, cotton, rubber, and tin. Export earnings from these and other commodities enabled Nigerians to purchase a wide range of imported goods on an unprecedented scale. Increased earnings also enabled the colonized people to meet their tax obligations to the colonial state. Furthermore, the occurrence of two world wars (1914–1918 and 1939–1945) placed increasing pressures on commodity producers in colonies like Nigeria, since Asian supplies were seriously disrupted by the Japanese action in that part of the world during World War II.

The first railway in Nigeria, from Iddo near Lagos to Otta, was started in 1896. This line reached the river Niger at Jebba in 1909. The building of the railway from Lagos to the Yoruba heartland in the southwestern part of the country greatly stimulated the cultivation of cocoa for the export market. For example, while 305 tons were exported during the period 1900–1904, the volume had jumped to 102,379 tons in 1940–1944. Nigeria remained one of the world's major cocoa producers.

Starting from the coast toward the end of the nineteenth century, the railway eventually reached the commercial city of Kano in the hinterland in 1911. With the extension of the railway into the interior, the export of groundnuts from northern Nigeria, which was initially hardly anticipated by the colonial government, blossomed. As rightly pointed out by McPhee (1971), "The export trade of ground nuts from Northern Nigeria was a creation pure and simple of the railway" (88). Originally, the colonial authorities in Nigeria had envisaged that with development of a railway line from the coast to the interior, cotton would be the dominant export product of northern Nigeria. However, various factors such as the low price offered for cotton, high transport cost, and high local demand militated against the development of cotton as the principal export at the initial stage of the railway's arrival in the north. Instead, groundnuts, being both a food and cash crop, became the producers' crop. While 475 tons were exported in the period 1900–1904, the volume had increased to 181,901 tons in the period 1940–1944. Nigeria remained the second leading producer of groundnuts after Senegal.

Palm products were among the oldest commodities exported from Nigeria to Europe. And with the suppression of the Atlantic slave trade in the nineteenth century, palm products became the most important export from the Nigerian area to Europe. The extension of the eastern railway line from Port Harcourt into the Igbo hinterland in 1913 facilitated the expansion of palm exports from Nigeria. During the period 1900–1904, 117,358 tons of palm oil were exported; between 1940 and 1944, the figure stood at 284,889 tons.

In the 1910s and 1920s, Nigerian cocoa and groundnut exports accounted for about a quarter of all exports from Nigeria, although palm produce still supplied half of the total. Besides cocoa, groundnuts, palm products, and cotton, the production of other important commodities such as rubber, gum arabic, hides, and skins was greatly stimulated by the development of the railway.

YAKUBU MUKHTAR

See also: **Nigeria: Industry, Oil, Economy; Nigeria: World War I; Nigeria: World War II.**

Further Reading

Adebayo, A. G. "The Production and Export of Hides and Skins in Colonial Northern Nigeria." *Journal of African History*. 33 (1992): 273–300.

Egboh, E. O. "The Nigerian Gum Arabic Industry, 1897–1940: A Study in Rural Economic Development under Colonial Regime. *Cahiers d'Etudes Africaines* 69–70, xviii, 1–2 (1977): 215–221.

Ekundare, R. O. *An Economic History of Nigeria, 1860–1960.* London: Methuen and Co., 1973.

Harrison, C., T. B. Ingawa, and S. M. Martin. "The Establishment of Colonial Rule in West Africa, c. 1900–1914." In *History of West Africa,* edited by J. F. Ade Ajayi and M. Crowder. 2nd ed. Vol. 2. Harlow: Longman Group, 1987.

Helleiner, G. K. *Peasant Agriculture, Government, and Economic Growth in Nigeria.* Homewood, Ill.: Irwin, 1966.

McPhee, A. *The Economic Revolution in British West Africa.* 2nd ed. London: Frank Cass, 1971.

Walker, G. *Traffic and Transport in Nigeria: The Example of an Underdeveloped Tropical Territory.* London: Her Majesty's Stationery Office, 1959.

Nigeria: Colonial Period: Christianity and Islam

Christianity and Islam antedated the establishment of British colonial rule in Nigeria. Islam filtered into northern Nigeria from across the Sahara through the Borno Empire in the eleventh century and was introduced to the Hausa states to the west by Wangarawa traders, from Mali further to the west, by the fourteenth century. By the end of the eighteenth century, most of the Hausa states and the Kanem-Borno Empire were officially Islamic in character. But from the opening decade of the nineteenth century, the outbreak of the Sokoto jihad opened a new phase in the spread of Islam in northern Nigeria and parts of Yorubaland to the south. By the end of that century, most communities in northern Nigeria had been incorporated in either of the major Muslim polities, the Sokoto caliphate, or the sultanate of Borno. The rest, the so-called pagan communities, maintained relations of conflict or coexistence with these states.

Christianity had been introduced to Warri and Benin in southern Nigeria as early as the sixteenth century but had not gained a strong foothold and was soon eclipsed. It was only from the late eighteenth century, following evangelical revival in England and the campaign against the slave trade, that Christian missions renewed interest in the evangelization of Africa. By the 1890s the Anglicans, Methodists, Presbyterians, Baptists, and Roman Catholics had established missions all over Southern Nigeria, notably at Badagry, Abeokuta, Ibadan, Onitsha, and Calabar. The religion made gains in large parts of southern Nigeria but did not in largely Muslim northern Nigeria.

By 1900 Britain had declared its rule over Nigeria. Initially, the British were hostile to the vanquished Fulani emirs of the Sokoto caliphate, a number of whom had resisted conquest militarily. But this changed when the British realized that the structures of the Islamic polities were indispensable to the success of their rule. The British, therefore, developed a protectionist attitude toward Islam, especially vis-à-vis Christianity. They allied with the emirs against a common threat: Mahdism, a brand of Islamic millenarianism. British preferential policy toward Islam was, however, limited to Northern Nigeria. It was not extended to Yorubaland, where the like of the Sokoto caliphate did not exist.

Most Muslims embraced the British when it became clear that they did not seek the overthrow of Islam. Nevertheless, there were hostile reactions to the new order, notably, *hijra* (planned withdrawal from the territory of the heathen), military confrontation, and Mahdist propaganda. *Hijra* and military resistance were demonstrated at Burmi in 1903 while the Mahdist challenge manifested at Satiru in 1906. Though Muslim resistance was crushed, the threat of Mahdism remained potent for the rest of the colonial period and drove the British and the indigenous ruling classes into a warmer embrace for mutual self-preservation.

Islam consequently spread phenomenally in northern Nigeria. First, with the establishment of peace under colonial rule, Muslim traders and scholars moved into the non-Muslim areas of northern Nigeria, plying their wares and spreading their faith. Their literacy in Arabic and Hausa, and their association with commercial prosperity, made a positive impression on the preliterate non-Muslim societies. The latter soon converted to Islam partly in order to join a wider commercial network and to share in its prosperity. Second, British officials strictly forbade Christian missions from establishing churches and stations within the emirates. This fulfilled their pledge to respect the sanctity of Islam and allowed Muslims to freely propagate and practice their faith unhindered.

Much more important was the colonial policy of placing non-Muslim communities under the emirates and appointing Muslims as their district heads. In time, Muslim control of commerce and the Native Administration (NA) system exerted pressure on non-Muslim subjects of the emirs who converted to Islam. The religion thus spread by peaceful means into areas where it could not be imposed by force in the previous century. Colonial rule had inadvertently achieved for Islam what the jihad had failed to do. Thus, the percentage of Muslims in the total population rose in Bauchi province from 50 per cent in 1920 to 75 per cent in 1952; from 74.9 per cent to 83.5 per cent in Borno; and from 43.5 per cent to 62.6 per cent in Ilorin, respectively.

In southern Nigeria, Islam did not fare as well partly because there was no corresponding colonial protectionism and partly because of the freedom granted Christian missions to operate in the region. Nevertheless, the government was sympathetic to Muslim rejection of Western education, which was seen as a ruse by the missions to proselytize their children. Government accordingly supported efforts by Muslims to establish their own schools so that their children could receive Western education without having to convert to Christianity. It gave limited grants and encouraged Muslims to develop curricula which integrated Western and Islamic education. The Ahmadiyya Movement, the AnsarUd-Deen Society, and the Anwar ul-Islam championed the development of Western education among Yoruba Muslims. The success of this blend of Western and Islamic education enabled Islam to hold its ground against the advance of Christianity in western Nigeria. The establishment of Muslim printing presses, increasing participation in the *hajj* (which exposed Western Nigerian Muslims to the wider world of Islam) and the distribution of Mahdist, Tijani, and Wahhabi literature also fostered the religious and intellectual growth of the Muslim community.

Christianity had made great inroads into southern Nigeria by 1900. Colonial rule, by enforcing law and order, enabled the Christian missions to spread into hitherto hostile territories. The defeat of the Ijebu in 1892 paved the way for the evangelization of that kingdom. The ability of the missions to offer Western education and modern health facilities enabled them to win converts in many communities under the protection of the British flag. They pioneered the establishment of secondary grammar school education between 1859 and 1881 and later expanded educational facilities wherever they had a foothold. The translation of the Bible into many indigenous languages also gave a great boost to the spread of Christianity during this period.

The emergence of "African Churches" especially among the Yoruba, was a major development during this period. Africans who had been discriminated against in the appointment to church offices or had deplored the denationalizing doctrines of the European missionaries (on marriage and membership of secret or title societies, for example) sought to establish Churches devoid of unnecessary Westernization. Most major denominations experienced schisms leading to the formation of various "African Churches" which differed from the mission churches in doctrine and liturgy. Of significance were the "Aladura" churches in Yorubaland, which indigenized Christianity by introducing African music and instruments in worship, African chieftaincy titles in church administration, and the wearing of uniform dresses.

The role of Christianity in the establishment of colonial rule has been controversial. It had been argued that the religion had been the handmaiden of colonialism and had thereby reaped benefits from of this association. Although the missions supported British colonization of Abeokuta and Ijebu, for example, their consent or prompting was not decisive to the "forward policy" of the British, which had its own dynamics. In any case, in northern Nigeria, where Islam could better serve the ends of the colonial state, Christianity was kept out of the Muslim communities. Hence, while the missions supported the colonial government in their own interest, they did not hesitate to castigate the excesses of colonial officialdom as occasion demanded.

Christianity and Islam spread in different parts of the country and for different reasons during this period. Both took advantage of the presence of the British while inadvertently serving the ends of the colonial state. By the end of the colonial period they had become the leading organized religious groups in Nigeria.

AYODEJI OLUKOJU

See also: **Religion, Colonial Africa: Conversion to the World Religions; Religion, Colonial Africa: Islamic Orders and Movements; Religion, Colonial Africa: Missionaries; Religion, Colonial Africa: Religious Responses to Colonial Rule; Sokoto Caliphate, Nineteenth Century.**

Further Reading

Ayandele, E. A. *The Missionary Impact on Modern Nigeria, 1842–1914: A Political and Social Analysis.* London: Longman, 1966.

Clarke, P. B. *West Africa and Islam: A Study of Religious Development from the 8th to the 20th Century.* London: Edward Arnold, 1982.

Gbadamosi, T. G. O. *The Growth of Islam among the Yoruba, 1841–1908.* Ibadan: Longman, 1978.

Hiskett, M. *The Development of Islam in West Africa.* London: Longman, 1984.

Kalu, O. U., ed. *Christianity in West Africa: The Nigerian Story.* Ibadan: Daystar, 1978.

Okafor, G. M. *Development of Christianity and Islam in Modern Nigeria (A Critical Appraisal of the Religious Forces of Christianity and Islam in Modern Nigera).* Religionswissenschaftliche 22 Wurzburg: Echter, and Altenberg: Oros-Verlag, 1992.

Osuntokun, A., and A. Olukoju, eds. *Nigerian Peoples and Cultures.* Ibadan: Davidson, 1997.

Nigeria: World War II

Nigeria was involuntarily sucked into World War II (1939–1945), given its status as a colony of Britain. Britain's economic, industrial, military, and air power were weakened by World War I, and thus Britain was less prepared for a world war in 1939 than it had been in 1914. This, coupled with a quick succession of reverses in Europe, North Africa, the Mediterranean, and the Far East, meant that Britain needed all the support it could muster from its colonies to prosecute the war. Nigeria, one of Britain's biggest African colonies, did not disappoint.

Britain mobilized Nigerian public opinion in its favor through assiduous propaganda. Hitler was demonized as "the harbinger of darkness," and the war itself was presented to the public as between bondage, represented by Hitler, and freedom for humanity, represented by Britain and the Allies. Hitler's racist theories, his foul massacres in Poland, and the millions of Jews who died in his concentration camps and gas chamber made the oppressive and exploitative British colonial rule in Nigeria seem benign. Not surprisingly, Nigerians unanimously affirmed their loyalty to Britain and the cause of the Allies. Influential Nigerian political leaders such as Nnamdi Azikiwe and Herbert Macaulay, hitherto critics of British colonial rule, reversed gear and appealed to all Nigerians to "rally round the Union Jack." Revered "royal fathers" used the influence of their esteemed offices to urge all Nigerians to support Britain and the Allies. The response was infectious, and seemingly overnight, win-the-war organizations mushroomed all over the country, propagating the gospel of a holy war against the force of Satan.

Verbal affirmation went hand in hand with concrete support. Barely a fortnight after the commencement of the war, the Nigerian War Relief Fund (NWRF) was launched due to the urging of Sir Bernard Bourdillon, governor of Nigeria. The fund was for the provision of relief to victims of the war in Britain and other Allied countries. A national committee to oversee and popularize the fund was formed, and was backed up by local committees across the country. Thanks to the efforts of the committees, donations soon began to flow into the fund from individual persons and corporate entities in all parts of the country. Entertainments of various sorts were staged to raise money for the fund. Some people donated voluntarily, while funds were also squeezed out of local communities, civil servants, and other people in the colonial establishment through compulsory levies. Among the war relief and charitable organizations that benefited from the fund were those in Britain, Malta, China, Yugoslavia, Holland, Burma, Russia, Greece, Poland, and Finland. In addition to the NWRF, there was also the Win the War Fund to which Nigerians contributed substantial amounts of money. Some provinces made additional donations to Britain's war effort for the purchase of weaponry. The Nigerian government on its own part made substantial interest-free loans to Britain.

Nigeria also contributed to the Allies' war effort in regard to the supply of agricultural and mineral resources needed by British industries. The closure of the Mediterranean sea-route to Britain was compounded in 1942 when Japan seized the Far East island colonies. Consequently there developed a frantic demand in Britain for almost everything west Africa could grow and mine. To ensure accelerated supplies to Britain's war industries by her West African colonies, Britain dispatched a resident minister of Cabinet rank, Sir Swinton, to West Africa. Nigeria was penciled as a major actor in the scheme with especial regard to palm oil, cocoa, groundnuts, and tin. Subtle as well as coercive administrative measures were adopted to get Nigerian farmers to increase their production of the export crops even at the expense of local food production. The rationing of essential imports such as bicycle and lorry tubes and tires was manipulated in favor of traders in export produce, and local trade in foodstuffs was restricted. London also reversed its laissez-faire policy and set up the West African Produce Control Board, which it made the monopoly purchaser of British West Africa's exports. The board fixed the prices it bought produce from farmers invariably far below open market prices. About 1,800 unwilling laborers were conscripted into the tin mines of Jos under appalling conditions and at low wages. Against the poor returns for his produce or wage labor, the Nigerian consumer was faced with escalating prices of imports arising from wartime scarcity. The government tried to mediate the situation by controlling the sale of essential commodities, but the measures merely aggravated the situation.

Falling living standards and harsh sacrifices thus inflicted on all Nigerians estranged relations between Britain and Nigerians, but not to the point of considering Hitler as an alternative.

When Mussolini and Hitler effectively closed the Mediterranean to the Allies, Nigeria suddenly became strategic in the Allies' military calculations. The country provided the Allies with take-off points for bombing missions in North Africa and the Mediterranean front. Young Nigerians were hurriedly mobilized and drafted into various military and paramilitary construction projects such as airports, harbors, barracks, and railways. The rough-and-ready methods used in prosecuting the projects meant that the laborers were stretched to their utmost. Apart from the Nigerians who fought the war at the home front, there were 100,000 others who took part in direct combat and acquited themselves heroically, in Eritrea, Abyssinia (Ethiopia), Sudan, India, and, especially, Burma.

Inevitably the war impacted Nigerian in various ways. Excessive imperial direction of the economy estranged relations between ruler and ruled, evident in a series of protests by farmers, traders, and wage earners. The General Strike of 1945 was the most publicized of the protests. When Prime Minister Churchill denied that the principle of self-determination for all subject peoples, espoused in the Atlantic Declaration, applied to Africa, relations between London and Nigerian political leaders were strained to the limits. Nigerians, however, returned from the war imbued with a new confidence in themselves and with the aura of their colonial overlords shredded. During the war they had had mingled with working-class, poverty-stricken, and barely literate Europeans, and they had killed many Europeans in the name of freedom and democracy. They started to question their own subject status and demanded a change in the status quo. It became increasingly difficult for Britain to deny freedom and democracy to Nigerians. The emergence of the United States and the Soviet Union as the world's leading powers—both anticolonialists—and the diminution of Britain as a world power weakened the cause of colonialism in Africa. The upshot of this was the radicalization of the nationalist struggle, which resulted in Nigeria's independence in 1960.

ONWUKA N. NJOKU

See also: **Azikiwe, Nnamdi; Macaulay, Herbert; World War II: North Africa.**

Further Reading

Amadi, L. O. "Political Integration in Nigeria, 1939–1945: The Role of Economic Developments During the Second World War." *Trans-African Journal of History.* 6–8 (1977–1978): 142–153.

Coleman, J. S. *Nigeria: Background to Nationalism.* Evanston: Northwestern University Press, 1965.

Crowder, M. *West Africa Under Colonial.* London: Hutchinson and Co., 1968.

Darwin, J. *Britain and Decolonization: The Retreat from Empire in the Post-War World.* Hampshire and London: Macmillan Education, 1988.

Hargreaves, J. D. *Decolonization in Africa.* London: Longman, 1988.

Mansergh, N. *Survey of British Commonwealth Affairs: Problems of Wartime Cooperation and Post-War Change, 1939–52.* London: Frank Cass and Co., 1968.

Njoku, O. N. "Burden of Imperialism: Nigeria War Relief Fund, 1939–1945." *Trans-African Journal of History.* 6–7 (1977–1978): 79–99.

———. "Export Production Drive in Nigeria During World War II." *Trans-African Journal of History.* 10, no. 1–2 (1981): 11–22.

Olusanya, G. O. *The Second World War and Politics in Nigeria, 1939–1953.* London: Longman, 1973.

Pearce, R. D. "Morale in the Colonial Service in Nigeria during the Second World War." *Journal of Imperial and Commonwealth History.* 11, no. 2 (1983): 175–196.

Nigeria: Colonial Period: Intelligentsia, Nationalism, Independence

Nigerian resistance to British rule began with the imposition of that rule, but the forces of nationalism really grew with the growth of the partially "detribalized" educated elite, one of whose remarkable members, Herbert Macaulay, is widely referred to as "the father of Nigerian nationalism." Many have seen him as a collaborator with the Europeans, yet despite his Bechstein grand piano and his "stand-up collars of an irreproachable whiteness," Macaulay left his "European post" as Surveyor of Crown Lands in 1898 and became the foremost critic of the colonial government, which could never live up to his high imperial ideals. His influence grew through his championing of the cause of Eleko Eshugbayi of Lagos. His deportation in 1925 united the traditional and educated elite as never before, and Macaulay's six-year legal wrangle, which resulted in the return of Eshugbayi in 1931, made him into a popular hero.

Macaulay's ascendancy in Lagos politics is also shown by the formation in 1923 of the Nigerian National Democratic Party (NNDP). A new constitution, which gave Lagos three elective seats for the first time, stimulated political activity in the capital. Two new political parties and five newspapers quickly made an appearance, but it was Macaulay's NNDP and his *Lagos Daily News* that prospered. Between 1923 and 1937 the party won all the elections for the Legislative Council and for the Lagos Town Council. It gained the support of the local aristocracy, the market women, the Muslim Associations, and the educated elite, thus translating modern political activity into traditional political language. Yet its policy, which endorsed that of the National Congress of British West Africa (set up in Accra in 1920), was undoubtedly reformist, calling for reform within the existing system, and it is best considered as a proto-nationalist body. Furthermore, it made no headway outside Lagos, partly because Macaulay wished to dominate its affairs personally; and after the early 1930s, when Eleko Eshugbayi's return removed its major grievance, it was clearly in decline.

The initiative passed to the Nigerian Youth Movement (NYM), formed as the Lagos Reform Movement in 1934 to protest that the new Yaba Higher College did not have university status. The college enrolled only eighteen students in its first year, and the highest annual total over the next decade was thirty-six. The NYM soon dominated the Lagos town council, and in 1938 its candidates won all three Lagos Legislative Council seats. By this time it had a membership of 10,000, with twenty provincial branches. It also called for the eventual ending of colonial rule. But its practical program was reformist, and it held regular meetings with Governor Bourdillon to bring about piecemeal changes.

During World War II, which saw the escalation of nationalism in many colonies, the NYM ceased to function effectively. It split in May 1941 over the choice of a candidate to contest a vacant legislative Council seat, and by 1943 it was moribund. The initiative passed to Nnamdi Azikiwe, the American-educated editor of the *West African Pilot*, who in 1944 formed the National Council of Nigeria and the Cameroons with the veteran Herbert Macaulay. Azikiwe's 1943 "Political Blueprint of Nigeria" called for a fifteen-year period of preparation for independence. Nationalist activity now heated up. Partly this was due to a new constitution, which allowed for northern participation in the Legislative Council for the first time. Partly it was due to the repressive stance of Sir Arthur Richards, governor from 1943 to 1947, who failed to grant a cost of living allowance before extensive strikes took place and who wanted to reduce the influence of the educated elite. It was also a reaction to Azikiwe's insistence that he spoke for the whole of Nigeria.

By 1948 the situation deteriorated. The Zikist movement clustered around Azikiwe became increasingly violent; the radical Nigerian National Federation of Labour was formed; and the National Church of Nigeria proclaimed Azikiwe as the new messiah. On November 18, 1949, twenty-one miners were shot dead during a strike at the Enugu colliery, leading the Zikists to seek Azikiwe's support for a violence campaign of revenge against the whites in Nigeria. After a day's reflection, however, Azikiwe decided to repudiate violence, and after an unsuccessful attempt to assassinate the chief secretary, Hugh Foot, the Zikists were banned. By this time the British had already announced that the Richards constitution would be revised, Nigeria having to keep broadly in step with reform in the neighboring Gold Coast. Violence would thus have been counterproductive. The door to rapid decolonization had been opened. But first the educated elite in Nigeria—who for so long had seemed to the colonial rulers out of touch with the masses outside the cities—had to learn to mobilize mass support.

The largely Igbo NCNC, strongest in the eastern region, was joined in 1950 by the Action Group, founded by British-educated Obafemi Awolowo from a Yoruba cultural association, the *Egbe Omo Odudua*, which was to control the western region, and in 1951 by the Hausa Northern People's Congress, set up by the Sardauna of Sokoto to prevent the better-educated southerners from gaining supremacy in northern affairs. Regional politics—and ethnic nationalism—dominated the political agenda. Nigeria's first general election was fought in the dry season of 1951–1952 between these three parties. It confirmed the dominance of each of the major parties in the region of its origin. The struggle for independence was now not so much against the British colonial power as between competing groups of Nigerian nationalists. What was at issue was the timing of independence and the form which a new self-governing state would take. That the road would be difficult was dramatically revealed by riots in Kano in May 1953, when at least thirty-six people, mostly Igbo and Yoruba, were killed. Henceforth Nigeria took the federal route. In 1956 the British sent out their last governor to negotiate the final hurdles to independence, which was completed in 1960.

ROBERT PEARCE

See also: **Azikiwe, Nnamdi; Macaulay, Herbert; Nigeria: Colonial Period: Federation.**

Further Reading

Ananaba, W. *The Trade Union Movement in Nigeria.* London: Hurst, 1969.

Awolowo, O. *Awo: The Autobiography of Chief Obafemi Awolowo.* London: Cambridge University Press, 1960.

Ayandele, E. A. *The Educated Elite in Nigeria.* Ibadan: Ibadan University Press, 1974.

Bello, A. *My Life.* London: Cambridge University Press, 1962.

Clark, T. *A Right Honourable Gentleman: Abubakar from the Black Rock.* London: Edward Arnold, 1991.

Cole, P. *Modern and Traditional Elites in the Politics of Lagos.* London: Cambridge University Press, 1975.

Coleman, J. *Nigeria: Background to Nationalism.* Berkeley and Los Angeles: University of California Press, 1958.

Pearce, R. *Sir Bernard Bourdillon.* Oxford: Kensal Press, 1987.

Nigeria: Colonial Period: Federation

"Nigeria is not a nation," concluded Chief Obafemi Awolowo, a front-line Nigerian statesman and scholar of federalism and constitution, "it is a mere geographical expression. There are no 'Nigerians' in the same sense as there are 'English' or 'Welsh' or 'French'; the word Nigeria is merely a distinctive appellation to distinguish those who live within the boundaries of Nigeria from those who do not" (*Path to Nigerian Freedom,* 47–48). The politics of federation are primarily designed to respond to the ethnic divisions in the country. A large and multiplural society, the difficulty of a direct government from one center in Nigeria partly dictated the choice of a federal system of government. Canada, Australia, and South Africa had provided a federalist model for the British, a way of keeping together disparate people. It was also a convenient politics of divide and rule, to prevent all ethnic groups from uniting against the colonial invaders, or of manipulating one large group against the others in order to gain some advantages. As the Nigerian experience unfolded, it became clear that federalism was an admission of disunity, the failure of integration, and the recognition of uneven development. The country officially became a federation in 1954, after seven years of experimentation with features of federalism and a long history of separate development.

The British conquest of Nigeria occurred in stages, leading to three protectorates, two in the south and one in the north. In 1906 the protectorates became two provinces, one each in the south and north. Both were amalgamated into one country in 1914 partly because there was no artificial boundary between them, and in order to use resources in the south to finance the north. Both regions were different in their levels of development and culture. The educated elite in the south was more assertive, anti-British, sought a role in government, and simply assumed that it would inherit the mantle of power.

A native Nigerian transports a member of the Chicago Field Museum's Africa Expendition across a river in the 1930s. © SVT Bild/Das Fotoarchiv.

In spite of the amalgamation, differences in education, administration, and progress continued to divide the regions, while many British administrators continued to promote a policy of separate development. By the late 1920s, a model of federalism was being discussed, with the possibility of Nigeria being divided into four regions—the East, West, North, and Middle Belt, each with its own legislature and budgetary independence.

In 1946, Governor Arthur Richards took the first decisive step in the federation of the country. Without any discussion with the Nigerian elite, Richards divided the country into three regions, North, West, and South, each with executive, legislative, and financial powers. For him, Nigerians had different languages, culture, and customs, and Nigeria was "still far from being one country or one nation socially or even economically." The 1946 constitution also created a Nigerian Legislative Council, to include representation from the North, although the body was purely advisory.

Although the elite and nationalists wanted unity, they had also come to realize after 1945 that unity would not work. Thus, from 1946 to 1954, debates about the form of a federal constitution were intense, but the idea of regional power was now taken for granted, with each developing at its own pace. The political conflict took a South-North divide: whoever controlled the center would determine the share of revenues and appointments and promotion to the civil service, police, and army. The political parties that emerged were regionally based: the Action Group (AG) controlled the West, the National Council of Nigerian and the Cameroons the East, and the Northern People's Congress (NPC) the North. After 1948, leading British officers served as umpires to mediate conflicts among the warring elite. Between 1948 and 1953, the Nigerian elite took the center stage in writing and modifying a federal constitution for the country, based on the assumption that regions and cultures were different. Debates and suggestions about the future of Nigeria reflected the tension between "nationalists" and "sectionalists," and revolved around the timing of independence, the distribution of political power and federal resources, and the form of government.

Hostility was deep and bitter, with politics revolving around regionalism. The NCNC lost its national appeal, nationalism was now fractionalized, and ethnic-cum-cultural organizations became the basis of political parties. Each region threatened secession, and the form that the federation would take became a matter of intense negotiation. At the Ibadan Constitutional Conference in 1950, the emirs of Kano and Zaria called for parity with the South in the membership of the Central Legislature if they did not want the North to secede. When the South demanded in 1953 that the country should become independent three years later, the North refused, fearing domination by the southern elite. A so-called enlightenment party by the AG to educate northerners ended in the Kano riots of May 1953. In the same year, the West threatened to secede if it was not given control of Lagos, the federal capital. Separatist tendencies were manifested in political cartoons, songs, and outright abuse of one another, as well as in policies and memoranda on the regionalization of the police, civil service, and judiciary. Forces of unity remained strong throughout the 1950s, laying the foundation for the crisis and eventual civil war of the 1960s.

The structure of Nigerian federation was faulty: there were three big regions, with the North as large in size and population as the two regions in the south combined. This anomaly made the fear of northern domination not just an imagination of the southern elite, but a real political threat. The northern region used its size and population to dominate the House of Representatives and the federal government.

Regionalism was enthroned, to the extent that it displaced nationalism. The regions were more powerful than the center. The leading political actors—Obafemi Awolowo, Ahmadu Bello, and Nnamdi Azikiwe—chose to be the executive heads of their regions and sent their deputies to the center.

Another defect was the difficulty of protecting the rights of minorities within the big regions. Each region comprised a big ethnic group and many minority groups. In the 1950s, as independence drew nearer and the dominant ethnic group gained more power, the representatives of the minorities began to form movements to demand political reorganization that would give them autonomy. These minorities complained of marginalization and domination. It was clear that the creation of additional states would have eased the problem; but only the AG was willing to tolerate the creation of the new states while the other parties and regional leaders were greatly opposed to the idea, thinking that it would undermine their contest for federal power. A commission was set up in 1957 to look into a series of complaints, but it accepted the imperfection of the federal arrangement, forcefully arguing against the creation of new states on the basis that they might not be viable, and that new minorities would actually be created within them. Better political management and time, argued the commission, would heal all wounds and the minority problems would disappear. If regional leaders insisted on new states, concluded the commission, the date of independence would have to change, a condition that the anxious leaders would not accept. The defects in the federal arrangement were to lead to the instability and civil war of the 1960s.

TOYIN FALOLA

See also: **Nigeria: Colonial Period: Intelligentsia, Nationalism, Independence.**

Further Reading

Adebayo, A. G. *Embattled Federalism: History of Revenue Allocation in Nigeria, 1946–1990*. New York: Peter Lang, 1993.

Akinyemi, A. Bolaji, P. D. Cole, and W. Ofonagoro (eds.). *Readings on Federalism*. Lagos: Nigerian Institute of International Affairs, 1979.

Awa, E. O. *Federal Government in Nigeria*. Berkeley: University of California Press, 1964.

———. *Issues in Federalism*. Benin City: Ethiope, 1976.

Awolowo, O. *Path to Nigerian Freedom*. London: Faber and Faber, 1947.

Falola, T. "The Evolution and Changes in Nigerian Federalism." In *Federalism in a Changing World*, edited by R. Olaniyan. Ile-Ife: Obafemi Awolowo University Press, 1989.

Nigeria: Conferences, Commissions, Nigerian Constitution: 1956–1960

The 1950s marked a period of decolonization in Nigeria culminating in the attainment of political independence on October 1, 1960. This decade witnessed the convening of constitutional conferences in Nigeria and Britain before each constitutional reform was promulgated. These conferences were characterized by divisive tendencies based on ethnic and regional rivalries. The division of Nigeria into three main administrative regions—north, east and west—each of which was dominated by a majority ethnic group, Hausa-Fulani, Igbo, and Yoruba respectively, as well as the colonial policy of divide and rule, helped to accentuate ethnic rivalries.

The dominance of each region by a majority ethnic group resulted in a situation where the constitutional conferences were dominated by parochial and divisive issues that would favor each region and its dominant ethnic group as opposed to issues of national interest. Thus the contentious issues at the 1950–1951, 1953–1954, and 1957–1958 constitutional conferences included the percentage of representation of each region in the central legislature, revenue allocation, the status of Lagos, agitation for state creation by ethnic minorities and the date for Nigeria's political independence. The 1954 constitution firmly entrenched federalism and regionalism in Nigeria and instituted the fiscal base of the regions through the regionalization of the marketing boards. This constitution established the institutional framework on which the independence constitution was based.

The period between 1956 and 1960 marked the final phase in the movement toward independence. It witnessed a number of amendments to the 1954 constitution most of which unfortunately intensified the strains and divisions between the different ethnic groups and communities in Nigeria. The first concrete step toward the granting of political independence to Nigeria was taken in 1957 when the western and eastern regions became self-governing in matters of regional competence. The granting of self-government to these regions was a compromise between their request for political independence for Nigeria in 1956 and the opposition to this request by politicians from the northern region. On March 31, 1953, Anthony Enahoro and Action Group (AG) member of parliament from the western region moved a motion demanding for self-determination for Nigeria in 1956. This motion received the support of politicians from the eastern and western regions but was opposed by politicians from the northern region who moved a counter motion that Nigeria should attain self-determination "as soon as practicable" rather than the specific date of 1956. This disagreement over the independence motion precipitated a crisis that led to the northern region threatening to secede from Nigeria. At the London constitutional conference of July–August 1953, politicians from the respective regions stood their ground on the self-determination issue. The British colonial authority therefore refused to commit itself to a date for Nigeria's independence but agreed that any region that so desired could become self-governing in 1956: the western and eastern regions became internally self-governing in 1957.

Agitation by ethnic minorities for the creation of more states was a significant issue that dominated the deliberations of the 1957 and 1958 constitutional conferences held in London. Since these conferences were to prepare the final framework for Nigeria's independence, the ethnic minorities were determined that their concerns be addressed. Since 1953 the ethnic minorities had become more vociferous in their demand for the creation of more states that would comprise the ethnic minority areas. The issue of state creation was raised at the 1954 constitutional conference but was not addressed because it was not included in the conference's agenda. The 1954 federal constitution, which granted greater powers to regional authorities dominated by the respective majority ethnic groups, accentuated the agitation of the ethnic minorities. At the 1957 constitutional conference, the agitation by the minority ethnic groups for the creation of more states could no longer be ignored.

The Willink Commission was set up to examine the allegations and demands of the minority ethnic groups. The commission was charged with ascertaining the facts about the fears of minorities in any part of Nigeria and to propose means of allaying the fears as well as recommending safeguards against the mistreatment of minorities to be included in the constitution. The commission could only make detailed recommendations for the creation of new states if no other solution could be found. It is clear from the terms of reference that the colonial administration was reluctant to create any new states in Nigeria.

The report of the commission, which, expectedly, recommended against the creation of new states and merely recommended policies for protecting the interests of minority ethnic groups, was presented before the 1958 constitutional conference. The representatives of the minority ethnic groups were very critical of the report while the leaders of the Northern Peoples Congress (NPC) who all along had been firmly opposed to state creation were very pleased with the report. The leaders of the National Convention of Nigerian Citizens (NCNC) who would have liked to have seen more states created, largely supported the report. However, the leaders of the AG who had been ardent advocates of states creation, and in fact, made it a campaign issue in the past, stridently criticized the report. But because the colonial administration threatened that the creation of new states would delay the granting of political independence, the AG dropped its opposition to the report.

With the attainment of consensus over the issue of state creation among the leaders of the main political parties, the conference directed its attention to other issues. The north agreed to become self-governing in 1959 while it was agreed that Nigeria would become politically independent in 1960. The constitutional conference decided that representation in the central legislature should be based on population in place of the previous practice of parity between the north and the south. On this basis, the north had 174 seats in the legislature while the east, west and Lagos combined, had 138 seats.

The issue of revenue allocation was contentious in the 1950s (and has remained so in postcolonial Nigeria). From 1946 the introduction of any new constitution was accompanied by a review of the revenue allocation formula. The first of such revenue allocation commission, was the Phillipson-Adebo Commission of 1946, which accompanied the Richards constitution. The main disagreements between Nigerian politicians centered on the factors should be given more weight in allocating revenue. The west, and to some extent the east, placed more emphasis on derivation while the north favored population and size as the most important factors.

The Hicks-Phillipson Commission of 1951 was the first to attempt to spell out the criteria on which revenue allocation should be based. The criteria included derivation, needs, national interest, population, and even development. It gave some weight to derivation by providing that 100 per cent of mineral rents and royalties be retained in the regions from where the minerals were derived. The Chick Commission, which was set up with the introduction of the 1954 federal constitution and the Raisman Commission of 1958, essentially followed the formula laid down by the Hicks-Phillipson Commission. However, the percentage of mineral rents and royalties to be paid to their regions of origin was reduced to 50.

In essence, the period between 1956 and 1960 marked the final phase of Nigeria's movement toward political independence. This period witnessed the organization of the final stage of constitutional conferences and the setting up of commissions that were to amend aspects of the 1954 constitution that essentially formed the basis of the 1960 independence constitution. However, two significant issues which were not effectively addressed by the conferences, commissions, and the independence constitution—the ethnic minority problem and revenue allocation—were to become sore points and the basis of some form of instability in postcolonial Nigeria.

J. I. DIBUA

See also: **Nigeria: Federalism, Corruption, Popular Discontent: 1960–1966.**

Further Reading

Adebayo, A. G. *Embattled Federalism: History of Revenue Allocation in Nigeria, 1946–1990.* New York: Peter Lang, 1993.

Akinyele, R. T. "States Creation in Nigeria: The Willink Report in Retrospect." *African Studies Review.* 39, no. 2 (1996).

Arikpo, O. *The Development of Modern Nigeria.* Middlesex, England: Penguin Books, 1967.

Dudley, B. *An Introduction to Nigerian Government and Politics.* Bloomington, Ind.: Indiana University Press, 1982.

Ezera, K. *Constitutional Developments in Nigeria.* Cambridge: Cambridge University Press, 1960.

Nwaubani, E. "Constitution-Making and the Nigerian Identity, 1914–1960." In *The Transformation of Nigeria: Essays in Honor of Toyin Falola,* edited by A. Oyebade. Trenton, N.J.: Africa World Press, 2002.

Okpu, U. *Ethnic Minority Problems in Nigerian Politics 1960–1965.* Uppsala: University of Uppsala, 1977.

Olusanya, G. O. "Constitutional Developments in Nigeria 1861–1960." In *Groundwork of Nigerian History*, edited by O. Ikime. Ibadan: Heinemann, 1980.

Nigeria: Federalism, Corruption, Popular Discontent: 1960–1966

Nigeria's First Republic reflected the strong regionalism enshrined in the colonial MacPherson Constitution of 1951. As a result, federal governance relied on alliances and coalitions between political parties with deep roots in the country's three regions. The three largest parties, the Northern People's Congress (NPC), the National Congress of Nigerian Citizens (NCNC) in the east, and the Action Group (AG) of the west each depended on its home region's ethnic majority for support, and exploited local patronage networks.

The regions, however, had minority populations who felt their interests largely overlooked by the strongly ethnic characters of the three major parties. The NCNC was the most nationally oriented of the three major parties, and the most successful in attracting support outside of its regional base. Nonetheless, its mostly Igbo leadership alienated many non-Igbos in the east, who reiterated longstanding demands for a Calabar-Ogoja-Rivers state. Similarly, the western region's Igbo minority joined with other non-Yoruba groups in demanding a midwestern state separate from the mostly Yoruba west. And in the northern region, religion played a part as the largely Christian and traditional Middle Belt felt alienated by the close relationship between the NPC and the Muslim Hausa-Fulani aristocracy of the far north. This led to the formation of the Tiv-led United Middle Belt Congress (UMBC), which agitated for a Middle Belt state. In Muslim parts of the north, opposition to the NPC came from groups like the Kano-based Northern Elements Progressive Union (NEPU) and the Borno Youth Movement (BYM) that appealed to subregional sentiments. Alliances (like the NCNC-NEPU and AG-UMBC pairings) tied the regions' dominant parties to opposition parties in other regions.

Each region also inherited the colonial Native Authority (NA) system of local government, which the ruling parties used to varying degrees to further their political goals. The NCNC and the AG each abused its power; the NPC, however, was particularly brazen in its use of NA police and local courts to harass and intimidate its NEPU, BYM, and UMBC opponents. In 1960, following UMBC electoral victories, violence erupted between UMBC supporters in Tivland and local authorities loyal to the NPC government of Premier Ahmadu Bello, the Sardauna of Sokoto. The "Tiv riots" lasted for four months, during which, authorities estimate, 30,000 houses were burned.

Since no party held a majority of seats in the federal House of Representatives, national power rested on a sometimes uneasy coalition between the NPC and the NCNC, into which the NCNC entered despite its longstanding partnership with NEPU, a rival of the NPC in the north. In Lagos, NCNC leader Nnamdi Azikiwe occupied the largely ceremonial office of head of state, while the NPC's Abubakar Tafawa-Balewa headed the government as prime minister. In 1962, under pressure from the coalition government, the opposition AG split, facilitating a political crisis in the western regional assembly. The NPC-NCNC government intervened, and further eroded the power of the AG, which remained popular with many westerners. Then, in 1963, the federal government imprisoned AG standard bearer and opposition leader Obafemi Awolowo on treason charges. The federal government also created a mid-western region out of non-Yoruba portions of the west. The NCNC captured both a regional parliamentary majority and the premiership of the midwest in regional elections in February 1964. Ironically, its victories came over the Mid-West Democratic Front, a party backed by the NPC, the NCNC's national coalition partner. Even as the NPC and NCNC excised the midwest from the west, they ignored demands for statehood in minority areas in the northern and eastern regions—regions they controlled, respectively.

Later that year, a major realignment of parties happened preceding national elections in December. The NPC broke its alliance with the NCNC and took as its major southern ally the new Nigerian National Democratic Party (NNDP). Dissident AG members and former western members of the NCNC had formed the NNDP after the 1962–1963 crisis, and the party controlled the western regional assembly. The NPC-NNDP alliance was called the Nigerian National Alliance (NNA). The NCNC joined with the AG and northern opposition parties to form the United Progressive Grand Alliance (UPGA).

The national elections of 1964 were awash in controversy. In the north, there was evidence that the NPC had used the Native Authority system to hinder the registration of UPGA candidates. Further complicating matters was controversy over the results of the national census of 1963. Parliamentary seats were allocated on the basis of population, and historically the north had a 50 per cent share. The new figures gave the north more than half, leading to accusations from the southern parties of manipulation. As a result, eastern Premier Michael Okpara of the NCNC called for a boycott of the December 1964 elections. Prime Minister Tafawa-Balewa of the NPC ordered elections to go ahead, but many UPGA strongholds, including the east, did boycott. Not surprisingly, the election results in the other regions were favorable to the NNA, and the UPGA called for the government to throw them out. The federal parliament had dissolved before the elections, and, faced with a major crisis, President Azikiwe of the NCNC had the option of appointing a caretaker government; instead, in January 1965 he called for new elections in the east only, and invited the prime minister to form a new government, thus ushering in another period of NPC-NCNC coalition.

The west, however, was to remain at the center of events. While the NNDP had taken control of the western government from the AG following the 1962–1963 crisis, it had limited mass support, and imprisoned AG leader Awolowo remained a popular figure in the region. The buildup to 1965 western regional elections was bloody, with open violence between the parties and their supporters in the streets of western cities and the federal capital Lagos. The NNDP declared itself victorious despite what many saw as clear victories for the NCNC-AG opposition in most districts. As 1965 ended, fighting continued, and the NNDP government of Premier Samuel Akintola teetered on the brink of collapse.

Public confidence in elected leaders was at a new low. Local and regional politicians across Nigeria, in addition to members of the federal government, had stood accused at various times of patronage and financial improprieties. The chaos in the west combined with these factors to set the stage for the introduction of the military into Nigerian politics in January 1966.

DOUGLAS A. ANTHONY

See also: **Nigeria: Biafran Secession and Civil War, 1967–1970; Nigeria: Army.**

Further Reading

Diamond, L. *Class, Ethnicity, and Democracy in Nigeria: The Failure of the First Republic*. London: Macmillan Press, 1988.

Nnoli, O. *Ethnic Politics in Nigeria*. Enugu: Fourth Dimension Publishers, 1978.

Post, K., and M. Vickers (eds). *Structure and Conflict in Nigeria, 1960–1966*. London: Heinemann, 1973.

Sklar, R., and C. S. Whitaker. *African Politics and Problems in Development*. Boulder, Colo.: Lynne Rienner, 1991.

Nigeria: Army

The history of the Nigerian army started in 1886 just after the Royal Niger Company was granted a charter. The charter authorized the company to raise the Royal Niger Constabulary. This quasi-military power was used to enforce the authority of this early British colonial administration. When the British colonial government expanded its influence into the hinterland and consequently came into conflict with the inhabitants, the government found it necessary to increase the size and improve the training of these forces. In 1892 the Niger Coast Protectorate Force numbered about forty ordinary ranks, but by 1900 this force had risen to a battalion with the strength of nearly one thousand men.

In 1901 the various regiments and dependencies of Great Britain along the West African coast (Nigeria, and Gold Coast—now Ghana, Sierra Leone, and Gambia) were merged to form the West African Frontier Forces (WAFF). In Nigeria the WAFF had two regiments, one in the north and the other in the south. On January 1, 1914, on the day that the north and south were amalgamated to form Nigeria the two WAFF regiments were merged. WAFF was changed to Royal West African Frontier Forces (RWAFF) in 1928. RWAFF became the Royal Nigerian Army in 1960.

Before 1949 there were no officers of Nigerian origin in the army. By January 1949, however, some Nigerian soldiers were selected for training as officers. Duke Bassey was the first Nigerian to be commissioned into the Officer Corp of the Nigerian Army in April 1949. David Jemibewon (1978) asserts that out of the 250 officers in the Nigerian army in 1956, only 15 were Nigerians. While the officer corps had few Nigerians, the other ranks were overwhelmingly staffed with Nigerians by 1958.

Between 1958 and 1960, 82 per cent of the officer's corps was still British. However, with the assumption of ministerial control by the prime minister of Nigeria in February 1960, efforts were made to ensure that ordinary ranks were recruited from all parts of Nigeria. The prevailing regional recruitment quotas of 50 per cent from the northern Nigeria and 25 per cent from the western and eastern Nigeria was agreed upon when Nigeria took over the control of the military in 1958.

Efforts were also made to recruit university graduates into the military in order to raise the quality of the Nigerian officer corps and the image of the military. This attempt to improve the image of the military and to secure its loyalty to the government in power led to large increases in army pay. Nigerian troops were sent for training to the United States, Canada, India, and Australia, thereby abandoning the practice during the colonial period of having such soldiers trained only in Britain.

The strength of the Royal Nigerian army in 1958 was only 7,600. The general officer commanding of the army announced the plan to increase the size in May 1964 by about 2,900. Of the 10,500 in April 1965, only a little over 500 belonged to the officer corps, 330 of whom were of combatant status. After 1963, all battalions were commanded by Nigerians. The composition of the military after that time reflected an agreed-upon regional quota system. Nigerian soldiers were recruited on the basis of 50 per cent from the northern region, and 25 per cent from the western and eastern regions, respectively. The same quota system prevailed in the recruitment of officers. On attainment of a republic in October 1963, the army changed its name to the Nigerian Army. Many Nigerians were trained and commissioned as officers to replace the outgoing British officers. The Nigerian administration seems to have followed the British pattern in locating military institutions after independence. The Military School was located in Zaria (1960); the Nigerian Defense Academy (1964) in Kaduna; the Command and Staff College at Jaji (1973), near Kaduna; the Institute of Policy and Strategic Studies (1976) at Bukuru, near Jos; and the Nigerian War College (1992) in Lagos. The Nigerian War College is the only military institution in the southern part of the country. The preferential location of facilities has led to the northern domination of the army's higher ranks for the last twenty-five years.

Postindependence military intervention in Nigeria's politics started when late Major Chukwuma Nzeogwu led the first military coup on January 15, 1966. In the course of the first military intervention, four out of five of the northern senior officers, two out of six Yoruba senior officers, and one out of ten of the eastern senior officers also were murdered. Among civilians, the deaths were equally one-sided. Major-General Ironsi escaped the coup in Lagos and later emerged as the new leader of Nigeria after the federal cabinet handed power to him in an effort to restore order.

As a result, the distrust, riots, and bloodshed that took place in various parts of the country led to a counter-coup organized by northern officers in July 1966. General Ironsi's regime was short-lived. He and the then–western region military governor, Colonel Francis Fajuyi, were kidnapped and killed by mutinous troops in late July 1966. After several days of anarchy, Colonel (later General) Yakubu Gowon, an officer from the middle belt of northern Nigeria, emerged as the new head of state. The reasons for intervention conform with the "internal characteristics model," which suggests that one can explain military intervention in politics mainly by reference to the internal organizational structure of the military (Janowitz, 1964, 27–29).

During riots in September and October 1966, 30,000 Igbos were killed in the north, in a slaughter far beyond the scale of previous riots in May of the same year. The mass killings forced easterners from all over the federation to migrate in search of refuge. Colonel Ojukwu the Military Governor of Eastern Nigeria in 1966 announced that the constitutional arrangements of the national government of Nigeria no longer represented a guarantee to the military government of the eastern region. Igbo lives and property could not be protected. The Igbos had lost confidence in a federated Nigeria and had no illusions about the chances of welding Nigerians into a single nation. Therefore, the Igbos seceded, and the consequence was a bloody and costly civil war that lasted thirty months, from July 1967 to January 15, 1970, and resulted in the defeat of the Igbo secessionists. The war was called the Biafra civil war.

Between 1967 and 1970 General Gowon directed the attention of the federal military government toward winning the Biafra civil war. In this process the size of the Nigerian military increased from its prewar level of about 8,000 to more than 250,000 men by 1970. General Gowon critics felt that he moved too slowly to curb corruption, inflation, and economic mismanagement. Much of the profit from Nigeria's oil boom of the early 1970s was squandered or stolen, and the return to civilian government was delayed.

The government of General Gowon was overthrown in July 1975 without bloodshed while he was attending an Organization of African Unity (OAU) summit in Kampala, Uganda. The new regime was headed by Brigadier Murtala Mohammed, with Brigadier Olusegun Obansajo as chief of staff, supreme headquarters and Brigadier Theophilus Danjuma as army chief of staff.

Within two months of assuming office, General Murtala Mohammed dismissed 150 military officers and 10,000 civil servants who were found guilty of corruption and abuse of office. Mohammed increased the number of states from twelve to nineteen and decided to move the federal capital from Lagos to Abuja. As a result, a group of army officers who feared for their own position attempted a coup on February 13, 1976. The attempt was unsuccessful, but General Mohammed was killed. His chief of staff, General Olusegun Obasanjo, a Yoruba, assumed power. As head of state, Obasanjo continued in the spirit of his predecessor. In October 1979, the military regime of General Obasanjo stepped down and ushered in a new democratically elected civilian government, called the Second Republic. On December 31, 1983, still another coup was staged by senior army officers, which brought the Second Nigerian Republic to an end.

The cost to the nation of military control of the government between 1966 and 1999 has been enormous, both in terms of professional preparedness and political stability and in loss of economic growth. The large number of coups and plots, abortive and successful, and their aftermaths, have made internal discord within the armed forces widespread. During the Babangida, Abacha, and Abubakar regimes the Nigerian army experienced constant purges, reshuffles, trials, and executions. These drastic actions have shaken the officer corps. The most notorious episodes after the abortive Vasta coup of 1985, the failed revolt in 1990, and the alleged conspiracy of 1995, prompted the execution of more than ninety officers and jail terms for many others. The Nigeria army has dismissed or forced the retirement of more than 350 officers since 1995, including sixty-four air force officers sacked in mid-1997. The chiefs of army and naval staff were dismissed in 1995, and the following year military administrators in the thirty-six states were relieved of their positions. The practice, inherited from the British, of retiring expensively trained military officers at the relatively young age of between forty and forty-five years has led to a decay in the nation's military readiness as well as being an enormous loss of funds to the Nigeria economy. In 1999 after only a few weeks in office, Obasanjo retired more than 100 senior military and police officers that had held political positions in previous regimes. The Nigerian army has now become an institution where officers raise money to seek political positions. The military management style has been such that they would use the nation's money to buy off members of the armed forces who were potential rivals as well as the civil elites who would otherwise be clamoring for early return to civil rule. Nusakhare Isekhure (1998) nicely describes the Babangida and Abacha regimes as those that used the most brilliant scholars to write speech using philosophical prose which the head of state themselves did not understand. In fact the Babangida and Abacha regimes could both be classified as periods of intellectual fraud, with characteristics of intellectual criminality.

Delegates from President Obasanjo's administration recently signed a contract with the United States military to help harmonize the Nigeria military into a more professional force that would respect the ongoing democratic process in the nation. The United States Military Professional Resource Initiative (MPRI), a private consultancy organization manned by retired U.S. senior military officers, has been mandated by the U.S. government to reorientate and reorganize the Nigerian military following the return to democracy in 1999.

Robert Dibie

See also: **Nigeria: Military Rule, 1983–1999.**

Further Reading

Aborisade, O., and R. Mundt. *Politics in Nigeria*. New York: Longman, 1998.

Achike, O. *Groundwork of Military Law and Rule in Nigeria*. Ibadan: University Press, 1990.

Amuwo K., R. Suberu, A. Agbaji, and G. Herault (ed.). *Federalism and Political Restructuring in Nigeria*. Ibadan, Nigeria: Spectrum, 1999.

Dibie, R. *Public Management and Sustainable Development in Nigeria: Military-Bureaucracy Relationship*. Ashgate Press, 2003.

Finer, S. *The Man on HorseBack: The Role of the Military in Politics*. London: Pall Mall Press, 1969.

Graf, W. *The Nigerian State, Political Economy, State Class and Political System in Post-Colonial Era*. Portsmouth: Heinemann Press, 1988.

Isekhure, N. *201 Solutions to Vision 2010*. Benin City, Nigeria: Oduna Communications, 1998.

Janowitz, M. *Military Institutions and Coercion in Developing Nations*. Chicago: University of Chicago Press, 1977.

Janowitz, M. *The Military in the Development of New Nations*. Chicago: University of Chicago Press, 1964.

Jemibewon, D. *A Combatant in Government*. Ibadan, Nigeria: Heineman, 1978.

Lewis, P., P. Robinson, and B. Bubin. *Stabilizing Nigeria*. New York: The Century Foundation Press, 1998.

Luckham, R. A. *The Nigerian Military: A Sociological Study of Authority and Revolt*. London: Longman, 1971.

Miners, N. J. *The Nigerian Army 1956–1966*. London: Methuen, 1971.

Peters, J. *The Nigerian Military and the State*. African Series Books. Tauris I. B. Compant, 1995.

Nigeria: Gowon Regime, 1966–1975

On January 15, 1966, a group of young army majors led by the charismatic Major Chukwumma Kaduna Nzeogwu overthrew the civilian government of Prime Minister Abubaka Tafawa Balewa. Their aim was to restore sociopolitical and economic stability and to eradicate corruption. Between 1962 and 1965, Nigeria had witnessed many crises, which ranged from the disputed census and the controversial federal elections to the inconclusive, violent western regional election of 1965, all of which collectively eroded Nigeria's stability and unity.

But the partial and selective manner in which the military operation was conducted left much to be desired. In Kaduna, Ibadan, and Lagos, the event was marked by much bloodshed and led to the assassination of both top military officers and leading politicians. The Igbo-controlled eastern and mid-western regions were left unscathed by the event. However, the forceful intervention of major general J. T. U. Aguiyi-Ironsi, General Officer Commanding, and other loyal officers like Lieutenant Colonel Yakubu Gowon, Commander, Second Battalion Nigerian Army, Ikeja and his men, aborted the assumption of office by those who masterminded the plot. At the end of the day, the loyal troops under Ironsi, assumed the reins of power. The overthrow of the civilian politicians was initially welcomed in the south and tolerated in the north. However, as events unfolded and the identity of the coup-makers and their victims became known, the event of January 15, 1966, began to be seen as an Igbo bid to dominate Nigeria. Consequently, every action of Ironsi, especially the enactment of the unification decree that abolished regionalism in place of unitary government and unified administration, became misrepresented as part of an Igbo grand design to rule the country. The nonprosecution of the plotters was another sore point the northern officers and men held against him. These views, whether founded or not, generated much disquiet in the north and culminated eventually in the violent May riots against the Igbo in various northern cities.

On July, 29, 1966, a countercoup took place, spearheaded by northern officers and soldiers who said they acted to forestall further Igbo attacks on them. Major-General Ironsi, Lt. Col. F. A. Fajuyi, (military governor of the western group of provinces), and many Igbo officers and men were killed in Lagos, Ibadan, and Abeokuta. For three uncertain days Nigerians had no head of state. The northern instigators of the countercoup chose the most senior northern officer, Lt. Col. Yakubu Gowon, Army Chief of Staff under Ironsi, as their candidate for the office of head of state.

On August 1, 1966, Lt. Col. Yakubu Gowon became the head of state and supreme commander of the Nigerian Armed Forces. Prior to his elevation, he was largely unknown to most Nigerians, but was popular with the army, where he had held important posts as adjutant general and army chief of staff positions that had endeared him especially among the northern officers corps and the rank and file. Yakubu Gowon had attended the renowned government (now Barewa) College Zaria and on graduation, joined the army in 1954 as an officer cadet, and by 1963 had risen to the rank of lieutenant colonel.

Gowon inherited a Nigeria that was politically unstable and on the verge of disintegration. His assumption leadership displeased Lt. Col. Odumegwu Ojukwu, military governor of eastern Nigeria, who refused to recognize. The armed forces, which had struggled with credibility issues since the January coup, faced total collapse. Furthermore, massacres of Igbo in northern cities, and the exodus that followed, made any prospects for "one Nigeria" highly unlikely, as far as the Igbo were concerned. Mutual trust was now replaced by ethnic suspicion and hatred. Though worried, Gowon did not allow these problems to overwhelm him. In an effort to win public acceptance for his regime, he abolished the unification decree and reverted to a federal structure. He won over the largely Yoruba population of the western region when he released political prisoners, including Obafemi Awolowo and his colleagues (who had been charged with treason in 1963).

The failure of Gowon and Ojukwu to reach amicable compromise necessitated the meeting of the Supreme Military Council (SMC) at Aburi Ghana on January 4–5, 1967. Gowon's political inexperience manifested itself when he agreed, with Ojukwu, to accept confederation. But, when the SMC met in Benin to ratify the draft decree of the Aburi agreement, Ojukwu refused to attend on security grounds and so disowned its provisions. With his mind already made up to secede from Nigeria, he hastily promulgated the Revenue Edict, which appropriated taxes from the east due to the federal government. Further attempts at peaceful resolution, by the National Reconciliation Committee under Awolowo, failed.

As a result, Gowon's attitude hardened and on May 27, 1967, he declared a state of emergency and split the country into twelve regional states. The creation of two states for the eastern minorities was intended to undermine support for Ojukwu and present an excuse for attacking the Igbo. On May 30 Ojukwu, as expected, declared the state of Biafra and the country was embroiled in civil war for 30 months.

On January 12, 1970, the Biafran forces formally surrendered to Nigeria. To allay the fears of Biafran returnees, Gowon declared his famous policy of "no victor no vanquished." He embarked on the "3R" program of reconstruction, rehabilitation, and reconciliation. In principle it was a laudable scheme but in practice it left much to be desired in its implementation. Winning the war was the high point of Gowon's administration, but he failed to win the peace. He lost what goodwill Nigerians had for him when he was unable to successfully implement his program.

Gowon reneged on his promise to return the country to civil rule in 1976, pronouncing the date unrealistic in 1974. Public confidence in his administration was further eroded when allegations of impropriety were leveled against his officials. The incidence of corruption reached a new height and he appeared both unwilling and unable to do anything about it.

On the international level, Gowon pursued the nonaligned policy by making Africa its main focus. He was a founder of the Economic Community of West African States (ECOWAS).

He was overthrown on July 29, 1975, in a bloodless coup, while attending the Organization of African Unity (OAU) summit in Kampala, Uganda. He went immediately to Britain and enrolled at the University of Warwick, where he graduated with a doctorate in political science. For a time, he was implicated in the 1976 Dimka abortive coup in which his successor, Murtala Muhammed, was assassinated. He was granted amnesty by President Shehu Shagari in1980. Despite his shortcomings, history will not forget the role of General Yakubu Gowon in keeping Nigeria united.

J. O. Ahazuem

Further Reading

Akinrinade, S., and A. Oghuma. "Gowon Clinches the Saddle." *Newswatch.* Special Edition, 3, no. 3 (January 20, 1986).

Elaigwu, J. I. *Gowon.* Ibadan: West Books Publishers, 1985.

Harneit-Sievers, A., J. O. Ahazuem, and Sydney Emezue. *A Social History of the Nigeria Civil War.* Enugu: Jemezie Associates and Lit Verlag Hamburg, 1997.

Jemibewon, D. M. *A Combatant in Government.* Ibadan: Heinemann, 1979.

Kirk-Greene, A., and D. Rimmer. *Nigeria since 1970.* London: Hodder and Stoughton, 1981.

Nigeria: Biafran Secession and Civil War, 1967–1970

Within five years of independence, Nigeria was subjected to a series of harrowing events. The country afflicted with regional and ethnic chauvinism, political intolerance, victimization, lawlessness, government ineptitude and corruption, and nepotism, which culminated in the military coup d'ếtât of January 15, 1966. The coup, aimed at rescuing the country from disintegration, was interpreted as an Igbo subterfuge to dominate Nigeria. The ineptitude of General Ironsi, head of state, and an Igbo, seemed to confirm northern fears of planned Igbo domination. A countercoup, which toppled General Ironsi on July 29, 1966, brought Lt. Col. Yakubu Gowon installed as head of state. This countercoup was followed by massacres of Igbo in the northern region, in September and October of 1966. At the end of this organized genocide over 10,000 Igbo people had been exterminated. Several thousand more were maimed, or dispossessed, while 1.5 million people were turned into refugees within their own country. The perpetrators of this heinous crime were not punished, nor was compensation made to the victims.

The government's failure to stop the massacres convinced the Igbo that their security could only be guaranteed in the eastern region, which was overseen by Lt. Col. Emeka Ojukwu, an Igbo. It was against this background that the eastern region refused to recognize Gowon as the head of state of Nigeria.

A combination of bad faith, mutual distrust, duplicity, and the incompatible styles of Ojukwu and Gowon scuttled all mediation efforts both within and outside Nigeria. For instance, a good opportunity for the peaceful resolution of the situation came in January 1967, when General Ankrah, the military head of state of Ghana, interceded in the crisis. He convened a meeting of the Nigerian Supreme Military Council at Aburi, Ghana on January 4–5, 1967 to iron out the differences between Ojukwu and Gowon's federal government. The Aburi conference passed the following resolutions: non-use of force in the settlement of the crisis; a confederal status for the regions without boundary adjustments; a veto power for all members of the supreme military council that would enjoin a unanimous concurrence of the regions before any major decision could be taken; the payment of salaries of all displaced persons until March 31, 1967; and finally, the head of the federal military government should assume the title of commander in chief of the armed forces.

However, the prospects for peace in Nigeria were short-lived. Federal civil servants, after thorough perusal of the Aburi accord, told Gowon that he had been outwitted by Ojukwu. Gowon started to demur on the agreement and on March 17, 1967, issued Decree No. 8, which rejected some of the resolutions of the Aburi agreement. Ojukwu, in turn, rejected Decree No. 8.

The stage was thus set for a conflict between the eastern region and the federal military government. At the end of March 1967, Ojukwu issued a number of edicts to safeguard the region's economic interest. The federal government imposed economic sanctions against the region. The face-off continued until

May 26, 1967, when Ojukwu summoned the Eastern Region Consultative Assembly and the Advisory Committee of Chiefs and Elders in Enugu. On May 27 the assembly issued a communiqué empowering Ojukwu to declare the eastern region an independent sovereign state to be known as the Republic of Biafra. The federal authority reacted swiftly on the same day by splitting Nigeria into twelve states. Gowon assumed sweeping powers under Decree No.14, which banned political activities and introduced press censorship.

The "cold war" reached its crescendo when on May 30, 1967, Ojukwu declared the Republic of Biafra. The federal government declared the action null and immediately made clear its determination to suppress the secession. It also embarked upon massive mobilization and procurement of military weaponry. In Enugu, the Biafran capital, Ojukwu embarked upon a propaganda campaign, declaring that no power in black Africa could overcome Biafra.

The federal government launched a two-pronged attack against Biafra on July 6, 1967. From the northern border at Nsukka, Biafra presented an initial stiff resistance against the federal onslaught, but faced a continuing problem of low supplies of ammunition. Within a fortnight, the federal forces had pushed the Biafra forces out of the university town of Nsukka. At the Garkem-Ogoja front, Biafrans offered feeble resistance to the artillery and firepower of the federal troops. Biafra continued to suffer because of insufficient weaponry. The federal government drew from its enormous human and material resources, while Biafra was handicapped by sea blockade, little international support, and internal division. Despite heroic displays by the Biafrans through technological innovation, and grim determination, the secession was doomed to failure. Starvation decimated much of the Biafra population. Early in the war, an estimated 3,000 to 5,000 people died daily in Biafra, and about 10,000 daily toward its close.

Biafra had lost most of its strategic and important towns by July 1968 to the federal government. However, Biafra won a consolatory victory when it recaptured Owerri in April 1969. Nevertheless, Biafra lacked the resources to follow up its victories. About this time Biafra had shrunk to one-third of its original size.

Biafra's insurrection collapsed on January 11, 1970 when General Ojukwu fled to Côte d' Ivoire. On January 15 General Gowon accepted the unconditional surrender of Biafra by Maj. Gen. Philip Effiong, declaring that there was "no victor and no vanquished." Gowon's post–civil war reconstruction was half-hearted, inconsistent with his government's declared aims, and mere window-dressing to calm the international community's fear of reprisals against the Igbo. The Igbo people were discriminated again in Nigeria during Gowon's regime and received harsh peace terms from the victorious federal government. Their properties were declared abandoned in several parts of the country at the end of the civil war. They were refused reinstatement in their previous places of employment. The fate of the Igbo people still hangs in the balance in post–civil war Nigeria.

PAUL O. OBI-ANI

See also: **Nigeria: Gowon Regime, 1966–1975.**

Further Reading

Achuzia, J. O. G. *Requiem Biafra.* Enugu: Fourth Dimension Publishers, 1986.

Ademoyega, A. *Why We Struck: The Story of the First Nigeria Coup.* Ibadan: Evans Brothers (Nigeria Publishers), 1981.

Elaigwu, J. I. *Gowon: The Biography of a Soldier Statesman.* Ibadan: West Books Publishers Ltd, 1982.

Forsyth, F. *Emeka.* Ibadan: Spectrum Books, 1982.

Gbulie, B. *Nigeria's Five Majors: Coup D'etat of 15th January 1966 First Insider's Account.* Onitsha: Africana Educational Publishers (Nig.), 1981.

Jorre, J. De St. *The Nigeria Civil War.* London: Hodder and Stoughton, 1972.

Madiebo, A. A. *The Nigerian Revolution and the Biafra War.* Enugu: Fourth Dimension Publishing Co., 1980.

Oluleye, J. J. "The Role of the Nigerian Army in the Crises and Civil War of 1966–1970: The Facts and the Lessons." In *Inside Nigeria History 1950–1970: Events, Issues, and Sources*, edited by Y. B. Usman and G. Amale Kwanashie. Ibadan: The Presidential Panel on Nigeria Since Independence History Project, 1995.

Nigeria: Murtala Muhammed, Obasanjo and Return to Civilian Rule, 1975–1979

The coup that brought the Murtala Muhammed/Olusegun Obasanjo regime to power in 1975 occurred against the background of general disenchantment with the corrupt and inept regime of General Yakubu Gowon. It was clear that Gowon could not check the excesses of his subordinates. The only solace that the public had was the promise Gowon made in 1970 to hand over power to civilians in 1976. But when, in 1974, he reneged on the promise, declaring that 1976 was no longer realistic, large sections of the public that had long suspected the sincerity of the military's promise to hand over power to civilians felt vindicated. Within the military, there were divisions over this issue of withdrawing from politics. It was against this background that a section of the military that favored withdrawal from politics and led by General Murtala Muhammed overthrew the Gowon's regime in a bloodless coup d'étât in July 1975.

Given the factors that influenced the coup, the primary concern of the new administration, which described itself as a corrective regime, was the improvement of the image of the military, ridding the society of corruption and perhaps more importantly setting in motion a democratization process. The first step the regime took was to carry out a massive retrenchment of corrupt and inefficient workers from various government departments, the judiciary, parastatals at both the federal and state levels, as well as the military. However, the primary program of the regime was the setting in motion of a transition to civil rule process. Hence on October 1, 1975, during the independence day broadcast, General Muhammed announced a five-stage program of transition to civil rule which was to last from 1975 to 1979. The program combined structural reforms with constitution making. The structural reforms involved the creation of new states and the reorganization of the local government system. The constitution making process included the setting up of a Constitution Drafting Committee (CDC), followed by a Constituent Assembly (CA) to deliberate on the draft constitution, lifting of the ban on politics, elections into state and federal legislatures, and the handing over of power to civilians on October 1, 1979. Muhammed stated that structural reforms had to be carried out along with the demilitarization process, in order to create a viable political system that will be stable and responsive to the needs and realities of the country. However, this transition to civil rule program had barely started when Muhammed was assassinated in an unsuccessful coup on February 13, 1976. Muhammed was succeeded by General Olusegun Obasanjo, his second in command, who committed himself to fully implementing the transition program.

Based on the report of the Irikefe Panel, on the creation of new states, seven more states were created in February 1976, bringing the total number of states in Nigeria to nineteen. It was believed that the creation of new states would bring government closer to the people, promote even development and allay the fears of minorities, thereby helping to enhance political stability in the country. The 1976 local government reforms introduced a uniform system of local governments and made local governments the third tier of government in the federation. Local governments were to promote development at the grassroots level, were entitled to revenue allocation and had areas of exclusive legislative jurisdiction. One effect of these structural reforms was to increase the financial dependence of the states and local governments on the federal government with the result that these two lower tiers of government became mere administrative agents and distribution outlets for federal resources.

The first step in the constitution-making process was the inauguration of the CDC in October 1975. The all-male fifty-member CDC, made up largely of professionals, academicians, and bureaucrats, was given the mandate of producing a draft constitution which would provide a sound basis for the continuing existence of a united Nigeria. The submission of a two-volume report by the CDC in September 1976 and the wide circulation of these reports, led to a nationwide debate on the draft constitution. Following the submission of the report of the CDC, a Constituent Assembly (CA) with majority of its members elected through the electoral college system and a few members nominated to represent special interests, was inaugurated. The main task of the CA was to deliberate on the draft constitution and produce a final copy of the constitution to the federal military government for ratification. Since most of the members of the CA were politicians, its deliberation was more partisan and controversy-ridden than the highly technical CDC. The issues that generated the greatest controversies, in particular, the establishment of a separate federal Shari'a (Islamic law) court of appeal and the formula for the creation of more states, reflected the religious and sectional differences among the members of the CA. The CA equally provided an avenue for the formation of political associations that metamorphosed into political parties when the ban on politics was lifted. However, the CA completed its task in August 1978 and submitted a copy of the constitution to the government.

The Supreme Military Council (SMC) deliberated on the constitution and made seventeen amendments before promulgating it into law in September 1978. Right from the beginning of the constitution making process, the military set down the framework of the type of constitution it desired. The final deliberation and amendments by the SMC ensured that the military had the final say regarding the nature of the constitution that was made law. This, together with the fact that the CDC and the CA were dominated by members of the elite, ensured that the constitution did little in the way of providing rights and privileges for the non-elite majority. However, the Federal Electoral Commission (FEDECO) which had been set up in 1976 to oversee the electoral process, registered five out of the over fifty political associations that applied for registration as political parties. FEDECO conducted elections at the state and federal levels between July and August 1979. After a bitterly contested and disputed presidential election, Shehu Shagari of the National Party of Nigeria was sworn in as the country's executive president on October 1, 1979, thereby marking the final stage in the transition to a program of civil rule. It was clear, however, that the Second Republic began on an uncertain foundation and was destined to face a number of serious challenges.

J. I. Dibua

See also: **Obasanjo, Olusegun.**

Further Reading

Bolaji, L. *Shagari: President by Mathematics.* Ibadan: Automatic Printing Press, 1980.

Falola, T. *The History of Nigeria.* Westport, Conn.: Greenwood Press, 1999.

Forrest, T. *Politics and Economic Development in Nigeria.* Boulder, Colo.: Westview Press, 1993.

Graf, W. D. *The Nigerian State: Political Economy, State Class and Political System in the Post-Colonial Era.* London: James Currey and Heinmann, 1988.

Odetola, T. O. *Military Politics in Nigeria: Economic Development and Political Stability.* New Brunswick, N.J.: Transaction Books, 1980.

Osaghae, E. E. *Crippled Giant: Nigeria Since Independence.* Bloomington: Indiana University Press, 1998.

Oyediran, O. (ed.). *Nigerian Government and Politics Under Military Rule, 1966–1979.* London: Macmillan, 1979.

Nigeria: Second Republic, 1979–1983

Nigeria's Second Republic started on a very shaky foundation. Four of the five political parties that were registered to contest the elections had the bulk of their support from specific ethnic groups and regions of the country. In fact some were reincarnations of the ethnic and regional based parties of the First Republic. The Unity Party of Nigeria (UPN) led by the frontline Nigerian politician, Obafemi Awolowo, was a reincarnation of the Action Group of the First Republic and had the bulk of its support among the Yoruba. The Nigerian Peoples Party (NPP) led by Nigeria's First Republic ceremonial pesident, Nnamdi Azikiwe, was a reincarnation of the National Convention of Nigerian Citizens (NCNC) and drew the bulk of its support from the Igbo (though it was able to capture Plateau state in the Middle Belt). The Peoples Redemption Party (PRP) was a reincarnation of the Northern Elements Progressive Union (NEPU) and drew the bulk of its support from Kano State (though by default it was able to capture the Governorship of Kaduna State). The Great Nigerian Peoples Party (GNPP) drew the bulk of its support from Borno and Gongola states. The National Party of Nigeria (NPN), which was more national in character and had a relatively large support in parts of the middle belt and the southern minority states, was more fully entrenched in the conservative Hausa-Fulani northern states. Even then, the NPN was a reincarnation of the Northern Peoples Congress (NPC).

In the 1979 elections, it was only the NPN that was able to achieve a national spread in terms of the plurality of votes, the parliamentary and governorship seats won, but it was not able to win majority of the seats in the national assembly. However, although Shehu Shagari, the presidential candidate of the NPN, was declared the winner of the presidential elections, this was bitterly contested in court by Obafemi Awolowo, the candidate of the UPN who came second. The basis of the challenge was that Shagari did not win one-quarter of the votes cast in at least two-thirds of the states of the federation as provided in the constitution. Before this election, two-thirds of the nineteen states was generally interpreted as thirteen states. But in a highly controversial decision Shagari was declared the elected President on the basis of the fact that he won at least two-thirds of the votes in twelve states and two-thirds of 20 per cent of the votes in the thirteenth state. This greatly angered Awolowo and his supporters who accused the military of bending the rules in other to install their favored candidate hence some critics referred to Shagari as "President by mathematics." This decision engendered serious opposition from the UPN, as its five elected governors championed the formation of an alliance by the twelve non-NPN governors, the so-called Progressive Governors who were constantly antagonistic and critical towards the federal government. This situation adversely affected inter-governmental relations and proved detrimental for the effective functioning of the Second Republic.

In the face of the opposition by non-NPN legislators, the federal government through various forms of patronage formed working alliances with legislators of the opposition parties in other to get its bills passed by the National Assembly. Up to 1981, when the alliance between the NPN and NPP was still in force, it was relatively easy for the federal government to mobilize the NPP legislators in support of its bills. But the collapse of the alliance in July 1981 resulted in the increased use of patronage and other corrupt practices. One factor that greatly contributed to the intraparty crisis that bedeviled the Second Republic was the competition for access to federal patronage.

The politicians were mainly members of the petty bourgeoisie that thrived on commerce, contracts, and political access. As a result the issue of whether or not to cooperate with the NPN became the most important source of intraparty disputes among the so-called opposition parties. Significantly, the anti-accord groups were usually led by State Governors who had access to state power and therefore patronage, while the pro-accord groups were usually led by federal legislators, who wanted patronage from the NPN federal government. Indeed the accord reached by the NPP with the NPN in 1979 was predicated on the appointment of NPP members as federal ministers and to positions in federal corporations and parastatals. It is important to note that the breakdown of the accord in 1981 was as a result of what the NPP perceived as discrimination in the award of contracts, import licenses, and distribution of offices. Even then while the NPP governors championed the breakdown of the accord, some of its ministers and legislators disagreed with the move. Two of the ministers therefore resigned from the party and continued to serve as ministers in the NPN federal government while Senator Anah formed a breakaway faction of the NPP. Similar disagreements over cooperation with the NPN resulted in splits in the GNPP led by Senator Mahmud Waziri and the PRP led by Senator Sarbo Bakin Zuwo.

Within the NPN itself, the issue of the extent to which members benefited from federal patronage became an important source of disagreement. In fact the primary concern with patronage and rent seeking led to the award highly inflated contracts many of which were never executed, or at best very poorly done, to members of the ruling party. The massive corruption of the Second Republic plunged the country into a serious economic crisis, with Nigeria, which had an external reserve of 5 billion Naira in 1979, incurring an external debt of 20 billion Naira by the end of 1983.

The serious political and economic crisis that the country faced had by 1983 greatly delegitimized the NPN federal government. In the face of widespread opposition, the regime resulted to the use of coercion and various forms of manipulation to remain in power. The 1983 elections were therefore conducted under a very charged atmosphere. The attempt of the opposition parties to form an alliance, the Progressive Parties Alliance (PPA) was not very successful. Though there was clear evidence of rigging of the elections by all the political parties, the NPN used its control of state power and institutions to manipulate the outcome of the elections that virtually turned the country into a one party state. Widespread frustration with this "electoral coup" resulted in massive violence in parts of the country, especially in Ondo and Oyo states. The increasing use of coercion by the NPN to keep itself in power created the conditions that led to the military coup of December 31, 1983, which brought the Second Republic to an end.

J. I. Dibua

See also: **Azikiwe, Nnamdi; Nigeria: Military Rule, 1983–1999.**

Further Reading

Adamolekun, L. *The Fall of the Second Republic.* Ibadan: Spectrum Books, 1983.

Ake, C. "Introduction." *Africa Development: Special Issue on Nigeria.* Dakar: CODESRIA, 1984.

Dibua, J. I. "Conflict Among the Nigerian Bourgeoisie and the Demise of the Second Republic." *Africa Development.* 13, no. 4 (1988).

Falola, T., and J. Ihonvbere. *The Rise and Fall of Nigeria's Second Republic, 1979–84.* London: Zed Books, 1985.

Joseph, R. *Democracy and Prebendal Politics in Nigeria: The Rise and Fall of the Second Republic.* Cambridge: Cambridge University Press, 1987.

Okpu, U. "Inter-Party Political Relations in Nigeria 1979–1983." *Africa Spectrum.* 2 (1985).

Turner, T., and P. Badru. "Oil and Instability: Class Contradictions and the 1983 Coup in Nigeria." *Journal Of African Marxists.* 7 (1985).

Nigeria: Agriculture, Irrigation, Rural Development

Traditionally, agriculture has been the mainstay of the Nigerian economy. At the expiration of colonial rule, it employed well over 80 per cent of the working population and accounted for 56 per cent of the Gross Domestic Product. Colonial agriculture had emphasized export produce, namely cocoa, palm oil and kernels, and groundnuts, neglecting domestic food production. In the first decade of independence, the colonial system was hardly changed as emphasis was still on the export crops while the marketing boards, a colonial heritage, continued as the monopoly purchasers of peasant exports. They consistently paid the farmers well below standard prices in the world markets.

In the 1970s, crude oil replaced agriculture as the country's chief revenue earner. This notwithstanding, successive governments have continued to recognize, at least in principle, the central place of agriculture in the nation's economy. Various national development plans have, accordingly, provided substantial portions of their budgets to the sector. With urbanization and escalating costs of foodstuffs, the policy thrust of government has shifted to the domestic front with two basic aims: (a) to effect self-sufficiency in food production and to meet the demands of a rapidly growing population, and (b) to provide raw materials for agro-based domestic industries. To this end, the authorities established some management instruments such as banks to give easy credit to farmers. The banks are encouraged to establish in the rural areas where the farmers live. In 1976 a wide range of schemes that came under the general rubic Agricultural Development Program was launched. In the same year, the Operation Feed the Nation was initiated by government with the aim of projecting to the national consciousness the need for all Nigerians, to contribute to increase food production by cultivating every piece of land within their reach. A directorate of food, roads, and rural infrastructure was also established and charged with providing essential infrastructure, especially all-season roads, for rural communities.

During the third NDP, government initiated the National Accelerated Food Production Program and used it as the principal tool with which to bridge the widening gap between food production and demand. The main thrust of the program was to make available to farmers fertilizers, pesticides, and credits through agricultural research extension services and timely distribution of high response seed varieties. The program was, however, marked by a high level of corruption and incompetence.

Among the agricultural instruments that government put in place were a number of river basin development authorities (RBDAs), each of which was charged with the task of harnessing the agricultural potentials of the river basin(s) under its jurisdiction. This involved creating extensive areas for year-round cultivation of cereals and vegetables. The RBDAs were large-scale capital intensive projects involving massive land clearing and dam construction. Under the scheme, it was projected that irrigated areas in Nigeria would jump from 13,000 hectares (1968) to 274,000 in a decade. The projects were costed in 1977 at $2.2 billion but by 1982 they had used up $2.7 billion. Much of the money went into providing lavish housing estates for the foreign contractors handling the projects.

There were little tangible results to show for the huge expenditures. In the southern parts of the country, the RBDAs were an abysmal failure. High-ranking officials in collusion with contractors ripped open the RBDAs. In the northern parts, a couple of dams were actually constructed and some land brought under irrigation, but the total acreage involved fell far below projections. In any case, the ecological and human costs have been disastrous. Water supplies from the dams are unstable and unpredictable. Flooding of farmlands, resulting in considerable loss of farm crops, has been a common occurrence. The Goronyo and Bakalori dams have diverted the flow of several rivers and drastically reduced water supply in several other basins. Rural self-sufficiency has been badly jettisoned. In 1980 frustration and starvation drove dislocated and unresettled peasants to violent demonstrations, which the government ruthlessly crushed. Government efforts in the field of agriculture have been a total failure. The contribution of agriculture to the GDP has continued to decline in absolute and relative senses. Food imports went up from a 1.6 per cent average between 1960 and 1970 to a 21 per cent average between 1971 and 1979. The high cost of food has created miseries for urban dwellers, who spend virtually all of their incomes on food. Since the 1980s, increasing numbers of agro-based industries have folded up or are working far below installed capacity because of inadequate raw materials supply. Sixty per cent of hides produced in Nigeria is eaten by humans as a source of protein because fish farming and animal husbandry have been grossly neglected.

A combination of factors explains the nonperformance of the agricultural sector. Soil deterioration has meant diminished output. Flight of youths to the city greatly diminishes the vitality of the agricultural labor force. Far much less has consistently been spent on agriculture per se than budgeted. And much of what remains to be spent is hijacked by government officials. Peasant farmers, the backbone of Nigerian agriculture, are denied the benefits of modern agriculture and continue to rely on traditional tools and techniques. Agricultural modernization has neglected the fund of empirical knowledge which rural farmers have accumulated over generations. Foreign "experts" often find that they have a lot to learn from rural farmers about their local milieu. Finally, successive governments have emphasized the centrality of agriculture in national life, but as long as farming remains financially unattractive and rural neglect continues without redress, official appeals in favor of farming will fall on deaf ears.

Agricultural decline has been accompanied by a degeneration of rural life. Although about 70 per cent of Nigerians are rural dwellers, less than 20 per cent of the national expenditure goes into rural development. Most rural dwellers live below absolute poverty line, and rural-urban income differential is staggering. The rural populations are denied access to basic social amenities like good roads, piped water, electricity, education, and health care.

Onwuka N. Njoku

See also: **Nigeria: Industry, Oil, Economy.**

Further Reading

Abba, A. Y. Abdullahi, et al. *The Nigerian Economic Crisis: Causes and Solutions.* Zaria: Academic Staff Union of Universities of Nigeria, 1985.

Gana, I. *Food for Nigerian Cities: A Mobilization Approach.* Abuja: MAMSER, n.d.

Ghonemy, M. R. E., ed. *Development Strategies for the Rural Poor.* Rome: Food and Agricultural Organization, 1984.

Heinecke, P. *Freedom in the Grave: Nigeria and the Political Economy of Africa.* Okpala, Nigeria: S. Asekome and Co., 1986.

Helleiner, G. E. K. *Peasant Agriculture, Government, and Economic Growth in Nigeria.* Homewood, Ill.: Richard D. Irwin, 1966.

Nigeria: Federal Ministry of Agriculture, Water Resources, and Rural Development. *Agricultural Policy of Nigeria.* Abuja: Directorate for Social Mobilization, n.d.

Osuntogun, A., and A. Adeleke, eds. *Policies for the Development of Agricultural and Rural Cooperatives.* Ilorin: Agricultural and Rural Management Training Institute, 1988.

Well, J. C. *Agricultural Policy and Economic growth in Nigeria, 1962–1968.* Ibadan: Oxford University Press, 1974.

Nigeria: Industry, Oil, Economy

At independence in 1960 Nigeria lacked modern industries worthy of note. Successive independent governments were determined to right this colonial neglect. The first step was to provide a conducive setting, through appropriates legislation and incentives to industrialists such as tax holidays to infant or pioneer industries, easy repatriation of profits by foreign investors, and industrial layouts, which would facilitate land acquisition to investors and also permit the advantages of industrial aggregation. Government also established industrial banks and other financial institutions, the leading one being the Nigerian Industrial Development Bank, to provide financial services to the industrial sector. In 1960 Nigeria had its Central Bank charged with the responsibility of giving the lead and direction to the banking sector. By the time the Nigerian civil war erupted in 1967, the industrial landscape had started to wear a new look and the contribution of the sector to the Gross Domestic Product (GDP) had moved from 4.37 per cent in 1962 to 18 per cent.

The first decade following the civil war witnessed prosperity, thanks to the rapid emergence of crude oil as Nigeria's leading foreign exchange earner. Bumper prices for crude oil, which hit the roof in 1973, inundated the national treasury with billions of dollars. Mesmerized and tempted by the huge foreign exchange reserves at its disposal, the government assumed a key role in direct economic activity, and got involved in a wide range of industrial ventures including iron and steal, oil refining, cement, vehicle assembling, brewing, textiles, fertilizer, and even pulp and paper. The government also dabbled directly into the service industry such as insurance; land, marine, and air transportation; and even hotel. The boom period attracted massive investments in industry from the private sector, too. The net result of all these was that by the early 1980s manufacturing and construction firms had blazoned the landscape of the major cities and accounted for over 70 per cent of the GDP.

Since the 1970s, petroleum has the key to the manufacturing sector. It is the fastest growing sector of the national economy, accounting for 58 per cent of export value in 1970 and over 97 per cent per annum since 1984. Crude oil provides a raw material base for the local production of bitumen, pharmaceuticals, cosmetics, and fertilizers. The country's three refineries are owned by the Nigerian National Production Corporation, a government parastatal enjoying total monopoly in oil refining. But oil prospecting and drilling are monopolized by foreign trans-nationals such as Royal Dutch Shell, Chevron, Mobile, Agip, and ELF. The industry is very capital-intensive, employs some of the country's best professionals, and pays the most attractive wages. But the colossal dominance of the entire industrial sector by the oil industry distorts the total economy and disguises its narrow and unstable base.

The era of economic boom in Nigeria was short-lived, for by the late 1970s, the early signs of hard times had started to appear. Oil prices began to decline, and then tumbled to their depths. The national treasury dried up. By the mid-1980s more manufacturing firms were going under than emerging, and the surviving ones were producing far below installed capacity. By the 1990s economic stagnation had degenerated to retrogression. Even the NNPC was strapped of funds and unable to maintain its refineries, thus leading to acute gasoline shortages in a country ranked fifth among the world's oil producing countries. Between 50 and 70 per cent of the country's banks and insurance firms collapsed, taking with them down the drain several billions of naira.

These developments had negative spread affects on the rest of the economy and the society at large. Unchecked unemployment, which had gone over the roof in the 1980s, hit hardest those in the between eighteenth and twenty five years old. Their future blighted, these youths have been driven to prostitution, drug, and armed banditry. Spiraling inflation made nonsense of the income of wage earners and pushed the living standards of most Nigerians beneath the absolute poverty line. A significant number of urban dwellers lived in squalid over-crowded conditions and could not afford one good meal a day.

With its national treasury empty, Nigeria joined the league of the world's eleven poorest nations. The military government of General Babangida turned to the World Bank and the IMF for loans but was required by these bodies to introduce a structural adjustment program as a precondition for obtaining the loans. Amid national outcry, SAP was introduced. The net result has been predictable: Nigeria got mired in a vicious debt-trap estimated in 1990 variously at between $35 and $46 billion. Servicing, let alone repaying, the loan has become too tall an order for the country.

A combination of factors explains the economic predicament of Nigeria. Wholesale reliance on crude oil, a diminishing resource, along with the neglect of agriculture, put the economy in jeopardy. Food imports took a substantial portion of scarce national reserves. Nigeria has adopted the import-substitution method in her industrialization efforts, which entails that the final stages in the manufacture of imported goods are carried out in the country. The implication is that the moving force of industrialization resides in the countries which produce the industrial machines and factories. Import substitution is a recipe for perpetuating strategic dependence because it denies the local economy the opportunity to initiate research and technical innovation.

At the root of Nigeria's economic woes is the involvement of government in direct economic activity. The government squandered the oil money, undertaking ego-boosting white elephant projects that had no relevance to the basic needs of the overwhelming majority of Nigerians. Overnight, government bureaucrats became managers of key industries. Sheer executive incompetence was compounded by overdeveloped kleptomania evident in the unrestrained pillage of the state by a handful of state officials. Contracts were routinely over-valued, the excess going into the pockets of the officials, mostly top military men, who had been in power for twenty-five out of Nigeria's twenty-nine years of independence. This strikingly rich minority live a life-style of unrestrained revelry, flaunting their ill-gotten wealth in the face of the pauperized majority. The several billion dollars in cash recovered from the private homes of Sani Abacha, former military head of state of Nigeria, and his government officials are believed to be only the tip of a monstrous iceberg.

ONWUKA N. NJOKU

See also: **Banking and Finance; Nigeria: Gowon Regime, 1966–1975; Nigeria: Agriculture, Irrigation, Rural Development; Oil.**

Further Reading

Achebe, C. *The Trouble With Nigeria.* Enugu: Fourth Dimension Publishing Co., 1987.

Ihonvbere, J. O., and T. Shaw. *Towards a Political Economy of Nigeria: Petroleum and Politics at the (Semi-) Periphery.* Aldershot: Avebury, 1988.

Njoku, O. N. "Broken Covenant: A Historical Reflection on the Nigerian Economy since Independence." In *Indian Journal of African Studies.* 6, no. 1 (1993): 67–86.

Nwankwo, A. A. *Can Nigeria Survive?* Enugu: Fourth Dimension Publishing Co., 1987.

Ogbonnaya, M. N. *Key Development Issues in Nigeria.* Lawrenceville, Va.: Brunswick Publishing Co., 1985.

Okongwu, C. S. P. *The Nigerian Economy: Anatomy of a Traumatised Economy.* Enugu: Fourth Dimension Publishing Co., 1986.

Sayre, P. S. "The Nigerian Economy since the Great Oil Price Increase." In *Africa Today.* 29 (1982): 33–44.

Williams, G. *Nigeria: Economy and Society.* London: Rex Collings, 1996.

World Bank. *Nigeria: Options for Long-Term Development.* Baltimore and London: The Johns Hopkins University Press, 1974.

Nigeria: Military Rule, 1983–1999

From 1960, when the nation gained independence, to 1998, Nigeria only experienced ten years of civilian, as opposed to military, rule. Following the collapse of the first republic in 1966, the civil war and subsequent military rule under Generals Gowon, Muhammed, and Obasanjo, Nigeria returned to civilian rule in 1979. The second republic under Shehu Shagari lasted from the elections of 1979 until the end of 1983 when the army, which by then had clearly acquired a permanent taste for political power, again seized control.

Major General Muhammed Buhari was the new military ruler. He emphasized the corruption and immorality of the National Party of Nigeria (NPN), which he had ousted, and dissolved or banned all political institutions and reinstated the Supreme Military Council (SMC). The coup met with widespread approval.

The economy was in faced serious problems, and in 1984 the military government broke off negotiations with the IMF and initiated its own austerity budget. Special tribunals dealt with former politicians and state governors, a number of whom were sentenced to prison for corruption.

Buhari became increasingly unpopular because of his inept handling of the economy, which reduced Nigeria to bartering its oil for imports, and because of his authoritarianism and the imposition of severe restrictions upon the media. In May 1985 Buhari expelled 700,000 "unauthorized foreigners" including 300,000 Ghanaians, positioning them as scapegoats for the declining state of the economy.

On August 27, 1985, the army declared Buhari deposed, the SMC was dissolved, and a new Armed Forces Ruling Council (AFRC) was set up with Major General Ibrahim Babangida as head of state. As with Buhari, Babangida faced a declining economy, with a static demand for oil (the country's principal export and foreign exchange earner). He was thus obliged to impose further austerity measures upon the nation.

In January 1986 Babangida announced that the army would hand back power to civilians in 1990. Unrest in northern Nigeria, mainly Islamic discontent, persuaded Babangida to apply for Nigeria to join the Organization of Islamic Conference (OIC) in February 1986. Continuing clashes between Muslims and Christians led the government to set up an Advisory Council on Religious Affairs (ACRA) in April 1987.

The next five years were taken up with a great deal of discussion about the form of a new constitution, and the government postponed the return to civilian rule to 1992. During these years the continuing decline of the economy and the way in which Nigeria could return to civilian rule dominated politics. In October 1989 Babangida rejected the credentials of all thirteen political parties that had emerged to take part in the elections. Instead, the government announced that it would create two parties which all politicians would be allowed to join. Antigovernment riots during 1989 focused upon desires for civilian rule and a strengthened economy.

In April 1990 middle-ranking officers mounted a coup attempt, attacked Dodan Barracks (headquarters of the ruling military), and took over Radio Nigeria. The coup, which collapsed after ten hours of fighting, highlighted north-south rivalries and Christian fears of Muslim domination. On July 27 Major Gideon Orkar, the coup leader, and forty-one other soldiers were executed.

The year 1991 saw further religious riots in the north but also moves toward a return to civilian rule. The number of states was increased to thirty and the two government-authorized parties, the Social Democratic

Party (SDP) and the National Republican Convention (NRC), held countrywide congresses in June to select delegates for primary elections. Early in 1992 dates were set for the elections: November 7 for the Senate and House of Representatives, and December 5 for the presidential elections. However, although the elections for the Senate and House of Representatives were advanced to July (the SDP won a majority of seats in both houses), the results of the first round of presidential primaries were thrown out in August due to allegations of corruption and other irregularities. Fresh elections were set for September but following further setbacks and cancellations, President Babangida postponed the return to civilian rule until August 1993.

Although 1993 began with preparations for elections, it would turn out to be one of the worst years for Nigeria since independence. In January, as an apparent move toward instituting a civilian government, a transitional council composed mainly of civilians was set up. Chief Ernest Adegunle Shonekan was named head of government, although the real power remained with President Babangida. At the end of March the two political parties selected their presidential candidates: the SDP chose Moshood Kashimawo Olawale ("M.K.O.") Abiola, while the NRC chose Bashir Othma Tofu. The elections were scheduled for June 12, and despite a legal attempt to stop them, they were held. By June 14 it was clear that Abiola was winning by a wide margin and on June 18, the Campaign for Democracy claimed that he had won outright in nineteen of thirty states. However, in June the National Defense and Security Council (NDSC), which had been set up the previous January ostensibly to oversee the elections, annulled the results "to protect our legal system and the judiciary from being ridiculed and politicized both nationally and internationally."

The United States described the annulment as outrageous; Britain cut off aid in protest. In August General Babangida stood down, handing power over to an interim national government led by Chief Shonekan that would rule through March 1994. Shonekan's defense minister was General Sani Abacha, who had played a key role in the 1983 coup and was generally considered as Babangida's right hand man. Abiola, meanwhile, had fled to London. On November 17, Abacha forced Shonekan to resign and made himself head of state. He dissolved the existing organs of state and set up a provisional ruling council (PRC). By the end of the year Abacha was presiding over a country where living standards were plummeting, inflation was soaring, and corruption was rife, while the price of oil stood at a ten-year low.

Nigeria was in a state of political crisis throughout 1994. In mid-June Abiola was arrested and despite calls by the courts to do so, the government twice refused to produce Abiola for trial. The awful state of the economy was emphasized in April when Nigeria was obliged to import 100,000 tons of petrol due to production problems at its refineries.

Throughout 1995 the political uncertainty continued with demands for a return to civilian rule. Abacha announced the extension of military rule until 1998. A low point in Nigeria's international relations was reached on November tenth when, at the beginning of the Commonwealth Heads of Government Meeting (CHOGM) in New Zealand, Abacha had nine Ogoni activists, led by Ken Saro-Wiwa (who had been protesting at the activities of the oil companies in the Delta region) executed. The Commonwealth suspended Nigeria's membership.

At odds with the Commonwealth over the Saro-Wiwa affair and his record on human rights, and widely criticized by Nigerians both inside and outside the country throughout 1996, Abacha paid scant attention to such criticisms, athough he did twice dismiss numbers of senior army officers, clearly pre-empting coup actions. New rules for eventual elections were announced by the National Electoral Commission of Nigeria (NECON) and five political associations were registered as political parties.

A rise in the price of oil enabled the Finance Minister, Anthony Ani, to increase budgets for rural development, education, and health in his January 1996 budget. In February General Abacha announced that he might stand in the 1998 presidential elections; he claimed that his program to return the country to civilian rule was on schedule. Registration of voters at over 100,000 centers took place in February, and local elections were held on March 15. The turnout was massive; these were the first elections to be held since the Abacha takeover in November 1993. The electoral timetable for a return to civilian rule was set as October 1, 1998. Abiola remained in prison and Nigeria remained at odds with the Commonwealth.

The death of General Sani Abacha on June 8, 1998, followed a month later by that of Chief Moshood M. K. O. Abiola, fundamentally altered the political outlook for Nigeria. The chief of the General Staff, General Abdulsalam Abubakar, succeeded Abacha as head of state; he promised to reinstate civilian rule. In August Abubakar announced a new electoral timetable for the elections, and in September he published the draft of a civilian constitution and invited public comments on it. Meanwhile twenty-five of thirty-two political parties had registered for the forthcoming elections and the former head of state, General Olusegun Obasanjo, announced his candidacy as leader of the People's Democratic Party (PDP).

On March 1, 1999, the Independent National Electoral Commission (INEC) declared General Obasanjo of the PDP winner of the presidential elections; in his victory speech General Obasanjo promised to continue Nigeria's transition back to democracy.

GUY ARNOLD

See also: **Nigeria: Army.**

Further Reading

Ekineh, A. *Nigeria: Foundations of Disintegration.* London: New Millenium, 1997.

Falola, T. *Violence in Nigeria: The Crisis of Religious Politics and Secular Ideologies.* Rochester, N.Y.: Woodbridge: University of Rochester Press, 1998.

Na'allah, A. R. (ed.). *Ogoni's Agonies: Ken Saro-Wiwa and the Crisis in Nigeria.* Trenton, N.J.: Africa World and London: Turnaround, 1998.

Osaghae, E. E. *Crippled Giant: Nigeria since Independence.* London: Hurst, 1998.

Saro-Wiwa, K. *Nigeria: The Brink of Disaster.* Epsom: Saros International, 1991.

Nigeria: Opposition, 1990s, to the Fourth Republic

The 1990s witnessed widespread opposition against the administrations of Ibrahim Babangida (1985–1993), Ernest Shonekan (August–November, 1993), and Sanni Abacha (1993–1998). The level of opposition was a product of the high degree of activism in civil society: indeed, civil society can be said to have come of age in Nigeria in the 1990s. This decade saw the proliferation of various nongovernmental voluntary organizations and associational groups, particularly human rights and pro-democracy organizations. The main opposition groups comprised human rights and pro-democracy organizations; students, acting mainly through their umbrella body, the National Association of Nigerian Students (NANS); professional associations; labor organizations mostly acting through their umbrella body, the Nigerian Labor Congress (NLC); primordial groups with predominantly ethnic and regional character; the press, particularly independent newspapers and magazines; and different categories of womens' organizations.

The dictatorial manner in which the Structural Adjustment Program (SAP) was introduced in 1986, and the manipulation of the transition to civil rule, which had become apparent in the late 1980s, provided the background for the emergence of an activist civil society in the 1990s. However, the authoritarianism of the respective military regimes was the catalyst for the widespread opposition of the 1990s. In particular, the authoritarian and uncompromising manner in which SAP and the transition program were implemented, made confrontation with the increasingly vocal civil society inevitable. The opposition of the civil society groups took the form of demonstrations, strikes, riots, revolts, sabotage activities, critical press reporting, and the operation of underground radio stations.

The introduction of SAP in June 1986, against popular opinion, as well as the debilitating consequences of SAP, generated a great deal of opposition from the civil society. The situation was not helped by the repressive manner in which the program was implemented and the failure to brook any form of opposition to SAP with the Babangida administration insisting that there were no alternatives to SAP. The suppression of alternative viewpoints, as well as the increasingly negative effects of SAP on the Nigerian economy and society, created a situation where segments of the society resorted to demonstrations, riots, and strikes, against the continued implementation of the program. The opposition to SAP was championed by students under the aegis of NANS, and in alliance with human rights groups and market women organizations, among others. In April 1988 students organized a nationwide demonstration against the SAP-induced removal of subsidies from petroleum products, and in May 1989 they organized a nationwide anti-SAP demonstration.

Students continued to champion the opposition against SAP in the 1990s. In April 1990 they organized mass demonstrations against the World Bank loan for the restructuring of the Nigerian educational sector mainly because the restructuring was to be based on policies associated with SAP. The most wide-ranging protest against SAP championed by students occurred in May 1992, when NANS decided to launch a nonviolent mass protest against the deteriorating material conditions of Nigerians occasioned by the continued implementation of SAP. The protest, which started in Lagos spread to other parts of Nigeria and attracted the participation of various human rights groups, workers, market women organizations, urban youths, and the unemployed people. The violent nature of the protest was such that many government properties were destroyed.

An area in which the opposition of the civil society was more effectively coordinated was the transition to civil rule programs of both the Babangida and the Abacha regimes. Babangida tried to win an initial legitimacy for his regime on coming to power in August 1985, by promising respect for human rights and the handing over of power to a civilian regime in 1990 (later extended to 1992 and subsequently to 1993). However, it soon became clear that Babangida's transition program was a ruse and that the "hidden agenda" of the program was to ensure that he succeeded himself in office. In an attempt to achieve this aim, the transition program was constantly manipulated. The manipulation of the program led to an intensified opposition by the civil society against Babangida's self-succession bid. Most of the civil society groups decided to coordinate their campaign against military rule by coming together to form an umbrella organization, the Campaign for Democracy

(CD) on November 11, 1991. The CD campaigned vigorously for the termination of military rule no later than October 1992 and persistently called for the convening of a sovereign national conference.

The CD played a vanguard role in the widespread opposition to the annulment of the universally acclaimed free and fair June 12, 1993, presidential election presumably won by M. K. O. Abiola. The annulment was seen as an attempt by Babangida to actualize his self-succession bid and was therefore greeted with widespread demonstrations in various parts of the country. The massive opposition forced Babangida to step down from office and hand over power to a hastily contrived Interim National Government (ING) under the leadership of Shonekan. The civil society regarded the ING as an illegal contraption and called for the declaration of the result of the June 12 presidential election. The ineffective ING was subsequently overthrown in a military coup led by Abacha in November 1993. It soon became apparent that Abacha was not prepared to restore the June 12 mandate; rather, he was interested in putting in place another transition program that would result in his perpetuating himself in office. The civil society reacted by organizing nationwide mass demonstrations and strikes that would hopefully cripple the regime and force it to declare the winner of the June 12 presidential election. The period from June to July 1994 can be said to have marked a high point of opposition to military dictatorship in Nigeria in the 1990s. The various groups of the civil society and sections of the political class were joined by the powerful oil workers unions, unions of bank workers, teachers, nurses and midwives, and academic staff, among others in organizing nationwide demonstrations, riots, and strikes that virtually brought the country to a standstill.

Abacha reacted to the highly effective 1994 mass actions by becoming more repressive. The executive committees of the various workers unions that participated in the strikes were dissolved and many of their leaders detained, various human rights and pro-democracy activists were detained, while some critical newspapers and magazines were proscribed with journalists detained. Abiola, the presumed winner of the June 12, 1993, election was subsequently arrested and jailed. The naked repression of the regime included the trial and jailing of some critical army officers and other members of the elite class over what most Nigerians regarded as a phantom coup attempt in 1995. Olusegun Obasanjo, a military head of state of Nigeria (1976–1979) and a vocal critic of the military regimes of Babangida and Abacha, was allegedly implicated in this phantom coup and sent to jail. There was also the outright assassination of individuals who were critical of the administration (including Kudirat Abiola, the activist wife of M. K. O. Abiola). In the face of this naked repression, most opponents of the regime went underground and resorted to clandestine opposition activities like the setting up of an opposition radio, Radio Kudirat, named after the assassinated wife of Abiola. Some members of opposition groups like the Nobel laureate, Wole Soyinka, and some leaders of the National Democratic Coalition (NADECO) fled abroad where they tried to mobilize international opposition against the Abacha regime.

Another form of opposition in Nigeria in the 1990s was that by minority ethnic groups, mainly from the Niger Delta oil producing areas, more ably exemplified by the Movement for the Survival of Ogoni People (MOSOP) led by Ken Saro-Wiwa. These movements were protesting the degradation of their environments and the marginalization of their communities in spite of the fact that the bulk of the oil wealth that sustained the country's economy comes from their land. The execution of Saro-Wiwa and eight other leaders of MOSOP on November 10, 1995, attracted widespread international condemnation and the imposition of various sanctions on the Abacha regime.

With the sudden death of Abacha in 1998, Abdulsalami Abubakar, who succeeded him, set in motion a transition to civil rule program. In March 1999 he released from jail the people who had been imprisoned by Abacha over the phantom coups of 1995 and 1997. Obasanjo who benefited from this amnesty won the presidential election on the platform of the Peoples Democratic Party (PDP), which equally won majority of the seats in the national assembly. The fourth republic has been characterized by a great amount of political instability, ethnic and religious conflicts, with, perhaps, the adoption of the Shari'a law by most of the Muslim-dominated northern states posing the greatest threat to the survival of the fourth republic. Agitations by the oil-producing minority Niger Delta communities have intensified and in some instances, as in the Odi massacre, the Obasanjo administration has adopted repressive measures.

The Obasanjo administration has not been able to come up with meaningful economic policies to resolve the debilitating economic situation it inherited, while the high level of corruption among Nigerian politicians and other members of the elite, in the face of massive poverty and misery, have created disaffection and resentment among the populace. Obasanjo's rather dictatorial style as in the periodic increase of the prices of petroleum products in the face of massive opposition has further helped to aggravate the level of disaffection. The threat of instability was equally heightened by the outcome of the 2003 presidential and general elections that returned Obasanjo to power for a second term while the PDP won massive victories in the national assembly, and the governorship and legislative elections at the state level. The opposition parties refused to accept the outcome of the elections claiming that they were massively rigged, a charge corroborated by both local and international observer missions.

The 1990s can be characterized as a decade in which postcolonial Nigeria experienced an unprecedented amount of civil society activism against military repression. The period between 1993 and 1994 during which a sustained and coordinated opposition was mounted against the annulment of the June 12, 1993, presidential election can be regarded as the pinnacle of opposition politics in postcolonial Nigeria. The opposition groups achieved some amount of success but could not really achieve much in the face of repression by the authoritarian military administrations. Ethnic, sectional, and religious divisions, as well as the failure of these largely elitist, urban-based opposition groups to form meaningful and creative alliances with the rural dwellers, negatively affected their effectiveness. Nevertheless, the eventual disengagement of the military from politics and the inauguration of the fourth republic after the death of Abacha can be attributed to the rather sustained opposition to military rule by the civil society. Unfortunately, the performance of the civilian administration under Obasanjo has not been encouraging. There is still rampant corruption in the midst of the worsening impoverishment of the overwhelming majority of the Nigerian populace while Obasanjo constantly exhibits dictatorial tendencies.

J. I. DIBUA

See also: **Nigeria: Industry, Oil, Economy; Nigeria: Military Rule, 1983–1999.**

Further Reading

Dibua, J. I. "The Structural Adjustment Program and the Transition to Civil Rule in Nigeria." In *Democracy, Democratization, and Africa*, edited by L. A. Thompson. Ibadan: Afrika-Link Books, 1994.

Momoh, A. "Some Associational Groups and the Transition to Civil Rule in Nigeria." In *Democratisation in Africa: African Perspectives*, edited by O. Omoruyi et al. Vol. 2. Abuja: Centre for Democratic Studies, 1994.

Naanen, B. "Oil-Producing Minorities and the Restructuring of Nigerian Federation: The Case of the Ogoni People." *Journal of Commonwealth and Comparative Politics*. 33, no. 1 (1995).

Osaghae, E. E. *Crippled Giant: Nigeria Since Independence*. Bloomington: Indiana University Press, 1998.

Shettima, K. A. "Structural Adjustment and the Student Movement in Nigeria." *Review of African Political Economy*. 56 (1993).

Nile Valley: *See* Stone Age (Later): Nile Valley.

Nilotes, Eastern Africa: Origins, Pastoralism, Migration

The Nilotic peoples of eastern Africa are conventionally placed in three separate groups on the basis of linguistic classification. These are Southern (or Highland), Eastern (Plains), and Western (Lake and Rivers) Nilotes, each of which is comprised of several individual languages and dialects. Linguists consider these three branches to be subdivisions of the language family known as Eastern Sudanic, which in turn is a subdivision of one of the primary branches of the Nilo-Saharan language phylum. Compared with the much larger Niger-Congo and Afroasiatic phlya, Nilo-Saharan is particularly diverse, which may indicate that it is the second oldest African language phylum after Khoisan. Based on the reconstructed distributions of earlier forms of Nilo-Saharan, this phylum probably first evolved in the area between the Ethiopian Highlands and the White Nile. Subsequent splintering and fusion of different groups as well as interaction with speakers of Afroasiatic and Niger-Congo languages led, over several millennia, to the different branches and subbranches found today.

In terms of modern ethnic groups, Southern Nilotes, with the exception of Tatog-speakers of the Loita-Mara/Serengeti area, are comprised mostly of the various Kalenjin communities of Kenya. The latter are divided into Southern Kalenjin (e.g., Kipsigis, Marakwet, Tugen, Nandi) and Northern Kalenjin, of whom the Pokot, who inhabit areas of the Central Rift to the west of Lake Baringo up to the modern Kenya-Uganda border, are the only representatives. The remaining Kalenjin speakers occupy much of the adjacent highlands to the west and south of the Pokot. Eastern Nilotes can be broadly divided into Bari and non-Bari speakers. The latter has a much more diverse composition, and includes the Maa, Teso, and Lutoko language clusters. With the exception of Lutoko speakers, who like the Bari are found in Equatoria Province, southern Sudan, most eastern Nilotes inhabit the central Rift Valley and parts of the adjacent highlands, between Lake Turkana in the north to the southern edge of the Masai Steppe in central Tanzania. They include the Jie, Teso, and Karimojong of western Uganda; the Turkana, Chamus, and Samburu of northern and central Kenya; and the Maasai, Arusha, and Parakuyo of southern Kenya/north-central Tanzania. Western Nilotes are believed to have originated between the Bahr el Ghazal and the White Nile. Today, they are concentrated in three main areas: southern Sudan, along the White Nile, the Bahr el Ghazal and adjacent wetlands (e.g., Nuer, Dinka, Shilluk); north-west Uganda and adjacent areas between Lake Albert, the Victoria Nile, and Lake Kyoga (e.g., Acholi, Padhola, Paluo); and on either side of the Winam Gulf, on the eastern side of Lake Victoria (Luo, Busoga).

Virtually all of these modern groups are associated with cattle and small-stock herding, either, as in the case of the Maasai, Dinka, Samburu, and Karimojong as specialist pastoralists, or, more widely, as mixed agropastoral groups. Since there is no evidence for local, indigenous domestication of either cattle or ovicaprids (sheep and goats), these species must have been introduced to the region from further north. The expansion of herding economies across eastern Africa, therefore, was probably intimately related to the southward movement of Nilotic speakers. The combined archaeological, historical, and linguistic evidence suggests that this took place in a gradual, piecemeal fashion rather than in a single or limited number of major population movements. Ecological variables, including the natural distribution of vectors that transmit livestock diseases such as Trypanosomiasis, Bovine Malignant Catarrhal Fever, and East Coast Fever, as well as climatic changes and the distribution of grazing lands would have provided a number of constraints and opportunities to newly immigrant populations, in addition to those offered by the social and historical contexts in which these occurred.

Linguistic evidence indicates that the earliest Nilo-Saharan speakers were food collectors, and it is conceivable that speakers of these early forms were the same pottery and stone-tool-using, gatherer-hunter-fishers whose settlement and burial remains have been found at numerous points along the Middle Nile in central Sudan. This material is generally attributed by archaeologists to the "Khartoum Mesolithic," and dates to between approximately 7,500 and 3,500BCE. The linguistic evidence also suggests that, within the Nilo-Saharan phylum, food production—in the form of cattle keeping and grain cultivation—first took place among proto-Northern Sudanic speakers, from whom all Nilotic languages were ultimately derived. In this regard, it is interesting that the presence of domesticated cattle and ovicaprids is attested at a number of sites in the Middle Nile area, including Kadero and Esh Shaheinab, by the fourth millennium BCE.

The earliest securely dated archaeological evidence for the presence of pastoralism further south comes from the site of Dongodien, east of Lake Turkana (Kenya), where a large assemblage of sheep/goat remains and some cattle bones have been recovered in association with Nderit pottery, in levels dated to about 2,000BCE. However, most archaeologists and linguistic historians consider that these initial pastoralists were Southern Cushitic rather than Nilotic speakers, originating from the Horn of Africa. At the site of Enkapune ya Muto, in the south-central Rift Valley, near Lake Naivasha, a few domestic ovicaprids and cattle remains have been recovered from a level dated to about 1,990BCE, raising the possibility that domestic stock were also present this far south some four thousand years ago. The majority of Pastoral Neolithic (PN) sites in central, southern, and western Kenya and northern Tanzania, however, date to around 3,000 to 2,000 years ago and so are significantly younger. Although many of these sites are broadly coeval, there is considerable variation between them in terms of the styles of pottery and stone tools in use, the relative proportions of wild to domesticated fauna being exploited, and preferred site location. All of this would imply the existence of a number of distinct communities possibly with different cultural and perhaps linguistic origins, and also different subsistence strategies.

Of the various PN traditions defined by archaeologists, the Elmenteitan is regarded by some scholars as attesting the initial presence of Southern Nilotic speakers in the area (always bearing in mind that linking archaeological entities to linguistic or ethnic groups is notoriously problematic). These sites are found in a broad band running south-westwards from the Naivasha/Nakuru area across the Mara plains, to the edges of Lake Victoria. Most sites date to between 2,300 and 1,300 years ago, with faunal remains indicative of intensive use of domestic stock, as at Ngamuriak, Sambo Ngige, and Maasai Gorge. Sites closer to Lake Victoria, however, such as Gogo Falls and Wadh Lang'o contain more mixed wild and domestic assemblages, including evidence for fishing. For dietary reasons, it is likely that plant foods were also exploited, although the archaeological evidence for the presence of domesticate cereals is extremely limited. By about 200CE, iron-using cultivators of Bantu-stock would have present within the general area from whom crops and iron may have been obtained in exchange for livestock, and possibly other products.

From about 500CE, there is increasing evidence for the adoption of iron by the various PN groups, which seems to have precipitated a marked qualitative decline in stone tool production, especially in the use of obsidian. Around the same time, there was a greater shift toward the type of specialized pastoralism that has often been held to characterize the economies Nilotic speakers in more recent times. This is best exemplified by the evidence from the site of Deloraine, on the edge of the Mau Escarpment (*c.*700–1000CE). At Deloriane, the remains of finger millet have also been recovered, although whether cultivated or obtained through trade with neighboring farmers is uncertain. Around 1200CE, another Iron Age pastoral tradition, characterized by Lanet Ware, appears. This pottery tradition has a widespread distribution, encompassing most of the areas previously occupied by Elmenteitan and Savanna PN groups. It is also commonly associated with a type of earthwork, comprising a sunken cattle pen and attached houses, known as "Sirikwa holes" after the presumed occupants, identified from surviving oral traditions as an early Kalenjin people. Not all scholars agree with this interpretation, however, arguing that the appearance of Lanet Ware correlates far better with the expansion of Maa (Eastern Nilote) speakers, who, to judge from their oral traditions probably reached the northern Rift valley during the ninth century CE, and the southern Rift by seventeenth, perhaps earlier. Another characteristic of these sites is the first attested presence of humped cattle (*Bos indicus* or *Bos indicus/taurus* crossbreed), as at Hyrax Hill and Lanet, both dated to the sixteenth century CE. These were probably obtained, initially, through a network of exchange partners stretching either north to the Horn of Africa where *Bos indicus* had been present since at least the second century CE, or perhaps east to the Swahili coast.

Finally, mention must be made of the expansion of the Western Nilotes that took place over 400 to 500 years, ending in the nineteenth century. The oral traditions suggest that these originated from series of population movements in plains around the White Nile and Bahr-al Ghazal Rivers, precipitated by an initial expansion of Nuer at the expense of their neighbors. Among the other Lwo speakers that were displaced some moved north, giving rise to the Shilluk kingdom by the sixteenth century. Other groups, such as the Pubungu, moved south along the Nile into the savanna around Lakes Albert and Kyoga. Here they encountered various Central Sudanic and Bantu speakers, and frequently managed to gain political power within these communities, with interesting results. For example, the absorption of a Western Nilotic elite by the Alur, resulted in a language shift from a Central Sudanic base to a Nilotic one. In contrast, the Lwo clan known as Bito established their hegemony within the emerging Banti Nyoro kingdom, which subsequently became the Bunyoro state. Other clans related to the Bito included the Hinda, who formed royal dynasties along the western side of Lake Victoria and the Hima who rose to political power in Rwanda and Burundi. In these contexts, however, despite gaining access to political power, the immigrant Nilotic speakers adopted the Bantu language of their host community. Not all Lwo-settled areas developed a royal tradition, however. The Padhola who settled the forests west of Mount Elgon, for example, had a lineage based system of social and political organization as did the Kenyan Luo. Despite these variations, in virtually all these societies cattle were held to be ritually and symbolically, as well as economically, important, and often had particular associations with leadership and the divinity.

PAUL LANE

Further Reading

Ehret, C. "Nilo-Saharans and the Saharo-Sudanese Neolithic." In *The Archaeology of Africa: Food, Metals and Towns*, edited by T. Shaw et al. London: Routledge, 1993.

Gifford-Gonzalez, D. "Early Pastoralists in East Africa: Ecological and Social Dimensions." *Journal of Anthropological Archaeology.* 17 (1998): 166–200.

Marshall, F. "The Origins and Spread of Domestic Animals in East Africa." In *The Origins and Development of African Livestock: Archaeology, Genetics, Linguistics and Ethnography*, edited by R. Blench and K. MacDonald. London: UCL Press, 2000.

Robertshaw, P. *Early Pastoralists of South-West Kenya.* Nairobi: British Institute in Eastern Africa, 1990.

Spear, T., and R. Waller, (eds.). *Being Maasai: Ethnicity and Identity in East Africa.* Oxford: James Currey, 1993.

Nilotes, Eastern Africa: Eastern Nilotes: Ateker (Karimojong)

Karimojong, the name of one particular community, has been used by some writers as a general designation (as in "the Karimojong cluster") for a larger group of peoples speaking closely related Eastern Nilotic languages in northeastern Africa. The name "Karamoja," for the district in northeastern Uganda where many of this group live, is also derived from it. Most Africanists now use the term *Ateker* as the generic name for the group.

From all indications, the Ateker were the last of the Nilotes to move south from the Sudan, apparently in the early or middle centuries of the second millennium. Typical of African origin sagas, many Ateker traditions which recount migrations from a mythical homeland, often called "Longiro," are highly stylized renderings containing elements of political charter and cosmological affirmation. Nevertheless, one can deduce that ancestral Ateker probably did move out of the southeastern Sudan in two separate streams. One, traveling via the wetter borderlands of western Karamoja, had close interactions with Central Sudanic-, Kuliak-, other Nilotic, and especially Luo-speaking peoples. Many became bilingual and most, although often keeping cultural attachments to livestock, developed a strongly agricultural economy, earning them the nickname *Ngikatapa*, "Bread People." The second stream pushed south through the drier grasslands of eastern Karamoja into the Koten-Magos hill country. Their economic outlook was mainly pastoral, although they also practiced hunting/gathering and dry grain cultivation.

By the early eighteenth century, the Koten-Magos group had begun to fragment, many pushing westwards into central Karamoja, apparently because of population increases linked at least in part to the development of more efficient pastoral systems featuring improved strains of cattle. These systems could be highly productive, but they were also, in many respects, inherently unstable. Their mobility could produce dynamic expansions resulting in fluid frontiers and constant interethnic contacts that might undermine group solidarity. Their livestock was vulnerable to a host of sudden disasters, such as drought, epizootics, and the raids of competitors. Therefore, broad and complex systems of livestock exchange between individual stockmen gave insurance against catastrophe and created bonds that gave some corporeal form to basically amorphous societies. Moreover, animals provided the essence of cultural outlooks, as well as political economies.

The western Ngikatapa groups, although less pastoral, were still open to natural calamities. Their more sedentary systems of cultivation, involving permanent concentrations of larger populations in areas of limited agricultural potential, could tax the resources of fragile ecosystems and bring on terrible famines. By the early eighteenth century, one such occurrence, a famine remembered by some as the Nyamdere, disrupted their communities and caused many to flee. In the course of these movements, Koten-Magos and Ngikatapa elements came into contact with each other in various parts of Karamoja, where some formed new communities, such as the Jie, Karimojong, and Dodos. Combining their agricultural and pastoral skills, they developed mixed farming economies better suited to the environment than either of the older systems had been. Some of the Ngikatapa, however, such as the Loser, Loposa, and Kapwor groups, abandoned Karamoja to migrate westwards to more fertile regions around Mount Otukei where they could maintain their primarily agricultural focus. The formation of the new societies in Karamoja entailed additional fissioning, as people who would become Toposa, Jiye, and Nyangatom moved back into the southern Sudan, and others, who formed Turkana and Iteyo elements, went east to the headwaters of the Tarash River below the Karamoja escarpment in Kenya.

Toward the end of the eighteenth century, another famine, the *Laparanat*, devastated the Ngikatapa around Mount Otukei, and many moved off even further to the west and southwest, some as far as the Nile. Here they formed sections of developing Iteso, Kumam, and Langi. While all retained many aspects of Ateker culture, the three latter groups adopted the Luo speech of neighboring peoples.

Up to about this point, Ateker groups had tended to favor decentralized, egalitarian political forms. In the more mobile communities of the east, political activity was exercised largely by ruggedly individualistic extended families, which functioned—at least ideally—as self-sufficient economic units. For most Ateker, age-class systems with strong generational principles crosscut kinship and territorial groups, however, and, through participation in common rituals, imbued them with their broadest sense of corporate identity. A degree of gerontocratic control was exercised by venerable congregations of senior elders, although some authority might be invested in a few outstanding individuals, too, especially among some of the western societies. Nevertheless, the age-systems could also foster fission, as bands of young age-mates often hived off from parent societies to pioneer new areas and establish new political identities.

During their initial expansions, Ateker communities sometimes had clashes with others, and livestock raiding among the more pastorally oriented was endemic. From the late eighteenth century such conflicts apparently were becoming more frequent. In far southern Karamoja, the Karimojong raided Southern Nilotic peoples and dispersed an earlier group of pastoralists, the Iworopom. Many defeated remnants were absorbed into developing Ateker communities, especially the Iteso, who were also making contacts with Bantu societies to the west and south. In central Karamoja, the Jie and Dodos destroyed a last remaining Ngikatapa group, the Poet, assimilating many. In the far west, the Langi fought a wide variety of peoples, including the Jopaluo, Alur, and Madi. By the latter part of the century they were pushing vigorously to the south and west against the Kumam, Iteso, and Acholi. By then they also had contacts with the powerful Bantu-speaking Nyoro kingdom, for whom many became mercenaries.

The most dramatic expansion of all was that of the Turkana in the east. From the upper Tarash, the Turkana decimated a multilingual confederation, the Siger, already stricken by a serious drought in the early nineteenth century. They then advanced relentlessly across the rugged, arid plains west and south of Lake Turkana against the previous occupants, the pastoral Kor, retreating elements of whom helped form Maa-speaking Sumburu and Cushitic-speaking Rendille. They also drove Southern Nilotes out of the plains and up into highland areas. In a remarkably short time, Turkana thus gained a vast territory and absorbed huge numbers of outsiders.

Competition for resources, especially in the more pastoral regions, became increasingly intense as the century progressed, and soon individual Ateker societies, especially in Karamoja and the Sudan, began battling each other. In the west, internal tensions developed within the Lango and Iteso, leading to further dispersions, and, in the case of the latter, hard fought civil wars by the end of the century.

All this escalating conflict was accompanied by political changes among many of the Ateker. Among some, such as the Jie, Toposa, and Dodos, hereditary firemakers provided a deeper corporate unity, although their authority remained largely religious. With the Iteso, powerful military leaders used territorial bases to forge large confederacies. Similarly, among the Lango, military leadership became greatly expanded and institutionalized. Among the Turkana, hereditary prophet/diviners became emergent centralizing figures who directed their territorial expansion. In addition to these general tendencies to consolidate power in the hands of individual "big men," some Ateker societies altered their age-class systems. Among the Lango and Iteso, gerontocratic functions apparently disappeared altogether. With the Turkana, principles of biological age became dominant over generational ones, facilitating the more effective mobilization of fighting men.

By the eve of the colonial conquest, Ateker peoples were thus having a tremendous impact on the whole course of East African history. They also were proving themselves extraordinarily adaptive, adjusting economic and political features to conform to local conditions, and thus providing a cultural and linguistic bridge between Bantu- and Luo-speaking riverine agricultural states in the west and Eastern and Southern Nilotic- and Cushitic-speaking pastoral nomads in the east.

JOHN LAMPHEAR

Further Reading

Dyson-Hudson, N. *Karimojong Politics.* Oxford: Oxford University Press, 1966.

Gulliver, P. H. *The Central Nilo-Hamites.* London: International African Institute, 1953.

Gulliver, P. H. *The Family Herds.* London: Routledge and Kegan Paul, 1955.

Lamphear, J. "The Evolution of Ateker 'New Model' Armies." In *Ethnicity and Conflict in the Horn of Africa*, edited by K. Fukui and J. Markakis. London: James Currey, 1994.

———. "The People of the Grey Bull: The Origin and Expansion of the Turkana." *Journal of African History.* 29 (1988).

———. "Some Thoughts on the Interpretation of Oral Traditions Among the Central Paranilotes." In R. Vossen and M. Bechhaus-Gerst, eds. *Nilotic Studies.* Berlin: Dietrich Reimer Verlag, 1983.

———. *The Traditional History of the Jie of Uganda.* Oxford: Clarendon Press, 1976.

Muller, H. *Changing Generations: Dynamics of Generation and Age-Sets in Southeastern Sudan (Toposa) and Northwestern Kenya (Turkana).* Soarbrucken: Breitenbach, 1989.

Tarantino, A. "Lango Wars." *Uganda Journal.* 13, no. 2 (1949).

Tosh, J. *Clan Leaders and Colonial Chiefs in Lango.* Oxford: Clarendon Press, 1978.

Vincent, J. *Teso in Transformation.* Berkeley: University of California, 1982.

Webster, J. B., ed. *The Iteso During the Asonya.* Nairobi: East African Publishing House, 1973.

Nilotes, Eastern Africa: Maasai

Maasai pastoralist society is a relatively recent development in the savanna areas of Kenya and Tanzania. The Maa language, today spoken by Maasai, Samburu, Tiamus, Parakuyo, and Arusha communities, is part of the Eastern Nilotic language group, historically found in the border areas of Sudan, Uganda, and Kenya. Linguists theorize that Maa-speaking peoples broke away at least three hundred years ago from an ancestral area near the western side of Lake Turkana, and migrated southward into the high grasslands of the Rift Valley. Maa-speaking society was rooted in cattle-keeping and a decentralized political system in which individuals were organized by age-class, with elders and age-set spokesmen sharing political influence.

Maasai family beside their huts, twine structures covered with clay. When the group moves on, the huts decay. In a new grazing area huts are built again. © SVT Bild/Das Fotoarchiv.

During the seventeenth and eighteenth centuries, Maa-speaking peoples occupied the Rift Valley savanna as far south as the Maasai Steppe in present-day Tanzania, perhaps through interaction and assimilation with indigenous groups such as the Sirikwa. Maa-speaking peoples formed several independent sections linked together by linguistic, cultural, and ecological affinities. The Purko and Kisongo sections occupied the center of Maa-speaking territory. To the north were the Laikipiak and Samburu, to the west the Uasin Gishu and Loosekelai, and to the south the Loogolala and Parakuyo. Maa-speaking society developed in at least two distinct ways: first, through the actual migration of people themselves, and second, through the emergence of new identities from within existing communities.

In the late eighteenth and early nineteenth centuries, a new Maasai identity radiated outwards from the central heartland, spurred perhaps by competition for limited resources of water, salt, and pasturage. This new identity quickly came into conflict with the other Maa-speaking communities. The resulting civil confrontations, known as the "Loikop Wars," saw the disbanding of some peripheral Maa-speaking sections, and the reorganization of others. For example, the Purko and Kisongo sections defeated the Loogolala in the 1840s and then the Laikipiak in the 1870s, scattering the defeated communities and effectively ending their existence as distinct sections. The Parakuyo section, on the other hand, was able to regroup and push further south, filtering into central and southern areas of Tanzania by establishing close relations with neighboring agricultural communities.

The new Maasai identity was grounded in a more specialized form of pastoralism, a more professionalized military use of the *murran* (warrior) age-class, and the increased authority of the *loibon*, the traditional prophet-diviner in Maa-speaking society. The Nkidongi family became the primary *loibon* lineage, producing in succession three of the most influential individuals in Maasai history: Supeet, Mbatiany, and Lenana. The *loibon* was able to gain influence by divining, healing, and overseeing the raids of the *murran*, and he attracted clientele by giving away cattle, acquiring wives for himself, or paying bridewealth for others. As the Loikop Wars dragged on throughout the nineteenth century, the *loibon* gained more effective political authority than ever before in Maa-speaking society.

Maasai themselves generally think of their history as beginning with the emergence of this new identity, or more specifically, with the birth of Supeet around 1778. Maasai remember historical events through reference to the chronological succession of age-sets, providing a source of shared cultural identity. For example, the first age-set widely recognized in Maasai oral history is Tiyioki, whose members were *murran* from 1791 until 1811, the time of the first Loikop Wars. Likewise, Supeet's death is remembered to have taken place during the time when the members of the first Nyankusi age-set were *murran* (1851–1871), and the last Loikop War, during which the Laikipia were defeated, is remembered to have taken place during the time of the Laimer age-set (1866–1886).

In the late nineteenth century, Maasai communities, which had barely begun to recover from the effects of the Loikop Wars, were hit by a series of devastating epidemics. These disasters, which Maasai refer to as *emutai* ("to finish off completely"), further destabilized the beleaguered pastoralists of the Rift Valley. The first two epidemics affected Maasai cattle: bovine pleuropneumonia, which swept through Maasailand between 1883 and 1887; and rinderpest, which arrived in 1891. The cattle diseases were followed quickly by an outbreak of smallpox in 1892, and then a severe famine. Some Maasai were forced to abandon pastoralism temporarily and take refuge with agricultural neighbors. Among the remaining Maasai pastoralists, intersectional cattle raiding became more desperate and violent as the intricate network of relationships built upon cattle loans fell apart. Another period of civil warfare began, but this time with a significant new element, since it coincided with the establishment of European colonial rule in East Africa.

The "War of Morijo" began in the early 1890s as a conflict between Loitai and Purko, two of the stronger Maasai sections which had managed to maintain their cohesion through the time of *emutai*. Added to this conflict was a succession dispute between Lenana and Senteu, the sons of the *loibon* Mbatiany, who had passed away in 1890. Lenana threw his services behind the Purko, while Senteu took sides with the opposing Loitai. But the decisive factor proved to be Lenana's alliance with the British, who were eager to name him a "paramount chief" as a means of consolidating their rule. To the south, Senteu could come to no such agreement with the Germans, who saw Maasai only as antagonists. In 1901 Senteu and the Loitai offered their unconditional surrender and were allowed to rejoin the victorious Maasai communities.

The Maasai-British alliance proved to be brief, as the two sides saw their mutual interests fade quickly after 1900. In 1904 and again in 1911, Maasai in Kenya were moved onto arid reserves, a crippling alienation of land which Maasai unsuccessfully tried to reverse in court. During the twentieth century, Maasai pastoralists on both sides of the Kenya-Tanzania border have seen their land base continue to shrink in the face of restricted wildlife areas and expanding agricultural land use.

CHRISTIAN JENNINGS

Further Reading

Berntsen, J. "Maasai Age-Sets and Prophetic Leadership, 1850–1912." *Africa*. 49 (1979): 134–146.

Kipury, N. *Oral Literature of the Maasai.* Nairobi: Heinemann Educational Books, 1983.

Spear, T., and R. Waller, eds. *Being Maasai: Ethnicity and Identity in East Africa.* London: James Currey, 1993.

Waller, R. "Emutai: Crisis and Response in Maasailand 1883–1902." In *The Ecology of Survival*, edited by D. Johnson and D. Anderson. Boulder, Colo.: Westview, 1988.

Nilotes, Eastern Africa: Southern Nilotes: Kalenjin, Dadog, Pokot

The Southern Nilotes were early arrivals in East Africa from a homeland in the Sudan. Indeed, some linguistic reconstructions place them in the area as far back as the fourth century BCE, although other scenarios have them arriving considerably later. Some suggest they were linked to the Elmenteitan cultural tradition that persisted in southwestern Kenya until the seventh century, and that they practiced a mixed economy of pastoralism and cultivation, augmented by hunting. Others argue that they were specialized pastoralists from an early date.

There is more general agreement that by the beginning of the second millennium, Iron Age Southern

Nilotes had established themselves well into East Africa, where they interacted with earlier Stone Age Southern Cushites, and from them adopted initiation rites involving circumcision, food taboos, and certain sociopolitical structures. Gradually, the Nilotes assimilated or displaced these earlier populations until only a few small pockets of Cushites remained. The Southern Nilotes also appear to have interacted with Kuliak-speakers in eastern Uganda, and, in various places, with Bantu agriculturalists who may have facilitated the emergence of a pastoral focus among Nilotes within broad systems of regional interaction.

By the early part of the millennium, if not before, Southern Nilotes had split into three distinct sub-groups. In the south were Dadog, a vanguard of southern penetration, who eventually pushed down into the grasslands of northern Tanzania. Behind them, in the uplands of western Kenya, emerged the Kalenjin, and, developing separately from them to the north, the Pokot. At this point, all seem to have had decentralized political structures based on similar cycling age-set systems.

By at least the middle of the second millennium, the early Kalenjin inhabited a region from Mt. Elgon and the Cherangany Hills in the north, down across the Uasin Gishn Plateau, to the Kericho-Lake Nakuru area in the south. Their origin traditions often picture a rather mysterious people, the "Sirikwa," as the earlier inhabitants of this area, and link them with the remains of "Sirikwa Holes," semisubterranean structures, found throughout much of it. Deep wells, dams, agricultural terraces, and irrigation systems are sometimes associated with the Sirikwa, as well, although traditions of Maa-speakers attribute them to another ancient people called Il Lumbwa.

Some observers identify the Sirikwa with the early Kalenjin themselves and argue that they were specialized pastoralists for whom milking was especially important. Certainly there are indications that some ancestral Kalenjin and Dadog (who also have Sirikwa traditions) had a strong pastoral focus. Other scholars believe the Sirikwa are better seen as multilingual confederacies of mixed farmers, the products of long interaction between Cushitic and Southern Nilotic elements, and, later, Maa-speaking Eastern Nilotes as well. As such, they may be perhaps better regarded as a cultural "phenomenon" than as an actual ethnic group. Certainly this seems to have been the case with Sirikwa-like groups such as the Oropom and Siger who inhabited the Karamoja-Turkana borderlands northeast of Mount Elgon.

In any case, it is clear that not all early Southern Nilotes were pastoralists. The Pokot branch, for instance, most probably had a decidedly agricultural economy, as apparently did some of irrigation-using Kalenjin of the Cherangany Hills. In addition, an important feature of this "Sirikwa era" were hunter-gatherers from whom were descended Southern Nilotic-speaking Okiek populations.

Many scholars believe that from about the seventeenth century the Southern Nilotes underwent profound transformations. The agents of these changes were in many cases Maa-speakers who began a series of significant expansions into areas previously held by Southern Nilotes and/or "Sirikwa." These advancing Maasai apparently practiced a "new," more vigorously mobile form of pastoralism, which combined with sophisticated military practices and the leadership of powerful prophets (*laibons*), led to the rapid assimilation or dispersal of Southern Nilotes. Sirikwa holes, which had provided defense against earlier raiding, were easily overwhelmed. Some Southern Nilotic traditions dramatically depict the cataclysm as a mountain falling from the sky to scatter earlier population. From this welter of activity, new Southern Nilotic communities were born; "Sirikwa" came to denote old-fashioned ways of earlier times.

By the mid-eighteenth century, agricultural Nandi and Kipsigis societies had been formed from Kalenjin elements to the southwest of Uasin Gishu, though excluded from the plateau itself by Maasai neighbors. To the west, closer to the shores of Lake Victoria, other Kalenjin interacted with Luo- and Bantu-speakers, sometimes adopting their languages while imparting Southern Nilotic cultural forms. In the Mount Elgon area, Kalenjin were forced from the grasslands below to the slopes of the mountain itself where some became plantain-cultivating Sebei. In the Cherangany uplands, Kalenjin-speaking Marakwet, Tuken, Endo, and Keyo agriculturalists, together with neighboring Pokot, were kept from the surrounding grasslands by pastoral neighbors.

To the south, Maasai displaced Dadog (known to them as Il Tatua) and their Cushitic allies from Lolindo, the Serengeti, and the Crater Highlands. Disintegrating into separate fragments, Dadog in small groups of migrating coevals gradually retreated throughout the nineteenth century into less desirable areas deeper into Tanzania, where they adapted themselves to a broad range of new environments. In recognition of their stubborn resistance, the Maasai gave them the nickname Il Mangat, "Respected Enemies." Meanwhile, in the Turkana-Karamoja borderlands to the north, the last of the old "Sirikwa" confederations were defeated and absorbed by other expanding Eastern Nilotes, the Ateker group, by the early nineteenth century.

From about that same time, however, the Maa-speakers began a series of devastating internecine quarrels. In the process, Maasai groups, especially those which contained "Sirikwa" elements such as the Segellai and Uasin Gishu, were crushed and eliminated as competitors with Southern Nilotes. This allowed the dramatic expansion of some Southern Nilotes into grassland environments, where, often absorbing remnant populations, they turned (or perhaps returned) to specialized pastoralism. By the later nineteenth century, for instance, both Nandi and Pokot had evolved strong pastoral sections that were competing successfully with their neighbors for control of pastoral resources.

Attending this reinvigoration, the sociopolitical structures of some Southern Nilotic communities underwent substantial changes. Nandi and Kipsigis borrowed the notion of powerful prophets, whom they termed *orkoiyots*, from defeated Maasai. The Sebei and Pokot developed similar prophets, apparently borrowing the idea from the Sirikwa-like Siger. In all cases, these functionaries became emergent centralizing figures who provided a stronger sense of community integration, and often more effective military leadership, as well. Nandi and Kipsigis also refined their *pororiet* territorial systems, and the Pokot altered their age-class system to an Ateker-like model, in each case to promote military efficiency.

By the eve of the colonial era, therefore, Southern Nilotic societies were among some of the most vigorous in all of East Africa. Over many centuries, they had displayed a remarkable resilience and the capacity to adjust to changing circumstances. As a result, their role in shaping the course of East African history had been profound.

JOHN LAMPHEAR

Further Reading

Ehret, C. *Southern Nilotic History.* Evanston: Northwestern University Press, 1971.
Gold, A. "The Nandi in Transition." *Kenya Historical Review.* 8 (1981).
Goldschmidt, W. *Culture and Behavior of the Sebei.* Berkeley: University of California Press, 1976.
Huntingford, G. W. B. *The Southern Nilo-Hamites.* London: International African Institute, 1953.
Lamphear, J. "The Persistence of Hunting and Gathering in a 'Pastoral' World." *Sparache und Geschichte in Afrika.* 7, no. 2 (1986).
Robertshaw, P., ed. *Early Pastoralists of South-western Kenya.* Nairobi: British Institute in Eastern Africa, 1990.
Sutton, J. E. G. "Becoming Maasailand." In *Being Maasai*, edited by T. Spear and R. Waller. London: James Currey, 1993.
Weatherby, J. M., B. E. Kipkorir, and J. E. G., Sutton. "The Sirikwa." *Uganda Journal.* 28, no.1 (1964).

Nilotes, Eastern Africa: Western Nilotes: Luo

The Luo occupy areas of eastern Lake Victoria, mostly on either side of the Winam Gulf, Nyanza Province, Kenya. Pockets of Luo settlement are also found in southeastern Uganda, northern Tanzania, and parts of Western Province, Kenya. The Luo are speakers of a Western Nilotic language who, according to their oral traditions, first settled in the Nyanza area toward the end of the fifteenth century, where they encountered a number of Bantu language speakers, including the ancestors of modern Abagusii and Logoli. The original homeland of these early immigrants is said to have been in southern Sudan between the White Nile and the Bahr-el-Ghazal, possibly around Wau at the confluence of the Meridi and Sue Rivers. Linguistically, they are closely related to the Dinka (Jiaang) and Nuer (Naath) of southern Sudan, who are also Jii-speaking groups. They also share linguistic and cultural ties with various Jii-speakers in Uganda, including the Acholi, Paluo, Lango, Padhola, and Alur, all of which are said to have migrated from the upper Nile zone at much the same time.

From the available clan histories and genealogies, it appears that Luo settlement of the Nyanza region took place in a number of phases, of which four principal ones are well established. These gave rise to the following four main clusters of Luo found in the area today.

The Joka-Jok (also known as Joka-Ramogi) from Acholiland, who are believed to have been the first Luo group to settle in the Nyanza area, between 1490 and 1600. Joka-Jok settled initially around Got Ramogi, before expanding into other areas including Alego, Uyoma, and Asembo.

The Jok'Owiny, which split from the Alur in northwestern Uganda, arrived in the region between around 1560 and 1625. Their initial area of settlement was around Samia-Bugwe, from where they expanded into Alego.

The Jok'Omolo, which broke away from the Padhola, arrived in the Nyanza area at about the same time as the Jok'Owiny, via Busoga and Ibanda (Uganda), before occupying parts of Samia and Central Nyanza.

A fourth, rather more heterogeneous group, known as the Luo-Abasuba, made up of refugees from Buganda and other neighboring areas, found mostly in South Nyanza and on the islands of Mfango and Rusinga, and who began arriving in the late eighteenth century.

Subsequent disputes and divisions between different sections of these larger groupings, and also responses to environmental change, led to further movements and the formation of various clans and similar descent groups, each with its own particular understanding of history and claims to a particular territory.

The reasons behind the successful expansion of Western Nilotic speakers into the Nyanza region are not well known. One possible explanation is that periodic droughts and famines across the region during the sixteenth and seventeenth centuries (for which there is a growing body of proxy environmental evidence), encouraged groups to move southward from the Sudan in search of new land. Being predominantly cattle-keepers, the early Luo settlers may have been able to colonize less productive areas more suited to livestock grazing than agriculture. Conversely, a period of higher rainfall in the late fifteenth century may have caused longer and higher seasonal flooding of the Bahr-el-Ghazal, thereby reducing the amount of pasture and land suitable for habitation (as happened in the more recent past). This too could have stimulated population movements southward. At present, there is insufficient evidence on which to assess either hypothesis, and it is quite possible that various social and economic factors also contributed to the establishment of Luo settlements in Nyanza.

The oral traditions suggest that, whereas the initial phases of settlement were relatively peaceful, by the time the Jok'Owiny and Jok'Omolo began to expand, relations with neighboring groups such as the Gusii, Logoli, and Kuria had worsened, giving rise to periodic cattle-raiding and warfare. The presence of numerous, potentially fortifiable, stonewalled and earthen ditch-and-bank enclosures across Nyanza may bear testimony to this. The former, known as *ohinga* (pl. *ohingni*) in Dholuo, occur mostly in South Nyanza. Their basic plan consists of an outer, dry stonewall, circular enclosure between two and four meters (approximately 6 and 13 feet) high and at least fifty meters (164 feet) in diameter. Inside this, traces of other structures, such as cattle enclosures and house floors, sometimes also survive. The largest and most impressive example is Thimlich Ohinga in the Macalder subregion. The main enclosure here is about 115 meters (377 feet) in diameter and contains the remains of at least five inner stock enclosures and numerous house platforms.

Over 520 *ohingni* are known in South Nyanza alone. Studies of their distribution indicate a preference for hill-top and upper slope locations, typically within three kilometers (approximately 2 miles) of a permanent water source. They also tend to occur in distinct clusters, with the highest density occurring around Thimlich. Their precise origin remains unclear. Many Luo oral traditions suggest that they were built by Bantu speakers before the Luo arrived. However, finds of pottery similar to that made by modern Luo, and the available radiocarbon dates from Thimlich (which place its occupation in the eighteenth century), indicate that they were also occupied by Luo if not actually originally built by them. Resolving this question requires further archaeological research.

Although a few stonewalled enclosures are known from the northern side of the Winam Gulf (especially in Asembo, Seme, and Alego locations), most of the enclosures in this area consist of a circular earthen bank with an outer ditch. A few more complex types, with outer and inner ditches and internal banks also occur. These are known as *gunda* (pl. *gundni*) in Dholuo, and like the *ohingni*, are believed to have been occupied initially by non-Luo. Some, however, were definitely occupied by Luo, and still in use in the early part of the twentieth century.

By the nineteenth century, and probably earlier, the Luo economy was based on small scale agriculture, cattle-herding and fishing. Land was owned by segmentary, exogamous, patrilineal descent groups. Traditionally, there was no central political authority, and political power was mostly vested in the male elders who headed the different patrilineal descent groups. These often formed alliances with one another, of which there were at least twelve or thirteen such larger associations at the beginning of the colonial period. Known as *ogendin*i (sing. *oganda*), these were composed of several of patrilineal clans or large lineages, and varied in size from 10,000 to 70,000 individuals and had its own leader, or *Ruoth*. Each *oganda* was also associated with a particular "territory." It seems likely, however, that the precise composition and spatial distribution of these changed several times over the centuries, and it maybe that the variable nature and distribution of the *ohingni* and *gundni* across Nyanza are a reflection of this.

PAUL LANE

Further Reading

Cohen, D. W., and E. S. Atieno Odhiambo. *Siaya: The Historical Anthropology of an African Landscape.* Oxford: James Currey, 1989.

Lofgren, L. "Stone Structures of South Nyanza." *Azania.* 2 (1967): 75–88.

Ogot, B. A. *History of the Southern Luo.* Vol. 1. Nairobi: East Africa Publishing House, 1967.

Nilotes, Eastern Africa: Western Nilotes: Shilluk, Nuer, Dinka, Anyuak

The Western Nilotes—the Shilluk, Nuer, Dinka, and Anyuak—form part of the greater Nilotic-speaking peoples of eastern Africa. They reside in southern Sudan with the exception of the Anyuak, who also extend into Ethiopia. Numerically the Dinka have the greatest population, numbering between three to four million. They speak an Eastern Sudanic language of the Chari-Nile branch of Nilo-Saharan.

Although linguistically connected, the migration histories of these Nilotes differ considerably. Shilluk oral tradition remembers that they were led north by their first king and culture hero, Nyakang. Around 1500 they arrived at their present location at the junction of the Sobat and Nile Rivers from a previous southern homeland remembered as "Dimo." The Anyuak, closely related to the Shilluk, also trace their origin to the "country of Dimo" southeast of their present homeland. They were led north by a powerful chief, Gila, a brother of the Shilluk king Nyakang. A quarrel led to a split between the Shilluk and Anyuak prior to Nyakang's arrival at the present-day Shilluk homeland on the White Nile, during which the Anyuak migrated east. Gila's grandchild Cuwai became their first king. The Dinka claim an ancient homeland in northern Sudan. This is supported by linguistic data which shows loanwords from the classical language of Nubia, *Nobiin,* suggesting a cultural and religious connection with the Nubian kingdom of Alwa (300–1300). The Dinka migrated into southern Sudan (*c.*1300–1600) along the eastern bank of the Nile as far as Bor, and then forged across the river three hundred miles northwest. At this juncture they had penetrated into the swamps of the southern Sudan and fully surrounded the Nuer. The Nuer claim they originated from a barren waterless country northwest of their present homeland in a region they identify as "Kwer-Kwong." It is remembered that a leader, Gau, married Kwong giving birth to Ġaa who became the most important Nuer leader, the Land Chief, acquiring the title of "Chief of the Leopard Skin." Some scholars suggest that the Nuer were formerly part of the mosaic of Luo peoples present in Southern Sudan prior to the Dinka arrival.

The politics of the Nilotes vary greatly. The Shilluk have been historically united in a single polity headed by a series of divine kings (*reths*) chosen by primogeniture. The Dinka have been less politically centralized than the Shilluk because of the vast geographical area they occupy. Their language is diverse and each group is internally segmented into small political units with a high degree of autonomy. During times of war, however, they have historically valued intra-group unity and tended towards political and military centralization. In the nineteenth century the Dinka amassed armies of thousands to fight the colonizing Turco-Egyptians whom they expunged permanently from their homeland. Politically the Nuer form a cluster of autonomous communities within which there is little unity. The basic social group is the patrilineal clan and in each community the men are divided into six age sets. Among the eastern Ethiopian Anyuak there is more dry ground available giving rise to closely connected villages and a wider political organization than that afforded the autonomous villages of the western Anyuak in Sudan. The Ethiopian Anyuak historically have had a royal clan and a king while western villages have not.

Religiously Dinka priests (*beny biths)* and Shilluk kings (*reths*) were believed to be divine and their physical and ritual well being were held to ensure the prosperity of the whole land. The large royal Shilluk clan traced descent from their first king Nyakang. Revered Dinka authority figures who were also rainmakers (Masters of the Fishing Spear) were derived from "aristocratic" clans who traced descent from a leader, Ayuel Longar. Dinka priests and Shilluk kings, as sacred leaders could never die a natural death; if severe illness was imminent they were ritually killed, most commonly by burial alive for Dinka *beny biths* and strangulation for Shilluk *reths*. Dinka priests tended to live much longer than Shilluk kings for there was no special stress laid on the maintenance of high standards of sexual activity which the Shilluk demanded of their royal leaders. Neither the Nuer or Anyuak have ritually killed their priests or kings.

Levels of social stratification differ widely among these Nilotes. Along with several classes of royalty the Shilluk are divided into commoners, royal retainers, and slaves. The Dinka possess "aristocratic" and "commoner" clans as do the Anyuak. The Nuer however, recognize only a limited aristocracy tending towards less social stratification than the Dinka, Shilluk, and Anyuak.

Culturally and economically all four groups are patrilineal and polygynous. Marriage among the Dinka and Nuer is marked by the giving of cattle by the bridegroom's kin and both are transhumant taking their cattle to the rivers during the dry seasons. The Shilluk are sedentary agriculturalists with strong pastoral interests (cattle, sheep, and goats). Unlike the Dinka, Nuer, and Shilluk the Anyuak keep some cattle but rely heavily on fishing, hunting, and agriculture. Among the Shilluk and Anyuak spears and sheep, and to a lesser degree cattle, have come to represent bridewealth.

Around 1770, slave raiders from the Islamic kingdoms of Wadai and Darfur forged south, plundering Dinka and Nuer communities in southern Sudan. This era marked the beginning of centuries of slave raids and instability in the region encouraging the Nuer, located on the inner periphery of the Dinka to forge east in large numbers to the Nile. The era was accompanied by drought intensifying ethnic stress and as the Nuer migrated into primarily Dinka and Anyuak territories wars ensued. During this period the Nuer ethnically absorbed many and expelled others. By the twentieth century 70 per cent of the Nuer comprised former Dinka peoples giving rise to the belief that the two were originally one ethnic group; an argument that no longer prevails among historians of the Dinka and Nuer. By the dawn of the Turco-Egyptian conquest of Sudan (1821) the Dinka, Nuer, Anyuak, and Shilluk lacked sharp ethnic boundaries.

STEPHANIE BESWICK

Further Reading

Beswick, S. F. "Violence, Ethnicity and Political Consolidation in South Sudan: A History of the Dinka and Their Relations With Their Neighbors." Ph.D. diss., Michigan State University, 1998.

Burton, J. W. *A Nilotic World: The Atuot Speaking Peoples of the Southern Sudan.* New York: Greenwood Press, 1987.
Crazzolara, J. P. *The Lwoo.* Part I, *Lwoo Migrations.* Verona: Missioni Africane, 1950.
Evans-Pritchard, E. E. *The Nuer.* Oxford: Clarendon Press, 1940.
———. *The Political System of the Anuak of the Anglo-Egyptian Sudan.* London: London School of Economics, 1940.
Hofmayr, W. *Die Schilluk.* St. Gabriel, Modling bei Wien: Administration des Anthropos, 1925.
Johnson, D. H. "History and Prophecy Among the Nuer of the Southern Sudan." Ph.D. diss. University of California, Los Angeles, 1980.
Kelly, R. C. *The Nuer Conquest: The Structure and Development of an Expansionist System.* Ann Arbor: University of Michigan Press, 1985.
Lienhardt, G. *Divinity and Experience.* Oxford: Clarendon Press, 1961.
Perner, C. *The Anyuak Living on Earth in The Sky.* Basel, Switzerland: Helbing and Lichtenhahn. 1994.
Riad, M. "The Divine Kingship of the Shilluk and its Origin." *Archiv Fur Volkerkunde.* Band XIV, 1959.
Santandrea, S. *A Tribal History of the Western Bahr El Ghazal.* Verona: Nigrizia, 1964.
Seligman, C. G., and B. Z. Seligman. *Pagan Tribes of the Nilotic Sudan.* London: George Routledge, 1932.

Nilotic Sudan: ***See*** **Nubia: Banu Kanz, Juhayna, and Arabization of the Nilotic Sudan.**

Nimeiri: ***See*** **Sudan: Nimeiri, Peace, the Economy.**

Njinga Mbande (1582–1663)

Queen of Ndongo

Njinga Mbande became Ndongo's most famous queen and remains a national heroine in Angola today. She was the eldest daughter of King Mbande a Ngola, a ruler who spent much of his long reign both fighting the Portuguese colonization of Angola (begun in 1575) and seeking to centralize power in Ndongo.

Njinga witnessed Ndongo's most serious crisis during her early life. Born in 1582 shortly after the war between Ndongo and Portugal, she saw her brother Ngola Mbande come to power around 1617; she also watched as the kingdom of Ndongo was crushed by the joint forces of the Portuguese governor Luis Mendes de Vasconcellos' army and its Imbangala mercenaries in 1617–1620. The Imbangala, brought from south of the Kwanza by the Portuguese after 1615, were ruthless cannibals who replaced their losses by recruiting new soldiers from among adolescent boys. In 1622, after the disastrous campaigns of Mendes de Vasconcellos, Ngola Mbande sent her from his new capital in the islands of the Kwanza river on a mission to Luanda to negotiate relations between the two countries. Later tradition maintained that when the governor did not offer her a seat (a sign of subjection) she sat on the back of her serving girl to stress the continued independence of her country. During this visit she was baptized as Ana de Sousa and promised to help Christianize her country.

When Ngola Mbande committed suicide in 1624, Ndongo faced a serious succession crisis. Ngola Mbande's son was too young to take up rule, and the primary goal of the previous two kings had been to centralize power and limit succession by primogeniture by eliminating some of the electoral elements in it, especially the role played by the nobility. Njinga, with the approval of the court and the royal officials, declared herself regent of the Ngola Mbande's young son, but soon, when the son was murdered (perhaps at her command) she assumed the royal dignity herself.

Portugal was interested not only in supporting a vassal candidate for the throne, but also in insuring that servile populations (both military and agricultural) once under Ndongo's authority did not flee to Njinga, but continued to provide their services to the new colony of Angola. In the following war both Njinga and Portugal relied heavily on bands of Imbangala mercenaries to fight. Njinga was initially defeated in 1625 and had to withdraw from Ndongo's capital in the Kwanza islands but soon returned to the islands, only to be driven out again in 1628–1629, when her Imbangala allies deserted her.

Njinga fled eastward with her army, and sought to join with Kasanje, the most powerful Imbangala band of the area. She was rebuffed, and underwent initiation as an Imbangala herself. Using Imbangala methods to augment her army, she conquered the kingdom of Matamba, which was to remain her base even when her forces recovered the islands of the Kwanza in the mid-1630s. By 1639 she had regularized relations with the Portuguese colony. In undertaking the Imbangala initiation, Njinga repudiated Christianity, but she never abandoned the idea that she was rightful ruler of Ndongo, and did not propose changes of her own government along those of the Imbangala bands.

During this whole period, Njinga was troubled by claims against her legitimacy, particularly the claim that women ought not to rule. She tried successively being regent to Ngola Mbande's child, and queen to a puppet male king whom she chose, but this was also without success, even though she married two such men in turn. She also played a male role, leading her troops in battle, dressing in men's clothing, and at one point ordering her servants to do similar dressing reversals, and even to sleep together without contact. She was, according to eyewitnesses, both an excellent commander and quite capable of handling weapons such as the battle-axe.

When Dutch forces occupied Luanda in 1641, Njinga sought an alliance with them against the Portuguese who remained grouped around Massangano. The Dutch provided only half-hearted support, but Njinga's army launched very successful campaigns, first into the "Dembos" regions lying north of her domains, and then against Massangano itself, which she narrowly missed taking in 1648. When the Dutch were driven from Angola in 1648, Njinga abandoned her offensive, but quickly fought the reinforced Portuguese army to a standstill, causing them to sue for peace in 1654. The final peace treaty, concluded in 1657 recognized Njinga's claims to Matamba and the islands of the Kwanza, called for the liquidation of some Imbangala bands, required her to return to Christianity, and returned her sister, captured in 1646, to her.

The last years of Njinga's reign were spent seeking a suitable succession to her rule. She had no children and sought to head off claims by either dissident nobles or the Imbangala elements in her army to replace the royal family of Ndongo as rulers. She sought compromise by readmitting missionaries and becoming a practicing Catholic herself, arranging a marriage with her sister, whom she named as successor, with Njinga Mona, the Imbangala leader, and by promoting another noble family, of Ngola Kanini to favorable positions. She negotiated Portuguese support for her plans in the treaty of 1657.

Her death in 1663 was followed by a struggle between Imbangala and Christian-legitimist factions, with occasional Portuguese interventions. After her sister died in 1666, partisans of Ngola Kanini and Njinga Mona contested the kingship, and it was not until 1681 that the line of Ngola Kanini finally won out. The descendants of this family, also known as the Guterres, ruled Njinga's kingdom for the next century. Njinga's struggle to be recognized as legitimate female ruler had significant implications, as some of her most important successors, such as Veronica I (1681–1721) and Ana II (1742–1756) were women.

JOHN THORNTON

See also: **Angola; Kongo; Ndongo, Kingdom of.**

Biography

Born in 1582. Sent to Luanda negotiate relations between Portugal and Angola in 1622. Baptized as Ana de Sousa and promised to help Christianize her country. Defeated in battle against the Portuguese in 1625. Sought an alliance with the Dutch forces against Portugal in 1641. Continued resisting the Portuguese until they agreed to a peace treaty in 1654, which was finalized in 1657. Died 1663.

Further Reading

Birmingham, D. *Trade and Conflict in Angola: The Mbundu and Their Neighbours under the Influence of the Portuguese, 1483–1790.* Oxford, 1966.

Heintze, B. *Studien zur Geschichte Angolas im 16 und 17. Jahrhundert.* Cologne, 1996.

Miller, J. C. "Nzinga of Matamba in New Perspective." *Journal of African History.* 16 (1975): 201–216.

Thornton, J. K. "Legitimacy and Political Power: Queen Njinga, 1624–1663." *Journal of African History.* 32 (1991): 25–40.

Nkomo, Joshua Mqabuko Nyogolo (*c.*1917–1999)

Zimbabwean Politician and Nationalist Leader

Joshua Nkomo is generally considered the founding father of Zimbabwe nationalism, from the generation of Nelson Mandela rather than Robert Mugabe. He officially began his political career in 1952, when he was elected an officer of the All-African Convention. In that capacity he accompanied Godfrey Huggins to meetings in London as a representative of African opinions concerning the proposed Central African Federation. He stood for election to the Federation Assembly in 1953 but lost. He continued to be politically active and in 1954 was elected president of the Bulawayo chapter of the African National Congress (ANC). In 1957 he became national ANC president.

In September 1959, while Nkomo was out of the country, Federation Prime Minister Edgar Whitehead banned the ANC and arrested many of its top leaders. Rather than face arrest by returning home, Nkomo remained in London where he established an ANC exile office. He was elected president of the new National Democratic Party (NDP), short-lived successor to the banned ANC, in October 1960. He led the NDP delegation to the Southern Rhodesia Constitutional Conference in London in 1960–1961. Initially accepting a United Federal Party (UFP) proposal granting Africans fifteen of sixty-five parliamentary seats, his party's rejection of it caused him to disassociate himself from the plan.

In December 1961, the Southern Rhodesia government banned the NDP. Again, Nkomo was out of the country, this time in Dar es Salaam. With the support of nationalist leader the Rev. Ndabangi Sithole, Nkomo formed and assumed the presidency of a new organization, the Zimbabwe African Peoples' Union (ZAPU) in 1962. Traveling widely to call attention to the Rhodesia problem, Nkomo won United Nations recognition of the issue of African rights and independence in Southern Rhodesia in 1962.

Shortly after Nkomo's his return to Rhodesia, in September 1962, the Whitehead government banned ZAPU. Nkomo was arrested in October and restricted for three months to Kezi, near Bulawayo. Throughout 1963, he was repeatedly rearrested and released. He and Sithole split over strategy during this time, with Nkomo taking the more hard-line stance in opposition to the rising power of the extremist, pro-white, Rhodesia Front (RF) Party. It was at this time that Sithole formed the rival Zimbabwe African National Union (ZANU), with Robert Mugabe and James Chikerema. Ian Smith and the RF came to power in April 1964 and a new wave of arrests, including Nkomo's, quickly followed.

Restrictions on his movement and long periods in jail and rural detention camps filled most of the next ten years, with brief releases in order to meet with British emissaries engaged in talks over Rhodesia's Unilateral Declaration of Independence (UDI) in 1966, 1968, and 1971. The Smith regime released him in December 1974, for a new round of constitutional talks in Lusaka.

Intense competition and bitter rivalries for leadership of the Zimbabwe nationalist movement erupted into the open during late 1974 and continued in 1975, as international pressures, including sanctions, on the Smith regime to agree to a settlement, mounted. Nkomo briefly joined other African leaders under the umbrella of a reconstituted African National Congress (ANC) for yet another round of inconclusive talks with the RF government at Victoria Falls. This arrangement soon collapsed, as ZAPU and ZANU factions fought among themselves. By late 1975, Nkomo's ZAPU was emerging as the moderate alternative, in contrast to ZANU under its new leader, Robert Mugabe.

From December 1975 to March 1976, Nkomo and Ian Smith held a series of inconclusive informal weekly talks, bringing Nkomo even sharper criticism from other nationalist leaders. Later that year, Nkomo and Mugabe formed the Patriotic Front (PF), in preparation for another round of negotiations with Smith at Geneva and the British and Americans at Malta. Their position was for an unconditional transfer of power to the African majority and the talks ended without an agreement and with an intensified armed struggle appearing likely. Nkomo set up ZAPU military headquarters in Zambia and used his authority to help arm and recruit Zimbabwe Peoples Revolutionary Army (ZIPRA) fighters, with Soviet support.

The Smith government's "Internal Settlement" agreement with Bishop Muzorewa, Sithole, and Chief Chirau preserved white minority power while granting token African political rights under a new "Zimbabwe-Rhodesia" constitution. In March 1978, Nkomo and Mugabe denounced it and declared that the armed struggle would continue. They also agreed to meet with British and American officials to set terms for another attempt at a negotiated agreement granting legal independence and full majority rule.

In 1979, under pressure from front-line presidents and Commonwealth leaders meeting in Lusaka, all parties agreed to a new constitutional conference under British sponsorship at Lancaster House in London, to begin in September 1979. The PF alliance between Mugabe and Nkomo held through three difficult months of negotiations leading to reluctant agreement to a less than ideal constitutional settlement in December.

Nkomo returned home in January 1980 to begin organizing and campaigning for scheduled February elections. Robert Mugabe announced that ZANU (PF) would contest parliamentary elections as a separate party, thereby ending the PF alliance and making ZAPU (PF) the main, de facto, opposition party. Drawing nearly all of its support from the minority Ndebele-speaking population of the south, Nkomo's ZAPU predictably finished a distant second in the elections.

Mugabe became prime minister of the new Republic of Zimbabwe and in March he formed a coalition government which included only four ZAPU cabinet appointments. Nkomo was offered and accepted the Home Affairs portfolio. In January 1981, Nkomo was demoted to Minister without portfolio. Conflict and rivalry intensified as Nkomo fought off pressures from ZANU to merge the two parties. In 1982 Nkomo was sacked from Cabinet after caches of illegal arms were discovered on his properties and he was accused of plotting a coup.

Nkomo continued to criticize Mugabe's increasingly forceful calls for creation of a one-party state in Zimbabwe, while complaining that the ZANU (PF) regime was persecuting and killing ZAPU members and supporters in Matabeleland. Mugabe charged that ex-ZIPRA "dissidents" were waging a divisive, anti-government terrorist campaign in the province and deployed elite, North Korean-trained soldiers from the Fifth Brigade to restore order. Nkomo charged that Fifth Brigade units were engaged in a politically and ethnically motivated extermination campaign against ZAPU. In March 1983, fearing for his safety, he fled to Botswana and then to Britain. Threatened with losing his seat in parliament, he returned to Zimbabwe in August. By then, he was ready to discuss the possibility of a ZANU-ZAPU merger, as part of a peace agreement for Matabeleland and in the interest of national unity.

Negotiations were slow and painful. In October 1984, with elections coming in 1985, ZAPU held its first party congress in ten years. Nkomo again rejected the idea of a one-party state and was reelected ZAPU leader. Following ZANU electoral gains, and ZAPU losses in June 1985, Nkomo agreed to reopen unity talks with Mugabe, eventually producing an agreement in December 1987. In 1988, Nkomo was appointed co-vice president, third-highest post in government, and minister of local government. ZAPU was merged into a unified ZANU-PF. Nkomo accepted this diminished status and used it to help supporters in Matabeleland during his remaining years in government and public life.

He had largely retired from public life by 1995. He died on July 2, 1999, leaving Zimbabweans debating the political future of the country in his wake.

JAMES J. ZAFFIRO

See also: **Mugabe, Robert Gabriel; Zimbabwe: Second Chimurenga, 1966–1979; Zimbabwe (Rhodesia): Unilateral Declaration of Independence, and the Smith Regime, 1964–1979; Zimbabwe (Southern Rhodesia): Federation; Zimbabwe (Southern Rhodesia): Nationalist Politics, 1950s and 1960s; Zimbabwe (Southern Rhodesia): Urbanization and Conflict, 1940s; Zimbabwe: Zimbabwe-Rhodesia, Lancaster House and Independence, 1978–1980.**

Biography

Joshua Nkomo was born in Matobo District near Bulawayo. Attended local mission schools and worked as a truck driver before going to South Africa in 1941 for secondary education at Adams College, Natal and post-secondary at the Jan Hofmeyer School of Social Science, in Johannesburg, where he trained as a social worker. Returned to Rhodesia in 1947. Hired as the first African social worker by Rhodesia Railways. Obtained a B.A. in social sciences from the University of South Africa in 1951. Appointed general secretary of the African Employees Association of Rhodesia Railways in 1951. Active in Zimbabwean national politics throughout his life. Contracted prostate cancer, and died July 2, 1999.

Further Reading

Davidow, J. *A Peace in Southern Africa: The Lancaster House Conference on Rhodesia, 1979*. Boulder, Colo.: Westview Press, 1984.

De Waal, V. *The Politics of Reconciliation: Zimbabwe's First Decade*. Capetown: David Philip, 1990.

Herbst, J. *State Politics in Zimbabwe*. Harare: University of Zimbabwe, 1990.

Kriger, N. "The Zimbabwean War of Liberation: Struggles Within the Struggle." *Journal of Southern African Studies*. 14, no. 2 (1988): 304–322.

Mandaza, I., and L. Sachikonye, eds. *The One-Party State and Democracy: The Zimbabwe Debate*. Harare: SAPES Books, 1991.

Martin, D., and P. Johnson. *The Struggle for Zimbabwe*. London: Faber and Faber, 1981.

Mitchell, D. *African Nationalist Leaders in Zimbabwe: Who's Who*. Salisbury, 1980.

Moyo, J. N. *Voting for Democracy: Electoral Politics in Zimbabwe*. Harare: University of Zimbabwe, 1992.

Nkomo, J. *The Story of My Life*. London: Methuen, 1984.

Sithole, M. "Ethnicity and Factionalism in Zimbabwe National Politics, 1957–1979." *Ethnic and Racial Studies*. 3, no.1 (1980): 17–39.

Stoneman, C., and L. Cliffe. *Zimbabwe: Politics, Economics, and Society*. London: Pinter, 1989.

Nkore: *See* Great Lakes Region: Karagwe, Nkore, and Buhaya.

Nkrumah, Kwame (1909–1972)

Kwame Nkrumah left for the United States in 1935. He studied there and in Britian. It was while he was in Britain that he received an invitation from the United Gold Coast Convention (UGCC) to return home to become its full-time secretary, which he accepted after some hesitation. He arrived in Ghana on December 16, 1947.

Five months before his arrival, the UGCC had been launched with the aim of ensuring that "by all legitimate and constitutional means, the control and direction of the Government shall within the shortest possible time pass into the hands of the people and their chiefs." Though led exclusively by the upper-elite of lawyers, business magnates, and intellectuals, the UGCC had nonetheless succeeded in arousing strong nationalist and anticolonial sentiment throughout the country and opened a number of branches.

Nkrumah became an instantaneous success and soon won over thousands to the fold of the UGCC. However, he broke away from the UGCC and formed his own party, the Convention People's Party (CPP), on June 12, 1949. By the end of 1950, the CPP had eclipsed the UGCC as the more dynamic party, and its leader had become the most popular nationalist leader the country had ever known. It is not surprising, therefore, that at the first general election held in February 1951 (when Nkrumah was serving a prison sentence for the "positive action" that he had declared on January 9, 1950), the CPP swept the polls, winning thirty-four out of the thirty-eight popularly elected seats. Nkrumah was released to head the government.

During his first administration, from 1951 to 1954, Nkrumah adopted a pragmatic and laissez-faire approach and succeeded in promoting social, economic, and political developments including infrastructure development (roads, railways, and communications), free and compulsory primary education for children between the ages of six and twelve, the opening of numerous primary and secondary schools, training colleges and the new University College of Science and Technology, and a new salary structure and daily wage for workers. Politically, Nkrumah introduced a new local government system which drastically reduced the powers of the traditional ruling elite and compelled the British government to introduce a new constitution in 1954 that granted internal self-government by the introduction of a parliament.

Independence would probably have been conceded in a matter of months after June 1954 but for the sudden rise of the National Liberation Movement (NLM) and the Togoland question, that is, the question of how the British Mandated Territory of Togoland was to be administered on the attainment of independence by Ghana.This was finally resolved by a UN-sponsored vote in 1956, which resulted in a majority vote in favor of the union of British Togoland with the Gold Coast (the former name of Ghana). In August 1956, the new parliament passed the motion for independence and on March 6, 1957, the Gold Coast was declared "free for ever" by Nkrumah.

Nkrumah introduced a number of measures to weaken the opposition parties and strengthen the CPP. Among them was the Deportation Act, under which a number of strong opposition party members supposed to be aliens were deported. The most notorious of these measures was the Preventive Detention Act (PDA) passed in July 1958, which empowered the government to detain anybody threatening the security of the state without trial for five years. Under this Act, sixty-seven opposition members were detained between 1958 and 1960.

Nkrumah's career from 1957 to 1960 was marked by a continuity of the pragmatic and laissez-faire approach of the previous period. He allowed foreign companies and firms to continue to dominate the import and export trade and the mining, insurance, and manufacturing sectors. No restrictions were placed on the transfer of profits abroad while more goods from the dollar areas and Japan were put on the open general license in 1959 and 1960. Thus, the economy of the country boomed, and many new industries were built that increased employment opportunities. But this economic growth was to the advantage of the expatriate firms and companies, while the open door policy resulted in more capital leaving the country than coming in, which in turn caused a steady depletion of the country's foreign exchange reserves.

It was in the field of foreign policy that Nkrumah is best remembered. His policies here were driven by three main objectives, namely, the total liberation of Africa from colonial rule, the union of all independent African states and the integration and cultural renaissance of all black peoples in Africa and the diaspora. He organized the Conference of Independent African States in Accra in April 1958. He followed this up with the All African Peoples' Conference at Accra in December 1958, the All-African Trade Union Federation Conference in Accra in November 1959, and the Conference on Positive Action and Security in Africa held in Accra in April 1960. In addition to these conferences, Nkrumah made the first concrete move toward the formation of African unity by forming a union with Guinea in November 1958, which he expanded into the Ghana-Guinea-Mali Union in April 1961. Finally, in pursuit of his pan-Africanist objectives, Nkrumah went on an official tour of the United States in June 1958.

The period from 1960 to 1966 witnessed an anticlimax of decline, fall, and tragedy. In the political field at home, Nkrumah introduced a new constitution in July 1960 that concentrated power in his hands and turned him into a constitutional dictator who could rule by decree, dismiss any public servant, and override the decisions of parliament. The second constitutional move was made in 1964 when, in conformity with his socialist principles, Ghana was turned into a one-party state. In 1965, in lieu of the planned party elections, he went on national radio to announce the names of the new politicians whom he had selected to represent the 104 constituencies.

In the economic field, Nkrumah abandoned his laissez-faire approach in favor of the socialist approach to economic development, which necessitated active state control and participation in all sectors of the economy and the establishment of a large number of state corporations. By March 1965, there were forty-seven state corporations in operation. Nearly all these corporations were running at a loss by the end of the 1965 due to a lack of trained personnel, lack of proper planning and feasibility studies, inefficiency, corruption, and nepotism. The country was also experiencing an acute shortage of food, manufactured and imported goods, spare parts, raw materials, inflation and acute unemployment.

By the beginning of 1966, the country had gone bankrupt and was on the verge of economic collapse. On February 24, 1966, a coup d'étât was staged through the combined efforts of the armed forces and the police, which led to Nkrumah's replacement by the National Liberation Council.

Nkrumah sought refuge in Guinea. He suffered from skin cancer and was flown to Bucharest, where he died on April 27, 1972. His body was flown to Guinea where it was given a state burial. However, it was later exhumed and flown to Ghana, where it was buried first at his village of Nkorful, and later transferred and buried at the polo ground in Accra where he had proclaimed the victory of the battle for his country's independence.

A. ADU BOAHEN

See also: **All-African People's Conference, 1958; Ghana.**

Biography

Kwame Nkrumah was born in Nkroful in the Western Region of Ghana in 1909. He was educated at the Government Training College at Accra and Achimota, 1926–1930, and taught before leaving for the United

States in 1935. He attended Lincoln University and the University of Pennsylvania, 1939–1943, graduating with bachelor's and master's degrees in economics, sociology, education, theology, and philosophy. In May 1945 he left the United States for Britain and registered as a Ph.D. student at the London School of Economics. On March 7, 1957, the Gold Coast won its independence under the name Ghana. From 1957 to 1966, Nkrumah devoted his energies to promoting the social and economic developments of Ghana; leading the struggle for the liberation of Africa from colonialism; and campaigning for the formation of African unity, an African high command, and an African common market, as well as for the cultural renaissance and unity of all black peoples both in the continent and in the diaspora. He was overthrown in a coup d'état in February 1966, died of skin cancer in Romania in April 1972, and was buried first in Guinea and then in Ghana.

Further Reading

Addo, E. O. *Kwame Nkrumah: A Case Study of Religion and Politics in Ghana*. Lanhanm University Press of America, 1999.
Boahen, A. A. *Ghana Evolution and Change in the Nineteenth and Twentieth Centuries*. London: Longman, 1975.
Nkrumah, K. *Africa Must Unite*. London: Panaf, 1970.
———. *The Autobiography of Kwame Nkrumah*. London: Thomas Nelson and Sons. 1957.
———. *Towards Colonial Freedom*. London: Heinemann, 1962.
Omari, P. *Kwame Nkrumah: The Anatomy of an African Dictatorship*. Accra: Moxon: Paper Backs, 1970.
Sherwood, M. *Kwame Nkrumah: The Years Abroad 1935–1947*. Legon: Freedom Publications, 1996.

Nkumbula, Harry Mwaanga (1916–1983)

Zambian Politician and Opposition Leader

In July 1951, Harry Mwaanga Nkumbula was elected president of the African National Congress (ANC), replacing the founder and president Godwin Akashambatwa Mbikusita Lewanika. As leader of the ANC, Nkumbula participated in several constitutional talks regarding the decolonization of Zambia. His popularity would eventually decline due to his position on the federation issue. African nationalists saw Nkumbula as too accommodating to the views of the colonial government over the question of federation. Although he opposed federation and was instrumental in the formation of the Action Plan in 1952 to fight against the introduction of federation, the Action Council proved futile in the face of government hostility toward the ANC.

The imposition of federation in 1953 lowered the morale of African nationalists for several years. During this period Nkumbula made a fatal mistake of supporting Sir Stewart Gore-Browne's idea of partitioning Zambia, which Nkumbula saw as the only hope for Africans to ever attain a measure of self-government. The idea was greatly opposed by African nationalist and further weakened Nkumbula's position in the ANC.

The coming of federation and Nkumbula's apparent lack of radicalism further cost him the position of number one political leader in Zambian nationalist politics. Kenneth David Kaunda, his secretary general, began to emerge as the next leader of the party. The two leaders began to drift apart during their trip to London in May 1957. While in London, Kaunda was not happy with Nkumbula, whom he accused of spending less time on the nationalist cause. Furthermore, Zambians in London also disapproved of Nkumbula's leadership. Kaunda was urged to take over the leadership of ANC when he returned home. Although Kaunda was not happy with Nkumbula's leadership, he was not willing to remove Nkumbula from the presidency of ANC.

However, events in the country decided Nkumbula's fate. Nkumbula's attempt to deal with dissent in the party led him to dismiss Munukayumbu Sipalo, his private secretary. The move backfired and the *African Times* publicized the unpopularity of Nkumbula and talked of Kaunda as the "man of the moment." Although Nkumbula managed to hold on to power, the rift between him and other leaders grew. Pressure on Kaunda to take over was also mounting. In May 1958 Kaunda went on an extended visit to Dar es Salaam for a World Assembly of Youth Conference. Nkumbula took advantage of Kaunda's absence and dismissed members of the provincial offices who he thought were disloyal to him. The move only served to worsen the impending split. During this period, Nkumbula grew close to Harry Franklin, a European representative for Africans in the Legislative Council in charge of education and social services. Nkumbula also joined the white, liberal-dominated club in Kabulonga and urged other African nationalists to do the same.

By August 1958, the foundations of a breakaway movement were firmly in place. In October Nkumbula was reelected as ANC president. Simon Mwansa Kapwepwe led a breakaway movement, which became the Zambia African National Congress (ZANC) and Kaunda became its president. Nkumbula's political leadership of the nationalist struggle was weakened and he never recovered. ZANC was short-lived and was superseded by the United National Independence Party (UNIP), which was formed after an amalgamation of a number of parties that had emerged following the ban of the ZANC. Kaunda led UNIP.

Meanwhile, in July 1961, Lawrence Katilungu took over ANC leadership when Nkumbula was imprisoned for a driving offence. Katilungu died in a car accident in the Congo in November 1961, and Nkumbula reclaimed his position in the ANC. By this time Nkumbula had lost the leadership of the nationalist struggle that was firmly in the hands of Kaunda's UNIP. However, Nkumbula still had a role to play in the nationalist struggle and this became evident after the December 1962 elections. Neither UNIP nor the white-led United Federal Party (UFP) had enough seats to form a government. It was inevitable that a coalition government was the only answer, and Nkumbula's ANC had the power to decide with which of the two parties to enter into a coalition. Nkumbula's decision demonstrated that he was an African nationalist who considered the interests of Africans to be of paramount importance. While he could have easily and legally entered into a coalition with the UFP, he chose to form a coalition government with the UNIP. The coalition government lasted until January 1964, when the UNIP formed an all-African government following its overwhelming victory in that month's election. The UNIP won fifty-five of the sixty-five main seats while Nkumbula's ANC won the remaining ten seats. From this time until December 1972, when the one-party state was declared in Zambia, Nkumbula remained the leader of the opposition in parliament.

Yet on January 22, 1969, the speaker of the National Assembly, Robinson Nabulyato, refused to recognize the ANC as an official opposition in the National Assembly because of its small number of members. The speaker, who was a founder member of ANC, argued that the ANC could neither form a quorum to execute the business of the House nor a government. Nkumbula, as leader of the opposition, was therefore denied a salary of the leader of the opposition, an official residence, as well as office space in the National Assembly building. Nkumbula ceased to be an important personage in parliament because the UNIP was running a de facto one-party state political system.

Nonetheless, UNIP required Nkumbula's signature to make Zambia a one-party state. While President Kaunda signed the bill on December 13, 1972, to make Zambia a one-party state, it took the Choma Declaration signed between Nkumbula and Kaunda to formally dissolve the ANC and for Nkumbula and his followers to join the UNIP. In June 1973 Nkumbula announced that he was joining the UNIP. In 1978 Nkumbula attempted to stand for the republican presidency, but he was disqualified on account that he had not been a member of UNIP for at least five years in line with a September 1978 amendment of the UNIP constitution. Nkumbula's appeal against the disqualification was turned down by the High Court in November 1978. From that time, Nkumbula's political career was over. In ill health, Nkumbula led a quiet life until his death in 1983 at the age of sixty-seven.

BIZECK JUBE PHIRI

See also: **Kaunda, Kenneth; Zambia: Nationalism, Independence.**

Biography

Harry Mwaanga Nkumbula was born in January 1916 at Mala Village in Namwala in the Southern Province of Zambia. He was educated at Methodist Mission schools and received teacher training at Kafue Methodist Training College, where he qualified as a school teacher in 1934. From 1934 to 1942 he taught at Namwala schools. In 1942 he moved to the Copperbelt where he joined United Missions as a teacher. He was offered a scholarship to study at Makerere College in Uganda. After completing his studies at Makerere he was given a government scholarship in 1946 to study at the University of London where he obtained a diploma in education. He later embarked on studies in political science at the London School of Economics. However, the scholarship was withdrawn because Nkumbula was actively involved in politics. He left London in 1950 and spent a year working as salesman in East Africa. He returned to Northern Rhodesia (Zambia) in July 1951 and settled in his birthplace at Mala as a rancher. In ill health, Nkumbula led a quiet life until his death in 1983 at the age of sixty-seven.

Further Reading

Gertzel, C., C. Baylies, and M. Szeftel, eds. *The Dynamics of the One-Party State in Zambia.* Manchester: Manchester University Press, 1984.

Hall, R. *Zambia 1890–1964: The Colonial Period.* London: Longman, 1976.

Makasa, K. *Zambia's March to Political Freedom.* Nairobi: Heinemann, 1985.

Mulford, D. C. *Zambia: The Politics of Independence, 1957–1964.* London: Oxford University Press, 1967.

Mwangilwa, G. *Harry Mwaanga Nkumbula: A Biography of the "Old Lion" of Zambia.* Lusaka: Multimedia Publications, 1982.

Phiri, B. J. "Zambia: The Myth and Realities of 'One-party Participatory Democracy,'" *Geneva-Africa.* 29, no. 2 (1991): 9–24.

Sikalumbi, W. K. *Before UNIP: A History.* Lusaka: Neczam, 1977.

Nobadia, Makurra and 'Alwa

In the mid-sixth century, a number of ecclesiastical historians wrote of the conversion of the inhabitants of the Nile valley south of Egypt's border at Aswan, thus informing us of the existence of three kingdoms in that region. Nobadia lay closest to Egypt, beyond the Third Cataract was Makurra, and to the south of the Fifth Cataract lay 'Alwa. Later sources, many of them Arab writers, called these peoples Nubians. As early as the third century BCE, the Hellenistic geographer Eratosthenes describes a people known as the Noba living on the west bank of the Nile. By the fourth century they appear to have infiltrated the Kushite empire and assumed dominance upon the collapse of the Kushite monarchy. The Noba who came to occupy Nobadia found themselves in conflict both with the Romans to the north and with the Blemmyes, desert tribesmen from the Eastern Desert who conquered part of the river valley. The Nobadians under their king Silko ousted the Blemmyes in the mid-fifth century and, like the Blemmyes, were alternately allies and protagonists of Roman Egypt.

In the sixth century, as part of the Byzantine emperor Justinian's plans to regain control of the former territory of the Roman Empire and extend the writ of the empire over the peoples beyond its borders, proselytizing missions were dispatched to Nubia. The royal family of Nobadia was converted to Christianity in 543, that of Makurra around 570, and the Alwan king in 580. Hostilities between the kingdoms of Nubia are reported in the accounts of these missionary missions; it appears that while Nobadia and Alwa enjoyed cordial relations, they were both at loggerheads with Makurra.

Between 639 and 641, Egypt was invaded and conquered by the Muslim armies of Amru b. al-As, breaking once and for all direct contacts between Nubia and its imperial Christian patron. The Muslim armies pushed on into Nubia but withdrew after meeting fierce and perhaps unexpected resistance. In 652 another Muslim army advanced as far as Old Dongola, the capital of Makurra to which it laid siege. However, no permanent conquests were made, and after the signing of a treaty known as the Baqt (a reciprocal treaty slightly biased against the Nubians), Egypt and Nubia coexisted until the twelfth century on relatively peaceful terms. In the accounts of the invasion of 652 no mention is made of Nobadia, and the Baqt was a treaty binding "on all the Nubians from the borders of Egypt until the borders of Alwa." This implies that by that date, Nobadia and Makurra were already united into one kingdom and the cultural dominance of the latter, certainly in the fields of art and architecture, are clear by the turn of the eighth century. The region of the former northern kingdom retained a degree of autonomy. It was known as the province of Maris and was governed by a high-ranking official, the eparch, known to the Muslims as the "Lord of the Mountain" or the "Lord of the Horses," who seems to have been primarily responsible for Nubian-Muslim relations. He was originally based in the old Nobadian capital at Faras but later his seat was moved to the hilltop fortress of Qasr Ibrim.

'Alwa remained independent, although links between the two Nubian royal families may have been close and the matrilineal succession practiced in both kingdoms seems to have occasionally placed an Alwan on the throne of Makurra, and vice versa.

The whole of Nubia shared a common culture united both by the Christian faith and by the use of common languages. Although the Meroitic language may have survived into the later fourth century, it was thereafter replaced by Greek as the official language, with Coptic used primarily in religious contexts. Eventually Old Nubian came into use, largely replacing the other languages by the late Christian period. Arabic was also employed, and became more common to facilitate interaction with Egypt and the Muslim traders in Nubia, and also as a result of an influx of Arabic speakers into the region.

The culture of the early pagan Nubians was firmly rooted in local traditions. In funerary culture and religion, one can readily recognize traits going back several thousands of years, to at least the Kerma culture. The arrival of Christianity, which gradually percolated down throughout the population, caused a fundamental change. The new ideology made obsolete the need to physically manifest one's worldly status through grandiose tomb monuments and grave goods. The earlier Nobadian kings, buried at Qustul and Ballana near Abu Simbel under massive tumuli, had been accompanied to the grave by sacrificed individuals, camels, dogs, horses, and abundant material possessions. In stark contrast, the insubstantial nature of later burials is highlighted by the fact than not one single royal burial has been identified and the one royal tombstone known—that of King David of Alwa—found at his capital Soba East near Khartoum, is on a small roughly hewn slab of marble.

Nubia's Christian culture drew heavily on the Middle East and Egypt for its inspiration, but eventually developed with a distinct character of its own. Among the clearest manifestations of Christianity are the abundant churches found throughout the Nile valley, from the First Cataract as far upstream as Sennar on the Blue Nile. Some of the earliest churches were inserted into preexisting temples that were modified to suit the needs of the new religious practices. The major Nubian centers showed great architectural vitality. At Faras a sequence of increasingly grandiose churches was built on the same site over a period of approximately 150 years, culminating in the Cathedral Church of Paulos dedicated in 707. At Old Dongola there is a similar situation, with several very large churches being constructed, demolished, and rebuilt within the first two centuries of Christianity. With the uniting of the two northern kingdoms, the architectural norms established at Old Dongola were applied to the north; the Paulus cathedral at Faras is a provincial copy of the Church of the Granite Columns at the metropolis. Similar churches were also constructed within the Alwan capital, although the relative importance of, and direction of influences between, the united northern kingdoms and its southern neighbor cannot at present be assessed, largely because of the very limited amount of archaeological work undertaken within 'Alwa.

A particular characteristic of Nubian churches was the profusion of paintings that adorned their walls, and after the introduction of vaulted roofs, their vaults.

Excavations of the Paulos cathedral at Faras in the early 1960s, a building that had been totally engulfed in sand in the late Christian period, revealed a treasure house of mural art, with over 140 individual compositions on up to four superimposed layers of plaster, spanning from the early eighth until the fifteenth centuries. The large number of paintings, together with the many inscriptions from the building, allowed a detailed chronology of artistic styles to be developed and, at least for the later period, the discovery of many more paintings in the Monastery of the Holy Trinity at Old Dongola is opening up new horizons of inquiry.

The Nubians excelled in the production of fine painted pottery. The earliest pottery in the north drew on late Roman stylistic traditions, while in 'Alwa the highly decorated polychromatic pottery, known as Soba Ware, copied designs from the repertoire of the wall painter. Pottery was produced in great quantities at a number of centers. Faras and Old Dongola may have dominated the scene, and their products seem to have been traded widely. The main economic base of the Nubians was agriculture, largely along the banks of the Nile, and with the aid of the newly introduced water wheel, the *saqia,* to allow large scale irrigation for much of the year. Trade in the staple products of central Africa—among which slaves figured prominently—was also important, particularly to the monarchy. The terms of the Baqt stated that the Makurran king was obliged to deliver 360 (or 400) slaves annually, along with produce, to the Muslims at the First Cataract.

Although the Baqt did much to stabilize relations between Makurra and Egypt, there was a number of outbreaks of hostilities between the two powers, the expedition of King Cyriacus in about 748 to Fustat (Cairo) showing that the Muslims did not always have the upper hand. However, with the rise to power of the Ayyubid dynasty, followed by the Mamluks in the thirteenth century, Muslim armies, aided and abetted by various claimants to the Makurran throne, operated extensively in northern Nubia. The first Muslim ruler occupied the Makurran throne in 1323, while the throne hall of the kings at Old Dongola was converted to a mosque in 1317. Old Dongola was abandoned as the capital in the later fourteenth century and the court was established at Derr. There, as the Kingdom of Dotawo, a Christian enclave survived at least as late as 1485 but had vanished by the time of the arrival of the Ottomans in the sixteenth century. The fate of Alwa is less easy to document. Many of its churches appear to have been in ruins by the thirteenth century, although a Kingdom of Soba was still in existence around 1500, when it was conquered by the Abdallab Arabs or the Funj.

DEREK WELSBY

See also: **Nubia: Relations with Egypt.**

Further Reading

Adams, W. Y. *Nubia: Corridor to Africa*. London: Allen Lane, 1977.

Vantini, G. *Christianity in the Sudan*. Bologna: EMI, 1981.

———. *Oriental Sources Concerning Nubia*. Heidelberg and Warsaw. 1975.

Welsby, D. A. *The Medieval Kingdoms of Nubia: Pagans, Christians, and Muslims along the Middle Nile*. London: The British Museum Press, 2002.

Nobel Peace Prize: *See* Luthuli, Albert; Mandela, Nelson; Tutu, Desmond.

Nok Culture: Terracotta, Iron

Nok has been described as one of the early centers of sculptural tradition, second only to Egypt. Its sculptures are terracotta figurines and iron implements, with the terracotta works being more extensive: while all the areas excavated thus far have produced terracotta figurines, only a few sites have yielded iron implements. The terracotta figurines and iron implements are widely distributed across northern Nigeria, covering an area of 500 × 150 kilometers. Within this space are found, in addition to the village of Nok, centers including Kegara, Katsina Ala, Tare, Jemaa, old Kafanchan, Wamba, Kachia, Rafin Dinya, Makafo, and Shere. These centers have yielded important objects or figurines that bear a striking resemblance to those found in Nok, which explains why they are all generally referred to under the umbrella term of the Nok culture area.

Terracotta Sculpture

Most of the terracotta sculptures were recovered from alluvial or water lain deposits and originally came to light in the tin mines near the village of Nok. The radiocarbon date of the deposits beneath the sculptures is 925BCE (plus/minus 70 years). This, combined with the specific dates for some of the sculptures in different parts of the Nok culture area, has led scholars to conclude that the date for most Nok sculptures ranges between about 900BCE and 200CE.

It is important to note that while some of the terracotta figurines are naturalistic, others are creative and artistic interpretations. Each terracotta figure was produced through a process or act of adding a little clay at a time, until the whole figurine was formed. In terms of style, both human animal figures shared similar eye shapes; the major features noticeable in all the figurines are the triangular or semi-circular shapes of the eyes. The human figurines are either cylindrical or conical in shape, and are usually adorned with headdresses. In all the large Nok figurines, the lips, ears, nostrils, and pupils are pierced. The piercing of the eyes in Nok culture resembles that of modern Yoruba "gelede" marks, which are stylistic features rather than functional ones. It has been suggested that the people of Nok used the holes deliberately as technical devices for the escape of air during the firing process.

The people of Nok were masters in the use of clay. Unfired clay contains air bubbles and moisture. When clay is fired, it shrinks by about one-tenth. The Nok people understood that the clay must not contain air bubbles to avoid expansion of the holes during the process of firing, which would automatically lead to the cracking of the objects. This sort of sophisticated understanding of the medium's innate qualities underscores the skill of Nok sculptors.

The details of dress and hair style found in Nok sculptures resemble those found today among some groups in the Plateau State of Nigeria and the Benue River Basin such as the Tiv, the Dakakari, the Ham, and the Jebba. Nok culture shares numerous similarities with Ife culture. Both cultures are the only ones in Africa that produced life-sized or nearly life-sized human figures. While Ife arts are characterized by an idealized naturalism in both human and animal representations, Nok art displays extreme stylization in human figurines and great naturalism for animal figures.

Iron Works

The earliest evidence of the use of iron in Nigeria is found at Taruga. Taruga is about thirty-five kilometers south of Abuja. It lies in a group of hills west of Gurara River, a tributary of the Niger River. Excavations carried out in the area indicate that smelting operations were carried out in the valley. The archaeological finds here include wrought iron, a quantity of iron slag, quantities of domestic pottery, a number of figurines, and a small concentration of charcoal.

The radiocarbon date of the excavated charcoal samples is 440BCE (plus/minus 140 years). The radiocarbon date of iron objects is 280BCE (plus/minus 120 years). A number of other iron smelting furnaces excavated from Taruga produced radiocarbon dates ranging from the fifth to the third centuries BCE. An occupation site in the village yielded ten furnaces. The charcoal sealed in the base of one of the furnaces yielded a radiocarbon date of 300BCE (plus/minus 100 years). The layer on which a terracotta figure was found in the same excavation yielded a radiocarbon date 440BCE (plus/minus 140 years), while the iron slab itself yielded a radio carbon date of 280BCE (plus/minus 120 years), thereby confirming the fifth through the third centuries BCE the iron age in the Nok culture area. Since no earlier evidence of iron technology has been found in Nigeria to date, there is reason to suspect that iron smelting spread to other parts of Nigeria from here.

The origin of iron smelting technology found in Nok has been a matter of enormous controversy. Some scholars have asserted that the knowledge of iron came from outside the culture area. One theory is that the iron technology in Nok originated from Meroe, in the present-day Republic of Sudan, the capital of the ancient empire of Kush, which was destroyed around 400. It had been argued that, following the destruction of the empire, some people migrated westward along the southern edge of the Sahara desert, carrying with them the knowledge of iron and iron smelting. From here, it has been postulated, the iron technology diffused into the Nok culture area. In view of the archaeological evidence, which convincingly demonstrates that Nok iron-smelting technology predates the fall of the Kush Empire, this theory seems untenable. Evidence may yet emerge of trans-Saharan diffusion from North Africa, but until conclusive evidence pointing to diffusion of iron into Nok from outside the culture area become available, it is reasonable to assume that the iron smelting technology may have evolved from within the region.

LEO C. DIOKA

See also: **Ife, Oyo, Yoruba, Ancient: Kingship and Art; Igbo-Ukwu.**

Further Reading

Fagg, B. "The Nok Culture in Prehistory." *Journal of the Historical Society of Nigeria*. 1, no. 4 (1959).

———. *Nok Terracottas*. London, 1979.

Shaw, T. *Nigerian Pre-history and Archaeology*. Ibadan: Ibadan University Press, 1975.

———. "The Nok Sculpture of Nigeria." *Scientific American*. 244 (1981): 154–166.

Tylecote, R. F. "The Origin of Iron Smelting in Africa." *West African Journal of Archaeology*. 5 (1975): 1–9.

Nonqawuse and the Great Xhosa Cattle-Killing, 1857

Little is known about the life of Nongqawuse, yet she has become one of the most famous figures in the history of the Eastern Cape and the Xhosa people. She was probably born sometime in the early 1840s. In 1856 the adolescent Nongqawuse was living with her uncle, Mhlakaza, near the Gxarha River, which was just outside the border of colonial British Kaffraria. In April of that year she and a younger girl named Nombanda were sent to drive birds away from the maize fields when two strangers called to them from a nearby bush. The strangers told the girls that the entire Xhosa community would soon be reborn but that all cattle must be slaughtered, as they had been raised by people contaminated by witchcraft. Furthermore, people should prepare for this rebirth by the building new gain pits, cattle enclosures, and houses. However, when the girls went home to report what they had been told, no one believed them.

The next day they returned to the same spot, and once again the strangers appeared and told Nongqawuse to go directly to her uncle and tell him that they wanted to see him after he had purified himself by slaughtering a cow. Mhlakaza followed the instructions and four days later accompanied Nongqawuse to the field where he heard voices which repeated the earlier prophecies. Mhlakaza then reported this to Sarhili, ruler of the Gcaleka state and nominal king of the Xhosa, who was eventually convinced to issue a formal command that all the people should follow the orders that the strangers had given to Nongqawuse.

The message then spread to other Xhosa rulers, including those living in colonial territory. Ravaged by years of colonial aggression and a recent outbreak of a lung sickness among their cattle, many Xhosa people partially obeyed the prophecies by slaughtering or selling some cattle. When the date for the expected rebirth (the full moon of June 1856) passed without incident, Xhosa society became more polarized, as those who believed the prophecies blamed those who did not, and had not followed its dictates, for its apparent failure.

In January 1857 Nonkosi, a young girl who lived in British Kaffraria, reported seeing strange people who repeated the prophecies to her. This gave the cattle-killing movement renewed momentum within the colonial territory. Violence between believers and nonbelievers disrupted the planting season, and more cattle were slaughtered. Some chiefs supported the movement; others opposed it. Opportunistic colonial officials took advantage of this chaos to seize thousands of Xhosa to work on settler farms and to imprison Xhosa rulers, such as Maqoma of the Rharhabe, who had fought against colonial conquest.

By June 1857 mass starvation caused the cattle-killing movement to fade away. The cattle-killing controversy left as many as 50,000 Xhosa dead and upward of 150,000 displaced. As many as 400,000 cattle had been slaughtered. Within British Kaffraria, 60,000 acres were taken from the Xhosa and given to white settlers. In 1858, the colonial police invaded Sarhili's weakened kingdom and drove him further east into Bomvanaland.

After the cattle-killing, Nongqawuse and Nonkosi were detained by the British, who forced them to dictate "statements" about their roles in this event. They were most likely released in 1859. For the rest of her life, Nongqawuse lived in obscurity; she died around 1898 near the Eastern Cape town of Alexandria.

There are many different opinions concerning the origins of this series of events. At the time, colonial officials justified their enslavement of the Xhosa and possession of their land by claiming that the chiefs, particularly Sarhili, had orchestrated the prophecies in the hopes their starving people would invade British territory. Today, Xhosa people believe a similar conspiracy theory, which maintains that colonial agents, perhaps Governor George Grey himself, hid in the bush and pretended to be Xhosa ancestors telling Nongqawuse the prophecies. The cattle-killing, therefore, is thought to be part of a colonial plot to destroy Xhosa resistance to colonial conquest. In some versions of this story, Nongqawuse is even portrayed as a colonial agent. It has become a common saying to describe a lie as a "Nongqawuse tale."

There are many other interpretations of the cattle-killing. As early as the 1930s, Elizabeth Dowsley identified the relationship between lung sickness and cattle-killing. In the 1950s and 1960s, it was seen as either the result of missionaries teaching biblical miracle stories or as a "pagan reaction" to the increased colonization. Jeff Peires, an historian of the Xhosa people, explains it in terms of Christian influence specifically emanating from Mhlakaza, who had once been a convert at a mission station. However, Helen Bradford has demonstrated that there is absolutely no evidence for this claim. Her explanation is that the cattle-killing movement, in which women played a prominent role, arose because Xhosa men had engaged in mass child abuse and incest. However, there is no compelling evidence for this conclusion, either. Jack Lewis points out that too much emphasis has been placed on explaining the ideology of the prophecies, but not enough on the material reasons explaining why people heeded them. According to Lewis, some chiefs attempted to use the movement to centralize their authority in the face of increasing colonial power. Tim Stapleton argues that the movement was, at least in part, directed against the traditional aristocracy, whose power was based on cattle patronage, which had been discredited by continual defeat at the hands of the British and weakened by cattle disease. Powerless, many chiefs sanctioned cattle-killing because they had no other choice. Julian Cobbing has pointed out that it is possible that colonial officials, whose records provide the bulk of evidence for historians, exaggerated the millenarian nature of the movement to conceal their destruction of Xhosa society as an irrational national suicide.

TIMOTHY J. STAPLETON

See also: **Hundred Years' War, 1779–1878.**

Biography

Born sometime in the early 1840s. In the mid-1850s she lived within the Gcaleka Xhosa state of King Sarhili, which was located just over the eastern border of British Kaffraria. She lived with her uncle Mhlakaza who was an advisor to Sarhili. In 1856 she reported being visited by long dead ancestors who promised a national rebirth of the Xhosa people if they slaughtered their cattle and refrained from planting their crops. After the cattle-killing she became an obscure figure and died around 1898 near the Eastern Cape town of Alexandria.

Further Reading

Bradford, H. "Women, Gender, and Colonialism: Rethinking the History of the British Cape Colony and its Frontier Zones, 1806–1870." *Journal of African History.* 37 (1996): 351–370.

Dowsley, E. D. A. "An Investigation of the Circumstances Relating to the Cattle-Killing Delusion in Kaffraria, 1856–1857." Master's thesis, Rhodes University, 1932.

Lewis, J. "Materialism and Idealism in the Historiography of the Xhosa Cattle-Killing Movement 1856–1857." *South African Historical Journal.* 25 (1991): 244–268.

Peires, J. B. *The Dead Will Arise: Nongqawuse and the Great Xhosa Cattle-Killing Movement of 1856–1857.* Johannesburg: Ravan Press, 1989.

Stapleton, T. J. "Reluctant Slaughter: Rethinking Maqoma's Role in the Xhosa Cattle-Killing (1853-1857)." *International Journal of African Historical Studies.* 24, no. 2 (1993): 345–369.

North Africa, Ancient: Urbanization

It is ironic to note that the roots of urbanization can be traced to the development of rural activities such as the domestication of animals and crop cultivation. Such a crucial change in lifestyle, from the hunter-forager to settled, and further to the creation of urban centers, marked a fundamental, irreversible step in human history. Additional factors that led to urbanization are many but they can be summed up as an adaptation to the acquisition of a new skill, such as metallurgy, or change in critical circumstances, for instance, environmental.

The domestication of animals and agriculture led to a food surplus for the first time in human history, which also allowed a number in the community to be relieved of food production duties, allowing for the development of other skills. In ancient Egypt, the surplus was achieved as a result of the population gaining an understanding of the Nile's annual cycle, and therefore knowing when to sow and harvest for the maximum gain. As a result of such advances people also began to recognize the advantages of living with others with whom there were neither blood ties nor a compulsion to live together, rather making a choice for mutual benefit. Simply put, without a surplus of food there would be no urban development.

The idea of creating towns because it could be for the benefit of nonkinsmen was a radical departure from any society up to that point, and yet the concept appears to have gained acceptance fairly rapidly, as soon as the material gain was obvious. Different forms of benefit existed, security perhaps being primary among them, after which location was the single most important question that had to be dealt with. The most prosaic of reasons would be taken into consideration first, such as the presence of a reliable source of clean, defensible water and a location that is free of disease. It is not by chance that Egyptian cities would be founded along the Nile, with the desert providing additional security from foreign attack.

Other factors that impacted on the setting included both the spiritual and the temporal. For instance, if a location was of some religious importance or the ruler had a residence there, that alone could persuade followers or subjects to live in the immediate vicinity. Along strictly economic lines, trade was another powerful deciding factor in a town's location, whether because it fell at a trading crossroads or a prominent terminus, such as a port, as was the case with Carthage.

Cities were built behind walls with a gate or gates to control access to the interior, with the wall itself becoming one way that a town could be defined, and any growth could be more easily regulated. Having people within also made the business of taxation an easier prospect, as did the charging of tolls to outsiders who wished to gain entry or to trade. The size of the walls themselves did not always exist solely for the purposes of security; often they were oversized to impress visitors, (potential) enemies, or for an aesthetic preference. Not to be underestimated too is the sense of belonging to a community that could be very powerful should the need to defend the town be required. With the security this guaranteed, trade also tended to flourish.

The growth in number of non-food-producing citizens was a matter that a king had to deal with carefully, so as not to offend the producers. Religion was often used to this end, giving the ruler an inherent power to demand that the citizens do as instructed. It also worked in the urban centers to persuade subjects to work on building projects that would benefit the town as a whole, such as the walls, roads, stores, temples, and palaces. Masons are, therefore, one of the earlier examples of a skilled worker removed from food production. They were soon followed by all those professions that became necessary to a functioning town or city: merchants, priests, craftsmen, public officials, and transport specialists.

Again it was the advent of surpluses that created a need for an organized transport system, whether to move the food to other parts of the kingdom or into storage. And linked to the storing of food was the growth of literacy and mathematics out of necessity to record details such as dates of floods, quantities harvested, exports, costs, and the like. Once the surpluses had been organized, and storage and transport were both available, then the possibility of regular trade arose, and with it the need for additional skills and skilled occupations. Also at this point there came into being a mercantile class, who in North Africa were fortunate to maintain some very lengthy trading contacts with foreign powers.

Profits from trade would go to the trader and the ruler, who now had to be supported by a ruling class, either political or religious, in order to assist with the day to day ordering of the town. Taxation, a concept alien before urbanization, was also needed to pay the public officials' wages. The erection of public buildings such as temples and stadiums helped to set the city apart from the village, an attempt to impress the food producers, and showed the people where the surplus money had been spent. Increased wealth also allowed citizens to enjoy leisure time, so that the arts also found an environment in which to flourish, creating a class of painters, sculptors, and so forth.

Memphis, the onetime capital of Egypt, was founded around 3100BCE and managed to maintain its importance for nearly two thousand years, until Thebes became the new capital. It is said to have been the largest city in the world with a population of more than 30,000. The other major city of ancient Egypt was Heliopolis, which was founded in 2900BCE. However, it was another five hundred years before it reached its maximum importance when it became the center of sun worship, with Ra moving up to become the state deity (which illustrates how important the role of religion can be upon the atmosphere and cultural life of a city).

Although it was in Egypt that urbanization had the best pedigree it seems not to have had more than a passing influence on the rest of the coast, or indeed Africa south of the Sahara. West along the coast, however, the Phoenicians founded Carthage around 800BCE. The city grew into a powerful trading city that had influence over most of northern Africa and the western Mediterranean. It was this influence that eventually brought it into conflict with the Roman Empire and led to its being razed in 146BCE. It was the consequent Roman conquest of North Africa that did most to promote the spread of urbanization in the region from one end of the North African coast to the other.

EAMONN GEARON

See also: **Carthage; Domestication, Plant and Animal, History of; Egypt, Ancient: Literacy; Hunting, Foraging; North Africa: Roman Occupation, Empire.**

Further Reading

Alston, R. *The City in Roman and Byzantine Egypt.* London: Routledge, 2002.

Anderson, D. M., and R. Rathbone (eds.). *Africa's Urban Past.* Oxford: James Currey, 2000.

Aufrecht, W. E., N. A. Mirau, and S. W. Gauley (eds.). *Urbanism in Antiquity: From Mesopotamia to Crete.* Sheffield: Sheffield Academic Press, 1997.

Cousins, A. N., and H. Nagpaul (eds.). *Urban Man and Society: A Reader in Urban Sociology.* New York: Alfred A. Knopf, 1970.

Hull, R. W. *African Cities and Towns before the European Conquest.* New York: W. W. Norton and Company, 1976.

O'Connor, A. *The African City.* New York: Africana Publishing Company, 1983.

Rich, J., and A. Wallace-Hadrill (eds.). *City and Country in the Ancient World.* London: Routledge, 1991.

North Africa: Roman Occupation, Empire

The coastal plains of North Africa, which ran across the shores of the Mediterranean Sea, had a favorable Mediterranean-like climate, which supported the production of forest fruits and attracted sedentary population traders and settlers from Greece, Phoenicia, and Rome. Behind the coastal plains were the Atlas Mountains, which provided a home for the pastoral Berbers, who were probably the descendants of survivors of the various phases of Sahara desert habitation periods and of the mysterious "C Group" invaders of Egypt of the Old Kingdom. The mountain communities were not easily accessible to foreign influence, thus they remained in their seclusion for centuries. Beyond the Atlas Mountains lay the seemingly limitless Sahara Desert, the domain of the indigenous

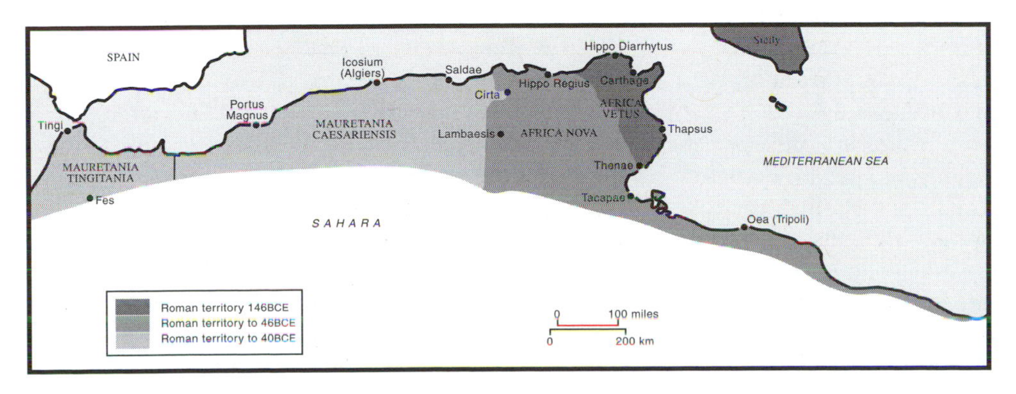

North Africa under Roman occupation.

Roman water conduit in Mohammedia, near Casablanca, Morocco. © Johann Scheibner/Das Fotoarchiv.

Berber tribes variously called Libyans, Nubians, and Moors.

The Berbers of the North Africa were patrilineal, with social organization based on family groups. Villages were conglomerations of families usually from the same ancestral descent. The several villages constituted themselves into a division capable of entering into ethnic confederation with others to ward off external aggression. The Berber confederacies were usually temporary arrangements, which broke up as soon as the common danger was removed. Berbers throughout history never formed a permanent union because each tribe jealously guarded its independence. In spite of their inability to form any formidable single front on a permanent basis, the Berbers were not easy prey to external forces. Invaders had the difficult task of defeating one Berber clan after another and so had to conquer be claimed.

The Phoenicians were one of the best-known foreign visitors to the North African coastal plains. As sailors and explorers, they established several notable colonies as trade stations on the shores of the Mediterranean Sea. The city of Carthage, which was known for its citadel, fine natural harbor, and an extensive hinterland, became the greatest and most prosperous city. Carthage was more than a trade port, it was a republic. Two s*uffetes* in the tradition of Roman consuls, ruled Carthage. The s*uffetes* were elected by the population to preside over the senate where they dispensed justice. By the end of the fourth century BCE, Carthage was a flourishing commercial center, with a population of over 700,000. The wealth of Carthage derived from trade, and tributes paid by vassal states and tithe payments. Carthage maintained a large and powerful army with an armada of seven hundred military ships.

In about 580BCE, a *suffete*, Malchus, led the Carthaginian army into Sicily and conquered almost the entire island. The continued interest of Carthage in Italy led to war with Rome. Rome dispatched an army into Sicily to oppose Carthage when it became obvious that a further delay would play into the hands of the ambitious Carthaginians. The series of wars that were fought intermittently between 262 and 146BCE between Carthage and Rome were called the Punic Wars. After 202BCE Carthage had lost some of its power and influence, although its trading ports along the Mediterranean coast kept it prosperous.

In 149BCE Rome imposed a military blockade against Carthage, and for three years the Carthaginians defended their city. Resistance to continued harassment by Rome failed, and the Carthaginian army was defeated. About 50,000 people were sold into slavery, and the city was razed to the ground. The rebuilding of the city was forbidden by the Roman conquerors.

The destruction of Carthage was the result of the rivalry for military and territorial supremacy between the two world powers. Rome saw Carthage as a dangerous rival to its dominant position.

Several attempts were made by Rome to move settlers to the old site of Carthage. In 122BCE, the Roman Senate unsuccessfully attempted to develop a colony on the site. Julius Caesar, pursuing the last retreating remnants of Pompeii's army under Sciopio II, encamped near the ruins of Carthage, where he claimed he dreamed of an army of men weeping bitterly and uncontrollably. This intimate experience made him appeal for land, resources, and men to rebuild Carthage.

It was, however, the adopted son and successor of Julius Caesar, Augustus, who rebuilt the city. Augustus was a military ruler who realized the strategic importance of Carthage on the Mediterranean shore, seeing it as a gateway to the manpower and material resources of black Africa. By the time of Sentius Sartuinuis, Carthage was once again a leading city, the headquarters of Roman Africa and one of the greatest and wealthiest of Roman cities.

The citizens of Rome's new experiment in Carthage fell into one of two broad categories: the wealthy class and the peasantry. The wealthy class produced the magistrates, the merchants, and the educated elite. They lived as the nobles of Rome and enjoyed more rights than the commoners.

Through interracial marriages, Roman-African families emerged. At least two of the best-known Roman emperors were Africans. The first, Septimus Serverus, was emperor for eighteen years, beginning from 193BCE. Severus was born at Letpis Magna, received a good education, and became a civil magistrate. He also enlisted in the army and rose to the position of commander. During his tenure as emperor, he paid particular attention to African affairs and encouraged the breeding of camels in Africa. He is remembered as a man of enormous energy who instituted the habit of touring the empire periodically to right wrongs done in the course of native administration by appointed consuls.

Roman rule in North Africa was based on a system of land appropriation. The government annexed large areas of land as state property and made grants of land to its citizens and ex-soldiers. The peasant cultivators under this system were taxed to defray government expenses on local administration, to the extent that many of them left Roman territory to farm in the less fertile mountainous country. Those who remained became wage laborers on lands that formerly belonged to their ancestors. The system concentrated the ownership of land in a few nobles who were absentee landlords.

In spite of this, Roman civilization, which was essentially urban, became noticeable in North African civic life. It was possible to see the characteristic Roman basilica, temple, and baths in all these areas. There was one culture, one official language, one law, one literature, and one architecture from the Atlantic to the Nile valley and from the Mediterranean to the Scottish border.

AKIN ALAO

See also: **Berbers: Ancient North Africa; Carthage; Egypt, Ancient: Old Kingdom and Its Contacts to the South: Historical Outline; Egypt, Ancient: Roman Conquest, Occupation: Historical Outline; Ibn Khaldun: History of the Berbers.**

Further Reading

McEwan, P. J. M. *Africa from Early Times to 1800.* Ibadan: Oxford University Press, 1968.

Bennett, N. R. *Africa and Europe from Roman Times to the Present.* London: Africana Publishing Co., 1975.

Davidson, B. *Old Africa Rediscovered.* London: Longman Group, 1970.

Northern Africa

The region of North Africa has been given many names throughout history. To the Greeks, it was all "Libya"; to the Romans, "Africa"; to the Arabs, "the island of the west" (*jezirat al-maghrib*), a term from which scholars derive "Maghrib" (meaning North Africa west of Egypt), and the term from which the Arabic name of Morocco comes (*al-Maghrib*). Geography serves to partially isolate North Africa—with the Atlantic Ocean on the west, the Mediterranean Sea on the north, and the Sahara desert to the south and west—from other parts of the world. It also has served to isolate areas of North Africa from each other. Although at different times in history the region has exhibited degrees of cultural unity, political unity has been elusive; there is no obvious portion of North Africa at which to base a North African empire, and the area's high mountains have resulted in difficult communication and transport across the region. Until relatively recently, North Africa's main economic and cultural contacts were to the north, with the Mediterranean world, rather than to the south, across the Sahara, and with the rest of the continent. This connection with the Mediterranean world and North Africa's involvement with and ties to literate, urban civilizations from a comparatively early period resulted in this region developing differently from the Sub-Saharan Africa.

The earliest African civilization from which we have extensive written records is ancient Egypt. Though urban culture arose in Egypt as far back as 4000BCE, Egypt was not politically united until 3100BCE under the first pharaohs. Geography facilitated Egyptian unification under the legendary pharaoh Menes (whose exact historical identity is uncertain, though scholars believe the actual pharaoh was either Aha or Narmer); the Nile River facilitated transport and communication, and most settlements were along this body of water. Egypt's isolation also aided the formation of a strong, centralized, and protected state: with deserts to the east and west of the Nile River basin and the Mediterranean to the north, potential invaders faced a daunting task in conquering the country. Ancient Egyptian civilization is typically divided by historians into several different periods, roughly corresponding to the following dates: the predynastic period (prior to unification in 3100BCE), the protodynastic period (from 3100–3000BCE), the early dynastic period (3000–2625BCE), the Old Kindgom (2625–2130BCE), the First Intermediate Period (2130–1980BCE), the Middle Kingdom (1980–1630BCE), the Second Intermediate Period (1630–1539BCE), the New Kingdom (1539–1075BCE), the Third Intermediate Period (1075–656BCE), the Late Period (664–332BCE), and the Greco-Roman (also Hellenistic or Ptolemaic) Period (332–30BCE).

Legend has it that Carthage was founded in 814BCE, though this is not confirmed by archaeology. Phoenician settlements in North Africa were initially dependent on their home cities. However, with the growing power of Greece in the eastern Mediterranean, Carthage gradually became an independent power; it was because of Carthaginian resistance to Greek expansion that Sicily and points west did not become Greek territories (though Greek settlements and Hellenistic culture were commonplace). By the middle of the sixth century BCE, the main city of Phoenicia, Tyre, was under Persian control; by the fifth century BCE Carthage was not only independent but was also founding its own North African empire. The Carthaginian Empire at its greatest extent covered North Africa from Morocco to the Egyptian border and extended across the Mediterranean into Spain, Sicily, Sardinia, and Corsica.

Carthage was an empire based on sea-going trade, although it never attempted to extend its control into areas distant from the North African coast. Its focus was on the Mediterranean world, and here it came into conflict with another great regional power of the era: Rome. In 508, 348, and 279BCE these conflicts were solved through treaty; by 264 the competition erupted into warfare. The first of the three Punic Wars began as a struggle for control over Sicily and Corsica. After more than twenty years of warfare, Carthage was defeated and forced to cede Sicily and the Lipari Islands to Rome and pay an indemnity (Carthage was later forced to increase its indemnity payments and cede Corsica and Sardinia to Rome as well). The Second Punic War (218–201BCE) further reduced the Carthaginian Empire's holdings. The attempts of the famous Carthaginian general Hannibal to defeat Rome in Italy proved fruitless; Roman troops arrived in North Africa in 204 and in 201 forced Carthage to pay yet another indemnity, surrender its entire navy, and cede Spain and its Mediterranean island possessions to Rome. Now limited to its North African territories, Carthage nevertheless continued its luckless struggle against Roman domination. Though the previous wars had deprived Carthage of its political and military power, it remained a prosperous trading state; it was (at least in part) Roman greed for the wealth of Carthage's trade that caused the Third Punic War. Again, Carthage was defeated, but by this time it had neither territories nor a military to cede to the victorious Romans. The Roman conquerors instead sold the 50,000 surviving inhabitants of the city (from a population of around a quarter million) into slavery, razed the city to the ground, and seized North Africa as a Roman province.

Egypt was incorporated into the Roman Empire in 30BCE, yet Egypt and the Maghrib experienced Roman authority differently. Egyptian social and economic organization remained much as it had been prior to Roman domination; the principal difference was that Egypt's wealth was now being channeled to a Roman, rather than a Greco-Egyptian, elite. Egypt became one of Rome's main suppliers of grain, Egyptian religion continued to exist (though now deities were often identified with their Roman counterparts, as they had been with their Greek counterparts previously), and Alexandria continued to be a center of educational, scientific, and cultural achievement, as it had been under the Greek Ptolemies. The rest of North Africa underwent significant social, economic, and cultural change.

After the conversion of the Roman emperor Constantine to Christianity in 313 and the subsequent favoring of Christianity in the empire from about 320, Egypt became the center of a number of doctrinal disputes. Alexandria, where Saint Mark had preached in the first century, had become a stronghold of Christianity in North Africa (and the location of Roman persecution of both Christians and Jews before Constantine), and as such attracted numerous religious scholars. Disputes over the nature of the Trinity arose in Alexandria (the "Arian controversy," settled at the Council of Nicaea in 325 is one such instance). Occasionally religious differences resulted in violence, as happened in 391 when the Coptic patriarch and his monks in Alexandria attacked centers of "paganism" and destroyed a subsidiary library of the museum complex in 391 (the original complex, including the library, was destroyed by civil war under the Roman emperor Aurelian in 272); earlier in 415 Hypatia, a noted female neo-Platonist scholar, was murdered.

The Alexandrian church also found religious doctrine as way to assert its independence from Constantinople, from which it was governed following the division of the Roman Empire in 364. Declaring its belief in monophysitism (the idea that Jesus had a single divine nature despite taking on human form), the Alexandrian church held fast to this belief even after the Council of Chalcedon rejected the view in 451. This atmosphere of religious dissatisfaction with Byzantine rule contributed to the ease with which Arab armies took the city in 642.

Though the Byzantines added North Africa to their domains in 533, it took more than ten additional years to pacify the region, as the Byzantines faced resistance from Mauritanian tribes and revolts within their own army (due to lack of pay and insufficient troops). Justinian's rule witnessed a campaign to restore, decorate, and build new churches in North Africa. However, these churches did not always agree with the eastern Church; they supported the efforts of the western Church against the Byzantine emperors prior to Arab conquest.

After the death of the prophet Muhammad in 632, Islam began to spread out of the Arabian peninsula and into other areas of the world, including North Africa. Under the second caliph (successor to the prophet), 'Umar ibn al-Khattab, Muslim armies succeeded in conquering most of the Middle East, including Egypt. In 639 the Arab general Amr ibn al-As and his army began their invasion of Egypt, bringing with them Islam and an end to Byzantine rule by 642. The general also created a new capital for Egypt at an interior site known as al-Fustat, near modern Cairo. The location of the new city was significant. No longer was the capital on the north coast, connecting Egypt symbolically and physically to the Mediterranean and thence to Europe; now the capital was farther south, at a new location not identified with Greek and Roman rule, and symbolically linking Egypt with other Muslim territories to the east. More broadly, the invasion of the armies of Amr ibn al-As inaugurated a new period in Egyptian history characterized by a break from past traditions and the Arabization and Islamization of Egypt.

From Egypt, the Arab armies continued their campaigns in the Mediterranean, to Nubia, and westward across North Africa. By 670 a new base for westward expansion had been established by Uqbah ibn Nafi at the conquered city of al-Qawrayan in modern Tunisia. The invasions and the incorporation of North Africa into the wider Islamic world resulted not only in an increased Arab presence in the region but also in the Islamization of North Africa and the almost complete elimination of North African Christianity (with the exception of Egypt). Islam, though, was not spread in the Maghrib through force or concentrated missionary activity; instead, it spread among the Berbers because it proved an attractive means (through doctrinal differences) by which these tribes could assert their independence from caliphal government.

From their base in Tunisia, Arab armies under Uqbah ibn Nafi and his successor, Abu al-Muhajir Dinar al-Ansari, launched campaigns against Berber tribes in Algeria and Morocco and brought North Africa under direct Arab rule. Yet the process was not smooth, and Arab authorities faced serious Berber revolts throughout the late seventh century, necessitating Egypt's sending of two significant military forces to put down the rebellions. In the meantime, Carthage had remained in the hands of the Byzantines. In 698 Hassan ibn al-Numan began building a new Arab town called Tunis near Carthage, and this, coupled with waning Byzantine and increasing Arab naval power in the Mediterranean led to a Byzantine evacuation of North Africa around the turn of the century. Not until 705 was the Maghrib administratively separated from Egypt, grouped together as *Ifriqiyyah*, made a province of the Umayyad caliphate, and governed from the caliphal capital of Damascus. Umayyad caliphal government did not sit well with the independent-minded Berber tribes, however, particularly given official policies that discriminated against the Berbers despite their conversion to Islam and the religious requirement of equal treatment for fellow Muslims.

At the same time as the Umayyads were facing North African revolts against their authority, they were also facing a revolt in the east that would eventually topple the dynasty and bring about the dawn of the Abbasid caliphate in 750. The Abbasid caliphs put an end to a brief period of local dynastic rule in the Maghrib (under the Fihrids and the Ibaites) when they reconquered eastern Algeria, Tunisia, and Tripolitania (Libya) in 761. However, after a revolt in 800 by factions of the predominantly Arab army of Algeria led by Ibrahim ibn al-Aghlab, the Abbasids ruled largely by relying the eponymous Aghlabid dynasty to actually govern North Africa in the name of the caliph. The remainder of the former Umayyad territory of *Ifriqiyyah* then fell to a number of smaller dynasties: the Rustamids in western Algeria, the Banu Midrar in southern Morocco, and the Idrisids, based in Fez.

By the late ninth century, the Abbasid caliphate had begun to lose its grasp on some of its provinces, and Egypt was no exception. In 868 Ahmed ibn Tulun began governing Egypt for his stepfather Babak, who had been given Egypt as an *'iqta* (administrative land grant) by the Abassid caliph. Ibn Tulun saw his mission a bit differently; however, he quickly established himself as the real ruler of Egypt, assembled his own army (based on slave service), wrested Syria from Abbasid control, and began minting coins with both the caliph's and his own name imprinted upon them. His reign was not only one of expansion and assertion of his own power but also one of prosperity (he left a sizeable budget surplus and larger agricultural yields) and beauty (as evidenced by the immense, splendid, and still-existing mosque he had built near Fustat).

Isma'ili Shi'ites in northern Syria under Ubayd Allah Sa'id had been attempting to undermine the Abbasid caliph's authority, and one way they sought to do this was by sending emissaries to North Africa to convert the inhabitants to Shi'ism and raise a revolt against Abbasid authority. Abu Abdallah al-Shi'i, one of those sent for this purpose, was able to interest enough of the inhabitants of Algeria in his mission to succeed in taking Algeria away from the Aghlabids in 907 before taking their headquarters at al-Qayrawan two years later. The new state, based at the newly built capital of al-Mahdiyyah in northern Tunisia, was named *al-dawla al-fatimiyyah* after the prophet's daughter Fatima.

The Fatimids sought nothing less than the replacement of the Sunni Abbasid caliphate with a Shi'ite Fatimid one, but they did not march at once upon Baghdad. Instead, the Fatimid caliphs turned their attention west and succeeded in seizing the capitals of the Rustamids and the Banu Midrar in 909; in 921 the Idrisids fell to the Fatimids as well. Yet Fatimid rule did not cover all of North Africa. Though they attempted to conquer western Algeria and Morocco, their influence extended little further than the former capitals of those areas—the northern Moroccan coastal cities of Ceuta and Melilla remained in the hands of the Umayyad rulers who had fled to Spain and established their own Umayyad dynasty after the Damascus branch fell to the Abbasid revolt, and Egypt remained within the bounds of Abbasid caliphal rule until 969.

In 969 the Fatimid general al-Jawhar and his Berber army removed Egypt from the Abbasid domain and proceeded to build al-Mansuriyyah, a walled city near the old, ill-planned, and sprawling Fustat. This new city underwent further alteration in 973 when the Fatimid caliph al-Mu izz renamed it al-Qahirah (Cairo, or "the Victorious") and designated it as the new Fatimid capital. Though the conquest of Egypt brought prestige and wealth to the dynasty, it also shifted the attention of the rulers to the east, and the result was the loss of real control over the rest of North Africa a few years later.

The Fatimids, eager to spread their brand of Islam, to establish themselves as focus of loyalty for the Shi'ites under Sunni Abbasid rule, to eventually eradicate the Abbasid caliphate, and to gain a reputation for (and legitimacy from) religious zeal, founded al-Azhar University in Cairo as a center of religious, linguistic, philosophical, and scientific advancement. The building of al-Azhar and the Fatimid desire to end Sunni Abbasid rule did not result in the repression of other religions in North Africa, however. Controlling most of the North African coast, the Fatimids were a dynasty known for their tolerance of non-Muslims, and Christians and Jews continued to serve in high government positions. Although Sunni Islam was officially outlawed under this Shi'ite dynasty, there was no significant persecution of Sunni Muslims either (with the exception of the arguably insane Fatimid caliph al-Hakim [996–1021], who vigorously persecuted all but Ismai'li Shi'ites and insisted all his subjects convert or leave his lands).

Yet even Fatimid economic prosperity could not maintain a firm grip on the Maghrib. With the decline in Fatimid authority in North Africa, the way was open for the establishment of alternative centers of power, and as usual, the Berbers were the primary opposition group. The Lamtuna (from the Sanhajah confederation of Mauritania) controlled the trans-Saharan trade routes, and in the mid-eleventh century, after enlisting the aid of an *'alim* from Morocco, began a drive to both return to the simplicity and purity of the early Muslim community and to conquer more territory in the western Sahara region. This group founded the Almoravid dynasty, one of two Berber dynasties in the Maghrib in this period that was able to (at least partially) unite the region.

By the late eleventh century, the Almoravid dynasty had expanded its authority into all of Morocco and parts of western Algeria and across the Mediterranean to Muslim Spain. The linking of Spain and Morocco was perhaps the most important long-term accomplishment of the Almoravids, as it meant that the relatively isolated Maghrib was now connected and open to European influences (evident in this period in architecture and art).

Despite their accomplishments, the Almoravids were a short-lived dynasty. In the early twelfth century, a new religious group (*al-muwahidun*, the unitarians) was gaining strength in the Maghrib and would go on to found the Almohad dynasty that replaced the Almoravids. The original emphasis of the religious movement was on the oneness of God and the need to return to religious fundamentals; its founder, Abdullah ibn Tumert, also emphasized the idea of an infallible redeemer (*mahdi*), and eventually claimed to be that redeemer. By the late twelfth century, the Almohads had annexed all Morocco, had taken Spain from the Almoravids, and had also extended their control over North Africa as far east as Tripoli and Tunis. Yet this too was a brief dynasty; internal strife and serious military losses to the Christians in Spain in the thirteenth century combined to put an end to Almohad rule, and by 1269, the capital at Marrakesh was taken by Berber nomads.

The Fatimid dynasty lasted longer but fared no better in Egypt, though here opposition came from a different source: its own slave warriors. Military uprisings in the mid-twelfth century led to the Fatimid caliph being de facto replaced by his own vizier and chamberlain, yet even these men could not hold onto the reins of power themselves and asked for assistance from Sunni Muslim leaders and from the Christian crusader states. In 1169 a Sunni army under the command of the Kurdish general Salah al-Din Yusuf ibn Ayyub (Saladin) from Syria staged an invited invasion of Egypt, and Salah al-Din became the Fatimid vizier. By 1171 he had formed his own dynasty (the Ayyubids), returned Egypt to the Sunni fold, and given nominal allegiance to the Fatimids' nemesis: the Abbasid caliph in Baghdad.

From 1171 until 1250, Salah al-Din and his successors ruled Egypt and proceeded to tie it once more to the Muslim world of the east (and hence away from the rest of North Africa). Under the Ayyubids, Egypt became a military force to be reckoned with, not only fighting against the crusaders in the eastern Mediterranean but also establishing once more an Egyptian empire that included parts of Syria and Mesopotamia as well as portions of Arabia (Yemen and the Hijaz), and Palestine (after the fall of Jerusalem in 1187).

From 1250 until 1517, the Mamluks led Egypt again to a position of social, religious, economic, and political prominence in North Africa and the Islamic world. Eight years after the Mamluk dynasty was founded, the last Abbasid caliph (to whom the Mamluks owed allegiance) was killed in Baghdad by the invading Mongol forces from east Asia. Three years later, in 1261, the Mamluks reestablished the Abbasid caliphate in Cairo. Though the caliph no longer had any real temporal or spiritual power, the action was important in that it indicated the Mamluks' desire to be the leader of the Arab Islamic world.

The Mamluks ruled Egypt through a rather peculiar system of semihereditary succession. Upon the death of a Mamluk sultan, one of his sons became sultan, but he did not long remain in that position. Rather, he was sultan only as long as it took for one of the amirs and his corps of mamluks to overthrow him; the system thus ensured the succession of the most qualified military man to the position of sultan. Thus, the Mamluk sultans rose through the ranks of the sultan's mamluks.

By the fourteenth century, the system that had worked so well in the beginning was starting to crumble, as advancement became based not on skill and strength but on family and connections. Egypt also suffered tremendously with the arrival of the bubonic plague in 1348, the Mongol conqueror Timur's gains in Syria in 1400, the growing naval strength of the Portuguese (who replaced Egypt as the dominant power in Indian Ocean trade in the fifteenth century), and the increasing strength of the Turks in southwest Asia. It was, in fact, the Ottoman Turks who brought an end to the Mamluk sultanate in 1517 and incorporated Egypt into the Ottoman Empire.

After the collapse of Almohad rule in the Maghrib in 1269, the region was again fractured into several smaller Muslim Berber dynasties: the Zayyanids (based in Tlemcen and ruling western Algeria), the Marinids (Morocco), and the Hafsids (in eastern Algeria, Tunisia, and Tripolitania). Conflict within and between these Muslim Maghribi states continued until the end of the fifteenth century.

The internal conflict of the Maghrib combined with continued assaults from Europe eventually brought an end to these dynasties. From 1471 to 1505, the Portuguese succeeded in taking a number of coastal ports in Morocco; in 1492, the last Muslim outpost (Grenada) in the Iberian peninsula was retaken by Spain; and from 1505 to 1510, the Spanish began establishing strongholds on the North African coast—most notably at Oran and Tripoli. The arrival of European Christian colonial control in parts of North Africa provoked a religious and political reaction that paved the way for the Sa'di *sharif* (claiming descent from the prophet) dynasty to seize power in Morocco. Expelling the Portuguese (1550) and conquering the state of Songhay (now Mali) in 1591 helped legitimate Sa'di rule, as did the rulers' claims of descent from Muhammad and the support they received from the now powerful Sufi movement. Yet Sa'di rule was soon replaced by the rule of another group claiming *sharif* status—the Alawite family—who established their own dynasty and who still rule Morocco today.

The rest of North Africa did not remain independent but was instead incorporated into the Ottoman Empire (at least nominally) after the fall of the Mamluks in Egypt to the invading Turks. The original Ottoman entry into the Maghrib came as a result of the privateer Khayr al-Din Barbarossa's confrontation with Spain; Barbarossa asked for Ottoman aid and swore allegiance to the sultan in 1518, thus bringing Algeria into the Ottoman realm. Algeria was governed by governors sent from Istanbul, but in 1689, Ottoman troops rebelled against their governor and forced the installation of an officer of their own choosing as governor, thus inaugurating a new period in Algerian history. The *deys* (governors) of Algeria continued to recognize the religious authority of the Ottoman sultan as caliph, yet they governed Algeria independently of Ottoman authority. Though the deys came from the class of Ottoman troops (and not the local population), they were acknowledged and accepted by the people because taxes were light (the government gaining most of its revenue through piracy) and local leaders did much of the actual governing of Algeria. By the eighteenth century, income from piracy was down and taxes were consequently raised, resulting in much internal unrest that contributed to the relative ease with which the French invaded and occupied Algeria in 1830.

Ottoman rule came to Tunisia briefly in 1534 (the Hafsids sought and obtained Spanish protection of their regime in 1535) and finally in 1574. In 1591 Ottoman troops in Tunisia did what those in Algeria would later do: they revolted against the Ottoman governor. This led to a system where Tunisia was governed by a *dey* (governor) and a *bey* (an official who collected taxes and maintained order). Gaining its income through piracy and trade, Tunisia recognized the religious authority of the Ottoman sultan as caliph, but not its political sovereignty. By 1705 the *bey* (Husayn ibn Ali) took control of the government from the *dey* and established a hereditary *beylik*, or dynasty (the Husaynids), that continued to rule Tunisia until its monarchy was abolished in 1957.

Libya was also herded into the Ottoman fold in the sixteenth century, when Ottoman forces seized the city of Tripoli from the Knights of Saint John of Malta. From this conquest in 1551 until 1711, all of Libya was governed as an Ottoman province. In 1711 Ottoman forces in Libya, like those in Algeria and Tunisia also revolted against their governor; cavalry head Ahmed Karamanli established his own dynasty (the Karamanlis) that ruled until an 1835 tribal rebellion, supported by the British, brought back direct Ottoman rule.

Meanwhile, in 1798, the French, concluding that an invasion of Britain was not feasible, sent their military, under the command of Napoleon Bonaparte, to invade Egypt—not so much because Egypt was valuable per se, but instead in order to disrupt British trade and access to India and to have a strong bargaining position in any future settlements with Britain. France occupied Egypt until 1805 (though Napoleon, evading a British blockade off Syria, returned to France in 1799 and took power there). Brief though it was, the French occupation of Egypt was significant and is often dated as the dawn of the modern period in Egypt. The incident began a trend of increasing European involvement and presence in Egypt, brought Egypt in particular and the Ottoman Empire in general into the power rivalry between Britain and France, resulted in the discovery of the Rosetta Stone (which proved the key to Champollion's decipherment of hieroglyphics), resulted in the publication of a massive work (*Description de L'Egypte*) on the country's ancient monuments, and highlighted not only the weakness of the Ottoman-Mamluk government (though under Ottoman control, the Mamluk class continued to do most tasks of government after 1517), but its reliance on foreign power to expel France (done with British assistance in 1803).

One member of this joint Ottoman-British effort to expel the French was a Turco-Albanian adventurer named Mehmet (Muhammad) Ali. In 1805, after quietly gaining the support of the *'ulama* and the elite, Mehmet Ali was installed as viceroy of Egypt during revolts in Cairo against the current Ottoman official. Mehmet Ali's reign in Egypt was characterized by intense activity abroad and at home. At the behest of the Ottoman sultan, Egyptian forces spent eight years (beginning in 1811) pacifying Arabia and putting down the rebellious Wahhabi movement (which posed a threat to Ottoman control of the holy cities of Mecca and Medina), conquered much of the northern Sudan (Nubia) in 1821 in accordance with Mehmet Ali's desire to acquire large numbers of slaves for his army, suppressed a revolt in Crete in 1822, unsuccessfully (due to European intervention) attempted to suppress a revolt in Greece in 1825, and then made a move to wrest Syria from Ottoman control. (The move on Syria was motivated by a number of factors, not least of which was the sultan's failure to honor his promise of make Mehmet Ali the governor of Syria in return for Egyptian aid in Greece.) Militarily defeated by Egyptian forces in 1839 (Sultan Mahmud II died two weeks later) and forced to recognize Mehmet Ali as the governor of Syria, the Ottoman government was in trouble. It was, however, saved from Mehmet Ali by the intervention of Europe. Mehmet Ali did gain one significant concession, however: the hereditary right of rule for his family in Egypt. It was the descendants of Mehmet Ali who governed Egypt until the revolution of 1952.

Internally, Mehmet Ali's reforms earned him the nickname "Father of modern Egypt." He was concerned primarily with making Egypt a military power and hence desired to build the institutions and infrastructure that would facilitate this. By the time he died in 1848, he had seized most of Egypt's productive land for the state, begun the cultivation of long-staple cotton as a cash crop to finance his other reforms, reorganized the military, founded schools, engaged Europeans to train his army and teach in the schools, sent Egyptian students abroad, founded a national press, and began translation projects of European works on the military, education, science, and medicine—all without incurring any external debt.

In 1830 France invaded Algeria, inaugurating the colonial period in Africa (though most colonial conquest did not take place until some fifty years later), setting up a colonial regime there that would last more than one hundred years and occasion one of the most violent conflicts of decolonization in the twentieth century. Resistance to French control was immediate and significant; French control over most of Algeria was not complete until 1872. Nonetheless, European immigration to Algeria, primarily from France, began almost as soon as Algiers was taken in 1830; eventually the French government began offering incentives of land, seed, and favorable trade terms to settlers, gradually transforming Algeria into a settler colony where the European 13 per cent of the population owned most all the productive land and had a virtual monopoly not only on political influence but on access to educational and social services.

By the late 1800s, Mehmet Ali's successors in Egypt had managed to squander most of the country's wealth and had become severely indebted to European creditors as a result of their misguided attempts to continue their ancestor's modernization schemes and to make Egypt more like Europe. European social and cultural influence was also significant, and the European population of Egypt was growing. The completion of the Suez Canal in 1869 meant further European penetration, as the canal was built by a French firm, its shares held in part by Europeans, and the canal itself used primarily for European trade. In 1882 a nationalist rebellion led by Colonel Ahmed Urabi provided Britain the excuse it sought to invade Egypt. Claiming to be protecting the canal, its financial interests, and the rights of the legitimate ruler (Tawfiq), Britain took unofficial control of the Egyptian government in an arrangement often referred to as the "veiled protectorate." Sir Evelyn Baring (later Lord Cromer) served as Britain's top official until 1907, and he reorganized Egyptian governmental policy to meet the needs of Britain. The Egyptian economy was reordered to ensure it met its debt payments to Europe, meaning export agriculture and European-led industry were encouraged and "unnecessary" expenses such as social services, education, and health services were kept to a minimum.

Beginning in the 1830s, under pressure from the French in Algeria and the Ottomans in Libya, the *beys* of Tunisia sought to modernize their state and thus stave off foreign invasion and domination. Yet, as was the case in Egypt, the *beys* did this by borrowing heavily and at extremely high interest rates from Europe; in order to meet its interest payments, the government had to raise taxes, causing unrest among its population. At the same time, Tunisia's foreign population (French, Maltese, and Italian) was growing and thus further disrupting Tunisian society and bringing more interference by foreign governments seeking to protect their subjects. Though the French were set to invade Tunisia in the 1860s to secure their financial interests, pressure from other European governments delayed this plan until the completion of the Berlin Conference, which set up procedures for the European countries to abide by in colonizing Africa, in 1881. The only significant difference between French control of Tunisia and British control of Egypt was that the French instituted a formal protectorate from the first, whereas the British protectorate over Egypt was not formally declared until the beginning of World War I.

Morocco took a different path. Instead of welcoming modernization and rushing headlong into the all too eager arms of Europe, the sultans decided to preserve Moroccan traditions despite the risks of not adopting modern military techniques. The balance of power in Europe helped Morocco for a time, as Britain protected the sultan versus the neighboring Spanish and French forces. Yet in the early twentieth century, the sultan began to move toward modernization, causing a revolt near Fez. This provided the European powers with an excuse to interfere in Morocco. France promised Britain it would not interfere in Egypt if Britain refrained from action in Morocco and promised Spain its own area of Morocco if it too would delay action. Meanwhile the French government loaned large amounts of capital to the sultan and offered its services in running Morocco's customs and postal departments. Internal resistance to the sultan's policies continued, which led to division of Morocco between France and Spain, though the sultan remained the official leader with European protection.

Libya also fell to Europe in the early twentieth century. Italy invaded Libya in 1911 with the goal of creating another Italian-based Mediterranean empire, similar to ancient Rome. Though the Ottomans signed a peace accord with Italy in 1912 recognizing Italian authority, this authority was mostly confined to coastal areas. Resistance to Italian colonialism and to earlier French pressures from French-governed Chad was led by the Sanuysiyyah Sufi order (founded in 1837 and preaching a return to the simple beliefs and lifestyle of early Islam). Yet the leaders of the order were willing to compromise to maintain some autonomy. In 1917 the Grand Senusi (leader of the order), Idris, secured an agreement with the Italians that recognized his own authority in Cyrenaica (the Peace of Arcoma) and two years later engineered another agreement that helped him set up a parliament and got Italian aid for his state. Thus, by the start of World War I, all of North Africa was thus under some form of European control.

During the Great War, most of the fighting in Africa was in the eastern portion of the continent (in German-controlled areas), rather than in the north. The Ottoman Empire was dismembered after the war, but since its North African territories had been only nominally a part of the empire for some time and had been governed by local leaders under European control, the dissolution of the empire brought little real change to the region. Though World War I did not have the impact upon North Africa that World War II did, the period surrounding the conflict witnessed significant change in North Africa. Beginning in the late nineteenth century, and in large part as a consequence of foreign (in this period, European Christian) domination, reformers in North Africa began confronting the issue of how to best change Muslim societies to cope with these new threats. Though the specifics of the ideas differed, one shared theme was that the Muslim world ought to unite against the common foreign enemy and that this sort of unification needed to be based upon a reformulated Islam. Cairo's al-Azhar University became a key center for the propagation of these pan-Islamist ideas, as Muslim students from a variety of African (and other) lands came to Egypt to study and returned to their countries ready to reform their own societies. These early religious reform movements were then transformed beginning in the 1930s into more modern, often secular, nationalist movements that organized political and military opposition to European colonialism.

The effects of World War II upon North Africa were significant. Unlike in World War I, North Africa became a hotly contested area and an important base of operations. Italian-controlled Libya became a target of the British after the fall of France to Nazi Germany in 1940, but the Germans were able to push British forces back into Egypt in 1942. France's colonies in North Africa were administered by the Vichy government after 1941, prompting an Anglo-American invasion of Morocco and Algeria in 1943 and another British drive westward from Egypt the same year. With the region firmly in Allied control by 1943, North Africa then became a base for Allied operations against Europe (Sicily, Italy, and Vichy France).

In Morocco in early 1944, the growing nationalist movement (newly coalesced as the Independence Party, *Hizb al-Istiqlal*) asked sultan Sidi Muhammad and the Allied forces for independence; this earned its leaders arrests on the charge of collaborating with Nazi Germany. Riots ensued, and the sultan gradually became a staunch advocate of nationalism, despite French attempts to keep him in the colonial camp. By 1953 the sultan was viewed as enough of a threat by France that the French authorities in Morocco deported him and his family and appointed a new puppet sultan (this despite the Sidi Muhammad's forced signing of a decree giving his legislative powers to a joint

Moroccan-French assembly). The deportation of the sultan made him a national hero, and Spanish public opposition to French actions in French Morocco made the Spanish zone of Morocco into a haven for Moroccan nationalists. Continued opposition to French power in Morocco and the outbreak of rebellion in Algeria prompted a change in French policy, culminating in the restoration of Sidi Muhammad as sultan and the proclamation of Moroccan independence in 1956. The Spanish, though surprised by the rather abrupt declaration, nonetheless shortly followed suit in Spanish Morocco, and the country was united under the authority of the sultan.

Tunisian independence was achieved with relatively little violence. The leaders of its nationalist movement, headed by the Neo-Destour Party under Habib Bourguiba, had been deported to France when World War II began in 1939; when the Nazis occupied France, the nationalists were first given to the Italian Fascist government (as Germany viewed Tunisia as Italian territory), before being released and allowed to return to Tunisia. When the Allied and Free French forces took Tunisia in 1943, Bourguiba fled to Egypt, whence he began mobilizing further support for independence. Though allowed to return to Tunisia in 1951, Bourguiba's attempts to establish a national parliament met with stiff French resistance, which in turn sparked rural and urban riots, almost paralyzing the economy. By 1954 France was forced to promise independence to Tunisia; the final agreements were signed two years later.

Algeria's struggle for independence was much different than its neighbors to the east and west, though all three had been under French control. As a settler colony with its own powerful lobby in Paris, a land officially made part of France (annexed as three *départements* in 1848), and a target of the French policy of total colonization, Algeria was one colony France could not let go easily; France's loss of Indochina (1954) and Morocco and Tunisia (1956) also affected its desire to retain Algeria. The Algerian war for independence began in 1954 under the leadership of the *Front de Libération Nationale,* or FLN (National Liberation Front), a group advocating social democracy within an Islamic framework. The struggle (including mobilization of international pressure on France, the French left's opposition to continued colonization, extreme violence on both sides, and several settler revolts against French authority in Algeria when the settlers feared France might give Algeria independence) lasted eight years. In 1962, after a national referendum, Algeria became an independent nation.

Egypt, struggling in the interwar years with formal independence but little formal autonomy, continued to have the same problems after World War II. The three-way struggle between the palace, the British, and the Wafd (the nationalist party founded by Saad Zaghlul) offered the country little stability, and both the Wafd and the king had been severely damaged by the 1942 Abdin incident when British Ambassador Sir Miles Lampson ordered British tanks into position near Abdin Palace and then went armed into the palace to inform King Faruq that he could choose between appointing a prime minister sympathetic to the British and abdication; Faruq chose to appoint a Wafdist minister, thus saving his throne but highlighting to the Egyptian people that the country, though formally independent, was in reality anything but. The creation of Israel in 1948 also spawned discontent, as it appeared to many Egyptians (and others in North Africa) to be yet another attempt at foreign colonization in the region. The end result was revolution in 1952, led by a small group of army officers under the leadership of Gamal Abd al-Nasir. The last vestiges of British authority in Egypt were removed in the 1950s with the final agreement on the evacuation of all British troops from the last remaining base at Suez (1954) and the nationalization of the Suez Canal Company in 1956.

Libya, occupied by the British in 1942, became a constitutional monarchy in 1951 under the formerly exiled Grand Sanusi Idris (who then became King Idris I). Yet despite the spiritual leadership of the Sanusiyyah brotherhood and its key role in resisting Italian colonialism, its leader did not function well as king. Though a strong ruler with total control of the military and strong influence with parliament, Idris was viewed as too conservative by the younger and more radical segments of Libyan society (young army officers and the urban middle class), and his government was seen as alienated from these groups, as it was made up of wealthy urbanites and strong tribal leaders. Idris had also refused to become involved in the pan-Arabist movement spearheaded by Abd al-Nasir, and this too affected his popularity. The discovery of vast oil reserves in 1959 also brought vast changes to Libyan society as the country was transformed from an extremely poor nation into one with immense wealth. The result of these divisions in Libyan society was a military coup in 1969 led by captain Muammar Gaddafi (also, al-Qadafi) while Idris was out of the country.

Since achieving independence, North African governments have continued to struggle with their colonial legacies. The colonial period resulted in the drawing of false borders, under or uneven development, the concentration of wealth in the hands of a small number of foreigners and indigenous elites, and political arrangements that facilitated authoritarian governments, and independent governments have variously taken advantage of these factors and struggled to overcome them. Internal problems and the failures of governments to effectively address them, coupled with a desire on the part of some elements in society to redesign their nations in a more culturally and religiously authentic (and less foreign and colonial influenced) manner, have resulted in the formation of various Islamist opposition groups that have attempted to gain power through both legal and illegal means. As majority Muslim an Arab states, North African countries since 1948 have also had to address (both rhetorically and practically) the issue of Palestine and Israel, and this issue has colored their foreign relations.

In Morocco, despite some constitutional changes, the monarchy has continued to govern more or less autocratically while facing attempted military coups in the 1970s and popular protests caused by poor economic conditions in the 1980s. Territorial disputes with Algeria and Mauritania have also caused conflict.

Tunisia, benefiting from the organizational abilities of the Neo-Destour Party, underwent a rapid series of reforms (including advances in education and women's rights and changes to the legal system) after achieving independence. Though a multiparty political system was begun with the 1981 elections, opposition parties have boycotted both national and local elections, and Islamist opposition to Tunisia's increasing secularization and reformist agenda has caused unrest.

Independence did not bring peace to Algeria. Many European settlers fled the country in 1962, including much of the educated class and most technical experts. Attempts to reclaim Algeria's national heritage after more than a century of French rule were complicated by the fact that most educated Algerians were educated in French schools and in the French language; Algeria thus had to import teachers from other Arab countries to teach its population their native language again. Though provincial elections were held in 1967, ten more years would elapse before national elections were held. The FLN-dominated government favored a centrally run, socialist economy; it also began a plan of land reform that included both the formation of state-run farms (from former French estates) and redistribution of lands to landless peasants. By the late 1980s, Islamist opposition to the government (led by the Islamic Salvation Front, *Front Islamique du Salut*, or FIS) had was significant. The FIS won local elections and the first round of national elections in 1991, prompting the government to cancel the second round of elections. The cancellation of elections resulted in waves of violence in Algeria, as the FIS targeted foreigners, governmental and military officials, and a variety of real and perceived opponents to their agenda and as the government responded in kind.

Since 1952, Egypt has changed as well. The socialist-oriented economic policies of Gamal Abdel Nasser were gradually replaced by Anwar Sadat's *infitah* (opening) policies in the 1970s, and the government of president Hosni Mubarak has continued to encourage foreign investment. The continued economic and cultural involvement of western countries in Egypt as well as Egypt's internal problems (including governmental corruption, economic problems, lack of arable land, and rapid population growth) has resulted in a growing Islamist opposition movement in this nation as well that has targeted public officials (including Sadat, who was assassinated by a member of one such group), foreigners, and Egyptian Christians. Governmental response has been repressive and occasionally effective, but the persistence of economic and social problems in Egypt guarantees that not all Islamist opposition will wither.

Libya under Gaddafi has undergone a series of domestic reforms (including nationalization of the lucrative petroleum industry, and bans on gambling and alcohol) in accordance with Gaddafi's dual socialist and Islamic agenda. Internationally, Libya's reputation is tied to Gaddafi's sponsorship of a wide variety of international extremist and terrorist groups, his mercurial style of leadership, and his confrontations with western countries. Libya was also involved in a series of border conflicts with its southern neighbor, Chad, that resulted in war in the 1980s.

AMY J. JOHNSON

See also: **Algeria; Arab and Islamic World, Africa in; Augustine, Catholic Church: North Africa; Colonialism, Overthrow of: Northern Africa; Education: North Africa (Colonial and Postcolonial); Egypt, Ancient; Egypt: Fatimids; Egypt: Mamluk Dynasty; Egypt: Ottoman, 1517–1798; Libya; Maghrib; Media as Propaganda; Morocco; North Africa, Ancient: Urbanization; Tunisia.**

Further Reading

Abun-Nasr, J. M. *A History of the Maghrib in the Islamic Period.* Cambridge: Cambridge University Press, 1987.

Brown, L. C. (ed.). *Imperial Legacy: The Ottoman Imprint on the Balkans and the Middle East.* New York: Columbia University Press, 1996.

Cherry, D. *Frontier and Society in Roman North Africa.* Oxford: Clarendon Press, 1998.

Entelis, J. P., ed. *Islam, Democracy, and the State in North Africa.* Bloomington: Indiana University Press, 1997.

Fairservis, W. A. *The Ancient Kingdoms of the Nile.* New York: Mentor, 1962.

Gordon, D. C. *North Africa's French Legacy, 1954–1962.* Cambridge, Mass: Harvard University Press, 1962.

Halm, H. *The Empire of the Mahdi: The Rise of the Fatimids* (translated from the German by M. Bonner). Leiden: E. J. Brill, 1996.

Joffe, G., ed. *North Africa: Nation, State, and Region.* London: Routledge, 1993.

Julien, C.-A. *History of North Africa from the Arab Conquest to 1830.* London: Routledge and Kegan Paul, 1970.

Long, D. E., and B. Reich, eds. *The Government and Politics of the Middle East and North Africa.* Boulder, Colo.: Westview Press, 1995.

Matar, N. I. *Turks, Moors and Englishmen in the Age of Discovery*. New York: Columbia University Press, 1999.
Morsy, M. *North Africa, 1800–1900: A Survey from the Nile Valley to the Atlantic*. London: Longman, 1984.
Picard, G. C., and C. Picard. *The Life and Death of Carthage*. New York: Taplinger, 1969.
Raven, S. *Rome in Africa*. London: Routledge, 1993.
Taha, 'Abdulwahid Dhanun. *The Muslim Conquest and Settlement of North Africa and Spain*. London: Routledge, 1989.

Northern Rhodesia: *See* Zambia: Nationalism, Independence; Zambia (Northern Rhodesia): British Occupation, Resistance: 1890s; Zambia (Northern Rhodesia): Colonial Period: Administration, Economy; Zambia (Northern Rhodesia): Copperbelt; Zambia (Northern Rhodesia): Federation, 1953–1963.

Ntusi: *See* Great Lakes Region: Ntusi, Kibiro, and Bigo.

Nubia: Relations with Egypt (Seventh–Fourteenth Centuries)

During the seventh century, the Christian Church in the Nubian kingdoms (Nobatia, Makurra, and 'Alwah) became aligned predominantly with the Coptic Church, thus strengthening ecclesiastical relations with Egypt. Following the Arab conquest of Egypt in 641, two military expeditions were sent by successive emirs into Nubia, reaching as far as Dongola, capital of Makurra. Neither was successful and in 651–652 a form of peace treaty was arranged, termed the *baqt*, which allowed the continued independence of the Nubian states. The *baqt* appears to have comprised a truce and an exchange of slaves (from Nubia) and certain goods (from Egypt). Ninth- and tenth-century accounts list wheat, drink (wine), horses, and cloth or clothing among the main items given.

Relations with Islamic Egypt were generally peaceful up to the reign of Cyriacus of Makurra. According to tradition, he invaded Egypt in 747–748 to obtain the release of the patriarch of Alexandria, who had been imprisoned by the emir. This invasion may have been of some importance because of the political support given to the patriarchate. Later in Cyriacus's reign, in 758, relations were strained temporarily due to the Nubians' nonpayment of the *baqt*. The Nubians again ceased paying the *baqt* from around 820. The Caliph al-Mu'tasim ordered King Zacharias II of Makurra, in 834, to pay the *baqt* and its arrears for fourteen years. Zacharias's son, George, went to Baghdad in 835–836 and negotiated successfully with the Caliph; the arrears of the *baqt* were canceled and a further pact of mutual nonaggression was made.

During the first half of the tenth century, Nubian-Egyptian relations continued to be peaceful. Burials and tombstones demonstrate Muslim settlement in Lower Nubia from this period onwards. However, during the second half of the century, the Nubians mounted two main offensives, in 956 and again in 962, after which they retained control over part of Upper Egypt into the eleventh century. The Fatimids conquered Egypt in 969. Their relations with the Nubian Kingdoms appears to have been quite close during most of the period they were in power, the Makurran rulers being able to intervene in some Egyptian affairs. One king, probably Solomon, aided the patriarch of Alexandria on one occasion and cooperated with the rulers of Egypt by handing over the Kanz ed-Dowla, leader of an Arab-Beja tribe, who had rebelled and fled to Nubia. During this period, both secondary sources and primary historical evidence indicate that Egypt carried on considerable trade with Makurra and some with 'Alwah, a Muslim quarter being established at Soba, capital of 'Alwah.

Salah al-Din overthrew the Fatimids in 1171. In this same year, the king of Makurra invaded Egypt, capturing Aswan and advancing north, either seeking plunder or in support of the Fatimids, but the Makourran army was forced to retire. Nubia was entered in the following year by Shams ed-Dowla, the brother of Salah ed-Din. Reasons for this seem to have been partly punitive but also to have been to gain control of the country for use as a base, should the latter be forced out of Egypt. Shams ed-Dowla ultimately became convinced that Nubia was unsuitable for this purpose, and neither Salah al-Din nor his Ayyubid successors attempted to conquer Makurra.

Makurra's peaceful relations with the later Ayyubid rulers of Egypt did not long survive the accession to power there of the Mamluks in 1250. 'Alwah, or perhaps its northernmost principality, el-Abwab, appears to have had better relations with the Mamluks, occasionally aiding them in conflicts with Makurra. However, the processes leading to the collapse of both the Christian kingdoms can be seen to have begun at this time. One aspect of these relates to the Mamluks' hostile policy toward the nomadic tribes in Egypt. Many either migrated or were forced to flee into Nubia. Furthermore, members of some tribes entered Nubia as auxiliaries in the successive armies dispatched during the late thirteenth and the fourteenth centuries. Within the next three centuries they seem to have intermarried extensively with the Nubians. According to Adams (1977, p.458), the interventions of the Mamluks eventually "tipped the balance of power in favor of the growing Islamic element in the population." This balance became significant when political and ecclesiastical institutions within the Christian states began to disintegrate.

King David took the throne of Makurra in 1268 by deposing his uncle, Abu'l Izz Murtashkar, who had converted to Islam. David attacked the port of Aydhab in 1272, thus adversely affecting Egypt's sea trade routes, then devastated Aswan. The Mamluk Sultan Baybars counterattacked in 1276, deposing David and installing Shakanda, another nephew of Abu'l Izz Murtashkar, on the throne. Shakanda had to take an oath that included swearing allegiance to Baybars in return for his support, and transferring the province of Maris (Nobatia) to him, but these conditions do not seem to have been enforced.

Several successive Mamluk nominees subsequently held the throne of Makurra. Their reigns usually were short, since they were either assassinated or deposed. Such fates befell Kings Amay (before 1304 to 1311), Kudanbes (1311–1316 and 1323), and Saif ed-Din Abdallah Barshambu (1316–1317 or 1319) in the following century. The last-named king was a Muslim; he turned the Throne Hall of the palace at Old Dongola into a mosque in 1317 but, otherwise, seems not to have undertaken extensive Islamization of the state.

Egypt again became embroiled in Nubian affairs in 1365, when an embassy arrived from the two rulers of a divided Makurra seeking assistance in resisting some nomad tribes. The sultan sent a force that, together with the Nubian army, successfully defeated them. The seat of the king of Makurra then moved to Daw in Lower Nubia. The latest attested contact between Nubia and the patriarch of Alexandria occurred in 1372 with the consecration of a bishop of Ibrim. Trade declined drastically. Although a king of "Nubia" sought asylum in Cairo as late as 1397, it appears that by this time the kingdoms of Makurra and 'Alwah had each broken up. Effectively, the political relations between Egypt and these Nubian states ended with the century.

LAURENCE SMITH

See also: **Egypt and Africa (1000–1500); Nobadia, Makurra and 'Alwa.**

Further Reading

Adams, W. Y. "The United Kingdom of Makouria and Nobadia: A Medieval Nubian Anomaly." In *Egypt and Africa: Nubia from Prehistory to Islam*, edited by W. V. Davies. London: British Museum Press/Egypt Exploration Society, 1991.

———. *Qasr Ibrîm: The Late Mediaeval Period.* 59th Excavation Memoir. Pt. 4. London: Egypt Exploration Society, 1996.

Munro-Hay, S. C. *Ethiopia and Alexandria: The Metropolitan Episcopacy of Ethiopia.* Bibliotheca Nubica et Aethiopica. Vol. 5. ZA-PAN, 1997.

Shinnie, P. L. "Trade in Medieval Nubia." In *Études nubiennes: colloque de Chantilly, 2–6 juillet 1975,* edited by J. Leclant and J. Vercoutter. Institut français d'Archéologie orientale du Caire, 1978.

Vantini, G. *Oriental Sources Concerning Nubia.* Warsaw: Polish Academy of Sciences, 1975.

Nubia: Banu Kanz, Juhayna and the Arabization of the Nilotic Sudan (Fourteenth–Eighteenth Centuries)

The Arabization of northern Sudan was a gradual process that started immediately after the Arab conquest of Egypt between 639 and 641. Although Nubia successfully resisted any military attacks from the north and was never annexed, Arab traders and settlers came to the country at an early date, and there is evidence of a progressive Arabization and Islamization of Nubia between the ninth and twelfth centuries.

In the later Middle Ages the stability of the Christian kingdoms was slowly undermined by forces from both within and beyond their borders. The fourteenth to sixteenth centuries saw the massive Arabization of the people of the Nilotic Sudan in connection with migrations of Arab groups into and within the Sudan. Intermarriage was one important vehicle of Arabization, especially in regard to the Nubian peoples along the Nile, whose matrilinear system led to the acquirement of rights of succession to leadership as well as share in land by sons of Arab fathers and Nubian mothers. The gradual conversion of the people to Islam was another important factor that resulted in the emergence of new Arab-Sudanese ethnic entities. Although at first sight the Arabic influence seems to be predominant—for example in the many language shifts from indigenous languages to Arabic that took place—an equally intensive Africanization of the immigrants can be reconstructed. In the post-Christian era, religious teachers invited into the country by the Funj Sultans became important to the emergence of the characteristic

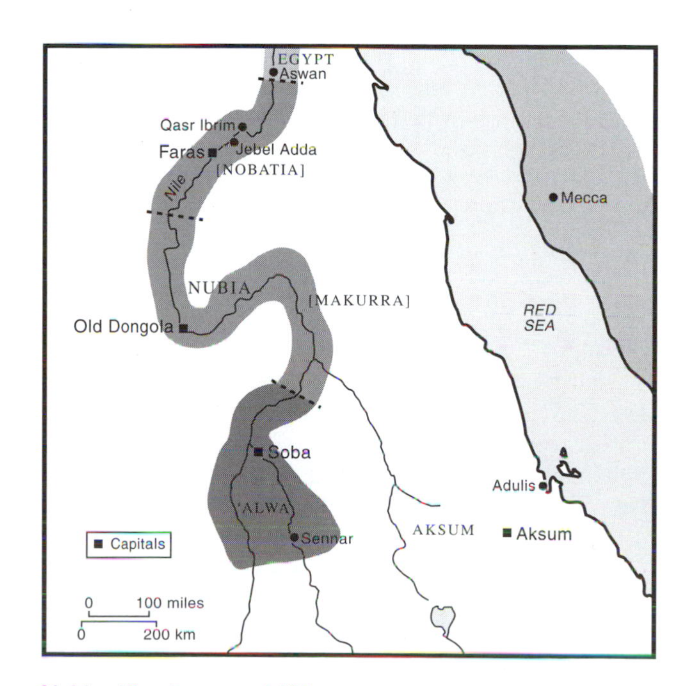

Nubian Kingdoms to *c.*1400.

Sudanese Islam that can be found until today. These teachers were mostly representatives of the mystical Sufi orders, and they spread a form of popular worship with local cults and belief in saints and miracles that has always been associated with Sufism, but which was also well known to the northern Sudanese peoples through their Christian faith since the early Middle Ages. Most of the non-Sufi teachers were Sudanese who had studied in Egypt or other Muslim religious centers. In the middle of the sixteenth century Mahmud al-'Araki as the first Sudanese Muslim scholar who had studied in Cairo and is said to have established seventeenth schools on the White Nile on his return. Ibrahim al Bulad ibn Jabir introduced the teaching of the Maliki textbooks in about 1570, which helped to establish the predominance of the Maliki rite in the northern Sudan.

An impressive early example of the process of intensive Africanization of an immigrant people that set off the simultaneous Arabization of the original population are the Banu Kanz, who originally formed part of the Rabi'a from the Arabian Peninsula. In the middle of the ninth century an extensive migration of Rabi'a to Upper Egypt took place, resulting in their settlement among the Beja of the Red Sea Hills. The new settlers intermarried extensively with the original inhabitants of the region and finally extended their influence and control over Aswan and adjacent parts of the Nile valley. In 1006 the chief of the Nile valley, Rabi'a, assisted the Fatimid caliph in the capture of a political rival and was rewarded with title Kanz ed-Dawla ("treasure of state"), which later became a hereditary title. The group as a whole became subsequently known as Banu Kanz, or descendants of the Kanz ed-Dawla. By the end of the thirteenth century the Banu Kanz were a powerful group in the northern part of Christian Nubia and their leader presumably held the important Nubian office of the eparch. They profited by the internal weakness that at that time was characteristic of the Christian Nubian kingdom, and in alliance with the Mamluk rulers of Egypt they were in the position to overthrow or appoint Nubian rulers as they wished. This political involvement in and around Dongola had the more peaceful effect of widespread intermarriage between the Banu Kanz and the local Nubian population. Although they retained and even spread their Islamic faith, the Banu Kanz became Nubianized in language and culture. A new ethnic entity emerged, which is known as Kenzi Nubian today. The ruler of the Kenzi and his family also became allied with the ruling house in Dongola by marriage and in 1323 the Kanz ed-Dawla resumed the throne as legitimate heir of his maternal uncle. The history of Kenzi reign over Dongola is short. Only forty years later they had to withdraw to their original area around Aswan, where they resettled permanently.

Most of the Arabic-speaking groups of the Sudan affiliate themselves with one of two comprehensive groups, Juhayna or Ja'aliyyin. The Ja'aliyyin are essentially Arabized Nubians whose homeland lies in the Middle Nile region south of the Fourth Cataract. At the beginning of the sixteenth century, parts of the Ja'aliyyin migrated west to Kordofan where they were absorbed by the local population, but preserved a memory of their original identity. The term Juhayna has both a wider and a more restricted meaning. One meaning includes all non-Ja'aliyyin nomadic groups, which are not necessarily connected historically with the Juhayna who originated from south Arabia. The Juhayna had migrated to Upper Egypt in the Fatimid period and later, presumably under Mamluk pressure, had moved to the Beja country and later south to the green plains of 'Alwa. Unlike the sedentary Ja'aliyyin they kept up a nomadic way of life, and they played an important part in the final blow against the decaying Christian kingdom. Sudanese traditions trace the final downfall of 'Alwa to a combined nomadic Arab and Funj attack. Actually, this process has to be attributed to Arab groups alone. During the second half of the fifteenth century, a confederacy of Arab groups under the leadership of 'Abdallah Jamma' (the Gatherer) succeeded in conquering the kingdom of 'Alwa. For a short time, 'Abdallah and his descendents, the 'Abdallabi, succeeded in establishing an independent state, but they were confronted and defeated by the Funj in 1504. They were reduced to the position of vassal of the Funj sultanate but continued to rule the northern part until the Turco-Egyptian conquest of 1820.

MARIANNE BECHHAUS-GERST

Further Reading

Adams, W. Y. *Nubia—Corridor to Africa.* London: Allen Lane, 1977.

Hasan, Y. F. *The Arabs and the Sudan: From the Seventh to the Early Sixteenth Century*, Khartoum: Khartoum University Press, 1973.

Holt, P. M., and M. W. Daly. *The History of the Sudan: From the Coming of Islam to the Present Day.* London: Weidenfeld and Nicolsen, 1979.

O'Fahey, R. S., and J. L. Spaulding. *Kingdoms of the Sudan.* London: Methuen and Co., 1974.

Nuer: *See* Nilotes, Eastern Africa: Western Nilotes: Shilluk, Nuer, Dinka, Anywa.

Nujoma, Sam (1929–)

First President of Namibia

A bitter hundred-year struggle against colonial rule came to a close on March 21, 1990, when Sam Nujoma was sworn in as the first president of independent Namibia. Cofounder and leader of the South West

Africa People's Organization (SWAPO), Sam Nujoma spearheaded a thirty-year military and diplomatic campaign attacking South Africa's illegal presence in South West Africa. By cleverly navigating the broader global politics of the Cold War, Nujoma converted SWAPO from an obscure nationalist movement into an internationally recognized voice of Namibian independence. In the process, he emerged as the personification of the independence struggle, assuring his own political primacy after liberation.

Samuel Daniel Nujoma worked a succession of jobs before emerging in 1959 as the leader of a protest against the government's apartheid-based policy of forcible resettlement. Arrested for his role in organizing the resistance, Nujoma went into exile and commenced an energetic campaign to thrust the plight of the Namibian people into the international spotlight. He was elected in absentia as president of SWAPO in 1960, working successfully to transform what had been primarily an ethnic and regionally based organization into a truly national one. He also set out to establish SWAPO as "the sole and authentic" representative of the Namibian people. Unwilling to share the spotlight with other Namibian nationalist movements, Nujoma lobbied and politicked to win for SWAPO exclusive backing from the Organization of African Unity and later from the United Nations General Assembly. Nujoma's success in garnering international legitimacy for SWAPO enabled him to consolidate positions of unassailable preeminence within the movement for himself and his closest associates.

Operating in an environment where numerous nationalist movements were preparing for armed struggle against white minority regimes across southern Africa, Sam Nujoma undertook a dual approach to achieving Namibian liberation. He orchestrated a campaign of international diplomacy directed at triggering United Nations entry into the Namibian political process. Aside from statements of sympathy and solidarity, early efforts at lobbying and petitioning produced few tangible results. As a result, Nujoma turned to armed struggle. The first clash between SWAPO and South African forces took place in August 1966, and although the inaugural battle proved a hopeless mismatch in favor of the South Africans, the skirmish proved a decisive propaganda victory for SWAPO. Thus began twenty-three years of low-intensity conflict that utilized military action as a form of propaganda to strengthen SWAPO's diplomatic and political bargaining position on the international stage.

With arms supplied by the Soviet Union and other Eastern-bloc countries, the People's Liberation Army of Namibia (PLAN) conducted localized and sporadic attacks against South African interests in Namibia. Faced with the logistical problems created by carrying out military strikes in Namibia from political headquarters in far away Dar es Salaam, Tanzania, Nujoma, and the SWAPO leadership moved their center of operations twice. From 1966 to 1974, PLAN's campaign of sabotage and assassination was conducted from Zambia, but with the collapse of Portuguese colonial rule in Angola in 1974, Nujoma negotiated the establishment of PLAN bases in southern Angola. Although Nujoma's earlier ties to Jonas Savimbi caused frictions with the Angolan government in Luanda, he worked hard in the late 1970s to repair relations with the victorious People's Liberation Movement of Angola (MPLA). With a stable base of operations and thousands of young Namibians crossing the border into Angola to join the ranks of SWAPO in exile, Nujoma stepped up the pressure with a more intense military campaign within Namibia itself from 1978 through 1984. In turn, South Africa escalated the conflict toward a more conventional war, leading to a series of PLAN defeats and questions about the competence of the liberation movement's military commanders and their continued commitment to armed struggle.

With PLAN casualties far outnumbering those of South African forces, Nujoma and the SWAPO leadership faced mounting criticism. Historically, problems within the organization had been countered by the diplomatic successes of Sam Nujoma, whose tireless presence on the world stage won for SWAPO considerable international goodwill and a level of financial support unequalled by other southern African liberation movements. But Nujoma's ability to exploit external assets only camouflaged the shortcomings that had plagued SWAPO from its inception. Nujoma and the leadership in exile developed a political culture that discouraged spontaneity and debate, increasingly defined criticism as disloyalty, and eventually focused considerable energies on maintaining security. This restrictive political climate aimed to silence criticisms of the leadership and to derail calls for democratization, accountability, and reform.

Nujoma proved adept at silencing dissent within the movement. When SWAPO members demanded more democratic procedures at a consultative congress in 1969, Nujoma undermined attempts at reform by adopting the militant language of his critics and by warning that party unity could never be compromised. A clear tilt toward authoritarianism occurred in the mid-1970s, when idealistic radicals of the SWAPO Youth League revolted against the leadership in exile in Zambia. Nujoma crushed the challenge to his authority by invoking Zambian military assistance to arrest and detain the dissidents. Strict hierarchy and party discipline were established.

Nujoma embraced Soviet-style phraseology on issues of security and, on occasion, raised eyebrows in the West when he touted his commitment to liberate Namibia through a mobilization of the broad masses. With military support flowing into SWAPO from the Eastern-bloc countries, and with Nujoma's visits to Cuba and the Soviet Union in 1976, fears arose that SWAPO had transitioned from a liberation movement to a Marxist revolutionary party. But those closest to Nujoma understood that the socialist rhetoric found in SWAPO's public utterances was designed for political effect. The movement's sweeping manifestos were kept sufficiently vague so that they could be tailored to audiences and circumstances. Labels of ideology during the liberation struggle were meaningless, for Nujoma's pragmatism made ideology expendable. SWAPO's revolutionary undertones would not be allowed to damage its diplomatic campaign.

The final settlement that led to Namibian independence, which came about through lengthy diplomatic and political wrangling, had less to do with SWAPO's struggle than with changes in international relations as a result of the end of the Cold War. With the Soviet Union scaling back its support for liberation movements around the globe, and with South Africa increasingly isolated, the Western Contact Group (the United States, Canada, Great Britain, France, and West Germany) devised a peace plan calling for a ceasefire, a phased withdrawal of South African forces, and one-person-one-vote elections under the supervision of the United Nations. Although the Reagan administration complicated the negotiations by linking the withdrawal of Cuban troops from Angola with independence for Namibia, a comprehensive agreement was finally reached in 1988.

Ending three decades in exile, Sam Nujoma returned to Namibia in September 1989 to enter the political struggle for the future of his country. During his long years in exile when he was dependent on Communist support, Nujoma often called for a socialist government for Namibia. Although he continued to insist that the new government undertake land reform and redistribute wealth to the black majority, during the election campaign he went out of his way to reassure whites that their rights would be protected and that he wound not impose one-party rule. SWAPO won just over 57 per cent of the total vote, ensuring that Nujoma would be chosen by the constituent assembly to lead Namibia into independence.

The politics of transition were far from easy. During the decades of struggle for liberation, little thought or planning had been given to the development of an independent Namibia under a SWAPO government. Upon assuming the presidency of independent Namibia on March 21, 1990, Nujoma proclaimed national reconciliation and nation building as his priorities. Facing the realities of running a state and governing a nation, Nujoma abandoned any hint of socialism by working to establish relations with Western financial institutions. Nujoma settled on a pragmatic, market-oriented strategy for national development. Over the years, he has established a bond with Namibian voters, and they have remained loyal to him. Despite high rates of unemployment, a troubled economy, and accusations of government corruption, Nujoma and his South West African People's Organization have dominated presidential and parliamentary elections, winning overwhelming victories in 1994 and again in1999. While praised for skillfully guiding Namibia through its early years of independence, Nujoma has been accused of adopting an increasingly authoritarian style.

W. Frank Robinson

See also: **Namibia: Independence to the Present; Namibia: Struggle for Independence, 1970–1990; Namibia: SWAPO and the Freedom Struggle.**

Biography

Samuel Daniel Nujoma was born May 12, 1929, in the Ongandjera district of Ovamboland in northern South West Africa. The son of farmworkers, he studied with missionaries and worked a succession of jobs before emerging in 1959 as the leader of a protest against the government's apartheid-based policy of forcible resettlement. Elected in absentia as president of SWAPO in 1960. Ending three decades in exile, returned to Namibia in September 1989. Assumed presidency of Namibia March 21, 1990.

Further Reading

Dobell, L. *SWAPO's Struggle for Namibia, 1960–1991: War by Other Means*. Basel: P. Schlettwein Publishing, 1998.

Emmett, T. *Popular Resistance and the Roots of Nationalism in Namibia, 1915–1966*. Basel: P. Schlettwein Publishing, 1999.

Katjavivi, P. *A History of Resistance in Namibia*. London: James Currey, 1988.

Leys, C., and J. S. Saul. *Namibia's Liberation Struggle: The Two-Edged Sword*. Athens: Ohio University Press, 1995.

Nujoma, S. *Where Others Wavered: The Autobiography of Sam Nujoma*. London: Panaf Books, 2001.

SWAPO. *To Be Born a Nation: The Struggle of the Namibian People*. London: Zed Books, 1981.

Nyabingi Cult and Resistance

The anti-colonial Nyabingi resistance movement had its origins in a secret society organization and was led by a woman called Muhumuza in southwestern Uganda between 1910 and 1930. The Nyabingi cult, however, dates much further back, to about 1700. The Nyabingi cult was one of the many religions in Kigezi in precolonial times. Many oppressed minorities sought and found sanctuary and refuge in the Nyabingi cult. Through the process of *Okutweija*, many priestesses (*bagirwa*, sing. *mugirwa*) or agents of Nyabingi (always women) dedicated their daughters to the cult, thus ensuring a pool of ready adherents. There were many such *bagirwa* in various parts of Mpororo and Rwanda proclaiming Nyabingi's edicts and wishes.

Oral tradition claims that Nyabingi, a sovereign queen, ruled the northwestern Tanzania kingdom of Karagwe (Omugole) about 1700. She was later married to Ruhinda, a chief of Mpororo in southwest Uganda, who remained in her kingdom as prince consort. Ruhinda subsequently overthrew his queen, had her killed, and took over the kingdom himself. Nyabingi's sprit brought untold woes to Ruhinda and his kingdom, including the annexation of the Ndorwa region by the Mwami of Rwanda. The sprit of Nyabingi then appeared in Kisiki, Rwanda. This new personification of Nyabingi in Rwanda was killed by Mwami Lwagera of Rwanda, seeking to negate any other famous or potentially powerful forces in his own kingdom.

Around 1860, another personification of Nyabingi appeared—again in Rwanda—during the reign of Mwami Lwabugiri Kigeri IV. This spirit possession was through Kahaya's daughter, one of Mwami's vassal chiefs. Kahaya's daughter, Kanzanira, was subsequently killed on her own father's orders, and her spirit ostensibly reincarnated in a destitute woman called Rutajira Kijuna (Rutajira Muhanda). Rutajira's personification of Nyabingi almost turned her into the ruler of Ndorwa. She toured the country, receiving salutations of "Kisinje" (a term of salutation only due to royalty), as she cured the sick by evoking the powers of Nyabingi. Again, another Mwami of Rwanda, Lubugiri, could not stand Rutajira's fame and on his orders, Rutajira was killed and was succeeded by her son Katondwe at Kyante Rutaji. For over two centuries, the Nyabingi cult had gained momentum and recognition, especially among the peasant Bakiga community, as a religion of the oppressed and disadvantaged. The cult remained anti-establishment and the main opposition was directed toward the ruling Tutsi class in Rwanda and its territories.

The Nyabingi cult took root particularly in Ndorwa, Mpororo kingdom, where most of the inhabitants were the subject Bahutu. Here the area was not very favorable for cattle and as such there were very few Batusi in Ndorwa. Mwami's authority here was almost nonexistent. The area was an outlaw territory of political dissidents and runaways fleeing the Mwami's authority.

This was the cultural and political environment in which Muhumuza, wife of Mwami Lwabugiri and mother to the heir apparent, found herself as an exile from civil wars in her native Rwanda. Mwami Lwabugiri had died in 1894 and left the throne to Muhumuza's son Bulegeya, at the time only an infant. Bulegeya's claim to the throne was challenged by the Bega clan, who also had a contender from their clan. Muhumuza and her son were forced to flee to Mpororo with the remnants of the royal guard.

She established herself on Mount Lutobo, northeast of Ndorwa in Mpororo kingdom. But Muhumuza, an obvious MuTutsi woman, former wife of Mwami Lwabugiri and also mother of the heir to the throne in Rwanda, was not readily accepted by the people of Ndorwa. Her flight from Rwanda did not lessen her desire to see her son become the next Mwami at some future date. She wanted to remain in contact with sympathizers back home. She realized that she needed political power, or some other type of awe-inspiring authority. She could only achieve all this by associating herself with the cult of Nyabingi. She first became a *Mugirwa* (Nyabingi priestess), and through her intelligence, force of character, and resolve, she gradually achieved leadership among *Bagirwa,* before claiming herself the reincarnation of Nyabingi. She thus claimed both religious and political legitimacy, and drew thousands of dedicated followers.

In 1903 Muhumuza intercepted a group of White Fathers missionaries near Lutobo on their way to found the Rivaza Mission in southern Ndorwa. She became increasingly anti-European and particularly hostile to the Germans, who were propping up Masinga on the Rwandan throne, creating the basis of their administration there. In 1908 Muhumuza was arrested by the Germans near Kaamwezi and jailed for two years in Bukoba. Upon her release from prison, she attempted to capture Rwanda for her son but was repulsed by the Germans and their Rwandan collaborators. She returned to Ndorwa, where she attempted to carve out a kingdom by declaring herself the queen of Ndorwa, and both as queen and the reincarnation of Nyabingi, she raised a large following of Bakiga and Banyarwanda, declaring herself the liberator of Ndorwa.

In 1911 Muhumuza and her forces attacked members of the Anglo-Belgian-German Boundary Commission constructing boundary pillars from Kamwezi to Mount Muhavura, through Ndorwa. A reprisal attack by British forces on Ihanga Hill was an ambush in which about forty of Muhumuza's men were killed and Muhumuza herself was shot in the foot and captured. As a military and political threat to British administration, Muhumuza was deported to Mengo where she died in 1944, without ever returning to Kigezi.

Her followers, the *Bagirwa*, continued the anticolonial struggle. Nyabingi priests and priestesses continued harassing the agents of British administration until 1928. In 1915 a Nyabingi priest, Ndochibiri, attacked a strongly guarded Anglo-Belgian post at Chahaji in Bufumbira with a two thousand-strong force; the battle lasted five hours. Between April and May 1917, Ndochibiri and his followers organized another secret rebellion against the British and Belgian agents and their works. This was supposed to be the final rebellion to oust Europeans from the entire district of Kigezi and Kabale. However, Ndochibiri and his followers were ambushed near Kabale, and the entire party was wiped out. Ndochibiri's head was cut off and sent to England; it is supposedly still held in the British Museum. His two-fingered hand was also cut off and for a time displayed in Kabale to prove that he had indeed been killed.

These military measures seem to have broken up the central organization of the Nyabingi cult. Although various Bagirwa claimed to be reincarnations of Nyabingi, they were not strong enough to cause concern for the authorities until 1928, when a rebellion led by a man called Ndungutsi attacked Kabale station and the Kabale mission. They later attacked and killed a Muluka chief and two Batongole chiefs before they were overtaken by government forces. Ndungutsi and about twenty of his followers were arrested and sent to jail. That was the last organized uprising under the aegis of the Nyabingi cult in southwest Uganda.

D. Kiyaga-Mulindwa

See also: **Religion, Colonial Africa: Religious Responses to Colonial Rule.**

Further Reading

Bamuhigire, O. "The Woman who Fought Colonialism." *The New Vision*. December 28, 1999.

Murindwa, R. *Nyabingi Movement: Peoples' Colonial Struggles in Kigezi 1910–1930.* Kampala: Centre for Basic Research.

Phillips, Captain J. E. T. "Nyabingi an Anti-European Secret Society in Africa, in British Ruanda, Ndorwa and the Congo (Kivu)." *Congo.* Revue Generale de Colonie Belge.

Nyanga Hills

The landscape of the Nyanga highlands of northeastern Zimbabwe, and adjacent regions to the west, bears extensive remains of agricultural terraces and cultivation ridges, water furrows, stone-walled homesteads and defensive forts, over an area of approximately 7,000 square kilometers. This complex dates from about the fourteenth to nineteenth centuries, and is unrelated to the contemporary and better-known ruins of the Great Zimbabwe tradition, or to the preceding Early Iron Age occupation of the first millennium.

The southern part of the Nyanga highlands forms a broad dissected plateau at around 1,800 to 2,000 meters, falling relatively gently to the west and rising to Mount Nyangani (2,592 m) to the east. Northward the plateau narrows to a high spine at around 2,000 meters, with steep escarpments on either side. To the west, granite inselbergs form often substantial hills, rising from a base level which declines from about 1,200 meters in the south to 900 meters in the north. The underlying geology is various granites, overlain by dolerites and some sedimentary rocks which cap the highlands, while dolerite sills and dykes also form lesser features in the lowlands.

The tentative sequence of development starts with nucleated sites covering several hectares on peaks and ridgetops over 2,000 meters on the northern range, dated to the fourteenth to fifteenth centuries. Ruined "pit structures" at a slightly lower altitude are dated to the seventeenth century; pottery artifacts indicate cultural continuity from the earlier sites. Here and subsequently the settlement pattern represents dispersed villages. Better-preserved pit structures are lower again and probably date from the eighteenth and nineteenth centuries. The pit structures have a large stone-lined pit for dwarf cattle surrounded by houses on an artificial platform. They occur down to an altitude of 1,400 meters, the lower ones associated with terraces. Below this level homesteads are stone enclosures with some geographical variation in design, also associated with terracing, and dating probably from the late seventeenth to nineteenth century. Imported items consist only of rather sparse glass beads throughout and the communities appear to have been relatively isolated. The whole complex was largely abandoned by 1900, but was almost certainly the work of the ancestors of the present populations.

Stone-faced terraces cover large areas of the highland escarpments and the slopes of foothills and detached hills mainly to the west. Some slopes have ranges of up to 100 terraces. The altitudinal range is from about 900 meters in the northern lowlands to around 1,700 meters on the escarpments and in the highlands, with very little above this level, which is about the upper limit for the cultivation of traditional grain crops at the present time.

Distribution favors dolerite rocks and soils that are of greater fertility than the sandy granite soils. However, they are often thin and very stony. Terracing is necessary to clear the stones and concentrate the soil for cultivation; it also protects against erosion and impedes drainage to allow water percolation. Terraces are not precisely leveled on the contour, allowing for longitudinal drainage, so that they could not have been intended to flood them either artificially or by rainfall. Stone-lined drains carried excess run-off down slope, while in some cases upstanding walls were pierced by drain holes. The majority of terraces were not irrigated.

Networks of cultivation ridges are extensive on the lower, less stony slopes below the escarpments and extending some sixty kilometers to the west, the total area probably equaling or exceeding that of the terracing. The features are parallel or subparallel linear banks, usually seven to ten meters wide between ditches up to a meter or so deep, and up to several hundred meters long, with a more or less shallow longitudinal gradient. These occur both in areas of impeded drainage (vleis) and on the valley sides or interfluves. One such system immediately below the western escarpment covers around 1,000 hectares. Ridge size, patterns, and orientation to slope vary even within a single localized drainage basin and must represent a flexible system of balancing drainage and water retention under varying conditions of soil, slope, rainfall, and seasonal water table.

Numerous old water furrows survive mainly in the highlands where they are better preserved by perennial grass cover. Many furrows serve groups of homesteads and would have been used for domestic purposes, livestock, and watering gardens. Some of these also traverse ranges of terraces. In the National Park area, furrows commonly run on substantial earthen banks and must have been used for irrigating unterraced fields.

There is no direct association between the earlier occupation sites and the agricultural works, and it is not yet known when these were initiated, although some rough granite terracing may be associated with the preceding Early Iron Age.

The agricultural systems integrated crops and livestock. Cattle were penned in the pits or small stone enclosures within the homestead, and small stock in the houses, many of which have low dividing walls. The central pens are larger in the highland pit structures, suggesting larger cattle holdings. There are no signs of dung heaps and little accumulation of domestic refuse, so these must have been used for fertilizing gardens and home fields. Seeds of traditional crops (millets, sorghum, cowpeas, ground beans) have been identified from lowland sites, and traditional root crops such as *Plectranthus esculentus* and *Colocasia* must also have been grown especially on the cultivation ridges. Some degree of intensification may be postulated in an inner zone around the homestead, but the cultivation of outlying terraced fields must have been less sustainable and a continuous process of terrace building is envisaged, with older terraces fallowed or abandoned as fertility declined. This process could account for the extent and density of the complex even with a relatively small overall population. Ultimately terraceable land may have run out and the fertility of homestead plots proved unsustainable, which, coupled with political events, may explain the abandonment of the complex.

ROBERT SOPER

See also: **Manyika of Eastern Zimbabwe.**

Further Reading

Grove, A. T., and J. Sutton. "Agricultural Terracing South of the Sahara." *Azania.* 24 (1989): 114–122.

Plug, I., R. Soper, and S. Chirawu. "Pits, Tunnels and Cattle in Nyanga: New Light on an Old Problem." *South African Archaeological Bulletin.* 52, no. 166 (1997): 89–94.

Soper, R. "The Nyanga Terrace Complex of Eastern Zimbabwe: New Investigations." *Azania.* 31 (1996): 1–35.

Sutton, J. "A New Look at the Inyanga Terraces." *Zimbabwean Prehistory,* 19 (1983): 12–19.

Nyasaland: *See* Malawi: Colonization and Wars of Resistance, 1889–1904; Malawi (Nyasaland): Colonial Period: Chilembwe Rising, 1915; Malawi (Nyasaland): Colonial Period: Federation; Malawi (Nyasaland): Colonial Period: Land, Labor, and Taxation.

Nyerere, Julius (1922–1999)

First President of Tanzania

The first president of Tanzania, Julius Kambarage Nyerere, was one of the most outstanding twentieth-century African statesmen. He worked first as a teacher and later was always called by the title Mwalimu, meaning "the Teacher" in Swahili. Born at Butiama in the Musoma District of Tanganyika, the son of a chief, he went to Muisenge Primary School and Tabora Government Secondary School in Tanganyika, and then to Makerere University College in Uganda, where he qualified as a teacher. Then he went to the University of Edinburgh where he obtained a Diploma in Education.

His political career began when, in 1953, he became president of the Tanganyika African Association (TAA), which concentrated initially on cultural matters, only to eventually play a key role in the development of the nationalism movement. On July 7, 1954,

The former President of Tanzania, Julius K. Nyerere. © Sebastian Bolesch/Das Fotoarchiv.

Nyerere joined others in revising the constitution of TAA to turn it into a very different body, the Tanganyika African National Union (TANU), a nationalist party calling for an end to British rule. The party built up an effective organization and won widespread support. Nyerere promoted the use of Tanganyika's common language, Swahili, from an early date, for example in TANU's slogan *Uhuru na Kazi,* "freedom and work." While Nyerere always rejected racism and his close colleagues for many years included a European (Derek Bryceson) and an Asian (Amir Jamal), TANU campaigned first for an end to the privileged position of Europeans and Asians, and for African majority rule. He served as a nominated TAA member of the Legislative Council but resigned in late 1957 because of the slow progress toward majority rule.

In 1958, however, Nyerere agreed to British proposals for elections under a new system, even though the three racial groups would each have ten elected representatives. In fact, TANU swept the board in elections in 1958 and 1959. Governor Turnbull now cooperated with TANU and, following a constitutional conference in 1959, elections were held for a new Legislative Council with an African majority on August 8, 1960; TANU was returned unopposed in fifty-eight seats out of seventy-one. Nyerere became chef minister in October 1960. Then, on December 9, 1961, Tanganyika became independent, with Nyerere as prime minister. But on January 22, 1962, he resigned, ostensibly to concentrate on the affairs of the party, TANU; Rashidi Kawawa became prime minister.

After a decision to make the country a republic, Julius Nyerere was elected president on November 1, 1962, winning 97 per cent of the vote; he was sworn in as president of the Republic of Tanganyika on December 9, 1962. A little over a year later, a revolution in newly independent Zanzibar brought the Afro-Shirazi Party to power, and it negotiated a union with Tanganyika, which came into effect on April 26, 1964, with the creation of the United Republic, soon afterward named Tanzania. Nyerere became president of the United Republic, whose Constitution of 1965 made it legally a one-party state. It was not until 1977 that the two ruling parties, TANU and the ASP, were merged into a single party, Chama Cha Mapinduzi (CCM), the "Party of the Revolution."

Julius Nyerere was a thoroughly authoritarian ruler, who defended the one-party system in theory as the best for Africa, as well as enforcing it in practice. In mainland Tanzania (i.e., Tanganyika) there were contested elections in which leading TANU or CCM politicians could and did lose seats. But in Zanzibar, where the revolution had involved large-scale killing, ruthless repression of a sort not seen in mainland Tanzania went on for years, as the island government was essentially semi-independent. Nyerere defended principles of respect for certain human rights. However, his ideology and that of his party was a form of socialism, and they believed that their principles must be enforced on the population for its own good. Nyerere summed up the official ideology in the term *ujamaa*, "togetherness." He always stressed the importance of the rural majority, and for them the idea of "*ujamaa* villages" on cooperative lines was launched. The Arusha Declaration of February 5, 1967, set out the basic policies of "Socialism and Self-Reliance." This included, as an early feature, large-scale nationalization of foreign businesses and state control over the greater part of the economy, including the retail trade.

Nyerere was an articulate speaker and writer who took care to explain his theories clearly and won widespread attention for them, including much admiration abroad. But within Tanzania, application of his theories had limited success. Tanzania did avoid the glaring inequalities of wealth seen in other African countries. But state control led to widespread shortages of goods, the "people's shops" often lying empty. Nyerere, who lived a simple and austere life himself and imposed a "Leadership Code" to avoid self-enrichment by those in power, fiercely condemned corruption, but it went on. His subordinates often failed to respect his principles. The call to establish "Ujamaa villages" on a voluntary basis met very little response. And in 1973–1975 the government carried out a drastic program of "villageisation," forcibly moving rural people from isolated hamlets into villages. Intended to make it easier to provide amenities for rural areas, this authoritarian measure caused great hardship and disruption. Nevertheless, amenities were extended widely over rural areas, and there was great progress in literacy and education, with Swahili generally used in schools.

President Nyerere was noted in Africa for his strong support for all action, including armed resistance, against the white minority and colonial regimes in South Africa, Rhodesia (Zimbabwe), and other territories. Tanzania was the main rear base for the struggle against the Portuguese in Mozambique, and Dar es Salaam was an important center for other liberation movement activity also. The OAU Liberation Committee was based at Arusha in Tanzania.

Unusually for Africa at that time, Nyerere said that oppression must be condemned whether it was by Africans or white people. On that principle he recognized Biafra during the Nigerian civil war, and later opposed the dictatorship of Idi Amin. Eventually Tanzania, after being attacked by Uganda, invaded that country in turn and drove Amin out in 1979. However, Nyerere then secured the return of Milton Obote who started another period of violent misrule in Uganda; meanwhile

Nyerere did not condemn the violent dictatorship in Burundi, another neighbor, as he did that in Uganda, though Tanzania gave shelter to thousands of Burundian refugees. In foreign relations, Nyerere favored African unity but wanted it to be approached cautiously through regional groupings, like the East African Community (Tanzania, Kenya, and Uganda), which he backed but which collapsed in 1977. After that Tanzania closed the border with Kenya for six years, to isolate its poorer socialist economy from the exploitative and richer economy of Kenya.

President Nyerere left office on November 5, 1985, having announced that he would not stand for reelection; he was succeeded as head of state by Ali Hassan Mwinyi, but remained chairman of the CCM until August 1990, continuing to defend the policies that he had followed but which now had to be gradually modified, as the economy was in a poor state and the majority had seen only limited improvement in their lives. In August 1990 he gave up the party leadership and retired altogether. The one-party system was abolished in 1992; after cautiously endorsing this change, Nyerere later said it had not improved matters. There were greater changes in the socialist economic system. Although the nation's political and economic systems were greatly modified from what they had been during his presidency, Julius Nyerere's personal standing remained high. He continued to travel and in 1995 became the official mediator in efforts to end the civil war in Burundi. In the midst of this peace effort he fell sick and was taken to a hospital in London, where he died on October 14, 1999. Half a million people thronged the streets of Dar es Salaam to witness the return of his body for burial, in a display of national mourning.

JONATHAN DERRICK

See also: **Socialism in Postcolonial Africa; Tanzania (Tanganyika).**

Biography

Born at Butiama in the Musoma District of Tanganyika in April 1922. Named president of the Tanganyika African Association (TAA), in 1953. His party, TANU, swept the elections of 1958–1959. Named Chief minister in October 1960. Named prime minister of newly independent Tanganyika on December 9, 1961. Resigned, January 22, 1962. Elected president on November 1, 1962. Stepod down from presidency on November 5, 1985. Gave up party leadership and retired from politics in 1990. Died October 14, 1999.

Further Reading

Duggan, W. R., and J. P. Civille. *Tanzania and Nyerere: A Study of Ujamaa and Nationhood.* Maryknoll, N.Y.: Orbis Books, 1976.

Hodd, M. (ed.). *Tanzania after Nyerere.* London and New York: Pinter Publishers, 1988.

Nyerere, J. K. *Freedom and Unity/Uhuru na Umoja: A Selection from Writings and Speeches 1952–1965.* London: CUP, 1967.

OAU: *See* Organization of African Unity (OAU) and Pan-Africanism.

Obasanjo, Olusegun (1937–)

President of Nigeria

Twice as the country's president and as a leading commander during the civil war (1967–1970), Olussegun Obasanjo has played a major role in the postcolonial history of Nigeria. Courageous, ambitious, and intellectual, his path to power owes to his skills, luck, and image as a nationalist, rather than as an ethnic leader. Unlike most other politicians and leaders, he has not fallen on his ethnic constituency as a source of support. A simple lifestyle and a commitment to his Baptist faith also separate him from the crowd of corrupt politicians and military generals.

In 1958 he enlisted in the Nigerian army, with military training in England and India. In 1959 he became a commissioned officer, rising to the rank of a general ten years later. Meanwhile, the army had begun its long and infamous incursion into politics, starting with the coup of January 1966. Obasanjo spent most of the 1970s in political roles, starting as a federal minister of works and housing in 1973, then a chief of staff (Supreme Headquarters) in 1975, and head of state from 1975 to 1979.

His period as head of state is now regarded as a redemptive moment in military rule, for providing a sense of direction, for an articulate and aggressive foreign policy, and for new domestic policies. His government failed, however, to lay the foundations for a strong economy and actually took a small external loan to which his successors added to substantially until a crisis point was reached. He pursued an honorable commitment to transition to a democratic government, becoming the first military leader to voluntarily relinquish power to a civilian.

After his retirement in 1979, his stature actually increased, to the extent that he became an international figure, a candidate for the office of the secretary general of the United Nations, and member and co-chair of the Commonwealth Eminent Persons Group on South Africa. In Nigeria, he was a member of the Inter-Action Council of Former Heads of States and Government and a leading critic of the government policies on economic reforms and military disengagement. He established the Africa Leadership Forum and Foundation, which convened conferences and published policy papers on African affairs.

He also became an author, with a major account of the Nigerian civil war, *My Command* (1980), and of his activities in government, *Not My Will* (1990). Both books generated considerable media interest and public controversy relating to his own original contributions to war and politics, and his bold and often condemnatory opinions of others. To many Yoruba, Obasanjo prevented the emergence of Chief Obafemi Awolowo, the leader of the Unity Party of Nigeria, as the country's president in 1979, a reason why he is unpopular among members of his own ethnic group. There is no justification for this accusation, but Obasanjo's denial has been made without humility, thus creating further antagonism. In many writings, he has criticized the collapse of moral and political leadership, the degeneracy of the civil service, the failure of the university system, and the collapse of professionalism in the armed forces. He is never shy in saying his mind, irrespective of who will be offended. He articulates a new vision for society, although he can be superficial in his recommendations. He is a federalist, with a passion for the development of his country as well as a belief that it should be the leading nation in Africa.

If the previous military regime of General Babangida could tolerate his acerbic criticisms, that of General

Sani Abacha which followed in 1993 was different. Abacha, an unrefined strongman and head of state, pursued a policy of incarcerating his political opponents and critics. Obasanjo was arrested in March 1995 for concealing information on a coup, an allegation without any evidence; he was tried in secret and sentenced to life imprisonment, which was later commuted to fifteen years after domestic and international pressure.

When Abacha died in 1998, a new government headed by Abdulsalam Abubakar released Obasanjo from prison. As with Nelson Mandela of South Africa, Obasanjo moved from prison to the state house. Despite his original desire to avoid politics and elections, he changed his mind, joined the People's Democratic Party (PDP), and became its flag-bearer after a keenly contested primary. He later won the election in February 1999. Ballot irregularities were many and his opponent went to court, but domestic and international opinions were very much in support of a new government.

Obasanjo assumed leadership as a civilian president on May 29, 1999, after fifteen years of military rule that generated grave political instability and ruined the economy. Although he lacks the power of the authoritarian military that he enjoyed in the 1970s, he remains decisive in some of his early actions. He has promised to combat corruption, which has destroyed the social fabric of society; to restore confidence in government and the civil service; to run an open government; to restore the country's image in international politics; to improve the standard of living of the people; and to settle the antigovernment protest in the oil-producing regions.

The milieu is different. Corruption has become institutionalized, poverty has spread with the country listed as one of the poorest, revenues have declined, external and domestic debts are enormous, agriculture has been devastated, unemployment and inflation rates are in double digits, youth are restless, and civil society recognizes the crucial role of violence. Although he has promised a new order, the majority of the politicians are motivated by greed and money, and the test of Obasanjo's regime will be how to keep the military in the barracks and change the orientation of politics. The future of Obasanjo and Nigerian politics are dependent on the extent to which he can move the country out of this depression.

TOYIN FALOLA

See also: **Nigeria: Murtala Muhammed, Obasanjo, and Return to Civilian Rule, 1975–1979.**

Biography

Olussegun Obasanjo was born in Abeokuta, a Yoruba city, where he also attended the Baptist Boys' High School. In 1958 he enlisted in the Nigerian army, with military training in England and India. In 1959 he became a commissioned officer, rising to the rank of a general ten years later. In the 1960s he participated in two wars, first in the Congo (now the Democratic Republic of the Congo) and in the Nigerian civil war. He was the commander of the Third Marine Commando Division, and the Biafran forces surrendered to him marking the end of the war in 1970. Obasanjo spent most of the 1970s in political roles, starting as a federal minister of works and housing in 1973, then a chief of staff (Supreme Headquarters) in 1975, and head of state from 1975 to 1979. He retired in 1979. Obasanjo was arrested in March 1995 for concealing information on a coup, an allegation without any evidence, and was tried in secret and sentenced to life imprisonment, later commuted to fifteen years after domestic and international pressure. When Abacha died in 1998, a new government headed by Abdulsalam Abubakar released Obasanjo from prison. Obasanjo assumed leadership as a civilian president on May 29, 1999.

Further Reading

Babatope, E. *Not His Will: The Awolowo Obasanjo Wager.* Lagos: Jodah Publications, 1990.

Falola, T. *The History of Nigeria.* Westport, Conn.: Greenwood, 1999.

Obasanjo, O. *Constitution for National Integration and Development.* Lagos: Friends Foundation, 1989.

———. *My Command: An Account on the Nigerian Civil War,* 1967–1970. London: Heinemann, 1980.

———. *Not My Will.* Ibadan: University Press, 1990.

———. *Nzeogwu: An Intimate Portrait.* Ibadan: Spectrum, 1987.

Obote, Milton (1925–)

First Prime Minister and Former President of Uganda

As independent Uganda's first prime minister (1962–1966) and executive president (1966–1971; 1980–1985) who was twice deposed by military coups (January 1971 and July 1985) and forced into political exile, Apolo Milton Obote occupies a unique place in Uganda's modern history. The controversial circumstances of his overthrow in each case and the general elections that returned him to power in December 1980 have generated considerable debate by scholars and other commentators. His contribution to the nationalist anticolonial struggle and the important role he played in founding the modern Ugandan nation in the first period of his rule seems almost indisputable. However, his overall life history and political career in particular will continue to exercise the minds of many scholars, journalists, and politicians, including both his detractors and admirers.

Upon leaving college, Obote went to neighboring Kenya where he secured temporary employment. After a brief period there, he returned to Uganda to work with the Mowlem construction company in their accounts department at Jinja. In 1952, Obote was back in Kenya again when the company transferred him to their Nairobi branch. He remained there till 1957 when he decided to return home for good.

In both Kenya and Uganda, the early 1950s was a period of nascent nationalism, when Africans began to organize modern political parties and demand self-government. The launching of the Uganda National Congress (UNC) by Ignatius Musazi and Abu Mayanja in 1952 had found Obote in Uganda. He joined the Jinja branch. However, the party's main area of concentration then was Buganda. In Kenya, Obote met Jomo Kenyatta briefly. Later he also met the lawyer C. Argwings-Khodek, whose Nairobi District African Congress he joined, and the trade union leader Tom Mboya. This was also the period during which the Mau Mau movement was active. Though never directly a participant, Obote apparently made his contribution to this and other African political causes quietly. His close association with Argwings-Khodek and Mboya, in particular, provided him with the opportunity for cutting his political teeth in the emergent nationalist struggle of the 1950s.

Obote returned to Uganda around the middle of 1957 and immediately became involved in the local politics of his home district of Lango. The burning political issue then was the question of land tenure. The colonial administration had recently passed the Land Apportionment Act through which it hoped to introduce African individual land ownership. This provoked considerable opposition from the Langi people. Obote's return coincided with widespread unrest in the district. When the British administration asked him to accompany the officials in their tours around Lango to explain the land reform legislation, he obliged. In the event, this turned out to be an opportunity for the young politician to become known among the Langi. He emerged as an articulate, eloquent, and very astute individual who seemed quite critical and completely unafraid of the British administration. When later in the year the incumbent Lango District representative in the Legislative Council (Legco) resigned, Obote decided to contest the election for his successor. The District Council duly elected him and in March 1958 he took up his seat in the Legco.

For Obote this marked the beginning of an active political life in the country's public affairs that was only interrupted by the two military coups of 1971 and 1985. His contribution to the debates in the Legco, in which he articulated issues concerning his constituency, the wider Northern Province, and Uganda as a whole, soon caught the attention of the colonial state. Although later in his career he was to clash with the Buganda kingdom and thus earn the wrath of Uganda's largest and most powerful ethnic group, at this stage he seemed quite preoccupied with ensuring its survival in a future independent Uganda. His biographer, Professor Kenneth Ingham, notes that Obote was then very sympathetic toward Buganda. When Uganda—except Buganda, which declined to participate—held its first direct elections later in 1958, Obote won the Lango seat with an overwhelming majority. He had stood as a UNC candidate. As the country moved toward self-government, the administration appointed him to serve on the country's constitutional committee that was to collect evidence from the Ugandan populace about Uganda's future independence constitution.

Obote's career as party leader began in early 1959 when the UNC split into two wings. One wing was led by him and the other by the veteran politician J. W. "Jolly Joe" Kiwanuka. Meanwhile, the newly elected Legco members from outside Buganda had formed a new political party, the Uganda People's Union (UPU), led by the Busoga District representative, William Nadiope. In March 1960 this party and the Obote wing of the UNC, which was far larger than Kiwanuka's, merged to form the Uganda People's Congress (UPC). Obote was elected president of the UPC and Nadiope became the vice president. It was this party, in alliance with the Buganda-based Kabaka Yekka (KY, or "King Only") political movement advocating Buganda's interests, that formed Uganda's first independence government in 1962. Despite losing power twice, Obote remained president of the party throughout his first exile in Tanzania (1971–1980) and has continued, even in his second exile in Zambia in 1999, to be the UPC leader.

Obote belongs to that group of African politicians often described as the "founding fathers" of their nations. They usually had to grapple with the formidable task of forging new African nations out of many nationalities within the boundaries of their newly independent countries. Having led his country to independence in 1962, he was a signatory to the Organisation of African Unity (OAU) charter in 1963. Four years later in 1967, with Presidents Kenyatta and Nyerere, he participated in the formation of the East African Community.

Internally, Obote attempted to unify Uganda in the mid-1960s by abolishing kingships, discouraging any centrifugal and divisive tendencies, and declaring Uganda a republic with a unitary system of government. In doing this he angered various political forces within the country. In pursuing African indigenous control of the Ugandan economy through nationalization, he antagonized several multinational companies and other external interests. He put Uganda on a sound economic footing during his first regime. This period saw an expanded secondary school system, the construction of an extensive road and railway network, and the introduction of a vastly improved rural health service throughout the country.

However, Obote faced enormous problems and made some serious errors of judgment in his internal political policies. His critics would probably point to the prolonged civil war of the early 1980s as a serious blot in his career, and might argue that his policies may have led to the militarization of politics in Uganda.

Obote also misjudged his chief of the army and air force, Idi Amin. Obote considered Amin one of his most loyal supporters and ignored rumors that he had tortured opponents. Idi Amin was able to build an extensive power base from his high position within Obote's government. In 1970 Obote finally recognized that Idi Amin had become too great a threat and demoted him. However, the following year, Idi Amin led a coup d'étât and declared himself president.

BALAM NYEKO

See also: **Museveni, Yoweri Kaguta; Uganda: Amin Dada, Idi: Coup and Regime, 1971–1979; Uganda: Buganda Agreement, Political Parties, Independence; Uganda: Obote's First Regime, 1962–1971; Uganda: Obote: Second Regime, 1980–1985; Uganda: Tanzanian Invasion, 1979–1980.**

Biography

Obote was born at Akokoro, a small village just north of Lake Kyoga, in Lango District, Northern Uganda, on December 28, 1925. Attended primary school locally in Lira before going on to Gulu High School in neighboring Acholi District. Moved on to secondary school at Busoga College Mwiri, near Jinja, Uganda's second largest town. In March 1947 at the age of twenty-one, Obote joined Makerere College to study English, geography, and general studies for the intermediate certificate. Served as Uganda's first prime minister, 1962–1966. Deposed by military coups in January 1971 and July 1985.

Further Reading

Gingyera-Pinycwa, A. G. G. *Apolo Milton Obote and His Times.* New York and Lagos: NOK Publishers, 1978.

Ingham, K. *Obote: A Political Biography.* New York: Routledge, 1994.

Mazrui, A. A. "The Social Origins of Ugandan Presidents: From King to Peasant Warrior." *Canadian Journal of African Studies.* 8, no. 1 (1974): 3–23.

Museveni, Y. K. *Sowing the Mustard Seed: The Struggle for Freedom and Democracy in Uganda*, edited by E. Kanyogonya and K. Shillington. Basingstoke: Macmillan, 1997.

Nyeko, B. "A. M. Obote Revisited: A Review Article." *Uganda Journal.* 44 (1997): 73–91.

Omara-Otunnu, A. *Politics and the Military in Uganda, 1890–1985.* London: Macmillan, 1987.

Uzoigwe, G. N. (ed.). *Uganda: The Dilemma of Nationhood.* New York and Lagos: NOK Publishers, 1982.

Odinga, A. Oginga (1911–1994)

Kenyan Nationalist

Jaramogi Ajuma Oginga Odinga was an African nationalist and a leading figure in Kenya's struggle for independence from Great Britain. He took center stage in the independence fight while Jomo Kenyatta was imprisoned. Shortly after independence, Odinga parted company with Kenyatta. His organizational skill and political brilliance were devoted to creating an opposition movement. He abhorred the single-party rule imposed on Kenya first by Jomo Kenyatta and later by Daniel Tirotich Arap Moi. Odinga promoted the ideal of democratic socialism, which he preferred to what he perceived as authoritarian rule. Many observers consider Odinga one of Kenya's most controversial leaders. Odinga accused post-independence Kenya of being a "neo-colonialist" state. He wrote: "The object of neo-colonialism is to ensure that power is handed to men who are moderate and easily controlled, political stooges. Everything is done to ensure that accredited heirs of colonial interest capture power. This explains the pre-independence preoccupation of the colonial power with the creation of an African Middle class and the frenzy to corrupt leaders at all levels with temptations of office and property and preferably both" (Odinga, 1967, p.256).

Odinga was especially concerned about mistreatment of "freedom fighters," including the official practice of denying them land. It angered Odinga that following independence Britain silenced militant Africans and promoted moderate Africans, who supported what he perceived as neocolonial arrangements.

Jomo Kenyatta recruited him to organize the Luo on behalf of a growing Kenya African Union (KAU) when it initiated the post–World War II independence struggle. Odinga and other liberal Africans attempted to unite disparate African political and social organizations into a broad national movement. They tried to make KAU's leadership reflect Kenya's ethnic diversity. Odinga's Nyanza branch of the KAU became one of the strongest in Kenya. Despite this, KAU's executive committee remained overwhelmingly Kikuyu.

Odinga went to India on a two-month study tour in 1953. After Kenya declared a national emergency due to the Mau Mau revolt, Odinga formed the Luo Union. This was one of many ethnic organizations encouraged by the British to keep Africans divided. Arrested and questioned for opposing British efforts to recruit Luo to fight during the Mau Mau revolt, this only added to his fame as a nationalist.

In 1958 Odinga shocked the British Colonial Office by openly referring to Kenyatta as the recognized leader of Kenya's independence movement and calling for his immediate release from detention. Kenyatta became the symbol of nationalism and freedom. This signaled to the British that their effort to use divide-and-conquer tactics with various African to delay independence had failed. The Kenya Legislative Council recognized Kenyatta as a genuine political leader, despite previous efforts to discredit him.

The Kenya African National Union (KANU) led by James Gichuru, Tom Mboya, and Oginga Odinga met with British officials at Lancaster House, in England, to discuss independence. KANU favored immediate independence and opposed the continued colonial occupation of Kenya. Another group, led by Ronald Ngala, together with Daniel Arap Moi and Masinde Muliro, was known as the Kenya African Democratic Union, or KADU. This group feared domination by the Luo and Kikuyu; they favored cooperation with the colonial regime and a delay of independence.

With Odinga and Mboya's help, KANU won a majority of seats in Kenya's first nonracial election. Odinga helped speed Kenya's advance to self-government. KADU favored *majimbo* or regionalism, while KANU favored centralism and the creation of a national identity as Kenyans. In election campaigns, KADU emphasized ethnic identity, while KANU appealed to a form of anticolonialism then termed "African socialism" as well as nationalism.

Odinga was vice president of KANU; he served as minister for home affairs from 1963 to 1964, and then vice president of Kenya. In 1960 Odinga visited China and Russia. Odinga's socialist views increasingly conflicted with Kenyatta's procapitalist stance. Odinga formed the Lumumba Institute, with the aid of socialist countries, to provide ideological training for Kenyan politicians. Kenyatta officially opened the institute at the end of 1964. Kenya's Ministry of Defense discovered guns in the basement of the Ministry of Home Affairs, headed by Odinga. British newspapers alleged that Odinga was plotting a communist revolution for Kenya. Odinga denied these charges, claiming that the arms had been ordered when Britain still maintained control over the region and the police force because he and Kenyatta wanted to be able to arm the police themselves.

Odinga held onto power from 1964 to 1966. Subsequently, he formed a radical political opposition party known as the Kenya People's Union (KPU). In April 1966, Odinga resigned from office to lead the KPU, thus making him the leading figure of Kenyan opposition. In 1967 he published an autobiography titled *Not Yet Uhuru*, became influential, and encouraged open opposition to the government. Fearing the spread of violence, the government banned the KPU following the assassination of Tom Mboya in 1969. The government arrested and detained Odinga in an effort to quell ethnic violence. In 1971 he announced his reconciliation with Kenyatta, but never again did he enjoy Kenyatta's confidence. Upon release from detention, Odinga rejoined KANU, but did not play a prominent role, as he was prohibited from running for a parliamentary seat.

Odinga continued to be an outspoken critic of the government and corruption. The end of the Cold War created international pressure for President Daniel arap Moi (in power since 1978) to agree to multiparty elections in 1992. During the election, he exposed major corruption. He easily won a seat in parliament, but lost his bid for the presidency, coming in last with 12 per cent of the vote. Again, he became the official leader of Kenya's parliamentary opposition, and chairman of the Public Accounts Committee. Odinga died in Kisumu, Kenya, in 1994.

DALLAS L. BROWNE

See also: **Kenya: Kenyatta, Jomo: Life and Government of; Kenya: Mau Mau Revolt.**

Biography

Jaramogi Ajuma Oginga Odinga was born at Nyamire in Sakwa location, in Central Nyanza province in 1911. Attended Maseno Secondary School and Kenya's Alliance High School. After graduating from high school, entered Makerere University in Uganda. Earned a diploma in education and began a career as a teacher of mathematics at the Church Missionary School in Maseno. Promotion to headmaster of the Veterinary School at Maseno in 1943. Odinga resigned the headmastership in 1946 to found the Luo Thrift and Trading Corporation. Appointed in 1947 to the Central Nyanza African District Council. Vice president of Kenya, 1963–1969. Died in Kisumu, Kenya, in 1994.

Further Reading

Elderkin, S. *The Passing of a Hero: Jaramogi Oginga Odinga*. Nairobi: Jaramogi Oginga Odinga Foundation, 1994.

Gertzel, C. J. *The Politics of Independent Kenya 1963–1968*. Evanston: Northwestern University Press, 1970.

Goldsworthy, D. *Tom Mboya, The Man Kenya Wanted to Forget*. Nairobi: East African Publishing House, 1982.

Kibaki, J. B. *Transtribal Politics and the Little General Election*. Dar es Salaam: University College Dar es Salaam. Dissertation. Political Science, Paper Number 6. 1968.

Leys, C. *Underdevelopment in Kenya: The Political Economy of Neo-Colonialism*. Berkeley: University of California Press, 1974.

Mazrui, A. A. *Nationalism and New States in Africa*. London: Heinemann, 1985.

Mboya, T. *The Challenge of Nationhood*. London: Andre Deutsch, 1970.

———. *Freedom and After*. London: Andre Deutsch, 1963.

Odhiambo, A. *Jaramogi Ajuma Oginga Odinga: A Biography.* Nairobi: East African Educational Publishers, 1997.
Odinga, O. *Not Yet Uhuru: The Autobiography of Oginga Odinga.* New York: Hill and Wang, 1969.
Oruka, H. O. *Oginga Odinga: His Philosophy and Beliefs.* Nairobi: Initiatives Publishers, Sage Philosophy Series (Number 1), 1992.
Schatzberg, M. G. (ed.). *The Political Economy of Kenya.* New York: Praeger, 1987.

Oil

Oil constitutes a major source of energy for any category of countries, rich or poor, industrialized or developing. All countries need it for different tasks, such as industry, transportation, or heating. Petroleum by-products are also used for a variety of products that are of importance to Africa, such as fertilizer. Oil's utility makes it an important source of revenue for countries that produce it. For countries that do not produce it, yet must use it, it constitutes a major import item that can be a drain on valuable foreign exchange if prices are high.

Apart from the fact that only a few countries in Africa are endowed with oil resources of any significance, Africa's known share of global reserves is much too small to make it a highly influential voice in global oil politics. Known reserves in the region were estimated to be around 10 per cent of the global total during the 1970s. Comparatively, Saudi Arabia alone accounts for 25 per cent of the world's reserves. In the 1980s, Africa's ratio of global oil exports was only around 4 per cent.

Oil production in Africa is concentrated in a few countries, the most significant of which are Libya, Algeria, Nigeria, Gabon, Angola, and the Democratic Republic of Congo. Production in these countries dates back to the late 1950s but did not become a driving force of their economies until the 1970s. Other producers of some significance include Cameroon, Egypt, and Tunisia. Major discoveries have also been made in Chad that would make that country the next new member of Africa's exclusive oil producing club, once production begins.

Oil did not become an issue of major contention in Africa (or, indeed, the world in general) until 1973. It was propelled to the forefront of domestic and global economic politics following the 1973 Arab-Israeli war when, in retaliation against the Western states that had supported Israel in the war, the Organization of Petroleum Exporting Countries (OPEC) succeeded in organizing an oil cartel, cutting back on production while raising prices. The 1973 cartel lasted until 1976. In 1979–1980, a second wave of restriction was put into effect.

Apart from its effects on the industrial capacity and household needs of industrialized countries, the OPEC cartel had two contradictory effects on the economies of Africa. African countries that do not produce oil were forced by the higher prices to divert important foreign exchange reserves to buy oil at the higher rate. The cartel affected the oil importing states in different ways. Those that waited to see if prices would return to the pre-cartel level ended up paying even more than they would have paid had they ordered their requirements when prices started rising. On the other hand, the countries that ordered their requirements as prices started rising ended up beating the price hikes that came with time. The cartel affected not just crude oil but also by-products of oil. Therefore, its effects were extensive.

The high oil prices increased the indebtedness of African states and contributed to the debt crisis that erupted in the region in the early 1980s. African governments were forced to contend with less oil at very high price. The terms of trade (the price of exports in relation to the price of imports) already worked against Africa, and many countries were compelled to borrow more to meet their energy needs and also have enough left to meet their need for imported manufactured products. The result was yet more debt, for which interest had to be paid as well.

For oil-producing African countries, OPEC's actions had quite the opposite effect. The high oil prices increased their revenue base and most raised production to take advantage of the higher prices and increased demand. The rise in oil revenue led oil-producing African states to deemphasize agriculture and encouraged the migration of people from rural areas to the cities to wok in oil-related positions. The net result was that three of the major oil-producing African states—Libya, Congo, and Gabon—became dependent on oil exports for more than 80 per cent of their export revenues in 1984–1985. The ratio for Nigeria was over 90 per cent, Angola 76 per cent, and Egypt 50 per cent. Only Algeria and Tunisia, with 36 and 40 per cent, respectively, maintained a degree of diversification within their export earnings.

The increased demand for their oil of the 1970s was only a short-lived blessing for African countries. By the early 1980s, prices had fallen to an all-time low, and prices have generally remained low. In the summer of 1998, prices fell further, before beginning to recover a year later. The legacy of nearly two decades of low oil prices continue to cause economic difficulties for African countries that depend on it for the bulk of their foreign exchange earnings.

Moses K. Tesi

See also: **Development, Postcolonial: Central Planning, Private Enterprise, Investment; Libya: Oil, Politics, OPEC; Nigeria: Industry, Oil, Economy; Sudan: Cotton, Irrigation, and Oil, 1970s.**

Further Reading

Baker, J. "Oil and African Development." *Journal of Modern African Studies.* 15, no. 2.
Hammeed, K. A. "The Oil Revolution and African Development." *African Affairs.* July 1976.
Johnson R. W., and E. J. Wilson, III. "The Oil Crisis' and African Economies: Oil Wave on a Tidal Flood of Industrial Price Inflation." *DAEDALUS.* Spring 1982.
LeVine, V. T., and T. Luke. *The Arab-African Connection: Political and Economic Realities.* Boulder, Colo.: Westview Press, 1979.
Wilson, E. J. III. "The Energy Crisis and African Underdevelopment." *Africa Today.* October–December 1975.

Oil Rivers Protectorate: *See* Lagos Colony and Oil Rivers Protectorate.

Old Kingdom: *See* Egypt, Ancient: Old Kingdom and Its Contacts to the South: Historical Outline.

Olduwan and Acheulian: Early Stone Age

Around 2.5 million years ago (hereafter *mya*), global cooling and drying from polar glaciation initiated a period of accelerated biological and behavioral readjustment and change across mixed habitats: in East Africa, major adaptive changes occur in protohuman diet and behavior. Earliest traces of the genus *Homo*, which is archaeologically defined by toolmaking, are left by its first species, *H. habilis* ("able man," the toolmaker), on the continent's rifted and uplifted eastern side, where a volcanic geology favors fossil preservation.

Both advanced gracile australopithecines and early habilines (*H. habilis* varieties) were omnivores occupying an expanding scavenging niche, so stone knapping began for hammers to extract bone marrow, and for a sharp edge for butchering and plant processing. The earliest intentionally flaked stone tools have been discovered at Gona, Ethiopia, dated 2.5 million years old (hereafter *myo*); they are multipurpose hand-sized choppers and flakes of simplest design, though not obviously more rudimentary than those 1.8 *myo* finds at Olduvai that named this entire earliest tool-making period "the Oldowan." It persists virtually unchanged for 1*my*, with chipping techniques gradually refined to bring in the first bifacial tools: the Developed Oldowan Industry 1.7 > 1.6 *mya*, now considered part of the early Acheulean complex, formerly thought to have appeared around 1.5 *mya*.

By classifying different Oldowan tool types, Mary Leakey implied that the makers could mentally image standard designs for specific tasks, but most researchers now believe this ability developed only later, with a larger-brained species: Oldowan technology is the basic minimum required for effectiveness, involving little more than detaching flakes from cores (mostly large "cobbles"). Though the choppers resulting from this core reduction are well known, the more abundant flake products were probably more important. All Oldowan artifacts were rudimentary enough to be mistaken for later traditions' byproducts, so their occurrences can only be dated by associated fauna, such as at Sterkfontein and Swartkrans (South Africa), where Oldowan toolmakers were living two *mya*.

It is probably the overall rarity of habiline fossil finds that accounts for tools having been found exclusively in association with early Homo's robust contemporaries the paranthropines. Though *P. robustus*'s brain size never crosses the "cerebral rubicon" of 600 cm^2, the robust species are otherwise anatomically candidate tool users in having had the same precision grip as Homo. Isotopic analysis of the Swartkrans paranthropine remains showed a remarkable protein intake for a vegetarian species, and when the site's fossil bone tools (some of the world's oldest) were reexamined, the wear patterns on these 13 > 19 cm-long straight splinters were found to result not from uprooting tubers, as initially proposed, but from digging into termite mounds. Year-round *insectivory* may have been as important as carnivory in the diet of habilines too.

Otherwise, direct evidence of non-toolmaking life is absent almost everywhere due to organic materials' ephemeral nature. And only East African sites (notably Olduvai and East Turkana) have sufficient excavation to allow some reconstruction of the life and culture of the several tool-making hominid species. Notably, everywhere the evidence for deliberate hunting (i.e., woodworking: spears), being perishable, is disadvantaged against evidence for scavenging (i.e., stone for butchering: hand-axes). But a recent Tanzanian hand-axe assemblage (Peninj west of Lake Natron) from 1.5 *mya* includes worn blades with traces of acacia-wood, suggesting woodworking was underway one million years earlier than previously imagined (from the oldest known wooden implements, from northern Europe 400,000 years ago, hereafter *tya*). This evidence that the tool kit was not limited to hand-held stone until around 500 *tya*, as formerly thought, but included shaped wooden implements, may revise present estimation of the habilines' foraging capacities.

Many sites show that Oldowan and later tools occur in localized concentrations (at Sterkfontein, for instance, cores from gravels close to the site were brought to be worked in the shade of trees growing at cave entrances). Since these artifact clusters are typically found near resources (water, plant foods, shade trees, rock outcrops), early studies took them to indicate camps ("home bases") consisting of "living floors" 20 > 60 feet across, where tool-manufacturing and other activities were centered. Being frequently located beneath or near groves of climbable trees, these accumulations of stone and bone refuse also possibly mark "tree-nest refuges," to which forage and scavenged meat (mainly long marrow bones) could be carried. This hypothesis is plausible if Oldowan hominids were still quasi-arboreal, but if they were not, it means they were able—despite lacking control of fire—to defend their safe places cooperatively against competitors. This implies a degree of reciprocity that now seems improbable this early on, as does the argument for food sharing.

For future ground-dwellers leaving the shelter of trees, however, predation by large carnivores would have encouraged large-group living and increased sociality. Coping with life in large social groups would have resulted in selection for increased intelligence, which was then applied in stone and other toolmaking; "curation" (retaining tools for future use rather than just shaping suitable materials at hand); and organized food procurement.

Major change in the tool kit leading to the more advanced Acheulean industry is seen first at Konso-Gardula in the southern Main Ethiopian Rift 1.9 > 1.3 *mya*, contemporaneous with the around 1.8 *myo* emergence of *H. ergaster*, early/African *Homo erectus*, who appears 1.6 *mya* at Koobi Fora. A stream-side site here yielded both the post-Oldowan "Karari" tool kit featuring serrated cutting flakes, and an arc of red patches indicating fireplaces: evidence of much earlier manipulation of fire than the 1.1 *myo* evidence from Swartkrans.

But fire was likely first managed for protection and warmth; only circumstantial evidence exists for a cooked rather than raw diet for *H. ergaster*. Her reduced chewing musculature, smaller molars, and less protective enamel compared to the habilines are thus more probably due to increased reliance on tools for processing tough foods than to cooking of new savanna edibles such as tubers. Certainly at some point the domestication of fire resulted in a diversification of diet that spurred *ergaster's* spread beyond the woodland mosaic, but until conclusive evidence of this appears, this critical range expansion should be attributed primarily to both her more modern anatomy (significantly, an increased cranial breadth) and improved tools. These were manufactured in great quantities in dedicated "workshops," with a preference for large (fist-sized) cobbles of hard-to-work quartzite, off which large flakes could be struck for the crafting of both scrapers and elaborate, standardized *bifaces* (almond-shaped *hand-axes* and *cleavers*).

The radical cognitive advance represented by this new technology (implying the toolmaker retaining a mental template) may have been due to a general increase in intelligence arising out of growth in size of the social group. As tool-carrying savanna gatherers, women made an enhanced contribution to group subsistence that was probably fundamental to the evolution of a more intense sociality. Acheulean toolmaking evidences the introduction of rules into society, with the pace of cultural evolution quickening beyond the proto-human when stoneworking came to form a *tradition*, probably along with other sets of rule-governed behaviors, forms, and procedures. (Stable pair-bonding and cooperative defense of food stores, however, may have arisen somewhat earlier, contrary to some recent speculation.)

Although bifaces vary in finish, with imposed patterns suggesting incipient symbolization (beliefs, aesthetic sense), they nevertheless do not show strong style trends in either time or space: hand-axe distributions indicate that the basic design concept was shared and transmitted down 1 *my*, and spanned the continent. There was no premium on innovation for what was, in the narrow niche of riverine wetlands and valley bottoms preferred by Acheulean biface-makers, the best design for a large, sharp hand-held tool.

The apparent predilection for semi-aquatic habitats explains the narrow, linear Acheulean geographic distribution, and why even with low population densities, it is found from the Cape to Morocco. The "Nariokotome/Turkana boy" fossil indicates *H. ergaster*'s locomotion may have been more efficient than that of modern humans skeletally adapted to birthing larger-brained offspring; he becomes a successful hunter by running his swift savanna quarry to ground but also by occupying and adapting quickly to new niches (riverine wetlands, beachcombing: Acheulean tools recently found embedded in Eritrean coral reef along with fossil shellfish and crustacea were obviously used to harvest marine food. Though little evidence can survive land-water interfaces, such data may justify renewed attention to the hypothesis that at least part of our history took place in wetland environments).

Over the Acheulean's million years of evolution in Africa, it spread into most habitats other than true desert and moist evergreen woodland (Kalambo Falls excepted): hand-axes have been found in Nigeria (Jos), upper Niger (Adrar Bous), at riverside sites in Volta and Senegal, in middle and lower Egypt and the oases of Dakhla and Kharga west of the Nile, at Casablanca and Rabat, and in surface scatters from Zambia to the Cape. Dates indicate these continental radiations from East Africa took place over 500 *ty*. At Kabwe and Elandsfontein, "Broken Hill man" (200 *tya*) and "Saldanha man" (400 > 300 *tya*) respectively are not *H. ergaster*, but rather a massively built (archaic) *H. sapiens* named *H. heidelbergensis*, who also occurs in central Tanzania (Eyasi) around 100 *tya*.

The Acheulean in Africa, as elsewhere, continued in use by archaic *H. sapiens* to 200 > 100 *tya*, when the bifaces disappeared and the flake-tool component evolved into lighter toolkits with stone hafted into wood—the regional variants of the Middle Stone Age (Africa)/Middle Palaeolithic (Eurasia).

ROBERT PAPINI

See also: **Humankind: Hominids, Early, Origins of.**

Further Reading

Asfaw, B., et al. "The Earliest Acheulean from Konso-Gardula." *Nature.* 360 (1992): 732–735.

Berthelet, A., and J. Chavaillon. *The Use of Tools by Human and Non-human Primates*. Oxford: Clarendon Press, 1993.

Clark, J. D. "The Earliest Cultural Evidence of Hominids in Southern and South Central Africa." In *From Apes to Angels: Essays in Anthropology in Honour of Phillip V. Tobias*, edited by G. Sperber. New York: Wiley-Liss, 1990.

Gibson, K., and Ingold (eds.). *Tools, Language, and Cognition in Human Evolution*. Cambridge: Cambridge University Press, 1993.

Kuman, K. "The Earliest South African Industries." In *Early Human Behaviour in Global Context: The Rise and Diversity of the Lower Palaeolithic Record*, edited by M. Petraglia and R. Korisettar. London: Routledge, 1998.

Nitecki, M. H., and D. V. Nitecki (eds.). *The Evolution of Human Hunting*. New York: Plenum, 1987.

Roche, H., et al. "Early Hominid Stone Tool Production and Technical Skill 2.34 Myr Ago in West Turkana, Kenya." *Nature.* 399 (1999): 57–60.

Schick, K. D., N. Toth. *Making Silent Stones Speak: Human Evolution and the Dawn of Technology.* New York: Simon and Schuster, 1993.

Semaw, S., et al. "2.5-Million-Year-Old Stone Tools From Gona, Ethiopia." *Nature.* 385 (1997): 333–336.

Wynn, T. "Tools and the Evolution of Human Intelligence." In *Machiavellian Intelligence: Social Expertise and the Evolution of Intellect in Monkeys, Apes and Humans*, edited by R. W. Byrne and A. W. Whiten, eds. Cambridge: Cambridge University Press, 1988: pp.270–284.

Olympio, Sylvanus (1902–1963)

Nationalist Leader and First President of the Togolese Republic

Born in Lomé on September 6, 1902, to an influential coastal merchant family, Olympio was educated at the University of Vienna and the London School of Economics. From an early age he was groomed for a leadership role among the Ewe-speaking people and the wider Togolese community. His charismatic style and authoritarian leadership proved the greatest threat to both French colonial control and postindependence political stability.

Sylvanus' father, Octavianus, was Lomé's leading citizen during the German, British, and French occupation. Sylvanus benefited from his father's favorable alliances in education and commerce. Upon returning to Lomé in 1926, Olympio joined the largest commercial firm, the British-oriented United Africa Company (UAC), and served with it in Nigeria (1926–1928), Gold Coast (1928), and French Togoland (1928–1938), becoming its general manager for Togoland and a prosperous merchant himself. A founding member and vice president of the Cercle des Amitiés Françaises, a pro-French cultural alliance association for the Lomé elite that later evolved into the Comité de l'Unité Togolaise (CUT), Olympio was imprisoned in 1942 in neighboring Benin, and only permitted to return with the end of the Vichy administration. In 1946 he led his nascent party to victory in the first elections for the new Assemblée Representative and became the Assembly's president (1946–1952).

His involvement in the pan-Ewe unification movement and links with the All-Ewe Conference in the neighboring Gold Coast Colony and British Togoland, coupled with his erudite petitions to the United Nations Trusteeship Commission, placed him at odds with the French administration. The French government saw the solution in his relocating to the UAC Paris branch, in an effort to curtail his political influence. When he refused to leave Lomé, he was arrested on trumped-up charges for currency trafficking and prohibited from running for office. The CUT was also subjected to political intimidation as part of a wider attempt by French authorities allegedly to promote political alternatives. The CUT, under Olympio's leadership, responded to this by boycotting all elections. This decision in turn led to Olympio's main rival Nicolas Grunitzky and his Parti Togolais du Progrès gaining control of the 1958 Togo (French Union) legislature.

The UN Trusteeship Council, however, disagreed with the French Union and its concomitant granting of autonomy to Togo. The UN supervised an election that effectively ended the union with Togo, and with it the administration of Grunitzky. Olympio was named prime minister (1958–1961). He was also elected mayor of Lomé (1959–1961). The frustratingly close 1956 UN-administered plebiscite in British Togoland that led to its amalgamation with the Gold Coast Colony, and the subsequent 1957 gaining of independence in Ghana, marked a shift in Olympio's political interests away from Ewe-centered concerns toward the new Togolese nation-state. After the merger of the two British zones, Olympio pressed for the independence of French Togo and appeared before the United Nations Trusteeship Commission. Independence was declared on April 23, 1960. Olympio engineered significant constitutional changes, however, and with the passing of a referendum on a presidential system, he became president of the republic (1961–1963). The new constitution has been described as having all the powers of a U.S. presidency and all the weaknesses of parliament in the Fifth French Republic (Prouzet, 1976, p.26).

After independence, Olympio's political trajectory and technique changed markedly. He adopted a style of leadership marked by authoritarianism and paternalism, and his personal political goals clashed with those of the Togolese nation and the population as a whole. The most obvious example of this was the widening gulf between Juvento, the youth wing of the CUT, and the CUT. Juvento had established itself as an independent party in 1959. After independence, however, Olympio criticized the Juvento leadership as subversive and disloyal and imprisoned many of its most prominent members. Olympio felt himself to be in the shadow of the great independence leader of Ghana, Kwame Nkrumah, and a clash over the integration of Togo within a greater Ghana led to the closing of the Ghana-Togo border. Further examples of this departure in style include the lack of attention given to northern leaders and northern concerns, the impact of the border closure on Lomé commerce, the pressures of taxation on cocoa producers, and a clash with the Catholic archbishop in Lomé.

This change in personal style in 1961 and 1962 was mirrored by an intensified drive against all organized political opposition. Leaders of other parties and internal threats were imprisoned for alleged plots, opposition parties disqualified from standing in elections, and excessively strict electoral laws provided the means for political leverage. This political despotism culminated in 1962, with the creation of a one-party state under which all parties were banned except the CUT.

The political terror of 1962 coincided with the first serious financial test of the former French colony's internal economy. Olympio unwisely pushed for a balanced budget, and in so doing awakened the hostility of the last few remaining sectors of the administrative hierarchy that had not already declared their opposition to him. Fiscal austerity led to conflict with the colonial military veterans' association, and this served as a means whereby serving officers enhanced their collegial credentials. The NCO and officer corps sought better pay and conditions for themselves and their veteran allies and led the assault on the president's private Lomé residence on January 13, 1963. Olympio was killed by a group of soldiers; it is widely acknowledged that the future president, Etienne Gnassingbé Eyadéma, fired the shot that killed Olympio as he attempted to scale the walls of the neighboring United States Embassy.

After Olympio's death, all imprisoned dissidents were released, and political activities resumed. Nicolas Grunitsky, recalled from exile to assume the presidency, convened a national assembly. The political situation continued to remain unstable until Eyadéma himself seized power in another bloody coup d'étât in 1967.

The memory of Olympio, although somewhat tarnished by his later activities, remains a common point for all opposition to the Eyadéma dictatorship. Two of Olympio's sons remain active in the exiled political community, and one, Gilchrist Olympio, is widely believed to have won the 1998 president election. The results, marred by irregularities, fraud, and political violence, are the subject of a 2001 UN/OAU report.

BENJAMIN NICHOLAS LAWRANCE

See also: **Togo.**

Biography

Born in Lomé on September 6, 1902. Educated at the University of Vienna and the London School of Economics. Led the CUT to victory in the first elections for the new Assemblée Representative. Became the assembly's president in 1946, served until 1952. Named prime minister in 1958, served until 1961. Elected mayor of Lomé in 1959, served until 1961. Served as president of the republic from 1961 to 1963. Killed in an assault on his private Lomé residence on January 13, 1963.

Further Reading

Dyke, F. A., E. Sylvanus. *Olympio, libérateur du Togo: essai biographique*. Lomé: Togo, 1994.

Kokouvi Agbobli, A. *Sylvanus Olympio, un destin tragique*. Abidjan, Côte d'Ivoire: Livre Sud, 1992.

Olympio, S. *Quelques discours importants du Président Sylvanus Olympio en 1961*. Lomé, Togo: République togolaise, 1962.

Wiyao, E. *13 Janvier 1963–1913 Janvier 1967. Pourquoi?* Lomé: Les Nouvelles Editions Africaines du Togo, 1997.

Omdurman: *See* Sudan: Omdurman and Reconquest.

One-Party States: *See* Political Parties and One-Party States.

OPEC: *See* Oil.

Orange Free State: *See* Boer Expansion: Interior of South Africa.

Organization of African Unity (OAU) and Pan-Africanism

The Organization of African Unity (OAU) was an outgrowth of several years of pan-African sentiments dating from 1900, when the First Pan-African Congress met in London. Its establishment in 1963 was the culmination of successive attempts at establishing an inter-African organization. The emotional impetus for OAU's birth was provided by the colonial situation.

The deep-rooted unity of African states manifested itself first in the development of Pan-Africanism as an expression of African cultural nationalism, and later in what was called the "African personality" in world affairs. Its genesis could be dated to the beginning of the twentieth century, when the term "pan-Africanism" first came into vogue. Between 1900 and 1927, five congresses met to promote black solidarity and protest organizations. Though the initiators and delegates were primarily West Indian and African American, they nevertheless made some progress in putting the African case to the world.

During the 1930s, the movement was almost nonexistent, but in 1944 several black organizations founded the Pan-African Federation, and by the time the sixth Pan-African Congress was organized in 1945, Pan-Africanism and African nationalism had found concrete expression. Africans were now in the majority and for the first time the necessity for well-organized, firmly-knit movements as a primary condition for the success of the national liberation struggle in Africa was emphasized.

The first conference of independent African states, initiated by the newly independent state of Ghana, was held in Accra in 1958, resulting in a great upsurge of interest in the cause of African freedom and unity. Conflicts of opinion, however, divided the governments of the newly independent African states, leading to the emergence, in the early 1960s, of two powerful blocs. The first was the Casablanca Group, which consisted of the more "radical" states. Created in January 1961 under the leadership of Dr. Kwame Nkrumah of Ghana, the group argued for rapid political unity. The second group, known as the Monrovia Group, consisted of the more conservative states. Founded in May 1961, it favored a program of gradual economic unity. There was yet a third group, the Brazzaville Group, consisting of representatives of former French colonies still under powerful French influence and indirect control. It was comparatively weak and was eventually absorbed by the Casablanca Group.

At any rate, despite the differences in interests and approach, the ideal of a continental organization remained, and African leaders continued to strive towards its realization. Primarily through the initiative of Emperor Haile Selassie I of Ethiopia, Sir Abubakar Tafawa Balewa (prime minister of Nigeria), and President Sekou Toure of Guinea, moves were commenced to resolve the differences between the Monrovia and Casablanca Groups. This culminated in a meeting of representatives from independent African states at Addis Ababa, the Ethiopian capital in 1963. The organization which the contracting parties agreed to establish was christened the Organization of African Unity and its charter was signed on May 25, 1963, by the thirty-two leaders of the then independent Africans states. After the formation of the OAU, the two ideological groups disbanded. Membership of the Organization was open to all independent African States and Islands surrounding Africa.

The broad aims and objectives of the OAU, as set out in articles II and III of its charter, were to:

(a) promote the unity and solidarity of the African States;
(b) coordinate and intensify efforts to achieve a better life for the peoples of Africa;
(c) defend their sovereignty, territorial integrity, and independence;
(d) eradicate all forms of colonialism from Africa; and
(e) promote international co-operation, having due regard to the Charter of the United Nations and its Universal Declaration of Human Rights.

Toward the above ends, the member-states pledged themselves to coordinate and harmonize their general policies by cooperation, especially in the following fields: politics and diplomacy; economics, including transport and communications; education and culture; health, sanitation and nutrition; science and technology; and defense and security.

Other provisions of the OAU Charter affirmed the principles of equality of all member-states with each other; noninterference in the internal affairs of states; respect for the existing frontiers of member states; and peaceful settlement of disputes. The charter equally condemned all forms of political subversion and assassination and pledged the member states to work for the liberation of African peoples then still under colonial rule and in South Africa. It declared the loyalty of member states to the policy of nonalignment by which African independent nations were implored to remain outside the "big-power blocs" into which the rest of the world was then divided, to forestall African nations loosing their newly won independence. The OAU Charter was indeed a reflection of a compromise between the various prevailing opinions, especially among the Casablanca and Monrovia Groups, envisaging a unity transcending ethnic and national differences. From 1963, therefore, the African continent possessed its own international forum which won the loyalty of all the states, including those that gained their independence thereafter.

To ensure the achievement of the OAU's aims and objectives, several institutions were created. This consisted of an assembly of heads of state and government, which was the policy-making body of the organization; a council of ministers appointed by the assembly; a general secretariat, which was the permanent administrative body of the OAU, based in Addis Ababa; and a commission to settle disputes. Peace-keeping efforts were made through the Commission of Mediation, Conciliation and Arbitration, and through ad-hoc committees. Technical research, mainly in agriculture, was conducted through a scientific and research commission. Revenue for the organization was derived from member states, each of which was requested to contribute on the same scale as its contribution to membership in the United Nations.

Once launched, the OAU gave Pan-Africanist ideas a supranational basis toward overcoming the rivalries of nationalism and the divisions which hitherto characterized interstate relations. Admittedly, the deep-seated misgivings were not completely overcome, yet on the heels of the Addis Ababa compromise, the perspectives of the Pan-Africanists were at least redefined.

The survival and relevance of the organization, however, had over the years been buffered by a myriad of crises, and shaken by numerous problems. Among several others, the organization had been threatened by severe internal political crises and civil wars within and among member states. In the opening years of the OAU, for example, the earlier division between "moderates" and "radicals" continued to exist. The difficulty consisted, really, in a strong neocolonial presence. The other main difficulty, especially during the formative years of the OAU, was that the Pan-African scope and nature of the organization came into conflict with regional organizations and groupings. There were multiple loyalties of member-states to different pro-imperialist international organizations. This explains why at inception the meetings of the OAU were at times reduced to little more than empty talk or even the echo of voices and interference from outside Africa. Ideological cleavages among its member states or, divergent leanings toward opposing ideological blocs in the international system, had to be acknowledged. The OAU was beset by crushing economic and financial problems. Moreover, the apprehensive weight of pressures placed on several OAU member states by external powers and forces had virtually relegated the continental body into functional irrelevance during its last years. The general orientation of the bulk of African states had been pro-imperialist while the institutional structure of the OAU itself remained largely superstructural and superficial. Thus the OAU was less effective in tackling the problem of neocolonialism.

The OAU settled several boundary disputes between various member nations. From its inception, the political liberation of Africa was its preeminent Pan-African concern and duty. Toward this end, the organization established a special fund to aid independence movements against colonial rule in Africa. This eventually culminated in independence in several African countries such as Guinea-Bissau in 1974, Angola, Mozambique, Cape Verde, and Sao Tome in 1975; Zimbabwe in 1980 and Namibia in 1990. The struggle against apartheid and white minority rule in South Africa was for long a major preoccupation of the OAU. It was a great triumph, therefore, for the organization when the new democratic South Africa joined the league in 1994, bringing the membership of the OAU to fifty-three.

On the economic front, where the purpose of the OAU was to achieve a better life for the peoples of Africa, it did not achieve as much, as Africa remains ravaged by famine and hunger and characterized by poverty, illiteracy, and a lack of economic growth. Admittedly, the OAU, concerned with Africa's economic problem, began to address itself frontally to the critical and important issue of economic cooperation and development, especially from the 1980s. A treaty establishing an African economic community by 2000 was signed in June 1991 at the Abuja OAU summit. However, it is still expected that in the twenty-first century, the liberation of the continent from economic domination should be the central Pan-African task.

That task has now fallen to the African Union. On September 9, 1999, the OAU issued a declaration now known as the Sirte Declaration, which officially called for the establishment of a new body, to be called the African Union (AU). At the Lomé summit in 2000, the Constitutive Act of the Union was adopted. In 2001 the Lusaka summit produced an outline of the implementation of the AU. Finally, in 2002 at the Durban summit, the African Union was officially launched, as the first assembly of the heads of states of the African Union was convened. The African Union focuses on the process of political and economic integration in Africa, while also addressing problems that have arisen as negative side effects of globalization. In its focus upon integration, the AU continues to uphold the ideals of Pan-Africanism. In its emphasis on economic matters, it addresses the most pressing problems facing African nations in the new millennium.

S. Ademola Ajayi

See also: **Du Bois, W. E. B. and Pan-Africanism; Nkrumah, Kwame.**

Further Reading

Agbi, S. O. *The O.A.U. and African Diplomacy, 1963–1979.* Ibadan: Impact Publishers, 1986.

Ajala, A. *Pan-Africanism: Evolution, Progress, and Prospects.* London, 1973.

Akindele, R. A. (ed.). "The Organization of African Unity, 1903–1988: A Role Analysis and Performance Review." *Nigerian Journal of International Affairs*. 14, no. 1. (1988).
Amate, C. O. C. *Inside the OAU: Pan-Africanism in Practice*. Basingstoke, U.K., 1986.
Cervenka, Z. *The Unfinished Quest for Unity: Africa and the OAU*. New York, 1977.
Geuss, I. *The Pan-African Movement*. New York, 1974.
Langley, J. A. *Pan-Africanism and Nationalism in West Africa, 1900–1945*. Oxford, 1973.
Legum, C. *Pan Africanism: A Short Political Guide*. New York, Praeger, 1965.
Thompson, V. B. *African and Unity: The Evolution of Pan Africanism*. Longman, 1969.
Wolfers, M. *Politics in the Organization of African Unity*. London, 1976.

Oromo: Origins, Social and Economic Organization

The Oromo (or Galla as they were formerly known) constitute one of the largest and most important ethnic groups of Ethiopia. The question of their ethnic genesis and origin has been subject of scholarly debates for a considerable period, and up to the present no general agreement on that problem has been reached. It seems an established fact that parts of the Oromo-inhabited regions are today occupied by Somali groups. Archaeological findings in the northern part of Somali country such as burials and funeral grounds are attributed to the Oromo. Essentially, however, evidence points to a highland origin in what is today the province of Ba'li, and contrary to a widely held belief of the past, the Oromo are a genuinely Ethiopian people. Correspondingly, it is now well known that the great Oromo migrations were not due to pressure of other peoples. Another biased perception of Oromo history and society concerns their description as primitive cattle-raisers with no knowledge of farming techniques. This incorrect assumption must be revised, since it has become evident that they practiced differentiated agriculture wherever they settled.

The Oromo consisted of genealogically connected groups and presumably as a result of a steadily growing population parts of these groups broke away and formed new independent subgroups. Initially, two major divisions existed that were named Borana and Barentu after their two mythical ancestors and assumed founders. As early as the sixteenth century, these groups were powerful confederacies that had integrated many different ethnic groups. It is therefore important to state that there probably never was anything like a "pure"' Oromo ethnic entity.

One important impetus for the massive expansion of the Oromo might have been the *gada* system as a central institution of social and political organization, which ruled every aspect of life for the Oromo. The *gada* system included a classification by age groups that succeeded each other in assuming military, economic, political, and ritual responsibilities every eight years. Every male member of the Oromo society was classified into generation-sets and *gada*-grades. The full cycle of the *gada* consisting of ten grades was divided into two periods of forty years each. Regardless of his actual age, each Oromo had to enter the children's class forty years after his father had done so, which meant that father and son were five grades apart at all times. During his lifetime every Oromo man had ideally to pass ten classes of eight years each. All those who entered a class together formed a *gada* group and remained a military fraternity all their lives. With membership of a certain class specific duties and rights were associated. The fifth and sixth classes constituted the leadership and warrior class. The political power was actually held by the *gada* class and selected officials were only representatives of the ruling set. It was expected that at least once during the eight years of the ruling gada class a fighting and killing expedition was undertaken against either big game or enemies which none of the ancestors had raided.

Another important feature of some of the Oromo societies was the *Qallu* institution. The *Qallu* was the spiritual leader of Oromo traditional religion and the first leader was believed to have been of divine origin. According to Oromo traditions, the *Qallu* was "the prophet of the nation" and guarded the laws of the *Waaqa,* who was both the sky god and the sky itself. Adult men went on a pilgrimage to the *Qallu* to receive its holy blessing.

The Oromo were characterized by a mixed economy with extensive farming. The status of cattle was high; beyond economic considerations, the people had a strong emotional and ritual relationship with the cattle. In the older anthropological literature, the Oromo were therefore regarded as typical exponents of the so-called cattle-complex. Cattle formed the basis of Oromo livelihood, and the Oromo myth of origin tells us that the first cattle and the first human being were created together. The importance of cattle is emphasized in another tradition according to which God exclaimed when creating the Oromo people, "Come forth, you owners of cattle!" In reality, the role of cattle within the mixed economy was determined by the natural environment of the different Oromo groups. Only where the arid climate led to less than ideal agricultural conditions did cattle-breeding predominate.

Another institution contributed to the dynamic character of the Oromo societies and might have facilitated the process of the migration. This institution consisted of the adoption of an individual or a group of Oromo or non-Oromo origin into an Oromo *gossa* (which is traditionally translated as "clan") or subgroup. Adopted individuals or groups collectively became the "sons" of the *gossa*. Mutual responsibility and obligation were promised, and the adopting *gossa* thereby increased their numbers. This institution of adoption was inspired by political, economic, and military considerations on both sides. In this way, the Oromo seem to have assimilated more than they were assimilated by other ethnic groups. It demonstrates that the Oromo ethnic entities were fluid groupings. Through the continual process of migration and conquest, as well as interaction and assimilation, old members were lost while new members were incorporated into the group.

MARIANNE BECHHAUS-GERST

Further Reading

Hassen, M. *The Oromo of Ethiopia: A History 1570–1860.* Cambridge: Cambridge University Press, 1990.

Lewis, H. S. "The Origin of the Galla and the Somali." *Journal of African History.* 7 (1966): 27–46.

Van de Loo, J. *Guji Oromo Culture in Southern Ethiopia.* Berlin: Dietrich Reimer Verlag, 1991.

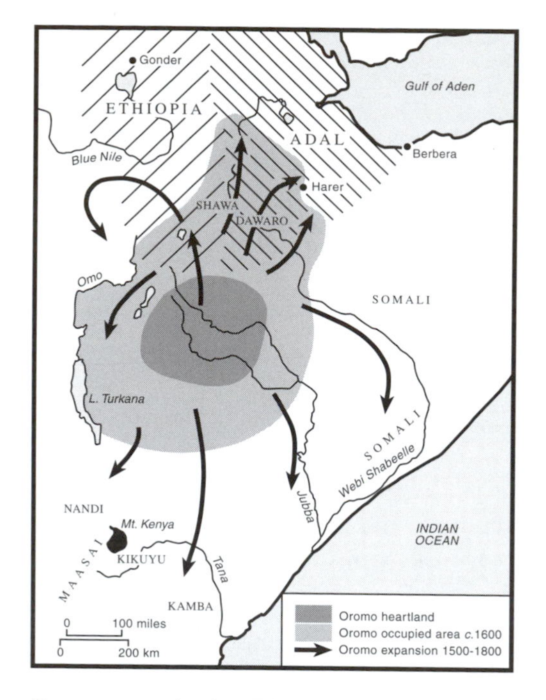

Oromo, expansion into Ethiopia, sixteenth–eighteenth centuries.

Oromo: Migration and Expansion: Sixteenth and Seventeenth Centuries

The massive expansion of the Oromo (or Galla as they were formerly known) at the beginning of the sixteenth century presumably was the result of multiple factors. One important impetus for the massive expansion of the Oromo might have been the *gada* system as the central institution of social and political organization, which ruled every aspect of life of the Oromo. An increase in population and demographic pressure also caused the leaving of former homelands of many of the Oromo groups. Oral traditions furthermore speak of great droughts at the time of their migration.

Originally there were two confederations of Oromo, called Borana and Barentu. During the first phase of their migration after 1530 the Oromo profited by the aftermath of the fierce warfare between Muslims and Christians and were advancing into regions virtually depopulated. The first land acquisition seems to have taken place as early as 1530 when the Borana Oromo invaded Bali. Between 1530 and 1538, in the period of the Mudana gada, the Oromo crossed the Wabi.

A tradition relates that even at this time a three-stage process could be discerned that consisted of scouting, surprise attack, and settlement. In the period of the Kiolole *gada* (1538–1546), they devastated the predominantly Muslim-populated country of Dawa'ro north of the Wabi river and the lowlands of the Hawas further north. The Christian emperor Galawdewos fought against the Barentu and the Borana during the Bifole Gada (1546–1554) but could not prevent them from attacking Waj, Fatagar, and other provinces.

Particularly important in the history of the Oromo migrations was the period of the Michelle *gada* (1554–1562), because it brought about a decrease in the power of both the Christians and the Muslims, which ended two centuries of struggle between the two groups. At the same time, the power of the Oromo dramatically increased, and Christians and Muslims united in their struggle against the common enemy for the next 150 years.

During the period of the Harmufa *gada* (1562–1579) the Oromo began migrating to the southwestern region of present-day Ethiopia. They attacked the provinces Angot, Amhara, and Bagemder, which were beginning to recover from the devastation of the war against the Muslims. Here the armies of the new emperor, Minas, confronted them. At the same time, Barentu Oromo groups attacked Adal, where famine and plague weakened any potential resistance. Only a few small groups of Muslims were able to flee to the Awsa Oasis in the Afar desert or survived within the fortified city. The greater part of the Muslim population of Adal was assimilated by the Oromo.

When Emperor Minas died in 1563, a third of the Ethiopian Empire was already occupied by Oromo groups. Their military strength was considerably improved by the introduction of the horse. During the first half of the seventeenth century, invasions by different Oromo groups were a permanent menace to the Ethiopian Empire. About 1617 the Borana attacked Bagemder and Gojjam, which were central regions of the empire. Between 1620 and 1660 the Ethiopian emperors had to constantly defend different parts of their territory but were unable to put a stop to the waves of advancing Oromo groups.

The main target of Oromo expansion was Gojjam, which was assaulted from the south by the Liban Oromo, and from the east by the Tulama. Simultaneously, the Tulama expanded from Shoa into Amhara and the Wallo and Azebo overran Angot, parts of Amhara and Waj, Bagemder, and Tigre. In 1642 the eastern Oromo nearly annihilated the Ethiopian army in Tigre.

Under the reign of emperors Fasiladas and Yohannes the Oromo seem to have been virtually unrestrained in their expansion. It was Iyasu I (1682–1706) who resumed the offensive against the Oromo while at the same time recruiting battalions of loyal Oromo groups whom he settled in conquered areas. Tulama and Liban Oromo were settled in northern Gojjam and Bagemder. They were encouraged to convert to Christianity. Some of their authorities were appointed to high offices in the army and in the administration of the provinces. In 1684–1685 Oromo groups fought against Emperor Iyassu I in Wollo and Gojjam. In 1694 the Gugru-Oromo attacked Gojjam and Bagemder.

Although the military expansion of the Oromo continued, many Oromo groups started to settle in Ethiopian territory and developed into a political power, which was utilized by the different secular and ecclesiastical groupings. By the end of the seventeenth century they were taking an active part in the political formation of the Ethiopian state. The process of mutual assimilation between the Oromo newcomers and other inhabitants of the empire was well under way.

MARIANNE BECHHAUS-GERST

Further Reading

Hassen, M. *The Oromo of Ethiopia: A History 1570–1860.* Cambridge: Cambridge University Press, 1990.

Lewis, H. S. "The Origin of the Galla and the Somali." *Journal of African History.* 7 (1966): 27–46.

Van de Loo, J. *Guji Oromo Culture in Southern Ethiopia.* Berlin: Dietrich Reimer Verlag, 1991.

Oubangui-Chari: *See* Central African Republic: Colonial Period: Oubangui-Chari.

Ovimbundu States

The great central highlands of Angola are characterized by fertile soil and a temperate climate. Since ancient times, the region has been regarded as the demographic center of west Central Africa. The Umbundu language is closely related to others of the western Bantu linguistic group, and was probably spoken throughout the central highlands in ancient times, as it is today. Even in the seventeenth century, outsiders recognized a common cultural identity among the Ovimbundu people of the highlands. This cultural and linguistic unity was not recognized at the political level, however, for the highlands were always divided into several polities of various sizes.

Its deeper past remains essentially unknown, with only a handful of archaeological sites having been excavated. Judging from these and comparisons with better known adjacent regions, the area was probably largely dependent upon agriculture as early as 500BCE, and was practicing ironworking by the start of the Common Era.

Complex societies had probably already been developed for a long time when the Portuguese first arrived in central Africa. In 1540, responding to information about copper production and exports, the Portuguese crown organized an expedition to seek relations with the "King of Benguela," a polity which probably dominated the northwestern part of the highlands, and the headwaters of the Longa River. This kingdom must have been fairly powerful and extensive, for the important kingdom of Ndongo was frequently at war with it in the mid-sixteenth century, and Portuguese reports suggest it was among the largest in the area. Ndongo reports suggested that the kings of Ndongo had forced Benguela to submit to it, although this submission was probably little more than formal recognition and perhaps payment of tribute.

More modern traditions often link founding houses of the Ovimbundu states to that of Ndongo, or to the Portuguese post of Pungo Andongo, which was built in and claimed authority over the heartland of Ndongo. But it is not clear whether these traditions reflected real sovereignty or simply a means of attaching origins to a prestigious ancient kingdom.

However, at some point toward the end of the sixteenth century, the area was overrun by bands of Imbangala warriors who destroyed the old kingdom of Benguela, and perhaps whatever other polities existed in the region. The Imbangala were a group of mercenary military bands, organized into companies with an intricate command structure, known for their fearsome pillaging habits. Rumors abounded of their cannibalism and their habit of killing all children born in their camps. They replaced their wartime losses and augmented their numbers by capturing and kidnapping adolescent boys and integrating them into their system, which was governed as a sort of religious cult. They were powerfully armed and feared throughout the area.

The origins of the Imbangala are uncertain. An account of the band commanded by Imbe Kalandula around 1600 said that this band descended from a "page" of Elembe, possibly one of the lesser known Ovimbundu states, and thus raises the possibility that they originated as a renegade faction of an official army. Later traditions linked them also to the central highlands, though their modern descendants trace their origin to the Lunda region, and some historians have seen a more ancient link there.

By the middle of the seventeenth century, the highlands were divided into a number of "provinces," each of which was in turn composed of a mixture of local political rulers and Imbangala bands. Some of these leaders, such as the ruler of Wambu, or Ngola Njimbo, acted as regional lords commanding the lesser leaders, but these organizations appear to have been alliances and nominal subordinations rather than real states. In many cases an Imbangala band or a combination of an Imbangala band and a regional lord might exert control.

The political alignments of the highlands began to change in the middle of the eighteenth century, however, as more firmly constituted states replaced the provincial organizations. The newer states grew out of the provincial politics of earlier times. The new kingdom of Viye, for example, was headed by an Imbangala band that had become a political authority and subordinated a host of lesser nobles (*osomas*) to their government. A professional army, perhaps drawn from the original band, combined with local levies to make Viye powerful enough to expand and dominate its neighbors, but at the same time the overall ruler was subject to electoral control by a group of fairly independent nobles.

In Mbailundu, which grew to be the largest of the Ovimbundu states, on the other hand, it was not the Imbangala element that prevailed, but that of older noble roots, manifested in what was called the "Impunga Court," some sort of collective decision-making body of several noble groups. In time, however, the kings of the new state, like their counterparts in Viye, had engrossed the power of the court, developed dependent armies, and conquered outlying areas.

The rise of these states was also connected with the emergence of a more aggressive Portuguese policy in the area. Portuguese traders had assisted the rise of the new states, and bought the many people enslaved through the wars of expansion. Some had become advisors, but now the Portuguese government wished to place them under its authority through a system of controlled markets. A series of military campaigns between 1773 and 1776 had succeeded in creating an alliance between Portuguese governors and African monarchs who swore "vassalage" to the Portuguese in exchange for their military assistance, or in the wake of defeat. The ruling dynasties of both Viye and Mbailundu were established during this period, establishing a special relationship with Portugal that did not necessarily impede the sovereignty of the Ovimbundu states but did help to bring trade under the control of these states and Portugal. The following period witnessed the increasing centralization of these states and the decline of local nobilities and Imbangala elements.

John Thornton

See also: **Angola: Chokwe, Ovimbundu, Nineteenth Century; Kongo; Ndongo, Kingdom of.**

Further Reading

Childs, G. M. *Ovimbundu Kinship and Character.* Oxford, 1949.

Heywood, L. M. *Contested Power in Angola: 1840s to the Present.* Rochester, 2000.

Miller, J. C. *Kings and Kinsmen: Early Mbundu States in Angola.* Oxford, 1976.